INTEGRAL
LOGISTICS
MANAGEMENT

Series on Resource Management

INTEGRAL LOGISTICS MANAGEMENT

THIRD EDITION

Operations and Supply Chain
Management in Comprehensive
Value-Added Networks

PAUL SCHÖNSLEBEN

Auerbach Publications
Taylor & Francis Group
Boca Raton   New York

Auerbach Publications is an imprint of the
Taylor & Francis Group, an informa business

Auerbach Publications
Taylor & Francis Group
6000 Broken Sound Parkway NW, Suite 300
Boca Raton, FL 33487-2742

© 2007 by Taylor & Francis Group, LLC
Auerbach is an imprint of Taylor & Francis Group, an Informa business

No claim to original U.S. Government works
Printed in the United States of America on acid-free paper
10 9 8 7 6 5 4 3 2 1

International Standard Book Number-10: 1-4200-5194-6 (Hardcover)
International Standard Book Number-13: 978-1-4200-5194-0 (Hardcover)

Visit the Taylor & Francis Web site at
http://www.taylorandfrancis.com

and the Auerbach Web site at
http://www.auerbach-publications.com

Foreword to the Third Edition

It is a great pleasure to release this third edition of *Integral Logistics Management — Operations and Supply Chain Management in Comprehensive Value-added Networks*. This is a dynamic field, in both theory and practice. As the revised subheading to the title of the book shows, issues in strategy have gained increasing importance. For this reason, the new edition contains:

- a section on facility location planning, for both production networks and distribution and service networks
- a section on strategic procurement
- a chapter with an overview of TQM and Six Sigma
- a chapter with an overview of system and project management
- new key figures for classification of planning methods in materials management

Also, additional interactive Macromedia Flash elements have been developed that are available for download from the companion Web site to this book at http://intlogman.ethz.ch/. The Web site is frequently updated with further learning materials that the reader may like to use. Readers are invited to send suggestions and comments to me at Paul.Schoensleben@ethz.ch. The comprehensive index of the book has been expanded in this edition. The material now covers almost all of the key terms in the five CPIM modules contained in the APICS *CPIM Exam Content Manual*.

In parallel to this third English edition of the book, Springer is publishing the fifth edition in German, *Integrales Logistikmanagement – Operations- und Supply Chain Management in umfassenden Wertschöpfungsnetzwerken* (ISBN 9783-540-68178-6). Readers of German may like to know Springer-Verlag has also published a treatment of a subject that complements this book (that is, integral information management) under the title *Integrales Informationsmanagement: Informationssysteme für Geschäftsprozesse — Management, Modellierung, Lebenszyklus und Technologie* (ISBN 3-540-41712-5).

Zurich, January 2007   Prof. Dr. Paul Schönsleben

www.lim.ethz.ch/schoensleben/index_EN

Foreword to the First Edition

Changes in the world outside the company alter the way that we look at problems and priorities in the company itself. This presents new challenges to company logistics and to planning & control of corresponding business processes.

While logistics was once understood as storing and transport, today — in the course of the reorganization of business processes — an integral perspective on company logistics is making headway. Naturally, products must still be stored and transported. But now these processes are seen as disturbing factors that should be reduced as greatly as possible. The current focus lies on that part of the logistics chain that adds value. This chain, from sales logistics to research and design logistics, production and procurement logistics, distribution logistics, service and maintenance logistics, and — a recent development — disposal logistics, now stands as a whole as the subject for discussion. We seek improvements at the level of the comprehensive, coordinated business process. Moreover, more and more networks of companies arise that develop and manufacture products in cooperation. The logistics of these coupled companies must work together closely and rapidly. This also demands integral management of logistics.

These recent tendencies do not only affect the logistics of the flow of goods itself, but rather also its planning & control, or, in other words, *administrative* and *planning logistics*. The term PPC (for production planning & control) has in reality long since been expanded to become planning & control of the entire logistics network.

Changing requirements in the world of practice often call for new theories and methods, particularly if earlier theories seem to have lost their connection to that world. This impression indeed often arises when we look at what is happening in company logistics. Close examination reveals that behind the methods and techniques that are sold on today's market with new and rousing catchwords there is seldom anything that is really new. It seems reasonable to assume that the attempt to match existing knowledge against the rapidly changing reality and — in the sense of continuous improvement — to expand and adapt it has met with failure. Here lies the crux of the challenge to company logistics today.

The methods and techniques implemented in planning & control are, interestingly enough, not dependent upon classification of the tasks and competencies in the organization of the company. For example, techniques of capacity planning do not change according to whether control tasks are executed by central operations planning and scheduling or, in decentralized fashion, by the job shops. The algorithms also remain in principle the same despite being either realized manually or with the aid of software. The algorithms in a comprehensive software package are also the same as those of a locally implemented planning board. In contrast, methods and techniques do indeed change in dependency upon the entrepreneurial objectives, which the choice of logistics should support. These objectives relate to key areas such as quality, costs, delivery, or various aspects of flexibility.

The present volume aims to present the differing characteristics, tasks, methods, and techniques of planning & control in company logistics as comprehensively as possible. Development and change in operational management for company performance should become transparent. However, we will not be content with a wide-ranging, general treatment of the subject at the cost of depth and scientific elucidation of the matter at hand. Due to the very fact that logistics and planning & control take place at the operational level of a company, competency in the details is absolutely necessary. Effective plans at the strategic level should not lead to contradictions and inconsistency at the operational level.

Consultants and the software industry, as well as widespread circles in educational institutions, produce constant pressure for novelty — which should not be confused with innovation. There is no need to allow ourselves to be irritated by such influences, which are often just short-lived trends. As always, after all, broad, detailed, methodological, and operational knowledge continues to lead to competency. It is this competency that makes it possible to classify and relate the various business processes and the tasks people in companies carry out and to continuously adapt this system of relations and categorizations to changing entrepreneurial objectives, market situations, product ranges, and employee qualifications.

Today, computer-aided planning & control enjoys a very high status in small- to medium-sized companies. And this is usually rightly so, for the large amounts of data can often not be handled quickly enough by another means. For this reason, presentation of the methods of planning & control in detail will include references to possible IT support.

The present volume is a textbook for industrial engineers, business managers, engineers and practitioners, and computer scientists as part of their studies. It also aims to serve the further education of professionals in business practice in industry and the service industries.

The book is a translation of my book *Integrales Logistikmanagement — Planung & Steuerung umfassender Geschäftsprozesse*, published in 1998 by Springer. The first edition has sold out. The second edition will appear simultaneously and with the same content as the English version.

You will find a part of the bibliography referring to German books or papers. This means that I am still looking for English literature on the specific topic. I would be grateful for any indication of additional English sources of such a specific topic.

In parts, the book reflects the work of my esteemed colleague Prof. Dr. Alfred Büchel, to whom I am greatly obliged. This is the case particularly with regard to the area of his great interest, statistical methods in planning & control. These are treated mainly in Chapter 9 and Sections 10.3, 10.4, and 12.2.

Zurich, January 2000   Prof. Dr. Paul Schönsleben

Acknowledgments (Third Edition)

My thanks go first of all to you, my readers, for your numerous suggestions. And then to my colleagues and fellow members of the APICS Curricula and Certification Council: you have enriched my work through your many ideas. Here, special thanks go to Merle Thomas and Roly White. I am grateful to Dr. Robert Alard, Dr. Matthias Schnetzler, Dr. Alexander Verbeck, Sören Günther, and Nikolai Iliev, members of my staff at the Center for Enterprise Sciences (BWI) at the Swiss Federal Institute of Technology Zurich (ETH), for their valuable input to the new sections and chapters. And I would like to thank my colleagues Hugo Tschirky, Hans-Peter Wiendahl and Markus Bärtschi for their continuing support of my work.

The work of translating and proofreading was again done by Ellen Russon, East Sandwich, MA (ellenrusson@ellenrusson.com), to whom I extend many thanks. Roger Cruz, Dipl. Ing., and his team again took on ready-to-print production of this edition. To them also I express my thanks.

Zurich, January 2007   Prof. Dr. Paul Schönsleben

Acknowledgments (First and Second Edition)

For the first and second edition, I wish to thank numerous scientific colleagues here and abroad, for valuable discussions and suggestions. Special thanks are due to many of the active and engaged experts in the APICS community.

In particular, I would like to thank:

- Barry Firth, CPIM, Melbourne, for his invaluable help in updating the classification of fundamental concepts in logistics management (branches in dependency on characteristic features, production types, and concepts for planning & control within the enterprise), as well as for many other contributions.

- Prof. Merle Thomas, CFPIM, Vermont State College, WV, for his ongoing support of my work.

- Prof. Dr. Alfred Büchel and Prof. Markus Bärtschi, my colleagues at the chair of Logistics and Information Mangement at ETH

- Paul Bernard, Rapistan Systems, Grand Rapids, MI

- Prof. Dr. Hans-Peter Wiendahl, University of Hannover, Germany

- Prof. Dr. Thomas M. Liebling, ETH Lausanne, Switzerland

For help with the manuscript, particularly for their critical questions, I wish to thank all previous and current scientific associates and post graduate students of the chair of Logistics and Information Management of the Department of Manufacturing, Industrial Engineering and Management at the Swiss Federal Institute of Technology ETH in Zurich. They make up far too great a number to list individually here. Instead, I am pleased to refer to many of their doctoral theses and further scientific works in the text and bibliography of this book.

And for their untiring help in creating, translating, and correcting the manuscript, I give hearty thanks to Dipl.Ing. Roger Cruz and all the many professionals and assistants that participated in this undertaking.

Zurich, April 2003 and January 2000   Prof. Dr. Paul Schönsleben

Overview of Contents

Table of Contents

At a first reading of the book, some sections are optional in the sense that they are not necessary in order to understand the material that follows. An asterisk (*) indicates these sections.

Detailed Table of Contents

At a first reading of the book, some sections are optional in the sense that they are not necessary in order to understand the material that follows. An asterisk (*) indicates these sections.

Part A. Concepts, and Fundamentals of Design of Integral Logistics Management

Logistics management is operational management. This means *implementing* ideas, concepts, and methods that have the potential to increase the effectiveness and efficiency of company performance. The symbol below aims to express the idea.

Magic formulas, catchwords, and simplifying theories do not stand much of a chance in logistics management. The complex reality of day-to-day operation of companies in industry and the service sector demands highly diligent detailed work. Here, in contrast to some strategic concepts in company management, the proof of truth — namely, effectiveness — shows up quickly and measurably. Errors in logistics management rapidly produce dissatisfied customers and employees, and thus poor business results. This immediacy and measurability do not make it easy to shift the blame to others.

On the other hand, logistics tasks offer a variety of possible solutions. This is an area that calls for human creativity, drive, and perseverance. Methods of planning & control in company logistics, and particularly computer-supported tools, are after all merely supporting aids. Moreover, experience has shown repeatedly that the successful use of methods and tools depends heavily upon the people who implement them.

The eight chapters of Part A of the book deal with logistics management as embedded in the entrepreneurial activities of developing, manufacturing, using, and disposing goods. The focus is on the objectives, basic principles, analyses, concepts, systems, and systematic methods of the management and design of logistics systems both within companies and in company networks. We introduce planning & control tasks and develop the methods used to fulfill those tasks in two simple but important cases: master planning and repetitive manufacturing. Part B, in eight further chapters, treats the methods of planning & control in complex logistics. These are the methods used in all temporal ranges of planning & control. In addition, the detailed discussion of methods to solve the planning & control tasks in Part B provides the reader with an in-depth methodological foundation for understanding the concepts in part A.

Some notes to the reader:

> • Definitions of key concepts and terms appear in text boxes, and the terms being defined always appear in *italics*.

- • The *definitions of terms* sometimes take the form of an indented bullet list. This form is useful particularly where one and the same characteristic has varying degrees of expression.

- • A gray background highlights important principles, examples, points to remember, prescribed procedures, steps of a technique, or solutions of selected scenarios and exercises. The reader will often find a reference to a figure.

- • Some sections of the book are not essential reading for an understanding of the subsequent material. An asterisk (*) identifies these optional sections.

- • Also optional in this sense are the additional definitions provided in footnotes. They appear for the sake of completeness or as information for practitioners or for readers coming from related disciplines.

We use the following abbreviations in the text:
- • *R&D* for "research and development"
- • *ID* for "identification" (for example, item ID)

For our interactive elements, as well as for additional teaching material, please refer to: http://www.intlogman.lim.ethz.ch/. In addition, a visit to our web site could be helpful: http://www.lim.ethz.ch/index_en.htm. Please direct questions or comments to Paul.Schoensleben@ethz.ch.

1 Logistics and Operations Management and Enterprise Performance

Logistics and operations management deal with the design and management of productive systems as well as with the planning and control of daily business operations within a company or in transcorporate networks, that is in supply chains. This chapter gives an overview of logistics management and logistics networks in and among companies.

In small companies, the operational management of daily production is often handled by human beings who, through intuition and on the basis of experience, find creative solutions. People have unique operational management abilities, in that they can fill in the blanks accurately and react flexibly to specific situations.

If, however, processes become more complex, frequent, and rapid, intuition alone does not suffice. Prior experience can also be misleading. In large companies and in supply chains, moreover, there are many people involved in the processes, both simultaneously and in sequence. They differ with respect to the level of experience, knowledge, and intuition at their disposal. It is here that the scientific handling of enterprise logistics comes into play.

> An *enterprise* is seen as a system in which people work together to reach an entrepreneurial objective. For the purpose of this book, we use *company* synonymously with enterprise.

Logistics and operations management stand in the field of tension of the various stakeholders of the company and its own contradictory objectives. After defining the basic concepts of logistics and operations management (in Section 1.1) as well as the related business objects (in Section 1.2), we will examine this field of tension in Section 1.3. Section 1.3 also presents fundamental principles of effective logistics networks. The principles concern the agility of a company as well as the integral treatment and the transcorporate objectives of the supply chain.

To measure the performance of logistics and operations processes, enterprises must select appropriate performance indicators that relate to the company's business objects and objectives. These measures allow a company to evaluate the degree to which objectives are reached and to analyze initial causes and effects. Section 1.4 discusses these performance indicators for logistics and operations management.

1.1   Basic Definitions

When confronted with practical problems requiring solutions, people are not generally concerned about definitions. Definitions become essential, however, when we seek to gain an understanding of the concepts and techniques of integral logistics management. First of all, definitions transmit a picture of the phenomena under study. They also clear up the misunderstandings that arise because people and companies make varying usage of technical terms. And, finally, definitions are indispensable for structured presentation of the material in a textbook that covers a subject in substantial detail. However, definitions should not detract from the pleasure of learning new concepts. For this reason, this chapter offers only those definitions that make clear the level at which the topics are being covered and that explain how the topics relate to overlapping issues in management.

1.1.1   Goods, Products, and the Product Life Cycle

A *good* is something that has an economic utility or satisfies an economic want ([MeWe03]). *Goods* (the plural form) stands for personal property having intrinsic value but usually excluding money, securities, and negotiable instruments. It is the noun form of an adjective that formerly had the meaning of "fitting in a building or human society," while today it can be defined as "suitable, serviceable, convenient, or effective."

Not all goods exist in nature as such. There are special terms for materials that are transformed by production functions into goods.

A *product*, according to [MeWe03], is something brought about by intellectual or physical effort. An *artifact*, according to [MeWe03], is something created by humans, usually for a practical purpose.

For logistics, these nuances of meaning are of minor importance. We therefore use "artifact" synonymously with "product."

Materials, according to [MeWe03], are the elements, constituents, or substances of which something is composed or can be made. Beside raw materials, also documents, evidence, certificates, or similar things may serve as materials.

A *component* is, according to [Long03], one of several parts that together make up a whole machine or system. With regard to a product, components are goods that become part of a product during manufacturing (through installation, for example) or arise from a product during disposal (for example, through dismantling).

Material and *component* are not completely synonymous terms. "Material" generally refers to rather simple initial resources or information, while "component" generally refers to semi finished products as well.

Goods may be classified according to several dimensions, such as:

The nature of goods:

- *Material goods* are produced or traded mainly by companies in the industrial sector

- *Goods of a nonmaterial nature (nonmaterial goods)*, such as information, tend to be produced, compiled or traded by companies in the *service industry*[1] sector.

The use of goods:

- *Consumer goods* are mainly intended for direct consumption.

- *Investment goods* are utilized mainly to develop and manufacture other goods.

In addition to the nature and use of a product, there is thus a further dimension of products based on the above and shown in Figure 1.1.1.1: the *degree of comprehensiveness of a product* is the way that the product is understood. According to the degree of comprehensiveness, the consumer sees and judges the quality of products, processes, and the organization.

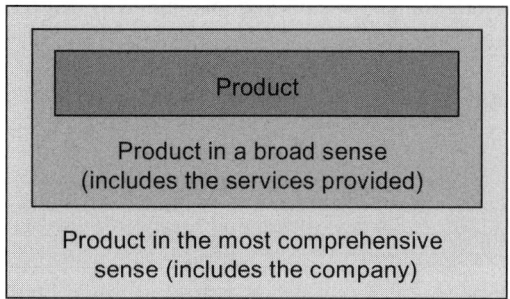

Fig. 1.1.1.1   Comprehensiveness of product understanding: the degree of comprehensiveness of a product.

---

[1] *A service industry* is an organization that essentially produces no material goods.

Firstly, during the phase of use, the end user may require service:

> *Service*, according to [MeWe03], is the performance of some useful function. With companies, service is customer service or customer support.
>
> *Customer service or customer support* is the ability of a company to address the needs, inquiries, and requests from customers ([APIC04]).

In many areas, service itself is more important than the products used to provide the service. For investment goods also, service is becoming increasingly important and often constitutes the key sales argument.

> A *product, in a broad sense,* is a product along with the services provided, where the consumer sees the two as a unit.

In addition, the company can also become a sales argument in and of itself.

> A *product, in the most comprehensive sense*, is comprised of the product, the services provided, and the company itself, with its image and reputation. Here, the consumer sees all three as a unit.

An example of product in the most comprehensive sense is the concept of *Total Care* in the insurance branch. The aim is to give the customer the idea that the company as a whole will provide all-encompassing care.

Products are made, according to the above definition, by converting goods. The use or utilization of products leads to their consumption or usage.

> *Consumption* of goods (by the *consumer*) means, according to [Long03], the amount of goods that are used (up).

Following consumption, a product must be disposed of properly. There is thus a life cycle to products.

> Put simply, the *product life cycle* consists of three time periods: *design and manufacturing, use (and ultimately consumption)* and *disposal.*[2]

---

[2]   This is one of several current definitions of the term ([APIC04]). See Section 3.4 for a second definition.

Figure 1.1.1.2 shows the product life cycle. Design, manufacturing, service, and disposal are seen as value-adding processes,[3] symbolized by the value-adding arrow pointing in the direction of value-adding. Use is itself a process; however, it is a value-consuming one.

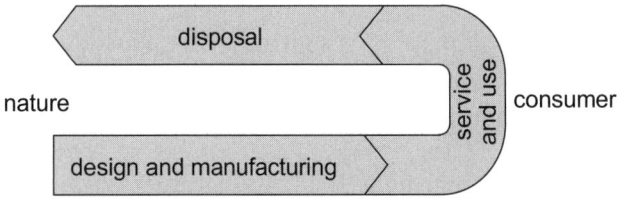

Fig. 1.1.1.2   The product life cycle.

The life cycle of *material products* generally begins with nature and leads from *design and manufacturing* to the consumer. A consumed product must then be disposed of. In the most general case, the life cycle ends once again with nature, in that the materials are returned to the earth.

The life cycle of *nonmaterial products* begins with a topic or issue about which something can be determined. This topic, in a broad sense, can also be seen as ultimately connected to things in nature, whether to objects or at least to human thinking about objects. Disposal ends with the information being erased or deleted. In the broadest sense, then, it is also returned to nature.

1.1.2   Basic Definitions in Logistics and Operations Management

Logistics is involved with products over their entire life cycle:

Logistics in and among companies is the organization, planning, and realization of the total flow of goods, data, and control[4] along the entire product life cycle.

Logistics management deals with efficient and effective management of day-to-day activity in producing the company's or corporation's output.

---

[3]   Even disposal is a value-adding process. After use (or being used up), a product has a negative value as soon as disposal involves costs, such as — at the very least — fees for trash disposal.

[4]   See Section 3.1.3 for definitions of flow of goods, data, and control.

The term "operations management" is very similar to the above definition of logistics management.

Operations, according to [RuTa05], is a function or a system that transforms input to output of greater value.

Operations management, according to [APIC04], is the planning, scheduling, and control of the activities that transform input into finished goods and services.

The term also denotes a field of study of concepts from design engineering to industrial engineering, management information systems, quality management, production management, accounting, and other functions as they affect the operation. According to [RuTa05], it denotes the design and operation of productive systems — systems for getting work done.

It also makes sense to view the other functional terms found all along the company's value chain, namely *procurement*, *production*, and *sales*, from the management perspective. In the literature, functional terms are usually defined clearly and distinctly. In contrast, for management terms — like procurement *management*, production *management*, and sales *management* — you will often not find formal definitions. In practical usage, however, these terms do not differ significantly from the definitions given above for logistics or operations *management*. This is not surprising, for it is impossible to conduct successful operations management if it is applied to only a part of the value chain. For this reason, we assume in the following that there are no significant differences among all these management terms (see also [GüTe97]).

Value-added management can thus be used as a generalized term for all the types of management mentioned above.[5]

Figure 1.1.2.1 shows a graphical representation of how the terms fit the company's internal and external activities.

Design and manufacturing logistics encompasses all logistics along the way to the consumer. *Disposal logistics* runs back from the consumer. *Service logistics* accompany the use phase.

---

[5]   "Value-added" is defined in Section 3.1.2.

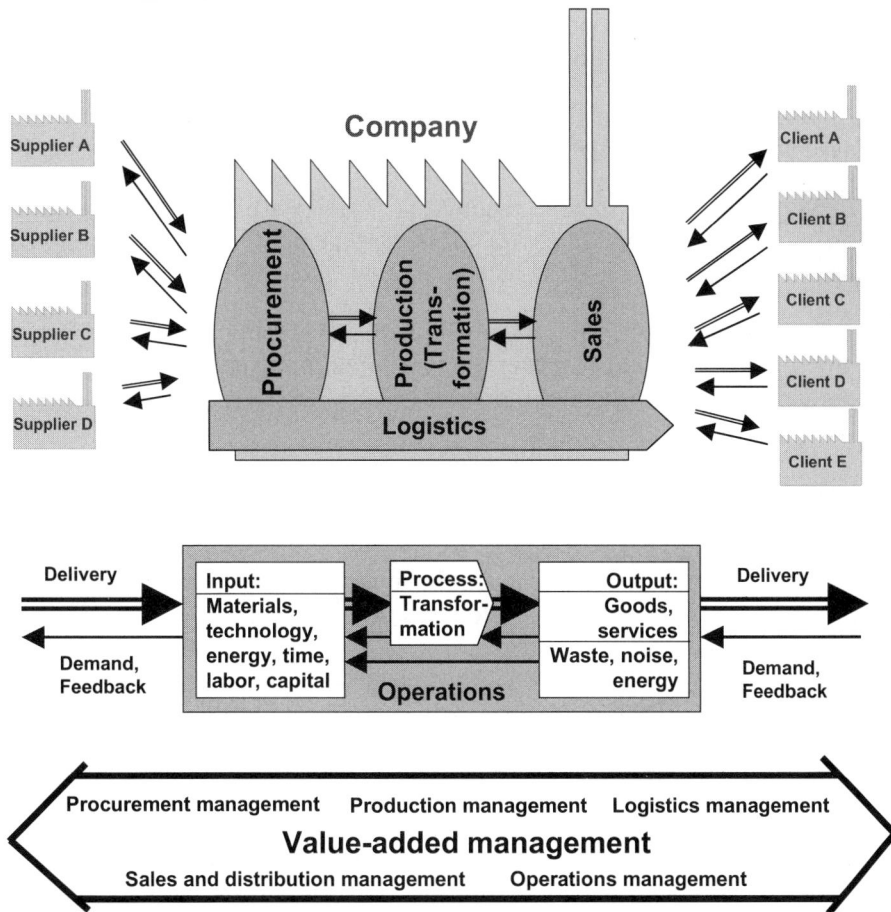

Fig. 1.1.2.1   Assignment of terms to value-added management.

In the following, we will examine manufacturing logistics in order to illustrate the most important principles of logistics. These same principles will apply to disposal logistics as well.

A fundamental problem in logistics is temporal synchronization between use and manufacturing. Here are some basic definitions:

Demand, according to [APIC04], is the need for a particular product or component. The demand could come from any number of sources, e.g., customer order or forecast, an interplant requirement, or a request from a branch warehouse for a service part or for manufacturing another product.

Actual demand is composed of customer orders, and often allocations of components to production or distribution (see [APIC04]).

Demand forecast is an estimation of future demand. *Demand prognosis* is used here synonymously (see [APIC04]).

Lead time is a span of time required to perform a process (or a series of operations). In a logistics context, it is the time between the recognition of the need for an order and the receipt of goods (see [APIC04]).

Delivery lead time is the total time required to receive, fill, and deliver an order; the time from the receipt of a customer order to the delivery of the product or the fulfillment of the service (see [APIC04]).[6]

Customer tolerance time, or *demand lead time* is the time span the customer will (or can) tolerate between from order release to the delivery of the product or the fulfillment of the service.

The *delivery policy* is the company's objective for the time to deliver the product after the receipt of a customer's order.

In a market-oriented economy, the consumer expresses a need as demand for a product. A manufacturer then attempts to fulfill the demand. In principle, design and manufacturing are thus controlled by demand: they should begin only when the need has been validly formulated.[7] In the world of practice, this ideal orientation of the producer towards the consumer is usually not possible:

- Design and manufacturing may be too slow: The delivery lead time may be longer than the customer tolerance time. Obvious examples are medications, groceries, or tools.

- Manufacturing may be too early: In nature, many basic materials for production are ready at a point in time that does not coincide with the timing of the consumer's need. Obvious examples are foodstuffs and energy.

---

[6] *Delivery cycle, delivery time,* or *time to delivery* are used synonymously for delivery lead time.

[7] In a market economy the producer, of course, attempts to manipulate the needs of the consumer. In contrast to a planned economy, sales are assured in a market economy only when the consumer places an order for the product. Risk-free production can begin only at this point. For the rest, the relationship between supply and demand determines whether customers can enforce their required delivery lead times.

Storage of goods over time plays an important role in solving this problem, allowing temporal synchronization between consumer and design and manufacturing.

Storage is the retention of goods (i.e., parts or products) for future use or shipment (see [APIC04]).

Warehouse, store, or — more precisely — *goods store* are possible terms for the infrastructure for the storage of goods.

Storage of goods at sufficiently high levels in the value-adding process may allow the company to meet the customer tolerance time. But there are also disadvantages to stocking. Stock ties up capital and requires space. Due to limited *shelf life* (that is, the length of time an item may be held in inventory before it becomes unusable), goods may perish, become obsolete, damaged, or destroyed. Keeping an inventory only makes sense where stored goods will be turned over rapidly enough. Accurate demand forecasting, where possible, helps to achieve this.

Stockpiling must therefore take place at the right levels in the logistics of manufacturing (and, analogously, in the disposal logistics). This means that goods to be stored should ideally involve none of the disadvantages mentioned above. In Figure 1.1.2.2, there are two stores within the logistics of design and manufacturing.

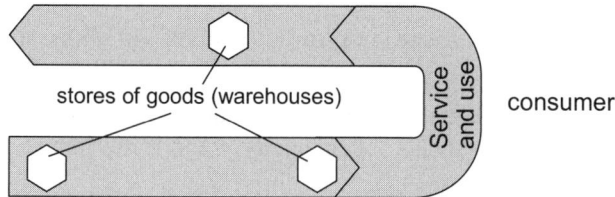

Fig. 1.1.2.2   Storage of goods within logistics.

A goods store decouples the processes upstream and downstream from this point, and therefore demand from supply. The following definitions reflect this point of view:

Decoupling is the process of creating independence between use and supply of material ([APIC04]).

Decoupling points are the locations along the value-added process, where inventory is placed to create independence between processes or entities.

> *Decoupling inventory* is the amount of inventory kept at a decoupling point.

The design of decoupling points is a degree of freedom in logistics and operations management. Their selection is a strategic decision that determines delivery lead times and the *inventory investment* — that is, the dollars that are in all levels of inventory [APIC04].

1.1.3 The Supply Chain — A Value-Added Network

For products of a certain complexity, it is not a single organizational unit that will handle design and manufacturing. Instead, the tasks are distributed among several companies or among different organizational units within a company. From the perspective of the individual manufacturer, the reasons for this are, for example:

- *Quality*: The individual manufacturer may not have the necessary technologies or processes at its command or may have not mastered them successfully enough (problem of *effectiveness*, that is, achieving the given or expected standard of quality).

- *Costs*: Certain technologies or processes cannot be implemented economically (problem of *efficiency*, that is, the actual output compared to the standard output expected, with regard to the use of means).

- *Delivery*: Some processes are not rapid enough, or they are unstable over time.

- *Flexibility*: Customer demand may show rapid variation; the company's own competencies or capacity cannot be adapted quickly enough.

As a result, a network is formed of the sub logistics of a number of companies, all along the way to the end user, that participate in design and manufacture. The simplest form of such a network is a sequence or chain. A tree structure leading to an assembled product is not uncommon.

> A *logistics network* is the joining of the logistics of several organizational units, that is, companies or parts of companies, to form comprehensive logistics. *Production network*, or *production system*, and *procurement network* can be used as synonyms of logistics network.
>
> The *end user* in a logistics network is the consumer.

Goods that can be stocked and have a large number of uses allow the formation of a supply chain with just a few partners. However, there must be agreement among all partners on the general usability of the goods. This is achieved through standardization, both within a company and through central standards organizations (for example, ISO or DIN). Economical service and industrial production are based, among other things, on such norms.

Figure 1.1.3.1 shows an example where three organizational units form a logistics network. Here it is a logistics chain.

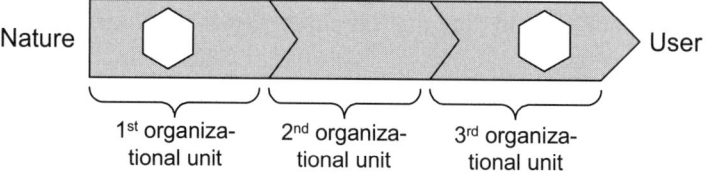

Fig. 1.1.3.1   Three organizational units in a logistics chain.

The logistics chain between two warehouses is crucial. The logistics of the second organizational unit in Figure 1.1.3.1 must not be viewed in isolation. Since there is no buffer between the store of the first organizational unit and the store of the third organizational unit, the logistics of the first organizational unit and the logistics of the third organizational unit will have a direct influence on the logistics of the second organizational unit.

From the perspective of the end user, distribution and service networks also belong to value-added, for only with distribution and possibly service is the customer order fulfilled.

A *distribution network*, or *distribution system*, is a group of interrelated facilities — manufacturing and one or more levels of warehousing — linking the production, storage, and consumption activities for spare parts and finished goods inventory [APIC04].

A *service network* is a group of interrelated facilities for performing all services in connection with material or nonmaterial goods.

This leads to the following comprehensive definitions:

A *supply chain*, or a *value-added network* is the global network used to deliver products and services from raw materials to end customers through an engineered flow of information, physical goods, and cash [APIC04].

Supply chain and value-added network are used today as general terms for all of the types of networks mentioned above.

Integral logistics management is the management of the comprehensive supply chain, that is, along the entire product life cycle.

Value-added networks take various forms. The organizational units involved can be independent companies, profit centers, or cost centers within a company. In addition, there are always varying strategies and forms of activity in a logistics network that lead to differing potentials. See Chapter 2 for more details. A particularly intensive form of cooperation between the organizational units involved is called "co-makership."

Co-makership: A *co-maker* has know-how of products at its disposal. In a supply chain, the co-maker works not only in production but also in research, development, and design.

An impressive example of "co-makership" is the Boeing Company in Seattle, WA. For some time now, Boeing has worked with co-makers in the Pacific arena, in particular in Japan. These companies manufacture the greater part of the airplane bodies. The cooperation was undertaken with the explicit view to the Asian market. Potential customers are airline companies that belong for the most part to national governments. For decision-makers, it is crucial that a part of the value-added chain take place in their own countries. Initial cooperation experience gained with the B747 was then applied to the successful and cost-effective manufacture of the B777. This airplane design was conceived from the start in co-makership — according to the principle of "simultaneous engineering."

Supply chain management is a well-known approach to strategic procurement by co-makers. See Section 2.3 for more details.

With investment goods, value-added networks do not appear in isolation. Figure 1.1.3.2 shows that in the design and manufacturing of investment goods *multidimensional value-added networks* arise. For the sake of simplicity, each network is shown as a chain.

- One *dimension* is the *multilevel* nature of the network. The user is a co-maker in another value-added network. That network may produce other investment goods, and so on. For example, with a tool machine, products may be manufactured that are used as tools or as components in the manufacture of other tool machines.

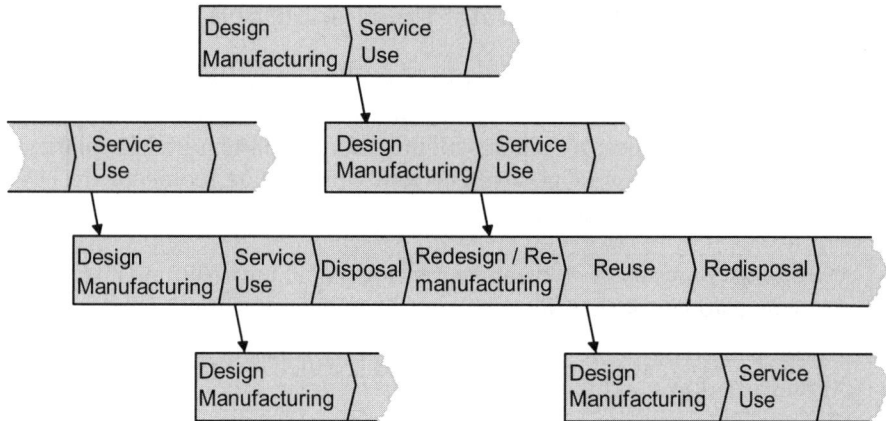

Fig. 1.1.3.2   Multidimensional logistics networks for the design and manufacturing of investment goods.

- Another dimension is *time*, or the product life cycle. A close look shows that partial disposal of the product, such as through taking back, disassembly, and recycling, can lead to a further life cycle — through *redesign* and *remanufacturing* to *reuse* — as another product, if need be.

1.2   Business Objects in Logistics and Operations Management

Long lists of definitions can be a problem for the reader, as mentioned above. The business objects handled in logistics and operations management will already be familiar to some readers due to their own professional experience. They as well as impatient readers may want to skim through Sections 1.2.1 to 1.2.6 and go directly to the sections under 1.3 that deal with the challenges the enterprise faces, keeping in mind that they can always return here for definitions of terms that require some explanation.

Business objects vary in complexity. Those that are important in logistics will be described below in principle, that is, as total objects. For complex logistics, it will be necessary to describe complex business objects later in greater detail.

1.2.1   Business Partner, Date, Time Period, and Order

The order serves as an instrument both in the legal sense and with regard to process organization, for logistics and operations management within and among companies. It contains all the information required for planning & control of the flow of goods. The following business objects are basic for the definition of an order.

A *business partner* of a company is a general term for an internal or external customer or supplier.

A *date* is a fixed point in time at which an event occurs. It is normally expressed as day and time of day ([MeWe03]).

A *due date* is a date on which something is scheduled, i.e., expected in the prescribed, normal, or logical course of events ([MeWe03]).

A *time period* is a period on the time axis. The *start date* is the beginning, and the *end date* is the end of the time period. In a logistics environment, it is mostly an end or completion date.

A representation of an order must address all order information and map it in an appropriate way.

An *order* is a complex business object. It consists at minimum of the simple business object *business partner* (in addition to the company itself) and a *date*. An order sets binding obligations with regard to the following:

- Who the business partners are (customer and supplier); each may serve as a holder of an order, that is, as a characteristic identifier of an order

- When the order is issued or what the *order validity date* is

- What the time period for order processing is, that is, *order start date* and *order completion date* or *order end date* (in general a due date, or the *order due date*).

Depending on the purpose, the order, with a number of *order position*s, also sets binding obligations with regard to:

- The products (identification and quantity) that must be manufactured or procured, and when

- The components (identification and quantity) that must be ready for use or building in

- The tasks that must be performed and in what sequence; this also includes transport, inspection, and other similar tasks

> • The nature of the order, meaning how order tasks are linked to other orders

The definition of order holds for all types of orders for part logistics, such as in sales, procurement, and production, as well as for all internal company orders (for example, design, maintenance, and so on) both in industry and the service sector.

An order becomes legally binding by order promising and confirmation.

> *Order promising* is the process of making a delivery commitment, i.e., answering the question: When can you ship how much ([APIC04])?
>
> An *order confirmation* is the result of order promising.

An order runs through several phases.

> *Order status* is a phase in the carrying out of the order. We can distinguish among four phases:
> 1. Planning or bid status
> 2. Order confirmation status
> 3. Order execution status
> 4. Billing status (calculation or invoice)

While in the first status (planning or bid) the order data represent projections. In the second and third status they are projections (budgets or cost estimations) that will be replaced gradually with real data. In the fourth status (billing), we find the effective data associated with a concrete order, tapped through some kind of recording of shop floor data.

> The *kind of order* classifies an order according to its business partners or the holder of the order.
>
> • A *customer order* or a *sales order* is an order from an *external* customer to the company.
>
> • A *procurement order* or a *purchase order* is an order from the company to an *external* supplier.
>
> • A *production order* or a *manufacturing order* or a *job order* or a *shop order* is a *company internal* order to manufacture an end product or a semifinished good.
>
> • An *overhead order* or a *work order* is a *company internal* order to manufacture items (such as tools) or for services that concern the infrastructure of the company (such as equipment maintenance).

Figure 1.2.1.1 shows an example of a simple sales order, an order form used by an Internet company. This order is a typical example of a sales order or also simple purchase order in all areas of business.

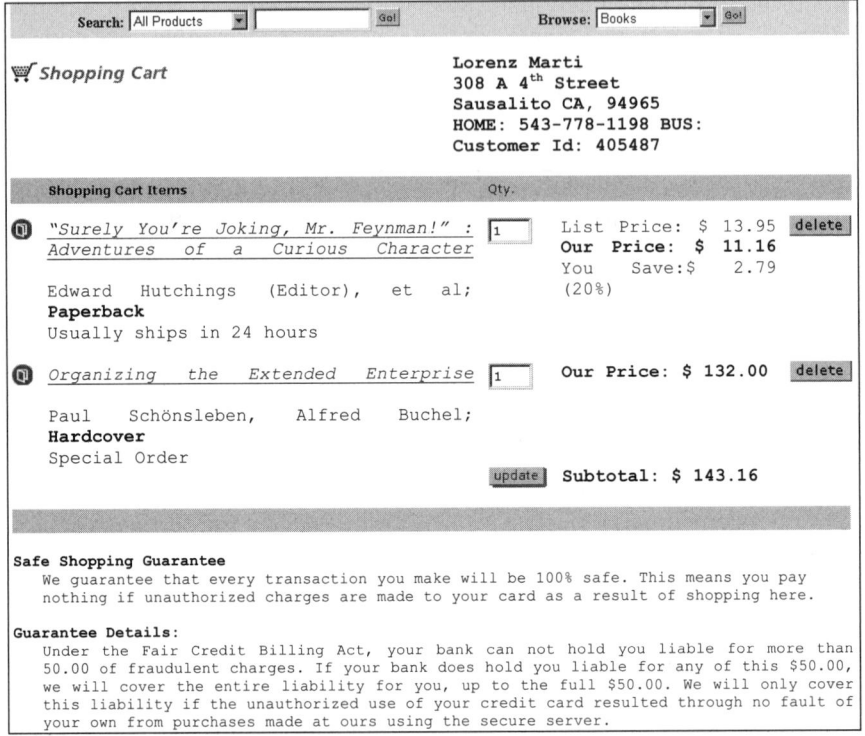

Fig. 1.2.1.1   Simple sales order form used by an Internet company: status "order."

- The upper portion, the heading, contains customer data (supplier data are the same as company data and are self-understood). Order date in this case is understood implicitly as the date the order is received by the company.

- The main body of the sales order represents its positions and lists the items to be delivered, that is, their identification and quantities.

- Finally, the footer contains the delivery address.

Here the delivery due date for the desired item is again implicit and is understood to be "as soon as possible." Thus, with very little data a practical order comes about. Because the supplier usually has the items in stock, this sales order serves as logistics control from the supplier to the customer. The invoice is usually produced — following successful delivery — within the same structure. Billing information, in most cases, will correspond to order information. Deviations might occur due to delayed deliveries or backorders.

A more complicated example, an invoice for auto repair, and thus from the service industry, is shown in Figure 1.2.1.2.

	405482	41030	

JOHN DOE
PO BOX 9999
W BARNSTABLE, MA
HOME: 508-362-9999
BUS:

INVOICE

PAGE 1

SEARS AUTO SALES INC.
JEEP / EAGLE
499 Rt. 6A
E. Sandwich, MA 02537
(508) 888-0175 * 775-7972

SERVICE ADVISOR: 112 PATRICIA STARBARD

COLOR	YEAR	MAKE / MODEL	VIN	LICENSE	MILEAGE IN / OUT	TAG
MAROON	1990	JEEP CHEROKEE	1J4FJ58L0LL205432	639BBW	138000 / 138000	

DEL. DATE	PROD. DATE	WARR. EXP.	PROMISED	PO NO.	RATE	PAYMENT	INV.DATE
01JAN1990			16:30 10MAY99		60.00	CASH	10MAY1999

R.O. OPENED	READY	OPTIONS:
		STK: / 1) CHEROK
07:54 10MAY99	16:20 10MAY99	

LINE OPCODE TECH TYPE HOURS	LIST	NET	TOTAL

A CHECK FOR NOISE IN LOWER PART OF ENGINE - USUALLY WHEN WARM - RATTLE -
        SEE BRAD
    00   REPLACED ALTERNATOR
            110   CP   1.00   60.00   60.00
            1 JR775126 REMAN-ALTERNTR-   175.00   175.00   175.00
PARTS: 175.00   LABOR: 60.00   OTHER: 0.00   TOTAL LINE A: 235.00

        ****

B TAILGATE HATCH HAS A WATER LEAK - ROOF HINGE HAS MOVED SO THERE IS A
        GAP WHEN CLOSE DOOR - MOSTLY ON RIGHT SIDE
    00   RESEALED LIFTGATE WINDOW
            110   CP   1.00   60.00   60.00
PARTS: 0.00   LABOR: 60.00   OTHER: 0.00   TOTAL LINE B: 60.00

        ****

CUSTOMER PAY SHOP SUPPLIES FOR REPAIR ORDER   3.95
                        THANK YOU FROM SEARS AUTO SALES INC.
                        FOR AN APPOINTMENT CALL 508-888-0175
                        FAX # 508-888-8841

ON BEHALF OF SERVICING DEALER, I HEREBY CERTIFY THAT THE INFORMATION CONTAINED HEREON IS ACCURATE UNLESS OTHERWISE SHOWN. SERVICES DESCRIBED WERE PERFORMED AT NO CHARGE TO OWNER. THERE WAS NO INDICATION FROM THE APPEARANCE OF THE VEHICLE OR OTHERWISE, THAT ANY PART REPAIRED OR REPLACED UNDER THIS CLAIM HAD BEEN CONNECTED IN ANY WAY WITH ANY ACCIDENT, NEGLIGENCE OR MISUSE. RECORDS SUPPORTING THIS CLAIM ARE AVAILABLE FOR (1) YEAR FROM THE DATE OF PAYMENT NOTIFICATION AT THE SERVICING DEALER FOR INSPECTION BY MANUFACTURER'S REPRESENTATIVE.	STATEMENT OF DISCLAIMER The factory warranty constitutes all of the warranties with respect to the sale of this item/items. The Seller hereby expressly disclaims all warranties either express or implied, including any implied warranty of merchantability or fitness for a particular purpose. Seller neither assumes nor authorizes any other person to assume for it any liability in connection with the sale of this item/items.	DESCRIPTION	TOTALS
		LABOR AMOUNT	120.00
		PARTS AMOUNT	175.00
		GAS, OIL, LUBE	0.00
		SUBLET AMOUNT	0.00
		MISC. CHARGES	3.95
		TOTAL CHARGES	298.95
		LESS INSURANCE	0.00
		SALES TAX	8.95
(SIGNED) DEALER, GENERAL MANAGER, AUTHORIZED PERSON (DATE)	CUSTOMER SIGNATURE	**PLEASE PAY THIS AMOUNT**	**307.90**

CUSTOMER COPY

Fig. 1.2.1.2   Example of a complex sales order of an auto garage: status "billing."

This invoice is the result of an order that was placed previously within the same structure: usually in verbal, sometimes in written form.

- The heading contains company data and customer data, complemented by the characteristic object related to the service (the car). The delivery of services date is registered in the upper portion. As this is an invoice, the billing date is also given.

- The main body of the document includes entries for labor performed (identified and billed) and parts supplied. Quantity and price relate to definite defined units, such as pieces and hourly labor rates. The parts list lists the items used to complete the labor performed. These items may be listed as in-stock shop supplies or items ordered specially for the job. Comments on the invoice aid communication between customer and service provider.

- The footer of the invoice contains specific billing information, such as the total amount, broken down into the various charges, conditions of sales, and sales tax. Bids and order confirmations, or, in other words, the first and second statuses that preceded the billing status, would contain similar data.

1.2.2   Item, Item Family, Product Structure, and Product Family

> *Item* is a collective term for any good that can or must be identified or handled in the logistics of distribution, production, procurement, or recycling/disposal. Compare [APIC04].

From the company's perspective, the collective term "item" thus includes the following types of goods:

- An *end product* or *end item* or *finished good* is a completed item that generally does not serve as a component of another product.

- An *intermediate product* or a *semifinished good* is stored or awaits final operations in the production process. It can be used in the assembly of a higher level product and is thus also a component.

- An *assembly* or a *(product) module* is an intermediate product and is composed of at least two components (parts or subassemblies).

- A *part* or *single part* is either produced in-house (*in-house part*) or purchased (*purchased part*) and is used in an end item. An in-house part is produced from only one component.

- A *raw material* is, for the company, a purchased item or an original material that is converted via the manufacturing process.

- A *service part* or a *spare part* is a component that can be used without modification to replace a part or an assembly.

- A *MRO item* is an item for maintenance, repair, and operating supplies. It is an item for supporting activities in the company and is, in general, not used as a component for products.

All these goods are similar business objects insofar as the majority of their basic descriptions (or attributes) are of the same type, such as identification, description, inventory, costs, and price. They are often grouped together in a generalized object called an *item*. Figure 1.2.2.1 shows goods objects as special cases of the *item*.

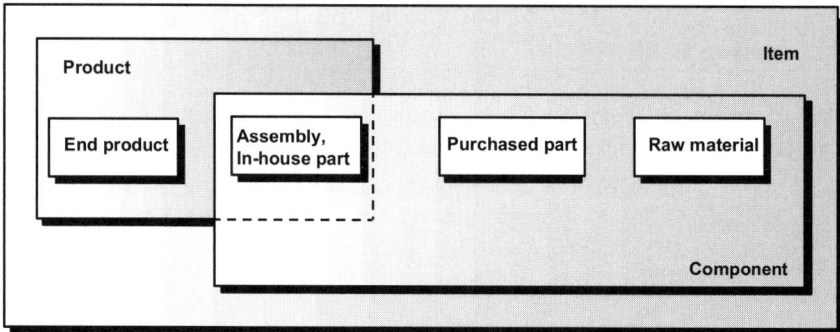

Fig. 1.2.2.1   The business object *item* as a generalization of various goods objects.

An *item family* is a group of items having similar features (such as form, material) or a similar function.

The total items belonging to an item family are seen as a (complex) business object, with the individual items as parts of the object. For example, different kinds of screws may be grouped together as an item family and viewed as the "family of screws."

Product structure is the structured list of components to be used in order to manufacture a product, understood as a whole-part hierarchy.

A *structure level*, or simply *level*, is assigned to every part or assembly in a product structure. It signifies the relative level in which that part or assembly is used within the product structure [APIC04].

The (structure) level stands in inverse relation to the relative depth of the components in the product structure. End products generally have the level 0. The direct components of an end product have the level 1. A component in an assembly has a level code one unit higher than the assembly.

> A *design structure level* is a structure level from the point of view of product design.
>
> *Bill of material* and *nomenclature* are other terms for a *convergent* product structure (in contrast to *divergent* product structure, where we usually speak of *recipes*; see also the definition of these differing concepts in Section 3.4.2).
>
> The *quantity required* or *quantity per* or *usage quantity* is the number of components per unit of measure of the next higher level product into which the component is built. The *cumulative quantity per* of each component in the end product is thus the product of quantities required along the product structure.

The example in Figure 1.2.2.2 shows a bill of material, that is, a convergent product structure with two (structure) levels.

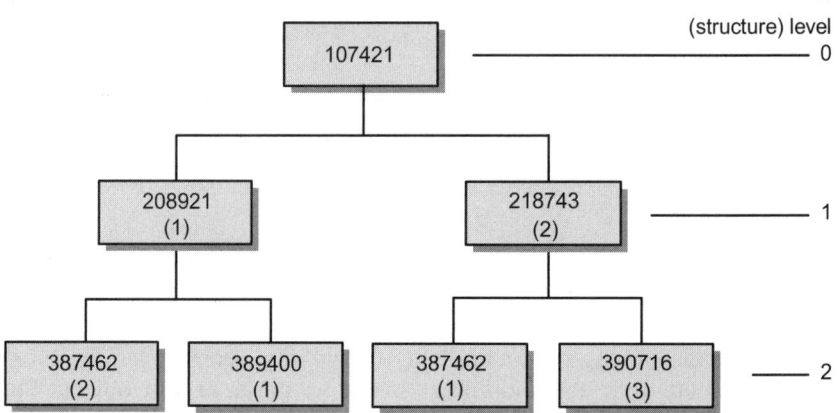

Fig. 1.2.2.2   A product structure (bill of material) with two (structure) levels.

Item 107421 is the end product composed of the two assemblies 208921 and 218743. Each assembly, in turn, has two components. The quantity required is given in parentheses. As an example of cumulative quantity per, in 107421 there are $2 \cdot 3 = 6$ components 390716.

The *low-level code* is a number that identifies the lowest level in any bill of material at which a particular component appears ([APIC04]).

The low-level code is generally calculated by a computer program.

A *product family* or *product group* or *product line* is a group of products having similar features (such as form or material) or similar functions, similar product structure with a high percentage of the same components or components from the same family, and a high percentage of the same processes in the process plan. Compare [APIC04].

A *variant*, a *product variant* or a *(product) option* is a specific product in a product family.

A *co-product* is a product that is usually manufactured together or sequentially because of product or process similarities ([APIC04]).

A *product hierarchy* is a division of products into families and subfamilies at various structure levels.

Product families are designed as such as early as the product design phase. Throughout its life cycle, it will be expanded where desired. The product structure of each variant is different, but according to its definition, it is based on a high percentage of the same components (modules). Product hierarchies are designed, in general, during sales planning.

1.2.3 Operation, Routing Sheet, Production Structure, and the Process Plan

Logistics is fundamental to an understanding of the problematic of delivery — particularly in terms of *short* lead times. The most detailed business object to examine is the operation. Factors affecting this building block of a business process have a strong influence on logistics.

An *operation* in logistics is a step in a process that is required for the design and manufacturing of a product. Another term used is *routing sheet position* or *basic manufacturing step*. Examples of operations are "cut," "stamp," or "bend" in industrial areas, or "serve," "maintain," "advise," or "repair" in service industries.

Setup or *changeover* is the work required to change or prepare the production infrastructure (machines, tools, and other resources) for the next order.

> *Operation time* is the time required to complete an operation. In the simplest case, operation time is the sum of:
>
> • *Setup time* or *setup lead time*, that is, the time required for setup, and
>
> • *Run time* for the actual work on the order.
>
> Run time is, in the simplest case, the product of:
>
> • The size of the *lot* or *batch*, that is, the number of the units of measure produced together, and
>
> • The *run time per unit*, that is, the total treatment time for one unit of the batch.

When the run times are planned as a series after setup time, the simplest formula for operation time is as shown in Figure 1.2.3.1.

> Operation time = (setup time) + (lot size) · (run time per unit)

Fig. 1.2.3.1   The simplest formula for operation time.

A length of time can refer to either planned or real manufacturing processes.

> *Standard time* or *standard hours* is the length of time that should be required to setup and run an operation. It assumes average efficiency of people and production infrastructure and is also frequently used as a basis for planning and incentive pay systems as well as a basis for allocating overhead costs.
>
> *Actual time* is the actual length of time for the execution of an operation in a particular order. It is often used as a basis for job-order costing

> The *routing sheet, operation sheet,* or *routing* of a product is a complex object; it is a list of the operations that are required to manufacture a particular item from its components. It includes information on the work centers involved (see the definitions in Section 1.2.4 and also [APIC04]).
>
> The *critical path* is the set of activities, or operations, that defines the (planned) duration of the network of operations. These activities usually have very little slack time, close or equal to zero.
>
> The *production lead time* or *manufacturing lead time* is the total time to manufacture an item, exclusive of lower level purchasing lead time.

Production lead time is measured along the critical path. It is made up of the three following categories of time:

- *Operation time*
- *Interoperation time*, which can occur either before or after an operation and may be
    - *Wait time*, that is, the time a job remains at a work center before or after execution of the operation, or
    - *Transportation time* (move time or transit time)
- *Administration time*, the time required to release and complete an order

Lead time projected on the basis of these three categories is a probable value only, because it is based on time averages, particularly for interoperation time. Wait times depend upon the current situation in production and its physical organization. In typical job shop production (see Section 3.4.3), interoperation time and administration time make up more than 80% of lead time and are thus its main determinants.

A sequence of operations is the simplest and most important order of the operations. A more complex order of the operations makes up a network or repeatedly executed sequences of operations (see Section 12.1.1).

> The *production structure* of a product is the combination of its product structure and the routing sheet for the product itself and for its assemblies and its single parts.

Through combining routing sheets with product structure in production structure, we gain a useful rationale for integration into a structure level, and thus for differentiating an intermediate product from a subsequent, higher structure level.

> A *production structure level* is a structure level that is determined by the arguments shown in Figure 1.2.3.2.

Within a production structure level there is no storage. A production structure level corresponds, therefore, to a logistics system whose part-processes are completed in the shortest possible lead time. This is the least amount of time required for value-adding. Components needed for this production structure level are drawn from storage or from the immediately preceding production structure level.

- The last operation results in a module, or semifinished good, that can be built into various further products as components.
- The last operation results in a semifinished good that is to be stored.
- The operations are required for a particular process technology.
- The last operation results in an intermediate state that is seen as an object or entity, that is, as a self-contained thing or object.

Fig. 1.2.3.2   Useful rationale for combining operations in a product structure level and thus for differentiating an intermediate product.

The *purchasing lead time* is the total time required to obtain a purchased item. Included here are order preparation and release time; the *supplier lead time* (that is, the amount of time that normally elapses between the time an order is received by a supplier and the time the order is shipped); transportation time; and receiving, inspection, and putting into storage (*put away time*) ([APIC04]).

The *cumulative lead time* or *aggregate lead time* or *critical path lead time* is the longest planned length of time to accomplish the value-adding activity in question, with respect to the time to deliver to the customer, the entire process plan — that is, the lead time for all production structure levels — as well as the purchase lead times.

Depending upon the context, *lead time* denotes either the cumulative lead time, the lead time required for one production structure level, or the purchasing lead time.

The *process plan* of a product is the total production structure on the time axis.

The process plan is a very complex business object that shows the cumulative lead time to manufacture a product. Figure 1.2.3.3 serves as an example for product P.

The process plan corresponds, as does product structure, to the way that the workers view customer order processing (their *scheme*, or natural conception of the process).

Lead-time offset is the moment of a resource requirement (component or capacity) relative to the completion date of a product, based on the lead time for that product ([APIC04]).

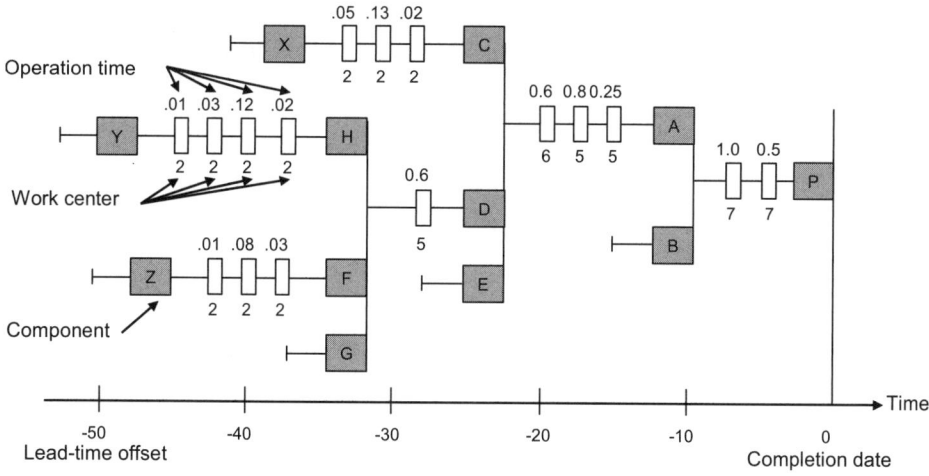

Fig. 1.2.3.3   Process plan for product P (detailed structure).

For each component, we can calculate the lead-time offset. To do this, the proportion of lead time must be calculated along the corresponding branch of the process structure. Throughout the total working process time, this time period is dependent upon batch size.

1.2.4   Employees, Production Infrastructure, Work Center, Capacity, and Utilization

Employees or *workers* in an enterprise are all those people involved directly and indirectly in a company's performance.

The *production infrastructure* is comprised of all available *production facilities*, that is factories and their workstations, as well as other production equipment.

A *workstation* is an assigned location where a worker performs the job; it can be a machine or a workbench ([APIC04]).

The *production equipment* includes machines, appliances, *devices* (such as jigs, fixtures), and tools.

Employees and the production infrastructure of an enterprise make up work centers:

A *work center* or *capacity center* or *load center* is an organizational unit of production within the chosen organization of the production infrastructure (see Section 3.4.3). It is comprised of the totality of employees and production infrastructure required to complete a quantity of work that is considered to be one unit for the purposes of higher level planning & control. Internal planning & control of a work center is not necessary or takes place autonomously under consideration of the higher level orders. Compare [APIC04].[8]

The *capacity* of a work center is its potential to produce output. This potential is always related to a time period. The unit of measure is called the *capacity unit*, and it is mostly a unit of time (hours of work).[9]

Theoretical capacity is the maximum output capacity, determined by the number of shifts, the number of workers or machines, and the theoretically available capacity per shift. Theoretical capacity can vary from week to week due to *foreseen*, overlapping changes, such as vacation time, additional shifts, overtime, or preventive maintenance requirements.

The *capacity profile* of a work center represents its capacity over time. Within a time period, this distribution may be represented graphically as rectangles rather than as along a continuum. This has proved to be a useful practice. See Figure 1.2.4.2.

Efficient use of capacity by workload is fundamental in logistics analyses and planning & control.

Load is the amount of work planned for or released to a facility, work center, or operation for a specific span of time, measured in capacity units.

To calculate load, we must first — once again, as in Section 1.2.3 — take a closer look at the detailed object *operation.*

Operation load is the work content of the operation, measured in the capacity unit of the work center carrying out the operation. In the simplest case, it is the sum of:

- *Setup load*, or the given work content of an operation independent of batch size, and

---

[8] The term *machine center* is used as a subset of work center, referring only to the machines and not to the totality of resources of a work center.
[9] There are other possible measures that could be used as the unit. See also Chapter 15 on activity-based costing.

- *Run load* of the actual batch size of the order.

The run load is the product of:

- The size of the *lot* or *batch*, that is, the quantity or number of the units of measure produced together, and
- The *run load per unit*, or the work content for one unit produced in the batch of the operation.

In analogy to the formula for operation time (Figure 1.2.3.1), the formula for operation load, in the simplest case, can be seen in Figure 1.2.4.1.

Operation load = (setup load) + (lot size) · (run load per unit)

Fig. 1.2.4.1   The simplest formula for operation load.

Load can refer to either planned or real manufacturing processes.

Standard load is the given, probable content of work.

Actual load is the actual content of work, the use of capacity by the content of work.

Standard load of an operation and actual load of an operation are defined in a similar way. The following definitions are again related to the work center.

Work center load is the sum of the load of all operations for orders processed by the work center.

The *load profile* or *load projection* of a work center is a display of work center load and capacity over a given span of time. See Figure 1.2.4.2.

(Capacity) utilization is a measure of how intensively a resource is being used to produce a good or service. Traditionally, it is the ratio of its actual load to its theoretical capacity.[10]

Figure 1.2.4.2 shows a typical picture of a load profile, under the assumption of continuous or rectangular distribution within a time period.

---

[10]   Here, capacity utilization refers to a work center. However, it can also refer to other resources and objects. See also the performance indicators in Figure 1.4.3.4.

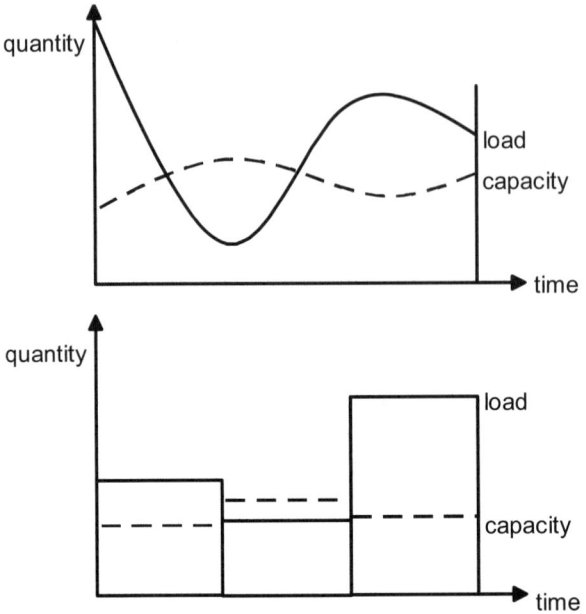

Fig. 1.2.4.2   The load profile of a work center (continuous and rectangular distribution).

Similar to product structure and the process plan, the load profile represents a schema, or natural conception, from the perspective of the people responsible for the processing of the production order.[11]

The lead time given in the process plan ignores the actual load of the work center, although capacity utilization can strongly influence queue times. But, for most planning methods, particularly for long-term planning, the "normal" lead time calculation based on the average duration of operations and interoperation times is sufficiently accurate. The shorter the planning term, the more important it is to consider load when calculating lead time.

For a more detailed analysis of the load profile, it is necessary to take a closer look at *capacity*.

Work center efficiency, or the *efficiency rate* of a work center, is a percentage, namely "standard load divided by actual load" or — equivalently — "actual units produced divided by standard units to

---

[11] It is also a common practice to set the capacity profile at 100%, that is, to make it the horizontal value and to express load as percentages thereof.

produce" (see [APIC04]). This is calculated as the average of all operations performed by a work center.

Rated capacity, or *calculated capacity*, is the expected output capability of a work center, that is, theoretical capacity multiplied by capacity utilization multiplied by work center efficiency.

An example of theoretical capacity and rated capacity, along with detailed explanations of the terms, is shown in Figure 13.1.1.1. The above definitions, however, provide a basis for understanding important aspects for planning & control:

Standard load to be scheduled should always refer to *rated capacity*. In order to compare capacity with *standard load*, the capacity profile should always show *theoretical capacity multiplied by efficiency*.

1.2.5 Rough-Cut Business Objects

Many tasks are so complicated that planning & control must make do with only general, rather than detailed, business objects. For example, in order to estimate the requirements for goods and capacity *quickly*, planning cannot reach the detail of the precise number of screws or the minutest task. For manufacturing purposes, sometimes only partial data are needed, because:

- Only relatively few purchased items, such as raw materials or semifinished goods, are expensive or difficult to procure (have very long procurement lead times).

- For a great percentage of work centers, load is not critical, because for technical reasons, over-capacity is the rule (for example, replacement machines or special machines that are not available with low capacity).

- Various processes are very short and do not affect the total load of a work center.

Furthermore, it can suffice to use item families or product families as the business object rather than individual items or products. In analogous fashion, the following rough-cut business objects may be defined:

Rough-cut product structure is the structured make-up of the product from its components, whereby both product and components may be an item or product family. For convergent product structure (see Section 3.4.2), the term *rough-cut bill of material* is also used.

A *rough-cut work center* is comprised of the total of work centers that do not have to be further differentiated by rough-cut planning & control.

A *rough-cut operation* is comprised of the total of operations, not further differentiated by rough-cut planning & control.

A *rough-cut routing sheet* for a product or product family is the overall chain of operations, not broken down further by rough-cut planning & control.

The *rough-cut production structure* of a product or product family is the combination of its rough-cut product structure and the rough-cut routing sheets of the product or product family itself, as well as associated (rough-cut) assemblies and single parts.

The *rough-cut process plan* of a product is the rough-cut production structure plotted on the time axis.

One way to derive a rough-cut resource requirement plan from a detailed resource requirement plan involves three steps:

1. Determine an item's item family. Determine the item families to be included for the rough-cut product structure.
2. Determine the work centers or rough-cut work centers to be included and assign the work centers to the rough-cut work center. Determine a time length for operation time under which a (rough-cut) operation can be omitted in a rough-cut structure. Instead, determine a percentage for the reduction of capacity that will be caused by these short operation times and use this percentage to take these into account.
3. Determine rough-cut product structure (rough-cut bill of material) and the rough-cut routing sheet for each product or product family, often by contraction of several structure levels into one.

Example: Figure 1.2.5.1 shows a rough-cut process plan that was derived from the detailed plan in Figure 1.2.3.3.

Taking the resource requirement plan in Figure 1.2.3.3, the following measures allowed formulation of the rough-cut process plan in Figure 1.2.5.1 (the numbered steps below refer back to steps one and two above):

1a. Purchased components X, Y, and Z form a single item family Y'.

1b. Component E is not included in the rough-cut structure.

1c. Components G and B form the single item family B'.

2a. Work center 6 is not included in the rough-cut structure.

2b. Work centers 5 and 7 join to form a single rough-cut work center 7'.

2c. All operations having an operation time of less than 0.1 hours are not included in the rough-cut structure.

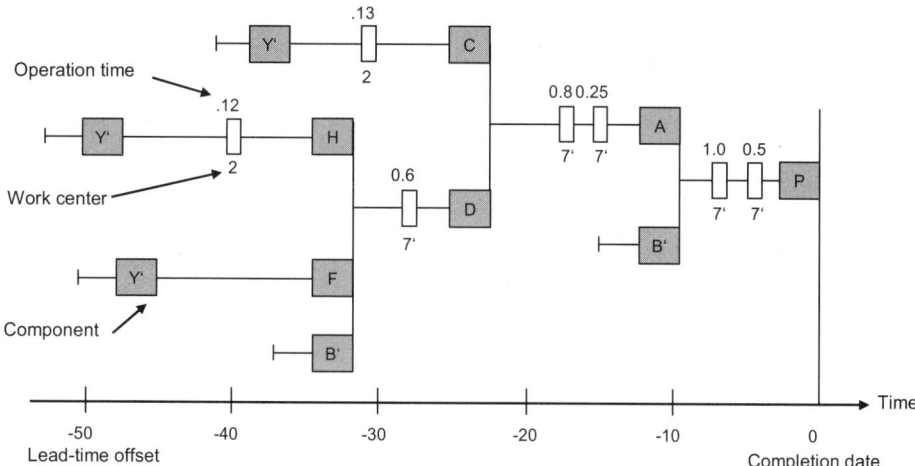

Fig. 1.2.5.1   Rough-cut process plan for product P.

The resulting rough-cut process plan must, of course, include (rough-cut) interoperation times, which are no longer apparent once individual (rough-cut) operations have been excluded. Otherwise, lead-time calculation will be unrealistic. Through including interim times, every (rough-cut) component gains realistic lead-time offset in relation to the completion date of the product. Setup time and setup load are divided by a norm batch size and added to run time and run load. The lead-time offset then refers to that batch size.

A *bill of resources* is a listing of the required key resources (components and capacities) needed to manufacture one unit of a selected product or product family.

A *product load profile* is a bill of resources where the resource requirements are defined by a lead-time offset.

In general, a product load profile is a one-level rough-cut bill of material and a one-level rough-cut routing sheet.

Example: Figure 1.2.5.2 shows two variants of a product load profile for the example in Figure 1.2.5.1. Notice the contraction to one structural level. To do this, lead-time offset must be calculated for each operation. The second variant additionally joins together all positions that load the same rough-cut resource within ten units of time. This further reduces the complexity of the rough-cut business object.

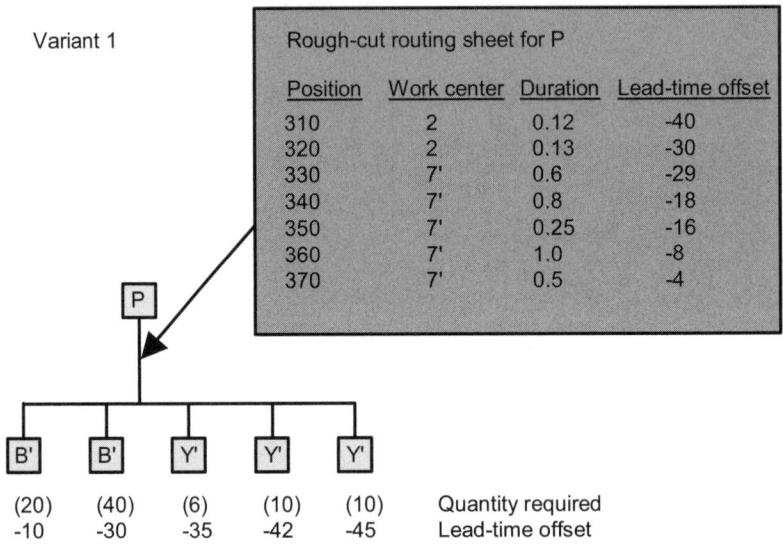

Variant 1

Rough-cut routing sheet for P

Position	Work center	Duration	Lead-time offset
310	2	0.12	-40
320	2	0.13	-30
330	7'	0.6	-29
340	7'	0.8	-18
350	7'	0.25	-16
360	7'	1.0	-8
370	7'	0.5	-4

(20)	(40)	(6)	(10)	(10)	Quantity required
-10	-30	-35	-42	-45	Lead-time offset

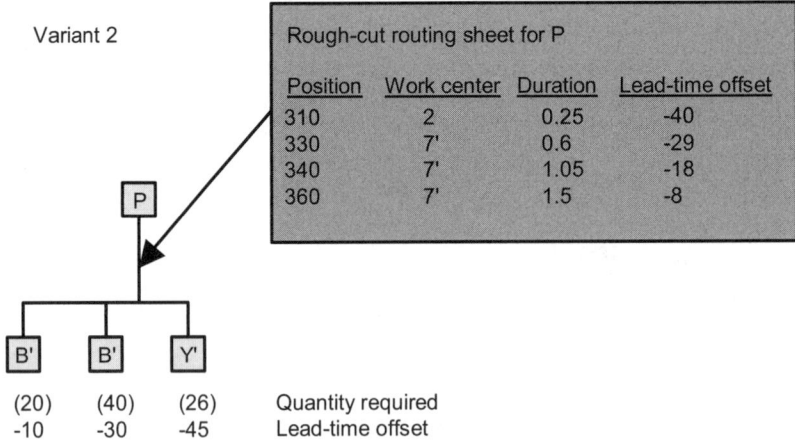

Variant 2

Rough-cut routing sheet for P

Position	Work center	Duration	Lead-time offset
310	2	0.25	-40
330	7'	0.6	-29
340	7'	1.05	-18
360	7'	1.5	-8

(20)	(40)	(26)	Quantity required
-10	-30	-45	Lead-time offset

Fig. 1.2.5.2   The product load profile: a one-level rough-cut bill of material and one-level rough-cut routing sheet.

In some cases it may be possible to derive rough-cut business objects from detailed business objects in a direct fashion. In difficult cases, this will require manual determination. In addition, rough-cut and detailed business objects must be modified synchronously. In terms of organization, this is difficult and expensive to accomplish. For this reason, rough-cut business objects are often kept so general that they will not be affected by changes in the detailed business object.

1.3   Logistics and Operations Management in the Entrepreneurial Context

Logistics, or operations management, is one of the management systems in the company[12] and can best be understood as a management system for performance. It is this aspect that is the special focus of this section. Particular attention will be paid to delivery, that is, high fill rate, delivery reliability, and short lead times. No other management system in the company focuses to this extent on this task.

As logistics, or operations, management accompanies the product life cycle companies, it is also seen as a process-oriented and therefore cross-department and cross-company task along the value-added chain, that is the supply chain.

In addition, logistics, or operations, management – like the other management systems in the company – is also concerned with how the various stakeholders of the company, in this case especially the business partners experience the way in which the tasks are handled.

1.3.1   The Contribution of Logistics and Operations Management to Resolving the Problem of Conflicting Company Objectives

A *company's performance* is comprised of the achievement of *company objectives* in the areas of quality, costs, delivery, and flexibility.

---

[12]   It is recommended that the reader refer to the introduction to Part C before reading this section.

In part, logistics has a significant influence on company objectives in all the four areas. This means that logistics affects a company's performance significantly.[13] Individual objectives are the same for logistics within a company and for all companies participating in a logistics network. Figure 1.3.1.1 identifies entrepreneurial objectives in these four areas, both main objectives and partial objectives.

• Target area quality:
• Main objective: to meet high demands for product quality
• Main objective: to meet high demands for process quality
• Main objective: to meet high demands for organization quality:
• Partial objective: high transparency of product, process, and organization

• Target area costs:
• Main objective: low physical inventory and low work in process
• Main objective: high capacity utilization
• Main objective: low cost rates for administration
• Partial objective: complete and detailed bases for calculation and accounting

• Target area delivery:
• Main objective: high fill rate (high customer service ratio or short delivery lead time)
• Main objective: high delivery reliability rate
• Main objective: short lead times in the flow of goods
• Partial objective: short lead times in the data and control flow

• Target area flexibility:
• Main objective: high degree of flexibility to enter as a partner in logistics networks
• Main objective: high degree of flexibility in achieving customer benefit, e.g., by product and process innovation (that is, by innovative power)
• Main objective: high degree of flexibility in the use of resources

Fig. 1.3.1.1   Company objectives affected by logistics.

A company's strategies and policies determine the relative weighting of target areas as well as individual objectives. These are strategies and

---

[13]   Performance includes more than *productivity* (that is, the actual output of production compared to the actual input of resources), measured by quality and costs, but less than *competitiveness*, which in addition includes the necessary economic environment.

policies with regard to product line, fill rate, partnership in a logistics network, "make or buy decisions," and distribution and supplier channels. The resulting *strategic plan* reflects company management's view of:

- The market and other companies in the market
- Product and service positioning[14] in the market segment
- The company's competitive advantages and product differentiation[15]
- Order qualifiers and order winners[16]
- The type of production and procurement

The surrounding systems that influence the company's perspective include economic considerations (such as the relationship between supply and demand), probable customer behavior (whether the products will be seen as investment goods or consumer goods, for example), competition, available suppliers, the costs of short- and long-term financing, and expected economic and political trends.

The actual quantitative weighting of these areas and objectives represents a challenge to the company. Objectives are not readily comparable. One method of comparison is to translate objectives outside of the area of costs into monetary values.

Opportuneness is the suitability of an action in a particular situation. *Opportunity cost* is defined by [APIC04] as the return on capital that could have resulted had the capital been used for some purpose other than its present use.

---

[14]   *Product* or *service positioning* is the marketing effort involved in placing a product or a service in a market for a particular niche or function ([APIC04]).

[15]   A *competitive advantage* is an edge, i.e., a process, patent, management philosophy, or system that enables the company to have a larger market share or profit than it would have without that advantage. *Product differentiation* is a strategy of making a product different — the best or unique — from the competition with regard to at least one feature or goal of a target area (compare [APIC04]).

[16]   *Order qualifiers* are those competitive characteristics that a firm must exhibit to be a viable competitor in the marketplace. This means that the firm has to be within a certain range in all four target areas, even when it may be leading in a specific target area. *Order winners* are those competitive characteristics that cause a firm's customer to choose that firm's goods and services. They can be considered as competitive advantages and focus on one, rarely two, of the four target areas (compare [APIC04]).

Opportunity costs arise when for some reason customer demand cannot be fulfilled. In this case, the invested capital is used for something other than the gain that would have been made through meeting customer demand. Such costs result if company objectives with regard to concrete demand have not been weighted appropriately.

As an example of translating non-cost objectives into monetary values in order to determine the opportunity cost, let us take the main objective of high fill rate. What does it cost to be unable to deliver? There can be loss of:

1. The non-deliverable order item.
2. The complete order, even though other items can be delivered.
3. The customer, even if other orders can be filled.
4. All customers, due to the company's resulting poor reputation.

This example shows how difficult it is to determine opportunity cost. Translating other non-cost objectives into monetary values is just as complex. Thus, the weighting of objectives is unquestionably a company-level matter that must be conducted within the framework of the normative and strategic orientation of the enterprise. Determining opportunity cost determines at the same time the relationship between company objectives in the four areas listed above and *primary company objectives* (such as to maximize return in investment or "shareholder value").[17]

In contrast to objectives in the areas of costs and delivery, logistics and planning & control, in particular, have only a limited influence upon the achievement of company objectives with regard to quality and flexibility.

- *Target area quality:* Whenever many people need to work together efficiently, products and services — and the processes producing them — have to be declared as explicit business objects, which is also a requirement for effective logistics. Products, processes, and organization then become transparent and understandable to all involved. But this is just one of the prerequisites to quality. Clearly product and process design as well as the choice of production infrastructure, employees, and partners in the logistics network are the main determinants of the quality of products, processes, and the organization.

---

[17] A particular goal in the four areas does not always support the company's primary objectives. For example, if efforts to reduce lead time do not result in increased demand or a larger share of the market, then return decreases rather than increases.

- *Target area flexibility:* The main objectives listed above are certainly the most significant with regard to the influence of logistics. The flexibility to enter as a partner into logistics networks is, first of all, a question of the total culture of an enterprise. The potential for flexibility in achieving customer value, as for quality, develops through product and process design and the choice of production infrastructure. Flexibility in the use of resources is determined initially by the qualifications of personnel and by the choice of product infrastructure. In each case, efficient logistics allows flexible use of the potentials developed in day-to-day production.

Some possible strategies, shown as example profiles in Figure 1.3.1.2, illustrate clearly that the four target areas result in a potential for conflicts among objectives. There are even conflicts within the area of costs itself.[18]

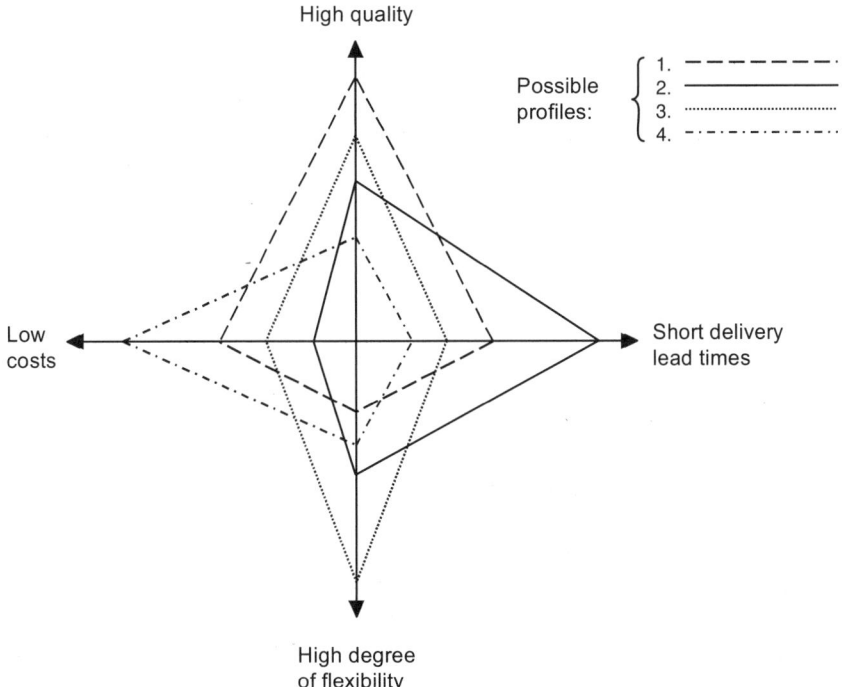

Fig. 1.3.1.2   Potential for conflicting entrepreneurial objectives.

---

[18]   Reduction of inventory and of work in process with a simultaneous increase of capacity utilization can result in goal conflict, as we will show later.

The four profiles in Figure 1.3.1.2 show the potential for conflicts among objectives:

1. High quality of product or process tends to result in high costs and long lead times. There is also a tendency towards repeatable processes, and thus to a low degree of flexibility.

2. The shorter the delivery lead times, the higher the costs: to achieve short delivery lead times, stock or over-capacity is a must. Short lead times can result in reductions in quality and flexibility (for example, scope of variants).

3. A high degree of flexibility in achieving customer value, through scope of variants for example, leads either to long delivery lead times (as little inventory can be stocked) or, due to unusable inventory of product variants, to high costs.

4. Low costs, due to high capacity utilization and simultaneous avoidance of stock, result in long delivery lead times and reductions in quality and flexibility in the range of goods.

Resolving the problem of the conflicting objectives of "high fill rate" versus "low costs for inventory on stock and in process" is one of the main tasks of logistics and operations management. In this well known conflict, the evaluation of the opportunity costs due to a lower fill rate leads to the determination of the (customer) order penetration point.

> The *(customer) order penetration point (OPP)* is a key variable in a logistics configuration; it is the point in time at which a product becomes earmarked for a particular customer. Downstream from this point, the system is driven by customer orders; upstream processes are driven by forecasts and plans ([APIC04]).

Figure 1.3.1.3 shows the situation applied to the process plan of Figure 1.2.3.3, reduced to the product structure in the time axis. The issue here is the relation of customer tolerance time to cumulative lead time.

If the customer tolerance time is at least as long as the cumulative lead time, the product can be engineered, procured, produced, or delivered when actual demand in the form of a customer order is placed. Otherwise, all goods (such as semifinished goods, single parts, raw materials, and information) from which the end product cannot be manufactured and delivered within the customer tolerance time must be ordered *before* there is known demand. The goods must all be procured and stocked on the basis of demand forecast. If the customer tolerance time is zero, the end product must be procured before demand is known. This is the same as stocking the end product in a warehouse.

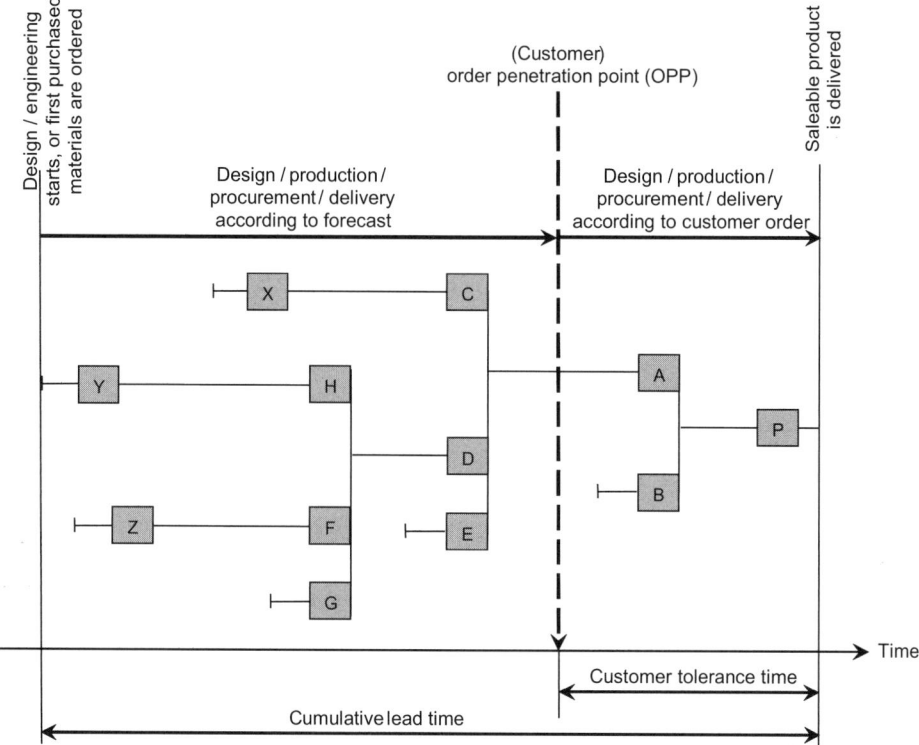

Fig. 1.3.1.3   The (customer) order penetration point.

Thus, the OPP corresponds to a level in the product structure where stocking occurs.

> The *level of stocking* defines that level in the bill of material above which a product can be engineered, procured, produced, or delivered within the customer tolerance time. For goods below and at the level of stocking, no exact demand is known. Demand forecast is required.

Therefore, the order penetration point entails decoupling points, each with its decoupling inventory. In general, decoupling points in the product structure are items downstream from the OPP with at least one direct component upstream from the OPP. In the example of Figure 1.3.1.3, item A is the only decoupling point. It is downstream from the OPP, whereas its direct components C, D, and E are upstream from the OPP.

1.3.2   The Target Area Flexibility – Agile Companies

Flexibility is the capability to adapt to new, different, or changing requirements [MeWe03].

In the literature, the above very general definition is specialized in various directions:

- Various subtypes of flexibility. The above definition of the target area of flexibility comprises three different subtypes of flexibility, which build up potentials so that later, objectives in the target areas quality, costs, and delivery can be better fulfilled. [APIC04] distinguishes six categories of flexibility. [Gots06] provides a comprehensive list of types of flexibility.

- Aspects of flexibility that mostly are meant to describe the company. It is common to use adjectives like lean, agile, adaptable, changeable, resilient (see [Shef05]) and the corresponding nouns. The examples that are given for these terms are all quite similar, and they can be understood as flexibility potentials. As an example, agility is discussed in the following.

Agility is defined in [MeWe03] as ability to move; dexterity. Agility according to [GoNa94] is the capability to take advantage of a competitive environment where insecurity dominates and that differs structurally from mass production.

Agile manufacturing refers to the building up of potentials or scope (or "play") in the right place at the right time and in the right amount.

Agile companies are companies that apply the principles of agile manufacturing to all areas in their organizations.

Increasingly, the predominant consumer market demands agile competitors and individualized production even of consumer goods. What the consumer buys is more solutions and values than pre-defined functions, whereby the product is ever more frequently defined only in direct interaction with the customer. The behavior of the consumer is more spontaneous and less predictable. Clearly identifiable market segments will disappear, and brand names will serve increasingly to reflect the personality of the customer instead of providing a function as they used to do.

Agile competitors [PrGo97] are competitors who understand how to remain competitive by means of *proactive* amassing of information, knowledge, know-how and competency.

Crucial factors for agile competitors are thus information, knowledge, know-how, and competency. Agile companies develop potentials and scope that the customer does not see (and thus does not recognize as value-adding). Here are some examples:

- *Short term*: Formation of multiple parallel executions of orders and running order coordination by the different partners in the logistics network linked by pull logistics (see Section 3.2.1); establishment of overlapping activities in part-processes to coordinate push logistics (see Section 3.2.2). Each of these makes possible rapid business processes of high quality.

- *Medium to long term*: Building a staff capable of qualitatively flexible work assignments by means of training qualifications and coordination in groups; setting up a production infrastructure that can be implemented flexibly. Both measures lead to flexibility in the use of resources.

- *Medium term*: Building over-capacity or quantitatively flexible capacity and/or goods in stock. Either of these measures allows a response to unplanned demand or shifts in demand with short delivery lead times. In the production of capital goods, capacity measures that reduce ordering deadlines take precedence.

- *Medium term*: Development of competency in proactive service. The producer gathers information on the product in the user phase. By evaluating this information, the maker is in a position to recognize changes in customer demands. He can — proactively — offer an upgrade or new product, even before the customer is aware of need. In this way, he sells to the customer a solution rather than a single product. The customer feels cared for (total care).

- *Long term*: Development of know-how and methods to develop and manufacture products in manifold variants. This knowledge allows flexibility in achieving customer benefit. The maker is able to give positive answers to customer requests at crucial moments, which increases bid proposal and order success rate.

- *Long term*: Developing know-how and methods in reconfiguring the organization. This knowledge allows the flexibility to enter into cooperation as a partner into a logistics network. According to the product, departments take on a new structure and cooperate with other organizations. Thus, for example, a company can become a partner of a virtual enterprise at just the right moment.

Automation with broad implementation of basic technologies allowing worldwide direct transfer of data supports agility. Useful here are fax and

EDI[19] — e.g., an EDIFACT interface[20] — but also the Internet and corresponding company-internal Intranets and transcorporate Extranets. Here are some examples:

- *Multiple parallel order execution by several independent partners in the logistics network:* E-mail (electronic mail) over the Internet is used for worldwide order coordination. One distribution mailbox can store all addresses of those involved in the logistics network. Informal inquiries to this mailbox as to order status — and answers — are thus immediately available to all partners in the logistics network.

- *Running order coordination:* Transport companies supply the customer with information on the exact location of their goods ("tracking and tracing") via the Internet and the World Wide Web. This occurs in the ideal case through self-identification of goods by means of attached transponders (e.g. the RFID technique).

- *Proactive service:* Automobile manufacturers have access to the product and service data bank of their customers via service centers. Their own data banks then allow effective evaluation of the "life data" of the product during the user phase.

- *Competency to develop and produce products in manifold variants:* In jeans or shoe stores, customer measurements are taken and transmitted directly to production workshops. A few days or weeks later, the customer receives the finished, made-to-order product. Or, a customer may configure a specific insurance policy directly on the web site of an insurance company. He simply types in the desired parameters, which he may then vary according to need.

- *Competency in reconfiguring the organization:* Partners within a specific logistics network transmit order data using mutually configured software. The data are used directly to control processes (such as in machines). In the manufacture of cars or airplanes, the partners represent their business objects in a standardized form. To this purpose, they long ago developed

---

[19] *Electronic data interchange (EDI)* is a term for the transmission of trading documents, such as purchase orders, shipment notices, and invoices, via telecommunications.

[20] *EDIFACT* (electronic data interchange for administration, commerce, and transport) is a set of United Nations rules for EDI. The data are standardized in such a way that all companies involved in the order exchange can process them in the same format.

special standards of EDI, among others IGES (later STEP, for engineering purposes) and EDIFACT with its variations (Odette in the automotive industry, for example) for sales order processing.

1.3.3   Logistics and Planning & Control within the Company

The importance of the following sublogistics will depend upon the type of company and its activities. The logistics will take the form of either business processes as such or as partial processes.

- *Sales and distribution logistics* begins and ends with the final user or consumer. It is comprised of, as partial logistics: (1) actual *sales logistics*, or tasks pertaining to offer and sales order;[21] (2) *distribution logistics*, encompassing tasks from the finished product to the final user; and (3) *service and maintenance logistics*, which follows investment goods, in particular, throughout their further life cycle.

- *Research and development logistics* (called R&D logistics) manages tasks along the chain of "research — design — product and manufacturing process development — conception and procurement of production facility — prototyping." The importance of research and design logistics is on the rise due to customer-order-oriented product and process design, which often makes up more than half of the delivery lead time of a customer order. To obtain a short lead time, product and process design must be included in the logistics design from the start. This is usually achieved in a project-oriented manner.

- *Procurement logistics* and *production logistics* are tasks in *purchasing* and in *production* up to the provision of saleable output. Traditionally, this has included all tasks and processes involved in moving (transporting, cargo handling, picking (putting together all items of an order), and storing goods,[22] but *not* tasks and processes that result in the physical transformation of the goods. This narrow

---

[21] Offer and sales orders require logistics processes that cost time and money: on the one hand, the customer receives information and, on the other, information is processed in order to provide the resources for subsequent production and procurement on time. Comprehensive logistics always extends "from customer to customer": bid processing and sales order processing are partial processes within this more comprehensive business process.

[22] This is, by the way, a possible definition of logistics — that is, logistics in the narrow sense, in contrast to the definition in a wide sense chosen for Section 1.1.2.

definition has survived. Actually, production processes that change goods physically or in content have a great influence upon the choice of logistics systems and their efficiency. With the demand for short total lead times, production processes must be a part of logistics planning — by the company producing the goods as well as by suppliers.

- *Disposal logistics* handles the flow to disposal-preparation maintenance, to taking back, to disassembly, and to recycling. For material goods, the importance of disposal logistics is currently increasing due to depleting resources as well as to overloaded waste depots. Companies differ in their motivation in this area. Some are forced to act by legislation, and others view action as a strategy towards success. Significant areas of disposal logistics are handled today more pragmatically than systematically. To a large extent, planning and control in practice and in research continues to be *ad hoc*.

A different categorization of logistics is based upon the content of the task.

Physical logistics includes the moving and storing of goods, but also physical control and content verification of the flow of goods (material and information) that lead to the saleable product. Automatic instruments are frequently used to control these processes.

Administrative and planning logistics, also known as *information logistics*, *logistics planning and control,* or simply *planning & control*:[23]

- *Administrative logistics* handles tasks in sales order processing with regard to documents, movement of goods, or inventory (projects, sales orders, stock, and so on). It also supplies the data for accounting and statistics.

- *Planning logistics* refers to decision tasks that affect physical and administrative logistics. When, how, and in what quantities will goods be produced or procured? Will inventory be inserted between storehouse and production factors? What personnel and what assets will be used? When will delivery take place to customers and subsidiaries?

---

[23] The term "control" should not be interpreted in a technical sense as complete mastery of a controlled process. In a company organization, the term indicates regulation or even just coordination. Due to the established use of the term (for example, "production planning and control"), however, we maintain it here. Transcorporate tasks in the logistics chain also require planning & control.

In the following, we will use the term *planning & control* for administrative and planning logistics.

Figure 1.3.3.1 shows the sublogistics discussed above.

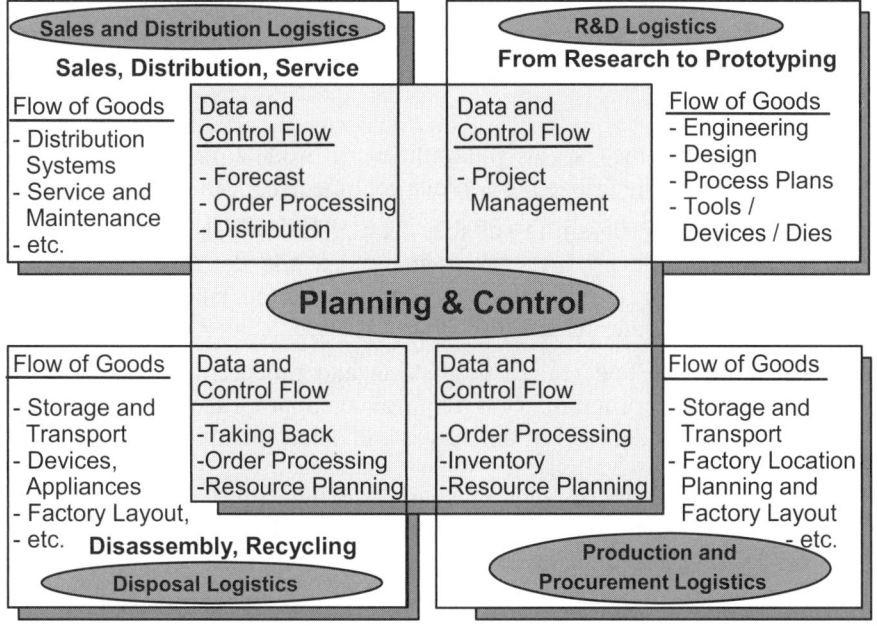

Fig. 1.3.3.1   Relation between logistics and planning & control.

A system for planning & control is frequently called *PPC*, or *production planning and control*. But this term is too restrictive. Because of the comprehensive nature of the task, the term *logistics* is more suitable than the term *production*.[24] The term *PPC* also leads to misunderstandings, because the term *PPC system* is used to refer both to the logistics task and to computer software supporting the task. These two meanings are often mixed deliberately. Upon the background of misplaced optimism with regard to logistics software, demagogues — when the use of logistics software fails — tend to declare that the entire scientific body of knowledge on planning & control is "useless." They overlook the fact that

---

[24]   MPC (manufacturing planning and control) is another classic abbreviation. In the world of practice, it is used, as is PPC, in a pragmatic, comprehensive sense for logistics. See [VoBe97].

the primary responsibility for understanding methods and their practical application always falls upon the people in the company. Chapter 8, on logistics software, will examine these issues in more detail.

As mentioned in Section 1.3.1, operations management has to weigh the various entrepreneurial objectives and implement them. Once this is done, planning & control in the logistics network and within a company entails a number of principles, methods, and procedures in order to accomplish the following tasks:

- Evaluate the various possibilities of production and procurement that may be utilized to achieve set objectives.

- Create a program in suitable detail. This will include decisions as to saleable products, their quantities, and deadlines. Such plans must be revised periodically in response to changing internal or external determinants.

- Elaborate and realize production and procurement plans derived from the program. This requires an appropriate degree of detail and consideration of objectives and determinants.

This is an integral task that must include the entire logistics network. Within the company and in all companies involved, all logistics partial processes must be integrated (logistics tasks in sales and distribution, research and development, procurement, production, service and maintenance, and disposal).

1.3.4   The Objectives of Transcorporate Logistics and Operations Management

Corporate logistics has a significant influence on enterprise objectives in the areas of quality, costs, delivery, and flexibility. In fact, most approaches to measuring logistics performance focus on these four target areas of company performance. Transcorporate, or inter-company, logistics management extends the perspective to performance of a supply chain, or a value-added network.

Three target areas for supply chain performance can be identified, following [Hieb01]:

- *Supply chain collaboration:* The ability to work together and act collaboratively in a win–win partnership to fulfill (final) customer demand in a logistics network. All activities should be directed towards overall optimization of the logistics network.

- *Supply chain coordination*: The ability of logistics network partners to coordinate and communicate efficiently in daily operations. Organizations, people, and systems must all have access to relevant logistics information regardless of organization, location, or company.

- *Supply chain changeability:* The ability to achieve high potential of flexibility in (re-)configuration of the supply chains among the partners in the network by means of practicing and sharing logistics know-how, capabilities, routines, and skills, as well as leveraging ideas and visions.

These network performance target areas aim to achieve the overall optimum of a logistics network. Ultimately they contribute to improvements in transcorporate as well as corporate logistics with respect to quality, costs, delivery, and flexibility. Figure 1.3.4.1 lists the fundamental objectives within each target area of supply chain performance.

• Target area supply chain collaboration:
• Main objective: to achieve a high degree of strategic alignment in the supply chain
• Main objective: to achieve highly integrated business processes, both in planning and in execution

• Target area supply chain coordination:
• Main objective: to achieve seamless goods, data, and control flow among the supply chain partners
• Main objective: to achieve a high degree of information transparency

• Target area supply chain changeability:
• Main objective: to achieve a high degree of flexibility in (re-)configuration of supply chains for customer responsiveness

Fig. 1.3.4.1   Performance target areas in supply chains (according to [Hieb01]).

The network-level objectives in Figure 1.3.4.1 aim to enable performance excellence (and are called *enablers* or *enabler objectives*). Like company objectives in the target area of flexibility, they are higher-level, or meta-level, objectives that set the direction of what is done; enablers are the approaches that drive the network towards performance. Enablers are ways to achieve the following *results* or *results objectives* at the network level:

- *Target area supply chain collaboration:* Focusing on overall optimization of the supply chain — rather than on local optimization within companies' boundaries — will contribute to reduced friction losses and thus to reduced supply chain lead times and reduced transaction costs.

- *Target area supply chain coordination:* Seamless flow will reduce total inventory levels and yield higher efficiency of resource utilization, higher inventory turns, higher delivery reliability, and faster logistics decision making at the network level.

- *Target area supply chain changeability:* The flexibility objective will cause quicker time-to-market, higher customer responsiveness, and maximized value delivered to the final customer.

These results objectives are of course similar to the results accomplished in the target area of flexibility at the company level: quality, cost, and delivery. In fact, these are aggregated objectives at the level of the supply chain.

The target areas of logistics networks thus extend the current perspective towards a more integral view. The network can best assess and measure progress in these areas using common transcorporate, or supply chain performance indicators. See Section 1.4.6.

In true profit centers, or decentralized organizations, the organizational units of a company act as independent companies in matters of logistics. It then makes no difference whether internal or external companies make up the logistics network. Accordingly, a planning and control system will suit for both an internal and transcorporate logistics network. Particularly appropriate for this case are systems for pull logistics.

In true cost centers, or centralized organizations, the organizational units act as parts of a single logistics system with regard to logistics requirements. Again, it makes no difference whether internal or external companies are involved in the supply chain. And, again, a planning and control system is appropriate for both an internal and transcorporate logistics network. Systems for push logistics are particularly suitable here.

In both cases, inventory processes can (or should) be fed into the logistics network (see also Section 3.2.3). From a process-oriented viewpoint, these should not, however, merely serve to correct disturbances or lack of flexibility in the logistics network, but rather — as described in Section 1.1.2 — should support synchronization between user and manufacturer. From this, it follows that (Figure 1.3.4.2):

In analyzing present logistics, one should view the supply chain in a comprehensive way, that is, over the entire chain from development and manufacture to the user. This way of proceeding evaluates automatically the necessity of stock and determines its correct place in the network.

Fig. 1.3.4.2   Rule for a comprehensive view of the supply chain.

Linkable planning and control systems become required as soon as cooperation increases in intensity. The demands again do not differ from those of purely internal company supply chains. In both cases, human beings must first of all work well together. Where there is computer support, logistics software must also be able to be linked and integrated — something that is also not always easy within one and the same company.

It follows, to take an exact position, that (Figure 1.3.4.3):

The choice of the system, methods, and concepts of planning and control is in principle not dependent upon whether a supply chain is realized only internally or among companies.

Fig. 1.3.4.3   Rule of choosing planning and control systems in a supply chain.

Thus, each of the concepts of planning and control can be implemented in the entire supply chain either within a single company or among companies. What is important is that all participants work according to the same principles. In the world of practice, problems result if the cultures in the companies participating in the supply chain differ, and a profit center, for example, must work with a cost center organization. The same problems arise for semi-autonomous organizational units, if the degree of autonomy in a supply chain differs too widely.

1.4   Performance Measurement in Logistics and Operations Management

A *performance indicator* or *performance criterion* is the specific characteristic to be measured for estimating the concerned performance.

A *performance measurement system* collects, measures, and compares a measure to a standard for a specific performance indicator.

> A *performance measure*, or *performance measurement*, is the actual value measured for the indicator ([APIC04]).

Appropriate indicators for the performance of a company are meant to show the degree to which enterprise objectives (see Figure 1.3.1.1) are fulfilled or not fulfilled.

> *Logistics performance indicators* analyze the effect of logistics on company objectives in the four target areas of quality, cost, delivery, and flexibility.

Descriptions of logistics performance indicators can be found in [OdLa93] or [FoBl91], Ch. 5. We discuss some of these in the following. Whenever possible, a logistics performance indicator will give direct indication of fulfillment of one of the individual objectives within a target area. A performance indicator relates to a logistics object and thus becomes an attribute of that object — and sometimes it becomes a logistics object in its own right.

> *Global measures* are a set of indicators to measure the overall performance of a company (such as cash flow, throughput, utilization, inventories).
>
> *Local measures* are a set of indicators that relate to a single resource or process and usually have a small influence on global measures (i.e., volume discount on an item, lead time for stock entries, utilization of a storage location).

In the following, we introduce a balanced set of *global* measures *from a logistics perspective*. This balance is one of the requirements of the *balanced scorecard*, an approach in finance that pointed out the prevalent one-sidedness of performance indicators in the financial sector, which (too) often only refer to primary objectives of the company in relation to return (see [KaNo92] and the discussion regarding opportunity cost in Section 1.3.1). A systematical derivation of the balanced set of performance indicators from the company's strategy can be found in [Schn07]. Together with indicators from other areas of the enterprise, such as finance, marketing, and research and development, the logistics indicators form a complete set of measurements of performance and provide a basis upon which company performance can be improved, via continuous process improvement (CPI).

1.4.1   The Basics of the Measurement, Meaning, and Practical Applicability of Logistics Performance Indicators

In actual practice, the *measuring of logistics performance* varies in difficulty and usually requires that certain aspects be counted. With the exception of local measures, it is generally not possible to assess these aspects without expending a lot of time and energy. In addition, integrating and compressing the local measures into global measures, covering several levels for example, can be very problematic.

The following sums up central problems in terms of the meaning and practical applicability of performance indicators in the form of practical methods. The problems are typical of any quality measurement system and, in part, costing systems as well.

- *General performance indicators:* Simple, measurable performance indicators are often so general and qualitative in meaning that no practical steps can be derived from them without making additional, non-quantitative, and implicit assumptions. An example of such a performance indicator is *customer satisfaction*.

- *Lack of comprehensive measurement methods:* Simple, applicable performance indicators often cannot be measured directly. They require various, sometimes complicated or inexact measurements that are then combined with non-measured, implicit methods to yield the desired performance indicator. A good example is flexibility potential.

- *Distortion of the processes:* Each measurement affects the process being measured. The disturbance can be so great that the process would behave differently under non-measurement conditions.

- *Meaning of the performance indicators:* The absolute value of a performance indicator has little meaning as such. Only repeated comparison of measurements of the same performance indicator over time can make the performance indicator an instrument of continuous process improvement (CPI).

- *Comparability of performance indicators:* Benchmarking, the measuring of a company's products, services, costs, and so on against those of competitors, has meaning only if the competitor has used the same bases of measurement. In practice, it is common to find that companies use different *reference objects*, the objects to which certain performance indicators refer. An example is *fill rate* or *customer service ratio* (see Section 1.4.4). Fill rate can refer to either order positions or items; its measurement can be based on quantity units or value units. Before making comparisons, therefore, it is essential to know how another enterprise defines the performance indicator.

- *Practical applicability in logistics networks:* Many performance indicators can be applied in the total logistics network as well as in the individual company. Because the companies forming a logistics network follow the same principal objectives, logistics performance indicators should be comparable in the main. However, careful confirmation of exact comparability remains indispensable.

It makes sense to weigh the value of the potential application of the measurement against the expenditure in time and effort required by measurement. In the world of practice, a few, simply measured performance indicators have proven worthwhile. Employees must then apply the measurement using a multitude of means that cannot be directly derived from the measurement.

1.4.2   Performance Indicators in the Target Area of Quality

The influence of logistics on the target area of quality is rather small. But some performance indicators arise from logistics itself, particularly scrap factors and complaint rates of all kinds. With scrap factors, mistakes are discovered during customer order processing. Complaints, however, come from the customer. In both cases, the causes can be many and difficult to pinpoint. They may be even caused by insufficient quality of information.

There is a relationship between complaint rate and scrap factor. The source of a complaint may turn out to be parts or components that, discovered sooner, would have qualified as scrap. Scrap can lead to customer complaints. The yield factor is complementary to the scrap factor. Hence, for a given reference object, the scrap factor plus the yield factor is equal to 1.

Indicator	Scrap factor (or yield factor)
Definition	Number of rejected (or accepted) facts divided by number of facts
Reason for measuring	A high scrap factor indicates insufficient quality and leads to opportunity cost
Reference object	(a) process, (b) components, (c) part logistics (e.g. production)
Fact to measure	For (a): item demand or order position For (b) and (c): order position or order

Fig. 1.4.2.1   The indicators *scrap factor* and *yield factor.*

Indicator	Complaint rate
Definition	Number of rejected facts divided by number of facts
Reason for measuring	A high complaint rate indicates insufficient quality and leads to opportunity cost
Reference object	(a) item, (b) business partner, (c) part logistics (such as sales)
Fact to measure	For (a): item demand or order position For (b) and (c): order position or order

Fig. 1.4.2.2   The indicator *complaint rate.*

1.4.3   Performance Indicators in the Target Area of Costs

The influence of logistics in the target area of costs is significant. Some performance indicators are the direct measure of the target objectives involved. For a discussion of the terms, definitions, and arguments, see Sections 1.2.1, 1.2.3, and 1.2.4.

Indicator	Stock-inventory turnover
Definition	Annual cost of inventory issues (i.e., sales) divided by average inventory
Reason for measuring	Carrying cost increases as average inventory increases or stock-inventory turnover decreases
Reference object	(a) item and item group, (b) time period
Fact to measure	Annual inventory issues and average inventory (e.g., based on standard cost)

Fig. 1.4.3.1   The performance indicator *stock-inventory turnover.*

Indicator	Work-in-process-inventory turnover
Definition	Sales divided by average work in process
Reason for measuring	Production infrastructure costs increase for high level work in process and low work-in-process-inventory turnover
Reference object	(a) work center, (b) time period, (c) combination of the two
Fact to measure	Sales and work in process (e.g., based on cost price)

Fig. 1.4.3.2   The performance indicator *work-in-process-inventory turnover.*

Indicator	Work center efficiency
Definition	Standard load divided by actual load = actual units produced divided by standard units to produce
Reason for measuring	High work center efficiency leads to lower costs through better use of investment costs
Reference object	(a) work center, (b) time period, (c) combination of the two
Fact to measure	Load by production orders (planned and actual, for setup and run)

Fig. 1.4.3.3   The performance indicator *work center efficiency.*

Indicator	Capacity utilization
Definition	Actual load divided by theoretical capacity (= standard load divided by efficiency rate divided by theoretical capacity)
Reason for measuring	High capacity utilization leads to lower costs through better use of investment costs
Reference object	(a) work center, (b) time period, (c) combination of the two
Fact to measure	Load by production orders (planned and actual, for setup and run), work center capacity

Fig. 1.4.3.4   The performance indicator *capacity utilization.*

A number of further performance indicators relate to administration costs for purchase administration, sales administration, administrative operations planning and scheduling, and so on. They are all of the following type:

Indicator	Administration cost rate (such as inventory control, purchasing)
Definition	Costs of administration divided by sales
Reason for measuring	Administration costs should be kept as low as possible
Reference object	(a) organizational unit, (b) time period
Fact to measure	Sales of the organizational unit, actual costs of the organizational unit for administration

Fig. 1.4.3.5   The performance indicator *administration cost rate.*

Such costs can vary according to order. If differences are large, it is usually in the operations area that a company will try to calculate variable administration costs per order. See activity-based costing in Section 15.4.

An important performance indicator, although influenced by logistics only to a limited extent, is the unit cost of an item itself. This is measured through exact cost estimating and job-order costing (see Sections 15.2 and 15.3). These calculations yield information on cost structure and the calculation schema on which it is based. If the unit cost changes greatly, a detailed calculation serves at the same time to check the validity of the bases of calculation and billing.

1.4.4   Performance Indicators in the Target Area of Delivery

As logistics has a direct effect upon the target area of delivery, the performance indicators here are very important. The first two performance indicators are direct measures of target objectives.

Indicator	Fill rate or customer service ratio
Definition	Number of products delivered on desired delivery date divided by number of products ordered
Reason for measuring	Poor fill rate results in opportunity cost and, depending on contract, penalty costs
Reference object	(a) item, (b) business partner, (c) part logistics (e.g., sales)
Fact to measure	For (a): item demand or order position For (b) and (c): order position or order

Fig. 1.4.4.1   The performance indicator *fill rate* or *customer service ratio.*

Indicator	Delivery reliability rate
Definition	Number of products delivered on confirmed delivery date divided by number of confirmed products
Reason for measuring	Poor delivery reliability rate results in opportunity cost and, depending on contract, penalty costs
Reference object	(a) item, (b) business partner, (c) part logistics (e.g., sales)
Fact to measure	For (a): item demand or order position For (b) and (c): order position or order

Fig. 1.4.4.2   The performance indicator *delivery reliability rate.*

The next performance indicators are connected with lead time. For terms, definitions, and arguments, see Sections 1.2.1, 1.2.3, and 1.2.4 and detailed discussions in Chapters 12 and 13.

Indicator	Lot size (batch size)
Definition	Average order quantity
Reason for measuring	Large batch size may result in longer lead time
Reference object	(a) process, (b) product
Fact to measure	Order quantity of the order position

Fig. 1.4.4.3   The performance indicator *batch size* or *lot size.*

Indicator	Capacity utilization
Definition	Actual load divided by theoretical capacity (= standard load divided by efficiency rate divided by theoretical capacity)
Reason for measuring	High loading of the work center may result in longer queue time
Reference object	(a) work center, (b) time period, (c) combination of the two
Fact to measure	Load by production orders (planned and actual, for setup and run), work center capacity

Fig. 1.4.4.4   The performance indicator *capacity utilization.*

Indicator	Value-added rate of lead time
Definition	Value-added part of lead time divided by lead time
Reason for measuring	Non-value-added parts of lead time should be reduced
Reference object	(a) process and product, (b) business partner, (c) part logistics (e.g., production)
Fact to measure	Value-added (e.g., operation time) and non-value-added parts (e.g., interoperation times, administration time) of lead time

Fig. 1.4.4.5   The performance indicator *value-added rate of lead time.*

Indicator	Variance in work content
Definition	Standard deviation of operation times
Reason for measuring	A high degree of variance in work content may result in longer queue time
Reference object	(a) work center, (b) time period, (c) product, (d) order
Fact to measure	Actual operation time for a reference object or combination of reference objects

Fig. 1.4.4.6   The performance indicator *variance in work content.*

And, finally, there are two performance indicators for data and control flow.

Indicator	Response time
Definition	Time from order entry up to order pre-confirmation divided by total lead time
Reason for measuring	Long response time results in long lead time, but also directly to opportunity cost
Reference object	(a) order, (b) business partner, (c) part logistics (e.g., sales)
Fact to measure	Time from order entry up to order pre-confirmation

Fig. 1.4.4.7   The performance indicator *response time.*

Indicator	Order confirmation time
Definition	Time from order pre-confirmation up to order confirmation divided by total lead time
Reason for measuring	Long order confirmation time results in long lead time
Reference object	(a) order, (b) business partner, (c) part logistics (e.g., sales)
Fact to measure	Time from order pre-confirmation up to order confirmation

Fig. 1.4.4.8   The performance indicator *order confirmation time.*

Additional performance indicators may reflect the time required for product design or maintenance time of the production infrastructure.

1.4.5   Performance Indicators in the Target Area of Flexibility

The target area of flexibility is influenced by logistics in only a few aspects. However, there are some performance indicators that have their roots in logistics, particularly the following success rates.

Indicator	Bid proposal success rate
Definition	Number of bid positions proposed divided by number of customer requests for quotations
Reason for measuring	A high bid proposal success rate demonstrates high flexibility to create customer value
Reference object	(a) item, (b) business partner, (c) part logistics (e.g., sales)

Fact to measure	For (a): items in bid position, or bid positions
	For (b) and (c): bid position, or bid
	The same for requests for quotations

Fig. 1.4.5.1   The performance indicator *bid proposal success rate.*

Indicator	Order success rate
Definition	Number of order positions divided by number of bid positions
Reason for measuring	A high order success rate is a measure of high flexibility in achieving customer value
Reference object	(a) item, (b) business partner, (c) part logistics (e.g., sales)

Fact to measure	For (a): item demand or order position
	For (b) and (c): order position or order
	The same for bid positions and bids

Fig. 1.4.5.2   The performance indicator *order success rate.*

The following performance indicators show flexibility potentials. Measurement of these values yields only the proportion that was actually exploited in the past. In order to determine potentials, additional considerations are required.

Indicator	Breadth of qualifications
Definition	Number of different operations that can be executed by an employee or a production infrastructure
Reason for measuring	Broad qualifications raise the potential for flexibility in the implementation of resources
Reference object	(a) workers and production infrastructure, organizational units
Fact to measure	The various operations executed by the reference object or combination of reference objects

Fig. 1.4.5.3   The performance indicator *breadth of qualifications.*

Indicator	Temporal flexibility
Definition	Short-term possible percentage of deviation from an employee's or a production infrastructure's average capacity
Reason for measuring	Temporal flexibility raises the potential for flexibility in resource use
Reference object	(a) workers and production infrastructure, organizational units
Fact to measure	Actual load in time periods of a reference object or combination of reference objects

Fig. 1.4.5.4   The performance indicator *temporal flexibility.*

As a further performance indicator of flexibility in achieving customer value, a measure for product complexity is conceivable (see [Albe95]). This is difficult to assess, however.

As performance indicators of the flexibility to enter as a partner into a logistics networks, the following are possible (see [HuMe95], p. 100); up to now, these have been "measured" only qualitatively:

- Reduction of the company's part in value-adding in the various logistics networks

- The number of logistics partnerships in a logistics network and its turnover

1.4.6   Transcorporate Supply Chain Performance Indicators

As mentioned towards the end of Section 1.3.4, aggregating objectives in the target areas of quality, cost, delivery, and flexibility at the level of the individual companies yields the objectives at the *transcorporate* supply chain level. The same can be done for the performance indicators.

In addition, some further performance indicators measure what has been achieved by the "enabler" objectives of supply chain that were introduced in Figure 1.3.4.1.

These additional performance indicators evaluate qualitative dimensions, however. The degree of achievement is not usually something that can be calculated. Mostly, the measure is a value ranging from "insufficient" to "perfect." Figure 1.4.6.1 shows a set of possible performance indicators[25] for enablers at the logistics network level, together with a possible representation of "quantification" of the degree of achievement. The representation was proposed in [Hieb01], where more details can be found.

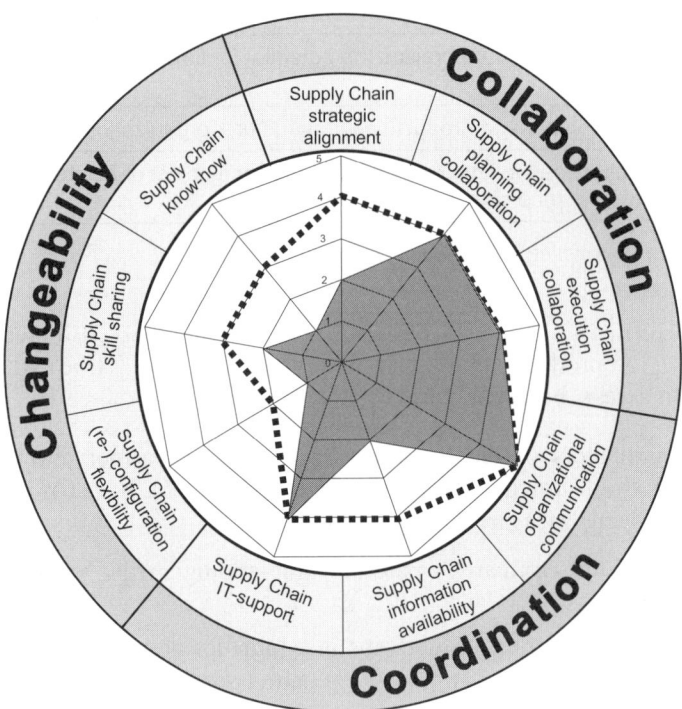

Fig. 1.4.6.1   Enabling-oriented performance indicators at the *transcorporate* supply chain level (according to [Hieb01]).

---

[25] In a first approximation, the performance indicator and the associated objective were given the same names. Practical application led to the definition of additional indicators.

1.5   Summary

The chapter defines basic terminology, including goods, product, and components. The product life cycle is comprised of the three fundamental time periods of "design and manufacture," "service and use," and "disposal." Goods inventories provide temporal synchronization between consumer and manufacturer. A logistics network is the combined logistics of several organizational units to form a comprehensive logistics system. Integral logistics management is the management of the logistics network for the design and manufacture of a product. In developing and producing investment goods, multidimensional logistics networks are formed.

Business objects correspond to the way the persons involved naturally envision them. In logistics there are relatively simple objects such as worker, business partner, date, time period, item, product, and product family. In addition there exist several quite complicated objects. To these belongs the order itself. Further complex business objects include *product structure*, *process plan*, and *load profile*. As a complement to these objects, we also introduced the similarly complex objects of operation, production infrastructure, work center, capacity, and load. Through reducing the degree of detail, we can also derive rough-cut business objects. Based on these objects, certain tasks can be processed more simply.

Logistics within and among companies is the organization, planning, and realization of the entire goods, data, and control flow along the product life cycle. There are logistics tasks in all areas of the company along the value chain, from bid processing to sales order processing, research and development, procurement, production, and distribution, as well as service, maintenance, and disposal. The flow of data and control for administrative and planning logistics is called planning & control. Logistics affects a company's objectives, such as the costs of the company's output, fill rate, and delivery reliability rate. Logistics has only a limited influence on quality and flexibility. There are basic conflicts among company objectives.

An important fundamental of effective logistics networks is the agility of the companies involved. Agile companies are able to remain competitive by means of the *proactive* development of knowledge and competence. This is, in the shortsighted view of the customer, not value-adding. Timely implementation of appropriate temporal, local, and quantitative potentials and degrees of freedom will be competitively decisive. A further fundamental of effective logistics networks is an integral view of the logistics network, that is, consideration of the entire chain from development to manufacture to user. Logistics network performance target areas are supply chain collaboration, supply chain coordination, and supply chain changeability.

Appropriate logistics performance indicators are connected to company objectives and business objects. Logistics performance indicators analyze the effect of logistics on company objectives in the four areas of quality, cost, delivery, and flexibility. The most important performance indicators for each target area were defined. The best-known indicators are stock-inventory turnover, work-in-process-inventory turnover, utilization, fill rate, and delivery reliability rate. All of these performance indicators can refer to various business objects or combinations of these objects. At a logistics network level, possible performance indicators evaluate "enabler" objectives. They refer to qualitative dimensions.

1.6   Keywords

1.7   Scenarios and Exercises

1.7.1 Improvements in Meeting Company Objectives

Review the discussion of company objectives in four target areas (quality, costs, delivery, and flexibility) in Section 1.3.1. Your company manufactures a single product from easily obtainable components in four operations with a batch size of 5. You determine the following problems:

- Your product does not meet the demands for product quality; returns of delivered products are frequent.

- When demand is high per period, you regularly run into delivery difficulties. In addition to the problem of insufficient quality — which results in frequent rework — delivery difficulties are being caused mainly by poor coordination of the manufacturing departments among themselves and with the sales department. Moreover, production at the first work center is too slow, and in-house transport cannot keep up the pace. In other company areas, there tend to be too many employees, particularly in sales and distribution and quality assurance.

- You think that there is a strong fluctuation of demand per period. However, you do not have the figures to back this up. You also do not know whether you can predict future demand reliably from the sales figures of past periods.

In other words, you determine a need for comprehensive improvement. Discuss with your team possible specific measures to achieve improvement in each of the four target areas.

For each specific measure proposed, consider the amount of investiture that will be required. Decide the order in which the specific measures will be realized.

1.7.2   Company Performance and the ROI

The following exercise was developed in communication with Prof. Dr. Peter Mertens, University of Nuremberg-Erlangen, Germany, to whom we express many thanks.

When we looked at opportunity cost in Section 1.3.1, we mentioned that a particular objective in the four target areas (quality, cost, delivery, and flexibility) does not always support the company's primary objectives, such as maximum return on investment or "shareholder value." For example, if investments to reduce lead time do not result in increased demand or a larger share of the market, then the return on investment (ROI) decreases rather than increases.

How can this be shown more exactly, correlating the objective *short lead time*, or *reduction of the lead time*, to factors in ROI? The ROI can be expressed as follows:

ROI	= earnings / (investment or assets)
	= (revenue – costs) / (circulating assets + fixed assets).

A possible solution is based on the following line of thinking: Reduction of lead time can have the following consequences:

- It can increase the number of customer orders and thus increase revenue.
- It requires the elimination of bottlenecks. This can have the following consequences:
    - It generally requires investitures, which increases fixed assets and therefore capital costs.
    - It can reduce inventories of work in order, which reduces circulating assets and therefore capital costs.

In this case, it is important to determine exactly whether the increase in revenue will be cancelled out by the increased costs (taking into account the increase and decrease in capital costs according to the line of thinking above). Since total assets appear in the denominator of the division, ROI decreases even when total assets increase with constant earnings.

Now, use similar arguments to try to elaborate the correlation of the following performance indicators in Section 1.4 (each corresponding to a different objective of the target areas in Section 1.3.1) to the factors in the ROI:

- Scrap factor (objective: meet high demands for product quality)
- Inventory turnover (objective: low physical inventory)
- Capacity utilization (objective: high capacity utilization)
- Fill rate (objective: high fill rate)
- Delivery reliability rate (objective: high delivery reliability rate)

1.7.3   Rough-Cut Business Objects

Determine the process plan, the rough-cut process plan, and a possible load profile for the following product P:

- P is produced from the components A and B (with quantity per equal to 1 for both components) by the same operations as in Figure 1.2.3.3 and consuming the same lead time.
- A is produced from component C only (with quantity per equal to 1) by the same operations as in Figure 1.2.3.3, consuming a lead time of 10 units.
- B is produced from the components X and Y (with quantity per equal to 1 for both components) by the same operations for producing C as in Figure 1.2.3.3, consuming a lead time of 10 units.
- C is produced from the components X and Z (with quantity per equal to 1 for both components) by the same operations for producing C as in Figure 1.2.3.3, consuming a lead time of 10 units.
- X, Y, and Z are purchased components, consuming a lead time of 10 units each.

Apply the technique presented in Section 1.2.5 using the same rules as shown in the example, but assuming that components C and B form the single item family B.

Solutions:

a) Process plan:

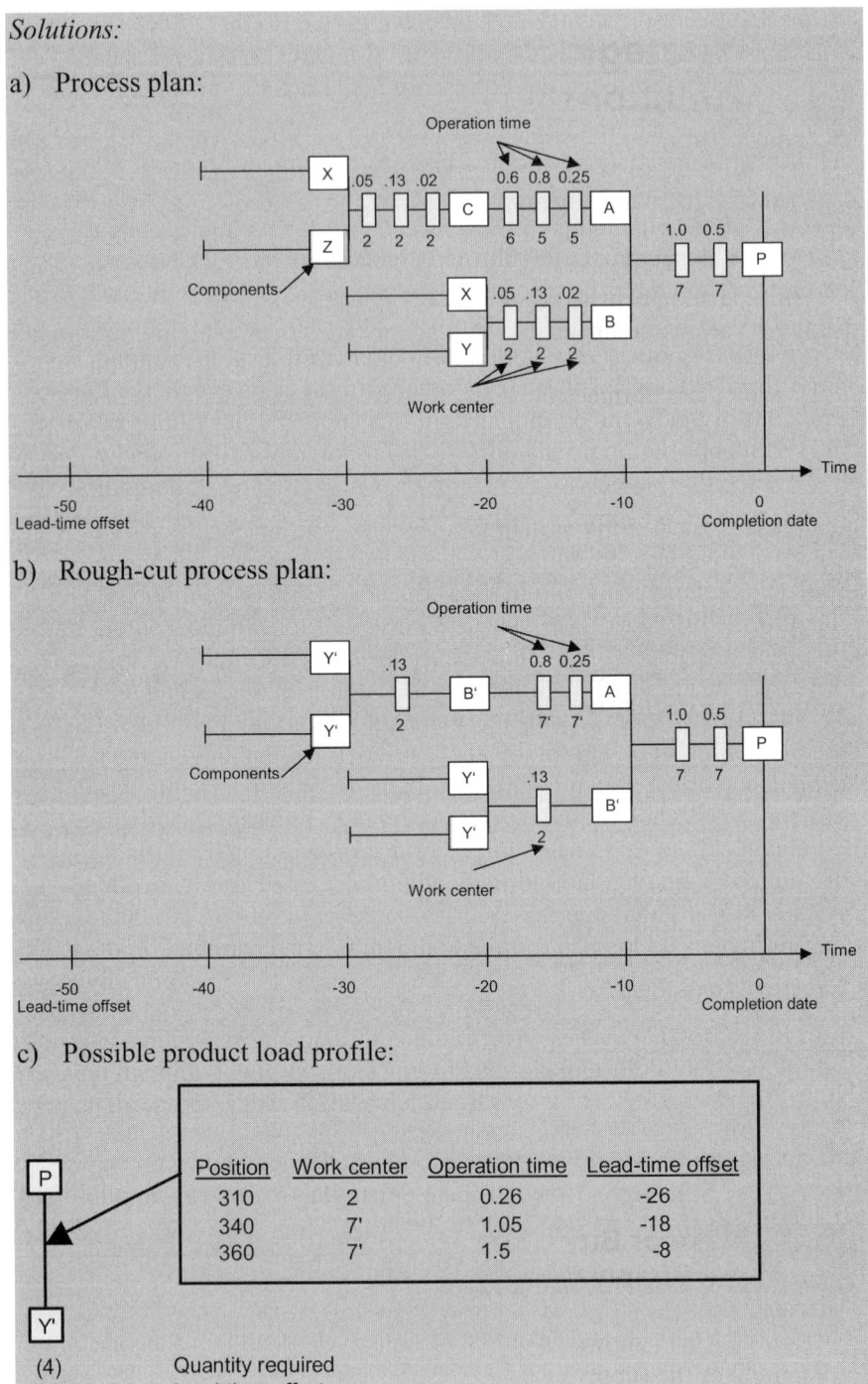

b) Rough-cut process plan:

c) Possible product load profile:

2 Strategic Decisions and Business Relationships in a Supply Chain

Individual companies today seldom possess all the necessary competence to develop and manufacture products of a certain complexity rapidly and efficiently with advanced technology. Single organizational units no longer handle development and manufacture. Instead, these tasks are distributed among various companies or among several organizational units within a company. Therefore, it is crucial to have an understanding of how companies are formed and also how their boundaries to the outside and their inner structures change.

Section 2.1 examines how a supply chain comes into being and changes and provides an introduction to various strategic design possibilities for internal company value-added and external procurement.

Sections 2.2 and 2.3 deal with strategic procurement. Section 2.2 shows typical criteria for and classical design possibilities for the relationships with and the selection of suppliers. Section 2.3 then delves into the designing of intensive cooperation with suppliers, and therefore actual Supply Chain Management, which is required when the focus is not on the company in competition with its direct suppliers but instead on the entire supply chain in competition with another supply chain for the favor of the *end* customer (the consumer).

Section 2.4 deals with the strategic decisions in company-internal value-adding. We look mainly at facility location planning in production, distribution, and service networks and introduce possible arrangements, location factors, and criteria of location selection, location configuration – that is, the assignment of products and services to a location – and qualitative and quantitative solution methods.

2.1 Make or Buy – The Strategic Process of Designing the Supply Chain

Figure 2.1.0.1 shows a possible strategic process for fundamental designing of the supply chain.

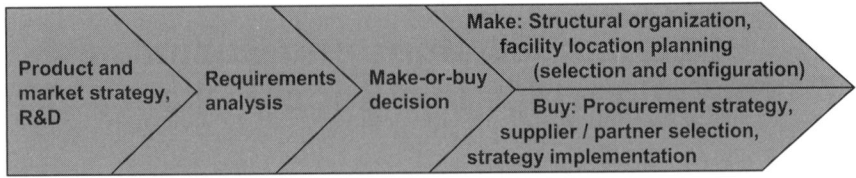

Fig. 2.1.0.1   Strategic process of designing the supply chain.

Here we will not discuss the development of product strategy and market strategy and the subsequent phase of product development (R&D). In the framework of sales planning, for the analysis of requirements, a demand forecast is worked out for each product and market and, if need be, using resource requirements planning (see also Section 4.1.2), the requirements in components, capacities (personnel and infrastructure), and finances are calculated.

We will look at the part-processes "make or buy" decision and "make" or "buy" in the following sections.

2.1.1   Transaction Costs as the Basis of Forming Companies

A *make-or-buy decision* is the choice between outsourcing and insourcing.

In *outsourcing*, parts of the value-added chain are turned over to other companies. *Insourcing* refers to the formation or expansion of companies by means of taking parts of the value-added chain into the company.

In what cases will an organization disband or become re-dimensioned by means of outsourcing? Keeping in mind the objectives of the enterprise outlined in Section 1.3.1, a company will choose outourcing whenever a product or product part can be produced on the whole in better quality and more cheaply, rapidly, reliably, and flexibly by a third party than when produced within the own company. If the contrary is the case, the decision is made to form or expand a company through insourcing.

In the following, we will assume that the same quality product may be procured on the market as could be produced by the company itself. The crucial factor in forming a company under this condition is transaction costs, according to Nobel Prize winner Ronald H. Coase ([Coas93]; this fundamental work was actually written in 1937). As for the *transaction-costs approach*, the reader is also referred here to [Pico82], p. 267 ff.

> The *transaction process* is the transmission of goods from seller to buyer. *Transaction costs*, or *market transaction costs* of goods, are the costs of the organization as a production factor. These include all costs of the transaction process that are not set in price by the market.

Transaction costs thus arise when price does not reflect all the necessary information on goods, for example due to inability, opportunism, uncertainty, or market distortions. Transaction costs are thus the cost of information and include the following types of costs:

- *Search and initiation costs:* These are, for example, the costs of locating and obtaining information on potential business partners and the conditions involved.

- *Negotiation costs* include the actual costs of negotiation and decision making, legal counsel, and fees.

- *Control costs* include expenditures necessary to coordinate orders so as to maintain quality, quantity, costs, and delivery dates as well as eventual costs to adapt to changes in orders. In addition, there are costs to ensure other contractual agreements, in particular patent protection, licensing and security agreements, and so on.

Transaction costs are thus comparable to various types of friction loss in the coordination of relations in a logistics network. Figure 2.1.1.1 takes as an example a network with five partners.

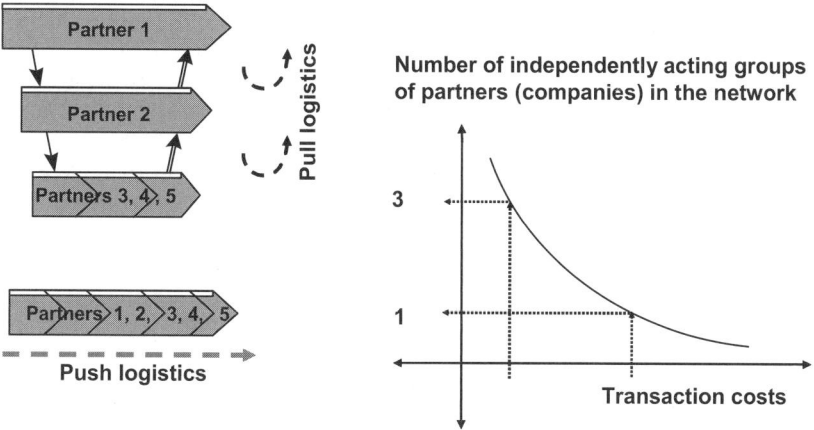

Fig. 2.1.1.1   Number of independently acting groups of partners in a logistics network with five partners in dependency upon transaction costs.

The example demonstrates that with increasing transaction costs or friction loss, the number of groups of partners in the network acting independently decreases. As a consequence, there is a tendency towards push logistics (see Section 3.2) and finally towards a decreased number of independent companies. Conversely, the number of independently acting partners within a logistics network increases with sinking transaction costs, which leads to an increased number of process levels (cascades) in the process model and to pull logistics and, finally, to an increased number of independent companies.

What *factors* influence transaction costs? These are factors of the "specificity" and "risk" type. The reader is referred here also to [Port98a] and [Port98b]. For each factor the following list contains examples that lead to a *buy decision*, or outsourcing, as well as examples that speak well for a *make decision*, or insourcing.

- *Specificity of product and processes or location:*
  - Outsourcing: Product and process are not specific. For development and production there are already a number of bidders on the market. Those companies already have specialists and specific infrastructures at their disposal. Moreover, transport is not a problem.
  - Insourcing: Whenever the development and production of a product requires specific investitures in production infrastructure and the qualification of employees, all types of transaction costs rise. The same is true whenever it is crucial for the supplier to be in a proximate location. On the other hand, product specificity creates better product differentiation and thus the building up of a trade name and share of the market.
- *Complexity of product and processes*, and *time-to-product:*
  - Outsourcing: The projects are too complex or too extensive to be realized by the company with its particular culture, the qualifications, and the capacities of its personnel. Small enterprises often face this problem, for customer-order-specific tasks in the value-added process.
  - Insourcing: Order coordination and control become more costly and more difficult. The danger of opportunistic behavior on the part of the supplier increases.
- *Core competencies, greater degree of innovation in product and process*, and *time to market (time to product innovation):*

- Outsourcing: Superior quality products require production technology that is ever more difficult to command. Moreover, there is time pressure: within increasingly shorter time periods, new technologies have to produce goods that succeed on the market. Procuring some of the company's competencies from a third party does not cause any critical problems, even if know-how that exists may be lost. In addition, the company desires access to the know-how of another organization.

- Insourcing: The development of core competencies and the achievement of innovation secure a lead in know-how and are thus keys to the survival of a company. A great store of know-how results in short lead times and flexibility. Continuing to give work to third parties involves too great a risk and high control costs.

- *Capital requirements and cost breakdown structure:*

  - Outsourcing: The company cannot afford the cash requirements for amassing and maintaining company know-how. Specialists do not fit into the payroll or do not fit into the company culture. Moreover, the company cannot fully utilize their specific abilities. The same holds for the infrastructure.

  - Insourcing: The cash requirements of amassing and holding on to the company's own know-how are affordable. The company's favorable size and structure permit the advantages of in-house development and production.

- *Lack of trust and lack of stability:*

  - Outsourcing: The single company is very highly dependent upon too few or even individual persons. It cannot build up a culture of sufficient capacity in the respective area. Remedial action, such as cooperating with several like-minded companies, is not possible.

  - Insourcing: Insufficient information on partners or frequent changes in partner relations within a logistics network lead to an increase in all transaction costs. For example: Are the human relationships stable? Are crucial individuals no longer part of the picture? Is quality maintained at a certain level? Does the supplier retain customer focus and user orientations? Do the supplier's prices reflect a *learning curve*, that is, the supplier's rate of improvement due to the frequently repeated transaction, and decrease?

In addition, outsourcing can be forced in the following contexts:

- *Counterdeals:* Corporations can be, with their various subsidiary companies, both potential customers and suppliers of a manufacturer. If a company wishes to gain them as customers, it may have to agree to a counterdeal stipulating that one of their subsidiaries will supply certain components, even if it could produce these itself.

- *Protectionism:* Certain markets elude the laws of a free economy. Political decisions can force manufacturers — in order to gain market access — to form "joint ventures" with companies in other countries. This type of cooperation then involves parts of the supply chain that manufacturers could actually process themselves.

Thorough evaluation of all factors thus helps to determine the *optimum value-added depth* of the company.

- *Vertical integration* is the degree to which a firm has decided to directly produce multiple value-adding stages from raw material to the sale of the product to the end user ([APIC04]).

- *Backward /forward integration* is the process of buying or owning elements of the production cycle and the channel of distribution (back toward raw material suppliers/forward toward the final consumer; see [APIC04]).

Parallel to this, similar scrutiny is needed at the level of the entire supply chain in order to set the number of partners. See also Section 2.3.1. The rule in Figure 2.1.1.2 holds.

> The optimum value-added depth of a partner in a supply chain is not necessarily optimal for the *total* supply chain. However, a balanced win–win situation for all companies involved is prerequisite to long-term or intensive cooperation in a supply chain.

Fig. 2.1.1.2   Rule for setting the optimum value-added depth for partners in a supply chain.

2.1.2   Make Strategies: Profit Center, Cost Center, and Semi-autonomous Organizational Units

The decision to make or buy must be based on *life-cycle costing*, that is, considering all costs, including acquisition, operation, and disposition costs, that will be incurred over the entire time of ownership of a product ([APIC04]). This also includes an estimation of internal friction losses. For products of a certain complexity, internal development and production must also be subdivided in an effective way. Companies have to set up an appropriate organizational structure.

> *The internal transaction costs* for goods are all costs related to the processing and handling of company-internal transactions among the organizational units involved. These are all internal processing costs that would not arise if one single individual could do the handling. Internal transaction costs arise from a lack of mutual information, that is, due to inability, opportunism, uncertainty, or diverging interests. Internal transaction costs are thus the price of information.[1]

Internal transaction costs include types of costs that are similar to market transaction costs. These are the costs of shaping an organization, the ongoing management of the organization and coordination of workers, planning and control costs, and flexibility costs, as well as costs of lead times.

The right form of organization can be decisive in supporting cooperation in the company-internal value-added processes, especially when the facility locations are at a great distance from one another or handle different product families or services. Various forms of organizational units are possible:

- *Profit center* within a *decentralized* or *product-focused organization:* In its pure form, a profit center plans and acts just like an independent company. It is thus a sub-company within the company, as for example in a holding. It carries comprehensive responsibility, but also has the authority to accept or reject orders from other organizational units of the company. In view of logistics, a profit center in its pure form would be considered under the aspects discussed in Section 2.1.1. This form of cooperation leads to pull logistics (see Section 3.2.1).

- *Cost center* within a *centralized* or *process-focused organization:* In its pure form, a cost center receives clearly formulated orders: due date, type and quality of products. A cost center does not form its own logistics system. Instead, the often complex and capital-intensive processes are triggered by order management — the central department — sensibly, within a system of push logistics

---

[1]   There are internal coordination costs as well. These include the cost of acquiring information by decision-makers in management and so-called "agency" costs. Agency costs are the costs of coordinating the interests of the owner with those of decision-makers in management. Similar costs are incurred in "outsourcing."

(see Section 3.2.2). The cost center then has the task of maintaining quality requirements. It also attempts to fulfill quantity and due date; it does not, however, carry responsibility for these, as it neither has its own resources (personnel and production infrastructure) nor does it manage resources procured from the outside (for example, information, semifinished goods, and raw materials).

- *Semi-autonomous organizational units* do not have full entrepreneurial responsibility. They obtain orders from other organizational units within the company upon the basis of company strategy for the entire logistics network. For procurement they are also linked to company-wide strategies. For example, they must procure certain components from other organizational units of the company or through a central procurement department. On the other hand, they are semi-autonomous with regard to their internal logistics. A semi-autonomous unit forms a system of logistics with its own order processing and fulfillment. It negotiates due dates, type, and quantity of goods with customers and suppliers and realizes order processing under its own direction. At the level of company strategies, however, clear framework conditions are set within which the unit has some degrees of freedom. This type of cooperation is usually viewed as pull logistics in dependency upon the degree of autonomy.

All three of the above forms appear in the world of practice, whereby the characteristics of the third form are by no means unambiguous. In dependency upon strategic framework conditions, semi-autonomous organizational units may act as profit centers or cost centers. For this reason, they are seldom stable in the long term. Internal transaction costs are particularly dependent upon the persons involved. Here the human factor — that is, the qualifications of those involved — has to be closely attended to with regard to cooperation with colleagues in other organizational units, know-how in logistics, planning and control, and flexibility in thinking and acting. The reader is referred to [Ulic05]. Two common mistakes result when all-too-human characteristics find expression:

- *"Kingdoms" within departments or foreman areas:* Decentralized organizational units take on authority without perceiving the conjugate, necessary responsibility. For example, they might set order due dates autonomously without taking the superordinate interests of the total logistics network into consideration. "Kingdoms" such as these also arise when decentralized organizational units are evaluated on the basis of isolated objectives, such as capacity utilization.

- *Centralistic kingdoms:* Central management delegates responsibility to decentralized organizational units without giving them the necessary authority. Holding companies, for example, may turn over cost and profit responsibility to subsidiaries and affiliated companies while maintaining the right to choose these companies' suppliers and customers.

Independently of the form of organization, it is important in all make strategies to pay particular attention to facility location planning. Section 2.4 goes into that topic.

2.1.3   Buy-Strategies: Overview on Strategic Procurement

A supply chain generally produces products with a certain degree of complexity. Procurement strategies in supply chains differ from simple business relationships in that here, it is best to take the product structure into consideration (see Fig. 1.2.2.2). The manufacturer attempts to realize a *supplier structure* that follows the product structure. From the view of the end product manufacturer, or *original equipment manufacturer*, the suppliers are arranged accordingly in tiers. Fig. 2.1.3.1 shows an example of this for end product A.

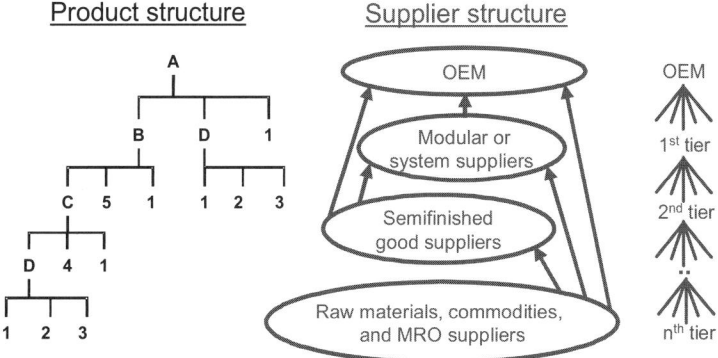

Fig. 2.1.3.1   Procurement strategy in a supply chain: the supplier structure follows the product structure.

- The *original equipment manufacturer (OEM)* produces the finished product, or end product (in the example, product A), and sells it to the consumer.
- *First tier suppliers*, or *modular* or *system suppliers*, are responsible for several structure levels that together yield a module, that is,

an assembly ready for final assembly, and supply this directly to the assembly line of the original equipment manufacturer.[2] In automobile manufacturing, for instance, this can be complete car door modules or instrument panels. In the example in Fig. 2.1.3.1, assembly B is this kind of module or system.

- *Second tier suppliers,* or *semifinished good suppliers*, supply simple semifinished goods, both to the OEM and also to the system suppliers. In the example in Fig. 2.1.3.1, assembly D is a semifinished good.

- *Raw materials, standard parts,* and *MRO suppliers* supply these items both to OEM and also to the system and second tier suppliers. In the example in Fig. 2.1.3.1, these are items 1, 2, 3, 4, and 5.

Procurement strategies in the supply chain are generally different for each of these levels of suppliers. The companies involved in such a channel of distribution[3] form customer–supplier links. With the exception of the end user, each customer is also a supplier within the supply chain.

The procurement strategies differ independently of the logistics characteristics of the goods that flow from supplier to customer.

- *Direct material* is material procured that becomes a part of the product or is required for the execution of an order. Typically, direct material includes components, documents, receipts, proofs, or similar materials, but also, in the broadest sense, external operations. As a rule of thumb, direct material is material that would not be procured if there were no production or selling.[4]

- *Indirect material* is all material that is not direct material. More specifically, indirect material includes all material that must be procured to maintain company performance and efficiency, e.g., maintenance, replenishment, and operating (MRO) materials.

---

[2] A distinction is frequently made between modular supplier and system supplier insofar as module suppliers tend to supply components that for the most part have been developed by the buyer; system suppliers do a great deal development work of their own.

[3] A *channel of distribution* is a series of firms or individuals that participate in the flow of goods and services from the raw material supplier and producer to the final user or customer ([APIC04]). A *distribution channel* is the route which products take along the channel of distribution.

[4] What is said in the following about direct material also holds – particularly in the case of services – for capacity that is to be procured externally and required for producing a product or carrying out a contract.

- *Commodities* are entirely standard and can come from a sufficient variety of sources. *Custom semifinished goods* are manufactured to spec. Printed circuit boards and injection-molded plastic pieces are good examples.

- Demand pattern: Items have *continuous demand* if demand is approximately the same in every observation period. Items have *discontinuous* or *highly volatile demand* if many observation periods with no or very little demand are interrupted by few periods with large, for example ten times higher demand, without recognizable regularity.

The following is a list of some of the frequently mentioned traditional procurement strategies. Combinations of these can also appear.

Multiple sourcing or *multisourcing* refers to the search for the greatest number of sources of a service. This strategy reduces the risk of too great a dependency upon another company. This is a common strategy in traditional market-oriented relations.

Single sourcing refers to the search for one single source of a certain service, such as a *single-source supplier*, i.e., a unique supplier per item or family of items. This strategy lowers transaction costs and speeds up order processing. It becomes imperative, if short lead times are important.

Dual sourcing plans for two suppliers for an item or an item family. This strategy can reduce the risk of disruption in production due to delivery difficulties on the part of the supplier, while retaining most of the advantages of single sourcing.

Sole sourcing refers to the situation where the supply of a product is available from only one supplier. Usually technical barriers such as patents preclude other suppliers from offering the product.

With modular or system suppliers, we also speak of *modular sourcing* or *system sourcing*. Here the buyer has the advantage of not having to assemble a great number of parts and components from various suppliers that have no contact with each other. The task of technical coordination and procurement of the required components is taken over by the modular or system supplier.

Global sourcing refers to the search for the best source worldwide of a particular service. This sourcing strategy may be necessary with products and processes involving high technology.

Local sourcing is the search for local sources of a certain service. Intensive cooperation entailing personal meetings or large transports may require this strategy.

However, strategies of this kind describe only one certain aspect. They are therefore generally embedded within more comprehensive procurement strategies. These can be differentiated in a portfolio as in Fig. 2.1.3.2 in dependency on the *duration of the supply contract* and the *intensity of cooperation according to win-win approaches*.

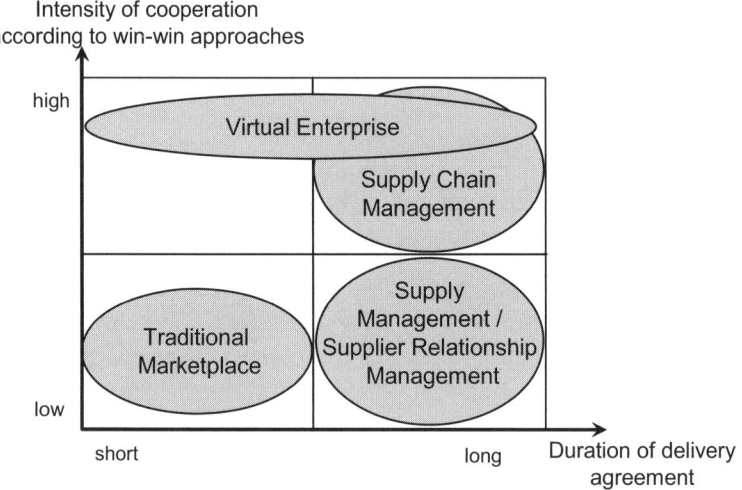

Fig. 2.1.3.2   Different extensive procurement and cooperation strategies in a value-added network by duration and intensity of collaboration.

Sections 2.2 and 2.3 discuss these extensive procurement strategies. See here also [Merl91] and [HuMe95].

2.2   Strategic Procurement

In the mid-1970s, there was a shift in many areas of the economy — caused by the law of supply and demand — from sellers' markets to buyers' markets. This phenomenon had decisive consequences for procurement and collaboration strategies in a value-added network. In this section we will compare procurement via the traditional marketplace with supply management and supplier relationship management. The following section will cover the supply chain management approach as well as other forms of company partnerships in the supply chain.

2.2.1   Strategic Procurement Portfolios

In the procurement system, the portfolio technique has become an established tool for classing strategies. See here, for example, [Alar02], [Kral83], [Bens99]. The material portfolio and the supplier portfolio are examples of familiar techniques. In both cases the attempt is to use simple visual mapping to distinguish between objects and suppliers that are "important" for procurement or have risks and objects and suppliers that are "less important" or associated with fewer procurement risks. The idea is to use this as a basis to derive, for the objects to be procured, strategies and recommendations to organizations and IT.

Today companies seldom procure single items from suppliers and instead procure entire item families or even more comprehensive material groups, or planning groups.[5] This is the case not only for high-cost items or high-turnover items (A items – see Fig. 10.2.2.1) but particularly also for low-cost items or low-turnover items (C items).

With this, the material portfolio shifts more and more to a material *group* portfolio. With regard to the entire material *group*, however, now only few groups of indirect material, such as office materials, are "less important." As companies generally work with a few or only one supplier per material group, *all* material groups are in addition associated with certain procurement risks. In such cases, the traditional material portfolio does not yield much information. If that is so, then the *supplier portfolio* becomes more useful. Figure 2.2.1.1 shows a possible supplier portfolio.

This supplier portfolio describes the degree of mutual dependence between buyer and supplier. As companies become aware of their dependence, they generally come to the recognition that a certain degree of cooperation is necessary and are then mostly willing to cooperate.

- In *market-oriented relationships*, that is, via the traditional market-place, goods or capacities are procured that are unimportant in the eyes of both the buyer and the supplier. Either side, buyer or supplier, can change business partners without great consequences.

---

[5]   Treating material groups instead of individual items is also called *material group management* and is generally carried out by teams.

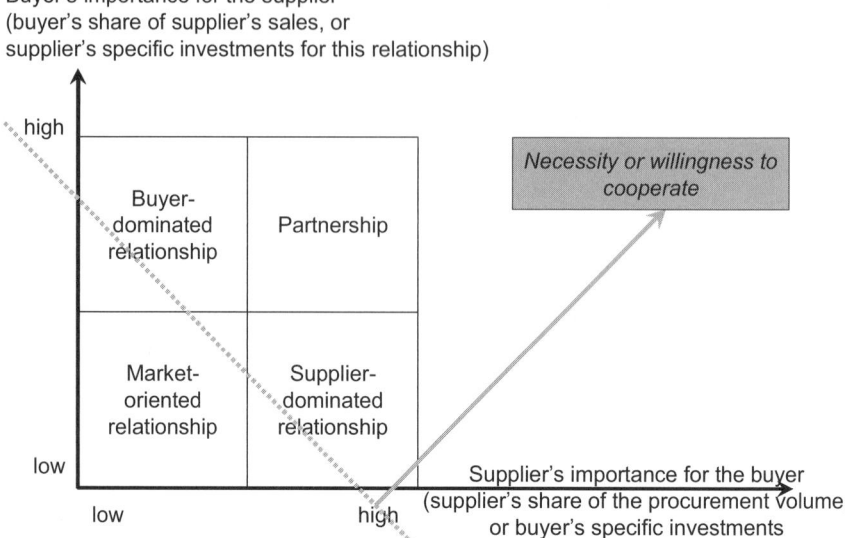

Fig. 2.2.1.1   Supplier portfolio.

- In *buyer-dominated relationships*, goods or capacities are procured that are important in the eyes of the supplier but not for the buyer. Or, the supplier must make one-sided investments of some kind that are related to only the one buyer. These can be, for example, buyer-specific devices, IT platforms, consignment inventories, or personnel that must acquire know-how on customer-specific processes and business practices. This type of relationship should in every case be designed for the long term, that is, via the supply management strategy, or supplier relationship management, which is explained below.

- In *supplier-dominated relationships*, goods or capacities are procured, with the one-sidedness of the investments on the opposite side: the buyer's side.

- In *partnership relationships*, goods or capacities are procured that are seen as important in the eyes of both buyer and supplier. Both parties make considerable and mutually demonstrable investments in this relationship to the one business partner. This type of relationship should in every case be designed for the long term, mostly with intensive cooperation. For this, there is supply chain management, presented below in Section 2.3.

Figure 2.2.1.2 shows that between one and the same pair of business partners, different procurement strategies of the types shown in Figure 2.1.3.2 can occur in dependency upon the logistics characteristics of the material group that the supplier delivers to the buyer (customer). Instead of a material portfolio, this yields a simple list of strategies for the procurement of the different material groups.

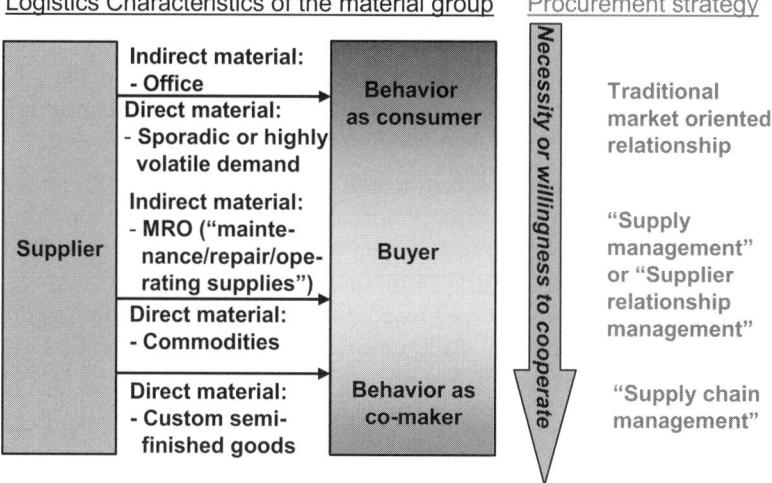

Fig. 2.2.1.2   Procurement strategies for material groups in dependency upon their logistics characteristics.

- The procurement of indirect material in the case of office supplies is usually handled via a market-oriented relationship. The behavior of the buyer is like that of any consumer: the buyer follows the classical law of supply and demand. The buyer will try to achieve a position of strength by bundling the requirements. If material of this type shows a sporadic pattern of demand, it is necessary to find especially inexpensive and rapid solutions for their operative procurement, called buy-side solution (see Section 2.2.5).

- The same can be said of the case with MRO items. However, here the buyer depends on high quality and on-time deliveries in order to maintain performance levels towards the buyer's own customers. For material groups of this type, companies will strive to design longer-term relationships in the sense of supply management or supplier relationship management, described below, and, depending on the conditions, a buyer-dominated or supplier-dominated relationship.

- For the procurement of direct material what was said about MRO items largely holds in the case of commodities. Experience has shown that suppliers are quite willing to enter into buyer-dominated relationships For example, suppliers of material groups of C items (like screws, nuts, and so on) invest in efficient delivery logistics such as kanban or vendor managed inventory (VMI) due to the large delivery volumes for an extensive range of products. Also, for the business of the buyer, long-term relationships are certainly important also in the case of a supplier-dominated relationship. A supplier-dominated relationship can occur, for example, in the case of use of patents or proprietary technologies of the supplier or with large suppliers of electronic components.

- In the case of custom semifinished goods, such as, for example, specific semifinished items or single parts, joint product innovation can also stand in the foreground. One example is assembly modules from system suppliers. Here it is best for the business partners to choose the partnership relationship. Collaborative principles following supply chain management can be applied (see Section 2.3).

- For direct material with highly volatile or sporadic demand, the buyer – in some circumstances also where there is a well-established buyer-dominated or even partnership relationship – may have to procure a part of the demand, sometimes the entire demand, via a market-oriented relationship, often with the aid of one or more brokers. Here the buyer is often not in a strong position.

Assigning the procurement items to material groups, evaluating suppliers in supplier portfolios, and choosing the procurement strategy are prone to errors. To *reduce* these *risks*, these tasks should generally be performed by a team made up of people from R&D, logistics, production, strategic and operative procurements, and quality assurance.

2.2.2   The Traditional Market-Oriented Relationship

The traditional *market-oriented relationship* is determined by the law of supply and demand. Suppliers are chosen on the basis of low prices. Cost reductions are achieved as suppliers play off against each other.

Customer–supplier relationships of this type show low intensity in terms of entrepreneurial cooperation. In principle, the duration of the relationship is indefinite, but in fact it is calculated to be short term: the supplier network is flexible, and any relationship may be replaced with another.

Related to the target areas of a company's performance, target area strategies arise between the producer as buyer and the producer's suppliers as shown in Figure 2.2.2.1.

• Target area quality:
• The supplier is responsible for meeting the customer's quality specification.   • The customer is responsible for the acceptance and must check the meeting of the specification.

• Target area cost:
• The customer chooses a supplier, where quality is sufficient, primarily according to the lowest prices, following the law of supply and demand.

• Target area delivery:
• The customer awards a contract stating desired product, quantity, and delivery due date.   • Safety stock is necessary in order to avoid the problems caused by delivery delays.

• Target area flexibility:
• The customer aims for multiple sourcing. This helps offset demand fluctuations and offers better protection against dependencies on individual suppliers.   • If transaction costs become too high, a make decision is made.

• Relationship between the companies in the supply chain:
• Starting from raw materials and standardized parts, it is the customer who develops all products and processes in the logistics network.   • The customer delegates the manufacturing of semifinished goods or parts for the manufacturing process to suppliers. The customer controls the quality particularly of first deliveries.

Fig. 2.2.2.1 Target area strategies for the traditional market-oriented relationship.

In sum, price and quality arguments, or productivity in the narrow sense, determine supply and demand. Where friction loss is too high, the customer tends to use insourcing. This is also why there has been a trend in the past towards large and even multinational corporations.

Risk management: The procurement strategy "market-oriented relationship" tends to have the following disadvantages and risks, which on the whole have to be smaller than the risk of over-dependence on one supplier:

- Relatively high costs for the order process, due to the great expense of frequent information gathering and contract negotiations. The selection of the supplier has to be able to be made within a short time and based on fewer criteria.

- For custom material, changing the supplier can result in significant adaptation costs on the buyer side, for example the cost of changing production or logistics processes. For this reason, companies should purchase only commodity material via the marketplace whenever possible.

- In a buyer's market, the suppliers can absorb the pressure to lower prices by drastically reducing costs on their side. They minimize costs in the area of quality or in the warehousing of goods, for example. This results in the *additional risks* of lower quality, long delivery times, and low delivery reliability, which can impact the buyer's service level. For this reason the buyer, even though dominant, can not push prices down too low.

2.2.3   Supply Management – Supplier Relationship Management

The term "supply management," along with the concept of "just-in-time" (see Chapter 5), originated in the 1980s. It stands for an approach to supply and demand that functions not only according to price and quality, for delivery unreliability on the part of supplier's results in opportunity cost for the manufacturer, if it is then unable to supply its own customers (compare Section 1.3.1). The term "supplier relationship management" arose in connection with consideration of the strategic tasks associated with e-procurement, and in principle it addresses the same contents as the term "supply management."

> *Supply management*, or *"Supplier relationship management,"* means the strategic and long-term reduction of the number of suppliers to achieve fast and easy operational order processing. The choice of a supplier is made in view of *total cost of ownership* that is, under consideration of all opportunity costs.

This type of cooperation with suppliers demands extensive preparations. For this reason, long-term relationships of this kind cannot be established and maintained with a large number of partners. Related to the target areas of company performance, target area strategies arise between the producer as buyer and the producer's suppliers as shown in Figure 2.2.3.1.

• Target area quality:
• The supplier achieves a minimum level of quality (according to its own quality evaluation or external certification). Defects and flaws are corrected immediately.
• In order to control the quality of the supplier, the customer has access to its production facilities. Both parties mutually improve quality in a logistics network.

• Target area cost:
• Through single sourcing, greater business volume and thus lower cost prices are achieved.
• (Long-term) blanket orders allow intermediate stores to be reduced.
• The choice of a supplier is made according to total cost of ownership, that is, in consideration of opportunity cost.

• Target area delivery:
• (Long-term) blanket orders reduce total lead time (supplier and customer).
• There is now direct delivery on demand to the production facilities of the manufacturer.

• Target area flexibility:
• In a buyer-dominated relationship, the buyers' market secures the robustness of the relationship: transaction costs are small, and it is relatively easy to secure a replacement supplier (buy decision).
• The result of a sole sourcing situation can be a supplier-dominated relationship. In this case in particular, a stable and long-term relationship is important for the buyer.

• Entrepreneurial cooperation in the supply chain:
• Demands on products and processes to be delivered are mutually defined.
• The supplier is consulted about each (further) development.

Fig. 2.2.3.1   Target area strategies for supply management or supplier relationship management.

Supply management, or supplier relationship management, in short-term order processing, leads to the elimination or reduction of friction loss caused by order negotiations or incoming inspection. With this, many of the advantages of company-internal production for fast lead time can be retained.

Quality goals are achieved through certification of the suppliers; cost goals are achieved through closing blanket order contracts across entire item families or material groups.

A *certified supplier* is a status awarded to a supplier who constantly achieves a minimum level of quality as well as other objectives in other target areas, such as cost or delivery (see also [APIC04]).

An *(item) family contract* is a purchasing order grouping a whole family of items or a material group together to obtain pricing advantages and a continuous supply of material ([APIC04]).

Relationships of this type are also called *customer–supplier partnerships* or simply *customer partnerships*. However, such partnerships show low intensity in terms of entrepreneurial cooperation. Thus, they can be checked again and again with regard to their validity.

The procurement strategy "supply management" or "supplier relationship management" tends to have the following disadvantages and risks, which must be smaller that the advantages mentioned in 2.2.3.1.

- Dependence on one supplier can prove to be too strong (delivery failures, lack of flexibility when demand fluctuates, changes in company ownership on the supplier side). If there is no sole sourcing situation, a switch to dual sourcing may be possible, which can lead to higher unit costs.

- The long-term nature of the relationship and the costs incurred for changing suppliers can lead to a lack of adjustment to pricing developments on the market. After a sufficiently long period, for this reason, continuance of the relationship must be examined and, if necessary, new terms must be negotiated.

- A buyer-dominated relationship can transition into a supplier-dominated relationship unexpectedly, that is, the buyer's market can become a supplier's market. This is, for example, the case with system suppliers if they take over technological leadership, but it can also occur in raw material procurement due to natural phenomena and catastrophic events or due to speculative manipulation. The relationships must then be renegotiated.

2.2.4   Strategic Selection of Suppliers

After establishing the procurement strategy, the task is to find appropriate suppliers. The process involved is called procurement market research.

Procurement market research is the systematic gathering of information for an object to be procured. It entails supply market analysis, identification of potential suppliers, and request for quotations.

Procurement market research leads to transaction costs. These are search and initiation costs, as mentioned in Section 2.1.1 as the first type on the list of transactions costs. They are incurred

- either ongoing, for example costs for updating or enlarging the existing market information,

- or due to a special occurrence such as a shortage of raw materials, bankruptcy of a previous supplier, the introduction of a new product, new regulations, or cost savings measures.

Once market research has been completed, the next steps are supplier evaluation and supplier selection. The supplier's quotations have to be analyzed and compared. Then it is time to conduct negotiations – and if necessary renegotiations – and to make decisions. The costs incurred here belong to negotiation costs.

Supplier evaluation is a method for evaluating the performance of a supplier generally and relative to the required object.

In the world of practice, there are various methods for evaluating suppliers. See here also [WaJo04]. One possibility is to measure the performance of a supplier in the same way that the company's own performance is measured, that is, by assessing performance in achieving targets in the areas of quality, cost, delivery, and flexibility (see here Figure 1.3.1.1). As a category in its own right, general working cooperation with the potential supplier is evaluated. Figure 2.2.4.1 shows possible evaluation criteria for each target area.

Supplier selection includes pre-selection of the supplier (or possible a number of suppliers) and possibly post-selection negotiations.

The best suppliers are generally *pre-selected* using a factor rating. First the criteria are weighted. The potential suppliers are then rated as to degree to which they fulfill the individual criteria. This fulfillment rating can be an absolute value (*scoring method*) or a relative value compared to a maximum possible value (*gap method*).

In many cases, post-selection negotiations are conducted with the best-rated suppliers in order to establish definitive prices or other conditions. This can change the degree of fulfillment of some of the criteria. Finally, the supplier with the highest total score (or possibly, several suppliers with the highest scores) is awarded the contract.

- Target area quality:
  - Existing quality infrastructure, guidelines, recording of data, quality certifications and awards, qualifications of personnel, programs for continuous improvement.
  - Product and process: Patents and licenses, mastery of product and process technologies, system supplier, results of examination of first samples.
  - Organization: Service (sales and technical support, handling of complaints, fair dealing), environment (standards, environmental performance evaluation, emissions certificate, location and transport, packing).

- Target area cost:
  - Unit costs, additional delivery costs, terms of acceptance, delivery, and payment. Ongoing efforts to reduce costs.
  - Stability of exchange rate, inflation in the procurement country.

- Target area delivery:
  - Service level, delivery reliability, short lead times in flow of goods, data, and control, terms of transport and delivery.
  - Ability to handle logistics concepts (such as blanket order processing, release orders, vendor managed inventory, Just-in-Time, Just-in-Sequence)

- Target area flexibility:
  - Customer benefit: product innovation capability, integration of external know-how, capability for custom production and for joint product innovation.
  - Use of resources: technology and production infrastructure, way of dealing with fluctuating order quantities.

- Business cooperation in the supply chain:
  - Importance of the buyer to the supplier and vice versa, location proximity.
  - Information on development of the company (for example, business development, financial stability, product range, organization, international support).
  - Reduction of total costs (for example, passing on cost savings to customers, joint value analyses, transparency on pricing changes).

Fig. 2.2.4.1　　Evaluation criteria for supplier evaluation.

Procurement market research, supplier evaluation, and supplier selection can be supported today in many cases by information technology. Here the transactions costs mentioned (search and initiation costs and negotiation costs) can be decisively lowered, especially in the case of global sourcing (see on this the next section below).

Figure 2.2.4.2 shows as an example the score and gap method with two potential suppliers and a limited number of criteria.

Criterion	Buyer's weighting 1=low,2=medium, 4=high	Degree of fulfillment 1=low, 2=medium, 4=high	
		supplier A	supplier B
Product technology	4	2	4
Process technology	2	4	2
Acquisition and additional costs	2	2	1
Delivery and payment terms	1	2	4
Service level and delivery reliability	4	2	4
Short lead times in flow of goods	2	4	2
Capability for custom production	1	4	2
Capability for joint R&D	2	2	4
Financial stability	4	4	2
Importance of buyer rather low	2	4	1
International support	2	4	2
Total score (number of points) Max. = 104 (= 26·4)		78	70
100% minus gap Max. = 100%		75 %	67 %

Fig. 2.2.4.2   Supplier evaluation: score and gap method with two suppliers.

Evaluation according to criteria as shown in Figure 2.2.4.1 is not a guarantee but rather an aid. There will still be risks entailed in the selection of suppliers. Some of the possible risks are the following:

- The factor rating does not yield an unambiguous decision. Robustness analysis can provide clarification here. On this, see also Figure 2.4.3.9 and the explanation in the text.

- The evaluation may base upon the wrong criteria. Team work can help here (second-set-of-eyes principle). It also makes sense to evaluate fewer criteria if the importance of the supplier is low for the buyer than in the case where the importance of the supplier is high (keyword one-factor comparison versus multifactor comparison).

- Conditions can change at the supplier company, particularly when key persons leave the company.

- If a supplier-dominated relationship is foreseeable or if this is a case of sole sourcing, supplier selection will already involve high costs. Here, personal relationships will be important from the start.

2.2.5   Basics of E-Procurement Solutions

E-procurement refers to electronic procurement solutions, particularly Internet-based solutions.

E-procurement solutions can be grouped in several categories according to the institutional provider of the application, as shown in Figure 2.2.5.1 (for detailed information, see also [AlHi01], [BeHa00]).

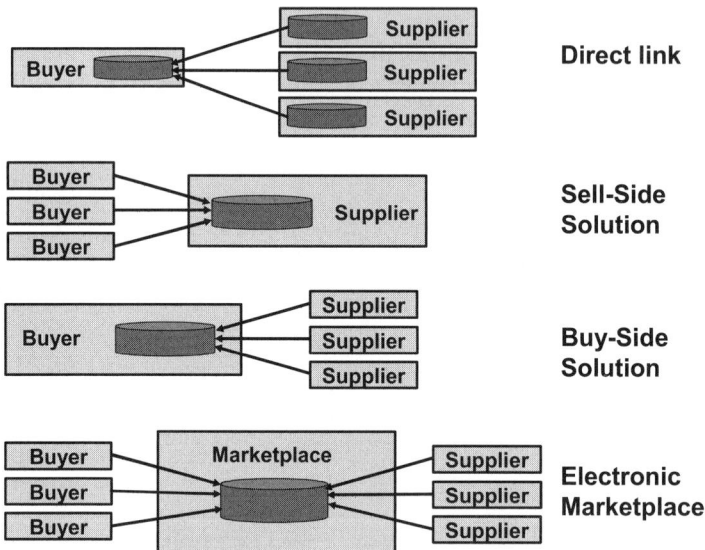

Fig. 2.2.5.1   Categories of e-procurement solutions (the cylinder stands for electronic procurement solutions of trading platform).

- A direct link connects the electronic procurement solutions of buyers and suppliers, when both sides already have them in place. With the introduction of MRP II / ERP software packages, modern IT-based systems were already redesigning communication between business partners on the supplier and buyer sides. EDI solutions, which used standards like EDIFACT, were also developed to support communication — to improve the exchange of data and information among strategic partners in the company network. But EDI solutions are complex and very expensive, both in terms of organization and finances. Internet-based solutions changed the scenario starting in the mid-1990s, not least due to the use of XML standard technologies (see here also [Schö01], p. 71).

- A *sell-side solution*, or shop solution, is initiated by a supplier. The supplier provides access to a catalog of products and ordering procedures on the World Wide Web. This is also typical of B2C applications in the area of consumer goods (for example, amazon.com and dell.com). However, for industrial procurement these applications are of only limited usefulness. They do not offer uniform accessibility to the offerings of various sellers and are therefore of limited value to the purchaser during the information-gathering phase. The purchasers themselves have to make sure that they do not overlook any potential suppliers in the decision-making process. This means taking the trouble to navigate through a number of vendor Web sites and having to become familiar with the interfaces used by each.

- A *buy-side solution* is a buyer's side application. Ariba and Commerce One are typical representatives here. Standard software is installed directly at the purchasing company. The purchasing department in the company uses the software to set up a uniform catalog of products from a number of suppliers. The user within the company can then select products directly from this catalog and, via an interface to ERP software, place orders and process the orders internally. Internal company procedures, such as obtaining approvals from the cost center, are also processed by the system. Direct integration with the company's back-end system eliminates the need for tedious and error-prone manual booking procedures. The systems thus simplify internal company processes and prevent individual orders from being placed with suppliers that are not in the company's preferred vendor pool (maverick buying). This reduces transaction costs, but actual purchasing costs remain essentially the same, excepting discounts that can be obtained by concentrating on a few suppliers. What the use of the pool of suppliers does *not* do is increase the number of suppliers that are considered in procurement decisions. Furthermore, the building and updating of company-internal catalogs can require major work efforts, and the required IT environment is comparatively deman-ding. For these reasons, buy-side solutions are more practicable for medium to large enterprises than for small enterprises.

- An *electronic marketplace* brings together a comparatively large group of participants and provides a high degree of transparency in real time to all taking part; in that sense, they come a step closer to optimal market conditions.

The types of electronic marketplaces are currently being differentiated according to the institutional provider:

- A *dependent marketplace* is financed and managed by a single company or a group of companies. It will therefore tend to be a buy-side or sell-side solution

- A *neutral, or independent, marketplace* is provided by an independent third party, meaning a neutral party, which can also aggregate and edit the data. In addition, it can add additional services to the marketplace.

- A *consortium marketplace* is built by a consortium and can take on any of the forms described above.

Marketplaces also have differing degrees of "openness":

- A *public marketplace* is open to any company and accessible without proprietary software. A valid e-mail address is often the only thing that is required.

- A *closed* or *private marketplace* is not open to all companies. Participation in these electronic marketplaces often hinges on certain conditions. Participating firms may be required to be members of a certain trade association, for example. In other cases, certain companies (such as partners in a supply chain) will exchange data like forecasts or cooperate in some other form (for instance, in the areas of product development, project planning, and project processing).

In the area of investment goods, a third distinguishing feature of electronic marketplaces is the range:

- A *horizontal electronic marketplace* cuts across industries to offer products and services to support general operations and maintenance in many sectors. As a rule, these marketplaces are channels for the buying and selling of indirect materials, such as MRO items (maintenance, repair, and operating supplies) or office supplies. Two examples are MRO.com and www.alibaba.com.

- A *vertical electronic marketplace* is sector specific. Companies in the same sector come together to conduct business, for communication purposes, or to call up industry-specific information. Some examples of vertical marketplaces are 1sync.org (consumer packaged goods), Chemfidence.com (chemical industry), Covisint.com and VWGroupSupply.com (automotive industry), and sourcingparts.com (manufacturing industry).

2.3   Strategic Procurement via a Partnership Relationship

According to Figure 2.2.1.1 a partnership relationship is based on considerable and mutually demonstrable investments of both sides – customer and supplier – in the relationship with this one business partner. This can be the case, for example, with products and services that are customized for the user. It is also the case where joint product innovation stands in the foreground – for example, with system suppliers. In any case, this type of relationship must be designed as long term. In contrast to the buyer-dominated and supplier-dominated relationships, the intensity of cooperation is significantly greater in partnership relationships. Therefore, for entrepreneurial partnerships, the social competency and thus objectives within the target area of flexibility stand in the foreground.

> The *social competency of a company* comprises the flexibility to enter as a partner into a logistics network and to link others into a logistics network.

This demands a high degree of social competency particularly of the leading partner in the supply chain. For many companies, acquiring such competency requires some changes in behavior: Similar to the way that individuals develop social competency for a balanced partnership, a company must develop, first, the ability to play a part in cooperation with others, and second, the ability to engage others as partners in a trustworthy way, that is without using coercion.

In the following, we introduce supply chain management (SCM) and other approaches to strategic procurement that base upon a partnership relationship. The discussions centers mainly on SCM implementation.

2.3.1   Supply Chain Management

> *Supply chain management (SCM)* is the coordination of strategic and long-term cooperation among co-makers in the total supply chain for the development and production of products, both in production and procurement and in product and process innovation. Each co-maker is active within its own area of core competence. The chief criteria when choosing co-makers is their potential contribution towards realization of short lead times.

Related to the target areas of a company's performance, target area strategies arise between the producer and his suppliers as shown in Figure 2.3.1.1. They are complementary to the strategies shown in Figure 2.2.3.1.

- **Target area quality:**
  - Each co-maker *feels responsible* for the satisfaction of the end user.
  - Quality requirements are developed and improved mutually.

- **Target area cost:**
  - All advantages of supply management are maintained. This leads generally to lower transaction costs.
  - Sharing of methods and know-how among co-makers reduces costs.
  - Each co-maker is active in its area of core competence. This yields the best possible return from the resources implemented (including time).
  - Modular sourcing or system sourcing results in fewer ordering processes, because instead of many items, only a few modules or systems have to be procured.

- **Target area delivery:**
  - The same logistics are necessary for all co-makers (same operational procedures, documents, and so on).
  - Planning & control systems are linked (for example, via EDI).
  - The choice of co-makers depends with chief importance upon speed, that is, the co-maker's contribution to short lead times.
  - Local sourcing increases speed and reduces unproductiveness due to misunderstandings.

- **Target area flexibility:**
  - All co-makers give impetus towards product development.
  - Customer and supplier invest considerably in the partnership relationship. In a buyer's market, a change in suppliers is possible, but it is connected with the associated costs.

- **Entrepreneurial cooperation in the supply chain:**
  - All co-makers are involved in product and process development as well as in planning & control from the start.
  - Friction losses due to procurement negotiations are eliminated or reduced. In principle, the advantages of a profit-center organization are carried over to independent companies.

Fig. 2.3.1.1   Target area strategies for supply chain management.

The demand for short product innovation times (time to market) has come to the fore especially in buyer's markets. Cross-company product and process development with co-makers can be advantageous. When product development becomes more and more costly, entrepreneurial risk may in this way be more widely distributed. Reducing the time for product innovation and production demands more intensive business collaboration with co-makers – and this, at all levels of the supply structure (see [Fish97]). That is the origin of the term supply *chain* management.

This type of cooperation gives co-makers insight into the participating companies. Entrepreneurial cooperation thus becomes intensive. One absolute prerequisite is the long-term formation of trust.

In order to support the comprehensive requirements placed on planning & control in a supply chain management concept, specific software called SCM software has been developed in recent years, and intensive development continues. See also Sections 3.5.5 and 8.2.5. As is the case in coping with many other recent issues in modern management, supply chain management requires organizational innovation as well as IT innovation. Good communication paths are necessary, both technical (telephone, fax, ISDN, and EDI) and personal (regular meetings at all hierarchical levels).

Figure 2.3.1.2 groups the tasks in which both supplier and buyer invest in different areas, namely, supply chain structure, supply chain organization, and the required information technology.

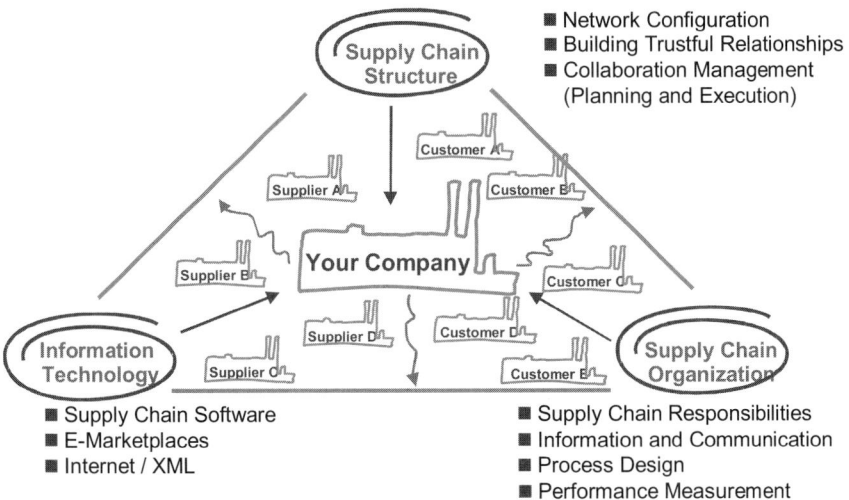

Fig. 2.3.1.2   Tasks and investment areas in supply chain management.

Supply *chain* management tends to have the following disadvantages and risks – in addition to those in supply management, which must be in total smaller than the advantages listed in Figure 2.3.1.1.

- Abuse of the knowledge gained from cooperation with co-makers in order to enter into business relationships with their competitors

- Investment by co-makers that — due to too brief cooperation periods — is not profitable

- Dependence on a system or modular supplier, due to the very close link, can prove to be excessively strong, but dual sourcing can not be considered.

- Local sourcing can result in higher prices, suboptimal product quality, and a lack of quantitative capacity flexibility.

Therefore, great care must be taken when implementing supply chain management. The following section presents a basic framework of the tasks entailed.

2.3.2   The Advanced Logistics Partnership (ALP) Model, a Framework for Implementation of Supply Chain Management

A distinguishing feature of a partnership relationship is its long-term and, at the same time, intensive in nature. The stability of such a relation is guaranteed only if each partner perceives the situation as "win–win." Achieving a win–win situation is the guiding design principle in implementing supply chain management. The *Advanced Logistic Partnership (ALP) model*[6] puts this basic principle into concrete terms. The ALP model is a framework that describes three management levels of interactions among suppliers and customers:

- At the *top management level:* building trust and establishing principal legal relationships

- At the *middle management level:* working out collaborative processes on the supply chain

- At the *operational management* level: order processing

The ALP further distinguishes among three phases in the relationship between suppliers and customers:

- *Intention phase:* choice of potential partners

- *Definition phase:* search for possible solutions, decision making

- *Execution phase:* operations and continuous improvements

---

[6]   The ALP model was developed at the Institute for Industrial Engineering and Management (BWI) of the Swiss Federal Institute of Technology (ETH) in Zurich in cooperation with several firms. See [AlFr95].

Figure 2.3.2.1 shows the nine fields that result from this structuring. Marked in the fields is the basic sequence of implementation of supply chain management.

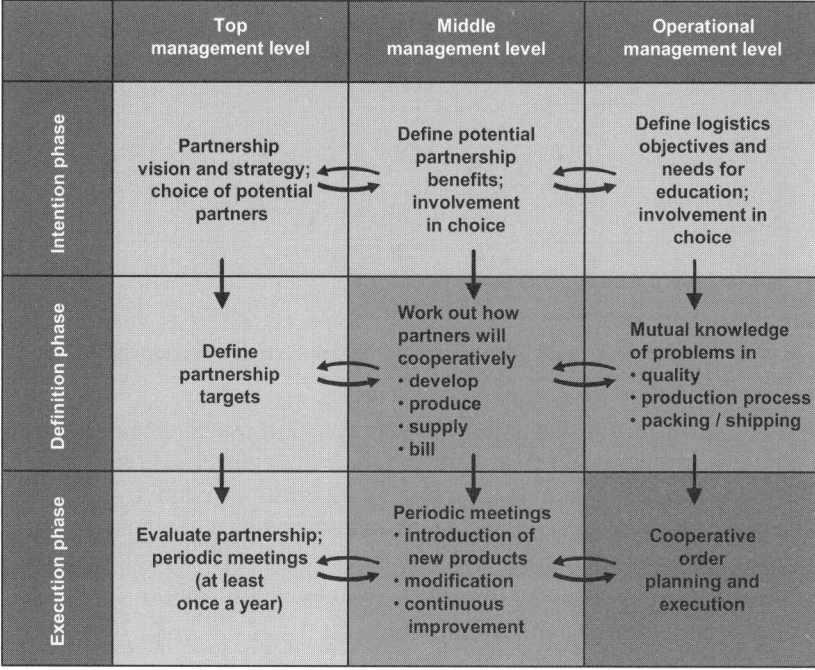

	Top management level	Middle management level	Operational management level
Intention phase	Partnership vision and strategy; choice of potential partners	Define potential partnership benefits; involvement in choice	Define logistics objectives and needs for education; involvement in choice
Definition phase	Define partnership targets	Work out how partners will cooperatively • develop • produce • supply • bill	Mutual knowledge of problems in • quality • production process • packing / shipping
Execution phase	Evaluate partnership; periodic meetings (at least once a year)	Periodic meetings • introduction of new products • modification • continuous improvement	Cooperative order planning and execution

Fig. 2.3.2.1 The ALP model: a framework for implementation of supply chain management.

Looking at the individual levels in more detail, the top management level in principle supplies the requirements for the middle level, while the latter in turn sets requirements for the operational management level. Because cooperation on all levels is the key condition for supply chain management, it is important to involve all participants early on. Only in this way will the consensus and team spirit, that are essential to transcorporate cooperation, develop within an organization. With this, the operational and middle management levels also influence the top level, as indicated in the figure by means of the thin arrow. Additionally, figure 2.3.2.2 indicates the core activities and potentially overlooked activities.

The crucial areas of supply chain management lie in the fields along the axis from the top left to the bottom right. The main work is performed for the relevant activities. The top right and bottom left fields enclose activities which are mostly overlooked in practice.

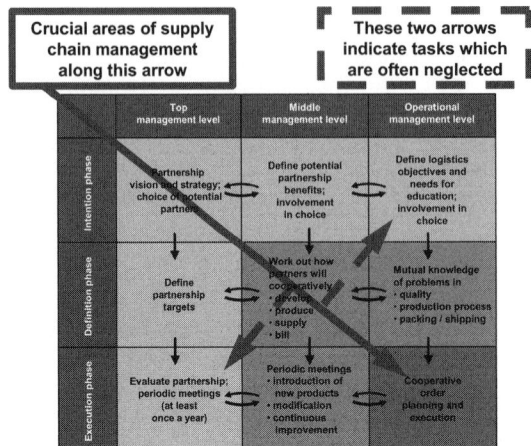

Fig. 2.3.2.2   The ALP model: core activities and potentially overlooked activities.

It is true that in recent discussion on supply chain management, attention has shifted to the four fields to the bottom right of Figure 2.3.2.1 (highlighted by dark shading). Through an integral perspective and a focus on all business processes in the value-added chain, a company aims to coordinate its own planning and execution with that of suppliers and customers in order to achieve the optimum in the entire supply chain.

All the tasks of supply chain management are oriented towards the darkest field, bottom right, of the nine fields in Figure 2.3.2.1, that is the cooperative order processing in the network. For that is where the value-adding takes place that is of interest to the end user. In general, also supply-chain-management software, manages only the tasks in this ninth field. Adequate and efficient implementation of IT support is a necessary, but by itself not sufficient, prerequisite for the success of all other components of supply chain management.

2.3.3   Top Management Level: Building Trust and Establishing Principal Relationships

In the selection of potential partners, the fundamental consideration is whether a co-maker can fulfill the required goals optimally. Partners must formulate these targeted objectives in a sufficiently clear manner, in order to successfully handle unplanned deviations in results from the contractual agreements. However, in order to cooperate long-term and intensively in a supply chain, our research found *trust-building measures* according to Figure 2.3.3.1 to have proven significance (see [Hand95]).

Create the required conditions in your own company first.
- The necessary mentality for a mutual win–win situation.
- Openness to suggestions from internal and external participants.
- Orientation towards procedures and value-adding tasks
- Delegation, teamwork, and the like.

Where possible, place emphasis upon local networks (local sourcing).
- Local proximity affects not only logistics favorably (speed, transport, and carrying cost), but also has a particularly favorable effect on relationships among the participants.
- The persons participating speak the same language and possibly also see each other outside the business relationship. Such informal contacts are often crucial to the success of a network.
- If there are no "world class suppliers" in the region, and none can be brought to locate in the area, it is sometimes advantageous to help a local company to become one. It is then called a "world class local supplier."

Do not exploit strengths in your company's negotiating position.
- Present all intentions openly (no hidden agendas).
- Formulate the objectives of the cooperative venture clearly for all. These objectives may include, for example, achieving a leadership position in a certain market segment or reaching a certain sales volume of an item group.
- The primary competition is competition of the entire supply chain against other supply chains for the favor of the user. Competition between buyer and supplier within the supply chain is of secondary importance.
- It is advisable to distribute gains from a cost reduction or increase in earnings equally, because it is the partnership that is the primary factor in success and not the individual contribution of a partner.

Fig. 2.3.3.1   Trust-building measures in partnership relationships.

Even this incomplete list points out the degree of social competency that is demanded of each partner in supply chain management. But exploiting strengths in the company's negotiating position in particular does accord with the traditional buyer/purchaser mentality. This shows that many supplier relationships that go under the term supply *chain* management do not actually deserve that name; they can be called at best supply management. However, in many cases the supplier will be positioned in the supplier portfolio accordingly, which will be correct with regard to its current business activity.

If, however, the importance of supplier and buyer are mutually high, only the partnership relationship will result in competitiveness of the entire supply chain. People working in procurement learn to become supply chain managers. And employees in sales, production, and logistics can also acquire the required knowledge from procurement and the other areas and successfully become supply chain managers.

For the selection of suppliers, the steps and evaluation criteria in Figure 2.3.1.1 are again useful. In supply chain management, supplier selection often takes place in steps:

- A first call for tenders can define the detailed product requirement specifications as well as the rules for detailed cooperation. This is described in the section 2.3.4. The result serves as the basis for the contractual details in the further requests for quotations.

- The next request can be a request for development and production of a prototype, or the first conducting of a service. Especially for service products or for software production, this can be the only way to test concrete feasibility as well as the validity of the rules and agreements.

- In the case of repetitive services or for large batch production of material goods, there may be one more selection process. Here the supplier that was responsible for the prototype will not automatically be selected again.

2.3.4   Middle Management Level: Working Out Collaborative Processes on the Supply Chain

At the middle management level, the task is to work out collaborative processes on the supply chain that fulfill the required objectives according to Figure 2.3.2.1.

> A *collaborative process* is a process in which supply chain trading partners collaborate.

Figure 2.3.4.1 shows processes in the supply chain in the company (value-adding entity) view. To optimize the *entire* supply chain, the processes have to be worked out jointly with the supply chain partners: that is, the customer chain – the customer and the customer's customers – and the supplier chain – the supplier and the supplier's suppliers.

- Designing a supply chain entails selection of partners in the network and facility location planning. This is a strategic task. It includes also trust-building measures. The definition of controlling processes in the supply chain serves evaluation of the degree of fulfillment of the postulated value. These processes can work out performance indicators of the kind introduced in Section 1.4. Both the design and controlling of the supply chain are processes that *determine* strategically the subsequent planning and operations processes all along the chain.

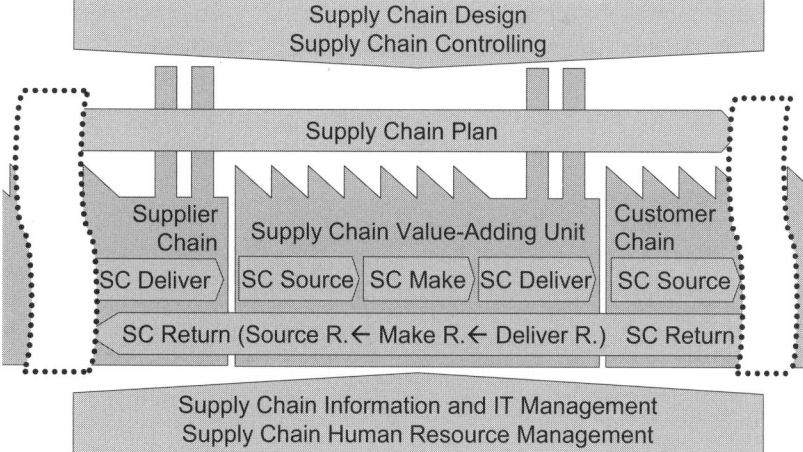

Fig. 2.3.4.1   Cooperative processes in the supply chain.

- In the figure, SC Plan means processes for comprehensive planning of demand and the resources in the network, in particular long-term planning. Also belonging here are also processes for cooperatively billing. SC Source, SC Make, SC Deliver and SC Return describe the specific, long-term and short-term planning and operations tasks in the relevant areas of a value-adding entity. To these tasks belongs also the influence and impact on the adjoining areas of the supply chain, on the side of the network of suppliers as well as the network of customers. The well-known Supply Chain Operations Reference model, SCOR, (see Section 3.5.5) treats these tasks in greater detail.

- Processes integrated across the entire network in the area of IT support are a further key to successful supply chains. A fundamental requirement is, in addition, the necessary education and training of employees at all levels, which includes both specialist competencies in the field and social competency. Both of these categories of processes are support processes that determine what the customer views as the value-adding planning and operations processes along the entire supply chain.

Figure 2.3.4.2 shows how the increased demands for speed result in special challenges for cooperative processes.

Co-makers must master the process of simultaneous development (*concurrent engineering*, or *participative design/engineering*). Co-makers have to possess know-how of the logistics processes in temporally coordinated production and delivery of components. The transparency of planning and control systems is crucial. All necessary information on the co-makership must be freely exchangeable among the partners.

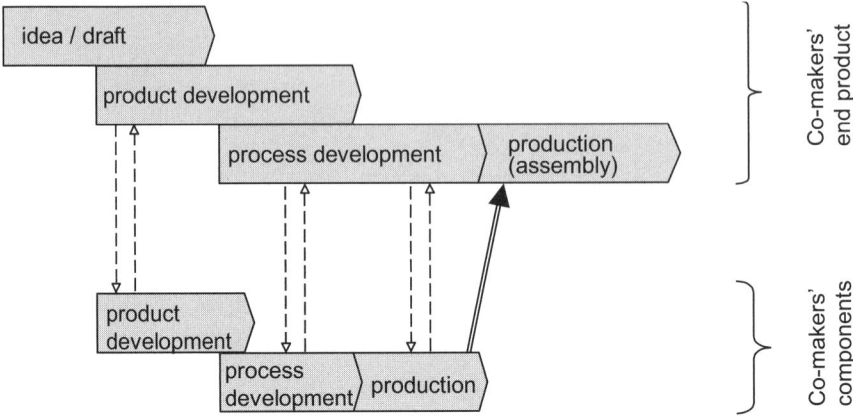

Fig. 2.3.4.2   Co-makership of products: collaborative processes.

With a view to long-term win-win collaboration, the processes as well as all further agreements should be documented in writing. Here, contracts should be drawn up that address the points outlined in Figure. 2.3.4.3:

- *Fundamentals:* Duration, procedure upon liquidation, confidentiality and secrecy, point of arbitration.
- *Quality:* Specification of products and processes,[7] quality management, and measures to handle deviation.
- *Costs:* Distribution of investments in facilities and communication systems.
- *Delivery:* Delivery procedures (normal and rush), batch size and packing, responsibility and cost distribution for warehousing.
- *Flexibility:* Performance indicators and improvement objectives with regard to quality, costs, and delivery.
- *Entrepreneurial cooperation:* Project management of new products and production technologies, copyrights and rights of ownership, liability and guarantees.

Fig. 2.3.4.3   Contract issues for co-makership of products.

---

[7]   A *specification* is a clear, complete, and accurate statement of the technical requirements of a material, a product, or a service, as well as of the procedure to determine whether the requirements are met ([APIC04]).

2.3.5   Operational Management Level: Collaborative Order Processing – Avoiding the Bullwhip Effect

To fulfill the objectives of the collaboration, not only must planning & control systems be linked, but close contact among the participants is also necessary.

> *"Collaborative planning, forecasting, and replenishment"* *(CPFR)* is a process whereby supply chain trading partners can jointly plan key supply chain activities from production and delivery of final products to end customers. Collaboration encompasses business planning, sales forecasting, and all operations required to replenish raw materials and finished goods (see [APIC04]).

Here, employee qualifications play a central role. Transcorporate teamwork with the highest possible degree of decentralized responsibility and powers of authorization for well-trained teams are typical of highly functional logistics networks. Such teams have a mutual understanding of problems with regard to quality, production sequence, and delivery, and they strive towards continuous improvement of order processing, following the idea of a learning organization.[8]

Further measures include techniques of transcorporate data accessing and data revising, particularly of inventory and capacity data. Examples:

- *Vendor-managed inventory (VMI)*, or *supplier-managed inventory (SMI)*: The supplier has access to the customer's inventory data and is responsible for managing the inventory level required by the customer. This includes in-time inventory replenishment as well as removal of damaged or outdated goods. The vendor obtains a receipt for the restocked inventory and invoices the customer accordingly. See [APIC04].

- *Continuous replenishment (CRP, continuous replenishment planning)*: The supplier is notified daily of actual sales or warehouse shipments and commits to replenishing these sales without stock-outs and without receiving replenishment orders. See [APIC04].

An implementation of such procedures entails a lowering of associated costs and an improvement in speed and stock-inventory turnover.

---

[8]   In a *learning organization*, each of the individuals of the group is engaged in problem identification and solution generation ([APIC04]).

The planning & control system for customer order processing is comprised of the tasks shown in Figure 2.3.5.1. Systemic aspects and the systematic of planning & control within a supply chain will be examined in later sections. Here, we present the terms without further definition or commentary.

Long- and medium-term planning:

- System of blanket orders either for development and production of products or "only" for capacities to be reserved, such as production infrastructure and staff members

  Procedures:
- Rolling planning and supplier scheduling
- Continual fine-tuning along the short term

Short-term planning and control:

- System of short-range blanket orders for products and capacities reserved by medium-term and long-term planning, now for concrete products or processes

  Procedures:
- Rapid data and control flow
- Blanket releases and delivery schedules to deliver directly on the production site
- In extreme cases, also delivery on the basis of unplanned demand

---

Fig. 2.3.5.1   Planning & control tasks in co-makership of products.

It is very important in supply chain management to implement countermeasures to prevent the bullwhip effect (also called the Forrester effect).

The *bullwhip effect* is an extreme change in the supply position upstream generated by a small change or no change in customer demand. Inventory can shift quickly from being highly backordered to being excess.

Observations show that the variation of inventory and order quantities increases up the supply chain from customer to supplier. In addition, the longer the lead times of goods, data, and control flow are, the stronger the bullwhip effect is. See [Forr58], [LePa97], and [SiKa03]. Figure 2.3.5.2 shows this effect.

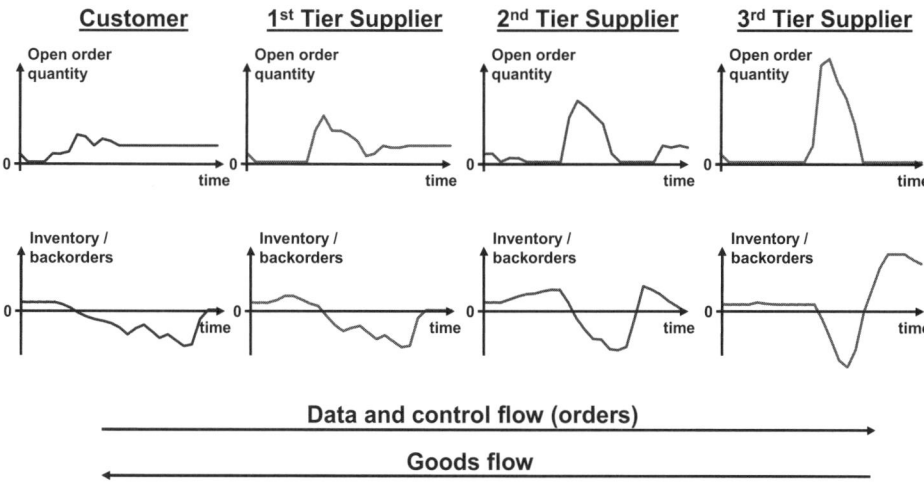

Fig. 2.3.5.2   Open order quantities and inventories/backorders in a supply chain: the bullwhip effect (or Forrester effect).

A famous example, analyzed and published by Procter&Gamble, is demand for Pampers disposal diapers. The bullwhip effect is caused mainly by information processing obstacles in the logistics network; the obstacles are information time lag and distortion (by the actual orders). An appropriate countermeasure is adapting manufacturing lead times (see here [SöLö03]), based on rapid information exchange on consumption, or demand, by point-of-sale scanning.

Point of sale (POS) is the relief of inventory and computation of sales data at the time and place of sale, generally through the use of bar coding or magnetic media and equipment ([APIC04]).

In distribution control, the term *quick response program (QRP)* stands for an information system that links retail sales along with the production and shipping schedules back through the distribution chain. At the point of sale, it employs electronic scanning and data transfer. It may use direct shipment from a factory to a retailer.

This type of information system can also transmit information on demand from end user back to the first link in the chain within a production network. All partners in the network can then rapidly adapt their capacities to current demand quantities and thus avoid large fluctuations in inventory. Experience has shown that this type of information can be exchanged only in networks characterized by complete trust.

2.3.6   An Example of Practical Application

Agie-Charmilles SA, a high-tech Swiss machine tool manufacturer with a world market presence (www.agie-charmilles.com), wanted to introduce the co-maker principle with suppliers of important assemblies. Its objective was to reduce the number of partners while improving quality, keeping costs the same, receiving reliable delivery, and gaining a more flexible response to its needs in terms of quantity and delivery date. Even more important to the company, however, was the creation of conditions that would allow it to focus on its core competencies in developing and assembling its products.

The various suppliers differed in terms of degree of independence and depth of value added. For example, the circuit board manufacturers were all pure subcontractors for performing single operations: the machine tool manufacturer provided not only development and design engineering of the circuit boards, but also the production materials required. The manufacturers of metal casing for the encasement of the benches for workpiece processing, while they procured their own materials, did not do their own development. At the foreground stood local suppliers, in most cases small firms with 50 or so employees and individual departments of medium-sized companies. The following outlines the relevant phases of the co-maker project.

Top management level

The firm's management met for several rounds of discussion of strategy with the management of each supplier. Some of the meetings also included various employees from affected offices and factory workshops. Great emphasis was placed on the win–win principle. A major strategic gain for the supplier was greater competitive advantage achieved through taking on additional competencies. Naturally, each supplier was free to participate or not. However, a supplier choosing not to participate had to reckon with the possibility that it would lose its client to a competitor willing to cooperate.

- The circuitboard manufacturer, in addition to building its own purchasing department, was to achieve delivery quality of virtually 100% while meeting delivery quantity and delivery timing demands. Successive steps towards reaching these objectives were planned out. The machine tool manufacturer promised complete assistance in transferring know-how in these areas.

- For the metal casing manufacturer, the step forward consisted in the choice of a co-maker strategy. The objective for the co-maker was to build up a research and development department having "time to market" priorities that matched those of the machine tool manufacturer. Prerequisites with regard to quality, cost, and delivery were defined more precisely.

Officials met four times a year to examine strategies and objectives. Management of the firms met once a year in order to monitor progress. A serious difficulty arose when the production manager of the machine tool manufacturer, who had lent strong ideological support to the project, left his company. Although unvoiced, serious doubts about the continuity of the project made themselves felt among the suppliers. Things calmed down only once a successor to the production manager was chosen who was known to support the chosen policy. This successor had been manager of procurement and would now take over as the new logistics director as well as manage production, distribution, and information technology. It became quickly apparent that such demanding forms of cooperation do not generally just continue to run at the operational level. Repeated confirmation by responsible officials at the participating companies is essential. Let's look at subsequent steps by taking as an example one particular circuitboard manufacturer and one metal casing manufacturer.

Middle Management Level

At this level products and processes must be developed and introduced. This is the level where it first becomes clear whether the trust-building measures were just talk or were instituted solidly.

- The *metal casing manufacturer* insisted upon a minimum sales quantity, set in advance for a period of several years, in order to have some measure of security in the face of the large investment in CAD for its development department. The machine tool manufacturer was not prepared to agree, as this did not accord with its own view of the meaning of the co-maker principle. A close look revealed that in this phase of defining the processes, it was the commercial director who set the tone, and not the technical director as before. And the commercial director of the supplier firm feared that his investment as co-maker would — due to possible too short cooperation periods — not be profitable. He did not trust the machine tool manufacturer *a priori*. In the discussion, the argument was brought to bear that the machine tool manufacturer itself was incurring an associated risk, namely potential abuse of the knowledge gained from cooperation by the co-maker in order to enter into business relationships with the machine tool manufacturer's competitors. Finally, after long and tough negotiations, the attempt at close cooperation had to be abandoned.

The supplier had reckoned with this result. This was not a problem, because its volume of business with the machine tool manufacturer made up only 4% of their turnover, and their very profitable main business was booming. And the machine tool manufacturer soon found other metal casing manufacturers with which it realized its co-maker concept very satisfactorily.

- The *circuit board manufacturer* saw the requirement to build up its own purchasing department as an opportunity to acquire know-how in qualified office work. Even though, or perhaps because, 80% of its turnover fell to the machine tool manufacturer, it became convinced by the argument that new know-how could in the future be used in connection with other clients as well. (Today, by the way, the machine tool manufacturer makes up only 20% of its turnover, proving the success of the strategy for the supplier.) The required investment was not without risk: hiring an additional employee who was only indirectly productive and 20 directly productive employees. As a result, the processes of shared production, procurement, delivery, and calculation could be defined.

  Throughout the entire design phase, officials of the two companies paid each other visits in order to better understand their partner's processes and associated problems. This led the circuitboard manufacturer to initiate a complete redesign of its procedures, including even the layout of its production infrastructure. But the machine tool manufacturer also had to modify some of its procedures.

Operational Management Level

For the machine tool manufacturer's orders to the circuitboard manufacturer, they chose as a planning and execution system a *supplier scheduling* system, that is, a system of long-, middle- and short-term blanket orders as well as blanket releases with quantities and time periods. This was a logistics method previously unfamiliar to the supplier. Formerly, the supplier had produced only to fixed orders, but it soon recognized that only improved planning on both sides would allow adherence to the drastically reduced delivery lead times that were now demanded. And only in this way could the supplier, for its part, procure the necessary electronic components from its own supplier in time.

In the example, the machine tool manufacturer orders the *exact* required quantity only for the next month, by placing a short-range blanket order. The exact points in time for individual blanket releases during the next month result in this case from a kanban control principle. In the course of the monthly period, requirements arise unpredictably, so that if the company has not given precise dates for probably delivery, the supplier will have to ready the entire quantity of the short-range blanket order at the start of the month.

A system like this, with continuous, ever more precise blanket orders and blanket releases, demanded significant investiture in logistics and planning & control between the company and its supplier. Rapid and efficient communication techniques, to exchange information and to update the planning data, had to be introduced as a condition of coordination.

2.3.7   The Virtual Enterprise and Other Forms of Coordination Among Companies

Are there any possible forms of temporally restricted and yet intensive cooperation, such as for non-repetitive production or a service that solves a customer's specific problem? A virtual enterprise is a potential answer. The reader is referred to [DaMa93] and [GoNa94].

The adjective *virtual* means, according to [MeWe03], "possessed of certain physical virtues." In reference to the business world, this means that a company functions as such, even though it is not a company in a legal sense.

The concept of virtuality aims to utilize the advantages of supply chain management as soon as the customer defines its individual needs. In order to fulfill those needs, several co-makers, with some of their departments, join together. Towards the customer, they stand as a single company, but later they will separate again. These same companies may then join with other companies to form a new virtual enterprise.

A *virtual enterprise* is a short-term form of cooperation for the development and manufacturing of a product among legally independent co-makers in a network of long-term duration of potential business partners. This is true for procurement and production as well as for product and process innovation. The co-makers cooperate on the basis of mutual values and act towards the third party as a single organization. Each co-maker is active within the area of its core competence. The choice of a co-entrepreneur depends upon the co-entrepreneur's innovative power and its flexibility to act as a partner in the logistics network.

The strength of virtual enterprises lies in their ability to form quickly. In the world of practice, co-makers must already be familiar with each other. Figure 2.3.7.1 illustrates this concept.

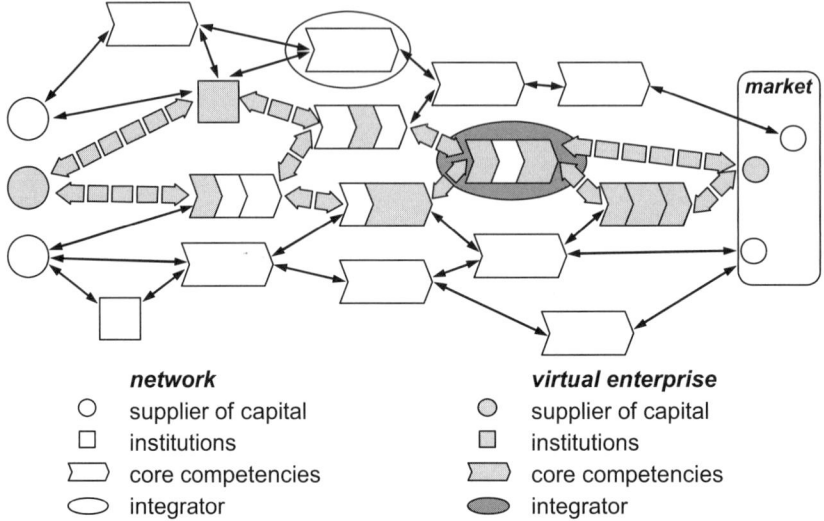

network		virtual enterprise	
○	supplier of capital	○	supplier of capital
□	institutions	□	institutions
⊐	core competencies	⊐	core competencies
◯	integrator	◯	integrator

Fig. 2.3.7.1   The virtual enterprise and underlying network of potential partners (from [Brue98]).

The co-makers of the most various types, that are potential partners in the virtual enterprise strive towards a community of interests in the form of a *long-term* network (see thin arrows in Figure 2.3.7.1) that gives each partner competitive advantages. Any obstructions to cooperation must be removed during this phase, so that the individual network participants can develop a relationship of trust. This requires, just as does supply chain management, the establishment of good communication channels, both technical and personal. For development cooperation, it makes sense in some cases to stipulate contractual terms.

Figure 2.3.7.2 groups the target area strategies with reference to the target areas of a company's performance (see Figure 1.3.1.1). These should be seen as complementing the strategies shown in Figure 2.3.1.1.

• Target area quality:
• Each co-maker is also co-entrepreneur that is, the co-maker shares the entrepreneurial risks within the entire supply chain. Thus, the co-maker carries *extensive responsibility* for end-user satisfaction. • Action guidelines, structures, and processes of the virtual enterprise are developed mutually, as is the basic network of potential partners.

• Target area cost:
• All advantages of supply chain management are retained. This leads to lowest costs.

• Target area delivery:
• The supply chain for a specific order is formed rapidly. • The same operational procedures, documents, etc. are prerequisites. • Identical information systems allow maximal exchange of information during mutual product development and production.

• Target area flexibility:
• Criteria for the choice of a co-entrepreneur are (1) its flexibility to enter as a partner into a logistics network; (2) its *innovative power*, that is, its flexibility in achieving customer benefit by product and process innovation; and (3) the extent of shared value orientations.

• Entrepreneurial cooperation in the supply chain:
• All potential partners form a long-term network. Friction losses that arise from procurement negotiations are eliminated or reduced. One partner has the role of a broker that puts together the virtual enterprise according to a concrete demand. • All co-entrepreneurs supply product and process development and planning & control from the start. They share mutual involvement and responsibility for success or failure.

Fig. 2.3.7.2   Target area strategies for a virtual enterprise.

Of all enterprise performance criteria, a company's flexibility is particularly important here. In addition, in order to form a virtual enterprise rapidly, the company boundaries of the potential co-makers in the network must already be open. In this way, entrepreneurial cooperation can be very intensive. Again, as an absolute prerequisite, trust must develop long term. As a general principle, competition within the network is usually ruled out.

A broker is required for the rapid formation of networks. In the case of non-repetitive production, the broker often serves also as a center for order processing, that is, for planning & control. If lead time must be very short, the planning autonomy of the participating companies must be curtailed. In terms of logistics requirements, the virtual enterprise then takes on the characteristics of a centrally managed cost center.

The other way around, cost center organizations can increase the efficiency of their internal logistics networks substantially by simple application of the principles of the virtual enterprise. The decisive factor here is the degree of flexibility of the cost center to contribute to the objectives of the total enterprise.

In addition to the risks of supply chain management, the procurement strategy via the virtual enterprise tends to have the following disadvantages and risks, which on the whole have to be smaller than the advantages listed in Figure 2.3.7.2.

- A lack of competition with regard to potential partners in the network means that certain orders cannot be taken on.

- Legal problems (loss and gain distribution, copyrights, and rights of ownership) can arise.

- The volume of business is too small to justify the long-term expense involved.

To reduce the risk of a lack of business volume, each of the partners must attempt to anticipate the customers' needs. This demand on agile companies requires study of the actual use of products in order to develop proactive proposals for the implementation of new products that have not even occurred to the customer. See Section 1.3.2.

There are many other forms of cooperation as well. For some of these, specific terms have been coined. The following outline places some of these in relation to the strategies and action plans presented here, in particular in relation to the virtual enterprise. See also [MeFa95].

- *Consortium:* Virtual enterprises are closely related to consortia, because both forms of organization are oriented towards temporally restricted shared objectives (products). Consortia, however, have a horizontal effect, as the member companies work on partial lots of a total order, but do not — as in logistics networks — supply each other. Examples of consortia are found in the building and construction industry. Banks may form a consortium for the issue of securities. *Supplier partnerships*, where several supplier organizations act as one, can also be a consortium.

- *Strategic alliance:* The strategic alliance focuses upon particular business areas and thus on identical or similar competencies. In contrast, the virtual enterprise goes deeper, as it is composed of multifarious abilities. Also, a strategic alliance is formed as an addition to a company's actual core business, while the virtual enterprise is related directly to a company's core competence.

- *(Company) group*: A group is characterized by dominating the companies of the group via contracts. Such contracts — as well as mutual financial participation — are not necessary in a virtual enterprise. However, some companies of a group can certainly take on the role of partners within a virtual enterprise.

- *Cartel:* A cartel serves to regulate or limit competition. Partners tend to be complementary. However, in a virtual enterprise, the goal is not to allow each partner to market the same products, but rather to allow cooperating companies to put a product on the market together.

- *Joint ventures:* Joint ventures involve re-formations and financial participation. These are not necessary in a virtual enterprise.

- *Electronic market:* The electronic market is currently being applied mainly to standard products. It is very conceivable, however, that the electronic market could be installed as a link between the end user and a virtual enterprise. But it would be important that — through parameterization — it could handle demands for individual service.

- *Keiretsu:* Keiretsu is a form of cooperation in Japan in which companies remain legally and economically largely independent, even though they are woven together in various ways. The difference between *keiretsu* and the virtual enterprise is that, in the Japanese variant, membership is permanent.

- *Virtual service organizations* apply the principle of the virtual organization to the structural installation of large international firms manufacturing machines and plant facilities to manage industrial services. See here [Hart04].

2.4   Facility Location Planning in Production, Distribution, and Service Networks

The term *facilities* refers to the physical production plant, distribution and service centers, offices, research and development laboratories, and related equipment [APIC04].

Facility location is the physical location (for example, a region or city) where the facilities come to be. In the following, we use the abbreviated term, location, synonymously.

Facility location planning, or *location planning*, is the planning of locations for company facilities.

Facility location planning is a strategic task, and it is closely associated with a "make" decision. The first steps in facility location planning sometimes make "make-or-buy" decisions at all possible (see Section 2.1.1). Location decisions also have to be reviewed periodically. Globalization in particular is leading companies to revise their location strategies. The reasons for this are, among others:

- Globalization of the targeted market segment requires the local presence of production and distribution facilities, due to official regulations, for example, or because the customer demands it.

- Entry into new market segments: the creation of new production facilities or a distribution center is necessary.

- Cost pressures due to competition and customers as well as a focus on core competencies and core businesses: due to these, individual steps in value added are moved to locations where there is specific know-how or where costs are lower.

- Increasing importance of the time factor in development, order processing, and service in order to achieve short delivery times in distant markets. One solution can be decentralized adaptation of products and services by completing them locally.

- Location disadvantages in the home market (personnel, finance, legal, aids for exports, taxes, patent system, customer basis, mentality, labor unions): moving can provide a remedy.

These reasons change continuously due to the changing global environment. Facility location planning is, however, a very long-term task. Generally, mistakes can not be rectified quickly, and they are very costly. Figure 2.4.0.1 shows the dynamics of the problem as revealed by a survey of medium-sized industrial companies in a country in Central Europe from 2001 to 2003 (see [Frau04]). The survey investigated reasons for moving production facilities to new locations (mostly to Eastern Europe or Asia) and reasons for moving them back.

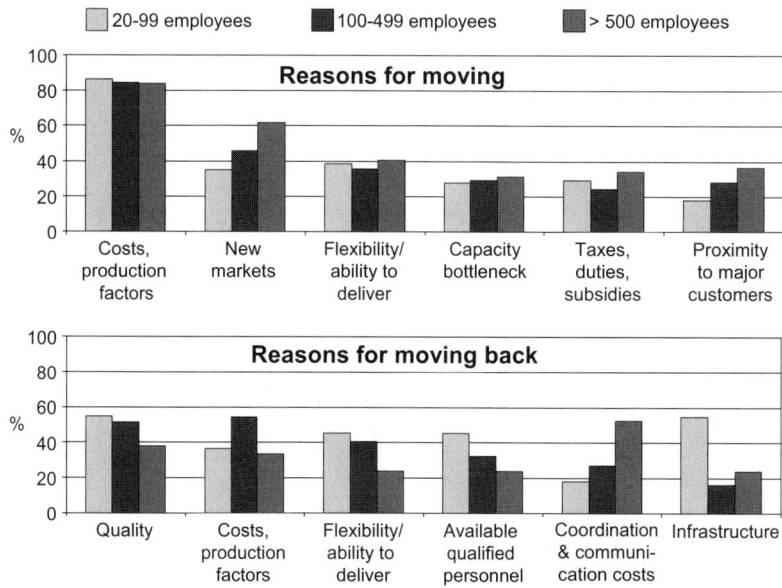

Fig. 2.4.0.1   Reasons for moving facilities to new locations / reasons for moving facilities back (taken from Fraunhofer ISI).

2.4.1   Design Options for Production, Distribution, and Service Networks

Production, distribution and service networks come under the generalized term *value-added networks* (see Section 1.1.3).

There are two fundamental types of production, distribution, and service networks:

- In *centralized production* a product is manufactured at only one location or through a chain of single locations, one location per operation. Analogously, in *centralized distribution* products are delivered to the customer directly from one or a few central warehouses, and in centralized service the customer receives the service directly from or a few central points of service.

- In *decentralized production* a product or certain operations of a product are manufactured at several locations. Analogously, a company operates several warehouses, as close to customers as possible, in *decentralized distribution* and several points of service in *decentralized service*.

Regarding decision variables in configuring locations in a production, distribution, or service network, the advantages that can be achieved by centralization (for example, economies of scale or consistent process quality) stand in fundamental competition with the proximity to the market and customers that a decentralized configuration offers. Here the company must make a strategic decision. Sometimes there are differences for each product family. Figure 2.4.1.1 shows various positioning options in this field of tension, taking the example of a product with four operations (or four production levels) and subsequent distribution.

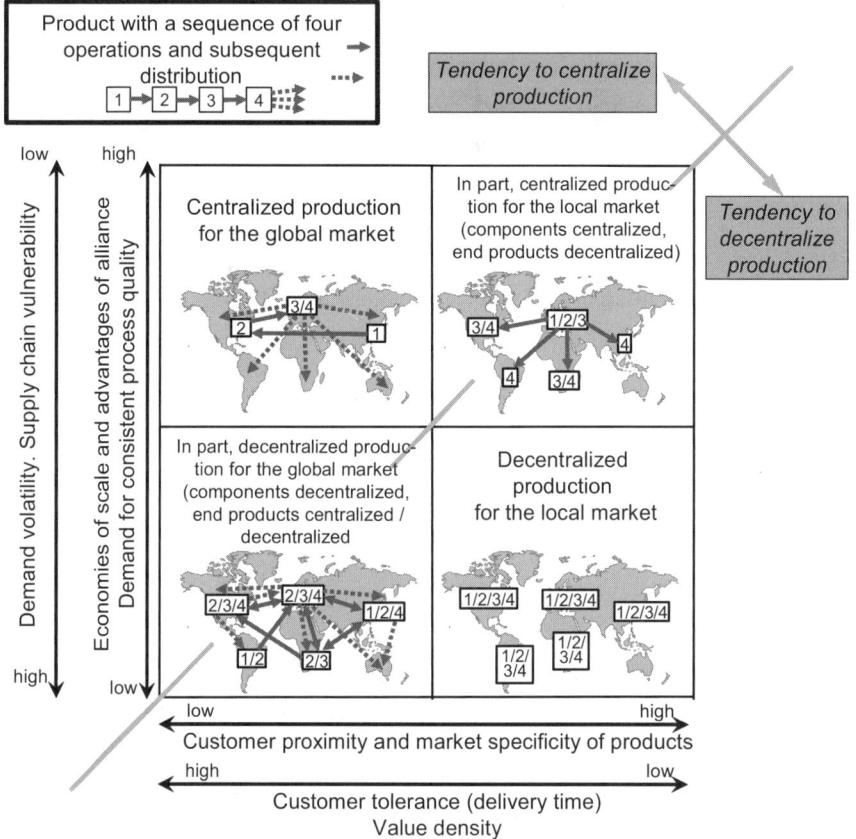

Fig. 2.4.1.1   Decision variables in designing production networks.

The following observations hold:

- *Centralized production for the global market* is advantageous where economies of scale are strong and, in addition, when there are advantages to having well-established, always identical partnerships for the added value of the various production levels. In this way, there is a greater possibility to maintain consistent process quality, which is important mainly for validation of production processes (keyword: GMP, Good Manufacturing Practices). Here it is not essential whether added value occurs via a company-internal supply chain or a cross-company supply chain. Distribution takes place from the location that manufactures the last production level, or last operation. Required for this is, in any case, high *value density*, that is, high product value per kilogram or cubic meter, as well as high customer tolerance regarding delivery time and low vulnerability of the (only) supply chain. The products tend to be standard products. Some examples here are electronic components, LCD displays, consumer electronics, chemicals and pharmaceuticals, fine chemicals, giant aircraft, standard machines and plants.

- *Decentralized production for the local market* is advantageous when high proximity to customers is required, when products must be modified for the local market, and when customer tolerance time and value density are very low. What is needed is a supply chain that is not strongly dependent on economies of scale. Qualitative differences, however, will result. Some examples here are household appliances, building materials (gravel, cement), and products connected with services.

- *In part centralized production for the local market*: If semiprocessed items are produced centrally, and if the last value added steps are performed at decentralized locations, important economies of scale can be exploited while at the same time having proximity to market. Examples here are strategies for local end production for all consumer goods, such as, for example, "mass customization" or "postponement" (see Section. 6.1.4).

- *In part decentralized production for the global market*: If the same components and/or end products are manufactured at different locations, and if at various production levels they can be moved to different locations and distributed globally, this brings advantages in the case of volatile demand as well as for a supply chain that is vulnerable to disruptions, in that the capacities in the network are utilized more evenly or can even substitute for one another. This makes sense, however, only for standard products with high value density and sufficient customer tolerance with regard to delivery times, such as, for example, for components or end products in the automotive industry, perishable foodstuffs, or important raw materials (such as steel).

There are, of course, mixed forms of production networks that lie between these four main designs. This is particularly the case when the characteristics are not significantly pronounced on the abscissa or ordinate of Figure 2.4.1.1.

A distribution network or also a service network – especially if facilities have no direct contact with customers – can potentially certainly develop into a production network or even have, in principle, the same characteristics as a production network. Here are some examples:

- A distribution location can transition to performing some individual operations locally, even if this is only packing and adding lists of contents/instruction booklets (keyword: "postponement" – see Section 6.1.4).

- A call center, travel office, or credit card billing company does not always need to have direct customer contact. These services are then often similar to the production of material goods. The locations of these facilities are then also selected similarly.

For this reason, in the following we will look first at location planning of production networks and then at the specific requirements of distribution and service networks.

For the reasons discussed in connection with Figure 2.4.0.1, facility location planning should be conducted systematically. Figure 2.4.1.2 shows a possible way to systematize the procedure by distinguishing between two different problems, location selection and location configuration.

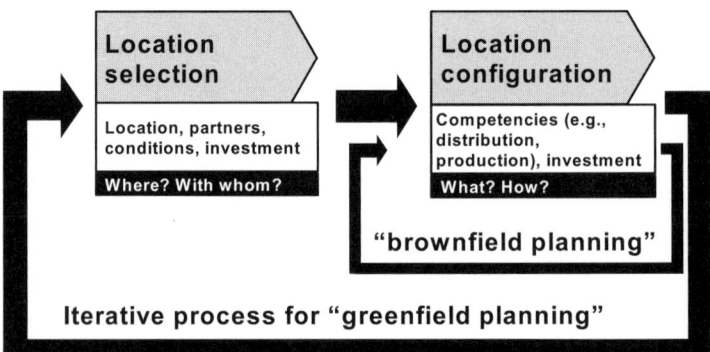

Fig. 2.4.1.2   Location selection and location configuration.

> *Location selection* is selection of new locations, also in the case of moving facilities from existing locations to new locations.

Location selection is a part of what is called "*greenfield planning*", that is, planning with new locations and therefore the fewest possible given framework conditions. Location selection involves investments in basic infrastructures as well as the building of possible company partnerships (for example, joint ventures). Official regulations often play a large role here.

> *Location configuration* is assignment of products to an existing location. The assignment is made for each new product, or service, and can be reviewed periodically. A certain product, or certain service, can be assigned to several locations, not only in distribution but also in production.

Location configuration is a part of what is called "*brownfield planning*", that is, planning with already existing locations and possibly also different framework conditions. Investments are also required for location configuration, this time in personnel, machines, and the necessary investment to build supplier relationships. Official regulations play a great role here.

This means that the starting points and the objectives of location *selection* and location *configuration* are not the same. As a consequence, the methods also differ.

- Location selection is often handled using catalogues of criteria, such as morphological schemes, followed by cost-benefit analysis (factor rating).

- In location configuration, optimization algorithms from operations research are often utilized, such as linear programming, non-linear programming, or heuristic methods.

The two problems will thus be treated in the following in separate sections.

2.4.2   Location Selection for Production Networks: Possible Location Factors and Procedure

Instead of listing all possible criteria for location selection, in the next section below we will discuss a specific case, namely, the evaluation of a joint venture in China by a European company that constructs plants.

It is best to conceive of location selection as a project, with the associated tasks of project initiation, project management, and project realization, that is, the steps of the procedure. Figure 2.4.2.1 shows the steps in the concrete case mentioned above. Noticeable in this specific case is the long time period for location selection. Almost two years were required for the evaluation.

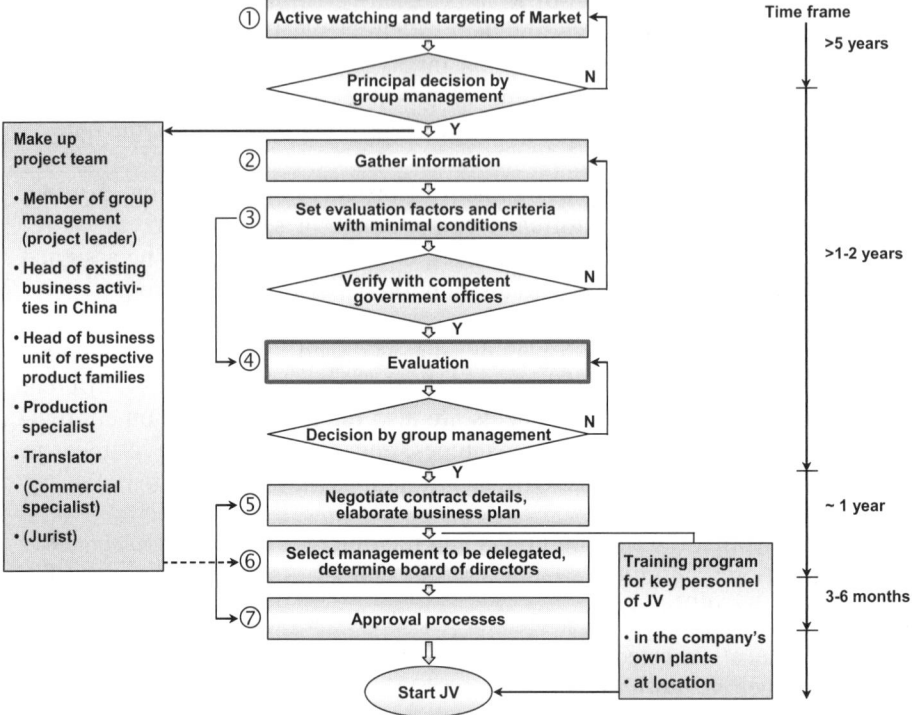

Fig. 2.4.2.1   Steps in location selection and evaluation of a joint venture partner in China.

In the world of practice there are many location factors critical to success. For a comprehensive view of the network, a complete set of location factors with individual criteria is required. Evaluating the degree to which the criteria are fulfilled is then dependent upon the strategy chosen in the specific case. Figure 2.4.2.2 shows the location factors examined.

In addition to five factors that relate to the actual location, three factors are shown that relate to the contemplated joint venture partner. The individual criteria in these three factors can implicitly also characterize – although not only – the location of the partner.

The individual criteria in each location factor and the ratings of each criterion identified in the specific case will be presented in the following section; they will be complemented by some additional possible criteria.

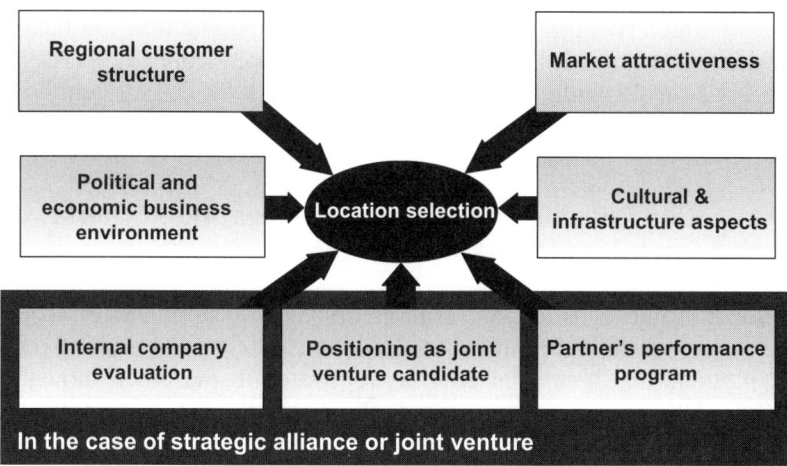

Fig. 2.4.2.2   Factors for facility location selection.

In order to proceed effectively and also efficiently, whereas as many locations as possible are considered, they are reduced as rapidly as possible to a few candidates through examination of an appropriate sequence of location factors. One model for this is shown in Figure 2.4.2.3.

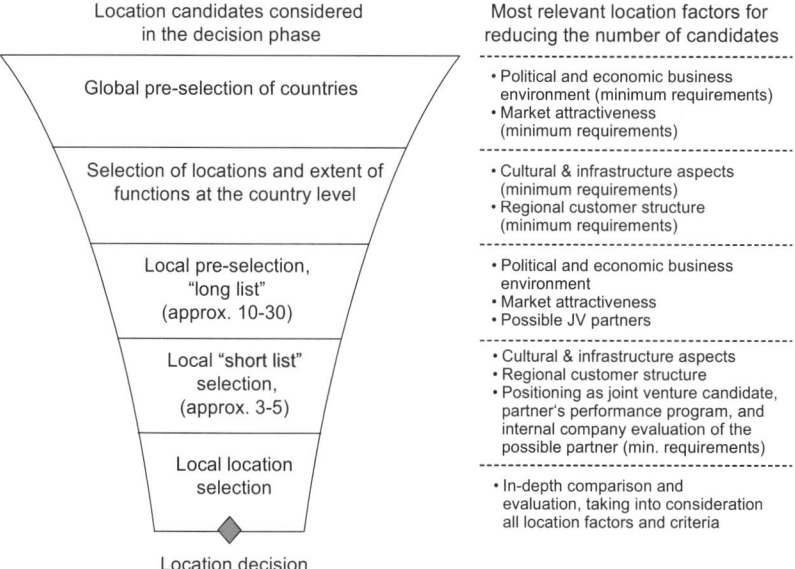

Fig. 2.4.2.3   Systematic reduction of possible locations / partners.

This funnel which was based on an idea in [AbKl06]. The location factors are considered in an order that allows systematic reduction of locations. Section 2.4.2 deals with the final step in Figure 2.4.2.3, treating the comprehensive list of location factors in Figure 2.4.2.2.

2.4.3 Location Selection for Production Networks: Criteria and Cost-Benefit Analysis

The following figures show the criteria for each location factor that a European plant manufacturer rated in the concrete case of evaluating joint venture partners in China. The criteria were rated in the order shown in Figure 2.4.2.1. Each criterion was rated. Of course, the range of values for the factors chosen here are just examples; in other cases, a different range of values might be used.

Figure 2.4.3.1 shows the criteria of the location factor "political and economic business environment."

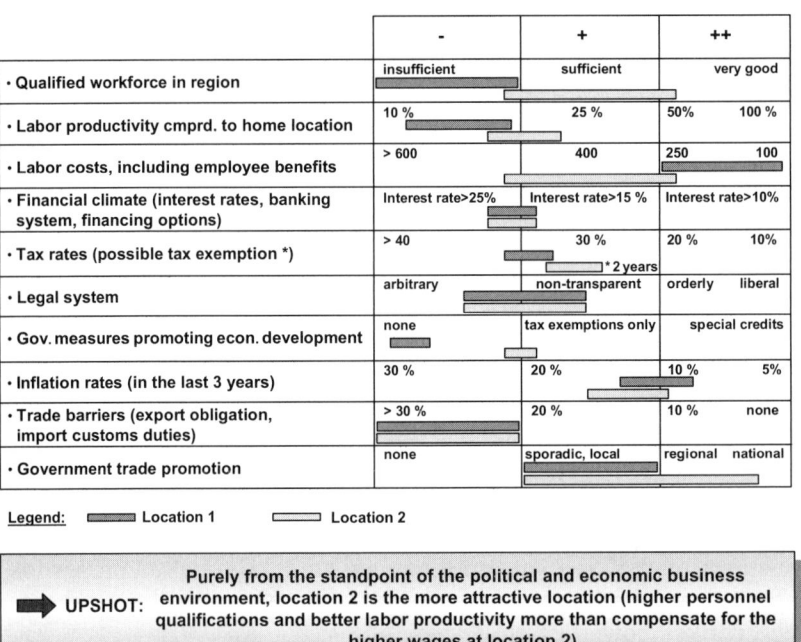

Legend: ▰▰▰▰ Location 1   ▭▭▭ Location 2

➡ UPSHOT: **Purely from the standpoint of the political and economic business environment, location 2 is the more attractive location (higher personnel qualifications and better labor productivity more than compensate for the higher wages at location 2).**

Fig. 2.4.3.1   Evaluation of a JV candidate in China: Criteria of the location factor "political and economic business environment."

As a further criterion for the location factor "political and economic business environment," political stability (unrest, corruption, and strikes) could be evaluated, for example.

Figure 2.4.3.2 shows the criteria of the location factor "cultural and infrastructure aspects."

	-	+	++
• Language (local dialect)	minority language	Cantonese	Mandarin
• Size of town (in thousand inhabitants)	100	1000	3000 >5000
• Number of other joint ventures at location	< 10	< 100	< 500 > 1000
• International schools	none	in planning	available
• Political influence in joint ventures at location	great	exists / manageable	not evident
• Personal relations with local management	problems	perceptible & improvable	full trust
• Personal relations with political authorities	none	problems improvable	good
• Connections to closest big city	train only	train, poor roads >24 h	train, highway 10 h <2h
• Energy availability at location (in part. electr.)	insufficient	some problems	no problems

Legend: ▬▬ Location 1   ▭ Location 2

UPSHOT: **Location 2 clearly offers better cultural and infrastructure conditions for a joint venture dominated by a foreign company.**

Fig. 2.4.3.2   Evaluation of a JV candidate in China: Criteria of the location factor "cultural and infrastructure aspects."

Other criteria under "cultural and infrastructure aspects" could also be work ethic, the availability and skills of workers, and the telecommunications infrastructure or water availability.

Figure 2.4.3.3 shows the criteria of the location factor "regional customer structure."

Further criteria under "regional customer structure" can be the proportion of customers in the region that already are being supplied by the home base, the market power of customers, purchasing power of customers, customer and buying behavior, and the specific product and delivery time requirements of the customers.

Figure 2.4.3.4 shows the criteria of the location factor "medium-term attractiveness of the market."

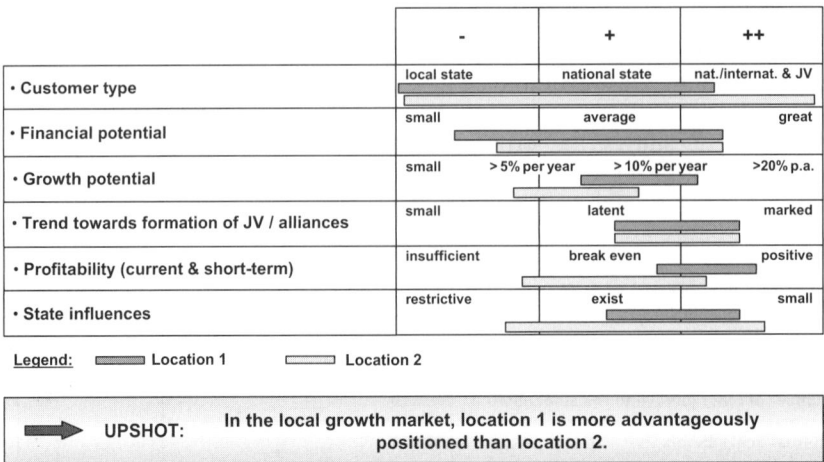

Fig. 2.4.3.3   Evaluation of a JV candidate in China: Criteria of the location factor "regional customer structure."

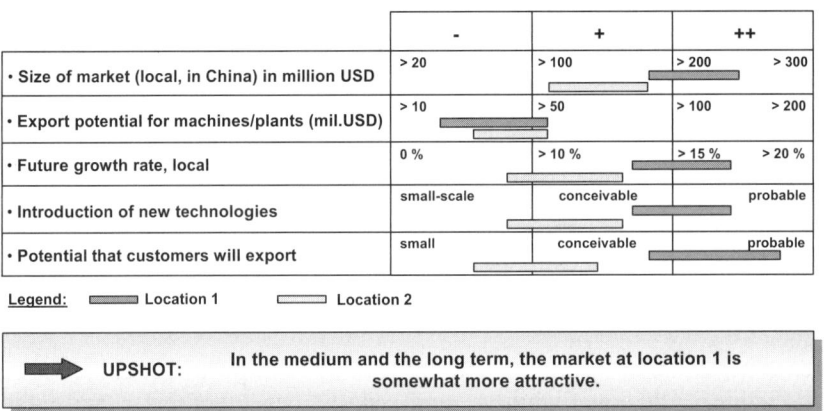

Fig. 2.4.3.4   Evaluation of a JV candidate in China: Criteria of the location factor "medium-term attractiveness of the market."

Further criteria under "medium-term attractiveness of the market" can also be examined: the expected market position, the origins of the competitors (possibly from home), the market segments, the company's own potential for exporting products (transport, customs duties, and so on), and possible substitution products by competitors.

Figure 2.4.3.5 shows the criteria of the location factor "internal company evaluation of a joint venture candidate."

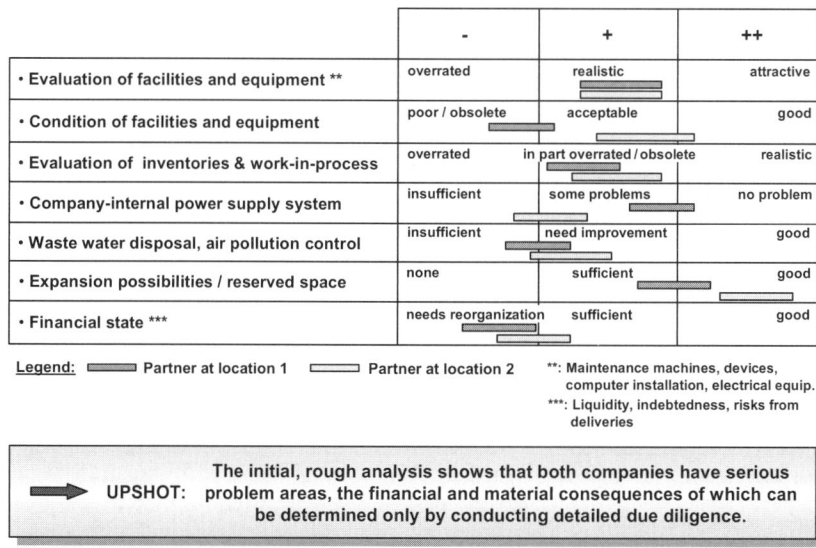

Fig. 2.4.3.5   Evaluation of a JV candidate in China: Criteria of the location factor "internal company evaluation of a JV candidate."

Figure 2.4.3.6 shows the criteria of the location factor "general positioning as joint venture candidate."

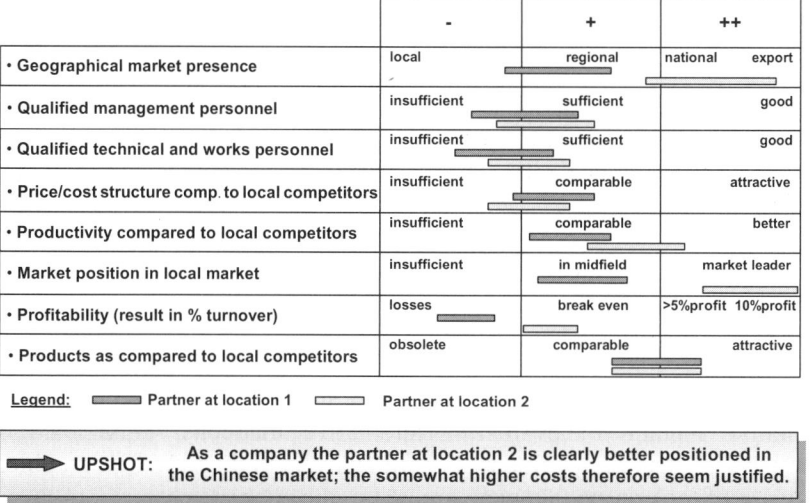

Fig. 2.4.3.6   Evaluation of a JV candidate in China: Criteria of the location factor "general positioning as joint venture candidate."

Further criteria of the location factor "general positioning as joint venture candidate" that can be rated are: regional presence (production / distribution / sales / service), innovation behavior, and strategic orientation.

Figure 2.4.3.7 shows the criteria of the location factor "performance program of the potential joint venture partner."

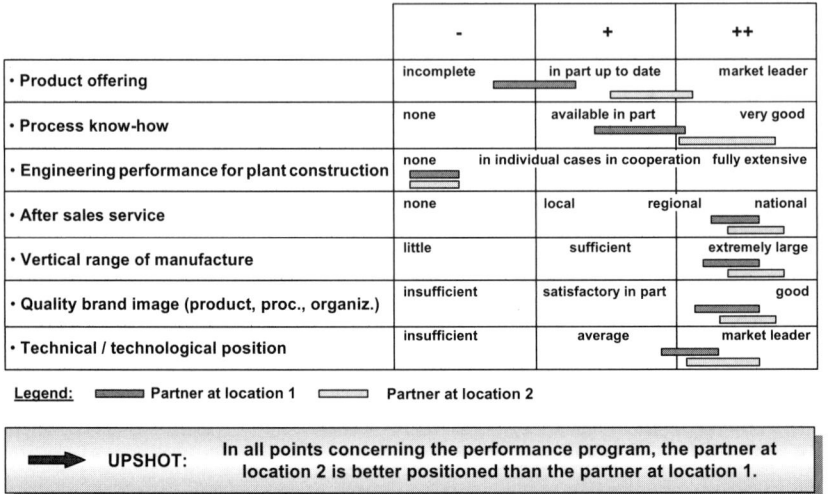

	-	+	++
• Product offering	incomplete	in part up to date	market leader
• Process know-how	none	available in part	very good
• Engineering performance for plant construction	none	in individual cases in cooperation	fully extensive
• After sales service	none	local regional	national
• Vertical range of manufacture	little	sufficient	extremely large
• Quality brand image (product, proc., organiz.)	insufficient	satisfactory in part	good
• Technical / technological position	insufficient	average	market leader

Legend: ▬▬ Partner at location 1   ▭▭ Partner at location 2

➡ UPSHOT: **In all points concerning the performance program, the partner at location 2 is better positioned than the partner at location 1.**

Fig. 2.4.3.7   Evaluation of a JV candidate in China: Criteria of the location factor "performance program of the potential joint venture partner."

Further criteria that can be examined under the location "performance program of the potential joint venture partner" are also the specific process know-how in individual areas of sales and distribution, R&D, production, installation.

Cost-benefit analysis also called *factor-rating system* [DaHe05, p. 382], is a decision method for evaluation of several possible solutions to a problem that can be characterized using factors or features.

Cost-benefit analysis, or factor rating, is generally considered to be a qualitative method of evaluating alternative locations. Figure 2.4.3.8 shows the results of a rough cost-benefit analysis in the form of a graphical summary of the criteria that were applied in the concrete case.

		POSITIONING	
	-	+	++
• Political and economic business environment			
• Positioning of the company as a JV-candidate			
• Cultural and infrastructure aspects			
• Internal company evaluation			
• Performance program			
• Customer structure			
• Medium-term market attractiveness			

Legend: ▬▬ Location 1, or partner at location 1   ▭▭ Location 2, or partner at location 2

Fig. 2.4.3.8   Results of cost-benefit analysis.

The overall rating can be determined qualitatively using the graphical representation in Figure 2.4.3.8 as an aid. First, starting from the rating of the individual criteria in Figures 2.4.3.1 to 2.4.3.7, simple graphical averaging, or interpolation, allows the determining of the positions in Figure 2.4.3.8. As the great majority of the values for location 2 are higher than the values for location 1 – also in both cases where better evaluations resulted for location 1, but were only insignificantly better than location 2 – the decision will be made that location 2 is the better location; in the case at hand, that was indeed the company's decision.

Generally, however, it is necessary in the last step to quantify the ratings and to assign weights to both the individual criteria within a location factor and the location factors in relation to one another (reflecting their relative importance to the company) in order to be able to compare the alternative locations. Instead of estimating the ratings qualitatively (from minus to plus to double-plus), we can determine the degree to which a criterion is fulfilled, expressed, for example, as a percentage of maximum fulfillment of the criterion. Suppose

- n is the number of locations,
- m_i is the number of criteria per location i, $1 \leq i \leq n$,
- $F_{i,j}$ is the degree of fulfillment of the criterion (i,j) of location factor i, $1 \leq j \leq m_i$, $1 \leq i \leq n$,
- $W_{i,j}$ is the weight assigned to the criterion (i,j), $1 \leq j \leq m_i$, $1 \leq i \leq n$,
- W_i is the weight assigned to the location factor i, $1 \leq i \leq n$.

The formula for calculating the overall benefit B for each location and thus the ranking of the locations is then the formula in Figure 2.4.3.9.

$$B = \sum_{i=1}^{n} W_i \cdot (\sum_{j=1}^{m_i} W_{i,j} \cdot F_{i,j})$$

Criterion $C_{i,j}$	Weight $W_{i,j}$	W_i	Alternative locations L_A	L_B	L_C	L_D
$C_{1,1}$	$W_{1,1}$	W_1				
$C_{1,2}$	$W_{1,2}$	W_1	Degree of fulfillment F_{ij}			
...	...	...				
C_{n,m_i-1}	W_{n,m_i-1}	W_n				
C_{n,m_i}	W_{n,m_i}	W_n				

Rank	Final score
1	Location L_B: B =432
2	Location L_D: B =328

Fig. 2.4.3.9   Cost-benefit analysis with degrees of fulfillment and weightings.

For greater certainty in ranking the alternative locations, in addition to determining the overall benefit, it is also necessary to analyze the robustness of the evaluation. This allows identification of locations that are close in the overall score. This robustness includes variation of both the degree of fulfillment and the weightings. Here the degree of variation of each parameter should be as well-founded as possible.

The quantification of ratings can also be set by considering costs and investments associated with the locations. This can, for example, concern the criteria under the location factor "internal company evaluation" (see Figure 2.4.3.5). In this case, to discount the benefits and costs over time, commonly used methods of investment analysis can be applied, such as the net present value technique, NPV (see Figure 18.2.5.3).

2.4.4   Location Selection for Distribution and Service Networks

The *distribution network structure* defines the planned channels of distribution of goods. Figure 2.4.4.1 shows an example.

The distribution network thus comprises:

- The number of *distribution structure levels* (e.g., central warehouse or distribution center → regional distribution center → wholesaler or distributor → retailer)
- The number of warehouses per distribution level
- The locations and delivery areas of warehouses

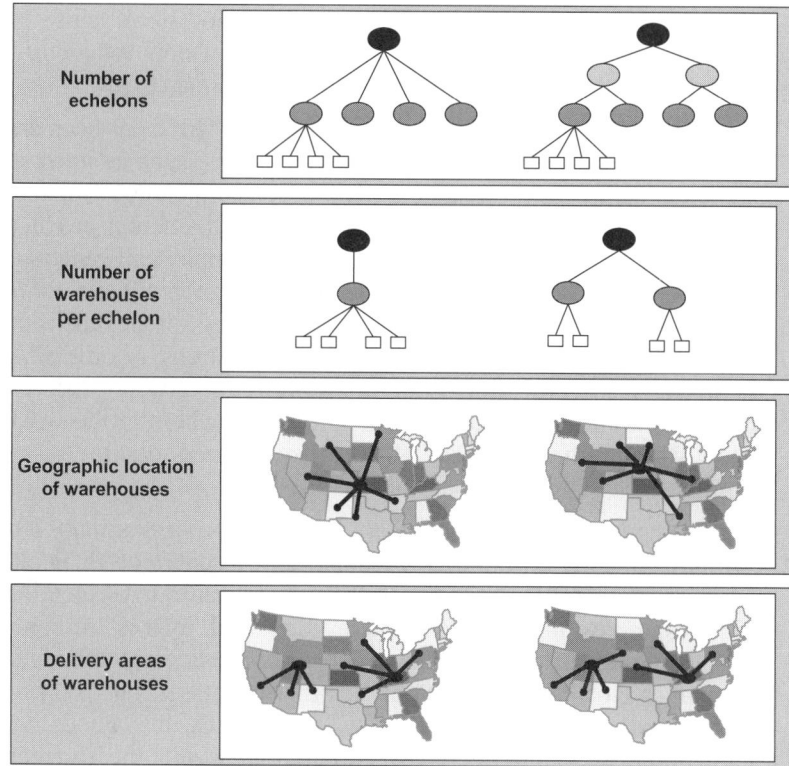

Fig. 2.4.4.1   Decision variables in the design & planning of the distribution
network structure. (Following [FIR00], p. 249.)

The result is a spatial distribution network, and several such networks can
become linked together through transfer stations.[9]

There is a dual consideration behind service networks. A *service* is a
process that mainly takes place in the presence of the customer. Due to
technological development and industrialization, however, (sub) processes
of the service as a whole have developed for which the extent of customer
contact differs:

- *Process with direct contact with customers*: These are the original
  services, such as services in hair salons, hotels, bank branch
  offices, supermarkets, and small stores. These sales locations,

---

[9]   In addition, at every distribution structure level, by a process called *break-bulk*,
truckloads of homogeneous items can be divided into smaller, more appropriate
quantities for use ([APIC04]).

therefore, must be located at convenient locations close to customers. The crucial point in the selection of new locations is prediction of the potential for feasible *points of sale* (POS).

- *Process with indirect contact with customers*: These services are, for example, the taking of reservations or orders, such as in travel agencies, car rental companies, mail order companies. But they can also deliver information and thus support the actual products or services, both before and after sales (for example, call centers or hot lines). The locations for these services do not have to be located in proximity to customers. Web sites often fulfill the purpose, at least for simple information, reservations, or orders. As the delivery costs of information do not differ greatly for different locations, the locations can in principle be anywhere in the world where the production costs – for the required quality – are minimal.

- *Process with no customer contact*: These are processes that – for example, due to efficiencies (economies of scale) or difficulty (economies of skill) – must be carried out at a centralized location. Some examples of these processes are the "back offices" of banks (for example, in the mortgage or loan business), insurance companies (for example, for policies that cover special risks), or credit card billing companies. In these cases the goods are nonmaterial, so that delivery costs do not play a role; these centers can in principle be located anywhere in the world, as long as quality is assured. Other processes that belong here are also centralized commissaries for catering businesses or – as mentioned above – processes along the distribution network structure for material goods; in these cases there are delivery costs in addition to production costs, so that the facilities can not be sited at just any locations.

With this, under certain conditions multi-level service networks will form, in which the individual locations are linked together through the definition of the entire process that defines the service.

Location selection for distribution and service networks depends essentially on customer relationship management.[10]

---

[10] *Customer relationship management* is a marketing philosophy based on putting the customer first ([APIC04]). Guidelines for the desired relationship to the customer are established (for a discussion of the more technical background of this term, see Section 8.2.6).

- For processes with no customer contact, the location factors and criteria are in principle the same as those described above in Section 2.4.3 for production networks.

- For processes with indirect contact with customers, there are often additional factors, such as the availability of lower-cost temporary personnel that can be flexibly (time) employed.

- For processes with direct contact with customers, in contrast, the main factors are criteria such as access routes (pedestrians, cars, public transportation), population density, size of families, and annual family income.

As a simple decision method for location selection, cost-benefit analysis can be used. If delivery and transport distances from a production location, an order picking store, or a commissary, to customers play a dominant role, and if the corresponding costs are proportional to volume, the method of choice can be the center of gravity approach. Although the postulated proportionality is generally not a permissible simplification, it is acceptable in the first approximation.

> The *center of gravity method* is a highly simplified quantitative methodology for locating service centers at approximately the location representing minimum costs for delivery or transportation from the production or distribution plants to the markets or customers.

Figure 2.4.4.2 shows the principle of the center of gravity approach. A company in the United Kingdom needs to find the optimum location for an order picking store, to serve six customer locations L_i, $1 \leq i \leq 6$ in London.

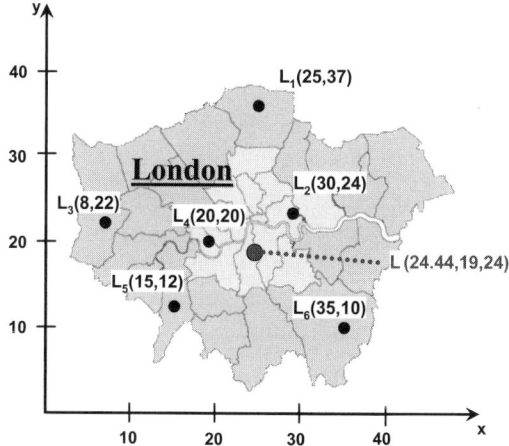

Fig. 2.4.4.2   The center of gravity method.

To put it simply, the geographical coordinates of the center of gravity L, that is, L_x und L_y, multiplied by the total volume V, correspond to the sum of the geographical coordinates of the customer locations L_i, that is, $L_{i,x}$ and $L_{i,y}$, multiplied by their volumes V_i , as shown in Figure 2.4.4.3:

$$L_x = \sum_{i=1}^{n}(L_{i,x}V_i) / \sum_{i=1}^{n} V_i$$

$$L_y = \sum_{i=1}^{n}(L_{i,y}V_i) / \sum_{i=1}^{n} V_i$$

Fig. 2.4.4.3   Formulas for the coordinates of the center of gravity.

That is where the term "center of gravity" comes from. The calculation can also be programmed using an MS Excel spreadsheet. If, for example, for the example in Figure 2.4.4.2 we select as volumes $V_1 = 100$, $V_2 = 20$, $V_3 = 40$, $V_4 = 100$, $V_5 = 80$, $V_6 = 160$, then the resulting sum is $V = 500$, and thus

$L_x = (25 \cdot 100 + 30 \cdot 20 + 8 \cdot 40 + 20 \cdot 100 + 15 \cdot 80 + 35 \cdot 160) / 500 = 24.44$
$L_y = (37 \cdot 100 + 24 \cdot 20 + 22 \cdot 40 + 20 \cdot 100 + 12 \cdot 80 + 10 \cdot 160) / 500 = 19.24$

The same method – with the same restriction as to general validity – can be chosen for location planning of a retail location, if the potential proceeds are proportional to sales volume in the residential areas to be supplied, that is, the number of potential customers in the residential area multiplied by the average expected sales revenue per customer.

However, generally the facility can seldom be located at the identified geographical center of gravity, and even so, it would be rather by chance the truly optimal location:

- It may not be suitable for physical reasons (for example, the center of gravity could be the middle of a lake) but also due to zoning laws (for example, it may be outside the building zones) or pure logistics reasons (far from transportation routes).

- In addition, the distance measure selected is implicitly right-angled: it is as if the delivery from the center of gravity to the customer would follow a right angle, first via the x-axis and then the y-axis, or vice versa. However, the actual geographical distance depends on the transportation routes.

- And then, as mentioned, costs and revenues are not always proportional to volumes. For with higher volumes, for example, a different means of transport can be chosen, and the same goes for long distances.

Nevertheless, the location can serve as an initial solution for further considerations: In the area around the center of gravity, we can look for a number of feasible locations, for example, locations that are near highway exits or where there is a high concentration of customers. The distance $D_{A,i}$ from candidate facility location L_A to customer location L_i can be determined using transport distance tables or geographic information systems (GIS), for which in many countries commercial software is available (for example, at http://www.mapinfo.com). Supposing that the volume to be delivered to customer location L_i is again V_i and the costs $c_{A,i}$ are proportional to the volume distances, then the total costs C_A, C_B, ... add together for the candidate locations L_A, L_B, ... as shown in Fig. 2.4.4.4.

$$C_A = \sum_{i=1}^{n} c_{A,i} * D_{A,i} * V_i$$

$$C_B = \sum_{i=1}^{n} c_{B,i} * D_{B,i} * V_i$$

Fig. 2.4.4.4   Formula for location selection in distribution and service networks.

The formula also has the advantage that for different distances to customer location L_i different means of transport can be implemented. This is expressed by the different cost factors $c_{A,i}$ and $c_{B,i}$ for two candidate locations L_A and L_B. Of course, an extended formula can take also conditions other than volume proportionality into consideration, if, for example,

- Different means of transport are selected for volumes above a certain amount.

- Minimum volumes determine the transport costs (which is often the case for a company's own transport capacities).

This simple method stands in contrast to complicated heuristic methods, which can possibly deliver better solutions. This difference is small, however, as compared to the difference that arises from the fundamental problem that new transport routes and concentration centers are always being built. Moreover, important customers can move away, or the political and economic business environment can change. Then, any once selected location can prove to be suboptimal. If the high building costs have not yet been written off, the facility can not simply be changed to fit the new data, or in other words, it can not simply be moved to a new location.

In distribution and service networks, sometimes location planning for multiple locations is required. Cluster analysis methods or other heuristic methods, which are not discussed here, can provide decision support. Also in this case, however, and for the same reasons, the observation above holds that any "optimum" solution at any given moment can become suboptimal in the medium term. Ultimately, simple and robust methods have advantages over complicated optimization methods.

2.4.5   Location Configuration with Linear Programming

Probably the most challenging configuration of a production network as shown in Figure 2.4.1.1 is *in part decentralized production for the global market*. In this case the task of location configuration is not trivial, but it is also not insignificant in the other cases. This is a master planning task, that is, it is determination of a global production plan: What products and – in the face of limits of capacity – how much of what product will be manufactured for what markets at what level at what locations? A similar question can also arise for *decentralized distribution* or *decentralized service*: What customers will be served by what distribution and service locations? Very many influencing variables can soon lead to a complex configuration problem.

Decision making can be supported – often with simplified model assumptions – by Linear Programming (LP). The following section deals with LP, and Section 2.7.4 presents a simple scenario. Solution of the problem using a non-linear objective function, or non-linear programming altogether, will not be discussed here.

In *Linear Programming* the task is to solve a problem that can be expressed as in Figure 2.4.5.1.

1. Objective function: $OF = max!$ *(maximize OF)*

2. Solve for vector of variables $\boldsymbol{x} = (x_1, x_2, x_3, ...)$,
   the decision variables are $x_1, x_2, x_3, ...$

3. Value of OF depends on $\boldsymbol{x}$, subject to restrictions / conditions as constraints for $\boldsymbol{x}$

   Matrix notation: $OF = c \cdot \boldsymbol{x} = max!$

   $$A \cdot \boldsymbol{x} \leq b$$

   and $\boldsymbol{x} \geq 0$

Linear programming:
Maximize OF subject to constraints and solve for $\boldsymbol{x}$

Fig. 2.4.5.1   Linear Programming.

Figure 2.4.5.2 shows another commonly used form with sum notation.

1. Objective function: $OF = max!$
2. Decision variables $x_i,\ 1 \le i \le n$
3. Restrictions/conditions as constraints for x_i
   Sum notation:

$$OF = \sum_{i=1}^{n} c_i x_i = max!$$

$$\sum_{i=1}^{n} A_{ij} x_i \le b_j \qquad ,1 \le j \le m$$

$$x_i \ge 0 \qquad ,1 \le i \le n$$

Fig. 2.4.5.2 Linear Programming: Sum notation.

If the number of decision variables is two, the problem can be solved using a simple graphical method. With a greater number of variables, the use of an algorithm is recommended, such as, for example, the Simplex algorithm. The complexity of the problem increases with increasing values of the number of variables (n) and the number of constraints (m). Computation time does not increase polynomially with n and m: the Simplex algorithm is what is called an "NP-hard" algorithm. With high values of n and m, also the procurement of data is a problem.

For some years now, MS Excel has offered a Solver tool that can be used to solve a Linear Programming problem with (in the current release) 200 variables. Scenario 2.7.4 uses this tool. In this section, the screen shots in MS Excel Solver also show a depiction and solution of an LP problem.

2.5 Summary

The transaction cost approach describes the primary factors in the formation of companies. Estimation of transaction costs leads to a make-or -buy decision. A make decision results in outsourcing: parts of the supply chain are turned over to other companies. A buy decision results in insourcing; here there are various possibilities of forming organizational entities within the company.

A buy decision requires subsequent setting of the procurement strategy. Concepts such multiple sourcing, single sourcing, and so on describe only one aspect. The objects to be procured are grouped into material groups. The supplier portfolio divides relationships with potential suppliers into market-oriented, buyer-dominated, supplier-dominated, and partnership relationships. Based on their logistics characteristics, the appropriate supplier relationships are determined for the material groups.

As procurement strategies, the following are described in this chapter: 1) for market-oriented relationships, the traditional marketplace with supply contracts of short duration and low intensity of cooperation according to win-win approaches; 2) for buyer-dominated or supplier-dominated relationships, supply management or supplier relationship management with long-term supply contracts but still low intensity of cooperation according to win-win approaches; 3) for partnership relationships, either supply chain management with long-term supply contracts and a high intensity of cooperation according to win-win approaches or the virtual enterprise more for non-recurring business but also with a high intensity of cooperation according to win-win approaches. In all cases, the target area strategies that develop between the producer as buyer and the producer's suppliers are discussed. Supplier selection is then performed via procurement market research, supplier evaluation, and the actual selection of suppliers. All of the steps of search and initiation and negotiation, in particular, can today be supported by e-procurement, for example by sell-side or buy-side solutions as well as horizontal and vertical marketplaces. In partnership relationships in particular there can be several requests for bids: a first one for product requirement specifications and the rules of cooperation, a second one for prototyping, and a third one for repetitive procurement. The Advanced Logistics Partnership (ALP) Model is a basic framework here for the implementation of supply chain management.

A make decision requires subsequent planning of facility locations. Arguments for centralized or decentralized organization (or combined forms of these) of production, distribution, and service networks are, among others, value density, customer proximity, customer tolerance time, markets requiring specific products, volatility of demand, the supply chain's vulnerability to disruptions, economies of scale, and other advantages of the close link. For the selection of new locations, the chapter introduces seven possible location factors (three of these for the selection of joint venture partners) with 5 to 10 criteria per factor and a procedure for systematic reduction of possible locations. Locations for distribution and service networks are selected according to the degree of customer contact. If only indirect contact, or even no contact at all, with customers is necessary (the case, for example, with "back offices"), the location criteria are basically the same as those for production locations. For selection of new locations, cost-benefit analysis is frequently used; also the center of gravity approach is used for distribution and service networks. For location configuration, that is, for assigning products or services to an existing location, Linear Programming can be used. Microsoft's MS Excel offers a Solver tool that can be used to solve problems with up to 200 variables.

2.6 Keywords

Advanced Logistic Partnership (ALP), 98

backward integration, 74

bullwhip effect, 106

continuous replenishment, 105

cost center, 75

CRP (continuous replenishment planning), 105

customer–supplier partnership, 88

direct material, 78

distribution network structure, 130

electronic marketplace, 93

facility, 115

forward integration, 74

global sourcing, 79

indirect material, 78

insourcing, 70

local sourcing, 80

location (syn. facility location), 116

make-or-buy decision, 70

multiple sourcing, 79, 85

outsourcing, 70

point of sale (POS), 107

process-focused organization, 75

product-focused organization, 75

profit center, 75

quick response program QRP, 107

single sourcing, 79

social competency of a company, 95

sole sourcing, 79

specification, 104

supplier relationship management (SRM), 86

supply chain management, 95

supply management, 86

transaction costs, 71

vendor-managed inventory (VMI), 105

virtual enterprise, 111

2.7 Scenarios and Exercises

2.7.1 Supply Management — Supply Chain Management — Advanced Logistics Partnership (ALP)

a. Figure 2.3.3.1 presented arguments for the emphasis on local networks (local sourcing with world class local suppliers) that is a feature of the ALP model. Do you know of any companies (including some in the service industry) that follow this principle? Do some Internet research and find out whether these companies address the issue of local sourcing on their web sites.

b. A supply chain processes a particular kind of timber with special
    characteristics that grows in a particular region. The following
    companies make up the supply chain: (1) a lumber mill with various
    forest owners as potential suppliers, (2) a wood planing mill, and (3) a
    company that provides surface treatments and finishes and handles
    distribution. For the wood planing mill, how would you take into
    consideration and hold in check the following risks involved in
    forming this supply chain:

    b1. There is a risk that the lumber mill could be bought out by a paper
        factory that requires the entire production for its own use. (*Hint*:
        Compare this situation with the argumentation in Sections 2.2.3
        and 2.3.1.)

    b2. Storms could cause widespread destruction of the forests, resulting
        in a sharp rise in the price of this type of wood on the free market.
        (*Hint*: Compare this situation with the argumentation on "non-
        exploitation of the strengths of a company's negotiating position"
        presented in Figure 2.3.3.1.)

2.7.2   Evaluate Company Relationships

Look at a supply chain in the wood and furniture industry. The IGEA
Company is a furniture company known mainly for its successful cash-
and-carry furniture retail business. Faced with enormous cost pressures,
IGEA management has decided to explore the possibility of forming a
supply chain. Internal company improvement measures simply do not
promise more than marginal cost savings, and prices paid to suppliers can
not be lowered any further without risking losing some suppliers, which
would mean that IGEA could no longer offer some of its products.

IGEA managers have read a study that you published on cost savings
achieved through transcorporate supply chain management. They believe
that the savings they could achieve through supply chain management
would give them an edge over their main competitor, the INFERNIO
Company. IGEA will therefore head the supply chain project, taking on the
role of integrator for the new form of supply management. Due to its
dominant position on the market, IGEA succeeds in convincing its main
suppliers and some of the affiliated sub-suppliers to join them in taking
this transcorporate step.

You are commissioned to conduct an analysis of a logistics network in the
wood and furniture industry. Figure 2.7.2.1 shows the interrelationships

among the companies concerned. The companies highlighted in gray will be integrated into the new supply chain described below. As of now, five companies have agreed to form the supply chain:

- Forest Clear Co.
- Wood Chips Co.
- Wood Flooring Co.
- Shelving Manufacturing Co.
- IGEA

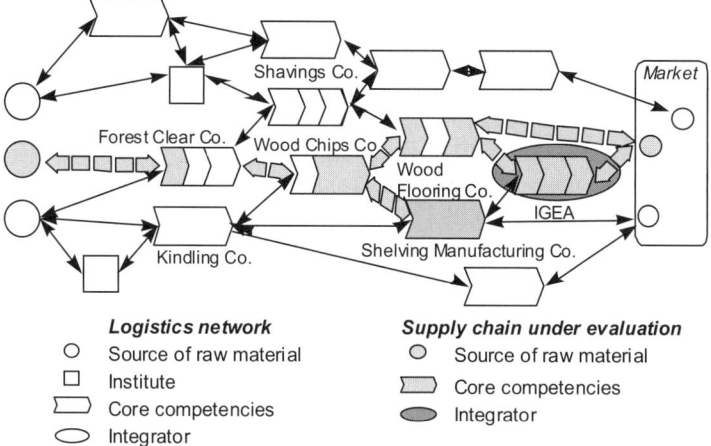

Fig. 2.7.2.1   Logistics network in the wood industry (compare Fig. 2.3.7.1).

For the following analyses and considerations, however, it is important not to lose sight of the other, existing company relationships, since it might make sense to include additional companies as partners in the cooperative project or to sever some of the existing company relationships (for example, Kindling Co., Shavings Co., and other possible companies).

You will need the following details of some of the company relationships in order to conduct your analysis and identify potential improvements:

- *Business relationship between Forest Clear Co. and Wood Chips Co.:* Forest Clear, based in Finland, is known for its bold dealings with its customer, the Wood Chips Co. Delivery agreements are very short term, which necessitates frequent, tough negotiations. Still, the excellent quality of the Forest Clear material forces Wood Chips to continue doing business with them. However, delivery delays are becoming more and more frequent, to the point that this is now affecting Wood Chips' own fill rate. The chief buyer at Wood Chips has invested many hours in meetings with the wood supplier in an attempt to improve the situation, but Forest Clear is resistant to showing its cards. The Forest Manager does not encourage visits, and the company will not reveal their long-term product and capacity planning. Although Forest Clear had been asked repeatedly to develop a concept for eliminating the problems, they have produced no proposals.

- *Business relationship between Wood Chips Co. and Wood Flooring Co.:* The relationship between Wood Chips and Wood Flooring is very tense. The delivery reliability of Wood Chips, as sub-supplier of high-quality boards, is seriously deficient, which is having an extremely negative effect on Wood Flooring's own service level. For this reason, Wood Flooring is often forced to procure products from another sub-supplier, Shavings Co., which entails considerable additional costs and effort. Another contributing factor is the tense relationship between the chief buyer at Wood Flooring and management at Wood Chips. Due to the very large volume of material purchased, Wood Flooring has not been able to find another, equivalent supplier. In addition, because it procures such vast amounts of material, Wood Flooring has a strong enough position in the market that it can often dictate prices. And naturally, over the years, it has frequently exploited this advantage. Blanket contracts with a 5-year duration thus contain a 2.5% discount annually, based on forecasted productivity increases and a learning curve on the part of the supplier. This is another reason why Wood Chips does not want to work with Wood Flooring.

- *Business relationship between Wood Chips Co. and Wood Shelving Co.:* Wood Shelving and Wood Chips enjoy a very friendly and constructive business partnership. Wood Shelving is one of Wood Chips' most important customers, and Wood Chips is willing to respond promptly and without complications to any special requests. The business relationship has advanced to the point where monthly product management meetings at Wood Chips are attended by a purchaser from Wood Shelving, who reports on forecasts and trends in the sales market. For delivery, 1- to 2-year contracts are concluded. There are some problems, however, with operational order processing. Orders are made by fax and by mail, but also by telephone, which results in a lot of redundant data, and no one is sure what the correct figures are. The business relationship is supported by the geographical proximity of the two companies (within 20 miles of each other in Sweden).

- *Business relationship between Wood Shelving Co. and IGEA Co.:* IGEA is known for its readiness to invest very heavily in new technologies. For instance, IGEA has already set up an EDI system with its main suppliers. As soon as a certain number of products are rung up at the cash registers or withdrawn from stock, automatic orders are placed with suppliers. The order quantity is then subtracted from the agreed-upon blanket order purchasing quantity. In selecting its suppliers, IGEA also has strict criteria: suppliers have to satisfy IGEA's environmental concept, but they also have to meet high quality standards. Wood Shelving Co. has been able to meet these initial demands, but it is experiencing considerable difficulties in fulfilling the quantity demanded and adapting to the strong fluctuations in the demand. The consequences for Wood Shelving are serious earnings losses, which have led to overtime and special shifts as well as enormous quantities of inventory. The two companies have engaged in heated discussions and mutual recriminations. Due to the unpredictable fluctuations, particularly for a product called PILLY, they have mandated a task force to examine the roots of the problem. Despite the frequent bottlenecks, IGEA wants to continue doing business with Wood Shelving. The product quality is high, and the company shows positive cooperation when it comes to new projects.

- *Business relationship between Wood Flooring Co. and IGEA Co.:* Wood Flooring and IGEA also have a mutual information exchange program. Because demand does not fluctuate and sales processing of these higher quality products are stable, the exchange of forecast information and planning is optimal. Advertising campaigns are planned cooperatively, and the two companies split the necessary costs as well as the additional earnings. However, as the product assortment of IGEA has a low demand for such high quality products, the companies cooperate mainly for short-term products or particular partnerships of convenience. For this reason, Wood Flooring is also very active in the international market, and, due to its flexibility, it is highly esteemed as a business partner.

- *Other company relationships, which are not being considered in the start phase of the new supply chain project (shown in white):* Kindling Co. and Shavings Co. have only recently entered into IGEA's supply chain conglomerate. They partially supply to

Wood Chips and Wood Flooring, but there are efforts underway to have them supply directly to Wood Shelving Co. IGEA has initiated this and wants to further expand its role as an integrator in the network.

Your task: Position the five interfaces (customer–supplier relationships) listed above and enter your results into the portfolio shown in Figure 2.7.2.2 below. Evaluate the individual companies' potential development opportunities and development strategies within this logistics network. Indicate the trend (using an arrow) that best describes the future directions of each company. Write a one-page explanation of the positions of the companies and the corresponding trends (customer–supplier strategies).

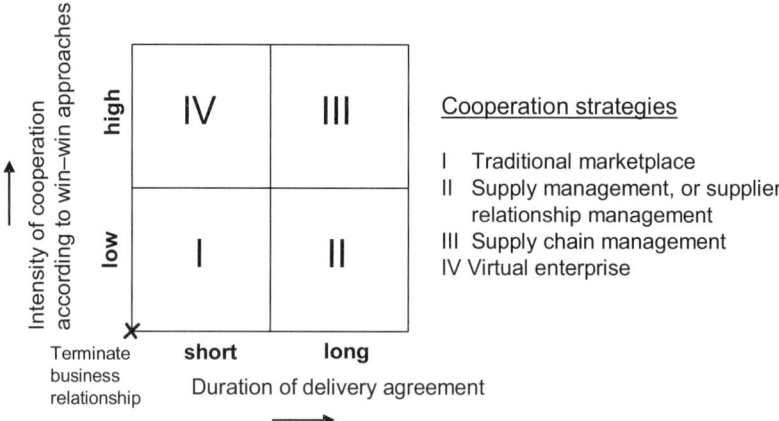

Fig. 2.7.2.2   Portfolio of customer-supplier relationships (compare Fig. 2.1.3.2).

2.7.3   The Bullwhip Effect

Figure 2.3.5.2 discussed the bullwhip effect (or Forrester effect) and its impact on open order quantities and inventories / backorders in a supply chain without communication of point-of-sale data. Discover this effect in a supply chain simulation on the Internet at

www.beergame.lim.ethz.ch

Play the beer distribution game — if possible, with up to 3 of your colleagues — and compare your results with the findings shown in Figure 2.3.5.2. What is the impact of lead time on the bullwhip effect?

2.7.4   Location Configuration with Linear Programming

The Ironer Company, a manufacturer of ironing machines, has its facilities at one single location. The Ironer Company markets two different products in two regions. Once a year, the company performs rough-cut capacity planning based on sales forecasts. In addition, it must answer the following important question for marketing: With the given capacity situation, what quantity of what product should be offered in which market in order to maximize the contribution margin? While demand for New Product P1 is increasing sharply in Market M2, sales of Predecessor Product P2 are declining as the market becomes saturated (decline stage). Here the assumed market demand reflects the maximum saleable number of pieces. The contribution margins of the two markets differ, in part considerably, due to the differing cost and price structures. Figure 2.7.4.1 shows the details:

Input data	Product P1	Product P2
Contribution margin Market M1	80	70
Contribution margin Market M2	70	40
Maximum demand Market M1	1000	3000
Maximum demand Market M2	5000	2000
Capacity required, in hours	4.00	2.40
Total capacity	15000	

Fig. 2.7.4.1   Input data for the planning problem at the Ironer Company.

Ironer Company requires 4 hours to manufacture Product P1 and 2.4 hours to manufacture Product P2. The total capacity in a year is 15,000 hours. Please answer the following questions:

1. What quantities of P1 and P2 should be put on the two markets in order to maximize the contribution margin?

2. A consulting firm is proposing, by introducing lean-/just-in-time concepts (lean/JIT), to increase the contribution margin by 5% and lower the capacity required for P1 by 60 minutes and the capacity required for P2 by 24 minutes. What should the maximum cost of introducing JIT concepts be? And how will this improve the company situation?

3. In addition, the marketing department decides to increase market penetration of P1 and, to maximize profits, to intensify the decline of P2. To do this, sales of P2 in Market M1 must rise to 4,000,

while for Market M2 complete product withdrawal is planned. What are the advantages and disadvantages of this strategy?

Proceed as follows:

Define the decision variables

- Possible solution: $X\_P_i\_M_j$, $1 \leq j \leq 2$, $1 \leq i \leq 2$ stands for the number of products P1 that will be delivered to Market M_j

Formulate the target function

- Possible solution: contribution margin = max!
$$= (DB\_P1\_M1 \cdot X\_P1\_M1) + (DB\_P1\_M2 \cdot X\_P1\_M2) + (DB\_P2\_M1 \cdot X\_P2\_M1) + (DB\_P2\_M2 \cdot X\_P2\_M2)$$

Figure 2.7.4.2 shows how you can perform these first steps utilizing MS Excel Solver, Microsoft Excel's tool for solving linear optimization.

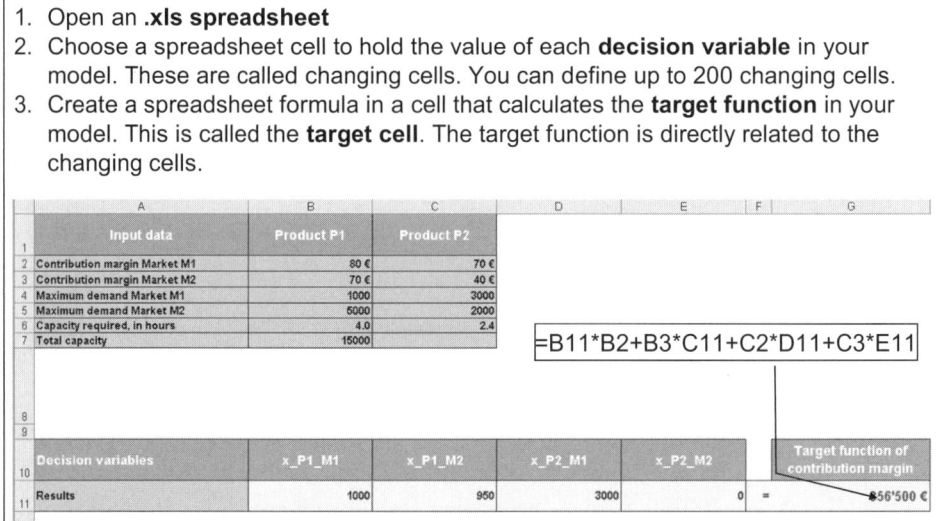

1. Open an **.xls spreadsheet**
2. Choose a spreadsheet cell to hold the value of each **decision variable** in your model. These are called changing cells. You can define up to 200 changing cells.
3. Create a spreadsheet formula in a cell that calculates the **target function** in your model. This is called the **target cell**. The target function is directly related to the changing cells.

Fig. 2.7.4.2   Solver tool in MS Excel, part 1.

Formulate all side conditions:

a) Demand: Maximum coverage of market demands

- $X\_P1\_M1 \leq$ maximum demand for Product P1 in Market M1=1000
- $X\_P1\_M2 \leq$ maximum demand for Product P1 in Market M2=5000

- X_P2_M1 ≤ maximum demand for Product P2 in Market M1=3000
- X_P2_M2 ≤ maximum demand for Product P2 in Market M2=2000

b) Capacity: Restricted total capacity

- X_P1_M1 · capacity required$_{P1}$ + X_P1_M2 · capacity required$_{P1}$ + X_P2_M1 · capacity required$_{P2}$ + X_P2_M2 · capacity required$_{P2}$ ≤ total capacity

c) Variable non-negativity

- X_P1_M1 ≥ 0
- X_P1_M2 ≥ 0
- X_P2_M1 ≥ 0
- X_P2_M2 ≥ 0

Figure 2.7.4.3 shows how MS Excel Solver handles the formulation of side conditions.

4. Create a formula in a cell to **calculate side condition** 1, the restriction you place on the changing cells. In the cell next to it, input the **max./min. constrain value of side condition** 1.
5. Repeat step 4 for each side condition, including the **non-negativity requirements** for decision variables.

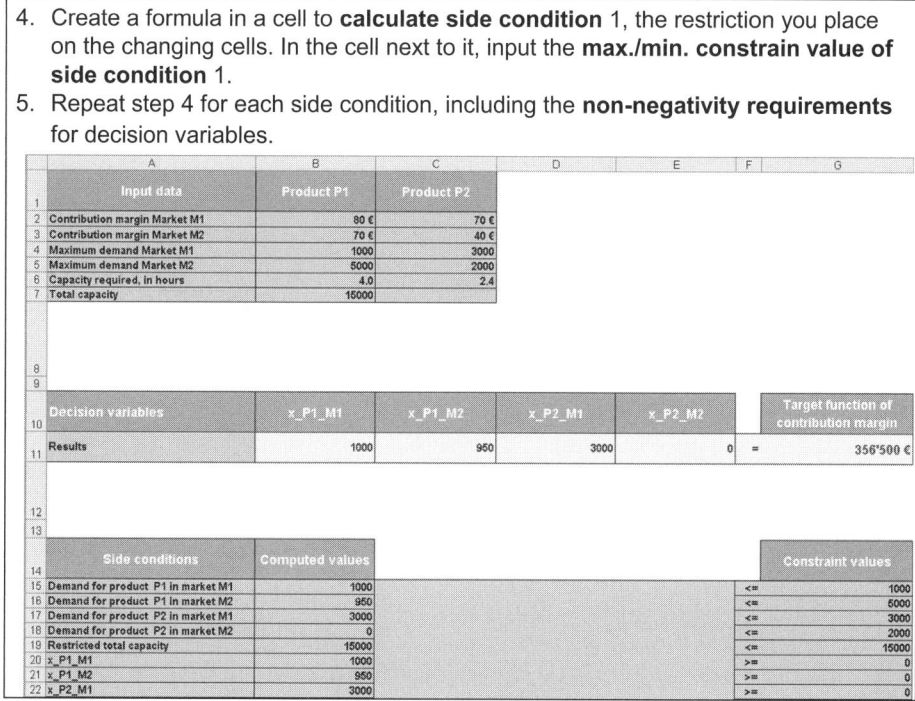

Fig. 2.7.4.3   Solver tool in MS Excel, part 2.

In Figure 2.7.4.3, the constraint operators (e.g. $\leq$, $\geq$) were entered only as text, for purposes of clarity to the reader. Figures 2.7.4.4, 2.7.4.5, and 2.7.4.6 show how you must actually enter the decision variables, target function, and side conditions using the Solver tool in MS Excel:

6. Run Solver by clicking **Solver** on the **Tools** menu. (To install Solver, click Add-Ins on the Tools menu, and then select the Solver Add-in check box. Click OK, and Excel will install the Solver.)

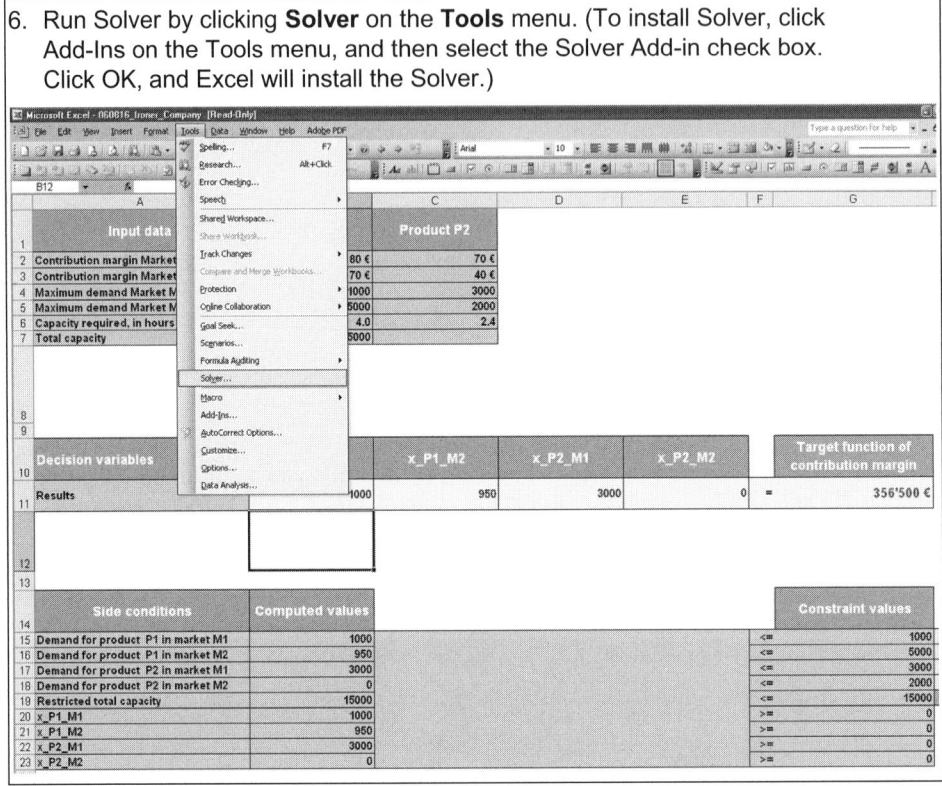

Fig. 2.7.4.4   Solver tool in MS Excel, part 3.

7. In the **Solver Parameters dialog box**, input the target cell, changing cells (decision variables), and side conditions that apply to your optimization model. Choose Max to maximize the target cell.

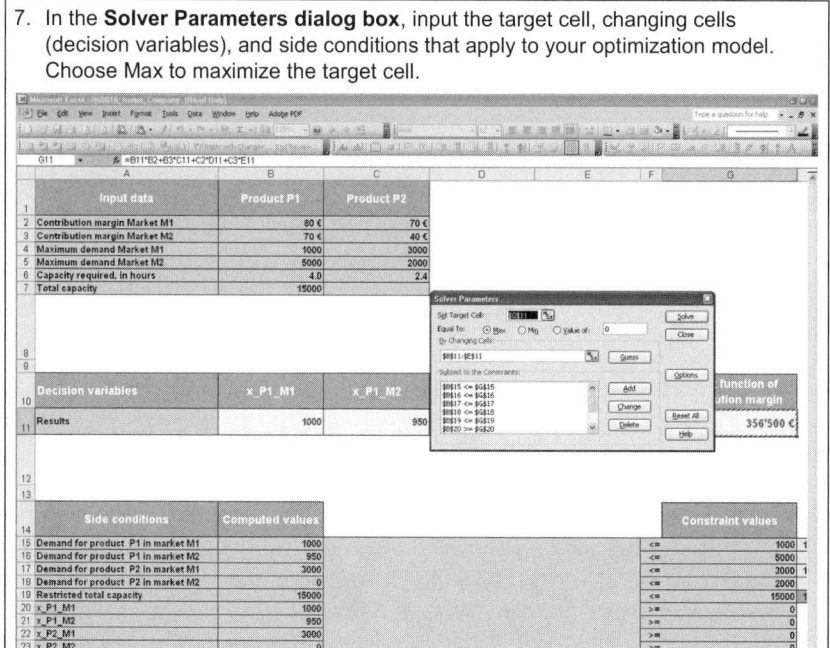

Fig. 2.7.4.5   Solver tool in MS Excel, part 4.

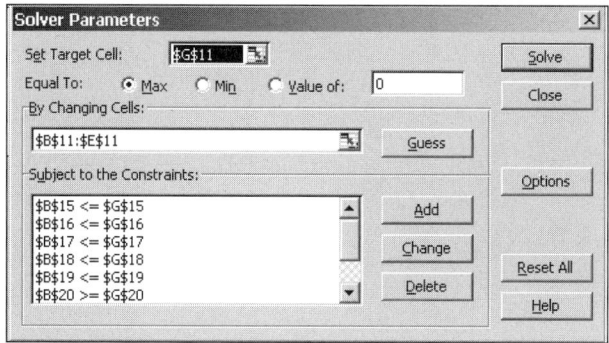

Fig. 2.7.4.6   Solver tool in MS Excel, part 5.

Solutions

Task 1):

- Click Solve (see Figure 2.7.4.6) to display the results. If you have entered everything correctly, the maximum contribution margin achievable should be 356.500€, as it is in Figure 2.7.4.2.

Task 2), the introduction of JIT:

- Start out from the basic case in Task 1, copying and pasting it into a new Excel spreadsheet. Now change the values accordingly.

- Through the higher contribution margins and lower capacity required, the total contribution margin and service level for P1 can be increased.

- If you have set everything correctly, you can determine the cost ceiling for introducing the JIT concept as the contribution margin difference: 451.500€ - 356.500€ = 94.900€.

Task 3), the additional marketing measure:

- Start out from the basic case in Task 2) (JIT), copying and pasting it into a new Excel spreadsheet. Now change the values accordingly.

- By intensifying the decline of Product P2, the total contribution margin can be increased even more, to 476.000€. The service level for P1, however, drops in comparison, since the available capacities produce Product P2 for Market M1. For this reason, it must be considered to what extent the increase in the number of pieces of P1 will take place and the extent to which P1 will at best replace Product P2.

3 Business Process Analysis and Fundamental Logistics Concepts

All management tasks and activities must support the objectives of an enterprise. Chapter 1 of this book showed how, and to what extent, logistics management and planning & control of daily processes can contribute to the fulfilling of company objectives.

Appropriate performance indicators are connected to individual company objectives (see Section 1.4). These measures allow a company to evaluate the degree to which objectives are reached and to analyze initial causes and effects. The present chapter presents an overview of the analysis and design of logistics systems. Figure 3.0.0.1 diagrams the individual steps in a systematic *procedure for analysis and design of logistics systems*.

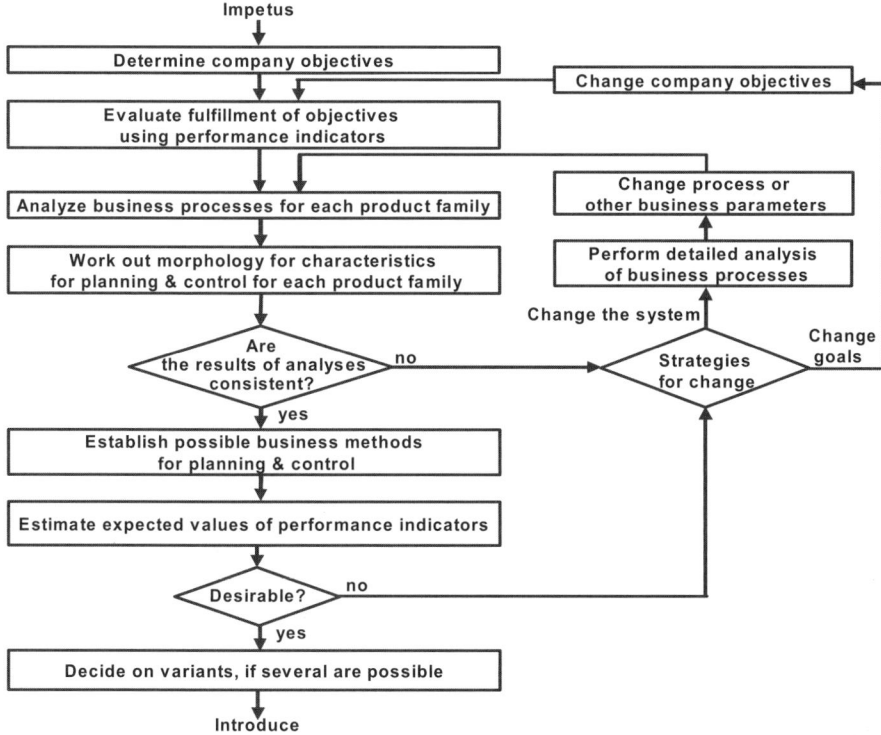

Fig. 3.0.0.1   Procedure for analysis and design of logistics systems.

As the first step in a logistics systems analysis and design project, company management must set the objectives of the enterprise. The basis of any improvement to the success and efficiency of an enterprise is analysis of the current situation. The following will introduce some methods of analysis that are also (and particularly) relevant to logistics, spotlighting different aspects of the situation.

- Logistics management has as its object company-internal and transcorporate business processes. The first sections below will therefore focus on the basics of process management.

- A next step is business process analyses. The processes, as well as further analyses, are usually worked out for each product family. Section 3.3 outlines possible methods of analysis of processes and procedures. For now, we will begin with less detailed representations, such as organization-oriented process charts.

- Finally, there are characteristic features that are relevant to planning & control in logistics networks. These are outlined in Section 3.4. Different product families, and sometimes even different products, will have varying values for these features. The features are related to company objectives and must be determined under consideration of the total management of the enterprise. Examination of the features allows us to discover inconsistencies with business processes as revealed by process analysis.

- Section 3.5 presents fundamental concepts in logistics and operations management. Here, a company has to position itself within a selection of different production types, and concepts for planning & control.

The results of the various analyses are checked with regard to consistency, both among themselves and in relation to company objectives and desired results. If no general consistency is found, either the system or the company's objectives must be changed.

- Change of the system first requires detailed process analyses, using e.g., layouts of the production infrastructure or process plans. Section 3.3 deals with these techniques. Then, in a design step, changes are introduced in the process or in design parameters (such as production infrastructure, qualifications of employees, product concept, or relationship to business partners). Chapters 5 through 7 discuss the possibilities in this regard.

- Changing the company objectives can be necessary, if current options involve too many inconsistencies (see Section 1.3.1).

- In either case, many steps of analysis may have to be repeated.

If the results are consistent, a design step can work out possible business processes and methods of planning & control. The principal methods and their dependency upon analysis results are discussed in Chapters 4 through 7. Chapters 9 through 14 outline more detailed methods.

Once concrete methods of planning & control have been worked out, a company can attempt to estimate the expected values of performance indicators. These estimates will be checked against desired values. If the result is negative, then once again either the system or the objectives of the enterprise must be changed (see above).

If the results are positive, the company may have a choice of various possibilities. For example, variants emerge as the result of a possible different view of the product family. In other cases, differing methods of planning & control may be implemented.

The approach proposed here is not dependent upon any particular type of project organization. However, logistics systems function satisfactorily only when the people who use them (want to) understand them well. For this reason, it is advantageous for the people who use the system to be actively involved in the design process.

3.1   Elements of Business Process Management

In recent years, the design of effective and efficient business processes has become a key issue with regard to a company's performance and has triggered wide discussion, such as in [Dave93], [HaCh01], and [JoHu93]. The link between process management and logistics management is evident. See [Stew97], for example. The following subsections under Sections 3.1 and 3.2 examine the elements and design of logistics processes.

3.1.1   Basic Definitions of Work, Task, Function, and Process

Concurrent to new understandings of business processes, there is (too) frequent confusion among the terms *task*, *function*, and *process* (as well as task orientation, function orientation, and process orientation). By referring to etymological dictionaries and dictionaries of related words and meanings, we can find out how people *normally* understand the terms. While some branches of science traditionally give terms their own definitions, such definitions are arbitrary. As a result, researchers within the same scientific field often give differing definitions to the same terms. However, process management, which takes its orientation from everyday understanding, must use definitions of terms that will be generally understood.

Figure 3.1.1.1 presents the basic term *work*, to which all other terms refer, as well as the terms *task, function, order, course of action* (procedure), and *process*.

Term	Word origin, definition	Related terms
work	<u>old</u>: travail, toil, drudgery, exertion of strength <u>new</u>: activity in which one exerts strength or faculties to achieve an object, means of livelihood <u>but also</u>: the product of work	job
task	assigned piece of work; work imposed by an employer or circumstances	function; order, work; assignment; quota
function	action contributing to a larger action; activity; effectiveness; carrying out	task; purpose
order	to give somebody the job to do something; directive, instructions	task; purpose
course of action	an ordered process or succession of actions; a procedure	process
process	something ongoing; proceeding; continuing action; series of operations conducing to a development	course of action; procedure

Fig. 3.1.1.1   Concepts in business process engineering and management [part 1].

The most important finding here is that the word *work* contains both the character of a course of action (a sustained effort) and of content and result. This duality seems to be fundamental. The content of work, that is its purpose or objective, is often expressed as *task*. The term *function* is clearly related to *task*. *Function* more strongly refers to the result of work, while *task* is more work's content and purpose, whereby each term includes the other. An *order* arises when a task is assigned to someone else. In commercial law, the order is a pivotal concept of trade between people.

Course of action and *process* are practically synonymous and stand in duality to the terms *task* and *function.* A close examination of a task, or function, reveals that it is seldom "nuclear" in the sense of *not* seen as a procedure. In most cases, a task or function can be structured as a consequence or as a net of subtasks, or subfunctions, and thus thought of as a process. Turned around, a process is usually seen as various tasks progressing in a certain sequence. Each of these tasks may be seen as a task or function, or as a part of such.

According to the dictionaries and due to the above duality, recursiveness results: parts of processes, tasks, and functions are themselves processes, tasks, and functions. So there is no reason to understand "subprocess" as anything other than "process," and the reverse is also true. On the other hand, there exist tasks and functions that are "nuclear" — they cannot be broken down further. We find this kind of task in the area of company strategy, for example, but also in product and process research.

3.1.2   Terms in Business Process Engineering

Figure 3.1.2.1 shows terms used in the engineering of business processes.

Term	Word origin, definition	Related terms
business	work; concern; purposeful activity; <u>new</u>: commerce, trade, industry	
object	something mental or physical towards which thought or action is directed; the goal or end of an activity or trade	thing
method	systematic procedure or techniques; orderly development, often in steps	procedure
state, status	mode or condition of being	composition; the way things stand
event	something that happens; archaic: outcome	occurrence

Fig. 3.1.2.1   Concepts in business process engineering and management [part 2].

Note that *business* refers to the central term *work*, whereby in today's usage, business means tradable work according to its new definition.

Looking at the pair of terms *state* and *event*, we see that each task or subprocess describes an *action state* within the whole process, in which the goods being processed (material or information) exist. Between two tasks or subprocesses, there is a transition. If processing does not continue immediately, the transition ends in a *waiting state*. An example would be a buffer or an in-box in an office. The *event* is then a special process through which a person or a sensor registers the waiting state and then triggers the next process or task.

The above definitions from dictionaries allow us to define important concepts in process management in terms that are natural and that accord with our everyday understandings. See Figure 3.1.2.2:

Term	Definition
value added	(1) a company's own output, including overhead; purchased products or services may complement this (2) value and usefulness of design and production as seen by the customer
business process	process performed to achieve a potentially tradable outcome that is value added as seen by the customer — internal or external — and that the customer is willing to pay for
core competency	significant or crucial ability, capability, or skill
core process	a process for which a company has competitive competencies
business object	an important object or thing, or a content of thought or planning, in connection with business
business method	an important method in connection with business
logistics system	a process with its trigger event and its order and process management

Fig. 3.1.2.2   Important new terms in business process engineering and management.

Value added varies in meaning according to the standpoint of either producer or customer. The traditional perspective is that of the manufacturer. From the manufacturer's standpoint, for example, the expense of keeping inventory or work in process is always value-adding. The customer, however, does not normally view such processes as value-adding. With the trend towards customer orientation, it has become increasingly important to take the customer's point of view.

A *business process* in one company is not necessarily a business process in another. The deciding factor is ultimately whether or not the organizational unit fulfilling the order does its own processing. The unit carries responsibility for and performs not only the value-adding process itself, but also the necessary planning & control of the process. It does not matter if the order connected with a business process comes from within the company or externally. If the degrees of freedom are there, the business process may be insourced or outsourced in a flexible manner (make or buy).

A company's *core competencies* are the total skills that make it competitive. It is generally easier to identify the core competencies of a company than to derive *core processes* from them. A core competency is not always related to clear tasks. A task cannot always be broken down or structured, that is, expressed as a process. For example, a core competency can be a strategy. It may also consist in a function that occurs in various business processes that themselves do not have to constitute core processes. Other functions of the business processes also do not have to be core competencies. Indeed, it is not always easy to distinguish between important and less important business processes.

Familiar *business objects* are, for example, customers, employees, products, production facilities, and equipment. With regard to logistics, an order is a business object, too. *Business methods* describe how tasks are performed or functions within the company can be achieved. In logistics, this will also include methods of order processing.

A *logistics system* is comprised of logistics tasks, functions and methods, processes, states, flow, and sublogistics. For each process, it encompasses not only the series of operations but also the event(s) that trigger the process. A logistics system, like an independent contractor, is responsible for fulfilling the order itself. It is precisely this control of the trigger events to the process that characterizes value-adding oriented organizations.

3.1.3   Order Management and Graphical Representation of Logistics Processes

The legal system (civil law, in particular commercial law) defines trade between a company and its partners through the instrument of the *order*. The customer, or client, formulates an order, and the supplier agrees to perform services or to deliver merchandise. A legally binding *contract* results. The supplier agrees to supply the services or goods specified by the order in a certain quantity at a certain price and is responsible for adequate order management. The customer agrees to pay for them. There are no stipulations as to the form of the order: it may be oral or written. In certain formal contexts, even shouts and gestures may serve the purpose (on the floor of the stock exchange, for example).

The order has become the main instrument of logistics, and the course and processing of a contract has become the control flow of logistics. This is the case both within and among companies. The form of the contract is unimportant: it may be a detailed written contract, a simple card in a pull system (a kanban), or a contract not on paper at all (in production, for example, an empty container may be sent from a work center as a previously arranged signal that parts are required from feeding operations).

Order processing can be compared to a freight train. The cars are coupled together, and the train moves along a certain route. As it goes, goods or information are added to the train. Stopping at certain stations, it signals to other trains to start out and supply goods or information. Before finally ending its journey, our freight train also delivers goods and information to trains traveling farther on. An observer could sit in the locomotive of the order train and observe the happenings. *MEDILS* (Method for Description of Integrated Logistic Systems) was designed from this observation point. MEDILS goes beyond the classical *flowchart*, which was introduced to better understand processes, showing flows, tasks, waiting states, storages, and so on. Figure 3.1.3.1 introduces the symbols used in MEDILS:

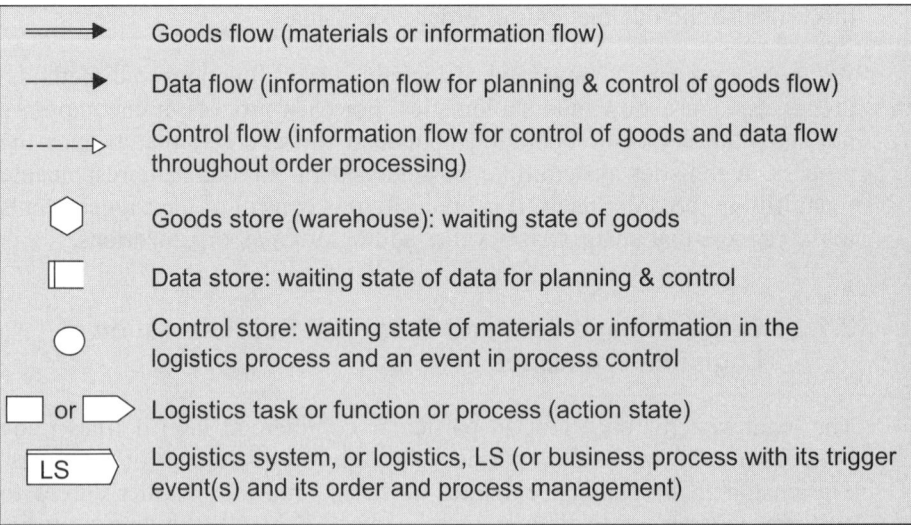

Fig. 3.1.3.1   MEDILS symbols.

- A double arrow represents the flow of goods. In the industrial sector, goods are usually material goods, but they can be information that belongs with the product from the start, such as drawings or specifications. In the service sector, goods are often non-material in nature. In banks and insurance companies, for example, goods are often comprised of information.

- A single arrow denotes the flow of data for planning & control. This is the flow of information required for administrative, planning, and material planning logistics. Data describe the characteristics of goods in an appropriate way. Every goods flow is a self-description and thus is also data flow, although it is not drawn separately as such.

- A broken arrow represents the control flow. This is made up of information that in logistics deals with control of the flow of goods and data throughout order processing. In principle, every goods flow and every data flow are self-controlled and thus also control flow, although they are not drawn separately as such.

- A hexagon stands for a goods store. Depending on the kind of goods, this may be a warehouse, information store, and so on. An object in this store stands for certain goods and thus represents a waiting state in the flow of goods. In principle, it may stay in this state for an indefinite length of time in the store.

- A rectangle with a double line on the left represents a data store. An object in this store stands for a certain quantity of data (for example, an order), and it is a waiting state in the flow of data. It may remain in store in this state for an indefinite period of time. The particular characteristics or structure of the object can be described in more detail by the symbol.

- A circle stands for a process store, a kind of intermediate store in the logistics process. An object here is control information that serves to select and initiate the next task. This waiting state in control flow derives from the preceding task, and so it can be understood without further description. We can think of a process store in the flow of data or non-material goods (information) as a mailbox. An object is the envelope addressed with control information, while the data are found inside the envelope. A process store in the flow of material goods can be seen as a buffer or transit camp. An object is a crate inscribed with control information, while the goods are found inside the crate.

- A process store stores tasks waiting in line to be processed. The impetus for processing an object is given by an event: a sensor, such as the human eye, registers a state and finds an envelope in the mailbox. Thus, the event is an implicit part of process storage.

- A rectangle represents a logistics task that may be described in detail within the rectangle. If the effect of a task is the most important aspect, then the rectangle stands for a function. If procedure according to plan is the focus, the rectangle stands for a method. If the focus is on the route of implementation, the well-known value-adding arrow, which stands for a process, is used instead of the rectangle. A task or process can be "nuclear" or comprise subtasks or subprocesses, which are connected via flows.[1]

- The rectangle in the shape of an arrow represents logistics, that is, a logistics system "LS" in the direction of the temporal axis. The logistics system includes logistics tasks, states, flows, and sublogistics. It has its own order and process management, which is indicated by the doubled top line. As compared to the simple value-adding arrow, a logistics system includes not only the process itself, but also the process store containing the trigger event(s), that is, the impetus to start the process. Control of process initiation is the key feature of value-adding organizations.

Logistics systems are represented in graphic form by using and connecting the symbols. Figure 3.1.3.2 shows the connections used conventionally in MEDILS.

- Goods or data along with control information or control information alone flow from storage into a task or function, or process. Execution of the task, function, or process transforms the goods or data, and they are then moved to new storage points. Multiple flows to a task must be coordinated at the start of the task. Depending upon the context, related flows may be combined in the sense of "and" connections. Flows that need to be separated in the sense of an "or" or "exclusive or" connection are handled separately. Flows leading out from the task are handled analogously.

---

[1] Due to the duality of content-oriented and effect-oriented terms (task or function) and the process-oriented concept (process) discussed in Section 3.1.1, there is no sense in arguing that the graphical symbol should be a process value-adding arrow or a traditional rectangle. Every *structured* task or function can be seen as a process, and by the same token, every process can be viewed as a function or task.

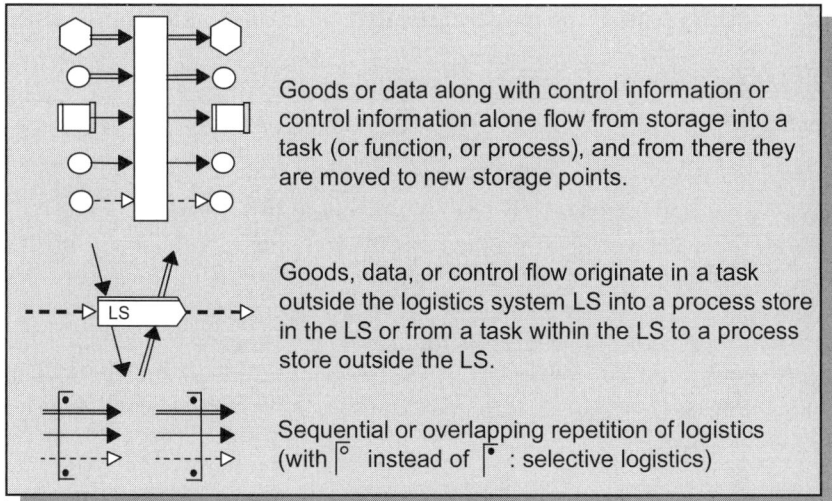

Goods or data along with control information or control information alone flow from storage into a task (or function, or process), and from there they are moved to new storage points.

Goods, data, or control flow originate in a task outside the logistics system LS into a process store in the LS or from a task within the LS to a process store outside the LS.

Sequential or overlapping repetition of logistics (with $\lceil^\circ$ instead of $\lceil^\bullet$: selective logistics)

Fig. 3.1.3.2   MEDILS: connecting the symbols.

- Goods, data, or control flow originates in a task outside the logistics system LS into a process store in the LS or from a task within the LS to a process store outside the LS. We can think of this as follows: goods or information in the order processing "train" are transferred to a transport "train" and delivered to another logistics systems "train". This takes place, for example, when production turns over a completed customer order to distribution.

- Special parentheses stand for sequential or overlapping repetition of (sub-)logistics, for as many times as demanded by the situation (even zero times). The flows leading into the parentheses must be of the same type as those leading out of the parentheses. The contents within the parentheses can also be executed selectively, that is, at most only once.

3.2   Push and Pull in the Design of Business Processes

3.2.1   Pull Logistics

Transitions between functions or processes arise when several people or groups work independently of one another within a business process. In general, for a value-adding process of any complexity, a business process must be divided into a number of subprocesses. Crucial to an efficient process cycle are the states of goods between subprocesses and particularly the event (see above) that detects the state, or momentary standstill. Two subprocesses must be connected by an interface. This guarantees that the two subprocesses cannot be torn apart in time, but will take place one right after the other.

We develop possible solutions looking at the example of a customer order that entails both design and manufacturing, which is common in the world of practice. Figure 3.2.1.1 emphasizes the fact that the customer's logistics are ongoing throughout this whole period.

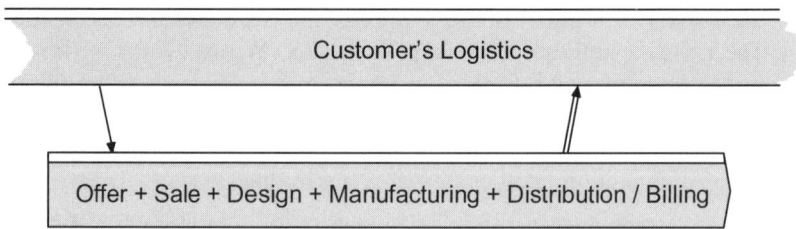

Fig. 3.2.1.1   Business process in the enterprise from order acquisition to fulfillment.

The customer keeps track of order fulfillment more or less intensively, as the goods ordered are needed for fulfilling the customer's own tasks (in design and manufacturing) or for use.

In most cases, more people are needed for order acquisition and fulfillment than can be incorporated into one single group. How should the business process be organized into subprocesses? There are several possible solutions. Experience has shown that each transition from subprocess to subprocess is critical. This is the reason why the design of the interfaces is so important.

Figure 3.2.1.2 shows a common solution to the problem. This example has been taken from a mid-sized company in the metals industry. Transitions are defined by the way that an order arises or is formulated between the persons or groups of persons involved.

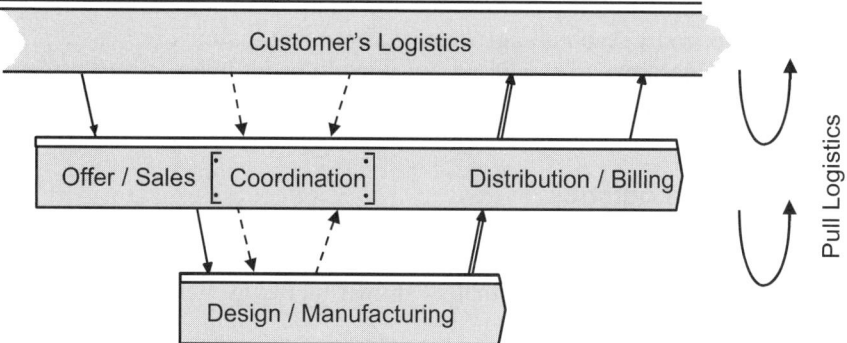

Fig. 3.2.1.2   Interface between subprocesses: "customer–supplier relationship with an internal order" model and pull logistics.

Design and manufacturing is viewed here as its own business process, as the sales department has issued a so-called internal order to the design and manufacturing departments. Sales, however, remains responsible to the customer for order fulfillment during the entire design and manufacturing period. Through continuing coordination, or in other words, the exchange of control information, the order is eventually fulfilled. The flow of goods from manufacturing via sales to the customer illustrates this. Here, the internal organization of the company is like the organization between the customer and the company. It is a customer–supplier relationship. The "customer," whether internal or external, places an order and "pulls" the logistics in such a way that the logistics produce the goods ordered for delivery. The customer remains an active monitor, at least potentially, throughout the entire delivery lead time.

This results in *cascades*, that is, a number of process levels in the process model. *Pull logistics* is the generalized name for this system: Value-adding takes place only on customer demand (or to replace a use of items). Its characteristic is that several parallel order processes arise. This means that several order managing persons concern themselves with the value-adding process simultaneously. With regard to delivery reliability rate, each customer, through coordination with the supplier, "pulls" the order on up through the process levels.

This kind of logistics ensures that nothing is "forgotten". Parallel order management in multiple levels is in itself, of course, not value-adding.

From a lean production perspective in a narrow sense, it may even be wasteful. However, from an agility perspective, this slack is necessary if logistics are to be effective in this model. The interface in the cascade model is formed mainly through the formulation of the order. Customer and supplier must reach an agreement. These negotiations represent slack, and thus unnecessary expenditure, but they do result in an overall effective business process.

3.2.2 Push Logistics

An alternative solution to the design of the business process in Figure 3.2.1.1 is a type of logistics that is shown in Figure 3.2.2.1 — a simple sequence of subprocesses.

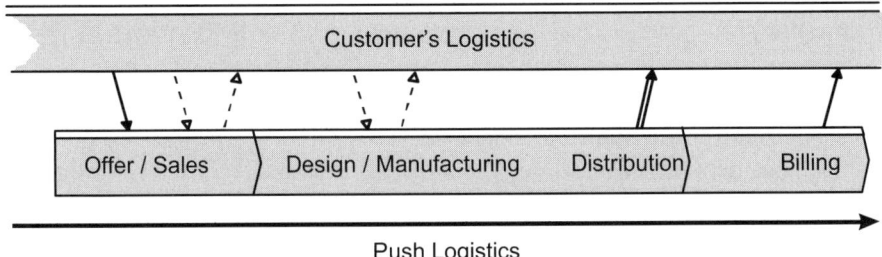

Fig. 3.2.2.1   Interface between subprocesses: the "simple sequence" model.

The "simple sequence" model is common and effective, as long as order management does not change and remains in the hands of the same person. This person is the supplier responsible for all subprocesses; he or she manages the executing organizational units in a central fashion, one after the other. This is the model of push logistics.

With *push logistics*, you push the order in the direction of the added value, without need of customer influence or a definite customer order.

However, if decentralized control by the executing organizational units themselves is desired, the "simple sequence" model can hardly be utilized. First, there are no indications of how states between the subprocesses might be registered so that the next subprocess will be initiated. Between subprocesses, as we know, order management must be shifted from one processing facility to the next. Responsibility then lies in the hands of the organizational unit that executes that next subprocess. Second, the customer in our example must first deal with sales and then later with design and manufacturing units. But how will the customer know when these transitions occur? Misunderstandings become inevitable. For these reasons, the "simple sequence" model — although "lean" — is bound to fail. Figure 3.2.2.2 shows that only careful designing of the transitions between subprocesses, that is, the interfaces, can make uninterrupted order fulfillment processing possible using push logistics.

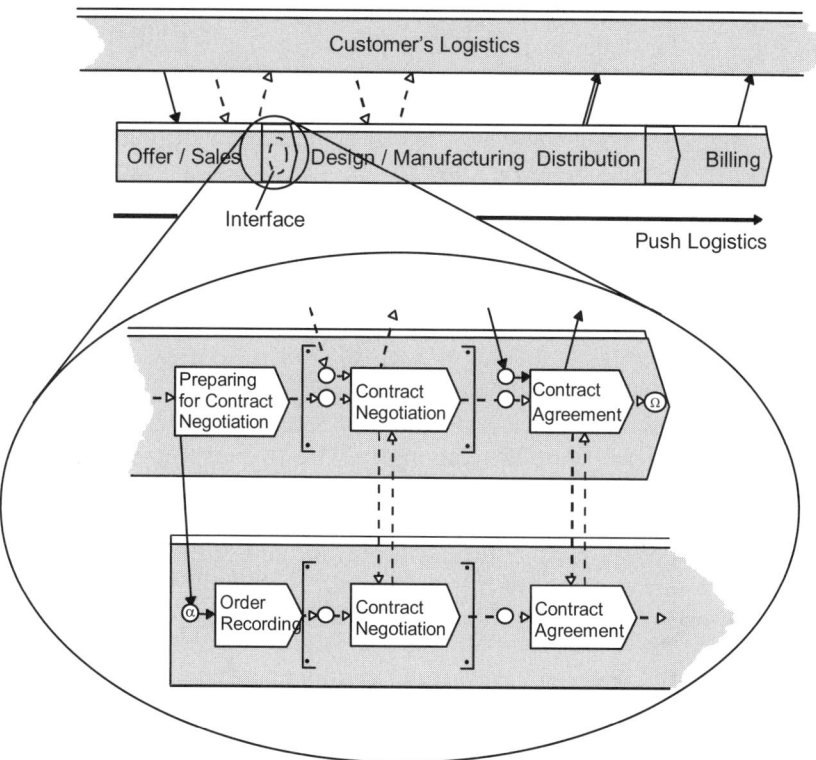

Fig. 3.2.2.2   Interface between subprocesses: "partner relationship with overlapping subprocesses for handing over the order" model.

The practical example in Figure 3.2.2.2 is taken from a consulting firm. In the company's past, salesmen had made agreements with customers that the executing units could not fulfill. This, of course, had a negative effect upon customer satisfaction. The company recognized that during contract negotiations, and also at the conclusion of the agreement itself, at least one person should take part that will actually perform the services. This type of organization ensures that nothing will be sold that cannot be produced. Conversely, the executing unit commits itself at the right point in time in direct contact with the customer.

With push logistics it is crucial that the two part processes overlap, that is, that the next part process begins parallel to the end of the preceding part process. This link is established by having people in the organizational unit handling the first part process conduct their last task in coordination with representatives of the organizational unit that will begin the second part process. This second group takes over process management — the responsibility as supplier with regard to quality, cost, delivery, and flexibility. At the same time, the party placing the order knows its "new" business partner, and order fulfillment can be coordinated.

In this model, the organizational units of subprocesses do not stand in a customer–supplier relationship, but rather stand in a partnership. The overlap of the subprocesses is the necessary slack. It is true that more persons than actually necessary perform certain subtasks. But it is this very redundancy that assures a smooth takeover of the order by one organizational unit from the other. The two subprocesses become sewn together, and this is what makes for an overall effective business process.

It is not necessary to play off the two models in Figures 3.2.2.1 and 3.2.2.2 against each other (the "customer–supplier relationship with an internal order" model and the "partner relationship with overlapping subprocesses for handing over the order" model). Both the multiple process levels model with its pull logistics and the flat model with its push logistics have their justifications. For fast, uninterrupted pull-through of complex value-adding processes, enough slack, or non-value-adding activity, must be built in at process transition points.

It is interesting to note that the greater the numbers of persons who are capable of handling "longer" processes, the faster and cheaper the processes become. The reason is that there is less necessity for slack times and redundant work in order to join subprocesses in smooth transition. The objection can be raised, of course, that qualifying employees to do this and coordinating them in the group entails costs. From this, we can derive guidelines for the design of process organization. Division into short subprocesses may be necessary in order to achieve certain quality demands. As soon as several people show competency in the handling of a number of related subprocesses, it is correct — with a view to reducing transition points — to make a long process out of the short subprocesses and to organize these persons into a group (see also [Ulic05]).

3.2.3   Synchronization between Use and Manufacturing with Inventory Control Processes

Section 1.1.2 introduced *temporal synchronization between use and manufacturing* as a fundamental problem in logistics. Warehouses serve the storage of goods when manufacturing or procurement is too slow or too early. Figure 3.2.3.1 shows the MEDILS notation for logistics with stocking. Depending upon the point of view, or the type of order (see Figure 3.4.4.1), the following cases of inventory control processes result:

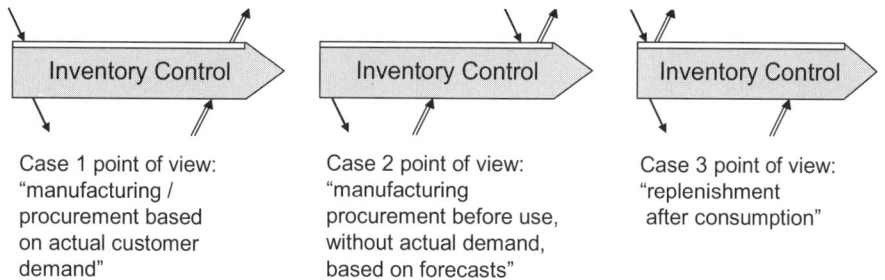

Case 1 point of view: "manufacturing / procurement based on actual customer demand"

Case 2 point of view: "manufacturing procurement before use, without actual demand, based on forecasts"

Case 3 point of view: "replenishment after consumption"

Fig. 3.2.3.1   Different inventory control processes for temporal synchronization between use and manufacturing / procurement.

1. Manufacturing / procurement takes place only upon actual customer demand. Storage is necessary only if order receipt is too early.

2. Manufacturing / procurement is released based on forecast, before there is a definite customer and without need to replace items taken for use. These products are then held in inventory until required by a user. They can then be delivered immediately.

3. Demand is filled immediately from inventory. The items taken for use will then be replaced by *stock replenishment* afterwards, and remain in inventory for an indefinite length of time.

Case 1 and 3 can be considered to be pull logistics. Case 2 is mostly solved by push logistics, as long as there is no definite customer. However, for each case it is clear that carrying inventory only makes sense if goods in stock will be used within a reasonably short period of time.

Figure 3.2.3.2 shows the example from the above section once again, this time incorporating inventory control for end products following the Case 3 point of view.

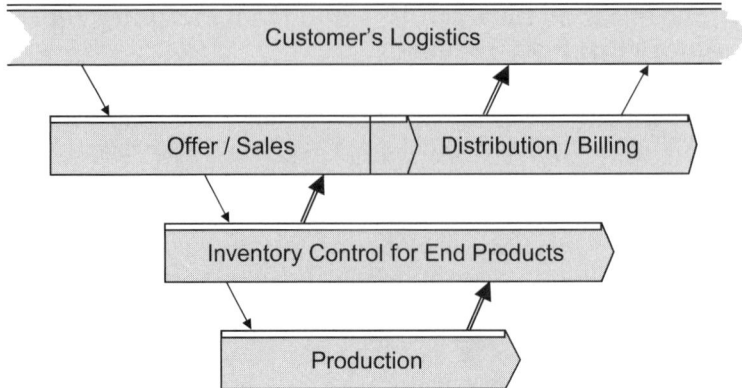

Fig. 3.2.3.2   Pull logistics with inventory: order processing with end product inventory.

Note that "design" is missing here: Because it is a requirement that products in inventory must be marketable, no design and manufacture of products according to customer specification are involved. Rather, these are goods demanded by users repeatedly, so that they can be produced without design changes. This is an example where the cascade model could include several levels, in that production will order components from intermediate stores that, in turn, will then be replenished.

3.3   Important Techniques of Analysis in Business Process Engineering

> *Business process engineering* is the discipline of design and improvement of business processes.

The term "engineering" underlines that this is an engineering science approach. This shows in the emphasis on the constructive aspect and on methods, models, and techniques.

An analysis forms the basis for all necessary changes both within and among companies. The analysis requires examination of processes and procedures with regard to their success (effectiveness) and their efficiency. Like any systems analysis, analysis of processes gives us a picture of ancillary constraints and yields initial suggestions for improvement.

Various techniques of process analysis yield different ways of viewing logistics contents. In addition, each technique has its own character with regard to the way data are collected (for example, interviewing experts and participants, observations throughout the course of order processing). These factors can influence the results. Redundant findings using various methods are desirable, for they ensure the soundness of the conclusions.

In the following, we will introduce simple and often-used techniques. They can be used for the description of every kind of output (service, product, or product family) in appropriate detail. Whenever possible, the findings should be complemented as early as this stage with information on:

1. Lead times of the processes
2. Frequency and periodicity of the processes
3. States that launch the processes or part processes

3.3.1   Organization-Oriented Process Chart

The *organization-oriented process chart* shows a process with its part processes, tasks, or functions (1) through the course of time (horizontal axis), and (2) in its embeddedness in the structural organization (vertical axis).

In practice, there are various ways to draw an organization-oriented process chart. Generally, the diagram will correspond to usual practice in the field or branch. We will choose an expanded version of the method introduced in Section 3.1.3, incorporating the constructs defined in Section 3.2 into the chart.

For pull logistics (Section 3.2.1), the cascading can be used again unaltered, for vertical cascades necessarily lead to the transition to another organizational unit. Figure 3.3.1.1 shows the example used in Figure 3.2.1.2 in an organization-oriented process chart.

Complex order processes are reflected in complex diagrams that include many organizational units or the same organizational unit involved repeatedly in the process.

For the push logistics in Section 3.2.2, it makes sense to put the part processes on the vertical as soon as the organizational unit changes. A vertical connection produces the connection in the model of the "simple sequence." The model "partnership relationship with overlapping part processes," on the other hand, shows two vertical connections. Figure 3.3.1.2 shows the example used in Figure 3.2.2.1 in an organization-oriented process chart. The transition from sales to design/production is represented as an overlapping part process, and the transition to invoicing is shown as a simple sequence. The chart shows parallel part processes for various organizational units involved in design and production.

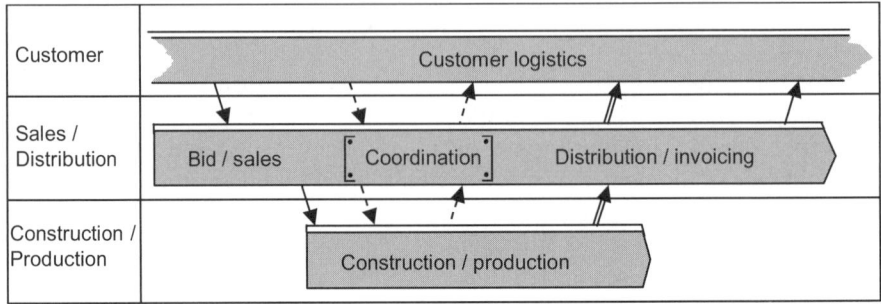

Fig. 3.3.1.1   Pull logistics: organization-oriented process chart.

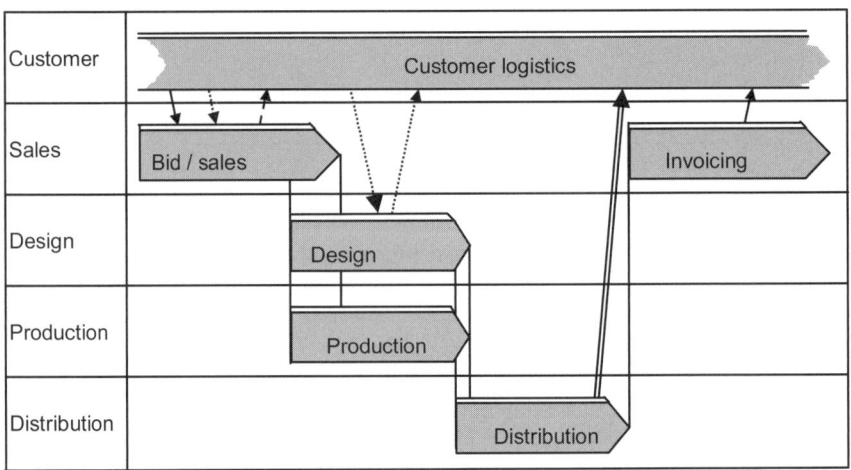

Fig. 3.3.1.2   Push logistics: organization-oriented process chart.

With the help of persons that are involved in the logistics network, you can use the organization-oriented process chart to analyze and chart the formal flow. Through interviews or brainstorming sessions with the employees involved, you can identify and chart processes, tasks, or functions, each with their incoming and outgoing flows and their origins and destinations. The findings of the various interviews can be placed in proper succession and integrated into a single diagram.

Employees generally make quick sense of the charts, for they can identify themselves within the structural organization. In a cooperative effort, the results can now be verified and improved. Employees can determine whether the part processes are indeed executed as diagrammed in the chart and whether goods, data, and control flow have been charted correctly.

One disadvantage is that the organization-oriented process chart may not correspond to reality if it was constructed on the basis of interviews and the know-how of the engineer doing the analysis. That is why additional on-site analyses are necessary.

The organization-oriented process chart is an old method. For an historical example, see [Grul28] on the "division of labor in the company" (note in particular Figures 156 and 157).

3.3.2 Manufacturing and Service Processes in the Company-Internal and Transcorporate Layout

A *manufacturing process* is the series of operations performed upon material to convert it from the raw material or a semifinshed state to a state of further completion ([APIC04]).

A *service process* is the series of operations performed for a customer service or customer support.

A *layout* shows the "geography" of resources involved in the manufacturing or service process — both company-internal and transcorporate.

One layout may show, for example, the "geography" of a logistics network, while another may depict company-internal "geography." The actual course of an order is then drawn into the layout. From this, it is easy to see intuitively the limits of the production infrastructure and to spot areas for improvement. After changing the layout, the new process is then charted. The "new" can now be compared to the "old." Figure 3.3.2.1 shows a company-internal layout.

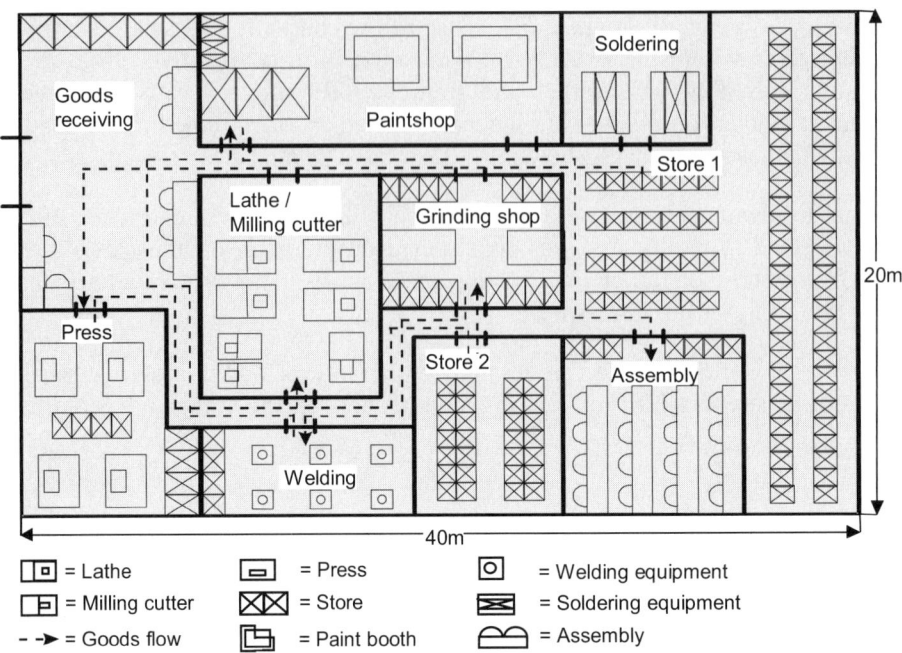

Fig. 3.3.2.1   Company-internal layout with an example process.

Transcorporate layouts are usually diagrammed as maps showing the various sites. The flow of an order is drawn in with arrows that connect the sites.

Service blueprinting is a technique used for analyzing service processes. The service blueprint usually makes a distinction between customer actions and service provider actions that are visible to the customer and service provider actions that are backstage, or not visible to the customer. Lines of interaction show the form of customer involvement and points of customer contact. Beyond that, using special symbols, the tool can identify frequently occurring fail points and important decisions in the service process. (Compare [APIC04]).

Figure 3.3.2.2 shows a "collaborative (service) blueprint" following [Hart04]. This type of service blueprint is especially useful when service delivery is distributed across several companies or cooperation partners, which is a development that is frequently seen today especially in service in the area of machinery and plant manufacturing.

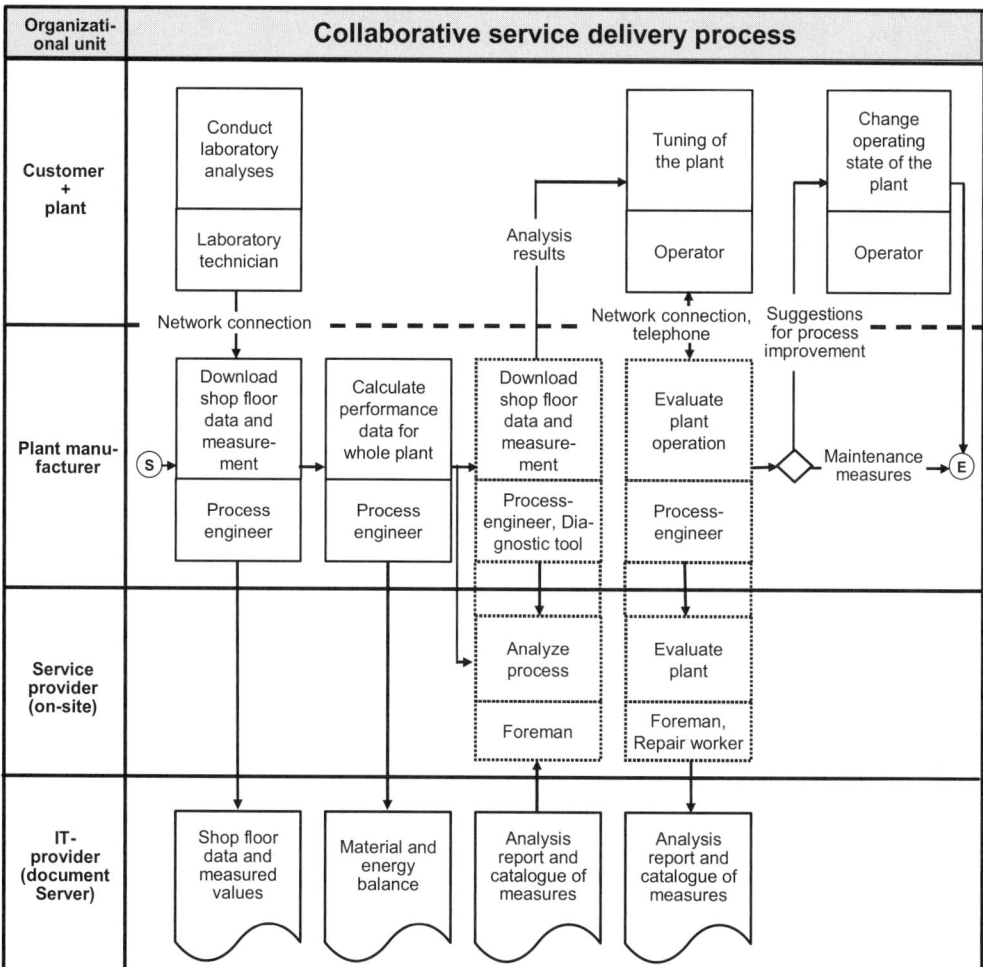

Fig. 3.3.2.2   Example of a service process represented graphically as a collaborative service blueprint following [Hart04].

The horizontal axis shows the course of service provision over time. The part-processes are assigned to the companies involved, the organizational units, on the vertical axis. The arrows between individual actions indicate the information flows. This creates transparency about the division of tasks between the companies involved in the service processes and their resource needs.

3.3.3   Detailed Analysis and Time Study of Processes

> A *time study* is a representation of the exact temporal sequence of the operations of a process.

Time study can be required in order to identify improvement or optimization potentials. Time study is one of the typical tasks of an industrial engineer. Actual stopwatch timing is often used to establish standard hours, or standard times. These are often needed also for capacity planning (see here also Chapter 12).

A suitable technique of detailed process analysis documents the results of a time study. The same technique can be used for the documentation of the process improvement.

> A *basic process analysis* is a detailed analysis of the process plan on-site that, operation by operation, explains the exact percentages of the total lead time.

Figure 3.3.3.1 shows an example of a basic process analysis. Its form has been chosen similar to [Shin89], and it thus belongs to the Toyota Production System.

(Design of the part)				Process ID	451		Batch size	20
				Part name	Transmission		Part ID.:	ABC-123
				Material:	AC-2			
				Inspector:	Smith		Inspect. date	2000.06.15
Quan-tity	Dis-tance	Time	Sym-bol	Process (place)	Opera-tor	Machine	Type of storage	Operating conditions, developments, etc.
		2 days	▼	Ware-house 1				
60	40 m		⬇		Trans-porter			
		3 h	▼	Pressing			Pallet on ground	
		20 s	●	Pressing	Opera-tor	Press		20% parts defective
		20 min	✸	Pressing			Pallet on ground	
	25 m		⬇		Trans-porter			
		3 h	●	Milling		Milling cutter		

✸ = batch-size-dependent wait time   ⬇ = transport
● = process   ▼ = wait time   ■ = control

Fig. 3.3.3.1   Example of a basic process analysis.

For purposes of illustration, we show only the most important columns. By this tool, the information from the more general tools can also be verified on-site. In a practical sense, this means that you must physically follow the course of the data flow and flow of goods of an order. At the same time, the people processing the order can give information on the flow. By gathering and comparing all this information, you also gain insight into the degree to which employees have mastered the process.

The "basic process analysis" technique was further developed mainly in the United States to what is today known as "value stream mapping."

Value stream mapping is a paper and pencil tool that helps you to see and understand the flow of material and information as a product or service through all of the value-adding and non-value-adding process steps.

Figure 3.3.3.2 shows an example of a value stream map of a mortgage company with normal priority.

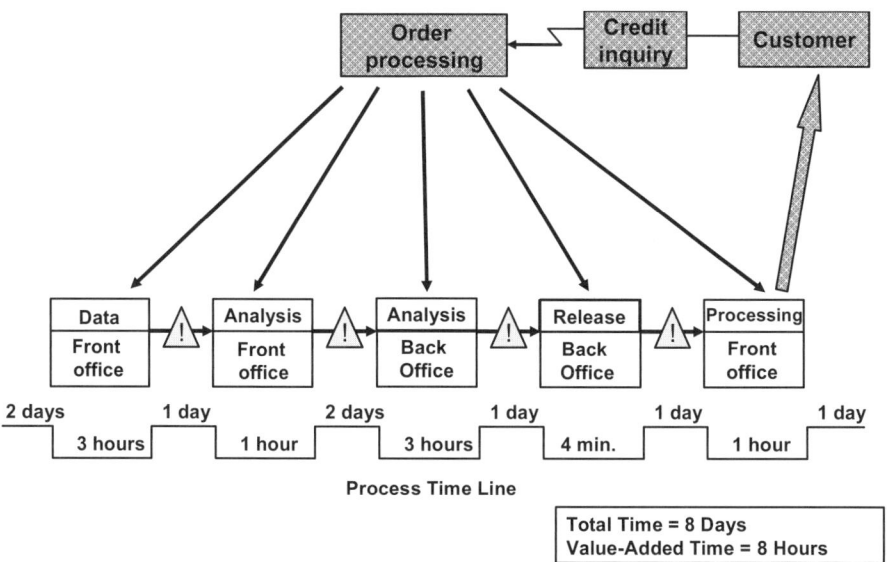

Fig. 3.3.3.2   Value-stream mapping.

• The value-adding activities are the procurement of all relevant data, analysis in the front office, and analysis in the back office required for larger business, followed by release and, finally, processing in the front office (that is, preparation of all documents and forms).

- The non-value-adding activities are shown together with their duration on the upper part of the typical *process time line*. They will be given special attention – as indicated by the triangular symbols As with basic process analysis, the objective is to identify non-value-adding activities that can be avoided and thus to identify "waste".

3.4   Characteristic Features in Logistics and Operations Management

3.4.1   Principle and Validity of Characteristics in Planning & Control

Any enterprise striving to reach its objectives cannot dispense with individual logistics. This alone is not satisfactory, of course, as it is safe to assume that there are principles common to whole branches of business. With the help of a morphological scheme, the weighting of company objectives can be translated into appropriate logistics.

> A *characteristic in planning & control* in a logistics network is the sum of all values, that is, one value per *feature in the morphological scheme*. It relates to a product or product family.

Each product or product family can have a different characteristic for planning & control. This type of schema can be found in [LuEv01]. Our discussion will include similar features and values. But we will also consider some important changes and additions in reference to transcorporate cooperation, non-repetitive production, and the process industry. The 18 features are divided into three groups, namely:

- Features pertaining to the user and the product or product family
- Features pertaining to logistics and production resources
- Features pertaining to the production or procurement order

The following describes each feature and its values and defines the terms. While the features are independent of each other, individual values can certainly relate to other values. For example, the value of a feature can result in a particular value of another feature or preclude that value. But there are cases where there are no such dependent relationships. The totality of all features and values therefore shows redundancies. This situation is actually desirable, for it allows, at least to some extent, testing for plausibility.

Logistics analysis works out a characteristic for planning & control for each product or product family. For each company in a logistics network, a company-internal analysis is carried out.

It is not always easy to determine the value of a feature. The decision is often the result of estimation, probability, or even an intuitive grasp of the situation. These decisions are a matter for strategic company management. Operations management must insist that company management make the decisions here. To do this, it will need the help of operations management in order to foresee the repercussions of the decision for one or the other value of a feature. Obviously, it is advantageous to have persons in upper management who are experienced in operations management. In small companies, a person may work in both upper management and operations management. This is one reason why such companies are very efficient with regard to logistics.

The results of the analysis can be used as follows:

1. A comparison of results in the supply chain reveals potential problems for efficient logistics.

- *Within the company:* If features for the product families are too different, differing business methods of planning & control will be used. The co-existence of differing methods causes problems and diminishes the efficiency of logistics.

- *Transcorporate:* As described in Sections 2.2.3 and 2.2.4, the same logistics and information systems should be implemented in a logistics network wherever possible. With this, the characteristic for planning & control should be the same all along the network. If not, inefficiency will result.

2. Once the characteristic has been determined, it will indicate the appropriate business methods and techniques for planning & control.

The following sections will derive business methods for planning & control from the features. They all have advantages and disadvantages as well as limits to their implementation. They cannot be employed for all types of business processes. They may be incompatible with the business processes determined through process analysis, making it necessary to change the business processes or to alter company objectives. This kind of feedback also shows whether enterprise objectives and actual business processes cohere.

Position with regard to the features and thus also the weighting of enterprise objectives must be examined continually, because the market changes. If planning & control in a company follows an outdated philosophy, this is often due to the fact that enterprise objectives have not been reviewed and given new weightings. Had the company used changed characteristics for planning & control, it would have been in a position to institute new business methods for planning & control in a timely fashion.

> 3. The features making up a characteristic have an influence on logistics performance indicators.

Various characteristics can result in varying values of performance indicators. To compare performance indicators among companies effectively, the features making up the characteristics must be taken into account.

3.4.2   Six Features in Reference to Customer, and Item or Product or Product Family

Figure 3.4.2.1 shows the first group of features.

Depth of product structure:

> The *depth of product structure* is defined as the number of structure levels within the total logistics network for the product, whether company-internal or transcorporate.

Product structure and structure level are defined in Section 1.2.2. The depth of product structure is dependent upon the product. A deep product structure is usually also "wide": in each structure level many components are put together. Such complex products usually entail complex planning & control. The depth of product structure is thus also a measure of the complexity of planning & control in the logistics network (see also [Albe95]). This complexity influences planning & control in each of the companies involved in the logistics network. See the feature *depth of product structure in the company* in Section 3.4.3.

Features referring to customer and item, product or product family				
Feature ➤➤	**Values**			
Depth of product structure ➤➤	many structure levels	some structure levels		one-level production
Orientation of product structure ➤➤	▲ convergent	▲ combination ▼ upper/lower structure levels		▼ divergent
Frequency of customer demand ➤➤	unique	discontinuous (lumpy, sporadic)	regular	continuous (steady)
Product variety concept ➤➤	according to (changing) customer specification	product family with many variants	product family	standard product with options	individual or standard product
(Item) unit cost ➤➤	low		high	
Transporta-bility ➤➤	not transportable	transportable	portable	digitally transmittable

Fig. 3.4.2.1   Important features and possible values referring to the user and the product or product family.

Orientation of product structure:

The *orientation of product structure* indicates whether in *one single* production process *a certain* product is manufactured from *various* components (symbol ▲ , convergent product structure), or whether in *one single* production process *various* products are made out of *a certain* component (symbol ▼ , divergent product structure).

- *Convergent product structure* is often used as a synonym for *discrete manufacturing*, that is, the production of distinct items such as machines or appliances. It is also called *assembly orientation*. The triangle pointing up symbolizes a *tree (or arborescent) structure*, as the product structure, such as that in Figure 1.2.2.2.

- *Divergent product structure* is often used as a synonym for *by-products* arising in continuous production (see Section 3.4.3). In chemical or oil production, which is a typical example from the process industry, processing of the basic material yields – in one single process – several active substances as well as waste or by-products. In the food industry there are by-products that, through recycling, can be used as basic materials in another production process (such as scrap chocolate). The triangle pointing down symbolizes an upside-down, arborescent structure as the product structure. Note that a divergent product structure should not be confused with the multiple use of a component in different products.

- "▲ on ▼": This is a product with divergent product structure at lower structure levels, and convergent product structure at higher structure levels. The (lower) chemical level of pharmaceutical products, for example, has a divergent product structure, while the (higher) pharmaceutical level has a convergent structure. Other examples are products made from sheet metals. Many semifinished goods arise simultaneously from the sheet metal through pressing or laser cutting, and they are then used for various end products.

Determining the values of this feature corresponds exactly to a part of the VAT analysis (the "VA part"):

VAT analysis is a procedure for determining the general flow of parts and products from raw materials to finished products. A V structure corresponds to the divergent product structure (the letter V has the same shape as the symbol ▼). An A structure corresponds to the convergent product structure (the letter A has the same shape as the symbol ▲). A T structure consists of numerous similar finished products assembled from common assemblies, subassemblies, and parts. See the feature *product variety concept* below.

A note on "▼ on ▲": This often symbolizes an end product having many variants and therefore addresses the T structure mentioned above. In the lower structure levels, semifinished items are put together as modules. In assembly, many variants of end products are built from the semifinished goods or subassemblies. This is the case with automobiles. But because final assembly is clearly based upon an assembly-oriented, convergent product structure, it should not be represented by the upside-down triangle. It is not the case that several products will arise from a particular semi-processed item. Although the symbol is used quite commonly in this case, it is used incorrectly. A separate feature for describing the variant structure is — as mentioned before — the product variety concept. See below.

Frequency of customer demand:

> *Frequency of customer demand* means the number of times within defined observation time periods that the entirety of the (internal or external) customers demand a product or product family.

The individual values are defined as follows. Demand is

- *Unique*, if it occurs only once within an observation period
- *Discontinuous*, *lumpy*, *sporadic*, or *highly volatile*, if many observation periods with no or very little demand are interrupted by few periods with large, for example ten times higher demand, without recognizable regularity
- *Regular*, if it can be calculated for every observation period according to a certain formula
- *Continuous* or *steady*, if the demand is about the same in every observation period (e.g., daily)

This feature determines the options for repetitive frequency of the corresponding production and procurement orders. This in turn will determine the basic business methods and procedures for planning & control.

If longer observation periods are chosen, the frequency of customer demand can change, tending towards continuous demand. However, shifts and dips in demand within the observation period in this case will be unknown. For its purposes, planning & control can assume that the total demand occurs at the start of the observation period.

Product variety concept:

> The *product variety concept* determines the strategy for developing the product and offering it to the customer. Where applicable, there may also be a product variety concept for semifinished goods.

The product variety concept allows the producer to respond to customer requests to varying degrees of *variant orientation*. The individual values of product variety concept are defined as follows:

- *Individual* or *standard product*: This is a product that is offered to the customer "in isolation," that is, with no reference to other products in the range. These are "off the rack" products, or "standard menus." These products have their own complete product structure.

- *Standard product with options*: Here, the number of variants is small, and a variant is an option or additional feature of one and the same basic product. Each option and addition has its own product structure along with that of the standard product. Many examples are found in the machine industry.

- *Product family*: Compare here the definition in Section 3.1.2. In gastronomy, this value of the product variety concept is comparable to combining various appetizers, main dishes, and desserts to form an individual menu. Example industrial products are appliances and tools.

- *Product family with many variants*: The potential number of various products that can be produced in a product family can lie in the thousands or even in the millions. Production starts with raw materials or various components, but with an identical process. Variability of the process is achieved by CNC machines or by the workers themselves. Representation of the product structure requires a generic structure in order to overcome data redundancy problems and to reduce the administrative efforts for defining orders and maintaining the product structure. Product families with many variants are comparable to *prêt-à-porter* in the fashion industry. Some examples are automobiles, elevators, appliances and machines with variable specifications, complex furniture, or insurance contracts.

- *Product according to (changing) customer specification:* In contrast to the product family, here at least some design work occurs during delivery lead time, according to customer specification. Usually, the product will be similar to a "mother product," meaning a product that has been delivered before. The product structure and the process plan will be derived and adapted from the "mother version." This value of the product variety concept is comparable to *haute couture*, whereby a creation is made to order for the individual customer. Examples can be found in the manufacturing of facilities (plants), such as the building of exteriors or refineries.

A subcategory of this value is the *degree of change in customer orders*, where product and process structures change *after* the start of production. This problem arises mainly in relation to the fourth value (at the far left in Figure 3.4.4.1) of product variety concept and is found in the table in parentheses.

Elaborating the values of the feature *product variety concept* can be considered to be a more detailed analysis of the T structure within VAT analysis.

T analysis describes the product variety. Qualitatively, the length of the cross-beam of the T stands for the number of product variants.

Figure 3.4.2.2 shows the idea of T analysis.

Product variety concept				
according to (changing) customer specification	product family with many variants	product family	standard product with options	individual or standard product
T analysis	⊤	⊤	T	T		

Fig. 3.4.2.2   T analysis within the VAT analysis and its relation to the product variety concept.

The product variety concept stands in relation to other features. This will be discussed in the next section. As a rule, the complexity of planning & control increases with the number of different products that are produced. It is not, however, dependent upon the number of variants, but rather on the number of product families having differing characteristics. Based on the definition of a product family, it is clear that all of its members can be described by one and the same characteristic. However, planning & control becomes more complicated with an increasing degree of product variety and, of course, with the degree of change in customer orders.

Unit cost:

An item's *unit cost* is defined as the total cost for producing or purchasing one unit of measure of the item, e.g. one part, one gallon, one pound. It includes labor, material, and overhead cost.

- A *high-cost item* is an item with a relatively high unit cost compared to the unit cost of a *low-cost item*.

For many important decisions in logistics and operations management, a very rough classification in low and high cost items is sufficient. However, an ABC classification considering sales and projected volume, would allow a finer distinction. See Section 10.2.2.

Transportability:

> The *transportability* of an item is actually a statement on the size and weight per unit of measurement. If the item is a service, transportability refers to the object on which the service is carried out.

- A *non-transportable item* is an item with a size or weight that permits no transport. These are items or objects, for example, of a size greater than 50 m^3 or a weight greater than 200 metric tons. An example here is manufacture or maintenance of large plants.

- A *transportable item* is an item with a size or weight that permits transport using technical aids, such as helicopters, heavy goods vehicles, airplanes, or several people working together.

- A *portable item* is an item with a size or weight that permits transport (over a longer period of time) by means of the strength of one person. These are items or objects, for example, of a size smaller than 0.01 m^3 or weighing less than 15 kg per unit. Letters sent out by courier are an example.

- *Digitally transmittable items* are items that may be transmitted, or transported, using a digital communication protocol. These non-material goods have size or weight zero.

The division of unit costs by the size or weight of the object leads to the concept of *value density*, that is, product value per kilogram or cubic meter. Digitally transmittable items have a value density approaching infinity. Value density plays a central role in the design of value-added networks. See here also Section 2.4.1 and [Senn04]. It is a challenge is, for example, if low-cost services are to be provided for non-transportable objects. This is the case with services for plants that have been installed worldwide. In designing the services, the proportion of services that can be transmitted digitally is particularly important.

3.4.3   Five Features in Reference to Logistics and Production Resources

Figure 3.4.3.1 shows the second group of features.

Features referring to logistics and production resources					
Feature ➡	**Values**				
Production environment ➡	engineer-to-order	make-to-order	assemble-to-order (from single parts)	assemble-to-order (from assemblies)	make-to-stock
Depth of product structure in the company ➡	many structure levels	few structure levels		one-level production	trade (including external production)
Facility layout ➡	fixed-position layout for site, project, or island production	process layout for job shop production	product layout for single-item-oriented line production	product layout for high-volume line production	product layout for continuous production
Qualitative flexibility of capacity ➡	can be implemented in many processes		can be implemented in specific processes		can be implemented in only one process
Quantitative flexibility of capacity ➡	not flexible in terms of time		hardly flexible in terms of time		flexible in terms of time

Fig. 3.4.3.1   Important features and their possible values in reference to logistics and production resources.

Production environment:

Production environment or *manufacturing environment* refers to whether a company, plant, product, or service is organized to fulfill orders downstream from a specific (customer) order penetration point (OPP). The organization involves methods and techniques of planning & control of development, procurement, production, and delivery.

This feature is naturally closely connected with the (customer) order penetration point (OPP) and the level of stocking (see Fig. 1.3.1.3):

- *Make-to-stock* is a store at the level of the end product. Delivery takes place from the *end products store* according to customer order.

  An *order picking store* or a *commissary* are special cases in the logistics flow that represent a status between actual stocking and use. Here all items or products are brought together that will be used for a certain production or sales order. They are stocked until final use in production or in the form of delivery to the customer. See Section 14.4.1.

- *Assemble-to-order*, or *finish-to-order* is stocking at the level of assemblies or single parts. Upon receipt of a customer's order, a customized product is assembled using key components from the *assemblies store* or from the *single parts store* (that is, from the *in-house parts store* or *purchased parts store*).

  Package-to-order is a production environment in which a good can be packaged during the customer tolerance time. The item itself is the same for all customers. However, (only) packaging determines the end product.

- *Make-to-order* involves stocking at the level of raw materials or direct purchasing of material from suppliers after receipt of a customer's order. The final product is produced to meet the special needs of the customer using materials from the *raw materials store* or acquired through customer procurement orders. In both cases, the starting point is completed design and manufacturing process development. Thus, we can speak of stocking at the level of product and process development.

  Consigned stocks, or *consignment inventory*, or *vendor-owned inventory (VOI)* are inventories of unpaid items. These are items that legally still belong to the supplier, but have already been physically moved to the company.[2]

- *Engineer-to-order* involves no stocking at all. At least parts of a customer order must be designed or developed prior to procurement and production.

Depth of product structure in the company:

The *depth of product structure in the company* is defined as the number of structure levels within the company.

This feature describes the degree to which the company's logistics resources must work towards the inside and towards the outside of the company. In regard to the logistics network within a company, the following possibilities result:

- In a pure *trading company* the number of structure levels, and thus the depth of product structure, is zero. Note: A company is still a

---

[2]   A *consignment* is the process leading to consigned stock.

trading company if it administrates a logistics network but contracts the production processes to third parties. Actually though, the underlying basis is a one-level process plan with all external operations.

- Pure *assembling companies* or *producers of single parts* generally have at least one-level production, with mainly outside suppliers.

- A *supplier* may produce pre-assemblies or single parts or perform individual operations (such as surface treatments). Here, again, one-level production is the general rule. Suppliers are forced, however, to depend on producers further along the logistics network. Sometimes they function as system suppliers.

- The greater the number of structure levels the company itself produces (make decision), the fewer components it will purchase from outside suppliers — and the greater the depth of product structure in the company.

This feature goes hand in hand with the feature *depth of product structure within the total logistics network* (Section 3.4.2). The less depth of product structure in a company as compared to that in the entire logistics network, the more strongly the company is bound to the transcorporate logistics network. In other words, with less depth of product structure, the greater the necessity for transcorporate cooperation. Depending upon position within the network, this may refer to procurement or distribution tasks. Experience has shown that deep product structure of the entire logistics network is also "wide," in the sense that many components enter into each structure level. This extends the range of procurement tasks.

With great depth of production structure, a company may attempt to reduce the complexity of the network by turning over structure levels to third parties (buy decision). This does reduce complexity within the company itself, but — and this is the important point — complexity is not reduced within the total logistics network. Each company should contribute towards mastering the total complexity. Outsourcing must result in lower transaction costs (see also Section 2.1.1). The general rule is that outsourcing replaces long push logistics with pull logistics, through augmenting the number of independent partners and thus the number of process levels in the process model. In consequence, more persons become involved in planning & control. As they stand closer to their part of the entire process, the quality of planning & control can increase.

Facility layout:

> The *facility layout* describes the physical organization of the production infrastructure (the spatial arrangement and grouping of production equipment in work centers), the degree of the division of labor among workers, and the course that orders take through the work centers.

The following values of this feature are generally distinguished:

- *Fixed-position layout* for *site production, project production,*[3] or *island production,* also called: Here one work center carries out all operations to produce a product. All persons involved work here. All the production equipment is found at this work center or supplied to it. From the outside, the sum of all operations has the appearance of one gross operation. Workers exercise extensive autonomous control at the construction site. Typical examples of fixed-position layout for site or project production include plant and facility construction, shipbuilding, large aircraft, very specific car production, automobile repair service, service at tables in a restaurant, operations in a hospital. Examples for island production include the production of prototypes[4] and specific product families, in particular with group technology.[5]

- *Process layout,* also called *job shop layout* or *functional layout,* for *job shop production,* or simply *job shop:* Similar production equipment is grouped together spatially at one work center. Only one operation is carried out at the work center, usually by one person (division of labor). The product moves from shop to shop in a variable, undirected sequence, that is, according to the particular process plan. The process plan lists all individual operations to be carried out. Certain persons are responsible for control. Typical examples include the production of appliances, electrical devices and electronics, furniture, pharmaceuticals,

---

[3] *Project manufacturing* is used synonymously with project production.

[4] A *production of prototypes* or a *pilot test* is the production of a quantity to verify the manufacturability, customer acceptance, or other requirements before implementation of the ongoing production ([APIC04]).

[5] *Group technology (GT)* identifies product families via a high percentage of the same processes in the process plan and establishes their efficient production. Group technology facilitates cellular manufacturing.

radiology and specific analysis in a hospital, and traditional forms of education.[6]

- *Product layout* for *single-item-oriented line production:* Here, the product moves through all work centers, which are ordered along the process, meaning the sequence of operations to produce the product. Depending on the product, individual work centers or operations may be omitted. Generally, the line processes several variants of a product family in rather small batches, or a large variety of variants in single items (lot size of 1), often with high value-added for each unit. The quantity produced by the line is determined by the actual demand. The fewer the number of variants that are produced, the more that production scheduling and control can be based on production rates.[7] Setup times between batches, if required, are very short. All the required production equipment is found along the line. Ideally, workers are capable of executing neighboring operations in the process, whereby they move along the line.[8] To the outside, the sum of all these operations looks like one rough-cut operation. If workers are organized in *group production*, the group itself exercises control to a large degree within the group. Sometimes, the offices for planning & control as well as those for product and process development can be found close to the line, too. Typical examples include the assembly of automobiles, catamarans, motors and axles, machines, personal computers, and — most recently — aircraft (the Boeing 717-200, for example). Other examples are a modern cafeteria line or office administration.[9]

- *Product layout* for *high-volume line production:* Here we find the same arrangement as in single-item oriented line production. However, the operations are generally more detailed. Whole sequences of operations are carried out in direct succession. At times, the course of the process is rhythmical, meaning that the

---

[6] *Intermittent production* is a term used by many people as a synonym of job shop production.

[7] A *production rate* is the rate of production expressed in simple quantity measures for a period of time, e.g., a day, week, or month. *Rate-based scheduling* is scheduling and controling based on production rates.

[8] *Process flow production* describes the case where queue time is virtually eliminated by integrating the movement of the product into the actual operation of the resource performing the work ([APIC04]).

[9] *Mixed-model production* is a term similar to single-item-oriented line production. It stands for a factory producing close to the same mix of different products that will be sold that day (see [FoBl91]).

course follows a strict time schedule. The work centers form a chain or a network with fixed, specifically designed facilities, sometimes linked by conveyors or pipes. Generally, the production line produces only a few different products, whenever possible in large batches of discrete units or non-discrete items (for example, liquids). That is, the line produces with long runs, but the material flow is discontinuous. Setup times between batches are typically very high, due to cleaning or major adjustments of the production equipment, for example. The facility is built in order to obtain very low unit costs. Typical examples include the production of food, general chemicals, and transportation.

- *Product layout* for *continuous production* or *continuous flow production* is an extreme form of line production, namely a lotless production system where material flow is continuous during the production process ([APIC04]). The process is halted only if required by the transportation infrastructure or if resources are unavailable. The production line generally processes a commodity such as sugar, petroleum, and other fluids, powders, and basic materials.

The latter three kinds of facility layout have a common spatial arrangement:

> A *line* is a specific physical space for the manufacture of a product that in a flow shop layout is represented by a straight line. In actuality, this may be a series of pieces of equipment connected by piping or conveyor systems ([APIC04]).

- The work centers are arranged along the process, that is, according to the sequence of operations required to produce a product or a product family. A line in the manufacturing environment is often called *assembly line* (particularly in the case of single-item-oriented line production) or *production line* (particularly in the case of high-volume line production).[10] In practice, a line can take any form or configuration, such as straight, U-shaped, or L-shaped (see Section 5.2.2).

From the term *line*, used to describe this particular spatial arrangement, stems the term *line production*. For high-volume line production or

---

[10]   A *dedicated line* is a production line permanently configured to run well-defined parts, one piece at a time, from station to station ([APIC04]) and is thus a simple kind of single-item-oriented line production.

continuous production, the terms *flow shop* or *flow manufacturing* are sometimes used synonymously.

The facility layout can be dependent upon the structure level. For example, facility layout may differ for assembling and parts production. In addition, a subcategory here is the *degree of structuring of the process plan*. This degree of structuring tells us the number of operations that are divided up in the process plan for one structure level. Site production and single-item-oriented line production generally have a low degree of structuring, as the operations defined are considerably less detailed.

Qualitative flexibility of capacity:

> The *qualitative flexibility of capacity* determines whether capacity can be implemented for various or for particular processes only.

A producer's capacity is made up of the capacity of its employees and of its production infrastructure. This is the feature that sets a company's possible range with regard to the target area of flexibility. If employees have broad qualifications and the production infrastructure can be widely implemented, there will be great flexibility in the use of resources. This is also the necessary prerequisite for a wide product range and thus for flexibility in achieving customer benefit.

In practical application, this feature can be broken down further into sub-categories, if the different types of capacity show differences in qualitative flexibility. The main differentiation is between the *qualitative flexibility of employees* and the *qualitative flexibility of the production infrastructure*.

The qualitative flexibility of employees deserves special attention (*job enlargement* is also often used). First of all, it can normally be achieved to a far greater degree than flexibility of the production infrastructure. Second, in contrast to the production infrastructure, employees do not simply represent a production factor, for they are themselves stakeholders.

Quantitative flexibility of capacity:

> The *quantitative flexibility of capacity* describes its temporal flexibility.

Temporal flexibility of capacity along the time axis is a significant factor in the target areas of delivery and cost. As follows, it even becomes a crucial feature when choosing planning & control methods, particularly in capacity management.

Once again, if different types of capacity show varying quantitative flexibility, it will be necessary to differentiate subcategories. The main differentiation is between the *quantitative flexibility of employees* and the *quantitative flexibility of the production infrastructure*.

People have far greater possibilities to achieve quantitative flexibility than machines. Quantitative flexibility of machines can only be reached by means of maintaining over-capacity. People, on the other hand, are to a certain degree able to adapt their efforts to the current load.

Moreover, if capacity has a qualitative flexibility that transcends the "home" work center (that is, employees can be implemented for processes outside the "home" work center), flexibility along the time axis is increased. For example, if workers can be moved from one work center to another, this is the same as flexibility in implementation of the employees at both work centers. Depending upon load in the areas, the employees can be implemented flexibly.

3.4.4   Seven Features in Reference to the Production or Procurement Order

Figure 3.4.4.1 shows the third group of features.

Reason for order release / type of order:

> The *reason for order release* is the origin of the demand. The *type of order* indicates the origin of demand that resulted in the order.

Conventionally, the following values are distinguished (compare to Figure 3.2.3.1):

- *Order release according to demand* and *customer production order* or *customer procurement order:* A customer has placed an order. It may be a classic (single) order, for a car, for example, or it may be a blanket order, such as for electronic components. In the latter case, customer production orders can follow at different points in time, released according to the delivery agreements. This is also called *demand-controlled materials management*, using pull logistics.

Features referring to production or procurement order			
Feature ➤	**Values**		
Reason for order release (type of order) ➤	demand / (customer production or procurement order)	prediction / (forecast order)	consumption / (stock replenishment order)
Frequency of order repetition ➤	production / procurement without order repetition	production / procurement with infrequent order repetition	production / procurement with frequent order repetition
Flexibility of order due date ➤	no flexibility (fixed delivery date)	not very flexible	flexible
Type of long-term orders ➤	none	blanket order: capacity	blanket order: goods
(Order) lot or batch size ➤	"1" (single item production / procurement)	Single item or small batch (production / procurement)	large batch (production / procurement)	lotless (production / procurement)
Lot traceability ➤	not required	lot / batch / charge	position in lot
Loops in the order structure ➤	Product structure without loops, and directed network of operations		Product structure with loops, or undirected network of operations

Fig. 3.4.4.1   Important features and possible values in reference to production or procurement order.

- *Order release according to prediction* and *forecast order:* Future demand has been estimated, such as demand for a machine tool. Customer orders for the machine tool have not yet been received. To meet forecasted demand, a production or procurement order is released. This is also called *forecast-controlled materials management* using push logistics.

- *Order release according to consumption,* and *(stock) replenishment order:* A customer places an order for a product in stock, for example in the retail trade. In response to the demand, stock must be reordered. Actually, this is a response to forecasting future need in the quantity that is reordered. This is also called *consumption-controlled materials management* using pull logistics.

The trigger for the release of orders can be different for end products, semifinished goods, and raw materials. It is dependent upon the (customer) order penetration point (OPP).

Frequency of order repetition:

The *frequency of order repetition* tells us how often within a certain time period a production or procurement order for the same product will be made. The time period chosen should be sufficiently long.

We differentiate among the following values:

- *Production without order repetition* or *procurement without order repetition* means that an order for the same physical product will practically never be placed again.

- *Production with infrequent order repetition* or *procurement with infrequent order repetition* means that, with a certain probability, an order for the same physical product will be placed again.

- *Production with frequent order repetition* or *procurement with frequent order repetition* means that orders for the same physical product will be very frequent.

Note: The adjective *physical* is used here to underline that this feature refers to the product level, and not to the product family level. Therefore, if an order produces a physically different product of the same family compared to another order, this is *not* considered to be production with order repetition.

Flexibility of the order due date:

The *flexibility of the order due date* indicates whether customers (internal or external) are flexible when stipulating the delivery due date.

The flexibility of the order due date is of great importance to methods of planning & control, particularly with regard to the target area of delivery. With regard to the target area of cost, it is connected to the quantitative flexibility of employees, the production infrastructure, and stored inventory and in-process inventory.

Type of long-term order:

The feature *type of long-term order* describes the manner in which long-term planning is done in the logistics network.

A *blanket order*, for example, is a long-term agreement for a great number of deliveries.

> A *minimum blanket order quantity* is — for a blanket order — a long-term minimum volume of business for a particular period of time

Long-term orders are in the best interests of both parties. The customer profits from more reasonable pricing and from a higher fill rate from the supplier. The supplier in turn can depend on a minimum blanket order quantity and gains the advantage of increased planning capability.

We distinguish the following values, which correspond generally to the values of the features *frequency of customer demand* and *product variety concept* in Figure 3.4.2.1:

- Blanket orders for goods are long-term binding commitments in the logistics network for products and their components. Assured sales are necessary and are guaranteed by continuous customer demand. If the minimum blanket order quantity is zero, then demand is only a forecast. If the forecast is relatively reliable, production planning for both partners in the logistics network will be better than without the forecast. For example, if customer demand is discontinuous, forecasts will be used for long-term planning.

- Blanket orders for capacity are long-term binding agreements on reserving capacity. This may be in reference to a product family, for example, for which at least regular customer demand is guaranteed and which is produced in the main according to the same production process. The products are ordered short term, and they are to be produced using the reserved capacity within the delivery lead time. Again, if the minimal order quantity is zero, the same applies as described above.

- "None" means that, in the logistics network, neither blanket orders nor forecasts are made. This is appropriate when actual customer demand is non-repetitive.

Lot size or batch size of the order:

> *Lot size* or *batch size* is the *order quantity* of an ordered item (and vice versa).

The following values are distinguished for batch size:

- *Single-item production*, or *single-item procurement*, or *lot size one*, or *batch size one* means that only one unit of the product is produced or procured for an order.

- *Small batch production* or *small batch procurement* indicates that for an order only a few units of the product will be produced or procured.

- *Large batch production* or *large batch procurement* means that a high quantity of units of the product will be produced or procured for one order.

- *Lotless production* or *lotless procurement* means that no specific quantity is linked with the order. Rather, after order opening, production/procurement continues until an explicit order stop is given.

Note: There is no correlation between the values in nearby columns of the feature *batch size* and of the feature *frequency of order repetition*. For example, single-item production with frequent order repetition is quite common (for example, in machine tool production). Conversely, there can be production (without order repetition) of exactly *one batch for the entire product life cycle*[11] (such as when an active substance in the chemical industry, for cost reasons, is produced only once in the product life cycle, or in the case of special components that are very difficult to procure).

Lot traceability:

> *Lot traceability* is information on the production and procurement of a product, in particular about the components used in the product.

Lot traceability is often required by law or can be important with regard to liability and problems associated with recalling a product. It generally asks for records about every production or procurement lot, batch, or charge:

- A *charge,* according to [APIC04], is the initial loading of ingredients or raw materials into a processor, such as a reactor, to begin the manufacturing process. It has become a synonym for a number or quantity of goods produced or procured together that, for the purposes of the lot traceability, are identical.

- *Position in lot* refers to the successive numbering of the individual items in a lot.

The lot traceability requirement makes planning & control considerably more complicated. Nevertheless, lot traceability plays a particularly important role in the process industry. See Chapter 7.

---

[11] Here, a 2nd definition of the term *product life cycle* is used: the market stages a new product goes through from the beginning to end, i.e., introduction, growth, maturity, saturation, and decline ([APIC04]). See Section 1.1.1 for the first definition.

Loops in the order structure:

> *Loops in the order structure* is a situation in resource planning, where business objects have to be considered an indefinite number of times.

- A *product structure with loops* means a situation where a product is its own component — either directly or via intermediate products. It plays an important role again in the process industry, where production yields important quantities of by-products that are reused, such as scrap chocolate or energy.

- An *undirected network of operations* means a situation where sequences of operations within the network may be repeated. It is found in the precision industry, where individual operations are repeated until the required degree of quality is reached. In addition, it plays an important role in the process industry, where a mixing operation may be repeated as often as is necessary to assure the desired level of homogeneity.

- A *product structure without loops*, as well as a *directed network of operations*, are free of the above mentioned effects.

Planning of loops in the order structure is relatively complicated. See Sections 7.1.3, 7.3.3, and 12.4.4.

3.4.5   Important Relationships between Characteristic Features

In some cases, there is a relationship among characteristic features, which can even be a positive correlation. For example, the feature *facility layout* is — according to Figure 3.4.5.1 — closely related to other features:

Features referring to logistics and production resources					
Feature	➤	Values			
Facility layout	➤	fixed-position layout for site, project, or island production	process layout for job shop production	product layout for single-item- oriented line production	product layout for high-volume line production	product layout for continuous production

Features referring to user and product or product family				
Feature	➤	Values		
Orientation of product structure	➤	▲ convergent	▲combination ▼upper/lower structr. levels	▼ divergent

Features referring to production or procurement order				
Feature	➤	Values		
(Order) lot or batch size	➤	"1" (single item production / procurement)	single item or small batch (production / procurement)	large batch (production / procurement)	lotless (production / procurement)

Fig. 3.4.5.1   Links among facility layout, orientation of product structure, and (order) batch size.[12]

The figure shows that, in a *first approximation*, the different values of the features in the same columns appear together. For example:

- *Site production, job shop production, and single-item-oriented line production have a tendency to appear together with:*
  - Convergent product structure
  - Production or procurement of single-items or small batches
- *High-volume line production and continuous production tend to appear together with:*
  - A combination of convergent product structure on upper levels and divergent product structure on lower levels, or a fully divergent product structure
  - Large-batch or lotless production or procurement

---

[12] The horizontal distribution of the values in the morphological scheme has been effected to indicate the correlation of the features.

Both observations also hold in the reverse direction. This means that in all the following figures in Section 3.5, we can replace the feature *facility layout* with one of the two features *orientation of product structure* and *(order) batch size.*

A further observation is that the product variety concept is — according to Figure 3.4.5.2 — closely related to other features:

Features referring to user and product or product family					
Feature	➡	**Values**			
Product variety concept	➡	according to (changing) customer specification	product family with many variants	product family	standard product with options	individual or standard product

Features referring to logistics and production resources					
Feature	➡	**Values**			
Production environment	➡	engineer-to-order	make-to-order	assemble-to-order (from single parts)	assemble-to-order (from assemblies)	make-to-stock

Features referring to production or procurement order			
Feature	➡	**Values**	
Frequency of order repetition	➡	production / procurement without order repetition	production / procurement with infrequent order repetition	production / procurement with frequent order repetition

Fig. 3.4.5.2   Links among the features product variety concept, production environment, and frequency of order repetition.

The figure shows that, in a *first approximation*, the different values of features in the same columns appear together. For example:

- *Product variety concept* versus *production environment*: A product variety concept according to customer specification (such as the manufacturing of plant facilities) means that part of the customer order has to run through design prior to procurement or production. This is the exact meaning of engineer-to-order. Product families with many variants are generally produced using raw materials (make-to-order). The variants in a product family concept with a restricted number of variants are normally produced during assembly (assemble-to-order). Standard products are stocked at the level of end products (make-to-stock).

- *Product variety concept* versus *frequency of order repetition*: Production / procurement without order repetition is generally typical for a product variety concept according to customer specification or for product families with multiple variants. Production / procurement with infrequent order repetition is found with product families. Production / procurement with frequent order repetition is the rule with individual or standard products and with a small number of variants.

On the basis of these observations, we can see that, in all following figures in Section 3.5, the feature *product variety concept* can be replaced with either of the two features *production environment* or *frequency of production or procurement order repetition*.

It is also interesting to compare the feature *frequency of customer demand* in Figure 3.4.2.1 (features related to user and product or product family) with the feature *frequency of order repetition* as shown in Figure 3.4.5.3. It is noteworthy that the values of the features in the same columns do not necessarily have to correspond.

Features referring to user and product or product family					
Feature	➡	**Values**			
Frequency of customer demand	➡	unique	discontinuous (lumpy, sporadic)	regular	continuous (steady)
Features referring to production or procurement order					
Feature	➡	**Values**			
Frequency of order repetition	➡	production / procurement without order repetition	production / procurement with infrequent order repetition	production / procurement with frequent order repetition	

Fig. 3.4.5.3   The features *frequency of customer demand* and *frequency of order repetition* do not necessarily need to correspond.

Indeed, procurement and production can be decoupled from demand on the basis of the type of stockpiling:

- To a certain degree, storage can provide a buffer for discontinuous demand, so that there can be more frequent production. For example, a product can be manufactured throughout the year that will be in demand mainly at a holiday time like Christmas. Through this, capacities can be utilized more evenly. On the negative side, carrying costs are incurred.

- On the other hand, if demand is continuous, delivery can also be made from storage, and usage can be replenished through less frequent orders in large batches. This course of action is sometimes unavoidable, due to both technical constraints (if, for example, such as in the process industry, certain production facilities allow production in specific batch sizes only) and economic reasons (if, for example, as is typical in procurement, the ordering of a small quantity makes no sense, because transport costs — or in production, setup costs — are too high in relation to the unit costs of the small quantity).

Usually, however, there is a connection between values of the features in the same columns: Unique demand occurs together with production or procurement without order repetition, discontinuous demand together with production or procurement with infrequent repetition, and continuous demand with production or procurement with frequent order repetition.

Similarly, the choice of the planning & control concept (see Section 3.5.3) as well as methods and techniques for materials management (see Section 4.3.2) must first be made on the basis of the frequency of customer demand. If a number of concepts and techniques are possible, the choice is determined by the selected frequency of production or procurement order repetition.

3.4.6   Features of Transcorporate Logistics in Supply Chains

Cooperation among all participants is the key prerequisite for effective operation of the supply chain (see Sections 2.2 and 2.3). For this reason the characteristic features of supply chains include various aspects of cooperation. A morphological scheme proposed in [Hieb01] encompasses three groups of features that are closely linked to the Advanced Logistics Partnership (ALP) model (see Section 2.3).

Figure 3.4.6.1 presents *features referring to supply chain collaboration.* They describe the degree and kind of partnership among the participants on a high level as well as the fundamental commitment of the companies to pursue a common "network strategy."

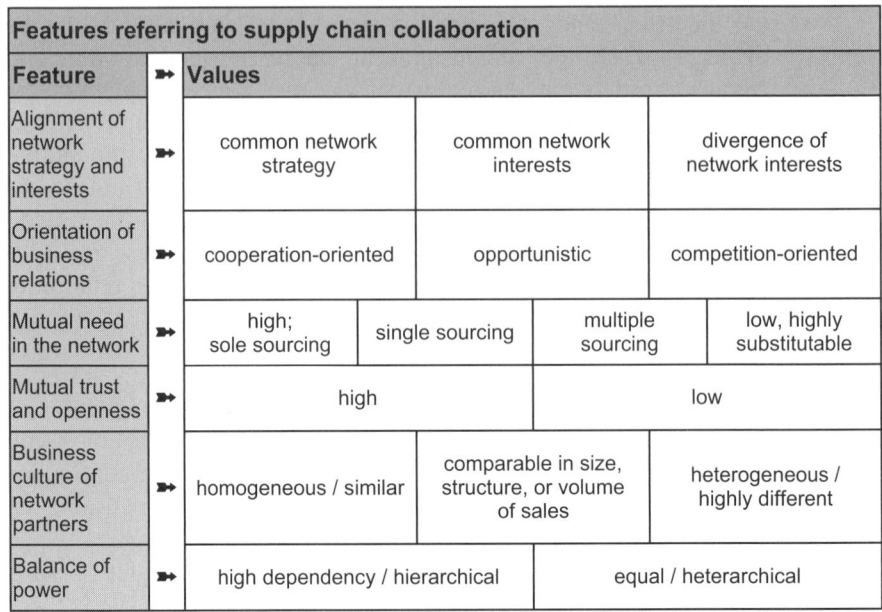

Features referring to supply chain collaboration			
Feature ➤	**Values**		
Alignment of network strategy and interests ➤	common network strategy	common network interests	divergence of network interests
Orientation of business relations ➤	cooperation-oriented	opportunistic	competition-oriented
Mutual need in the network ➤	high; sole sourcing	single sourcing	multiple sourcing	low, highly substitutable
Mutual trust and openness ➤	high		low
Business culture of network partners ➤	homogeneous / similar	comparable in size, structure, or volume of sales	heterogeneous / highly different
Balance of power ➤	high dependency / hierarchical	equal / heterarchical

Increasing complexity of supply chain collaboration.

Fig. 3.4.6.1   Important features, possible values, and increasing complexity of supply chain collaboration.[13]

The columns to the left contain values that indicate that the companies have already expended efforts towards strategic collaboration or that there is an inherent alignment from the start. The columns at the right contain values that indicate increasing complexity of the common operation of value-added processes.

Figure 3.4.6.2 presents *features referring to supply chain coordination* that describe the type of the daily operations in shared transcorporate processes and methods.

---

[13]   The horizontal distribution of the values in the morphological scheme indicates their relation to the increasing degree according to the given criterion.

Features referring to supply chain coordination					
Feature	➡	**Values**			
Intensity of information sharing	➡	limited to needs of order execution	forecast exchange	order tracking and tracing	sharing of inventory / capacity levels	as required for planning and execution processes
Linkage of logistics processes	➡	none, mere order execution	integrated ex-ecution, (e.g., consigned inventory)	vendor-managed inventory	collaborative planning	integrated planning and execution
Autonomy of planning decisions	➡	heterarchical, local independent, autonomous		local, with central guidelines		hierarchical, led by strategic center
Variability of consumption (execution)	➡	low / stable consumption	variability in time	variability in amount	high variability in time and amount	
Extent of formalization (long-term orders)	➡	none; regular purchase orders	blanket order: capacity		blanket order: goods	
Degree of communica-tion among multiple tiers and channels	➡	single contact for the transaction	regular network meetings (e.g., supplier days)	central coordination (e.g., supply chain manager)	multiple contacts among levels and channels	
Use of information technology (IT)	➡	IT use only to support internal business processes	IT use to support network coordination mechanisms (e.g., EDI)		IT use to support execution and planning mechanisms; SCM-software	

Increasing complexity of supply chain coordination.

Fig. 3.4.6.2 Important features, possible values, and increasing complexity of supply chain coordination.

Figure 3.4.6.3 presents *features referring to the configuration of the supply chain*. They describe the modeling of the existing business relationships among the network entities and the setup, meaning the physical structure as well as temporal and legal business relationships. The values of these features determine supply chain changeability to a great extent.

Just as in Figures 3.4.2.1, 3.4.3.1, and 3.4.4.1, the features are – as a whole — independent of each other. However, individual values can certainly relate to other values.

Features referring to the configuration of the supply chain			
Feature ➡	**Values**		
Multi-tier network (depth of network) ➡	2 value-adding tiers	3–5 value-adding tiers	>5 value-adding tiers
Multi-channel network (breadth of network) ➡	1–2 logistics channel(s)	3–5 logistics channels	>5 logistics channels
Linkage among the partners ➡	simple relationship, segmentation		complex relationship, ramifications
Geographical spread of network ➡	local	regional	national	global
Time horizon of business relationship ➡	short-term, less than 1 year	mid-term, 1–3 years	long–term, >3 years
Economical and legal business involvement (financial autonomy) ➡	independent business partners	alliances, joint ventures	group / combine

Increasing complexity of the configuration of the supply chain

Fig. 3.4.6.3   Important features, possible values, and increasing complexity of the configuration of the supply chain.

[Hieb01] defines all of these features in detail. Some of the definitions are readily understood in a common sense, but others have a very specific meaning. However, what is important is that all partners in a logistics network seeking jointly to start a supply chain initiative examine the morphological scheme — including the exact definition of each feature. The scheme must be discussed, completed, and agreed upon. This can culminate in common performance metrics for the entire network. It can be the first step towards a common understanding of the network and deeper knowledge of the interactions among its members.

Often, a supply chain is already in place when morphological schemes are applied. In that case, the scheme proposed above can support achievement of network objectives. It can also be a very helpful tool when replacing a partner in the supply chain.

3.5   Fundamental Concepts in Logistics and Operations Management

3.5.1   Branches of Industry in Dependency Upon Characteristic Features

A *branch* of industry is the sector or segment of business a company engages in.

Definitions of various branches of industry and areas of business can be found in governmental statistics on economics and industry, for example. Typical industrial branches include the chemical industry, plastics industry, electronics and electrical industries, aircraft and automobile industries, engineering and metal industries, watch-making industry, paper industry, and textile industry. Typical branches in service-providing businesses include banking, insurance, consulting, computer software, trust companies and private management, and care agencies (for people and things). The branch will basically determine the classification of a product or service according to the three dimensions of *nature, use* and *degree of comprehensiveness* discussed in Section 1.1.1.

An obvious approach is to seek branch-dependent concepts.

A *branch model* of planning & control groups together with concepts appropriate to specific branches, including suitable types of business processes and business methods.

The branch of industry or service is indeed related to many of the characteristic features of planning & control. The corresponding business methods, however, are usually too general to be ideally suited to a particular branch. For this reason, it has been useful to go beyond those concepts and develop branch models.

Figure 3.5.1.1 shows different branches in dependency upon two characteristic features:

- *Facility layout* from Figure 3.4.3.1 (features related to logistics and production resources)

- *Product variety concept* from Figure 3.4.2.1 (features related to user and product or product family)

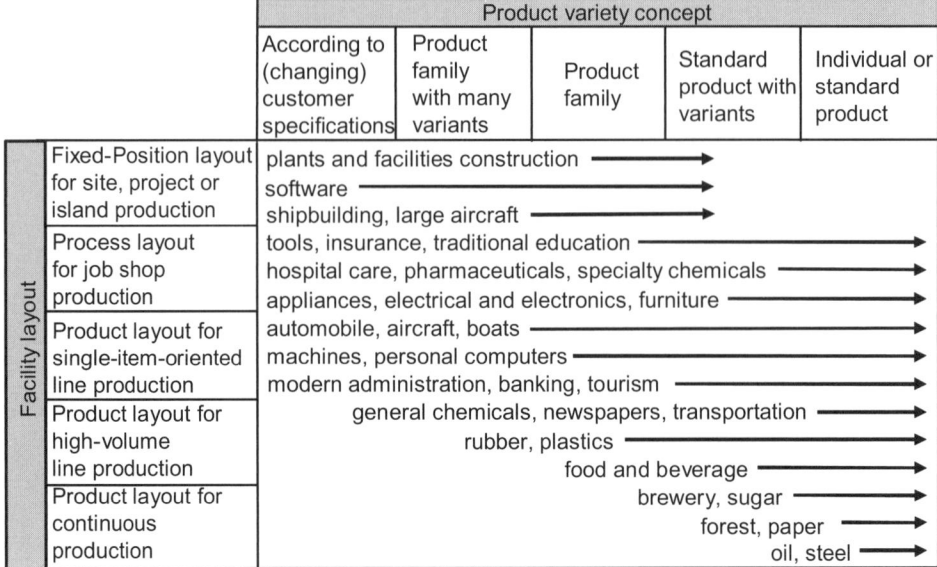

Fig. 3.5.1.1   Different branches in dependency upon the two features *facility layout* and *product variety concept*.

The figure shows that:

- In a first approximation, branches can be readily positioned according to the feature *facility layout*. This indicates that there is a clear relation here.

- A number of branches, particularly those in the process industry (branches producing "stuff" rather than "things," as some would say), can be distinguished along the values of the feature *product variety concept* relatively clearly. In nearly all branches, however, we find product variety concepts of "according to (changing) customer specification" all the way to "individual or standard product" — with some exceptions. Exceptions are the production of plants and facilities, shipbuilding, large aircraft, and software: there are no examples positioned in the top right-hand corner of the matrix. Other exceptions are the production of rubber, plastics, food and beverage, brewery, sugar, forest, paper, oil, steel: there are no examples positioned in the bottom left-hand corner of the matrix. The relation here, therefore, is less clear than the relation to the feature facility layout.

It is interesting that the feature *product variety concept* is therefore largely independent of the feature *facility layout* (as well as of volume, understood as batch size).[14] This important observation leads to the matrix. The following are some examples that support this important observation:

- Take a company producing standard machines. This is done with frequent order repetition, but in single units, either according to arrival of a customer order, or in advance (because it is a standard machine, inventory risk is small: the machine will be sold sooner or later). This is the "nearly top" right-hand corner in the matrix: job shop production or single-item-oriented line production.

- Another company produces standards screws. Again, this is done with frequent repetition, but each time in large batches. This is the bottom right-hand corner in the matrix (as lotless is also very possible): high-volume line production or continuous production.

- A company in the chemical branch produces a large batch of a specific active substance only once for the whole life cycle of the product, due to the high setup and order administration costs. This is the nearly bottom left-hand corner in the matrix: high-volume line production.

- Still another company produces a plant as a single unit and only once, according to customer specification. This is the top left-hand corner in the matrix: site or project production.

3.5.2 Production Types

A *production type* encompasses a particular set of manufacturing technologies and methodologies, having specific importance with regard to logistics management and planning & control.

In the world of practice, the understanding of the different values of the feature *facility layout* introduced in Figure 3.4.3.1, namely:

- Fixed-position layout for site, project, or island production
- Process layout for job shop production
- Product layout for single-item-oriented line production
- Product layout for high-volume line production
- Product layout for continuous production

---

[14] A dependency exists, as mentioned, in the top right-hand corner and in the bottom left-hand corner of the matrix — that is, in the blank areas in the figure.

is not limited to the physical organization of the production infrastructure or the process design. Beyond this, from a systems capability viewpoint, these values are often also seen as production types.

However, a number of new terms have come into use in recent years, each standing for a specific process technology and methodology.

- *Batch production* or *batch processing* is production or procurement of a generally wide variety of standard products or variants of a product family that are manufactured in batches either to order or to stock (see [FoBl91], p. 700). Due to batching, precise timing and sizing of component lots are essential.

- *Mass production* is high-quantity production characterized by specialization of equipment and labor ([APIC04]).

- *Repetitive manufacturing* is "the repeated production of the same discrete products or families of products. Repetitive methodology minimizes setups, inventory, and manufacturing lead times by using production lines, assembly lines, or cells. Work orders are no longer necessary; production scheduling and control are based on production rates (*flow control*). Products may be standard or assembled from modules. Repetitive is *not* a function of speed or volume" ([APIC04]).

- *One-of-a-kind production* is the production or procurement of an engineered-to-order or made-to-order product, generally according to customer specification or configured out of a product family with a very large variety of products.

- *Mass customization* is a production or procurement principle that emphasizes customized products that do not cost more than mass-produced products. According to [APIC04], it is "the creation of a high volume product with large variety so that a customer may specify his or her exact model out of a large volume of possible end items while manufacturing cost is low because of the large volume." Having some characteristics of repetitive manufacturing with regard to the facility layout, mass customization could be seen as "high volume repetitive manufacturing with high variety" [PtSc03]. In this context, "high volume" means either "high number of orders" or "high work content," but *not* (!) "large batch." It is repetitive manufacturing on the family level, but *not* on the product level: each product (unit) produced is, while belonging to the same family, generally physically different. Therefore,

- Techniques of repetitive manufacturing can be used for those aspects of planning & control that refer to the product family as a whole.

- For those aspects of planning & control that refer to a specific product variant, the techniques of repetitive manufacturing can *not* (!) be used. In particular, a specific work order is required for each product produced. The work order includes the configuration of the customer-ordered variant from its specific components as well as variations on the process (omissions or insertions of operations, for example). Furthermore, long lead times may entail the increasing use of project management techniques rather than rate-based scheduling techniques.

It is simply not possible to line up all of these additional production types according to a single feature. In fact, in a systems capability perspective, many of them overlap, just as do some of the different facility layouts already mentioned. Fortunately however, as Figure 3.5.2.1 demonstrates, all of these additional production types can be shown in dependency upon the same characteristic features as in Figure 3.5.1.1, that is, *facility layout* and *product variety concept*.

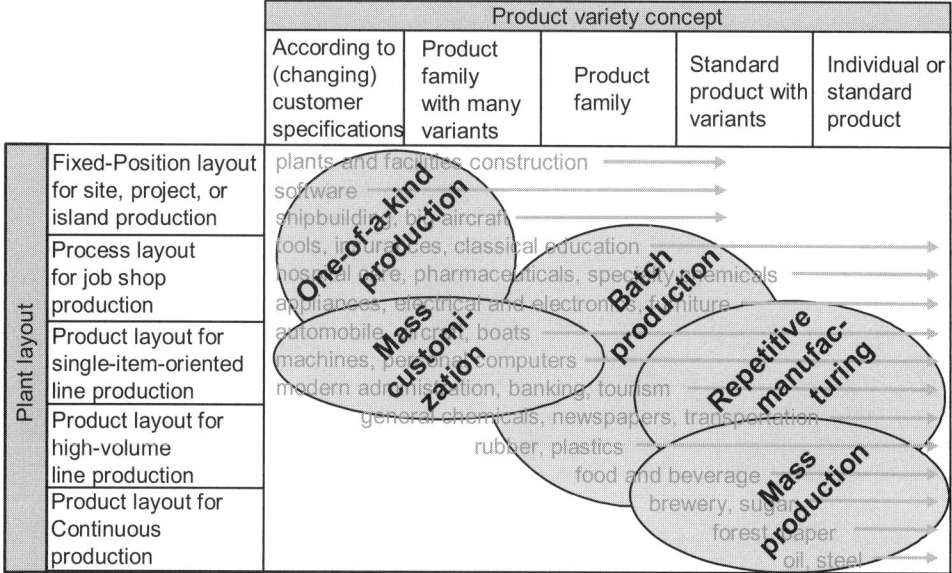

Fig. 3.5.2.1   The different kinds of facility layouts seen — from a system capabilities viewpoint — as production types together with other production types.

3.5.3   Concepts for Planning & Control within the Company

> A *concept for planning & control* is made up of particular types of business processes and business methods for order planning and fulfillment.

Recent decades saw the development of different concepts of planning & control in logistics networks. Each was developed in a particular area and so represents to a certain degree a model for a branch of industry. Some of the concepts arose in powerful industries, such as the automobile or machine industry. The concepts were systemized and given brand names.

- The *MRP II concept (manufacturing resource planning)*[15] originated in North America in the late 1960s. See [Wigh95] and [VoBe04]. MRP II was developed in branches of industry having clearly *convergent product structures,* such as for the construction of big machines and in the automobile and aircraft industries. Three temporal ranges of planning & control (short, medium, and long range) were basic to the MRP II concept that quite early on went beyond matters of production. Further development of the concept led to the *ERP (enterprise resources planning) concept* in order to include all areas of a company. See Chapter 4.

- The Japanese *just-in-time concept*, today also known as lean/JIT (*lean production*), aimed at improving the flow of goods. Marketed in the late 1970s as a contrasting alternative to the MRP II concept, the lean/JIT concept has turned out to be also generally valid and fundamental to planning & control in ERP when *delivery* becomes a targeted company priority. The kanban technique, often linked with lean/JIT, however, is applicable — as well as other simple techniques for repetitive manufacturing — only to standard products or product families with very few variants. The lean/JIT concept and all these techniques form an important *extension* to the MRP II concept and its techniques. See Chapter 5.

The details of resource management developed by the MRP II / ERP concept remain fundamentally valid in the extended concepts below. These extensions differ from the classic MRP II / ERP concept mainly in the modeling of logistics business objects and, accordingly, in order configuration, order processing, and order coordination in all temporal ranges of planning.

---

[15]   Important note: The MRP II concept should not be confused with the MRP method of material requirements planning. See Section 4.3.2 and Chapter 10.

- Various *variant-oriented concepts* originated particularly in Europe in the late 1970s. They were developed in connection with the product variety concept of *product family*, with *one-of-a-kind production* and *production without order repetition*. They are necessary *extensions* of previous concepts. See Chapter 6. Depending on the product variety concept, different characteristics of planning & control arise often and typically together, namely:

  - *Standard product with (few) options*: → Repetitive manufacturing; production with frequent order repetition; make-to-stock or assemble-to-order (from assemblies); small batch production possible.

  - *Product family*: → Repetitive manufacturing or mass customization; production with infrequent order repetition; assemble-to-order (from single parts or subassemblies); mostly single item production to customer order.

  - *Product family with many variants*: → Mass customization; tendency towards production without order repetition; make-to-order; single item production to customer order.

  - *According to (changing) customer specification*: → One-of-a-kind production; production without order repetition; engineer-to-order or make-to-order; single item production to customer order.

- In the late 1980s, *processor-oriented concepts* were developed in North America for process industries. These concepts *extended* the MRP II concept, but they have not yet found complete systematization. They come under the concept called *process flow scheduling*. Besides concepts for continuous production and campaign concepts (to handle high setup costs), processor-oriented concepts consider *divergent product structures*, a phenomenon that was not covered adequately by earlier concepts. See Chapter 7.

Figure 3.5.3.1 summarizes the different concepts. It is interesting to see that they, again, can be shown in dependency upon the two characteristic features of planning & control in logistics networks that were already showcased in Figure 3.5.1.1, that is, *facility layout* and *product variety concept*.

The colored areas indicate the areas of application of the underlying basic MRP II concept and the extended concepts mentioned above.

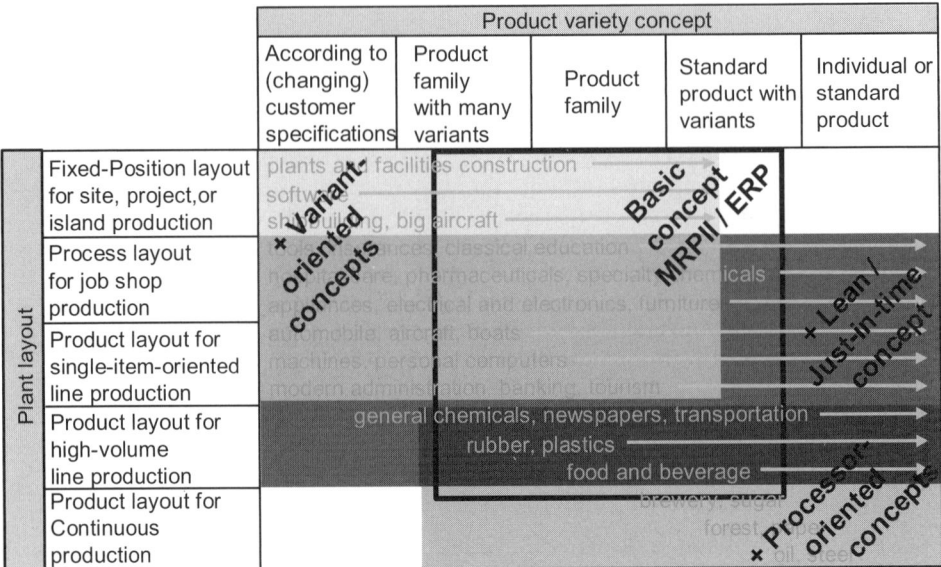

Fig. 3.5.3.1   Different concepts of planning & control in dependency upon the features *facility layout* and *product variety concept*.

A rough-cut comparison of Figure 3.5.3.1 with Figure 3.5.1.1 shows that the different concepts for planning & control within the company — in a *first approximation* — can be applied to the production types in the following way:

- The basic MRP II / ERP concepts are well suited to batch production for all facility layouts with the exception of continuous production.

- The lean / just-in-time concept applies to nearly all production types. It is a prerequisite for mass customization and for repetitive manufacturing. However, the kanban technique and other simple techniques for repetitive manufacturing that are often linked with lean/JIT, are applicable only to standard products or product families with few variants.

- Variant-oriented concepts apply to batch production and all facility layouts designed for single items or small batches. They are prerequisites for one-of-a-kind production and mass customization.

- The processor-oriented concepts apply to continuous or (discontinuous) high-volume line production, in particular to mass production.

3.5.4   Selecting an Appropriate Branch Model, Production Type, and Concept for Planning & Control

As the figures in the previous sections show, the branch of industry or service is indeed related to many of the characteristic features of planning & control. *Facility layout* and the *product variety concept* thus prove to be the most important features with regard to the pragmatic development of concepts for planning & control in logistics.

The positioning of the branches in those figures suggests that it would make sense to seek branch-dependent concepts in logistics and operations management with the aim to discover a branch-specific production type and concept for planning & control.

A *branch model* in logistics and operations management encompasses concepts appropriate to specific branches, including suitable types of business processes and business methods.

Do such branch models really exist? Let us take as an example the company ABB Turbo Systems (www.abb.com/turbocharging) near Zurich, Switzerland. ABB produces turbo-chargers for ship motors, each unit according to customer order. A turbo charger is *de facto* a machine with high value-added. ABB produces many production structure levels in-house. What we find is that the application of a unique production type or a unique concept for planning & control would lead to problems in many domains of the enterprise operations:

- The main business is the sale of customized machines with multiple variants. The appropriate production types are one-of-a-kind production and — from a systems capability viewpoint — single-item-oriented line production. Thus, variant-oriented concepts have to be applied for planning & control.

- Many components and semifinished goods are variant independent and can be produced for a large span of the value-adding chain independent of any customer order, that is, make-to-stock, with frequent order repetition. The appropriate production type is batch production, or — from a systems capability viewpoint — job shop production. The appropriate concept for planning & control can be a simple pull principle (reorder after consumption), which is listed in the figure above under the lean / just-in-time concepts.

- The service parts business, finally, is considered to be just as important as the main business, and this with reason. There, characteristic features are important, such as for example backtracking down the history of the machine configuration to the one used for the original production order. The availability of service parts stands in the foreground. The service parts are often just one production structure level above the components and semifinished goods for the main business. But, in contrast to those, the consumption of service parts is lumpy. Thus, the simple pull principle cannot be applied for planning & control. MRP, or the time-phased order point technique of the MRP II concept, based on appropriate forecasting techniques, can be used here. Again, job shop and small batch production is an appropriate production type.

This example clearly illustrates that it is not possible to simply identify a branch model with a specific production type and a specific concept of planning & control. Generally, several production types and concepts for planning & control have to be implemented in parallel in a given company.

Vice versa, a specific production type or concept of planning & control is generally valid in different branches. This is one of the reasons why researchers and professionals emphasize the standardization of these production types and concepts of planning & control rather than encourage branch models.

Of course, for a given branch it can be useful to adapt some of the terminology to the common usage in that branch, as well as to further develop the general planning & control techniques with a view to the specific needs and terminology of that branch.

Chapter 8 will present a similar discussion with regard to MRP II and ERP software. At present, there seems to be no simple software available that covers all kinds of production types or concepts for planning & control. Moreover, simple reorder for the components after consumption can be controlled by the kanban technique (see Section 5.2), which in the eyes of many professionals requires no software at all. As is the case for the underlying production types and concepts for planning & control, a specific MRP II / ERP software package — such as SAP R/3 — can generally be used by different branches. Again, branch packages are available — for example, for furniture production — where specific techniques are implemented in a "branch-customized" way, using branch-customary terminology and graphical user interfaces that represent familiar business objects in the branch.

3.5.5 Concepts of Transcorporate Planning & Control of the Supply Chain

Chapter 2 introduced concepts of transcorporate partnerships in a supply chain. On the global scene, the 1990s have seen further expansion of the existing concepts of planning & control into *transcorporate* planning & control. They have been termed *supply chain management (SCM) concepts*, or *advanced planning and scheduling (APS) concepts*. A new generation of software supporting the planning of logistics and production networks is on the market today (see Section 8.2.5), and implementation is in progress. We can expect to see further development of concepts of planning & control in the near future, improving supply and demand chain planning.

In 1996, the Supply Chain Council (SCC) was founded in the United States (see www.supply-chain.org). With the SCOR model (supply chain operations reference), this organization created an aid to standardization of transcorporate process chains. Its objective is to foster a common understanding of processes in the various companies participating in a logistics network. This transcorporate view is well represented by level 1 of the actual SCOR model, shown in Figure 3.5.5.1.

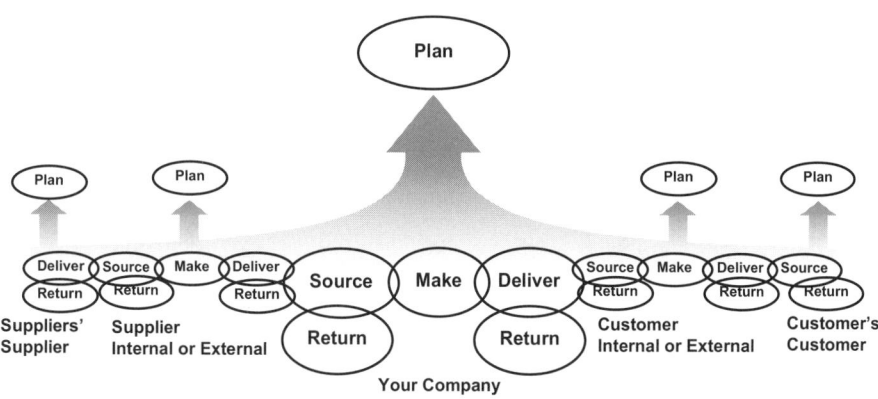

Fig. 3.5.5.1   The SCOR model, version 8.0, level 1.

Figure 3.5.5.2 shows the 6 process categories and 25 reference processes defined by level 2 of the actual SCOR model.

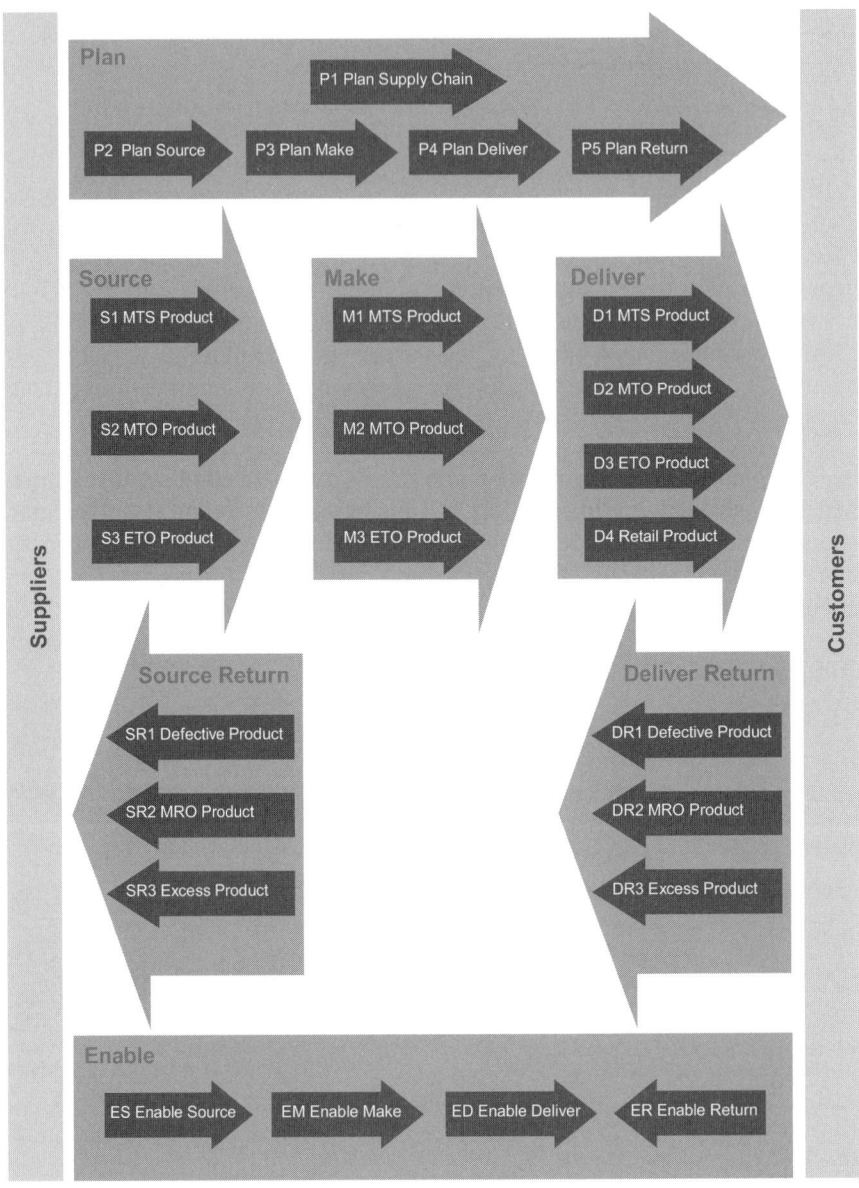

Fig. 3.5.5.2   The 6 process categories and 25 reference processes of SCOR version 8.0, Level 2, toolkit.

The process categories in the SCOR model are differentiated according to the *production environment* (refer to the definitions in Sections 3.4.3). According to Figure 3.4.5.2, there is a close correlation between the two features *production environment* and *product variety concept*. Therefore, the same characteristic feature that already in Figure 3.5.3.1 allowed the differentiation among the various concepts of planning & control now differentiates also process categories in Figure 3.5.5.2.

Figure 3.5.5.3 shows the task handled by the SCM concept of planning & control in supply chains:

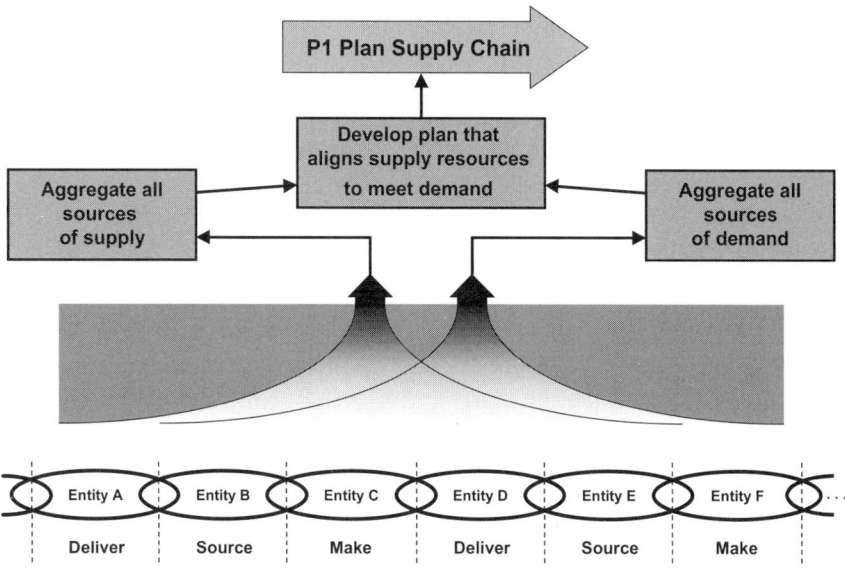

Fig. 3.5.5.3   Task handled by the SCM concept (based on the SCOR model).

The main task of the SCM concept is continuous synchronization of value-adding in the entire network and continuous reconciliation with user demand. This is based upon the internal chain of "source," "make," and "deliver" in each of the companies involved. All requirements and possibilities of fulfilling them are carried by the network as a whole and reconciled jointly. The planning & control methods actually required to do this coincide in the main, of course, with the methods used in company-internal planning & control.

3.6   Summary

The fundamental elements of process management are based on the terms *work*, *task*, *function*, and *process*. The event is a special process that determines the states of goods. Definitions of the terms *business process*, *business object*, and *business method* are derived.

A logistics system encompasses both a process and the order and process management connected with it. Together with business processes, logistics systems form the focus of the logistics perspective. Whether linked or integrated, business processes result in the characteristic pattern of the logistics of a company. Push logistics are distinguished from pull logistics. Temporal synchronization between manufacturer and user is realized by means of inventory control processes. In the network of customer orders, production orders and procurement orders, inventory and lead times are the classic design elements of logistics.

Instruments of logistics analysis make up business process analyses in differing degrees of detail. The organization-oriented process chart is an old method that corresponds closely to the way people naturally view the processes. Layouts of the production infrastructure are useful aids to visualizing restrictions and new possibilities. The detailed analysis of the process plan, the basic process analysis, finally, allows more precise mapping of the facts and thus helps to qualify the natural view of the processes held by the persons involved.

Logistics analysis works out a characteristic for the planning & control of each product or product family. For each company within a logistics network, a company-internal analysis must be carried out, and final comparisons will reveal areas for potential improvement.

Comparison of the findings within a company and in the transcorporate logistics network shows potential hindrances to effective logistics, both within the company and in the logistics network as a whole. By establishing the characteristic features in planning & control, we already gain indications for appropriate business methods. The characteristic features can also be seen as influences on logistics performance indicators. The chapter discusses six features referring to the user and the product or product family, seven features in reference to logistics and production resources, and seven features of the production or procurement order.

Using the three morphological schemes describing features of trans-corporate logistics in supply chains we can obtain an overview of the current state and the specific type of the supply chain and gain some insights into the appropriateness of transcorporate methods and concepts.

Fundamental concepts in logistics and operations management can be distinguished within a matrix of two dimensions: the product variety concept and the facility layout. A first example showed the branches in dependency upon these two characteristics, in a first approximation. The second example, as an extension to the production types already defined by the facility layout, positions additional production types — mass production, repetitive manufacturing, batch production, mass customization, and one-of-a-kind production — using the additional dimension of the product variety concept. The third example positioned four different concepts for planning & control within the matrix. Each comprises particular types of business processes and business methods for order planning and fulfillment: the basic MRP II / ERP concept, and — as extensions — the lean / just-in-time concept, variant-oriented concepts, and processor-oriented concepts.

3.7   Keywords

advanced planning and scheduling (APS) concept, 215
assemble-to-order, 186
assembly line, 190
basic process analysis, 174
batch production, 208
batch size, 195
batch size one, 195
blanket order, 194
branch model, 205
business process engineering, 168
consigned stocks, 186
continuous demand, 181
continuous production, 190
core competency, 156
core process, 156
customer production order, 192
dedicated line, 190

depth of product structure, 178
discontinuous demand, 181
discrete manufacturing, 179
divergent product structure, 179
engineer-to-order, 186
facility layout, 188
fixed-position layout, 188
flow manufacturing, 191
forecast order, 193
high-volume line production, 189
island production, 188
job shop production, 188
large batch production, 196
layout, 171
line production, 190

logistics system, 156
lot traceability, 196
lotless production, 196
make-to-order, 186
make-to-stock, 185
mass customization, 208
mass production, 208
one-of-a-kind production, 208
order, 154
order quantity, 195
process, 154
process layout, 188
process store, 159
product layout, 189
product life cycle, 196
product variety concept, 181
production environment, 185
production line, 190
project manufacturing, 188

3.8   Scenarios and Exercises

3.8.1   Concepts for Planning & Control within the Company

a. Figure 3.5.3.1 showed different concepts for planning & control in dependency upon the features *facility layout* and *product variety concept*. Using the Internet, try to find three different companies together with their products or product families, where (1) the lean / just-in-time concept, (2) variant-oriented concepts, and (3) processor-oriented concepts would be adequate for planning & control. As you browse the companies' web sites, try to base your reasoning on *facility layout* and *product variety concept*.

b. For the three companies that you found in (a), what branch of industry, as shown in Figure 3.5.1.1, is the company in? What production type(s), as shown in Figure 3.5.2.1, does the company implement for these products or product families? In reference to the discussion in Section 3.5.4, try to decide whether these companies implement in parallel several production types and concepts for planning & control.

Present your findings for group discussion.

3.8.2   Synchronization between Use and Manufacturing with Inventory Control Processes

Figure 3.2.3.1 discussed stocking with different inventory control processes for temporal synchronization between use and manufacturing. Using that kind of process chart, represent decoupling of procurement or production from demand for the two examples discussed with Figure 3.4.5.3, namely,

1. Manufacturing throughout the year to meet demand occurring mainly at a holiday time
2. Manufacturing in large batches where demand is continuous; delivery can be made from storage

3.8.3 Basic Process Analysis and Manufacturing Processes in the Company-Internal Layout

Figure 3.8.3.1 shows the company-internal layout at Pedal Works Company, a bicycle manufacturer.

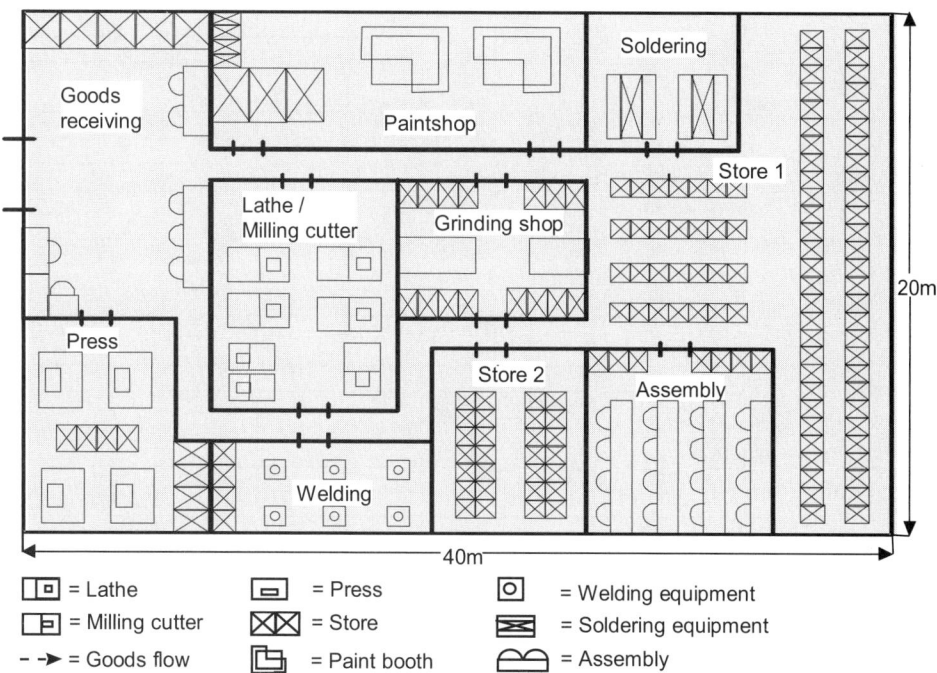

Fig. 3.8.3.1   Company-internal layout with an example process.

Based on the basic process analysis shown in Figure 3.8.3.2, pencil in the paths an aluminum bicycle frame will take through the layout.

Solution:

Compare your results to the result in Figure 3.3.2.1.

ProcessID	451		Batch size	20
Part name	Frame		Part ID:	ABC-123
Material:	AC-2			
Inspector:	Smith		Inspect. date	2000.06.15

Quan-tity	Dis-tance	Time	Sym-bol	Process (place)	Opera-tor	Ma-chine	Type of storage	Operating conditions, developments, etc.
60 fittings		5 days	▼	Store 1				
	40 m		⬇		Trans-porter			
		3 h	▼	Pressing			Pallet on ground	No 100% control; 20% parts defective
		20 s	●	Pressing	Opera-tor	Press		Tool change takes 40 minutes
		20 min	✱	Pressing			Pallet	
	25 m		⬇		Trans-porter			
		3 h	▼	Milling				
		20 min	●	Milling	Opera-tor	Milling cutter		
		20 min	✱	Milling				
	20 m		⬇		Trans-porter			
		16 h	▼	Store 2				
		2 min	●	Store 2				
		20 min	✱	Store 2				
20 fra mes	5 m		⬇		Trans-porter			
		20 s	●	Grinding	Opera-tor			
		20 min	✱	Grinding		Template		
	20 m		⬇		Trans-porter			
		2 h	▼	Welding				
		10 min	●	Welding	Welder	Weldin g tool		
		3.5 h	✱	Welding	Welder			
		2 min	■	Welding				Random sampling inspection of welding joints
	30 m		⬇		Trans-porter			
		3 min	●	Washing				
		1 min	■					Control if frames clean
		20 min	✱	Washing				
		3 h	▼	Paintshop	Painter			
		30 min	●	Paintshop	Painter	Oven		
		6 h	✱					
	30 m		⬇		Trans-porter			
		3 h	▼	Assembly				
		10 min	●	Assembly				

✱ = batch-size-dependent wait time ⬇ = transport
● = process ▼ = wait time ■ = control

Fig. 3.8.3.2   Basic process analysis of an aluminum frame.

4 The MRP II / ERP Concept: Business Processes and Methods

Sections 3.4 and 3.5 introduced characteristic features and different concepts of planning & control for logistics systems. This chapter takes a closer look at the first fundamental concept of planning & control, the MRP II / ERP concept.

> The *enterprise resources planning (ERP) concept* is comprised of a set of processes, methods, and techniques for effective planning and control of *all* resources needed to take, make, ship, and account for customer orders in a manufacturing, distribution, or service company ([APIC04]).

The APICS Dictionary ([APIC04]) also provides a definition of the term *ERP system*, emphasizing the system capability of the ERP concept as an accounting-oriented information system assisted by *ERP software.* Beyond the MRP II concept and other concepts of planning & control for logistics systems, the ERP concept deals in particular with financial management, controlling, and human resource management. In this book, however, these themes are only considered marginally.

Section 4.1 presents definitions of the different tasks within these processes and then derives a reference model for business processes and tasks in planning & control. The chapters in Part B of the book follow the structure of this model.

Section 4.2 shows business objects and business methods in the business process of long-term planning. Long-term planning is a fundamental requirement of long-term business relations in the logistics network. In most cases, long-term planning takes the form of rough-cut planning.

Section 4.3 presents an overview of business methods for medium and short-term planning & control in the areas of distribution, production, and sales. These business methods will be examined in more depth in later chapters.

Section 4.4 treats business methods for planning & control in research and development. An interesting task is the linking of the information systems supporting these areas.

Challenges to logistics have brought about certain tendencies that are understandable in a historical context. Many logistics phenomena are also simply too complex to be represented in complete form in a formal model. Models can thus never eliminate the need for well-qualified personnel. Rather, the purpose of using model concepts is to encourage people in the enterprise to think and act methodologically in order to expand and improve their effectiveness.

4.1   Business Processes and Tasks in Planning & Control

4.1.1   The MRP II Concept and Its Planning Hierarchy

The *MRP II concept (manufacturing resource planning)*[1] encompasses a set of processes, methods, and techniques for effective planning of all resources of a manufacturing company ([APIC04]).

The APICS Dictionary definition in [APIC04] goes on to explain that MRP II "is made up of a variety of functions, each linked together: business planning, production planning (sales and operations planning), master production scheduling, material requirements planning, capacity requirements planning, and the execution support systems for capacity and material. Output from these systems is integrated with financial reports such as the business plan, purchase commitment report, shipping budget, and inventory projections in dollars."

A fundamental idea underlying the MRP II concept is that development and production must be planned in part long before there is customer demand or demand from higher structure levels, as we emphasized in Sections 1.1.2 and 3.4.3. Figure 4.1.1.1 proposes a *planning hierarchy*, namely *three-level planning according to temporal range*, a typical feature of the MRP II concept.

Long-term planning takes place several months to a year prior to realization. The aim is to forecast the total demand for products and processes that will be placed on the enterprise or on the logistics network from the outside. The company can then derive quantities and gain the

---

[1]   Important note: The MRP II concept should not be confused with the MRP method of material requirements planning. See Section 4.3.1 and Chapter 10.

resources – persons, production infrastructure, or deliveries from third parties – necessary to fulfill demand.

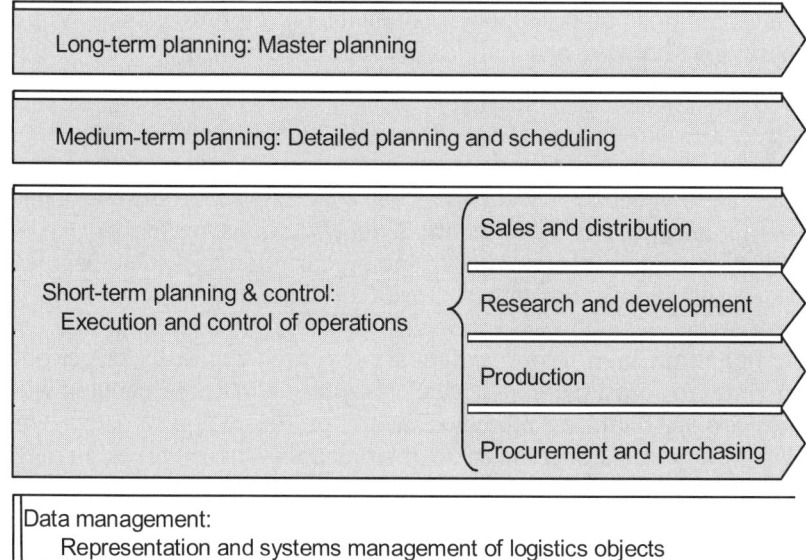

Fig. 4.1.1.1   Business processes in logistics and operations management of an enterprise, structured according to temporal range, with data management.

- *Master planning* is another term used for long-term planning. Both terms emphasize that this type of planning sets the cornerstones for logistics. These cornerstones determine the marginal conditions and limitations of shorter-term planning.

Medium-term planning concerns the months or weeks to come. Its purpose is to forecast demand more precisely along the time axis. Demand for resources must correspond to the resources probably available at certain times. As a consequence, sourcing agreements that were reached during long-term planning might have to be precision-tuned or modified.

- *Detailed planning and scheduling* is another name for medium-term planning. It reflects the fact that medium-term planning considers information on a more detailed level. In addition, it often involves only areas of production — assembly or parts production, in industry, for example — and areas of procurement. But detailed planning and scheduling may also involve the areas of design and manufacturing process development — particularly for customer order production.

Short-term planning and control concerns the actual servicing of orders. It represents the short-term temporal horizon — the days or weeks during which physical logistics take place. Data and control flows in the producing enterprise at this point accompany the flow of goods. Within this short time horizon also fall capital-intensive investiture in bought goods and value added from the consumer's perspective.

- *Execution and control of operations* is another name for short-term planning & control. During the execution phase, the controlled system does yield feedback to the persons controlling the system. Thus, control takes the form of coordination, which is performed by all persons involved. With a view to the organization as a sociotechnical system, however, more apt terms are "coordination" or "regulation."

Long-term and medium-term planning are reviewed cyclically or periodically, in order to adjust planning to the changing estimates of demand with regard to product families, products, quantities, and delivery dates. This does not say anything about the issue of structural organization or, in other words, nothing about who will execute this planning. It is important to ensure, however, that planning can be executed in a way that is appropriate for each department. This is particularly true of short-term planning, for short-term planning must take account of the actual flow of goods (e.g. in distribution, R&D, production (shop-floor), or purchasing). A natural solution for the three temporal ranges of planning is to distribute the associated tasks among different persons. This ensures that the various perspectives are taken into account in the planning and that all aspects that can contribute to quality and feasibility of the planning are considered.

The different temporal ranges in planning are not equally important in all logistics networks. Although the tasks are basically the same, they vary in content, and thus business processes will also vary.

Strictly speaking, the concept of degree of detail in planning is not the same as the temporal ranges in planning.

Rough-cut planning refers to rough-cut business objects. *Detailed objects planning* refers to detailed business objects.

Rough-cut planning of goods aids rapid determination of the procurement situation for critical item families. Rough-cut planning is indispensable where there are numerous orders to plan. It allows quick calculation of different variants in long-term planning.

In general, the degree of planning increases with decreasing temporal range. Rough-cut planning is usually conducted in long-term planning, while planning in the short term refers to detailed objects. This is not always the case, however. At least some short-term planning can be conducted in a rough-cut manner. In sales, for example, checking the load on rough-cut work centers and the availability of item families of raw materials allows quick decisions on whether to accept customer order production. Conversely, long-term planning in process industry must often refer to detailed objects.[2]

Rough-cut and detailed business objects are also objects of data management. See Section 1.2, in particular Section 1.2.5, and Chapter 16.

Data management ensures that the necessary data on objects is available at all times in a detailed and up-to-date form.

Data management addresses basic problems that arise particularly in computer-aided planning & control: How can the business objects in the logistics of an enterprise be represented in the information system in such a way that they reflect reality? This task can prove difficult. See also [Schö01].

4.1.2   Part Processes and Tasks in Long-Term and Medium-Term Planning

Figure 4.1.2.1 shows the sequence and tasks in *long-term planning* in MEDILS form (for an explanation of MEDILS symbols, see Section 3.1.3).

Definitions of the tasks in Figure 4.1.2.1 follow here. For the methods and techniques used for long-term or master planning, see Section 4.2.

Bid processing handles a customer *request for quotations* and determines delivery (labor or product or product family, quantity, and due date). (For details see Section 4.2.1.)

A *customer blanket order* determines the delivery quantity. It can then be described by rough-cut business objects, or through product families or rough-cut work centers. In that case, the order due date is defined only as a time period. (For details see Section 4.2.1.)

---

[2]   The term *fine planning* has been avoided. In practice, this term has been applied to both short-term and detailed planning and has led to confusion and misunderstandings.

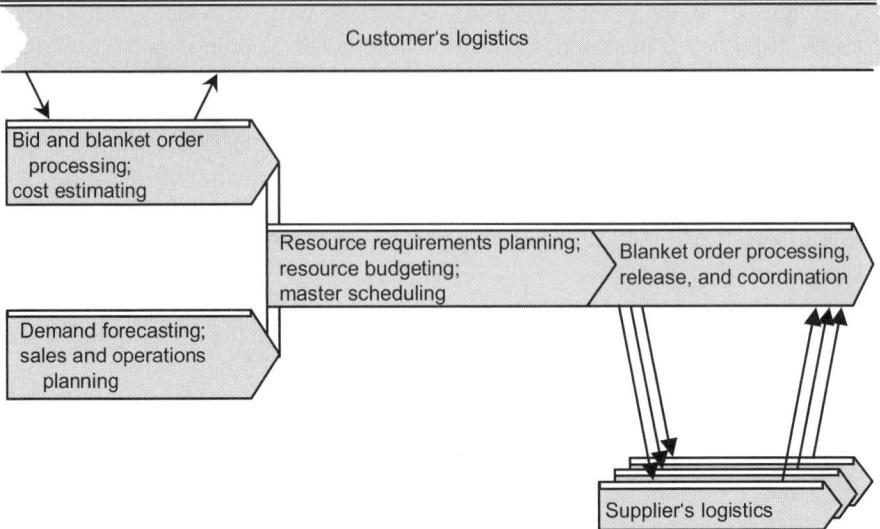

Fig. 4.1.2.1   Long-term planning: master planning.

Demand forecasting was defined in Section 1.1.1. It estimates future demand. A synonymous term is *demand prognosis*. (For details see Section 4.2.1 and Chapter 9.)

Sales and operations planning brings together all the plans for the business (marketing, development, sales, manufacturing / production, sourcing, and financial) in one integrated set of plans. It is performed at least once per month and is reviewed by management at an *aggregate* (product family) level ([APIC04]). (For details see Section 4.2.2.)

Resource requirements planning (RRP) or *resource planning* calculates the components requirements and the capacity requirements (persons and infrastructure),

- Based on the production plan (one of the outputs of sales and operations planning), generally — but not necessarily — divided up along the time axis, and

- Through analytical explosion of (generally — but not necessarily — rough-cut) product structures (also called *explosion of bill of materials*) and routing sheets.

RRP is *gross requirements planning*; inventory and open orders are *not* taken into consideration. (For details see Section 4.2.2.)

The output of RRP includes in particular a *procurement plan for components and materials*.

Resource budgeting calculates the procurement or materials budget, the capacity budget (direct costs and overheads), and the budget for other overheads. (For details see Section 4.2.2.)

Thus, master planning yields the quantities of the resources to be used in the long-term planning horizon and calculates financial implications.

The *planning horizon* is the future time period included in planning.

The planning horizon for master scheduling must be at least as long as the cumulative lead time to manufacture all units in the master schedule. This lead time encompasses production, procurement of all components, and customer-specific design.

Master scheduling is establishing a plan to produce *specific* products or provide *specific* services within a *specific* time period.

See Section 4.2.3. The most important output of master scheduling is the disaggregated version of a production plan, expressed in specific products, configurations, quantities, and dates. It serves as input for rough-cut capacity planning (RCCP) as well as for calculating the available-to-promise (ATP) quantity (for details see Section 4.2.4).

Blanket order processing, release, and coordination turn over the procurement plan for saleable products, components, and materials as well as the requirements for external capacities to suppliers in the logistics network. This task includes selection of suppliers, call for bids, blanket order release, and continued checks and precision tuning.

For details see Section 4.2.5. In data management, each blanket order is a business object, an *order* (see Section 1.2.1). If the minimum blanket order quantity on the blanket order is zero, the blanket order is a prediction only.

Figure 4.1.2.2 shows the process and tasks of *medium-term planning* in MEDILS form. The individual part processes and tasks in medium-term planning are similar to those in long-term planning. Precision-tuning accomplishes more exact determination of bids (particularly blanket orders) as well as the schedules (particularly the *production schedule* and the *purchase schedule*, that is the plan that authorizes the factory to manufacture — or the purchasing department to purchase — certain quantities of specific items within a specific time (compare [APIC04])).

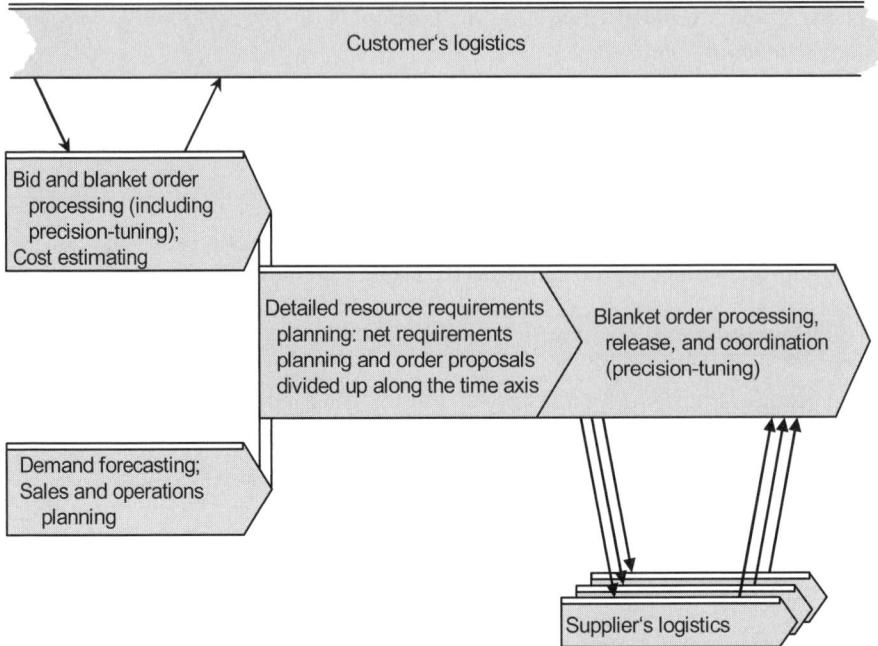

Fig. 4.1.2.2   Medium-term planning & control: detailed planning and scheduling.

Detailed resource requirements planning calculates detailed material and components requirements and detailed capacity requirements (persons and infrastructure), divided up along the time axis, and works out *order proposals* for R&D, production, and procurement for covering these requirements,

- Usually based on the master production schedule (the disaggregated version of a production plan), divided up along the time axis, and

- Through analytical explosion of detailed product structures (also called *explosion of bill of materials*) and routing sheets, or — using another term — of the process plan (see Figure 1.2.3.3).

This is *net requirements planning*; inventory and open orders *are* taken into consideration.

An *order proposal*, or *planned order*, sets the goods to be produced or procured, the order quantity, the latest (acceptable) completion date, and — often an implicit given — the earliest (acceptable) start date.

On the basis of the order proposals, blanket order planning can be defined more precisely.

4.1.3   Part Processes and Tasks in Short-Term Planning & Control

Figure 4.1.3.1 shows, in MEDILS form, part processes and tasks in *short-term planning and control*, or *execution and control of operations*.

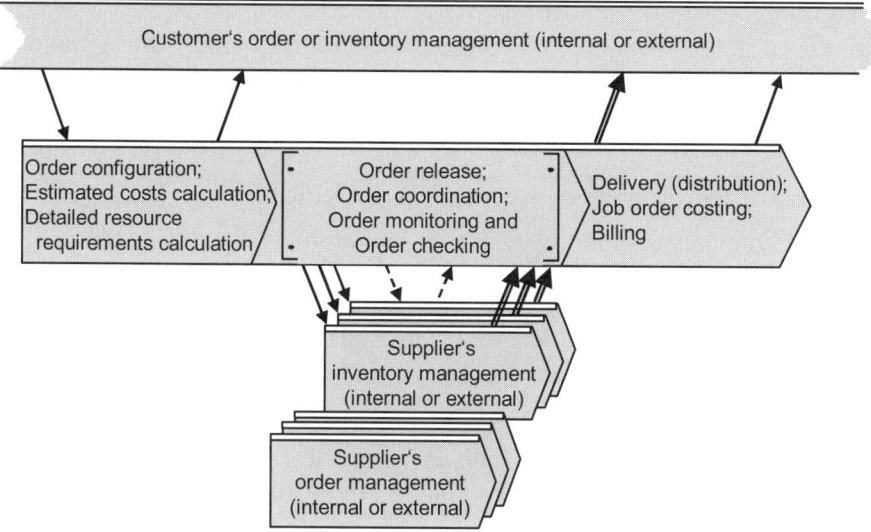

Fig. 4.1.3.1   Short-term planning & control: execution and control of operations.

The first two part processes have a certain similarity to the three part processes in long- and medium-term planning. The second part process can be repeated. For a production order, for example, first all components will be procured. Then all operations can be executed. Orders can be released either separately for each part process or all together. Order coordination can also be repeated (broken arrows in Figure 4.1.3.1). Execution and control of operations for a production structure level result in push logistics and should therefore be performed by only one person per order.

The figure shows only one production structure level in the logistics network. The order originates from a sales, production, or procurement department of an internal or external customer. The production structure level itself places orders to suppliers — either components warehouses or lower production structure levels — thus initiating production at that level. The linking of several production structure levels results in pull logistics, such as the pull logistics shown in Figure 3.2.3.2.

Order configuration handles an order proposal from medium-term planning or an order from an external or internal customer. It determines delivery (work, or product, quantity, and due date).

Order configuration compares the order to any existing bid or blanket order.

In the case of research and development orders, order configuration consists in *planning the volume of the release*. This is part of engineering change control (ECC). See Section 4.4.

Detailed resource requirements calculation calculates:

a. For an unplanned order (usually a customer order), the detailed material and components requirements and the detailed capacity requirements (persons and infrastructure), divided up along the time axis, required for the development and manufacture of an unplanned order, and works out *order proposals* for covering requirements,

• Based on the unplanned order

• Through analytical explosion of detailed product structures and routing sheets, or — using another term — of the process plan (see Figure 1.2.3.3).

b. For a planned order (an order proposal), the availability of resources, by double-checking that materials and components requirements and the requirements for internal or external capacities are covered.

If resources are not available at the required times, lead time must be increased:

• Sales orders require a check on the availability of stock (see the discussion on order promising in Section 4.2.4). In some cases, however, further capacities may be required, such as for on-site assembly.

• With production orders, the executing organizational unit may treat the individual operations as "small" production orders. *Dispatching* and *sequencing* then assign the individual operations to work places, workers, and machines in the most appropriate way (see Section 14.2.3).

• For some procurement orders, bids must be solicited, suppliers chosen, or existing blanket orders identified.

Resource requirements calculation is usually seen as a part task in order releasing.

Order release is the decision of the supplier to execute order proposals or orders originating from higher-level logistics. It produces all administrative documents required for order confirmation, order execution (for example, in production), or for communication with suppliers. Necessary transportation means will also be secured.

A *released order* is a production or procurement order with ongoing production or procurement (in contrast to a planned order).

Order coordination coordinates the order and all other connected orders in an integrated manner. For example, a customer order may require a development order and several levels of production and procurement orders. These make up further short-term processes of the type shown in Figure 4.1.3.1, arranged in a multilevel cascade. Figure 1.4.1.2 shows a simple example. Normally there are several levels and, at each level, several parallel part processes to coordinate.

Order monitoring and *order checking*: *Progress checking* monitors execution of all work according to plan in terms of quantity and delivery reliability. (If deviations from the plan are too great, this may lead to recalculation of the rest of the process plan.) *Quality control* means checking the quality of all incoming goods from production and procurement. Quality control has become an extensive process that is based upon specific quality control sheets.

In data management, all types of orders each are business objects, of the *order* class (see Section 1.2.1).

For *delivery*, or *(physical) distribution*, the products are issued from stock (*order picking*) and prepared for shipment; the required transportation means and accompanying documents are made available; and delivery is executed.

Job-order costing evaluates data captured by shop floor data collection (that is, mainly resource use).

Billing transmits the results of cost accounting to the customer (for example in the form of an invoice) and, where required, adjusts data management's projected values for the business objects.

4.1.4   Reference Model of Processes and Tasks in Planning & Control

Figure 4.1.4.1 summarizes the concepts presented in the previous sections, showing the relation between the planning processes and their planning priorities within the temporal ranges. This type of representation is common in teaching materials explaining the MRP II/ERP concept.

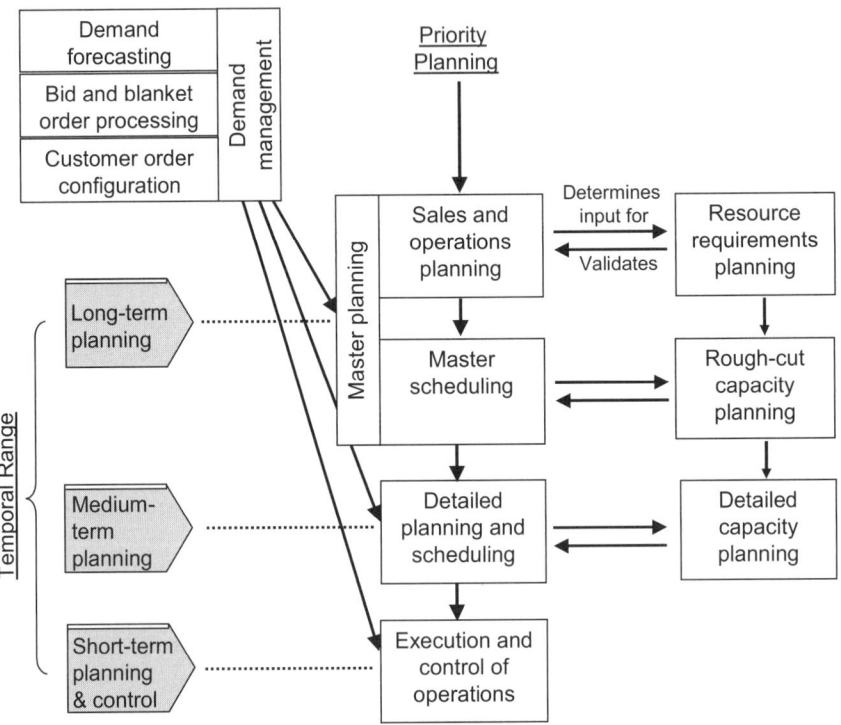

Fig. 4.1.4.1   Manufacturing planning & control processes within the temporal ranges in the MRP II concept.

Figure 4.1.4.2 summarizes the sections above and presents an overview of the planning processes according to — vertically — temporal range (long, medium, and short term) and — horizontally — all the planning & control tasks.

The processes and tasks are shown in the logical temporal sequence that derives from Figures 4.1.2.1, 4.1.2.2, and 4.1.3.1.

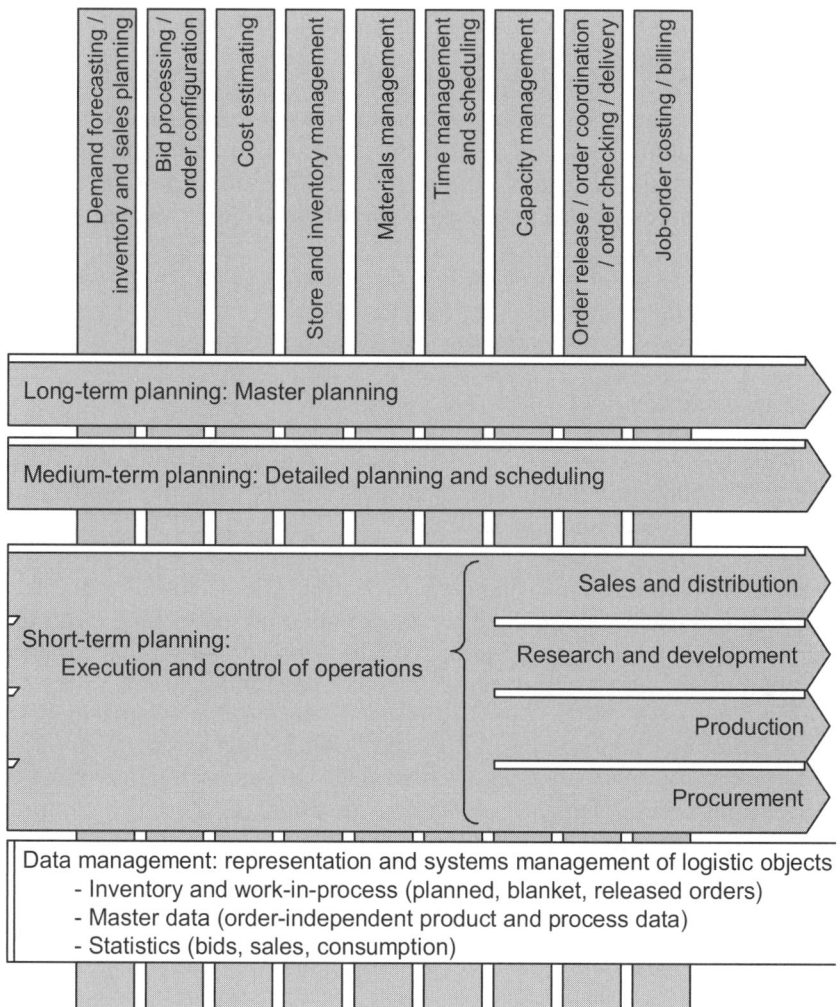

Fig. 4.1.4.2   Reference model of business processes and tasks in planning & control.

This reference model is an extension of the classical MRP II/ERP concept. Representing the processes in this condensed form allows us to conceive of planning & control tasks as *cross-sectional tasks*. Although there are some deviations, in principle cross-sectional tasks, appearing in all time ranges and in all kinds of orders, have the same forms. However, a particular task may not arise in every time frame or in every business process. Also, during execution of a particular task, not every logistics object is required in data management.[3]

Demand forecast, stock planning and sales planning, bid processing and order configuration, and cost estimating accord with the definitions in Sections 4.1.2 and. 4.1.3. Furthermore, the model breaks down resource planning into three classical planning & control tasks.

---

1. *Materials management* ensures that the goods required by demand are provided cost effectively and according to schedule (such as end products, semifinished goods, single parts, raw materials, and information).[4]

2. *Time management and scheduling*, as well as

3. *Capacity management*, ensure cost effective and timely provision of the capacities needed to cover the load on persons and the production infrastructure as determined by orders.

The distinction among these planning & control tasks is based on the fact that goods can usually be stocked for an extended period of time (with the exception of continuous production; see Chapter 7), whereas this is generally not the case for time and capacity (see the end of Section 4.3.3). As a natural consequence, the business methods for these resources differ.

The term *management* keynotes the fact that our perspective has broadened from pure requirements or costs considerations to the more comprehensive task of improving company performance (see Section 1.2.2).

Goods management would actually be a more appropriate term than materials management, for this task also handles finished products.[5] But as *materials management* is the term commonly used, we retain it here.

Order release, order coordination, order checking, and delivery correspond to the definitions in Section 4.1.3.

---

[3] At the same time, the reference model characterizes the elements of a planning & control system as well as various options for forming part systems — either along the business processes or along equal tasks.

[4] Some authors, for example [ArCh03], use the term *materials management* in a larger sense, equivalent to the overall concept of logistics or operations management. However, in this book, the term is used in the restricted sense, related only to goods and materials.

[5] In accounting, the term *materials* relates to purchased materials and production materials rather than to semifinished and end products. See also the distinction between the terms materials and components in Section 1.1.1.

Stores management is comprised of the tasks involved in storing goods as well as in handling inventory transactions, such as delivering stocked goods to user sites or receiving goods from suppliers.

Inventory includes all physical items in any form that can be found in the company. Inventory appears as:

- *Stored inventory*, that is inventory of actually stored items, for example items used to support production (raw materials); customer service (end products or service parts); and supporting activities (MRO items).

- *In-process inventory* or *work-in-process (WIP)*, meaning goods in various stages of completion throughout the plant.

Inventory management is the branch of business management concerned with planning and controlling inventories ([APIC04]). It includes all tasks involved in the inventory control process within the logistics network.[6]

Inventory control includes the activities and techniques of maintaining the desired levels of items, such as those shown in Figure 3.2.3.2.

Figure 4.1.4.2 does not show explicitly the process of store and inventory management itself; instead, it defines the *task* in these processes, or *store and inventory management*. In data management, all inventories of stored items or work-in-process items each build a business object. Depending on the degree of detail of inventory management, the business object type assigned may be *item* (see Section 1.2.2) or *order* (see Section 1.2.1).

Figure 4.1.4.2 also introduces two further categories of objects in data management.

The collective term *master data* is comprised of all order-independent business objects, as described in Section 1.2.

The term *statistics* refers to appropriately combined data on consumption, as well as data on bid and sales activity.

---

[6] Some authors, for example, [Bern99], use the term *inventory management* in a larger sense, equivalent to the overall concept of logistics or operations manage-ment. However, in this book, the term is used in the restricted sense, related only to goods and materials.

The values of performance indicators in Section 3.2 can be derived from certain statistical data. For details, see Chapter 10. For an in-depth description of master data, see Chapter 16.

As we examine business processes and methods in more detail in the following, we will refer again and again to the reference model on planning & control shown in Figure 4.1.4.2. Moreover, the reference model serves as the starting point for a detailed look at the individual planning & control tasks in Chapters 9 through 16.

4.1.5   Beyond MRP II: DRP II, Integrated Resource Management, and the "Theory of Constraints"

Distribution planning is an important component of the ERP concept that goes beyond MRP II.

Distribution planning covers the planning activities associated with site and location planning, transportation, warehousing, inventory levels, materials handling, order administration, industrial packaging, data processing, and communications networks to support distribution [APIC04].

Distribution planning determines the distribution network (see Section 2.4.4). This structure is often multilevel. For example, production or procurement supplies a central warehouse. From there, inventory is shipped to regional distribution centers, which supply wholesalers. Wholesalers supply retailers, and, finally, retailers supply the customers. Inventory management in this chain can be handled in principle in the same way that it is for the chain from raw material to final product, via the various distribution structure levels.

A central task of distribution planning is resource management in the distribution system, in particular inventory management.

Distribution inventory is inventory, usually spare parts and finished goods, located in the distribution system (e.g., in warehouses and in-transit between warehouses and the consumer [APIC04]). The terms *pipeline inventory* or *pipeline stock* are used simultaneously.[7]

---

[7]   In contrast to these terms, *in-transit inventory*, or *transportation inventory*, is limited to inventory that is moving between locations.

> *Distribution resource planning (DRP II)* is distribution planning of the key resources contained in a distribution system: warehouse space, workforce, money, trucks, freight cars, etc. ([APIC04]).

The term *DRP II* developed as an extension of *DRP* (*distribution requirements planning*; see Chapter 11.2.1), which stands for a deterministic method of *management of distribution inventory*. The term *DRP II* was coined in analogy to the term *MRP II*, an extension of MRP.

The techniques of management of distribution inventory do *not* differ essentially from inventory management in production and procurement. For this reason, they will not be treated in a separate section. However, distribution control is examined in Section 14.4. There you will find a description of important distribution planning tasks and results, such as transport planning and scheduling.

> *Resource management* is, according to [APIC04], the effective identification, planning, scheduling, execution, and control of *all* organizational resources to produce a good or service.

Today, the ordered sequence of the three classical tasks as shown in Figure 4.1.4.2 — materials management, time management and scheduling, and capacity management — is used mainly for teaching purposes only. Originally, this sequence came about because materials management takes temporal priority in the planning process with non-time-critical production or procurement. In the classical MRP II concept, the tasks are differentiated so sharply that in materials management, there is no routing sheet. For materials management, there exists only the attribute "lead time," which is assigned to all goods. This perspective also made concessions to the very limited processing capacity of computers of the day, when the materials management planning process of large firms (the so-called "MRP run") often took an entire weekend. It took that much time again to then complete the planning process for scheduling and capacity management (the so-called "CRP run"). This meant that it had to be possible to perform this process separately from materials management.

With short procurement times, however, all tasks must be performed in parallel fashion, in dependency upon each other, with a comprehensive perspective: as *integrated resource management*. Two examples illustrate why:

- For components to be available on time for assembly, we need to have a basic assumption about the lead time to produce an in-house manufactured component. For materials management in the framework of the classical MRP II concept, this assumption is one (single) number. Starting from the completion date of the assembly to be manufactured, all components are planned according to the lead-time offset. But this technique is not always precise. There certainly are cases where components are not required at the start of production of an assembly, but instead are needed during the course of the lead time, at the start of an operation. Thus, the date at which a component must be available must be derived ultimately from time management and scheduling.

- Storage of components at lower levels (semifinished goods) has the advantage that several structure levels can be planned independently of one another in scheduling and capacity management. However, this is appropriate only under certain conditions. Pending and delayed orders for replenishing stock can be compounded by components requirements for subsequent, higher level orders. It will then be necessary to find these requirements in materials management and to manage and shift higher level orders in scheduling and capacity management. In this way, a whole chain of shifts and changes in providing arrangements can be set off in materials management.

It is therefore not surprising that all the more recent concepts, including the lean / just-in-time concept, variant-oriented and concepts, and processor-oriented concepts, as well as supply chain management (SCM) or the advanced planning and scheduling (APS) concept, handle resource management in an integrated manner. Moreover, the earlier limitations on computer capacity no longer exist, so that the new, integrated approach is also possible in a MRP II framework.

There is also another impetus for the integrated resource management approach, namely, the more in-depth consideration of throughput and bottlenecks and — finally and more comprehensively — the theory of constraints:

> *Throughput* is the total volume of production passing through a facility ([APIC04]).

> A *bottleneck*, or a *bottleneck capacity*, is a work center where the required capacity is greater than the available capacity. Compare [APIC04].

As potential factors, capacities cannot — in general — be stocked, but rather are available for a certain period of time. If capacity is not used, it is basically lost. See the discussion toward the end of Section 4.3.2.

Well-utilized capacity is not only cost-advantageous; it also represents a bottleneck. Whenever capacity is not available to work, it directly reduces the throughput of the company and thus its output, its performance. Therefore, effective *bottleneck management* (and also the TOC approach) proposes:

- Utilization of the bottlenecked work center during breaks and with the greatest possible overtime. In addition, buffer stores, both downstream and upstream of the work center, should buffer the bottlenecked work center. On the one hand, this allows maximum utilization, because the bottlenecked work center does not have to wait for delayed delivery of materials. On the other hand, if downtime occurs in the bottlenecked work center, this will not directly affect the fill rate. In addition, through some increased administrative effort, various customer orders for the same item can be produced together at the bottleneck, which increases batch size, so that machine setup time and thus load are reduced.

- That production take place at non-bottlenecked work centers only when there are actual customer orders. Work centers should not make to stock. This keeps work in process as low as possible. The reason for this is that too early order releases do not improve capacity utilization; as a result, the work center simply does not work at a later time. In addition, goods will pile up that are not immediately required, implying carrying cost.

> The *theory of constraints (TOC)* is an approach to integrated resource management that addresses the problem of bottlenecks in a logistics system, or — more generally — the factors that limit or constrain the throughput in the system.

The TOC was developed in the 1980s and early 1990s in North America by E. M. Goldratt ([GoCo04]). The basic premise of a theory views the planning problem in logistics and operations management as a problem-solving area limited by constraints.

> A *constraint* is any element or factor that prevents a system from achieving a higher level of performance with respect to its objective ([APIC04]).

Constraints can take the form of limited capacity, a customer requirement such as quantity or due date, or the availability of a material, for example. They can also be managerial.

The concept of a problem-solving area limited by constraints originated in operations research, which also supplies algorithms for solutions. However, the difficulty often does not lie in the algorithms, but rather in the constrained problem area itself, which may not allow for reasonable solutions. This is the point where the TOC attempts to expand the problem-solving area, successively and in targeted fashion, according to the steps shown in Figure 4.1.5.1. This method represents continuous process improvement (CPI) of the flow of goods.

1. Identify the most serious constraint — that is, the constraint that is unduly constraining the problem-solving area. This can be a bottleneck, for example.
2. Exploit the constraint: For example, a bottleneck capacity should be utilized during breaks by rotating crews so that the capacity is never idle.
3. Subordinate everything to the constraint: For example, good utilization of other than bottleneck capacities is secondary.
4. Elevate the constraint: Make capacity available, for example.
5. Return to step one — that is, to the next iteration.

Fig. 4.1.5.1   Iterative procedure in the theory of constraints (TOC) approach.

In principle, this iterative procedure allows the logistics system to assign the correct resources in the current order situation. The resources may be — according to the integrated resource management approach — materials, capacity, or time. Special attention is given to capacity, which in this approach is handled according to capacity utilization priorities. The production control techniques include *drum–buffer–rope*[8] and an older technique called *OPT* (optimized production technology). See Section 13.3.3.

---

[8]   Drum–buffer–rope represents a synchronized production control approach. *Synchronized production* is a manufacturing management philosophy that includes a coherent set of principles and techniques supporting the global objective of the system (compare [APIC04]).

4.2   Master Planning — Long-Term Planning

This section jumps ahead to highlight the long-term business process in planning & control or, in other words, long-term planning or master planning. There are two reasons for this:

- Part A of this book also treats aspects of logistics management that are closely related to general management. Long-term planning, due to its temporal range, belongs here.

- Presenting the long-term business process here makes it possible to explain how the planning & control tasks in Figure 4.1.4.2 act together without having to resort to an overly complex method of presenting the material.

This section contains detailed information on the different tasks presented in Figure 4.1.2.1 — that is, the long-term planning or master planning process. The reader may wish to review the task definitions that appear below that figure.

4.2.1   Demand Management: Bid and Customer Blanket Order Processing and Demand Forecasting

Demand management is, according to [APIC04], the function of recognizing all demands for goods and services to support the marketplace.

According to Figure 4.1.4.1, this task is comprised of — among others — the following part task and processes of long, middle, and short-term planning (see Section 4.1):

- Bid and blanket order processing
- Demand forecasting
- Order entry and order configuration

A *customer order* is a deterministic independent demand. Quantity, due date, and other facts arc completely known.

One important factor when scheduling customer demand is the organization's distribution network structure. See Section 11.2.1.

What precedes the status of order confirmation of a customer order are — in the case of investment goods — various bid statuses.

A *customer bid* is a *quotation*, a statement of price, terms of sale, and description of goods or services given to a customer in response to a customer request for quotations.

The bid statuses are of differing duration, during which requirements are defined more and more precisely. In this case, the requirements are not absolutely definitive, but they will guide the planning of production and procurement. For customer order production (often single-item production), there is a certain probability that a bid will lead to an order as it is already defined at this point. The simplest technique of including bids in planning is to multiply the requirements by the probability of their success.

Order success probability devalues the demand defined by the customer bid. Only demand reduced in this way will be planned as independent demand for resource requirements planning.

This technique is similar to the stochastic technique of trend extrapolation (see Section 9.4.1). Continuous adaptation of order success probability to real conditions with decreasing temporal range of planning is crucial to this simple technique. In addition, bids must be confirmed, or removed, early enough that definitive orders can be scheduled even if bottlenecks occur in procurement. For this, an *expiration date* must be assigned to the order, from which time onward the confirmed delivery date may be postponed or the order termed inactive. This function can be automated in a computer-aided system.

If bottlenecks occur in procurement or production, it is difficult to set a reliable delivery date for a bid that is to be planned. If many other bids have been planned, a completion date that has been calculated by placing the new bid in this limited resource situation is only a probable completion date. This date needs to be complemented by a latest (maximum) completion date, calculated on the assumption that all bids, or at least the majority of them, will be realized. To do this, the portion of demand not reserved for each bid on the basis of order success probability is totaled up and used in the resource requirements management of capacity. The lead time for required but not available components yields the "maximum" completion date for the new bid. While this method, described here only in its rudiments, involves a great deal of complex calculating in detailed planning, it is often an appropriate technique for rough-cut planning with acceptable levels of calculation.

A customer bid often concerns and results in a *customer blanket order*. Here, the delivery quantity is often set by a long-term minimum and maximum blanket order quantity for a particular period of time.

If the minimum blanket order quantity is zero, it is merely a forecast.

- *Uncertain quantities* in a blanket order can be handled in a way similar to bids, that is, through continuous precision-tuning of their success probability with decreasing temporal range. In short-term planning, a certain quantity is ordered through a short-range blanket order for a defined period of time, but exactly when and in what breakdown the blanket releases will be made is left open.

- For *uncertain dates*, some additional information is usually available. This information will express, for example, the quantities that will be called for in the future, together with an estimate of the deviation factor in percent. These values allow partial demand to be distributed along the time axis. Here again it is important to continue to adapt the breakdown of the demand to reality or at least to the customer's increasingly precise requests. For more on blanket orders, see Section 4.2.5

Demand forecasting is, according to Section 1.1.2, the process that estimates the future demand.

Demand forecasting is a necessary process as soon as items upstream from the (customer) order penetration point (OPP) must be procured or produced (see Section 3.4.3).

The need for forecasting varies throughout the course of time and depending on the industry, market, and product. Examples of buyers' markets with a great need for forecasting include trade in consumer goods or the provision of components needed for a service or for investment goods. Before a customer places a definitive order, for example, single parts of a machine or "frameworks" containing data descriptions and programs for a software product must have already been produced or procured.

There are simple techniques of forecasting, including those based on judgment and intuition, but there are also some very complicated techniques. A whole set of techniques is presented in Chapter 9.

Finally, a further part of demand management is order service.

(Customer) order service, according to [APIC04], encompasses order receiving, entry,[9] configuration, and confirmation of orders from customers, distribution centers, and interplant operations.[10]

Order service is responsible for responding to customer inquiries during delivery lead time as well as for interacting with master scheduling regarding the availability of products.

4.2.2   Sales and Operations Planning and Resource Requirements Planning

When executed properly, the *sales and operations planning* process (see definition in Section 4.1.2) links all the *tactical plans* for the business (i.e., sales, development, marketing, manufacturing, sourcing, and financial plans) with its execution (see [APIC04]).

With a view to logistics and operations management, the following results of the process are of particular interest: the sales plan, the stock inventory plan, the production plan, and the procurement plan.

A *sales plan* is a time-phased statement of expected customer orders anticipated to be received (incoming sales, not outgoing shipments) for each major product family or item ([APIC04]).

A sales plan is more than a forecast. It represents sales and marketing management's commitment to achieve this level of customer orders and can be dependent on forecast. It is expressed in units or in gross income, on an aggregate level.

A *production plan* is the agreed-upon plan that comes from the overall level of manufacturing output planned to be produced ([APIC04]). *Production planning* is the process of developing the production plan.

The production plan is usually stated as a monthly rate for each product family. Various units of measure can be used to express the plan: units, tonnage, standard hours, number of workers, and so on.

---

[9]   *Order entry* is the translation of the customer order into terms used by the manufacturer or distributor.

[10]   *Interplant orders* are orders received by another plant or division within the same organization.

> Similarly, a *procurement plan for saleable products* is the agreed-upon plan for product families or products to be purchased, that are intended to be sold directly, that is, without being used by the company itself or built as components into products.

Generally, a sales plan does not reflect a steady demand. However, the capacities (workers and production infrastructure) tend to be available at a steady rate. Therefore, if the demand pattern cannot be changed — by offering complementary products or price incentives or simply changing the due dates, for example — there are in principle two possible manufacturing strategies[11] (or a combination of them) to manage supply:

- Augment the quantitative flexibility of capacity in order to match the demand fluctuations.

- Store products in order to meet peak demand, even while continuing production at a steady rate.

Choosing the first option incurs so-called costs of changing production rhythm, or production rate change costs. These may include the costs of overtime and undertime, more facilities and equipment, part-time personnel, hiring and releasing employees, subcontracting, or agreements to use infrastructure cooperatively. See the detailed discussion in Section 13.2.3.

The second choice incurs — as already discussed in Section 1.1.2 — carrying costs, in particular costs of financing or capital costs, storage infrastructure costs, and depreciation risk. For details, see Section 10.4.1.

> An *inventory policy* is a statement of a company's objectives and approach to the management of inventories ([APIC04]).

An inventory policy expresses, for example, the extent to which either one or both of the above options will be followed. The policy can include a decision to reduce or increase inventory in general.

> An *inventory plan* determines the desired levels of stored items, mostly end products, according to the company's inventory policy.

The production plan can thus be obtained from the sales plan via the desired inventory plan. Or turned around, a desired production plan

---

[11] A *manufacturing strategy* is a long-term decision on the definition and use of manufacturing resources.

implies a corresponding inventory plan. By changing the inventory policy iteratively, a different production plan as well as the corresponding inventory plan (or vice versa) can be obtained.

Once the production plan is established, the process of *resource requirements planning* (RRP) begins. Resource requirements are calculated for each product family in the production plan through simple explosion of product structures (bills of material) for components requirements (dependent demand) and routing sheets for capacity requirements. To do this, the process uses bills of resources or product load profiles (see Figure 1.2.5.2).

If gross requirement for each purchased item calculated in this way is weighted by purchase price, the result is a good approximation that can serve as the procurement budget. Other resource requirements can be estimated analogously. For the planning horizon covered by the production plan, there now result:

- Components requirements, procurement plan for components and materials, and the corresponding procurement or materials budget
- Capacity requirements and the capacity budget (direct and overhead costs)
- Budget for overhead costs (overhead budget)

> In the case of rough-cut planning, sales and operations planning produces an *aggregate plan* that is based mainly on aggregated information (rough-cut business objects such as product families, rough-cut product structures, *aggregate forecast and demand* [that is, forecast and demand on product groups or families]) rather than on detailed product information.

It is in the case of rough-cut planning in particular that long-term planning lends itself well to the simulation and the what-if analysis of several variants of the production plan.[12] For this, company management (or a team caring about supply chain coordination) comes together for a half-day meeting, for example, in order to simulate the various possible patterns of demand and to examine their repercussions with regard to the physical realization of production and procurement in the supply chain. As some components or operations have not been considered, the budgets can by

---

[12] A *simulation* is a model-based reproduction of various conditions that are likely to occur in the actual performance of a system. A *what-if analysis* is the evaluation of the consequences of alternative strategies, e.g., of changes of forecasts, inventory levels, or production plans.

multiplied by historical figures to obtain expected budgets. In a similar process, sensitivity analysis can take into consideration the effect of demand variation and thus control the whole process with regard to feasibility.

In addition, simulation of different variants is an aid to estimating the consequences of different manufacturing strategies for total production.

Management will then choose and release one of the variants calculated in the above manner and initiate the necessary measures to fulfill the production plan in a timely fashion:

- For capacity, blanket orders can be given to external production, and orders can be made for the purchase of new machinery and buildings or for the acquisition of personnel.

- To procure goods or capacity, blanket orders can be placed with suppliers, or existing supply agreements can be modified.

Figure 4.2.2.1 shows a typical algorithm used within sales and operations planning to determine the production plan and the procurement plan for saleable products. It accords with the concept of integrated resource management, because all resources are planned simultaneously.

1. *Sales plan:* Determine forecast or demand pattern.
2. *Production plan, procurement plan for saleable products, and inventory plan:* Set inventory policy with regard to change of production rhythm and inventory level. Determine the inventory levels and calculate the corresponding production plan (analogically, the procurement plan for saleable products) or vice versa.
3. *Resource requirements planning and budgeting:* Calculate the procurement budget for components and materials, the capacity budget, and overhead costs budget. Take into account macro costs due to change of production rhythm and inventory.
4. Compare budget figures with actual possible realization and, if necessary, begin again with steps 1, 2, and 3 for each desired variation.

Fig. 4.2.2.1   Iterative master planning: integrated resource management.

As mentioned above, this technique usually handles rough-cut business objects of the type discussed in Section 1.2.5, so that various iterations can be calculated relatively rapidly. Resource requirements planning of this kind (rolling planning) must be repeated regularly (for example, monthly), and must include the whole planning horizon.

The example in Figures 4.2.2.2 through 4.2.2.4 illustrates iterative planning of this kind. Using forecasted sales figures, the objective is to produce an optimal production plan. To estimate the consequences of different manufacturing strategies for total production, different variants are calculated. Thus, only steps 2 and 3 of the steps shown in Figure 4.2.2.1 are iterated.

Many products, such as toys or lawnmowers, have a seasonal demand pattern like the one shown in the example. Should planners choose regular production, which will create inventory, or should production be a function of the demand, which will incur the costs of changing production rhythm? These costs go beyond micro costs, such as machine refitting costs. Macro costs will be incurred, such as the costs of making changes to personnel or machinery. In the example, planners should calculate the following three production plans:

1. Maintain the production rhythm throughout the whole year.
2. Change production rhythm frequently — in this case, four times a year.
3. Attempt to find an optimal compromise between plans 1 and 2.

Month	Sales		Production		Inventory
	monthly	cumulative	monthly	cumulative	at end of month
December					200
January	500	500	1000	1000	700
February	600	1100	1000	2000	1100
March	600	1700	1000	3000	1500
April	800	2500	1000	4000	1700
May	900	3400	1000	5000	1800
June	1000	4400	1000	6000	1800
July	600	5000	1000	7000	2200
August	400	5400	1000	8000	2800
September	600	6000	1000	9000	3200
October	600	6600	1000	10000	3600
November	1800	8400	1000	11000	2800
December	3000	11400	1000	12000	800

Fig. 4.2.2.2   Plan 1: production plan at a constant level.

Month	Sales		Production		Inventory
	monthly	cumulative	monthly	cumulative	at end of month
December					200
January	500	500	600	600	300
February	600	1100	600	1200	300
March	600	1700	600	1800	300
April	800	2500	900	2700	400
May	900	3400	900	3600	400
June	1000	4400	900	4500	300
July	600	5000	600	5100	300
August	400	5400	600	5700	500
September	600	6000	600	6300	500
October	600	6600	1900	8200	1800
November	1800	8400	1900	10100	1900
December	3000	11400	1900	12000	800

Fig. 4.2.2.3   Plan 2: production plan with four changes in production rhythm per year.

Month	Sales		Production		Inventory
	monthly	cumulative	monthly	cumulative	at end of month
December					200
January	500	500	800	800	500
February	600	1100	800	1600	700
March	600	1700	800	2400	900
April	800	2500	800	3200	900
May	900	3400	800	4000	800
June	1000	4400	800	4800	600
July	600	5000	1200	6000	1200
August	400	5400	1200	7200	2000
September	600	6000	1200	8400	2600
October	600	6600	1200	9600	3200
November	1800	8400	1200	10800	2600
December	3000	11400	1200	12000	800

Fig. 4.2.2.4   Plan 3: production plan with two changes in production rhythm per year.

The planners can now compare the three variants with respect to budget, assuming the following cost rates:

- Number of hours required to manufacture one unit: 100
- Cost per hour: $100
- Carrying cost: 20% of inventory value
- Cost of changing production rhythm: $800,000 (at least once a year, according to the new sales plan)

Figure 4.2.2.5 shows that the third solution results in the lowest total costs.

	Average inventory (in hours)	Average inventory (in 1000s of $)	Carrying cost (in 1000s of $)	# of production rhythm changes	Cost of change	Total costs
Plan 1	200000	20000	4000	1	800	4800
Plan 2	65000	6500	1300	4	3200	4500
Plan 3	14000	14000	2800	2	1600	4400

Fig. 4.2.2.5   Comparison of the three production plans.

4.2.3   Master Scheduling and Rough-Cut Capacity Planning

Sales and operations planning works mainly with product families, that is, at an aggregate level of information. However, there will be a need for more specific information for individual products.

> The corresponding planning process at the level of the individual product is called *master scheduling*.[13]

The most important output of master scheduling is the master production schedule.

> A *master production schedule (MPS)* is the disaggregated version of a production plan, expressed in specific products, configurations, quantities, and dates.

Figure 4.2.3.1 shows an example of a MPS as derived from a production plan (shown here only for the first four months of a year).

As the figure shows, the MPS is not only more detailed for individual products rather than product families, but it also yields much more detail for the time period for which the quantities are aggregated. It is thus a link between the production plan, which is relatively close to the sales plan, and the products the manufacturing department will actually build. The MPS is the input to all planning actions in the shorter term.

---

[13]   *Scheduling* is the act of creating a schedule, such as a master, shipping, production, or purchasing schedule (compare [APIC04]). The *master schedule (MS)* is the result of master scheduling.

Product family \ Month	Jan.	Feb.	March	April
...				
P	100	100	150	120
...				

Product \ Week	1	2	3	4	Total
P_1	25	25			50
P_2			25	5	30
P_3				20	20
Total	25	25	25	25	100

Fig. 4.2.3.1   The MPS as a disaggregated version of the production plan (an example of a product family P with three different products P_1, P_2, P_3).

> The *planning time fence* corresponds to the point in time denoted in the planning horizon of the master scheduling process that marks a boundary inside of which change to the schedule may adversely affect customer deliveries, component schedules, capacity plans, and cost ([APIC04]).[14]

Planned orders outside the planning time fence can be changed automatically by a software system the planning logic. Changes inside the time fence must be changed manually by the master scheduler.[15]

Establishing a master production schedule entails a number of tasks:

1. *Selection of the master schedule items*, that is, the items managed by the master scheduler and not by the computer. Taking the example in Figure 4.2.3.1, if the difference between the products

---

[14] In general, a *time fence* can be understood as a policy or guideline established to limit changes in operation procedures. In contrast to this, the term *hedge* is used in logistics and operations mangement similar to safety stock, in order to protect against an uncertain event such as a strike or price increase. It is planned beyond some time fence such that, if the hedge is not needed, it can be rolled forward before major resources must be committed to produce the hedge and put it in inventory ([APIC04]).

[15] The *master scheduler* is the person charged with the responsibility of managing the master schedule for select items.

of the family P is due to three different variants (options) of a subassembly (namely, V_1, V_2, and V_3) and if the delivery lead time allows assembling to customer order, then the best choice for the (customer) order penetration point (OPP) is the subassembly level. The final products P_1, P_2, and P_3 are then produced to customer order, according to the final assembly schedule (FAS) (see Section 6.1.5). If the usage quantity is 2 for each variant, then Figure 4.2.3.2 shows the MPS corresponding to the production plan.

Subassembly \ Week	1	2	3	4	Total	%
V_1	50	50			100	50
V_2			50	10	60	30
V_3				40	40	20
Total	50	50	50	50	200	100

Fig. 4.2.3.2   The MPS on the level of subassemblies V_1, V_2, and V_3.

2. *Break down the production plan quantity for a product family into quantity for each product of the family* (possibly respecting the product hierarchy). We often do not know the exact percentage for splitting the total product family demand into individual product or variant demands. To cover this uncertainty, we increase the percentage of each option. This percentage is called the *option percentage* in Section 9.5.4, where the detailed systematic procedure for its determination is explained. This procedure results in overplanning, which yields protection in the form of *safety demand*. Figure 4.2.3.3 shows example overplanning in the MPS, assuming an uncertainty of 20%.

Subassembly \ Week	1	2	3	4	Total	%
V_1	60	60			120	50
V_2			60	12	72	30
V_3				48	48	20
Total	60	60	60	60	240	100

Fig. 4.2.3.3   The MPS for the first four weeks on the level of subassemblies V_1, V_2, V_3, including overplanning due to variant uncertainty.

This safety demand is in effect safety stock, or reserved stock, for the entire planning horizon to be covered. For details, see Section 9.5.5. The safety demand has to be planned at the beginning of the planning horizon. If the forecast indicates a large demand in one of the subsequent periods, the additional safety demand can be planned for that planning period. Figure 4.2.3.4 shows the first overplanning for January. An additional overplanning takes place for March, but only for the part that is not already overplanned in January.

Product family \ Month	Jan.	Feb.	March	April
...				
P	100	100	150	120
...				

Subassembly \ Month	Jan.	Feb.	March	April
V_1	100+20	100	150+10	120
V_2	60+12	60	90+6	72
V_3	40+8	40	60+4	48
Total	200+40	200	300+20	240

Fig. 4.2.3.4   The MPS on the level of subassemblies V_1, V_2, and V_3, including safety demand (due to variant uncertainty) during the planning horizon.

For the rest of the planning period, the safety stock in the system corresponds to the safety demand for the maximal monthly demand. Due to the general uncertainty in the system, it is sometimes easier to plan the whole quantity at the start of the planning period. A coordinated final assembly schedule (FAS, see Section 6.1.5) maintains the service level at 100%, meaning that consumption of the subassemblies stays within the limits of the safety stock. For more details, the reader may refer to Sections 6.2.1 and 6.2.2, where it is also explained that this kind of master scheduling is valid only as long as the number of variants to be planned in the MPS is significantly lower than the total demand quantity for the product family. Otherwise, a (customer) order penetration point (OPP) more upstream must be chosen.

3. *Verify the feasibility of the MPS* by rough-cut capacity planning.

> *Rough-cut capacity planning (RCCP)* is the process of converting the master production schedule into *required capacity*, that is, capacity of (key) resources to produce the desired output in the particular periods. Comparison to available or demonstrated capacity (with regard to feasibility) is usually done for each key resource ([APIC04]).

As the planning is more detailed, RCCP yields more precise information on the work centers and the capacities to be used than does resource requirements planning (RRP). It therefore allows more precise control of the feasibility of the production plan. Figure 4.2.3.5 shows the (average) load of the MPS in comparison to the weekly (average) capacity of a work center called WC-A.

Week Subassembly	1	2	3	4	Load per unit	∅ Load / capacity
V_1	60	60			0.75	
V_2			60	12	0.6	
V_3				48	0.5	
Load (in h) (= capacity required)	45	45	36	31.2		39.3
Capacity (in h)	40	40	40	40		40
Over-(+)/under-(–)capacity (in h)	–5	–5	+4	+8.8		+0.7

Fig. 4.2.3.5   RCCP on the level of subassemblies V_1, V_2, and V_3: load and capacity on work center WC-A.

For balancing load with capacity, the following strategies are possible:

- *Chase production method*: A production planning strategy that maintains a stable inventory level that corresponds to load. To do this, the quantitative flexibility of capacity — as is the case in Figure 4.2.3.5 — must be quite high.

- *Level production method*: A production planning strategy that maintains a *level schedule* (a master production schedule that generates a load that is spread out more evenly over the time period) corresponding to capacity. This can go as a far as requiring *linearity*, or the production of a constant quantity (or the consumption of a constant quantity of resources) in every period (such as daily). Figure 4.2.3.6 shows a possible solution.

Subassembly \ Week	1	2	3	4	Load per unit	∅ Load / capacity
V₁	54	54	12		0.75	
V₂			50	22	0.6	
V₃				48	0.5	
Load (in h) (= capacity required)	40.5	40.5	39	37.2		39.3
Capacity (in h)	40	40	40	40		40
+= Over / - = under (in h)	-0.5	-0.5	+1	+2.8		+0.7

Fig. 4.2.3.6   RCCP on the level of subassemblies V_1, V_2, and V_3: load and capacity on work center WC-A, load leveled.

- *Hybrid production method*: Companies can combine chase and level production methods.

- It is a question of an *overstated master production schedule*. The quantities are greater than the ability to produce, given current capacity and material availability (compare [APIC04]). The MPS has to be modified.

Figure 4.2.3.6 shows that load leveling is a time-consuming procedure even for just one work center. In real cases, several (rough-cut) work centers may be involved. Finite loading algorithms, often developed within operations research (such as linear programming), have to be used. In the face of the degree of uncertainty of the (mostly forecast based) production plan as well as of the demand breakdown from the family level to the level of individual products, it is often not worth putting too much effort into more detailed calculation. If there is (as in our example) a 20% uncertainty in the distribution of the demand of the family among the single products or subassemblies, a deviation of 10% of the average capacity (as in Figure 4.2.3.5) is probably precise enough. Investing great efforts in detailed calculation will be often useless at this (long-term) level of planning. In contrast, the importance of investing in quantitative flexibility of the capacities increases with a growing degree of variability of the product concept.

In more complicated cases, the MPS must divide the production plan into individual production or procurement lots. Then, just as in medium-term planning, net requirements planning over the time axis, rather than gross requirements planning, is needed. An example of this is long-term planning that aims explicitly to achieve high-capacity utilization, particularly in the process industry. In that case, RCCP (rough-cut capacity planning) seems to be a good solution:

- Quick calculation of alternative order quantities or subdivisions in part orders with shifted completion dates is possible.

- The number of planning variables is small, and sometimes the whole plan can be displayed on a large monitor. This provides excellent support to the human ability to make situation-appropriate decisions intuitively even when the data are incomplete and imprecise. These intuitive decisions take into account a multitude of non-quantifiable factors and implicit knowledge. This is a very important aspect of future-oriented forecasting techniques. Knowledge about the development of a forecast can influence our evaluation of planning results, particularly interpretations of capacity overload and underload.

See Section 13.4 for a detailed description of rough-cut capacity planning techniques.

4.2.4   Verifying the Feasibility of a Master Production Schedule: Available-to-Promise and Order Promising

The *master production schedule (MPS)* is the main output of long-term planning, and it is a primary input to medium- and short-term production and procurement planning. It is therefore important to verify the feasibility of the MPS as early as possible. One way to do this is through rough-cut capacity planning (RCCP), as discussed above.

Another way to do this is by looking ahead and simulating some tasks of medium and short-term planning, namely available-to-promise (ATP) and order promising.

(Order) backlog is all the customer orders received but not yet shipped. Sometimes referred to as *open customer orders* or the order board ([APIC04]).

> *Available-to-promise (ATP)* is the uncommitted – that is not yet assigned to an open customer order – portion of a company's inventory and planned production ([APIC04]).

The ATP quantity is maintained in the master schedule to support customer-order promising. It is normally calculated for each event or each period in which an MPS receipt is scheduled ([APIC04]). However, it is cumulative ATP that is of practical importance. Figure 4.2.4.1 illustrates the definition and calculation of discrete ATP and cumulative ATP.

Product PR

Physical inventory	= 12
Safety stock	= 0
Batch size	= 30
Lead time	= 3 periods

Period	0	1	2	3	4	5
Master production schedule			30		30	
Allocated to customer order		5	3	25	20	10
Projected available inventory	12	7	34	9	19	9
Cumulative ATP	7	7	9	9	9	9
ATP per period	7		2			

Fig. 4.2.4.1   Determination of ATP quantities.

We will begin formal calculation of ATP with some definitions:

For $i = 1, 2, \ldots$, let

$ATP_i \equiv$ ATP of period i.

$ATP\_C_i \equiv$ cumulative ATP of period i.

$MPS_i \equiv$ MPS quantity of the period i.

$QA_i \equiv$ quantity allocated to customer orders in period i.

Now, let ATP_C_0 and ATP_0 be equal to the physical inventory. According to the definition above, the following algorithm, done subsequently for $i = 1, 2, \ldots$, yields the ATP quantities.

$ATP\_C_i = ATP\_C_{i-1} + MPS_i - QA_i$.
$j = i$
While $ATP\_C_j < ATP\_C_{j-1}$ and $j > 0$, revise the ATP quantities as follows:
  $ATP\_C_{j-1} = ATP\_C_j$
  $ATP_j = 0$.
  $j = j-1$
end (while).
If $j > 0$, then $ATP_j = ATP\_C_j - ATP\_C_{j-1}$.
If $j = 0$, then $ATP_0 = ATP\_C_0$.

In our example, for the product PR, seven units are available-to-promise from stock. Two additional units become available-to-promise in period 2.

An MPS is feasible only if for the backlog, any projected available inventory (and therefore any ATP quantity) is at least 0. Because customer demand is known for the short term only, it becomes evident that the feasibility refers only to the near future.

Determining ATP quantities supports decision making regarding whether an order can be accepted or should be refused:

- For make-to-stock-items, order promising is a direct consequence of comparing the order quantity with the ATP quantities.

   A small exercise: Taking the example in Figure 4.2.4.1, determine whether 8 units can be promised for period 1. Furthermore, how would you promise delivery of an urgent order of 10 units to an impatient customer waiting on the phone for your answer?

- For make-to-order or assemble-to-order items, order promising requires a check of the ATP quantities for all necessary components at the (customer) order penetration point (OPP), as well as a check of the availability of capacity for assembling the components.

For more detailed information on availability and calculating projected available inventory, see Section 11.1.

4.2.5   Supplier Scheduling: Blanket Order Processing, Release, and Coordination

The objective of resource requirements planning in long-term, or master, planning, is not to release production or procurement orders, but rather to prepare the channels for later procurement. In the case of goods, the challenge is to determine what suppliers can fulfill the company's requirements in terms of quantity, quality, delivery, and delivery reliability. It is in this phase that the purchasing budget should also be set.

Experience in recent years — particularly in connection with the demand for faster delivery at lower procurement costs — has shown that for efficient logistics, a company must work together more closely with its suppliers.

> *Supplier scheduling* is a purchasing approach using blanket agreements, discussed below when viewing the company as a customer (it has a corresponding significance to the company in its role as a supplier in a logistics network).

The supplier has to have some knowledge of the company's master planning so that its own master planning can allow fast delivery. This exchange of information is a matter of trust, and it cannot be practiced with all or even very many suppliers (see Section 2.2.2).

Gross requirement calculated by resource requirements planning is, after all, a forecast that can be placed with suppliers as blanket orders. A *blanket order* is, in non-binding cases, a "letter of intent." A minimum blanket order quantity for a planned time period, together with a maximum quantity, increases the binding nature of the agreement and thus also raises planning security.

In medium-term planning, blanket purchase orders are defined ever more precisely, step by step. In agreement with the supplier, a company sets procurement quantities per period in medium-term planning (such as for three months hence, for two months hence, for the next month) with a decreasing range of deviation. From a certain point in time onwards, the part of the blanket order planned for "next month" becomes a short-range blanket order.

> A *short-range blanket order* is only for a set quantity. A company gradually sets due dates for parts of the order by means of an appropriate technique of execution and control of operations.
>
> A *blanket release* is the authorization to ship and/or produce against a (short range) blanket agreement or contract ([APIC04]). It sets the maximum quantity per week or per day, for example.

> A *delivery schedule* is the required or agreed time or rate of actual delivery of goods. A systems supplier, for example, may be requested by the company to deliver to the assembly line of an automobile manufacturer or machine builder in synchrony with production.

Figure 4.2.5.1 shows an example system of blanket orders and blanket releases. In this case, the two overlap.

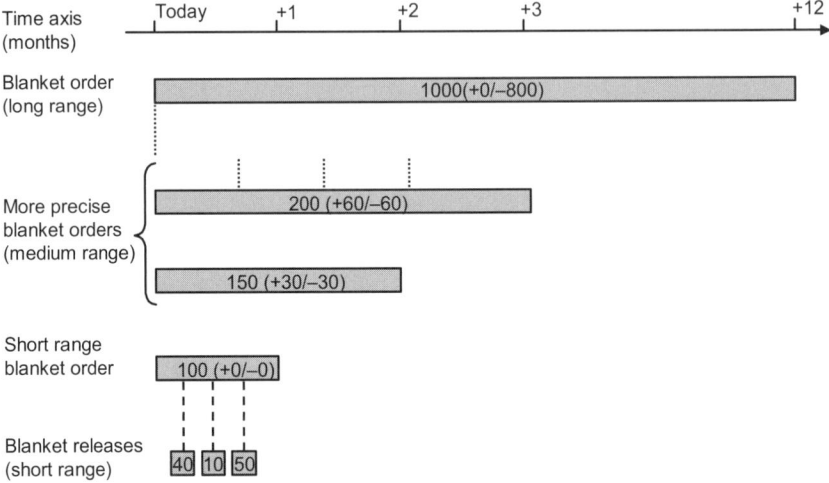

Fig. 4.2.5.1   Systematics of blanket orders and blanket releases with quantities and time periods (example).

The idea is that both the long-range blanket order and the medium-range, more precise blanket orders will be brought up to date on a rolling basis. In the example, the rolling cycle is one month. Blanket orders are given a plus or minus deviation. Each month's continuation of the blanket order must not contradict earlier agreements as to the acceptable range of deviation.

In this example, the company orders the exact required quantity for the next month, or, in other words, it places a short-range blanket order. The delivery schedule during the next month will be determined by a control principle such as a kanban. In the course of the monthly period, requirements arise unpredictably, so that if a company has not given precise dates for probably delivery, the supplier will have to ready the entire quantity of the short-range blanket order at the start of the month. Additional quantification of a short-range blanket order could also set maximum requirements for blanket releases in that month.

A system like this, of continuous, ever more precise blanket orders and blanket releases, demands investiture in logistics and planning & control between a company and its suppliers. Therefore, the system is economically feasible only with a certain number of suppliers. Rapid and efficient communication techniques for information exchange and for updating the planning data are not only an advantage, but also often a requirement of coordination. In some cases, a supplier may even have access to the company's database, while the company may check the status of the supplier's planning and implementation of procurement orders. See also Section 2.2.3.

4.3   Introduction to Detailed Planning and Execution

This section gives a brief overview of logistics business methods and techniques used for detailed planning & scheduling, as well as for execution and control of operations in the areas of distribution, production, and procurement. We will show the basic considerations that lead to various methods of solving the tasks presented in the reference model in Figure 4.1.4.2. The methods themselves will be the subject of more detailed, later chapters.

4.3.1   Basic Principles of Materials Management Concepts

Materials management must provide the goods required by demand both cost effectively and according to schedule. The objectives of materials management are similar for logistics networks in industry and in the service sector. The objectives are (see also Section 1.2.2):

- Avoidance of disruptions in delivery or production due to shortages
- Lowest possible costs for the administration of production and goods purchased externally
- Lowest possible carrying cost caused by goods procured too soon or even unnecessarily

The more exact our knowledge of inventory in stock and of open orders and due dates, the better the problem can be solved. It is even more important, however, to have exact information on demand. There are two possible ways to classify demand: with respect to accuracy or with respect to its relationship to other demand.

Classification of demand according to accuracy is defined as follows:

- *Deterministic demand* is demand downstream from the (customer) order penetration point (OPP).

- *Stochastic demand* is demand upstream from the (customer) order penetration point (OPP).

Classification of demand according to accuracy is thus dependent upon the (customer) order penetration point (OPP), or, in other words, upon the relationship between the customer tolerance time and (cumulative) lead time, as shown in Figure 1.3.1.3. Accordingly, the following sections will discuss two classes of methods and techniques in materials management.

Deterministic materials management utilizes a number of deterministic methods and deterministic techniques. In principle, these methods and techniques take demand as their starting point to calculate the necessary resources requirements on the basis of current conditions.

Stochastic materials management involves a number of stochastic methods and stochastic techniques. The methods and techniques utilize demand forecasts and buffer forecasting errors by building safety stock into the resource requirements.

Classification of demand according to its relationship with other demand is defined as follows:

- *Independent demand* is the demand for an item that is unrelated to the demand for other items.

- *Dependent demand* is demand that is directly related to or derived from the demand for other items ([APIC04]).

Company-external demand, or (customer) demand for end products or service parts, is independent demand, as is also a company's own internal demand for office supplies or — partly — indirect materials. The demand for assemblies, semifinished goods, components, raw materials, and — in part — auxiliary materials are examples of dependent demand.

There is an important subclass of stochastic materials management:

Quasi-deterministic materials management utilizes stochastic methods to determine independent demand. However, it utilizes deterministic methods and techniques to determine dependent demand, e.g. the bill-of-material explosion.

For stochastic demand, the practice is to avoid quasi-deterministic materials management whenever possible and to employ pure stochastic materials management. Here the fill rate plays a decisive role.

The *fill rate* used here is that percentage of demand that can be satisfied through available inventory or by the current production schedule.

This is the definition used as in Figure 1.4.4.1, whereas item demand is measured.

A s*tockout* is a lack of materials, components or finished goods that are needed ([APIC04]).

A *backorder* is an unfilled customer order or commitment, an immediate (or past due) demand against an item whose inventory is insufficient to satisfy the demand ([APIC04]).

The *stockout quantity* or *backorder quantity* is the extent of demand, that is, the quantity that cannot be covered during a stockout condition.

The *stockout percentage* or *backorder percentage* is the complementary percentage remaining when the fill rate is subtracted from 100%.

The *cumulative fill rate* is the probability that several different components will be available simultaneously on demand.

If the fill rate for a component is not very close to 100%, then the probability that several items of a product will be available from inventory simultaneously will be very low. For example, if we need to have ten components from inventory for an assembly, and the fill rate is 95%, the cumulative fill rate is only 60% ($\approx 0.95^{10}$), which usually will not suffice. Figure 4.3.1.1 illustrates this phenomenon.

Complex products such as machines are very often made up of a large number of components. In this case, avoiding planning errors means assuring a high fill rate for each component. Materials management, both in techniques and in form, is very dependent upon the characteristic features of planning & control.

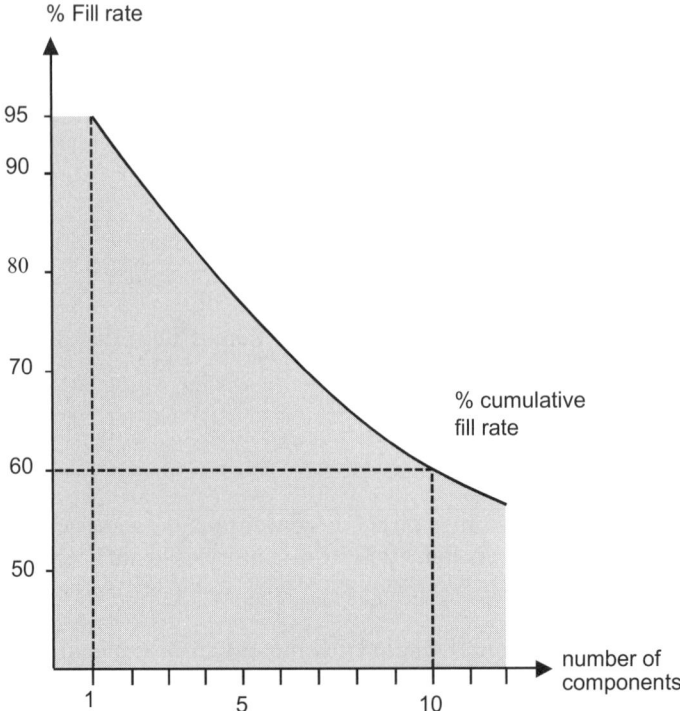

Fig. 4.3.1.1   Cumulative fill rate with components required simultaneously.

4.3.2   Overview of Materials Management Techniques

Figures 4.3.2.1 and 4.3.2.2 distinguish among the common techniques of detailed planning techniques in materials management. Firstly, figure 4.3.2.1 classifies planning techniques according to the characteristic features *frequency of customer demand* and *unit cost* of items (as defined in Figure 3.4.2.1).

Demand for low-cost items (with the exception of unique demand) or *demand for high-cost items with a continuous or regular demand pattern* is determined using stochastic techniques.

- In general, forecasting techniques determine future demand analytically or intuitively. From this perspective, demand forecasting is a *technique for determining stochastic independent demand* and is thus part of stochastic materials management. Once demand has been forecasted, different stochastic planning techniques exist, all being relatively simple. They are described at a first glance below.

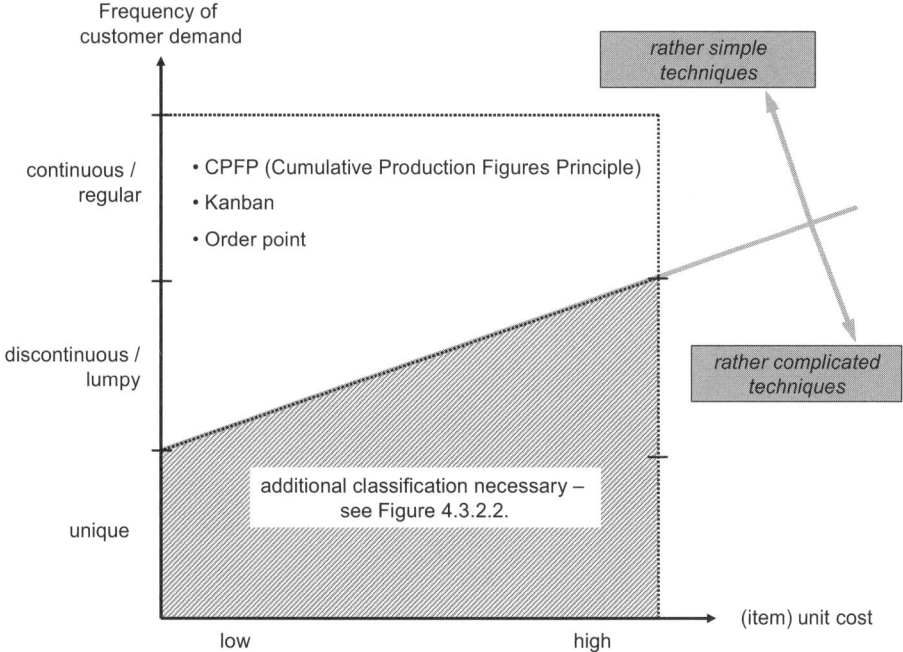

Fig. 4.3.2.1   Classification of detailed planning techniques in materials management.

- Dependent demand is calculated as if it were independent demand – that is, ignoring its possible derivation from independent demand.

- For low-cost items, a very high service level has priority. This holds especially in the event where the item appears on the bill of material with many components (see the case mentioned previously in Fig. 4.3.1.1). Low stock inventory is, due to the low carrying cost involved, of secondary importance.

- For high-cost items, short lead times in the flow of goods, meaning rapid value-adding and administrative processes, take priority, requiring simple data and control flow. Inventory is possible: the continuous or regular demand pattern guarantees a future demand (for end products: a customer order)[16] within a short time.

---

[16]   Downstream from the order penetration point (OPP), the customer order can also show specific features that lead to a custom-made product (keyword "mass customization"). See here also Section 6.1.4 and the concepts "generic Kanban" and "postponement". The demand for this custom-made product is then actually sporadic, while the demand for the underlying product family is continuous.

However, because of the high unit cost, the inventories should be low, which generally requires small batch sizes.

For all other kinds of demand, that is for *unique demand* or demand for *high-cost items with a lumpy demand pattern,* Figure 4.3.2.2 shows an additional classification of planning techniques, this time according to the accuracy of the demand and its relationship with other demand (see the definitions above).

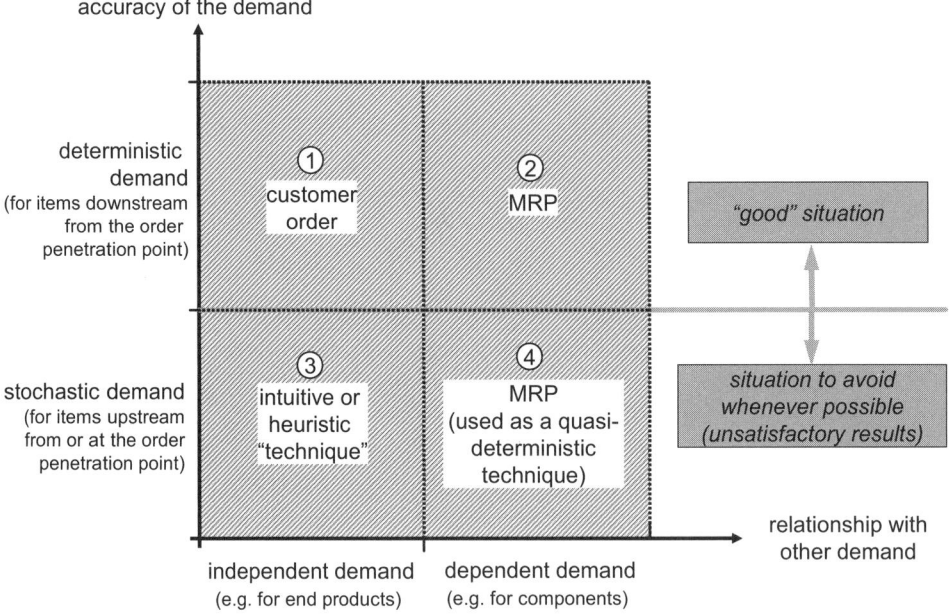

Fig. 4.3.2.2   Additional classification of detailed planning techniques in materials management for unique demand or demand for high-cost items with a lumpy demand pattern.

1. *Deterministic independent demand* can be met according to the actual demand, that is, according to the customer order.

- From this perspective, customer order processing and customer blanket order processing are *techniques for determining deterministic independent demand* and thus in a sense also belong to deterministic materials management.

2. *Deterministic dependent demand* can be calculated from higher level independent demand.

- The algorithm called MRP uses "explodes" of the bill of material, that is, the product structure, into its components.

- This type of demand calculation is a relatively complicated procedure. However, due to the priority of both high delivery reliability rate and low or even no inventory, it is appropriate.

Thus, while sometimes being rather complicated, planning techniques for items downstream from the order penetration point with unique demand or – for high-cost items – with a lumpy demand pattern present no great difficulty. However, planning of such items upstream from the OPP generally leads to unsatisfactory results:

> 3. *Stochastic independent demand* is determined more or less intuitively.

- As demand is lumpy, forecasting techniques tend to be inaccurate, and therefore ask for a lot of additional intuition. The materials management "technique" is often a manual procedure performed by the scheduler using a very personal heuristic. It is often a risky technique that should be avoided whenever possible.

> 4. *Stochastic dependent demand* is derived by quasi-deterministic techniques.

- Here, independent demand is determined using demand forecast techniques. Calculation of dependent demand is then based on independent demand by means of explosion of the bill of material. This is called *quasi-deterministic explosion of the bill of material.*

- As this demand pattern requires forecasting, there is a risk of a low service level or high carrying cost due to capital costs or depreciation as a consequence of technical obsolescence or expiration due to perishability. As a consequence, any materials management technique handling this case will generally yield unsatisfactory results. Therefore, it should be avoided whenever possible. However, for many businesses, being in that situation is a fact of life.

- It is interesting to consider that, due to the dependent nature of the demand, the value-adding processes are under the control of the company. A thorough analysis of these processes can lead to appropriate modifications that entail more items downstream from the OPP, or a more continuous demand pattern – both situations being desirable. See Chapter 5 on the just-in-time / lean concept.

Forecasting techniques will be discussed in Chapter 9. The planning techniques mentioned are explained in detail in different chapters. At a first glance, they are described in brief as follows.

- *Kanban* is a simple technique for stochastic materials management, but it requires invested capital. The objective is to work as quickly as possible with small batch sizes and with small buffer storages, which are kept at the user operation. These stores will contain, for example, a maximum number of standard containers or bins holding a fixed number of items. The order batch size will be a set of containers. The kanban card is a means to identify the contents of the container and to release the order. One or more empty containers are either sent directly by work center employees to the supplier or collected by one of the supplier's employees. The supplier executes the implied stock replenishment order and delivers it directly to the buffer. The kanban feedback loop is then closed. One of the tasks of long- and medium-term planning is to determine the type and number of kanban cards for each feedback loop. See Section 5.3.

- The *cumulative production figures principle* (CPFP) is another simple technique. In the manufacturing process of a certain product, the technique in essence counts the number of intermediate products or states in the flow at particular count points. It compares this amount to the planned flow of goods, through putting the two cumulative production figure curves, or whole cumulative production figure diagrams — the projected diagram and the actual diagram — one on top of the other. The object is to bring the actual diagram closer to the projected diagram, which can be accomplished by speeding up or slowing down the manufacturing process. See Section 5.4.

- The *order point technique* is probably the most well-known technique in stochastic materials management. It compares goods on hand — plus open orders and, sometimes, minus allocated quantities (reservations) — with a certain level called the *order point*. If the quantity calculated in this manner is no greater than the order point, the system generates orders to replenish stock. These replenishment orders can then be released. The order point is normally calculated as average usage (a forecast!) during the replenishment lead time plus safety stock, or reserved stock, to compensate for forecast errors. The "optimum" order quantity or batch size, called the economic order quantity (EOQ) can be determined through comparing ordering and setup costs to carrying cost. See here Chapter 10.

- *MRP* (material requirements planning) is a well-known set of techniques for deterministic materials management.[17] Starting from higher-level deterministic or stochastic independent demand, dependent demand is calculated by exploding the bill of material. The individual dependent demands are grouped together according to certain batch sizing policies and planned for timely production or procurement. In the deterministic case, the safety stock of components can be very small; inventory is kept to a minimum. In the quasi-deterministic case, safety demand at the level of the independent demand determines the safety stock of components. Deterministic materials management produces order proposals and the information required to control the processing of those orders. See Chapter 11.

Section 5.5.2 discusses further a possible strategy for choosing one of these techniques and gives tips for implementing procedures.

4.3.3   Basic Principles of Scheduling and Capacity Management Concepts

The type of business or company makes no difference when it comes to time management and scheduling and capacity management. Industrial and service companies alike face essentially the same challenges:

- How can individual order processing tasks be synchronized in time?

- What capacities must be available in order to realize master planning?

- Where and when must special shifts and overtime (or short-time work or part-time work) be put in place? What jobs, or whole orders, must be turned over to subcontractors (due to overload) or taken over from them (due to underload)?

- Where can the rhythm of production be brought into balance? Can short-time work in one area be compensated for by overtime in another?

- When and where can capacity or orders be shifted? For example, what shifts can be made from one shop, production line, office group, team, and so on to another?

---

[17]   It is important not to confuse the MRP technique with the MRP II concept (manufacturing resource planning).

- Can lead times and the number of orders in process be reduced?

The objectives of the tasks of *time management and scheduling* and *capacity management* are similar to the objectives of *materials management* (see Section 1.2.1):

1. High service level, short delivery times, high delivery reliability rate, and, at the same time, flexibility to adapt to customer requests
2. Low invested capital, that is, minimal inventory of work in process; optimization of wait times
3. Efficient use of available capacity through good utilization at a constant level; prediction of bottlenecks
4. Flexibility and adaptability of capacity to changing conditions
5. Minimal fixed costs in production administration and in production itself

Finding solutions for these issues requires consideration of large bodies of data from various open or planned orders. Computer-aided handling of the problem is often necessary. The planning problem becomes more complicated due to the fact that some of the above objectives, such as the first and the third, contradict each other.

Figure 4.3.3.1 shows the consequences of *not* planning capacity. If capacity is inadequate (here, too low) to begin with, a vicious circle of actions results. To gain an understanding of how this can arise, begin with "increased number of orders in the factory" at the bottom right of the figure.

1. If the number of customer orders increases, the number of orders released to production also increases, thus increasing the load on capacity
2. If the number of orders exceeds capacity, queues will form behind the work centers
3. In consequence, orders must wait and their actual lead times lengthen. Orders cannot be met at their due date, that is, not within the customer tolerance time
4. Standard lead times, particularly the interoperation times, are prolonged in order to gain more realistic planning

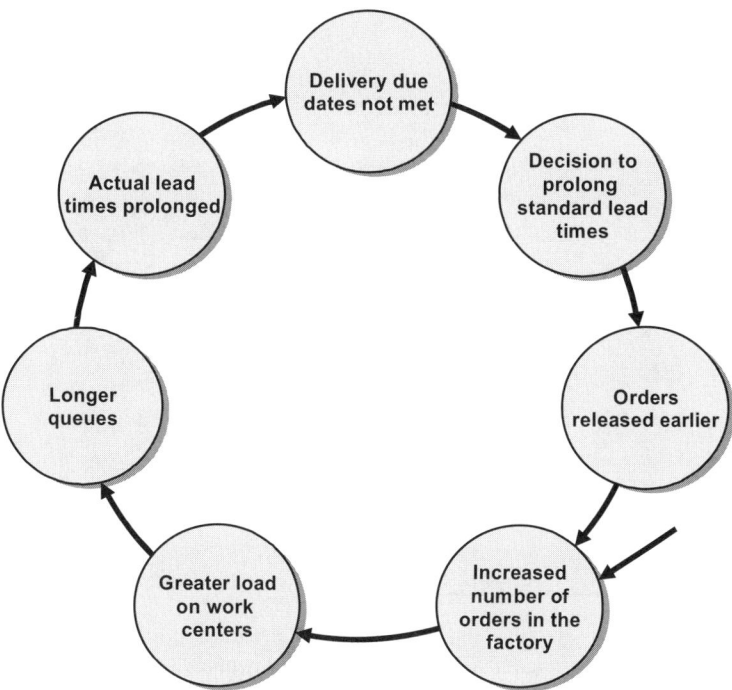

Fig. 4.3.3.1   A vicious circle caused when capacity bottlenecks prolong the planned production lead time. (From [IBM75].)

5. As a consequence, orders are released earlier, which in turn causes additional load in the form of released orders. The "game" begins all over again at point 1.

In this example, increasing the capacity could be a way to break out of the vicious circle.

The *overall objective* of scheduling and capacity management is to *balance load* arising through orders with *capacity available* to process those orders. Figure 4.3.3.2 shows a chance-produced situation through the course of time (above) and, in contrast, an idealized conception of the possible result of planning (below).

The problem to be resolved is basically the same in any of the temporal ranges of planning & control. However, the measures taken for capacity planning — such as procuring additional capacity — are very different in master planning and detailed planning and scheduling.

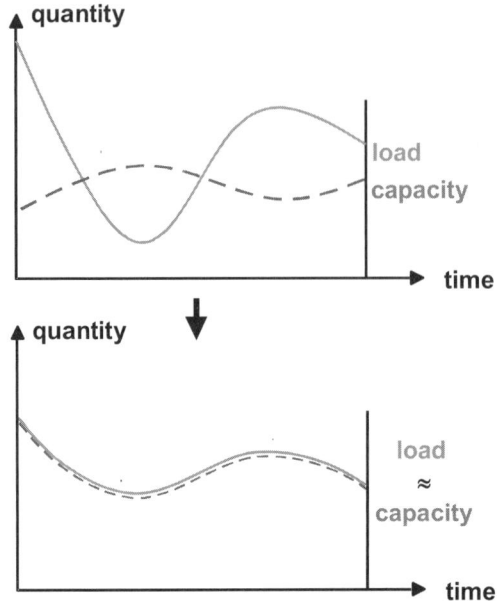

Fig. 4.3.3.2   Objective of time management and scheduling and of capacity management: balancing load with capacity available.

- In long-term planning, the company can procure additional production means, such as production facilities or persons. In addition, it can make comprehensive arrangements to subcontract to the outside. Or, if capacity must be reduced, this can all be accomplished in reverse.

- In medium-term planning, on the other hand, a company will attempt to gain at least some measure of elasticity of capacity through scheduling overtime or arranging rush subcontracts to the outside. Medium-term planning, however, cannot correct major errors in long-term planning. These planning errors result in late deliveries.

Capacity is a potential factor. Can capacity be stored? The company may think that this can be accomplished by producing ahead, thus creating inventory. However, inventory cannot be reconverted into capacity. Therefore, a company has to be very sure to produce ahead only those items that will be used within a reasonably short time frame. There are capacity management techniques that use this strategy, such as Corma. In other cases, however, producing ahead in order to "store capacity" may simply be a manifestation of a "just in case" mentality. As a result, the wrong items will be produced, and eventually the capacity is lost.

Somewhat "storable" is capacity in the form of personnel — if employees' presence along the time axis is somewhat flexible. For instance, say that an employee has to work only five hours instead of the usual eight on a specific day. If she or he is willing to go home but to work the three hours on another day where there is overload, you could say that three hours of capacity were stored. While this strategy is quite common, it is very limited with regard to the total capacity. Moreover, a company normally has to pay the employee for the quantitative flexibility of her or his capacity.

Generally, capacity cannot be stored effectively. Because this is so, planning must address two dimensions simultaneously; capacity (quantity axis in Figure 4.3.3.2) and dates (time axis) must be planned *together*.

4.3.4   Overview of Scheduling and Capacity Management Techniques

Depending on the main objectives of the enterprise (see Section 1.2.2), the values for some of the characteristic features of planning & control as in Figures 3.4.3.1 and 3.4.4.1 will differ.

- If a company puts the focus on flexibility in the utilization of resources, then *qualitative flexibility of capacity* (employees and the production infrastructure) is absolutely necessary.

- If high capacity utilization is required, there will be no *quantitative flexibility of capacity*. This is particularly the case for the production infrastructure.

- If high service level and delivery reliability rate are required, there will be no *flexibility of the order due date* of the production or procurement order.

If there is qualitative flexibility in capacity, meaning that capacity can also be applied for processes outside a particular work center, this can increase its quantitative flexibility, or temporal flexibility regarding assignments. For example, if employees can be moved from one work center to another, this is the same as if each work center showed quantitative flexibility in assigning employees.

There are various techniques for scheduling and capacity management. The techniques can be grouped into two classes based on the two planning dimensions shown in Figure 4.3.3.2: infinite and finite loading.

- *Infinite loading* means calculating the work center loads by time period, at first without regard to capacity. The primary objective of infinite loading is to meet dates as scheduled, with greatest possible control of fluctuations in capacity requirements. Therefore, infinite loading is most useful when meeting due dates must take priority *over* high capacity utilization, such as is the case in customer order production in a job shop production environment. The planning techniques are rather simple.

- *Finite loading* considers capacity from the start and does not permit overloads. To prevent overloads, the planner changes start dates or completion dates. The primary objective of finite loading is good use of the capacity available through the course of time, with greatest possible avoidance of delays in order processing. Therefore, finite loading is most useful if limited capacity is the major planning problem, such as in the process industry in a continuous production environment. Often, this condition is given in very short-term planning, in execution and control. The planning techniques are rather complicated simple.

In addition to these *two classes of techniques*, Figure 4.3.4.1 groups techniques for scheduling and capacity management in *nine sectors* in dependency upon quantitative flexibility of capacity and flexibility of the order due date. The techniques can be compared with respect to their overall capacity planning flexibility.

> *Overall capacity planning flexibility* is defined as the "sum" of the quantitative flexibility of capacity along the time axis and the flexibility of the order due date.

- Note that there is no technique in the three sectors at top right: Here, the overall capacity planning flexibility is high enough to accept and execute any order at any time. This case is very advantageous with regard to capacity planning, but it is usually too expensive due to overcapacity.

- Note the numerous techniques in the three sectors from top left to bottom right. Here, there is *sufficient* overall capacity planning flexibility in order to allow a computer algorithm to plan all the orders without intervention by the planner. After completion, the computer program presents unusual situations to the planner as selectively as possible in the form of lists or tables. The planner will intervene in order to execute appropriate planning measures — perhaps daily or weekly.

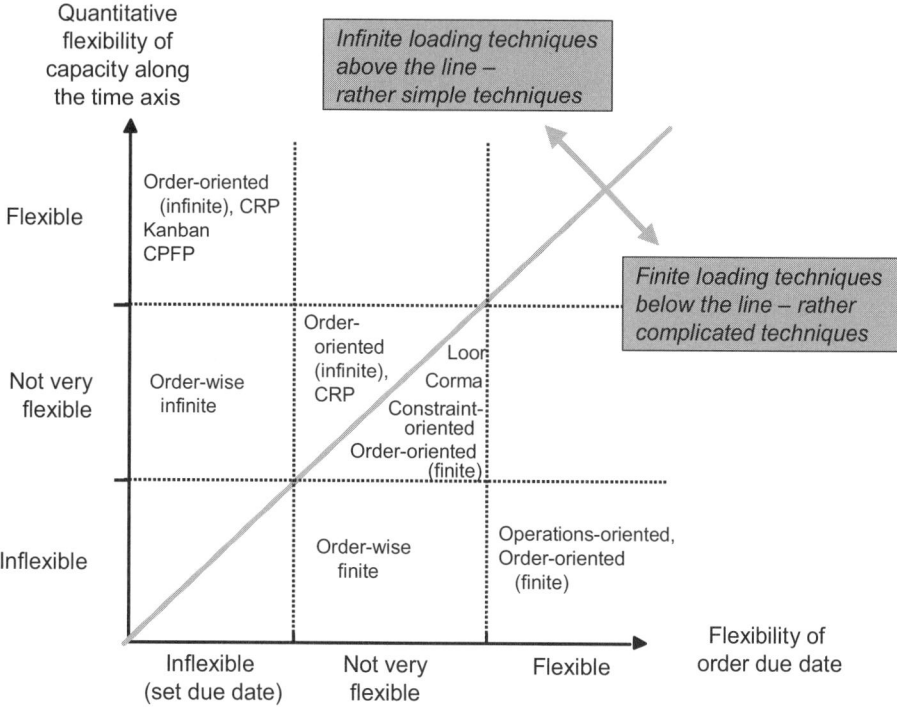

Fig. 4.3.4.1   Classes of techniques for capacity management in dependency upon flexibility of capacity and flexibility of order due date. The abbreviation "CPFP" stands for cumulative production figures principle (see text).

- Note that there are few techniques in the two sectors above and to the right of the bottom left sector. Here, there is no flexibility on one axis and only low flexibility on the other. Thus, there is *little* overall capacity planning flexibility. Planning takes place "order for order" (order-wise). Each new order must be integrated individually into the already planned orders. The planner may, in extreme cases, have to intervene following each operation and change set values for planning (completion date or capacity). Already planned orders may have to be re-planned. This procedure is usually very time consuming and is therefore efficient only for orders with considerable added value.

- Finally, note that there is no technique in the sector at bottom left. Here, there is no flexibility of capacity or due date. As a consequence, there can be none of the required balancing, and the planning problem cannot be resolved.

The following describes infinite loading techniques. Infinite loading is frequently the best capacity planning method. In many companies it is possible to modify labor capacities within one day by more than 50%.

- *Order-oriented infinite loading* aims to achieve a high delivery reliability rate, or to meet the due date for production or procurement orders. Overcapacity is often maintained intentionally for strategic reasons (meeting due dates). After scheduling (backward or forward, for example) all the orders, each scheduled operation represents a load at the specified work center and in the time period containing its start date. The sum of all these loads is compared to the available capacity for each time period. This yields load profiles showing the overcapacity or undercapacity for each work center and time period. The subsequent planning then attempts to balance capacity against load. This commonly used technique for infinite loading is also called *capacity requirements planning (CRP)*, particularly in connection with software for capacity management. There exist also some variations of CRP. See Section 13.2.

- *Kanban* and the *cumulative production figures principle* (CPFP) were introduced above in Section 4.3.2. It is noteworthy that these two simple materials management techniques serve at the same time as simple capacity management techniques. Execution control by the kanban technique is a form of infinite loading, as it assumes a very high level of flexibility of capacity in the immediate term. See Sections 5.3 and 5.4.

- *Order-wise infinite loading* (order for order, individually): For companies handling small numbers of high value-adding orders, such as for the production of special-purpose machines, planning takes place after loading each new order, or even after each new operation. As soon as an overload is detected, all work centers are checked, and load and capacity are adjusted until a feasible schedule is obtained. See Section 13.2.

The following describes finite loading techniques:

- *Operations-oriented finite loading* aims to minimize possible delays in individual operations and thus average potential delay in the entire production order. The individual operations are planned time period by time period on the basis of orders, starting from the start date determined by lead-time scheduling. This means establishing meaningful rules of priority for the sequence in which operations are scheduled (sequencing rules), with the aim of achieving maximum throughput. The queues waiting upstream of the work centers are monitored and adjusted. This type of planning provides a production simulation, that is, an actual working program for the coming days, weeks, or months, according to the planning horizon. See Section 13.3.1.

- *Order-oriented finite loading* ensures that as many orders as possible are executed on time with low levels of goods in process. Orders are scheduled in their entirety, one after the other, in the time periods. The objective is to find priority rules that will enable as many orders as possible to be scheduled. Those orders that cannot be scheduled for completion on time by a computerized algorithm are highlighted for attention by the planner, who may decide to change order completion dates. This technique is a commonly used technique for finite loading. See Section 13.3.2.

- As bottlenecks control the throughput of a production system, *constraint-oriented finite loading* plans orders around bottleneck capacities. It follows a theory of constraints (TOC) approach. An application of this is *drum–buffer–rope*. Work centers feeding bottlenecks should be scheduled at the rate the bottleneck can process. A time buffer inventory should be established before the bottleneck. A space buffer should be established after the bottleneck. Work centers fed by the bottleneck have their throughput controlled by the bottleneck. Another application is the *optimized production technology (OPT) technique*. First, only orders with a minimum batch size are generated. These lots then come together at bottleneck capacities, but are kept separate for the upstream and downstream operations. Then, operations at the bottleneck capacities are scheduled. Operations before the bottleneck are then scheduled backward, while later ones are scheduled forward and planned using normal lead times. See Section 13.3.3.

- *Load-oriented order release (Loor)* has high load as its *primary objective*. Equally important are its *secondary objectives* of low levels of work-in-process, short lead times in the flow of goods, and delivery reliability. The aim of this heuristic technique is to adapt the load to the capacity that is actually available. Thanks to a heuristic, the matching of load to capacity can be limited to one time period. See Section 14.1.2.

- *Capacity-oriented materials management* (Corma) is an operations management principle that enables organizations to play off work-in-process against limited capacity and lead time for customer production orders. Corma makes intelligent use of critical capacity that is available short term, by releasing stock replenishment orders earlier than needed. This in turn provides for optimal sequencing, which reduces set-up time. All in all, Corma follows the natural logic of production management as it is implemented in practice in many medium-sized companies. In principle, stock replenishment orders are viewed as "filler" loadings. The achievement of flexible utilization of capacity demands a price, however, as work-in-process increases. It is important that the total costs for capacity and work-in-process and inventory in stock be kept to a minimum. See Section 14.1.3.

- *Order-wise finite loading* (order for order, individually): In practice, this can be considered to be identical to order-wise infinite loading, with more flexibility in time axis.

All of these techniques can be used independently of company-organizational implementation of planning & control. Thus, they can be found in software packages of many kinds (logistics software or electronic planning boards [Leitstand], simulation software, and so on). In one and the same enterprise, it is quite possible that the company will use different techniques for short-term planning and long-term planning.

4.4   Logistics Business Methods in Research and Development (*)

Planning & control in the research and development area is basically project management. The individual processes do repeat themselves, but always with new products. This section will present some important concepts and methods common to planning & control in this area. The concepts will be treated later in the book only with regard to computer-supported processes (in Section 16.5), so that the material in this section is more extensive than that in Section 4.3 with regard to distribution, production, and procurement.

4.4.1   Integrated Order Processing and Simultaneous Engineering

Time-to-market is the total lead time through research and development logistics for new products. It is the time required for *product innovation*, that is, from product concept to introduction of the product to the market.

Short lead time through research and development is seen today as a strategy towards success. Due to pressure from competitors and the fact that significant product ideas will be made ripe for the market by competitors in a similar way, either at the same time or with only slight delays, just a few months' difference in the time required for research and development can be crucial to the success of a new product. An additional issue is the innovation process within a global network with its requirements of transnational R&D project organization. See [BoGa00].

In addition, there is also the concept of time-to-product:

> *Time-to-product* is the total time required to receive, fill, and deliver an order for an existing (that is entirely developed) product to a customer, timed from the moment that the customer places the order until the moment the customer receives the product.

This definition corresponds to the concept of delivery lead time. More and more, customers demand shorter delivery lead times, not only for products with a solid place in the market that are endlessly repeated, but also for custom orders, such as single-item or non-repetitive (one-of-a-kind) production orders. In many cases, such orders involve some design. Figure 4.1.1.1 shows, for example, the departments such an order (and related design and manufacturing orders) must pass through during processing.

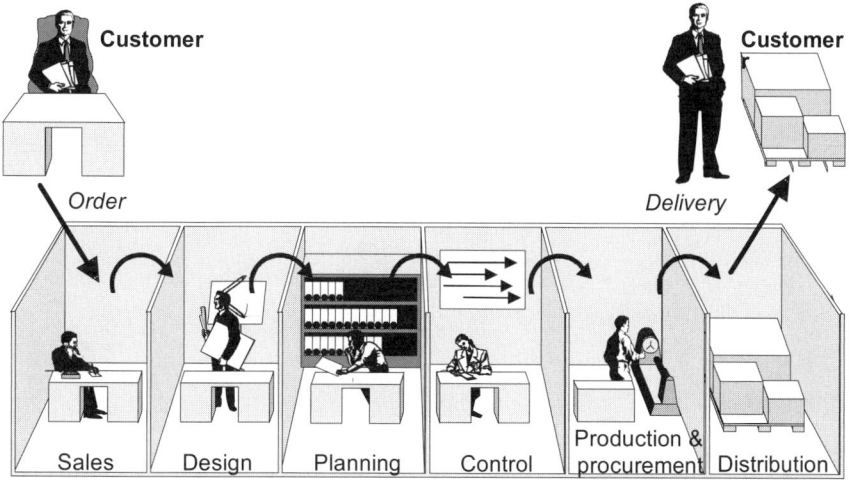

Fig. 4.4.1.1   Order processing of customer orders with specific research and development, production, and procurement (see also [Schö95]).

If the delivery lead time required by the customer allows enough time, most companies tend towards serial processing of the various research and development, production, and procurement orders required by the customer order. Individual departments are informed about the order only when it is passed along by the upstream department. The information available is limited to the original order data and the specifications followed to date, as well as any documents on previous orders that may exist in the department. Similar observations can be made in research and development activities during the time-to-market.

Figures 4.4.1.2 and 4.4.1.3 show how this way of proceeding must change if the customer tolerance time does not allow enough time for serial processing.

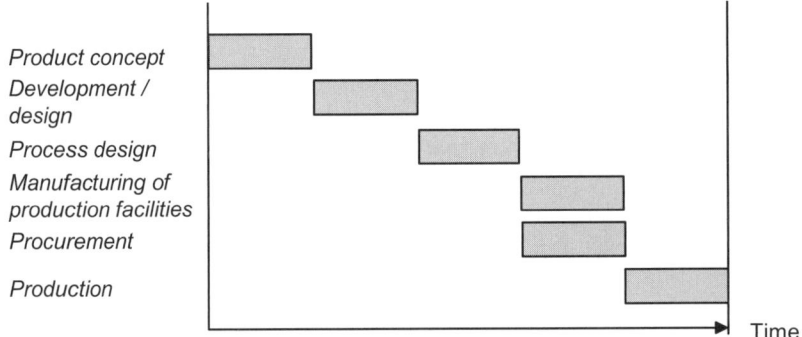

Fig. 4.4.1.2   Order processing via serial processing.

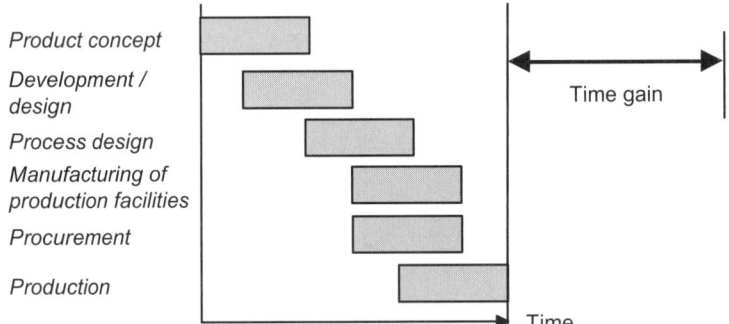

Fig. 4.4.1.3   Time gained through integrated order processing.

Simultaneous engineering, or *concurrent engineering*, or *participative design/engineering* refer to an overlapping of the phases in research and development logistics and, in addition, an overlapping with earlier phases of procurement and production logistics.

For overlapping processing of the individual phases in order processing, there are some prerequisites:

- The walls between the departments shown in Figure 4.4.1.1 must come down. All persons involved in the customer order, whether in sales, development, or production, must be grouped "around the product." This means that the organization must be business-process oriented.

- Integrated order processing is necessary all along the business process. Any site receiving information should immediately make that information available to all others participating in the business process. Computer support systems in individual areas of the company will have to be integrated, so that there will be a common, or at least commonly accessible, database.

Figure 4.4.1.4 shows four aspects of the necessary integration.

Social aspects
- Individual learning and acting
- Cooperative learning and acting

Organizational and management aspects
- Structural organization
- Process organization and control
  - Flow of goods, data, and control

Conceptual (logical) aspects
- Modeling of objects and facts in the system
  - Process, task, and function oriented modeling
  - Data- and object-oriented modeling (facts and rule model)

Technical (physical) aspects
- Memos and files
- Computer-aided databases and document systems
- Hardware / system software / networks

Fig. 4.4.1.4   Four aspects of integrated order processing.

- For rapid business processes, the social and organizational aspects demand appropriate structural organization and process organization. If several organizational units participate in a process, integration means that a unit must process data that another unit will require. The design engineer, for instance, must include data on the blueprints that allow identification for the bill of material. And, conversely, data must be kept on the item that is of relevance to design management. See further discussion in Section 4.4.3.

- The conceptual–logical aspect requires that the content of information systems must be linked in a way that allows the exchange of data or even allows for commonly shared data management.

- The technical–physical aspect demands that the various hardware and software components be linked. For a discussion of this requirement, see Section 16.5.

Such demands are actually not new. In many small- and mid-sized companies work has always been done in this way. This has been the case particularly where there is a large proportion of "one-of-a-kind" production orders, such as in plant and facilities construction or in structural and civil engineering. Companies specializing in these areas have been leaders in the integration of organization and in the integration of their computer-aided information systems as well. See Section 1.4.2 in [Schö01].

4.4.2   Release Control and Engineering Change Control

> *Release and engineering change control (ECC)* is an organizational concept for the process of the design and manufacture of a new product or of a new release of an existing product.

Release control and engineering change control (ECC) coordinate the production or modification of all blueprints, bills of material, routing sheets, and all other common documentation on a product and its manufacture. The procedure is project oriented and *releases, step-wise,* new developments or changes to existing products to production. Figure 4.4.2.1 shows an example with two steps — in this case, between design and production.

Project management of this kind includes the following tasks:

- *Coordination of development and design:* Planning the volume of the release, labeling of all items; Stopping the use of these items for planning & control; Request for change or new concept of products, quality control; Design release of individual items; Design release of all items belonging to the volume of the release.

- *Procedures for production release*: Transfer of bills of material and routing sheets; Release of all items belonging to the volume of the release.

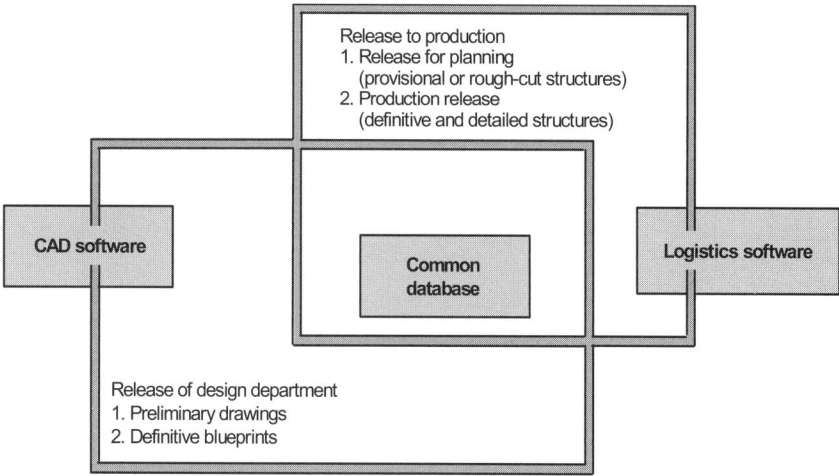

Fig. 4.4.2.1   Step-wise release between design and production.

Step-wise release is particularly important in order to provide for the principle of simultaneous engineering (see Figure 4.4.1.3). As we have seen, simultaneous engineering attempts to overlap individual steps in the product and process conception and to execute product or process conception in an overlapping fashion with the production or procurement of already fixed components. For this reason, we often distinguish between:

- *Rough-cut release for the production of a new development project or a new release:* The data released pertains only to the most important products and rough-cut bills of material and routing sheets. They include the most important components which allows activation of the procurement and production process at lower design structure levels. Depending on work progress, several rough-cut releases are conceivable.

- *Detailed production release with detailed documents:* Project management of the new release ensures that all required documents, such as blueprints, bills of material, routing sheets, and numerical control programs, are available in detailed form. Project management then releases individual items, or all items, to detailed production.

This kind of step-wise release corresponds to common practices in planning & control, which works with various temporal ranges of planning and rough-cut or detailed structures.

Figure 4.4.2.2 presents the different tasks and phases that must be handled by the (systems) engineering (see Section 18.1) for a new product or a new release of a product.

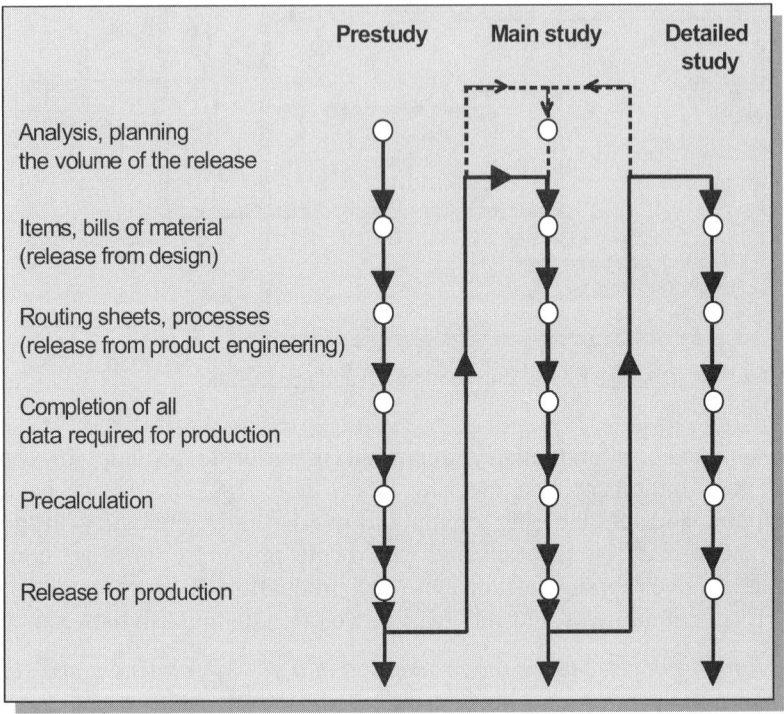

Fig. 4.4.2.2   Procedures in engineering for new product development or a new product release.

Pre study and main study can result in provisional releases, while detailed study leads to final release.

4.4.3   Different Views of the Business Object According to Task

The people involved in a business process generally have different viewpoints with regard to the business objects the process handles. Their particular viewpoints depend on the specific tasks their departments must perform. This becomes very apparent whenever persons are moved from their departments to new forms of organization based on a business-process orientation. Problems in mutual understanding arise immediately, and they can only be overcome by means of appropriate training and qualifications combined with a heavy dose of good will. It is important that such problems are resolved by the time that a common database is created for purposes of integration of computer-aided tools. The business objects described by the data are, after all, often the same, such as end products, components, production facilities, and so on. However, individual viewpoints in terms of use and task result in only partial descriptions of these objects.

For example, the design department will describe a particular, clearly identified item in terms of its geometry, while the manufacturing process development department — in connection with computer-aided production machines — will describe the same item in terms of numerical control techniques. Figure 4.4.3.1 shows another example, the object "operation."

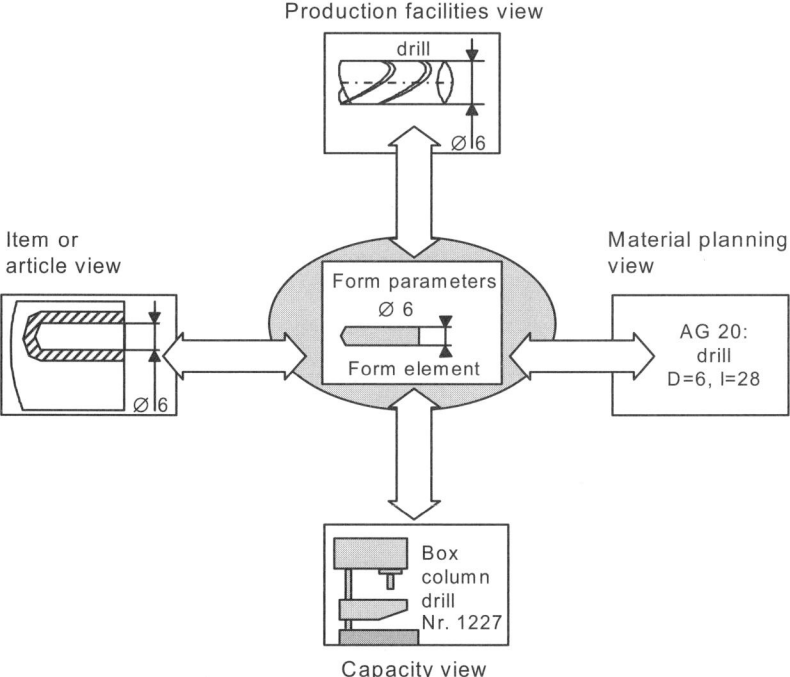

Fig. 4.4.3.1   Examples of different views of a business object (see [Schö95]).

- The item or article viewpoint shows the state and extract of the product to be manufactured according to the operation.

- The material planning aspect gives the order of operations as well as a description of the operation.

- The production facilities view shows the tools or facilities to be used.

- • The capacity viewpoint describes the workstation as a whole at which the operation will be executed.

Figure 4.4.3.2 illustrates the above with objects from design, release control and engineering change control, and planning & control. In many cases, the business objects are identical. Only the points of view differ.

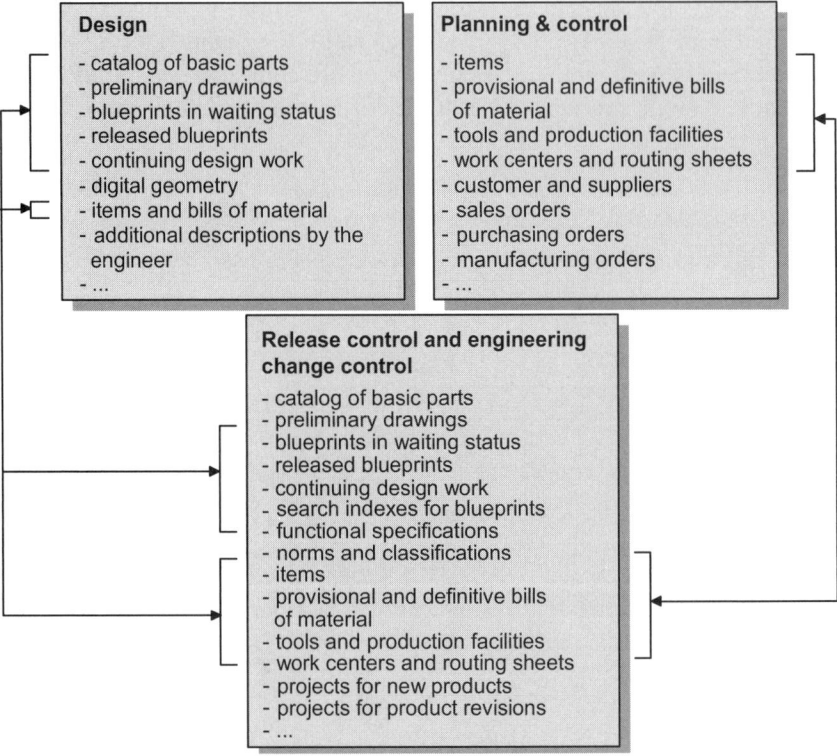

Design

- catalog of basic parts
- preliminary drawings
- blueprints in waiting status
- released blueprints
- continuing design work
- digital geometry
- items and bills of material
- additional descriptions by the engineer
- ...

Planning & control

- items
- provisional and definitive bills of material
- tools and production facilities
- work centers and routing sheets
- customer and suppliers
- sales orders
- purchasing orders
- manufacturing orders
- ...

Release control and engineering change control

- catalog of basic parts
- preliminary drawings
- blueprints in waiting status
- released blueprints
- continuing design work
- search indexes for blueprints
- functional specifications
- norms and classifications
- items
- provisional and definitive bills of material
- tools and production facilities
- work centers and routing sheets
- projects for new products
- projects for product revisions
- ...

Fig. 4.4.3.2   Business objects and attributes in the areas of design, release control and engineering change control, and planning & control.

To integrate business processes within the company, these viewpoints must become linked. All departments require access to data from the other areas. For example:

- • For the sake of cost and flexibility, the design engineer should preferably select for his or her design components that are already being used in the current product family as semifinished goods, single parts, or raw materials (see Section 15.4). To do this, the design engineer needs to have a classification system for items that already exist in the planning & control database.

- Bills of material drawn up by the design department should be automatically entered into the planning & control database in all phases as discussed in Section 4.4.2.

- Conversely, when production orders are released, planning & control may request blueprints from design in order to add them to the work documents. With parametrically described items, all necessary parameter values on the customer order are passed along to the design department, so that it may create new blueprints according to the parameters for a specific order.

In spite of these differing viewpoints, can the same business objects be represented applicably and comprehensively for all the departments? While there is usually no great difficulty in agreeing upon the definition of the objects, this is not the case for attributes of the objects, for attributes contain the actual information. The same content of information may be represented from the one viewpoint with two attributes, but from another aspect the information may be represented by three or four attributes. Redundant listings of attributes are generally not a reasonable solution, because this leads to consistency problems when modifying the data. Only a common definition reached by everyone involved in the business process can remedy the matter. This serves again to underline the importance of choosing an appropriate form of structural organization that is oriented towards business processes.

4.4.4   The Concept of Computer-Integrated Manufacturing

CIM (computer-integrated manufacturing) is understood as a concept for information technology support of integrated business processes, based on the integration of the total manufacturing organization through information technology (IT).

Figure 4.4.4.1 shows the areas to be integrated in an earlier form of representation that later became the well-known CIM "Y" (see [Sche95]).

- Integration of design- and product-related areas (the operations–technological process chain)

- Integration of production-related areas (the operations–planning process chain)

- Integration of the two operational process chains themselves and with processes in the areas of company management, planning, and administration (the strategic, planning, and administrative process chains)

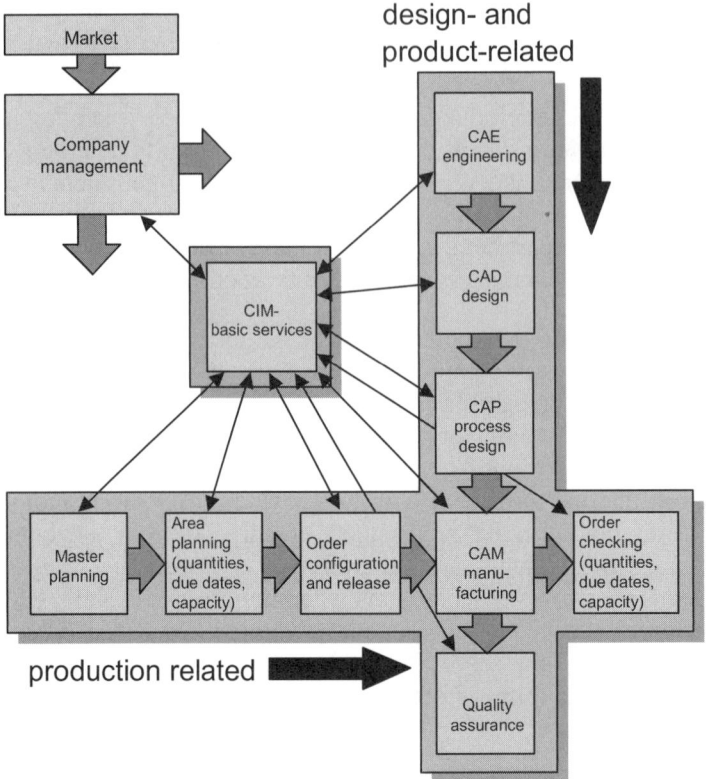

Fig. 4.4.4.1   The CIM concept: an overview.

The following computer-aided technologies are used in areas related to design and product:

- *CAE (computer-aided engineering)*: Computer tools to generate and test specifications, used in the product development phase.

- *CAD (computer-aided design)*: Computer tools to design and draw.

- *CAP (computer-aided process design)*: Computer assistance in defining production processes/routing sheets as well as in programming numerically controlled machines, facilities, and robots.

- *CAM (computer-aided manufacturing)*: The use of computers to program, direct, and control manufacturing through numerically controlled machines, robots, or entire flexible work cells.

- *CAQ (computer-aided quality assurance)*: Computer-aided quality assurance of the manufacturing process.

In production-related areas, there exist the following technologies:

- Computer-based planning & control systems, often called in shorthand logistics software or PPC software, refer to Chapter 8
- Computer-aided costing

Utilizing computer-aided information technology presents a challenge in itself to each of the areas of the organization. Moreover, all the various "CIM islands," or CIM components (the "CAs," or logistics software and costing), are now supposed to be integrated. See here Section 16.5.

4.5   Current State of Knowledge of Logistics Management (*)

4.5.1   Historical Overview

Due to demands for quality, short lead times, and flexibility, production methods and logistics have become linked. This is true in all kind of supply chains, both within a company and transcorporate. On the one hand, the processes transforming goods have a strong influence on the choice of logistics systems and on their efficiency — for example, on lead times. On the other hand, from the management point of view, it is not enough to aim for a zero-defect rate in the product-transforming production process if, at the same time, an defect rate of 30% can be expected in the logistical surround of sales, production, and purchasing. Warehousing and transport, moreover, are viewed increasingly as non-value-adding part processes to be avoided. There is a trend towards continuing production during these part processes, in that, for example, some stage of processing will be executed during transport. It is no longer possible to differentiate strictly between processes of logistics in the narrow sense and processes of production. For this reason, they must be designed and improved in a comprehensive manner.

The planning & control techniques proposed through the course of many decades stressed at the time one target area of a company's performance in Section 1.3.1 over others. This was not due simply to fashions and trends within the companies (microeconomy), but rather was mainly due to the macroeconomic surround, the requirements of national economic conditions.

Following World War II, for example, there was a worldwide demand for new — mainly material — goods, both consumer and investment goods. As at the same time financial means and capacity were short, emphasis was placed on quality and good capacity utilization. Traditionally, this meant serial production, combined with automation in highly specialized part processes in production (Taylorism). This achieved the best possible depreciation of the high costs of procuring machinery. The priority of the target area of *high capacity utilization* was faced with large inventory and long lead times. For the planning & control of operational business processes, therefore, techniques had to be developed that would control large and numerous warehouses and long lead times of orders with the aim to achieve high-capacity utilization. Techniques perfected in the 1950s, 1960s, and 1970s in connection with computer support are still used today whenever similar economic conditions reign.

The scene remained relatively constant until around 1975, when a most fundamental and increasingly rapid change set in. The reasons for the shift can be found in several parallel developments:

- The first far-reaching effects of the post-war boom suddenly changed previous conditions. Utilized capacity no longer stood in the foreground, but was replaced by shorter delivery lead times and delivery reliability, smaller inventories, and thus greater turnover. This was meant to increase liquidity at the same time as decreasing the risk of unsaleable products. In the 1980s, this tendency was magnified by more rapid cycles of development and marketing. The customer as "king" demanded more and more products that would resolve his specific problems. Serial production decreased to make way for more multiple variant products.

- Industrial production shifted increasingly to locations previously insignificant, especially to Asia. Development and production processes were viewed from a different mental perspective. Not least thanks to a different kind of readiness of workers in those countries, different planning and particularly control methods were possible. Successes achieved in terms of reduced lead times, small work-in-process inventories, and self-regulating principles began to reach Europe and North America.

- Mid-sized, and later even small, companies bought their own computer capacity, thanks to an enormous improvement in the cost effectiveness of computer hardware. This was also true for companies that worked in small-sized and single-item production whose basis of existence was fulfillment of special customer requirements. These users discovered that the program packages available for planning & control had not been developed for their needs. Optimized manual solutions for operational organization in these companies turned out to be a treasure chest of ideas for innovation in the form of improved or even novel techniques in computer-aided planning & control.

4.5.2 The Problem of Knowledge Continuity and the Role of APICS

Since the 1970s there has been an observable, growing gulf between needs in the real world of practice on the one side, and theories and methods on the other. Initially, theories and methods had been developed in the field, but more and more development and improvement became the realm of universities and large computer companies. Unfortunately, the tie to the pragmatically oriented user, acting in real practice, became ever weaker. Over time, practitioners set themselves in opposition to the theorists and began to develop their own methods that corresponded to their needs. The situation, highly charged with emotion, led to a split or gulf between the needs of the user and the theories that had been developed, as Figure 4.5.2.1 illustrates.

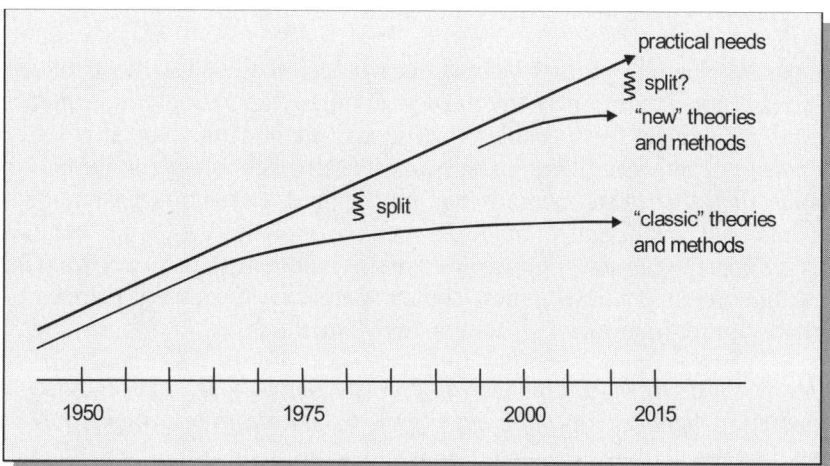

Fig. 4.5.2.1   The drift of theories and methods away from needs of the world of practice.

As a result, "new" theories and methods proliferated. Some of these moved gradually into the foreground as a result of clever or massive marketing efforts and the efforts of consulting companies. Characteristic of all these methods, principles, and thought patterns marketed with catchwords and slogans is that they sold themselves as new alternatives to inadequate earlier products. This development was magnified by the fact that scientists came under pressure to "publish or perish" and to produce new findings.

In many cases, close examination proves that the knowledge presented as "new" actually addressed issues that earlier theories and methods treated in a much more comprehensive theoretical manner. It is just that now they turn up in a more current and fitting practical surround, and they present themselves from a practical-applications perspective. The danger is that lots of knowledge will be constantly found anew. This underlines the fact that earlier findings were not transmitted to the new generation very successfully, thus representing a lack of knowledge transfer.

The tendency towards drift between the needs of practice and theoretical research and the development of methods results in a fundamental problem for research in applied areas. At some point there is always the danger that applied research will begin to develop into basic research. This is positive in and of itself, up to the point when basic research loses contact with ever-changing practical applications (or no longer finds it necessary to take changes in practical application through time into account). The chasm is all too often filled with novelties that represent nothing more than the reinvention of the wheel.

To ensure that the split does not ever reoccur, all sides must take on responsibility. Practitioners involved in company operational management should not neglect to study the "traditional" methods developed in earlier decades. For one thing, it is always possible that economic conditions will change such that those methods will be required. For another, some niche markets and even entire branches behave exactly the same as ever. Furthermore, classical principles often suddenly provide valuable contributions to solutions in new contexts, and they frequently reappear — perhaps in modified forms — within "new" methods.

It is not possible to emphasize strongly enough the importance of cooperation between research/development endeavors and those "on the shop floors" of industry. It is the responsibility of companies to make available the resources necessary for such cooperation. Research and development firms and institutes, for their part, have a responsibility to conduct their projects directly within the companies, so that there, at the pulse of activity, they will become versed not only in creative and systematic thinking, but also in creative and systematic action. In this way it will be possible not only to be in command of the current state of knowledge, but also to apply it to new situations and adapt it accordingly. Innovation can occur at the right location, namely at frontiers new to science, and the knowledge base will expand organically. This would spell success in meeting the challenge of conserving knowledge as well as — and more importantly — transmitting it to the next generation.

It is here that *APICS*, the American Association for Operations Management (the former American Production and Inventory Control Society), has an important role to play. This society of business people maintains the body of knowledge on planning & control in logistics and trains people from everywhere in the world. Concerned with standardization of the MRP II concept, APICS must integrate the additional concepts as shown in Figure 3.5.3.1 into the body of knowledge in a timely fashion. This cannot be done without also taking a critical look at, and changing, the existing knowledge base. This process is rather slow, but it is important to remember that standardization endeavors do not anticipate new developments in a field, but rather make them comprehensible.

European societies associated with APICS have joined to form the *FEPIMS* (Federation of European Production and Industrial Management Societies). The very choice of the term *management* in the name of the European federation, rather than the original *control*, is an indication of the continual changes being made in interpretations of the current body of knowledge.

4.5.3   New Trends and Challenges

Polarization in many areas of life has characterized recent times. Trouble-free, effortless patent remedies promised instant success. Production and its management were neglected, as even industrial companies increasingly achieved company success on the stock market — with dramatic speed and profit. Production lost its shine. From the sales perspective, it could not be fast enough, and from the financial perspective not cheap enough.

This proved to be fertile soil for the growth of "success prophets." The new techniques soon found avid champions and advocators: Each new technique for the production area could after all — at least potentially — strengthen production's position relative to finance and sales. New techniques are attractive *a priori*, because blame for failure can be placed on the insufficient techniques of the past. Unfortunately, the new techniques also prove to have their shortcomings:

- Heuristic techniques prove to be only more or less "clever": they hit upon the process to be simulated with better or worse success.

- Analytic methods are not comprehensive enough. They take insufficient account of real factors and parameters.

- The methods function only under certain company prerequisites, such as certain product, order, or personnel structures.

Glorified methods also lose steam if recession occurs. The choice of planning & control methods then has limited influence on company success.

Uncertainty has also developed in recent years on the academic front. Supporters of particular methods began to advocate that method as the best and only choice and so came into conflict with fellow researchers making the same claims for other methods. As a result, polemics and trench warfare have entered into the literature and the universities. Under these conditions, how can logistics and planning & control be studied with attention to the core matter in an atmosphere of relaxed communication? We need to have the insight that all methods do indeed work under certain conditions, but that under differing conditions they may turn out to be faulty. They may even turn out to be wrong in a strictly formal sense. Why are no overall valid methods found? As mentioned above, many aspects in the temporal behavior of the market and the production process can be determined at best qualitatively — and can certainly not be captured in quantitative data. In addition, the number of parameters relevant to planning & control is so large that the parameters can simply not be handled with exact algorithms. One method may handle a particular part well, while a second method is well suited to deal with another.

Moreover, even sub-optimal methods, applied consistently in everyday operations, have often brought about no worse results. A method may be called outdated, a dinosaur, but besides being inexact it may be robust. Such methods often do a better job than methods that are precise, offer safeguards at all ends, but are applicable only if whole sets of prerequisites are met (non-robust). It is important to compare all methods and apply them to the concrete company situation. Frequently, method knowledge that has been gathered in a certain connection will suddenly prove applicable in a very different context, perhaps in modified or expanded form. This has proved to be a source of ideas for innovation and improvement in the management of logistics systems.

Another problem lies in people's expectations of what planning & control software can do (see Chapter 8). Logistics software has not been used in an optimum way not least due to the false hope that computer aids can solve organizational problems — and all the human problems connected with them — without the company having to deal with such issues. However, planning & control can only be supported by information technology if — were resources in time and personnel unlimited — it could also be performed manually. That is why planning & control must be defined first as a company-internal and external system. Organizational processes, that is, operational organization, must first be studied and determined *completely* and *precisely* before any decisions can be made as to possible types of computer support.

This requirement has been emphasized clearly for decades. Approaches such as *total quality management* (TQM) or *business process reengineering* demand that, as a first step, business processes be rethought, so that structural or operational organization can be changed if necessary. Redefined organizational units may result that reflect differences in the requirements of their logistics systems. Only then can sensible decisions be made about information technology support. The software implemented can even vary from organizational unit to unit. In such a case, the software would probably be of a simpler type than "integral," comprehensive software designed to serve all units of an organization. Of course, each of the individual software program packages would have to — in a CIM sense — be able to communicate with all other programs in the entire logistics network.

All this underscores the need for qualified employees. Engineers and economists must have a good command of methods applied in logistics, planning & control, and ultimately logistics software. Thorough understanding of these methods will allow them to make competent decisions and, if required, to design the necessary software. Qualified employees are also less susceptible to the polarizing propaganda of proponents of certain methods or logistics software sales representatives. The knowledge that qualified employees possess will also supply them with the necessary factual arguments if faced with the polemics of sales and finance departments, and they will be able to make logistics improvements transparent as well as to justify clearly the remaining lead times and costs.

4.6   Summary

Operational business processes of planning & control in the MRP II/ERP concept can be classified as long, medium, or short term. There is an additional distinction between rough-cut and detailed planning. The tasks involved in the business processes are demand forecasting, bid processing and order configuration; resource management; and order release, order coordination, and order checking, as well as delivery and billing. The processes and tasks are shown in a reference model.

An important subtask of master planning is sales and operations planning and resource requirements planning. In the case of rough-cut planning, sales and operations planning produces an aggregate plan, which is a plan based on aggregated information (such as rough-cut business objects like product families, rough-cut product structures, gross requirement) rather than on detailed product information. This allows quick calculation of different possible variants of the production plan.

Another important subtask of master planning is master scheduling and rough-cut capacity planning. This task involves more effort, for the master production schedule (MPS) is the disaggregated version of a production plan, expressed in specific products, configurations, quantities, and dates. The appropriate level for scheduling — end products or assemblies — has to be chosen. Rough-cut capacity planning is a means to control the feasibility of the MPS. In addition, available-to-promise (ATP) verifies whether the actual customer demand can be covered by the MPS.

Customer blanket orders and blanket orders to suppliers are important instruments of planning & control in logistics networks. These agreements set intervals for delivery dates and order quantities. In their most non-binding form, they are purely forecasts. The intervals will be made more precise with decreasing temporal range. In the short term, precise short-range blanket orders replace blanket orders. Their quantities are set, and delivery dates will be set and confirmed by blanket releases as this becomes possible.

Business methods for detailed planning and scheduling as well as for execution and control of operations, include — in the area of distribution, production, and procurement — tasks in materials management, scheduling, and capacity management. In materials management, techniques are classed as deterministic or stochastic. Scheduling and capacity management should be integrated, because capacity can generally not be stored. In dependency upon the quantitative flexibility of capacity as well as the flexibility of the order due date, techniques can be classed as infinite and finite loading. Individual techniques, however, handle either quantity (capacity) or time (dates).

Business methods of planning & control in the area of research and development in essence comprise project management. Of particular interest here is the integration of the various tasks all along the business process — even overlapping execution (simultaneous engineering) — both during the time to market and time to product. The different viewpoints of all those involved in the business object make integration difficult. The concept of CIM treats information technology support of integrated business processes. Here, logistics software and the "CAs" (CAE, CAD, etc.) should be linked together.

Recently the market environment has had an increasing influence on logistics and planning & control. Moreover, examination of the historical development of recent decades reveals that transmitting knowledge from one generation to the next is a difficult problem. This problem cannot be handled in the realm of facts and knowledge alone.

4.7   Keywords

4.8   Scenarios and Exercises

4.8.1   Master Scheduling and Product Variants

Your company produces scissors for left- and right-handed customers. While both models have the same blades, the handles differ. Blade and handle are assembled after you have received customer orders. You can assume that approximately 12% of your customers are left-handed. If you produce 100 blades, how many handles for each type of scissors should you produce?

Solution:

Since the actual option percentage is not known in advance, overplanning in the master production schedule (MPS) is necessary to cover the uncertainty. A safety demand of 25% would result in $12 * 1.25 = 15$ handles for left-handled scissors and $88 * 1.25 = 110$ handles for right-handed scissors to be produced. Because only 100 blades are produced, it makes no sense to have more than 100 handles of either type. Thus, a good decision would be to produce 15 handles for left and 100 handles for right-handed scissors.

4.8.2 Available-to-Promise (ATP)

Sales employees in your company would like to know whether their customers' orders for can openers can be fulfilled or not. In long-term planning for the next half-year, you have put up the master production schedule provided below. Furthermore, your sales department has given you a list of customers' orders that have already been promised. At the beginning of the year, you have 800 can openers in stock.

Master Production Schedule:

January	February	March	April	May	June
600	600	600	600	450	450

Promised orders: 1200 pieces on February 14, 1400 pieces on April 5, 450 pieces on June 10.

a. How many can openers can your sales employees promise to customers in the next six months? (Assume that the amount planned to be produced in the master production schedule is available at the beginning of each month.)

b. Is the master production schedule feasible?

c. On January 7, a customer asks for 600 can openers to be delivered instantly. How do you react?

Solution:

a.

		January	February	March	April	May	June
Master production schedule		600	600	600	600	450	450
Allocated to customer orders			1200		1400		450
Inventory available	800	1400	800	1400	600	1050	1050
Cumulative ATP		600	600	600	600	1050	1050

b. Yes, because in each period cumulative ATP is greater zero.

c. Though the amount the customer asks for is generally available, fulfilling this order would mean that the company would not be able to accept any further orders for four months, from January to April. Your decision will depend on how likely it is that this would result in the loss of long-term customers.

4.8.3 Theory of Constraints

You produce two products A and B, which use the machine capacity of your production according to the following table:

Machine / Product	I	II	III
A		1.5 hours	2.0 hours
B	1.6 hours	1.0 hours	

a. If per working day (eight hours), you start producing three products A and five products B, what will happen? What will the buffer in front of machine II look like after one week (five working days)? What measures do you suggest to take if you cannot invest any money?

b. A consulting firm offers to speed up your machines, so that the time it takes to machine any product is reduced by a quarter of an hour. To which machine would you apply this measure first, to which next? (Your only objective is to increase the amount of production.)

Solution:

a. The capacity of machine II is not sufficient: (3 * 1.5 hours) + (5 * 1.0 hours) = 9.5 hours. Therefore, the buffer in front of machine II will fill with the speed of 1.5 hours of workload per day, which is equivalent to five products A per week. To reduce work-in-progress, the company should decide to release less production orders, e.g., for two products A and five products B, per working day only.

b. The bottleneck is machine II, so it would be desirable to increase its speed. After implementing the consulting firm's measures, the work on products A and B takes (3 * 1.25 hours) + (5 * 0.75 hours) = 7.5 hours. Machine I with a workload of 5 * 1.6 hours = 8 hours will become the new bottleneck.

4.8.4 Master Planning Case

On the basis of a long-term sales plan of a company in the wood industry, your task — with regard to resource management — will be to work out various variants of the production plan and inventory plan as well as the resulting procurement plan.

The case: The Planing Co. manufactures wood paneling in many different variants. Variants occur, of course, in the dimensions, but also in the profiled edges and the wood finishes. The company offers panels in both natural wood and in painted finishes. The Planing Co. has only one timber supplier, Forest Clear Co. in Finland.

As manager of the Planing Co., you are faced with the task of producing a master schedule for one year in preparation for a management meeting tomorrow morning. You are expected to provide information on capacity load and, in addition, on the quantities of raw material to be procured from your timber supplier.

Your job is to do the planning only for the four most important final products in Planing Co.'s varied product assortment. These four products are shown in Figure 4.8.4.1 below and fall into two product segments: painted finish panels (panel "tradition") or natural wood panels (bio panel).

Product segment	End product	width	length	height
Panel "tradition"	Top finish (profile 4)	97 mm	5 m	20 mm
Panel "tradition"	Top resin (profile 9)	97 mm	5 m	13 mm
Bio panel	Nordic spruce (profile 4)	97 mm	5 m	20 mm
Bio panel	Nordic spruce (profile 9)	97 mm	5 m	13 mm

Fig. 4.8.4.1   Final products requiring master planning.

These panels, already precut to size, are planed down to specific profiled panels at a number of processing centers. As Figure 4.8.4.2 shows, during the planing process there is a material loss of 3 mm to the width and of 2 mm to the height of a precut panel.

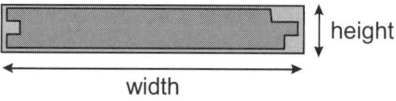
height

width

Fig. 4.8.4.2   Profiled edge of a finished panel.

The Planing Co. has machines to plane down the precut panels to specific profiled panels for a total of 2.7 million square meters of precut panels per year. The capacity unit, which comprises several machines, is given as square meters of material to be planed. You can assume that the same amount of material is processed every month.

a. *Production and inventory plan:* You will base your master planning on available data in the cumulative sales plan for the next 12 months (see Figure 4.8.4.3):

Product family	End product	Sales plan, June – Nov. (m²)					
		June	July	Aug.	Sept.	Oct.	Nov.
Panel "tradition"	Top finish (profile 4)	62,085	65,269	46,166	76,413	85,964	63,6
Panel "tradition"	Top resin (profile 9)	59,943	63,017	44,573	73,776	82,998	61,4
Bio panel	Nordic spruce (profile 4)	48,969	51,480	36,413	60,269	67,803	50,2
Bio panel	Nordic spruce (profile 9)	70,392	74,002	52,343	86,637	97,466	72,1

Product family	End product	Sales plan, Dec. – May (m²)					
		Dec.	Jan.	Feb.	Mar.	Apr.	May
Panel "tradition"	Top finish (profile 4)	41,390	42,982	52,534	58,901	50,942	63,6
Panel "tradition"	Top resin (profile 9)	39,962	41,499	50,721	56,869	49,184	61,4
Bio panel	Nordic spruce (profile 4)	32,646	33,901	41,435	46,457	40,179	50,2
Bio panel	Nordic spruce (profile 9)	46,928	48,733	59,563	66,783	57,758	72,1

Fig. 4.8.4.3   Sales plan for the next 12 months.

Taking into account the loss of material during the planing process, calculate the load profile according to Figure 1.2.4.2 and enter it into Figure 4.8.4.4. Discuss the result: Is there sufficient capacity?

Based on the load profile, create for the four products the following three variants of the production plan and enter them into Figure 4.8.4.4:

1. Each month the quantity produced is exactly the planned load that results from the planned demand. As a result, no inventory stock is produced, but costs are engendered for quantitative flexibility of capacity (see the definition in Section 3.4.3).

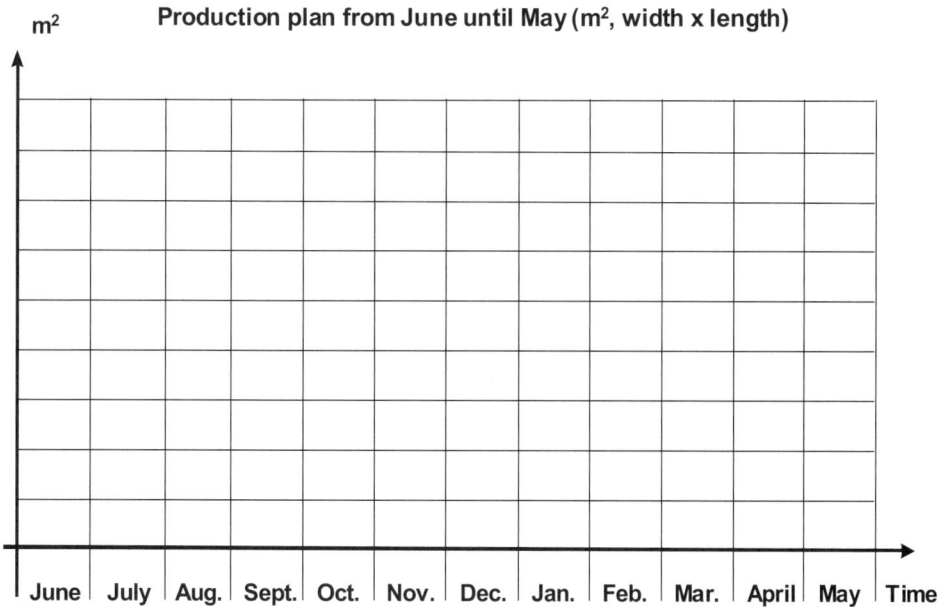

Fig. 4.8.4.4   Production plan for the next 12 months.

2. Each month the quantity produced is the average load. Fluctuations in demand have to be covered by inventory. To assure delivery reliability, initial inventory stocks of 180,000 m^2 must be carried (for the sake of simplicity, assume that there is appropriate inventory for all four final products). However, no costs arise for quantitative flexibility of capacity.

3. Half of the capacity is adapted to the load. This means that each month, the quantity produced is one-half the difference between planned load (that results from the planned demand) and the average load. To assure delivery reliability, initial inventory stocks of 90,000 m^2 must be held. Again, costs are engendered for quantitative flexibility of capacity, but the costs are lower than in variant 1, above.

Conduct a qualitative comparison of the total costs of the three solutions above, by comparing the following two aspects:

*   Inventory carrying cost:
    *   Unit cost: $2 per m^2
    *   Annual carrying cost rate: 30%

- Costs for flexibility of capacity:
  - Labor cost: $1 per m^2
  - Flexibility percentage required =
    (maximum monthly load – average load) / average load
  - Flexibility costs = flexibility percentage * labor cost per year

b. *Procurement plan:* The management at Forest Clear Co. has asked you to give them a rough estimate of the quantity of raw material that Planing Co. will order from them in the next 12 months. As upper management at Planing Co. has just recently decided to build a partnership relationship with this timber supplier, they expect you to respond to Forest Clear by tomorrow at the latest. Your answer will depend on which of the three variants of the production plan that you decide is the best.

The raw material, the timber, is the same for all four final products. It is procured and calculated in units of cubic meters. However, as Forest Clear supplies boards of 100-mm width, 50-mm height, and 5-m length only, Planing Co. has to cut the boards to precut panels (see Figure 4.8.4.1) before the precut panels can be planed. Due to the dimensions of the final products, two to three precut panels can be obtained from each raw board (see Figure 4.8.4.5). The raw material must be available in the same month as the final products.

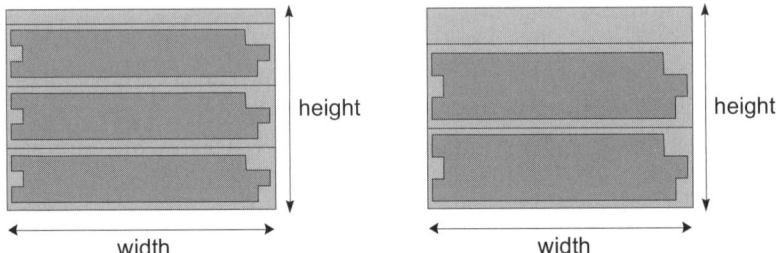

Fig. 4.8.4.5   Possible ways to cut the raw boards into panels.

Create a formula for calculating the raw material requirements for a given production plan. *Hint:* Derive the quantity of raw material in cubic meters (the wood boards) in dependency upon the specific final product, which is given in units of square meters. Company management is only interested in the total raw material requirements per month in Figure 4.8.4.6 (the raw material requirement per product is important only to establish the subtotals).

Raw material requirement for product	Procurement plan June – Nov. (m²)					
	June	July	Aug.	Sept.	Oct.	Nov.
Top finish (profile 4)						
Top resin (profile 9)						
Nordic spruce (profile 4)						
Nordic spruce (profile 9)						
Total raw material requirement						

Raw material requirement for product	Procurement plan, Dec. – May (m²)					
	Dec.	Jan.	Feb.	Mar.	Apr.	May
Top finish (profile 4)						
Top finish (profile 9)						
Nordic spruce (profile 4)						
Nordic spruce (profile 9)						
Total raw material requirement						

Fig. 4.8.4.6   Procurement plan: raw material requirements.

Solution:

a.   The average load per month is about 237,000 m², exceeding slightly the capacity available of 225,000 m². Therefore, overtime of about 5% will be necessary to fulfill the demand (about 2,844,000 m² per year).

- Variant 1 results in flexibility costs of about $1,300,000. The maximum load is in October (about 345,000 m²); its production requires a flexibility percentage of $(345,000 - 237,000)/237,000 = 46\%$.

- Variant 2 of the production plan (production of 237,000 m² each month) results in a carrying cost of about $80,000. Carrying cost is calculated in the basis of the inventories at the beginning of each of the 12 months in the inventory plan.

- Variant 3 results in a carrying cost of about $40,000 and flexibility costs of about $650,000. Maximum production is in October (about 291,000 m²), which requires a flexibility percentage of $(291,000 - 237,000)/237,000 = 23\%$.

You can view the solution, implemented with Flash animation, on the Internet at URL:

http://www.intlogman.lim.ethz.ch/master_planning.html

For all calculations, click on the "calculate" icon.

- Variants between the two extremes of Variant 1 and Variant 2 — as well as the variants themselves — can be produced by entering a value for alpha between 1 and 0 in the formula Av + alpha * (Load$_i$ – Av), where Av is the average load. Load$_i$ is the planned load that results from the planned demand.

- To calculate the costs of each variant, the parameters for carrying cost and flexibility cost can be changed:

b. For Variant 2 of the production plan, production per month will be one-twelfth of the total annual demand. This results in raw material requirements of about 4900 m^3 per month.

A mouse click on the icon "go to procurement plan" takes you to calculation of the procurement plan for the chosen variant; once there, click on "calculate." The upper section shows the production plan for all variants; the lower section shows the raw material requirements. Run the mouse over the product identification numbers in the left-most column to see whether two to three precut panels can be cut out of a raw board.

To create another variant of the production plan, you can click again on the icon "return to production plan" and the raw material requirement can be calculated for that plan as well.

5 The Lean / Just-in-Time Concept and Repetitive Manufacturing

In the 1970s, the seller's market changed to a buyer's market in many branches of the capital goods market. As a consequence, the weighting of company objectives (see Section 1.3.1) changed from stressing best possible capacity utilization to a focus on short delivery lead times. At the same time, however, companies had to avoid physical inventory. Inventory proved to be increasingly risky, because technological advances turned goods into non-sellers often overnight. Thus, *short lead time* became a strategy towards success in entrepreneurial competition.

To handle all of these aspects, concepts were developed — mainly in Japan — and grouped together under the term just-in-time, or JIT (pronounced as one word). More recently, the contents of JIT were re-launched under the new catchphrase "lean." Lean/JIT aims towards the fastest possible flow of goods while eliminating waste of resources.

The lean / just-in-time concept has advantages for all other concepts and all characteristics of planning & control in Section 3.5.3. For this reason, we will give the methods associated with the just-in-time philosophy preferential treatment. The well-known and simple production and purchase control technique in this connection is the *kanban technique*. Kanban, however, takes care of only short-term planning & control and can be used only in production or procurement with frequent order repetition – that is, in the manufacture of standard products, if need be with a few options.

The Lean/JIT concept is not only an aid but is indeed a prerequisite for efficient use of all simple planning & control techniques in logistics. Figure 5.0.0.1 shows some of the characteristic features of planning & control, taken from Section 3.4. The values of the features as arranged from left to right correspond to an increasing degree of the suitability for simple techniques of planning & control in logistics. On the table showing the most important features, the characteristic value is marked with a black background.

Simple techniques of planning & control are therefore particularly well-suited for manufacture of standard products, if need be with a few options, and thus for *repetitive manufacturing*. As kanban and the cumulative production figures principle are probably the most easily understood control techniques, they are discussed here in Part A. Moreover, the two techniques are techniques for short-term planning of materials, schedules, and capacity, whereby capacity must adapt to load. For long-term planning in these cases, methods appropriate to the MRP II concept (see Section 4.2) are used. If medium-term planning is necessary at all, methods will correspond to simple techniques of long-term planning.

Features referring to user and product or product family					
Feature	➽	**Values**			
Frequency of customer demand	➽	unique	Discontinuous (lumpy, sporadic)	regular	continuous (steady)
Product variety concept	➽	according to (changing) customer specification	product family with many variants	product family	standard product with options	individual or standard product

Features referring to logistics and production resources					
Feature	➽	**Values**			
Production environment	➽	engineer-to-order	make-to-order	assemble-to-order (from single parts)	assemble-to-order (from assemblies)	make-to-stock
Quantitative flexibility of capacity	➽	not flexible in terms of time		hardly flexible in terms of time		flexible in terms of time

Features referring to production or procurement order					
Feature	➽	**Values**			
Reason for order release (type of order)	➽	demand / (customer production (or procurement) order)		prediction / (forecast order)		use (stock replenishment order)
Frequency of order repetition	➽	production / procurement without order repetition		production / procurement with infrequent order repetition		production / procurement with frequent order repetition

Increasing degree of suitability for simple techniques of planning & control

Fig. 5.0.0.1   Degree of suitability for the simple techniques of planning & control.[1]

---

[1]   The horizontal distribution of the values in the morphological scheme indicates their relation to the increasing degree according to the given criterion.

5.1 Characterizing Lean / Just-in-Time and Repetitive Manufacturing

5.1.1 Just-in-Time and Jidoka – Increasing Productivity Through Eliminating Waste

The origin of the Just-in-Time concept is in the Toyota Production System.

> The *Toyota Production System* (TPS) is a framework of concepts and methods for increasing productivity and quality.

Increased productivity is to be achieved primarily by eliminating waste.

> *Waste* (Jap. *"muda"*) is seen as all activities in development and manufacturing within the entire supply chain, extending to and including the consumer, that are non-value-adding from the customer's point of view.[2]

Waste includes unnecessary inventory, wait times, moving activities, and physical work not suited to human beings. See here also [Ohno88].

Just-in-Time and Jidoka are the two pillars of the Toyota Production System.

> The *Jidoka concept* comprises approaches and techniques for immediately halting production when abnormal conditions occur.

Jidoka therefore is aimed at the elimination of production of defective products by building quality into the production process. This way of thinking stems from 1902, when Sakichi Toyoda, who later founded the Toyota Motor Corporation, patented a device to stop a weaving loom as soon as a thread broke. This prevented the weaving of defective fabrics and allowed operators to fix the problem itself, strand breakage, as soon as possible. Section 17.2.5 shows some of the techniques of the Jidoka concept.

> The *just-in-time (JIT) concept* encompasses a certain set of approaches, methods, and techniques for planned elimination of all waste. The primary elements are to have only the required inventory when needed; to improve

---

[2]   *Value-added from the customer's view* is the benefit view . This is different than value-adding from the view of company accounting, or costs view. See Sections 3.1.2 and 15.1.4.

quality to zero defects; to reduce lead times by reducing setup times, queue times, and lot sizes; and to incrementally revise the operations themselves. See [APIC04].

The just-in-time concept thus increases the potential for short delivery lead times, for all types of production and for many service lines of business.[3]

The terms *stockless production* or *zero inventories* as synonyms for just-in-time are misleading and thus not used in this work. After all, the kanban technique does require inventory in buffers at all production structure levels. The misunderstanding resulting from this misrepresentation is probably also responsible for the fact that JIT was frequently understood and applied incorrectly and that, finally, the new catchword "lean" took the place of the term JIT.

[APIC04] defines *lean production* as the minimization of all required resources (including time) for the various activities of the company. It involves identifying waste (see definition above) and eliminating them.

A *lean enterprise* applies the principles of lean production to all areas within the organization.

Since the time it was introduced, the philosophy of lean production [WoJo91] has often been taken to extremes. It served as a convenient justification for firing and not replacing staff members. Some people postulated polemically that the contradictory objectives of the company, as outlined in Section 1.3.1, could be resolved. They did not consider at all explicitly the target area of flexibility, for its objectives are usually long term in nature. The customer does not readily recognize that the building of such competencies is value-adding. This view led to company anorexia and resulting paralysis. It proved to be wrong at the very latest when companies became no longer capable of achieving innovations.

The JIT concept originally introduced by the Japanese corresponds most extensively with the current concept of "lean," which once again gives the target area of flexibility the consideration that it deserves. See here also Section 1.3.3. In any case, the aim is still to eliminate waste. As to

---

[3]   The term JIT has been somewhat unjustly, in its exclusiveness, assigned to the kanban technique. Even a deterministic technique such as MRP aims to — and without inventory — procure and produce what is required at the moment, just in time.

reducing inventory, Figure 5.1.1.1 shows the change in view of inventory that took place between 1970 and 1990.

Conventional view   Japanese view

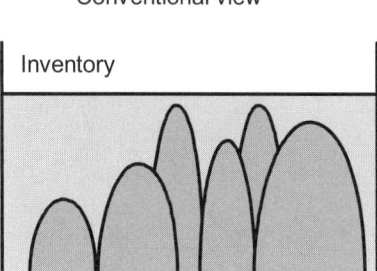

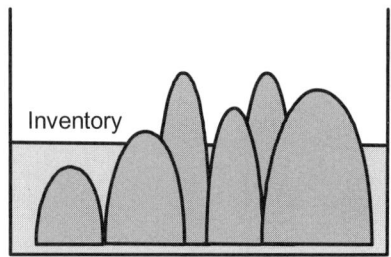

→ Inventory makes possible: → Reduced inventory reveals:
- bridging of disturbances   - the processes susceptible to disturbances
- high load   - unbalanced load
- economical batch size   - lack of flexibility
- protection against waste/scrap   - waste/scrap
- friction-free production   - unreliable suppliers
- high service level   - lack of delivery reliability

Fig. 5.1.1.1   Alternative views of inventory.

High inventory acts as a high water level (light background) in a lake that has shallows and shoals (dark background). If the water level falls, the obstacles will be felt and must either be removed or avoided through a change in course. Reducing inventory exposes problems that must be corrected by means of appropriate concepts. Japan gained this insight early on (see also [Suza89]).

5.1.2   Characteristic Features for Simple and Effective Planning & Control Techniques of Repetitive Manufacturing

Figure 5.1.2.1 reproduces Figure 4.3.2.1, which pointed out the reasons for simple or rather complicated techniques in materials management.

Simple planning & control techniques require, as shown in Figure 5.1.2.1, low cost items or at least continuous frequency of customer demand. In the case of dependent demand for expensive components, more continuous demand can be achieved through, for example, reducing lot sizes but also through a product concept with fewer variants or even standard components. More simple techniques can then be implemented in the place of more complicated techniques of materials management. To do this, some important methods were developed within the JIT concept. They lead to production or procurement with frequent order repetition – that is, to *repetitive manufacturing*.

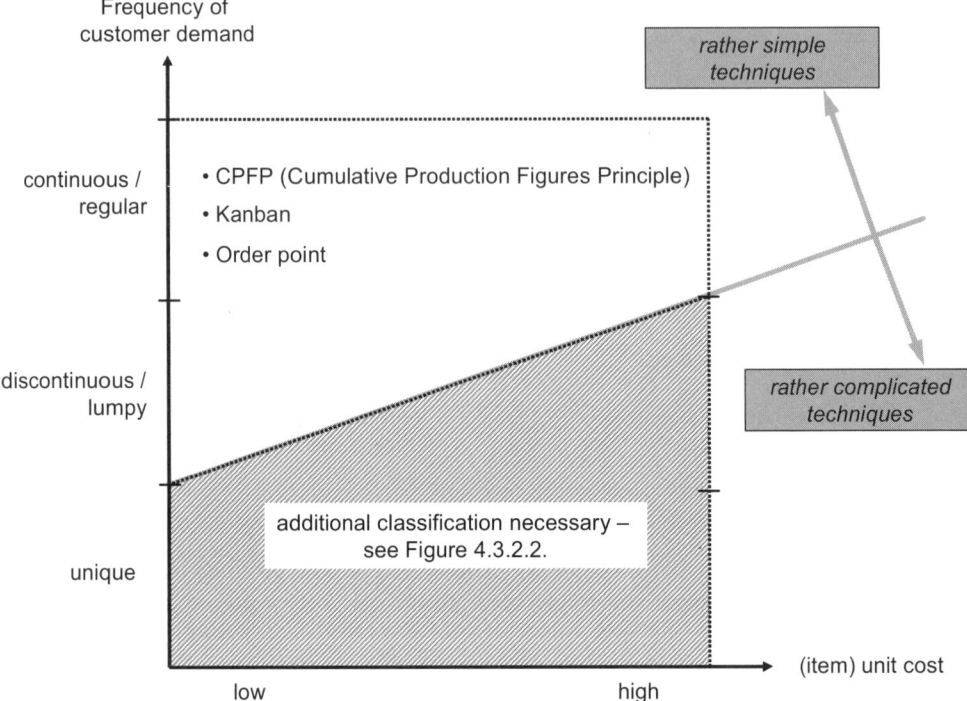

Fig. 5.1.2.1   Reproduced from Fig. 4.3.2.1 – Classification of detailed planning techniques in materials management.

The repetition of the same processes creates a potential for automation in administration. Continuous frequency of customer demand allows production or procurement with order release according to consumption, or a simple (stock) replenishment.

Figure 5.1.2.2 reproduces Figure 4.3.2.2, which pointed out the reasons for a "good" situation or a situation that should be avoided whenever possible in materials management.

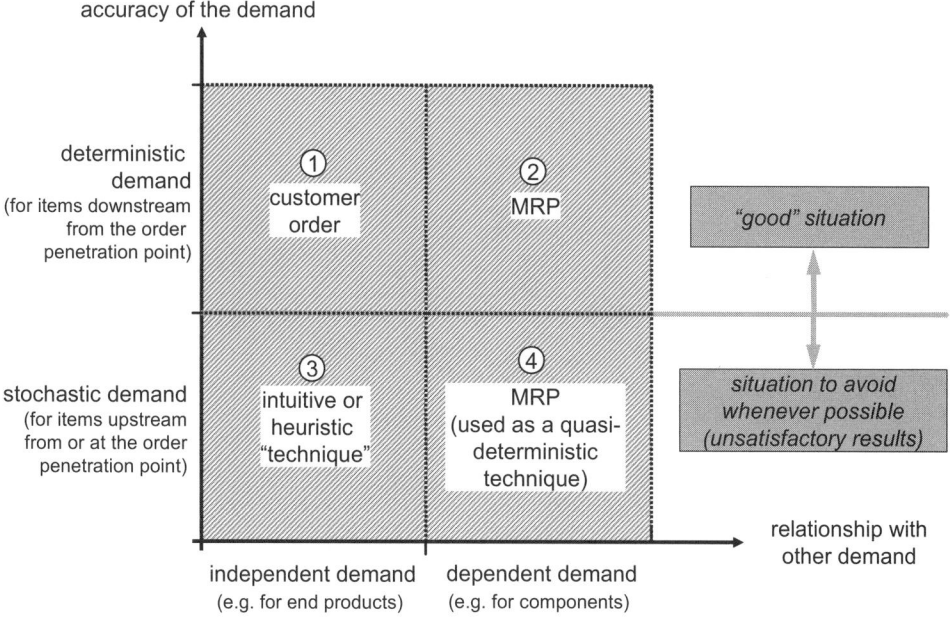

Fig. 5.1.2.2   Reproduced from Fig. 4.3.2.2 – Additional classification of detailed planning techniques in materials management for unique demand or demand for high-cost items with a lumpy demand pattern.

Following Figure 5.1.2.2, the situation becomes "better" the further upwards that the order penetration point (OPP) can be set. As the assumption must be that the customer tolerance time does not lengthen, the cumulative lead time must be reduced. Some of the best-known JIT/Lean methods are precisely those that increase the potential for short lead times.

Figure 5.1.2.3 reproduces Figure 4.3.4.1, which pointed out the reasons for simple or rather complicated techniques in capacity management.

As Figure 5.1.2.3 shows, simple planning & control techniques require flexibility of capacities along the time axis. Accordingly, the JIT concept contains important methods and guiding principles for increasing the quantitative flexibility of capacities.

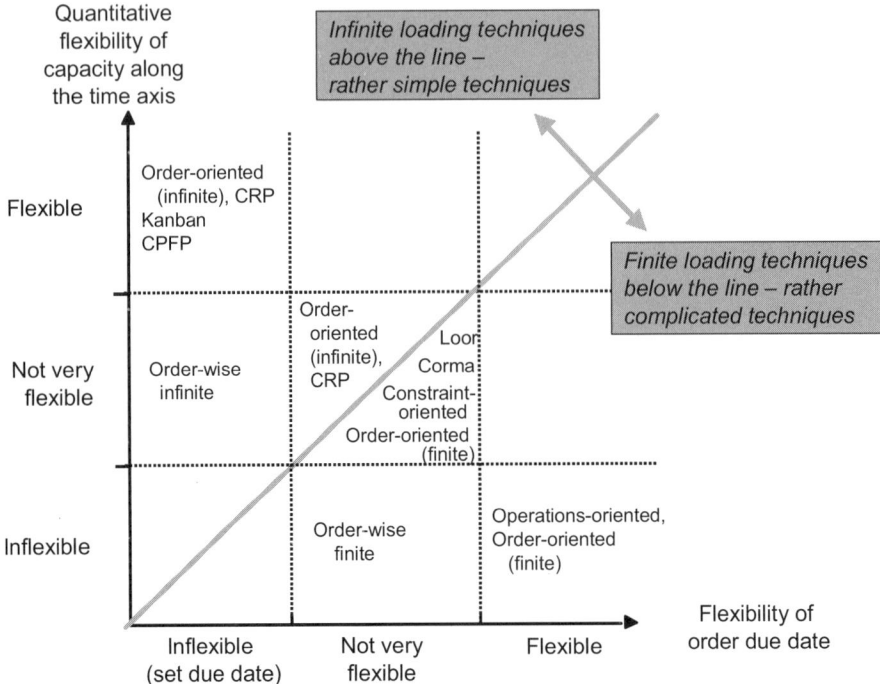

Fig. 5.1.2.3   Reproduced from Fig. 4.3.4.1 – Classes of techniques for capacity management in dependency upon flexibility of capacity and flexibility of order due date.

5.2   The Lean / Just-in-Time Concept

The following discusses the most important of the methods and techniques of the lean / just-in-time concept.

5.2.1   Lead Time Reduction through Setup Time Reduction and Batch Size Reduction

Most simply reckoned, lead time is the sum of *operation times* and *interoperation times* plus *administration time*. In job shop production, operation time determines in part queue time at a work center, which makes up a significant portion of interoperation time.[4] Reducing operation time, therefore, has both a direct and indirect effect. The simplest definition of operation time can be expressed as the formula in Figure 5.2.1.1. This definition appeared in Figure 1.2.3.1, but here the figure shows commonly used abbreviations that will be useful later on.

$$\text{(Operation time)} = \text{(setup time)} + [\text{(lot size)} \cdot \text{(run time per unit)}]$$
$$\text{or} \quad OT = ST + (LOTSIZE \cdot RT)$$

Fig. 5.2.1.1   The simplest formula for operation time.

The simplest way to reduce operation time is through reduction of batch or lot size. A company can even aim at batch sizes that fulfill only the demand of a day or a few days. Then, the same order is repeated at short intervals, which leads to processes that can be better automated.[5] Smaller batch size, however, does result in more setup and thus greater capacity utilization, which in turn increases lead time. Increased setup also causes higher costs. Lead time reduction on a large scale therefore requires a significant reduction in setup time. The following shows how this is achieved.

1. Setup-friendly production facilities:

The construction of specific devices (such as gauges or dies) for setup sometimes allows drastic reduction in setup time even where there are existing specialized machines. Another possibility is to use the machines by means of programmable systems such as computer numerical control (CNC) machines, industrial robots, or flexible manufacturing systems (FMS).

2. Cyclic planning:

Cyclic planning attempts to sequence the products to be manufactured by a machine in such a way that keeps total setup time at a minimum.

Cyclic planning is an example of *sequencing*, the planning of optimum sequences. Cyclic planning yields a basic cycle, as Figure 5.2.1.2 shows.

---

[4]   For definitions of these terms, see Sections 1.2.3 and 12.1. For detailed explanations of the following relationships, see Sections 12.2.2 and 10.3.

[5]   From this idea stems the concept of *one less at a time*, that is, the process of gradually reducing the lot size to expose, prioritize, and eliminate waste ([APIC04]).

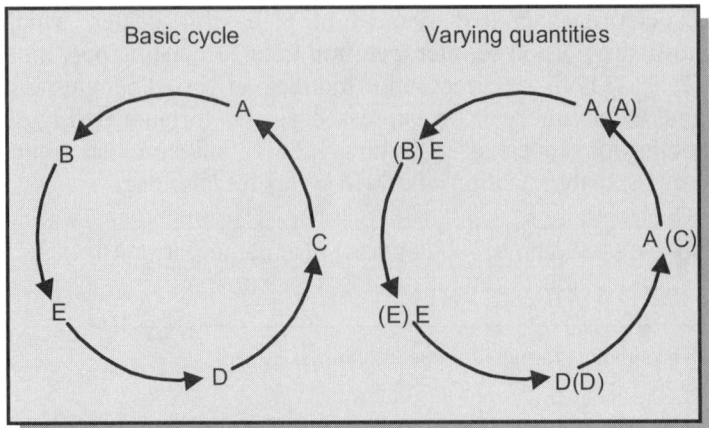

Fig. 5.2.1.2   Cyclic production planning.

In a cyclic manner, batches of parts A, B, E, D, and C are manufactured. It is simple to introduce variations in order quantities; additional batches are planned for a part at the same point that has been planned for that part in the basic cycle. Varying the quantity according to current requirements could also result in a cycle of A, E, E, D, and again A.

3.   Harmonizing the product range through a modular product concept:

Harmonizing the product range is reducing the number of different components and process variants required to manufacture a range of products, at times involving the reduction of the product range itself.

Harmonizing the product range thus means *reduction of variants*. The cost advantage is a reduction in overhead (see Section 15.4). Moreover, it simplifies logistics, because it leads to a more balanced flow of goods. A reduction in product variants results namely in goods production in sequences of similar operations. With identical goods, this reduction will even result in production with frequent order repetition. Each of these allows successive orders to be processed without major change in equipment, such as machines, for example. *Setup times* in the system decrease. In addition, due to fewer different processes, setup tasks become easier, because they repeat themselves and can be better automated. A modular product concept can achieve a reduction of variants.[6]

---

[6]   In addition to reduction of variants, the term *variant management* is also used (see [Schu89]).

A *modular product concept* is based on standardizing the components and operations as well as building product families.

Product variants are decided upon on the basis of a concept already defined in marketing, development, and design. At or upstream from the (customer) order penetration point (OPP), it is important to keep the number of product variants small. The manufacturer must be able to make the diverse variants within the customer tolerance time, that is, in customer-specified fashion. The number of significantly different process variants has to be kept small.[7]

4. *Reducing idle time of production facilities:*

The term *single-minute exchange of dies (SMED)* refers to methods aimed at reducing idle time of production facilities, according to Figure 5.2.1.3.

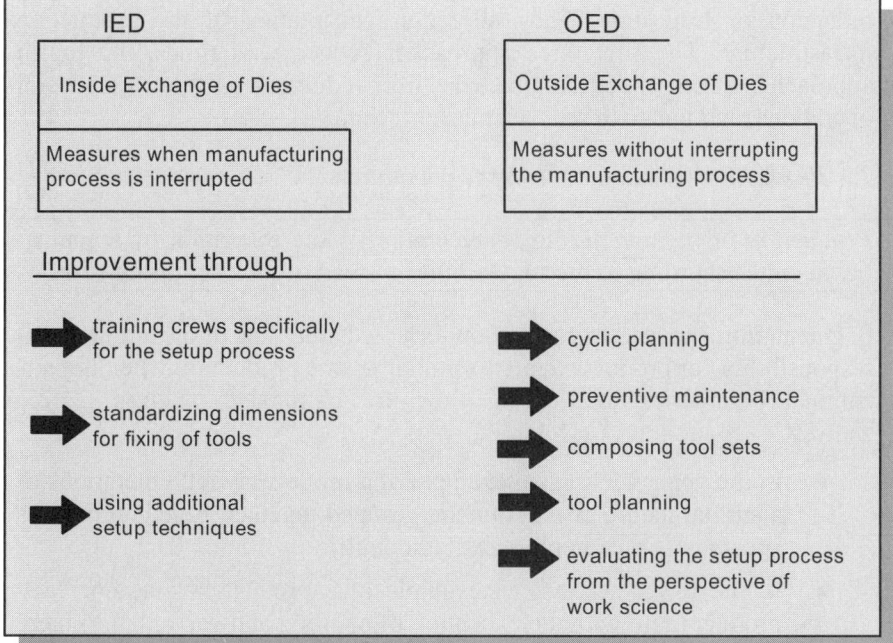

Fig. 5.2.1.3   Concepts of reducing setup time. (Source: [Wild89].)

---

[7]   As to the management of product families with many variants, see variant-oriented concepts in Chapter 6.

These methods were developed primarily in Japanese industry (see [Shin85]). In principle, there are two kinds of setup operations:

- *Internal setup (time)* or *inside exchange of dies (IED)* takes place when the workstation is stopped or shut down.

- *External setup (time)* or *outside exchange of dies (OED)* takes place while the workstation is still working on another order.

SMED is comprised of the entire setup process, including insertion and removal of special setup devices, or dies. SMED reduces idle time of the system by means of shifting portions of IED to OED. This method is comparable to a pit stop during a formula-one race.

5.2.2   Further Concepts of Lead Time Reduction

In addition to batch size reduction, there are further approaches to reduction of lead time. They all require adaptation of the production infrastructure. The first three approaches reduce wait times, the fourth approach reduces operation time, the fifth reduces lead time for several operations, and the sixth reduces transport time.

1.   Production or manufacturing segmentation:

> *Production* or *manufacturing segmentation* is the formation of organizational units according to product families instead of job shop production.

Segmentation can lead to goods-flow-oriented areas and allow autonomous responsibility for products to arise (similar to line production when organizational boundaries interrupting flow are eliminated). Figure 5.2.2.1 shows:

- In the upper section, an example of a process layout: Operations of a similar nature or function are grouped together, based on process specialty (for example, saw, lathe, mill).

- In the lower section, an example of a product layout: For each product (here with the exception of painting and galvanizing) there is a separate production line, or manufacturing group, but no longer any central job shop for each task.

There are cost factors that restrict the splitting of certain areas (such as galvanizing, painting, tempering), but an appropriate total layout and capacity reserves will ensure rapid throughput. Small- and medium-sized companies are often faced with the problem of special treatments for which they must rely on external refining and finishing companies. Because of the recent weight placed on setup time, however, ever more new facilities for such areas are being offered, such as paint shops that set up lacquer colors in a matter of minutes.

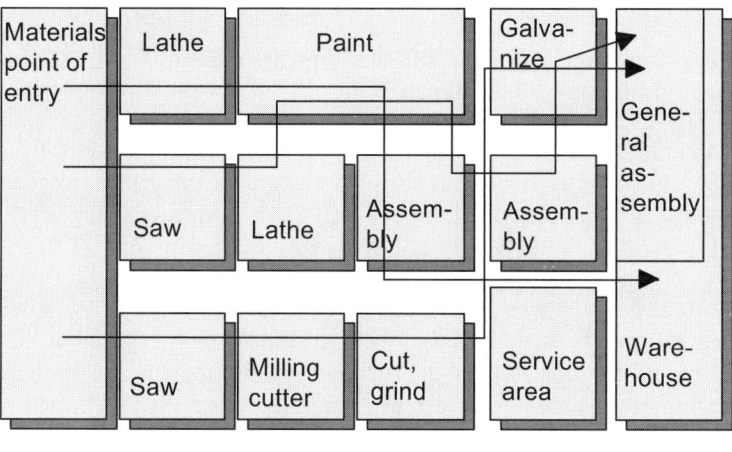

Fig. 5.2.2.1   Production or manufacturing segmentation. (Example taken from [Wild89].)

Applying production or manufacturing segmentation consistently leads to a set of focused factories.

A *focused factory* is a plant established to focus on a limited set of products or product families, technologies, and markets, precisely defined by the company's competitive strategy and economics (see [APIC04]).

2. Cellular manufacturing:

A further consistent application of production or manufacturing segmentation leads to cellular manufacturing.

A *work cell* is, according to [APIC04], a physical arrangement where dissimilar machines are grouped together into a production unit to produce a family of parts having similar routings.

The process of cellular manufacturing is closely linked with work cells.

In *cellular manufacturing,* workstations required for successive operations are placed one after the other in succession, usually in an *L-shaped line* or *U-shaped line* configuration. The individual units of a batch go through all operations successively, without having to wait for the other units of the batch between any two operations.

Near-to-line production can be used as a synonym to cellular manufacturing.

Figure 5.2.2.2 illustrates this concept, showing the change from job shop production to cellular manufacturing.

As cellular manufacturing may require multiple machines, it is not unusual to find older machines, retrieved from the "cellar" so to speak, in these lines. While this is specialized machinery that has a dedicated capacity,[8] it is inexpensive enough, for generally it has already been depreciated.

Efforts to identify business processes and reorganize them (business process reengineering) can also lead to the distributing of machines in lines that correspond to the new business processes. Cellular manufacturing is, moreover, significantly easier to control than job shop-type production. And, in many cases, less space is required for the machines.

---

[8]   A *dedicated capacity* is a work center that is designated to produce a single item or a limited number of similar items. Equipment that is dedicated may be special equipment or may be grouped general-purpose equipment committed to a composite part ([APIC04]).

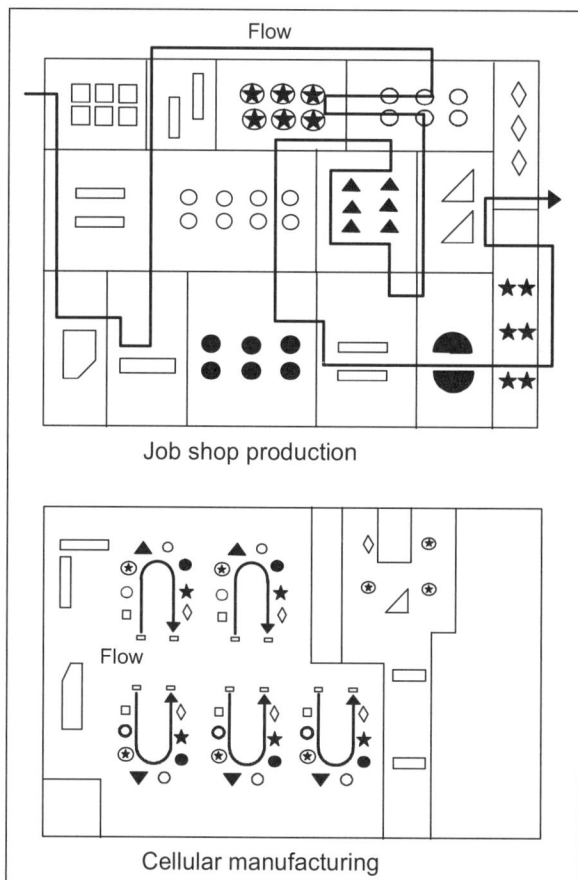

Job shop production

Cellular manufacturing

Fig. 5.2.2.2   Changeover to cellular manufacturing.

Cellular manufacturing can achieve a lasting reduction of lead time. On the one hand, interoperation time can be reduced to zero. On the other hand, it is similar to the principle of overlapping operations (Section 12.4.2), as shown in the following.

Using the definition in Figure 5.2.1.1, the lead time of an order — assuming a *sequence of operations* and omitting interoperation times and administration times — is the sum of all n operation times, as shown in Figure 5.2.2.3 (for details, see Section 12.3.2).

$$LTI = \sum_{1 \le i \le n} OT[i] = \sum_{1 \le i \le n} \{ST(i) + LOTSIZE \cdot RT[i]\}$$

Fig. 5.2.2.3   Formula for lead time with a sequence of operations.

With cellular manufacturing, the following estimate is calculated:

$$\max_{1 \le i \le n}\{ST(i)+LOTSIZE \cdot RT[i]\} \le LTI \le \max_{1 \le i \le n}\{ST[i]+LOTSIZE \cdot RT[i]\} + \sum_{1 \le i \le n^*}\{ST[i]+RT[i]\}$$

*but without the longest operation

Fig. 5.2.2.4   Formula for lead time with cellular manufacturing.

To understand this formula intuitively, consider the following: The longest operation, the so-called *cell driver*, provides the minimum lead time. The other operations overlap. Lead time then increases at most by setup and *one* run time per unit of all other operations. In concrete cases, lead time will fall at some point between the minimum and the maximum.

3. Standardizing the production infrastructure and increasing the qualitative and quantitative flexibility of capacity:

Close-to-maximum capacity utilization results in a strong increase in wait time.[9] Overcapacity brings load variation under control and allows short lead times. If capacity is costly, however, overcapacity must be carefully reviewed. First, the following measures should be examined:

- Can we standardize the machinery, tools, and devices — either through greater versatility or by means of standardizing operations? This would allow broader implementation of personnel, which would result in fewer workstations and simpler planning. Airlines, for example, strive towards identical cockpits in their fleets of planes.

- Can the qualitative flexibility of personnel be increased through training and broader qualifications? If so, employees can be implemented in a more balanced fashion along the time axis, because if there is underload at their own work centers, they can be moved to overloaded work centers.

- Can we increase the availability of production facilities, particularly tools? The employees at a work center can also be trained to do their own repairs and maintenance jobs, as the necessity arises.

---

[9]   Section 12.2.2 explains this important phenomenon in detail.

4. Structuring assembly processes:

In the assembly process, staggered supply of components reduces lead times, as shown in Figure 5.2.2.5. This is a well-known measure, especially in connection with customer order production.

The inbound deliveries in Figure 5.2.2.5 may be preassemblies or assemblies. Preassembly made parallel to assembly reduces the number of storage levels. If quality control is integrated into assembly, lead time can be reduced even further.

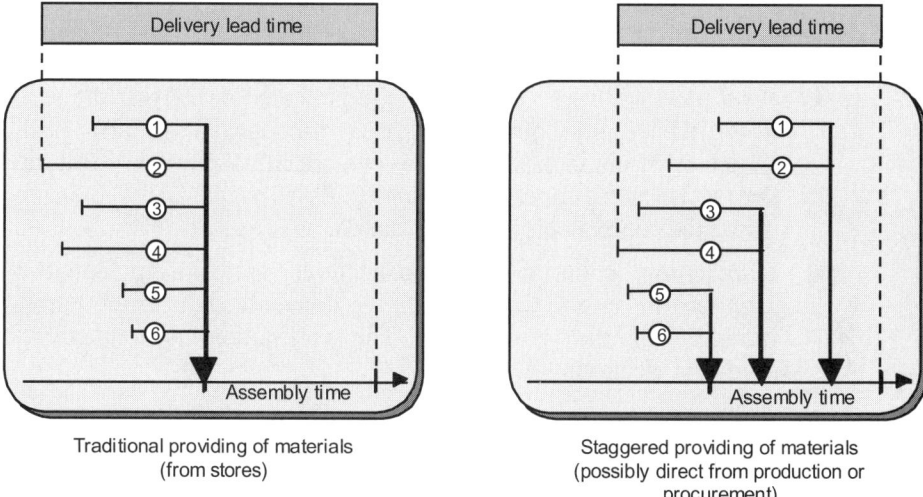

Traditional providing of materials
(from stores)

Staggered providing of materials
(possibly direct from production or
procurement)

Fig. 5.2.2.5   Assembly-oriented providing of components.

5. Complete processing:

> *Complete processing* is the execution of several different operations at a stretch — if possible, all the way up to completion of the product.

The newer tool machines often allow complete processing. With computer numerical control (CNC, DNC), they are versatile in implementation. Moreover, they are more independent in terms of cost as well as output and quality of employee performance.

There are fewer stations to run through with complete processing, so that there are no interoperation times. Reduced lead times should result. But for this to have a true advantage over the segmentation in approaches 1 and 2, the complete processing duration must be significantly shorter than the sum of operation times with a sequence of machines. Otherwise, the result would be simply that several, shorter wait times would be replaced with one single wait time. This time would be just as long as the sum of the shorter times, however.

For complex workpieces, a company could investigate the possibilities of automation of production with flexible manufacturing systems (FMS) and automation of transport and handling. Modern technological machines are designed to reduce setup time and achieve greater variant flexibility. Automated processes also reduce the problems of 24-hour shift work.

6. *Organizing supply and buffer storage to support the flow of goods:*

The *point of use* is in the focus of delivery and storage.

- *Point-of-use storage*: Buffer storage is placed directly at the spot where the components will be used (inbound stockpoint). Each container of components has its own specified physical location. On the assembly line, for example, it will stand at the location where the components will be installed.

- *Point-of-use delivery*: Fast connections are set up between suppliers and users. Components are delivered right to the buffer storage at the user workstation. The workstation can transmit its needs via electronic mail.

5.2.3   Line Balancing — Harmonizing the Content of Work

Line balancing balances the assignment of the tasks to workstations in a manner that minimizes the number of workstations and the total amount of idle time at all stations for a given output level ([APIC04]).

Line balancing is particularly important for *line manufacturing*, that is, repetitive manufacturing performed by specialized equipment in a fixed sequence (i.e., an assembly line). Line balancing can be realized by harmonizing the content of work.

Harmonizing the content of work means to design the following so that they require the same length of time: (1) the various production structure levels, and (2) the times required for individual operations within a production structure level.

This concept can — by the way — also be very useful in a job shop production environment.

With regard to (1), production structure levels must be designed or redefined in such a way that lead times at the individual levels are either identical or multiples of each other. Harmonization thus demands close cooperation between design and product engineering (simultaneous engineering). Product and process must be designed together from the start. Figure 5.2.3.1 illustrates this principle at the levels of assembly, preassembly, and parts production. The lead time for parts production is half as long as that for the levels of preassembly and assembly. In the example, the batch size at the part production structure level comprises half the usage quantity for a batch in preassembly or assembly.

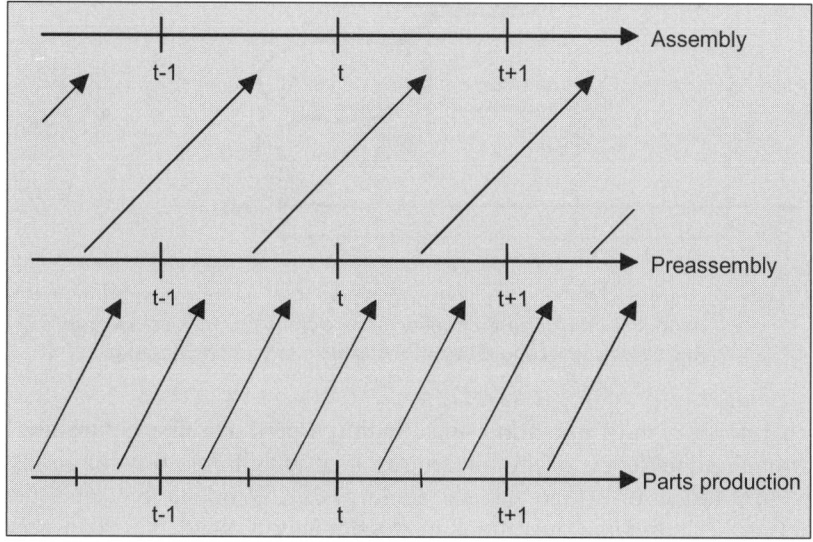

Fig. 5.2.3.1   Harmonizing the content of work: tasks of the same duration at each production structure level result in the rhythmic flow of goods.

With regard to (2), the following should be of the same approximate duration: the various operations at a workstation for all the products, and all the operations for a single product. Figure 5.2.3.2 illustrates this principle.

There will be little variation of the operation time, and this results in turn in a reduction of lead time. Queue time, except for its dependency on capacity utilization and average operation time, is namely a function of the variation coefficients of operation times.[10] In job shop production, queue

---

[10]   For a detailed explanation of this important phenomenon, see Section 12.2.2.

times at the workstations to a large part determine interoperation times, which themselves have a significant effect on lead time.[11]

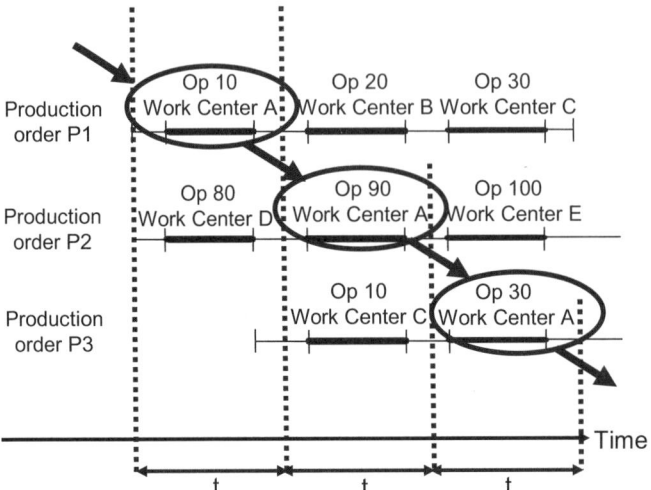

Fig. 5.2.3.2   Harmonizing the content of work: the various operations at a workstation (for all the products) as well as the various operations for a single product should be of the same approximate duration.

Such harmonization of operation times within a production structure level and throughout all levels of production results in a rhythmic flow of goods. Batch size reduction alone cannot achieve this. Workstations and the content of the individual operations must be newly defined. This is a very difficult task that can only be surmounted when product engineering cooperates with development and design. New technologies may be used for certain operations in order to change lead time at the very location where harmonization is required.

To complete the task, product engineering in cooperation with design must repeat the following two steps until sufficient results are achieved:

1. Determine the *production measure*, that is, the duration of a harmonized operation including necessary interoperation times before and after the (internal or external) operation. To start, experienced personnel in product engineering determine a production measure empirically. For further iterations, the new

---

[11]   These phenomena are explained in Sections 12.2.1, 12.1.3, and 12.1.1.

production measure will result from correction of a previously unsatisfactory result. The shorter the production measure is, the more flexibly processes can be put together.

2. Perform measures to change lead times of operations, chosen from the various possible measures in Figure 5.2.3.3.

Due to measures connected with suppliers, harmonizing work contents leads to closer cooperation with other companies. Products are increasingly manufactured by an affiliation of different companies that together have suitable infrastructures or that have the flexibility to establish such infrastructures.

- Combine operations through automation, thus reducing total lead time of previous operations. Or, analogously, split an operation, thus lengthening the lead time of the operation.

- Change the process by changing the production technique (sticking instead of screwing, a different surface hardening technique, etc.)

- Reduce setup times in order to reduce batch sizes. If capacity is not being utilized, batch size can also be reduced directly. The advantage of harmonizing, however, must supersede the resulting increase in setup costs.

- Purchase different components that allow for a different process, where, in a targeted fashion, operations will be longer or shorter. The components will be either more or less expensive.

- Purchase semifinished goods in order to avoid operations that do not allow harmonization. Possibly the supplier can perform such an operation better within its own order and production infrastructure.

- Assign operations to subcontractors or take over operations from subcontractors, if this results in a better production measure. Change subcontracting concepts and subcontract to subcontractors that are better suited with regard to better lead time.

Fig. 5.2.3.3   Measures for changing lead time of operations.

Because control must no longer observe priority rules, the advantage resulting from all these measures to harmonize the content of work is very simple management of queues.

Such detailed and comprehensive measures to harmonize the content of work are comparable to the design of a railway timetable of departures at regular intervals: Investiture in new lines takes place as a function of postulated rhythms in the regular interval departure plan. As a result, processes in the railway net can be automated, and there is maximum throughput through the net.

The strategic considerations underlying these measures are long term in nature and can be put into practice only if a company's financial policies are in agreement with them. Investiture in capital assets will not accord well with savings. Whenever possible reduction of delivery lead time is projected, the response of the customer to the improvement becomes the important factor. Estimating possible effects of this kind is a matter for decision making at the company level. It is for this reason that traditional profitability calculations generally fail here. However, the calculations are often not necessary at all. A company attempting to stay in competition will be forced to make the investment.

5.2.4   Just-in-Time Logistics

Just-in-time logistics is comprised of the measures to reduce lead time discussed in Sections 5.2.1 to 5.2.3. Beyond these, comprehensive concepts and measures will be required in the following areas:

Motivation, qualification, and empowerment of employees: In a just-in-time environment, operators' jobs no longer include only direct productive labor, but also planning and control tasks. As a consequence, their jobs are enriched (this is best described by the term *job enrichment*), but the importance of training and motivation increases. In Japan, a complicated system of bonuses, public commendation, promotions, and so on supports personnel motivation. The result of this type of personnel management, rarely seen in Europe or in North America, is devotion of employees to their duties and to their companies. In the framework of JIT logistics anywhere, a Japanese way of thinking appears. This Japanese approach is summarized in brief in Figure 5.2.4.1.

This kind of motivation leads ultimately to comprehensive *quantitative flexibility of employees* through the course of time. This allows some control of fluctuations in a logistics system set up for continuous demand. There are cases where 25% of overload can be handled by "normal" overtime by employees, 25% by "special" overtime, and 50% by scheduling employees' hours according to need.

Quality assurance is performing actions to ensure the quality of the goods:

- *Quality at the source:* As buffers at user sites are minimal and the order quantities correspond exactly to the demand, no faulty products may leave the producer.
- *Quality circles* of employees build quality consciousness and achieve the desired level of self-control of quality. They evaluate

the measures set to assure quality and the objectives achieved. Employees are thus encouraged to identify with their tasks and the quality of items that they produce and thus develop a feeling of responsibility for the products they manufacture.

The group takes priority (the individual "disappears" within the group).

- A "sense of the whole" makes conflict among different areas much less frequent than, for example, in Europe or in North America. At Toyota, for example, university graduates in all fields undergo a 2-year training program through all areas of production.

- *Employee involvement (EI)* — such as in quality circles — promotes acceptance of innovations and expands the quality concept to total quality management (TQM).

- All employees cultivate a problem-solving orientation in their thinking.

- Continuous improvement involving everyone (*kaizen*; [Imai94], [Maas92]) is a major element. This may be supported by a corresponding system for improvement suggestions.

- Waste or *non-value added* is eliminated, and this forms the basis for increased profit.

- Shortages and defects become visible (preferably by means of sensors), so that they can be eliminated.
  - In the case of defects, production stops.
  - Continuous process improvement eliminates the causes of defects.

- Simple, "foolproof" techniques (poka-yoke) are preferred; visual control systems (andon) are more effective than numbers and reports.

- Order and cleanliness improve the morale of the operators. White work uniforms are worn on the shop floor.

- "Even small details are important."

Fig. 5.2.4.1   Japanese approach.

Integrated procurement logistics and supply chain management: These are measures to reduce purchasing lead time. Suppliers are included in procurement logistics, sometimes as early as the development phase (co-makership; see Section 2.3.3). The flow of information to suppliers includes long-term components, such as blanket orders (see Section 4.2.5), and short-term components for blanket release (see Section 5.3). To be able to issue blanket orders, the user must have reliable long-term planning for the components and work to be purchased. Suppliers are no longer selected only on the basis of the lowest prices, but also according to the criteria of delivery reliability, quality, and short delivery lead times. There is an advantage to having local suppliers (distance, strikes, etc.).

5.2.5   Generally Valid Advantages of the Lean / Just-in-Time Concept for Materials Management

If the (customer) order penetration point (OPP) is close or at the level of the end product — the accuracy of the demand forecast will determine the validity of each technique of stochastic materials management. As forecasts get worse, quasi-deterministic techniques in particular will have considerable disadvantages. A company will have to reckon with delivery bottlenecks or safety stocks just below or at the level of stocking, at a great risk of technically obsolete or spoiled inventory. All efforts must be made to:

- Bring the order penetration point (OPP) lower in the product structure in order to reach a more deterministic situation.

- Achieve continuous demand in order to reduce safety stocks or even to allow implementation of a purely stochastic technique, such as the order point or kanban technique.

The lean / just-in-time concept discussed in Sections 5.2.1 and 5.2.2 can also aid the MRP technique (see Section 11.3), which often does not achieve satisfactory results in the quasi-deterministic case. Lean/JIT corresponds exactly to the above two demands. Thus, production and procurement costs decrease.

1. *Reduction of batch or lot size* through reduction in setup time results in combining fewer requirements in production or procurement batches at all levels. This is particularly important for lower production structure levels, where forecast errors will affect orders for components that will be required for end products far in the future. Figure 5.2.5.1 shows the positive effect that results if a batch sizing policy of *lot-for-lot* — every requirement is translated into exactly one order — can be achieved (see also Section 11.4.1).

   On the one hand, demand at lower production structure levels becomes more continuous, which with any stochastic technique results in smaller safety stocks. In the quasi-deterministic case, it is sometimes even possible to change over to purely stochastic techniques. On the other hand, the probability of production or procurement errors due to forecast errors decreases, because time buckets are reduced and orders are released only for requirements forecasted for the near future.

   With product families with many variants (and thus non-repetitive production to customer order), the prerequisite is a batch size of 1.

Here, companies have always been faced with the problem of how to reduce setup time. Lean/JIT is thus also advantageous for deterministic materials management.

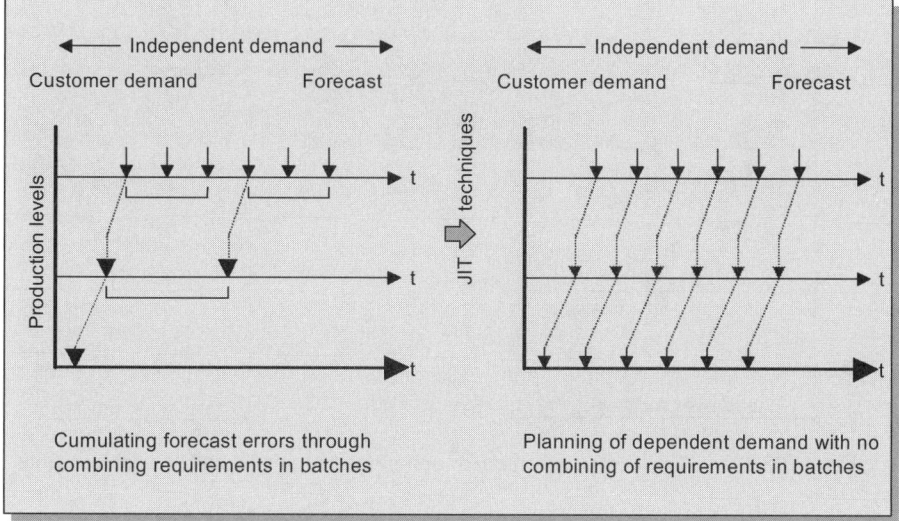

Fig. 5.2.5.1   Effect of forecast errors through the combining of requirements in batches across many production structure levels.

2. *Lead time reduction* allows a (customer) order penetration point lower in the product structure. Figure 5.2.5.2 shows this positive effect.

   The customer tolerance time now corresponds to a greater portion of the — now shortened — cumulative lead time. With this, a larger part of value-adding processes lie within a deterministic area. Forecast errors affect a smaller part of the value-adding chain. Because forecasts pertain to the near future, forecasted demand is also smaller.

   Through increased production within the required delivery lead time, certain orders can now be produced — thanks to lead time reduction — for which there can be no stockpiling for economic reasons. This is the case with non-repetitive production. In this way, additional sales can be realized. This is a further example of the advantages of the lean / just-in-time concept for deterministic materials management.

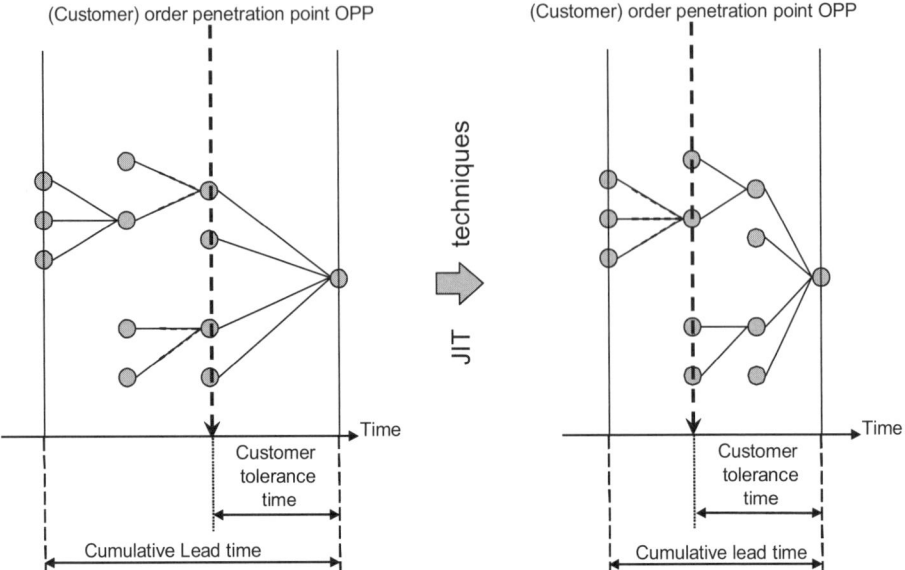

Fig. 5.2.5.2   (Customer) order penetration point with longer and shorter lead time.

5.2.6   Generally Valid Advantages of the Lean / Just-in-Time Concept for Capacity Management

The setup time reduction in Section 5.2.1 can achieve sufficiently short setup times even without cyclic planning. In this case, it is no longer necessary to reduce setup times by forming groups of orders for which a queue and thus some buffer inventory is required. Because priority rules for the waiting orders before the workstations are less necessary or fall away altogether, control in job shops becomes less complex.

Increasing the quantitative flexibility of capacity was discussed in the third part of Section 5.2.2 as the lean / just-in-time concept. What is meant is the practice of scheduling extra capacity or flexible capacity that can continually adapt to load. This measure has the following positive consequences:

- It reduces queue time over-proportionally. This is crucial if the focus is on delivery reliability. In addition, queue time is one of the least predictable factors in job shop production. If queue time varies little or is very short, this improves planning for several production structure levels. Decreased size of production areas represents, thanks to smaller inventory in queues to the workstations, a further advantage that has been too little emphasized.

- It allows for simpler control techniques, such as the kanban technique, where the control flow is achieved by the flow of goods itself. But any technique at all of capacity planning will function better and more simply. In general, when a computer-aided control technique with logistics software is introduced, there will be external costs of at least $100,000 and total costs of at least three times that amount. In view of these high costs, increasing capacity can prove to be a viable alternative, particularly when it can be implemented more rapidly than a computer control technique. In a medium-sized Swiss electronics manufacturing company, for example, the purchase of two additional coiling machines resolved a bottleneck in capacity. In this way, the company was not only able to avoid investing in an expensive control technique, but also chose a technique that could be put into effect immediately.

5.3   The Kanban Technique

Kanban is a production control technique that is consistent with the JIT concept. The Toyota Corporation began to develop the technique in the 1960s, and it became well known in connection with the "Toyota production system" (see here [Ohno88], or [Shin89]). Orders to withdraw required parts from suppliers and feeding operations are released directly by the work centers. The technique represents the control portion of a planning system that is often not mentioned in the literature. The prerequisite for a kanban technique is that demands be as continuous as possible along the entire value-adding chain. In other words, this should be production or procurement with frequent order repetition.

5.3.1   Kanban: A Technique of Execution and Control of Operations

The name *kanban* comes from the name of the document used for control.

> *Kanban* (Japanese for card, or visible record) is a reusable signal card that passes back and forth between two stations. It is thus a kind of traveling card.

Buffers are kept at the user operation. These stores will contain, for example, a maximum number of standard containers or bins (A) holding a fixed number of items (k). The order batch size will be a set of containers (A). The *kanban card* is a means to identify the contents of the container and to release the order. The card will look similar to the one in Figure 5.3.1.1.

STOCK LOCATION : *5E215*	SUPPLIER
ITEM ID. : *366'421'937*	(OPERATION):
DESCRIPTION : *gear*	*lathe*
MODEL TYPE : *Z 20*	USER

CONTAINER CAPACITY	CONTAINER TYPE	CARD NUMBER	(OPERATION):
20	*B*	*4 of 8*	*cutter*

Fig. 5.3.1.1   Example kanban card. (Taken from: [Wild89].)

The term kanban, meaning signboard, is formed from the characters for "to look at closely" and for "wooden board," as shown in Figure 5.3.1.2. Kanban was the word used for decorated shop signs that came into use in merchant towns in the late 1600s in Japan.

kan   看   to look at closely

ban   板   wooden board

Fig. 5.3.1.2   The word kanban (explanation by Tschirky; see footnote).[12]

---

[12] In a personal communication, Prof. Hugo Tschirky (Swiss Federal Institute of Technology ETH Zurich) kindly explained the origin of the Japanese word *kanban*. The character "kan" is made up of the symbols hand and eye and is derived from the pictograph of a man holding his hand to the brow to shade the eyes in order to better look at something. "Ban," meaning wooden board, contains the symbols for tree, wood, and wall (a wooden board supported against a wall).

The *kanban technique* is defined as a kanban feedback loop and rules for kanban use.

Figure 5.3.1.3 defines a *kanban feedback loop*, between parts production and preassembly as well as a *two-card kanban system*:

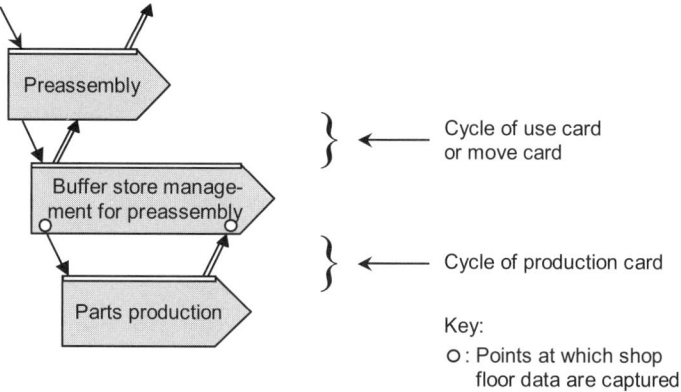

Fig. 5.3.1.3   Basic principle of the kanban technique: the kanban feedback loop.

1. If in preassembly the contents of the container have been used up, an employee goes with the container and the *use* (or *move*) *card* to the buffer and takes a full container of the required items. He removes the *production card* attached to the full container and places it in a mailbox. He attaches the move card from the empty container to the full container. The empty container remains in the buffer, while the full container with its move card goes to assembly.

2. An employee in parts production routinely goes to the buffer and collects the production cards and empty containers. The kanbans collected are the orders for manufacturing the corresponding number of items (an order may also comprise several containers). The release of the order is registered by passing through a shop floor data collection device, such as a bar code scanner. There is no due date on the kanban, for each order is to be filled immediately.

3. Once the items have been manufactured, the production card is attached to the full container and the container is moved to the buffer. Again, passing through a shop floor data collection device serves to register entry of the order.

The buffer usually stands at the *inbound stockpoint* of the user, that is, a defined location next to the place of use on a production floor. The buffer only seldom stands at the *outbound stockpoint* of the manufacturer, that is, a defined location next to the place of manufacturing on a production floor.

As a variant, there may also be a *one-card kanban system*, where the kanban remains fixed to the container. Another variant transmits the kanban of the empty container by fax or by an automatic scanner via tele-communications. This avoids transport time for the return of the empty container in the case of spatially remote sites. Here, the essence of the traveling card is lost: As it becomes "copied" in each cycle, it does not remain the identical physical card. This creates the danger of duplicate orders.

The *kanban rules* or *rules for kanban use* are defined in Figure 5.3.1.4 as a process strategy.

The user operation may never
- Order more than the required quantity.
- Order at a point in time earlier than required.

The supplying or producing operation may never
- Produce more than what has been ordered.
- Go into production before an order is received.
- Not produce, or produce late, what has been ordered.
- Deliver scrap or insufficient quality.

The planning operation (usually organized as a planning center) takes care of
- Medium- and long-term balancing of load and capacity.
- Keeping a suitable number of kanban cards in the feedback control system (the smallest number possible) by means of adding and removing cards.

Fig. 5.3.1.4   Kanban rules of order release and control of the feedback control system.

The kanban rules ensure, in their pure application, that no reserves will form and that orders are processed *immediately*. The order is registered immediately as an event, and it sets off the production process.[13] This means, however, that adequate capacity must be available and that it can adapt flexibly to load.

---

[13]   Kanban represents a synchronized production control approach. *Synchronized production* is a manufacturing management philosophy that includes a coherent set of principles and techniques supporting the global objective of the system (compare [APIC04]).

The kanban technique can be applied across numerous production structure levels or operations. This results in chains of kanban feedback loops. A comprehensive system includes external suppliers, so that close cooperation with producers is required. For purchased parts, the order to the supplier is a move card. Here again, the kanban card can be registered and transmitted by means of bar codes.

The kanban technique causes a consumption-oriented production. Because user work centers withdraw components from feeding operations or suppliers, it is also described as a pull system. Another term calls kanban the *supermarket principle*, as the user serves himself with the things he needs; once the shelves are emptied, they are refilled (see [Ohno88]). Due to standard locations for the containers and their contents, goods provision does not involve a lot of effort. This allows small production batches.

5.3.2   Kanban: A Technique of Materials Management

As each container must be accompanied by a kanban, the number of kanban cards in the feedback loop determines the amount of work in process. We can make the following status distinctions:

- Containers in issue by the user operation
- Containers in buffer at the user operation
- Containers in transport
- Containers being filled by work at the feeding operation
- Containers queued at feeding operation[14]
- Containers that represent safety stock

To calculate the optimum number of kanban cards in a feedback control system, the data are first defined in Figure 5.3.2.1.

---

[14] According to kanban rules, this queue should be of length zero. Orders received are filled on the same day. See the kanban rules in Figure 5.3.1.4.

–	A:	number of kanban cards
–	k:	number of parts (units) per container
–	UP:	usage during the statistical period (= expected value of demand)
–	TP:	length of the statistical period
–	LTI:	lead time (or procurement deadline)
–	SF:	percent needed as safety factor (for fluctuation of demand and delivery delays)
–	w:	number of containers per transport batch (=1, if possible)
–	SUMRT:	sum of the run times per unit
–	SUMST:	sum of setup times (independent of batch size)
–	SUMINT:	sum of interoperation times plus administrative time

Fig. 5.3.2.1   Basic data for calculating the number of kanban cards.

How many kanbans must flow in a feedback control system in order to guarantee the availability of components? Figure 5.3.2.2 examines the role of all kanbans that lie "in front of" an emptied container and illustrates the situation formulated below:

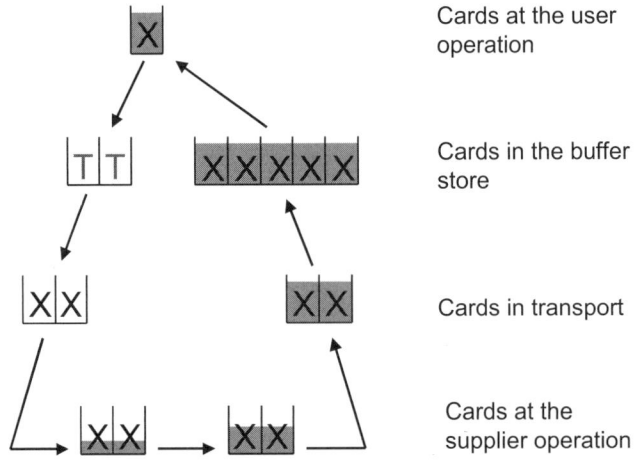

Cards at the user operation

Cards in the buffer store

Cards in transport

Cards at the supplier operation

X: usable kanbans during the lead time of transport batch (T)

Fig. 5.3.2.2   Number of kanban cards in the system.

At the moment an order is signaled (the sending of a transport batch of empty containers), the entire quantity in the buffer and in process — that is, number of kanban cards multiplied by the contents of a container — must correspond to *the expected usage during lead time*. To the number of cards calculated in this way, the number of containers of the transport batch itself is added.[15]

The value of A can thus be calculated using the formula in Figure 5.3.2.3. Here, w*k is the transport batch size, which is also the batch size of procurement or production. Batch size can therefore be larger than the quantity that fills one container.[16] The value of w is at least 1, and for high-cost items, it should not — if possible — be any larger than 1.

Notice the similarity of this formula to a further technique of order release according to consumption: the order point technique (Figure 10.3.1.3). The way that the kanban feedback loop functions, the kanban rules, and now also the formula to calculate the number of kanban cards, all indicate a technique of stochastic materials management.

$$
\begin{aligned}
A \cdot k \quad &= \frac{UP \cdot LTI}{TP} \cdot (1 + SF) + w \cdot k \\
&= \frac{UP \cdot (w \cdot k \cdot SUMRT + SUMST + SUMINT)}{TP} \cdot (1 + SF) + w \cdot k
\end{aligned}
$$

Fig. 5.3.2.3   Formula to calculate the number of kanban cards.

To avoid large safety stocks due to demand fluctuations, such techniques must be as continuous as possible at all production structure levels.[17] The kanban technique allows no large safety stock. For that reason alone, buffers are set up right on the shop floor and have to be kept to small dimensions. The number of kanban cards can also not be changed frequently because of the great administrative effort involved. Moreover, kanban rules allow no degrees of freedom for delivery delays. This results in the following:

The kanban technique guarantees availability only if there is the most continuous possible demand, that is, with limited fluctuations in all kanban feedback loops. The same holds for customer demand. Thus, this is production or procurement with frequent order repetition and small batch sizes.

---

[15] If, in addition, the order rhythm of the kanban order does not consider the exact point in time, but only time periods, then the period length must be added to the lead time (administrative wait time).

[16] Measures to reduce batch size were described in Section 5.2.

[17] See also a detailed discussion in Section 10.3.3.

The most interesting products when it comes to improving logistics techniques are, of course, those that add high value added. Such products are often A items in an ABC classification. The ABC classification can be complemented by an XYZ classification, which yields a measure of the continuity of demand (see Section 10.2.3). X items are those items having the greatest continuity, and Z-items are those in lumpy demand. Kanban items are therefore typical A and X items.

5.3.3   Kanban: Long- and Medium-Term Planning

The last rule for kanban use in Figure 5.3.1.4 indicated that kanban requires some long- and medium-term planning tasks. This planning is independent of the kanban feedback loop. In detail, planning must fulfill the following tasks:

- Devise a long-term plan (and, if required, a medium-term plan) for resources according to an MRP II concept (manufacturing resource planning).
  1. Determine the master plan (independent demand) based on forecast (*ad hoc* or using techniques described in Chapter 9) or based, occasionally, on customer demand (see Sections 4.2.1 and 11.2.1).
  2. Calculate gross requirement to determine required resources in the form of purchased goods and capacity (Section 4.2.2).
  3. Develop long-term contracts with suppliers (blanket orders; see Section 4.2.5). If necessary, fine-tune release quantities in medium-term planning.
- Determine the type and number of kanban cards for each feedback loop (see Section 5.3.2). Analyses of deviations will reveal those feedback loops that require reexamination of the number of kanban cards so that overstock in buffers and interruptions in the loop can be corrected. This is done by means of the targeted addition or removal of kanbans.
- Control actual load through the kanban systems by, for example:
  - Registering kanbans dispatched from the buffer (order releases).
  - Registering incoming kanbans in the buffer (incoming material in the buffer).

As mentioned in Section 5.2.4, kanban techniques cannot be simply grafted onto an existing organization of production (such as job shop production). JIT principles, listed below in brief, must be implemented first:

- Clear layout of the organization; that is, the workstations and machines required to make the product are located close together and in the sequence that corresponds to the flow of goods (see Section 5.2.2, approaches 1 and 2).

- Small batch sizes, connected with a drastic reduction in setup times (see Section 5.2.1).

- Adherence to exact quantities. The scrap factor aims toward a "zero defects" program, with workstations personally responsible for quality control of components they produce (see Section 5.2.4 on quality assurance).

- *Preventive maintenance* forestalls machine downtime. It should increasingly eliminate the need for repairs that traditionally take place only once the machine breaks down (endangering delivery). Interdisciplinary troubleshooting teams provide help here (see Section 5.2.2, approach 3).

- *Adherence to short delivery lead times*. This demands adequate capacity and operator flexibility (see Section 5.2.2, approach 3).

5.4   The Cumulative Production Figures Principle

The cumulative production figures principle originated, like the kanban technique, within the automobile industry. It aids control of a logistics network with regard to deliveries by system suppliers and to coordination among different manufacturing companies. It is a simple technique that combines long-term resource management with short-term materials management and scheduling. In essence, in the manufacturing process of a certain product, it counts the number of intermediate products or states in the flow at certain *count points* and compares this amount to the planned flow of goods. Depending upon the result, the work system can be sped up or slowed down.

For the manufacture of different products, and different variants of products, a particular quantity of cumulative production figures is required. The cumulative production figures principle is best suited to a product concept of standard products or standard products with a few options and to serial production. The most important prerequisite is the same as that for the kanban technique: continuous demand along the value-added chain, or production and procurement with frequent order repetition.

The following discussion of the cumulative production figures principle is based mainly on [Wien04].

A *cumulative production figure* (abbreviated below as CPF) is the cumulative recording of the movement of goods over time.

Figure 5.4.0.1 shows an example of cumulative production figures along a sample manufacturing process. The process has been divided into the part processes, also called *control blocks*, which in this case are parts production and assembly.

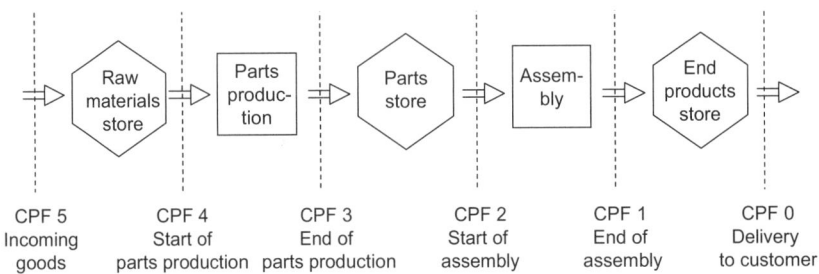

CPF 5	CPF 4	CPF 3	CPF 2	CPF 1	CPF 0
Incoming	Start of	End of	Start of	End of	Delivery
goods	parts production	parts production	assembly	assembly	to customer

Fig. 5.4.0.1   The   definition   of   cumulative   production   figures   along   the manufacturing process.

At the start and end of each part process, a cumulative production figure is defined: the entry cumulative production figure and the issue cumulative production figure. This is based on the assumption that there is always a process store, or buffer, between two part processes. For processing time within a part process, or control block, planning uses average lead time. In planning this is also called the *control block time offset*.

The *cumulative production figures curve* is a graph of the measurement of a cumulative production figure along the dimensions of amount and time.

A *cumulative production figures diagram* is a summary of cumulative production figures curves throughout the manufacturing process for a particular product.

Each product or product variant has its own pair of cumulative production figures diagrams:

- The *target cumulative production figures diagram* describes the planning based on demand forecast or blanket order and the subsequent resource requirements planning on the time axis. Batch size need not be taken into account, so that between two points in time a cumulative production figure will take a linear course. The difference in amount corresponds to gross requirement during the time period defined by the two count points. The rest follows long- and medium-term planning in the MRP II concept.

- The *actual cumulative production figures diagram* describes the measurement of the actual manufacturing process. The diagram shows the actual, current progress in production, lead times, and inventory in work-in-process and in buffers. Jumps in the lines are caused by batch sizes.

Figure 5.4.0.2 shows an example of a possible target and actual cumulative production figures diagram for the manufacturing process in Figure 5.4.1.

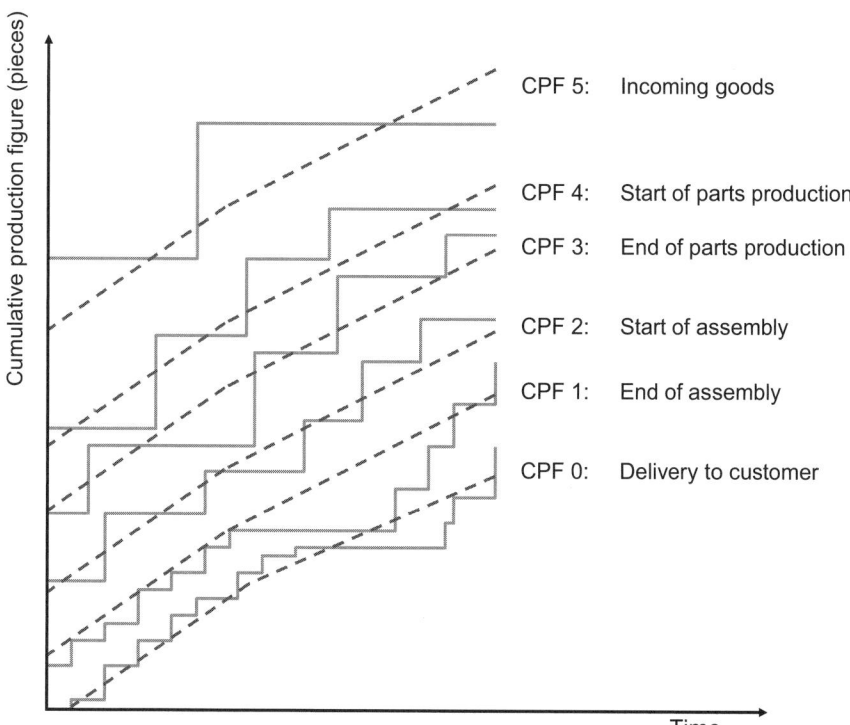

CPF 5:	Incoming goods
CPF 4:	Start of parts production
CPF 3:	End of parts production
CPF 2:	Start of assembly
CPF 1:	End of assembly
CPF 0:	Delivery to customer

Fig. 5.4.0.2   Cumulative production figures curves and target (dotted) and actual cumulative production figures diagram. (Example is based on [Wien04].)

The *cumulative production figures principle* (CPFP) is the planning & control of the manufacture of a product by means of comparing the target cumulative production figures diagram to the actual cumulative production figures diagram.

Through putting the two cumulative production figures curves, or whole cumulative production figures diagrams, one on top of the other, it is possible to bring the actual diagram closer to the target diagram through speeding up or breaking the manufacturing process. However, the following must be kept in mind:

- The diagrams give no information on the actual operation times and the current load on the work system: Incoming goods to a part process do not necessarily start the process immediately. In addition, there may be several different products being manufactured in the system. Therefore, the cumulative production figures principle cannot provide the basis for capacity management.

- Thus, for capacity management, the accuracy of the lead times, particularly interoperation times, is an absolute prerequisite.

- Count points must be placed in a way that guarantees accurate counts. A good point in time is at quality control: Here, both the amount of scrap and yield or good quantity are registered. The actual cumulative production figures can now be corrected accordingly at the already measured points, or appropriately marked special demand orders can be released.

In practice it becomes clear that in order to keep to the target diagram, sufficient capacity reserves, or capacity that can be implemented flexibly in time, must be available. This is even more the case due to the fact that capacity management in short-term planning (that is, control) is not possible with the cumulative production figures principle. Only continuous demand along the entire value-added chain will ensure that these reserves will not have to be tapped often.

5.5   Comparison of Techniques of Materials Management

We have introduced two techniques of materials management: the kanban technique and the cumulative production figures principle. Two further important techniques, the order point technique and the MRP technique, will be discussed in detail later in Sections 10.3 and 11.3. There are also techniques in connection with capacity management, such as Corma, that influence materials management (see Section 14.1).

Important principles behind these techniques, however, have already been introduced (for example, stochastic versus deterministic techniques). Now we will compare these very principles and, at the same time, compare the particular techniques themselves. We advise the reader to return to these comparisons again after reading the detailed sections mentioned above.

5.5.1   Comparison of Control Principles behind the Techniques

Push logistics and *pull logistics* are described in Section 3.2 as two different principles for the design of business processes. The control principles behind the techniques of materials management can be assigned to these two basic principles.

1. Push logistics:

The cumulative production figures principle, like the MRP technique, results in push logistics (see Figure 5.5.1.1).

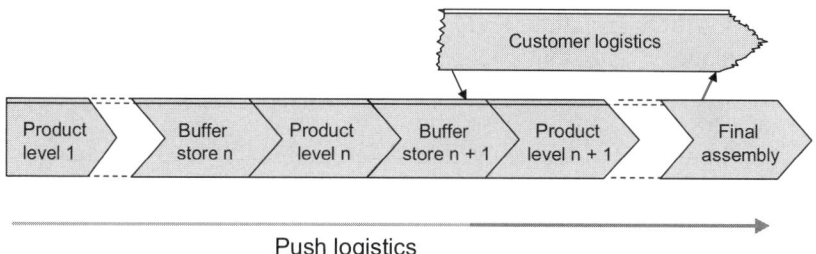

Fig. 5.5.1.1   Production logistics following the cumulative production figures principle (or the MRP technique): push logistics with central control superordinate to production.

- *In principle, there is only one single business process.* With this one process, goods are pushed through all production structure levels. The customer order can only affect push logistics in the final phase.

- *The order net already exists — as planned orders — in medium-term planning over the entire value-added chain.* In the *quasi-*

deterministic case, customer orders affect release of the production and procurement orders only in the area of delivery. It is the forecasts that ultimately determine quantity and point in time of order releases — individually and according to production structure level "from bottom to top" or from left to right as shown in Figure 5.5.1. As a result, the medium-term planning process is closely interwoven with the short-term control process, and it is difficult to uncouple them for decentralized planning structures.

With the MRP technique, in addition to the above, there are the following characteristics. They are discussed in more detail in Section 11.3.

- *MRP handles orders having contents that are very specific and difficult to plan, usually where there is no continuous demand.* In this case, the organizational units executing the work have too little knowledge to exercise independent control over the part orders they handle. In addition, any slack time in the order cycle is usually too short to allow for decentralized planning autonomy. For these reasons, the MRP technique is generally connected with central order releases for all production structure levels. The autonomy of the organizational units executing the work does not exceed the limits set by the planning data.

- *The classic MRP technique is used in medium-term planning.* The process of planning & control compares gross requirement at each production structure level with inventory and open orders and manages events that change inventory levels along the time axis. For the resulting net requirements, order proposals, or planned orders, are issued. These allow later order release of production and purchase orders as well as determination of load on capacities and dependent demand for components at lower production structure levels.

- *In a continuous process, planning adapts long-term forecasts to the medium term and charges incoming customer orders against the forecast.* Using a second MRP calculation, planning modifies the order proposals, if necessary. If the start date of the planned order falls in the present, orders are released. This triggers short-term planning and the control that will accompany the flow of goods.

2. Pull logistics:

The kanban technique leads — as does the order point technique — to pull logistics as shown in Figure 5.5.1.2.

- With decentralized planning, there are in principle as many (small) business processes as there are kanban feedback loops or production structure levels. From each of their buffers, the required components are ordered from the suppliers. The kanban rules, or the coordinating personnel, look to ensure timely delivery. They "pull" the components from a lower level to the buffer. The same type of pull logistics is found between customer and final assembly.

- *With the exception of blanket orders, there are no planned orders.* The planning variable is the forecast for each item. This is derived independently of the demand for other items from, for example, usage statistics. Planning is restricted to providing the infra-structure and setting up basic contracts. Actual control is conducted independently of planning.

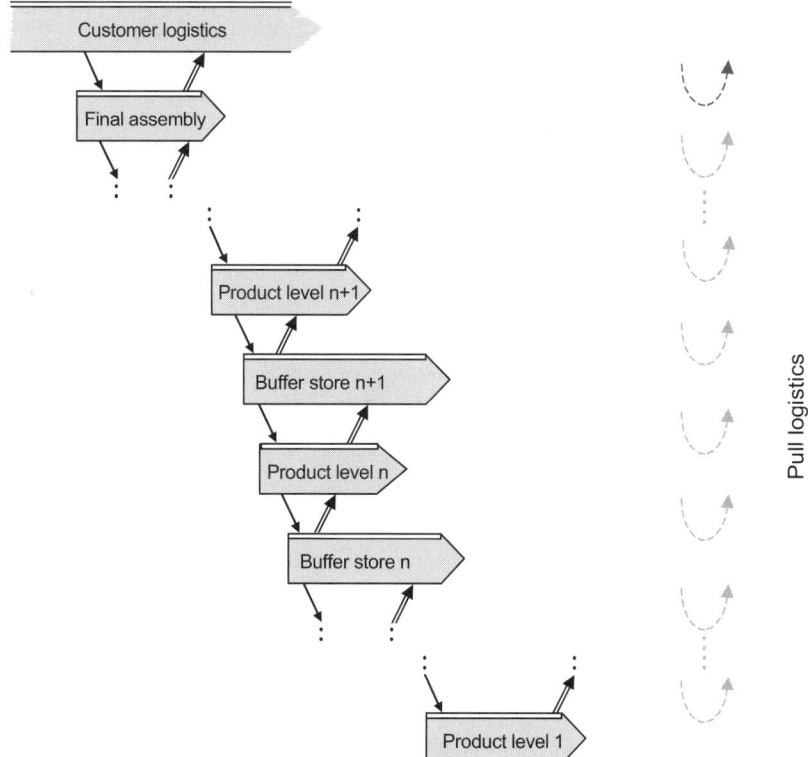

Fig. 5.5.1.2   Production logistics using the kanban technique (or the order point technique): pull logistics with control and inventory at each production structure level.

- *Kanban orders are repeated frequently:* Material planning for the orders can be tested and then turned over to the executing organizational units. Order release occurs decentrally. This autonomy is, however, restricted by the rules of kanban use. The design of the system (adding and removing kanban cards, for example) stays within the realm of central planning, as does control of the start-up and phase-out of production (see Section 5.3). The connection to the operator sites in production and to suppliers takes place when empty containers are sent, marked with a kanban card. Telecommunications can simplify this rather cumbersome transport, whereby the empty container is sent back to the supplier separately. In order to avoid duplicate orders, however, their kanban cards have to be specially marked.

Due to the fact that the production system downstream from the (customer) order penetration point (OPP) can be pulled directly by the customer order, the associated kanban card can clearly state very specific customer parameters. This is called a "generic kanban." See Section 6.1.4.

Pull logistics and repetitive frequency also basically characterize the order point technique. The differences are discussed in Section 5.5.3 below.

5.5.2   Strategy in Choosing Techniques and Implementing Procedures

Figure 5.5.2.1 lists as features some important prerequisites and effects that can be used as criteria when choosing one or the other of the techniques of materials management discussed above. The cumulative production figures principle does not appear as a separate technique. Its effects are approximately analogous to the kanban technique with continuous demand.

Figures 5.5.2.2 and 5.5.2.3 show strategy and a way of proceeding when implementing effective production and procurement logistics. This is based upon the JIT concepts in Section 5.2 and the comparison of techniques in Sections 5.5.1 as well as Section 4.3.2. The considerations shown in the figures hold for the entire value-adding chain, independently of whether the chain is within a single company or is a transcorporate chain.

The lean / just-in-time concept should be implemented first and independently of the technique to be chosen for materials management. The points raised in Figure 5.5.2.3 then serve to distinguish among the individual techniques of materials management.

Feature	Order point technique	Kanban	MRP
Prerequisites: •Frequency of demand: •Batch size: •Prod. levels linked: •A system must be set up for ... :	regular/continuous -- no (decoupled) .... control of inventory and goods on order	continuous small (f. high cost art.) via kanban chains ..... harmonic goods flow planning	-- -- via bills of material ... planning of orders at all structure levels
Measures to undertake if demand fluctuates:	increase safety stock	adapt capacity to load; increase safety factor	change safety requirements; frequent net change or recalculation
Risk incurred if demand is much lower than forecast:	inventory at all levels in the magnitude of the batch	inventory in all kanban feedback loops in the magnitude of the batch	inventory at all levels below or at the level of stocking
Risk incurred if demand is much greater than forecast:	medium stockout risk at all levels	medium stockout risk at all levels	high stockout risk below or at the level of stocking
Realization: •Conception (organizational / technical): •IT aids: •Execution/control:	simple simple simple	complicated to difficult simple very simple	simple complicated complicated

Fig. 5.5.2.1   Features of various techniques of materials management.

Implementation procedures for effective logistics (part 1): lean / just-in-time concept

1. *Introduce measures to raise the level of quality.* Processes must be so precise that no scrap will be delivered to the site executing the order.

2. *Examine the number and frequency of processes, particularly layouts.* Set up segmented or cellular manufacturing and implement logistics that reduce administration and transport times.

3. *Reduce batch-size-independent production or procurement costs, in particular setup time.* This latter must be very carefully checked at capacity-critical workstations. Implement modern setup technology.

4. *Consider the implementation of CNC machines, industrial robots, and flexible manufacturing systems (FMS).* These allow several operations to be combined into one (complete processing). The opposite may also prove advantageous, particularly in connection with segmenting; consider the use of several simple machines in various segments instead of a single-operation machine that transcends the segments.

5. *Achieve realization of rhythmic and harmonious production.* Production structure levels should be designed in such a way that lead times for the various levels are identical or multiples of one another.

6. *Determine batch size.* As small as possible. (Using the kanban technique, the batches should cover one day or just a few days.)

Steps 3, 4, 5, and 6 do not have to be performed in strict order.

Fig. 5.5.2.2   Procedures in implementing effective logistics: lean/JIT.

Implementation procedures for effective logistics (part 2): materials management techniques

7. For low-cost items or items with continuous or regular demand:

    a. Install the cumulative production figures principle if a number of successive levels were designed at point 5, through which large batches of relatively few products are manufactured according to forecast or blanket orders and for which capacity can be adapted to actual load despite mild fluctuations.

    b. Set up a chain of kanban feedback loops if a number of successive levels were arranged at point 5, which can — if, at the same time, demand is sufficiently regular — all be controlled according to use and for which capacity can be adapted to actual load.

    c. Otherwise, use the order point technique, together with the various techniques of scheduling and capacity management.

8. For items where demand is unique or for high-cost items with no regular demand — even after having implemented points 1–6:

    a. If the article can be produced at a rate downstream from the (customer) order penetration point (OPP) for a number of levels, planning & control should be deterministic, and as based on the customer order using a configuration of the customer production order over various levels with the MRP technique (material requirements planning).

    b. If the item lies at or upstream from the (customer) order penetration point (OPP) and demand is independent, a procedure that makes intuitive sense should be followed.

    c. Otherwise, the MRP technique can (must) be used in the quasi-deterministic case. The calculation should be updated daily or as often as several times per day ("online").

Fig. 5.5.2.3   Procedures in implementing effective logistics: choosing techniques of materials management.

5.5.3   Comparison of Techniques: Kanban versus Order Point Technique (*)

The implementation of the JIT concept entails advantages also to the order point technique (see Section 10.3). Indeed, short setup times result in smaller batch sizes, shorter lead times, and thus a lower order point. Smaller batch sizes lead to more frequent repetition of the same orders (which will increasingly overlap). Defining work contents of approximately the same length per production structure level improves the flow of goods.

Figure 5.5.3.1 shows the physical inventories on several production structure levels.

The symbol Δt stands for the necessary reaction time between reaching the order point (or, in kanban, registering that a container is empty) and withdrawing components from the next lower production structure level. With the lean / just-in-time concept, Δt is as small as possible, due to direct communication between supplier and user operation. T_p is the wait time of the item in the buffer or intermediate store. With just-in-time production, the buffer is located directly at the workstation, or user operation. T_p is thus time in storage.

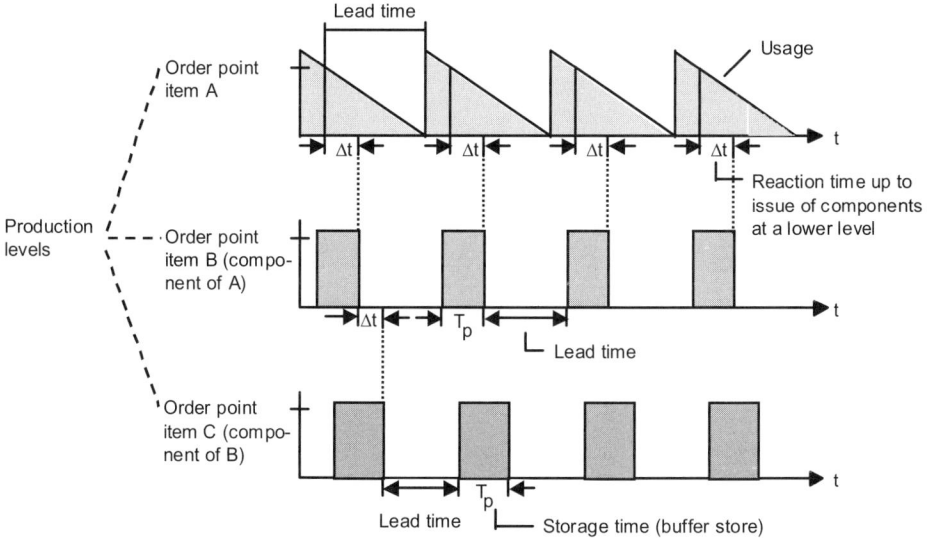

Fig. 5.5.3.1   Development of the buffers when production is rhythmic.

Order release according to consumption, is common to both techniques. Storage time functions as a time buffer. If usage is smaller than forecasted over a longer period, the production or procurement cycle will be triggered less often. In the kanban technique, fewer and fewer containers will be sent back and forth. But inventory in the buffer increases. From this, the same effect results as with the order point technique. In the reverse case, if usage is greater than predicted over a longer period, safety stock in the buffer ensures delivery capability. The percentage of stock for safety stock in the formula in Figure 5.3.2.3 and the number of kanban cards must then be increased.

So much for the common effects of both techniques. Now let's look at the *differences*. One feedback loop in the kanban technique will usually encompass only a few operations. There is a buffer between each loop.

Consequently, a production structure level controlled by the order point system is divided into a number of kanban feedback loops, ideally of the same length, as illustrated in Figure 5.5.3.2.

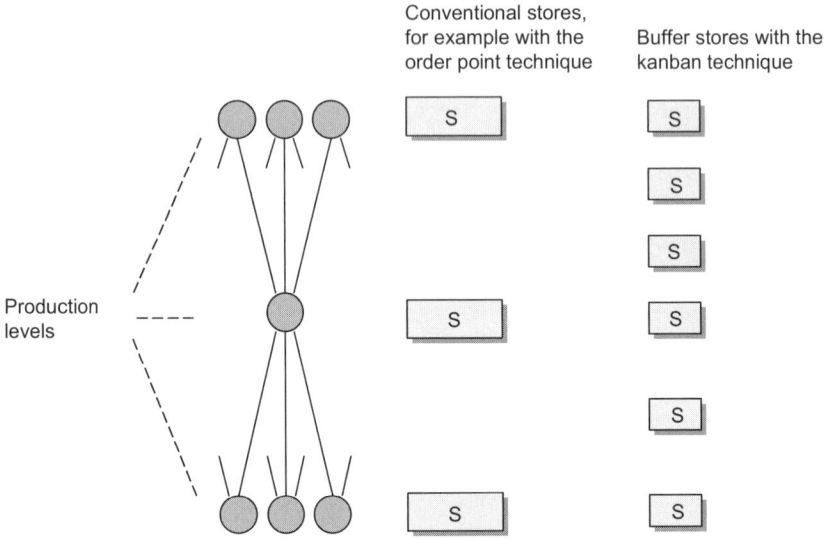

Fig. 5.5.3.2   Definition of production structure levels and (buffer) storage: order point technique versus kanban technique.

This results in the following advantages of the kanban technique:

- Inventory tends to be shifted to lower production structure levels, which is important for items with great added value. These are usually high-cost items, too (A items).

- Lead time through a kanban feedback loop is reduced for two reasons. First, a kanban feedback loop includes only a few operations. Second, there are no administrative expenses, as the buffers are located directly at the user operations.

- It is a *visual control system*, i.e. stockkeeping takes place "at a glance," and there is no paperwork or need for any other organizational unit to intervene.

- The process can be automated, because approximately the same quantities are produced again and again in short, sequential periods of time.

- Batch size in each feedback loop is small, because there are fewer operations and less setup time to consider.

It would be possible to design production structure levels controlled by the order point technique whose value-adding would equal that of the kanban feedback loops. However, due to the large number of small orders being processed all at once, the amount of administrative effort required controlling production remotely (away from the flow of goods) — through consulting computer lists, for example — would be prohibitive. The sensor that registers the kanban order (an event) to be released (state) is namely the simplest, most natural and rapid sensor imaginable: the human eye.

The large number of intermediate stores with the kanban technique can, of course, be seen as a disadvantage, as in the extreme case a buffer must be set up for each operation. However, the large number of stores is only a problem if an external agent or expensive measuring devices (such as tallying by hand) must be used to perform inventory control. Figure 5.3.1.3 has already suggested that automatic data collection is a good way to register the kanban process, including both open kanban orders and inventory in the buffers.

There are further important differences between the order point technique and the kanban technique with regard to flexibility and to assigning requisition control tasks:

- With kanban, control is consistently decentralized. The executing units take over requisitioning activities, which at first glance seems to encourage their autonomy. But one of the rules for kanban use demands that capacity be absolutely adapted to load, which is infinite capacity planning. The due date for all kanban orders is, without exception, "now" — which actually restricts autonomy.

- The order point technique can be implemented with either centralized or decentralized organization of control. The more temporal reserves that there are in the lead time and that can be planned infinitely, the more that requisitioning with the order point technique can be turned over directly to the work units.[18] If the available interoperation times are short, or if capacity limits must be considered, possible resulting interruptions in the order cycle could affect the entire value-adding chain. If the value-adding

---

[18]   There is no strict line dividing this from the kanban technique if stocks below order point are no longer checked according to lists, but rather are registered "visually" right at the buffer.

chain is made up of many executing organizational units, central coordination of control (with central order release) may be more flexible, but it also involves greater effort.

5.6   Summary

Lean/JIT aims to reduce lead time and, at the same time, to minimize stored and in-process inventory. The most significant measure to reduce lead time is setup time reduction. If setup time reductions result in decreased setup costs, batch sizes can become smaller. This reduces average operation times and wait times. Concepts for setup time reduction can be grouped under the term *SMED* (single-minute exchange of die), but also under the terms *setup-friendly production facilities*, *cyclic planning*, or *modularization*.

Further concepts for lead time reduction are production or manufacturing segmentation, cellular manufacturing, complete processing, and structuring of the assembly process. Harmonizing the product range and work contents helps, in addition, to achieve repetitive processes and a balanced flow of goods in production. This increases the degree of automation and reduces wait times.

Additional lean / just-in-time concepts ensure high quality as well as rapid administrative connections between feeder and user operations, for example, combined with blanket order processing. And, there is also the availability of resources: over-capacity of machines and tools as well as flexible personnel. Further elements of the Japanese way of thinking include group thinking, elimination of waste, *kaizen*, *poka-yokero*, order, and cleanliness.

Lean / just-in-time concepts improve the quality of all techniques of resource management. Shorter lead times allow the (customer) order penetration point (OPP) to be set lower in the product structure, thus increasing the potential for use of deterministic methods in requirements planning. Through smaller batch sizes, or even "make to order," inexact forecasts of requirements upstream from or at the (customer) order penetration point (OPP) lead to fewer long-term materials planning errors.

Simple techniques of planning & control are possible with production or procurement with frequent order repetition. The best-known technique is kanban. Between each user operation and supplier operation, a certain number of kanbans pass back and forth. Each kanban refers to a container that stands at the user operation in a clearly marked location. It is managed visually and sent back to the supplier operation as soon as it is empty. It is important to follow the kanban rules of use. The number of kanban cards must be determined on the basis of medium- or long-term planning according to the MRP II concept. The cumulative production figures principle represents another simple technique of materials and scheduling management. Work progress is recorded at set count points.

The cumulative production figures principle and the MRP technique are push logistics, while kanban and order point systems are pull logistics. In the first, planning is linked to control; with the latter, they are separate. For this reason, control with MRP is felt to be more complicated. Kanban is a usage-controlled technique of materials management that functions optimally with continuous demand. It is similar to the order point system, with the difference that control, in particular order release, is always decentralized. This allows for significantly more orders than with centralized control. The kanban cycles generally are comprised of fewer operations at a product level than the order point system, which tends to result in less (buffer) inventory. Consideration of these comparisons is a sensible strategy when choosing techniques and means of implementation in production and procurement logistics. Special considerations are necessary where different techniques coexist.

5.7   Keywords

cellular manufacturing, 322
complete processing, 325
cumulative production figures, 344
dedicated capacity, 322
external setup (time), 320
flexible manufacturing systems (FMS), 351
harmonizing
  the content of work, 326

the product range, 318
inside exchange of dies (IED), 320
internal setup (time), 320
jidoka concept, 311
job enrichment, 330
just-in-time concept, 311
just-in-time logistics, 330
kanban, 335

kanban feedback loop, 337
kanban rules, 338
kanban technique, 337
line balancing, 326
modular product concept, 319
move card, 337
near-to-line production, 322
outside exchange of dies (OED), 320
preventive maintenance, 343

5.8   Scenarios and Exercises

5.8.1   Operation Time versus Operation Cost, or the Effect of Varying Setup Time and Batch Size

This exercise will help to illustrate the need to find a balance between (1) short lead time, and (2) low cost, for any operation. These two factors are determined by setup time and batch size. You will find the effect of setup time and batch size on

a. The operation time, which is a measure of the lead time of the order.

b. The *operation time per unit* (that is, operation time divided by batch size), which is a measure of the cost of the operation and therefore of the cost of the production or procurement order.

Solve the following tasks:

(0) First, suppose a setup time of 200, a run time per unit of 100, and a batch size of 4. Calculate the operation time and the operation time per unit.

(1) If batch size is increased to 20, what are the effects on operation time and operation time per unit? In your opinion, what effects are positive or negative?

(2) Suppose that due to the hard work of the process engineers (e.g., by applying SMED measures), setup time could be reduced to 100. What is the effect of this, if the batch size is maintained at 20?

(3) To what extent can the batch size be reduced after the reduction of set-up time to 100, so that the operation time does not exceed the original operation time of 600? What will the operation time per unit be?

(4) To what extent can the batch size be reduced after the reduction of setup time to 100, so that the operation time per unit does not exceed the original time per unit of 150? What will the operation time be?

Solution:

(0) Operation time: 600; operation time per unit: 150.

(1) Positive: operation time per unit clearly reduced to 110. negative: operation time very much extended to 2200.

(2) Positive: operation time per unit slightly reduced to 105. negative: operation time only very slightly reduced to 2100.

(3) Batch size = 5; operation time per unit = 120.

(4) Batch size = 2; operation time = 300.

You can view the solution, implemented with Flash animation, on the Internet at URL:

http://www.intlogman.lim.ethz.ch/operation_time.html

Try out different values for setup time, run time per unit, and batch size.

5.8.2 The Effect of Cellular Manufacturing on Lead Time Reduction

Figure 5.8.2.1 shows a possible routing sheet for production of shafts. The batch size is 10.

Operation	Setup time	Run time per unit
Millcut	0.02	0.02
Lathe	0.6	0.06
Millcut nut	1.6	0.6
Pre-grinding	1.2	0.12
Final grinding	1.2	0.16

Fig. 5.8.2.1   Routing sheet for production of shafts.

a. Calculate the lead time in traditional job shop production. *Hint*: For job shop production, lead time has to be calculated assuming a sequence of operations. Therefore, you can use the formula in Figure 5.2.2.3.

b. Calculate the maximum lead time for the case of cellular manufacturing, that is, using the formula in Figure 5.2.2.4. (*Hint*: First determine the cell driver).

c. For the given routing sheet shown in Figure 5.8.2.1, and for cellular production, find a temporal order of operations that yields minimum lead time.

d. For the given routing sheet shown in Figure 5.8.2.1, and for cellular production, find a temporal order of operations that yields minimal load (or minimum allocated time for the operation, that is, operation time plus wait time between the units of the batch) at the workstations.

Solution:

a. 14.22.

b. 10.98 (the cell driver is the operation "millcut nut" with an operation time of 7.60; setup time plus run time of all the other operations is 3.38).

c. Minimum total lead time is 7.88. The setup and the first unit of the batch of operations "millcut" and "lathe" can be fully executed during the setup of the cell driver. The setup of the operations "pre-grinding" and "final grinding" can be executed during the setup of the cell driver. Each unit of the batch can be run directly after its run on the cell driver operation. Thus, the run times for one unit for "pre-grinding" and "final grinding" have to be added to the cell driver operation time, or $0.12 + 0.16 + 7.6$, making 7.88.

d. Lead time with minimum load is 8.24. Again, the setup and the first unit of the batch of operations "millcut" and "lathe" can be fully executed during the setup of the cell driver. For "pre-grinding," in order to be ready to execute the last unit of the batch just after the completion of the cell driver operation, the 9 units of "pre-grinding" must have been just completed at point 7.6 in the time axis. Thus, the latest start date of "pre-grinding" must be $7.6 - 9 * 0.12 - 1.2 = 5.32$. For "final grinding," the first unit of the batch can be executed directly after the first unit of "pre-grinding" has been executed, that is, at $5.32 + 1.2 + 0.12 = 6.64$. This implies that the latest start date of "final grinding" is at $6.64 - 1.2 = 5.44$, and its completion date is at $5.44 + 1.2 + 10 * 0.16 = 8.24$.

You can view the solution, implemented with Flash animation, on the Internet at URL:

http://www.intlogman.lim.ethz.ch/cell_driver.html

By modifying setup and run times of the operations, change the cell driver. Try to find a combination where the variant "minimum total lead time" tends towards the "maximum lead time" value of the lead time formula for cell manufacturing.

5.8.3   Line Balancing — Harmonizing the Content of Work

Figure 5.8.3.1 shows a possible routing sheet for parts production out of sheet metal. Three different products are produced: items 1, 2, and 3. All have a similar routing sheet. For the different operations, the number in the table is the operation time, and the number in parentheses is the setup time.

Product ID	1			2		3	
Lot size / Process	400	?	?	50	?	10	?
Cut / work center A	10 (2)			5 (1)		6 (1)	
Press / work center B	6 (2)			15 (1)		6 (1)	
Bend / work center C	2 (2)			20 (2)		12 (2)	
Treat surface / work center D	18 (10)			--		9 (7)	
Test / work center E	2 (2)			9 (5)		--	
Preassemble / work center F	16 (0)			3 (1)		--	
Σ operation times	54 (18)			52 (10)		33 (11)	
(Σ setup times) / (Σ operation times)	1/3			1/5 (ca.)		1/3	

Fig. 5.8.3.1   Harmonizing the content of work: routing sheets for three products.

In accordance with the discussion in Section 5.2.3, assume a production measure of 12 time units. The task is to perform measures to change lead times of operations, chosen from the various possible measures to line balance or harmonize the content of work listed according to Figure 5.2.3.3.

a. Suppose that the first two operations can be combined into one (why is this a feasible assumption?). Item 3 seems — at first glance — to fit quite well into 3 units of the production measure. Therefore, according to the first one of the measures listed in Figure 5.2.3.3, try to change lot sizes of items 1 and 2 (use the empty columns in Figure 5.8.3.1), in order to obtain for each of them a total operation time on the order of 36 units of time.

b. Is it possible, in practice, to combine the last two operations into one, fitting them into one production measure?

c. For item 1, the third and the fourth operations do not fit into one production measure, despite significant changes to the batch size. What other possible measures listed in Figure 5.2.3.3 could be implemented?

d. After implementing all these measures, are there still problems?

Possible solution:

a. There are machines that perform both operations in one step (e.g., laser cutting machines). Changing the lot size for product 1 to 200 results in a total operation time of 36, with 18 units of time for setup. Furthermore, the length of the combination of the two first operations is now 10 (or even less, due to complete processing), and this fits well into one production measure. Changing the lot size for item 1 to 100 would result in a total operation time of 27, with 18 units of time for setup. Thus a batch size of 200 is the better choice. In addition, changing the lot size for product 2 to 25 results in a total operation time of 31, with 10 units of time for setup. Again, the combination of the two first operations fits well into one production measure, its total length being 11.

b. Yes. Testing and preassembly can be done at the same physical work center. Furthermore, with a lot size of 200 for item 1, the combination of the two last operations would fit well into one production measure.

c. Considering the very small run time per unit, the bending operation seems to be very simple (also, the second operation, pressing, appears to be rudimentary, as compared the process for item 2). Thus, it might be possible to purchase sheet metal that is already profiled (bent). Another solution would be to combine this short process into the same production measure together with cutting and pressing, using a dedicated (simple, but cheap) machine that could be installed not at work center C, but close to work center B.

Surface treatment is most likely a subcontracted process. This is probably the reason behind the long setup time, which may actually reflect transportation time rather than setup time at the supplier's site. If so, why not look for a faster transportation vehicle or for a sub-contractor in greater geographical proximity to the factory?

d. Yes. For product 1, setup time is now 50% of the operation time. If setup time is not reduced significantly with the measure in point c, then additional measures must be found to reduce the setup time (e.g., by implementing SMED techniques).

5.8.4   Calculating the Number of Kanban Cards

An automotive company has implemented a JIT program using kanbans to signal the movement and production of product. The average inventory levels have been reduced to where they are roughly proportional to the number of kanbans in use. Figure 5.8.4.1 shows the data for three of the products.

Item ID.	Lead time	Length of the statistical period	Usage during statistical period	Number of parts (units) per container	Safety factor (%)	Number of containers per transport batch
1	36	20	600	200	0	1
2	36	20	100	25	0	1
3	36	20	50	10	0	1

Fig. 5.8.4.1   Data on three products for calculation of the number of kanban cards.

a. The process engineers have been hard at work improving the manufacturing process. They have initiated a new project to reduce lead time from 36 days to 21 days. What would the percentage change in average inventory be, for each item?

b. Calculate the number of kanban cards using other data values. Try to answer the following questions:

- What is the minimum number of kanban cards required in any case?

- How do the safety factor and the number of containers per transport batch influence the number of kanban cards required?

Solution for a:

Using the formula in Figure 5.3.2.3, calculate the required number of kanban cards before and after the process improvement. As inventory is proportional to number of kanbans, the inventory reduction corresponds to the reduction of the number of kanban cards.

- Item 1: before, 7; after, 5   →   Inventory reduction: 29%
- Item 2: before, 9; after, 6   →   Inventory reduction: 33%
- Item 3: before, 10; after, 7   →   Inventory reduction: 30%

You can view the solution, implemented with Flash animation, on the Internet at URL:

http://www.intlogman.lim.ethz.ch/kanban_principle.html

6 Concepts for Product Families and One-of-a-Kind Production

In buyer's markets, customers ask for meeting their specific requirements with regard to product composition and quality. Customers do not want to have to adapt their own processes to standard products. Instead, they demand adaptation of the product to their own specific requirements. This has given rise to a tendency towards product *families* and one-of-a-kind production which requires appropriate product and process concepts as well as logistics concepts. Traditional MRP II concepts did not suffice. New concepts had to be developed.

> *Variant-oriented concepts* do not aim towards reduction of the number of product variants, but instead aim towards mastering a variety of variants.

For many companies, particularly medium-sized companies, being *market driven*, that is, fulfilling customer specification, through flexibly offering product families with many variants is the main market strategy, as the following excerpts from sales brochures of some European companies illustrate:

"All fire dampers are manufactured to customer order to any desired widths and heights." (Trox-Hesco, Inc., 8630 Rüti, Switzerland)

"Collets from 6 to 20 mm for any desired diameter, to the exact tenth of a millimeter." (Schäublin, 2800 Delémont, Switzerland)

"The type of power supply system could not be determined until the last minute. In spite of late specifications, we delivered on time." (Knobel AG, 8755 Ennenda, Switzerland)

"Every exterior door is manufactured individually according to your specifications and measurements in single-item production. We could show you over a hundred thousand of our exterior doors already installed, but yours would not be one of them." (Biffar, Inc., 6732 Edenkoben (Pfalz), Germany)

Service industries show similar tendencies and selling points. In the insurance sector for instance, in addition to mass business that focuses on low costs, "custom" insurance policies are offered with flexible terms and customer design ease. Similar features are found in the banking industry. Mass customization is the corresponding production type that emphasizes custom products that do not cost more than mass-produced products.

An approach to fulfilling this demand is realization of the lean / just-in-time concept in the case of production with infrequent or without order repetition, as mentioned in Section 5.2.5. With short lead times, the (customer) order penetration point (OPP) can be set as low as possible in the product structure. This reduces the necessity of forecasting and thus also of forecast errors. However, the corresponding simple kanban technique, which belongs to lean/JIT, requires production with frequent order repetition. In all cases, *variant-oriented* concepts form the prerequisite.

Figure 6.0.0.1 shows some of the characteristic features of planning & control, taken from Section 3.4.

Features referring to user and product or product family					
Feature	➤ **Values**				
Orientation of product structure	➤	▲ convergent		▲combination ▼upper/lower structr. levels	▼ divergent
Frequency of customer demand	➤	unique	Discontinuous (lumpy, sporadic)	regular	continuous (steady)
Product variety concept	➤	according to (changing) customer specification	product family with many variants	product family	standard product with options	individual or standard product
Features referring to logistics and production resources					
Feature	➤ **Values**				
Production environment	➤	engineer-to-order	make-to-order	assemble-to-order (from single parts)	assemble-to-order (from assemblies)	make-to-stock
Features referring to production or procurement order					
Feature	➤ **Values**				
Reason for order release (type of order)	➤	demand / (customer production (or procurement) order)		prediction / (forecast order)		use / (stock replenishment order)
Frequency of order repetition	➤	production / procurement without order repetition		production / procurement with infrequent order repetition		production / procurement with frequent order repetition
Flexibility of order due date	➤	no flexibility (fixed delivery date)		not very flexible		flexible

Increasing degree of suitability for variant-oriented concepts

Fig. 6.0.0.1   Degree of suitability for variant-oriented concepts.[1]

---

[1]   The horizontal distribution of the values in the morphological scheme indicates their relation to the increasing degree according to the given criterion.

Values of these features are arranged from left to right in such a way that the suitability of implementing variant-oriented concepts is the greatest to the *left* of the table. For the feature most important with regard to these concepts, the characteristic value is shown with a black background. Compare also Figure 3.5.3.1.

The difficulties of variant production do not show up in logistics alone. The problem affects the very concept of the product, as well as computer-aided design. In many cases, customer order-specific drawings must be completed as early as the bidding phase. In actual production, the problem to be faced is how to set up the machines rapidly for a new variant. Moreover, variant-specific work documents must also be produced.

Variant-oriented concepts are also called *product family orientation*, *variant orientation*, *variant production*, and *customer order production*. They affect virtually all planning & control tasks (see Figure 4.1.4.2), particularly the representation of logistics objects like master data and orders. Other tasks, serving to process these data, must be expanded, such as for sales bids and orders, determination of independent demand, and planning and release of production or procurement orders.

6.1   Logistics Characteristics of a Product Variety Concept

We find the tendency towards non-repetitive production in many branches, as the examples above show. What stands to the fore, however, is discrete manufacturing, or *convergent product structure*. Flexibility to fulfill customer demands varies in degree. In the fashion industry, for example, there are "off the rack" products, *prêt-à-porter* (ready-to-wear) products, and actual *haute couture*, or creations made for individual customers. In gastronomy, there are standard dinner menus, *à la carte* concepts, and even customer-specific menu creations. Other industries and service industries distinguish similar levels of adapting to customer demands using their own specific terminology.

With regard to the variety of the product assortment, we can distinguish — in a first attempt — three well-known characteristics:

1. Standard product manufacturing
2. Low-variety manufacturing
3. High-variety manufacturing

While standard product manufacturing is not the subject of the present chapter, it will be used for comparison purposes as we examine differences in logistics management for these three types.

In the following sections, the characteristics in the figures beginning with 6.1.1.1 also include some of the characteristic features of planning & control, taken from Section 3.4. The values shown in black are the main values, while values shown in gray are frequent values for each of the order processing types.

6.1.1   Standard Product Manufacturing

Figure 6.1.1.1 shows the characteristics of *standard product manufacturing*.

Features referring to user and product or product family					
Feature	➡	**Values**			
Product variety concept	➡	according to (changing) customer specification	product family with many variants	product family	standard product with options	individual or standard product
Features referring to logistics and production resources					
Feature	➡	**Values**			
Production environment	➡	engineer-to-order	make-to-order	assemble-to-order (from single parts)	assemble-to-order (from assemblies)	make-to-stock
Features referring to production or procurement order					
Feature	➡	**Values**			
Reason for order release (type of order)	➡	demand/ (customer production (or procurement) order)		prediction / (forecast order)		use / (stock replenishment order)
Frequency of order repetition	➡	production / procurement without order repetition		production / procurement with infrequent order repetition		production / procurement with frequent order repetition
Type of long-term orders	➡	none		blanket order: capacity		blanket order: goods

Fig. 6.1.1.1   Values of characteristic features for standard product manufacturing.

Customer tolerance time with standard product manufacturing is zero or possibly so short that at most the last production structure level (final assembly) can be produced according to a customer order. This means that products must be manufactured, in the entire logistics network, *prior to* customer demand and stored. Close examination of processes and tasks in long- and medium-term planning reveals their high degree of importance for standard product manufacturing. The processes and tasks match almost exactly those presented in the generalized model in Section 4.1:

- *Long-term planning* determines the master plan for anticipated production and breaks it down for the production structure levels. The master plan must take into account forecasts at each structure level or forecasts for end products.

- Blanket orders at all production structure levels of the logistics network result in more accurate planning.

- *Medium-term planning* first determines criteria for order release and batch sizes, as a basis for calculating order proposals.

- If we view the minimum blanket order quantity as a kind of demand, we can speak of customer order production.

Short-term planning & control for standard product manufacturing involves processes and tasks that are of medium importance. For these tasks, Figure 6.1.1.2 shows a specialized form of the presentation in Figure 4.1.3.1.

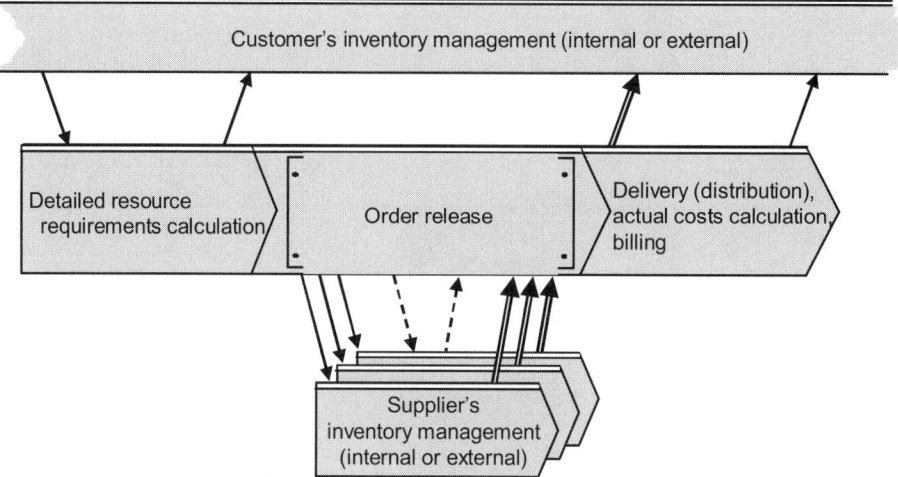

Fig. 6.1.1.2   Short-term planning & control for standard product manufacturing.

- An inventory control process of a customer starts the logistics of a manufacturer in the logistics network by a stock replenishment order. The manufacturer withdraws the ordered products from his (intermediate) store. The logistics of the various production structure levels are thus no longer linked. Moreover, order processing now involves "only" the release of order proposals.

- Resource management is restricted to renewed checking of the availability of the planned resources in the planned orders.

- Order coordination between production structure levels is only necessary if there are great deviations from planning, because (buffer) stores lie between the intermediate products. All orders are thus (one-level) stock replenishment orders or forecast orders.

- The manufacturer has to work to coordinate its capacity, particularly if capacity utilization is high.

6.1.2   High-Variety Manufacturing

Figure 6.1.2.1 shows the characteristics of *high-variety manufacturing*. In the extreme case, this is *manufacturing according to (pure) customer specification*.

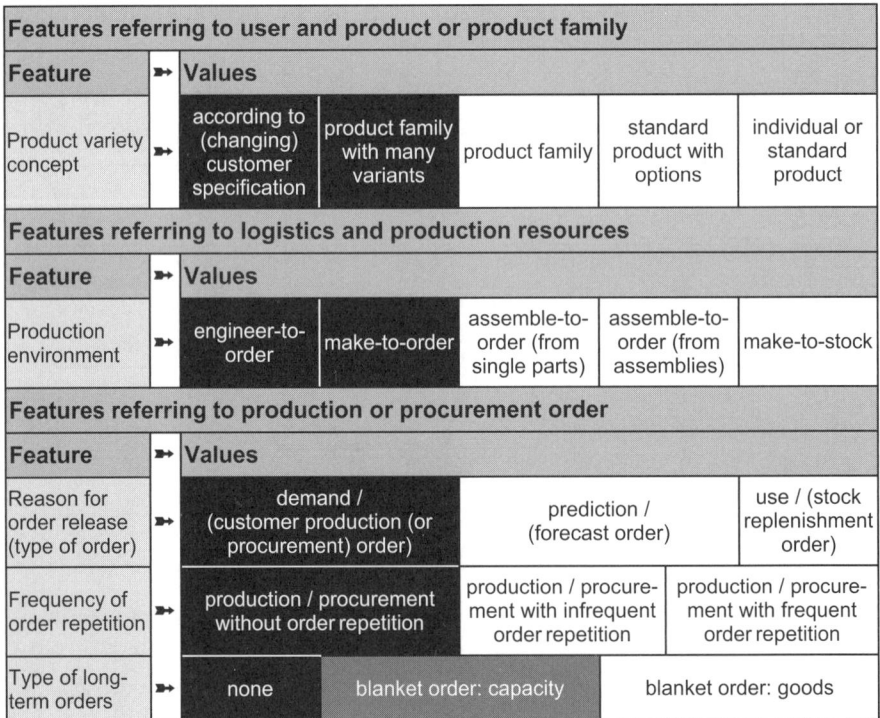

Features referring to user and product or product family					
Feature	➡ **Values**				
Product variety concept	➡ according to (changing) customer specification	product family with many variants	product family	standard product with options	individual or standard product
Features referring to logistics and production resources					
Feature	➡ **Values**				
Production environment	➡ engineer-to-order	make-to-order	assemble-to-order (from single parts)	assemble-to-order (from assemblies)	make-to-stock
Features referring to production or procurement order					
Feature	➡ **Values**				
Reason for order release (type of order)	➡ demand / (customer production (or procurement) order)		prediction / (forecast order)		use / (stock replenishment order)
Frequency of order repetition	➡ production / procurement without order repetition		production / procurement with infrequent order repetition		production / procurement with frequent order repetition
Type of long-term orders	➡ none	blanket order: capacity		blanket order: goods	

Fig. 6.1.2.1   Values of characteristic features for high-variety manufacturing.

For high-variety manufacturing there is usually enough time up to delivery to manufacture all production structure levels (except for general-use raw materials and purchased parts) for the customer order. Thus, products are manufactured in almost the entire logistics network according to demand, with no stockkeeping. Inventory, in the form of raw materials and purchased parts, is replenished as it is consumed.

Close examination of processes and tasks of high-variety manufacturing in long- and medium-term planning reveals that they have a medium to low degree of importance. Again, we can revise the generalized presentation in Section 4.1 to make it more exact and specialized (not all tasks are equally important or pronounced). Figure 6.1.2.2 shows this revised form.

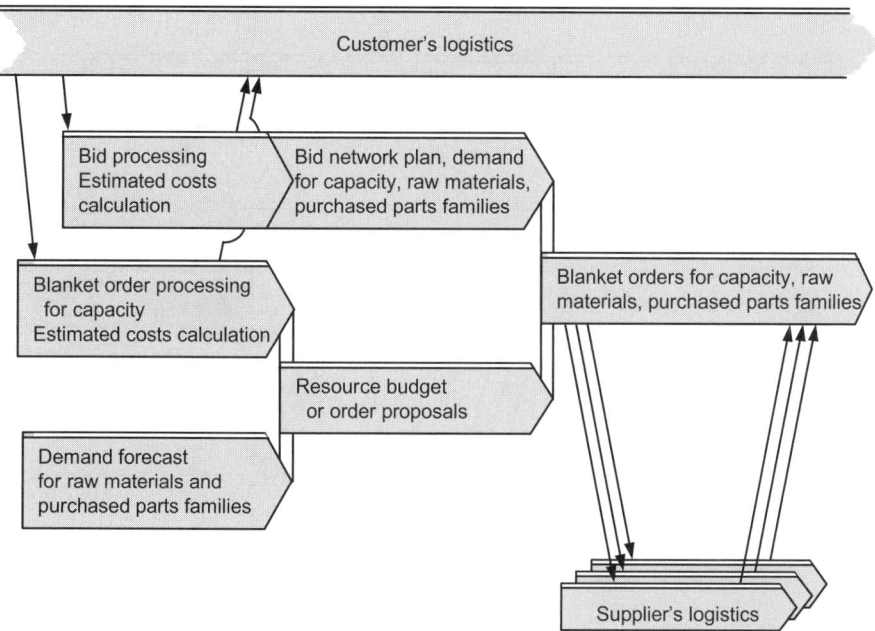

Fig. 6.1.2.2   Long- and medium-term planning for manufacturing according to customer specification or of product families with many variants.

- In *long-term planning* a master plan does not make any sense. At best, forecasts can be made for raw materials or purchased parts families.
- Forecasts for capacity are necessary, however. Blanket orders for capacity at all production structure levels of the logistics network result in improved planning power.

- An order must first be translated into a process plan for the planning of capacity, raw materials, or purchased parts families. This is usually a process network plan, such as is commonly used in project management.

- *Medium-term planning* is at most a fine-tuning of the long-term planning network plans for the orders.

Close examination of processes and tasks of manufacturing according to customer specification or of product families with many variants in short-term planning & control reveals their great importance. Order processing and subsequent resource management are complex. Let us again revise the generalized table in Figure 4.1.3.1 and show the more exact, specialized form in Figure 6.1.2.3.

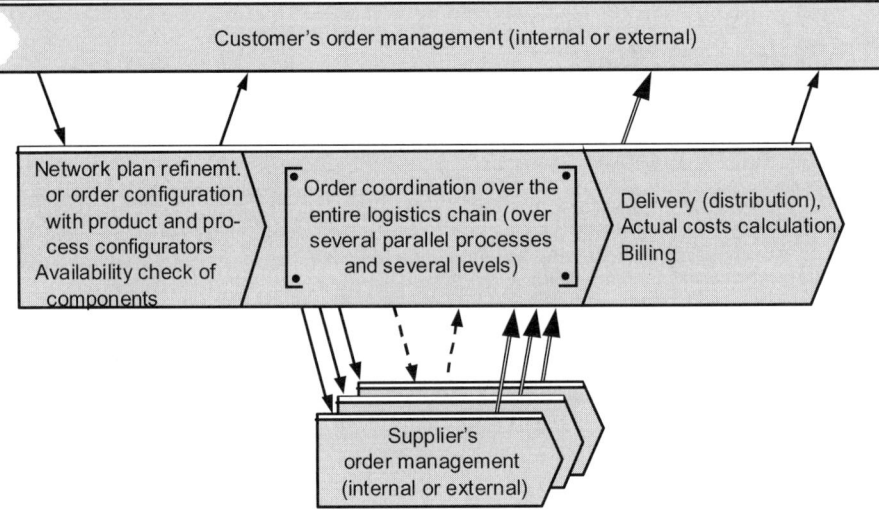

Fig. 6.1.2.3   Short-term planning & control for manufacturing according to customer specification or of product families with many variants.

- For orders according to customer specification, first the process network plan must be refined (see, for example, Section 13.4). Raw materials or purchased parts must be made available.

- A multilevel order must be configured with all its production documents, often including the drawing and process plans (see Section 6.2.3). In the case of variant-rich product families, this should happen quickly, due to the low value added. Rule-, case-, or constraint-based product and process configurators for order configuration with many variants are used here (see Section 6.3).

- Order coordination is required for all part orders over the entire logistics network, that is, over all parallel orders for components or processes at a lower level and over several production structure levels. Order coordination is thus complex. Generally there is no flexibility with regard to start and completion date for part orders. Any small disturbances on the user side or in the production infrastructure of a co-maker have rapid repercussions within the entire logistics chain.

6.1.3   Low-Variety Manufacturing

Figure 6.1.3.1 shows the characteristics of *low-variety manufacturing*.

Features referring to user and product or product family					
Feature	➡	**Values**			
Product variety concept	➡	according to (changing) customer specification	product family with many variants	product family	standard product with options	individual or standard product
Features referring to logistics and production resources					
Feature	➡	**Values**			
Production environment	➡	engineer-to-order	make-to-order	assemble-to-order (from single parts)	assemble-to-order (from assemblies)	make-to-stock
Features referring to production or procurement order					
Feature	➡	**Values**			
Reason for order release (type of order)	➡	demand / (customer production (or procurement) order		prediction / (forecast order)		use (stock replenishment order)
Frequency of order repetition	➡	production / procurement without order repetition		production / procurement with infrequent order repetition	production / procurement with frequent order repetition	
Type of long-term orders	➡	none	blanket order: capacity		blanket order: goods	

Fig. 6.1.3.1   Values of the characteristic features for low-variety manufacturing.

For low-variety manufacturing, delivery lead time is generally long enough that some of the highest production structure levels can be manufactured for the customer order. This is particularly so for production structure levels above which the variants of the product family appear. Ideally, this involves only pre-assembly and assembly. The processes and tasks of low-variety manufacturing in the logistics network are a combination of the two previous types, standard product manufacturing and high-variety manufacturing.

- Products downstream from the (customer) order penetration point (OPP) are manufactured according to customer order with no stocking. Order processing has the character here of that of manufacturing according to customer specification or of product families with many variants. However, as shown in the figure, there is production with infrequent order repetition, as there are only a limited number of variants. On the other hand, it makes sense to produce as often as possible with a batch size of 1, that is, in single-item production.

- Upstream from or at the (customer) order penetration point (OPP), products are manufactured and stored prior to customer demand. Here, order processing has the character of that of manufacturing standard products manufacturing. If variants are produced downstream from the order penetration point, production upstream from the order penetration point is production with frequent order repetition. Otherwise, it is production with infrequent order repetition.

- Triggers for order release and the type of long-term orders are mixed and differ in whether a product lies downstream or upstream from (or at) the order penetration point. Downstream from the order penetration point, we find the character of that of manufacturing according to customer specification or of product families with many variants. Upstream from or at the order penetration point, order processing has the character of that of manufacturing standard products manufacturing. Forecast and blanket orders refer here to product families.

6.1.4   Different Variant-Oriented Techniques, the Final Assembly Schedule, and the Order Penetration Point

In operations and logistics management, techniques for the planning & control of product variety concepts with options or variants are called *variant-oriented techniques*.

Sections 6.2 and 6.3 will present different variant-oriented techniques. They can best be grouped in *two classes*.

> *Adaptive techniques* entail two steps. The first step determines a suitable "parent version" from the existing variants. In the second step, the parent version is adapted, or specified in detail, according to the requirements of the variant.

Adaptive techniques are expensive in terms of administrative cost and effort. For use of these techniques to be economically feasible, the value added must be high. The techniques are implemented in the product variety concepts *standard product with options*, *product family*, and *product according to (changing) customer specification*. See Section 6.2.

> *Generative techniques* are variant-oriented techniques that configure the process plan for each product variant during order processing from a number of possible components and operations. Generative techniques use rules that already exist in an information system.

With generative techniques, order administration is quick and inexpensive, so that the product variety concept *product families with many variants*, despite value added that is often low, can be handled efficiently in terms of operations. See Section 6.3.

For further details with regard to the principles of adaptive and generative approaches and techniques, see [Schi01].

The principal characteristics of adaptive and generative techniques are closely associated with those of the four product variety concepts (standard product with options, product family, product family with many variants, and product according to changing customer specification).

Figure 6.1.4.1 summarizes four sets of characteristics. Each set of characteristics that is typically and commonly found together with a particular product variety concept has:

- A production type
- Values for the planning & control characteristics *frequency of order repetition*, *production environment* and *order batch size*

Product variety concept	...and typically associated characteristics and production types
Standard product with (few) options	Repetitive manufacturing Production with frequent order repetition Make-to-stock or assemble-to-order (from assemblies) Small batch production possible
Product family	Repetitive manufacturing or mass customization Production with infrequent order repetition Assemble-to-order (from single parts or subassemblies) Mostly single-item production to customer order
Product family with many variants	Mass customization Tendency towards production without order repetition Make-to-order Single-item production to customer order
Product according to (changing) customer specification	One-of-a-kind production Production without order repetition Engineer-to-order or make-to-order Single-item production to customer order

Fig. 6.1.4.1   Typical sets of characteristics and production types that arise frequently with the four product variety concepts.

Figure 6.1.4.2 offers a preview of additional criteria that the variant-oriented techniques address. The values of the criteria (high, low, short, and so on) associated with the techniques will only become clear when the various techniques are explained in more detail in the following sections.

Class of techniques	Adaptive	Generative	Adaptive
Product variety concept Criteria	Standard product with few options / product family	Product family with many variants	Product according to (changing) customer specification
Customer tolerance time	Short	Medium	Long
Value-added / feasible administrative costs	Low	Low	High
Expenditure of planning & control			
- Representing the logistics objects	Low	High	Medium
- Planning	High	Low	Medium
- Control (order and project management)	Low	Low	High

Fig. 6.1.4.2   Some additional criteria addressed by variant-oriented techniques.

As the production environment is closely associated with the product variety concept (see Figure 3.4.5.2), so too is the concept of *final assembly schedule*.

A *final assembly schedule (FAS)* is a schedule of end items to finish the product for specific customers' orders in a make-to-order or assemble-to-order environment ([APIC04]).

The FAS is also referred to as the *finishing schedule* because it may involve operations other than just the final assembly. Also, it may not involve assembly, but simply final mixing, cutting, packaging, etc. ([APIC04]).[2]

The type of FAS depends on the selection of items to be part of the master production schedule (MPS; see Section 4.2.3) and the production type, as follows:

- Make-to-stock: The MPS comprises end products. In effect, the FAS is the same as the MPS.

- Assemble-to-order, or package-to-order: The MPS is comprised of (sub-)assemblies. The FAS assembles the end product (a variant of a product family) according to customer order specification.

- Make-to-order: The MPS includes raw materials or components. The FAS fabricates the parts or subassemblies and assembles the end product according to customer order specifications.

In general, the MPS tends to concern the highest structure level still having a small number of different items. If this level corresponds to the (customer) order penetration point (OPP), only a minimum number of different items have to be stocked — certainly a desired effect.

Postponement, or *late customization*, is a product design approach that shifts product differentiation closer to the customer by postponing identity changes, such as assembly or packaging to the last possible facility location [APIC04].

Refer also to [SwLe03]. Figure 6.1.4.3 shows this situation together with the corresponding FAS and MPS levels:

---

[2]   *Finishing lead time* is the time allowed for completing the good based on the FAS.

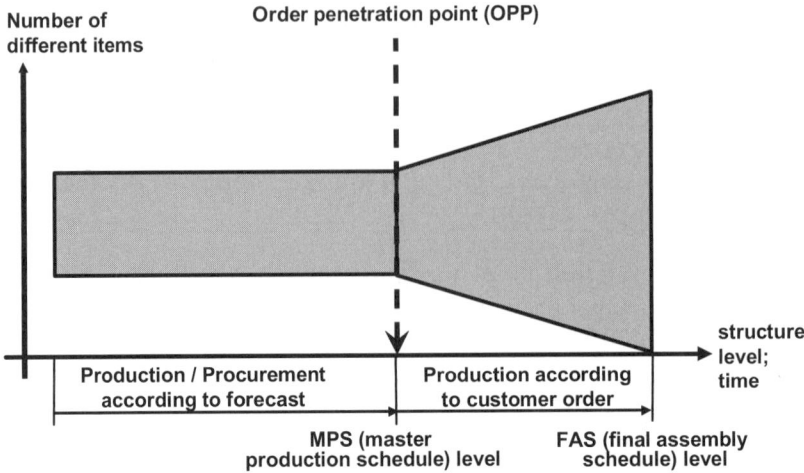

Fig. 6.1.4.3   The MPS concerns the highest structure level still having a small number of different items.

Figure 6.1.4.4 shows typical different patterns of MPS / FAS level and order penetration point in dependency upon on the product variety concept, or the four different classes of variant-oriented techniques: These patterns correspond to the different pattern of the T analysis within the VAT analysis.

In the case of the product variety concept, *"product according to (changing) customer specification,"* an engineer-to-order production type may mean that no MPS can be established. The planning activities then address capacities (personnel hours) rather than parts or material (compare Figure 6.1.3.2).

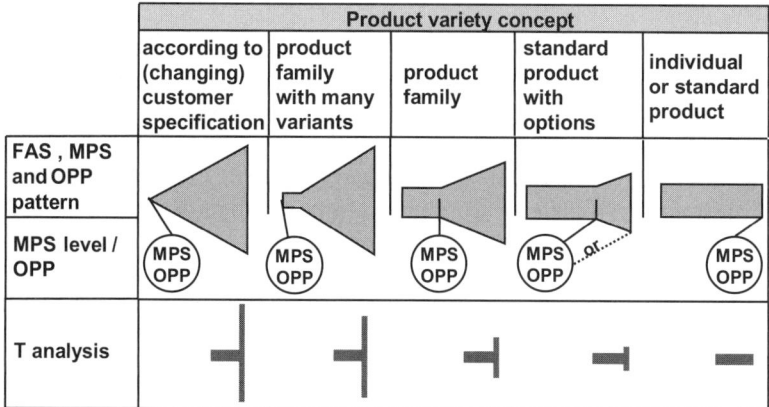

Fig. 6.1.4.4   FAS / MPS / OPP patterns in dependency on the product variety concept and their relation to the patterns of the T analysis. The FAS level is at the right of each pattern.

By the way, because the production system downstream from the order penetration point can be pulled directly by the customer order, it is possible that the associated kanban card will list very specific customer parameters.

Generic kanban is a kanban card that contains very specific customer order parameters. This is a kind of generative technique, where end product variants are generated from a set of possible components and operations.

This means that, in effect, even product variety concepts from a product family with many variants on up to products manufactured according to (changing) customer specification can be controlled by (generic) kanbans.

6.2   Adaptive Techniques

6.2.1   Techniques for Standard Products with Few Options

A *variant bill of material* is the bill of material for a product family containing the necessary specifications indicating how the bill of material for a variant of the product family is derived.

> A *variant routing sheet* is defined analogously.[3]

Conventional representations of product structure using bill of material and routing sheets can be used if there are few options, such as those produced repetitively and possibly stored. Figure 6.2.1.1 shows that an option or a variant in stock corresponds to a different *item*. Option-specific components are grouped in their own variant assembly, called V_1, V_2, ..., while the general components form their own assembly G. Options in stock (P_1, P_2, ...) contain as components the general assembly G and the corresponding option-specific assembly V_1 or V_2.

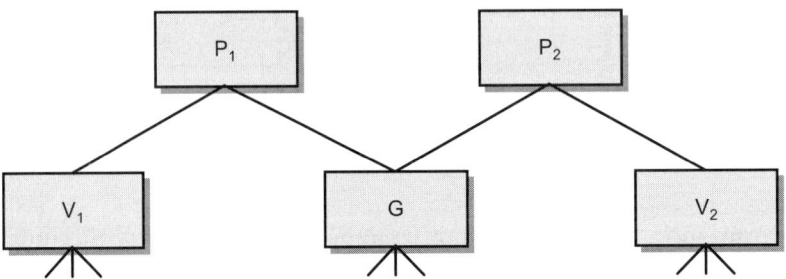

Fig. 6.2.1.1   Conventional variant structure for a few, stockable options.

The (independent) demand for the product family, weighted by the *option percentage*, results in the independent demand for options P_1, P_2, ... For the exact determination of this percentage, see Section 9.5.4. The option percentage, like independent demand, is a stochastic variable. Due to a necessary safety calculation (see Section 9.5.5), the sum of the independent demand for the variants is greater than the independent demand for the product, or product family. To put it another way: The sum of the option percentages, under consideration of a safety factor, is greater than 1.

Deriving dependent demand for the general assembly G thus yields an amount that is too large. This is corrected by entering negative independent demand for general assembly G. This negative number equals the sum of the safety demand for the options P_1, P_2, ... minus the safety demand for the product family.

---

[3]   These two definitions are deliberately more comprehensive than is usually the case, and they are not restricted to methods for simple variant problems. The aim is to encompass also the newer methods for product variety concepts of product families with many variants or of variants according to customer specification, using the same terminology.

For planning aspects, variant-oriented techniques may use different kinds of particular bills of material:

- Both the general assembly G and the variant assemblies V_1, V_2, ... can be phantom assemblies, which are transient (non-stocked) subassemblies.

  > A *phantom bill of material* represents an item that is physically built, but rarely stocked, before being used in the next step or level of manufacturing ([APIC04]).[4]

- A position of a variant-specific assembly can also (or partly) represent the subtraction of a position of the general assembly. This can be achieved through a negative quantity per in the variant-specific assembly, for example.

  > A *plus-minus bill of material* is a variant bill of material with added and subtracted positions. A *plus/minus routing sheet* is defined analogously.

- Both the general assembly G and the variant assemblies V_1, V_2, ... can be — and in particular the "parents" of a plus/minus bill of material are — pseudo items.

  > A *pseudo bill of material* is an artificial grouping of items that facilitates planning ([APIC04]).

- Phantom and pseudo bills of material facilitate the use of common bills of material.

  > A *common bill of material* or *common parts bill* groups common components of a product or product family into one bill of material, structured to a pseudo parent number ([APIC04]).
  >
  > A *modular bill of material* is arranged in product modules or options. It is useful in an assemble-to-order environment, i.e., for automobile manufacturers ([APIC04]).

The technique described so far is quite easy to apply to a range of several dozen variants, which can be found, for example, in the manufacture of large machinery.

---

[4] Linked with the concept of phantom bill of material is the *"blowthrough" technique*. See Section 11.4.1.

> A *variant master schedule* is a master (production) schedule for products with options or product families.[5]

There are two possibilities for the level of the variant master schedule. Figure 6.2.1.2 shows an example MPS at the end product level, supposing a quantity per of 1 for the general assembly G and an equal share in the demand — with a deviation of 20% — of the two variants at the product family P level. For teaching purposes, the example does not take into consideration safety demand for the product family P.

Product family \ Month	Jan.	Feb.	March	April
..				
P	100	100	150	120
..				

Product \ Month	Jan.	Feb.	March	April
P₁	50+10	50	75+5	60
P₂	50+10	50	75+5	60
Total	100+20	100	150+10	120
Assembly G	−20		−10	

Fig. 6.2.1.2   The production plan and its corresponding MPS at the end product level (example of a product family P with two different products, P_1 and P_2).

Note the negative demand on the level of the general assembly G, as discussed above. As for distribution of the deviation in the two periods of January and March, the reader can refer to Figure 4.2.3.4.

The associated final assembly schedule (FAS) modifies the MPS according to the actual customer orders. If in January the actual demand is 60 units of P_1 and 40 units of P_2, then the MPS for February must be revised to replenish first the excess use of P_1 in January (20 units). Figure 6.2.1.3 shows this situation, extended for several months.

---

[5]   The term *mixed-model master schedule* can be used synonymously.

FAS / Month	Jan.	Feb.	March	April
P	100	100	150	120
Actual P_1	60	45	60	
Actual P_2	40	55	90	

Product / Month	Jan.	Feb.	March	April
P_1	60	20+40	70+5	45
P_2	60	40	10+70+5	30+45
Total	100+20	100	150+10	120
Assembly G	−20		−10	

Fig. 6.2.1.3   Revision of the MPS according to actual splitting of family demand as given by the FAS.

Figure 6.2.1.4 shows the second possibility for the level of the master production schedule (MPS): the MPS at the subassembly level. We suppose a quantity per of 2 and, again, an equal share — with a deviation of 20% — for each option-specific assembly V_1 or V_2. Again, for teaching purposes, the example does not consider safety demand for product family P.

Product family / Month	Jan.	Feb.	March	April
P	100	100	150	120
..				

Subassembly / Month	Jan.	Feb.	March	April
G	100	100	150	120
V_1	100+20	100	150+10	120
V_2	100+20	100	150+10	120
Total $V_1 + V_2$	200+40	200	300+20	240

Fig. 6.2.1.4   The production plan and its corresponding MPS at the subassembly level (example of a product family P with two variants, V_1 and V_2).

In this case, there is no need to deal with the (tricky) negative demand of general assembly G.

The revision of the MPS according to actual splitting of family demand given by the FAS would result in a table similar to the one in Figure 6.2.1.3.

A planning bill of material can facilitate the management of a variant master schedule.

> A *planning bill of material* is an artificial grouping of items that facilitates master scheduling and material planning ([APIC04]).

A planning bill of material may include historical option percentages of a product family as the quantity per.

> A *production forecast* is a projected level of customer demand for key features (variants, options, and accessories).[6]

A production forecast is calculated by using the planning bill of material.

> A *two-level master schedule* uses a planning bill of material to master schedule an end product or product family, along with selected key features (options and accessories).
>
> A *product configuration catalog* is a listing of all upper level configurations contained in an end-item product family. It is used to provide a transition linkage between the end-item level and a two-level master schedule ([APIC04]).

6.2.2   Techniques for Product Families

Generally, a product family can have hundreds of variants. In this case, a super bill of material is an appropriate planning structure.

> A *super bill of material* is a planning bill of material for product family P, divided in one common and several modular bills of material. The common bill of material G, together with one of the modular bills of material V_1, V_2, ..., V_n, forms one possible product variant. The quantity

---

[6]   Disaggregating a product group forecast into production forecast (or in individual item forecasts) is also called the *pyramid forecasting technique*.

per (x_i) of each modular bill of material (V_i) is then multiplied by the expected value of the option percentage corresponding to the variant, plus safety demand for the deviation of the option percentage (as was also necessary in the case with few options).

Figure 6.2.2.1 illustrates the example in the definition above.

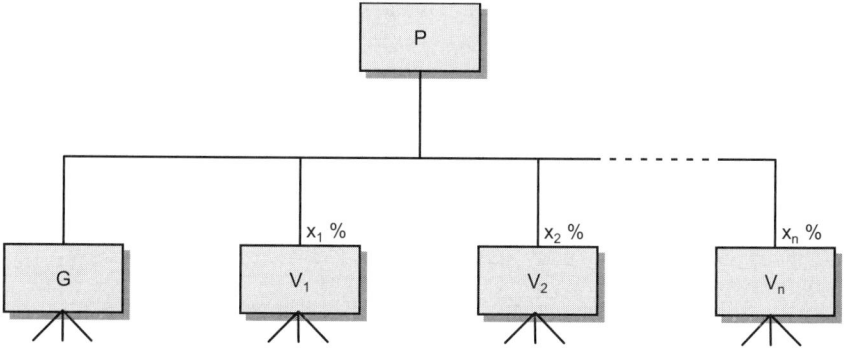

Fig. 6.2.2.1   Super bill of material with option percentages $x_1, x_2, ..., x_n$.

The (independent) demand for the product family is the forecast for the entire product family plus eventual safety demand (see Section 9.5.5). In general, the sum of all demand on variant assemblies is — even with a quantity per of 1 — by far greater than the demand for the product family.

A structure like this is also called *one-dimensional variant structure* (variable bill of material and variable routing sheet), because the variants are simply counted *de facto*. V_1, V_2, ..., V_n may lie in the form of a plus/minus bill of material.

In contrast to the case with few options in Section 6.2.1, requirements planning now yields *dependent* demands. In order configuration, a variant number must be added to the product family, so that the correct product variant can be selected and put into a production order.

The number of variants per product family that can be managed practicably with this technique is as high as several hundred. For larger numbers of variants it becomes very difficult to determine the correct variant. Administrative search efforts become unwieldy, and there is the danger that one and the same variant will be stored as master data more than once. Moreover, many of the bill of material positions and routing sheet positions saved under the variant assemblies are redundant; they exist in the various variants in multiple fashion. In most cases, there is a multiplicative explosion of the quantity of the positions in the bill of material and routing sheet; the same components and operations appear — often except for one — in almost every variant. This redundancy causes serious problems for engineering change control (ECC).

Figure 6.2.2.2 shows an example of the variant master schedule at the subassembly level. For this case, let the quantity per for each variant be only 1. In addition, let the number of variants be 100, and let the demand quantity of the whole family P be 100, too. Again, we suppose an equal share — with a deviation of 20% — of the variants of the demand at the product family P level. Again, for teaching purposes, the example does not take into consideration safety demand for product family P.

Month / Product family	Jan.	Feb.	March	April
P	100	100	150	120
..				

Month / Subassembly	Jan.	Feb.	March	April
G	100	100	150	120
V_1	1+1	1	2	1
V_2	1+1	1	2	1
...				
V_{100}	1+1	1	2	1
Total $V_1 + V_2 + \ldots + V_{100}$	100+100	100	200	100

Fig. 6.2.2.2   The production plan and its corresponding MPS at the subassembly level (example of a product family P with a number of variants in the order of the total demand quantity for the product family).

The revision of the MPS according to actual splitting of family demand given by the FAS would result in a table similar to the one in Figure 6.2.1.3, but it is more complicated to calculate.

Furthermore, the example reveals that if the number of variants becomes as high as the total demand quantity for the product family, the option percentages become small. In addition, their deviation from the mean becomes so large that no forecast for the variant assemblies with economically feasible consequences is possible. For each variant, demand tends to be lumpy. For this reason, it will be necessary to apply one of the deterministic techniques that are described in the following.

6.2.3   "Ad Hoc" Derived Variant Structures with One-of-a-Kind Production According to Customer Specification

In the plant manufacturing industry, many areas of a plant facility are customer specific and produced in non-repetitive production. With an intelligent product concept, however, it is usually possible to determine similarities of the plant facility to previously produced plants.

During processing of an order, the salesman recalls previous, "similar" problems. Derivation can thus often be performed on the basis of a previous customer order. As a "parent version," this order will be taken from the historical order file, copied into the order entities for the current order, and then changed to fit the customer specification for the current order.

For the same customer order, the starting point may also be a copy of the original, brought up to date with the most recent mutations, or a *template* that is used to create the new and specific bill of material and the routing sheet. Figure 6.2.3.1 shows the procedure.

The order configuration algorithm stops wherever a "?" is encountered and asks for entry of the attribute value specific to the current customer order. This will be the case, for example, for the quantity per for the components C_1, C_2, ..., C_n. Furthermore, single positions can be added, modified, or deleted.

If there are very many bill-of-material and routing-sheet positions, this will entail a high administrative load on qualified employees. In addition, the administrative lead time is long. This procedure is thus only justified for high-value-added products.

In the plant manufacturing industry, there have been attempts to restrict *ad hoc* derivations to a minimum and to use generative techniques for the larger part of the customer order (see also Section 6.3 below). This has worked well in the exterior construction business, for example, where certain elements of building exteriors are selected from a preset range of variants. Combining the elements themselves, however, may well be a variant derived *ad hoc* from a previous, similar customer order.

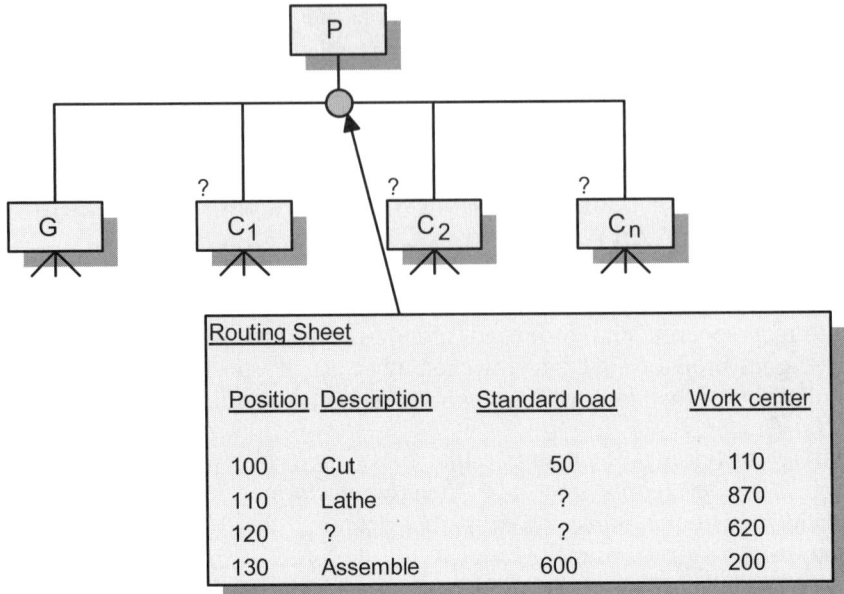

Fig. 6.2.3.1   Template for bill of material and routing sheet used to work out similar variants.

6.3   Generative Techniques

Generative techniques prove to be appropriate for *production with many variants*, that is, where there may well be millions of possible variants, but where the entire range of variants can be determined from the start. In addition, the variance through a combination of possible values has relatively few parameters. Although each product variant results in a different product, all stem from the same product family (see definition in Section 1.2.2). The production process for all product variants is principally the same.

6.3.1   The Combinatorial Aspect and the Problem of Redundant Data

Let us examine the problem using the example of a fire damper built into a ventilation duct, as shown in Figure 6.3.1.1. In the case of fire, the damper automatically stops the ventilation that would promote the spread of the fire. Because ventilation ducts must fit the building, fire damper manufacturers must be able to offer a damper for every conceivable cross-section of "width times height times depth," even to non-metric measurements (inches). All specifications such as damper type, height, width, depth, and type of connection profiles are called *parameters*, or *product features*. The customer can specify any combination of parameter values. A group of parameters like this must clearly determine all possible components and operations. This is usually possible in practical cases.

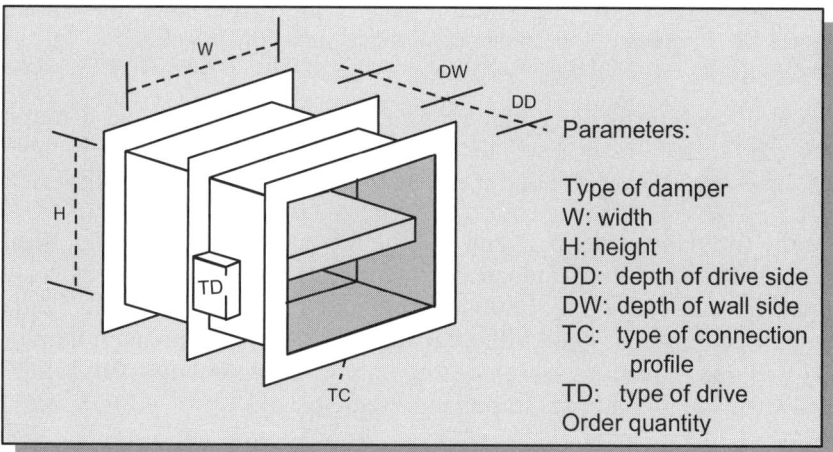

Fig. 6.3.1.1   Setting the parameters of the fire damper.

To reach flexibility in achieving customer benefit, the damper is manufactured only to customer's order. Only certain semifinished goods, such as side pieces, strips, and drive kits, are pre-manufactured according to frequently requested parameters in small-sized production. There are approximately 30 to 50 bill-of-material positions. However, with the individual parameters, the type and quantity of required components (such as sheet metal, strip, connecting, and drive materials) change. Operations can also change with regard to production facilities and setup and run time (or load), and even with regard to description (for example, the number of fastening holes and the distance between holes in the connection profiles).

Two types of dampers are offered with widths from 15 to 250 cm and heights from 15 to 80 cm. With measurement increments of 5 cm, there would already be over 1000 variants (2 * 48* 14). A free combination of parameter values results in a theoretical number of about 10,000 variants, but the number of different dumpers in the practical world reaches about 1000.

Let p(i) be the parameter of i (for example, type, width, height, depth, options, accessories) and $|p(i)| \geq 1$ be the number of possible values of the parameter p(i). The formula for the number of theoretically possible combinations is shown in Figure 6.3.1.2.

$$\prod_{1 \leq i \leq n} |p(i)| = |p(1)| \cdot |p(2)| \cdot \ldots \cdot |p(n)|$$

Fig. 6.3.1.2   Number of possible combinations with n parameters.

Of these, each possible combination has a bill of material and a routing sheet and differs — as a whole — from all others. A certain component can, however, be used to build many of these combination possibilities.

For the fire damper, let p(1) and p(2) be the parameters width and depth. As a semifinished good independent of the other parameters, sheet metal pieces are cut to a width of 800 mm and a depth of 240 mm. This item is used as a component in all bills of material for dampers having a width of 800 mm and a depth of 240 mm. The number of these bills of material is calculated according to the formula in Figure 6.3.1.3.

$$\prod_{3 \leq i \leq n} |p(i)| = |p(3)| \cdot |p(4)| \cdot \ldots \cdot |p(n)|$$

Fig. 6.3.1.3   Example for number of identical bill of material positions.

All bills of material and routing sheets for the product family are similar. Their being nearly identical is typical of this type of production. If you were to keep a bill of material and a routing sheet for every single possible combination of parameter values, the greater part of the stored data would be redundant.

Classical aids to product configuration with the business objects item, bill of material, routing sheet, and work center (see Section 1.2, or as detailed objects in Section 16.2) do not allow the definition and storing of parameters and dependencies.

In such traditional systems, it would be possible — starting from a copy of the last mutation of the original, or a template, constantly brought up to date — to create a new bill of material and routing sheet for an order with its own parameters (see Section 6.2.3). However, with very many positions on the bill of material and many operations, this would place a heavy administrative burden on qualified employees. This is not feasible for products with low value added.

If, however, bills of material and routing sheets were created from the start in all their possible combinations, for example, as one-dimensional variant structures (see Section 6.2.2), the multiplicative explosion of quantities of the positions on bills of material and routing sheets to be saved as data would make relocating efforts enormous and unfeasible. Engineering change control (ECC) for these thousands of bills of material and routing sheets would be highly problematic.

6.3.2 Variants in Bills of Material and Routing Sheets: Production Rules of a Knowledge-Based System

The key to a solution is to extend the business objects by adding a suitable representation of the knowledge about when certain components are built into a variant of a product family and when certain operations become part of the routing sheet.

This is accomplished by implementing knowledge-based information systems or expert systems; see [Apel85] and [Schö88b]. For a detailed description of these tools, see Section 16.3.1. For the sake of simplicity, let us explain these systems using our introductory example of the fire damper.

From the perspective of product design, a product family is a single product. For example, there is one single set of drawings for the entire product family. There is one single corresponding bill of material, and it contains all possible components (such as raw materials and semifinished goods) just once; in similar fashion, the single routing sheet contains all possible operations listed just once. By inserting tables or informal remarks, the documents will indicate that certain components or operations will occur only under certain *conditions*. This characteristic is expressed in design rules or process rules.

A *design rule* is a position of the bill of material that is conditional as specified by an *if-clause,* which is a logical expression that varies in the parameters of a product family.

A *process rule* is a position on the routing sheet that is defined analogously.

Following these definitions, the rules in the fire damper example may be structured like those in Figure 6.3.2.1.

Design rule:

"Component X (such as a sheet metal semifinished good) in quantity per of 1 is used in the product,
• if the product width is 800 mm and depth is 240 mm."

Design rule:

"Component Z (for example, for an option) in quantity per of 1 is used in the product,
• if type = 2 and option = x, or type = 1 and option = y."

Process rule:

"Operation 030 (for example, a cutting operation) is carried out
• with description d(1), time t(1), at work center wc(1),
    • if type = 2 and order quantity ≥ 100 and width ≥ 400,

or
• with description d(2), time t(2), at work center wc(2),
    • if type = 2 and order quantity < 100,
    • or type = 2 and width < 400,

or
• with description d(3), time t(3), at work center wc(3) in all other case."

Fig. 6.3.2.1   Design or process rules.

A position of the bill of material or the routing sheet thus becomes a production rule in the actual sense, that is, of a product to be manufactured. These rules are applied to facts, such as the data on item, facilities, and work center in the production database or on parameter values in a query (for example, for a current customer order for a specific product of the product family).

Product designers and process planners in the company function as experts. When they put their rules on paper for variant bills of material and variant routing sheets, they use — unconsciously — expressions that are very similar to production rules. It is evident that these are experts expressing expert knowledge, for no two product designers will deliver precisely the same design for a particular product. In the same way, two process planners will seldom produce exactly the same routing sheet.

The users of the system are those persons who release, control, and produce the orders.

The exact realization of production rules in an information system is treated in Section 16.3.2.

6.3.3   The Use of Production Rules in Order Processing

Figure 6.3.3.1 shows an excerpt from the product structure of the fire damper in Figure 6.3.1.1. This part of the bill of material lists some attributes and if-clauses important to an understanding of production rules.

Position	Variant	Quantity per / unit	Component identification	Component description
130	01 condition	2 PC if type = 1 and width ≥ 150	295191	Distance pipe FD1 D8/10/40
130	05 condition	2 PC if type = 2	295205	Damper axle FD2 D14/18/18
140	01 condition	2 PC if type = 2	295477	Sealing plate FD2 60/6/64
150	01 condition	1 PC if type = 1 and height < 150	296589	Angular console H100 FD1
150	03 condition	1 PC if height ≥ 150	295108	Angular console general FD 1/ 2
150	05 condition	2 PC if type = 2 and width > 1300	295108	Angular console FD 1/ 2
155	01 condition	1 PC if type = 1 and height < 150	494798	Pivot form B galvanized
160	01 condition	1 PC if type = 1 and drive = "left"	295167	Bearing fixture left FD1
160	03 condition	1 PC if type = 2 and drive = "left" and width < 1300 or type = 2 and width ≥ 1300	295183	Bearing fixture left FD2
160	07 condition	1 PC if type = 1 and drive = "right"	295175	Bearing fixture right FD1
160	09 condition	1 PC if type = 2 and drive = "right" and width < 1300	295191	Bearing fixture right FD2

Fig. 6.3.3.1   Excerpt from the parameterized bill of material for the fire damper.

For the query, the facts — the product identifiers, order quantity, and all parameter values — have been added. Through comparison of the facts (created by assigning the parameter values) with the rules stored for the product family, program logic determines for each position the first variant of the bill of material or routing sheet for which evaluation of the rule results in the value "true."

Try the following exercise: In Figure 6.3.3.1, what variants are selected, given the following parameter values: Type = 1, drive = left, width = 400, height = 120?

Solution: Position/variant: 130/01, 150/01, 155/01, 160/01. Compare also the exercise in Section 6.6.2.

Storing parameterized positions on the bill of material and routing sheet in the form of production rules has key advantages over conventional positions. Each potential position is, in *one* comprehensive, *maximal bill of material* or in *one* comprehensive, *maximal routing sheet*, listed exactly *once*, but it is listed together with the condition under which it will appear in a concrete order. This means that there is no longer the stored data redundancy found in the classical case without parameterizing. In terms of the combinatory aspect, rather than having a storage problem growing multiplicatively, we now have just additive increases. For a detailed comparison of data storage complexity, see [Schö88], p. 51 ff.

Figure 6.3.3.2 shows actual, rounded comparative numbers for the data storage necessary for the fire damper in our example.

Version	Number of item identifications	Number of positions (bill of material or routing sheet) or number of production rules
Classical	200 + 1000*	10,000**
Parameterized	200 + 1	400

* The number of 1000 is more or less the number of combinations produced during the observation period. The theoretically possible number is >15,000, when increments of only 5 cm are considered. The number of 200 is more or less the number of semifinished goods in stock.

** Theoretically >30,000. Through intelligent choosing of a phantom bill of material, or intermediate products with no operations, this can be reduced to 10,000.

Fig. 6.3.3.2   Comparing data storage complexity for the fire damper example.

With minimal data storage problems, any number of orders with all possible combinations of parameter values can be transposed into production orders in a simple manner. One only needs to enter the values of the parameters. All these orders contain the correct components and operations, each with correctly calculated attribute values. Moreover, all possible combinations have been defined previously and automatically.

Engineering change control (ECC) is also very simple. If, for example, a new component is introduced, with a typical bill of material mutation the component identification is added as a position to the (unique) bill of material. If it is a variant, its use dependent upon parameters will be given an if-clause. Qualified employees familiar with the design and production process perform all of these tasks.

There may be an advantage (not yet evaluated conclusively) to the use of knowledge-based product configurators when logistics software is used in connection with CAD and CAM (see the CIM concept in Section 4.4.4). With CAD, only one unique drawing is produced for all variants, but as above, it is parameterized. Within CAM, there is also only one unique, parameterized program controlling the machines. With this knowledge-based representation, planning & control also now keeps only one unique bill of material and routing sheet for all variants. If there is a suitable, parameter-based CAD program package, a parameterized bill of material with a drawing can be exported from CAD to the logistics software. More important, however, is the reverse direction with an order. The parameter values of the production order can be exported from the order to CAD in the bid phase (or at the latest at order release). CAD then produces an order-specific drawing. In the world of practice, this option is used in bids for products in the construction industry, for example. A description of such coupling is found in [Pels92], p. 53 ff. In analogous fashion, linking an order to CAM means that the same set of parameter values can serve as input to a CNC program.

And, finally, the generative technique is used successfully in the service industries, such as in the insurance branch and in banking. A family of insurance products can be seen as a product with many variants. Here, again, we find a clear case of non-repetitive production. The setting up of a policy, or order processing, is at the same time the production of the product. The parameters are the features of the insured object as well as the types of coverage to be provided. The production rules of the configurator assign the elementary products to possible contracts. Concrete entry of a set of parameters ultimately yields a concrete insurance policy and includes all calculations, mainly the premium. See here [SöLe96]. Those readers interested in banking applications may wish to refer to [Schw96].

6.4   Summary

Variant-oriented methods are required when the market demands flexibility in meeting customer specification. Today, this is frequently the case for the investment goods market. Variant-oriented techniques always require small batch sizes or single-item production. Some of the techniques also support production without order repetition, in particular the production types *mass customization* and *one-of-a-kind-production*.

With regard to variety of the product assortment, in a first approach, one can distinguish three well-known characteristics in logistics management:

1.   Standard product manufacturing
2.   Low-variety manufacturing
3.   High-variety manufacturing

For low-variety manufacturing, that is for standard products with options or for product families, the customer tolerance time is generally long enough that some of the upper production structure levels can be produced following the customer order, especially those where the variants in the product family appear. Ideally, this should affect only preassembly and assembly. The master production schedule (MPS) is best established at the level of the (customer) order penetration point (OPP). Downstream from this point, a final assembly schedule (FAS) is a possible tool to make or assemble the end items according to specific customers' orders.

In the simplest instance there are standard products with only a few options (in the dozens). This results in production with order repetition and a tendency towards a order penetration point relatively high in the product structure, but small-sized or single-item production. The demand for the options is more difficult to forecast than the total demand for the product family. For each option, an option percentage, a percentage of the total demand, is predicted. Because this is also a stochastic variable, the standard deviation of the demand for an option is greater than that of the demand for the product family. The sum of independent demands for the options is thus greater than the independent demand for the product family.

In the more difficult case of product families, the number of manufactured products is still much greater than the number of options or variants, which, however, can lie in the hundreds. This case can be handled in a manner similar to the first case above. However, data redundancy in the representation of products and processes increases, and this also raises the efforts required to search and maintain master data and order data.

For high-variety manufacturing, that is, for products to customer specification or for product families with many variants, the number of variants increases to the magnitude of the demand. The use of stochastic methods would lead to high safety demand in variants and thus high inventory. Because of the fact that, in the best case, there remains only potential repetitive production, we must move from stochastic to deterministic methods. However, the customer generally allows a delivery lead time long enough so that practically all production structure levels (except for generally used raw materials and purchased parts) can be produced following the customer order. Through almost the entire logistics network, the products are manufactured according to demand, with no stockkeeping. Inventory in raw materials and in purchased parts is replenished after use.

The first of these deterministic techniques applies to the case where products are manufactured according to customer specification, mostly with prior research and development logistics, such as in construction of plant facilities. One-of-a-kind production also demands the time-consuming, specific working up of a bill of material and routing sheet. Here, adaptive techniques are generally used, in that the bill of material and routing sheet are derived from previous orders through expanding, modifying, and deleting. It is also possible to build a template (a "parent version") that is then expanded or modified for specific orders.

The second of the deterministic techniques is implemented where — typically for mass customization — the order can be produced directly, because all possible variants of the product have already been included in product and process design. There can be millions of physically possible variants of a product family, that is, production with many variants. Each variant results in a different product. However, in characteristic areas, all product variants and also the production process are the same. Such product families are based on a concept in which the manifold variants are generated through combination of possible values of relatively few parameters. In principle, there is only one (maximal) bill of material and only one (maximal) routing sheet. To select positions for an order and to check compatibility of parameter values, knowledge-based techniques are used. Production rules then contain an IF-clause, which is a logical expression that varies in the parameters.

6.5   Keywords

adaptive technique, 375
common bill of
   material, 381
customer order
   production, 367
design rule, 391
final assembly schedule
   (FAS), 377
generative technique,
   375
generic kanban, 379
high-variety
   manufacturing, 370
low variety
   manufacturing, 373

modular bill of
   material, 381
phantom bill of
   material, 381
planning bill of
   material, 384
plus-minus bill of
   material, 381
process rule, 391
product configuration
   catalogue, 384
product family
   orientation, 367
standard product
   manufacturing, 368

super bill of material,
   384
two-level master
   schedule, 384
variant bill of material,
   379
variant master
   schedule, 382
variant orientation, 367
variant production, 367
variant-oriented
   concept, 365

6.6   Scenarios and Exercises

6.6.1   Adaptive Techniques for Product Families

Figure 6.2.2.2 showed an example of the variant master schedule. The example revealed that in practice, this technique would not be applied for that case, because the number of variants turns out to be too high. However, the present exercise is aimed to aid better understanding of the technique, and it is thus useful for all cases where the number of variants is significantly smaller than the total demand quantity for the product family.

a. Suppose that the demand of the product family P for January was 200 instead of 100. Again, suppose an equal share — with a deviation of 20% — of the variants of the demand at the product family P level. What would have been the total number of variants $V_1 + V_2 + \ldots + V_{100}$ in the master production schedule for January?

b. For the month of March, where the demand of the product family was 150, can you explain why two units have to be considered in the MPS for each variant?

c. For April, where the demand of the product family was 120, can you explain why only one unit has been considered in the MPS for each variant?

Solution:

a.   300. In fact, for 100 variants, an equal share would result in 2 units per variant. If a deviation of 20% has to be considered for each variant, an additional (safety) demand of 0.4 units must be added. Because no fraction of a unit can be ordered, this value has to be rounded up to the next integer value, which is 1. Therefore, for each variant, 3 units will be in the MPS for January, or 300 in total.

b.   An equal share would result in 1.5 units. The deviation of 20% can be included in the calculation before we round up to the next integer value. Thus, the deviation, that is, 20% of 1.5, equals 0.3, resulting in a total of 1.8 units per variant. This value is rounded up to the next integer, or 2 units.

c.   An equal share would be 1.2 units. The deviation, that is, 20% of 1.2, equals 0.24, resulting in a total of 1.44 units per variant. As the units were rounded up by 0.8 in January and 0.2 in March, the 0.44 units in April are covered in any case. Therefore, it is sufficient to have only 1 unit in the MPS for April.

6.6.2   Generative Techniques — The Use of Production Rules in Order Processing

Look at the excerpt from the parameterized bill of material for the fire damper in Figure 6.3.3.1. What are the positions/variants selected in Figure 6.3.3.1 with the following parameter values?

Type = 2, drive = right, width = 1000, height = 200

Solution:

Position/variant: 130/05, 140/01, 150/03, 160/09

6.6.3   Generative Techniques — Setting the Parameters of a Product Family

Figure 6.6.3.1 shows a product family (umbrellas) with some of the possible individual products.

Questions:

a.   What are the parameters that generate the product family, if they should generate the five variants at the least?

Many individual products:

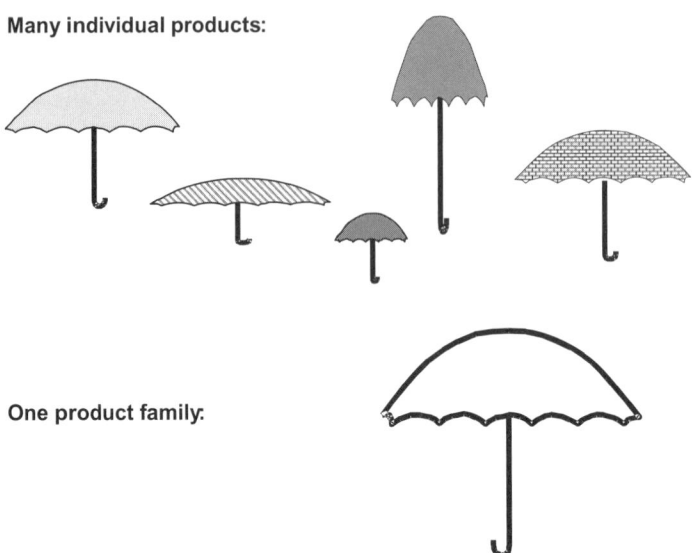

One product family:

Fig. 6.6.3.1   A product family and five product variants of this family.

b. What are possible ranges of values for these parameters?

c. How many physically different umbrellas can be generated within that product family?

d. Are there incompatibilities, that is, ranges of values that a parameter can assume, that are partly dependent on other parameters?

Problem-solving hints:

a. There are at least 6 parameters. The diameter of the umbrella is one parameter, for example.

b. For "continuous" parameters (e.g., diameter), assume reasonable increments (e.g., 10 cm), as well as a reasonable minimum (e.g., 60 cm) and maximum (e.g., 150 cm). For parameters representing a set of discrete values (e.g., pattern), assume a reasonable number of different values (e.g., 30).

c. Combine each value of a parameter with each value of another parameter (compare Figure 6.3.1.2). Your result depends on the number of parameters you detected in question a as well as the ranges of values you determined in question b. Thus, your answer will be different from your colleagues' results.

d. For example, if the diameter of the umbrella is greater than 120 cm, then the handle of the umbrella must be longer than 100 cm.

7 Concepts for the Process Industry

The data and control flows for logistics purposes were first organized on a systematic basis in the fields of mechanical and apparatus engineering and in the automobile and aircraft industries. The MRP II concept, which has been supported by logistics software for nearly 40 years, originated in these industries. With MRP II and logistics software, *a de facto* standard emerged, consisting in common terminology, use of similar representations of the logistics objects, and similar implementations of the principal planning & control methods. However, for repetitive manufacturing as well as for one-of-a-kind production, the MRP II concept has already required extensions through new terminology, new representations of the logistics objects, and additional methods. The same is now taking place for process industries.

Process industries or *basic producer industries* are manufacturers that produce products by process manufacturing.

Process manufacturing is production that adds value by mixing, separating, forming, and/or chemical reactions ([APIC04]).

Process manufacturing may be done in either batch production, that is, production in batches, or in lotless, or continuous, production.

Process industries are comprised of manufacturers of chemical products, paper, food, mineral oil, rubber, steel, and so on. In these industries it became increasingly clear that the terminology, logistics objects, and fundamental methods of the MRP II concept could not always be applied without adaptation. Many aspects of process manufacturing are simply not comparable to the production of aircraft, cars, or machines ([Hofm92]). It is interesting, however, that no uniform standard had been accepted within the process industry ([Kask95]) and that efforts towards standardization have been made only in the past 10 to 20 years. Clearly, there is a need for more scientific research in this area.

A *processor* in the process industries is the processing unit, or production infrastructure, that is, the production equipment (machines, appliances, devices) and the capacities.

Processor-oriented concepts aim towards mastering pronounced high-volume line or continuous production and specialized, expensive production equipment (or processors) with a focus on maximizing processor capacity utilization.

Figure 7.0.0.1 shows some of the characteristic features for planning & control in logistics networks, taken from Section 3.4. The characteristic values of the feature of greatest importance for this concept are highlighted in black. The further to the *right* that these values appear in the table, the better candidate the industry is for the use of processor-oriented concepts.

Features referring to user and product or product family				
Feature ➡	**Values**			
Orientation of product structure ➡	▲ convergent		▲combination ▼upper/lower structr. levels	▼ divergent

Features referring to logistics and production resources				
Feature ➡	**Values**			
Production environment ➡	engineer-to-order	make-to-order	assemble-to-order (from single parts)	assemble-to-order (from assemblies)	make-to-stock
Facility layout ➡	fixed-position layout for site, project, or island production	process layout for job shop production	product layout for single-item- oriented line production	product layout for high-volume line production	product layout for continuous production
Qualitative flexibility of capacity ➡	can be implemented in many processes		can be implemented in specific processes		can be implemented in only one process

Features referring to production or procurement order				
Feature ➡	**Values**			
Reason for order release (type of order) ➡	demand / (customer production (or procurement) order)		prediction / (forecast order)		use (stock replenish-ment order)
(Order) lot or batch size ➡	"1" (single item production / procurement)	single item or small batch (production/procurement)		large batch (production / procurement)	lotless (production / procurement)
Lot traceability ➡	not required		lot/batch / charge		position in lot
Loops in the order structure ➡	Product structure without loops, and directed network of operations			Product structure with loops, or undirected network of operations	

Increasing suitability for processor-oriented concepts.

Fig. 7.0.0.1   Degree of suitability for processor-oriented concepts.[1]

---

[1]   The horizontal distribution of the values in the morphological scheme indicates their relation to the increasing degree according to the given criterion.

The features of the production or procurement order, in particular, suggest that kanban techniques could also be used by the process industry. However, for this, capacity must be flexibly balanced against load, and in the process industries this is often not possible. Process manufacturers make significantly larger investments in specialized, often single-purpose production equipment. This makes utilization of capacity the key criteria for planning & control purposes, capacity taking precedence over materials, components, and the fastest possible flow of goods.

After identifying the characteristics of the process industry, the next step is to derive appropriate processor-oriented concepts for planning & control.

7.1 Characteristics of the Process Industry

7.1.1 Divergent Product Structures and By-Products

One of the characterizing features of the processor-oriented concept is *divergent product structure*. This type of product structure is an *upside-down arborescent structure* with by-products.

A *primary product* is the product that the production process is designed to manufacture. A *by-product* is a material of value produced as a residual of or incidental to the process producing the primary product. A *waste product* can be seen as a by-product without any value.

Manufacture of by-products is the simultaneous creation — that is, in the same manufacturing step — of further products in addition to the primary product.

The process often starts with a single commodity (raw material or intermediate product), although sometimes several commodities are processed together. The resulting products can be either intermediate products or end products. In some cases, a number of by-products (frequently steam or power) arise in addition to the primary product(s). By-products do not go directly into other products, but they can be recovered, utilized, and recycled in subsequent production processes. In contrast to by-products, that can reenter into the production process either directly or after appropriate treatments, waste products must be disposed of. Waste treatment and disposal engender additional costs.

Three examples will illustrate the manufacture of by-products. In the first example, from the chemical process industry, the production of by-products is the result of physical and chemical reactions, or occurs through the changeable operating states of the production equipment. The processor shown in Figure 7.1.1.1 can produce three grades (A, B, and C) of a certain fluid product. Basic material G moves from a feed tank (buffer) to the reactor. The chemical reaction produces the desired material and, in addition, by-product N, which is separated out through the aid of a distillation column, by supplying heat and generating vapor. N exits the distillation column and the production unit.

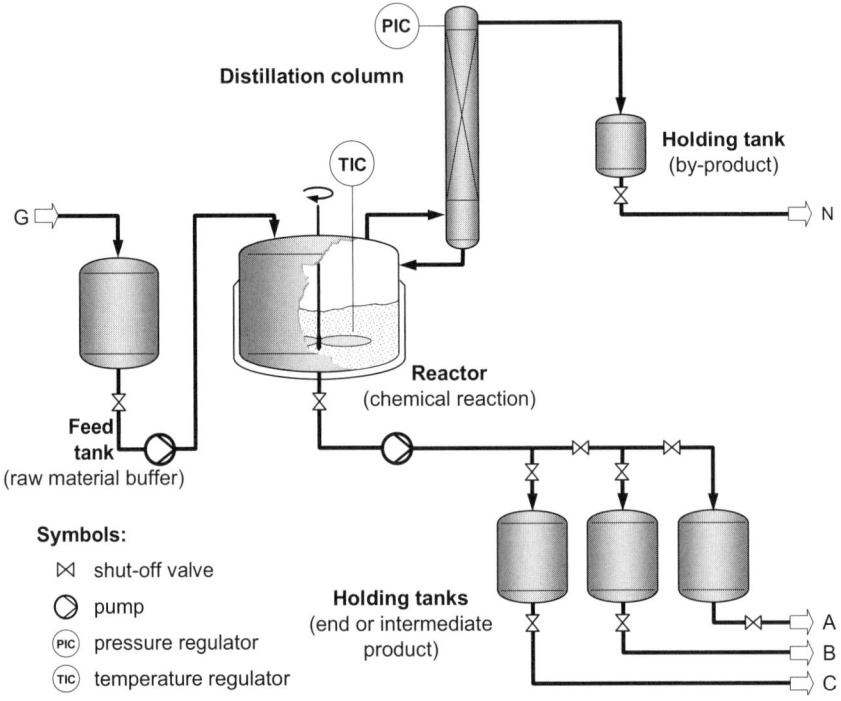

Fig. 7.1.1.1   Chemical production process: reactor with distillation column.

A change of product from one grade to another without shutting down the reactor involves resetting temperature and pressure. Transitional materials are obtained as a result of these changes. These materials are of a lesser quality, and later they will have to be mixed with a sufficient quantity of high-grade materials, which will be produced once operations reach a stable state. This means that a large quantity of each grade must be produced before the next change of product. Figure 7.1.1.2 shows the flow of goods using MEDILS notation (see Section 3.1.3).

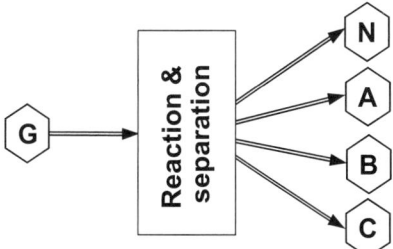

Fig. 7.1.1.2   The manufacture of by-products in chemical production.

The second example is taken from sheetmetalworking. Here, washers are stamped from a strip of metal. In this case, beyond the technical process itself, by-product production makes economic sense: it allows the fullest possible utilization of the raw material. Figure 7.1.1.3 shows a section of the metal strip after a typical stamping operation.

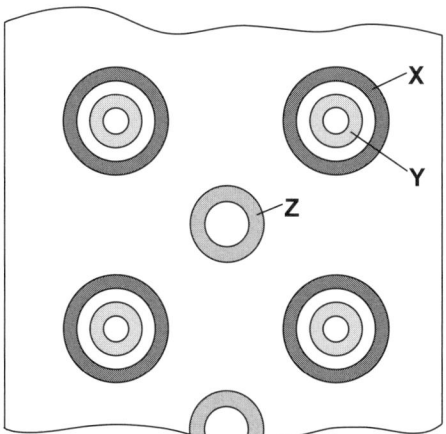

Fig. 7.1.1.3   Washers stamped from a strip of sheet metal by a stamping press.

In order to utilize more of the strip when producing washer X, a small washer Y is stamped inside each large washer. In addition, the press stamps other washers, of a size determined by the honeycomb principle, between the larger washers. As a result, 5 parts are obtained from each pass of the stamping machine: 2 each of part X and part Y and 1 of part Z. This can be expressed as the goods flow shown in Figure 7.1.1.4. The waste product obtained is the stamped sheet metal strip B'. There is an interesting parallel here to our first example: This stamping procedure makes sense only if the washers are separated out according to size. In the first example, it was necessary to separate the primary products (A, B, and C) from by-product (N).

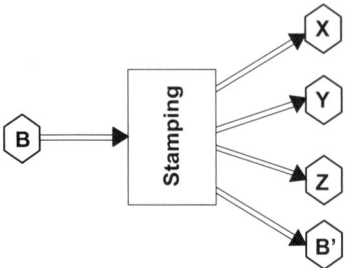

Fig. 7.1.1.4   The manufacture of by-products in the sheetmetalworking industry.

The third example shows the production of split steel collets, which are used for tool holding and disengaging. Figure 7.1.1.5 shows a typical production process that yields a number of different sizes of collets. Here, reasons of economy dictate the production of by-products.

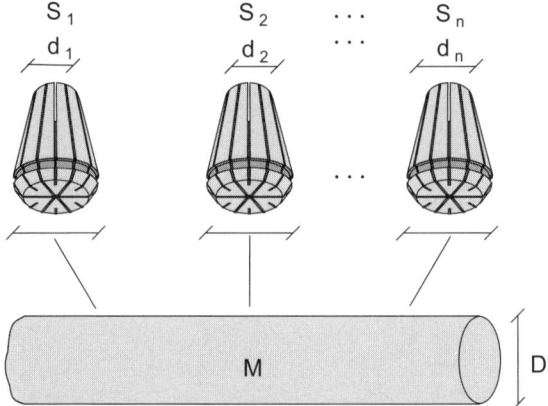

Fig. 7.1.1.5   Production of collets from a steel cylinder.

Collets S_1, S_2, ..., S_n, each of different diameter d_1, d_2, ..., d_n, can be produced from a round bar M of diameter D. Here, again, the decision to produce by-products is based on economy. Once production has been set up, collets of various diameters can be produced with negligibly short setup times. Since various collet diameters are produced together, the possible batch size is relatively large. This minimizes the share of setup for each collet. At the same time, only a few collets of each size are produced, which keeps down the carrying cost for each size and for production as a whole. Figure 7.1.1.6 shows the flow of goods for collet production.

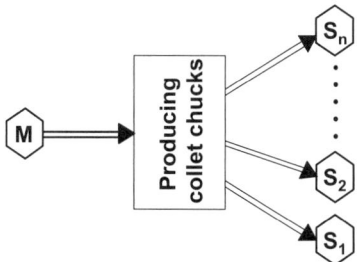

Fig. 7.1.1.6   Production of collets from a steel cylinder.

The fourth and last example is *temporary assembly*, taken from the manufacture of precision machines. Here, components at low production structure levels may have to be put together for mutual adjustment, disassembled again, and sent on for further processing. At the latest at final assembly, the fitted components are rejoined. This is the typical "saucepan and lid" problem, as formally shown in Figure 7.1.1.7. The saucepan and the lid have to be produced at the same time since they have to be matched to one another. However, they may then pass through other, quite different orders before they are finally assembled.

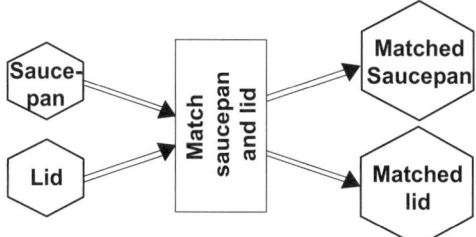

Fig. 7.1.1.7   Temporary assembly: the "saucepan and lid" problem.

The first example from chemical processing is a case of *variable manufacture of by-products*. In the case of chemical reactions, or in the food processing industry, it is not always possible to quantify the ratio of by-products or waste products to starting materials. This is due to the fact that either the process has a long start-up phase (in which the very first products produced are scrap, or waste) or the process control is unreliable, or due to a number of external factors (such as climate, quality of the raw materials, and so on) that cannot be controlled. We will examine this effect in greater detail in Section 7.3.3.

The second example, washers cut from sheet metal, describes *rigid manufacture of by-products*. In this case, specific quantities of products X,

Y, and Z and waste material B' are produced from a given quantity of starting material B. The third example again involves rigid manufacture of by-products. Although the amount of starting material is determined on an *ad hoc* basis from the number of products ordered, it is nevertheless possible to accurately calculate the amount of starting material M from a given variety of products S_1, S_2, ..., S_n and the quantities to be produced. The fourth example also describes rigid manufacture of by-products.

On the other hand, we can also call this third example a case of *flexible manufacture of by-products*. This is because through controlling production, we can change the proportional amounts of the different by-products. From a given variety of products S_1, S_2, ..., S_n and the amounts we wish to produce, we can predict accurately the quantities of raw materials needed.

There are thus a number of reasons for producing by-products in the process industries. In many cases, the reason lies in the nature of the chemical, biological, or physical processes in the various stages of processing. However, there may be economic factors that demand appropriate processing techniques.

7.1.2   High-Volume Line Production, Flow Resources, and Inflexible Facilities

The following values of characteristic features indicate processor-oriented concepts as the appropriate business methods for planning & control:

Production environment: In the process industry, *end products stores*, and thus make-to-stock are widespread and important. Chemical, pharmaceutical, or grocery products are, ultimately, stocked at the shelf in retail shops. Upstream added value stages are also kept in stock, where efficient.

Facility layout: Here, we find high-volume line production, and — in particular — continuous production. Production processes in process industries (producing chemicals, paint, oil, and so on) usually have to carry out an entire sequence of operations (a process stage; see the definition below), that is, one operation after another in a continuous fashion.

> *A flow resource* F is an intermediate product that should not or cannot be stored during the process stage and therefore flows through the process continuously.

An intermediate product becomes a flow resource mainly due to its physical nature or condition. An example is the active substances produced in the chemical industry. As a data element in the product structure, a flow resource is at the same level as the component materials for the subsequent operation or (basic) manufacturing step, and it facilitates modeling and monitoring of the balance of material inputs and outputs of individual manufacturing steps. Figure 7.1.2.1 shows an intermediate product Z produced from starting material G.

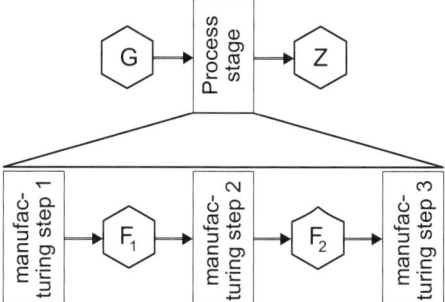

Fig. 7.1.2.1   Flow resources within a process stage.

The intermediate states F_1 and F_2 "flow," meaning that they are not, or cannot, be stored in containers or tanks. Thus, they cannot be in buffers at these work centers.[2] This also means that storable work in process cannot build up at these work centers. This reduces the degree of freedom for capacity planning (that leeway is utilized in the conventional MRP II concept; see the comments on queues in Section 12.2).

Qualitative flexibility of the production infrastructure: Single-purpose facilities were common in chemical production for a long time. For very large-scale mass production, there are sound economic reasons for this type of structure. However, in order to adapt capacity to load more flexibly and particularly in order to facilitate change of product on the same production resources, multipurpose facilities composed of modules became more frequent. Nevertheless, the process industry is still a long way from achieving the flexibility of mechanical production. The old, inflexible facilities still exist, not least because of conditions imposed by government regulations. See also [Hübe96], p. 23 ff. Food and drug production are subject to strict quality control by bodies such as the FDA (U.S. Food and Drug Administration). Production of foodstuffs and drugs must follow a

---

[2]   Actually, many technical plants for continuous production have buffers at work centers. However, as a rule, their main purpose is not to maintain degrees of freedom for planning & control. Instead, they serve to assure process stability.

set of guidelines known as Good Manufacturing Practices, or GMP (also known as Quality System Regulation). Under GMP, manufacturing practices are inspected and approved at each plant, which means that is it not possible to simply switch production between facilities in response to temporary capacity shortages or mechanical faults, for example. The production process would also have to be validated at the alternative facility.

7.1.3 Large Batches, Lot Traceability, and Loops in the Order Structure

In most cases, the *reason for order release* is a *forecast*, as customer tolerance time is minimal, and the lead time is often extremely long. This applies particularly to the chemical and pharmaceutical industries, but food production is similarly affected. The long lead times make any planning system extremely susceptible to fluctuations in demand. Another problem is that value is quite often added at the early production stages, which makes incorrect predictions particularly expensive. On the other hand, if there is a continuous usage on a production structure level, the prediction can be related directly to this level and does not have to be derived quasi-deterministically from the predictions for higher production structure levels. In this case, the reason for release is *consumption*, leading to a *stock replenishment.*

Batch or lot size of an order: Some processes require large quantities to be produced in order to obtain the desired quality. Preparation and setup times (such as for cleaning reactors) are generally very long in the process industry, and, strictly speaking, the process startup should be included in the setup time. Furthermore, the quantities required by the market are sometimes extremely large, as is the case in the food production industry, for example. Here the products are essentially mass produced.

Lot traceability is required by the governing regulations, but also due to product liability and problems associated with recalling a product. Control of lots, batches, or charges or even *positions in lots* serves this purpose. For further information on lot control, see Section 7.2.3. Lot control is also practiced for the following reasons:

- Active substances have a limited shelf life. If a batch results in various units, such as different drums of fluids, they must be labeled for identification (numbered individually in ascending order, for instance). For further processing, this procured or produced material must be identified by means of this relative position.

- In order to assure uniform quality within a batch. This is frequently the case in the chemical and pharmaceutical industries and sometimes in the metal or steel working branches. It is particularly useful if the product characteristics change from one pass through the process to the next, or if products are produced by mixing or merging different materials, and the starting materials do not affect the characteristics of the end product in a linear manner. One example of this is the mixing of fuels, where the addition of high-octane materials does not have a linear effect on the increase in the octane level.

Another feature of the process industry is a *product structure with loops*. The chemical reactor example shown in Figure 7.1.1.1 might use catalyst[3] K to influence the reaction rate. Catalyst K does not get used up, and it becomes available again as soon as the reaction has ended. This creates the goods flow shown in Figure 7.1.3.1. As the output and input store for catalyst K are the same, a loop results.

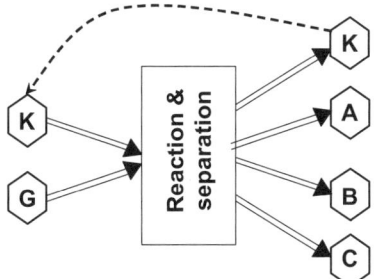

Fig. 7.1.3.1   Product structure with loops.

Another example of a product structure with loops is when waste products or co-products are treated, and the recycled waste reenters the processor as a starting material. In another case, amounts of product that have already been mixed in a mixing process stage can be returned to the process as often as is necessary to assure the desired level of homogeneity. An *undirected network of operations* results. This is typical in the production of paints or pharmaceutical products.

---

[3] *Catalysts* are used in chemical reactors for increasing production, improving the reaction conditions, and emphasizing a desired product among several possibilities.

7.2   Processor-Oriented Master and Order Data Management

Section 1.2 discusses business objects in logistics and operations management and their interrelationships. Important objects include the order (Section 1.2.1), the item and the product structure (Section 1.2.2), and the production structure and the process plan (Section 1.2.3).

In Section 1.2, the product structure, production structure, and process or resource requirement plan were each "attached" to a product. This is the conventional, assembly-oriented arrangement of product structure, production structure, and process plan. Section 16.2 discusses this kind of arrangement in detail. However, it is not suitable for the process industry. As will become clear in the following, the process industry requires extended business objects that essentially reflect an order structure with various possible products. This section introduces some new business objects and extensions to objects already discussed. Detailed modeling of these business objects is discussed in Section 16.4.

7.2.1   Processes, Technology, and Resources

In the process industry, product development also means the development of processes. There is no clear separation between these two steps, as is the case for mechanical production, for example. Product development is based entirely on the knowledge of the technologies that can be used in production processes. In mechanical production, there are technologies and machines for cutting, milling, electroerosion, and other operations, but the technologies involved in the process industry utilize biological, chemical, or physical reactions.

> The object *technology* describes process-independent properties and conditions, that is, all the knowledge contained in a given technology.
>
> The object *process*, on the other hand, describes the possible input, the effect of the process, and the resulting output independently of a given technology.

See also Section 16.4.1. A process may be implemented using different technologies, and, conversely, a technology may be used in various processes.

> The object *process with technology* describes the technique that can be implemented during the actual production process.

It is this business object in logistics that ultimately appears in the production structure as a basic manufacturing step.

> *Resources* are all the things that are identified, utilized, and produced in a value-adding process. The term is used in a generalized way here, that is, to represent products, materials, capacities (including personnel), facilities, energy, and so on.

One peculiarity of the process industry is that all resources are regarded as being of equal value. There are no priorities. Thus, materials are no more important than capacity or production equipment. This is reflected in the fact that a production structure is expressed solely in terms of resources, and all the possible types of resources are described in greater detail by appropriate specialization. Figure 7.2.1.1 shows the business object *resource* as a generalization of the business object *item* in Figure 1.2.2.1 and the business objects discussed in Section 1.2.4.

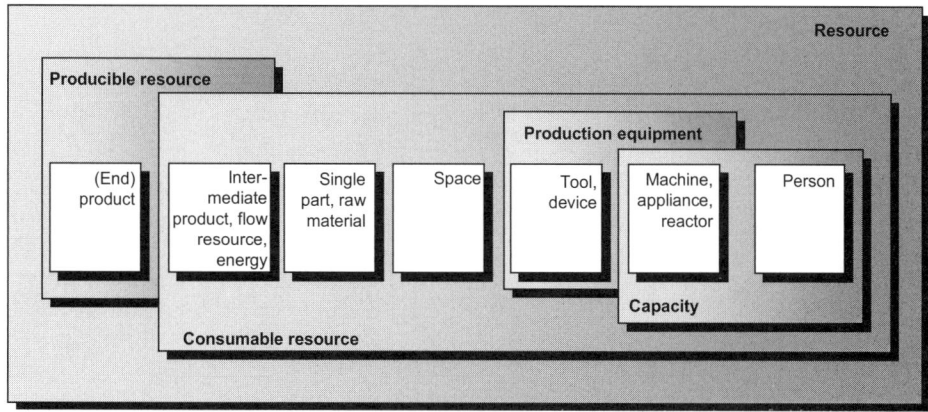

Fig. 7.2.1.1   Processor-oriented master data: examples of resources.

As the business object *item* is a specialization of the object *resource*, an *assembly* is a specialization of the object *intermediate product*. A *product* is a specialization of a *producible resource*, and a *component* is a specialization of a *consumable resource*. *Capacity*, as described in Section 1.2.4, is also shown as a further specialization of the object *resource*. Capacity can mean employees or automated equipment, such as machines and reactors. The latter resources are grouped with tools, devices, and the like, under the term *production equipment*. They describe the investment in physical plant that is required for the manufacturing process. A further resource is *energy*, such as electricity, steam, and so on. These resources can also be described as items. They are often produced as by-products.

7.2.2   The Process Train: A Processor-Oriented Production Structure

In the process industries, the conventional production structure consisting of bills of material and routing sheets (see Sections 1.2.2 and 1.2.3) has been replaced today, as mentioned above. Close examination of the new structure in current use reveals it to be a more generalized form of the conventional bill of material and routing sheet concept. See also [TaBo00], p. 178 ff, [Loos95]; and [Sche95].

Figure 7.2.2.1 shows, as an example, a typical production structure in chocolate production.

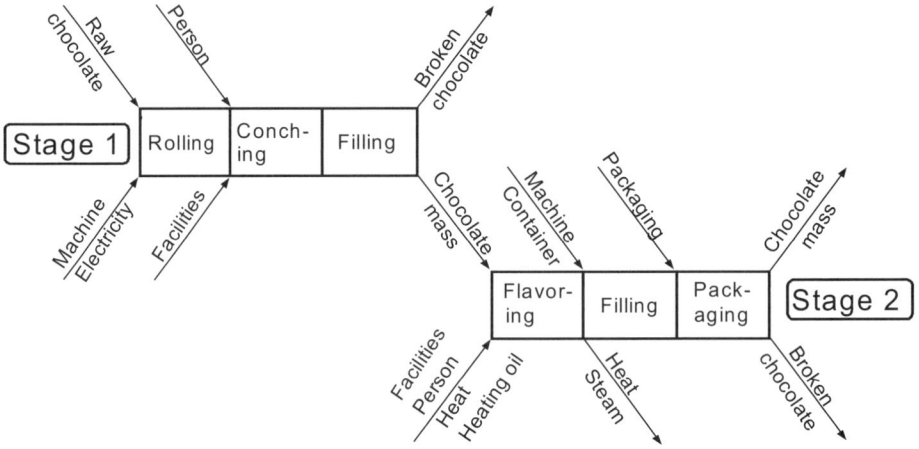

Fig. 7.2.2.1   A process train, here in chocolate production.

The first stage of processing consists of rolling the raw material between rollers, conching,[4] and filling. The resources consumed during rolling are the cocoa mass, the machines required, and power. This stage results in an

---

[4]   Conching is a process of rolling and kneading chocolate that gives it the smoother and richer quality that eating chocolate is known for today. The name "conching" comes from the shell-like shape of the rollers used. Typically the process takes the best part of 24 hours. It is judged to be complete when the required reduction in size of the sugar crystals has been achieved — this is what makes the chocolate "smooth."

intermediate product, in this case a chocolate mass that is subsequently used for further processing. The by-product is broken chocolate.

The second stage is comprised of the processes of producing the flavored mass, filling, and packaging. The primary product is the packed, semifinished, flavored product (again a chocolate mass). By-products as broken chocolate and energy (heat, steam) are also produced. In addition to the material used, the consumed resources include capacity and equipment.

Figure 7.2.2.2 represents the process train concept in a formalized way. This structure is the basic concept behind the data management of both master data objects and order objects in the process industries.

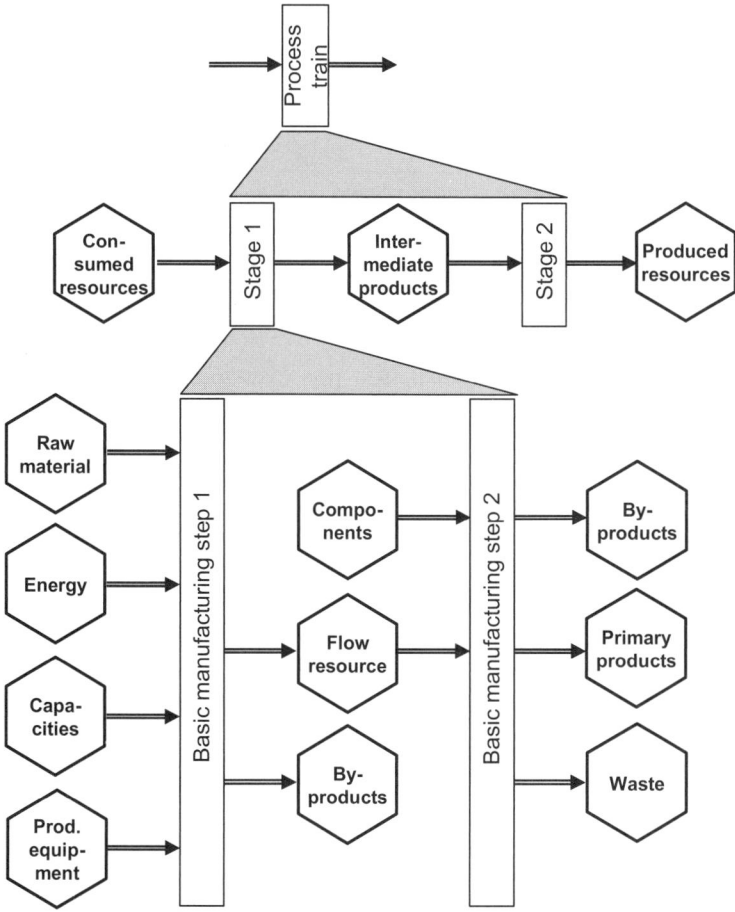

Fig. 7.2.2.2   Process train (formalized) with stages and basic manufacturing steps.

> A *process train* is a representation of the flow of materials through a process industry manufacturing system that shows equipment and inventories ([APIC04]).
>
> The term *process unit* stands for the (production) equipment that performs a basic manufacturing step, or operation, such as mixing or packaging.

Resources such as incoming and outgoing items, capacity, and production equipment are allocated to the basic manufacturing steps.

> A *process stage* is a combination of (generally successive) process units.

Several (generally successive) stages are combined into process trains. Inventories in intermediate stores decouple the scheduling of sequential stages within a process train. However, if there is an intermediate product between two successive manufacturing steps of a stage, it is "only" a flow resource, which cannot or should not be stored.

> *Processor-oriented production structure* and *production model* are other terms used for process train.
>
> *Recipe* or *formula* is the term commonly used to describe the content of a processor-oriented production structure.[5]
>
> A *processor-oriented order structure* is a processor-oriented production structure associated with a specific (production) order, that is, an order in which quantities and dates are specified.

The process train thus defined can be regarded as an extension of the production structure underlying the process plan shown in Figure 1.2.3.3, but without showing the individual time periods that make up the lead time along the time axis.

As is every production structure, a process train may be the object of cost estimating. The corresponding processor-oriented order structure will then be the object of job-order costing. One special feature of such a calculation is that the costs incurred are distributed among the various resources produced, that is, primary and by-products. In the simplest case, this involves allocating a predetermined percentage to each resource produced by the production structure.

---

[5]   For work on standardizing the terminology used, see also [Namu92], AK 2.3.

7.2.3   Lot Control in Inventory Management

As mentioned in Section 7.1.3, many process industries require a lot traceability for the ingredients used in a product in order to satisfy the governing regulations. This requirement is most frequently met by assigning an identification number to every lot, batch, or charge that is produced or procured. The batch thus becomes an object in the company. In the production of by-products, products that are produced at the same time using the same resources may be given the same identification.

> *Lot control* establishes production batch identification for each resource taking the following steps:

1. Each batch is given a *lot number* or *batch identification*, or batch ID, at the time that it is produced. The batch ID is also recorded as a "completed resource transaction" and entered as a receipt into stock. Apart from the batch ID, the attributes of this object include resource identification, quantity moved, order ID, position of the process in the order structure, and transaction date.

2. The physical inventory of a particular resource consists of the batches described in step 1 minus any quantities already issued from these batches in accordance with step 3.

3. The batch identification for an issue from stock is determined by allocating the issue to a physical inventory as per step 2. The batch ID (determined originally in step 1) assigned to this stock also becomes the batch ID for the issue from stock. The issue from stock is also a "completed resource transaction." The attributes are then the same as those described under step 1. If the quantity issued originates from different receipts into stock, then the same number of issues from stock must be recorded, each with the associated batch ID and the corresponding quantity issued from stock.[6]

See Section 16.4.2 for discussion of the objects used for administering batches.

---

[6] However, in many cases, the requirement for clear lot traceability prevents an issue being made up from different batches.

7.2.4   Overlaying of Production Structures

Section 7.1.1 pointed out that there are economic reasons for the manufacture of by-products. Figures 7.1.1.5 and 7.1.1.6 show an interesting
example. There, manufacture of by-products occurs because the
production of different collet sizes is combined, even though the different
collet sizes could be produced separately. The result is an overlaying of the
production structures, as shown in Figure 7.2.4.1. See also [Schö88],
Ch. 6.

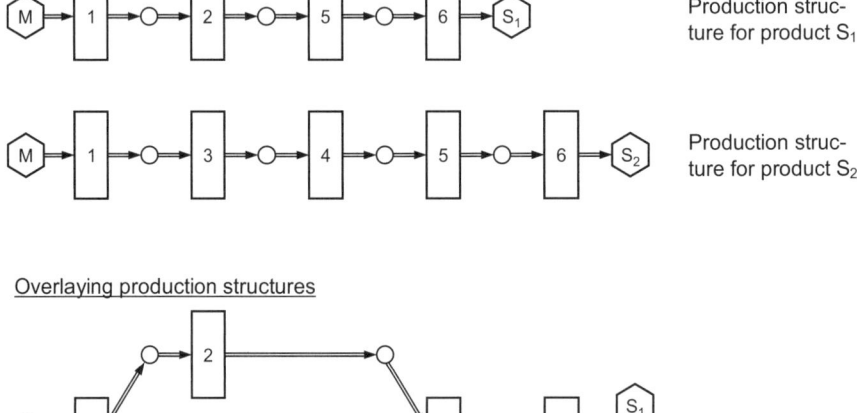

Separate production structures

Production struc-
ture for product S_1

Production struc-
ture for product S_2

Overlaying production structures

Overlaying pro-
duction structures
for S_1 and S_2

Fig. 7.2.4.1   Combination of production structures.

In the *overlay of production structures*, all the resources, (process) stages,
and processes are combined for production orders for various products.
The other resources must still be kept apart.

This example can be extended to include further collet sizes — S_3, S_4, and
so on. This would result in a single networked process plan, rather than in
several linear plans. In practice, however, this is a simple structure to
manage. The most flexible option is to first convert the individual partial
lots into linear production structures in separate order structures. The

orders are then combined using a supplementary algorithm that identifies identical resources and processes or operations and transfers them to a single object. It also specifies the way in which they are interlinked with previous or subsequent process steps. The run times required for a combined operation (actually, an overlay of identical operations) are added together, whereas the setup time is counted only once. Indeed, this is the economic reason for combination. The scheduling is then based on the networked process plan.

It can, however, be difficult to allocate costs to the batches produced in this way. The simplest option is to allocate costs proportionately to the quantities. Even if just one item ID is produced, all the manufacturing costs will be distributed evenly among the individual items (see also Sections 15.1.4 and 15.2.1). It could be argued that identical operations, but for different products which run in overlay, can give rise to different costs. In practice, however, there will be no overlaying of production structures unless the benefits of such an overlay (particularly the reduced setup costs) are greater than the difference between the operation costs for the individual products. In this case, allocation of costs proportionately to quantities is sufficiently accurate. Another reason for overlaying production structures is its potential for significantly reducing investment costs.

7.3   Processor-Oriented Resource Management

7.3.1   Campaign Planning

Section 7.1.2 describes large lots as a consequence of setup or tooling costs. In the process industry this applies particularly to stopping, cleaning, and restarting processes. The changeover processes for transporting flow resources are of lesser significance. In processor-oriented resource management, the objects concerning capacity management and production control are not equivalent to materials management objects.

- For control, the primary planning unit is the machine or facility, such as the reactor, which thus also becomes the actual planning object. The *technically feasible batch size* is calculated by the quantity of goods that should ideally be processed by this facility. The batch thus produced is also used for accounting, stockkeeping, and archiving information for the subsequent lot traceability, for instance.

- From the materials management viewpoint, the emphasis is placed on demand. For technical reasons, a production lot can only be a multiple of a production batch. "Optimum" batch sizes, whether calculated using stochastic or deterministic methods (see Sections 10.3 and 11.2), often have to be rounded up considerably due to the high setup costs and the required utilization of capacity. Such hidden formation of batch sizes results increasingly in block demand for, and thus a decidedly quasi-deterministic form of, materials management.

A *campaign* is an integer multiple of production batches of a certain item, the batches being produced one after another.

A *campaign cycle* is a sequence of campaigns during which all the important products are produced up to a certain capacity and in the quantity required by demand.

The sequence of campaigns is used in order to reduce setup costs. As soon as the optimum batch size from the materials management viewpoint consists of several batches, it is then combined to form a campaign. Under certain circumstances, it is then advisable to produce a batch of a different product immediately afterwards, if this will avoid the need for a cleaning process, for example. The formation of campaigns in this way is a characteristic feature of processor-oriented resource management. This means that the entire campaign must be considered, rather than just the individual batches, when scheduling capacity. A campaign can, of course, be split back into its constituent batches if necessary.

Campaign planning aims to create optimum campaign cycles.

Campaign planning is one type of *sequencing*, or the combination of optimum sequences. Optimization can target various areas: production costs, manufacturing time, or product quality. Figure 7.3.1.1 shows the example introduced in Figure 7.1.1.2, with the addition of a packaging process. The example is taken from [TaBo00], p. 18 ff.

The three grades A, B, and C produced at a plant are packed into two different drum sizes (4 liters and 20 liters) in the subsequent packaging process. The demand is for the 6 end products (3 grades times 2 packaging sizes). To simplify the example, the minimum batch is assumed to be one day's production. The demand for an end product is specified in relation to the overall demand: A4, 30%; B4, 20%; C4, 10%; A20, 20%; B20, 10%; and C20, 10%. Bill of material explosion results from the proportionate demand for the intermediate products obtained from the reactor: 50% A, 30% B, and 20% C.

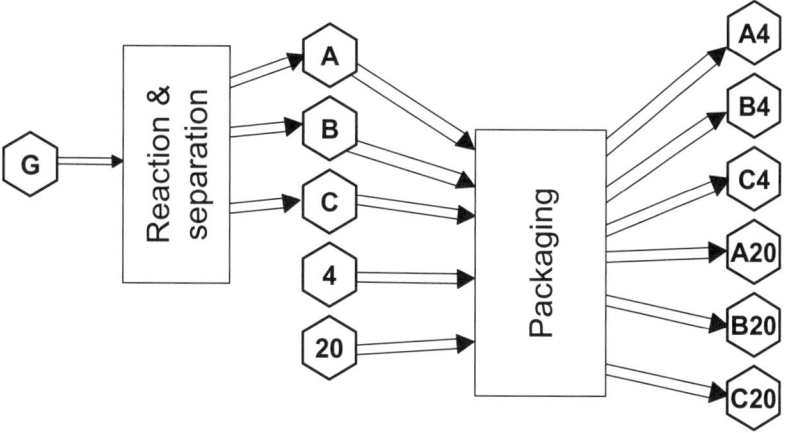

Fig. 7.3.1.1   Example of a process chain in chemical production (see Figure 7.1.1.2).

Assuming that the long time required to set up the packaging process arises when the packaging size is changed and that the reactor setup costs can be minimized by the sequence A, B, and C, as well as the specification of a minimum campaign of one day's production, the campaign cycles shown in Figure 7.3.1.2 result.

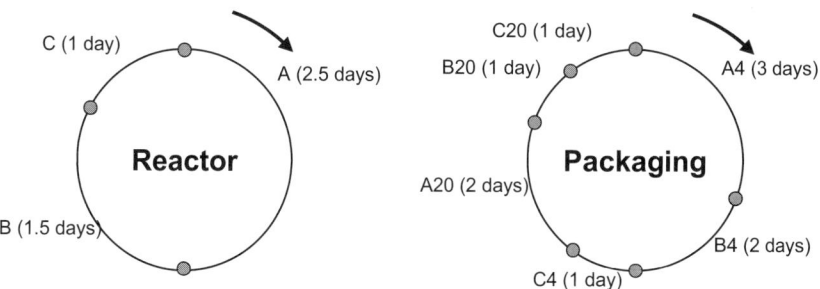

Fig. 7.3.1.2   Campaign cycles for the example in Figure 7.3.1.1 (see Figure 5.2.1.2) and a minimum campaign of one day's production.

The rhythm at which the reactor operates is determined by the minimum proportion of the demand, namely, 20% for C. The campaign cycle thus lasts 5 days. The packaging rhythm is determined by the minimum proportion of the demand of 10% for C4 or C20. This campaign cycle thus lasts 10 days.

The ideas behind processor-oriented resource management thus correspond in some respects to those of the lean / just-in-time concept (see Section 5.2), in which the optimum sequence of operations is important with a view to maximum reduction of the setup times (see also Figure 5.2.1.3). The reduced setup times should result in small lots and, therefore, continuous demand. Only then will it be possible to totally separate the processes that make up the various production structure levels, which will allow the use of the kanban technique in the process industry.

If continuous demand cannot be achieved, then quasi-deterministic techniques will still be required. In this case, the response to a net demand will be to schedule at least one campaign for production, rather than just a batch. A batch also results in by-products. Both of these contradict the simple pull logistics of goods flow-oriented resource management using the kanban technique, since production is determined by the technical process and savings in terms of setup time, rather than in response to consumption. The dominating factor is capacity management.

The conventional MRP II concepts of resource management do not incorporate processor-oriented concepts, such as manufacture of by-products and campaigns, making them less suitable for the process industry. Campaign planning enables demand to be synchronized in terms of quantities with the goods to be produced at all production structure levels, particularly with respect to end products. Where synchronization is not possible, buffers must be kept to absorb any shortfall. The aim of campaign planning is thus to minimize the inventories that have to be kept in the intermediate stores by synchronizing the various (process) stages as accurately as possible. Figure 7.3.1.3 shows how the two (process) stages (or production structure levels) could be synchronized for the above example.

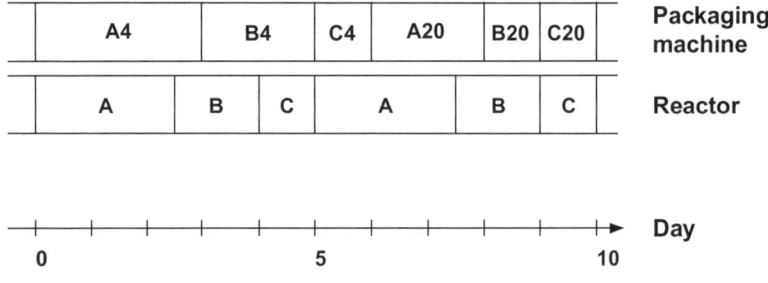

Fig. 7.3.1.3   Campaign planning: how the (process) stages could be synchronized.

The diagram shows the start and end of the overall campaign for each product, but not the individual batches. It can be used to calculate the resulting stock curves for the end and intermediate product stores for given quantities. The inventory curves are of the type discussed in detail in Chapter 11 for determining the available stock. They are used as the basis for troubleshooting, particularly for determining the buffers that will be needed.

The campaign planning technique described here is modified finite capacity planning (see also Section 13.3) that requires continuous intervention by the scheduler. The planning diagrams are similar to the Gantt charts or planning boards used in finite capacity planning (see the illustrations in Sections 13.3 and 14.2.2). The only difference is that they include — as well as individual batches — entire campaigns or even campaign cycles.

7.3.2   Processor-Dominated Scheduling versus Material-Dominated Scheduling

Processor-dominated scheduling (PDS) is a technique that schedules equipment or capacity (processor) before materials. This technique facilitates scheduling equipment in economic run lengths and the use of low-cost campaign cycles ([APIC04]).

See also [TaBo00], p. 30ff. The campaign principle outlined in Section 7.3.1 is an example of processor-dominated scheduling. Indeed, capacity management has priority over materials management for scheduling. Finite loading is used as the scheduling principle. Materials are planned according to the results of finite loading.

Processor-dominated scheduling is characteristic of processor-oriented concepts. It is typically used to schedule manufacturing steps within a process stage. However, the process industry does not use it in every situation.

Material-dominated scheduling (MDS) is a technique that schedules materials before processors (equipment or capacity). This technique facilitates the efficient use of materials ([APIC04]).

Material-dominated scheduling can be used to schedule each stage within a process train. Typically, the MRP II / ERP concept as well as the lean / just-in-time concept use material-dominated scheduling logic. In the process industry, they have their significance as well.

The problem in the process industry is to identify the point at which processor-oriented concepts replace the other concepts. Figure 7.3.2.1 provides a simplified rule of thumb.

This line of reasoning is similar to that followed in [TaBo00]. In addition, see also Figure 3.5.3.1.

MRP II / ERP concepts or the lean / just-in-time concept may be used if
- Materials are expensive related to cost of goods manufactured.
- There is over-capacity.
- Setup times and costs tend to be negligible.
- There is job shop production rather than line or flow shop.

Processor-oriented concepts may be used if
- Capacity is expensive related to costs of goods manufactured.
- There are capacity bottlenecks.
- The one-off costs for each lot produced are relatively high.

Fig. 7.3.2.1   Use of the MRP II / ERP concept or of the lean / just-in-time concept compared to processor-oriented concepts.

7.3.3   Consideration of a Non-Linear Usage Quantity and of a Product Structure with Loops

In the process industry, the quantity per, or usage quantity, corresponds to the selective use of starting materials to produce intermediate, end, or by-products.

The *operation/process yield* is the relationship of usable output from a process, process stage, or operation to the input quantity (compare [APIC04]).

Operation/process yield can often be expressed by a ratio, usually as a percentage. However, chemical and biological processes are subject to conditions that cannot always be predicted accurately (for example, external influences like the weather). In addition, the technologies and production processes used, as well as variations in the quality of the raw materials, have an effect on the consumption of resources that is not quantifiable in every respect. For example, excessive use may be made of certain materials in the startup phase of a process or in the course of the process — namely, as the produced quantity increases. In such cases, the usage quantity ceases to be a linear function of the quantity produced.

A *non-linear usage quantity* is an operation/process yield that cannot be expressed by a linear function of the quantity produced.

Just as with the usage quantity, the duration of the process is no longer proportional to the quantity produced. Thus, the effective consumption could change, as shown in Figure 7.3.3.1. See also [Hofm95], p. 74 ff.

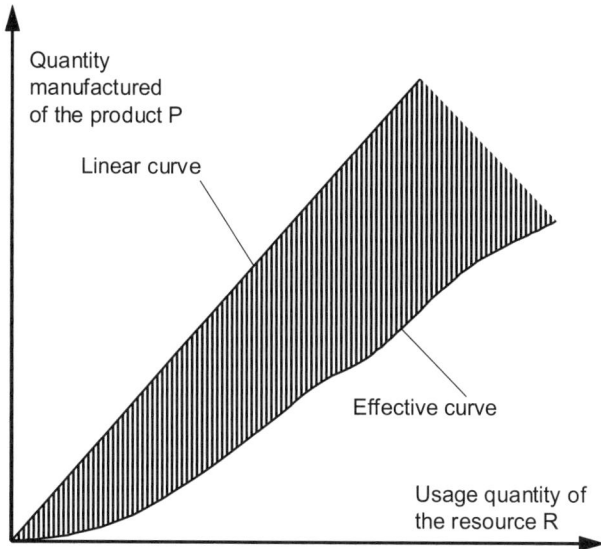

Fig. 7.3.3.1   Quantity of a manufactured product P as a non-linear function of the usage quantity of a resource R.

In some cases, the non-linear function for calculating the non-linear usage quantities may be known in advance. The problem is then solved using an appropriate formula as a parameter, rather than as a constant value for the *usage quantity* or *quantity per* attribute. In the event of a transition from the production structure to an order structure, the formula is evaluated using the parameter values associated with the order (including the batch size), and the appropriate demand for the resource is thus determined. This procedure is exactly the same as described in Section 6.3 for one-of-a-kind production of products with many variants. There, formulas are linked also with attributes, and not just with the usage quantity and the operation load.

Most products with a *product structure with loops* are those that can be returned to the production process. These may be by-products (such as broken chocolate or energy in the form of steam or heat) or processing aids (catalysts, for example) that can be used for further production. It thus follows that the by-products or waste products are not subject to external demand, and their use can therefore be optimized internally. There are, however, certain quantity or time-related marginal conditions concerning usability (spoilage, deterioration) or storability, shelf life. Most of the software packages based on the conventional MRP technique, as described in Section 11.2, do not allow loops. This is because the technique deals with the individual items in the order of their low-level code. In a production structure with loops, the low-level code would be regarded as "infinite."

One possible solution to this problem is to identify such items (by-products or waste products) and then to omit them from the structure level code calculation or to allocate to them a maximum structure level code. The MRP technique should then be used to schedule such by-products or waste products only at the end. At this time, all the demand is already known, as are also all the planned receipts in response to planned orders. Any net requirements for such by-products or waste products would then have to be produced or procured. Consequently, an additional production structure without further by-products should be allocated to each of these products. This is then converted into an order structure.

7.4   Special Features of Long-Term Planning

7.4.1   Determining the Degree of Detail of the Master Production Schedule

Companies that process basic materials (basic producers) manufacture a number of different end products from relatively few raw materials. The number of end products is small, however, when compared to the number of products that are manufactured by assembly-oriented production companies. For example, in the chemical industry, part of the pharmaceutical division (formerly Ciba-Geigy) of the Novartis Group produces "only" about 150 active substances, and they are produced from just a few raw materials. There are, however, a large number of process stages, and some of these active substances have a cumulative lead time of up to two years. There are also large safety stocks in intermediate stores along the process chain. The number of different work centers that have to be scheduled corresponds roughly to the number of products and intermediate products. The number can be counted in the hundreds, but not in the thousands, if we consider all the process chains.

Experience shows that with such quantities there are no meaningful rough-cut business objects. Long-term planning (master planning) is therefore carried out using detailed production structures (see Section 4.1.1). This is unavoidable, since resource requirements planning cannot be carried out using gross figures. Even at the long-term planning stage, the campaigns must be offset against the available capacity because, as mentioned above, a campaign cannot simply be interrupted or partly outsourced for economic reasons. This cannot happen at all for batches. In addition, with flow resources, successive processes cannot be interrupted.

In this situation, demand forecasts are absolutely essential, for this type of production involves a stocking transaction at the end product level. The demand for raw materials must also be derived quasi-deterministically, because the components are required block-wise, and there are limits on their use in other products. More and more companies in the process industry are faced with having to review their logistics costs, so that their stocks and lead times must also be reduced.

The loss of buffers resulting from this reduction makes any interruptions very visible, particularly if demand for the end products fluctuates greatly. Deterministic resource management models can then result in a shortfall of resources, particularly with respect to capacity. The robustness needed due to changing demand and rescheduling also asks for increased flexibility — again, capacity flexibility in particular. Increasingly, capacity has to be adapted to demand. As a result, finite loading in the sense of comprehensive advance planning is no longer possible. It must be replaced by a greater ability to respond, that is, control in response to changing situations. Greater emphasis is thus placed on the interaction between all the people involved in production and in planning and executing the process.

The software supporting the planning process must be able to take this into account. There is no point in spending a lot of time and effort drawing up the "optimum solution" if marginal conditions — particularly customer demand — are not stable. Instead, robust continuous rescheduling techniques are needed so that a new and reliable schedule can be created. In this context, "robust" also means easy to understand (transparent) and easy for the user to manipulate.

7.4.2 Pipeline Planning across Several Independent Locations

Globalization of the world's market has meant that companies now operate at different production locations around the world. There are many different reasons for this: For example, trade barriers may force companies to establish production facilities in countries with important markets (see Section 2.1.1). The buying up of foreign companies is an increasingly frequent phenomenon. New production facilities and the validation requirements of the FDA have combined to encourage the centralization of certain production facilities at a single location.

All these conditions result, however, in major disadvantages for efficient logistics: Intermediate products and active substances have to be moved from one location to another and also from one country to another. Figure 7.4.2.1 shows a practical example of a production structure called, in technical jargon, a *production pipeline*. See also [HüTr98].

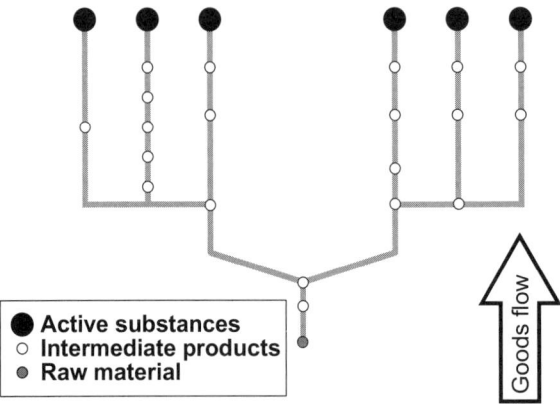

Fig. 7.4.2.1   A typical production pipeline.

The different process stages in this pipeline involve different volumes and process units. Some stages produce large volumes in dedicated single-purpose facilities. Others result in small volumes and take place in multi-purpose facilities. Figure 7.4.2.2 shows the same pipeline with the various production locations highlighted in different shades of gray.

This distributed production system can be regarded as a customer-supplier relationship among the individual production locations. In the example, the pipeline even links production sites in different countries. Each of these locations has its own planning process for its logistics systems, which makes it more difficult to schedule the entire pipeline efficiently, since each location aims to optimize different aspects when creating its long-term plan. Products that simply pass through the location (in the pipeline) are not taken into account in this optimization, with the result that, for pipeline products, large stocks build up in the intermediate stores, and long lead times are required.

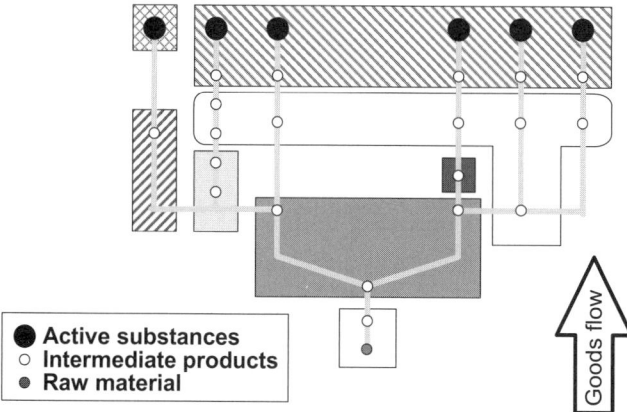

Fig. 7.4.2.2   A typical production pipeline showing its production locations.

This structure is not comparable with a company and its departments, because, in this case, the "departments" are independent companies or profit centers within a group of companies. The principles of supply chain management apply here, particularly the following:

- Information systems must be networked, in order to exchange forecasts and other planning data. The results of the central, coordinating pipeline planning process must be fed back to the companies involved in the pipeline. See Section 2.3.5.

- The people involved must regard one another as partners. This applies to the schedulers at the company that manufactures the active substances (the pipeline products) as a whole, and also to schedulers at the companies involved in producing the product. There is no point in any of the parties overplaying their negotiating position, since the entire pipeline is under the control of people. Mutual respect and consideration do not simply foster good relationships among all parties involved; they also increase people's willingness to attempt to understand specific problems. See also Section 2.3.3.[7]

---

[7]   In the world of practice, production of the desired pipeline products frequently goes hand-in-hand with the production of smaller or larger quantities of by-products and waste products. The economic efficiency of the main process and thus its feasibility often depend upon efficient distribution of the by-products. It follows that in addition to the companies directly involved in producing the pipeline products, planning must certainly also take into account the buyers of the by-products and waste products.

Figure 7.4.2.3 shows the process for master planning.

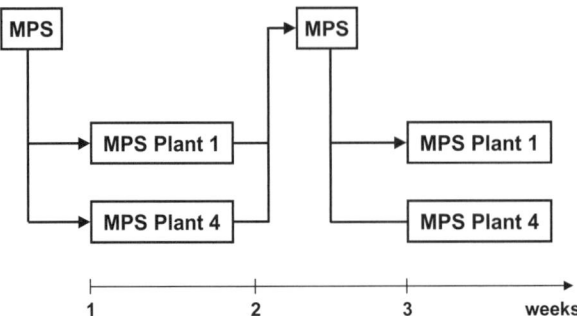

Fig. 7.4.2.3   Master production scheduling process for several locations that operate independently of one another.

The central planning office sends the result of master planning, that is, the master production schedule (MPS) for the entire pipeline, to the individual companies involved, where it will be adjusted to suit local scheduling needs. The result of this process is then returned to the central pipeline planning department, and so on. The planning process is organized on a rolling basis, and the planning horizon may be as long as one or two years hence. Figure 7.4.2.4 shows suggested scheduling groups.

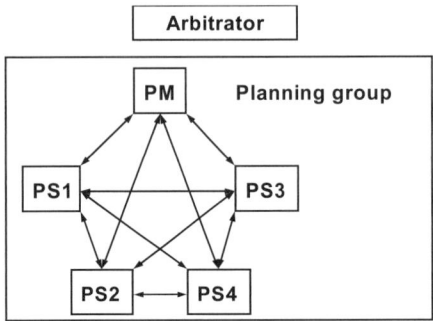

Fig. 7.4.2.4   Planning group for several production locations operating independently of one another.

The scheduling group comprises a (central) pipeline manager (PM) and representatives from the scheduling groups of all the plants involved (plant schedulers, PS). It is important to ensure that all the schedulers constantly exchange information with one another. It can also be useful to have an independent arbitrator. The presence of an arbitrator is a typical indicator of the weakness of every model of this kind, whenever the pipeline or network develops no self-understood culture of cooperation.

7.5   Summary

The ERP / MRP II and lean / just-in-time concepts that are now standard practice in mechanical and apparatus engineering companies and in the automobile and aircraft industries are unable to fully handle the special requirements of the process industry. Manufacture of by-products, high-volume line or continuous production, large batch or lotless production, mass production, and production structures with cycles are just some of the typical characteristics of the process industry.

Conventional concepts for master data and inventory management must therefore be extended. Materials and capacities become resources of equal value within the process, and processor orientation is the dominating factor. Process trains are therefore defined. A process train comprises several process stages that, in turn, are broken down into several basic manufacturing steps, or operations. A manufacturing step is linked to the resources required, particularly to the equipment. Lot control is indispensable in order to meet the product traceability requirements imposed by government bodies (especially the FDA).

Manufacture of by-products is not simply the consequence of certain chemical or physical aspects of the process (for instance, the simultaneous production of two substances during a chemical process by means of parallel or overlying chemical reactions during a production process). By-products can also be produced in a targeted fashion for reasons of economy. For example, a single production process may manufacture different products from sheet steel or steel bars in order to save setup costs.

The decisive factors for planning added value are often the actual production process and the required capacity, rather than the materials used. Such processes typically require a few, but significant, active substances, which are often kept in stock in large quantities. The value of the basic raw materials is often tiny compared to the overall production costs, which essentially means that adding value can only be economically viable if production facilities are utilized efficiently. Processor-dominated scheduling, the campaign principle in particular, respects this situation. The considerable setup costs that are often associated with production facilities for large batch production give rise to campaign cycles. Loss of materials caused by start-up and shut-down processes, shifting operating conditions in the production plant, or variations in the quality of raw materials result in non-linear functions for the quantity of resources required in relation to the quantities of the product produced. The scheduling of production structures with cycles presents yet another challenge.

Long-term planning generally involves detailed data structures on account of the relatively small number of products to be scheduled and in order to incorporate high-volume line or continuous production and campaigns. One particular feature is known as pipeline planning, or scheduling across different locations that operate independently of one another. This type of planning environment is a frequent occurrence due to the cost of capacity and the regulation of the markets associated with the process industry.

7.6   Keywords

7.7   Scenarios and Exercises

7.7.1   Batch Production versus Continuous Production

As a producer of fine chemicals, your company plans to introduce a new type of solvent to the market. It is suitable for use in the production of adhesives for the automobile industry. The corporate marketing department estimates that 5000 to 10,000 tons of the product can be sold per year.

The product development process with laboratory tests has been completed. But the industrial production concept for the product remains to be determined. While most of the production processes are actually done on the batch principle (discontinuous or batch production), your engineers now suppose continuous production for this product.

a. What are the differences between these two concepts? What criteria are important for the decision for one or the other of these concepts?

b. What is your suggestion regarding the new solvent? Explain the reasons for your decision.

Solution:

a.

Continuous production	Discontinuous production (batch)
Production facility (apparatus, reactor, ...) allows steady flow through by feed material and product.	Production time intervals — filling, process (e.g., chemical reaction), discharge.
Products (flow resources) are not stored under normal conditions.	Products are often stored between process steps.
Hardly flexible regarding production volume and other products.	Facilities and equipment are relatively flexible (e.g., in multipurpose plants).
Start-up and shut-down processes cause product loss.	Proof of origin for single batches is procurable.

In selecting the appropriate production principle, the following points have to be considered:

- Production volume and regularity of demand
- Need for flexibility
- Requirements in terms of proof of origin and quality control
- Technological conditions and safety requirements

b. In the case of the solvent, the preferred principle could be continuous flow production. The production volume is of adequate size for small facilities for continuous production. Furthermore, it can be assumed that the consumption of the new product will run relatively regularly. At least a proof of origin is not necessary.

7.7.2 Manufacture of By-Products

In the production of 300 kg per hour of an active substance for the manufacturing of photographic paper, 20 tons of sewage water accrue per day. The sewage flow is contaminated with an organic dissolver, which is needed for the production of the active substance. The purchase price of the dissolver is $1.30 per kg.

The current production process has about 6000 operating hours per year and runs on the principle of continuous production. The sewage water needs to be disposed of as waste product. Due to dissolver contamination of approximately 5% (mass percent), extra costs of $5.50 per m^3 are caused in comparison to waste water without organic impurities.

On the basis of thermodynamic calculations and laboratory tests, it was estimated that it would be possible to separate almost all of the dissolver by adding a simple distillation column as a further process step. For the distillation, 80 kg heating steam (cost: $20 per ton) is needed per m^3 of sewage water. The regained dissolver can be reintroduced into the production process without any additional effort.

The plant engineer now attempts to estimate how much money can be invested in the distillation device, if management sets a limit of 2 years maximum for payback on this kind of investment. Can you help?

Solution:

- 6000 operating hours equals 250 days (continuous production!)
- $20*250 = 5000$ tons of sewage water accrued per year
- Loss of dissolver: 250 t/a, → savings from recovery: $325,000/a
- Savings from lower cost for waste water treatment: $27,500/a
- Additional cost for heating steam: $8000/a
- Total savings: $344,500 per year
- Payback time: max. 2 years → about $689,000 available for investment

7.7.3 Production Planning in Process Industries

For the production in a 3-step batch process of 500 tons of an active substance for use in pharmaceutical products, chemical reactors of different sizes come into operation. Figure 7.7.3.1 describes the production sequences with batch size and yield in each process step. Please note that the figure does not show a mass balance or a bill of material.

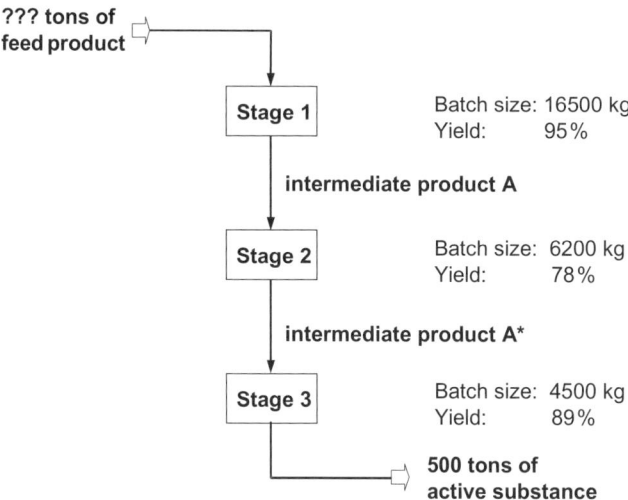

(Remark: The scheme does not show a mass balance!)

Fig. 7.7.3.1 Batch size and yield in each process step for an active substance.

Determine the needed quantity of feed product and the required number of batches per stage for the production of the desired quantity of the active substance. Please be aware that only complete batches can be produced.

Solution:
- Production quantity of active substance: 500 t
- Stage 3:
    - Yield: 89% → demand for A*: 562 t
    - Batch size: 4.5 t → number of batches: 124.9 → 125
    - → Actual demand for A*: 562.5 t
- Stage 2:
    - Yield: 78% → demand for A: 722 t
    - Batch size: 6.2 t → number of batches: 116.5 → 117

- $\rightarrow$ Actual demand for A: 725.4 t
- Stage 1:
  - Yield: 95% $\rightarrow$ demand for feed product: 764 t
  - Batch size: 16.5 t $\rightarrow$ <u>number of batches: 46.3 $\rightarrow$ 47</u>
  - $\rightarrow$ <u>Actual demand for feed product: 775.5 t</u>

8   Logistics Software

One aim of the logistics function is to ensure short lead times (see Section 1.3.1), with the ancillary objective of reducing lead times in the information flow for planning & control. Small companies can successfully and economically incorporate the information flow into their logistics without having to resort to computerization, although they will quickly find that they have to process large quantities of data. It is therefore not surprising that software designed to support logistics tasks started to be developed at a very early stage. Today, planning & control tasks are almost always computer-aided in companies above a certain size.

In practice, people (whether intentionally or unintentionally) often draw no distinction between the actual planning & control system and the computer-aided information system for planning & control, i.e., the logistics software. In recent years, this has led to unnecessary misunderstandings, and even to arguments and decisions based on prejudice. This chapter focuses on the main possibilities and limitations of the computerization of tasks and processes associated with planning & control. We shall first consider the historical development of logistics software and the extent to which it is used at present. This will be followed by a discussion of the types of software available and an attempt at classification. The chapter ends with some important notes concerning the implementation of logistics software.

8.1   Software Used for Logistics Purposes: An Introduction

8.1.1   Definitions and Three Types of Software Used for Logistics Purposes

> *Informatics* are the studies of techniques used to automatically process information.

On a computer, i.e., on the data storage components of a computer system, *software* is used to describe information in a suitable manner and to process this information by means of appropriate algorithms, with the aim of sending information to other locations, converting it into another format or obtaining new information from it.

> A *computer-aided information system* is an information system supported by information technology.

An information system cannot be computer aided unless all the information to be contained in that system is available in a clear and quantifiable form, i.e., unless (1) the system elements or objects can be represented on a computer using IT techniques, and (2) the information flow can be expressed by algorithms that handle such objects (i.e., the information flow is "programmable").

In the world of commercial systems, a system for planning & control is known as an *information system* because it contains information in a structured form concerning future, current, and past events associated with the provision of goods. Since it largely fulfills the requirement expressed above, it is unsurprising that computerization started at a very early stage. This first type of software used for logistics purposes is called "logistics software" in the rest of this chapter.

> *Logistics software* is used to computerize planning & control, i.e., it supports the comprehensive and integrated data flow required for administrative logistics and the control flow associated with scheduling and materials planning logistics.
>
> *PPC software* and *SCM software* or *APS software* are terms frequently used to describe different kinds of logistics software.

A second type of software for logistics purposes is used to model and simulate logistics processes. This is called *process modeling* and simulation software below.

> *Process modeling and simulation software* is used to develop organizations and processes and to dimension production infrastructure. It is also used to raise awareness and for training in both cases.

This type of software concentrates on the *strategic* aspects of logistics. For example, process simulation software is used for factory planning, whereas process modeling software is intended to analyze and modify the organization of structures and processes. Process modeling and simulation software was not, however, developed to assist *operational* planning & control of the goods flow, so it will not be discussed further in this chapter.

Since the late 1980s, we have seen a rapid explosion in the number of software packages for modeling and designing processes, developed in response to the trend towards business process reengineering. Some of these are drawing packages for modeling business processes. Typical examples include Proplan and CIMOSA, and the MEDILS software mentioned in Section 3.1.3. Other packages are also used to calculate the characteristic variables of such processes, such as costs and lead time. The most well-known package from this category is ARIS (see [Sche94]). One aim of this type of software is to identify the following weak points in existing business processes:

- Wasted time (waiting and transportation times)

- Redundant work and information, unused information (dead files)

- Excessive time spent on communication and coordination between different departments

- Concentration on standard situations, lack of skills needed to cope with special circumstances

- Tasks distributed between too many organizational units, too many interfaces working across the business process

- Frequent gaps in the flow of information or organization, responsibility not clearly allocated

Business process modeling can also be used to design logistics software. Here, again, a company's processes must be described so as to facilitate their transfer to the program. If such models are sufficiently accurate, they can also be incorporated directly into the workflow in the logistics software.

If the package is able to project events along the time axis, as well as modeling and calculating the process, then we use the term *process simulation*. The first attempts to develop software for simulating processes occurred as early as the 1960s, although they did not become generally accepted until the graphical user interface became available in the late 1980s. It was only then that logistics and production specialists could really give free rein to their imagination. One example of this type of package is Simple++ and its successors. Simulation software allows the logistics and production infrastructure to be sensibly designed by evaluating different variants, although it is only able to generate a limited number of events. This means that only relatively simple situations can be simulated. Nevertheless, the simulation provides valuable knowledge that can then be applied to more complex processes and, in straightforward cases, the software provides a quick and reliable aid to decision making.

The third type of software for logistics purposes is intended for developing new software.

Software development software, or a CASE-tool, is primarily a tool that helps the IT experts and management engineers to communicate with one another. It also supports the software development process and, in particularly suitable cases, also generates the actual program code.

Software development or engineering software also started to gain acceptance in the late 1980s. These "upper CASE tools" for model processes and functions work on a principle similar to the software used to model processes. There are also data modeling and object-oriented modeling modules, up to the modeling of the entire information systems architecture. See [Schö01], Chapters 3 and 4. A "lower CASE tool" converts the model in the upper CASE tool into an executable program. A typical upper CASE tool is "System Architect," and one example of an upper and lower CASE tool suitable for large-scale applications is "IEF/IEW." This type of software falls outside the scope of this chapter.

8.1.2   Scope and Range of Logistics Software

Logistics software was originally designed for modeling products and production processes, administering orders, and preparing accounts. These tasks were soon supplemented with planning functions for resource management (goods and capacity). In contrast, the software still only plays a supporting role in planning & control since the condition for computerization mentioned in Section 8.1.1 is less likely to be fulfilled as the period under consideration moves further into the future. In such cases, the information is often imprecise or cannot be described in qualitative terms.

Between 1960 and 1980, many companies developed their own company-specific software that was precisely tailored to their needs. Data was then transferred from forms to punched cards and processed in batches at computer centers. The range of such software was generally just a few years. The major breakthrough occurred in the late 1970s, with the development of the computer monitor (character format with 24 rows * 80 characters). Relational databases that could handle large volumes of data first appeared at roughly the same time. These provided users with direct and simple access to the data and to the programs that process this data (online or interactive techniques). In addition, a number of new logistics software packages appeared in quick succession. The software generation from this period is still in use today, although it is gradually being replaced by the graphical user interface introduced in the late 1980s. This change is much slower, however, than the change that occurred at the end of the 1970s due to the introduction of online techniques.

Computerization was only seen in large companies up until the mid-1970s. The most common applications could be found in companies with logistics characterized by convergent product structures, serial production, and production with order repetition and with high utilization of capacity as their logistics objective. The first generation of standard logistics software, such as the COPICS package, was also developed for this user profile. Since then, standard software gradually improved to meet at least partially also the needs of small- and medium-sized companies and their flexible forms of organization.

Planning & control software is still surprisingly long-lasting. The typical lifespan is 10 years or more, and 20 years is not unusual. What is the reason for this longevity? One answer may be that, since the online and interactive processing techniques were introduced, no new hardware or software technology has become available that would simplify or add to the way the user works sufficiently to justify the cost of such a change. Indeed, a change of hardware or software is both expensive and full of risks: for integrated packages, in particular, it would affect every operational order processing system — and thus a large number of users and a wide range of computer-aided processes. Any mistakes would immediately have a detrimental effect on the company's ability to add value and thus to do business. In addition, the logistics software developers who have recently entered the market take too little notice of the logistics specialists, with the result that packages created using the latest technology have inadequate data models and functionality.

8.2   Contents of Logistics Software Packages

Every logistics software package has developed in a slightly different way; some were designed for specific branches of industry, products, or production characteristics but now have to meet the needs of other branches or production characteristics. The developers also learned their craft in a certain type of company environment, which shows in the features of the software.

8.2.1   Logistics in a Comprehensive Information System within the Company

Figure 8.2.1.1 shows a comprehensive information system for an industrial company. See also [Schö01]. Other types of companies, including service companies, have systems that exhibit some of these features, although the tasks often have different names.

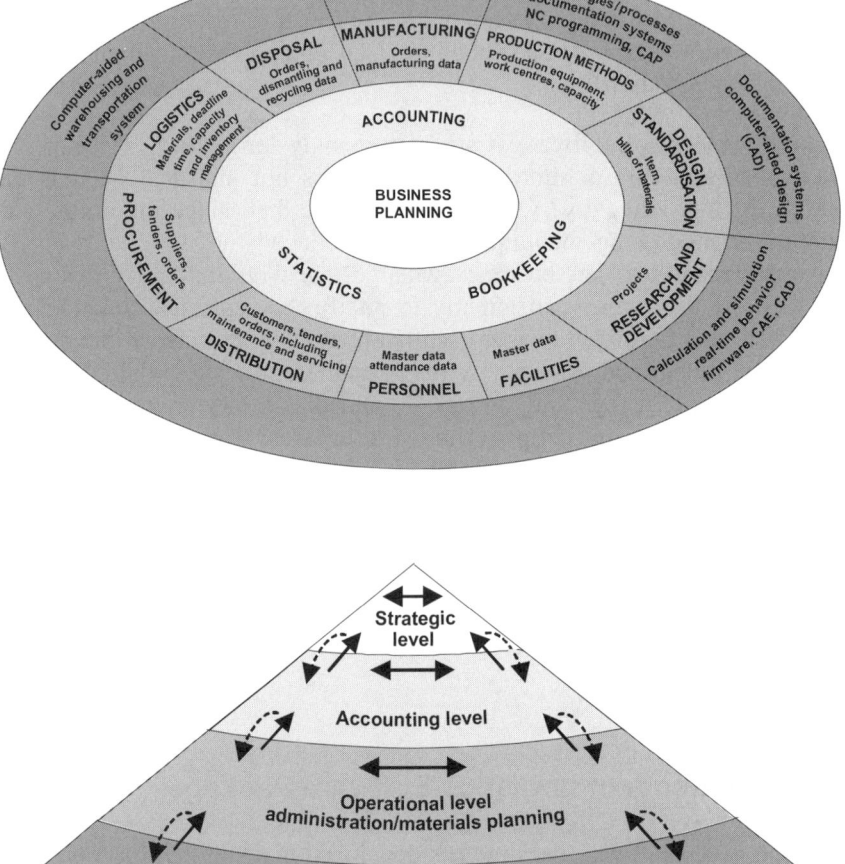

Fig. 8.2.1.1   The comprehensive information system of an industrial company.

The information system takes the form of a pyramid. The *strategic level* is at the top of the pyramid and represents the company-wide planning function. The next level contains the accounting systems (e.g., financial and cost accounting). At the *operational level* are the administrative and planning information systems for planning & controlling day-to-day business processes in the various functional areas. Short lead times require the short-term planning function to be closely linked to the actual operation; in the ideal situation, the two tasks would be performed by the same person. Short-term planning tasks are therefore situated at the operational level.

The systems described above are *company information systems.* The operational level also contains the *technical/industrial information systems*, as typically used in industrial companies. They can be broken down into the areas of R&D, design, production methods, production, and logistics. These systems for processing data in order to support technical processes are part of a company's comprehensive information system.

The information system may focus on different functional areas, according to the type of company. In addition, the various business processes within the same company may be emphasized differently in different areas.

Integration is the ability of a comprehensive information system to exchange information.

Integration of a comprehensive information system is a main challenge.

- *Horizontal integration* is the ability of an information system to exchange information at the same level. This is particularly important for fast business processes.

- *Vertical integration* is the ability of an information system to exchange information between levels. Much more information flows from the bottom to the top of the pyramid than from top to bottom. Large quantities of data are compressed to convert them into management variables for the higher levels. Fewer data flow from a higher to a lower level, although the information tends to be very important — generally parameters for controlling planning functions. It is not always possible to generate this type of para-meter automatically, so the qualitative strategies established by the company management have to be converted into quantitative data.

8.2.2   Logistics Software to Support Comprehensive Information Systems within the Company

Logistics software was developed in response to the needs of large mechanical engineering and automobile construction companies. Their logistics were primarily characterized by discrete manufacturing and by serial production and production with order repetition, with high utilization of capacity as their logistics objective. Extension of this functionality to cover all business processes from start to finish resulted in what we now know as *MRP II software* or *ERP software*. This type of software essentially supports the concept described in Chapter 4.

The first package in this category was the COPICS software from IBM. Other companies also developed software of the MRP II type, and these packages are still in use today, including MAPICS from IBM, Cincom, TPS from Burroughs, Manufacturing from Oracle, J.D. Edwards, Bpics, and many others. The market leader for some years has been SAP, with its R/2, R/3 and mySAP™ software and the follow-up products. It is not surprising to learn that the person who founded SAP came from IBM. The aim of the major software houses such as SAP is to incorporate logistics software into a comprehensive and integrated package that supports all the business processes carried out within a company. Figure 8.2.2.1 contains an overview of the R/3 structure.

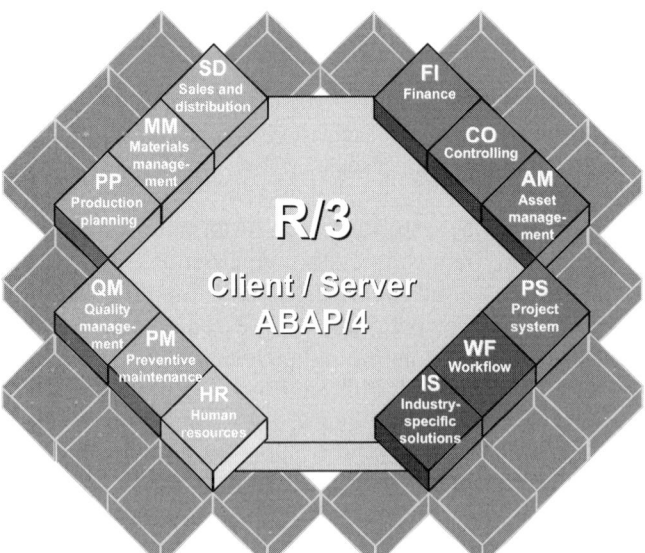

Fig. 8.2.2.1   The structure of SAP R/3 as a typical example of a generally applicable logistics software package.

The abbreviations that designate the modules, which are oriented towards specific functions within a company, consist of two letters. There are three modules at the top left for company logistics: SD for distribution logistics, MM for procurement logistics and stochastic materials management, and PP for deterministic materials management, scheduling and capacity management as used in production logistics. The modules contain sub-modules for the three temporal ranges (long, medium, and short term) and for the individual tasks. The functional separation between the MM and PP modules emphasizes the distribution of users between trade and production. It also betrays the fact that R/3 started out as an MRP II package.

SAP developed R/3 with a view to covering and integrating every function within a company. Most other logistics packages have not yet achieved this level of integration, particularly with respect to accounting. The finance and accounting functions have always been the driving force behind the development of logistics software, since detailed cost-center accounting requires efficient administration of all types of order within the company. The order administration functions of the logistics package and their integration into the accounting function are thus of particular importance to anyone with responsibility for procuring logistics software. This fundamental aspect of corporate policy explains why the emphasis always has to be placed on certain areas when developing logistics software. The decision will ultimately depend on whether the finance function can be integrated, rather than on the quality of support provided for planning & control.

SAP R/3 is a generally applicable and fully integrated logistics package, and is thus extremely complex. The software is configured by setting a large number of parameters and spreadsheet values. This requires special R/3 expertise. It is not enough just to have a thorough knowledge of logistics, planning, control, and the actual company, which means that R/3 is rather suitable for medium-sized and large companies.

A package such as R/3 can be customized to take account of different values for the features relating to planning & control described in Section 3.4. Since the software was developed from the MRP II concept, the limitations of usability indicated in Figure 3.5.3.1 also apply. In fact, most of the software packages were developed on the basis of MRP II, so the same restrictions will apply in almost every case.

The lean / just-in-time concept and all the techniques for production with frequent order repetition are oriented towards the needs of manual organizations. In the best-case scenario, such organizations can manage without software altogether, even if they have a large number of orders and require an extremely fast data and control flow. Logistics software can then be introduced when the volume of data becomes too large, in which case the package can run on a PC with a simplified master data management system. This will enable the number of kanban cards to be calculated, for example. It could also be a logistics software package extended to include this type of function.

In contrast, variant-oriented and processor-oriented concepts require appropriate software, as discussed in the rest of this chapter. These concepts, together with the software for the MRP II concept, also provide fundamental typologies for logistics software for planning & control.

8.2.3   Software for Customer Order Production or Variant-Oriented Concepts

Software for customer order production and variant-oriented concepts, i.e., for products according to (changing) customer specification or for product families with many variants, has been specially designed for and developed in conjunction with make-to-order producers. Such companies always produce their goods in response to a customer's order. Bills of material are not always created independently of their customers — they may also be customer-specific or order-specific. These companies need variant-oriented concepts for single-item production or non-repetitive or "one-of-a-kind" production. The four different techniques identified in Sections 6.2 and 6.3 all place different requirements on the software and, in the most extreme situation, could even lead to four different sub-types of logistics software for variant-oriented concepts. Equally, a package may only be suitable for one of these techniques within the variant-oriented concepts.

Software for customer order production or variant-oriented concepts was mainly developed in Europe. The software developed for small- and medium-sized companies (SME) includes Piuss from PSI, ProConcept von ProConcept SA, MAS90 from IBM, Diaprod from Seitz, and, in the past, IPPS from NCR, AFS, and many niche products. Packages that are particularly suitable for product families with a wide range of variants include Baan (formerly Triton) and Expert/400 developed by the author. There are also a number of industry-specific products, e.g., for window and furniture production.

Figure 8.2.3.1 shows, by way of example, the Piuss software module for product families with a wide range of variants. It also provides an overview of the level of detail below that illustrated in Figure 8.2.2.1.

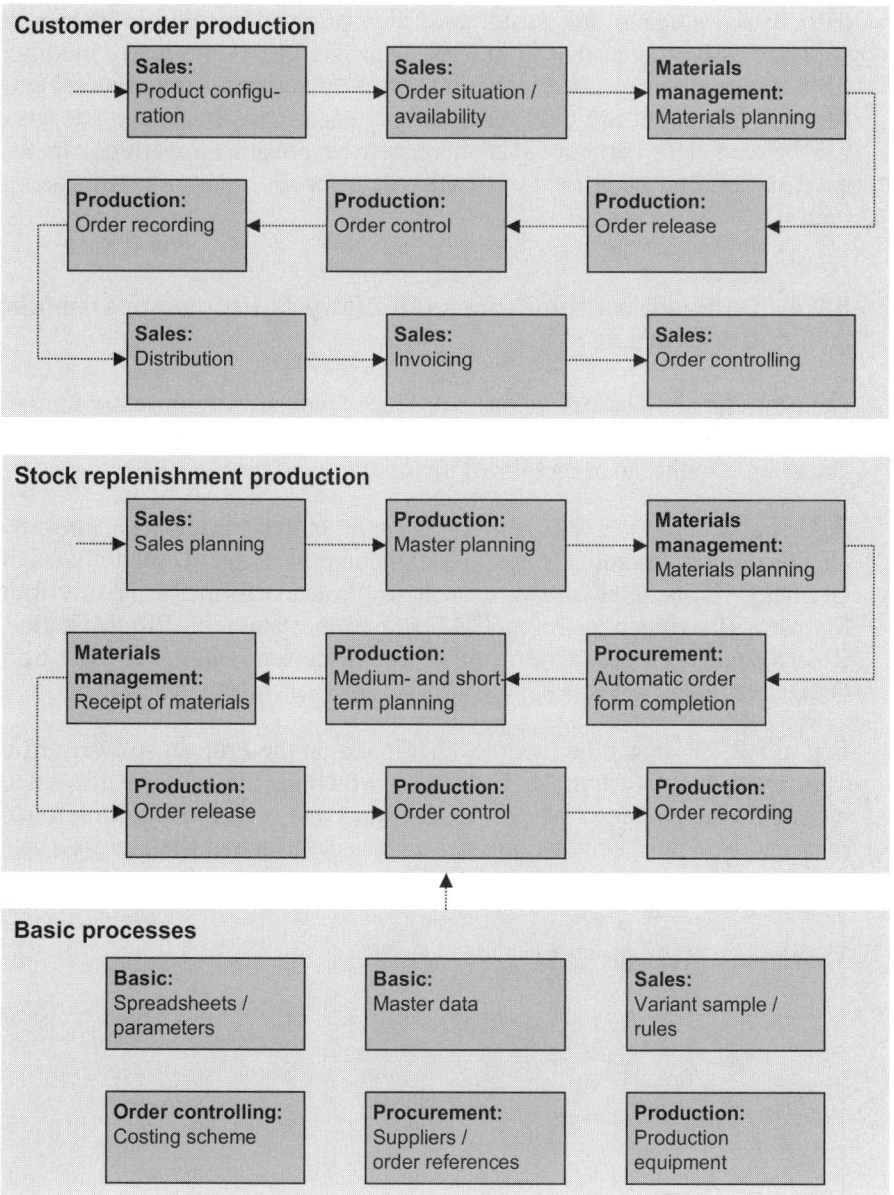

Fig. 8.2.3.1 Typical software for customer order or variant-specific production: the Piuss modules.

Some of the modules, such as "Customer order archive," "Create order package," and "Network planning module," suggest that the software is particularly suitable for customer order production. Within the order structure, the product that is ordered or offered may be greatly modified for a particular customer. One particular characteristic is the processing of "exotic" items that are only needed for a specific order and for which it can be said with certainty that there will be no order repetition. In this case, there is no need to store master data for the item or to allocate an item ID.

8.2.4 Software for the Process Industry or Processor-Oriented Concepts

Concepts for the process or basic producer industries require appropriate logistics software, i.e., in which the emphasis is placed on mixing ratios and recipes, rather than on bills of material.

Software for processor-oriented concepts largely originates from the chemical, pharmaceuticals and food industries in the United States or Germany. It includes software such as Protean (formerly Prism) from Marcam, Blending von Infor, CIMPRO from Datalogix, PROMIX from Ross Systems, Process One from Arthur Andersen, and MFG-PRO from QAD.

Figure 8.2.4.1 shows the modules that make up the Protean software from Marcam by way of example. The way in which the modules are divided up highlights the emphasis placed on resources and on the production model (processor-oriented production structures as described in Chapter 7).

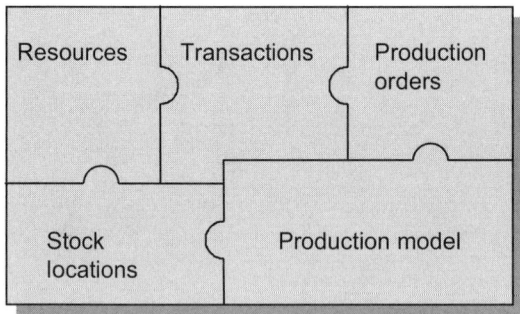

Fig. 8.2.4.1   Software for the process industry: some of the Protean modules.

The problems specific to the process industry that are covered by Protean include:

- Different lots of a bought-in product have different characteristics and must therefore be handled in different ways (e.g., production of tomato products: addition of sugar according to the sugar content of the tomatoes, the use of different grades for different products).

- The process industry often uses by-products, recycled products, or waste products. The traditional representation of product structures in the form of bills of material is not suitable for such cases.

- Planning & control do not just apply to materials — they are of equal importance for capacity and production equipment (e.g., mold for manufacturing chocolate bars).

Electronic planning boards (Leitstand) software packages such as Schedulex from Numetrix and Rhythm from i2 Technologies are used to computerize master production scheduling for processor-oriented concepts. These packages take account of the limited capacity typical of such industries and, by changing these limitations, allow reliable and appropriate production schedules to be created (constraint-based techniques, often using ILOG modules).

8.2.5   Software for Transcorporate Planning & Control in a Supply Chain

Chapter 2, in particular, presented some concepts for partnerships between companies within a supply chain. Section 4.2.3 added some associated concepts for transcorporate planning & control, and the terms "supply chain management concept" (SCM concept) and "advanced planning and scheduling concept" (APS concept) have already been discussed.

> The term *SCM software* or *APS software* is used to describe software that supports the SCM or APS concept for transcorporate planning & control.

SCM software has been available for several years and will be intensively developed in the years to come. Developments are moving in three different directions:

1. Electronic planning boards (Leitstand) software supplemented with modules for logistics and production networks. These include the modules for Numetrix, Rhythm from i2 Technologies, and SynQuest. Software such as Manugistics places particular emphasis on distribution networks, i.e., the distribution of end

products produced by different companies via various sales channels (e.g., national companies).

2. Conventional MRP II software or ERP software supplemented with company-specific or bought-in modules. These include APO (advanced planner and optimizer) from SAP or the equivalent products from Baan (by the take-over of CAP Logistics and the Berclain Group) or PeopleSoft (by the take-over of Red Pepper). The "problem solver" software kernels from ILOG are often integrated for scheduling tasks. These modules work using constraint propagation techniques.

3. Niche software specially designed for transcorporate planning & control.

Figure 8.2.5.1 illustrates the concept and some of the tasks of SCM software.

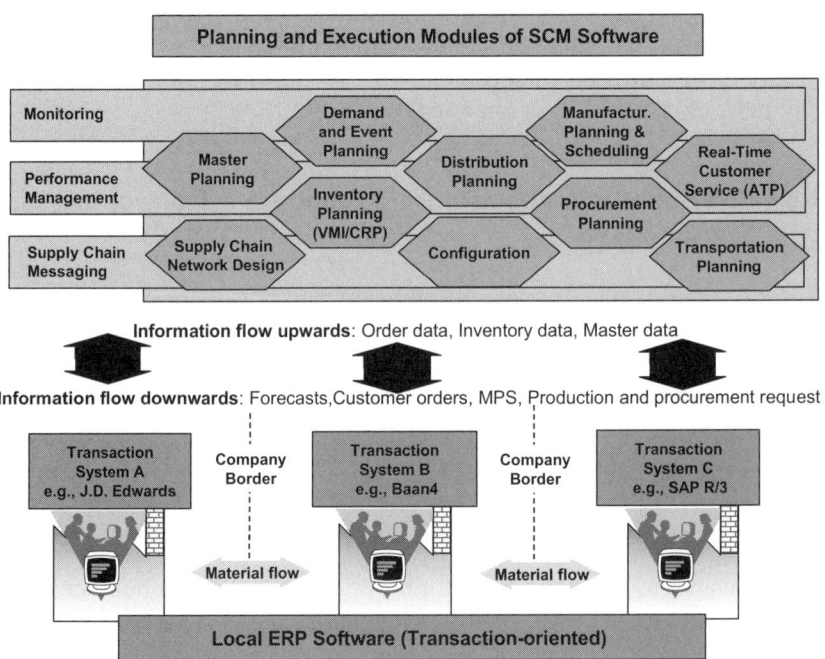

Fig. 8.2.5.1   Concept and some of the tasks performed by SCM software.

The master and order data are still administered by the local planning & control software of the individual companies involved in the logistics and production network. The data are periodically downloaded by the SCM software. The network planning then takes place and the results are returned to the local software.

The actual planning functions of SCM software are similar to those of traditional PPC and control center software, supplemented with new modules that meet the typical needs of networks:

- *Supply chain network* design in order to describe the logistics and production network

- *(Network) inventory planning* for tasks such as replenishment of the customer's stocks by the supplier (VMI, vendor-managed inventory; CRP, continuous replenishment planning). To be able to do this, the supplier must have access to the customer's inventory and order data (and the data of any customers downstream in the network).

- *Real-time customer service* in order to be able to assess the fill rate of open orders with suppliers in advance. To be able to do this, the customer must have access to the supplier's inventory and order data (and the data of any suppliers upstream in the network).

These concepts are still at the field trial stage, but the sales network software is likely to be implemented first. This is not surprising since the organizational concepts for sales networks are older than those for joint development and production. In this context, the author of [Nien04] presents an approach for designing SCM-Software that also considers aspects like robustness, tangibility, and efficiency.

8.2.6   Software for Customer Relationship Management (CRM)

Customer relationship management (CRM) is the collection and analysis of information designed for marketing, sales, and service decision support (as contrasted to ERP information) to understand and support existing and potential customer needs ([APIC04]).[1]

CRM applications integrate the relevant data and make them available company-wide. Beyond achieving cost savings through faster access to information, CRM aims toward individually designed, long-term, and thus profitable relationships with customers.

---

[1]   Refer also to the more philosophical background of this concept in chap. 2.4.4.

> *CRM software* is software that supports customer relationship management.

CRM software development began in the 1980s, when companies for which distribution is paramount first used computer-aided selling (CAS) software for rationalization purposes. The shift from this focus on rationalization to an emphasis on quality improvement of customer relationships required an extension to include marketing and services and led to today's generation of software (e.g. Siebel from Oracle).

CRM software provides functionality in two areas:

- The functions of operational CRM facilitate the business processes behind interactions with customers at the point of contact ("front office"). Tasks arising from the interaction processes and the required information are delivered to appropriate employees ("back office") for processing, interfaces are provided for further applications (word processing, e-mail client), and customer contacts are documented.

- Analytical CRM solutions, on the other hand, analyze the data created on the operational side of CRM, particularly for purposes of customer analysis and segmentation of the customer base (for instance, identifying potential failures of customer retention) or to exploit cross- and up-selling potentials.

CRM software supports all staff interactions with the customer in a number of ways (see Figure 8.2.6.1):

- CRM software provides a representation of all interactions between staff and customer. Staff members are always informed about who is responsible for supporting a customer and whom they should inform about contacts with the customer.

- CRM software supports staff in organizing, executing, and documenting customer contacts. These may be contacts with an individual customer (in person or by telephone, e-mail, or fax/letter), the sending of marketing content addressed to several customers, or a sales promotion event to which many customers are invited.

- CRM also provides functions for product-related interactions, such as customer service inquiries or sales opportunities. The system captures the probability that a sales opportunity will lead to a sale and the possible sales income that will be generated, allowing the company to forecast expected sales.

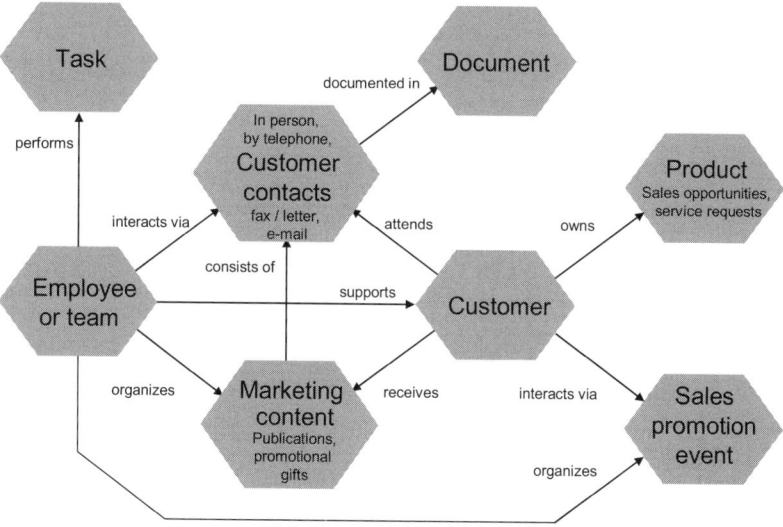

Fig. 8.2.6.1 CRM software representation of the objects and their interrelationships.

The data required by CRM software for the most part already exist in the company, but they are located within various applications:

- Product-related data (such as customer orders) in ERP software or legacy systems

- Customer addresses in personal information management (PIM) software — sometimes at decentralized workplaces; the PIM file may also document some of the interactions (appointments, e-mail)

- Customer-related documents (such as bids, invoices, invitations) produced by word processing and sometimes administered by document management systems

When implementing CRM software, the challenge is to integrate all of the data and the available interfaces. It is important to evaluate whether the systems work together in a coherent and consistent way. Today, many of the complete CRM software systems are being replaced by applications that make use of a company's existing PIM applications as the basis or by applications that are components of enterprise software packages.

8.2.7   Standard or Company-Specific Software?

Which is better for logistics applications — standard software or company-specific software?

Standard software is software designed to meet the needs of different companies. It is developed and sold by a specialist software house. *Company-specific software* is created for a specific company and thus precisely meets the needs of that company. It is either developed within the company or the work is commissioned from a software house.

Many companies had their own company-specific software by the end of the 1980s, including ABB, Siemens, Sulzer, and many others. Even some medium-sized companies developed their own software since the original packages, which were solely MRP II oriented, did not meet their needs.

In time, more logistics packages with most of the required functionality became available on the market. It was also recognized that the cost of maintaining company-specific software is extremely high. As a result, there has been a massive trend towards the use of standard software over recent years, even in large companies, which has contributed to the success of SAP R/2 and R/3. Nevertheless, some companies still need company-specific software for various reasons:

1.   *Unsuitable processes:* When standard software is implemented companies often find, particularly with respect to order processing, that they have to cut down processes forming part of their core processes and not just their antiquated legacy procedures. If core processes have to be adapted to conform to the "standard", then the company is likely to lose its competitive edge. If this is the case, the software must be examined to determine just how modular it is, i.e., whether the data model and process model have interfaces that will allow a company-specific program to be integrated in place of the unsuitable module supplied with the standard software. That is, only some modules would then be company specific, rather than the entire package. Such changes are expensive, and often time consuming and difficult.

2.   *Inadequate functionality:* Certain object classes or attributes may be missing from or inappropriately defined in the data model. This means that additional classes or attributes must be added or existing ones changed in order to modify the function model to suit the desired functionality. Today, this type of change can

usually be carried out by simply generating the code from a definition language.

3. *The user interface cannot be integrated into the company's processes and way of working:* For example, a variant generator of a well-known software package is very awkward to use and requires IT expertise and a programming-oriented approach. In one case, careful reprogramming of the user interface provided the design engineers with a simple interface that works well in their language. They are now able to provide all the necessary IT support as part of their job description. This means that it is not necessary to bring in the specialists, which would result in unnecessary process interfaces, thus making the processes slower and more unreliable. However, the need for a simpler process must be offset against the increased cost of adapting the user interface. Such modifications are often not difficult to implement, but are "merely" time consuming and thus expensive.

To summarize, a standard software package can rarely be implemented without adaptation if the entire logistics task is taken into consideration. A commercial decision must be taken to set the priorities: will the benefits of greater user friendliness, greater transparency, and faster lead times for the data and control flow outweigh the longer implementation time and higher costs?

There are two other aspects that should be taken into account when choosing between standard and company-specific software:

- *Risk of error:* The number of man years invested in the production of company-specific software will be less than that required to produce standard software of the same scope. It is also likely that the former will contain more bugs than the latter. On the other hand, standard software is not always completely stable; new software releases often have to be installed in quick succession, even though most of the changes are not relevant to a particular company. This is usually regarded as an unnecessary expense. Poor standard software can contain more bugs than good company-specific programs.

- *Continuity:* Here, again, it is not possible to give generally applicable advice. The pros and cons must be considered in each case. Although the teams involved in developing company-specific software are generally smaller, they also tend to be more committed to their program. Experience shows, however, that practically none of the companies that have produced logistics software packages have managed to issue a second generation of their successful package without going into liquidation or being taken over by another company. Both situations have direct consequences on the continuity of standard software packages.

New basic technologies offer great potential for the development of both company-specific and standard software. The benefits of *standard PC software*, such as word processors, spreadsheets, project planning software, etc., can already be used to implement much of the functionality provided by logistics software. See also [MöMe96], for example. The Internet, the Java programming language, and a standard for a company's objects (such as CORBA) enable software modules from various sources to be linked to one another.

8.3   Factors for Successful Implementation of Logistics Software

Logistics software has been available on the market for several decades. It is designed to contribute to the operational management of a company's output by systematizing and automating the data and control flow within that company's logistics. For nearly as many years, contradictory opinions have been expressed about the success of this project, and these have been carried over into views concerning the efficiency of logistics software. This contradiction can be illustrated by two extreme and opposite views:

- "There is no satisfactory logistics software package."
- "Every logistics software package is good."

If we examine these two statements in greater detail, we discover some interesting and somewhat surprising results that show that the contradictory views are due to different starting positions. The first statement concerns the limitations of any logistics software package, whereas the second relates to the essential success factors. A short digression into the history of data processing will help us to understand the limitations and possibilities of logistics software from the historical context.

The following illustrations relate to both company-specific and standard software, although some of the comments concerning the choice of logistics package will of course apply only to the standard software.

8.3.1   History and Origin of Logistics Software

Logistics software first gained acceptance in the late 1950s, as soon as data could be stored on suitable media, rather than having to "plug in" the computer programs every time they were used. During this period, the computer world was dominated by a single company – IBM (International Business Machines).

IBM was founded by an American named Hollerith who had introduced a system to classify the data obtained from the American census in the second decade of the 20th century. This was based on light and electrical circuits (and subsequently electronic circuits). It was also the origin of the term "electronic data processing." The medium used to store the data was the famous punched card. The way in which information was encoded on a punched card was a clever invention, as were the machines for punching and then reading the punched card. Essentially, every character (or "byte"), whether it was a letter, number, or special character, was assigned a unique sequence of six holes. The two states, "hole" or "no hole," thus formed the smallest unit of information — a binary number (0 or 1) known as a "bit" This sequence of 6 bits could be combined in $2^6 = 64$ different ways, enabling 64 different characters to be represented (which had to include the control characters for processing). Figure 8.3.1.1 shows an extract translated from *Hollerith-Mitteilungen* (*Hollerith News*), 1913 ([IBM 83]). The reference list shows that the system had quickly gained wide acceptance also in Europe because of its ability to perform logistics tasks within a company. The "Hollerith variations" show two possible applications. The second example also directly highlights implicitly an important problem associated with data processing, i.e., data protection.

Here is a list of just some of the major companies that use the Hollerith system to **organise their workshops**:

Allgemeine Elektrizitätsgesellschaft,	Jones & Laughlin Steel Comp.
Kabelwerk Oberspree, Berlin	Link Belt Co.
Siemens & Halske A.-G., Berlin,	Lodge & Shipley Mach. Tool Co.
Askanischer Platz 3	McCaskey Register Co.
Farbwerke vorm. Meister Lucius &	Marshall Wells Hdw. Co.
Brüning, Höchst/Main	
Accumulatoren-Fabrik Akt	
schaft, Hagen/Westf.	
Waldes & Ko., Prag-Wrs	
Brown Boveri & Cie. A.-	
Baden/Switzerland	
Gebr. Sulzer, Winterthur/	
Aktienbolaget Seperator,	
Sweden	
Bell Telephone Manufactu	
Antwerp	
Deutsche Gasglühlicht-Ak	
schaft (Auergesellschaf	
Städt. Elektrizitätswerke,	
Kaiserliche Werft, Kiel	
Witkowitzer Bergbau- und	
hütten-Gewerkschaft, V	
Central Foundry Compan	
Crucible Steel Company	
Miehle Ptg. Press and Mg	
Scully Steel & Iron Co.	
American Can Co.	
American Fork and Hoe	
American Iron & Steel Co	
American Radiator Co.	
American Sheet and Tin	
American Steel Foundries	
Bridgeport Brass Co.	
Bullard Machine Tool Co.	
Carnegie Steel Co.	
De Laval Separator Co.	
Illinois Steel Co.	

Hollerith variations.

Counting individual and specific cards. For the internal waterways statistics kept by the Imperial Statistical Office in Berlin, a card is punched for each consignment of freight and only the first consignment from a certain ship's cargo is punched with the load-bearing capacity of the ship. To determine the number of ships, the return cable of the load-bearing capacity counter is connected to a card counter so that the card counter only moves on one if a load-bearing capacity is actually added. It does not move on for cards in which no load-bearing capacity is added. This means that the cards do not have to be sorted, which would otherwise be necessary in order to separate those cards on which the load-bearing capacity is punched, i.e., which represent ships, from the others that only represent consignments.

Separation of abnormal cases. At the Statistical Bureau in Copenhagen, under the management of its Director, Mr Koefoed, an extremely sensible precautionary measure was taken by the head of the Hollerith Department, Mr Elberling. This has eliminated the need to sort 4.7 million cards. Around 100,000 people in Denmark were classified as abnormal because they fell into one of three different categories — with respect to affliction, religion and military situation. Using the normal sorting method, all the cards would have to be sorted three times in order to separate out the three abnormalities. Since Denmark has a population of around 2½ million, this would have meant sending around 7½ million cards through the sorting machine.

A special sorting machine brush holder was therefore produced. Instead of just one brush, this had three brushes, arranged so that they touched the three columns of the abnormal categories. Since the sorting machine then always sorted by the hole that closed the current circuit first, the consequence of this arrangement was that, even though the 2½ million cards were only sorted once, those with no abnormalities, i.e., which were not punched in the three rows, fell into the "R" hole, while the others were sorted into one or the other compartment. After that, the 100,000 abnormal cards had to be sorted three times because they were all muddled from the first sorting process. As a result of producing this device, it was only necessary to sort 2.8 million cards, rather than 7.5 million.

Fig. 8.3.1.1   Early logistics software: use of the Hollerith system.

Right from the start, Hollerith's idea was intended to process large quantities of data quickly and accurately. This saved an incredible amount of time, resulting in greater productivity and ultimately a new industrial revolution. The basic idea was perfected over the following decades. For example, the character code was extended from 6 to 7 or 8 bits, i.e., 256 possible combinations per byte (ASCII[2] or EBCDIC[3] code) so that lower case and special characters could be included. The hole in the card was gradually replaced by a two-digit state on a magnetic disk or tape, which resulted in the development of suitable searching and reading devices.

Since the introduction of data processing in the early years of this century, the *quantity of data and the speed with which it can be processed* have increased dramatically. However, the *logical principle used to display and process information* and the *conditions for computerization of an information system* (see Section 8.1.1) have not changed at all.

These facts are important if we are to understand the possibilities and limitations of data processing.

This ingenious idea combined with Hollerith's business sense enabled IBM to hold the monopoly of the commercial use of this technology for many years. The early logistics software also originated from IBM. COPICS (Communication-Oriented Production Information and Control System) was the most well-known standard software package of the 1960s, and for a long time was the standard for further developments in this field. See also [IBM81]. This software was designed, in particular, to meet the needs of the major industries of that period — mechanical engineering and automobile construction. Finally, IBM was, and still is, a multinational manufacturer of mainframe computer systems.

8.3.2   Possibilities and Limitations of the Computerization of Planning & Control

"There is no satisfactory logistics software package." Within companies, this type of view is generally expressed in departments involved in the strategic or overall management of the company, rather than operational management. The problem is often that such people have the wrong expectations of what logistics software can and cannot do.

These unrealistic expectations may be explained by the abbreviation *PPC*, which stands for $\underline{P}$roduction $\underline{P}$lanning & $\underline{C}$ontrol, and by the term *PPC system*. These are used to describe both the actual task of planning & control and the software used to support this task. An opinion about one

---

[2]   Abbreviation for "American Standard Code for Information Interchange," 7-bit code.

[3]   Abbreviation for "Extended Binary Coded Decimal Interchange Code," IBM's 8-bit code.

cannot be applied to the other. The same is true for the abbreviation *SCM*, which stands for <u>S</u>upply <u>C</u>hain <u>M</u>anagement, and by the term *SCM system*. The same problem arises for *APS*, which stands for <u>A</u>dvanced <u>P</u>lanning and <u>S</u>cheduling, and by the term *APS system*.

The mistake is still made, however, often unintentionally but sometimes intentionally, as well (for both positive and negative purposes). The term *software* is therefore used below in association with computerization.

The acronyms PPC, SCM or APS can nevertheless be misleading when used in association with computerization, i.e., the software. This misunderstanding may even be encouraged by the software vendors, but unfortunately it leaves a large area open to attack by anyone looking for an argument.

- The first letters in PPC and in SCM have extended meanings. PPC software packages no longer relate solely to production or supply, but rather as ERP software to the entire logistics chain from sales, production, and procurement, right through to distribution and maintenance. In addition, new requirements have arisen in association with reuse and recycling. Thus, it is logistics, rather than just production, that represents the overall function within the company. For this reason we now speak of logistics software, by which we mean *comprehensive* computerization of the way in which the data and control flow is handled within a company's logistics function. It is also no longer possible to equate PPC software with MRP II packages since it incorporates just-in-time, variant-oriented, and processor-oriented concepts and with varying levels of quality, just like the MRP II concept. Similarly, SCM software is as useful for demand chain planning.

- The letter "P" in PPC or APS for "planning": Neither a PPC software nor an ERP software nor a SCM software nor an APS software does planning in the strict sense of the word. It simply supports the planning function, for example, by showing the availability of components and capacity along the time axis. Then comes the planning, e.g., action to change stocks, capacity, or order dates. Every attempt to hand this planning step over to the computer, e.g., through the use of simulation software, has ultimately failed, because the software is unable to cope with the day-to-day problems of decision making, either because the relevant parameters were not all known or because they could not be reliably shown along the time axis.

- The letter "C" in PPC for "control" or "S" in APS for "scheduling": Neither PPC software nor ERP software nor SCM software nor APS software controls or schedules anything in the strict sense of the word. In the best-case scenario it merely provides a snapshot of the current status of order processing in the various domains in the company and recommendations options for control or regulation. The actual control or scheduling task still has to be carried out by people. Production and procurement in the manufacturing and service industries cannot be compared to the control of a machine or production system, since the equation inevitably includes people whose behavior finally cannot be predicted or simulated. On the other hand, although the inclusion of people as a production factor appears to be a disadvantage, it is also an advantage: no automated control system will ever be able to match the capabilities and potential of a human in control or scheduling, however flexible and autonomous it might be.

The last two paragraphs concerning the use of software to plan and control production and procurement apply equally to all logistics packages. So what are the consequences with respect to the influence of logistics software on a company's ability to fulfill the company objectives? Figure 8.3.2.1 lists the four target areas discussed in Figure 3.1.1.1 and shows the aims that can be pursued when implementing logistics software. It also shows, for each primary and secondary objective, the extent to which logistics software can help to fulfill the objective.

If we consider the extent to which logistics software influences the various objectives, we see that the objectives aimed at improving the company's performance can only partly be affected by the software.

- *Quality:* The advantage of using logistics software is that a company has to explicitly store its products and services, and the processes by which they are created, in the form of master data or, more precisely, in the form of bills of material, routing sheets, or master data on technology and the logistics network. In this way, products, processes, and organization are made transparent and easy to understand for all employees. However, this is only an aid to description and thus has only a minor influence over quality. The quality of products, processes and the organization is more substantially improved by design, development of processes, and through the choice of production infrastructure, employees, and partners in the logistics network.

Possible strategic objectives	Influence*
Target area quality	
To improve the transparency of product, process and organization	++
To improve product quality	+
To improve process quality	+
To improve organization quality	+
Target area costs	
To improve input for calculation and accounting	++
To reduce cost rates for administration	++
To reduce physical inventory and work in process	+
To increase capacity utilization	+
Target area delivery	
To reduce lead times in the data and control flow	++
To reduce lead times in the goods flow	+
To increase delivery reliability rate	+
To improve fill rates or customer service ratios, or the potential for short delivery lead times	+
Target area flexibility	
To increase flexibility to enter as a partner in logistics networks	+
To increase flexibility in achieving customer benefit	+
To increase flexibility in the use of resources	+

* The influence of logistics software over the strategic objective:
    ++: high / direct
    +: some / indirect / potential

Fig. 8.3.2.1   Influence of logistics software on the extent to which corporate objectives are fulfilled.

- *Costs:* Reduction of stocks in store and in work and increasing the utilization of capacity lead to conflicting objectives. Logistics software cannot resolve these conflicts, but it makes the processes faster, more comprehensive, and also transparent to more people. As indicated above, decisions concerning scheduling and materials planning and the actual control cannot be left to the software, so the increased transparency must be converted into better decisions by the people involved. The software thus has only an indirect influence.

The influence of software on basic costing and accounting methods arises from the requirements for complete and accurate management of master and order data. The software thus has a direct influence. To reduce administration costs, the processes must be automated, making this another area which can be directly influenced by the software.

It is worth repeating here that stocks and utilization are also subject to macro-economic influences, such as the employment market and the competitiveness of an entire national economy. These effects can far outweigh the influence of logistics.

- *Delivery:* Information on orders in progress or stocks can be quickly called up by anyone involved in the process. Logistics software thus directly reduces lead times within the data and control flow. Experience shows, however, that this does not necessarily affect lead times within the goods flow.

   This can be illustrated by an example in which it took just a few seconds to identify the physical location of a delayed order within the factory. The check demonstrated that the information was correct and reliable, but the goods had been left there because the operator was unavailable. This meant that the promised delivery date could not be met.

   Shorter overall lead times and increased delivery reliability therefore require a firm foundation within the company's internal organization. Simply holding the data on the computer is not enough to improve fill rates or customer service ratios — action must be taken in practice, as well. The software thus has only an indirect influence also in the target area delivery.

- *Flexibility:* As a first aspect of flexibility, today's logistics software allows product families with a wide range of variants to be managed efficiently. In fact, this is essential in order to be able to respond flexibly to customers' requirements. However, as with quality, the potential for flexibility is determined more by the way processes and the production infrastructure are designed and planned. Logistics and logistics software are a less important factor.

   The same applies to the other aspect of flexibility — the utilization of resources. Logistics software quickly provides comprehensive information on the needs and options arising from a given situation within the company. It will rarely be able to make the decision to move resources without human input, however. It is worth repeating that, the ability to use people flexibly and the capacity of machines to be used flexibly will essentially depend on the qualifications of those people and on the way in which the production infrastructure was planned.

If we consider these points together with Figure 8.3.2.1, we can draw the following conclusion:

Logistics software provides IT *support* for planning & controlling the way in which a company provides its services. However, a logistics software packages is used first and foremost — and in most cases successfully — for representing products and their production and procurement processes (make or buy) and to administer orders, and thus for administration and preparing accounting.

Logistics software ultimately links people together by the way it uses information. If we assume that sufficient numbers of people have been adequately trained and are given enough time, then they could manually do everything that the logistics software can do.

Logistics software can be used to good effect in situations where human skills and capabilities are insufficient, typically because of:

1. The increasing complexity of products and the product mix
2. Increased volumes of data and frequency of orders (or processes)
3. Greater requirements placed on the speed of process administration

To summarize, logistics software will always be able to do exactly what Hollerith intended data processing to do right from the start, i.e., fast and accurate processing of large quantities of data. It is thus not a replacement for the internal task of "logistics," i.e., systems and systematization. It is merely used to automate this task. It would be wrong to expect any more of it, however tempting this might sound. Implementing a logistics package will not automatically result in good logistics. It would be more accurate to say that successful implementation of the software is dependent on prior systematization.

The right choice of production infrastructure, combined with the correct use of logistics, will result in a mix of complexity and frequencies and will meet the need for speed. In many cases, it will be important, or even essential, to computerize the data and control flow by using logistics software, although, even in these situations, the software on its own will not be sufficient to achieve the primary objectives set within a company.

All logistics software packages have roughly the same influence over whether corporate objectives are achieved. This means that if a certain package does not fulfill the objectives that a company has set itself, then these objectives will not be achieved by using a different package. If the software is then investigated as the cause of failure, people will be all too ready to say that, "There is no satisfactory logistics software package." They will view this as a welcome opportunity to pass the buck outside the company.

If the logistics function has to be reorganized, it is therefore advisable to divide the procedure into two steps, each with its own break-even analysis. This procedure requires attention to be paid to the training of people who will carry out the task within the company.

- The first step is to devise one or more logistics methods that will be suitable for the various product families and their production and procurement processes (make or buy). Is reorganization desirable? Can the existing organization actually be carried over to the new? Can the new logistics be implemented? What will this cost? Computerization should intentionally be left out of the equation because, as mentioned above, all the tasks of logistics software can, at least theoretically, be carried out by people. If computerization is intended, it should merely be clarified at this point whether *in principle* logistics software with the necessary functionality is available on the market. The break-even analysis for this first step must then consider the cost of the training required to cope with all aspects of the new logistics. Consideration should also be given to how the company's objectives (e.g., to reduce lead times in the goods flow) can actually be achieved by the changed logistics.

- Only then comes the second step and thus the second break-even analysis, in which the precise value of computerization with standard logistics software is considered. Here, again, there will be costs associated with training employees in the correct use of the hardware and software. On the other hand, in this case it will also be possible to reduce staffing numbers since the flow of information will no longer be processed manually.

This type of procedure can disprove the view that there is no suitable logistics software (which is sometimes used as a convenient excuse). The problems really arise because the people involved have insufficient knowledge of logistics and the associated tools.

8.3.3   Factors that Influence Individual Acceptance and the Range of Implementation of Logistics Software

It is not easy to quantify the success of implementing a logistics software package. Figure 8.3.2.1 has already shown that success should not be measured against explicitly worded corporate objectives, since these are influenced by the logistics used, the product design process, and factors outside the company's control, rather than by the software. One study [Mart93] adopted "PPC acceptance" and "Range of PPC implementation" as its measured variables. Here, PPC means PPC software and, more broadly, logistics software in general. Many of the factors can as well be transferred to SCM software. Consequently, it is better to speak of the acceptance and range of implementation of logistics software below.

The study was carried out in 100 companies and 900 people were surveyed, particularly those who regularly work with the software at the operational level. Analysis of the questionnaires revealed extremely high acceptance of logistics software at the individual level: the people questioned felt that the package more or less met their expectations. Figure 8.3.3.1 shows the factors that influence individual acceptance.

Under *personal features*, education, vocational training, experience, and position within the company had no significant influence over the individual acceptance of logistics software, whereas it was affected by general data processing knowledge and experience and the support of colleagues.

Of the factors that influenced the *support for employees during implementation*, the duration and breadth of training, satisfaction with the training and the opportunity for participation all had significant influence over acceptance, which rose steadily as the number of days of training increased. No "saturation point" was identified, even with a high number of training days ([Mart93], p. 102). It also appears that certain deficits in the software can be overcome with the aid of training.

The most important factors appeared to be information on the reasons for implementing logistics software, combined with cooperation between departments, planning and organization, and the time available out of normal daily work. The extent, to which the data had to be revised and, unexpectedly, supported from senior management, appeared to be much less important.

Factors that influence individual acceptance	Influence*
Personal features	
School education	+
Vocational training	+
Number of years in the job	
Position within the company	+
General data processing knowledge	+++
Data processing experience	++
Support from colleagues	++
Support for employees during implementation	
Training: duration	++
Training: breadth of training	++
Training: satisfaction	++
Information concerning the reasons for implementation	+++
Participation: range	++
Participation: opportunity to put forward suggestions	++
Participation: desire for opportunity to put forward suggestions	+
Extent to which data had to be revised	+
Cooperation between departments	++
Planning and organization	++
Time available out of daily work	++
Support from senior management	+
Internal contact	
User's opinion of the logistics software	
General suitability for own work	+++
System availability	+
Relevance of information on screen	+
Relevance of information in lists	
Scope for action: in determining time	+++
Scope for action: in determining processes	++
Scope for action: changes	+++
User friendliness: help functions	+
User friendliness: error messages	++
User friendliness: familiarization period	+
User friendliness: error correction	+

* Extent of influence over individual acceptance

+++:	High
++:	Significant
+:	Insignificant
(blank):	Minimal or no influence

Fig. 8.3.3.1   Factors that influence individual acceptance of logistics software. (From [Mart93].)

For the *user's opinion of the logistics software*, the most important factor was whether the individual agreed that the adopted software was generally suitable for his or her own work. Work psychology concepts expressed by the scope for action also played a central role. This means that users are given the freedom to decide the order in which they perform their tasks and the sequence of activities within each task, even after implementation. On the other hand, the layout of screens and lists and, with the exception of error messages, other components associated with user friendliness (help functions, familiarization period, error correction) appeared to be less important.

To summarize, the reasons for implementation, good training, freedom of choice in work, and suitability for an employee's own work are all important factors in the acceptance of a logistics software package.

The range of implementation of the logistics software was then identified with reference to the factors of "time since implementation started," "number of functions implemented," and "degree of distribution." For the first factor, the sobering result from the questionnaire was an average time of 4.3 years, even though all the companies questioned were either in the process of implementation or had just completed this phase. The number of functions implemented was derived by counting the number of modules, such as Sales, Stockkeeping, etc. Thirteen such functions were implemented on average. The degree of distribution was calculated by dividing the number of people working with the logistics software by the total number of people working in the operational departments. The range of implementation was derived from the combination of the three values. Figure 8.3.3.2 shows a selection of the factors that might influence the range of implementation.

The *company features* (total number of employees, influence from the group level, company type, and branch of industry) had just as little influence over the range of implementation as the data processing equipment used (hardware, operating system, or cost of software). The selected logistics software also had no influence over the range of implementation, although it did appear to matter whether it was the first implementation of such software or a replacement for an existing package. This result is particularly interesting in view of the opinion that, "Every logistics software package is good."

Of the *project features*, the importance of "ownership" of the project was key. The most successful projects were those in which responsibility was held solely by the Organization and Data Processing department, rather than by a specialist department or two or more departments. This is one of the most unexpected results of the survey. It can be explained by the fact that, in an SME environment (small- or medium-sized enterprise), responsibility for the logistics software probably lies with employees in the Organization and Data Processing department, rather than the specialist departments.

The number of levels of the management hierarchy that receive training is also very important. Training must be received by at least the top level (board) and the bottom level (group leader).

Factor of influence (brief description)	Influence*
Company features	
Number of employees	
Influences from the group	
Features of the type of company, branch of industry	
Data processing equipment	
Hardware, operating system	
Cost of software	
Initial situation	++
Logistics software	
Project features	
Project leaders and time they are able to devote to the project	+
Reason for implementation (e.g., replacement, guideline, improvements)	
Control committee	++
Project team	++
Number of project teams	
Number of team members	
Number of departments represented	
Regular project team meetings	++
Project "owner" (specialist dept. / mixed / Organization–Data Processing)	++++
External consultants and number of consultants	
Reference customers visited	++
Vendor tests using company's own data	++
Current situation analyzed	++
Weak points documented	+
List of requirements drawn up	+++
Employees appointed to project	++
Number of trained hierarchical levels	+++
Board trained	+
Departmental manager trained	+++
Section manager trained	++
Project leader trained	++
Group leader trained	
Average acceptance of the logistics software in the company	++

* Extent of influence over the range of implementation

++++:	Very high
+++:	High
++:	Significant
+:	Insignificant
(blank):	Minimal or no influence

Fig. 8.3.3.2   Factors that influence the range of implementation of logistics software. (From [Mart93].)

It is also important to adopt a professional procedure for evaluating over-the-counter software (visiting reference customers, vendor tests using the company's own data, analysis of the current situation, list of requirements) and clear project management (appointing employees for the project, establishing a control committee and project team). On the other hand, the number of project teams, team members and represented departments, and the project leaders and the amount of time they are able to devote to the project are less important.

The average acceptance of the logistics software within the company, which is derived from the individual acceptance scores, also has a significant influence over the range of implementation.

To summarize, the survey clearly shows that, for the acceptance and range of implementation of logistics software, the characteristics of the software are not particularly important, with the exception of two points. First, individuals must believe that it is suitable for their own work and that they will retain freedom of choice in their work. Equally important is the support provided during implementation, the employee training, and the quality of the project management in general. If these requirements are fulfilled, it is clearly possible to gain acceptance for and implement any of a number of logistics software products, which ultimately leads to the view that, "Every logistics software package is good." This opinion is normally expressed by those who work with the logistics software every day and is not necessarily applicable to people who only use it sporadically.

8.4   Summary

Three types of software are used for logistics purposes. *Logistics software* is used to computerize planning & control, i.e., it supports the comprehensive and integrated data flow required for administrative logistics and the control flow associated with scheduling and planning logistics. *Process modeling and simulation software* is used to develop organizations and processes and to dimension the production infrastructure. It is also used to raise awareness and for training in both cases. Software development software is primarily used to support the software development and generation process.

With the benefit of Hollerith's ingenious idea and business sense, IBM long held the monopoly over the commercial use of data processing technology. The early logistics software also originated from IBM. Between 1960 and 1980, many other companies developed both company-specific and standardized packages for the computerization of planning & control. Today, logistics software is in widespread use. Indeed, it is currently used in over 80% of all medium-sized and large companies. The most widely used logistics software packages are based on the MRP II concept and, increasingly, incorporate just-in-time and both variant-oriented and processor-oriented concepts. Although the trend is towards standard software, company-specific packages are still very important in many situations.

If we consider the question of the quality of logistics software, it is easy to draw different conclusions, depending on the initial viewpoint. Many misunderstandings are caused by the terms *PPC* and *PPC system*, which are used for both the task of logistics and for the software used to support it. It is also unlikely that people who hold one viewpoint will change their opinion without further evidence. It is therefore important to understand the background behind the arguments used to defend the positions that are adopted — which can lead to totally contradictory views.

Thus, many businesspeople will find it difficult to understand how a logistics software package, which is an expensive tool, is unable to influence their most important corporate objectives. This is still largely attributable to the vendors who promise the businessman too much in this respect because they know it is exactly what he wants to hear. It is important not to raise any false expectations concerning the possibilities of logistics software. Its strengths are that it can be used to represent products and their production and procurement processes (make or buy) and to administer orders, and thus for administration and preparing accounting. By recording and processing the data (and compressing it statistically), logistics software thus provides the information needed to make decisions concerning planning & control.

Acceptance and the range of implementation of logistics software depend on the way in which the software is implemented, the support given to employees during implementation, and the training they receive. Employees must feel that the actual software is suitable for their own work and that they will retain freedom of choice in their work. People who work with the logistics software every day must not assume, however, that it is sufficient just to master the IT aspects. They must also have a thorough understanding of logistics and continuously adapt the company's processes to the needs of the market and individual products. Only then can it help (to a greater or lesser extent) a company to maintain its performance in the face of strong competition.

8.5   Keywords

8.6   Scenarios and Exercises

8.6.1   Factors that Influence People's Acceptance of Logistics Software

Look again at Figure 8.3.3.1 and recall the three main areas that have an influence on a person's acceptance of logistics software. Please describe for each area the factors that have the greatest effect on acceptance. If you are a practitioner or a consultant, does your personal experience match the findings presented in Figure 8.3.3.1? Please discuss this with your colleagues.

Solution:

a. *Personal features:* In this area, general knowledge of data processing and experience and support from colleagues have the highest impact on acceptance.

b. *Support for employees during implementation:* In this area, the most important factor is being informed of the reasons for implementing the logistics software. Other factors that influence employee acceptance are duration and breadth of training and satisfaction with training. Also important are cooperation between departments, planning and organization, and time to learn the software aside from normal daily work activities during the implementation phase.

c. *User's opinion of the logistics software:* From the user's point of view, the most important factor is whether the user feels that the adopted software is generally suitable for his or her own work. Another factor with high impact is the "scope for action," meaning that the software gives users the freedom to decide the order in which they perform their tasks and the sequence of activities within each task.

8.6.2   Standard or Company-Specific Software

Today, standard packages like mySAP™ ERP or J.D. Edwards' ERP are used to computerize planning & control activities, i.e., to support the comprehensive and integrated data flow required for administrative logistics and the control flow associated with scheduling and materials planning logistics. However, a lot of company-specific software is still being produced in this field. Can you explain why?

Hint for finding the answer: Ask people in companies using company-specific software about this issue and compare their responses to the arguments given in Sections 8.1.2 and 8.2.7.

8.6.3   Software for Transcorporate Planning & Control

Figure 8.2.5.1 illustrated the SCM software concept and some of the tasks it performs. In this exercise you will examine this concept further and look at some success factors.

How do you evaluate the claim of some SCM software salespeople that SCM software at last solves the problems that ERP could not handle, such as:

a. Taking into account capacity constraints when creating production schedules. (*Hint*: Compare especially the planning principles of processor-oriented and variant-oriented concepts.)

b. Finding the correct solution. (*Hint*: Look very carefully at the structure of Figure 8.2.5.1)

c. Finding best solutions rapidly (real-time planning).

Finally, consider the more general question that is raised in Section 8.3.2, which discussed possibilities and limitations of the computerization of planning & control:

d. What are the real reasons for the success of SCM software implementations?

Solutions:

a. When proclaiming the advantages of modern SCM software, salespeople often contrast SCM to older, outdated versions of ERP software. Ask a salesperson if he or she is familiar with any software for internal enterprise planning & control besides MRP II. Many software packages for variant-oriented concepts (for example, also project management software) and particularly for processor-oriented concepts, subsumed under ERP software, do indeed take capacity constraints into account.

b. Figure 8.2.5.1 shows that SCM software must get the planning data from a company's ERP system. This means that the same errors in master and order data are generated in enterprise planning with SCM that were generated using ERP software. Ask the software salesperson about the consequences of erroneous data on lead time and product load in the master data of ERP software for the quality of planning through SCM software. After all, the following principle will hold: "garbage in, garbage out." And, by the way, any claims that SCM software eliminates the need for ERP software (the lower section of Figure 8.2.5.1) are true only in theory or in very specific cases. Ask the salesperson for examples that correspond closely with your own company's situation.

c. Rapid planning through the use of SCM software is generally only the case for variants of a plan that has already been calculated. Ask the SCM software salesperson how long it takes to transfer greatly changed master or order data from ERP to SCM software. Ask for a reference from a company similar to your own in order to learn about their experience with the data transfer.

d. As in the case of ERP software, the decisive factors in success with SCM software lie in the company culture and the organization of supply chain collaboration. For implementation, therefore, the task is to find appropriate measures for all of the nine fields in the framework of Figure 2.3.2.1, and not for the ninth field alone.

Part B. Methods of Planning & Control in Complex Logistics Systems

The chapters in Part A examined logistics management as embedded in the entrepreneurial activities of designing, manufacturing, using, and disposing goods. The focus was on the objectives, basic principles, analyses, concepts, systems, and systematic methods of the management and design of logistics systems. We introduced essential business objects and business processes and presented an overview of the methods used for planning & control tasks. The business objects themselves were set in relation to the characteristics of planning & control.

Part A then took a closer look at the methods in two simple cases:

- The process of master planning was the first case. Although this business process is mostly carried out as gross requirements planning, it encompasses a number of methods that serve as examples in the following discussion.

- The second case examined was planning & control with a very simple characteristic feature, namely repetitive manufacturing, or production with frequent order repetition. The benefits of the kanban technique serve this task well. A look at this method, along with the underlying lean / just-in-time concept, gave the reader some insight into the ways of thinking in logistics management.

Chapters 9 through 16 in Part B turn to planning & control methods in complex logistics systems. These are methods used in all the temporal ranges of planning & control, and they provide solutions to the tasks outlined in the reference model in Figure 4.1.4.2. (reproduced below). The more detailed discussion will give the reader a deeper methodological foundation for understanding the kanban and master planning methods introduced in Part A. A look at cost object accounting in Chapter 15 also includes the more recent ABC approach, or activity-based costing. An advantage of ABC is that is based on the same type of data management as the ERP concept.

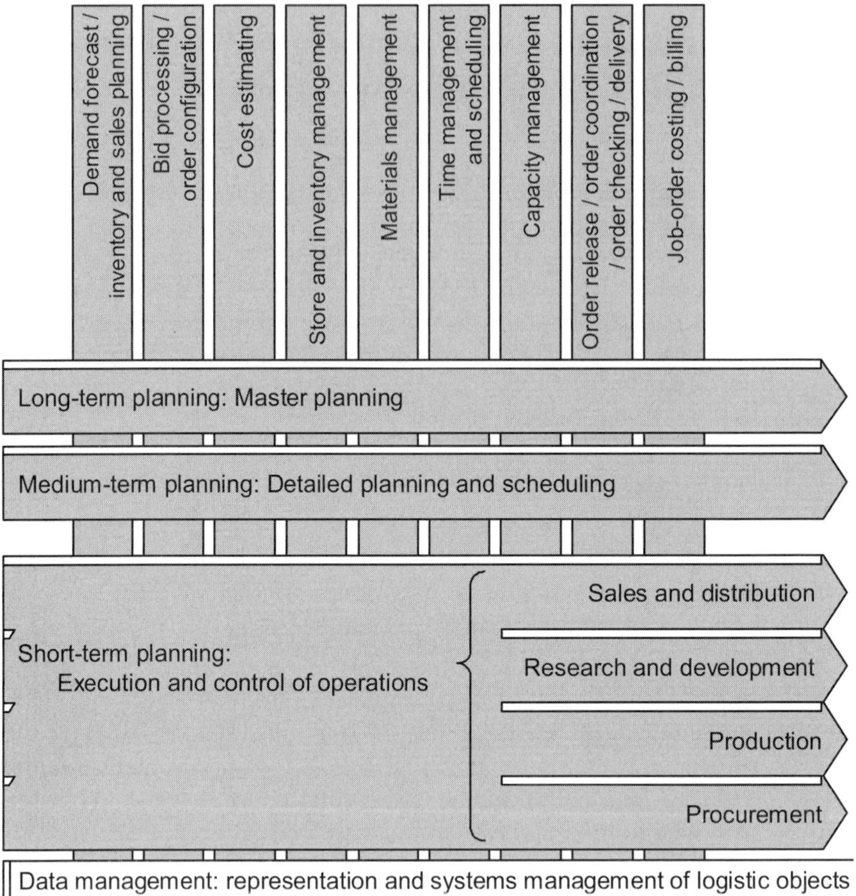

Fig. 4.1.4.2   A reference model for business processes and planning & control tasks (reproduced from Chapter 4).

Chapters 9 through 16 will examine the individual tasks in succession, with some exceptions: The discussion of bid processing and customer order configuration began in Section 4.2.1 and continues in Section 11.1, and Chapter 15 discusses cost estimating together with job-order costing. The introduction to each section will refer back to the reference model and show the task together with the temporal ranges of planning for which the task is particularly pertinent.

The in-depth discussion will also provide a deeper methodological basis for understanding various concepts introduced earlier (in more and less detail) in Section 4.3 and Chapters 5, 6, and 7. These concepts were shown in Figure 3.5.3.1, which is reproduced below.

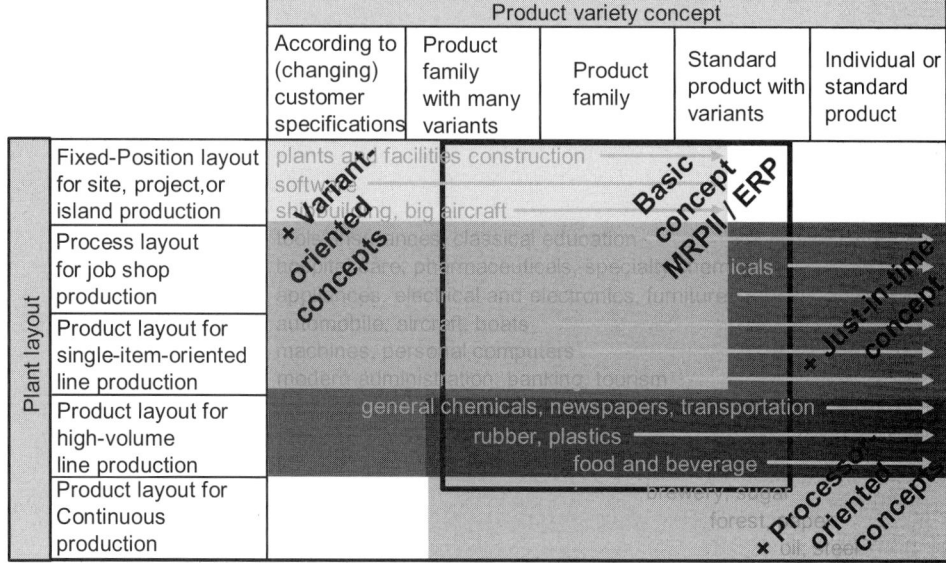

Fig. 3.5.3.1   Different concepts of planning & control in dependency upon the features *facility layout* and *product variety concept* (reproduced from Chapter 3).

The methods and techniques in Chapters 9 through 16 thus comprise all that is required for designing the logistics of production that is not characterized by frequent order repetition. Many of these techniques have their origins in the MRP II and ERP concepts. However, they also apply to the process industry as well as to non-repetitive production and non-repetitive procurement, whereby they, of course, are applied to the business objects of those processes. And, finally, Section 12.2 provides an in-depth methodological explanation of the lean / just-in-time concept.

9 Demand and Demand Forecast

Production or procurement of an item must take place on the basis of a demand forecast whenever its cumulative lead time is longer than the customer tolerance time. The planner can determine future demand using either analytical or intuitive forecasting techniques. The dark background in Figure 9.0.0.1 shows the task of demand forecasting and the planning processes that require forecasting.

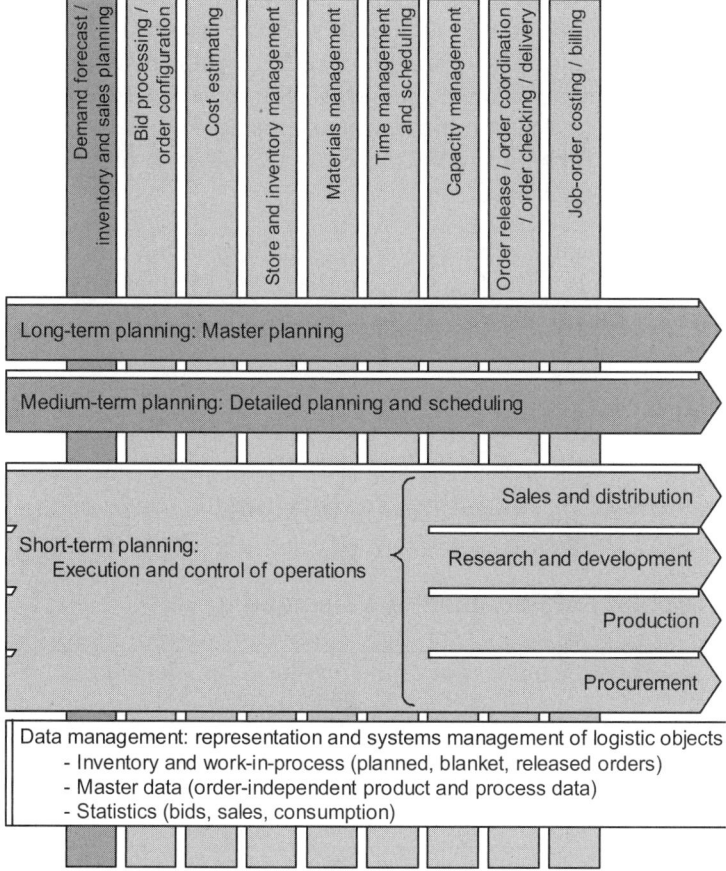

Fig. 9.0.0.1   The darker background shows the tasks discussed in this chapter.

Figure 9.0.0.1 reproduces the reference model for business processes and planning and control tasks presented in Figure 4.1.4.2. Sections 4.3.1 and

4.3.2 provide a good basis for the material in this chapter,[1] for they present demand forecasting as a *technique for determining stochastic independent demand*. Demand forecasting is, in that way, a part of stochastic materials management in the broader sense. The need for forecasting varies over time depending on the industry, market, and product. Examples of buyers' markets with a great need for forecasting include trade in consumer goods or provision of the components needed for a service or for investment goods. Before receiving any definite customer orders, the company must produce or procure, for example, machine parts or the "frameworks" of data descriptions and programs for a software product in advance.

The following sections will classify forecasting techniques and describe the procedures in principle. They will also describe and compare individual techniques in detail and define the consumption distribution as an overlay of the distribution of consumption events and the distribution of the quantity consumed per event. This will allow us to derive safety demand and the limits of determining independent stochastic demand. We will also take a look at the transition from forecast values to independent demand and how this is managed.

The material in this chapter is both qualitative and quantitative in nature. In many parts it demands not only intuitive or basic knowledge, but also an understanding of at least elementary statistical methods.

9.1   Overview of Forecasting Techniques

9.1.1   The Problem of Forecasting a Demand

Demand forecasting is the process of estimating the future demand.

A *forecast error* is the difference between actual demand and demand forecast. It can be stated as an absolute value or as a percentage.

A *forecasting technique* is a systematic procedure for forecasting demand according to a particular model.

---

[1]   We recommend that you reread Sections 4.3.1 and 4.3.2 before studying Chapters 9 to 11.

A certain degree of uncertainty and therefore forecast errors characterize every forecast, regardless of whether people or computer-aided stochastic forecasting techniques do the forecasting. In forecasting, information-technology-based forecasting techniques are a complement to human intuition and creativity. We should make appropriate use of both according to the situation.

If there are only a few items and only a limited amount of information that can be stated explicitly, human forecasting tends to be more precise. This is because human intelligence can process fragmentary information as well as knowledge derived by analogy directly, thus taking many further factors necessary for forecasting into account. This can be particularly important, for example, in rough-cut planning, where we need only forecast relatively few demands for item families or rough-cut items.

On the other hand, when there are many items, or when we can use information on demand that is expressed explicitly, a computer-aided forecasting technique generally provides more precise forecasting. This is due to the capacity of computers to process large quantities of data rapidly and accurately.

- Tendencies or trends, such as seasonality, can be calculated from consumption statistics. The length of the time frame to be observed makes this a difficult task for human beings.

- People tend to weigh unusual events too heavily. In this case, a computer-aided forecasting technique is more neutral in its "reactions."

- People tend to focus overly on the recent past. If a forecast proves too high for the current period, they tend to forecast a demand that is too low for the next period, even though this is not justified from the medium-term perspective.

Techniques of demand forecasting are always based upon certain fundamental assumptions and constraints. Parameters are used in order to keep their selection as general or flexible as possible. If the demand situation changes, demand management should reexamine the choice of both parameters and technique and change them if necessary.

Forecast management is a procedure for choosing the forecasting technique and its parameters (see Figure 9.1.1.1).

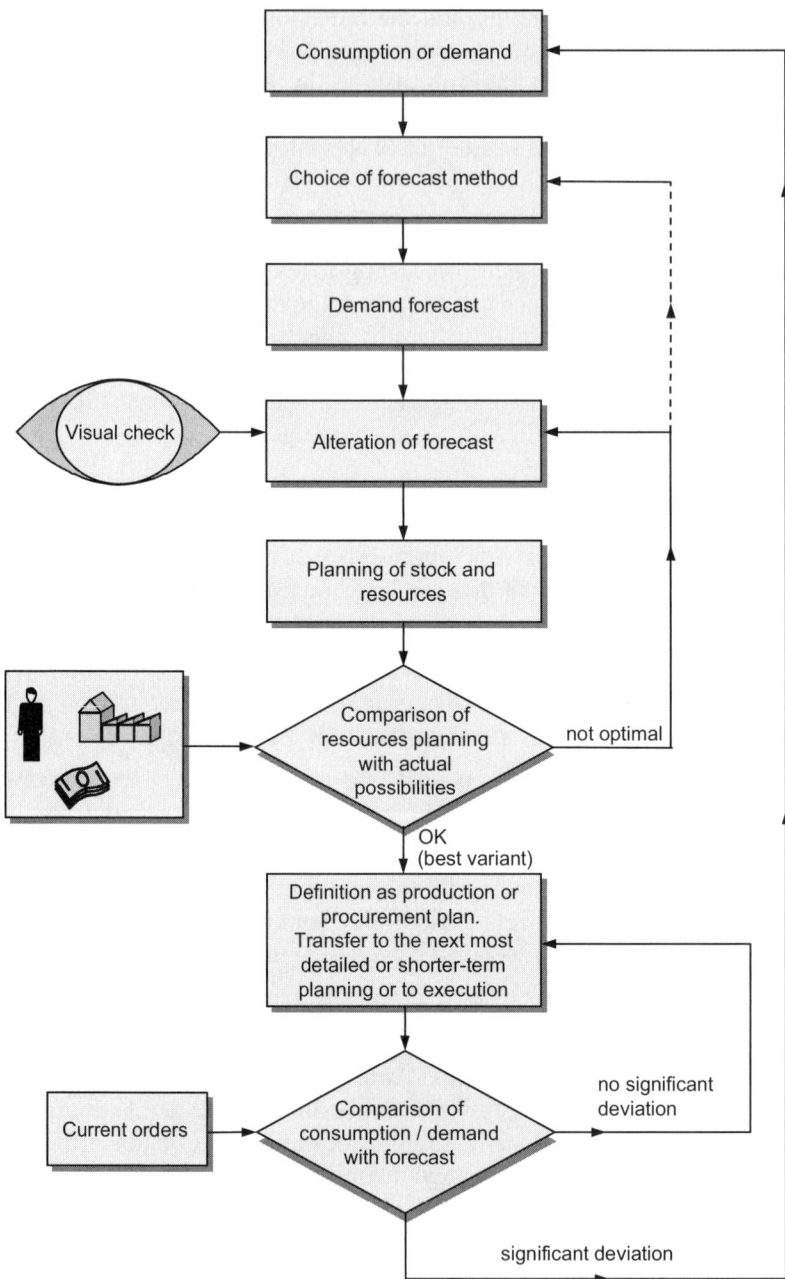

Fig. 9.1.1.1   Forecasting procedure.

- Chose a demand forecasting technique based on existing consumption or on partially known demand figures.

- Produce a forecast for future demand by applying the technique.

- When possible, make a visual check of the forecast and, if necessary, correct forecast values that vary too widely from intuitive assumptions. This check allows input of human knowledge of the behavior of the market into automated forecasting techniques.

- Break the demand forecast down into the needed resources — goods and capacity — according to temporal range and level of detail. This allows planners to estimate the consequences of implementing a forecast and to work out better variations if necessary.

- Adopt the optimal variant of the forecast as the production plan or procurement plan. These plans represent the independent demand; they are subsequently provided either to the next most detailed or shorter-term planning or to execution.

- At certain intervals in time, perform an analysis to see whether the course of the demand or consumption agrees with the forecast. If the analysis of deviation reveals too great a difference, repeat the cycle.

9.1.2   Subdivision of Forecasting Techniques

Figure 9.1.2.1 shows one possible subdivision of forecasting techniques:

- *Historically oriented forecasting techniques* predict future demand based on historical data, for example, on consumption statistics. If a forecast can be made only for an item family or a rough-cut item, then the predicted quantity must subsequently be applied to the detailed items with the use of an allocation key. Historically oriented forecasting techniques can be further subdivided into:

  - *Mathematical forecasting techniques*, predominant among which is the extrapolation of a time series. Future demand is calculated by extrapolating a series of demands in the past. Such procedures are used widely.

  - *Graphical forecasting techniques*, where a time series is represented graphically; a mean course and width of deviation are judged by "eyeballing" and are projected into the future based on past experience.

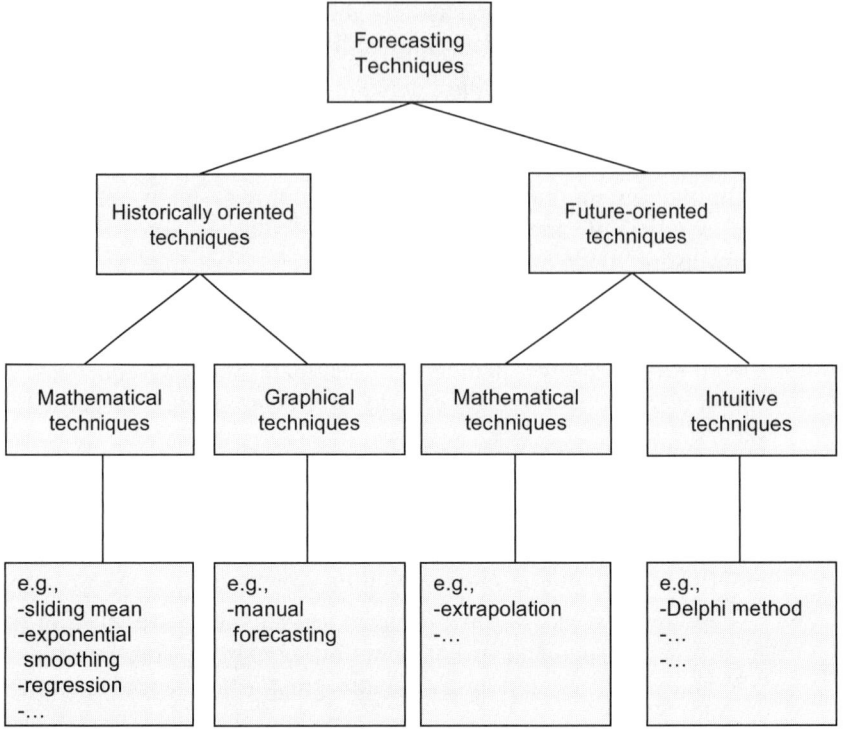

Fig. 9.1.2.1   Breakdown of forecasting techniques.

- *Future-oriented forecasting techniques* take information already at hand about future demand into account, such as bids, firm orders, orders in the concluding phases, or surveys of consumer behavior. Such techniques are further subdivided into:

  - *Mathematical forecasting techniques*, for example, extrapolation. Beginning with confirmed orders, future order volume is calculated empirically.

  - *Intuitive forecasting techniques*, such as surveys, juries of executive opinion, or estimation. Relevant information can be provided by the sales department, the sellers, or markct research institutes that use surveys to assess customer behavior, or by customers themselves (direct contact).

A *combination* of these techniques is also conceivable. For example, forecasts produced using a mathematical technique may be "eyeballed" for accuracy using a graphical representation.

Another possible subdivision of forecasting techniques is the following (see [APIC04]):

- *Qualitative forecasting techniques* based on intuitive expert opinion and judgment (manual forecast or Delphi method, for example)

- *Quantitative forecasting techniques* using historical demand data to project future demand; these techniques are further subdivided as follows:

  - *Intrinsic forecasting techniques* are based on internal factors, such as an average of past sales, and are useful for individual product sales.

  - *Extrinsic forecasting techniques* are based on a correlated *leading indicator* (a business activity index that indicates future trends), such as estimating sales of disposable diapers based on birth rates or estimating furniture sales based on housing starts ([APIC04]). Extrinsic forecasts tend to be more useful for large aggregations, such as total company sales.

9.1.3   Principles of Forecasting Techniques with Extrapolation of Time Series and the Definition of Variables

Particularly for forecasting based on historical data, statistical techniques are used that are based upon a series of observations along the time axis. The following values are fundamental to the determination of stochastic requirements:

A *time series* is the result of observation and measurement of particular quantifiable variables at set observation intervals equal in length.

The *statistical period* or *observation interval* is a time unit, namely the period of time between two measurements of the time series (e.g., 1 week, 1 month, 1 quarter).

The *forecast interval* is the time unit for which a forecast is prepared ([APIC04]). This time unit best corresponds to the statistical period.

The *forecast horizon* is the period of time into the future for which a forecast is prepared ([APIC04]). It is generally a whole number multiple of the statistical period.

As an example, Figure 9.1.3.1 shows the frequency distribution[2] of the observed variable "customer order receipts" during the most recent statistical period as a histogram.[3]

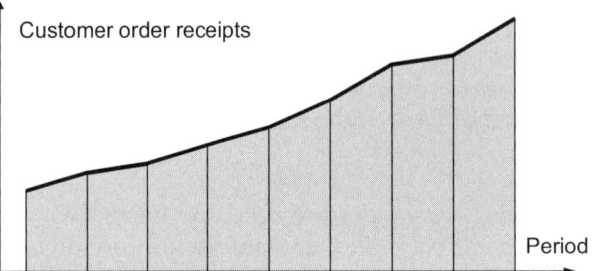

Fig. 9.1.3.1   Example of a time series.

A *demand model* attempts to represent demand by drawing the curve that shows the least scattering of the measured values.

Curve fitting is the process performed to obtain that curve, by means of a straight line, polynomial, or another curve.

We assume that the scattering (dispersion) of values is random and, most often, distributed normally. This presupposes that while demand values do indeed have a fluctuating pattern, it is possible to make fairly good approximations. Figure 9.1.3.2 presents some common cases of demand models.

Matching a particular demand model to a particular time series leads to the choice of a forecasting technique. The forecasting technique is thus based on a concept or a model of the course of demand. This concept forms the basis for the perception of regularity or a regular demand, and the model is

---

[2]   A *frequency distribution* indicates the frequency with which data fall into each of any number of subdivisions of the variable ([APIC04]).

[3]   A *histogram* is a graph of contiguous vertical bars representing a frequency distribution. The subdivisons of the variable are marked on the x axis, and the number of items in each subdivision is indicated on the y axis ([APIC04]).

- Either an *econometric model*, mostly defined by a set of equations, formulating the interrelation of collected data and variables of the model of the course of the demand as a mathematical regularity,

- Or an *intuitive model* as an expression of the perception of an intuitive regularity.

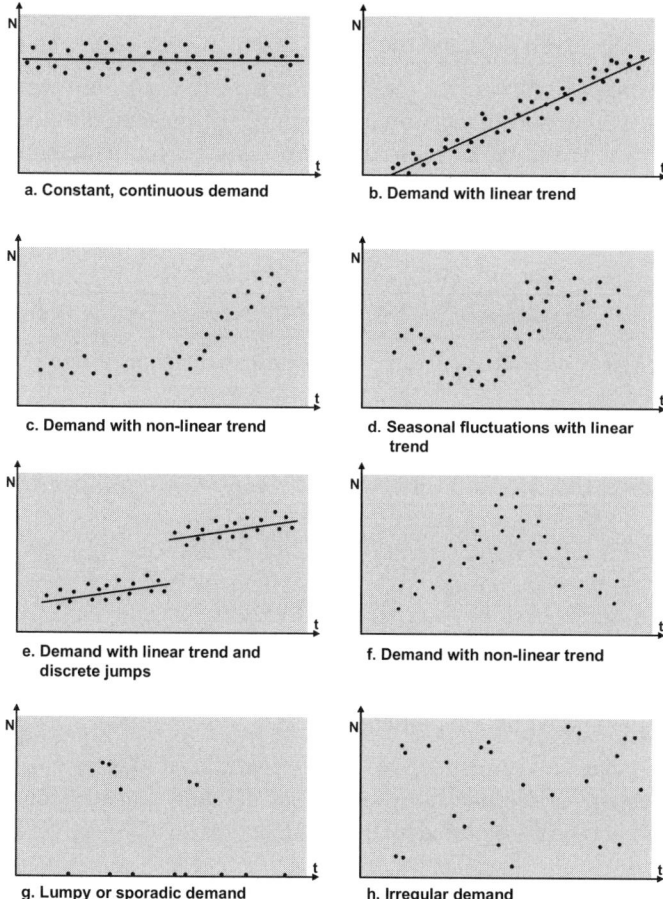

Fig. 9.1.3.2   Possible and common demand models.

It is quite possible that for a single time series several models will overlap.

(Statistical) decomposition or *time series analysis* is a breakdown of time series data into various components of demand by analysis, for example, into:

- (Long-term) trend component

- Seasonal component

- Non-seasonal, but (medium-term) cyclical component

- Marketing component (advertising, price changes, etc.)

- Random component (non-quantifiable phenomena), for example, due to *noise*, that is random variation or a random difference between the observed data and the "real" event.

Mathematical statistics offers various methods for determining the mean, deviation, expected value, and dispersion (scattering)[4] of measured values for a time series. Their ability to reproduce the demand for a demand model accurately depends upon the situation. Figure 9.1.3.3 shows a morphology of possible statistical features and the statistical methods that they characterize.

Degree of freedom	➡	Expressions	
Calculation of dispersion	➡	Extrapolation from the past	Determination of forecast error
Measure of dispersion	➡	Mean square deviation	Absolute deviation
Weighting of historic values	➡	Equally weighted	Exponentially declining

Fig. 9.1.3.3   Statistical methods to determine mean and dispersion.

1. *Calculation of dispersion.* Two basic methods are used:

   - *Extrapolation*, or estimation by calculation of deviations of individual values in the previous statistical periods from the mean, postulated by the demand model.

   - Direct, that is, retrospective *determination of the forecast error* as the difference between actual demand and projected demand according to the demand model.

2. *Measure of dispersion.* There are two standards here:

   - *Mean square deviation*: σ (*sigma*) (i.e., standard deviation)
   - *Mean absolute deviation (MAD)*

---

[4] A (arithmetic) *mean* is the arithmetic average of a group of values. The *deviation* is the difference between a value and the mean, or between a forecast value and the actual value. An *expected value* is the average value that would be observed in taking an action an infinite number of times. *Dispersion* is the scattering of observations of a frequency distribution around its average ([APIC04]).

3. *Weighting of values.* Most commonly encountered are:

- *Equal weighting* of all measured values

- *Exponential weighting* of measured values in the direction of the past

In most cases, we only measure *satisfied demand* for all models. This equates consumption with demand. The basic problem with this measurement is that real demand is not taken into account. The customer order receipts mentioned in Figure 9.1.3.1 may have been higher, for example, if a better demand model had resulted in better availability. Strictly speaking, the customer orders that could not be filled should have been measured as well. The problem with this, however, is that the customer orders may be filled at a later time period. At that time, there may be other orders that will then be unfilled, etc. Determining the exact amount of demand in the past by employing a "what would have happened if" method rapidly proves itself redundant; later demand on the time axis is most likely dependent on satisfied demand in the preceding periods on the time axis.

The following sections use the variables defined in Figure 9.1.3.4. The nomenclature was chosen in such a way that the index always shows the point at the end of the statistical period in which a value is calculated. The period to which the value refers is shown in parentheses.

M_t	=	Mean value, calculated at the end of period t
$P_t(t+k)$	=	Prediction (or forecast value) for period t+k, calculated at the end of period t
$\sigma_t(t+k)$	=	Forecast error for period t+k, calculated at the end of period t
N_i	=	Demand in period i, calculated at the end of period i
t	=	Current period or period just ended
n	=	Constant number of periods (the smaller the n is chosen to be, the more quickly the forecast will react to demand fluctuations)
k	=	Distance of a future period from the period just ended

Fig. 9.1.3.4   Definitions of variables, each calculated at the end of a statistical period.

9.2   Historically Oriented Techniques for Constant Demand

In a *forecasting model for constant demand*, planners obtain the forecast value for a future period using a mean from past consumption.

Figure 9.2.0.1 shows the forecast curve resulting from two techniques discussed in the following. The actual events — "damped" or "smoothed"[5] — are projected into the future. However, smoothing always lags one statistical period behind, since it is a historically oriented forecast.

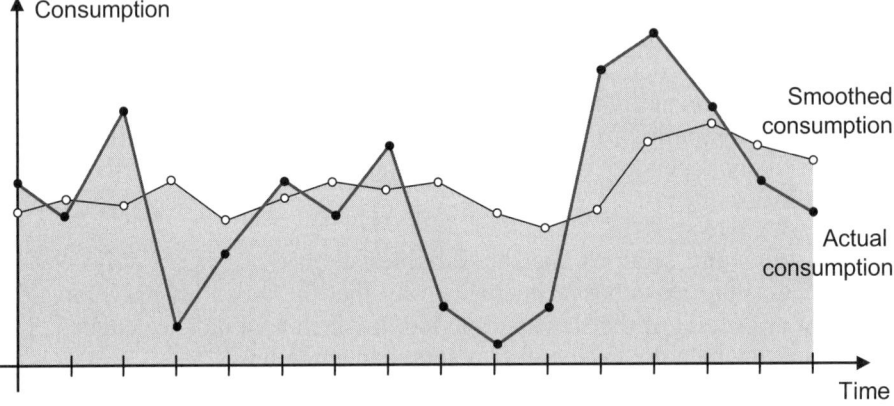

Fig. 9.2.0.1   Smoothing of consumption.

Despite the assumption of constant demand, we should always reckon that demand changes over the course of time. In order to take this into account, the mean is recalculated at the end of every statistical period, although the characteristic parameter of the mean calculation, that is, the number of the periods in the past included in the calculation or the smoothing constant, is usually kept constant.

---

[5]   *Smoothing* means the process of averaging data, by a mathematical method, for example.

9.2.1   Moving Average Forecast

> The *moving average forecasting technique* considers the individual values of a time series as *samples* from the *universe*, or parent population, of a *sample distribution* with constant parameters and performs periodic recalculations according to the principle of the moving average.[6]

The technique uses the classic repertoire of mathematical statistics, that is, the mean of a sample and, as a measure of dispersion, the standard deviation.

Figure 9.2.1.1 shows the calculation of *mean* and *standard deviation* in the moving average forecasting technique. The variables are set according to the definitions in Figure 9.1.3.4. The formulas are independent of k; that is, we interpret the determined parameters as the expected value and dispersion of forecast demands. These remain valid for any periods of time in the future.

$$P_t(t+k) = M_t = \frac{1}{n}\sum N_{t-i}$$

$$\sigma_t(t+k) = \sqrt{\frac{1}{n-1}\sum (N_{t-i} - M_t)^2}$$

where $0 \le i \le n-1, 1 \le k \le \infty$

Fig. 9.2.1.1   Mean and standard deviation in the *moving average forecasting* technique.

The average age of the observed values included in the calculation is shown in Figure 9.2.1.2. The larger the value chosen for n, the more exact the mean becomes, but because the moving average reacts more slowly to alterations in demand, so does the forecast; n should be set so that a rapid adaptation to systematic changes is possible, without causing a significant reaction to a purely random variation in demand. See also Section 9.5.3.

---

[6]   *Moving average* is the arithmetic average of a certain number (n) of the most recent observations. As each new observation is added, the oldest observation is dropped ([APIC04]).

$$\overline{n} = \frac{1}{n}\left(0 + 1 + \ldots + (n-1)\right) = \frac{n-1}{2}$$

Fig. 9.2.1.2   Average age of the observed values.

Figure 9.2.1.3 shows an example of moving average calculation that includes nine periods in the past.

Period	Forecast value	Actual demand	$\sum_{j} (N_{t-1-j} - M_{t-1})^2$	Forecast error	Confidence interval 95.44%
t	$P_{t-1}(t)$	N_t	$0 \le i \le n-1$	$\sigma_{t-1}(t)$	$I_{t-1}(t)$
1		104			
2		72			
3		110			
4		108			
5	Ø=91	70	3036		
6		86			
7		85			
8		66			
9		118			
10	91	115	3036	19.48	52 – 130
11	92	85	3430	20.71	50 – 134
12	94	105	3055	19.54	55 – 133
13	93	90	2913	19.08	55 – 131
14	91	75	2665	18.25	54 – 128
15	92	130	2477	17.60	57 – 127
16	97	—	3700	21.51	54 – 140

Sample calculation :

$$P_{15}(16) = \frac{85 + 66 + 118 + 115 + 85 + 105 + 90 + 75 + 130}{9} = \frac{869}{9} = 96{,}6 \approx 97$$

$$\sigma_{15}(16) = \sqrt{\frac{(85-97)^2 + (66-97)^2 + \ldots + (130-97)^2}{8}}$$

$$= \sqrt{\frac{3700}{8}} = 21{,}51$$

$$I_{15}(16) = P_{15}(16) \pm 2\sigma_{15}(16) = \langle \frac{54}{140}$$

Fig. 9.2.1.3   Example: determining the forecast value using moving average (n = 9).

The calculation formulas and results are valid independent of the underlying consumption distribution, although a particular distribution is assumed for implementation. Forecast calculations often assume a normal distribution as probability distribution.[7] We discuss this assumption in Section 9.5.3.

The statement in the last column of Figure 9.2.1.3, that the demand value N_t has a 95.4% probability within the confidence interval "forecast value (= mean) $\pm\ 2\ *$ forecast error (= standard deviation)" is only valid in a normal distribution.

9.2.2   First-Order Exponential Smoothing Forecast

If we wish to adapt the forecasting technique to actual demand, the demand values for the last periods must be weighted more heavily, according to the principle of the weighted moving average.[8] The formula in Figure 9.2.2.1 takes this weighting into account; the variables were chosen according to the definitions in Figure 9.1.3.4 and include an indefinite number of periods. G_{t-i} always expresses the weighting of demand in the period (t–i).

$$M_t \ = \ \frac{\sum G_{t-i} \cdot N_{t-i}}{\sum G_{t-i}} \quad 0 \le i \le \infty$$

Fig. 9.2.2.1   Weighted mean.

In the *first-order exponential smoothing forecast technique*, or *single (exponential) smoothing*, the weights are in an exponentially declining relationship and adhere to the definitions in Figure 9.2.2.2.

Figure 9.2.2.3 shows the calculation of

- *Mean smoothed consumption* as measure of mean
- *Mean absolute deviation (MAD)* as measure of dispersion

---

[7]   A *probability distribution* is a table of numbers or a mathematical expression, that indicates the frequency with which each event out of a totality of events occurs. The mathematical *probability* is a number between 0 and 1 that expresses this frequency as a fraction of all occurring events.

[8]   *Weighted moving average* is an averaging technique in which the data are given values according to their importance ([APIC04]).

See also the definitions of indexes and variables in Figure 9.1.3.4.

$$G_y = \alpha \cdot (1-\alpha)^y$$
where
y = age of the period, $0 \le y \le \infty$ (whole number)
G_y = weight of the period demand with age y
α = smoothing factor, $0 < \alpha < 1$
$$\sum_y G_y = \frac{\alpha}{1-(1-\alpha)} = 1, \quad 0 \le y \le \infty$$

Fig. 9.2.2.2   Exponential demand weighting.

$$M_t = P_t(t+k) = \underbrace{\alpha(1-\alpha)^0 \cdot N_t + \alpha(1-\alpha)^1 \cdot N_{t-1} + \alpha(1-\alpha)^2 \cdot N_{t-2} + \ldots}_{(1-\alpha) \cdot M_{t-1}}$$

$$= \alpha \cdot N_t + (1-\alpha) \cdot M_{t-1}$$

$$MAD_t(t+k) = \underbrace{\alpha(1-\alpha)^0 |N_t - M_{t-1}| + \alpha(1-\alpha)^1 |N_{t-1} - M_{t-2}| + \alpha(1-\alpha)^2 |N_{t-2} - M_{t-3}| + \ldots}_{(1-\alpha) \cdot MAD_{t-1}(t)}$$

$$= \alpha \cdot |N_t - M_{t-1}| + (1-\alpha) \cdot MAD_{t-1}(t)$$

$$\sigma_t(t+k) \approx 1.25 \cdot MAD_t(t+k) \quad \text{where } 1 \le k \le \infty$$

Fig. 9.2.2.3   First-order exponential smoothing: mean, MAD, and standard deviation.

Since the weighting G_y follows a geometric series, the recursive calculation indicated in the formulas is self-evident. These formulas allow us to perform the same calculation as in moving average using only the past values for mean and MAD and the demand value for the current period instead of many demand values. With a normal distribution, standard deviation and mean absolute deviation (MAD) stand in the same relationship as that given in Figure 9.2.2.3.

Figure 9.2.2.4 shows the average age of the observed values.

$$
\begin{aligned}
\overline{n} \; &= \; 0 \cdot \alpha (1-\alpha)^0 + 1 \cdot \alpha (1-\alpha)^1 + 2 \cdot \alpha (1-\alpha)^2 + \ldots \\
&= \; \sum y \cdot \alpha \cdot (1-\alpha)^y, \; 0 \le y \le \infty \\
&= \; \frac{(1-\alpha)}{\alpha}
\end{aligned}
$$

Fig. 9.2.2.4   Average age of the observed values.

The choice of *smoothing constant* α or *alpha factor* determines the weighting of current and past demand according to the formula in Figure 9.2.2.3.

Figure 9.2.2.5 shows the effect of the smoothing constant with $\alpha = 0.1$, a value often chosen for well-established products, and $\alpha = 0.5$ for products at the beginning or the end of their life cycles.

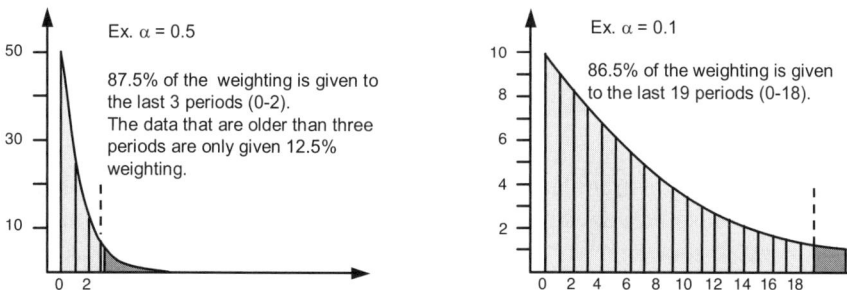

Fig. 9.2.2.5   The smoothing constant α determines the weighting of the past.

Figure 9.2.2.6 shows the behavior of the forecast curve with various values of the smoothing constant α. A high smoothing constant results in a rapid but also nervous reaction to changes in demand behavior. See also Sections 9.5.2 and 9.5.3.

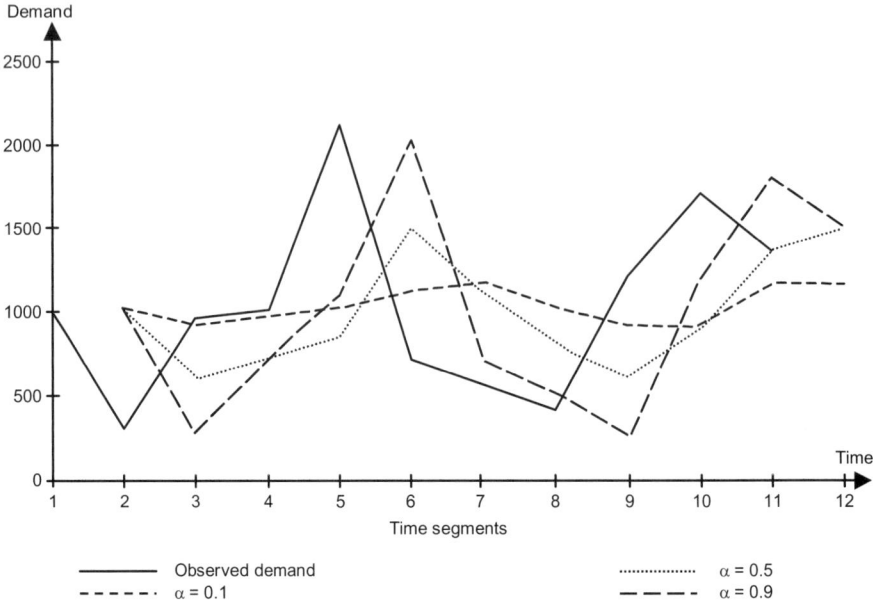

Fig. 9.2.2.6　　Forecasts with various values of the smoothing constant α.

Using exponential smoothing techniques, we can determine the uncertainty of a forecast by extrapolating the forecast error. To do this, we calculate the mean absolute deviation (MAD). Figure 9.2.2.7 is an example of exponential smoothing with smoothing constant α = 0.2. It was chosen in a way similar to the example of moving average calculation in Figure 9.2.1.4.

Period	Forecast value $P_{t-1}(t)$	Actual demand N_t	Deviation $N_t\text{-}P_{t-1}(t)$	Forecast error $MAD_{t-1}(t)$	Confidence interval 95.44% $I_{t-1}(t)$
⋮					
10	91	115	24	17	48 – 134
11	96	85	–11	18	51 – 141
12	94	105	11	17	51 – 137
13	96	90	–6	16	56 – 136
14	95	75	–20	14	60 – 130
15	91	130	39	15	53 – 129
16	99	70	–29	20	49 – 149
17	93	100	7	22	38 – 148
18	94	95	1	19	46 – 142
19	94	120	26	15	56 – 132
20	99	—	—	17	56 – 142

Sample calculation:

$$P_{14}(15) = P_{13}(14) + 0.2 \cdot \left(N_{14} - P_{13}(14)\right) = 95 + 0.2 \cdot (-20) = 91$$

$$MAD_{14}(15) = MAD_{13}(14) + 0.2 \cdot \left(\left|N_{14} - P_{13}(14)\right| - MAD_{13}(14)\right) = 14 + 0.2 \cdot 6 = 15$$

Fig. 9.2.2.7   First-order exponential smoothing with smoothing constant $\alpha = 0.2$.

9.3 Historically Oriented Techniques with Trend-Shaped Behavior (*)

Forecast values produced by techniques for a constant demand do not reflect actual demand in cases where the demand follows a trend.[9] For this reason, a number of trend forecasting techniques have been developed.

A *trend forecasting model* takes into account stable trends in demand.

---

[9]   A *trend* is a general upward or downward movement of a variable over time.

In Figure 9.3.0.1 all demand values fluctuate within the confidence limit around the calculated mean. Nevertheless, there is a systematic error (δ_v) in extrapolation of the mean. Regression analysis shows a rising demand trend. We can avoid the systematic error by extrapolating the regression lines.

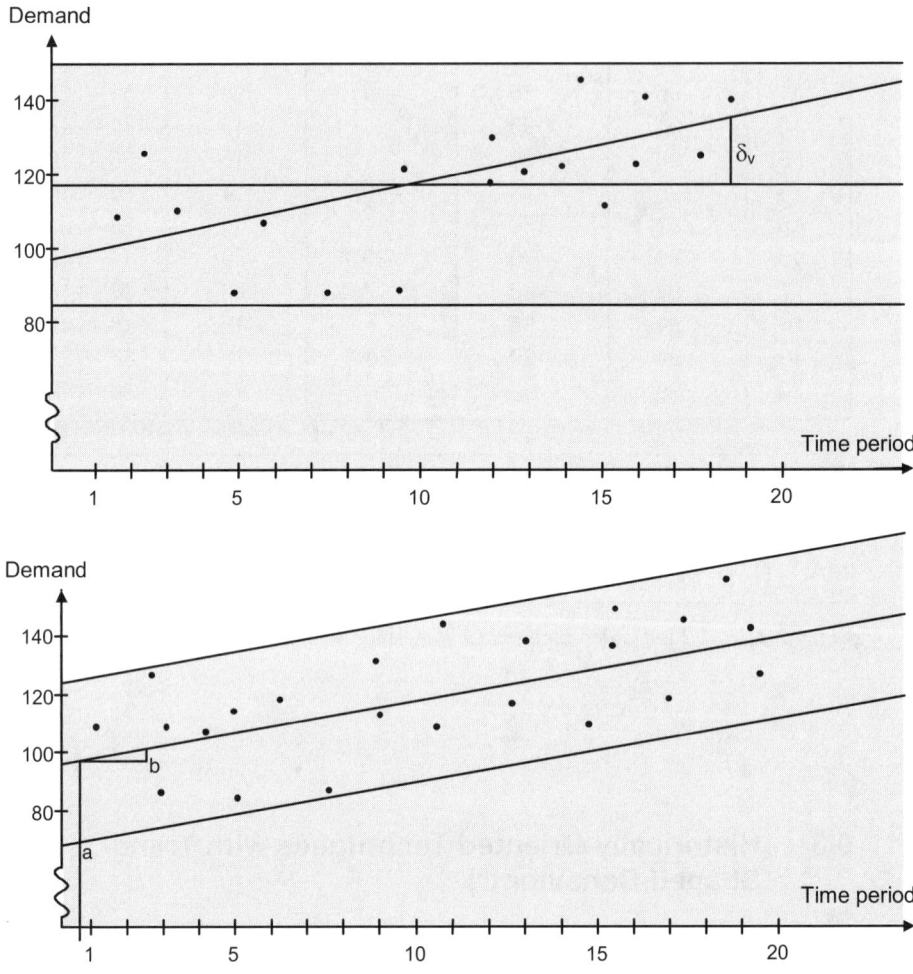

Fig. 9.3.0.1   Demand with linear trend: comparison of extrapolation of the mean with that of regression.

In order to detect a trend in advance, we could, for example, tighten the control limits, (+/– 1 * standard deviation). As soon as the limits have been exceeded a particular number of times, a correction is made.

9.3.1 Regression Analysis Forecast

Regression analysis or *linear regression* is often described as trend analysis. It is based on the assumption that demand values appear as a particular function of time, such as a linear function.

This means that a number of points represented on the *x–y* plane can be approximated by a line. Figure 9.3.0.1 shows demand as a function of time period. Given a *y*-axis value of a and a slope of b, we can determine the mean line (regression line) sought between the two pairs of values. Figure 9.3.1.1 provides the formulas for determining this, along with the values a and b. In order to perform the calculation, we need to know the values for at least n periods preceding time t. See also the definitions of indexes and variables in Figure 9.1.3.4. The derivation of the formulas is taken from [Gahs71], p. 67 ff.

$$P_t(t+k) = a_t + b_t \cdot (n+k)$$

$$a_t = \frac{1}{n}\sum_i N_{t-i} - b_t \frac{n+1}{2}$$

$$b_t = \frac{12 \cdot \sum_i\left((n-i)\cdot N_{t-i}\right) - 6(n+1)\sum_i N_{t-i}}{n(n^2-1)}$$

$$s_t = \sqrt{\frac{1}{n-2}\sum_i\left(N_{t-i} - P_t(t-i)\right)^2}$$

$$\sigma_t(t+k) = s_t \cdot \sqrt{1 + \frac{1}{n} + \frac{3\cdot(n+2k-1)^2}{n(n^2-1)}}$$

where $0 \le i \le n-1$ and $1 \le k \le \infty$

Fig. 9.3.1.1   Mean, standard deviation, and forecast error in linear regression.

Due to uncertainty in the determination of a and b, the forecast error is larger than the standard deviation, as shown in Figure 9.3.1.1. The term 1/n in the formula for forecast error represents the uncertainty in determining a, while the other term represents slope b. The influence of the slope b increases with increased forecast distance k. In this situation, therefore, we determine the forecast error by extrapolation of the deviations of individual values from the past value of the regression curve. Figure 9.3.1.2 shows a sample calculation of linear regression with $n = 14$.

Period i	N_t	a_{t-1}	b_{t-1}	$P_{t-1}(t)$	s_{t-1}	$\sigma_{t-1}(t)$
1	110					
2	120					
3	100					
4	85					
5	100					
6	120					
7	90					
8	130					
9	120					
10	90					
11	140					
12	120					
13	135					
14	125					
15	150	98.1319	2.011	128.2969	24.58	32.292
16	130	89.945	3.4835	142.1975	35.1365	46.3345
17	110	90.6588	3.4835	142.911	34.7262	45.7935
18	140	96.3165	2.7363	137.363	29.8761	39.3977
19	130	104.1208	2.3077	138.7363	26.7943	35.3336
20	150	109.7249	1.8462	137.4179	24.4796	32.2813

Sample calculation: estimated values for period 19 (in period 18)

1st step: $\sum N_{t-i} = 1700$, $\sum((n-i)\cdot N_{t-i}) = 13275$

2nd step: $b_{18} = \dfrac{12\cdot 13275 - 6\cdot 15\cdot 1700}{14(14^2-1)} = 2.3077$

3rd step: $a_{18} = \dfrac{1}{14}\cdot 1700 - 2.3077\cdot\dfrac{14+1}{2} = 104.1208$

4th step: $P_{18}(19) = 104.1208 + 2.3077\cdot(14+1) = 138.7363$

Fig. 9.3.1.2   Linear regression: sample calculation with n = 14.

9.3.2 Second-Order Exponential Smoothing Forecast

Second-order exponential smoothing forecast technique extends first-order exponential smoothing to create a technique capable of capturing linear trend.

Second-order exponential smoothing starts out from:

- The mean, calculated using first-order smoothing
- The mean of this first-order means, calculated according to the same recursion formula

These two means are the estimated values for two points on the trend line. Figure 9.3.2.1 shows an overview of this technique, which is elaborated in the following discussion. The exact derivations can be found in [Gahs71], p. 60 ff, and in [Lewa80], p. 66 ff.

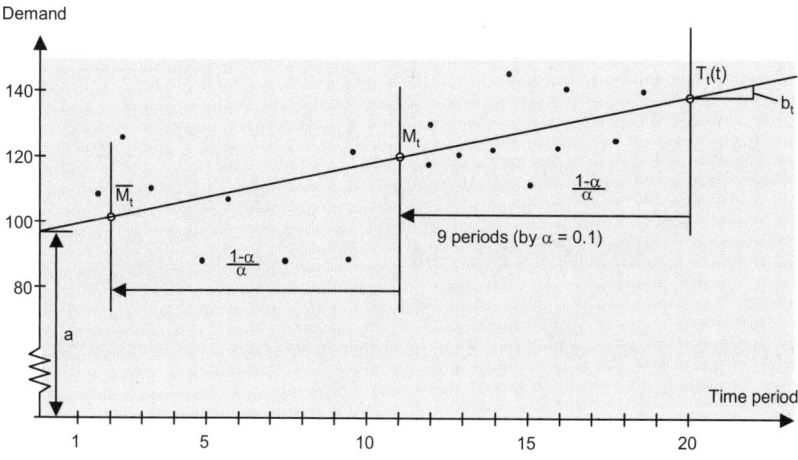

Fig. 9.3.2.1   Determination of trend lines in second-order exponential smoothing.

Figure 9.3.2.2 shows the formulas necessary for calculating the trend line; this gives us the second-order forecast value for subsequent periods as well as the corresponding forecast error. See also the definitions in Figure 9.1.3.4.

The following numbered explanations correspond to those presented in Figure 9.3.2.2:

1. The previous formula to determine first-order mean.
2. The new formula to determine the second-order mean, as the mean of the first-order means. The second-order mean lies at the same distance from the first-order mean as does the latter from the current period.
3. Slope of the trend line to time t, when two means are given.
4. Starting value T_t for the forecast at time t.
5. Forecast for subsequent periods.

6. Forecast error for the next period $t + 1$. Because a linear trend entails that the forecast error is dependent on k, the same formula does not automatically hold for period $t + k$, although it is often used.

7. The determination of the starting value that can be calculated, for example, by means of regression analysis.

1: $M_t = \alpha \cdot N_t + (1-\alpha) \cdot M_{t-1}$ mean age : $\dfrac{1-\alpha}{\alpha}$ periods before t

2: $\overline{M_t} = \alpha \cdot M_t + (1-\alpha) \cdot \overline{M_{t-1}}$ mean age : $2 \cdot \dfrac{1-\alpha}{\alpha}$ periods before t

3: $b_t = \dfrac{M_t - \overline{M_t}}{1-\alpha\big/\alpha} = \dfrac{\alpha}{1-\alpha} \cdot \left(M_t - \overline{M_t}\right)$

4: $T_t = \overline{M_t} + 2 \cdot \left(M_t - \overline{M_t}\right) = 2M_t - \overline{M_t}$

5: $P_t\left(t+k\right) = 2 \cdot M_t - \overline{M_t} + b_t \cdot k,$ $1 \le k \le \infty$

6: $MAD_t\left(t+1\right) = \alpha \cdot \left|N_t - P_{t-1}(t)\right| + (1-\alpha) \cdot MAD_{t-1}\left(t\right)$

7: $a, b, T_t = a + b \cdot t$ (calculate from linear regression)

   $M_t = T_t - b \cdot \dfrac{1-\alpha}{\alpha}$

   $\overline{M_t} = T_t - 2 \cdot b \cdot \dfrac{1-\alpha}{\alpha}$

Fig. 9.3.2.2   Trend line and forecast error in second-order exponential smoothing.

Figure 9.3.2.3 provides an example of the determination of the forecast value using second-order exponential smoothing for the smoothing constant $\alpha = 0.2$. We calculated the same demand value as the one in linear regression for the first 14 periods in order to obtain the same starting values.

Period	Actual demand	First-order mean	Second-order mean	Slope of trend line	Trend line value	Second-order forecast value
t	N_t	M_t	$\overline{M}_t$	b_t	$T_t(t)$	$P_{t-1}(t)$
1	110			Calculation of the beginning value for period 14 using regression analysis:		
2	120					
3	100			$b = \dfrac{12*12345 - 6*15*1535}{2730} = 2.01$		
4	85					
5	100			$a = \dfrac{1}{14}*1585 - 2.01*\dfrac{15}{2} = 98.14$		
6	120					
7	90					
8	130			$T_{14} = 98.14 + 2.01*14 = 126.3$		
9	120					
10	90			$M_{14} = 126.3 - 2.01*\dfrac{1-0.2}{0.2} = 118.3$		
11	140					
12	120			$\overline{M}_{14} = 126 - 2*2.01*\dfrac{1-0.2}{0.2} = 110.2$		
13	135					
14	125	118.3	110.2			
15	150	124.6	113.1	2.9	136.1	128.3
16	130	125.7	115.6	2.5	135.8	139.0
17	110	122.6	117.0	1.3	128.2	138.3
18	140	126.0	118.8	1.8	133.2	129.5
19	130	126.8	120.4	1.6	133.2	135.0
20	150	131.4	122.6	2.2	140.2	134.8
21						142.4

Sample calculation:
1st step: M_{18} = 122.6 + 0.2 * (140 – 122.6)   = 126.0
2nd step: $\overline{M}_{18}$ = 117.0 + 0.2 * (126.0 – 117.09)   = 118.8
3rd step: b_{18} =   = 1.8
4th step: T_{18} = 2* 126.0 – 118.8   = 133.2
5th step: $P_{18}(19)$ = 133.2 + 1.8   = 135.0

Fig. 9.3.2.3   Determination of forecast value using second-order exponential smoothing ($\alpha = 0.2$).

9.3.3   Trigg and Leach Adaptive Smoothing Technique

Adaptive smoothing is a form of exponential smoothing in which the smoothing constant is automatically adjusted as a function of forecast error measurement.

A good forecasting technique is not biased:

> A *(forecast) bias* is a consistent deviation of the actual demand from the forecast in one direction, either high or low.

If forecast values exceed the control limits of, for example, +/− the standard deviation from the mean several consecutive times, we must alter either the parameters or the model. Trigg and Leach suggest the following method for continuous adjustment of the exponential smoothing parameter:

> The *smoothing constant* γ or *gamma factor* smoothes forecast errors exponentially according to the formula in Figure 9.3.3.1.

$$MD_t(t) = \gamma \cdot \left(N_t - P_{t-1}(t)\right) + (1-\gamma) \cdot MD_{t-1}(t-1) \qquad 0 \le \gamma \le 1$$

Fig. 9.3.3.1   Forecast errors and exponential weighting (mean deviation).

A mean calculated in this way is also referred to as *mean deviation*.

> The formula in Figure 9.3.3.2 defines the *tracking signal* and its standard deviation.

$$AWS_t = \frac{MD_t}{MAD_t}$$

$$\sigma(AWS_t) = \frac{\sigma(MD_t)}{MAD_t} = 1.25 \cdot \sqrt{\frac{\gamma}{2-\gamma}}$$

Fig. 9.3.3.2   Tracking signal following Trigg and Leach.

Lewandowski shows the non-trivial result of the standard deviation ([Lewa80], p. 128 ff). According to that source, the deviation signal is a non-dimensional, randomly distributed variable with a mean of 0 and the standard deviation described above. Due to the manner of its calculation, the absolute value of the deviation signal is always ≤ 1.

Trigg and Leach also developed forecasting techniques that use the deviation signal to adjust the smoothing constant α automatically. Particularly when the mean of the process to be measured changes, a large deviation signal results. In that case, we should choose a relatively large smoothing constant α, so that the mean adjusts rapidly.

In first-order exponential smoothing, it is reasonable to choose a smoothing constant that is equal to the absolute value of the deviation signal, as in Figure 9.3.3.3. The result is a forecast formula with the variable smoothing constant α_t. The factor γ used to smooth forecast errors remains constant and is kept relatively small, between 0.05 and 0.1 for example. This forecasting technique is not only adaptive but also simple from a technical calculation standpoint.

$$\alpha_t = |AWS_t|$$

Fig. 9.3.3.3   Determination of the smoothing constant in first-order exponential smoothing.

9.3.4 Seasonality

Seasonal fluctuations in the demand for specific items are brought about by factors such as weather, holidays, and vacation periods. Restaurants and theaters experience weekly and even daily "seasonal" variations.

The best way to forecast and take seasonality into account is to compare the pattern of demand over multiple years.

We speak of *seasonality* or a *seasonal demand pattern* when the following three conditions hold:

1. Growth in demand occurs in the same time frame for every seasonal cycle.
2. Seasonal fluctuations are measurably larger than the random demand fluctuations.
3. A cause that explains demand fluctuations can be found.

Seasonality does not always have a yearly pattern. In the retail trade, particularly in the grocery industry, there is a commonly observed effect at the end of each month when people receive their monthly salary payments.

Figure 9.3.4.1 shows the definition of the *seasonal index*, which is necessary to accommodate seasonal effects.[10]

---

[10] The operation "mod z" upon a number x calculates the remainder when x is divided by z.

SZ = Length of the seasonal cycle
S_f = Seasonal index, $0 \le f \le (SZ-1), f = (t+k)_{\text{mod SZ}}$

Fig. 9.3.4.1   Seasonal index S_f.

The term *base series* stands for the succession of the f seasonal indices. Their average value will be 1.0.

Figure 9.3.4.2 shows the two basic models that superimpose the base series upon the trend in demand (that is, without respecting seasonality) for an item in question. *Additive seasonality* refers to an influence independent of the level of sales, whereas *multiplicative seasonality* refers to an influence that increases with the mean of sales.

additive : $P_t(t+k) = M_t + S_f$
multiplicative : $P_t(t+k) = M_t \cdot S_f$

Fig. 9.3.4.2   Forecasting that takes seasonality into account.

Figures 9.3.4.3 and 9.3.4.4 provide qualitative examples of demand adjusted for additive and multiplicative seasonality, respectively.

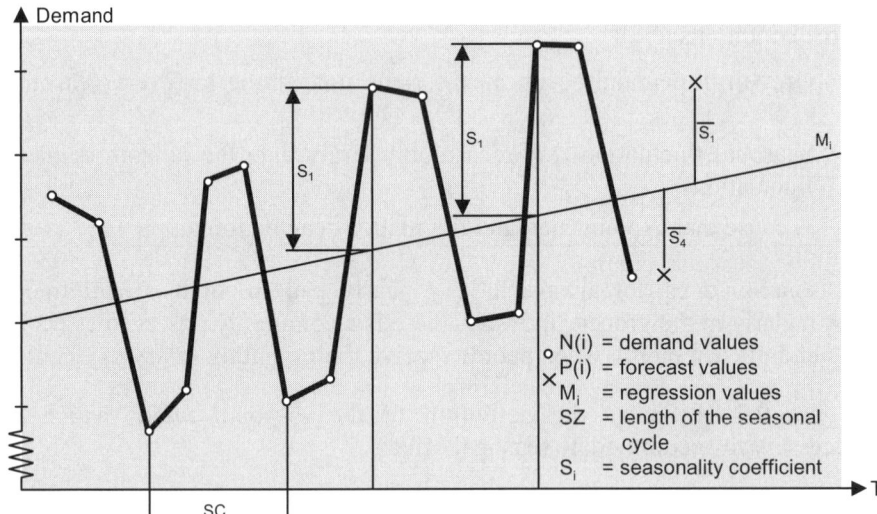

Fig. 9.3.4.3   "Additive seasonality" formulation.

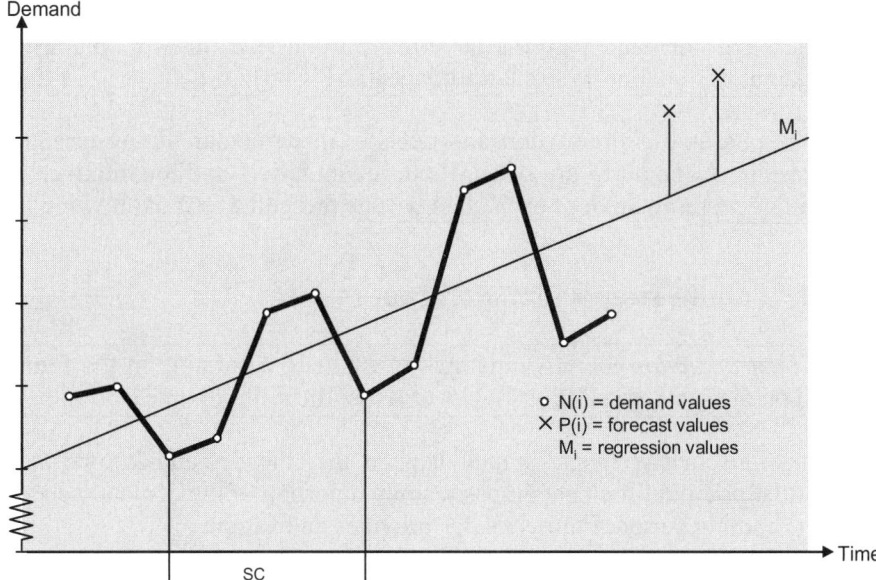

Fig. 9.3.4.4   "Multiplicative seasonality" formulation.

Various techniques that account for seasonal influences can be found in the literature. The following is an example of a simplified procedure:

1. Calculate the seasonal mean.
2. Calculate the trend line from the seasonal means.
3. Determine the base series or the succession of seasonal indices as the average deviation of demand from the trend lines for mutually corresponding periods.
4. Calculate the forecast value from the trend lines and the seasonality coefficient for the corresponding periods in the seasonal cycle.

9.4   Future-Oriented Techniques

During the different phases of the product life cycle, different forecasting techniques can be used.

> *Life-cycle analysis* bases on applying to a new product (in a quantitative manner) past demand patterns covering introduction, growth, maturity, saturation, and decline of similar products ([APIC04]).

For the phases of introduction and decline, in particular, future-oriented forecasting techniques are used, both quantitative and qualitative. A technique representative of each class will be presented in the following.

9.4.1   Trend Extrapolation Forecast

> *Trend extrapolation forecast* attempts to estimate a variable in the future based on the same variable as known at a specific point in time.

In materials management, it may happen that the demand known at a particular point in time t encompasses only a portion of the demand needed for the coming period. Figure 9.4.1.1 provides an example.

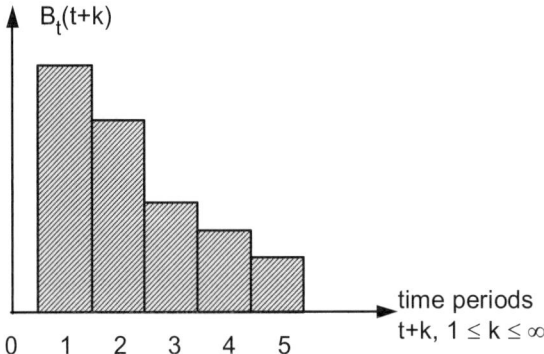

Fig. 9.4.1.1   Demand B_0 for period t known at time 0.

Extrapolation calculates the total anticipated demand from the demand already known for a product or product family. It compares the *base demand* $B_t(t+k)$, $1 \leq k \leq \infty$, known at time t to the demand N_{t+k} observed after the closing of a delivery period t+k. This is shown in Figure 9.4.1.2. The variables for the calculation are chosen either as defined in Figure 9.3.1.5 or in a similar fashion. k stands for the *forecast distance*.

The quotients resulting from this process are either standardized or smoothed over multiple periods. Let $\lambda_t(k)$ be the mean after period t for forecast distance k, so that $1 \leq k \leq t$. The previous mean is used to calculate the new mean using exponential smoothing with smoothing constant α according to the formula in Figure 9.4.3.1.

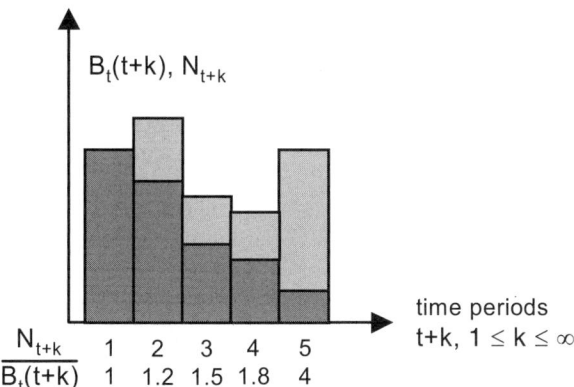

Fig. 9.4.1.2   Actual demand N_{t+k}, divided by base demand $B_t(t + k)$.

$$\lambda_t(k) = \alpha \bullet \left[\frac{N_t}{B_{t-k}(t)} \right] + (1-\alpha) \bullet \lambda_{t-1}(k), \quad \text{where } 1 \le k \le t, \ 1 \le t \le \infty$$

Fig. 9.4.1.3   Smoothing of quotient means for extrapolation.

The quotient standardized in this way is also called the *extrapolation constant*. It is defined in this way for every forecast distance and can be used to extrapolate total demand, at the moment not completely known, from the base demand. The formula in Figure 9.4.1.4 gives the forecast value $P_t(t+k)$ for the forecast distance k at the end of period t.

$$P_t(t+k) = B_t(t+k) \bullet \lambda_t(k) \quad \text{where } 1 \le k \le t, \ 1 \le t \le \infty$$

Fig. 9.4.1.4   Extrapolated forecast values for forecast distance k.

The technique described here assumes that the customers' basic order behavior does not change on the time axis or that it does so very slowly. This means that from a change in customer orders on hand, we can infer a proportional change in total demand. Since this assumption is often invalid in the average case, the technique will yield useful results only when used in combination with other forecasting techniques, such as intuitive ones.

The planner can use this same technique to forecast seasonal components. In the grocery industry, for example, the retailer must give orders to the producers early enough to ensure that shipments arrive on time. Assuming that the retailers' order behavior does not change significantly from year to year, the producer can derive standardized quotients from sales over multiple years; the probable total demand for the season in a future year can be extrapolated from the demand already known at a specific point in time.

9.4.2   Intuitive Forecasting Techniques

Intuitive forecasting techniques attempt to estimate the future behavior of target customers in an intuitive way, based on surveys or expert opinions for example.

These techniques are particularly useful when new or significantly enhanced products are introduced to the market. The problem with surveys lies in formulating the right questions, quantifying the answers, and filtering out extreme, non-representative responses.

In the *Delphi method forecast* (the name refers to the oracle at Delphi in antiquity), "expert opinion" is gathered through several structured anonymous rounds of written interviews.

The experts are chosen from various areas of an organization, including the sales and marketing units. They are selected for their competence in the field and their broad vision, not for their hierarchical position within the company. The composition of the group should remain anonymous so that the experts cannot identify and be influenced by the responses of other individuals.

The method generally proceeds in various iterations. Figure 9.4.2.1 shows the desired progression during the successive rounds of questioning. The mean of the answers shifts in a specific direction. At the same time, when the dispersion of the answers narrows, there is an increase in the consensus about the direction taken. In order to arrive at this result, a single iteration should include the following steps:

- The questionnaire is meaningfully constructed or altered. The questionnaires are distributed and completed once again.
- The answers are statistically evaluated by determining mean and dispersion. The results of the evaluation are sent to the experts.

- All the experts are asked to defend their views against extreme arguments. Those who change their opinions as a result of this procedure must provide justifications. The "extreme" respondents must either support their theses with arguments or abandon them.

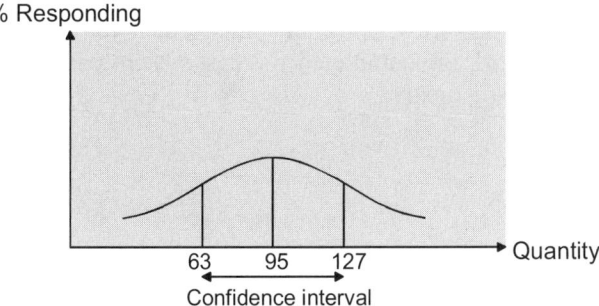

Distribution of answers after the first questionnaire

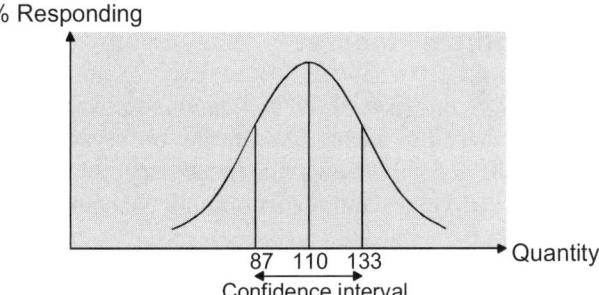

Distribution of answers after the second questionnaire

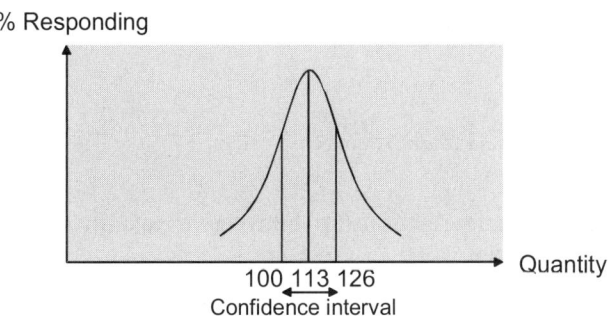

Distribution of answers after the third questionnaire

Fig. 9.4.2.1   Delphi forecasting method: increasing consensus.

Besides the Delphi method, the planner may also introduce other intuitive techniques, such as expert systems, jury of executive opinion, neuronal networks, decision support systems (DSS), or other statistics and operations research techniques that take additional factors into consideration. These may, for example, evaluate corrections made to the last forecast. In order to make the corrections accessible to an expert system, however, implicit knowledge must be transformed into explicit arguments. If this is successful, the completed forecast system can predict demand in the future more realistically.

9.5   Using Forecasts in Planning

9.5.1   Moving Average Forecast versus First-Order Exponential Smoothing Forecast

The results of *moving average* and *first-order exponential smoothing* are comparable, to the extent that the mean age of the observed values corresponds mutually. Figure 9.5.1.1 shows the necessary relationship between the number of observed values and the smoothing constant α.

$$\frac{1-\alpha}{\alpha} = \bar{n} = \frac{n-1}{2}$$

$$\alpha = \frac{2}{n+1}$$

$$n = \frac{2-\alpha}{\alpha}$$

Fig. 9.5.1.1   Formulas for the relationship between α and n.

Figure 9.5.1.2 shows the same relationship between α and n, using a tabular comparison of individual values.

Number of periods n	Smoothing constant α	Reactivity	Adaptation to systematic changes
3	0.50	rapid	rapid
4	0.40	nervous	↑
5	0.33	reaction	
6	0.29	↑	
9	0.20	↕	↕
12	0.15		
19	0.10	↓	
39	0.05	leveling reaction	slow

Fig. 9.5.1.2   Relationship between α and n in tabular form.

9.5.2   Comparison of Techniques and Choice of Suitable Forecasting Technique

In Figure 9.5.2.1 the techniques discussed in this section are compared according to a number of criteria.

Technique	Demand Model					Weighting of data	Understandability of the technique	Storage required for necessary data	Processing time
	constant	with linear trend	with non-linear trend	with seasonal component	discontinuous, irregular	according to immediacy			
Moving average	x					no	easy	large	short
1st order exp. smoothing	x					yes	easy	very little (2 values)	very short
2nd order exp. smoothing	(x)	x				yes	average	very little (2 values)	very short
Trigg & Leach adaptive smoothing		(x)	x			yes	average	very little (2 values)	very short
Exp. smoothing with seas. influences				x		yes	difficult	little	short
Linear regression	(x)	x				no	easy	large	long to determine parameters, otherwise short
Extrapolation	x					no	easy	large	short
Delphi					x	—	easy	large	long

Fig. 9.5.2.1   Areas of applicability of forecasting techniques.

When choosing a forecasting technique, it is crucial to find that technique (reasonable in use) that will provide the greatest accuracy of alignment to the demand structure.[11] The following criteria also play a role:

- Adaptability to demand performance
- Possibility of forecast errors
- Aids required
- Expense for data collection and preparation for analysis
- Ascertainability of parameters that describe the performance of the system to be forecast
- The purpose of the forecast and the importance of one material position
- Forecast time frame
- Transparency for the user

9.5.3   Consumption Distributions and Their Limits, Continuous and Discontinuous Demand

The *distribution of forecast errors* is a tabulation of the forecast errors according to the frequency of occurrence of each error value ([APIC04]).

The errors in forecasting are, in many cases, normally distributed, even when the observed data do not come from a normal distribution. Therefore, we now take a closer look into the origin of the observed values.

A *consumption distribution*, such as a statistic for order receipts allocated by time periods, can be understood as an aggregation of multiple individual events during each period. These individual events can be described by:

- The *distribution of the frequency of the events* themselves
- A *distribution of characteristic values for an event*, that is, order quantities

A combination of these two distributions results in consumption distribution.

---

[11]   *Focus forecasting* is a system that allows the user to simulate and evaluate the effectiveness of different forecasting techniques ([APIC04]).

Given the definitions in Figure 9.5.3.1 and a constant process (e.g., for constant demand), the formulas contained in Figure 9.5.3.2 are valid according to [Fers64]. Here, E stands for the *expected value*; VAR stands for the *variance*.[12]

$E(n), VAR(n)$	Distribution parameters describing the frequency of events per statistical period
$E(z), VAR(z)$	Distribution parameters of the characteristic values (here, the order quantity)
$E(x), VAR(x)$	Parameters of the consumption distribution per period

Fig. 9.5.3.1   Definitions for a consumption distribution.

$$E(x) \quad = \quad E(n) \cdot E(z)$$
$$VAR(x) \quad = \quad VAR(n) \cdot E^2(z) + E(n) \cdot VAR(z)$$

Fig. 9.5.3.2   Expected value and variance of the consumption distribution.

In a purely random process, the number of events per period has a Poisson distribution with distribution function P(n) and expected value = variance = λ. Knowing this, we can derive the formulas in Figure 9.5.3.3, where CV corresponds to the *coefficient of variation* for the distribution, i.e., the quotient of standard deviation and expected value.

$$P(n) = e^{-\lambda} \cdot \frac{\lambda^n}{n!}$$
$$E(n) = VAR(n) = \lambda$$
$$E(x) = \lambda \cdot E(z)$$
$$VAR(x) = \lambda \cdot \left[E^2(z) + VAR(z) \right]$$
$$CV^2(x) = \frac{1}{\lambda} \left[1 + CV^2(z) \right]$$

Fig. 9.5.3.3   Distribution function, expected value, and variance of the consumption distribution under the assumption of a Poisson distribution for the frequency of events.

---

[12]   In statistics, *variance* is a measure of dispersion, here the square of the standard deviation.

A few large issues can greatly influence the coefficient of variation for the *order quantity*. The square can very well take on a value of 3. If all issues are equally large, then the value is clearly at its minimum of 0 (for example, the order quantity for service parts may always equal 1).

Even if the measured values of the consumption distribution allowed, based on the rules of statistics, the assumption of a normal distribution as such, a coefficient of variation of $CV \leq 0.4$ is a pre-requisite for effective procedures in the stochastic materials management. From the formula in Figure 9.5.3.3, it is possible to say how many issues are necessary, so that such a small coefficient of variation results. Specifically, if 1 is assumed as the mean for the coefficient of variation of the distribution of the *order quantity*, then at least 12.5 orders or issues per period are needed, which can be high for a machine manufacturer $(\lambda \geq (1+1) / 0,16 = 12,5)$.

The value for λ may vary very widely and may be quite small, particularly in the capital goods industry. This type of demand is referred to as *discontinuous* or *lumpy demand*. It is different from both *regular* demand (regularity as described in Section 9.3.1) and *continuous* (steady) demand. (See the definitions in Section 3.4.2).

From above observations we can establish qualitatively that:

- The *discontinuous character* of a distribution is the result of a limited number of issues per time unit measured. With this, it is very difficult to calculate a forecast. Large coefficients of variation arise not least due to individual, perhaps rather infrequent, large issues. Wherever possible, large issues should be considered as outliers or as abnormal demand and should be taken out of a stochastic technique by a demand filter[13] and made available to deterministic materials management. This could be achieved by increasing delivery periods for large orders, for example.

- In the case of a stationary process, for example, constant demand, the relative forecast error depends heavily on the number of events, such as the number of orders. Generally, the actual forecast error is larger than that calculated by extrapolation. This is so because changes in the underlying regularities increase error, given that the number of events is small.

---

[13] A *demand filter* in the forecast model is expressed by some factor times +/− the standard deviation.

Whether demand will appear as continuous or discontinuous also depends upon the choice of the length of the statistical period. Figure 9.5.3.4 shows this effect.

If the statistical period chosen is too short, this quickly results in discontinuous demand values. These fluctuations are exaggerated and can be leveled by extending the statistical periods. However, the result in materials management may be an increase in levels of goods in stock or work in process, especially if the lead times are shorter than the statistical periods. For practical reasons, a unified length of the statistical period for the entire product range is required. Often, a period of one month is chosen.[14]

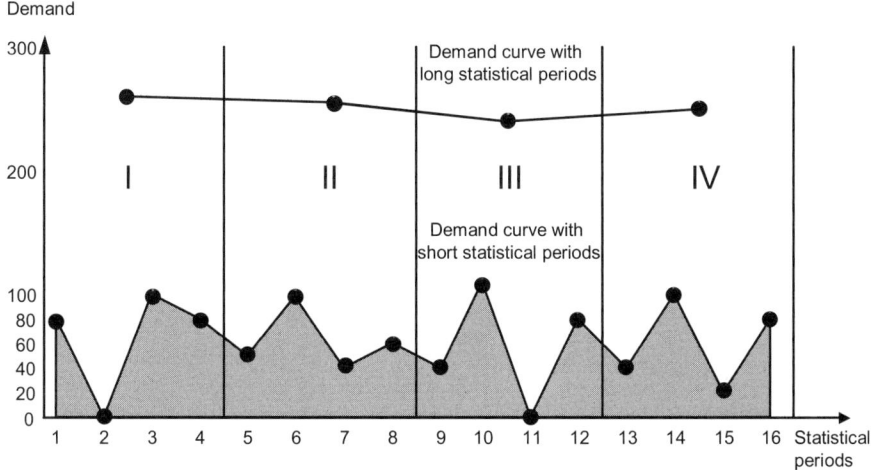

Fig. 9.5.3.4   Effects of length of statistical period on demand fluctuations.

Even if there is rather discontinuous demand for an individual item, demand for the entire item family may be continuous. In this circumstance, the forecast would be accurate enough for rough-cut planning. If the need for more detailed information should arise, the allocation of the forecast to the various items of the family may be difficult. See also Section 12.2.

---

[14]   The leveling of demand fluctuations is necessary, for example, for simple control techniques such as kanban, in which continuous demand is a prerequisite for their functioning. Enlarging the statistical period may sometimes be sufficient.

9.5.4   Demand Forecasting of Options of a Product Family

Often variants of a product are derived gradually from one basic type, a standard product with options or a product family. Often, a forecast can predict the total demand for a product family. Deriving the demand for components that are the same for all variants is no longer very difficult.

Demand forecasting for options or variants is more difficult. When the number of delivered variants of a product family is large enough, the use of variant items — related to 100 units of the product family, for example — can be recorded in a statistic and used for management.

> The *option percentage* OPC is the frequency with which a variant item is used within a product family.

This percentage varies from time period to time period and is therefore a stochastic variable that can be described with expected value and variance.

Often, in practice, the dispersion of the option percentage is not taken into consideration; that is, $E(PF)$ is treated as a quasi-deterministic value. This increases the risk of stock failures. To calculate option percentages, sales are subdivided by statistical period. For each period, we determine the actual frequency of use and calculate mean and standard variation from the results of multiple periods. Linking the forecast for the product family with the option percentage for demand for variants is achieved by using the formulas in Figure 9.5.4.1. These formulas are used for every periodic demand.

$$E(OD) = E(PFD) \cdot E(OPC)$$
$$CV^2(OD) = CV^2(PFD) + CV^2(OPC) + CV^2(PFD) \cdot CV^2(OPC)$$
where   OD = option demand
         PFD = product family demand
         OPC = option percentage

Fig. 9.5.4.1   Forecasting demand for options or variants.

The proportional-factor-weighted demand (expected value and variance) for the product family is the independent demand for a variant. Due to safety demand calculation, the sum of variant demands is greater than the demand for components not dependent upon variants.

For a more in-depth consideration of the formulas in Figure 9.5.4.1, see the footnote.[15]

9.5.5   Safety Demand Calculation for Various Planning Periods

A *planning period* represents the time span between "today" and the point in time of the last demand that was included in a specific planning consideration.

Figure 9.5.5.1 provides a few definitions required for the following discussion.

---

[15]   The following derivation of Prof. Büchel's formula for multiplicative coupling x of two independent distributions y and z, x= y*z, provides a more in-depth consideration of the matter. See also [Fers64]. Multiplication of a particular value Y of y by z results in a linear transformation of z with the following parameters:

$$E(Y*z) = Y * E(z), \quad VAR(Y*z) = Y^2 * VAR(z).$$

The distribution obtained in this way is weighted by f(y) and summed (or, with continuous distributions, integrated) to create a mixed distribution. The zero moments are to be applied for this. The result of the individual linear transformations for the second zero moment — defined as $E(u^2) = E^2(u) + VAR(u)$ — are as follows:

$$\begin{aligned}E((Y*z)^2) &= E^2(Y*z) + VAR(Y*z) = Y^2 * E^2(z) + Y^2 * VAR(z) \\ &= Y2 * (E^2(z) + VAR(z)) = Y2 * E(z^2).\end{aligned}$$

The summation produces the following result:

$$E(x) = E(y) * E(z), \quad E(x^2) = E(y^2) * E(z^2), \text{ and so the following hold:}$$
$$\begin{aligned}VAR(x) = E(x^2) - E^2(x) &= E(y^2) * E(z^2) - E^2(y) * E^2(z) \\ &= [E^2(y) + VAR(y)] * [E^2(z) + VAR(z)] - E^2(y) * E^2(z) \\ &= E^2(y) * VAR(z) + VAR(y) * E^2(z) + VAR(y) * VAR(z).\end{aligned}$$
$$\begin{aligned}CV^2(x) &= VAR(x) / E^2(x) \\ &= [E^2(y) * VAR(z) + VAR(y) * E^2(z) + VAR(y) * VAR(z)] / [E^2(y) * E^2(z)] \\ &= CV^2(z) + CV^2(y) + CV^2(y) * CV^2(z).\end{aligned}$$

Note: The formulas in Figure 9.5.3.2 can be derived analogously. Linear transformations are replaced by the distributions for the sum of multiple issues per period (so-called convolutions), whose parameters are determined as follows:

$$E(n*z) = n * E(z); \quad VAR(n*z) = n * VAR(z)$$

A general statement as to the form of the distribution cannot be made; a log-normal distribution (which becomes a normal distribution with small coefficients of variation) represents a useful approximation for practical application. When there are many periods with zero issues (low issue frequency), special consideration of the choice of "risk" may be required.

This is also true for Section. 9.5.3. However, the planning periods are decisive, not the statistical periods.

SP	=	Length of the statistical or forecast period (in some time unit)
PP	=	Length of the planning period
E(DSP)	=	Expected value of the demand in the statistical period
E(DPP)	=	Expected value of the demand in the planning period
σ (DSP)	=	Standard deviation of the demand in the statistical period
σ (DPP)	=	Standard deviation of the demand in the planning period
Z	=	Issue quantity (designated as in Section 9.5.3)
λ	=	Number of issues in the statistical period

Fig. 9.5.5.1   Definitions of variables for safety calculations.

In a forecast calculation we determine expected value and standard deviation for a particular statistical period, for example the SP. In materials management, however, it is necessary to have values for various planning periods. If, for example, the planning period is the lead time, then we have to take the total forecast demand during the lead time into consideration. Usually this is up until the receipt of the production or procurement order.[16]

We can infer the formulas shown in Figure 9.5.5.2 on the basis of the models developed in Section 9.5.3; the formulas are also valid for the non-integral proportions of PP:SP.

$$\text{Number of issues during the planning period} = \lambda \cdot \frac{PP}{SP}$$

$$E(DPP) = \lambda \cdot \frac{PP}{SP} \cdot E(z) = \frac{PP}{SP} \cdot E(DSP)$$

$$\sigma(DPP) = \sqrt{\lambda \cdot \frac{PP}{SP} \left[E^2(z) + VAR(z) \right]} = \sqrt{\frac{PP}{SP}} \cdot \sigma(DSP)$$

$$\overbrace{VAR(DSP) = \lambda \cdot \left[E^2(z) + VAR(z) \right]}$$

Fig. 9.5.5.2   Expected value and standard deviation with continuous demand.

In a non-stationary process, different expected values or standard deviations arise for various time periods in the future. Assuming independent

---

[16]   The planning horizon is a further example of a planning period.

forecast values in individual periods, the expected values and variances of demand can be added during the planning period. For n statistical periods, this produces the formulas shown in Figure 9.5.5.3.

$$E(DPP) = \sum_{i=1}^{n} E(DSP(i))$$

$$\sigma(DPP) = \sqrt{\sum_{i=1}^{n} \sigma^2(DSP(i))}$$

Fig. 9.5.5.3   Expected value and standard deviation over n statistical periods.

We can also use these formulas for certain periods, usually in the near future, where the demand has been established deterministically, that is, through customer orders, for example. The demand for these periods demonstrates a 0 variance. Similarly, a linear interpolation of the expected value and variance is used to determine intermediate values during a period.

9.5.6   Translation of Forecast into Quasi-Deterministic Demand and Administration of the Production or Purchase Schedule

The (stochastic) independent demand to be considered for further planning steps, results as the total demand from adding the expected value to the safety demand for the planning period to be covered.

The *safety demand* is the product of the safety factor and the standard deviation during the planning period to be covered.

Figure 9.5.6.1 shows the total demand to be considered as a function of the planning period to be covered.

For products manufactured in-house, this total demand belongs to the *production schedule*. For purchased items, the independent demand belongs to the *purchase schedule* for saleable products.

If the total demand is subdivided into various partial demands later (for example, the annual demand into 12 monthly demands), a larger share of the safety demand needs to be included in the earlier partial demand. The order point technique discussed in Section 10.3 adds the safety demand to the first partial demand. This technique is not only used for items with independent demand, but also for items with dependent demand, to the extent that they occur either continuously or regularly. Dependent demand is then considered as if it were independent demand (see Section 4.3.1).

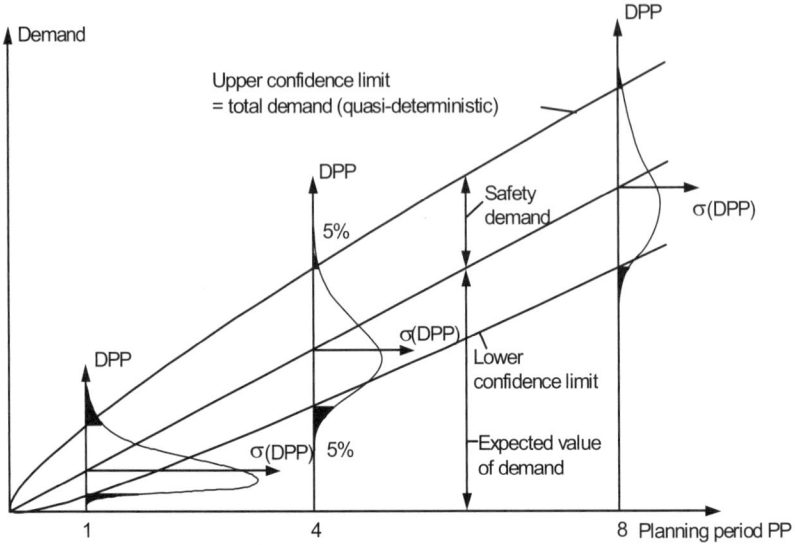

Fig. 9.5.6.1   Independent demand as total demand, taken as a function of the planning period to be covered.

Note: As presented in connection with Figure 4.3.2.2, the first step in determining high-cost dependent, but discontinuous or unique demand for an item is to stochastically determine the independent demand belonging to it. After this, the dependent demand is calculated using quasi-deterministic bill of materials explosion. In this way, the dependent demand contains the safety demand needed to produce the safety demand for the independent demand.

For *administrating independent demand,* an order-like *object class forecast demand* or *independent demand* is used, with at least the following attributes:

- Forecast or independent demand ID (similar to an order ID)
- Item ID or item family ID
- Planning date for the demand or its periodicity
- Forecast quantity (an item issue)
- Quantity of the forecast already "consumed" by orders (see Section 11.2.2)

A negative forecast demand is also conceivable; this would express receipt of an item. The negative forecast demand serves, for example, as a substitute for a purchase system that is lacking, or it serves to eliminate an overlap effect on lower structure levels from higher structure levels (see, for example, Section 6.2.1).

There are a number of ways to change or delete a forecast demand:

- By manual administration.
- Through periodic re-calculation, e.g., according to the principle contained in Figure 9.1.1.1. This is particularly important for demand serving as input to subsequent stochastic materials management.
- With independent demand in the true sense: by successive reduction due to actual demand (e.g., customer orders). If the actual demand reaches the forecast, or if the forecast lapses into the past and is no longer to be considered, the corresponding forecast demand object is automatically deleted. See also Section 11.2.2.

9.6   Summary

A demand forecast is an expression of the probable future course of demand along the time axis. An individual demand must be forecast if the cumulative lead time is longer than the customer tolerance time. Such a situation occurs, for example, in trade in consumer goods, in components for services, or in single parts of investment goods.

Forecasts are transformed into demand for resources later and then compared with the organization's supply capacity. However, every forecast is associated with uncertainty. Therefore, forecasts must be compared to demand continually, e.g., in a rolling manner. A significant deviation in demand may require the selection of a different technique.

We distinguished two basic types of forecasting techniques: historically oriented and future-oriented. Both basic types are further subdivided into mathematical, graphical, or intuitive techniques. The selection of a technique is made according to a series of criteria intended to produce a reasonable alignment of the forecast to the demand, at reasonable expense.

Historically oriented techniques calculate demand based upon consumption with the help of mathematical statistics (extrapolation of time series). There are simple techniques for continuous demand, such as moving average or first-order exponential smoothing. For linear trends, we may make use of linear regression or second-order exponential smoothing. In addition, the Trigg and Leach adaptive technique examines and adapts the parameters used in exponential smoothing. All the techniques may be expanded to account for the effect of seasonality. Extrapolation and the Delphi method were discussed as future-oriented techniques, although these also contain historically oriented elements.

The more discontinuously consumption occurs, the more difficult it is to forecast reliably. The definition of consumption distributions as an overlay of the distribution of consumption events and the distribution of consumption quantities per event helps describe discontinuous conditions. A suitable length of the statistical period, can lead to a smoothing of demands.

Where there are few options and repetitive production, forecast for variant demand of a product family may be calculated using option percentages. This is a stochastic variable with an expected value and standard deviation.

In all cases, larger fluctuations in demand lead to safety demand, which is calculated on the basis of standard deviation. The expected value and standard deviation are related to the statistical period, while independent demands are related to the planning period. The conversion of expected value is proportional to the ratio of the two time periods, whereas in the standard deviation the conversion is proportional to its square root. The expected value of the demand increased by safety demand is set as independent demand per planning period; the latter is then available as stochastic demand for further handling in the context of materials management. When dependent demand is calculated later, using a quasi-deterministic bill of materials explosion, it will contain the corresponding safety demand.

For each independent demand, the item ID, the forecast quantity, and the quantity of the forecast already "consumed" by orders are recorded, as well as the planning date. The total of all independent demands belongs to the production schedule, or, when referring to trade items, the purchase schedule. Independent demand can be re-calculated or canceled by rolling planning, either manually or with automated techniques. In general, independent demand successively replaces or reduces actual demand.

9.7   Keywords

adaptive smoothing, 503

consumption distribution, 514

curve fitting, 486

Delphi method, 510

demand model, 486

distribution of forecast errors, 514

expected value, 488

first-order exponential smoothing, 493

forecast error, 480

forecast horizon, 486

forecast interval, 485

forecasting, 480

forecasting model for constant demand, 490

forecasting technique, 480

graphic forecasting techniques, 483

historically oriented forecasting techniques, 483

intrinsic forecasting techniques, 485

intuitive forecasting techniques, 484

life-cycle analysis, 508

mean, 488

mean absolute deviation (MAD), 493

mean deviation, 504

moving average, 491

moving average (forecasting technique), 491

option percentage, 518

planning period, 519

probability, 493

qualitative forecasting techniques, 485

quantitative forecasting techniques, 485

regression analysis, 499

safety demand, 521

seasonal fluctuations, 505

seasonal index, 505

seasonality, 505

second-order exponential smoothing, 500

single (exponential) smoothing, 493

smoothing, 490

smoothing constant α, 495, 504

standard deviation, 491

statistical period, 485

time series, 485

tracking signal, 504

trend, 497

trend extrapolation, 508

trend forecasting model, 497

variance, 515

weighted moving average, 493

9.8   Scenarios and Exercises

9.8.1   Choice of Appropriate Forecasting Techniques

Figure 9.8.1.1 shows historical demand curves for four different products. What forecasting technique for each product do you propose to apply to forecast future demand?

Solution:

- Product 1: demand with linear trend → linear regression
- Product 2: constant demand without trend → moving average forecasting or first-order exponential smoothing
- Product 3: seasonal fluctuations with trend → linear regression or second-order exponential smoothing with seasonality

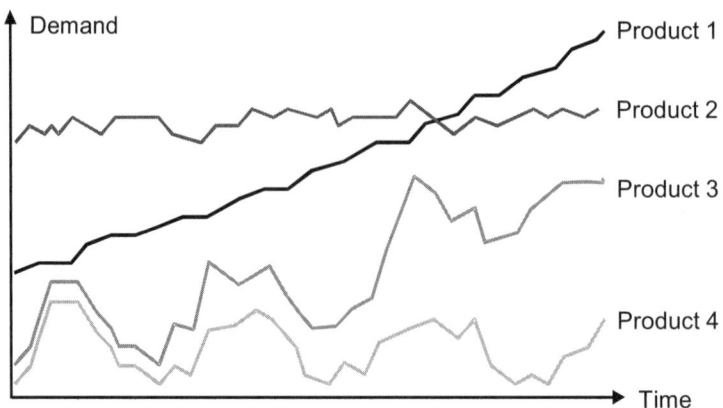

Fig. 9.8.1.1   Historical demand curves for four products.

- Product 4: constant demand with seasonal fluctuation → moving average forecasting, or first-order exponential smoothing, with seasonality

9.8.2   Moving Average Forecasting Technique

The person in your firm responsible for forecasting has been absent for three months, so your supervisor asks you to forecast the demand of the most important product. The information you get is a table (see Figure 9.8.2.1) showing the historical data on the demand for the product (January to October) and the forecast for the period January to July based on the moving average forecasting technique.

	Jan.	Feb.	Mar.	Apr.	May.	Jun.	July.	Aug.	Sept.	Oct.
Demand	151	135	143	207	199	175	111	95	119	191
Forecast	183	195	177	155	159	171	181			

Fig. 9.8.2.1   Demand and forecast with moving average forecasting technique.

Moreover, your supervisor asks you to:

a. Forecast the demand just as your colleague does. Therefore, you have to calculate the parameter n from the historical forecast data.

b. Calculate the forecast for August, September, and October as well as for the following month, November.

c. Compute the standard deviation σ of the forecast from January to October and decide if the applied technique fits this product.

Solution:

a. n = 4

b. Forecast August = (207+199+175+111) / 4 = 173; forecast September: 145; forecast October: 125; forecast November: 129.

c. σ = 53.87 and variation coefficient = 53.87 / 152.6 ≈ 0.35. A variation coefficient of 0.35 stands for a relatively low quality of the forecast. Therefore, the applied technique is not appropriate for this product. Try a value other than n = 4, or with additional seasonal index.

9.8.3 First-Order Exponential Smoothing

When you report to your supervisor that the moving average forecasting technique is not suitable for the product, he remembers that your colleague in charge of forecasting had been working on introducing the first-order exponential smoothing technique for this product. Therefore, your supervisor gives you the information in Figure 9.8.3.1, showing the demand for the product (January to October) and the forecast using the first-order exponential smoothing technique with $\alpha = 0.3$ of the product (January to July).

	Jan.	Feb.	Mar.	Apr.	May.	Jun.	July.	Aug.	Sept.	Oct.
Demand	151	135	143	207	199	175	111	95	119	191
Forecast	187	176	164	158	172	180	179			

Fig. 9.8.3.1   Demand and forecast using first-order exponential smoothing technique.

In order to evaluate your supervisor's suggestion, you execute the following steps:

a. Compute the forecast for August, September, and October and for the following month, November.

b. Calculate the mean absolute deviation (MAD) for November assuming MAD(Jan) = 18 and the smoothing parameter α.

c. In the preceding exercise, could you have obtained a result comparable to the one for the parameter α calculated above by changing n, that is, the number of observed values?

d. Decide whether or not the chosen first-order exponential smoothing technique with parameter α calculated above is appropriate for this product.

e. What can you say in general about the choice of α depending on the product life cycle?

Solution:

a. Forecast August = $0.3*111+0.7*179 \approx 159$; forecast September: 140; forecast October: 134; forecast November: 151.

b. MAD(Feb) = $0.3*(187 - 151)+0.7*18 \approx 23 \rightarrow$ MAD(Mar) = 29, MAD(Apr) = 26, MAD(May) = 33, MAD(Jun) = 31, MAD(Jul) = 23, MAD(Aug) = 37, MAD(Sept) = 45, MAD(Oct) = 37, MAD(Nov) = 43.

c. Yes, by choosing a value of $n = (2 - 0.3)/0.3 = 5.67$ (see the formula in Figure 9.5.1.1).

d. Since the demand fluctuates, it would be better to increase α. Moreover, the first-order exponential smoothing technique does not fit this demand curve well. Therefore, it is worth considering another forecasting technique, e.g., with short-term seasonality.

e. At the beginning and the end of the product (market) life cycle, α should be relatively high, e.g., $\alpha = 0.5$. For a well-established product, the α often chosen is around 0.1.

9.8.4   Moving Average Forecast versus First-Order Exponential Smoothing Forecast

Figure 9.2.2.6 showed the effect of different values of the smoothing constant α. Figure 9.5.1.1 shows the necessary relationship between the number of observed values and the smoothing constant α. You can view the comparison, implemented with Flash animation, on the Internet at URL:

http://www.intlogman.lim.ethz.ch/demand_forecasting.html

In the red section at the top of the web page, you can choose different values for the smoothing constant α. In the lower, green section you can choose either a different value for the smoothing constant α for comparison with the red curve or choose the number of values for the moving average forecast and compare the results of the technique with exponential smoothing (the red curve). Clicking on the "calculate" icon executes your input choice.

10 Inventory Management and Stochastic Materials Management

Inventory has a buffer function, in order to achieve synchronization between use, on the one hand, and design and manufacturing, on the other. This makes *inventory management* another important instrument for planning & control. Inventory transactions are the basis for usage statistics. Together with ABC analyses, XYZ analyses, and other evaluative procedures, usage statistics build the foundations of techniques of stochastic materials management — and demand forecasting in particular.

This chapter deals with the translation of forecasted demand into production or procurement proposals through the function of *materials management in the stochastic case*. The relevant tasks and processes are shown on a dark background in Figure 10.0.0.1. They refer back to the reference model for business processes and planning & control tasks in Figure 4.1.4.2. Sections 4.3.1 and 4.3.2 provide an introduction to the material in this chapter, in particular Figures 4.3.2.1/4.3.2.2.[1]

For goods upstream or at the order penetration point, production or procurement orders must be released prior to customer demand. Inventory in stock or work in process must cover total demand up to the point when newly proposed orders will be filled. Here, due to its simplicity, the order point technique is widely used. Although this technique is not intended for use with discontinuous demand, frequent recalculations can produce satisfactory results, particularly in the case of regular demand. The order point technique proposes orders with a quantity and a completion date. In medium-term planning the proposals serve to reconcile inventory to blanket orders. In short-term planning they trigger order releases. In the case of a production order, the proposal yields the requirements for components that, in turn, come under the direction of materials management.

Due to the inexact nature of demand forecasting and lead time, safety stock is carried to protect against the differences between forecast and actual usage and fluctuations in lead time. The level of safety stock thus affects stockout probability, carrying cost, and eventually the fill rate (percentage of demands that were met at the time they were placed, which is also called customer service ratio).

---

[1] We recommend that you read Sections 4.3.1 and 4.3.2 again before continuing to study this chapter as well as Chapter 11.

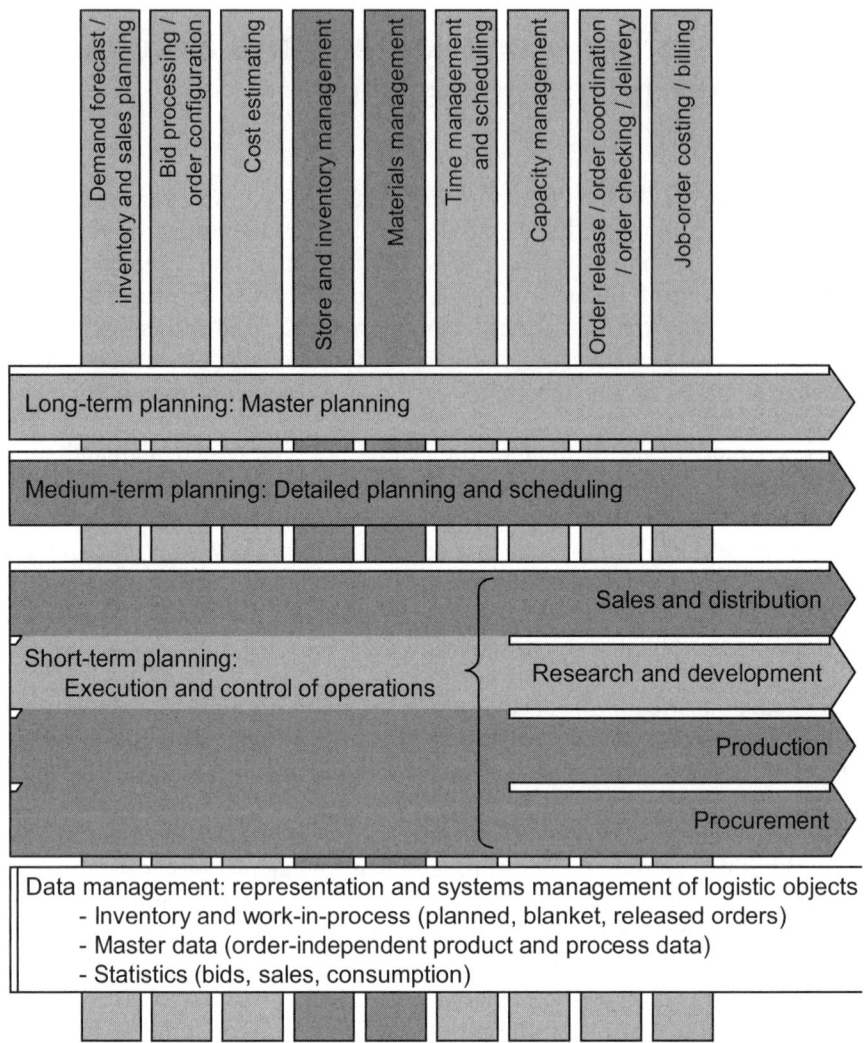

Fig. 10.0.0.1   The parts of the system discussed in Chapter 10 (shown on darker background).

In materials management, lot or batch size mainly affects costs. In scheduling and capacity management, additional considerations reveal the effect of batch size on lead time and flexibility. In the stochastic case, the composition of customer demand over time is unknown. This leads to imprecise proposals. The stochastic calculation technique presented in this chapter is robust at least in the face of forecast errors and incomplete parameters.

10.1   Stores and Inventory Management

Inventory is one of the most important instruments of logistics planning & control. Although inventory of work-in-process items is sometimes linked to the production process, such physical inventory as well as stored inventory is — from the standpoint of value adding — often unnecessary (considered a non-value added or a waste) and costly in terms of time and money (tied-up capital). As discussed in Section 1.1.2, inventory is unavoidable if customer tolerance time is shorter than the cumulative lead time. A further reason for stockkeeping, however, lies in planning & control itself. Stocks provide for the storage of goods over time. They create degrees of freedom that allow for the matching of capacity (humans, machines, tools) to the demand for goods.

10.1.1 Characteristic Features of Stores Management

Stores management, in particular, determines the values of characteristic features related to storage of goods. The choice of values is heavily dependent upon the characteristic features of planning & control within logistics networks listed in Section 3.4, but particularly upon the order penetration point.

> The *stockkeeping unit (SKU)* is an inventory item at a particular geographic location.

For example, a shirt in six colors and five sizes would represent 30 different SKUs. A product stocked at the plant and at six different distribution centers would represent seven SKUs. See [APIC04].

Figure 10.1.1.1 presents specific characteristic features of stores management. Definitions of some of the features and values follow.

- The *identification* or *storage location* usually identifies the geographic place of storage to facilitate storage and retrieval of stock. This will generally refer to the layout in a warehouse and include identification of the warehouse, its different floors, and, for each floor, the coordinates row (x-axis), shelf (y-axis), and level (z-axis).

- *Storage type* describes the infrastructure available for physical storage: floor storage, refrigerated storage, storage in special tanks, silos, and so on.

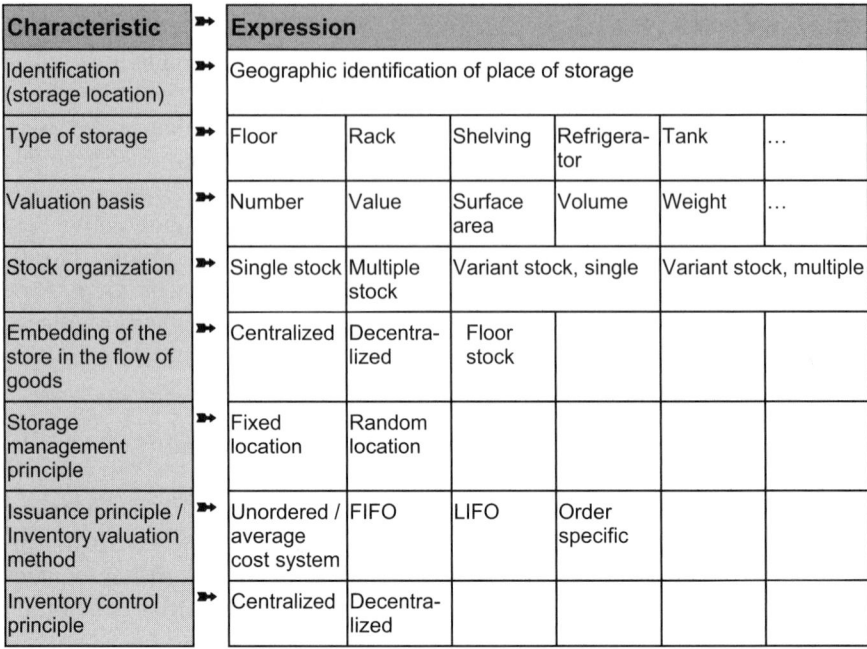

Characteristic ➤➤	Expression					
Identification (storage location) ➤➤	Geographic identification of place of storage					
Type of storage ➤➤	Floor	Rack	Shelving	Refrigera-tor	Tank	...
Valuation basis ➤➤	Number	Value	Surface area	Volume	Weight	...
Stock organization ➤➤	Single stock	Multiple stock	Variant stock, single		Variant stock, multiple	
Embedding of the store in the flow of goods ➤➤	Centralized	Decentra-lized	Floor stock			
Storage management principle ➤➤	Fixed location	Random location				
Issuance principle / Inventory valuation method ➤➤	Unordered / average cost system	FIFO	LIFO	Order specific		
Inventory control principle ➤➤	Centralized	Decentra-lized				

Fig. 10.1.1.1   Characteristic features for stores management.

- The *valuation basis* identifies the type of storage for purposes of cost accounting. It is important to allocate the costs of storage to their source, the stored goods, as accurately as possible. This feature yields information for costs distribution that is based upon the physical characteristics of the stored goods.

- *Stock organization*:

  - *Single stock organization* stores the entire stock of a particular item, or good to be stored, at one single stock location. It is also possible to store — provided the stock site is large enough — several different items at the same stock location, that is, under the same geographic identification.

  - *Multiple stock organization* keeps the inventory of a particular item at various stock sites. Each partial inventory corresponds to a different stockkeeping unit, according to the definition of this term.

  - *Variant stock organization* uses a concept that provides for storage of all variants of the same item family under one item identification. If, for example, the varying dimensions of a particular type of screw make up a family of screws, then every dimension of the screw is one variant of the same item family. The item family as a whole is then stored at one or several stock sites, while stock levels for each variant are maintained separately.

- *Embedding (of the store) in the flow of goods*:

  - A *centralized store* is usually remote from the flow of goods. Between the centralized warehouse and the user operations, inventories are transferred on the basis of a so-called inventory issue slip. Inventory receipts also generate a stock receipt slip. The responsibility for the inventory rests with an organizational unit (usually centralized) created for that purpose.

  - A *decentralized store* is located directly at the shop floor or production line. Consequently, the (decentralized) responsibility for and management of this store lies with production.

  - A *floor stock* is a stock of low-cost items held in the factory, from which production workers can draw without requisition.

- *Storage management principle:*

  - *Fixed-location storage*, or "on sight" storage, is arranged according to a particular sequence. All items that logically belong together can be picked up one after the other.

  - With *random-location storage*, any one storage location can hold the stock of one item or another. Warehouse personnel do not try to find logical locations for new stock to be stored, but simply place it in the next available location. While this method requires a locator file to identify parts locations, it often requires less space than a fixed-location storage principle.

- *Inventory issuance principle* and *inventory valuation method:*

  - With an *unordered issuance principle* it makes no difference what portion of stock should be issued. An appropriate valuation method is the *average cost system*: When a new order is received, a new *weighted average* unit cost value is computed as follows: (1) The value of the order is added to the value of the on-hand balance (valued at the current average unit cost value), and (2) the resulting value is divided by the sum of the units on hand plus those just received.

- The *FIFO issuance principle / valuation method (first in, first out)* or a *LIFO issuance principle / valuation method (last in, first out)* results in the removal from stock of that partial quantity that was received first — or last, respectively. For this we need proof of the time at which each quantity was placed into stock. Lot control, as described in Section 7.2.3, provides such data.

- The order *specific issuance principle* issues items that have been produced or procured by specific order. The corresponding *order-specific valuation method* assigns to these items a value that equals the actual costs of the respective order. For this, lot control has to be provided, too.

- *Inventory control principle:*

  - With *centralized inventory control*, one office or department is responsible for inventory decision making (for all SKUs) for the entire company.

  - With *decentralized inventory control*, inventory decision making (for all SKUs) is exercised at each stocking location for SKUs at that location (see [APIC04]).

Optimal inventory organization is tuned to the characteristic features of planning & control currently valid in the logistics network. Just as the value of each of these features may change with the organization's policies, the value of each inventory management feature can also change. Inventory organization must therefore remain flexible. Rather than forming a constraint for logistics, it must ensue from the type of logistics chosen.

10.1.2 Inventory Transactions

Inventory management includes — among other things — the tasks involved in the handling of inventory transactions.

An *inventory transaction* alters the stored or in-process inventory. This can be a planned or executed inventory transaction.

Perpetual inventory is an inventory recordkeeping system where each transaction in and out is recorded and a new balance is computed.

> *Book inventory* is an accounting definition of inventory units or value
> obtained from perpetual inventory transaction records rather than by actual
> (physical) count [APIC04].

Figure 10.1.2.1 shows an overview of the types and origins of important
inventory transactions in an industrial organization, both planned (for
example, an allocation) and executed.

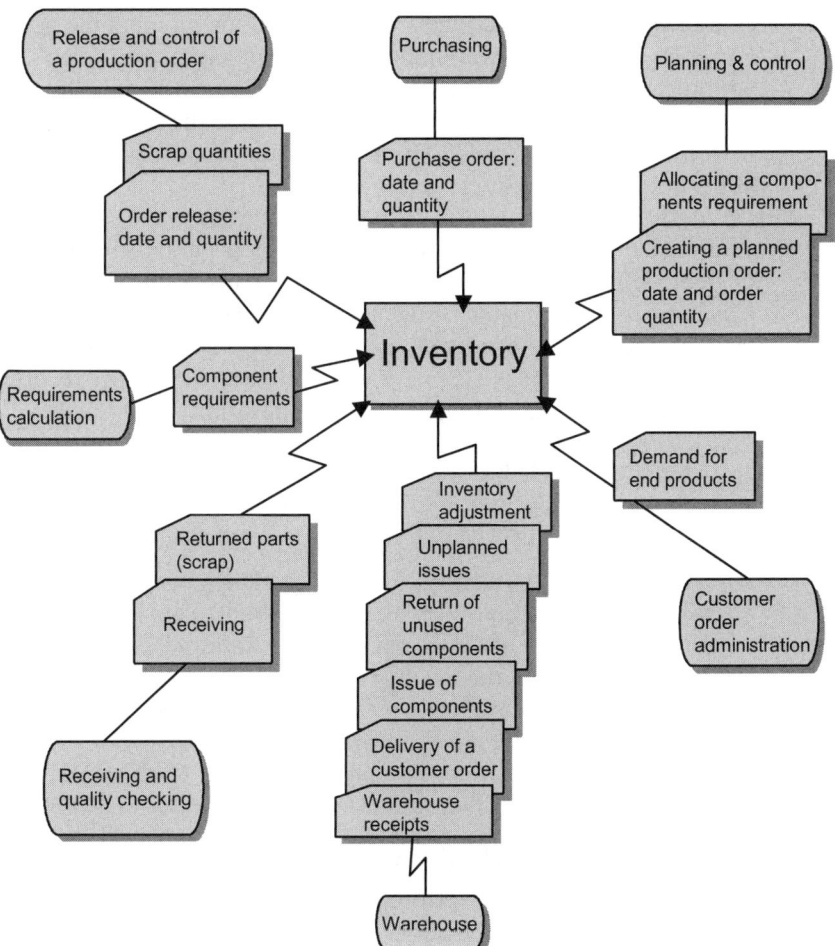

Fig. 10.1.2.1   Overview of the sources of planned and actual inventory transactions.

An exact and well-documented book inventory recording system is the
basis of all inventory management. Appropriate organizational measures
must make it possible to record accurate, up-to-date information on book

inventory, even with thousands of transactions per week and numerous employees. Book inventory should either equal physical inventory or deviate from it in a controllable and traceable manner. Measures to this purpose include:

- Ensuring that there are no uncontrolled *inventory issues* or *receipts*. Generally, this means that there will be "closed," or separate, warehouses or accurately controlled buffers, such as in container units. Transactions are recorded at the moment the goods leave or enter the warehouse. It is important to keep the administrative costs of putting into and issuing from stock low for inexpensive parts (screws, nuts, springs, and the like). For this reason, decentralized small parts stocks are often located directly at the production facilities.

- Guaranteeing the identification of goods by accurate specification of item identification and storage location. This is one of the main purposes of automated inventory organization through, for example, computer-aided warehouse transport systems. Interactive verification guarantees accuracy without the use of paper records. Inventory management should perform plausibility tests, such as:

  1. Test for correct item identification. If this is a number, it can contain control digits. This will avoid recording errors such as reversed digits or data entry of, say, a 2 rather than a 3.

  2. Test for correct quantity. The transaction quantity (receipt or issue) should be below a particular amount. This limit quantity should either be defined manually or adjusted continually in dependency upon the average inventory movement (receipts or issues). In doubtful cases, a computer-aided system can request explicit double entry of quantities.

With material goods, bar codes can collect item identification. However, if the transaction quantity deviates from the planned quantity, it must be registered manually. This contrasts with product sales in the grocery or clothing industries, where each issue represents exactly one unit quantity, making quantity recording unnecessary.

In order to avoid recording long lists of components for a production order (picking lists), recording is required only for deviations from the picking list. The other positions are booked automatically by using the allocated quantity as the issued quantity as soon as the picking list is designated as issued.

10.1.3 Physical Inventory and Inventory Valuation

> *Inventory accounting* is the branch of accounting dealing with valuing inventory ([APIC04]).
>
> *Physical inventory* is the process of determining inventory quantity by actual count. ([APIC04]. Note: The term *physical inventory* can also mean the actual inventory itself. See Section 11.1.1.)
>
> *Inventory adjustment* is a change made to an inventory record to correct the balance, to bring it in line with actual physical inventory balances.
>
> *Inventory valuation* involves determining the value of the inventory at either its cost or its market value ([APIC04]).

Physical inventory, inventory adjustment, and inventory valuation are needed to assure goods on hand, for example. Furthermore, inventory is a company asset: one of the entries on the assets side of the balance sheet is the *value of stored* and *in-process inventory*. Tax authorities demand an exact physical inventory as well. Figure 10.1.3.1 presents an example of an inventory list that shows the value of the inventory stocks.

Part ID	Description	Unit of measure	Stock	Entry	Issue	Available	Ordered	Allo-cated	Cost / unit	Inventory value	Stock range (months)
1348	Control-box	Pc	1499		850	649		600	1.45	941.05	
1349	Control-box	Pc	3314		1700	1614	560		0.59	952.26	
1414	Bolt with nut	Pc	6374		3600	2774	300	80	0.07	194.18	
1418	Hose 1 IN	Pc	715		575	140	485		0.26	36.40	
1425	Tank	Pc	2224		800	1424	2150	400	3.61	5140.64	1
1427	Tank	Pc	1712		550	1162	862	600	3.61	4194.82	1
1444	Horn	Pc	550	100	500	150			2.35	352.50	
2418	Hose 3 IN	Pc	7499		4200	3299	250		0.16	527.84	
2419	Hose 2 IN	Pc	7799	500	4400	3899		125	0.13	506.87	
2892	Closure	Pc	3058			3058	200	100	0.08	244.64	30
3010	Plate	Pc	918	315	525	708	175	110	0.15	106.20	1
3011	Gasket	Pc	5082	100	3185	1997	175		0.15	299.55	
3012	Spring	Pc	13500		7500	6000	100	500	0.07	420.00	
3021	Cartridge	Pc	1575		750	825	110		1.85	1526.25	1
3024	Cylinder	Pc	1978		1100	878		400	0.05	43.90	
3025	Pump	Pc	4			4			23.25	93.00	
3370	Motor	Pc	1350		750	600	3100	1200	7.25	4350.00	
3462	Pedal	Pc	100			100			1.53	153.00	999

Fig. 10.1.3.1   Example of a stock inventory list.

The lists generally class items according to group. Additional statistics at the end of the list, not shown here, group product range items according to certain other criteria.

Even with a very precise recording of book inventory, errors are possible
— particularly in the case of unplanned, or unannounced, transactions:

- Errors in the data media recording inventory transactions

- Recording of erroneous quantity numbers

- Duplicate entry or failure to record a transaction

- Incorrect physical counts at the time of stock receipt

- Errors in the physical assignment of storage areas (stock sites are
  entered into the computer that in reality contain no stock)

- *Shrinkage*, or the reduction of actual quantities in stock by
  pilferage, deterioration, or misuse of items

These errors are relatively difficult to detect. Physical inventory counts are
necessary if users are to retain their trust in *record accuracy*, that is, the
accuracy of the data in the computer. Depending upon the results of
physical counts of inventory, new controls may be established, or controls
that have proven to be unnecessary may be dropped.

Particularly difficult is the inventory of items like coffee beans, leaves,
seaweed, or gasoline. Such items change their weight or volume
significantly over time due to moisture or temperature.[2]

Periodic inventory is a physical inventory taken at a recurring, fixed
interval, usually at the end of the organization's fiscal period (for example,
the end of the calendar year).

Periodic inventory follows the procedure outlined in Figure 10.1.3.2.

- Shut down the warehouse.
- Physically count the stock quantities of randomly selected partial item
  quantities or all items. Check the results.
- Compare physically counted quantities to the quantities recorded in the
  inventory accounting system. Perform a deviation analysis.
- In the case of significant deviations, first verify correct entry of inventory
  quantities. If this produces no results, re-perform the entire physical
  inventory, including the deviation analysis.

Fig. 10.1.3.2   Periodic physical inventory procedure.

---

[2]   Even roasted coffee shows a loss in weight over time. It gives off carbon dioxide,
or "outgases," until it is stale.

The partial quantities of items to be inventoried are chosen in such a way that any deviations within these partial quantities will be representative of deviations in the entire quantity of the items.

For some companies it is too costly to shut down the warehouse entirely, even for a few days. Sometimes the production rhythm does not permit it, or there is a lack of qualified employees for the physical inventory. Here, cycle counting, or even perpetual inventory, is important.

Cycle counting is, according to [APIC04], an inventory accuracy audit technique where physical inventory is counted on a cyclic schedule, a regular, defined basis (often more frequently for high-value or fast-moving items and less frequently for low-value or slow-moving items).

The items determined by the cyclic schedule are mostly counted at the end of a workday, by a procedure similar to the one outlined in Figure 10.1.3.3.

- Count every item periodically, in fixed cycles. The length of a period may vary, depending on the type and importance of the item. Logically, count high-cost items more frequently than inexpensive ones.

- During the counting procedures, put a transaction freeze on only those items that are being inventoried at that particular moment. This will be a minimal percentage of all items. Furthermore, generally perform the physical count at the end of the working day, in other words, at a time at which the inventory transactions for the current day have already been executed.

- Select employees for the task who are trained and experienced. This reduces the probability of errors.

Fig. 10.1.3.3   Cycle counting procedure.

The method of comparison is the same as the one described above. A deviation analysis is performed for every counting cycle. It is also possible to count a random selection of all items for each cycle. After correction of any counting errors, the analysis is accepted, and the items can once again be released.

Some companies close the warehouse at the end of a working day for half an hour. They then inventory the random partial quantity of items and perform the deviation analysis. Generally, the same employees who have worked with receipts and issues during the day perform the counting.

10.2   Usage Statistics, Analyses, and Classifications

10.2.1 Statistics on Inventory Transactions, Sales, and Bid Activities

Statistics on particular events can provide an important basis for various calculations in requirements planning and inventory management.

Usage statistics analyze the quantity of all inventory transactions.

For each transaction, the following attributes should be recorded:

- Date of transaction
- Identification of the item or the item family
- Moved quantity
- Employees responsible for the recording of the transaction
- The two customer, production, or purchase orders or inventory stock positions (target and actual, "before" and "after" position of the transaction)

As the number of recorded transactions is usually very large, in practice it is often impossible to make older transactions available for online queries. Moreover, too much time would be required to process certain queries, particularly those pertaining to particular groups of items.

Turnover statistics condense the most important data on inventory transactions in order to gain rapid information about an item's movements.

Turnover statistics are updated, for example, daily, to include all trans-actions for that day. Managers maintain sales records for every item over the last statistical period, for example, the last 24 months and also over the three previous years. For all these periods, the following data are recorded:

- Total inventory issues, that is, items released from an inventory for use or for sale
- Partial inventory issues
- Inventory issues that were sold
- Total *inventory receipts*, that is, items released from an inventory for use or for sale
- Partial inventory receipts
- Inventory receipts that were purchased or produced

For each of these attributes, depending upon need and the data storage capacity of the system, the following can be recorded:

- Number of transactions
- Turnover expressed in quantity
- Turnover expressed in value

Why record the additional attribute *partial issues*? (The same arguments apply to the additional attribute *partial receipts*.)

An *outlier* is a data point that differs significantly from other data for a similar phenomenon.

For example, if the average sales for a product were 10 units per month, and one month the product had sales of 500 units, this sales point might be considered an outlier ([APIC04]).

Abnormal demand — in any period — is demand that is outside the limits established by management policy (see [APIC04]).

This demand may come from a new customer or from existing customers whose own demand is increasing or decreasing.

In general, outliers and abnormal demand should not be taken as a basis for demand forecasting. Care must be taken to evaluate the nature of the abnormal demand: Is it a volume change, is it related to the timing of some orders, or is it a change in product mix?[3]

Usage and turnover statistics do not provide a sufficient basis for certain calculations in requirements planning. This is always the case when a relatively large time span lies between estimated demand and measured usage. A good example is capital goods having a considerable lead time of several months. In this case we need statistics that are constructed in principle in the same way as the usage and turnover statistics above, but relate to more current events. A favorite measurement time point is the moment of sale or — even more up-to-date — the moment of bidding.

A *sales transaction* of an item records the sending of the order confirmation and thus the moment the customer order is accepted. *Sales statistics* analyze all sales transactions.

---

[3]   The *product mix* is the proportion of individual products that make up the total production or sales volume ([APIC04]).

Sales statistics are more up to date than usage statistics — by the amount of the lead time for the order. However, the corresponding sales data files tend to be less precise, for customers may cancel or alter placed orders. This causes problems if corrections to sales data are recorded incompletely, or at an inopportune time, such as when the canceled sales have already been used to determine demand.

> A *bid transaction* of an item records the sending of a bid to the customer. *Bid statistics* analyze all bid transactions.

Bid statistics are even more up to date than sales statistics due to the time that on average lapses between the formulation of the bid and the sale. But again, the corresponding data are less precise. The order success probability (see Chapter 4.2.1) shows the approximate percentage of bids that translated into sales. This uncertainty will be greater if order success percentage cannot be ascertained reliably for every individual product, or even for every individual product family.

10.2.2 The ABC Classification

Up to now we have stressed the "importance" of an item in relationship to all items as a whole. Turnover, which generally refers to past usage, can yield the importance of an item. However, forecasts rather than turnover may also yield this information.

In all types and sizes of organizations, it can be observed that a small number of products make up the largest portion of the turnover.

> *ABC classification* divides a set or group of items into three classes, specifically A, B, and C.[4]

Figure 10.2.2.1 illustrates the principle of this classification and possible limits for a change of class (break points):

- In the example, *A items*, that is the A class, is composed of 20% of the items, which account for 75% of total turnover.
- *B items*, that is the B class, is made up of 30 to 40% of the items, which comprise approximately 15% of total turnover.

---

[4]   ABC classification is an application of *Pareto analysis* to inventory management. Pareto analysis is "the concept that 20 percent of any entity represent the very important few and the remaining 80 percent are less important" (see [APIC04]).

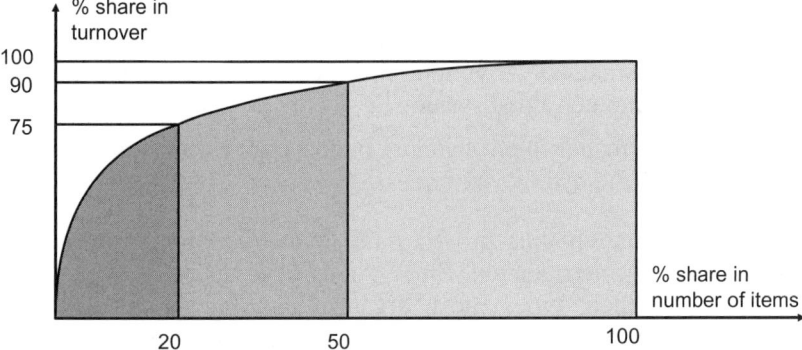

Fig. 10.2.2.1   The principle of the ABC classification.

- *C items*, that is the remaining items, which make up a large part of the product range, here 40 to 50% of the items, only account for approximately 10% of total turnover.

The precise shape of the Pareto curve and the break points between classes will vary among firms, but the point that a small percentage of items make up most of the importance (or value) remains generally true. Using ABC analysis to classify items is an aid to inventory control, because it prioritizes the items.

Not all items warrant the same level of attention by management. Prioritizing inventory items according to the ABC classification allows targeted implementation of appropriate materials management and control measures.

- It is much more important to reduce inventory stocks and goods in process for A items than for C items. In addition, since A items are more limited in number, close follow-up is much easier.

- Management orders A items in frequent small batches and places purchase orders only after intensive evaluation. Production orders are closely reviewed and expedited with high priority. Naturally, all these measures increase ordering costs and administrative costs.

- It is important that C items are always available. Under no circumstances should an item that costs only a few cents be allowed to delay the delivery of a machine that may have a value of hundreds of thousands of dollars. Management releases procurement orders very early, with ample margins as to quantity and time. This increases storage costs only slightly, since the items are inexpensive ones.

- Ordering costs for C items are very low, since large quantities are ordered at one time. It may sometimes even be possible to trigger orders automatically, without the intervention of a planner, by using a computer-aided system.

- Generally, management handles B items with a medium priority, between the above two extremes.

The ABC classification thus provides the foundation for various parameters in materials management. Since goods have different importance, depending upon their type, most organizations have separate ABC classifications for each type of item, as outlined in Section 1.2.2 (final products, intermediate products, sub-assemblies, individual parts, raw materials, and so on). This is especially important when the value added is high. In that case, a sole ABC classification for the entirety of the item range would tend to classify all final products as A items and all purchased items as C items. However, this would defeat the objective of the ABC approach.

> The *ABC category* is the identification of the set or group of items grouped together for an ABC classification.

Therefore, first all items are assigned to an ABC category. Then, the ABC classification is completed in two stages, as outlined in Figure 10.2.2.2.

In a first stage, sort all items of an ABC category to calculate 100% of the selected classification criterion (a measure of importance, or value), such as turnover.

In a second stage, handle all the items in the class in descending order of the chosen criterion. Compare the partial sums according to the selected classification criterion of the items handled to the 100% figure.

- All items that are handled at the beginning in accordance with this descending order receive the classification A.

- If, for example, the partial sum exceeds 75% (A break point) of the total quantity of 100% that was determined in the first stage, assign the items that follow to classification B.

- If the partial sum exceeds, say, 90% (B break point) of the total quantity of 100% that was determined in the first stage, assign the items that follow to classification C.

Fig. 10.2.2.2   The ABC classification for each ABC category.

10.2.3 The XYZ Classification and Other Analyses and Statistics

XYZ classification distinguishes items with regular or even continuous demand (X items) from those with completely irregular, lumpy or unique demand (Z items). Y items lie between the two extremes.

The decision about the assignment of an item results from analysis of the demand quantities per statistical period. Thus, the dispersion of the demanded quantities is a measure for the classification. For example, for an item in the X class we could require that the deviation from average consumption should not be larger than 5% per week or 20% per month.

Materials management sets its policies according to the XYZ classification. It also determines whether important materials management parameters should be calculated automatically (for example, using forecast data) or set manually.

An *exception list* contains goods that do not "normally" pass through the company.

Exception lists can be based on inventory transactions, such as:

- Items that have not moved during a period of a certain number of months (non-saleable goods)
- Items that do not show a sufficient turnover
- Items whose inventory value exceeds a particular total

Exception lists serve to sort out items that are in an exceptional state according to a particular criterion. Even in the case of computer supported planning & control systems, users can usually define such exception lists themselves.

We will discuss the entire category of exception messages that affect production and procurement orders in the course of this chapter as well as in Chapter 11.

10.3   Order Point Technique and Safety Stock Calculation

10.3.1 The Order Point Technique

The *order point technique* or *order point system* is used for items with stochastic demand that is relatively continuous along the time axis. The characteristic inventory curve is the *saw-toothed curve* as shown in Figure 10.3.1.1.

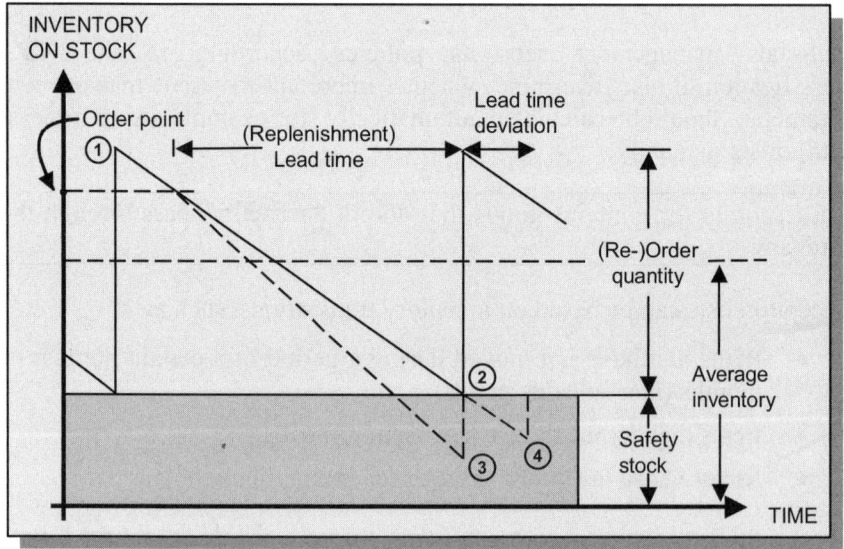

Fig. 10.3.1.1   Characteristic data for the order point technique.

- After stock entry (point 1), the stock falls gradually until it is below a quantity that is called the *order point*. At this point in time, a production or procurement order is generated.

- The inventory level sinks continually during the *replenishment lead time*, that is, the total period of time from the moment of reordering until point 2, where the *reorder quantity* or *replenishment order quantity* is available for use (determining this batch size is the subject of Section 10.4). After the stock entry, the cycle begins anew at point 1. The decline between the points 1 and 2 represents the demand during the lead time. This demand is a stochastic value.

- If the actual demand is larger than the expected (forecast) demand, the inventory level curve corresponds to the dashed line that leads to point 3. If no safety stock was maintained, there will be a stockout.
- If the actual lead time is longer than the (expected) lead time, then the inventory stock curve corresponds to the dashed line that leads to point 4. If no safety stock was maintained, there will be a stockout.

The *order interval* or *order cycle* is the time period between the placements of orders.

Cycle stock is the component of inventory that depletes gradually as customer orders are received and is replenished cyclically when supplier orders are received ([APIC04]).

Safety stock is the component of inventory that serves as a buffer to cover fluctuations in lead time and in the demand during the lead time. Statistically, we need to draw upon safety stock in half of all procurement cycles. For definitions, see Section 10.3.3.

This system is more difficult to manage in the case of non-continuous but regular demand (the case, for example, with seasonal components). The saw-toothed curve then has a shape that reproduces the seasonality of the demand (see Section 9.3.4).

The area under the saw-toothed curve, multiplied by a cost rate, yields the carrying cost for this item per time unit. This corresponds to the storage costs for the mean stock per time unit.

We can derive *average inventory* for the order point technique in Figure 10.3.1.1 by using the following formula (Figure 10.3.1.2):

$$\text{average inventory} = \text{safety stock} + \frac{\text{order quantity}}{2}$$

Fig. 10.3.1.2   Average inventory.

The *order point* or *reorder point* is calculated from safety stock and expected (forecast) demand during the procurement period according to the formula in Figure 10.3.1.3.

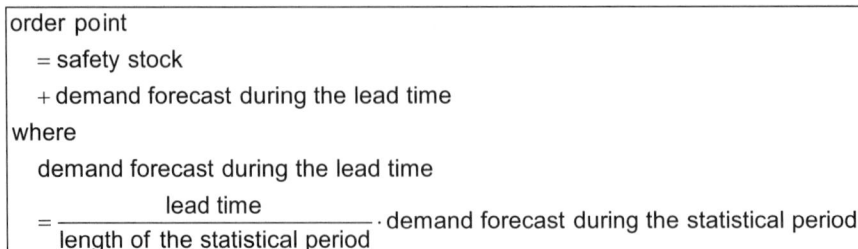

order point
  = safety stock
  + demand forecast during the lead time
where
  demand forecast during the lead time

$$= \frac{\text{lead time}}{\text{length of the statistical period}} \cdot \text{demand forecast during the statistical period}$$

Fig. 10.3.1.3   Order point calculation.

Calculation of the order point is executed after calculation of the demand forecast and always at the end of a statistical period. Order point calculation should be executed more frequently in cases of discontinuous demand, longer statistical periods, and shorter lead times, because the forecast may change significantly over the course of time.

In addition to physical inventory, we also include *scheduled receipts* in the coverage of demand during the lead time. These include firmly ordered quantities or quantities of released orders (see the definition in Section 11.1.1), since these will all arrive during the lead time. If the formula contained in Figure 10.3.1.4 holds, a new production or procurement order should be released.

$$\text{Physical inventory} + \sum \text{Scheduled receipts} < \text{Order point}$$

Fig. 10.3.1.4   Criterion for the release of a production or procurement order.

For management purposes it is important to periodically produce a list that contains and classifies all the items for which the criterion in Figure 10.3.1.4 is satisfied and to generate an order proposal for every item on that list. The order proposal contains all the required information, such as the predicted receipt to stock, the batch size, and information regarding earlier productions or procurements. In the case of procurement, the order proposal also serves to specify purchase blanket orders more precisely. Since the procurement decision must be made without delay, the proposal also contains bids from suppliers.

10.3.2 Variants of the Order Point Technique

If the customer allows a *minimum delivery lead time*, then we know all the *allocated quantities* or *reserved quantities* (in other words, the demand that is linked to released customer orders or assigned to production orders; see the definitions in Section 11.1.1) during the relevant time frame in the near future. This is true for all customer or production orders that require the corresponding items. Thus, we can choose the time to release according to the formula in Figure 10.3.2.1.

Physical inventory $+$ $\sum$ Scheduled receipts

  $-\sum$ Allocated quantities during minimum delivery lead time $<$ Reduced order point

where

  Reduced order point $= f($reduced lead time$)$

  Reduced lead time $=$ lead time $-$ minimum delivery lead time

---

Fig. 10.3.2.1   Criterion for the release of a production or procurement order, if the customer allows a minimum delivery lead time.

Since the demand that is to be determined stochastically must now cover only a reduced lead time, the technique becomes more deterministic and precise — particularly in the case of trends that are not considered by the forecast model.

Production or procurement orders can be released earlier than necessary:

The *anticipation horizon* refers to the maximum anticipated time for consideration of early release of a production or procurement order.

Figure 10.3.2.2 shows a formula to determine the items that are candidates for an early release. For a discussion of procedures with an early issuance of production orders, see Section 14.3.1.

Physical inventory $+ \sum$ Scheduled receipts

 $- \sum$ Allocated quantities during the anticipation time $<$ Order point

---

Fig. 10.3.2.2   Criterion for an early issuance of a production or procurement order.

The saw-toothed curve — which provides for the optimal functioning of the order point technique — is attained in its ideal form if the issue quantities are relatively small in relationship to the production or procurement batch size. If instead they are relatively large, a chopped-off saw-toothed curve results. For issue quantities on the order of the production or procurement batch size, the resulting curve looks more like the shape of human teeth with gaps between them. At that point, the order point technique no longer yields satisfactory results. See here also Section 11.3.1.

A variant of the order point technique described above is the min-max (reorder) system.

With the *min-max (reorder) system*, the "min" (minimum) is the order point, and the "max" (maximum) is the "order up to" inventory level. The order quantity is variable and is the result of the max minus physical inventory minus scheduled receipts. An order is recommended when the sum of the physical inventory plus scheduled receipts is below the minimum Compare [APIC04].

The advantage of the min–max (reorder) system lies in the clear definition of maximal storage space requirements. This is particularly important for racks and shelves in supermarkets, for example.

Another variant of the order point technique is a system that is used frequently for management of distribution inventory.

The *double order point system* has two order points. The smallest equals the traditional order point, which covers the demand forecast during the replenishment lead time. The second, higher order point is the sum of the first order point plus the demand forecast during the replenishment lead time *of the preceding structural level*, most usually the production lead time or the purchasing lead time. Compare [APIC04].

Figure 10.3.2.3 shows the principle for applying the double order point system. RLT1 is the replenishment lead time of the traditional order point technique, and RLT2 is the replenishment lead time of the preceding structural level.

As soon as inventory at the regional distribution center drops and reaches order point 2, the information is sent to the central warehouse as an order proposal, which the regional distribution center would have to release at about this time if it were ordering directly from the manufacturer or supplier instead of from the central warehouse.

The central warehouse has now got advance warning that an order is pending. It enables the central warehouse to forewarn the manufacturer of future replenishment orders. The advantage is that in theory, no safety stock needs to be held at the central warehouse.

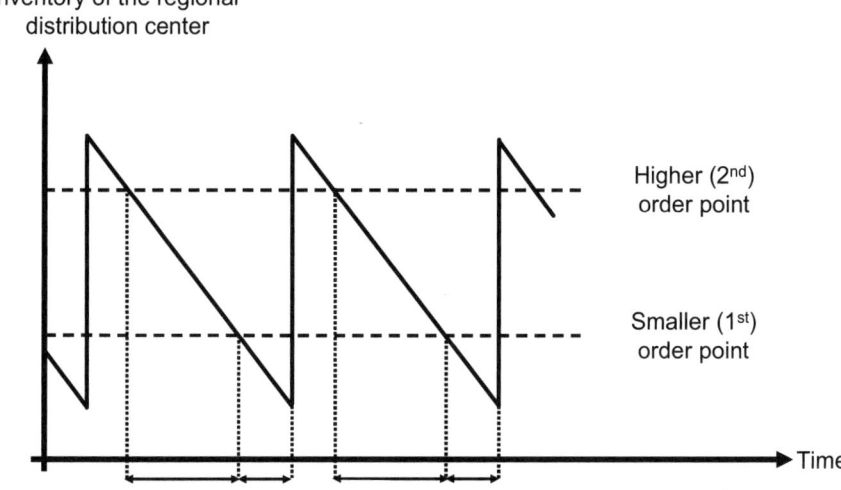

Fig. 10.3.2.3   The double order point system.

10.3.3 Safety Stock Calculation with Continuous Demand

Figure 10.3.1.1 indicates that without safety stock, there will be a stockout in half of the cycles defined by the saw-toothed curve. This results in backorders.

Safety stock or *buffer stock* serves to cushion the impact of forecast errors or deviations in the lead time as well as in the demand during the lead time.

Anticipation inventories is a similar term, used in the management of distribution inventory. It means additional inventory above basic pipeline stock to cover projected trends of increasing sales, planned sales promotion programs, seasonal fluctuations, plant shutdowns, and vacations ([APIC04]).

Figure 10.3.3.1 shows different techniques for determining safety stock depending on the nature of the item.

Technique	Safety stock	Typical use
Fixed	Set (manually) quantity	New and old items, discontinuous or lumpy demand patterns, low-cost items
Time period	Determine by forecasts for future periods	Critical components, new and old items, discontinuous or lumpy demand patterns
Statistical	Calculate via statistical method based on history	Mature items, continuous or regular demand patterns, deviations in predictable range

Fig. 10.3.3.1   Different techniques for determining safety stock.

The first two techniques determine safety stock in a largely intuitive manner. For the statistical derivation, however, there are formal techniques available, as described in the following:

1. *Statistical Fluctuations in the Lead Time*

Fluctuations in the lead time due to unplanned delays in production or procurement, for example, are absorbed by a safety lead time.

The *safety lead time* is an element of time added to normal lead time to protect against fluctuations. Order release and order completion are planned for earlier dates (before real need dates), according to the time added.

Safety stock due to fluctuations in lead time is calculated simply as the demand forecast during this safety lead time. This technique is often used, because it is easily understood.

2. *Statistical Fluctuations in Demand*

For purposes of absorbing demand fluctuations, safety lead time is not a sufficient basis for calculation.

Fluctuation inventory, or *fluctuation stock*, is inventory that is carried as a cushion to protect against forecast error ([APIC04]).

Figure 10.3.3.2 shows the pattern of demand for two items with the same demand forecast, but different demand fluctuations.

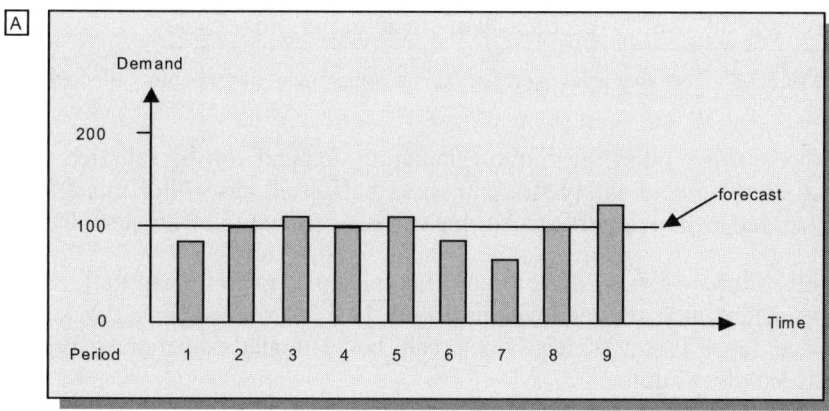

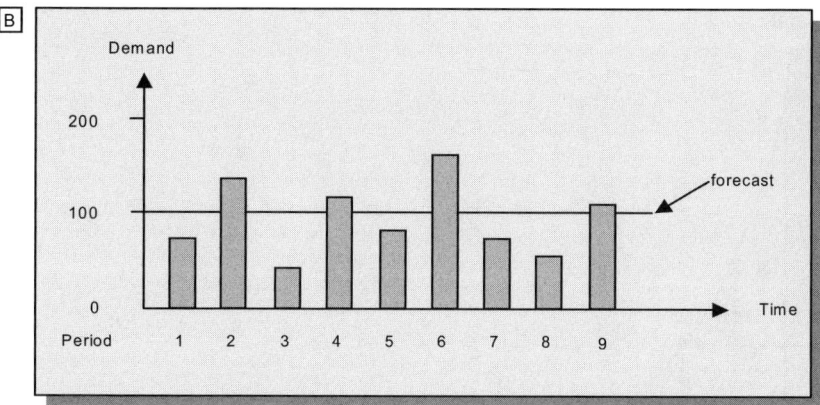

Fig. 10.3.3.2   Different patterns of the deviation of demand from forecast.

The fluctuation inventory for the item in Situation B must be larger than that for the item in Situation A. A pattern of demand that has only a small dispersion around the demand forecast will result in a smaller quantity of safety stock; one with large variation will require a larger quantity of safety stock.

The *service level*, or *level of service*, is the percentage of order cycles that the firm will go through without stockout, meaning that inventory is sufficient to cover demand.

The *probability of stockout* is the probability that a stockout will occur during each order cycle before a replenishment order arrives.

According to these definitions, the following relationship holds (see Figure 10.3.3.3):

| service level = 100% - probability of stockout per order cycle |

Fig. 10.3.3.3   Service level expressed as the complement of probability of stockout.

With the order point technique fluctuating demand can be satisfied from stock even without safety stock in about half of all cases. For this reason, the service level using this technique can be assumed to be at least 50%.

Safety stock — and with it carrying cost — grows quantitatively in dependency upon service level, as Figure 10.3.3.4 shows. Once the desired service level is set, safety stock can be estimated accurately through statistical derivation.

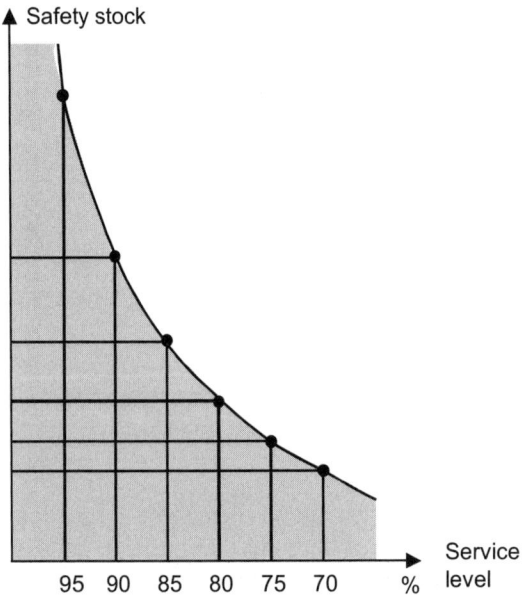

Fig. 10.3.3.4   Safety stock — and thus carrying cost — in relation to service level.

The *safety factor* is the numerical value, a particular multiplier, for the standard deviation of demand.

The *service function* is the integral distribution function, for which the integral under the distribution curve for demand up to a particular safety factor s corresponds to the service level.

If demand follows a *normal distribution*, or a bell-shaped curve, the service level corresponding to the safety factor s is the area shown in gray in Figure 10.3.3.5.

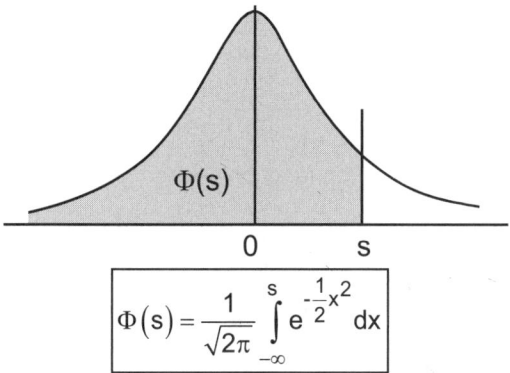

$$\Phi(s) = \frac{1}{\sqrt{2\pi}} \int_{-\infty}^{s} e^{-\frac{1}{2}x^2} dx$$

Fig. 10.3.3.5   Normal integral distribution function (service function).

Therefore, the safety factor is also the inverse function of the integral distribution function. It is the numerical value used in the service function (based on the standard deviation of the forecast) to provide a given level of service.

Figure 10.3.3.6 reproduces examples for corresponding values of the service level and the safety factor. They can be read from tables, such as the following table from [Eilo62], p. 26.

Safety factor	Service level %	Service level %	Safety factor
0	50.00	50	0
0.5	69.15	65	0.385
1	84.13	80	0.842
1.5	93.32	90	1.282
2	97.73	95	1.645
2.5	99.38	98	2.054
3	99.86	99	2.326
4	99.997	99.9	3.090

Fig. 10.3.3.6   Service level and safety factor when demand follows a normal distribution. (From [Eilo64], p. 26.)

The resulting formula for safety stock is shown in Figure 10.3.3.7. With a normal distribution, it is possible to use 1.25 * MAD (mean absolute deviation) instead of the standard deviation.

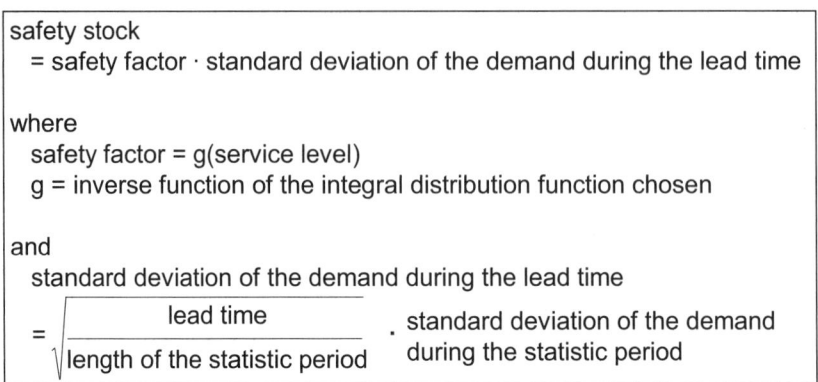

Fig. 10.3.3.7   Formula for safety stock.

In particular for small demand quantities, we can not always assume that demand is normally distributed. Sometimes, we could assume a Poisson distribution instead. However, with a mean value (average demand quantity) of merely 9 units, the upper part of the Poisson distribution curve is very close to the curve of the normal distribution. This is particularly true for larger safety factors and high service levels. See also Figure 9.5.6.1.

Figure 10.3.3.8 provides an example of the *Poisson distribution* and its integral function. A different curve and also a different inverse function will result, depending upon the mean value λ.

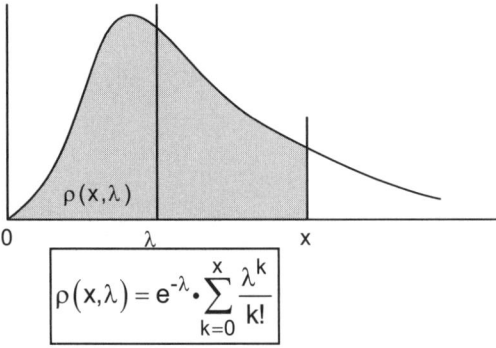

Fig. 10.3.3.8   Poisson distribution integral function.

Figures 10.3.3.9 and 10.3.3.10 show pairs of values of the service level and safety factor for means of $\lambda = 4$ and $\lambda = 9$, respectively.

Safety factor	Service level %	Service level %	Safety factor $\approx$
0	43.35	50	0
0.5	62.88	65	0.6
1	78.51	80	1.1
1.5	88.93	90	1.6
2	94.89	95	2.1
2.5	97.86	98	2.7
3	99.19	99	2.9
4	99.91	99.9	3.9

Fig. 10.3.3.9   Table of values for the Poisson cumulative distribution with a mean demand value of $\lambda = 4$ and standard deviation $\sqrt{\lambda} = 2$ units per period. (From [Eilo62], p. 84 ff.)

Safety factor	Service level %	Service level %	Safety factor $\approx$
0	45.57	50	0
0.5	64.53	65	0.5
1	80.30	80	1.0
1.5	89.81	90	1.5
2	95.85	95	1.9
2.667	98.89	98	2.4
3	99.47	99	2.8
4	99.96	99.9	3.8

Fig. 10.3.3.10   Table of values for the Poisson cumulative distribution with a mean demand value of $\lambda = 9$ and standard deviation $\sqrt{\lambda} = 3$ units per period. (From [Eilo62], p. 84 ff.)

For small consumption quantities, the cost of a stockout often does not depend so much upon the quantity not delivered as upon the fact that there is a failure to meet the full quantity of demand. Therefore, with small usage quantities the tendency is to choose a high service level, which in turn results in a high safety factor. The calculated safety factor that is based upon a Poisson distribution is then generally fairly equivalent to the one based upon a normal distribution.

However, based on *probability* of stockout alone, we cannot say anything about the stockout *quantity*, the stockout *percentage*, or backorder *percentage*. Thus, service level is not the same as *fill rate*, which only measures what actually happens when demand occurs. See also [Bern99], p. 345.

Like fill rate (see the definition in Section 4.3.1), service level is the quantitative application of the answer to the following question: What are the costs of not meeting customer demands from stock? Both measures, fill rate and service level, are thus estimates of opportunity cost. In order to achieve a specific fill rate, however, it is generally sufficient to set a smaller number as the service level, or desired probability that demand can be met from stock. The relationship between the two measures fill rate and service level as well as ways of determining the appropriate service level are examined in Section 10.3.4.

10.3.4 Determining the Service Level and the Relation of Service Level to Fill Rate (*)

Figure 10.3.4.1 shows a typical order cycle using the order point technique shown in Figure 10.3.1.1, in which the *length of order cycle*, that is the length of time the batch size will provide stockout coverage, is a multiple of the lead time. The batch size itself is a multiple of the expected demand during the lead time.

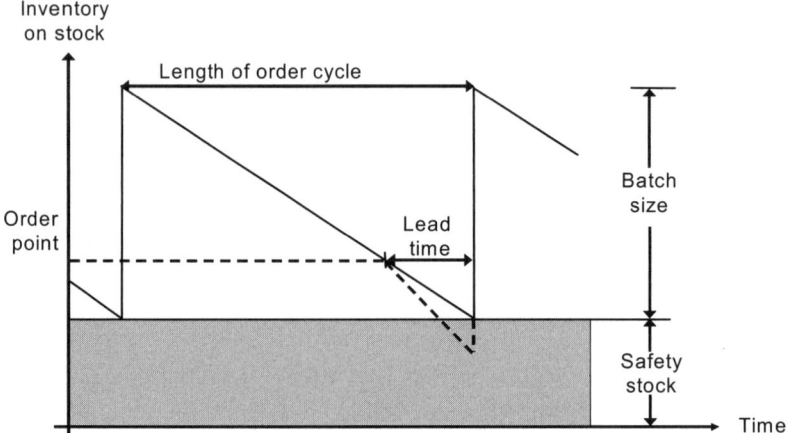

Fig. 10.3.4.1   Order point technique with an order cycle where the length of order cycle provided by the batch size is a multiple of the lead time.

If the length of order cycle divided by lead time equals 10, for example, and demand is not too discontinuous, then 90% of the batch size can be covered without stockout. Stockout will only occur for demand during the lead time, or for 10% of the batch size. If no safety stock were carried (safety factor is 0, that is, a service level of only 50%), the fill rate would be approximately 90% and higher. This shows that service level can usually be a percentage that is significantly smaller than the desired fill rate (which in most cases must be set at close to 100%; see the discussion in Section 4.3.1).

As mentioned above, determining the desired fill rate and service level has to be the quantitative application of the qualitative answer to the question of what stockouts will cost. Thus, fill rate and service level express an estimation of opportunity cost.

Stockout costs are the economic consequences of stockouts.

Stockout costs can include extra costs for express/emergency production or procurement or customer delivery, but also penalty costs, loss of sales, loss of contribution margin, loss of customer goodwill, and all kinds of associated costs. See the discussion in Section 1.3.1.

The following shows the derivation of two methods of determining the desired service level:

1. The first method bases on the assumption that opportunity costs can be assigned directly to each unit not filled.
2. The second method is based on the assumption that the total opportunity costs can be assigned to the fill rate during a particular time period (a year, for instance).

1. *Determine service level on the basis of stockout costs for each unit of an item not filled.*

Where stockout costs can be expressed as costs per (mass) unit not delivered, [Cole00], [SiPy98], and [Ters88] offer the following direct calculation of the *optimum probability of stockout* (see Figure 10.3.4.2). Because a stockout can only happen at the end of an order cycle, the number of stockouts can not be greater than the number of order cycles. Often the period chosen for the calculation is one year.

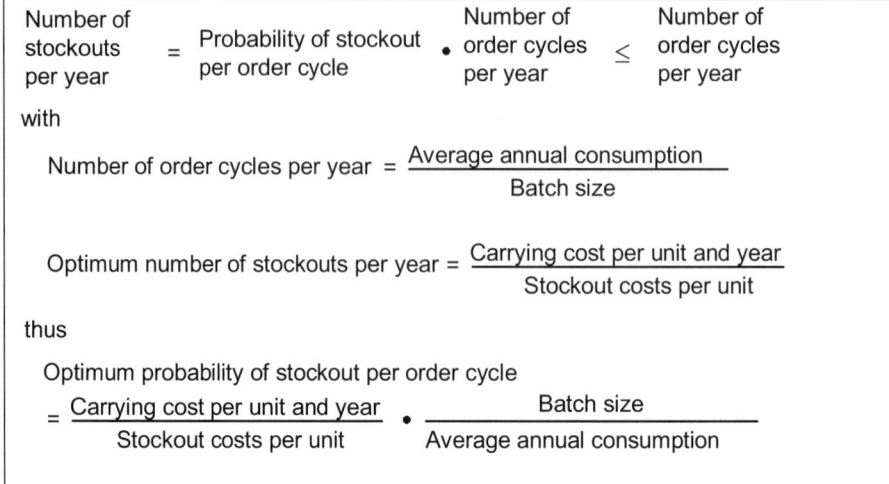

Fig. 10.3.4.2   Probability of stockout in dependency on stockout costs per unit.

As a consequence, the *optimum service level* results directly from the relation in Figure 10.3.3.3. Section 10.4 discusses determination of batch size, which often precedes safety stock calculation.

For example, if there are five order cycles per year (and the average annual consumption is five times the batch size) and stockout costs per unit are four times greater than carrying cost per year, the resulting optimum probability of stockout is 0.05 and the optimum service level is 95%.[5]

2. Determine service level on the basis of fill rate.

If a certain stockout percentage or backorder percentage has been set on the basis of estimated annual stockout costs, then the service level can be derived from the fill rate by estimating the stockout quantity per order cycle. See also [Brow67] and [Stev02].

For a *particular safety factor*, from now on called s, the stockout quantity is the product of all possible not filled quantities and their probability of occurrence. A specific not filled quantity is the quantity m, which exceeds the expected quantity of demand plus s times the standard deviation of demand during the lead time. Proportional to the standard deviation, this

---

[5]   In cases where the formal probability of stockout calculated in this way should be greater than 0.5, the lowest reasonable service level should be assumed (usually 50%).

quantity can be expressed as (t – s) times the standard deviation σ, for each
t ≥ s. p(t) is then the normal probability density function as shown in
Figure 10.3.3.5. Instead of the quantity itself, the factor of proportionality
with its probability of occurrence yields a *stockout quantity coefficient*.[6]

> The *stockout quantity coefficient* P(s) is the factor that, multiplied by the
> standard deviation of demand per lead time, yields the expected stockout
> quantity in dependency on the safety factor s.

The stockout quantity coefficient corresponds to the *service function*, that
is, to the integral of the factor of proportionality (t – s) of the standard
deviation of demand, during lead time for all possible t ≥ s, having the
density function according to the formula in Figure 10.3.4.3.

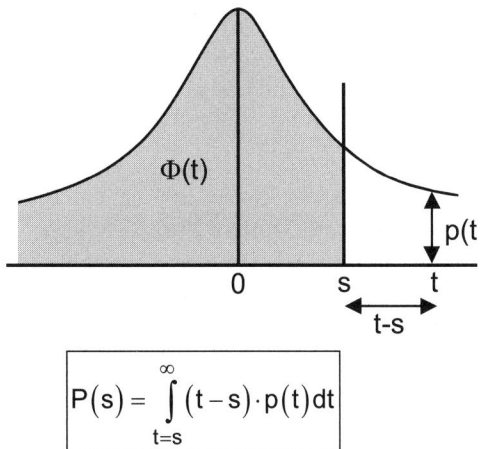

$$P(s) = \int_{t=s}^{\infty} (t-s) \cdot p(t)\,dt$$

Fig. 10.3.4.3   Service function (of the stockout quantity coefficient) P(s) in
dependency upon the safety factor s.

Figure 10.3.4.4 shows examples of corresponding values of safety factor s
and stockout quantity coefficient P(s). The values can be determined by
table look-up; see, for example, tables in [Brow67], p. 110, or [Stev02], p.
569.

---

[6]   This transformation of the quantity m can be confusing: m becomes (t – s) · σ. The
formula for calculating t, belonging to a specific m, is then t(m) = (m + s · σ) / σ.
This unusual method may be one of the reasons why, in the literature, the relation
between service level and fill rate is often explained only superficially or not at all.

Stockout quantity coefficient P(s)	Safety factor s	Service level in %		Service level in %	Safety factor s	Stockout quantity coefficient P(s)
0.8	−0.64	26.11		30	−0.52	0.712
0.4	0	50		50	0	0.399
0.2	0.5	69.15		65	0.385	0.233
0.1	0.9	81.59		80	0.842	0.112
0.05	1.26	89.61		90	1.282	0.048
0.01	1.92	97.26		95	1.645	0.021
0.005	2.18	98.53		98	2.054	0.008
0.001	2.68	99.63		99	2.326	0.003
0.0001	3.24	99.95		99.9	3.090	0.0003

Fig. 10.3.4.4   Safety factor s and stockout quantity coefficient P(s) with normally distributed demand. (Following [Brow67] or [Stev02].)

Thus, the expected stockout quantity per order cycle can be calculated from safety factor s via the stockout quantity coefficient P(s).

According to the definition in Section 4.3.1, the stockout quantity per order cycle is also the product of batch size and stockout percentage (that is, the complement of fill rate). This yields formulas, shown in Figure 10.3.4.5, that relate *service level* to *fill rate*.

Let us look at an example that illustrates the relation between fill rate and service level. Say the batch size is 100 units, and the standard deviation of demand during the lead time is 10 units. What safety stock should be carried to provide a desired fill rate of 99.9%? The stockout quantity coefficient P(s) is 0.01 (Figure 10.3.4.5), and the safety factor is thus 1.92 (Figure 10.3.4.4). Therefore, the resulting safety stock is 1.92 times 10 = 19.2 units (Figure 10.3.3.7).[7]

---

[7]   It is interesting to note that setting a low service level results in a safety factor of less than 0 (as Figure 10.3.4.4 shows).

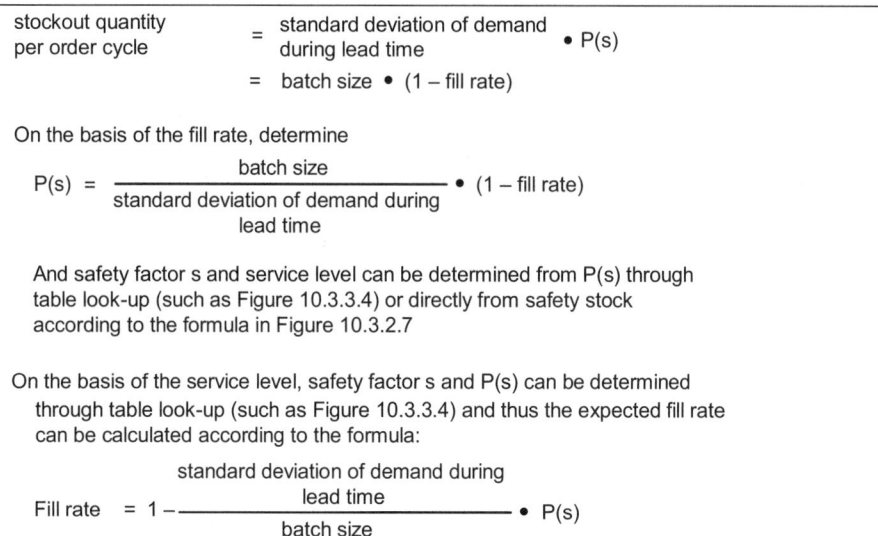

Fig. 10.3.4.5   Relation between fill rate and service level.

Figure 10.3.4.6 shows that the quotient resulting from the standard deviation of demand during lead time divided by batch size (following Figure 10.3.4.5) has a leverage between service level and fill rate. The smaller this quotient is, the higher — at a constant service level — the expected fill rate. That means that with a service level of 50% (that is, no safety stock) and a quotient of 1/5, a fill rate of over 92% is achieved, while with a quotient of 1/10 (as in the example above), the fill rate achieved is about 96%. With a service level of 80%, a quotient of 1/10 results in a fill rate of over 98.8%.

Service level in %	Standard deviation of demand during lead time / batch size	Fill rate in %
50	1/5	92.05
50	1/10	96.01
50	1/100	99.60
50	1/200	99.80
80	1/5	97.76
80	1/10	98.88
80	1/100	99.89
80	1/200	99.94

Fig. 10.3.4.6   Examples of the relation between service level and fill rate.

And finally, consider an example that links stockout costs per unit, via the optimal service level derived using method 1 above, with the fill rate calculated with method 2 above. In this example, annual carrying cost per unit is 1, the batch size is 100, average annual demand is 500, and the standard deviation of demand during the lead time is 10. What is the expected fill rate based on the given carrying cost per unit of 4? The optimum probability of stockout in each order cycle is 0.05 (Figure 10.3.4.2), which results in an optimum service level of 95% following Figure 10.3.3. Following Figure 10.3.4.4, this corresponds to the stockout quantity coefficient P(s) = 0.021. Following Figure 10.3.4.5, this yields a fill rate of 99.79%.

According to the formulas in both method 1 and method 2 above for calculating the desired service level, the service level and safety stock both decrease with increasing batch size. For this reason, it would be desirable to set the batch size as large as possible. For production orders in particular, however, as Chapter 12 will show, the cumulative lead time often grows over-proportionately as batch size increases, making it necessary to apply stochastic models of demand and to include the standard deviation. From this perspective, a small batch size is desirable. In practice, then, batch sizes and safety stock must be determined simultaneously (*de facto* in iteration).

10.4   Batch or Lot Sizing

Batch sizing or *lot sizing* is the process of, or techniques used in, determining batch or lot size ([APIC04]).

10.4.1 Production or Procurement Costs: Batch-Size-Dependent Unit Costs, Setup and Ordering Costs, and Carrying Cost

Lot-size inventory is inventory that results whenever quantity price discounts, shipping costs, setup costs, or similar considerations make it more economical to purchase or produce in larger lots than are needed for immediate purposes ([APIC04]).

Batch sizes that are not specified by the user lead to longer lead times and procurement deadlines and should therefore be avoided, as discussed in Chapter 5. Even so, batch sizes have to be accepted due to setup costs. In this section, we will examine the arguments that tend to favor either smaller or larger batch sizes.

There are *batch-size-dependent production or procurement costs* for every produced or procured unit of measure of the order, that is the *batch-size-dependent unit costs*.

Batch-size-dependent production or procurement costs are:

- In the case of external procurement, acquisition cost per procured unit quantity plus eventual additional costs that are proportional to quantity (for example, customs, shipping, and so on).

- In the case of in-house production, the sum of:

  - Costs of the components needed to produce a unit quantity

  - Standard quantity • batch size • cost rate for internal labor costs, whereby the cost rate generally includes full costs (fixed and variable costs).

Batch-size-independent production or procurement costs are incurred with the order, even with a batch size of one.

Batch-size-independent production or procurement costs are:

- In the case of external procurement, mainly the *ordering costs for procurement*, which are the administrative costs of purchasing divided by the number of purchases. Also:

  - Administrative costs of purchasing also include the costs of receiving stock and stock control.

  - Batch-size-independent procurement costs also include all costs per order that are independent of quantity, such as shipping, handling costs, and so on. In the extreme case, these are dependent upon the suppliers and the delivered items. In order to avoid large volumes of data, however, these costs are often added to purchasing costs.

  Procurement costs can also be tapped by item class, such as according to the ABC classification. This results in varying batch-size-independent procurement costs for each item class (for example, higher costs for A parts than for C parts). For a more precise determination, see Section 9.4 (activity-based costing).

- In the case of in-house production, the costs are mainly:

    - *Ordering costs for production*, that is, the administrative costs of planning & control and other office functions.

    - Possible indirect costs of production that are independent of quantity (transportation, control, putting into and issuing from stock). Usually, they also count as part of the ordering costs.

    - *Setup costs* (= setup load · the cost unit rate for internal labor costs) for the various operations (machine adjustments, tool assembly, start-up process, loss of materials at start-up, and so on). For this, management must decide whether to include full costs or only variable costs (essentially wages) in the calculations; this may influence the batch sizes.

Carrying cost or *holding costs* are all the costs incurred in connection with holding inventory.

Carrying cost rate or *holding cost rate* is the rate for the carrying cost, usually defined as a percentage of the dollar value of inventory per unit of time (generally one year).

See also Section 1.1.2. Carrying cost includes:

- The *costs of financing* or *capital costs:* Inventory stocks tie up financial resources. Calculation using an interest rate yields the costs of immobilizing money in inventory. This rate corresponds:

    - To the percentage of the mean return on investment if the inventories are financed using internal capital resources.

    - To the bank interest rate, if the inventories are financed by a third party. For calculation purposes, take interest rate values between 5 and 15% of the average value of the inventory.

- The *storage infrastructure costs:* These incur for the infrastructure necessary to store a particular product: buildings, installations, warehouse employees, insurance, and so on. The costs for inventory transactions, on the other hand, are seen as ordering costs.

    The first cost driver for storage infrastructure costs is batch size, as enough surface area or volume for the whole batch size must be provided. In a first approach, it is possible to express storage infrastructure costs proportionally, as a percentage related to the average inventory, because the average inventory corresponds —

apart from safety stock — to half of the batch size, according to the formula in Figure 10.3.1.2. More commonly used is a percentage related to the mean inventory value. In the machine tool industry, percentages between 1 and 3% are common.

Further cost drivers are storage type and valuation basis (see Section 10.1.1). The storage infrastructure costs rate can be much higher for inexpensive and voluminous products (insulation materials and other construction materials) than for very expensive and possibly easy-to-store products. For more precise figures, then, the calculation should include at least some separate values, such as for information and documents, raw materials, purchased parts, semifinished goods, and end products. However, there are limits to diversifying storage infrastructure costs into as many different storage unit cost rates as possible, due to the expense:

- Involved in recording the incurred costs per separate category

- For data maintenance, if, for example, a separate storage cost percentage were kept for each item

A large part of these costs is out of proportion to the value of the stored goods. Since warehouses involve specialized constructions, building a warehouse represents a long-term investment. A company will make the investment if it has exhausted existing warehouse volumes. This leads to a jump in costs. On the other hand, reducing inventory value does not automatically lead to a reduction in the personnel needed for warehouse management. Nonetheless, in practice, a proportional relationship is common.

- The *risk of depreciation*: This is again expressed as a percentage of the inventory value and includes:

  - *Technical obsolescence* that results from changes in standards or the emergence of improved products on the market.

  - Expiration due to *perishability:* Certain items can be stored only for a particular, limited period of time (shelf life). This is the case with "living" products such as groceries or biological pharmaceuticals, but also with "non-living" products such as certain electronics items.

  - *Damage, spoilage,* or *destruction* due to unsuitable handling or storage such as, for example, the rusting of sheet metals.

The percentage of the risk of depreciation may be very large under certain circumstances. For short-lived items it must be set at 10%

or more. However, the percentage is generally dependent upon the duration of storage.

It is not unusual for the carrying cost rate to be on the order of 20%. For goods with a high risk of depreciation, it may reach 30% and higher.

10.4.2 Optimum Batch Size and Optimum Length of Order Cycle: The Classic Economic Order Quantity

Most methods for determining batch sizes minimize the expected total costs. In dependency upon batch size, these are essentially composed of the costs mentioned in Section 10.4.1:

1. *Batch-size-dependent unit costs.* Usually the price per produced or procured unit quantity does not change with increasing batch size. However, this is not true in case of allowance for discounts or changes in the production process from a certain batch size upwards

2. *Inventory costs.* These are all the costs incurred in connection with ordering *and* holding inventory. Thus, inventory costs are the following costs:

   a. Setup and ordering costs:

   - These are incurred only once per production or procurement event. In the simplest and most common case, they are independent of the batch size. Thus, the larger the batch size, the smaller is the share in such costs that accrues to each unit.

   - However, there may be an upward jump in costs if a certain batch size requires the choice of another production procurement structure (such as a different machine or means of transport).

   b. Carrying cost:

   - With increasing batch size, the average physical inventory increases, together with carrying cost. For the sake of simplicity, these costs are often set as proportional to batch size, that is, proportional to the value of goods in storage. As was shown in Section 10.4.1, this is of limited validity, however. There are situations where the following assumptions are not valid:

     - The carrying cost is independent of the storage duration.

     - An entry in stock occurs following the issue of the last piece. Issues occur regularly along the time axis. Thus, if X is the batch size, on average X/2 pieces are in stock.

- There is sufficient warehouse space. This means that the size of the batch does not necessitate new installations.

In the simplest case, application of these principles leads to the so-called economic order quantity.

> The *economic order quantity (EOQ)* or the *optimum batch size* or the *economic lot size* is the optimal amount of an item to be purchased or manufactured at one time.

The economic order quantity is calculated with respect to a particular planning period, such as one year. The variables for its calculation are listed in Figure 10.4.2.1.

CU = batch-size-dependent unit costs	$ / unit
CS = setup and ordering costs per production or procurement	$
p = inventory interest rate = i + s + r	1 / year
i = interest rate used in calculating (capital costs)	1 / year
s = storage infrastructure costs rate	1 / year
r = depreciation risk rate	1 / year
X = lot or batch size	unit
AC = annual usage	unit / year
C1 = batch-size-dependent unit costs per year	$ / year
C2 = carrying cost per year	$ / year
C3 = setup and ordering costs per year	$ / year
CT = total costs of production or procurement per year	$ / year

Fig. 10.4.2.1 Variables for the EOQ formula.

The equation for calculating total costs is shown in Figure 10.4.2.2.

$$CT = C1 + C2 + C3,$$
where
$$C1 = AC \cdot CU$$
$$C2 = \frac{X}{2} \cdot \left(CU + \frac{CS}{X} \right) \cdot p \approx \frac{X}{2} \cdot CU \cdot p$$
$$C3 = \frac{AC}{X} \cdot CS$$

Fig. 10.4.2.2 EOQ formula: total costs equation.

Since the objective is to minimize the total costs, the target function is as shown in Figure 10.4.2.3:

CT = min!

Fig. 10.4.2.3   EOQ formula: target function.

The economic order quantity X_0 is the lot size with the minimum of total costs, and it results from deriving the target function and setting it to zero, as shown in Figure 10.4.2.4.

EOQ (economic order quantity) formula is another name for the X_0 formula.

$$\frac{dCT}{dX} = \frac{CU}{2} \cdot p - \frac{AC}{X^2} \cdot CS$$

For the optimum batch size X_0, the following holds:

$$\frac{dCT}{dX} = 0$$

$$\Rightarrow X_0 = \sqrt{\frac{2 \cdot AC \cdot CS}{p \cdot CU}}$$

Fig. 10.4.2.4   EOQ formula: determining the optimum batch size.

Figure 10.4.2.5 shows the cost curves that correspond to the values for C1, C2, C3, and CT as a function of batch sizes.

These cost curves are typical of the EOQ formula. The minimum point for total costs lies exactly at the intersection of the curves for setup and ordering costs and carrying cost.

Instead of an optimum batch size, we can also calculate an optimal time period for which an order or a batch covers demand.

The *optimum order interval* or *optimum length of order cycle* is an optimum period of time for which future demand should be covered.

This length is defined according to the formula in Figure 10.4.2.6. From this formula it is immediately apparent that the optimum length of the order cycle — and the optimum batch size in Figure 10.4.2.4 — rises less than proportionally with increasing setup costs and declines less than proportionally with increasing turnover. Thus, for example, if we set the value for the root of $(2 \cdot CS/p)$ at 40, the characteristic figures for optimum length of order cycle as a function of the value of turnover are those in Figure 10.4.2.7.

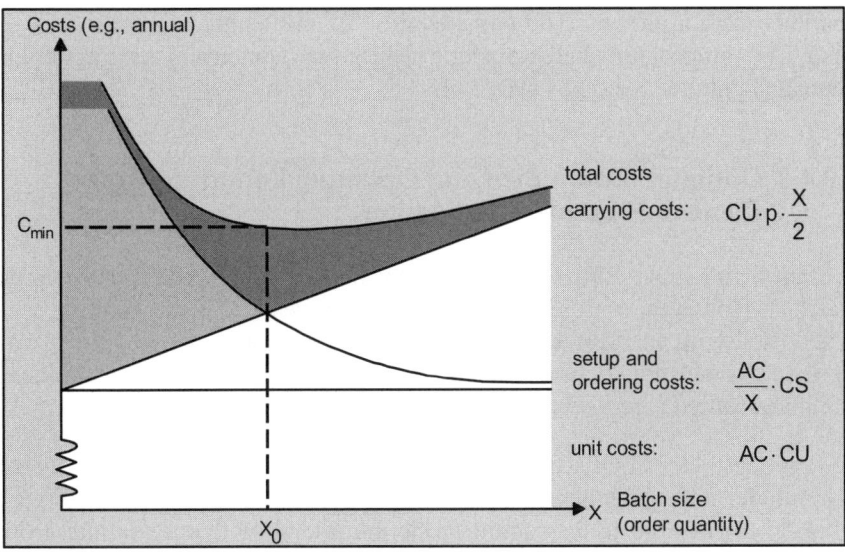

Fig. 10.4.2.5   Cost curves as a function of batch size.

$$LOC_0 = \frac{X_0}{AC} = \sqrt{\frac{2 \cdot CS}{p \cdot CU \cdot AC}} = \sqrt{\frac{2 \cdot CS}{p}} \cdot \frac{1}{\sqrt{C1}}$$

Fig. 10.4.2.6   Optimum length of order cycle.

C1 ($)	LOC_0 (years)
400	2.0
1600	1.0
6400	0.5
25600	0.25

Fig. 10.4.2.7   Sample characteristic figures for length of order cycle as a function of the value of turnover.

Unless we can reduce setup costs decisively, a very large length of order cycle will result in low turnover. In practice, however, when the range of demand coverage is very long, the depreciation risk increases disproportionally. For this reason, upward limits are set for the length of the order cycle, and thus as well for the batch sizes, for items with a small turnover value. This is, incidentally, the simplest and most common method in practice to control non-linear patterns of carrying cost. Carrying cost that jumps steeply when inventory exceeds a particular volume, for example, exhibits such a pattern. The consideration of the length of order cycle is also an important batch-sizing policy in deterministic materials management (see Section 11.4).

10.4.3 Optimum Batch Size and Optimum Length of Order Cycle in Practical Application

Unfairly, the EOQ formula has recently been held responsible for large batches. However, a closer look at practice reveals that the formula was often used with carrying cost unit rates that were much too low, or it was applied to deterministic materials management, for which other techniques are better suited (see Section 11.4).

In any case, the EOQ formula basically provides "only" an order of magnitude, not a precise number. The total costs curve shown in Figure 10.4.2.5 is very flat in the region of the minimum, so that deviations from the optimum batch size have only a very small effect upon costs. The following *sensitivity analysis* shows this "robust" effect. Beginning with a quantity deviation as given in Figure 10.4.3.1, and the fact that the formula in Figure 10.4.3.2 holds for the optimum batch size X_0, the cost deviation formula is shown in Figure 10.4.3.3.

$$v = \frac{X}{X_0} \quad \text{or} \quad v = \frac{X_0}{X}$$

Fig. 10.4.3.1   Sensitivity analysis: quantity deviation.

$$a \equiv \frac{X_0}{2} \cdot CU \cdot p \equiv \frac{AC}{X_0} \cdot CS$$

Fig. 10.4.3.2   Sensitivity analysis: carrying cost rates for optimum batch size.

$$b = \frac{C2 + C3}{C2_0 + C3_0} = \frac{\dfrac{v \cdot X_0}{2} \cdot CU \cdot p + \dfrac{AC}{v \cdot X_0} \cdot CS}{\dfrac{X_0}{2} \cdot CU \cdot p + \dfrac{AC}{X_0} \cdot CS} =$$

$$= \frac{v \cdot a + \dfrac{1}{v} a}{2a} = \frac{v + \dfrac{1}{v}}{2}$$

Fig. 10.4.3.3   Sensitivity analysis: cost deviation.

For example, a cost deviation of b = 10% results for v = 64% as well as for v = 156%, which means that the relationship shown in Figure 10.4.3.4 is valid:

$$64\% \leq v \leq 156\% \Rightarrow b \leq 10\%$$

Fig. 10.4.3.4   Sensitivity analysis: quantity deviation given a cost deviation of 10%.

This sensitivity analysis reveals the surprising robustness of the calculation technique, which indeed rests on very simplified assumptions. Extending batch size formulas to include additional influencing factors produces an improvement in results that is practically relevant only in special cases. In any event, we may round off the calculated batch size, adapt it to practical considerations and, in particular, make it smaller if a shorter lead time is desirable.

This robustness increases even further if we include not only C2 and C3, but also the actual costs of production or procurement C1 in the division for b given in Figure 10.4.3.3. If C1 is much larger than C2 + C3 — which is usually the case — even bigger changes to batch size do not have a strong effect upon the total production or procurement costs.

In a similar way, we can show that errors in determining setup and ordering costs, the carrying cost rates, or the annual consumption in the cost deviations make as little difference as a quantity deviation does. Among other things, the EOQ formula is thus not very sensitive to systematic forecast errors. This means that very simple forecasting techniques, such as moving average value calculation, will generally suffice when determining batch sizes.

In the case of produced items, the reduction in costs for in-process inventory achieved through smaller batches is thus negligible in most cases. Much more significant is the fact that smaller batches may lead to *shorter lead time*. In addition to this improvement in the target area of delivery, there are also positive effects in the target area of flexibility and on important aspects in the target area of costs. The positive effects discussed in Chapter 5 are lacking in the classic EOQ formula. However, as we will show in Section 12.2, smaller batches only result in shorter lead time if:

- The run time is long in relation to the lead time, particularly in line production (in classic job shop production this proportion is likely to be of the order of magnitude of 1:10 and less).

- The saturation of a work center does not have the effect of creating longer queues for the entire collection of batches.

Thus, the longer the run times — often required when much value is added — the higher the costs for goods in process are. In such cases we should choose rather lower values for batch sizes than those recommended on the basis of the EOQ formula (see also lead-time-oriented batch sizing in Section 10.4.4). For work-intensive operations especially, shorter operation times can contribute to harmonizing the content of work, which in turn leads to a further reduction in wait times, and thus lead times, as explained in Section 12.2.2. As Figure 5.2.5.2 illustrated, at lower production structure levels a reduction in lead time is likely to result in lower safety stocks, and thus *cost savings*. If for some reason storage is not possible at all, shorter lead times can even achieve additional sales.

A practical implementation scheme, which takes both total costs *and* short lead time into account, is provided in Figure 10.4.3.5.

1. Determine the optimum batch size using the EOQ formula by using a sufficiently large carrying cost rate. For not fully utilized work centers, consider only variable costs (essentially wages) in the calculations.

2. If production is not fully utilized: Due to the low cost sensitivity of the EOQ formula at the optimum, we can vary the batch sizes generously by x % where x is variable for every item category and can be chosen freely to be on an order of magnitude of 64 to 156%.

3. For manufactured articles, we should instead round off the batch sizes. In the case of large run times and larger value added, we may also choose a smaller percentage due to the effects of shorter lead times, even less than 50% under certain circumstances.

4. Include differentiated considerations concerning the minimum and maximum (see below).

Fig. 10.4.3.5   Practical implementation of the EOQ formula.

The *minimum order quantity* (or *maximum order quantity*) is an order quantity modifier, applied after the lot size has been calculated, that increases (or limits) the order quantity to a pre-established minimum (or maximum) ([APIC04]).

Differentiated considerations concerning the minimum and maximum order quantity can be found in Figure 10.4.3.6, as for example related to item groups or even individual items.

> - Space requirements in warehouse (maximum)
> - Length of order cycle (maximum)
> - Product shelf life: obsolescence, perishability (maximum)
> - Blocking of machine capacities (maximum)
> - Limits of tool use (maximum)
> - Liquidity problem (maximum)
> - For purchased items: shortages or price increases to be expected (minimum)
> - For purchased items: minimum order volumes (minimum)
> - Coordination with transport and storage units (maximum or minimum)

Fig. 10.4.3.6   Several factors that influence a maximum or minimum order quantity.

In the literature there are models that take additional operating conditions into consideration. We will present several of these in Section 10.4.4. Due to its simplicity, however, the EOQ formula is used frequently in current practice. Even if the simplified model assumptions that underlie it are not given in the concrete case, the formula is very robust in the face of such deviations, as we have shown. Before applying another, more complicated calculation method, materials management should clarify whether the more costly batch size determination truly offers crucial advantages over the simple implementation considerations outlined above.

10.4.4 Extensions of the Batch Size Formula (*)

> 1. *Lead-time-oriented batch sizing* is a generalization of the simplified approach using the EOQ formula for production, taking the cost of work in process into consideration.

As a complement to the variables in Figure 10.4.2.1, we add the variables shown in Figure 10.4.4.1. Most of these data come from the route sheet.

CU_M = materials costs per unit	\$ / unit
FD = flow degree = lead time / operation time	dimensionless
SUMRT = sum of run times per unit = $\sum_{1 \le i \le n} RT[i]$	working days / unit
NBRWKD = number of working days per year	working days / year

Fig. 10.4.4.1   Additional variables for lead-time-oriented batch sizing.

The EOQ results according to the formula given in Figure 10.4.4.2. For details of the derivation, see [Nyhu91], p.103. The denominator under the radical is significantly larger than the one in classic batch sizing only for a long manufacturing lead time.

$$\Rightarrow X_0 = \sqrt{\frac{2 \cdot AC \cdot CS}{p \cdot \left(CU + (CU + CU_M) \cdot AC \cdot FD \cdot \frac{SUMRT}{NBRWKD}\right)}}$$

Fig. 10.4.4.2   Lead-time-oriented batch sizing: determination of the minimum.

2. Batch size formation considering discount levels is a generalization of the simplified approach using the EOQ formula.

Figure 10.4.4.3 illustrates the decreasing batch-size-dependent unit costs as a function of the lot size, as well as the resulting total costs curves.

Batch-size-dependent unit costs CU are dependent upon the purchased quantity. This is particularly valid for procured goods.

A *quantity discount* is a price reduction allowance on orders over a certain minimal order quantity or value.

For example, a supplier may offer a quantity discount for the whole order quantity, as soon as this quantity exceeds X_m2. This results in reduced batch-size-dependent unit costs (CU2).

Every total costs curve for the various values of cost per piece demonstrates a minimum within the range of its validity. This is either the minimum of the corresponding total costs curve (X_02 in Figure 10.4.4.3), or it lies on the border of a discount level curve (X_m3 in Figure 10.4.4.3). If discounts are not large, we may also argue that the batch sizes for the different discount levels according to the EOQ formula will lie very close to each other. We may thus calculate the optimum batch size by selecting a particular mean cost per piece, and then rounding it up to the next discount level.

A similar line of thinking is followed when evaluating economical efficiency and batch sizing in the case of alternative (less expensive) production processes using larger batch sizes.

3. Joint replenishment is joint planning for a group of related items, treating them as an item family.

Two examples of management of sets of items follow.

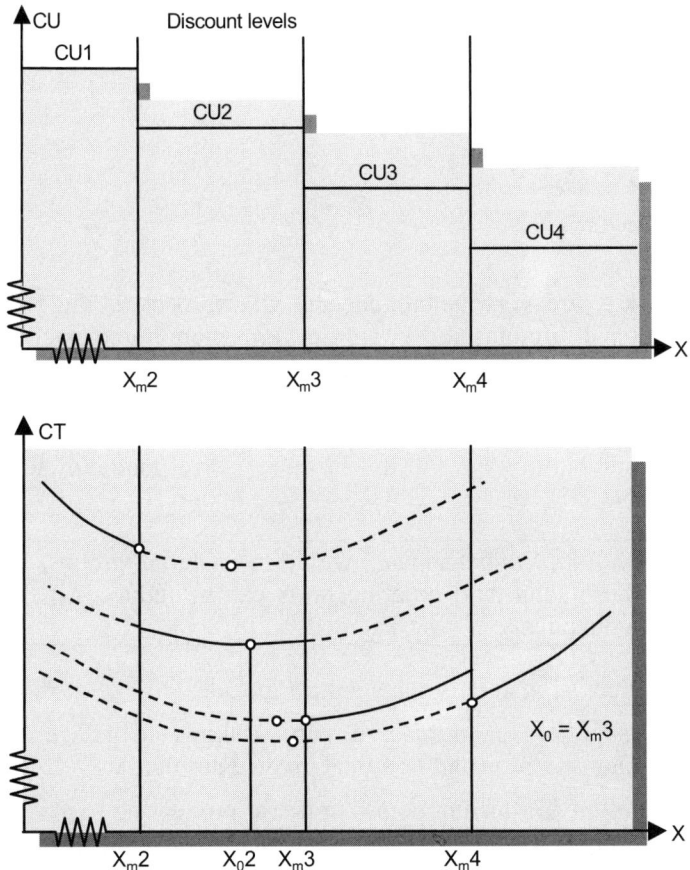

Fig. 10.4.4.3   Total costs curves, taking discount levels into consideration.

3a. In *kit materials management*, various goods are combined into a so-called *(material) kit* (because of their joint use in particular assemblies or products) and managed as a group.

The individual optimum batch size for an element i from a kit S with annual consumption AC of S results from the formula in Figure 10.4.4.4.

$$M_i := \text{Number of parts per element } i \text{ in kit S}$$

$$X_i = \sqrt{\frac{2 \cdot M_i \cdot AC_S \cdot CS_i}{p \cdot CU_i}} = \sqrt{\frac{2 \cdot AC_S}{p}} \cdot \sqrt{\frac{M_i \cdot CS_i}{CU_i}}$$

Fig. 10.4.4.4   Individual optimum batch sizes for an element i of kit S with annual consumption AC_S.

Instead of these individual batch sizes, we may determine a kit batch size X_S using the compromise formula in Figure 10.4.4.5.

$$X_S = \sqrt{\frac{2 \cdot AC_S}{p}} \cdot \sqrt{\frac{\sum (M_i \cdot CS_i)}{\sum CU_i}}$$

Fig. 10.4.4.5   Kit batch size X_S.

If the component kits are very heterogeneous with respect to the two factors in the batch size formulas above, we can form more homogeneous planning subgroups that are then used for separate batch sizings. Another possibility is to form an economic batch for the most value-intensive components. We then set the batch size of less value-intensive materials positions as whole-number multiples of this batch for correspondingly less frequent procurement.

3b. In *collective materials management*, we form material groups, or planning groups, whose setup and ordering costs can be reduced, if the batches are ordered collectively.

Valid criteria for collective materials management include:

- The same supplier for purchased parts (taking advantage of simplified administration and/or a total invoice discount)
- The same production technique for in-house production (e.g., for one product family), whereby simplified machine setup achieves a reduction in the total setup costs

In the case of collective materials management, within a planning group materials managers must determine an average reduction in the setup and ordering costs as a percentage. As soon as an item is to be ordered, a check is made of all other items of the same planning group. If the order of a batch is due in the near future anyway, it can be ordered now through an *early order release*. This should be a reduced batch size, which is calculated by using the reduced setup and ordering costs.

10.5   Summary

Inventories form buffers for logistics within and among organizations. Inventory management is thus another important instrument for planning & control. Categorizing and typing storage and warehouses facilitates detailed inventory management. A physical inventory count of stored and in-process inventory verifies the accuracy of book inventories as a prerequisite of accurate inventory valuation.

An important basis for various calculations in demand forecasting and in materials management is provided by statistics that analyze particular events such as inventory transactions, sales, and bid activities. These statistics contain information on quantities and values as well as on the number of transactions.

The ABC classification according to various measures of value, such as turnover, determines the importance of items in a product line. For this, the item range is first divided into different ABC categories. The XYZ classi-fication distinguishes items with regular or even continuous demand from those with lumpy/erratic or discontinuous or unique demand. Additional statistics sort out items that are exceptions according to some criterion.

Stochastic materials management aims to produce production or procurement proposals prior to actual demand resulting from customer orders. In most cases, a demand forecast is the sole basis for both the proposed quantity (the batch) and the proposed time of receipt.

The most familiar technique for stochastic materials management — particularly for continuous demand — is the order point technique. The order point is the expected value of demand during the lead time. Safety stock is carried to absorb deviations from the expected value, and safety lead time, which is also translated into a safety quantity, is used to absorb deviations from the lead time. If forecast parameters change, both order point and safety stock must be recalculated.

In the simplest case, materials management determines the batch size that will yield a minimum of setup and ordering costs and carrying cost. However, in the *stochastic case* there is as yet no concrete customer demand, so that the optimum batch size can only be derived (the economic order quantity EOQ) from a long-term forecast of total demand. In the final reckoning, however, this calculated quantity merely indicates the order of magnitude, and thus it can be rounded up or down generously. The order of magnitude is robust in the face of errors in quantity or cost forecasts. However, the formula does not take into account the effects of shorter lead times with smaller batches. In practice, other constraints exert an important influence on the final selection of minimum or maximum batch size. These include storage space requirements, storability, minimum order volumes, speculation, and so forth. Extensions to the simple batch size formula arise when taking into account lead time, quantity discounts, and kit or collective management.

10.6   Keywords

ABC category, 544
ABC classification, 542
abnormal demand, 541
anticipation horizon, 549
average inventory, 547
batch sizing, 564
bid statistics, 542
carrying cost, 566
carrying cost rate, 566
cycle counting, 539
double order point system, 550
economic order quantity (EOQ), 569
fixed-location storage, 533
inventory accounting, 537
inventory adjustment, 537
inventory costs, 568
inventory issuance principle, 533
inventory valuation, 537

issuance principle, 533
lot sizing, 564
lot-size inventory, 564
maximum order quantity, 574
minimum order quantity, 574
min–max (reorder) system, 550
multiple stock organization, 532
optimum length of order cycle, 570
optimum probability of stockout, 559
optimum service level, 560
order point, 547
order point technique, 546
Pareto analysis, 542
periodic inventory, 538
perpetual inventory, 534
physical inventory, 537

random-location storage, 533
replenishment lead time, 546
replenishment order quantity, 546
safety factor, 554
safety lead time, 552
safety stock, 551
sales statistics, 541
service function, 554
service level, 553
setup costs, 566
single stock organization, 532
stock organization, 532
stockkeeping unit (SKU), 531
stockout costs, 559
turnover statistics, 540
unordered issuance principle, 533
usage statistics, 540
valuation method, 533
XYZ classification, 545

10.7 Scenarios and Exercises

10.7.1 The ABC Classification

This exercise refers to Section 10.2.2. Perform an ABC classification for the items shown in the table in Figure 10.7.1.1, separately for two ABC categories 1 and 2. Class A accounts for 75% of sales turnover, and items in the B class account for 90% of turnover. Why does it often make sense to perform separate classifications for two or more ABC categories? Is your classification of the items as A, B, or C the only possible solution?

Item ID	Sales ($)	ABC category
4310	10	1
4711	1	2
5250	0	2
6830	6	2
7215	30	1
7223	2	1
7231	84	1

Item ID	Sales ($)	ABC category
8612	70	1
8620	13	2
8639	1	2
8647	3	2
8902	4	1
8910	0	1
9050	1	2

Fig. 10.7.1.1   Sales and ABC categories of some items.

Solution:

ABC category	Item ID	Sales ($)	Sales cumulated	% Share on cum. sales	ABC classification
1	7231	84	84	42	A
	8612	70	154	77	A
	7215	30	184	92	B
	4310	10	194	97	C
	8902	4	198	99	C
	7223	2	200	100	C
	8910	0	200	100	C
2	8620	13	13	52	A
	6830	6	19	76	A
	8647	3	22	88	B
	4711	1	23	92	B
	8639	1	24	96	C
	9050	1	25	100	C
	5250	0	25	100	C

The division of the items into two categories for a meaningful ABC classification is necessary so that like items can be compared; the categories will
reflect different types of items, such as individual parts and final products.

The classifications in the solution above do not represent the only possible
solution. Certain classifications can be problematic around the break
points. For example, why should item 4711 receive the classification B,
while items 8639 and 9050 are assigned to classification C?

10.7.2 Combined ABC–XYZ Classification

A combined ABC–XYZ classification allows decision making as to the
appropriate method of materials management for individual items. Mark
the areas (items) in the matrix in Figure 10.7.2.1 for which kanban control
would be appropriate. Explain the reasoning behind your answer.

Continuousness of demand	Consumption value		
	A High	B Medium	C Low
X High	high value continuous demand	medium value continuous demand	low value continuous demand
Y Medium	high value regular, or fluctuating demand	medium value regular, or fluctuating demand	low value regular, or fluctuating demand
Z Low	high value discontinuous demand	medium value discontinuous demand	low value discontinuous demand

Fig. 10.7.2.1   Combined ABC–XYZ classification.

Solution:

The prerequisite for the kanban technique is continuous demand along the entire value chain. X items are particularly suitable for production in a kanban system. For the Y group, A items should not be controlled by kanban, for their consumption value is high, and fluctuating demand leads to lower stock-inventory turnover and thus longer storage time. For the same reason, kanban control is as a rule not appropriate for Z items, whereby an exception can be made for C items, as carrying costs for C items may be lower than the costs of a more expensive control technique.

10.7.3 Safety Stock Variation versus Demand Variation

True or false: The safety stock level increases with increasing demand.

Solution:

As the formula in Figure 10.3.3.7 shows, this statement is generally not correct. The safety stock depends on the *standard deviation* of the demand during the lead time. Increasing demand does not automatically increase either the standard deviation during the statistical period or the lead time.

10.7.4 Batch Size Depending on Stockout Costs (*)

The carrying costs for a certain article are 2 per unit and year. Stockout costs are 5 per unit. The average annual consumption amounts to 1000, and the standard deviation of demand during lead time is 10. No safety stock is intended. Normal distribution is assumed.

a. How large should the batch size be, considering the optimum stockout probability? Can the fill rate target of 99% be met? What are the carrying costs per year?

b. Assume a batch size of only 250. What are the values for safety stock and fill rate corresponding to the optimum probability of stockout per order cycle?

c. Now assume a safety stock of 20 units. Again, the batch size is 250. What are the values for service level and fill rate?

Solution:

a. Zero safety stock entails a service level of 50% (see Figure 10.3.3.6, for example) and — by Figure 10.3.3.3 — a probability of stockout per order cycle of 50%. Because stockout can be expressed as cost per unit, the formulas in Figures 10.3.4.2, 10.3.4.4, and 10.3.4.5 apply. Therefore,

- Batch size = 1000 * 50% * (5/2) = 1250.
- Stockout quantity coefficient P(s) = 0.399.
- → Fill rate = 1 − ((10/1250) * 0.399) = 99.68% > 99%.
- Average inventory = 1250/2 = 625.
- → Carrying costs per year = 625 * 2 = 1250.

b. Again, the formulas in Figures 10.3.4.2, 10.3.4.4, and 10.3.4.5 apply:
- Optimum probability of stockout = (2/5) * (250/1000) = 10%.
- → Optimum service level = 1 − 10 % = 90%.
- → Safety stock = 1.282 * 10 {note: the standard deviation} ≈ 13.
- → Stockout quantity coefficient P(s) = 0.048.
- → Fill rate = 1 − ((10/250) * 0.048) = 99.81%.

c. Applying the formulas in Figures 10.3.4.4, 10.3.4.2, and 10.3.4.5:
- Standard deviation = 10; => safety factor = 20/10 = 2.
- → Service level ≈ 98%.
- → Stockout quantity coefficient P(s) = 0.008.
- → Fill rate = 1 − ((10/250) * 0.008) = 99.97%.

10.7.5 Effectiveness of the Order Point Technique

Figure 10.3.1.1 shows the famous saw-tooth shaped curve that is characteristic of the order point technique. You can view the curve on the Internet, implemented with Flash animation, at the following URL:

http://www.intlogman.lim.ethz.ch/order_point_technique.html

Explore the changing shape of the inventory curve for continuous and less continuous demand (moving your cursor over the gray icon executes your input choice). Try out different parameters to calculate lot size and service level. Try other consumption values. Observe the effect of the consumption values on the order of the production or procurement batch size. Again, touching the "calculate" icon executes your input choice. The initial demand values are automatically reentered by moving your cursor over the gray demand shape icon.

11 Deterministic Materials Management

Deterministic techniques are used in materials management whenever portions of the cumulative lead time remain within the customer tolerance time. This is the case, for example, with the assembly stage during the manufacture of capital goods. During this time, production, procurement or services are dependent upon customer demand. Figure 11.0.0.1 shows the relevant planning & control tasks and processes on a dark background. They refer back to the reference model in Figure 4.1.4.2.

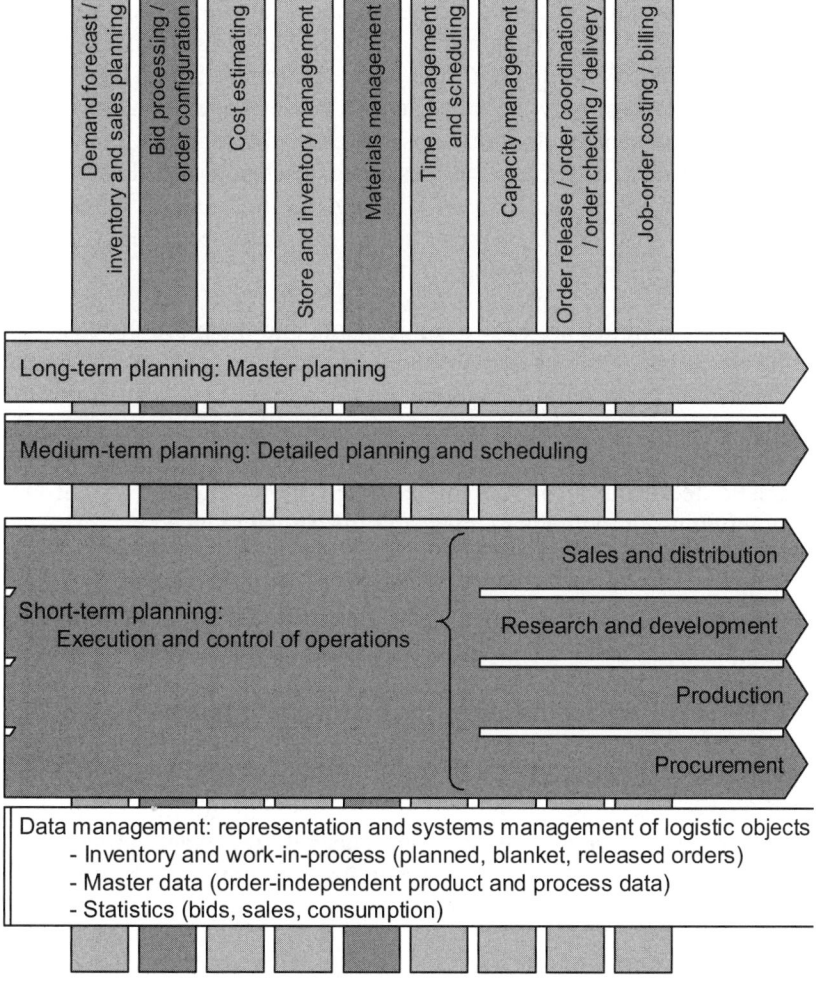

Fig. 11.0.0.1   The parts of the system discussed in Chapter 11 are shown against a darker background.

Sections 4.3.1 and 4.3.2, in particular Figures 4.3.2.1 / 4.3.2.2, provide an introduction to the material in this chapter.[1]

So called quasideterminstic techniques are used in a stochastic case, which is upstream from or on the order penetration point. For high-cost discontinuous dependent demand, the purely stochastic techniques outlined in Chapter 10 carry the risk that procured goods may not be used in time or that excessively large safety stock levels will have to be maintained. Quasideterministic materials management is also used for long-term planning, particularly for budgeting personnel and other resources and for determining blanket contracts.

Section 4.2 presented deterministic techniques for *long-term* materials management. The present chapter sets out the techniques for medium and short-term planning. What distinguishes these techniques is that the demand for an item cannot simply be regarded as an average demand that is approximately constant over time, as is the case in long-term planning or stochastic materials management as described in Chapter 10. Instead, you know the exact point or limited period along the time axis at which each requirement will arise and then make use of this knowledge. This enables you to manage even lumpy demand efficiently.

Deterministic techniques are easy to understand, and the more the customer is willing to accept a longer delivery lead time, the easier they are to use. This is particularly true in a manufacturer's market, but also holds for production or procurement orders that are customer specific, e.g., for in special mechanical engineering and plant construction or in services. Also, deterministic techniques can be implemented more often if — through carefully thought-out methods — the lead time can be reduced.

11.1   Demand and Available Inventory along the Time Axis

Both long-term management of resources, as outlined in Section 4.2.2, and stochastic materials management allow the demand for an item to be regarded as a scalar variable, i.e., as a total, because the exact time at which the demand arises is either not relevant or was not the object of the

---

[1]   We recommend that you read Sections 4.3.1 and 4.3.2 again before continuing to study this chapter.

estimate. What is estimated is the requirement quantity over a given time period. Thus, the shorter the selected period, the greater the scatter. At this level of inaccuracy, it is more sensible to assume that demand is uniformly distributed across the entire period.

However, when the exact point in time at which demand will occur within the customer tolerance time is known, it makes sense to utilize this information. Instead of relying on the order point technique, (see Section 10.3), which only takes stock levels into account, you can now also consider future demand and deliveries.

> *Time phasing* is a technique that divides the future time axis into time periods and considers stock levels for any desired point in the future [APIC04].
>
> *Time bucket* is the chosen period for time phasing. It contains all relevant planning data summarized into a columnar display (for example, a weekly or monthly time bucket).
>
> *Time-phased order point (TPOP)* is a concept that was used in the early version of the MRP (material requirements planning) technique as described in Section 13.1.2.

Considering time periods makes the technique easier to teach and learn. Also, calculation of the technique by hand is such a time-consuming procedure that it makes sense to produce a rough calculation according to time periods. This also held in the early days of logistics software, when access to the data media was very slow. Today, however, software packages produce calculations that are accurate at the event level.

The projected available inventory calculation described below forms the basis for deterministic materials management.

11.1.1 Projected Available Inventory

> *Physical inventory* is the actual inventory quantity determined by physical counting ([APIC04]).[2]
>
> Physical inventory is often also called *stock on hand* or *on-hand balance*.[3]

---

[2]   This is one of two possible meanings. The other meaning is the process of determination of inventory quantity. See Section 10.3.1.

Precise physical inventories on their own are not enough to allow efficient inventory management, as the following example shows:

- "A customer orders a certain quantity of a product for delivery in one week's time. A check of the inventory shows that there is sufficient stock, and the order is confirmed. One week later, however, it emerges that the product cannot be delivered, because in the meantime the stock has been delivered to another customer."

Solving the problem requires taking future demand into consideration.

An *allocated quantity* is a quantity of items assigned to a specific customer or production order. It is also known as *reserved quantity*.

- A quantity ordered in a new customer order is thus not only compared against the physical inventory. It must also be compared against the physical inventory minus the sum of all reserved quantities. The customer requirements in question may only be confirmed if the result is sufficiently large.

On the other hand, it is also necessary to take quantities ordered through current *procurement orders* or *production orders* into account.

An *open order* is either a released order or an unfilled customer order.

An *open order quantity* is the quantity of an open order that has not yet been delivered or received.

A *scheduled receipt* is the open order quantity of an open production or procurement order with an assigned completion date.

- The customer demand in question can thus be confirmed on the date of the next scheduled receipt, provided that this date is sufficiently reliable and the expected quantity is sufficiently large.

This example gives us a definition for projected available inventory.

Projected available inventory or *projected available balance* is defined in Figure 11.1.1.1 for every future transaction or event that changes stock levels. The calculation also includes the *planned demand*, i.e., the requirement for planned customer or production orders and *planned receipts*, i.e., (anticipated) receipts associated with production or procurement orders that have not yet been released.

---

[3] In practice, for the following calculations, physical inventory is often replaced by book inventory, assumed to be more or less accurate.

Projected available inventory$(t)=$

  Physical inventory $+\left(\sum \text{scheduled receipts}\right)(t)-\left(\sum \text{allocated qty.}\right)(t)$

  $+\left(\sum \text{planned order receipts}\right)(t)-\left(\sum \text{planned gross requirements}\right)(t)$

where

$\left(\sum \text{scheduled receipts}\right)(t)$	$:=$	the sum of all scheduled receipts where date of receipt $\leq$ transaction date.
$\left(\sum \text{allocated qty.}\right)(t)$	$:=$	the sum of all allocated quantities where issue date $\leq$ transaction date.
$\left(\sum \text{planned order receipts}\right)(t)$	$:=$	the sum of all planned order receipts where date of receipt $\leq$ transaction date.
$\left(\sum \text{planned gross requirements}\right)(t):=$		the sum of all planned gross requirements where issue date $\leq$ transaction date.

Fig. 11.1.1.1   Projected available inventory.

Projected available inventory is thus neither a scalar value nor an individually and directly manageable attribute. It changes with every planning-related event. Figure 11.1.1.2 shows the various planning processes or planning-related events or transactions that change the values of the four totals and may also change the physical inventory (see also Figure 10.1.2.1):

Transaction	Physical inventory	Σ Scheduled receipts	Σ Allocated quantity	Σ Planned demand	Σ Planned receipts
1. Increase in production plan				+	
2. Receipt of customer order			+		
3. Delivery of customer order	–		–	(–)	
4. Creation of a planned order					+
5. Creation of dependent demand				+	
6. Release of an order		+			(–)
7. Allocation of a components requirement			+	(–)	
8. Issue of an allocated quantity from stock	–		–		
9. Unplanned return or issue	+/–				
10. Scrapping during production		–			
11. Checking of goods received	+		–		
12. Inventory adjustment	+/–				

Fig. 11.1.1.2   Planning-related events and their effect on available inventory.

1. *Increase in production plan:* Every forecast is a planned demand.

2. *Receipt of a customer order:* Every item ordered results in an allocated quantity.

3. *Delivery of a customer order:* Stock quantity is reduced. Reserved quantity and, if necessary, a forecast quantity are also reduced (see also Section 11.2.2).

4. *Creation of a planned production or procurement order:* The planned receipts total is increased.

5. *Creation of (dependent) demand for each component of a planned production order:* The total of planned demand is increased (see also Section 11.3.3).

6. *Release of a production or procurement order:* The scheduled receipts total is increased. If the order already exists as a planned order, then the planned receipts quantity is reduced.

7. *Allocation of a components requirement*: Planned demand in planned production orders is translated into allocated quantities.

8. *Removal of an allocated quantity from stock:* The stock quantity and the allocated quantities total are reduced when an allocated quantity is issued or removed from stock.

9. *Unplanned returns or issues*: Such transactions occur during distribution and procurement, as well as during production. They may relate to equipment overheads for offices and workshops or to items for research and development, or may be sent as samples, and so on.

10. *Scrapping during production:* Quality control determines the scrap quantity, which reduces scheduled receipts.

11. *Checking of goods received:* Physical receipts into stock raise the stock quantity and reduce the scheduled receipts total.

12. *Physical inventory* alters the stock quantity in both directions.

It is important that available inventory be changed by only one of the transactions listed above. For this reason, the physical inventory or the four summed quantities are never simply corrected. This conforms to the principles of financial accounting, which in turn adhere to the legal requirements.

11.1.2 Projected Available Inventory Calculation

As described above, projected available inventory changes with every transaction, so there are as many projected available inventory figures as there are transactions for one item.

> The *projected available inventory calculation* considers future changes in the projected available inventory, beyond a time horizon that incorporates at least the cumulative lead time.
>
> The *inventory curve* is another term for the graphical representation of the projected available inventory calculation.

Figure 11.1.2.1 shows the conventional graphical representation, the spreadsheet, depicting the availability of an item along the time axis. It generally takes the following form:

Date	Entry	Issue	Balance	Text	Order ID
06.01.			1200	Physical inventory	
06.19.		500	700	Bernard	26170
07.31.	3000		3700	Stock replenishment	86400
08.02.		300	3400	Dow	27812
08.04.		2500	900	Sosa	26111
08.18.	3000		3900	Stock replenishment	87800
08.19.		2000	1900	Thomas	26666
09.24.		1000	900	Zoeller	25810

Fig. 11.1.2.1   Projected available inventory calculation (spreadsheet representation).

- The first row provides the current physical inventory.
- The other rows list the various transactions one after the other, in ascending order of transaction date. Quantities received and issued are recorded in the second and third columns. The fourth column shows the balance, that is, the quantity available after the transaction. The other columns describe the transactions.

Example problem: Using the spreadsheet in Figure 11.1.2.1 describing a possible actual situation for projected available inventory calculation, find an answer for the following important questions:

• What partial quantity is available on a particular date? The aim here is to determine the minimum available quantity — starting from the specified date.

• When will the entire quantity be available? Identify the earliest date after which the available quantity will no longer be smaller than the required quantity.

The contents of the graph shown in Figure 11.1.2.2 are exactly the same as in Figure 11.1.2.1. This qualitative view, however, allows fast, intuitive answers to the two questions addressed above. The necessary planning decisions can be made in a fraction of the time required when viewing the spreadsheet version.

The projected available inventory calculation presented in this section corresponds to the calculation of the ATP quantity (available-to-promise) presented in Section 4.2.4.

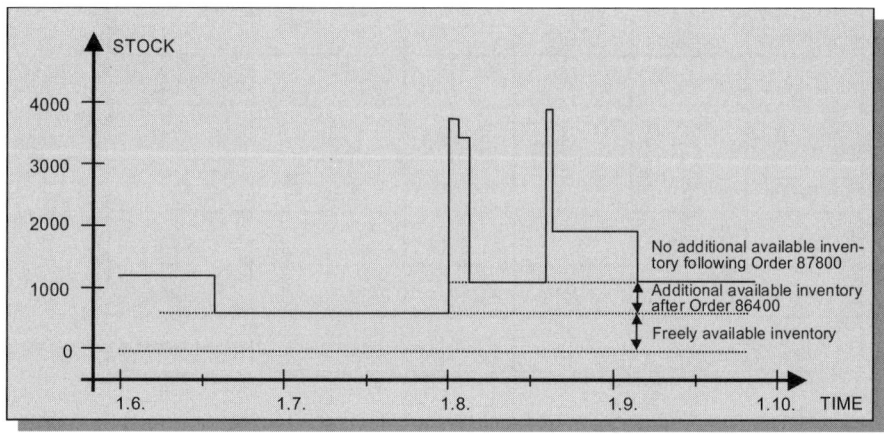

Fig. 11.1.2.2   Projected available inventory calculation (graph) or inventory curve.

11.1.3 Scheduling and Cumulative Projected Available Inventory Calculation

The *scheduling projected available inventory calculation* attempts to assign the associated scheduled or planned receipt to every requirement.

Figure 11.1.3.1 shows the previous example using this type of calculation, where customer order 25810 has been moved forward to June 10.

*	Date	Entry	Issue	Balance	Text	Order ID
	06.01.			1200	Physical inventory	
	06.10.		1000	200	Zoeller	25810
*	07.31.	3000		3200	Stock replenishment	86400
	06.19.		500	2700	Bernard	26170
	08.02.		300	2400	Dow	27812
*	08.18.	3000		5400	Stock replenishment	87800
	08.04.		2500	2900	Sosa	26111
	08.19.		2000	900	Thomas	26666

Fig. 11.1.3.1   Scheduling projected available inventory calculation (spreadsheet).

Again, demands are listed in order by date. Receipts, on the other hand, are sorted by the date on which they will be needed in order to have projected available inventory. The following situations result in lists of exceptions (only the first one appears in Fig. 11.1.3.1):

- A demand can only be covered by bringing forward a corresponding receipt. Two receipts of this kind indicated by an asterisk (*) in the first column in Figure 11.1.3.1.

- A receipt can be deferred, since the associated requirements have a later date than the date of the receipt.

- There are demands without corresponding receipts, so an order proposal should be generated.

- Planned or released orders without assigned demands may be canceled, if necessary.

Thus, the scheduling projected available inventory calculation also creates a link between materials management and scheduling by providing proposals to speed up or slow down production or procurement orders.

Conversely, if the production or procurement orders cannot be speeded up, the scheduling projected available inventory calculation indicates which requirements will have to be delayed. The orders associated with these demands should then be slowed down temporarily and then speeded up again as soon as the demands become available.

The scheduling projected available inventory calculation can also be shown in graph form. The graph in Figure 11.1.3.2 has the same contents as the spreadsheet in Figure 11.1.3.1. Negative projected available inventory corresponds to a backlog and is shaded accordingly, and the two extreme responses — delaying an allocated quantity or speeding up a production or procurement order — are shown as examples.

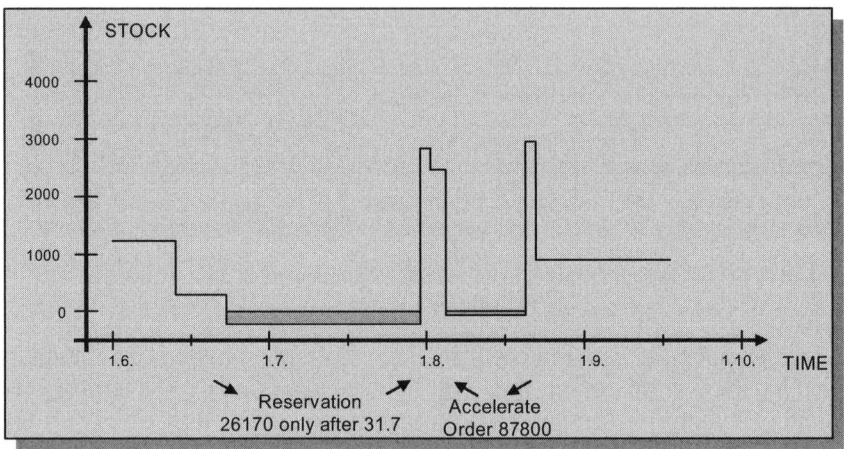

Fig. 11.1.3.2   The scheduling projected available inventory calculation (graph).

The *cumulative projected available inventory calculation* contains the same information as the non-cumulative calculation, but it also provides the cumulative totals for entries and issues along the time axis.

Store throughput diagram is another name for the graphical representation resulting from the cumulative projected available inventory calculation.

This is illustrated in Figure 11.1.3.3. It is more difficult to represent, because the values along the vertical axis are sometimes very large.

The expected projected available inventory is shown as a vertical difference. If the cumulative issues curve is higher than the cumulative receipts curve, then we should expect a negative projected available inventory. This will correspond to the expected backlog and is again shaded accordingly.

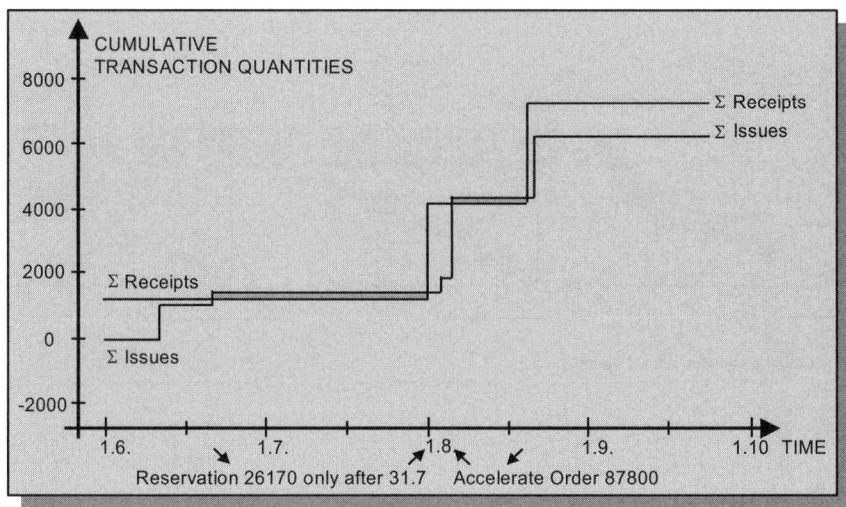

Fig. 11.1.3.3   The cumulative projected available inventory calculation (graph) or store throughput diagram.

11.1.4 Operating Curves for Stock on Hand

Operating curves for stock on hand describe delivery delays and time in storage in relation to the inventory.

Operating curves for stock on hand are created by representing different inventory statuses in condensed form as a curve. Figure 11.1.4.1 shows how the operating curves for the stock on hand of an item can be derived from the store throughput diagram (see Figure 11.1.3.3). See also [Wien97].

Inventory stock at a given point in time corresponds to the vertical distance between the stock receipts and stock issues curves. By considering the size of these areas, we can then calculate performance indicators such as mean inventory stock, mean time in storage, and mean delivery delay. See also [Gläs95].

Figure 11.1.4.1a shows the store throughput diagrams for three different inventory statuses. These statuses differ primarily with respect to mean inventory stock.

- Inventory status I has a high stock level. There are no delivery delays, because any demand can be fulfilled immediately. The mean time in storage is very long, however.

a) Store throughput diagrams for various inventory statuses

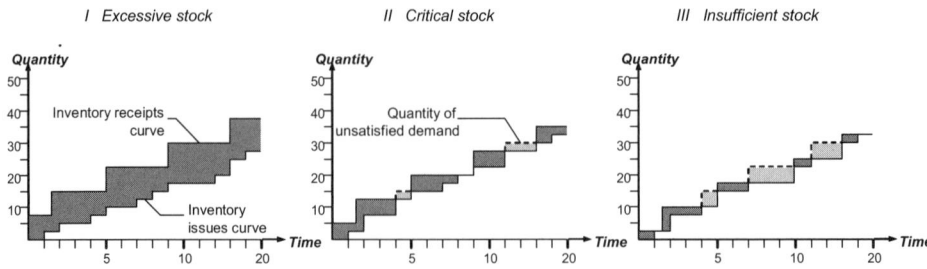

b) Operating curves for stock on hand

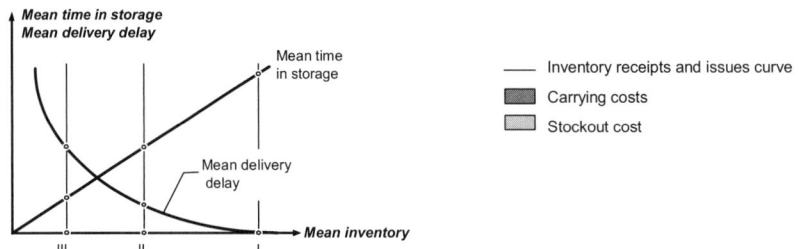

Fig. 11.1.4.1   Derivation of an operating curve for stock on hand from the store throughput diagram (see [Wien97], p. 173).

- For inventory status II, the mean time in storage is much shorter than for inventory status I. However, there are occasional supply bottlenecks, that is, periods in which demand cannot be satisfied.

- In inventory status III, no stocks are available over relatively long periods. Further demand cannot be satisfied, which leads to very long delivery delays.

Let us now consider Fig. 11.1.4.1b. Applying the three inventory statuses and their performance indicators – mean time in storage and mean delivery delay — to inventory stocks, we obtain the associated operating curves for stock on hand by joining up the points. This type of curve can be created in practice using analytical methods or by simulation. See [Gläs95].

The use of operating curves for stock on hand thus enables us to represent the interdependencies between quantitatively determinable logistic performance indicators in graph form. Operating curves for stock on hand enable us to derive target values for the important cost factor of inventory stock for the purposes of inventory control. This is analogous to the use of logistics operating curves for work stations (see Section 12.2.4). This form of graphical representation is useful for evaluating and improving procurement processes, analyzing capability when selecting suppliers, and comparing the power of different inventory control techniques. Typical examples include:

- The flatter the increase in the mean time in storage curve, the higher the stock-inventory turnover.

- The closer the mean delivery delay curve is to the two axes, the more closely inventory entries mirror inventory issues (and thus demand).

11.2   Deterministic Determination of Independent Demand

11.2.1 Customer Order and Distribution Requirements Planning (DRP)

Deterministic independent demand is independent demand where quantity, date, and physical characteristics are all known (see also Section 4.2.1).

For demand external to the organization, this means end products or service parts on order, that is, the individual positions on a customer order. The following are usually handled in a manner similar to the handling of customer demand:

- *Warehouse demand*, that is, demand for replacing inventory in a warehouse

- *Interplant demand*, that is one plant's need for a part or product that is produced by another plant or division in the same organization

A specific position in the customer order exists at least until it is delivered and invoiced during distribution control. If the items or their components are not available from stock, then the "life span" of a position in the customer order incorporates the "life spans" of all the production and procurement orders needed to cover this deterministic independent demand. It should be possible to establish a connection between these orders and the underlying independent demand at any time, so that control of operations can respond to any deviations from the schedule. The consequences that production or procurement delays or changes in quantities will have on customer orders must be apparent.

Strictly speaking, deterministic independent demand arises only when the order is confirmed, since this is the first document to contain a legally binding description of the items ordered, their quantities, and delivery dates. Nevertheless, despite its legally binding nature, independent demand is still not deterministic as defined above at this point. Depending upon supply and demand, the customer is still in a position to vary the quantity or defer the due date, despite divergent legally binding agreements. Here, the customer may be required to pay a previously agreed-upon penalty.

One important factor when scheduling customer demand is the organization's distribution network structure as determined by distribution planning. The due date for the independent customer demand is the date of shipment. The distribution network structure determines how far in advance this date is of the delivery date to the customer.

In-transit lead time is the time between the date of shipment (at the shipping point) and the date of receipt (at the receiver's dock) ([APIC04]).

In-transit lead time includes preparation for delivery from the plant, transportation to distribution warehouses, and distribution to the customer. These times are determined by distribution planning. For a distribution network structure with limited capacity, such as truck fleets, the date of an independent demand is often determined by the cycles used to cover certain routes. For very large or high-cost items in particular, route planning also determines the order in which parts are assembled (for customer production orders) or commissioned (for customer orders from stock), in addition to the delivery dates. See also Section 14.4.

The duration of the data flow accompanying the customer order is another important aspect of the distribution network structure. This applies to delivery documents and transportation documentation, such as for customs purposes. This aspect of the data flow should be planned very carefully, as there are cases in which the data flow can last longer than the associated goods flow, particularly with respect to service parts. Solutions based on the latest communications technology help to speed up the process. Examples include fax, EDIFACT, and so on.

With a multilevel distribution network structure (for example, central warehouse or distribution center → regional distribution center → wholesaler → retailer → customer) customer demand at each intermediate level can be handled as independent. For management of distribution inventory, the order point technique can be used. However, if demand fluctuates widely the distribution requirements planning technique has proved practical.

Distribution requirements planning (DRP) translates planned orders of the various levels of warehouses in the distribution network directly into planned orders of the central distribution warehouse.

Figure 11.2.1.1 shows distribution requirements planning for an example item with the item identification 4211.

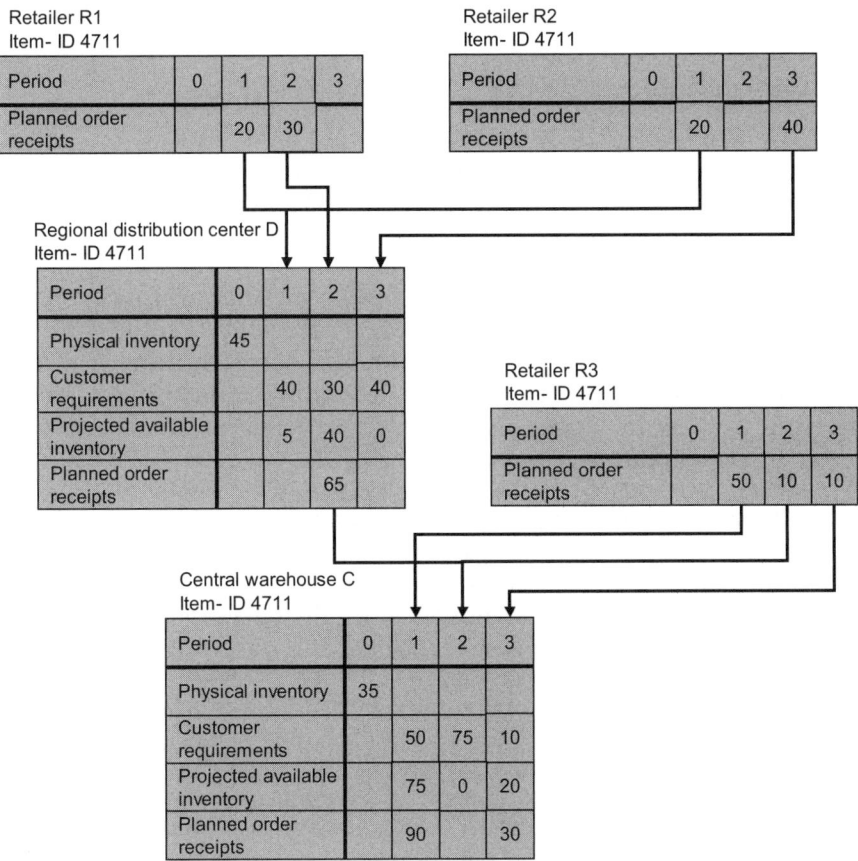

Fig. 11.2.1.1 Distribution requirements planning DRP (example).

Planned receipts of the central distribution warehouse — in the example in Figure 11.2.1.1 the 90 units in period 1 and the 30 units in period 3 — are the same as the gross requirements on the production source or sources that supply the central distribution warehouse.

The advantage of the DRP technique over multilevel application of the order point technique along the distribution chain is the elimination of safety stock at the individual levels. With this, however, all demand — on the distribution chain and on the supplying sources — in principle becomes dependent demand. The DRP technique thus corresponds to the MRP technique described in Section 11.3. For that reason, we will not go any further into the logic and the details of the DRP technique, such as determination of planned receipts from the projected available inventory.

11.2.2 Consuming the Forecast by Actual Demand (*)

Consuming the forecast or *forecast consumption* is the process of reducing the forecast by customer orders or other types of actual demand as they are received ([APIC04]).

Independent demand determined by stochastic methods, that is, a forecast, can be used as an alternative to customer demand not yet received. Viewed quasi-deterministically, it enables deterministic dependent demand to be calculated at lower product structure levels by exploding the bills of material in order to trigger production or procurement of these items in good time and in sufficient quantity.

The forecast is gradually replaced or "consumed" by actual demand, that is, by customer orders. The actual (deterministic) demand thus "overlays" the stochastic independent demand, which either immediately precedes it along the time axis or is the earliest forecast along the time axis that has not yet been completely replaced by customer demand.

The resulting forecast consumption rules are as follows:

1. If a customer demand is canceled, the demand forecast remains unchanged.
2. If a customer demand is issued, it "overlays" the corresponding forecast and thus "consumes" its open quantity, which is then regarded as "issued." There are two variations of this:
    - Variation 2.1: The demand forecast that immediately precedes it on the time axis is reduced.
    - Variation 2.2: All the forecasts preceding the customer demand whose forecast quantities have not yet been reduced — in chronological order — are reduced.

3.   Option overplanning: If the sum of the customer demands is too large, the quantity by which it exceeds the forecast quantity is regarded as net requirements.

The adjustments yield the value of the remaining forecast for each period. Figure 11.2.2.1 shows the principle of forecast consumption, both before and after the issue of two customer demands. This is variation 2.1.

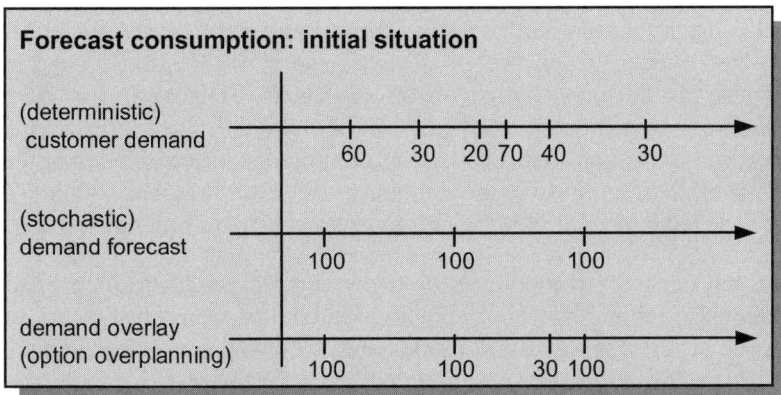

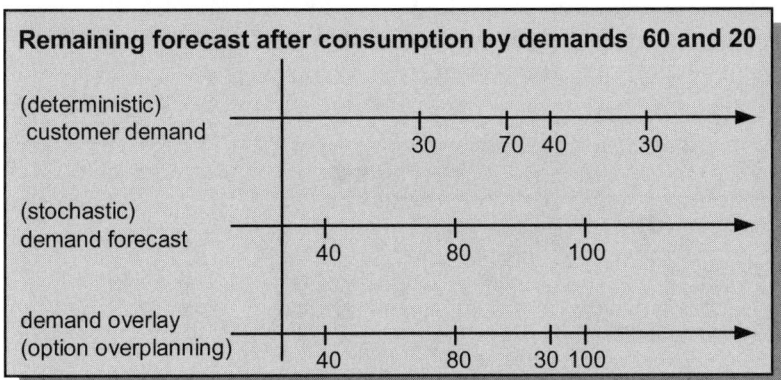

Fig. 11.2.2.1   The principle of forecast consumption.

The *demand time fence* (DTF) is that point in time inside of which the forecast is no longer included in total demand and projected available inventory calculations. Inside this point, only customer orders are considered ([APIC04]).

With option overplanning, an order quantity may only be planned in the period where new customer orders are currently being accepted. This is typically just after the demand time fence.

11.3   Deterministic Determination of Dependent Demand

11.3.1 Characteristics of Discontinuous Dependent Demand

If dependent demand is continuous or regular, analytical forecasting techniques may be used to determine demand, and, if necessary, the (stochastic) order point technique may be used for materials management. This applies to purchased parts, such as screws and nuts, or raw materials, such as sheet metal, which are of a very general nature and appear as components in various higher level products. Demand for such commodities is very frequent, sometimes extremely high, and is distributed along the time axis such that a relatively continuous pattern of demand is obtained overall. The individual demands are also relatively small in relation to the batch size of the production or procurement order.

However, the need for components of manufactured products often arises discontinuously, rather than continuously. Under these circumstances, we will first see several periods with no demand, followed by a large demand resulting from a production or procurement batch for the product at a higher structure level, as Figure 11.3.1.1 shows. In this case, the quantities issued will typically be of the same order of magnitude as the production or procurement batch for the component.

Period	0	1	2	3	4	5	6
Physical inventory	35						
Safety stock	5						
Customer demand		10	12	12	14	12	12
Planned order receipts				30		30	
Component requirements			30		30		

Fig. 11.3.1.1   Lumpy dependent demand due to batch sizes at higher structure levels.

Where the demand for components can be derived from the requirements for higher level subassemblies, the order point technique is unsuitable for control purposes, because the carrying cost is too high. Figure 11.3.1.2 illustrates this point (the shaded areas represent the carrying cost).

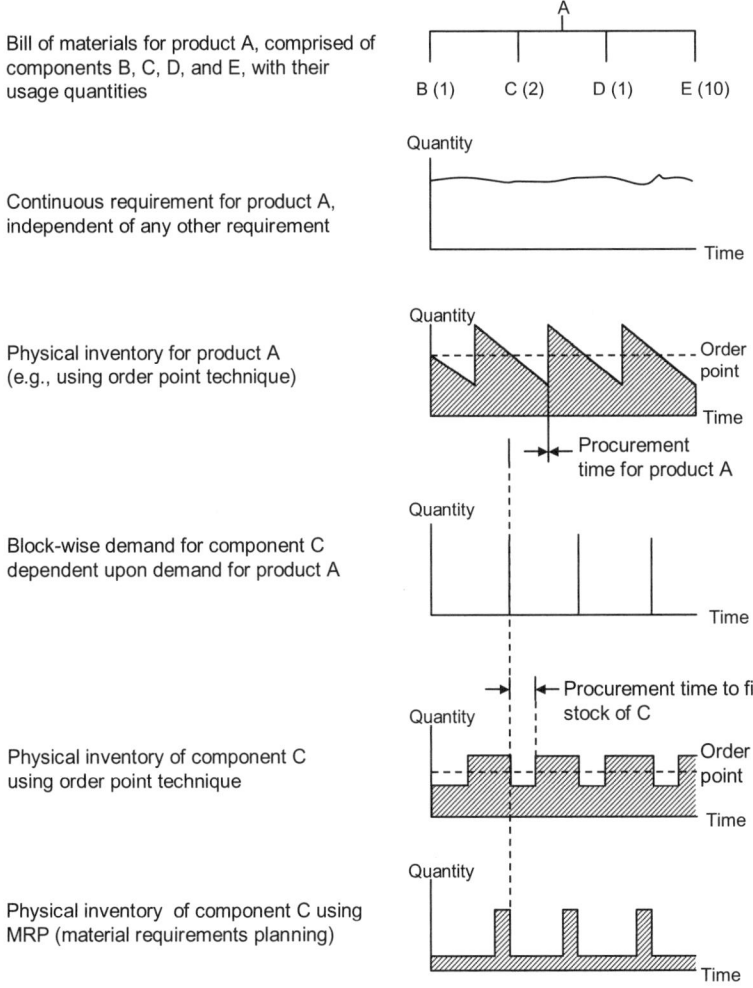

Fig. 11.3.1.2   Two techniques for inventory management of components with lumpy demand.

- There is a demand for component C as soon as an order for assembly A is received. As a result, the demand for component C is not continuous. There is no point in maintaining a safety stock of 20 units of C, for example, if the lumpy demand is for 100 units.

- The order point technique results a large physical inventory of C, which must be kept until the next order is received for higher level assembly A.

- • The ideal situation is the one shown at the bottom part of Figure 11.3.1.2. The production or procurement order for C should occur immediately before the demand for component C arises. In this case, component C is stored in the warehouse either for a very short time or not at all. This type of planning is the explicit objective of the MRP (material requirements planning) technique.

The MRP technique calculates dependent demand on the basis of higher level independent demands. In principle, this technique requires no safety stock to be kept in the stock. On the other hand, a safety lead time must be incorporated into the lead time in order to absorb the effects of late deliveries.

If a small safety stock of components is kept to cover such fluctuations, its purpose is to enable any parts that have to be scrapped during production of higher product structure levels to be replaced as quickly as possible. Similarly, scrap and yield factor can also be considered for every batch that is released. For example:

Batch size (= expected yield):	100
Scrap factor:	5%
$\Rightarrow$ Yield factor:	95%
$\Rightarrow$ Order quantity to be released:	$100/95\% = 105.26 \to 106$

However, if the demand is a *stochastic independent demand*, that is, a forecast, then a safety demand will already have been included in the (quasi-deterministic) independent demand, as described in Section 9.5.6. In this case, the bills of material explosion transfers this safety demand to the lower structure levels.

11.3.2 Material Requirements Planning (MRP) and Planned Orders

The *MRP technique (material requirements planning)* for calculating dependent demand is defined below. *Net requirements planning* is another term for MRP (see also Section 4.1.2).

Four steps are carried out for each item, *in ascending order of their low-level code* (see Section 1.2.2). The four steps thus start with the end products and finish with the raw materials and purchased parts. Repeating the four steps for every item results in a multilevel procedure, as shown in Figure 11.3.2.1.

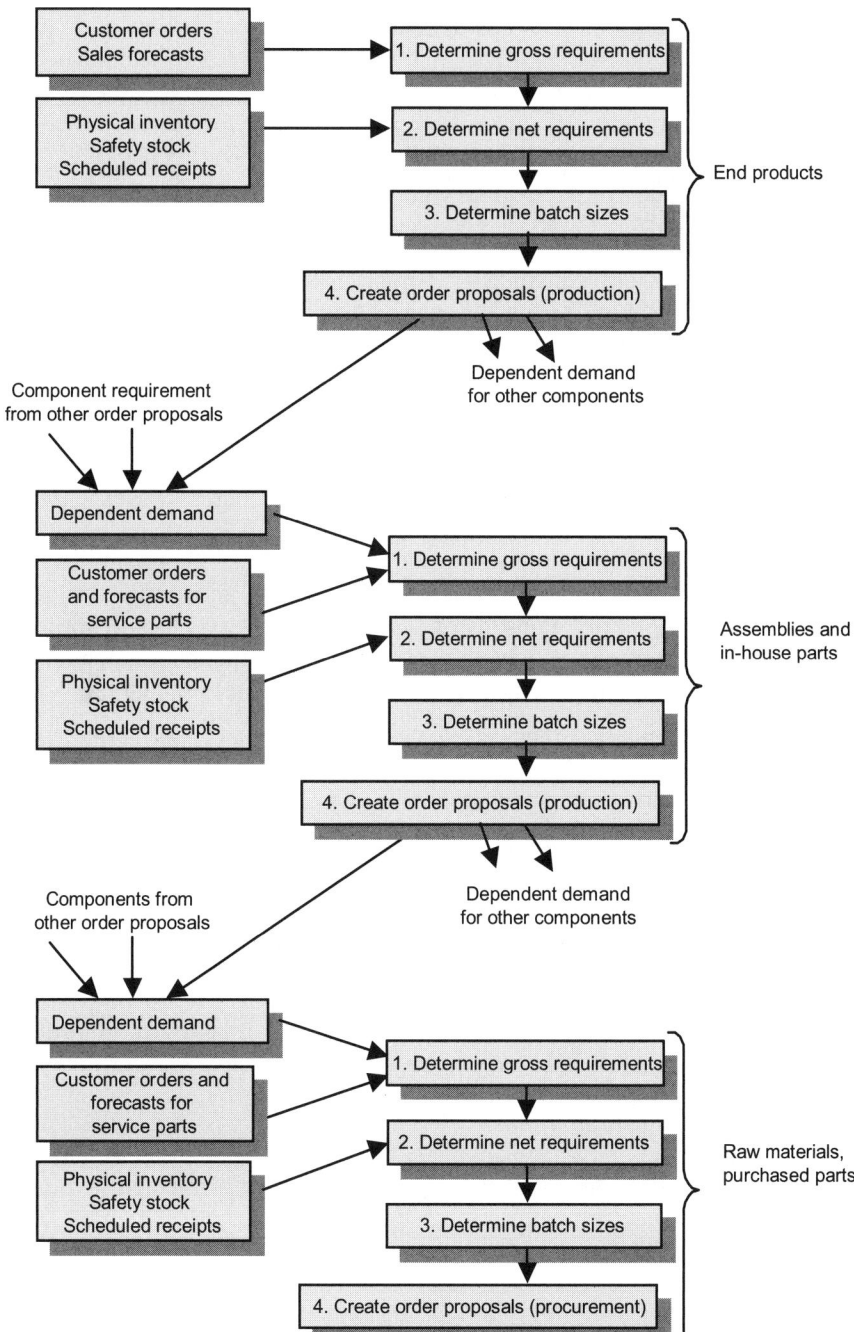

Fig. 11.3.2.1 Schematic representation of the MRP technique.

Let us now consider the four steps in detail:

1. *Determine gross requirements:*

> *Gross requirement* is the time-phased sum of independent and dependent demand of the respective period.

- At the highest level, that is, for end products, the gross requirement is independent demand. This main input for the MRP technique stems, in general, from the master production schedule (MPS) and is made up of:
  - Customer orders (the "original" requirement). This is *deterministic independent demand.*
  - Sales forecasts (the supplementary requirement). This is *stochastic independent demand,* which entails *quasi-deterministic materials management.*

- At the lower levels, that is, for assemblies and parts, the gross requirement often consists of just one of the two classifications of demand, namely of independent demand or dependent demand. For service parts, for example, it will be made up of both classes.
  - The so-called *service parts demand* is demand for service parts that are sold as such. Thus, it is forecasted independent demand.
  - Demand for service parts that are integrated into higher level products is calculated as dependent demand derived from the demand for the higher-level product in step 4. Thus, it is derived by a deterministic technique, in the case of stochastic independent demand by a quasi-deterministic technique.

  If the gross requirement consists of both classes, a multilevel master schedule may have to be used.[4]

2. *Determine the net requirements:*

> *Net requirements* are the time-phased negative projected available inventory.

---

[4]   A *multilevel master schedule* allows management of components at any level of an end product's bill of material as master schedule items ([APIC04]).

- Figure 11.3.2.2 shows a common situation for any given item. The safety stock is subtracted from projected available inventory right at the start. As a result, production or procurement orders are then scheduled such that they enter into stock when the projected available inventory falls below zero.

Period		0	1	2	3	4	5	6	7	8	9
Physical inventory	(+)	50									
Safety stock	(−)	20									
Scheduled receipts	(+)				65						
Allocated quantities	(−)		15	0	10	0	0	0	0	0	0
Planned gross requirements	(−)		5	0	40	25	0	20	15	0	10
Projected available inventory	(=)	30	10	10	25	0	0	0	0	0	0
Net requirements (negative projected available inventory)	(+)		0	0	0	0	0	20	15	0	10
Batch size / planned receipts									35			35
Planned releases						35			35			

Fig. 11.3.2.2   Determination of net requirements and batch sizes (example).

- It is assumed that receipts occur at the beginning of a time period and that issues occur during a period. Receipts and issues are now added or subtracted over time, and the available quantity is calculated along the time axis. This results in the net requirements: a series of negative available inventories after each period. The sum of all these negative available inventories along the time axis is known as *net requirements*.

- Step 3 of the MRP technique (see Figure 11.3.2.1), determination of batch sizes, has already been carried out by way of example. In step 4 planned orders are generated from the batch sizes. *Planned release*, that is, the scheduled release of a planned order, is thus the planned receipt brought forward by the lead time (here, by three periods).

- Of course, it would also be possible to use the same graphical representation, in this case listing every planning-related event individually, rather than in a *bucketed system*, that is combining them in periods or time buckets. Such a *bucketless system* could result in a very large list, however (or a large number of columns in Figure 11.3.2.2).

3. *Determine the batch sizes:*

   • There are a number of batch sizing policies for combining net requirements into batch sizes. These are described in Section 11.4.

4. *Create an order proposal, that is, a planned order for every batch:*

   • The first step is to calculate the lead time in order to determine the point in time at which the order should be released.

   • For a planned production order, the next step is to determine — from the routing sheet of the product to be manufactured — the planned operations and thus the planned load of the work centers (see also Section 11.3.3).

   • For a planned production order, this also includes a requirements explosion to schedule the demand for components (see also Section 11.3.3). This (dependent) demand is the batch size multiplied by the usage quantity. It is also the gross requirement for the component and is one of the quantities to be determined in step 1 for the component in a subsequent MRP stage. This is the final MRP planning stage.

If the order proposals are not subsequently released, they are automatically adapted to take account of the current situation the next time that requirements are calculated. This generally means deleting all the planned orders and then recalculating them in a comprehensive rerun of the MRP algorithm.

If the independent demand changes only slightly, the *net change MRP technique* is usually faster. This technique attempts to consider only those net requirements that have changed. The four-step procedure is applied only to those articles whose projected available inventory has changed since the last MRP run. If planned production orders are changed, this will also affect the dependent demands for components, so that the MRP procedure must be repeated for each component. If a large number of items are affected, the entire order network will have to be recalculated — effectively a comprehensive rerun of the MRP algorithm.

11.3.3 Determining the Timing of Dependent Demand and the Load of a Planned Order

Order proposals are compared against the net requirements, which are broken down into meaningful batch sizes. For a purchased item, generating an order proposal essentially means calculating the order point with due regard to the lead time (which is part of the master data for the item). For an item produced in-house, the start date can also be determined by subtracting the lead time from the completion date. The dependent demands for all the components will be needed on the start date. This is how the MRP technique is normally used.

A more appropriate, detailed, and comprehensive technique also calculates the *process plan* for the item's final production stage (see Section 1.2.3). At the same time, planning data are generated for materials management, time management, and scheduling and capacity management:

- The load that this order will generate at the various work centers: by multiplying the order quantity by the operation load for each operation (see also Chapter 13).

- The time at which a load arises: by means of a lead-time calculation starting with the order completion date (see also Chapter 12).

- The start date for the order (see also Chapter 12).

- The dependent gross requirement (or dependent demand): by multiplying the order quantity by the usage quantity for each position on the bill of material.

- The time at which a dependent demand arises, taking into account the start date for the operation that processes the demand.

Figure 11.3.3.1 compares the conventional MRP technique, that is, the mean lead time, with the proposed, more comprehensive technique. The example calculates the timing of the dependent demands for a product A, which is made up of components B and C.

In variation 1 (the conventional MRP technique), it is assumed that the average lead time for producing A is two months. The timing of the dependent demands for components B and C is thus the planned order completion date for A minus its average lead time.

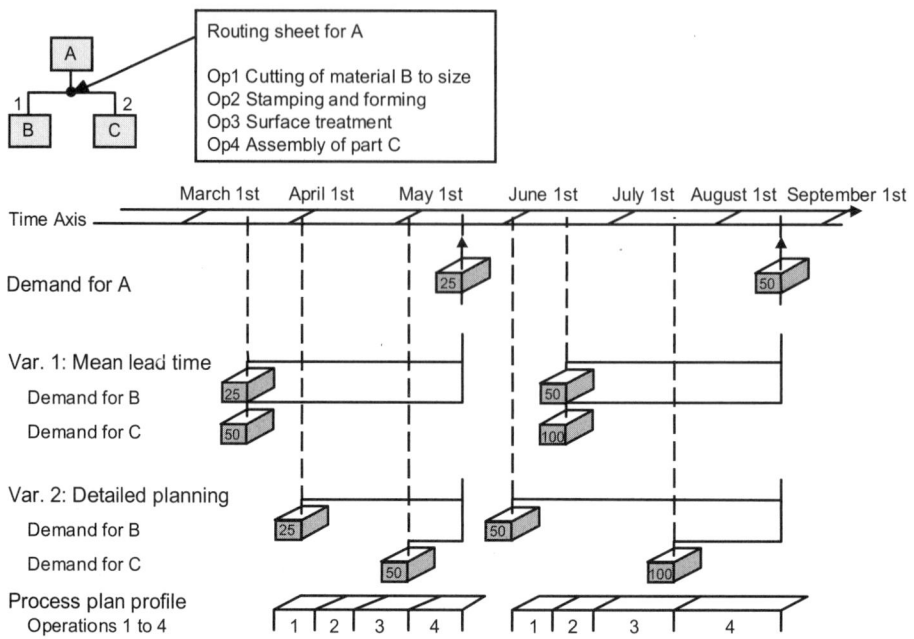

Fig. 11.3.3.1   Calculating the timing of dependent demands.

Variation 2 shows the more comprehensive and detailed technique. The process plan for product A was included in the calculation. The first difference is that the lead time for batches of 25 is just 1.5 months, whereas it rises to 2.5 months for batches of 50. In addition, demand for C does not arise until the fourth operation, which should start half or one month before the order completion date, depending upon the batch size.

Figure 11.3.3.1 shows how this affects the way in which the timing of dependent demands is calculated in variation 2. If B and C are very high-cost items, the detailed procedure would help to allow the components to be channeled into production exactly when they are needed. This can reduce both the volume and the value of goods in process.

If we compare the two variations, we can see that the more general variation 1 is very suitable both for (long-term) master planning and for medium-term or short-term planning for inexpensive and low-volume components. In all other cases, variation 2 is more suitable, although calculation requires much more processing power and more complex algorithms, which may also be more prone to error.

11.4   Batch or Lot Sizing

11.4.1 Combining Net Requirements into Batches

A *batch-sizing policy*, *lot-sizing policy*, or *order policy* is a set of techniques that create production or procurement batches from net requirements.

In practice, there are various possible batch sizing policies:

1. *Lot-for-lot*: This lot-sizing policy translates every net requirement into just one planned order.

    *   Variation: if the component batch sizes fall below a certain quantity, a "blowthrough" of the component requirements right into the requirements given by its bill of material and its routing sheet may take place (see description below).

2. A dynamic lot size, made up of an *optimum number of demands* taken together. If this number is 1, then the situation is again one of make to order.

3. A dynamic lot size with an *optimum number of partial lots*. This policy suggests splitting the demand into several orders. Another attribute determines the minimum deferral time between two of these orders.

4. A *fixed order quantity*, known as the *optimum batch size*, either determined manually or calculated using the EOQ (economic order quantity) formula, for example (see Section 10.4.2). If two orders are closer together than the specified *minimum deferral time*, they are procured in a single batch (multiples of the EOQ).

5. A *dynamic lot-sizing* technique, known as *period order quantity*, which combines various demands into one batch over the course of an optimum number of time buckets. This corresponds to the optimum period of time for which future demand should be covered, that is, the *optimum order interval* or the *optimum length of order cycle* in Fig. 10.4.2.6. It is calculated, in principle, by dividing the optimum batch size by the average annual consumption.

6. *Part period balancing*, another dynamic lot-sizing technique. For the first period's demand, an order is planned. For every further period's demand, the carrying cost that will be incurred from the time of the last planned order is calculated. If these costs are lower

than the setup and ordering costs, then every further period's demand is added onto the last planned order. Otherwise, a new order is scheduled for every further period's demand.

7. *Dynamic optimization* (as described by [WaWh58]). This relatively complicated technique calculates the various totals for set-up and carrying costs resulting from different combinations of net requirements to form batches and determines the minimum costs from these totals. This technique for identifying minimum costs is illustrated in the example below.

All batch-sizing policies, except the fourth, result in so-called discrete order quantities.

> A *discrete order quantity* is an order quantity that represents an integer number of periods of demand. That means that any inventory left over from one period is sufficient to cover the full demand of a future period.

The following additional aspects of the various batch-sizing policies should be considered:

- *The "blowthrough" technique linked with the lot-for-lot sizing policy:* Designers tend to define structural levels that correspond to the modules of a product. However, in the production flow the modules are not always meaningful, since some products are manufactured in one go, with no explicit identification or storage of the intermediate product levels. This is often the case with single-item production, where an additional objective is to create as few order documents as possible, and results — *de facto* — in phantom items and extended phantom bills of material. The blowthrough technique, however, drives requirements straight through the phantom item to its components and combines the operations in a meaningful order. Applying the technique means that several design structure levels can be converted to a single production structure level.[5] At the same time, the multilevel *design bill of material* is transferred to the associated single-level *production bill of material*. Figures 11.4.1.1 and 11.4.1.2 show as an example product X, which is made up of two longitudinal parts L and two transverse parts Q, each made from the same raw material. The information is shown before and after the "blowthrough" of requirements through L and Q. See also [Schö88], p. 69 ff.

---

[5]   See the definitions of these terms in Sections 1.2.2 and 1.2.3.

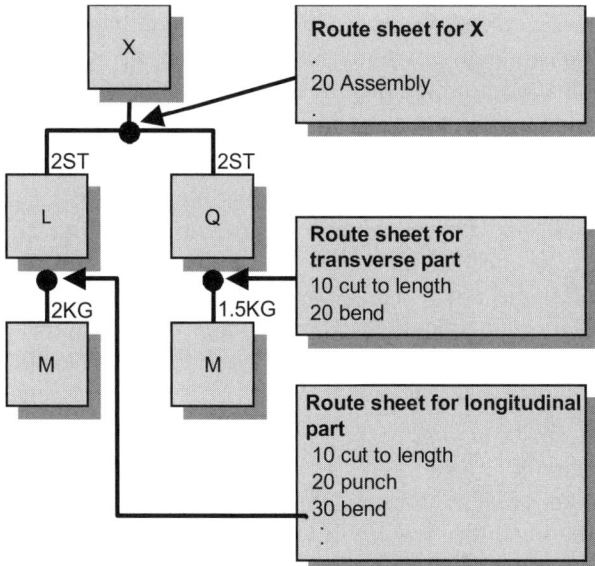

Fig. 11.4.1.1   Bills of material and route sheets for a product X from the viewpoint of design.

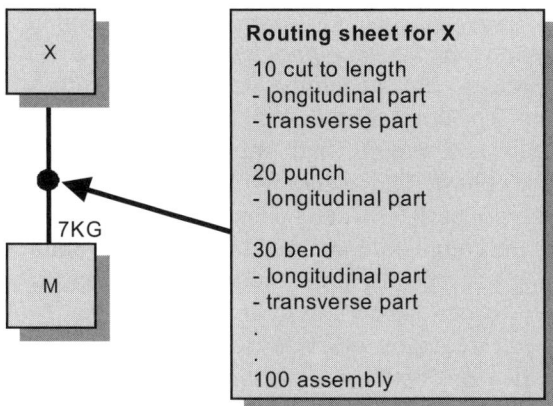

Fig. 11.4.1.2   Bills of material and route sheets for a product X: structure from the production viewpoint, after "blowthrough" of requirements through L and Q.

- *For the second to the fifth batch-sizing policies,* you can also specify whether the optimum sizes should be calculated or set manually. Maximum and minimum values can be assigned in order to restrict these optimum sizes if the calculation returns unusual values.

- *The second and the third batch-sizing policies* are particularly important for harmonious or rhythmic production, in which a certain quantity leaves production during each unit of time. The components should be procured at a similar rate.

- *The third batch-sizing policy,* or batch splitting, is used if the specified requirement in total is not needed all at the same time. For an assembly batch of 100 machines, for example, not all the components will be needed at once, since the machines are assembled one after the other. Thus, two partial batches could be created, if necessary, for producing or procuring components, and the second partial batch could be channeled into the assembly process some time after assembly starts.

- *With the fourth batch-sizing policy,* or fixed order quantity, physical inventory is inevitable, since more items are generally procured than are needed to satisfy demand. This policy should therefore only be used if the inventory level will actually be reduced, that is, when it is safe to assume that demand will really occur in the future. This is the case if future demand can be determined on the basis of past consumption — at least where demand is regular. This batch sizing policy is therefore not economically viable for lumpy demand.

- *Fifth, sixth, and seventh batch-sizing policies:* The fifth and the sixth batch-sizing policies are generally used in deterministic materials management. The seventh policy is the most complicated and, although it produces a precise and optimum solution, it is unfortunately not very robust. The accuracy obtained and thus the economic viability of policies 5, 6, and 7 increase in ascending order. Unfortunately, the complexity and processing power required also increase accordingly, especially if the techniques are applied to precise events, rather than time periods. On the other hand, the robustness decreases in ascending order, which means that, if the quantity or date of a demand within the planning horizon changes, the seventh policy will require complete re-calculation, while a change in demand will not necessarily have severe consequences for the fifth policy.

- *Seventh batch-sizing policy:* Figure 11.4.1.3 shows the steps of the dynamic optimization technique described by [WaWh58]. They should be studied in conjunction with the example in Figure 11.4.2.1.

1. The first batch should be determined at the start of the first period.

2. In every subsequent period, a new batch should be established as an alternative. The initial costs are determined from the minimum total costs for all variations to date (rows in the table) in the preceding period, plus the batch-size-independent production or procurement costs for establishing a new batch for the current period.

3. The minimum cost is the minimum value of the total costs in the previous period.

4. Starting from this minimum value, the lots are put together "backwards," by seeking the way to achieve this minimum.

5. To reduce the processing required, the following simplification can be applied to each variation (row in the table): When the carrying cost for a demand in a given period exceeds the batch-size-independent production or procurement costs, it is no longer worth adding this demand to the batch. It will not be possible to establish a minimum value, even if this variation (row) is subjected to more extensive calculation of the total costs for a subsequent period.

Fig. 11.4.1.3   Dynamic optimization technique as described by [WaWh58].

11.4.2 Comparison of the Different Batch-Sizing Policies

Batch sizing policies 7, 6, 5, and 4 described in Section 11.4.1 are compared below. These policies are:

- Dynamic optimization

- The cost leveling technique

- Comparison of the carrying cost for a single net requirement per period with the batch-size-independent production or procurement costs

- Comparison of the cumulative carrying cost with the batch-size-independent production or procurement costs

- The optimum length of order cycle or the optimum order interval

- The optimum batch size (economic order quantity, EOQ)

The following assumptions apply:

- Net requirement: 300 units of measure divided between six periods (for example, 2-month periods) giving 10, 20, 110, 50, 70, 40 units

- Batch-size-independent production or procurement costs: 100 cost units

- Carrying cost
  - Per unit of measure and period: 0.5 cost units
  - Per unit of measure over six periods: 3 cost units
- An order receipt is assumed at the start of a period. Carrying cost is always incurred at the start of the next period.

Based on these assumptions, you can thus calculate the following values:

- Optimum batch size using the economic order quantity (EOQ) (see Figure 10.4.2.4):

$$X_0 = \sqrt{2 \cdot 300 \cdot \frac{100}{3}} = \sqrt{20000} = 141.42 \approx 140$$

- Optimum length of order cycle or the optimum order interval (see Figure 10.4.2.6):

$$
\begin{aligned}
LOC_0 &= \frac{141.42}{300} \cdot 6 \, \text{periods} \\
&= 0.47 \cdot 6 \, \text{periods} \\
&= 2.83 \, \text{periods} \\
&\approx 3 \, \text{periods}
\end{aligned}
$$

In Figure 11.4.2.1, the total setup and ordering costs as well as the carrying cost are calculated for the various batch-sizing policies.

Every policy yields a different result in specific cases, although this is not necessarily so in the general case. The results obtained with these techniques tend to improve in the order given above. Indeed, the optimum batch-size technique can be used only if the quantity of the last batch does not exceed the net requirement. But, even under these circumstances, the technique produces unsatisfactory results when applied deterministically.

	Period	1	2	3	4	5	6	Total costs	
								per lot	cumu-lative
	Net require-ments	10	20	110	50	70	40		
Dynamic optimization	Cumulative carrying and set-up costs	100	110	220	295				
			200	255	305	410			
				210	235	305	365		
					310	345	385		
						335	355		
	Batch sizes	30		160		110			355
Part period balancing	Carrying cost per net requirement	0	10	(110)				110	
				0	25	70	60	255	
	Batch sizes	30		270					365
Optimum length of order cycle	Cumulative carrying and set-up costs	100	110	220				220	
					100	135	175	175	
	Batch sizes	140			160				395
Economic order quantity	Cumulative carrying and set-up costs	100	110	220				220	
					100	135	155	155	
							100	100	
	Batch sizes	140			140		140 (20)		475

Fig. 11.4.2.1   Comparison of various batch-sizing policies.

11.5   Analyzing the Results of Material Requirements Planning (MRP)

11.5.1 Projected Available Inventory and Pegging

The projected available inventory along the time axis, as defined in Section 11.1, is of relevance to every item. In the case of dependent demand calculations, planned receipts and requirements should be taken into account in addition to open orders and allocated quantities. The projected available inventory calculation extended in this way forms the basis for all exception reports (flagging deviations) and analyses.

Pegging or *requirements traceability* determines the independent demands that give rise to a dependent demand or a production or procurement order.

Pegging is one of the most important analyses for delayed orders, for example. It can be regarded as active where-used information. It determines the source of demand requirements, determining whether the underlying independent demands are customer orders or whether they stem from uncertain forecasts in the master plan.

In order to carry out this type of investigation, objects are created in the course of MRP for order connection purposes, specifically between item issues (demand positions in an order) and item receipts (positions for demand coverage). These objects can then be used to derive the desired pegging.

Pegging is equivalent to an allocation algorithm that assigns demand (item issues) to orders (item receipts). It is sometimes possible to cover every demand with several positions from different production or procurement orders. Conversely, every position in a production or procurement order can be used for several demand positions in various orders.

Creating the *order connection* object during MRP results in four types of action messages, or exception messages:

- Order to be pushed forward (speeded up)
- New order proposal
- Order to be deferred (slowed down)
- Superfluous order

The *rescheduling assumption* assumes that it is more promising to speed up an order already in process than to create a new order, since the remaining lead time is shorter.

As a consequence of this assumption, MRP logic tends to push forward orders that have already been released before it proposes a new order:

For the purposes of pegging, the order identification concerned is entered. One of the algorithms corresponding to the multilevel where-used list (see

Section 16.2.3) calculates all the independent demands that are affected by this order. This results in multilevel pegging which identifies all the intermediate demands and orders. The "leaves" of the resulting tree structure are then independent demands: forecasts, genuine customer demands, or unplanned orders for end products or service parts. For example:

- For *bottom-up rescheduling*, the planner uses pegging to solve material availability or similar problems. This can entail compressing lead time, cutting order quantity, or making changes to the master schedule.

For quick decision making in procurement situations, it may be necessary to identify the types of independent demand that give rise to a dependent demand, without the help of a pegging algorithm. A possible technique to solve this problem can be found in [Schö88], p. 117 ff.

The structure of the *order connection* object can also be used for the opposite purpose.

Demand coverage traceability specifies all the (dependent) demands or orders that are at least partly caused by a particular (independent) demand.

A demand coverage list may be needed if, for example, you have to change the date or quantity for an independent demand (such as a customer order) and want to assess the consequences of this change. The algorithm is thus equivalent to the algorithm that generates a multilevel bill of materials (see Section 16.2.3).

11.5.2 Action Messages

An *action message* or *exception message* is an output of a system that identifies the need for and the type of action to be taken to correct a current or potential problem ([APIC04]).

The MRP technique essentially yields planned orders with planned gross requirements for their components and loads at the work centers. The order completion date is calculated so that at least part of the batch will be used in a higher level order or for a sales order as soon as it is produced or procured. For this reason, the start date of the production or procurement order should always be met. Exception messages should thus report the following problems associated with orders:

- Planned orders whose start date has passed

- Planned orders whose start date will pass in the immediate future, such as within a week

- Open orders that should be speeded up or slowed down due to changes in the projected available inventory or too fast or too slow progress of the production or procurement order

The main problem with exception messages is that there are so many of them. Sorting and selection of exception messages is important to ensure that the right people receive the right messages. The most urgent messages should arrive first. Sorting and selection can be performed at the least according to the classification of items into groups and subgroups that reflect the structural organization of the planners. The ABC classification is another possible sorting criterion.

Some dependent demand is not due at the start date of an order, but at the start date of a later operation. Therefore, to obtain accurate dates for dependent demands, a scheduling technique should be used that calculates the start date of each operation. This will also reveal the planned load at the work centers, which can then be compared against planned capacity. See also Chapters 12 and 13.

The planners check the number and order quantity of the proposed orders. If the proposals relate to purchased items, they also select the suppliers. Proposals for new orders must then be released — see Section 14.1.

11.6   Summary

This chapter describes the deterministic materials management technique for medium-term and short-term planning. The unique aspect of this technique is that the demand for an item is not simply regarded as a total that, *de facto*, can be evenly distributed along the time axis, as is the case with long-term planning or even stochastic materials management. In contrast, you take advantage of the fact that you know the precise time of every demand and thus the limited period it will take up along the time axis. Lumpy demand can be managed particularly efficiently in this way.

Purely deterministic materials management requires the independent demands to be precisely known. Dependent demands are then derived from them by exploding the bill of materials. Since the cumulative lead time remains within the customer tolerance time, the exact demand for procured and produced goods is known.

An attempt should be made to use quasi-deterministic materials management techniques if components at lower levels have to be stored, but demand is only discontinuous. The independent demand is then calculated using stochastic techniques. On the other hand, dependent demand is again calculated by exploding the bill of materials.

The starting point for deterministic materials management is the projected available inventory. This is not a scalar variable — it changes after every transaction or every future event that changes stock levels. At any given time, the projected available inventory is defined as the physical inventory plus all open and planned receipts minus all allocated quantities minus all planned demands up to this point.

The projected available inventory calculation thus shows the projected available inventory defined in this way along the time axis. This is useful, for it provides information on the possible demand coverage (quantity and timing, and partial demands, if necessary) for any new demand. The scheduling projected available inventory calculation attempts to bring forward or put back orders in process or allocated quantities so as to maintain a positive projected available inventory at all times. Operating curves for stock on hand describe delivery delays and time in storage in relation to inventory.

Lumpy dependent demand often arises as a result of batch size creation at higher levels, often regardless of whether the independent demand was determined stochastically or deterministically. If stochastic materials management techniques were to be used in this situation, they would result in excessively large inventory stocks and carrying cost. The deterministic MRP (material requirements planning) technique ensures minimum stocks for production or procurement orders that are received in good time.

The MRP technique consists of four steps that are applied to every item in ascending order of their low-level code — starting with the end products, followed by the assemblies and semifinished products, through to the purchased goods.

- The first step is to determine the gross requirement, which may be made up of independent and dependent demands. The gross requirement is a dataset, rather than a scalar variable. If the calculation is applied to precise periods, there will be exactly one gross requirement per period. If the calculation is applied to precise events, every demand corresponds to a gross requirement.

- The second step is to determine the net requirement by offsetting the physical inventory, safety stock, open orders, and allocated quantities. The net requirement can be made up of individual net requirements. If the calculation is applied to precise periods, there will be exactly one net requirement per period. If the calculation is applied to precise events, every demand may give rise to a net requirement.

- The third step is to combine the individual net requirements to form batches. The conventional EOQ formula is not suitable here, because its batch sizes are fixed. Techniques that use dynamic lot sizes are much more appropriate here, since the demands are known.

- The fourth step is to convert the batch sizes into order proposals. The start date is determined by scheduling. For in-house production, the work center load and the quantity and date of each component demand are determined from the routing sheet and bill of materials. These are dependent demands and can thus be used to calculate the first of the four MRP steps for each component.

MRP generates exception lists containing orders to be released, speeded up, slowed down, or canceled, in addition to order proposals. Pegging and a demand coverage list help to identify orders that are interdependent within the order network.

11.7   Keywords

action message, 619
allocated quantity, 588
batch-sizing policy, 611
blowthrough, 612
consuming the forecast, 600
cumulative projected available inventory calculation, 594
demand coverage traceability, 619

demand time fence, 601
discrete order quantity, 612
distribution requirements planning, 599
DRP (distribution requirements planning), 599
exception message, 619

fixed order quantity, 611
forecast consumption, 600
interplant demand, 597
multilevel master schedule, 606
net change MRP technique, 608
net requirements, 606
open order, 588

11.8   Scenarios and Exercises

11.8.1 Projected Available Inventory Calculation

Complete the grid in Figure 11.8.1.1.

Date	Entry	Issue	Balance	Text	Order ID
01 Jan			1000	stock on hand	
05 Jan	100		?	replenishment	101 2897
14 Jan		1050	?	customer Smith	102 8972
15 Jan	?	?	500	?	102 9538
16 Jan		150	?	customer Adams	103 2687

Fig. 11.8.1.1   Projected available inventory calculation.

a.   What is the available inventory without any restrictions along the time axis?

b.   What is the additional available inventory after order 102 9538?

c.   Which receipt could be deferred?

d.   Furthermore, the following orders are planned:

   •   Customer order ID 104 2158 of 500 units on January 20

   •   Stock replenishment order ID 104 3231 of 500 units on January 22
   Does this situation lead to a problem? If so, how can it be solved?

Solutions:

Date	Entry	Issue	Balance	Text	Order ID
01 Jan			1000	stock on hand	
05 Jan	100		1100	replenishment	101 2897
14 Jan		1050	50	customer Smith	102 8972
15 Jan	450		500	replenishment	102 9538
16 Jan		150	350	customer Adams	103 2687

a. 50

b. 300 (= 350 – 50)

c. Stock replenishment order ID 101 2897 could be deferred to Jan. 14.

d. Yes, there will not be enough available inventory on Jan. 20. Expediting order ID 104 3231 by at least two days could solve this problem.

11.8.2 MRP Technique: Determining Net Requirements and Planned Release

Following the example in Figure 11.3.2.2, determine net requirements and planned releases for item ID 4711. Assume an optimum order interval (or optimum length of order cycle) of 3 periods. The production or procurement lead time for item ID 4711 is 2 periods.

Given data or assumptions: a physical inventory of 700 (no safety stock) and the planned gross requirements by period of time as in Figure 11.8.2.1.

Period	0	1	2	3	4	5	6	7	8	9	10	11	12	13	14	15
Planned gross requirements		250	200	125	150	150	175	200	220	225	240	250	250	225	225	210

Fig. 11.8.2.1   Gross requirements.

As for the planned available inventory, please enter the result including the planned receipts in each period.

Solution:

Period	0	1	2	3	4	5	6	7	8	9	10	11	12	13	14	15
Physical inventory	700															
Planned gross requirements		250	200	125	150	150	175	200	220	225	240	250	250	225	225	210
Projected available inventory without order receipts	700	450	250	125	0	0	0	0	0	0	0	0	0	0	0	0
Net requirements (negative projected available inventory)		0	0	0	25	150	175	200	220	225	240	250	250	225	225	210
Batch size / planned receipts					350			645			740			660		
Planned releases			350			645			740			660				
Projected available inventory with order receipts	700	450	250	125	325	175	0	445	225	0	500	250	0	435	210	0

11.8.3 Order Point Technique versus MRP Technique

Section 11.3 presents the MRP technique. It is clear why, in the comparison in Figure 5.5.2.1, the MRP is rated to be complicated with regard to the order point technique or the kanban technique. Section 11.3.1 explained why discontinuous demand is a main reason for the need of the MRP technique for determining stochastic dependent demand (or quasi-deterministic demand). We created an example using Flash animation that will give you a sense of how discontinuity or lumpiness of the demand influences the sum of carrying costs and setup and ordering costs, comparing the MRP technique with the order point technique. You can view the animation at URL:

http://www.intlogman.lim.ethz.ch/order_point_vs_mrp.html

Note that in order to compare the two techniques, a safety stock of the same size as for the order point technique has been introduced for the MRP technique. It is correct to do so, because in the quasideterministic case, a safety demand has to be introduced for the independent demand at the end product level (see Section 9.5.6). Through the MRP algorithm, this safety demand is — in fact — always present at some stage on the value chain, just as the safety stock is present in the order point technique for a specific component. Therefore, for comparison of the two techniques, we can assume the safety demand on the component — like a safety stock.

Now, find out how the shape of the of the inventory curve according to the two techniques changes for continuous and less continuous demand (running your cursor over the gray icon shape bar will execute your input choice).

Try out different parameters to calculate the lot size or choose a different initial inventory or service level. Running the cursor over the gray icon either leads you to a specific window where you can enter your input data or executes your input choice.

The "costs" icon opens a window with the carrying costs as well as the setup and ordering costs for the two techniques. Discuss whether for the given demand pattern with less continuous demand there is sufficient reason to prefer the MRP technique. Consider that the calculated costs do not take into account either the batch-size-dependent unit costs — which is the same for both techniques, but generally by far higher than the sum of carrying, setup and ordering costs — or the administration costs for the implementation and use of the specific materials management technique.

Try out other demand values. Observe the effect of issue quantities on the order of the production or procurement batch size. Again, use the "calculate" icon to execute your input choice. The initial demand values are automatically re-entered by touching the gray demand icon. Note what happens with the curves as you continue to enter sequences of two or more periods with zero demand, interrupted by one or two periods with very high demand. You will see that the order point technique will not be able to handle this demand pattern. The projected available inventory level will sometimes fall below zero, engendering opportunity costs that we did even not consider in the costs comparison.

12 Time Management and Scheduling

Planning & control in organizational logistics aims to deliver products and orders reliably by the specified due date. Time management and scheduling are first and foremost a matter of medium-term and short-term planning (during order release), although there are some long-term elements. Figure 12.0.0.1 shows the reference model for business processes and the tasks of planning and control introduced in Figure 4.1.4.2, highlighting the tasks and processes in time management and scheduling on a darker background.

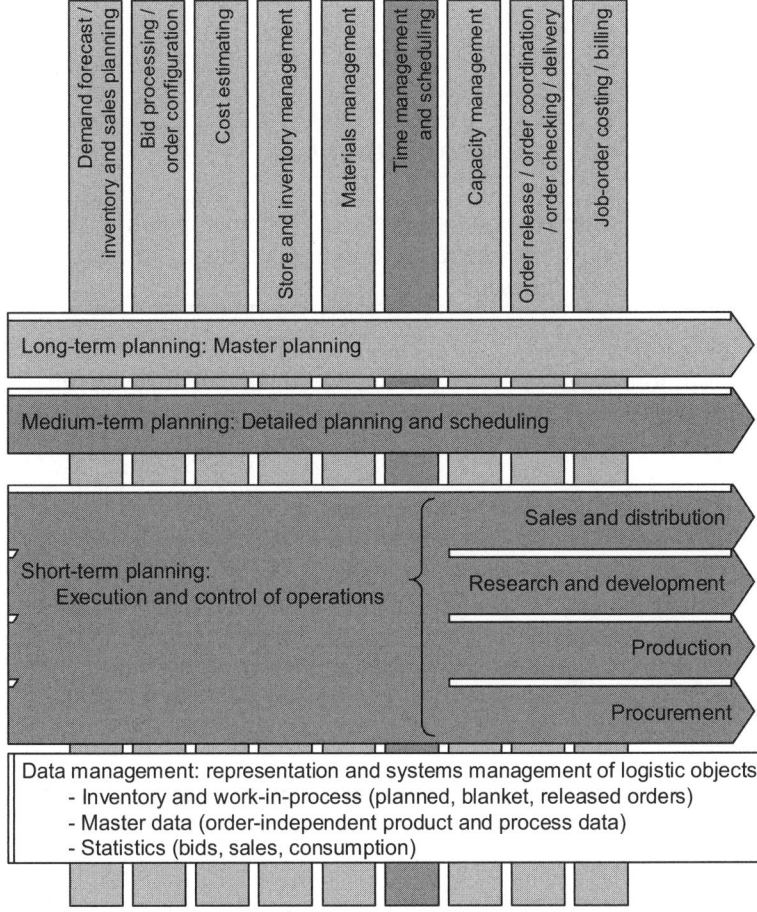

Fig. 12.0.0.1   The part systems examined in Chapter 12 are shown on a darker background.

For an overview of the material in this chapter, see also Sections 1.2.3, 4.3.3, and 4.3.4. (We suggest that you reread these sections before studying Chapters 12, 13, and 14.)

The first step in time management and scheduling is to estimate the lead time for an order. This chapter views and analyzes lead time as a composite of time elements. We will pay particular attention to unproductive interoperation times and examine difficult-to-estimate wait times for work centers statistically. From the results we will derive means to reduce wait times. This chapter also presents various scheduling techniques and their areas of application — specifically, forward, backward, central point, and probable scheduling — and discusses effects such as splitting and overlapping.

12.1   Elements of Time Management

Time management is the observation, control, and manipulation of time elements. *Time elements* are the duration of operations, interoperation times, and administration times.

In typical job shop production, the focus is on interoperation times, since they make up more than 80 % of the total lead time. However, in line production observation of the duration of the operations themselves is also of particular interest.

12.1.1 The Order of the Operations of a Production Order

In materials management, *lead time* (see Sections 1.1.2 and 1.2.3) is a basic attribute of both manufactured and purchased products. With this data, the start date of a production or procurement order — starting from the due date — can be calculated, and rudimentary scheduling can be performed.

The value for lead time can be a value based on prior experience. However, for effective planning, particularly of production orders, such more or less arbitrary values are often not precise enough:

- Some components do not need be reserved for the start date of an order, as they are only needed for a later operation.

- For exact capacity planning we need to know the point in time at which the work center will be loaded by work to be executed and thus a start date for each operation.

For a detailed calculation of *manufacturing lead time*, the essential elements are attributes of the bills of material and routing sheets. We can develop the process plan from these elements (see also Figure 1.2.3.3). Manufacturing lead time is the sum of the three different time elements that are defined in Section 1.2.3:

- *Operation time* (see Section 12.1.2)
- *Interoperation time* (see Section 12.3.1)
- *Administrative time* (see Section 12.1.4)

Lead time calculated on the basis of the lead times for individual operations is only an estimated value, since — especially for interoperation times — it is dependent on assumed average values. In this case, lead time calculation does not take into account the definite capacity utilization of work centers, which can dramatically affect wait time estimates (see also Section 12.2.). However, the "normal" lead time calculated in this way is accurate enough for several planning methods, and especially for rough-cut planning.

Lead time calculation is based on the *order of the operations* of the routing sheets.

> A *sequence of operations* is the simplest order of operations. It is illustrated in Figure 12.1.1.1. In the simplest case, lead time is merely the sum of the time elements.

Besides the simple sequence of operations, there are also more complex structures, which can be portrayed as networks.

- In a *directed network of operations* no operations are repeated. We can identify the operations in ascending order (in a semi-order). Lead time corresponds to the longest path through the network.

- In an *undirected network of operations* sequences of operations within the network may be repeated. In this case we can calculate lead time only if we know the number of repetitions or other constraints.

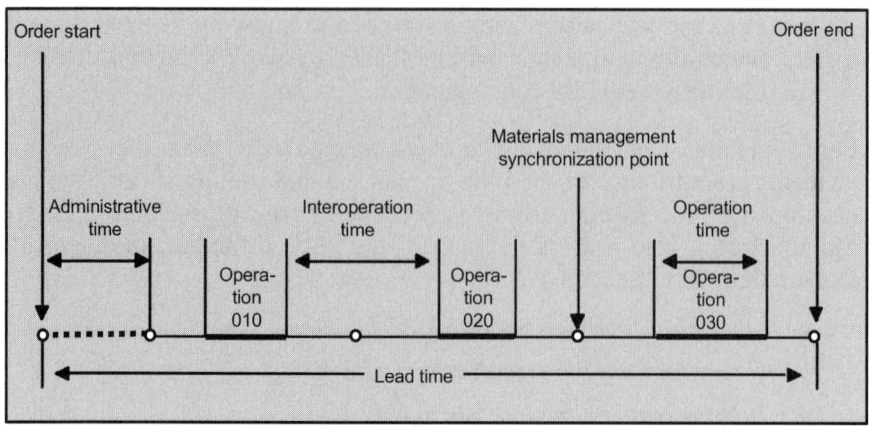

Fig. 12.1.1.1   A sequence of operations.

Figure 12.1.1.2 shows a typical example. In a *directed network of operations* the lead time corresponds to the longest path through the network.

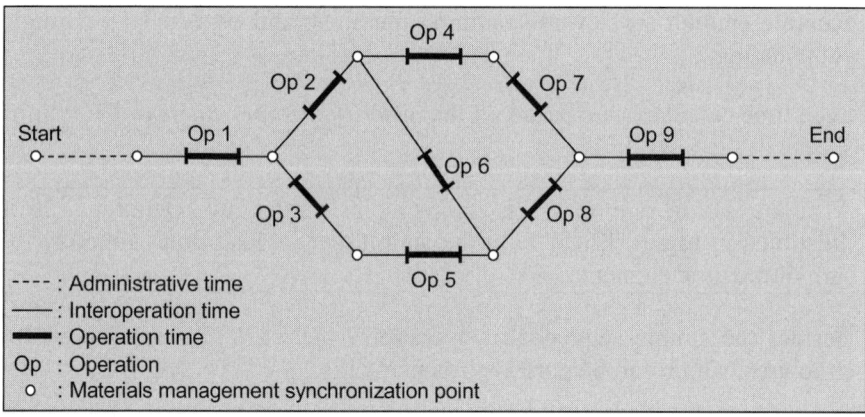

Fig. 12.1.1.2   A network of operations.

A process plan for multistage production, such as in Figure 1.2.3.3, corresponds to a directed network if a joint start event links together the open arborescent structure at the left.

A *synchronization point* is a link between the routing sheet and the bill of material, and thus between time management and materials management.

In Figures 12.1.1.1 and 12.1.1.2, circles designate the synchronization points at transitions between individual operations. At these points, we may channel in goods taken from a warehouse, directly procured, or taken from another, synchronous production order. At the same time, the circles represent an *intermediate stage* of the manufactured product. This can also be a partially completed product stage stocked as an in-house item. This means that these points in time on the time axis are also the planning dates for the necessary components.

12.1.2 Operation Time and Operation Load

Operation time is the time required to carry out a particular operation. It is defined in Section 1.2.3 as the sum of *setup time* for machines and tools and the *run time* for the actual order lot.[1] The latter is the product of the number of units produced (the *lot* or *batch*) and the run time for a unit of the lot produced (the *run time per unit*). The simplest formula for operation time occurs when run times are scheduled serially following the setup time, as in Figure 1.2.3.1.

Figure 12.1.2.1 shows the same formula for operation time as a graphic representation.

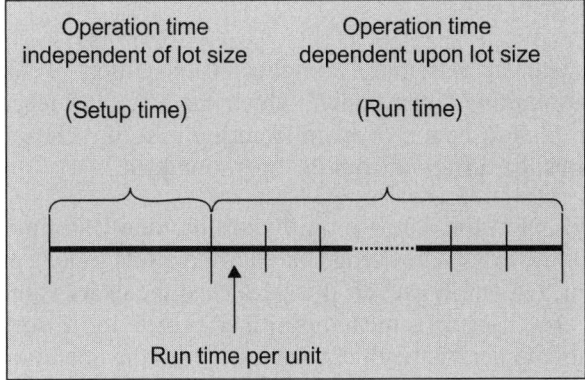

Fig. 12.1.2.1   The simplest formula for operation time (graphic representation).

---

[1]   Setdown time also belongs to operation time. In practice, however, it is generally short and therefore ignored.

The formula for calculating operation time becomes more complicated when we include special effects such as splitting or overlapping. See also Section 12.4.

Operation load is the work content of the operation, measured in the capacity unit of the work center used for the operation. In Section 1.2.4 we saw that operation load is the sum of the *setup load* — the work content that is *independent of batch size* — and the *run load* for the actual order lot.[2] The latter is the product of the number of units produced (the *lot* or *batch*) and the *run load per unit* for a unit of the lot produced. The formula for the operation load shown in Figure 12.1.2.2 repeats the simplest case of the formula given in Figure 1.2.4.1.

Operation load = (setup load) + lot•(run load per unit)

Fig. 12.1.2.2   The simplest formula for operation load.

Often, the capacity unit for the work center used for the operation is a unit of time. In these cases, setup time and run time are generally identical with setup load and run load. There are, however, instances in which the operation time bears no relationship to the operation load.

- For subcontracted operations, for example, a cost unit may be chosen as the capacity unit.

- For operations with an extremely complicated execution or for purely fictitious "waiting operations," which have no influence upon the load of a work center or manufacturing cost, the chosen operation time must be different from the operation load.

If the interoperation times exert the dominant influence on total lead time, scheduling does not require exact knowledge of the operation time. For purposes of capacity management, however, planners need the exact value of the operation load in order to gain a meaningful load profile for a work center. If they are now able to derive the operation time from the operation load, they can calculate the precise operation time as well as the operation load.

---

[2]   Setdown load also belongs to standard load. In practice, however, it is generally short and therefore ignored.

12.1.3 The Elements of Interoperation Time

Interoperation time occurs before or after an operation (see definition in Section 1.2.3). Figure 12.1.3.1 shows the *elements of interoperation time*:

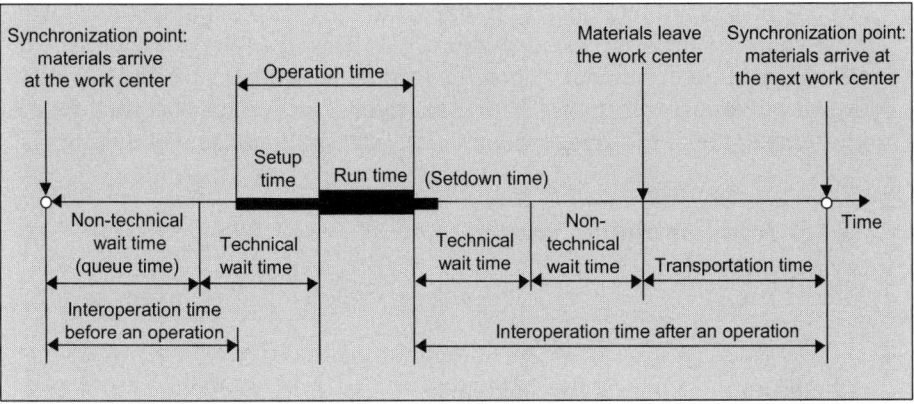

Fig. 12.1.3.1   The elements of interoperation time.

- *Technical wait time after an operation* describes the time required to complete testing, a chemical reaction, a cool-down period, or other things. It is an attribute of the operation. As is true of the operation itself, it is not generally possible to shorten this wait time in order to, for example, accelerate the order.

- *Non-technical wait time after an operation* is the wait time incurred before the lot is collected for transport. It is dependent on the work center and can be an attribute of this object or be included in transportation time.

- *Transportation time*, also called *move time* or *transit time*, is the time needed to transport the lot from the current work center to the work center that will carry out the subsequent operation. This time is dependent on both work centers. There are various techniques for determining this time (see Section 12.1.5).

- *Non-technical wait time before an operation* is made up of the so-called *queue time*, that is, the amount of time a job waits at a work center before setup or work is performed on the job. This includes preparation time for the operation, as long as it is not counted as a part of the actual setup time. This time is dependent on the work center and is an attribute of that object (see Section 12.2).

- *Technical wait time before an operation* is made up of the operation-specific preparation time, such as a warm-up process which does yet not load the work center. In practice, this time is of minor significance. It is an attribute of the operation.[3]

All components of interoperation time, with the exception of technical wait times before and after the operation, are "elastic": We can lengthen or shorten them in dependency upon the load at the work center and the order urgency (compare Section 12.3.6). Therefore, the values specified in the master data are only average values, and they can fluctuate widely.

12.1.4 Administrative Time

Administrative time is the time needed to release and complete an order (see definition in Section 1.2.3).

Administrative time at the beginning of an order is required for order release. This comprises availability control, decision making as to type of procurement, and the preparation time that the production or purchasing office needs for the order. It is also a lead time for the data or control flow (i.e., without flow of goods).

Buffer times added to this administrative time wherever possible will serve to control fluctuations in the effective loads of work centers. This will keep the capital-intensive lead time for goods as short as possible. Schedulers can use the play resulting from this buffer to move the entire order forward or backward on the time axis, according to the load of the work centers at the time of order release.

In addition, schedulers should plan administrative time for coordination purposes for each partial order. This time can also include a "normal" stock issue time for components, as long as it has not already been accounted for in the routing sheet as an independent operation, called "stock issue," for example.

Similarly, at the end of each partial order there is administrative time that generally includes time to place the completed order in stock or to prepare it for shipping. This time may also include a "normal" control time, provided that schedulers do not want to account for this in the routing sheet as an independent operation, called "final control," for example.

---

[3]   Technical wait time is also called *technical idle time*.

12.1.5 Transportation Time

There are different techniques to determine transportation time between work centers (also called move time or transit time):

- *Simple, but inexact:* As a *scheduling rule*, planners use one, single time that is not dependent on the work centers.

- *Exact, but complex:* A matrix of transportation times contains an entry for every combination: "preceding work center ⇔ following work center." This matrix should be maintained in the form of a table in a separate entity class. It is a square matrix containing zeros on the diagonal. If it is not dependent on the direction of the transport, the matrix will be symmetrical (see Figure 12.1.5.1). The difficulty with this technique lies in maintaining the two-dimensional table, since the number of work centers and the transportation times are continually changing.

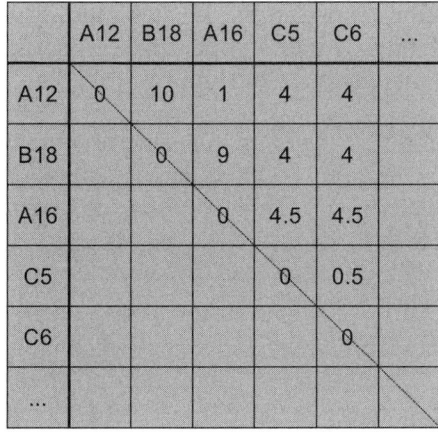

	A12	B18	A16	C5	C6	...
A12	0	10	1	4	4	
B18		0	9	4	4	
A16			0	4.5	4.5	
C5				0	0.5	
C6					0	
...						

Fig. 12.1.5.1   Transportation times matrix.

An efficient compromise between these two extremes is to use an approximation based on an analysis of transportation times and that experience has shown to be reliable, as in Figure 12.1.5.2.

- *Within a plant,* planners define a fictitious center and assume that each shipment must pass through this center. With this, the transportation time from one work center to another becomes the sum of the transportation time from the first work center to the fictitious center and the transportation time from the fictitious center to the other work center. As a result, you only have to register two attributes for every work center, and their values are not dependent on the other work centers.

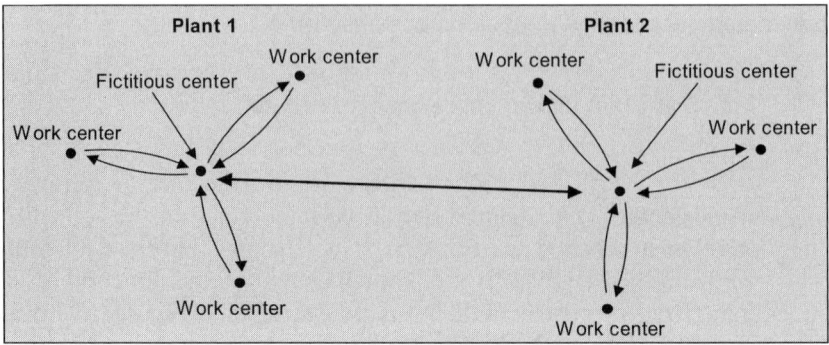

Fig. 12.1.5.2   Approximation of transportation time.

This approximation is reliable, because the *loading and unloading* of the means of transportation comprise the greatest portion of transportation time. Actual transportation time from one work center to another varies little in relation to this.

- *Between* the fictitious centers of *two plants,* planners assume an additional transportation time. Again, for production facilities *in the same region,* this approximation is reliable, because loading and unloading of the means of transport make up most of the additional move time. In relation, the actual transportation time between the plants varies little.

- Characterizing plants by the attribute "region" will distinguish among plants in differing geographic areas. This allows differentiation among regional and interregional or even national and international shipments.

12.2   Buffers and Queues

Non-technical wait time before an operation is a difficult element of interoperation time to plan. It arises if the processing rhythm of the operations of a work center does not correspond to the rhythm of the receipt of the individual orders. This can happen in job shop production, for example, if the work center receives orders randomly from preceding operations. Queuing theory is a collection of models to deal with the resulting effects — buffers and queues.

A *buffer* or a *bank* is a quantity of materials awaiting further processing.

A buffer can refer to raw materials, semifinished stores or hold points, or a work backlog that is purposely maintained behind a work center ([APIC04]).

A *queue* in manufacturing is a waiting line of jobs at a given work center waiting to be processed.

As queues increase, so do average queue time (and therefore lead time) and work-in-process inventory ([APIC04]).

Queuing theory or *waiting line theory* is the collection of models dealing with waiting line problems, e.g., problems for which customers or units arrive at some service facility at which waiting lines or queues may build ([APIC04]).

12.2.1 Wait Time, Buffers, and the Funnel Model

Scheduling may deliberately plan in buffers and wait times before a work center for organizational purposes.

Inventory buffer is inventory used to protect the throughput of an operation or the schedule against the negative effects caused by statistical fluctuations ([APIC04]).

Such buffers should absorb potential disturbances in the production process, that occur, for example, in line production or kanban chains. Figure 12.2.1.1 considers two adjacent workstations.

If both workstations were perfectly synchronized, a waiting line would be unnecessary. However, a disturbance may occur at either of the two work systems as a result of, for example:

- Overloading, scrap, or reworking
- Material shortage, breakdown, or absence of workers

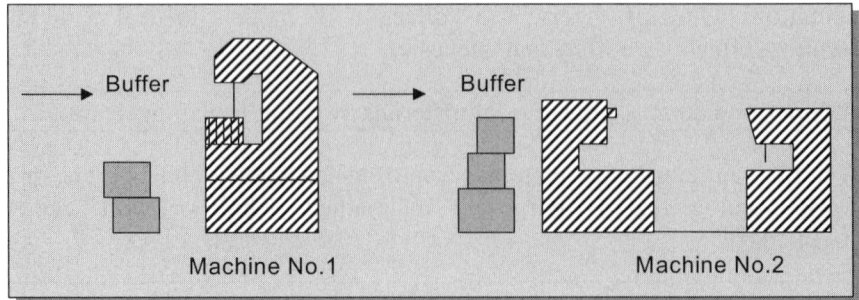

Fig. 12.2.1.1   Inventory buffers to cushion disturbances in the production flow.

The size of the inventory buffer in front of a work center depends on the degree of synchronization that can be maintained with the previous workstation in practice.

- If the work process on the first machine is disrupted, the queue waiting for the second machine is reduced. In this case, the second machine may become idle.[4]

- If the work process on the second machine is disrupted, the queue waiting for the second machine increases, as does the buffer before the second workstation. This may lead to a bottleneck at the second machine.

Scheduling may also plan buffers for *economic reasons*. By skillfully sequencing operations from the buffer inventory, you can save valuable setup times. Such setup time savings may occur, for example, in processing products from a single product family. Depending on the circumstances, it is possible to provide directly for such sequencing in detailed planning and scheduling. In practice, however, order lead times of unequal length or highly varied order structures limit the extent to which you can plan. As a result, you can often only optimize the sequence of operations at the workstation itself via finite forward scheduling.

Another *economic reason* for having a buffer in front of a work center is the psychological effect of the buffer on the efficiency of the workers:

- If the buffer is too small, the workers begin to slow down, fearing that their hours will be cut or even that they will not be needed at

---

[4]   *Idle time* is time when operators or resources (e.g., machines) are not producing product because of setup, maintenance, lack of material, lack of tooling, or lack of scheduling ([APIC04]).

the work center. Small buffers make it look like there is not enough work. Therefore, efficiency decreases.

- Up to a certain point, long queues have a positive influence on efficiency. However, if the queue is too long, it can have a demoralizing effect on workers. The quantity of work to be performed seems insurmountable. Efficiency sinks.

In summary, a buffer in front of a work center is often tolerated or even planned deliberately. However, in evaluating buffers, and in particular their economic repercussions, it is important to take into account the double negative effect of buffers, specifically:

- Increase in lead time
- Increase in work in process and thus tied up capital

> *The buffer model* and the *funnel model* below are concepts of the levels of work in process that are waiting at the workstations.

Figure 12.2.1.2 shows the buffer as a reservoir. This conceptualization is quite old (see [IBM75]).

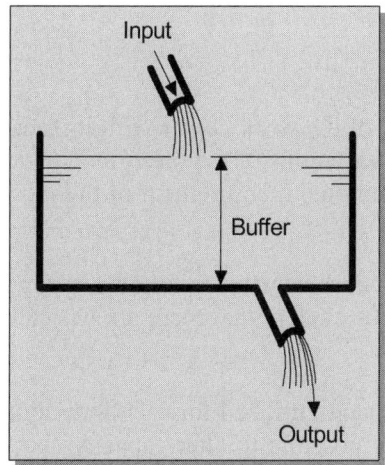

Fig. 12.2.1.2   Reservoir model.

A more recent conceptualization of the buffer is the funnel model (see [Wien94]). Each work center is viewed as a funnel, as illustrated in Figure 12.2.1.3.

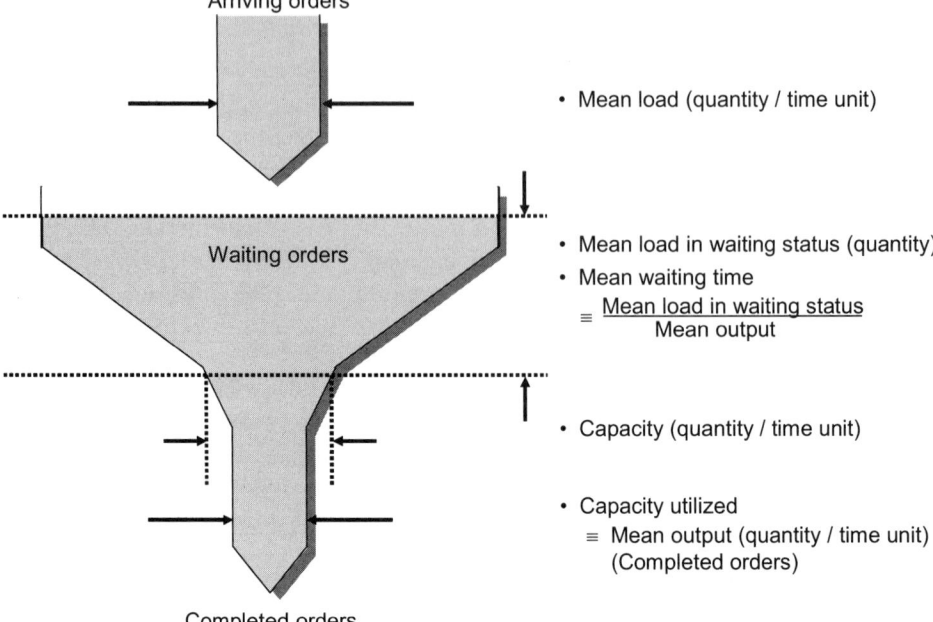

Fig. 12.2.1.3   Funnel model.

The objective is to align the mean output of the work center with its mean load. The funnel volume is used to bring variations of the mean load under control. This means that there must be continual measurement of the mean load, its variation, and the mean output.

If we see total production as a system of work centers, or funnels, that are linked together by output flows, it becomes evident that there are basically two ways to adjust the system:

- Change capacity, or rather the capacity utilized for each individual funnel. However, it is not always possible to alter capacity short-term.

- Regulate the number of orders that enter into the system. If too many orders are on hand, individual funnels can overflow, resulting in blocked shop floors and poor delivery reliability. In this case schedulers should decide what orders to withhold from production. Again, this measure is not always possible.

12.2.2 Queues as an Effect of Random Load Fluctuations

With the exception of continuous production, there is no production type in which the capacities of machines and workstations following one another in the process are completely synchronized. As Figure 12.2.1.1 shows, even in other cases of line production, synchronization is not always possible. Thus, to a certain extent, buffers serve to balance the differing output rates of the work centers and to ensure continual load of the individual work centers over a certain period of time.

These buffers are queues formed in front of a workstation; the size of the queues changes over time. Particularly in job shop production, there is great variation in the behavior of the buffer, since a queue is fed from many locations. We can view job shop production as a network with work centers as nodes, as represented in Figure 12.2.2.1.

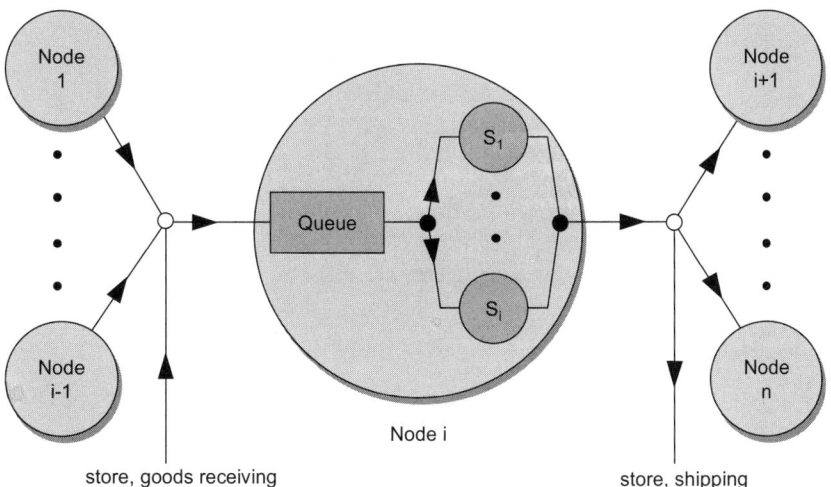

Fig. 12.2.2.1   Job shop production as a network with work centers as nodes.

In the figure, the nodes represent work centers, which are classified as homogeneous. The arrows represent the flow of goods or information bet-ween these work centers. In the discussion below, the focus is on 'Node i' of this network.

Input enters from various nodes and sometimes also from the outside (from a store or a receiving department, for example). This input arrives at a joint queue in front of one of the various workstations (S_1, S_2, ..., S_i) of work center i.

After completion of the operation in Node i, the orders flow to other nodes or toward the outside, either in part or in their entirety (after a final operation), depending on the specification in the routing sheet. In line production, there is essentially a sequence of nodes rather than a network.

As mentioned above, determining the size of a buffer is an optimization problem. Queuing theory provides some fundamental insights into the way that job shop production functions and, to a certain extent, how line production functions as well. Here we limit our discussion to the stationary state of a queue, that is, the state after an infinite time period and with fixed constraints.

For the following discussion, Figure 12.2.2.2 sets out several definitions of variables from queuing theory.

s	= Number of parallel stations (e.g., workstations per work center)
ρ	= Capacity utilization of the work center ($0 \leq \rho \leq 1$) = $\dfrac{load}{capacity}$
CV	= Coefficient of variation (ratio of standard deviation to mean) of a distribution
OT	= Operation time
WT	= Waiting time per order in the queue

Fig. 12.2.2.2   Definitions of queuing theory variables.

To simplify the discussion, assume the following:

- Arrivals are random; that is, they follow a Poisson distribution with the parameter λ. λ is the average number of arrivals per period under observation.

- Arrivals and the operation process are independent of one another.

- Execution proceeds either in order of arrival or according to random selection from the queue.

- The duration of the operations is independent of the order of processing and is subject to a determinate distribution with mean M(OT) and coefficient of variation CV(OT).

Figure 12.2.2.3 shows the average wait time as a function of capacity utilization for a model with one station (s = 1, where a queue feeds only one operation station, i.e., one workstation or one machine). We assume the coefficient of variation CV(OT) for the distribution to be 1, which is the case with a negative exponential distribution, for example.

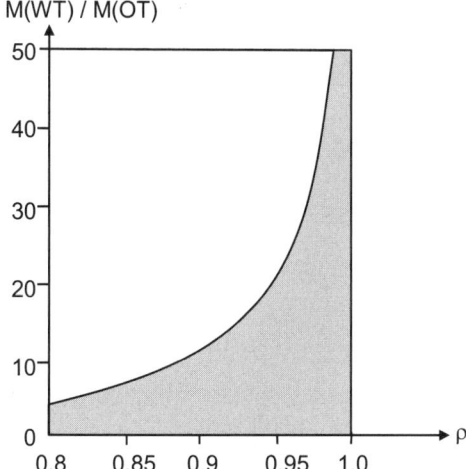

Fig. 12.2.2.3 Average wait time as a function of capacity utilization: special case $s = 1$, $CV(OT) = 1$.

Figure 12.2.2.4 presents the relevant formulas of queuing theory for the average case, with references to their original sources in the literature, specifically [GrHa98], [Coop90], and [LyMi94], including page and formula numbers. For further aspects of theoretical mathematics the reader can consult [Fers64] and [Alba77]. It is important to note, however, that for multiple-station models ($s = $ arbitrary), the relationships based upon numerical calculation only approach validity under conditions of extensive capacity utilization.

	$s = 1$ $0 \le \rho \le 1$	$s = $ arbitrary $\rho \to 1$
$CV(OT) = 1$	$M(WT) = \dfrac{\rho}{1-\rho} \cdot M(OT)$ [Gros85], p. 77, formula (2.30)	$M(WT) \approx \dfrac{\rho}{1-\rho} \cdot \dfrac{M(OT)}{s}$ [Coop90], p. 487, formulas (5.22), (5.23), (5.36) and $\rho = a/s$
$CV(OT) = $ arbitrary	$M(WT) = \dfrac{\rho}{1-\rho} \cdot \dfrac{1+CV^2(OT)}{2} \cdot M(OT)$ [Gros85], p.256, formula (5.11) or [LyMi94], p. 191, formula 6	$M(WT) \approx \dfrac{\rho}{1-\rho} \cdot \dfrac{1+CV^2(OT)}{2} \cdot \dfrac{M(OT)}{s}$ [Coop90], p. 508, formula (9.3)

Fig. 12.2.2.4 Summary of relevant formulas in queuing theory.

Figure 12.2.2.5 shows wait time as a function of operation time for selected values of s and CV(OT).

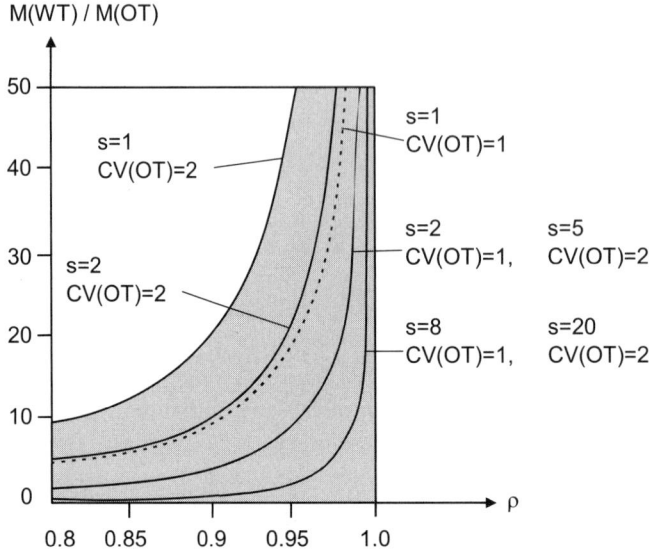

Fig. 12.2.2.5   Average relative wait time as a function of capacity utilization: selected values (following Prof. Büchel).

12.2.3 Conclusions for Job Shop Production

It is not possible to apply quantitative results of queuing theory to job shop production directly, since some of the specified conditions are not satisfied. For example:

- The arrival process may be *short term*, a purely random process. However, scheduling can shield production from large capacity utilization peaks, and the delivery rates of supplying nodes will limit arrival rates at a work center (= network node). Therefore, medium-term fluctuations will be somewhat smaller than in the case of a purely random process.

- There is no independence between the execution and the arrival process. Since the negative consequences of large queues are undesirable, scheduling will spare no effort to avoid extreme situations. It manipulates the processes by:

  - Subcontracting individual orders
  - Subcontracting individual operations

- Raising the capacity of operating facilities with overtime or shift work
- Advancing or postponing individual operations

The result is not a stationary state, but rather a series of transitional states, which are characterized by varying values of the parameters and distributions that specify a queuing process. Nevertheless, queuing theory yields qualitative findings for job shop production and, in part, for line production:

1. *High capacity utilization ⇔ large queues:* In a rigid queuing system, particularly with a one-station model, it is not possible to achieve both good utilization of the capacities and short lead times simultaneously. The higher the capacity utilization desired (in the absence of capacity adjustments from planning interventions), the larger the average queue must be.

2. *High capacity utilization ⇔ wait time >> operation time:* Wait time in the queue is significantly larger than operation time in the case of high capacity utilization.

3. *Shorter lead time ⇐ fewer operations:* Fewer operations mean fewer queues. In industrial production this is achieved by a greater versatility of machine tools, such as numerically controlled machines or machining centers, and in services and administration by a reduction of extreme division of labor. However, it is important to ensure that the total operation time with a reduced number of operations is shorter than that with a larger number of operations. Otherwise, no positive effect will result, since wait time increases with prolonged operation time.

4. Large queues result from
   - Prolonged operation time
   - Extremely varied operation times
   - Few parallel workstations, or only one workstation

The qualitative findings of queuing theory indicate the following measures:

- *A reduction of setup time, which will reduce batch sizes and hence cut the average operation time.* However, direct reduction of batch size without reducing setup time increases manufacturing costs. It is only productive if the work center is not fully utilized, that is, if the larger setup time resulting from splitting the operations does not lead to overloading or nearly full utilization of the work center.

- *Equal contents for all operations, in order to avoid markedly different operation times.* Schedulers can reduce the coefficient of variation for operation times, that is, the difference in the duration of operations, by, for example, splitting up orders with long standard times. This results in a reduction in the mean operation time as well. However, in fully utilized production, increased setup can negate the positive effect.

- *A reduction in utilization*, which can be achieved by holding over-capacity. Schedulers may also transfer employees to those work centers where capacity utilization threatens to become too large.

All these measures are starting points or basic principles of the lean / just-in-time concept. The general, dominant tendency today is to move away from production as a system with fixed constraints. The more successful this move is, the shorter the wait times resulting from the queuing effect will be. As a result, organizational intent — rather than chance — increasingly determines lead times.

12.2.4 Logistic Operating Curves

Logistic operating curves are ways to summarize the facts of an operation as shown in Figure 12.2.4.1 (see [Wien94]).

Logistic operating curves aid evaluation of production processes in the framework of production control. Logistic operating curves express a comparison of logistic performance indicators.

- In Figure 12.2.4.1, *performance* is the output, that is, the load processed by the work center (see also [Wien94]). Thus, the performance curve corresponds to the *capacity utilization* curve (see also Figure 1.4.3.4 or Figure 1.4.4.4). A particular output is achievable only if the waiting work in process is of a particular size. As output approaches its maximum, you can only increase it if you increase the inventory of work in the queue over proportionally. This logistic operating curve shows in its upper part roughly the same situation as in Figure 12.2.2.3, where the axes are reversed.

- The *range (of inventory)* is the length of time required to process the inventory at the workstation. Accordingly, the *mean range* is the mean of the wait time, as in Figure 12.2.2.4, plus the operation time. This mean has a minimum, which is influenced, among other things, by the operation times and their variances. For job shop production the level of waiting work determines the inventory or work in process to a large degree. See also the performance indicator *work-in-process-inventory turnover* in Figure 1.4.3.2.

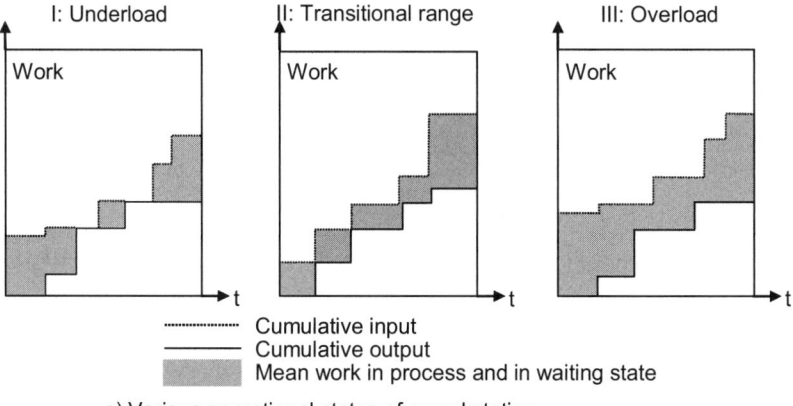

a) Various operational states of a workstation

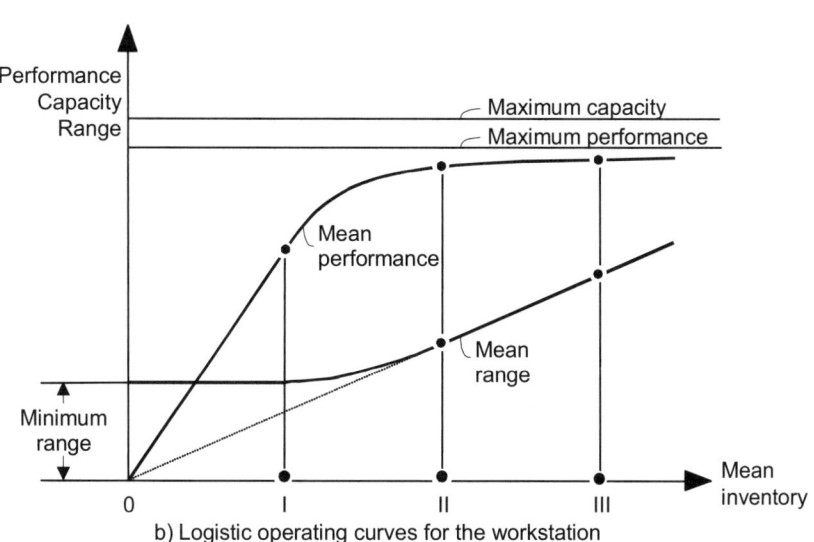

b) Logistic operating curves for the workstation

Fig. 12.2.4.1 An example of logistic operating curves (following [Wien94]).

From capacity utilization, then, we arrive at work-in-process and from there to the mean wait time (which, in job shop production, makes up a large proportion of lead time). The three inventory levels I, II, and III represent, respectively, an underloaded work center, an appropriately loaded work center, and an overloaded work center. Thus, the logistic operating curves indicate how much play there is to reduce queues, and hence wait times, without endangering capacity utilization.

In the following, we present suitable measures to alter the logistic operating curve so that the dangerous curve occurs as late as possible. In addition, the slope of the straight lines representing mean work on hand should be as small as possible. JIT concepts (see Chapter 6), for example, can create the potentials for achieving these aims. Through the use of these potentials, the logistic operating curves change, and new degrees of freedom arise that allow for a decrease in orders waiting to be processed.

12.3   Scheduling of Orders and Scheduling Algorithms

Scheduling of orders starts from customer-set order deadlines and determines the other required deadlines for feasibility decisions, loading of capacity, and reservations of components.

A *scheduling algorithm* is a technique of calculation designed to support scheduling of orders.

Scheduling of orders is mainly the job of the personnel involved in the placing and execution of the order. For these purposes, they should have access to appropriate tools, such as to information technology in the form of logistics software.

Scheduling of orders is based on knowledge of and calculations of lead time. However, time management reveals that there are limits to the accurate estimation of lead times. Not all time elements can be estimated precisely, and perhaps most difficult to assess is queue time. Of additional concern are unanticipated factors that may arise during actual production. Rescheduling is often the necessary consequence.

Rescheduling is the process of changing order or operation due dates, usually as a result of their being out of phase with when they are needed ([APIC04]).

In spite of the fact that it is important to build up potential for reactive rescheduling, we also need some approximation of cumulative lead time to set in relation to delivery lead time. We need this information proactively, that is, during scheduling of orders. In the short term, this allows decisions to be made to accept or refuse orders. In the medium term, we can get an idea of the probable utilization of the work centers along the time axis.

12.3.1 The Manufacturing Calendar

Measures of the load and capacity of a work center are often in units of time. In other cases as well, time quantities are necessary rather than load, at least for calculating lead time. It is a problem, however, that according to the Gregorian calendar, a week does not always contain the same number of working days.

The *manufacturing calendar* or *shop calendar* counts working days only and omits non-working days, such as vacations, holidays, or weekends.

The *manufacturing date* of the manufacturing calendar begins on day "zero," which corresponds to a particular Gregorian date. For each working day, you add the value of one.

Figure 12.3.1.1 shows an excerpt from a manufacturing calendar.

Gregorian Date	Day	Type of Day	Manufacturing Date
2003.05.09	Sunday	Weekend	879
2003.05.10	Monday	Work day	880
2003.05.11	Tuesday	Work day	881
2003.05.12	Wednesday	Work day	882
2003.05.13	Thursday	Holiday	882
2003.05.14	Friday	Work day	883
2003.05.15	Saturday	Weekend	883
2003.05.16	Sunday	Weekend	883

Fig. 12.3.1.1   The manufacturing calendar.

A manufacturing calendar allows addition or subtraction of a certain number of working days to or from a given Gregorian date. Scheduling of orders often uses these calculations.

In addition, in order to gain the load profile of a work center when we want to compare the load over a particular time period with the capacity available, this calendar takes only working days into consideration.

For efficient calculation, two conversion functions are needed:

- GREG-DATE (manufacturing date) yields the Gregorian date for a given manufacturing date.
- MANUF-DATE (Gregorian date) yields the manufacturing date corresponding to a Gregorian date.

In general, these two functions are carried out by reading entities of the "manufacturing calendar" class, whose attributes correspond to the columns in Figure 12.3.1.1. The two types of calendar are simply two different views of this entity class, either of the Gregorian date or of the manufacturing date. Evaluation of these functions gives:

- GREG-DATE(MANUF-DATE(x) + n) adds n working days to the Gregorian date.

- |MANUF-DATE(x) – MANUF-DATE(y)| yields the number of working days between two Gregorian dates. (Note: |x| is the absolute value of x.)

Some organizations publish the manufacturing calendar officially. It generally runs from 0 to 999 and then begins again with 0. This is impractical for the following reasons:

- Additional non-working days can appear at some point in time, which will necessitate alterations to the published calendar.

- The transition from 999 to 0 generally creates major problems for various sort routines that are based on the manufacturing calendar.

Therefore, we recommend maintaining the manufacturing calendar as an internal date in the computer and determining it on the basis of the attribute "type of day." Thus, when a working day changes into a non-working day, you can calculate a new internal manufacturing calendar easily, beginning with day "1" on a particular date, which usually lies several months in the past.[5] Only Gregorian date attributes should appear in the classes of entities for orders.[6]

12.3.2 Calculating the Manufacturing Lead Time

Let us assume that there is a production order with n operations. They are numbered throughout with the numerator i, where $1 \leq i \leq n$. The following abbreviations stand for the elements of *manufacturing lead time* introduced in Section 12.1 (generally measured in industrial units, i.e., hundredths of hours):

---

[5]   Incidentally, we have to recalculate the manufacturing calendar periodically in order to account for elapsed time and to provide the Gregorian calendar with future manufacturing dates.

[6]   Century and millenium must be included in the date in order to avoid sorting problems such as those encountered in the transition from 1999 to 2000.

The *operation time* for operation i:

LOTSIZE	≡	lot size ordered
ST[i]	≡	setup time for operation i
RT[i]	≡	run time per unit produced for operation i
OT[i]	≡	operation time for an operation i = ST[i] + LOTSIZE * RT[i]

The *interoperation times* for operation i:

INTBEF[i]	≡	interoperation time before the beginning of operation i (zero, if two successive operations are performed at the same work center) = transportation time from the fictitious center to the work center + non-technical wait time before the beginning of the operation (queue time)
INTTEC[i]	≡	technical interoperation time after the completion of operation i
INTAFT[i]	≡	non-technical interoperation time after the completion of operation i = transportation time from the work center to the fictitious center + transportation time from the fictitious center to the subsequent work center

The *administrative times*:

ADMPORDBEG	≡	administrative time for the partial order at the beginning = administrative time for the order release + (possible) materials requisition
ADMPORDEND	≡	administrative time at the end of the partial order = administrative time at the end of the partial order + (possible) time for final control + (possible) time for stocking or preparing the order for shipment
ADMORD	≡	order administrative time for release of the entire order

Fig. 12.3.2.1   Definitions for the elements of operation time.

In practice, we distinguish between two different values for ADMPORDBEG and ADMPORDEND: that which takes the possibilities mentioned in Figure 12.3.2.1 into account and that which does not.

For a *sequence of operations* as the order of the operations, the lead time for an order (abbreviated by LTI) is equal to the sum of all operation times, interoperation times, and administrative times, as the formula given in Figure 12.3.2.2 expresses:

$$LTI = \sum_{1 \leq i \leq n} \{INTBEF[i] + OT[i] + INTTEC[i] + INTAFT[i]\}$$
$$+ ADMORD + ADMPORDBEG + ADMPORDEND$$

Fig. 12.3.2.2   Lead time formula (first version).

LTI corresponds to the lead time for a product with lot size LOTSIZE. The lead time will vary if the lot size is different. If we sum up the elements according to the formula in Figure 12.3.2.3, the result is LTI as a linear function of lot size, as shown in Figure 12.3.2.4.

$$SUMINT = ADMPORDBEG + ADMPORDEND + \sum_{1 \leq i \leq n} \{INTBEF[i] + INTEND[i]\}$$
$$SUMTEC = \sum_{1 \leq i \leq n} INTTEC[i]$$
$$SUMST = \sum_{1 \leq i \leq n} ST[i]$$
$$SUMRT = \sum_{1 \leq i \leq n} RT[i]$$

Fig. 12.3.2.3   Partial sums for the lead time formula.

$$LTI = ADMORD + SUMINT + SUMTEC + SUMST + SUMRT \cdot LOTSIZE$$

Fig. 12.3.2.4   Lead time formula (second version).

You can save as data the partial sums from the lead time formula as attributes of the product. They can then be recalculated following each modification of the routing sheet by summing up all the values for the individual operations.

This procedure is the most efficient way to recalculate the lead time for a production order of any particular order quantity. Instead of having to read the operations, you need only refer back to the product data. For a rapid calculation of secondary requirements, you can now calculate lead time simply according to the formula in Figure 12.3.2.4 and plan all reservations for components on the basis of the start date for the order as in Figure 12.3.2.5:

Start date = completion date - LTI

Fig. 12.3.2.5   Start date as a function of completion date.

In a *directed network of operations* as the order of the operations, the lead time for the order is the sum of the operations along the critical, that is, the longest, path. In some cases this is dependent on lot size. Thus, the partial sums of the lead time formula are relevant for a particular lot size interval. This upper, or lower, limit of the lot size for a simplified calculation of lead time must be part of the product data.

Also, the meaning of the following terms is similar to manufacturing lead time, even though their formal definition differs:

- *Cycle time*: This is the time between completion of two discrete units of production. For example, the cycle time of motors assembled at a rate of 120 per hour would be 30 seconds ([APIC04]). Cycle time is an important variable in connection with single-item-oriented line production, particularly with control via production rates.[7]

- *Throughput time* (sometimes also called "cycle time"): In materials management, throughput time refers to the length of time from when a material enters a production facility until it exits ([APIC04]). Throughput time plays a role in connection with logistic operating curves and the expected value of wait time in the context of production controlling (see Section 12.2.4).

12.3.3 Backward Scheduling and Forward Scheduling

For every production order the planner should know the load of each operation and the point in time at which the work center will be loaded. To determine these factors, planning uses lead-time scheduling techniques.

In *lead time scheduling,* a schedule is developed by calculating the lead time. This calculation includes the duration of all operations, interoperation times, and administrative times.

---

[7]   *Takt time* is a *set* cycle time to match the rate of customer demand. *Flow rate* is the inverse of cycle time. In the example above, "120 units per hour" or "two units per minute" is the flow rate.

The *latest date* is a date that we cannot exceed in execution and control of operations. Similarly, we cannot allow a date to fall before the *earliest date*.

A *set date* is set "externally" and cannot be changed by means of the scheduling algorithm.

The two most important scheduling techniques are the following:

Backward scheduling or *back scheduling* begins with the set (that is, the *latest* acceptable) *completion date* for the order (that is, the *order due date*), and calculates — for each operation — the latest (acceptable) completion date (that is, the *operation due date*) and the latest (possible) start date (that is, the *operation start date*), as well as the *latest (possible) start date* for the order.

Forward scheduling begins with the set (that is, the *earliest* acceptable) *start date* for the order and calculates the earliest (acceptable) start date and the earliest (possible) completion date for each operation, as well as the *earliest (possible) completion date* for the order.

Figure 12.3.3.1 illustrates the two principles.

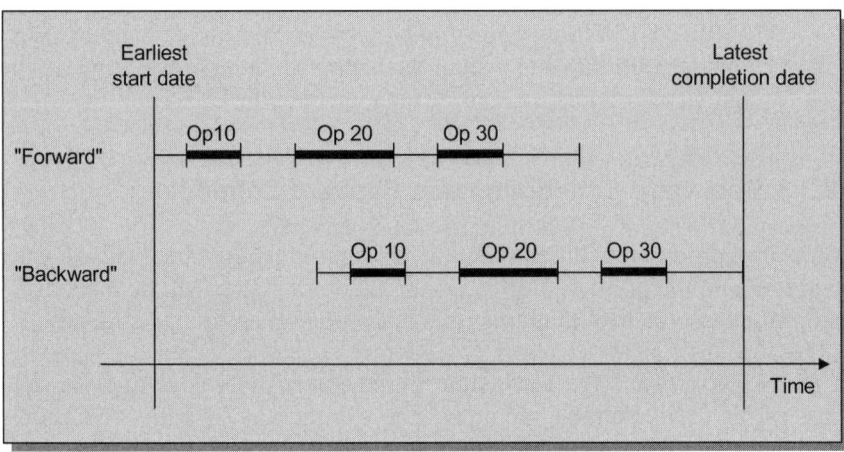

Fig. 12.3.3.1   Forward scheduling and backward scheduling.

Figure 12.3.3.2 shows the simplest algorithm for backward scheduling (the algorithm for forward scheduling has a similar structure):

1. The order of the operations is assumed to be a sequence of operations.

2. The production order consists of one single partial order.
3. All n operations are included in the lead time scheduling; i.e., the order has not yet begun.
4. The interoperation times are weighted with a factor of 1; that is, they are assumed to be "normal."

The formal description of this scheduling task is as follows:

- Take a production order consisting of one partial order with n operations i, $1 \leq i \leq n$, and m components j, $1 \leq j \leq m$, as given. The operation numbers stand in a semi-order; if, for example, $i_1 < i_2$, then operation i_1 is performed before operation i_2.

- Beginning with the set (that is, the latest acceptable) order completion date, we calculate the following "latest" dates:
  - Start and completion dates for the individual partial order
  - Start and completion dates for the individual operations
  - Reservation dates (= start date) for the components
  - Start date for the order, with an exception message if it is earlier than a set (earliest) start date

As data specifications, the following notations are used:

- x $\equiv$ order, partial order, or one position in the partial order (component or operation)
- LCD[x] $\equiv$ latest completion date for x
- ECD[x] $\equiv$ earliest completion date for x
- LSD[x] $\equiv$ latest start date for x
- ESD[x] $\equiv$ earliest start date for x
- OT[i] $\equiv$ operation time for operation i
- INTBEF[i] $\equiv$ interoperation time before operation i
- INTAFT[i] $\equiv$ interoperation time after the end of operation i
- INTTEC[i] $\equiv$ technical interoperation time after operation i
- ADMPORDBEG $\equiv$ administrative time for the partial order at the beginning
- ADMPORDEND $\equiv$ administration time for the partial order at the end

Remarks:

- For comparing the date attributes with one another, we will use the standardized "ISO" format, that is, YYYYMMDD.

- A date is calculated either by the scheduling algorithm or given as a set date. We distinguish the latter from the former by the addition of (set), for example, LCD(set)[x].

---

0   Initialize the start date for the order:
- ESD[order] := max{ESD(set)[order], "today"

1.   At the beginning of the partial order:
- a.   Calculate the completion date for the partial order:
  - LCD[partial order] := LCD(set)[partial order].
  - If LCD(set)[order] < LCD(set)[partial order], then
    - LCD[partial order] := LCD(set)[order].
- b.   Calculate the completion date of the last operation:
  - LCD[n] := LCD[partial order]-ADMPORDEND-INTAFT[n]-INTTEC[n]
  - If LCD(set)[n] < LCD[n], then LCD[n] := LCD(set)[n].

2.   Loop: for operation i, n ≥ i ≥ 1, in descending order:
- a.   Calculate the start date for the operation:
  - LSD[i] := LCD[i] - OT[i].
- b.   If i > 1, then calculate the completion date for the preceding operation:
  - LCD[i-1] := LSD[i] - INTBEF[i] - INTAFT[i-1] - INTTEC[i-1]
  - If LCD(set)[i-1] < LCD[i-1], then LCD[i-1] := LCD(set)[i-1]
- c.   Otherwise (i = 1) calculate the start date for the partial order:
  - LSD[partial order] := LSD[i] - INTBEF[i] - ADMPORDBEG

3.   At the end of the partial order:
- a.   Calculate the start date for the order:
  - LSD[order] := LSD[partial order] - ADMORD
  - If LSD[order] < ESD[order], then message: *start date too early*
- b.   Loop: For all components j, 1 ≤ j ≤ m, calculate the reservation date (the start date):
  - i := operation for which the components j will be needed
  - ESD[j] := LSD[i] - INTBEF[i] - ADMPORDBEG

End of algorithm

Fig. 12.3.3.2   Simple algorithm for backward scheduling.

12.3.4 Network Planning

Site production, or project manufacturing, uses mainly scheduling techniques proper to project management.

Network planning is a generic term for techniques that are used to plan complex projects ([APIC04]).

Project routings, a project task or a work package have directed networks of operations, such as in Fig. 12.1.1.2, instead of simple operation sequences. For network planning, the simple algorithm in Fig. 12.3.3.2 will not do.

The *critical path method (CPM)* is used for planning and controlling the activities in a project. It determines the *critical path* that is the path with the longest duration, which identifies those elements that actually constrain the cumulative lead time (or critical path lead time) for a project [APIC04].

Scheduling is done forwards <u>and</u> backwards. Figure 12.3.4.1 shows the results of scheduling the network in Figure 12.1.1.2 with set values for ESD and LCD. The difference between ESD and LSD is the lead-time margin.[8] On the critical path, it always has the same value (generally close to or equal to zero) and is also called *path float* or *slack time*.

Further network work techniques are:

- The *program evaluation and review technique (PERT)* is a network analysis technique in which each activity is assigned a pessimistic, most likely, and optimistic estimate of its duration. The critical path method is then applied using a weighted average of these times for each node. PERT computes a standard deviation of the estimate of project duration ([APIC04]).

- The *critical chain method* is an extension of the critical path method that was introduced in the theory of constraints, which considers not only technological precedence but also resource constraints.

---

[8]   In the critical path method, slightly different terms are used instead of ESD, ECD, LSD, and LCD: *early start date (ES)*, *early finsh date (EF)*, *late start date (LS)*, and *late finish date (LF)*.

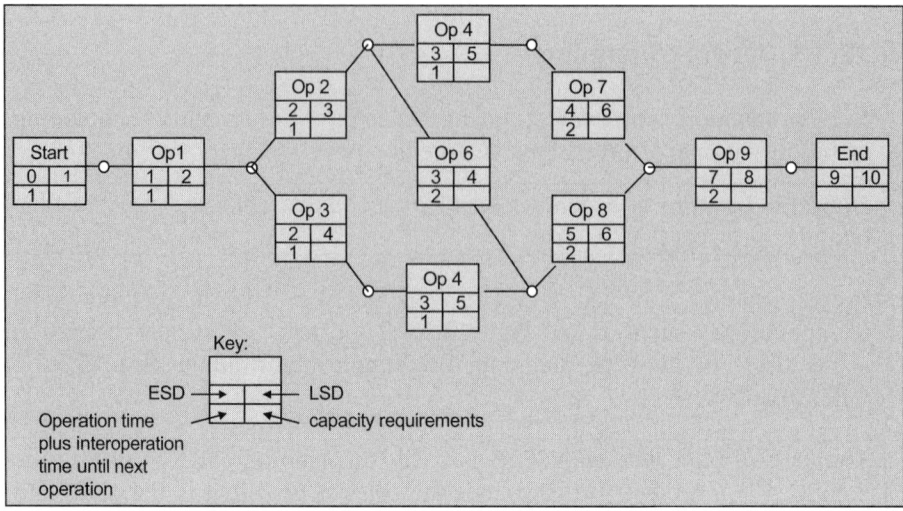

Fig. 12.3.4.1   Scheduled network.

Figure 12.3.4.2 shows an effective network algorithm for backward scheduling. It is formulated as a generalization of the algorithm in Figure 12.3.3.2. If BEGIN is the start and END the conclusion of the routing sheet, then:

- prec(i) designates the quantity of all operations which precede operation i or END.

- succ(i) designates the quantity of all operations which follow operation i or BEGIN.

An operation that precedes (or follows) a particular operation i bears a smaller (or larger) operation number than i. Thus, we can treat operations in an ascending (or descending) order. Usually this type of semi-order establishes itself naturally. Otherwise, it can be calculated easily by using the function prec(i) (or succ(i)).

Omitting all set dates, the above network algorithm is also able to calculate the critical path. For each operation i, the attribute CRIT[i] specifies the operation following i on the critical path. An analogous attribute specifies the first operation on the critical path in the item master data. In step 1b, all the last operations are assigned CRIT[i_1]= "END". Wherever the "<" condition appears in step 2b, CRIT[i_1] is replaced with "i".

0. Initialize the start date for the order:
- ESD[order] := max{ESD(set)[order],"today"}.

Initialize the completion date for the partial order and all operations:
- LCD[x] := min{"9999.99.99", LCD(set)[x]}.

1. At the beginning of the partial order:

a. Calculate the completion date for the partial order:
- If LCD(set)[order] < LCD(set)[partial order], then
   - LCD[partial order] := LCD(set)[order].

b. For each previous operation $i_1 \in$ {prec(END)}, calculate its completion date:
- LCD[i_1] := LCD[partial order]-ADMPORDEND-INTAFT[i_1]-INTTEC[i_1]
- If LCD(set)[i_1] < LCD[i_1], then LCD[i_1] := LCD(set)[i_1].

2. Loop: for operation i, n ≥ i ≥ 1, in descending order:

a. Calculate the start date for the operation:
- LSD[i] := LCD[i] - OT[i].

b. For each operation $i_1 \in$ {prec(i)}, $i_1 \neq$ BEGIN, calculate its completion date:
- LCD'[i_1] := LSD[i] - INTBEF[i] - INTAFT[i_1] - INTTEC[i_1].
- If LCD'[i_1] < LCD[i_1], then LCD[i_1] := LCD'[i_1].

c. For $i_1 \in$ {prec(i)}, i_1=BEGIN, calculate the start date for the partial order:
- LSD[partial order] := LSD[i] - INTBEF[i] – ADMPORDBEG.

3. At the end of the partial order:

a. Calculate the start date for the order:
- LSD[order] := LSD[partial order] - ADMORD
- If LSD[order] < ESD[order], then message: *start date too early*.

b. Loop: For all components j, 1 ≤ j ≤ m, calculate the reservation date (of the start date):
- i := operation for which the components j will be needed
- ESD[j] := LSD[i] - INTBEF[i] – ADMPORDBEG.

End of algorithm

Fig. 12.3.4.2   Network algorithm for backward scheduling.

12.3.5 Central Point Scheduling

Central point scheduling is a combination of forward and backward scheduling. Figure 12.3.5.1 shows the underlying concept.

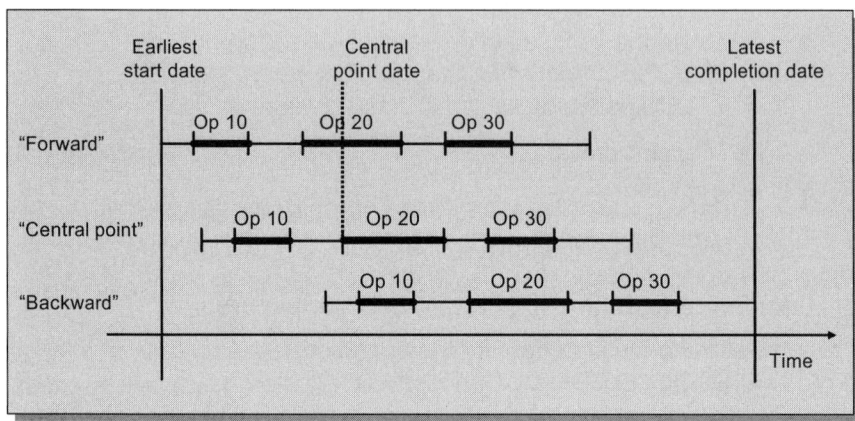

Fig. 12.3.5.1:   Central point scheduling.

The central point date is the start date for a particular operation. This is usually a critical operation (i.e., an operation at a fully utilized work center – often a bottleneck capacity). The critical operation determines the order schedule and therefore both the start and the completion dates. The relationship of this technique to the two scheduling techniques introduced earlier is as follows:

- For the critical operation and all subsequent operations, we use forward scheduling; for the operations previous to the critical operation, we use backward scheduling.

In this way, central point scheduling provides the latest start date and the earliest completion date. This proves to be quite simple in the case of a sequence of operations with exactly one central point as shown in Figure 12.3.5.1.

Other cases are more complicated and lead us to several possible solutions. For example:

- If a sequence of operations has more than one central point, it is unclear whether planning should apply forward or backward scheduling between any two central points.

In a directed network of operations there are several possible solutions:

- If there is one central point and it lies on the critical path, the latest start date and the earliest completion date appear as they do in a sequence of operations. Planners schedule the network operations that are not time critical using either forward scheduling beginning with the latest start date or backward scheduling beginning with the earliest completion date.

- If there is a central point lying on a path that is not time critical, it will affect either the forward scheduling branch or the backward scheduling branch of the time-critical network path. Here, the simplest procedure is to choose between the following two basic options:

  - Backward scheduling beginning with the central point. This will provide a latest start date, and the entire network is scheduled forward from this date.

  - Forward scheduling beginning with the central point. This will provide an earliest completion date, and the entire network is scheduled backward from this date.

- Where there are multiple central points located arbitrarily within the network, central point scheduling becomes more complex.

In order to eliminate ambiguities in central point scheduling within networks, it is useful to determine a so-called mid-level rather than a central point. The mid-level consists of a number of operations for which a start date is chosen in such a way that, without these operations, the beginning and end are no longer connected.

12.3.6 The Lead-Time-Stretching Factor and Probable Scheduling

In practice, the urgency of an order is often more important than an absolute date.

> *Order urgency* is the urgency of the order's operations in compared to those of other orders.

A possible measure for order urgency is the lead-time-stretching factor, which is introduced in the following.

For backward scheduling, *slack time* is the difference between the latest (possible) start date and the earliest (acceptable) start date; for forward scheduling, it is the difference between the earliest (possible) completion date and the latest (acceptable) completion date.

Therefore, slack time provides an element of flexibility in planning. Positive slack time allows an increase in lead time, while negative slack time requires that it be shortened.

In *probable scheduling* we take slack time into account to increase or decrease lead time.

Figure 12.3.6.1 illustrates the principle of probable scheduling using an example with three operations ("op") and positive slack time. In contrast to forward or backward scheduling, the operations are distributed evenly between the earliest start date and the latest completion date. Then, the start or the completion date of each operation is its *probable start date* or *probable completion date*.

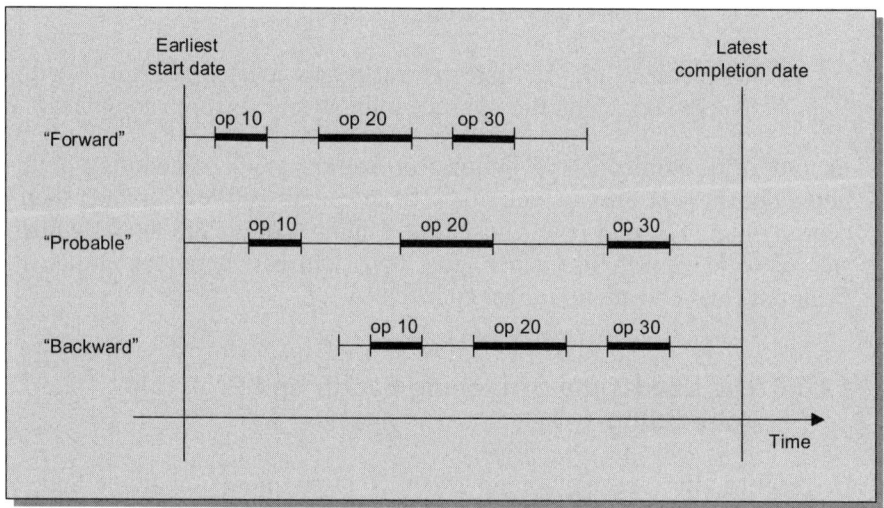

Fig. 12.3.6.1   Forward, backward, and probable scheduling.

Since the technical process itself determines the duration of operations and the technical interoperation time, we can only modify slack time by increasing or reducing either the non-technical interoperation times or the administrative times. All of these time elements are attributes of the product's master data, its routing sheet, and the work centers. Their values are averages, determined through measuring or estimating.

> The *lead-time-stretching factor* is a numerical factor by which the non-technical interoperation times and the administrative times are multiplied.

The choice of the lead-time-stretching factor has the following effects on the scheduling algorithm:

- A factor greater than 1 results in increased lead time.

- A factor equal to 1 results in "normal," or average, lead time.

- A factor between 0 and 1 results in reduced lead time.

- A factor equal to 0 results in a minimal lead time, in that only the duration of the operations and technical interoperation times are strung together.

- With a factor of less than 0, the operations overlap.

Probable scheduling takes the latest completion date and the earliest start date as givens and calculates the lead-time-stretching factor. This is the starting point in the cases that follow.

- *Customer production orders with a set due date:* This due date is the latest acceptable completion date for scheduling. Because delivery dates are often very short term, the earliest start date becomes *de facto* "today." The scheduling algorithm calculates the lead-time-stretching factor (less than 1) needed to shorten the interoperation times so that the order can be completed between "today" and the delivery date. In this case the lead-time-stretching factor indicates the feasibility of completion of the order cycle (where sufficient capacity is available, of course).

- *Orders in process:* The earliest start date for the first of all remaining operations is "today." The latest completion date is generally the date specified when the order is released. Rescheduling calculates the lead-time-stretching factor required for order completion on time. This is very useful if, for example, there are delays after the order is released. A lower lead-time-stretching factor gives this order immediate urgency.

- *Early released orders*: The earliest start date is provided by the date the order is released; the latest completion date is the date on which warehouse stocks will probably fall below the safety stock level. Again, probable scheduling will calculate the lead-time-stretching factor required for timely order completion. This factor can then serve as a priority rule for queues at the work centers (see also Section 14.3.1).

The lead-time-stretching factor is calculated using an iterative forward or backward scheduling process as follows:

0   Choose a lead-time-stretching factor, such as 1 (randomly) or the last valid factor used (in a previous scheduling process).

1   Schedule forward (or backward) using the chosen lead-time-stretching factor. At the same time, calculate the earliest completion date (or the latest start date) using the lead-time-stretching factor 0, and thus the lead time required for the duration of operations and technical interoperation times.

2   If the difference between the earliest completion date and the latest completion date in forward scheduling (or the earliest start date and the latest start date in backward scheduling) is approximately zero, then we have found the appropriate lead-time-stretching factor and the process is finished.

3   If the difference is not approximately zero, choose a new lead-time-stretching factor according to the formulas in Figure 12.3.6.3. Begin again with step 1.

Figure 12.3.6.2 shows the result of each iteration in Step 3, in *forward scheduling*.[9]

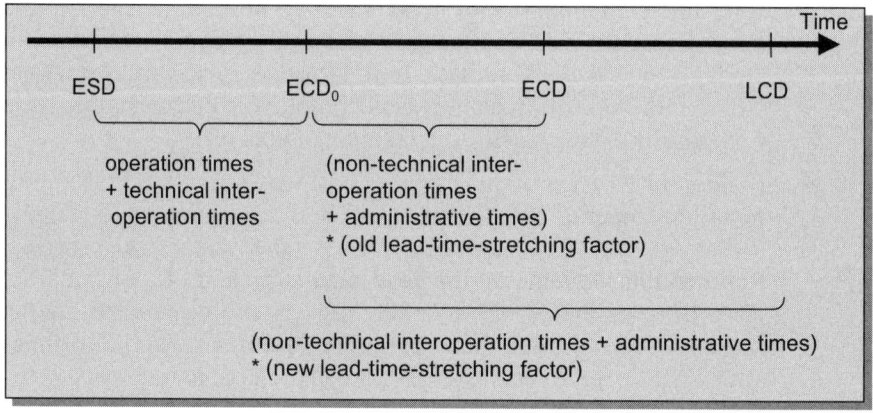

Fig. 12.3.6.2   The role of the lead-time-stretching factor in probable scheduling.

---

[9]   Key: ESD stands for the earliest start date, ECD for the earliest completion date, ECD_0 for the earliest completion date calculated with lead-time-stretching factor 0, and LCD for the latest due date (see definitions in Section 12.3.3).

Iteration of the forward scheduling algorithm calculates the earliest completion date using the currently valid lead-time-stretching factor. The same iteration of the algorithm calculates the earliest completion date using the lead-time-stretching factor 0. The result yields the minimum load time without an overlapping of the operations. The objective of probable scheduling is, by recalculation of the lead-time-stretching factor, to eliminate the difference, that is, the slack time, between the earliest completion date and the latest completion date. This is shown in Figure 12.3.6.2. Since this involves a multiplication factor, the equation is a proportional relationship, as shown in Figure 12.3.6.3.[10]

Backward scheduling	$\dfrac{STREFAC\ [new]}{STREFAC\ [old]} = \dfrac{LSD_0[order] - ESD[order]}{LSD_0[order] - LSD[order]}$
Forward scheduling	$\dfrac{STREFAC[new]}{STREFAC[old]} = \dfrac{LCD[order] - ECD_0[order]}{ECD[order] - ECD_0[order]}$

Fig. 12.3.6.3   Equation for recalculation of lead-time-stretching factor.

For a production contract with a limited number of serially executed operations, probable scheduling using the formula in Figure 12.3.6.3 usually yields the exact solution after only one iteration subsequent to the initial step. In a network structure, however, there may be a different number of operations with varying interoperation times in each branch of the network. In any case, there are always situations where one iteration alone does not produce an immediate, exact solution with a slack time of approximately zero. The reasons for this and some suggestions for solving the problem are as follows:

- The lead-time-stretching factor was too inexact. Another iteration of the process will yield a more exact result, namely, a slack time close to zero.

- The calculations were inexact, which we can correct by, for example, calculating to finer units, such as to tenth-days instead of half-days.

---

[10]   Key: STREFAC is the lead-time-stretching factor, LSD is the latest start date, LSD_0 is the latest start date (calculated with lead-time-stretching factor 0), and LCD is the latest completion date (see the definitions in Section 12.3.3).

- Because of the new lead-time-stretching factor, another path in the network of operations has become time critical; that is, it is now the longest path. A further iteration of the algorithm would yield precise results, provided that the critical path remains the same.

- There is a negative lead-time-stretching factor, and the scheduling algorithm cannot accommodate the operations between the earliest start date and the latest completion date. It is even possible that one of the operations itself is longer than the difference between these two set dates. In both cases, only lengthening the time span will resolve the situation.

12.3.7 Scheduling Process Trains

Process trains were introduced in Chapter 7. A process train is a representation of the flow of materials through a process industry manufacturing system that shows equipment and inventories.

To schedule the process train, we need to know the order in which to schedule the stages of the process train. Take, for example, a process train with three consecutive stages 1, 2, 3. There are three possible scheduling techniques:

- *Reverse flow scheduling* (3, 2, 1) starts with the last stage and proceeds backward (countercurrent to the process flow) through the process structure. It supports demand-based planning.

- *Forward flow scheduling* (1, 2, 3) starts with the first stage and proceeds sequentially through the process structure until the last stage is scheduled. It supports supply-constrained planning, such as short harvest cycle in the food industry.

- *Mixed flow scheduling* (2, 1, 3 or 2, 3, 1) supports planning where stage 2 is the logical focus of attention for scheduling because of processing capacity or material supply constraints. In general, detailed scheduling starts at each bottleneck stage and works toward the terminal process stages or another bottleneck stage.

It is easy to see that these three scheduling techniques have much in common with backward, forward, and central point scheduling.

12.4   Splitting, Overlapping, and Extended Scheduling Algorithms

12.4.1 Order or Lot Splitting

Order splitting or *lot splitting* means distributing the lot to be produced by an operation among two or more machines or employees at a work center for processing. This implies *split lots*.

Splitting reduces lead time, but it incurs additional setup costs, since employees must set up multiple machines. Figure 12.4.1.1 shows the situation.

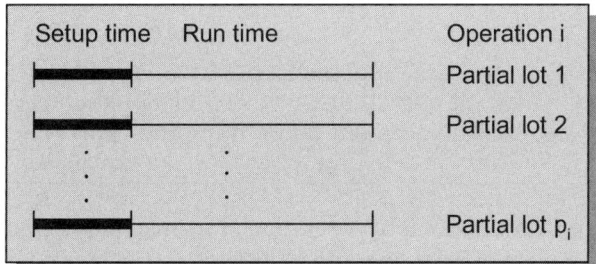

Fig. 12.4.1.1   Reducing lead time for operation i by using a splitting factor > 1.

The *splitting factor* for an operation expresses the degree of its potential splitting.

The initial value of the splitting factor is 1, that is, "no splitting." Where a splitting factor > 1 is given, run time is divided by this value. To calculate the costs of the operation, however, setup load must be multiplied by the splitting factor.

The split lots may be worked on in parallel or be finished at points that are offset in time.

A *split offset factor* expresses the possible temporal shift of the split lots, according to the principle illustrated in Figure 12.4.1.2.

The split offset factor is expressed as a percentage of the operation time after splitting. The initial value of this factor is zero, that is, "no split offset."

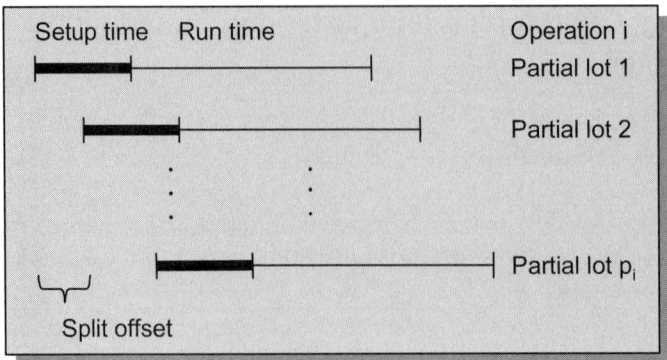

Fig. 12.4.1.2   The split offset factor offsets the split lots in time.

12.4.2 Overlapping

We speak of *overlapping within an operation* when the individual units of a lot are not produced sequentially, or one after the other, but rather overlap one another.

Consider the example of an assembly operation for machines. The operation may comprise several partial operations. A later partial operation on the first machine of the lot may be worked on parallel to the first partial operation on a subsequent machine of the lot. Figure 12.4.2.1 shows the situation for the lot as a whole.

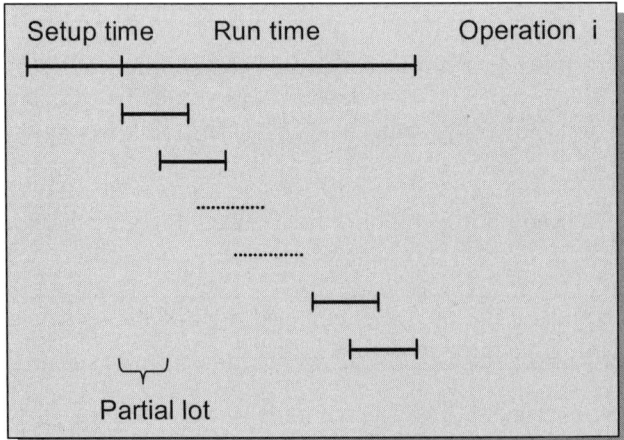

Fig. 12.4.2.1   The principle of overlapping within an operation.

The *run time offset* or *offset of the next run time* is a measure for the overlapping within an operation.

Run time offset is expressed as a percentage of run time. The standard value for run time offset is 100%, or "no overlapping."

For some production processes, you can overlap entire operations.

In an *operation overlapping* or an *overlapped schedule* we begin the next operation on a portion of the lot before the entire lot is completed with the previous operation.

Figure 12.4.2.2 shows an example. Schedulers can use operation overlapping to accelerate a production order.

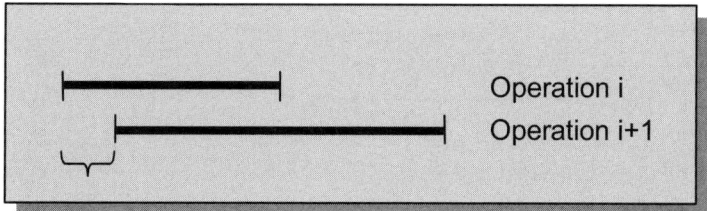

Fig. 12.4.2.2   The principle of operation overlapping.

The *maximum offset of the next operation* is a measure of operation overlapping. It is based upon one operation and shows the maximum lapse of time before the next operation begins.

In practice, the next operation begins immediately after the setup time and run time for the first unit (or first units) of the order lot. (See, for example, near-to-line production in Figure 5.2.2.2).

The initial value of the maximum offset of the next operation is infinite, i.e., "no overlapping." If the time we calculate (based on operation time and interoperation times) until beginning the next operation is smaller than the actual value, we take the smaller time as the new offset time.

12.4.3 An Extended Formula for Manufacturing Lead Time (*)

The following lists the definitions set out in Section 12.3.2 for the components of operation time. Here we have added the following abbreviations for the elements defined above.

LOTSIZE   := lot size ordered
ST[i]   := setup time for operation i
RT[i]   := run time per unit produced for operation i
STREFAC   := lead-time-stretching factor
SPLFAC[i]   := splitting factor for operation i
SPLOFST[i]   := split offset factor expressed as a percentage
RTOFST[i]   := run time offset for operation i expressed as a percentage
MAXOFST[i]   := maximum offset of the operation immediately
                  following operation i (a duration)

We can express the operation time for an operation i, OT[i], by the formula shown in Figure 12.4.3.1. This formula is much more complex than the one in Section 12.3.2.

$$OT[i] = \left\langle ST[i] + RT[i] \cdot \left(1 + \left(\frac{LOTSIZE}{SPLFAC[i]} - 1\right) \cdot \frac{RTOFST[i]}{100}\right)\right\rangle \cdot \left\langle 1 + \left(SPLFAC[i] - 1\right) \cdot \frac{SPLOFST[i]}{100}\right\rangle$$

Fig. 12.4.3.1   Extended operation lead time.

For a *sequence of operations* as the order of the operations, the formula in Figure 12.4.3.2 yields the lead time for the order.

$$LTI = STREFAC \cdot \left(ADMORD + ADMPORDBEG + INTBEF[1]\right)$$
$$+ \sum_{1 \le i \le n-1} \min\left(MAXOFST[i]; OPD[i] + INTTEC[i] + STREFAC \cdot \left(INTAFT[i] + INTBEF[i + \right.\right.$$
$$+ OT[n] + INTTEC[n] + STREFAC \cdot \left(INTAFT[n] + ADMPORDEND\right)$$

Fig. 12.4.3.2   Extended lead time formula (first version).

LTI represents the lead time for LOTSIZE and will vary when lot sizes are different. In Figure 12.4.3.3 we attempt to define partial sums in order to express lead time as a linear function of lot size.

As in Figure 12.3.2.3, we can store the partial sums in the lead time formula as attributes of the product and recalculate them after each modification of the routing sheet. Correspondingly, the formula according to Figure 12.3.2.4 holds.

$$\text{SUMINT} = \text{ADMPORDBEG} + \text{ADMPORDEND} + \sum_{1 \le i \le n} \left[\text{INTBEF}[i] + \text{INTEND}[i]\right]$$

$$\text{SUMTEC} = \sum_{1 \le i \le n} \text{INTTEC}[i]$$

$$\text{SUMST} = \sum_{1 \le i \le n} \left\langle \text{ST}[i] + \text{RT}[i] \cdot \left(1 - \frac{\text{RTOFST}[i]}{100}\right) \cdot \left(1 + \left(\text{SPLFAC}[i] - 1\right) \cdot \frac{\text{SPLOFST}[i]}{100}\right)\right\rangle$$

$$\text{SUMRT} = \sum_{1 \le i \le n} \left\langle \text{RT}[i] \cdot \frac{1}{\text{SPLFAC}[i]} \cdot \frac{\text{RTOFST}[i]}{100} \cdot \left(1 + \left(\text{SPLFAC}[i] - 1\right) \cdot \frac{\text{SPLOFST}[i]}{100}\right)\right\rangle$$

Fig. 12.4.3.3   Extended partial sums for the lead time formula.

$$\text{LTI}' = \text{STREFAC} \cdot \left(\text{ADMORD} + \text{SUMINT}\right) + \text{SUMTEC} + \text{SUMST} + \text{SUMRT} \cdot \text{LOTSIZE}$$

Fig. 12.4.3.4   Extended lead time formula (second version).

Due to the overlapping of operations, which is expressed in the formula for LTI in Figure 12.4.3.3 as a minimization, LTI is not equivalent to LTI': For either one or the other operation, the *maximum offset of the next operation* is smaller than the sum of the other time elements (the "normal" time period until the beginning of the next operation).

Figure 12.4.3.5 shows a possible plotting of the two lead times as functions of lot size.

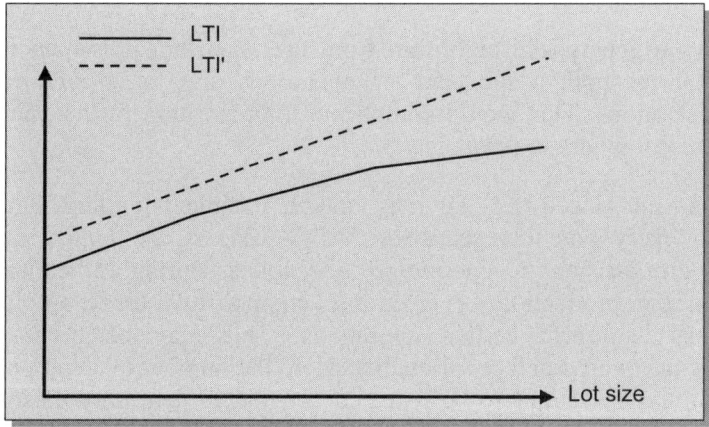

Fig. 12.4.3.5   Influence of overlapping of operations upon lead time.

In most circumstances LTI' is precise enough and certainly suffices for rough-cut planning. If necessary, we can set a *lot size limit for the lead time formula*. If the lot size is less than or equal to this quantity, we calculate lead time according to the "quick" lead time formula (the second version in Figure 12.4.3.4). Otherwise, we apply the more involved, "slow" formula in Figure 12.4.3.2.

In a *directed network of operations* as the order of the operations, similar considerations to those examined in Section 12.3.2 apply.

12.4.4 Extended Scheduling Algorithms (*)

We can now extend the scheduling algorithms presented in Section 12.3.3 to include the definitions introduced in the subsections above. These include:

- The introduction of a lead-time-stretching factor that multiplies interoperation times
- The introduction of splitting and overlapping and an expanded formula for lead time
- The inclusion of multiple partial orders for each production order
- The inclusion of divergent product structures, as – for example – the case of temporary assembly
- Ongoing planning for released orders with work remaining to be done

We can derive a generalized algorithm from the algorithm presented in Section 12.3.3, for both a sequence of operations and for a *directed* network of operations. This would complicate the algorithm further, and we will not present it here in detail.

The extensions introduced thus far may not be sufficient for lead time scheduling in every potential scenario. A first case is the *undirected network of operations* with a *repetition of operations*. During a chemical process or in the production of electronic components, for example, production has to repeat certain operations. This may be because inspection has uncovered defects in quality. Here the number of iterations and the individual operations to be repeated become evident only during the course of work and cannot be planned in advance. In this case, it is not possible to calculate lead time precisely. Instead we have to use expected mean values for the number of iterations and accompanying deviation. However, we have to take into account that each calculation of lead time itself is based on estimations of the time elements, particularly wait time in front of the work center.

Another case we will mention here arises in process industries. The processor-oriented concepts implemented in these industries may require sequencing or, more precisely, the planning of optimum sequences of operations, as early as the phase of long- and medium-term planning. Due to the extremely high setup costs, planners should establish suitable lots even prior to order release in order to keep changeover costs at a minimum. To this category belong, for example, cut optimizations for glass, sheet metals, or other materials. The scheduling of an individual order will depend on whether it may be combined with other orders and with what orders, in order to achieve optimal usage of the raw material, the reactors, or processing containers.

12.5 Summary

The ordering party sets the latest acceptable completion date and sometimes the earliest acceptable start date for a production order. The planner must establish start and/or due dates of the operations as well as the latest possible start date and the earliest possible completion date in advance, in order to obtain an initial estimate of feasibility and in preparation for work center loading and the setting of reservation dates for components.

For this, time management divides the lead time into meaningful time elements that can be measured or estimated relatively simply. Planners make use of the order of the operations (sequence or network of operations) of the product to be manufactured. Each operation has an operation time, and there are interoperation times before and after the operation. In addition, there are administrative times for each partial order and for the order in its entirety.

In job shop production, unproductive interoperation times make up the major proportion of total lead time. Simple models for estimating transportation times allow sufficiently precise estimates to be made without expending a lot of time and effort on data management. However, it is difficult to determine the adequate size of buffers or queues at the work centers. Statistical analysis of queues as the effect of random load fluctuations yields useful information with regard to reducing wait times: High loading as well as long or highly varied operation times lead to long wait times. This underlines the conflict between the entrepreneurial objectives of "low costs" and "short lead time" as set out in Section 1.3.1.

Scheduling management starts out from the dates set by the ordering party and calculates the other dates required for determining feasibility, loading capacity, and reserving components. The following list shows the scheduling techniques discussed in the chapter (for sequences as well as directed networks of operations), comparing data input with data output:

- Forward scheduling:
  - *Input*: earliest order start date, lead-time-stretching factor
  - *Output*: earliest order completion date, earliest start and completion dates for each operation, earliest reservation date for each component

- Backward scheduling:
  - *Input*: latest order completion date, lead-time-stretching factor
  - *Output*: latest order start date, latest start and completion date for each operation, latest reservation date for each component

- Central point scheduling:
  - *Input*: central point date, lead-time-stretching factor
  - *Output*: latest order start date and earliest order completion date; latest start and completion date for each operation as well as latest reservation date for each component *before* the central point, earliest start and completion date for each operation as well as earliest reservation date for each component *after* the central point

- Probable scheduling:
  - *Input*: earliest start date and latest completion date for the order
  - *Output*: lead-time-stretching factor, probable start and completion date for each operation, probable reservation date for each component.

Splitting and overlapping are techniques that are frequently used to reduce lead time. Their incorporation into the lead time formula, as well as the attempt to include other effects, reveals the limits to lead time estimation. Not all time elements can be estimated accurately, and only a modest degree of complexity can be expressed as a formula. Moreover, there are unforeseen factors that can always arise during actual production. On the other hand, planners must have a fair idea of cumulative lead time so that they can set it in relation to the customer tolerance time. With this, in the short term, the basic decision can be made to accept or decline an order. In the medium term, it allows planners to sketch out a possible load profile for the work centers along the time axis.

12.6 Keywords

backward scheduling, 654
buffer, 637
central point scheduling, 660
cycle time, 653
earliest date, 654
forward scheduling, 654
funnel model, 639
idle time, 638
inventory buffer, 637
inventory range, 646
latest date, 654
lead-time scheduling, 653
lead-time-stretching factor, 663
manufacturing calendar, 649

move time, 633
network planning, 657
non-technical wait time
    after an operation, 633
    before an operation, 633
operation overlapping, 669
order splitting, 667
overlapping
    of operations, 669
    within an operation, 668
probable scheduling, 662
queue, 637
queue time, 633
queuing theory, 637
run time offset, 669

scheduling algorithm, 648
sequence of operations, 629
set date, 654
slack time, 662
splitting, 667
synchronization point, 630
takt time, 653
technical wait time
    after an operation, 633
technical wait time
    before an operation, 634
throughput time, 653
transit time, 633
transportation time, 633

12.7 Scenarios and Exercises

12.7.1 Queues as an Effect of Random Load Fluctuations (1)

Answer the following questions using the relevant formulas in queuing theory (refer to Figure 12.2.2.4):

a. How many parallel workstations are needed to have an expected wait time of less than 10 hours, if capacity utilization is 0.95, the mean of the operation duration is 2 hours, and the coefficient of variation of the operation duration is 1?

b. The capacity is 10 hours. How much does the expected wait time increase if load rises from 4 to 8 hours?

c. How is the expected wait time affected when the coefficient of variation increases from 1 to 2?

Solutions:

a. $s = 0.95 / (1 - 0.95) * (1 + (1 * 1)) / 2 * 2 / 10 = 3.8$. Thus, with *four* workstations, the expected wait time will be 9.5 hours.

b. Capacity utilization increases from 4/10 to 8/10. Therefore, the respective factor in the formula for the expected wait time increases from $0.4 / (1 - 0.4) = 2/3$ to $0.8 / (1 - 0.8) = 4$. The new factor is $4 / (2/3) = 6$ times greater than the old factor. Thus, the expected wait time increases by a factor of 6.

c. The respective factor in the formula for the expected wait time increases from $(1 + (1 * 1)) / 2 = 1$ to $(1 + (2 * 2)) / 2 = 2.5$. Thus, the expected wait time increases by the factor 2.5.

12.7.2 Queues as an Effect of Random Load Fluctuations (2)

Figure 12.2.2.3 shows the average wait time as a function of capacity utilization in a job shop environment with random arrivals, execution of operations in order of arrival (or according to random selection from the queue), as well as operation times (OT) subject to a determinate distribution with mean M(OT) and coefficient of variation CV(OT). We reproduced the effect shown in Figure 12.2.2.3 by means of a Flash simulation, which you can view at URL:

http://www.intlogman.lim.ethz.ch/queuing_theory.html

Start the simulation by clicking on the given arrival rate and execution (service) rate on the gray button to the far left at the bottom of the figure and watch the number of elements in the system. Stop the simulation by clicking on the middle of the three buttons (or empty the system by clicking the button to the far right). Now change the input rate to bring it closer and closer to the execution rate and observe the rising number of elements in the queue. You will see the exploding number of elements in the system as soon as, for an execution rate of 60 per unit of time, the arrival rate is 58 and higher.

12.7.3 Network Planning

Figure 12.7.3.1 shows a scheduled network with incomplete data for 6 operations and a start operation (administration time).

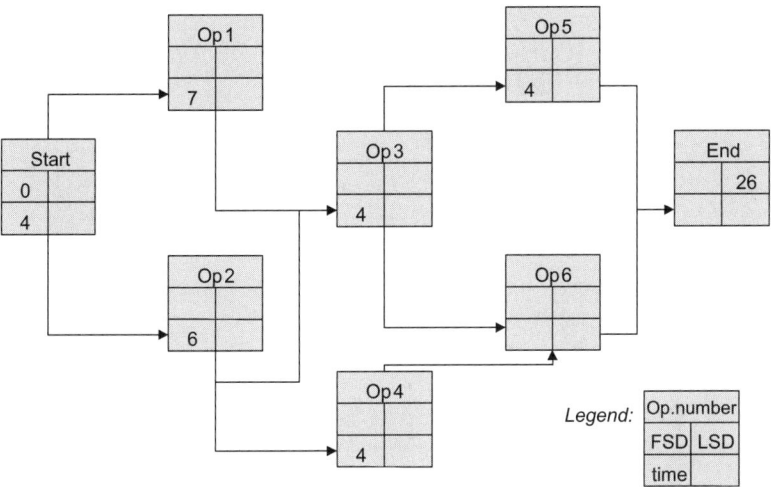

Fig. 12.7.3.1   Scheduled network (for you to complete).

a. For each process, please fill in the earliest start date (ESD) and the latest start date (LSD) in the scheduled network. What is the critical path, that is the path with the longest duration? What is its lead-time margin, that is the slack time?

b. The operation time for operation 6 has not yet been determined. What is the longest possible time for operation 6 (lead-time margin = zero)?

Solutions:

a. For the time being, as long as the time for operation 6 is still open, the longest path is (start – op1 – op3 – op5 – end). Lead-time margin = 7.

b. As soon as the time for operation 6 is greater than 4, the longest path is (start – op1 – op3 – op6 – end). The longest possible time for op6 is 11.

12.7.4 Backward Scheduling and Forward Scheduling

Here, you will practice some backward and forward scheduling. Figure 12.7.4.1 presents a simple network, including a legend showing the lead-time elements used.

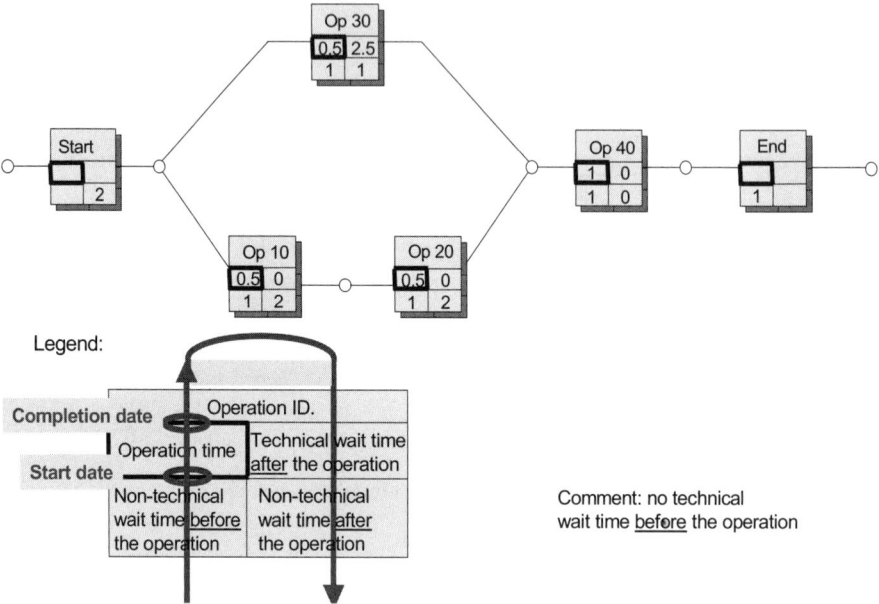

Fig. 12.7.4.1   Scheduled network.

Solve the forward and backward scheduling problems (calculation of start and completion dates for the order and each operation, as well as the critical path and lead-time margin) listed in Figure 12.7.4.2:

a.   Common forward scheduling.

b.   Common backward scheduling.

c.   Forward scheduling with different lead-time-stretching factor, that is a different order urgency, in order to accelerate or slow down the order.

d.   Forward scheduling with lead-time-stretching factor $= 0$, which results in the lead time as the sum of operation times plus the technical interoperation times.

Some common problems in the calculation process lead to the following potential errors:

- Calculating incorrect start date and due dates, not respecting inter-operation times multiplied by stretching factor
- Multiplying technical waiting time by stretching factor
- Not calculating correctly the longest path in a network
- Not understanding the principle of forward or backward scheduling

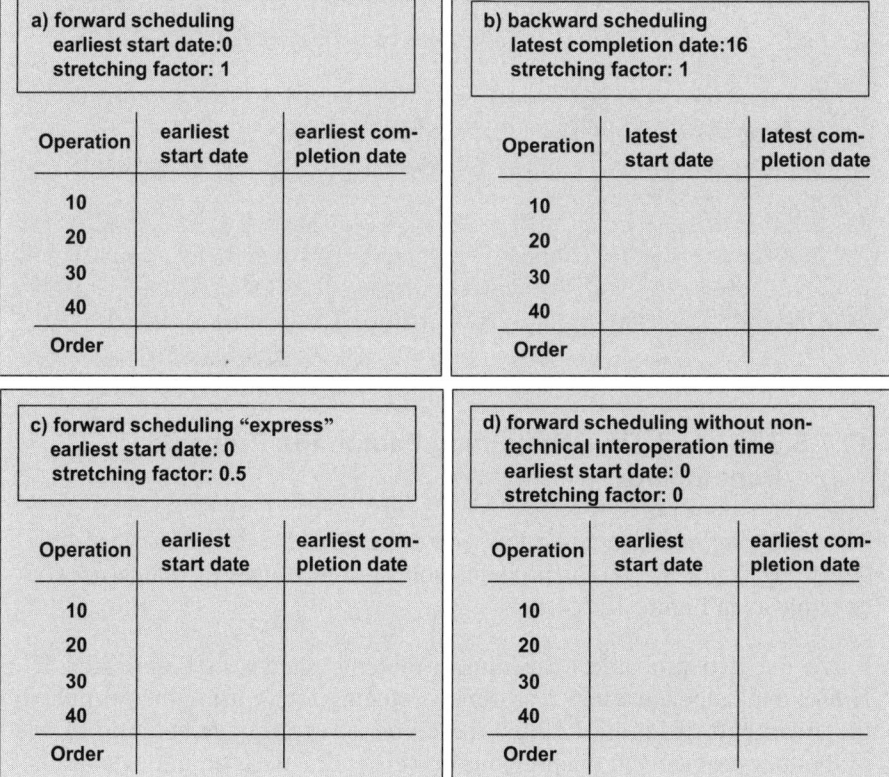

Fig. 12.7.4.2   Various forward and backward scheduling problems.

Solutions:

(ESD stands for earliest start date, ECD for earliest completion date, LSD for latest start date, LCD for latest completion date.)

a. ESD(op10) = 3, ECD(op10) = 3.5; ESD(op20) = 6.5, ECD(op20) = 7; ESD(op30) = 3, ECD(op30) = 3.5; ESD(op40) = 10, ECD(op40) = 11; ESD(order) = 0, ECD(order) = 12. Note the critical path in determining the ESD(op40): The *lower* path is critical. The lead-time margin of the *upper* path is 2.

b. LCD(op40) = 15, LSD(op40) = 14; LCD(op30) = 9.5, LSD(op30) = 9; LCD(op20) = 11, LSD(op20) = 10.5; LCD(op10) = 7.5, LSD(op10)=7; LCD(order) = 16, LSD(order) = 4. Note that — again — the *lower* path is critical. The lead-time margin of the *upper* path is again 2.

c. ESD(op10) = 1.5, ECD(op10) = 2; ESD(op20) = 3.5, ECD(op20) = 4; ESD(op30) = 1.5, ECD(op30) = 2; ESD(op40) = 5.5, ECD(op40) =6.5; ESD(order) = 0, ECD(order) = 7. Note that both paths are critical.

d. ESD(op10) = 0, ECD(op10) = 0.5; ESD(op20) = 0.5, ECD(op20) = 1; ESD(op30) = 0, ECD(op30) = 0.5; ESD(op40) = 3, ECD(op40) = 4; ESD(order) = 0, ECD(order) = 4. Note that the critical path has changed. The *upper* path is now critical. The lead-time margin of the *lower* path is 2.

12.7.5 The Lead-Time-Stretching Factor and Probable Scheduling

The following exercise will allow you to practice the use of the lead-time-stretching factor as well as probable scheduling. It uses the same network example as in Figure 12.7.4.1.

Solve the two probable scheduling problems shown in Figure 12.7.5.1. *Hint*: First, calculate a new lead-time-stretching factor using the formula in the lower part of Figure 12.3.6.3, based on an appropriate solution of one of the four problems in the previous exercise (12.7.4) as an initial solution.

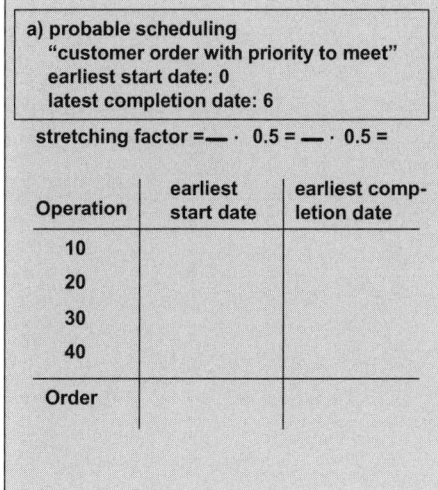
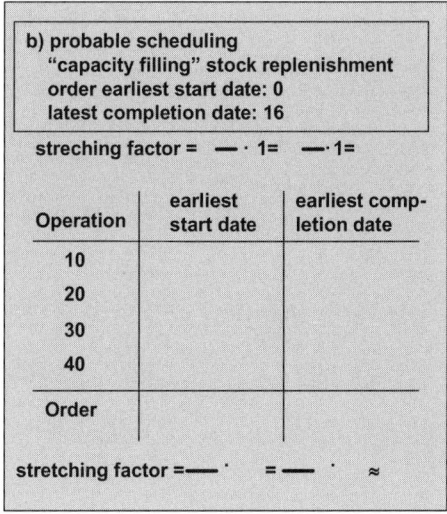

Fig. 12.7.5.1   Two probable scheduling problems.

Some common problems in the calculation process that can lead to errors are:

- Not understanding the goal and principles of probable scheduling
- Not understanding the formula for recalculation of the lead-time-stretching factor in probable scheduling
- Not choosing the most appropriate last calculation as initial solution for recalculation of the lead-time-stretching factor

Solutions:
(Again, ESD stands for earliest start date, ECD for earliest completion date, LSD for latest start date, LCD for latest completion date, STREFAC for lead time stretching factor.)

a. Use problem (c) in the previous exercise (12.7.4) as an initial solution. STREFAC(new) = (6 − 4) / (7 − 4) * 0.5 = 2/3 * 0.5 = 1/3.   =>
ESD(op10) = 1, ECD(op10) = 1.5; ESD(op20) = 2.5, ECD(op20) = 3;
ESD(op30) = 1, ECD(op30) = 1.5; ESD(op40) = 4.7, ECD(op40) = 5.7;
ESD(order) = 0, ECD(order) = 6. Note that the *upper* path is critical. The lead-time margin of the *lower* path is 2/3 = 0.667.

b. Use problem (a) in the previous exercise (12.7.4) as an initial solution. STREFAC(new) = (16 − 4) / (12 − 4) * 1 = 12/8 * 1 = 1.5.   =>
ESD(op10) = 4.5, ECD(op10) = 5; ESD(op20) = 9.5, ECD(op20) = 10;

ESD(op30) = 4.5, ECD(op30) =5; ESD(op40)=14.5, ECD(op40)=15.5; ESD(order) = 0, ECD(order) = 17 (!). Note that the *lower* path is critical. The lead-time margin of the *upper* path is 4. Because the desired ECD(order) of 16 has not been met (can you say why this is the case?), an additional iteration is necessary: recalculation with STREFAC(new) = (16 − 4) / (17 − 4) * 1.5 = 12/13 * 1.5 ≈ 1.4 will yield the desired solution.

13 Capacity Management

Unlike delivery lead time and delivery reliability rate, the efficient use of capacity is not directly observable by the customer. Nonetheless, it is an extremely important factor, since it enables the company to cut costs, ensure prompt delivery, and increase flexibility.

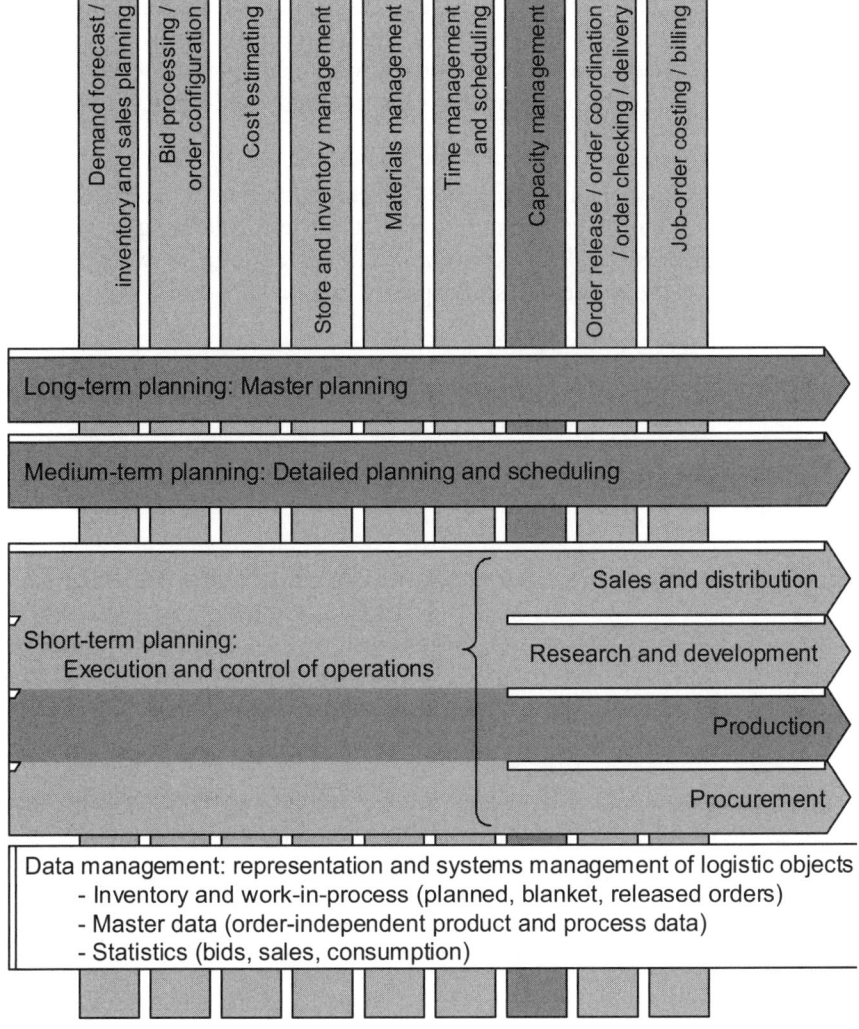

Fig. 13.0.0.1   The parts of the system discussed in Chapter 13 (shown on darker background).

Work center capacity utilization, like levels of inventories in stock and work-in-process, increases the flexibility of logistics planning & control. Capacity resources have to be estimated for every planning term. Flexibility in medium- and short-term planning often requires long-term arrangements. In Figure 13.0.0.1, the tasks and processes covered in this chapter are shown against a darker background, referring back to the basic model introduced in Figure 4.1.4.2. Sections 1.2.4, 4.3.3, and 4.3.4, in particular Figure 4.3.4.1, also provide useful overviews for this chapter.[1]

We will begin by reexamining the basic concepts presented in Chapters 3 and 4 on the nature of capacity and on well-known types of capacity management. A detailed look at well-known techniques follows, broken down by objectives, basic characteristics, methods and procedures, range of application, and other factors.

Rough-cut capacity planning deserves special attention. It can be used for both long- and short-term planning. For short-term planning it supports rapid order promising. The techniques differ according to whether they give greater weight to due dates or capacity limits.

13.1   Fundamentals of Capacity Management

13.1.1 Capacity, Work Centers, and Capacity Determination

Section 1.2.4 presents basic definitions of *work center*, *capacity*, *theoretical capacity*, and *rated capacity*, together with the factors that mediate them, namely *capacity utilization* and the *efficiency* of a work center (or *efficiency rate*).

Depending upon the type of work center, different capacities will be used *as the primary basis* for capacity management and for allocating costs:

- *Machine capacity* (referred to as *machine hours*, when using hours as the capacity unit), that is, the capacity of machines and equipment to produce output, is frequently used for parts manufacturing.

---

[1]   The reader may find it useful to go back over Sections 1.2.4, 4.3.3, and 4.3.4 before going on to the rest of this chapter.

- *Labor capacity* (referred to as *labor hours*, when using hours as capacity unit), that is, the capacity of workers to produce output, is frequently used for assembly or stores.

These factors and relationships form the basis for *capacity determination*, as shown in Figure 13.1.1.1.

Shift no.	No. hours per shift	No. machines	No. workers	Daily capacity machines hours	Daily capacity workers hours	Correction factor
1	8	10	6	80	48	
2	8	10	6	80	48	
3	4	10	1	40	4	

Theoretical capacity	200	100

(multiplied by) capacity utilization, subdivided in

- availability (in capacity)	90 %
- tactical under-utilization (desired):	75 %

Subtotal:	135	67.5

(multiplied by) work center efficiency:	120 %

Rated capacity:	162	81

Fig. 13.1.1.1 Determination of capacity. Rated capacity is the product of theoretical capacity, capacity utilization, and work center efficiency.

Theoretical capacity is the maximum output capacity, with no adjustments for unplanned downtime, determined by the number of shifts, the capacity theoretically available for each shift, and the number of machines and workers. The value thus determined applies up to a given boundary date, after which the calculation factors may change.

Theoretical capacity can also vary from one week to the next in response to *foreseen*, overlapping changes that must be taken into account, such as:

- *Scheduled downtime*, that is, downtime due to individual workers' vacations or for preventive maintenance, for example.
- *Scheduled overtime* due to additional shifts, for instance.

Capacity utilization is a measure of how intensively a resource is being used to produce a good or service. Traditionally, it is the ratio of actual load to theoretical capacity. There are two distinct factors in capacity utilization:

- *Availability (in capacity)*: All the possible downtime due to breaks, cleaning tasks, clearing up, unplanned absences, breakdowns, etc., must be considered for each work center. These losses are considered by the *availability factor* (hours actually worked / hours available).

- *Tactical underload* or *under-utilization*: To avoid long queue times (see Section 12.2.3) or for non-bottleneck capacities or non-constraint work centers, the desired capacity utilization should generally be less than 100%.

Taking the above into account results in *planned capacity utilization*. The measurement of *actual capacity utilization* cannot as a rule be broken down according to the two factors. This is the main reason for capturing availability and tactical underload in one factor, namely, capacity utilization.

The *efficiency of a work center* (or *efficiency rate*) is the ratio of "standard load to the actual load," "standard hours produced to actual hours worked," or "actual units produced to standard units to produce in a time period" (see [APIC04]), averaged over all the operations performed at a work center.[2]

Rated capacity is the expected output capability of a work center. The equation for rated capacity is theoretical capacity times capacity utilization times work center efficiency.

We should therefore consider *standard load* to be scheduled (that is, load on the basis of standard setup and run loads) to *rated capacity*, and not to theoretical capacity.

In principle, rough-cut planning uses the same attributes, usually applied to fully utilized work centers at the level of the department or entire plant. The capacity of a rough-cut work center is thus not necessarily equal to the sum of all the individual capacities concerned.

There are other capacity-related terms that are useful for capacity management. Figure 13.1.1.2 shows possible relations among the terms. The definitions are based mainly on [APIC04]. Barry Firth, Melbourne, contributed the figure and the explanations.

---

[2]   This factor can be greater than, equal to, or less than 1. The actual choice reflects different worker motivation concepts. Cost unit rates for load standards thus also differ accordingly.

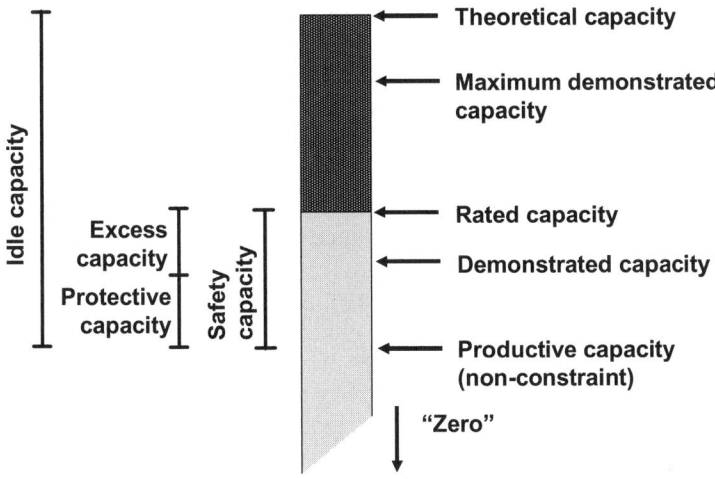

Fig. 13.1.1.2   Some capacity definitions and their relationship to each other. (Figure contributed by Barry Firth, Melbourne.)

Demonstrated capacity is proven capacity calculated from actual performance data, expressed in standard hours (for job shop) or production rate (for flow shop).

Maximum demonstrated capacity is the highest amount of actual output produced in the past, when all efforts have been made to optimize the resource.

Demonstrated capacity is the most practical measure of capacity available in the job shop manufacturing environment. The alternative of working with rated capacity (see below) is not as easy as it seems, because there are practical difficulties in measuring the utilization and efficiency factors.

Productive capacity is the maximum of the output capabilities of a resource (or series of resources) or the market demand for that output for a given time period.

Where the productive resource or system of linked resources is identified as the system constraint, its productive capacity is its maximum achievable output and should usually be based on 168 hours of available time per week (24*7); otherwise, TOC (theory of constraints) practitioners would say that this is not a true constraint. Where the system constraint is the market demand, productive capacity may be relative to a smaller number of hours per week.

Protective capacity is quantifiable capacity that is or can be made available at a non-bottleneck capacity to protect against fluctuation (idle time) of the bottleneck capacity. Technically, protective capacity provides contingency against unplanned events only, such as breakdowns and rework requirements.

Safety capacity is quantifiable capacity that is available over and above productive capacity that includes an allowance for planned events, such as on-shift plant maintenance and short-term *resource contention* (that is, simultaneous need from a common resource), and for unplanned events. It includes "protective capacity."

Excess capacity is defined as output capability at a non-constraint resource that exceeds the productive and protective capacity required.

Idle capacity is defined as capacity that is generally not used in a system of linked resources. It consists of protective capacity and excess capacity.

Activation is defined as the use of non-constraint resources to produce above the rate required by the system constraint, in this context a bottleneck capacity.

Budgeted capacity is the volume and mix of throughput on which financial budgets were set, for the purpose of establishing overhead absorption rates for calculating standard costs of products, expressed in standard hours. This really should be called *budgeted load*.

13.1.2 Overview of Capacity Management Techniques

Figure 13.1.2.1 (identical to Figure 4.3.4.1) shows capacity management techniques, subdivided into two classes in relation to quantitative flexibility of capacities and flexibility of the order due date. We show the figure here again, for it determines the structure of the present chapter.

The values of the typical characteristics for planning & control outlined in Section 3.4 will vary depending on which of the company objectives discussed in Section 1.3.1 are emphasized. From the values we can derive appropriate techniques from the two classes *infinite loading* and *finite loading*. If the quantitative flexibility of the capacity along the time axis is greater than the flexibility of the order due date, than infinite loading techniques should be used. In the reverse case, finite loading techniques are more appropriate.

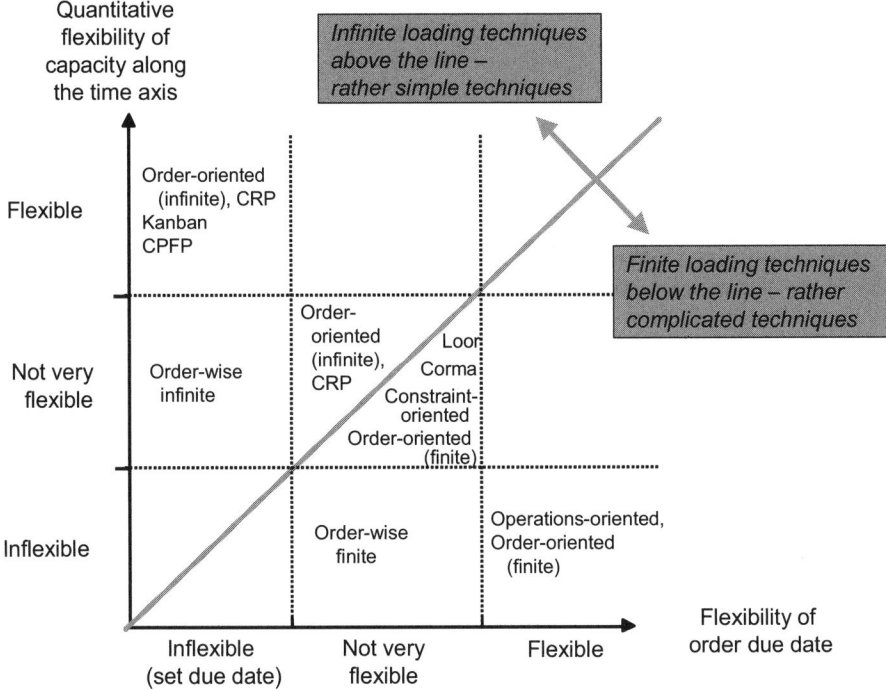

Fig. 13.1.2.1   Reproduced from Fig. 4.3.4.1 – Classes of techniques for capacity management in dependency upon flexibility of capacity and of order due date.

If there is *sufficient overall capacity planning flexibility* — that is, in the three sectors from top left to bottom right — a computer algorithm can generally load all the orders in question with no regard to their sequence using a batch program, i.e., with no interaction by the planner. The planner becomes involved only after the loading has been assigned, in order to schedule capacities on a daily or weekly basis, for example. Exceptional situations will be brought to the planner's attention selectively in lists or graphs.

If there is *little overall capacity planning flexibility* — that is, in the two sectors of the two [lower left] sectors where there is no flexibility on one axis and only limited flexibility on the other — planning takes place "order for order" (order-wise). Each new order is individually integrated into existing scheduled orders. The planning process is thus "interactive"; i.e., in extreme cases the planner may intervene after each operation and change set planning values (completion date or capacity). Existing scheduled orders may have to be replanned.

The techniques shown in Figure 13.1.2.1 are discussed in Sections 5.3 (kanban), 5.4 (cumulative production figures principle, CPFP), 13.2 (order-oriented infinite loading), 13.3 (operations-oriented, order-oriented, and constraint-oriented finite loading), and 14.1 (Loor, Corma). They can all be used regardless of what organizational unit carries out planning & control. Thus, they can be found in all types of software packages (logistics software, electronic planning boards [*Leitstand*], simulation software, and so on). Entirely different techniques are possible for short-term and long-term planning.

It is becoming increasingly important to plan machine tool capacities due to the increasing use of CNC and robot-controlled production. The methods are the same as those used to manage machine and labor capacities. On the other hand, tools to be produced or procured should be regarded as goods and represent a position on the order bill of materials.

13.2 Infinite Loading

The primary objective of *infinite loading* is to achieve a high delivery reliability rate, i.e., to meet the due date for production or procurement orders. Secondary objectives are low levels of goods in stock and work in process and short lead times in the goods flow. High capacity utilization is less important. Indeed, there can be good strategic reasons for maintaining overcapacity (meeting due dates).[3]

Overview: Section 5.3 examined the popular *kanban* technique, where due dates are fixed, i.e., inflexible, and capacities are always modified to suit the load. The kanban method can be used only for production or procurement with frequent order repetition.

This section describes the generally applicable order-oriented method. Load profiles are calculated for all the orders together after scheduling, and each scheduled operation represents a load at the specified work center and in the time period containing its start date. The sum of all these loads is compared to the available capacity for each time period. This yields load profiles showing the overcapacity or undercapacity for each work center

---

[3]   An example is *surge capacity*, which is the capacity to meet sudden, unexpected increases in demand (compare [APIC04]).

and time period. Subsequent planning then attempts to balance capacity against load.

This most commonly used *order-oriented-infinite-loading* technique is also called *capacity requirements planning (CRP)*.

Planning strategy: The objective is to manage fluctuating capacity requirements by having flexible capacities available. Both long-term and short-term actions are possible.

13.2.1 Load Profile Calculation

For *load profile calculation* we assume, as an approximation, that operations will be executed as scheduled (see Section 12.3). Thus, in the simplest case the method places the operation load in the time period that contains the start date of the operation.

The *load profile* is a display of the work center load and capacity over a given span of time.

Figure 13.2.1.1 shows a load profile over two time periods for six production orders, P1, ..., P6, each with operations at two different work centers, work center A and work center B.

At the top of Figure 13.2.1.1, we can see the orders corresponding to the results of lead-time calculations. Each operation has a start date, which may be the earliest, latest, or probable date, depending upon the scheduling technique used.[4]

The bottom of the figure shows the loads for these operations along the vertical axis. The "preload" represents operations for orders that were loaded *before* orders P1, ..., P6. The method then adds together the operation loads in each time period on the planning horizon to create a load profile.[5]

---

[4]   We could also create load profiles for all the scheduling techniques discussed in Section 12.3, as long as the corresponding scheduling calculations have been executed.

[5]   The time periods on the planning horizon are not necessarily of the same length. They may vary according to the type of work center. For example, some planners may use shorter time periods for the near future and longer periods for the more distant future.

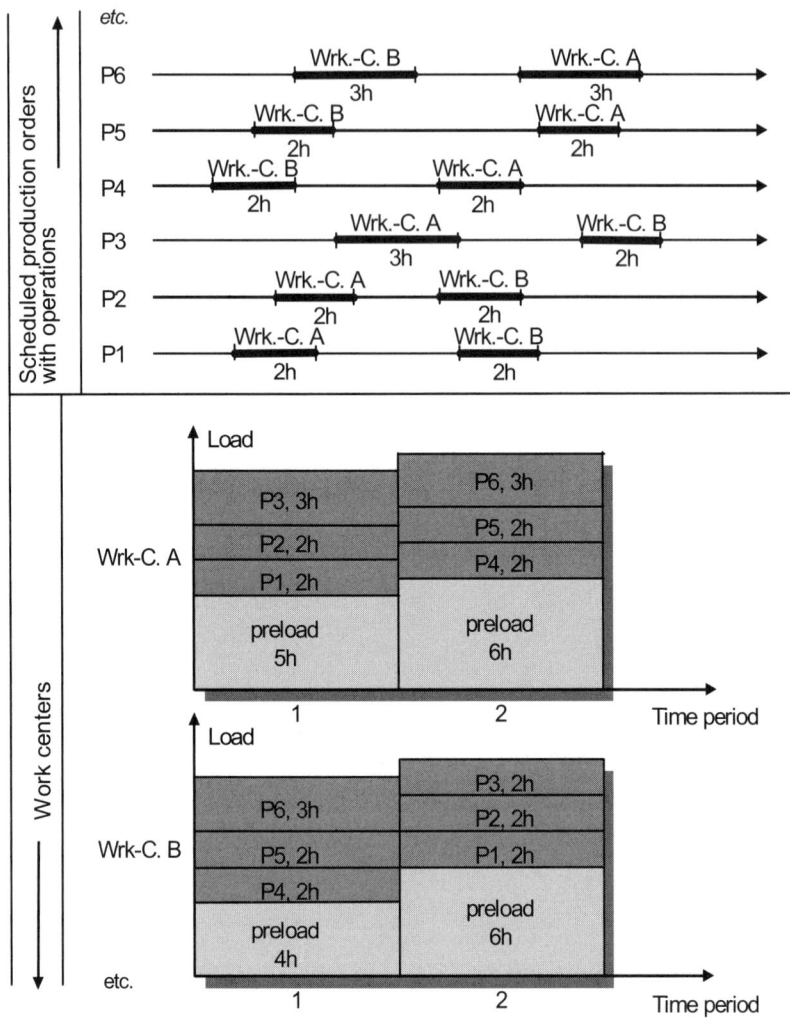

Fig. 13.2.1.1   Example of a work center load profile.

Figure 13.2.1.2 provides an example of a load profile known as an *overload* or *underload* curve along the time axis.[6]

---

[6]   In this example, the capacities are of equal size for each period. The horizontal line is always obtained when capacity is viewed as equal to 100% in each period.

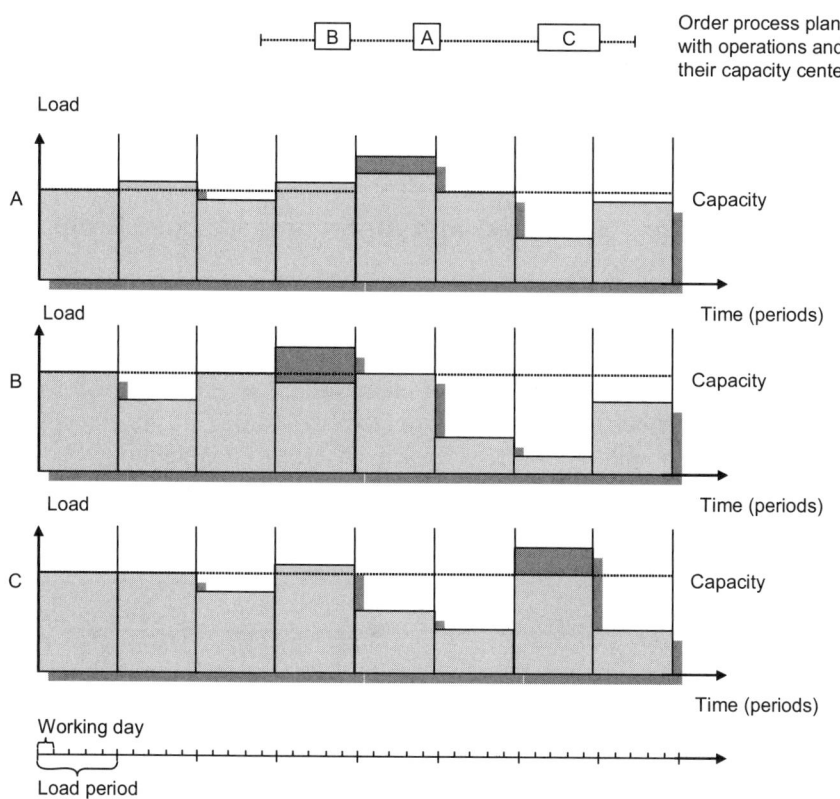

Fig. 13.2.1.2   An example of a load profile.

The use of different colors or hatching patterns make individual orders stand out in the profile. This can also highlight partial sums for particular order categories, such as:

- *Scheduled load*, caused by released orders (released orders with *provisional completion date* can be highlighted by an additional category)
- *Firm planned load*, caused by planned orders with fixed completion dates
- *Planned load*, caused by planned orders with provisional completion dates

The information may change according to the length of the chosen periods, that is,

- When selecting shorter load periods, the overload and underload curve is more precise
- Longer time periods reveal a longer-term trend, with the short-term fluctuations evened out

13.2.2 Problems Associated with Algorithms for Load Profile Calculation

A load profile calculation is not more than an approximation and must be interpreted as such. Thus, if interoperation times fluctuate widely (see Section 12.2), it will be difficult if not impossible to execute the operations as scheduled. Further inaccuracies arise from the quality of the algorithms employed, even with logistics software or electronic planning boards. Figure 13.2.2.1 shows a first problem associated with algorithms: assigning capacities to each time period on the planning horizon.

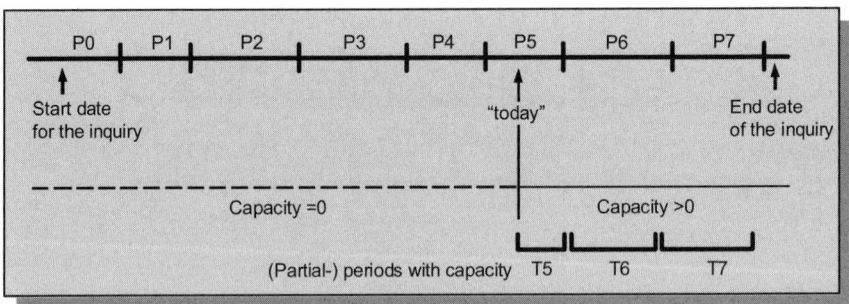

Fig. 13.2.2.1   Calculating capacity per load period.

The number of periods and the lengths of the periods may vary. Also, we need flexible selection of the start date for the first period and the end date for the last period under consideration. If, however, some of these loads lie in the past, we cannot compare them against capacities, since the capacities are available only from the date "today" onwards. "Today" may also fall within one of the time periods, in which case capacity is available only for the time remaining from "today" to the end of the time period.

Another problem is that a simple but imprecise method will assign the load to the time period containing the start date for the operation. An operation can extend across several load periods, however. Figure 13.2.2.2 shows this problem and offers an improved procedure.

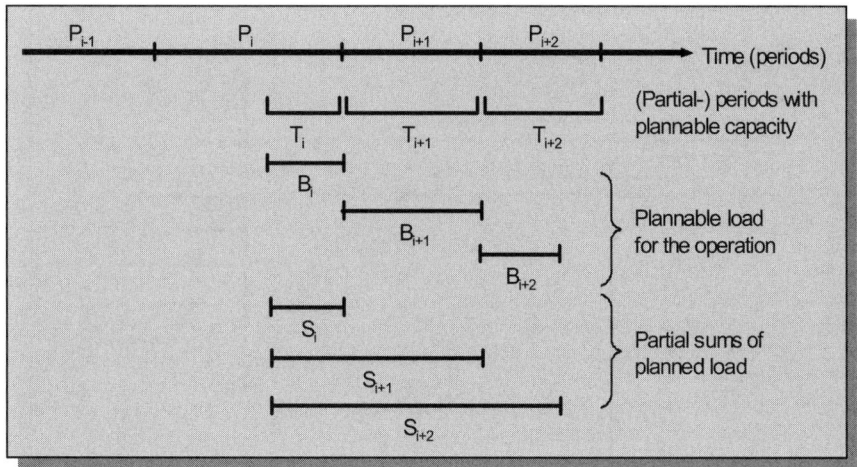

Fig. 13.2.2.2   Load assignment for one operation during the load periods.

The possible load per unit of time is obtained from the capacity master data (number of shifts, capacity per shift, number of machines or workers) and from the operation (splitting factor). The start date falls within a given period i. From this we can determine the time remaining until the end of period i and calculate the possible load B_i. The partial sum S_i is thus the sum of all the operation loads B_j, with $j \le i$ of the operations that have already been assigned to the periods up to and including i. The load for the last period in which part of an operation occurs corresponds to the remaining load for the operation. At this point, S_i represents the entire load.

A third problem is how to determine all the operations that occur in a given time period [start, end]. Figure 13.2.2.3 shows that various operations occur only partly within the time period.

In practice, we construct a view of the open (or open and planned) operations, arranged by start date. We consider any operation whose start date is earlier than the end date of the time period. The ratio between the load occurring within the time period and the total load for the operation is assumed to be proportional to the ratio between the lead time occurring within the time period and the total lead time.

We are only interested in those operations whose completion dates are later than the start date of the load period. As you can see in Figure 13.2.2.3, however, the algorithm starts by "reading" some operations unnecessarily, i.e., operations with completion dates earlier than the start date of the time period.

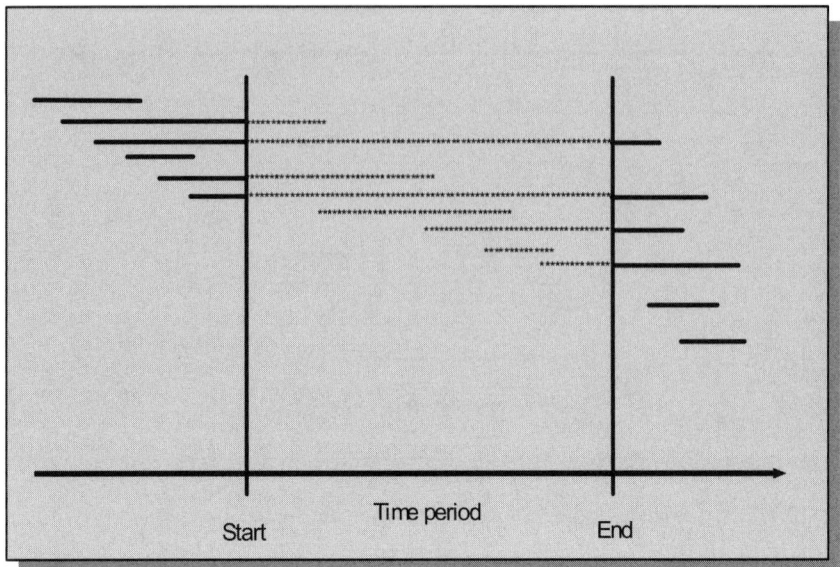

Fig. 13.2.2.3   Operations to be included in the load for a work center.

13.2.3 Methods of Balancing Capacity and Load

The load profile displays easily, directly, and accurately the overload and underload that would arise if our scheduling assumptions were totally accurate. Everything covered up to this point is not capacity planning, strictly speaking. In the simplest case, one response would be to plan to increase or reduce capacity.

The cumulative illustration of loads and capacities along the time axis presented in Figure 13.2.3.1 is also suitable for analyzing the load profile. We can see the overload or underload along the vertical axis, between the curves for capacity and load. The maximum possible movement of the load in one or the other direction can also be seen along the horizontal axis.

With forward scheduling in the case of bottleneck capacities, underload leads to financial losses. However, the farther into the future we can identify the underload, the less it need occur in reality, since the calculated operation start dates may be incorrect as a result of upstream bottleneck capacities, unplanned reworking, or unplanned operations due to rush orders, for example.

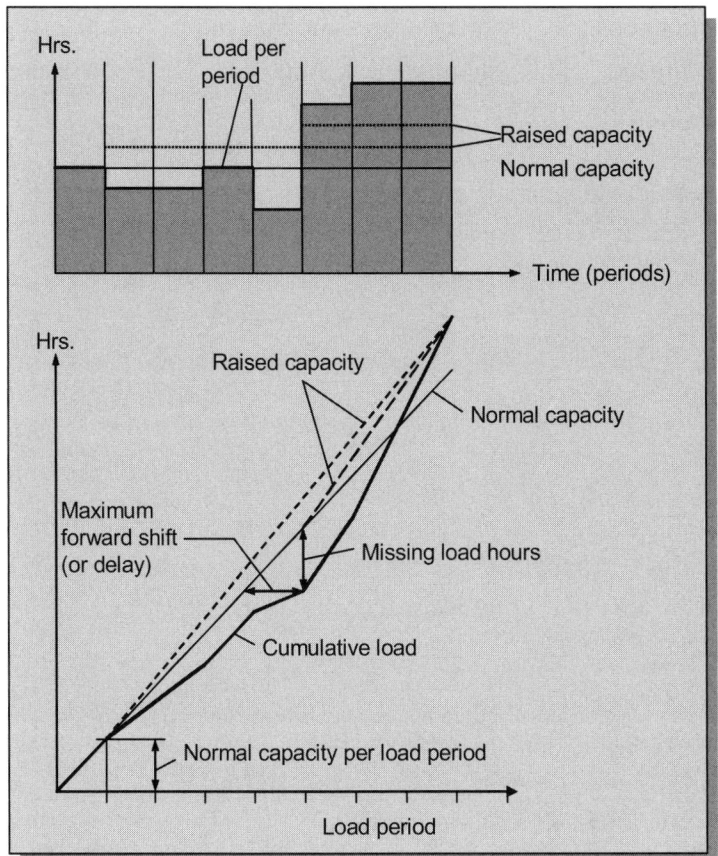

Fig. 13.2.3.1   Analysis of the load profile.

Figure 13.2.3.2 shows possible methods of balancing capacity and load.

Finally, a list of available work supports analysis of the individual operations as well as *priority control*, that is, the communication of start and completion dates for execution in the shop floor.

> *Available work* or *work on hand* or *load traceability* for a work center is a list of the operations to be carried out at that work center over a given time period.

This list is sorted according to a suitable strategy, which should also mirror the order in which the operations are carried out. Possible strategies include:

- Anticipated start date for the operation

- Operation time (SPT, shortest processing time rule)
- Order urgency (SLK, shortest slack time rule; see also Section 12.3.6)
- *Order priority*, that is the preferred status of the customer

1. Frequent self-compensating fluctuations, meaning that the interoperation times are longer than or roughly equal to the fluctuation frequency. No action is required. The time buffer can absorb these fluctuations without jeopardizing dates.

2. Trend towards *persistent overload*:
   2a. Long-term action (in the master planning): acquire additional production infrastructure (workers or machines) in good time. Other typical long-term responses are blanket orders to *subcontractors*, that is, sending production work outside the company ("extended workbench" or "outsourcing" principle) or arrangements with employment agencies (temporary workers).
   2b. Short-term action: arrange overtime or implement long-term blanket agreements as mentioned above.

3. Trend towards *persistent underload*: in principle, the action required is the opposite of that described under point 2.
   3a. Long-term action: cut back production infrastructure or reduce blanket agreements (insourcing).
   3b. Short-term action: cancel overtime, arrange short-time working, or cancel outsourced work.

4. Infrequent self-compensating fluctuations, meaning that the interoperation times are shorter than the fluctuation frequency:
   4a. Flexibly adapt capacity to load, alternating the steps described under points 2 and 3. For example, in the short-term case, this could mean arranging for and then cutting back on overtime.
   4b. *Load leveling*, that is, spreading orders over time so that the amount of work tends to be distributed evenly, resulting in a *level schedule*. This measure is associated with inflexible capacity, however, and thus actually belongs to finite loading. With a computerized system, we can move an operation forward or back and immediately see the consequences in a revised load profile. However, we must also take into account the work centers for the upstream and downstream operations for the order. Overload situations may now arise at other work centers precisely because the order was moved. Since the completion date is not flexible, this may require considerable manual replanning, order by order. See also Section 13.2.4.

Fig. 13.2.3.2   Possible strategies for capacity planning.

Evaluation of the technique: The following *prerequisites* must be satisfied before we can use planning methods for infinite loading:

- Capacities must be quantitatively flexible. Loads occur randomly according to the order situation. Replanning orders is time consuming and far too expensive given the often limited value-added.

- The technique only produces good results if the collected shop floor data tracks work progress precisely. In addition, no large load should lie in the past; otherwise, the backlog will be so great in the first period that the load profile no longer makes sense.

The following *limitations* also apply:

- The further we plan into the future, the lower the likelihood that the planning forecasts will be accurate; unforeseen breakdowns or variance in actual quantities will already affect accuracy. The technique merely predicts the probable capacity utilization so that sufficient capacity can be made available.

- The less that we know about the actual progress of the order, the more that actual control will have to be *ad hoc* on-site in response to the constantly changing dates and the mix of the orders.

The following are typical *areas of application*:

- For customer order production or where the mix of orders fluctuates, i.e., in a *buyer's market*. Today, this is typically the case in the manufacture of capital goods or in discrete production and services in almost any industry.

- For all planning periods, particularly the long term. For execution and control of operations, this does not provide a precise program of work, but rather acts as a basis for situational planning of capacities and priorities at the work floor level.

13.2.4 Order-Wise Infinite Loading

Order-wise infinite loading loads the orders individually, order by order. The necessary planning measures are determined continuously, during, or after the loading of an order.

Order-wise infinite loading is necessary where there is little flexibility in terms of capacity and, at the same time, order due dates are inflexible.

As Figure 13.2.1.2 shows, particular emphasis is placed on the new order. Planning takes place after loading of the entire order or after each operation. As soon as an overload occurs, it is important to check all the work centers concerned and take the steps outlined in Figure 13.2.3.2.

Order-wise infinite loading is extremely time consuming, especially if there are lots of operations or if starting with step 4b in Figure 13.2.3.2 (moving operations). It is possible that operations of other orders will also have to be moved. Capacity may even become saturated and thus inflexible, after a certain time. In this case, if the order due dates are inflexible, no further planning will be possible.

It thus follows that this type of planning is suitable only for companies working with a few, and thus high value-added, orders. One example is special machine construction in small and medium-sized companies.

13.3   Finite Loading

The primary objective of *finite loading* is high capacity utilization (see Section 1.3.1). The main target is not low levels of goods in stock and work-in-process, short lead times in the flow of goods, high fill rates, and delivery reliability rates. These are secondary objectives (see Section 1.3.1). With finite loading, the customer must be prepared to accept a longer delivery lead time and possible changes in the agreed-upon dates.

Essentially, there exist one *operations-oriented* and several *order-oriented* techniques. The operations-oriented technique is actually a simulation of the possible production processes that assumes — hypothetically — that all the planning data are correct. Some of the order-oriented techniques yield practically the same results as the operations-oriented technique. Others, however, tend to assume that capacities are not always fully utilized, which increases the delivery reliability rate and reduces levels of work in process.

13.3.1 Operations-Oriented Finite Loading

Operations-oriented finite loading aims to minimize possible delays to individual operations and thus the average potential delay of the entire production order.

Operations sequencing and operations-oriented finite loading are synonymous.

Overview: The individual operations are planned time period by time period on the basis of orders, starting from the start date determined by lead-time scheduling (Section 12.3.3).

Planning strategy: This means establishing meaningful rules of priority for the order in which operations are scheduled, with the aim of achieving maximum throughput. The queues waiting upstream of the work centers are monitored and adjusted.

Technique: The planning horizon is divided into time periods. The operations to be scheduled are then assigned to work centers, period by period, until the capacity limit is reached, regardless of the order to which they belong. Figure 13.3.1.1 demonstrates the principle of the resulting algorithm. This includes the following aspects:

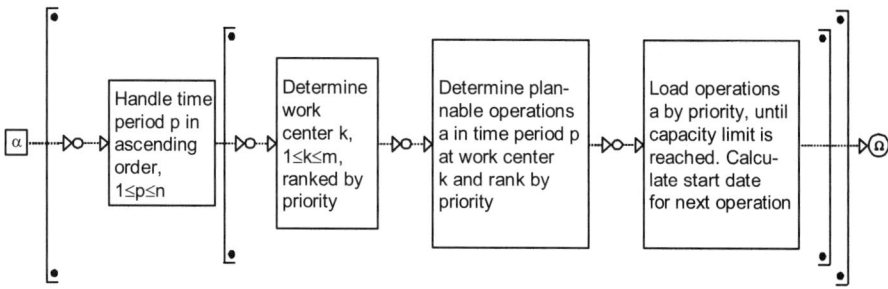

Fig. 13.3.1.1   Technique (algorithm) for operations-oriented finite loading.

- *Work center priority:* The order of the work centers becomes important as soon as there is more than one operation to be scheduled for an order in each time period. Possibly, the subsequent operation then relates to a work center whose planning has already been carried out for this period and now must be revised.

- *Determine the operations to be scheduled in the first time period;* typical operations are:

  - Every (subsequent) operation waiting for execution, for orders already started. The data on order progress identifies these operations.

  - Every first operation for orders not yet begun whose start date — calculated using a scheduling method (Section 12.3) — lies within the first time period.

- *Determine the operations to be scheduled in time period i, 2 ≤ i ≤ n;* typical operations are:
  - All operations not scheduled in the previous time periods.
  - Those operations for which the previous operation was scheduled in an earlier time period and whose start dates lies within time period i.
  - Every first operation for orders not yet begun whose start date — calculated using a scheduling method (Section 12.3) — lies within the time period i.

- *Arrange the plannable operations by priority.* The following secondary objectives may be applied to the selected order:
  A. Minimize the number of delayed orders
  B. Apply an equal delay to all orders
  C. Minimize the average wait time for operations
  D. Minimize the number of orders in process

- The following priority rules may be applied:
  1. The order in which the operations arrive (FIFO, "first in, first out")
  2. Shortest processing time rule (SPT)
  3. Proximity of the order due date (EDD, earliest due date)
  4. The ratio "remaining lead time for the order divided by the number of remaining operations"
  5. The ratio "remaining lead time for the order divided by the time still available for the order" (SLK, shortest slack time rule, ≈ order urgency; see also Section 12.3.6)
  6. The ratio "remaining lead time for the order divided by the remaining operation time for the order"
  7. (External) order priority
  8. Any combination of the above

Rules 1 and 2 are the easiest to apply in control of operations, because the information is immediately available, i.e., it is physically visible "locally." It is not necessary to consult a computer or a list. The other rules may require complicated calculations.

Every priority rule takes into account one or another secondary objective. Rule 1 is often used, since it minimizes the wait time upstream of the work center and thus the average order delay (objectives A and B). If capacity is utilized more fully, the strategy changes, and rule 2 is chosen. This accelerates the largest possible number of orders and thus reduces the value of goods in process (objectives C and D).

- *Load the operations in order until the capacity limit is reached:* If an operation exceeds the capacity limit, we transfer any as yet unscheduled operations to the next time period. The capacity used for the overlap load for the last operation is then no longer available in the next time period.

  One variation is not to schedule the operation that exceeds the capacity limit. However, this will use up remaining capacity only if an operation with a smaller load can be scheduled. This variation requires a more complicated algorithm.

- *Calculate the start date for the next operation:* After loading the operation, we calculate its completion date and the start date of the next operation on the basis of the interoperation time. To avoid problems with the algorithm, (see "priority of the work centers" above), it may be useful to use the start of the next time period as the earliest start date.[7]

Figure 13.3.1.2 shows the result of operations-oriented finite loading with reference to the orders in Figure 13.2.1.1, specifically P1, …, P6, and with the same work centers, namely work center A and work center B. Priorities were assigned in ascending order of order ID. Again, "preload" represents operations for orders that were loaded *before* orders P1, …, P6.

In contrast to the load profile in Figure 13.2.1.1, in finite loading we display the loads rotated 90° towards the time axis, whereby the height of the bar is equal for all work centers. The period length is then standardized at 100% capacity over the time period. This technique is only possible because the load does not usually exceed capacity. We can then enter a number of work centers along the vertical axis. Utilization of the entire system is then evident at a glance.

Evaluation of the technique: The following *prerequisites* must be met to use this technique:

---

[7]   If each operation is allowed a specific time period, such as a day or a week, we speak of *block scheduling*.

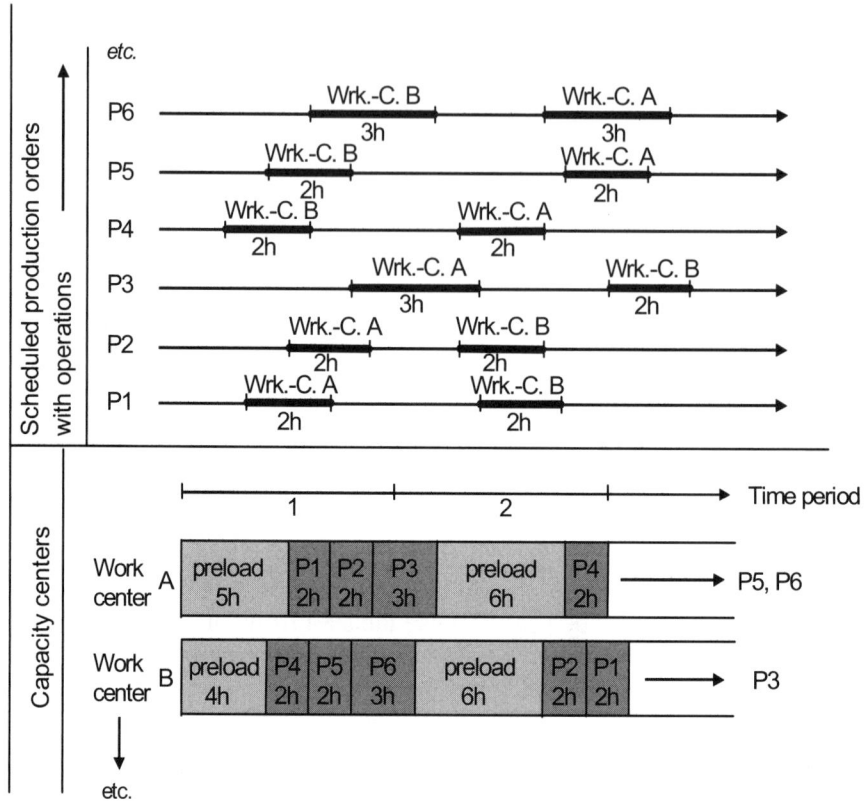

Fig. 13.3.1.2   Example of operations-oriented finite loading.

- Capacities and loads must be sufficiently reliable, i.e., the planning data and reported work progress must "tally." Otherwise, errors can accumulate very rapidly in the calculated dates.

- Due dates must be sufficiently flexible: We set the completion date for an order randomly on the basis of the existing utilization of production capacity. Lead times can be considerably longer than originally planned, however.

- It must be possible to limit the optimization of set-up times to the operations within a given period.

This creates the following *limitations:*

- The further we plan into the future, the smaller our chances that the planning forecasts will prove correct, if only due to unforeseen breakdowns or incorrect load specifications. For this reason, the technique is only sufficiently exact for short planning horizons, and it must be repeated at regular intervals.

- To be able to work to schedule in subsequent periods, any scheduled operations must be completed during this period. The technique does not allow reactive replanning locally.

- The level of goods in process is of secondary importance, both financially and with respect to volume. The planner monitors and adjusts the queues upstream of the work centers. Capacity is relatively inflexible, however, so orders must be held back, i.e., not released in good time. With long lead times in particular, however, order release can occur at the first identification of a bottleneck. This will physically hold up the production plant. Choosing a "neutral" priority rule will distribute the delay more or less evenly among all the orders.

The following are the typical *areas of application*:

- For *serial production* over a long period or in a *monopoly situation* i.e., in a *seller's market*. In such cases the date of delivery, e.g., to the end products store or to the customer, is less important. Some typical industries that belong here today are the chemical and food processing industries and niche capital goods markets.

- The operations-oriented finite loading technique *simulates* a situation that may arise in job shop or even line production. The operations for an order are executed in a more or less random order, in competition with other such orders. For execution and control of operations, this type of planning provides a production simulation for the coming days and weeks, i.e., an actual working program.

13.3.2 Order-Oriented Finite Loading

Depending on the technique that is used, *order-oriented finite loading* achieves maximum capacity utilization or ensures that as many orders as possible are executed on time with low levels of goods in process.

Overview: Orders are scheduled in their entirety, one after the other, in the time periods. If the period begins with an empty load, any orders that have already started are scheduled first, and only those operations that have not yet been carried out are considered.

Planning strategy: The objective is to find priority rules that will enable as many orders as possible to be completed. Special attention is given to those orders that cannot be scheduled, and whose start and completion dates must be modified as a result.

Technique: The planning horizon is once again divided into time periods. Individual orders (and all their operations) are scheduled in the order determined by the specified priority, without intervention by the planner. If the capacity limit for an operation is already exceeded, there are three possible responses: load the operation, defer it, or refuse the order. Once every order has been either planned or rejected, the planner handles the exceptions. The algorithm then attempts to plan rejected orders or those whose completion dates have been altered. Figure 13.3.2.1 illustrates the principle of the resulting algorithm.

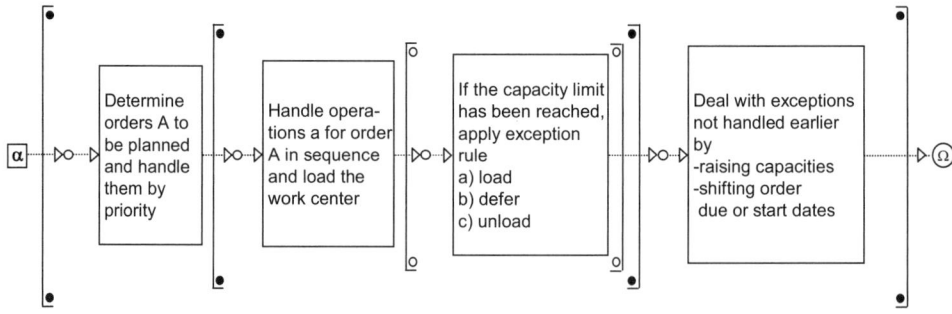

Fig. 13.3.2.1   Technique (algorithm) for order-oriented finite loading.

The details of the individual steps of the algorithm are as follows:

- *Determine the orders to be scheduled and treat them according to priority;* typical orders are:

  - All orders already begun. We know what operation is waiting to be carried out next from the order progress data.[8] All outstanding operations should be scheduled.

  - All orders not yet begun whose start dates lie within an arbitrarily chosen time limit. This limit defines the anticipation horizon, which should ideally be smaller than or equal to the

---

[8]   If the delivery date was promised on the basis of earlier planning and cannot be changed, no new scheduling can be performed. Probable scheduling (see Section 12.3.6) is one exception to this rule.

planning horizon. The start date should also be set or calculated using a scheduling method.

- The possible *priority rules* are similar to those presented in Section 13.3.1, although here they apply to the entire order and not just to the individual operations:

  1. Proximity of the start date for the order (orders with fixed start dates can be loaded first)

  2. Proximity of the order due date (EDD, earliest due date)

  3. The ratio "remaining lead time for the order divided by the time still available for the order" (SLK, shortest slack time rule, ≈ order urgency; see also Section 12.3.6)

  4. The ratio "remaining lead time for the order divided by the number of remaining operations"

  5. (External) order priority

  6. Any combination of the above

- *Handle and load operations in order:* All operations are loaded at the corresponding work centers for the time period in question, working forward, beginning with the earliest start date, or backward, beginning with the latest completion date. Interoperation times are also considered, *but queue times are not.*

- *Deal with exceptions:* If an operation falls within a time period during which the associated work center's capacity is already fully utilized, the following three possibilities can be applied:

  a. Load without considering available capacity: This option is suitable for orders already begun or for relatively short operation times. Some general reserve capacity is thus kept free for the latter operations.

  b. Defer the operation until the next period with available capacity (defer with forward scheduling, move forward with backward scheduling).

  c. Unload the entire order, to give priority to other orders.

- *Deal with all exceptions that could not be handled earlier:* If the steps described above have been carried out for all orders, the following contingencies requiring action may arise, depending upon which exception rule is applied:

a. For every capacity that is overloaded in a particular time period, either provide more capacity or unload orders accordingly.

b. (1) Backward scheduling: The resulting latest start date for an order lies before the earliest start date. Unload this order and then try again using forward scheduling, beginning with the earliest start date. (2) Forward or probable scheduling: The resulting earliest completion date for an order lies after its latest completion date. If the order due date is flexible, defer the order accordingly. Otherwise, it may be necessary to deliberately increase the critical capacity in order to first unload the order.

c. For every unloaded order: It may be possible to bring forward the start date. If the order due date is flexible, defer the order. If the critical capacities have at least some quantitative flexibility, they may be increased accordingly.

The unloaded orders are then scheduled in another iteration of these steps of the algorithm. This technique could quite conceivably be applied interactively, i.e., "order by order": If an operation falls within a time period in which the capacity limit is already exceeded, the planner can immediately decide upon the appropriate action.

Figure 13.3.2.2 shows the results of order-oriented finite loading after the first iteration, using exception rule (c). This example uses the same orders as in Figures 13.2.1.1 and 13.3.1.2, specifically P1, ..., P6, and the same work centers, namely work center A and work center B. Priority was assigned in ascending order by order ID. Again, "preload" represents operations for orders that were loaded *before* orders P1, ..., P6.

Exception rule (b) would have produced results similar to those in Figure 13.3.1.2, i.e., similar to operations-oriented finite loading. The more that exception rule (a) is applied or capacities are increased in the last step, the more infinite loading is obtained.

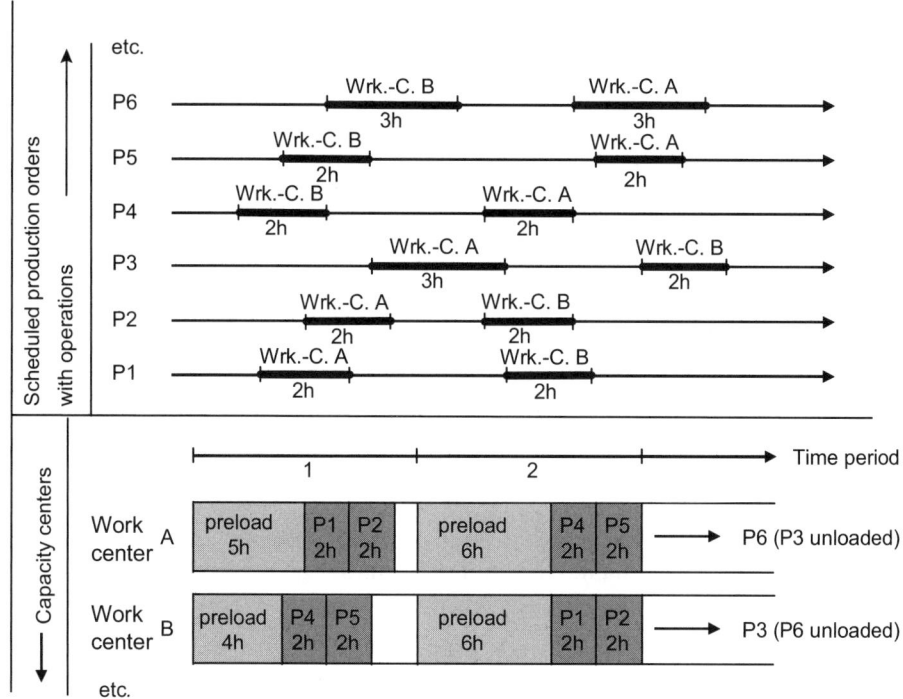

Fig. 13.3.2.2   Example of order-oriented finite loading, exception rule c): unloading.

The following *prerequisites* must be met to use this planning technique:

- Capacities and loads must be sufficiently reliable, i.e., the planning data and reported work progress must "tally." Errors can accumulate very rapidly in the calculated dates if this is not the case.

- Due dates must be sufficiently flexible — especially for exception rule (b). The order completion date results randomly on the basis of the existing utilization of production capacity. Lead times can sometimes be much longer than normal.

- Exception rules (a) and (c) are suitable for order due dates that are relatively inflexible. For these, however, the capacities must have some flexibility; otherwise, the administrative effort needed to regularly change dates would become unmanageable or so imprecise that capacities would be poorly utilized.

This creates the following *limitations:*

- The farther we plan into the future, the smaller our chances that the planning forecasts will prove correct. For this reason, the technique is only sufficiently exact for short planning horizons, and it must be repeated at regular intervals.

- In long-term planning, the technique calculates a *permissible* plan, in the full knowledge that it will change in the short term. Regular and efficient replanning is thus needed as the term becomes shorter.

- In short-term planning, for exception rule (b), any scheduled operations must once again be completed during this period. The technique does not allow local, reactive re-planning. Exception rules (a) and (c) do, however, allow some potential degrees of freedom for reaction if capacity is not fully utilized.

- Exception rule (b) leads to the best possible utilization of capacity. As with operations-oriented finite loading, long queues may arise. Goods in process then tie up capital and even hold up the entire production plant. Choosing a "neutral" priority rule will distribute the delay more or less evenly among all the orders.

- Exception rule (c) loads production only with the orders that it is capable of processing. It thus results in lower levels of work-in-process and shorter lead times. Successfully planned orders are completed on time. Exception rule (c) essentially uses the model of the queue presented in Section 12.2.1, i.e., the reservoir or open funnel model. If the funnel does not overflow, the production plant will not be held up. Thus, if further processing of an order is delayed excessively (e.g., over at least one time period), it should be rejected, rather than loaded.

- With inflexible capacities, on the other hand, exception rule (c) leads to lower utilization of capacity as soon as completion dates have to be deferred. This is because the load that would have been caused by operations earlier along the time axis is now missing. If there are no other orders, the capacity is wasted. Deferred orders will have long delays, and it may even become impossible to accept new orders.

- If the time between the earliest start date and the latest completion date is longer than the required lead time, then a start date and an end date that falls between these two extremes may be more suitable for the overall mix of orders. It is worth considering the load-oriented order release and capacity-oriented materials management (Corma) techniques outlined in Sections 14.1.2 and 14.1.3. Load-oriented order release, in particular, can actually be regarded as a generalization of order-oriented finite loading with exception rule (c).

- Interactive planning, i.e., order by order, is only efficient if relatively little effort is needed to load an order compared to its value added. In addition, we need continuous knowledge of the total load on the work center resulting from previous orders, so that a very fast database is required. We also have to keep load *totals* for each time period. To create sufficiently simple and rapid algorithms, the length of the time periods for each work center and along the time axis must then be defined as fixed.

Typical *areas of application* are as follows:

- As with operations-oriented finite loading, exception rule (b) is suitable for *serial production* over a long period or in a *monopoly situation* or *seller's market*. Typical industries here are chemical and food processing industries and niche capital goods markets.

- Exception rules (a) and (c) are suitable for many discrete manufacturing industries, wherever there is the minimum required level of quantitative flexibility. This is more often the case than we might at first suppose, even in short-term planning.

- For short-term planning and control. For this planning range, the technique provides:

  - With exception rule (b): An actual work program for the next few days.

  - With exception rules (a) and (c): An acceptable work program that also allows a degree of situational planning. The horizontal bar chart provides a rapid overview of all work centers and all orders, as it requires little space. It corresponds to the familiar "planning board" in production control. Individual orders can often be replanned very efficiently — in the case of the electronic planning board (*Leitstand*) through the click of the mouse.

- For long-term planning of few orders with high value-added and regular planning and replanning. For replanning individual orders, the advantages are again the clear display and ease of manipulation mentioned above.

13.3.3 Constraint-Oriented Finite Loading

In *constraint-oriented finite loading*, orders are planned around *bottlenecks*, or *bottleneck capacities*, which are work centers with a capacity utilization of 100% or more.

Bottlenecks depend on the given order volume and not upon the master data for the work center.

The drum–buffer–rope and the OPT techniques are techniques of production control that accord with the theory of constraints (TOC). See also Section 4.1.5 and [GoCo04].

The *drum–buffer–rope technique* includes the components shown in Figure 13.3.3.1.

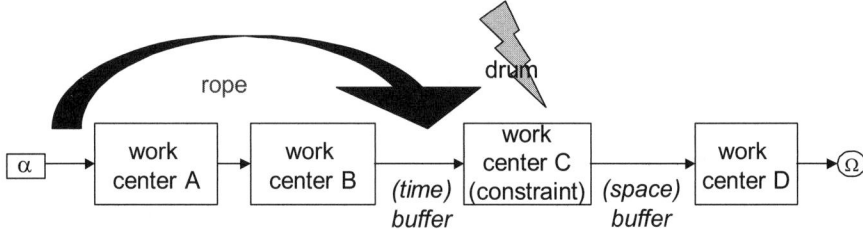

Fig. 13.3.3.1   The drum–buffer–rope technique.

- The *drum* stands for the rate or pace of the system. The "drumbeat" results from the *drum schedule*, that is, the master production schedule for the system, set by the throughput of the constraint, which should be balanced with the customer demand. The constraint controls the throughput of all products that it processes. *Feeder workstations*, that is, work centers feeding bottlenecks, should be scheduled at a rate that the bottleneck can process.

- A *buffer* in front of the constraint absorbs potential disturbances during a certain period of time. *Buffer management* expedites material in buffers in front of constraints and helps to avoid idleness at the constraint. In order to avoid idle time due to disturbances of the succeeding operations, buffer management can also include the maintenance of a (space) buffer after the constraint.[9]

- The *rope* is an analogy for the communication process: the set of planning, release, and control instructions for bringing the necessary material for production to the constraint in due time. This can be achieved using any technique: pull (kanban or order point type, for example) or push (MRP type, for example, by releasing material at the right time into the system), or any other appropriate intuitive or heuristic technique for the specific case.

The *OPT technique* (*optimized production technology*, see [Friz89] or [Jaco84]) is comprised of the following steps: First, only orders with a minimum batch size are generated. These lots then come together at bottleneck capacities, but they are kept separate for the upstream and downstream operations. Operations before the bottleneck are then scheduled backward, while later ones are scheduled forward and planned using normal lead times.

Planning strategy: Bottlenecks determine the order lead times and levels of goods in process. OPT does not give preference to either time limits or capacity limits.

Technique: Figure 13.3.3.2 illustrates the principle of the OPT method.

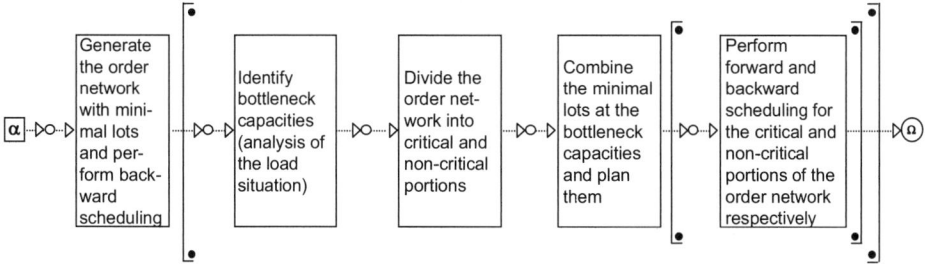

Fig. 13.3.3.2   Algorithm for constraint-oriented planning (OPT technique).

---

[9]   Compare here Figure 12.2.1.1.

Let us take a look at the individual steps of the OPT technique:[10]

- *Generate the order network with minimum batch sizes and perform backward scheduling:* Starting with customer orders, generate the minimum production batch sizes, based on minimum requirements using the logic of MRP (material requirements planning). In practice, these correspond to the smallest meaningful transport units and are thus also called *transport lots.* Then perform backward scheduling for infinite loading.

- *Identify bottlenecks, or bottleneck capacities, and divide the network into a critical and a non-critical part:* The critical part contains the bottleneck and subsequent capacities, especially assembly. The non-critical part is comprised of the operations preceding the bottleneck capacities. By way of example, Figure 13.3.3.3 shows the typical situation in the OPT algorithm after breaking down the order network.

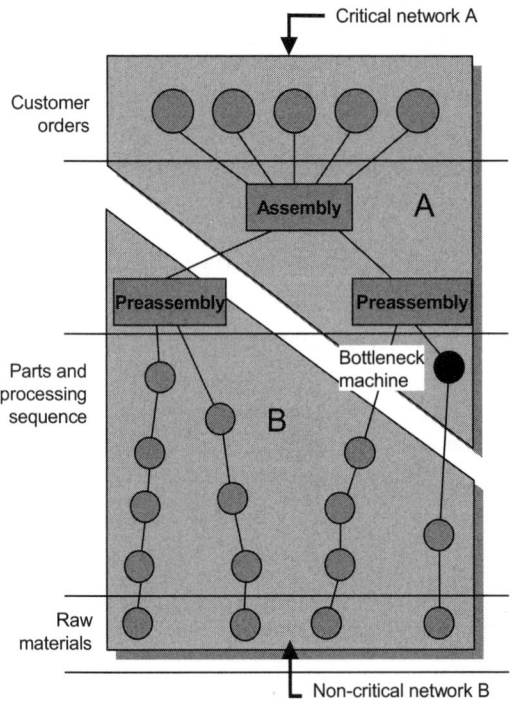

Fig. 13.3.3.3   Breakdown of the order network into two parts in the OPT algorithm.

---

[10]   The literature on the OPT technique usually offers only a broad outline.

- *Combine the minimum batch sizes and schedule them at the bottleneck capacities:* Unfortunately, the OPT technique does not provide exact criteria for this step. Using the largest possible lots and placing them in the optimum order should minimize setup times and thus maximize throughput. We also perform finite loading.

- *Forward and backward schedule the critical and non-critical parts:*

  - Perform forward scheduling for the critical part, i.e., after bottleneck capacities and particularly during assembly. Relatively small lots are recommended for these operations, created by further breaking down large bottleneck batch sizes. This step may be repeated several times, altering the parameters until an optimum delivery plan is obtained.

  - For both parts, we can generally use infinite loading.

- *Repetition:* If we change the timing of the production lot compared to its original backward scheduling, we may need to replan and even consider other bottleneck capacities (see below).

Evaluation of the drum–buffer–rope and OPT techniques: The following *prerequisites* must be satisfied for use of these planning techniques:

- Our picture of the capacities and loads must be very accurate, i.e., the planning data and reported work progress must "tally."

- It is essential to know the customer order volume and be sure that it will remain stable, since any change in volume requires further planning.

- The order due dates must have a degree of flexibility, since the completion date for an order is determined by the way in which the orders come together at bottleneck capacities and by the subsequent forward scheduling.

- In fact, most capacities require a degree of quantitative flexibility, or they would all become bottleneck capacities.

The following *limitations* apply:

- There must not be too many bottleneck capacities. In particular, the technique is unsuitable for situations where for a single order there are multiple bottleneck capacities, which may not follow in succession or may even be located at other production stages. In these cases, it would be difficult to determine the two separated parts of the order network for OPT. With the drum–buffer–rope technique, it would become difficult or even impossible to determine the "rope" part of the technique in detail. This means that the techniques are applicable mainly for simple — e.g., one-level — product structures.

- Identified bottlenecks can shift *de facto* due to changing of the completion dates in subsequent steps. In particular for job shop production, this means that the entire planning procedure may have to be repeated several times.

Typical *areas of application* are the following:

- The techniques are suited to mature line production running at a fixed rate, e.g., simple chemical products, food processing, or production of simple parts.

- The techniques are particularly suited for *machine-limited capacity*, or a production environment where a specific machine limits throughput of the process ([APIC04]).

13.4   Rough-Cut Capacity Planning

Rough-cut planning allows quick establishment of feasible variations of the master plan for many orders in *long-term planning* and quick determination of delivery dates for customer orders in *short-term planning*.

Efficient scheduling in the short term requires long-term overall coordination of load and capacity. If all the rough-cut structures are correct and sufficiently detailed and include all the goods to be procured through blanket contracts, then rough-cut planning of resources is entirely sufficient for long-term planning. At times it can even make shorter-term planning unnecessary or more straightforward.

Very simple rough-cut planning is possible wherever the total load for an order is sufficient for rough-cut planning.

With *capacity planning using overall factors (CPOF)*, the quantities of master schedule items are multiplied by the total load required by each item. This yields the total load of the master schedule. Historical percentages for each work center then provide an estimate of the required capacity of each work center to support the master schedule.

Figure 13.4.0.1 shows the (average) load of the master schedule with three items, I_1, I_2, and I_3. Suppose that two work centers WC-1 and WC-2 are involved. Historical percentages allow quick assignment of the total load to the two work centers.

Subassembly \ Week	1	2	3	4	Load per unit	Histori-cal %
I_1	60	60			0.75	
I_2			60	12	0.60	
I_3				48	0.50	
Total load (in h)	45	45	36	31.2		100
Required capacity on WC-1	29.25	29.25	23.4	20.28		65
Required capacity on WC-2	15.75	29.25	12.6	10.92		35

Fig. 13.4.0.1   Rough-cut capacity planning using overall factors: total load and estimation of the required capacity on work centers WC-1 and WC-2.

However, if knowledge of the load on each individual work center is necessary, rough-cut capacity planning gets more complicated. We look at this case in the following section.

13.4.1 Rough-Cut Network Plans and Load Profiles

> The *rough-cut process plan* for a product is the rough-cut production structure along the time axis.

Section 1.2.5 introduced rough-cut bills of material and rough-cut routing sheets. These are either derived from the detailed structures of a product or determined and maintained "manually." These rough-cut structures allow us to derive a rough-cut process plan with lead-time setoff for components or operations. As Section 12.3.3 also shows, a rough-cut process plan can easily form a directed network of operations.

Figure 13.4.1.1 shows a production order in a form similar to the familiar network plan. Rough-cut order structures are often represented in this way. In our example, we have combined the work centers into two rough-cut work centers.

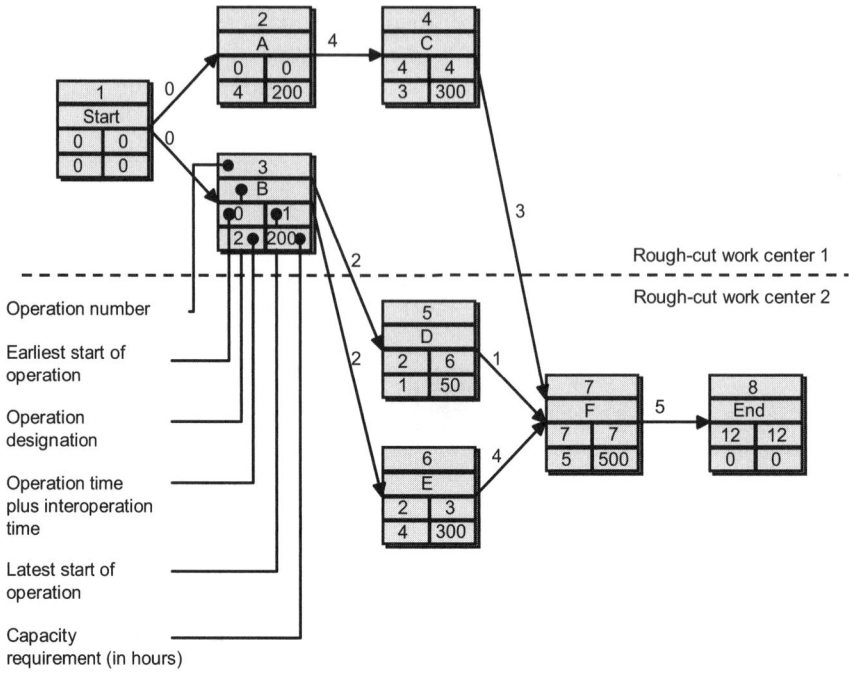

Fig. 13.4.1.1   Rough-cut network plan with two rough-cut work centers.

A *resource profile* is essentially a load profile, that is, standard hours of
load placed on a resource by time period, for rough-cut capacity planning.

Figures 13.4.1.2 and 13.4.1.3 show the resource profile derived from the
rough-cut process plan or from the *rough-cut network plan*.

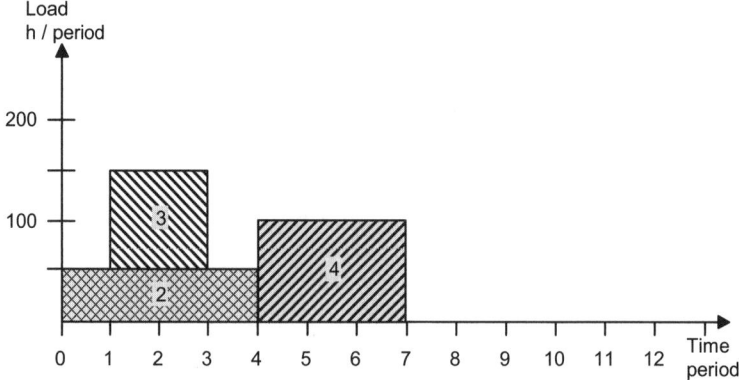

Fig. 13.4.1.2   Resource profile for rough-cut work center 1 as shown in Figure
              13.4.1.1.

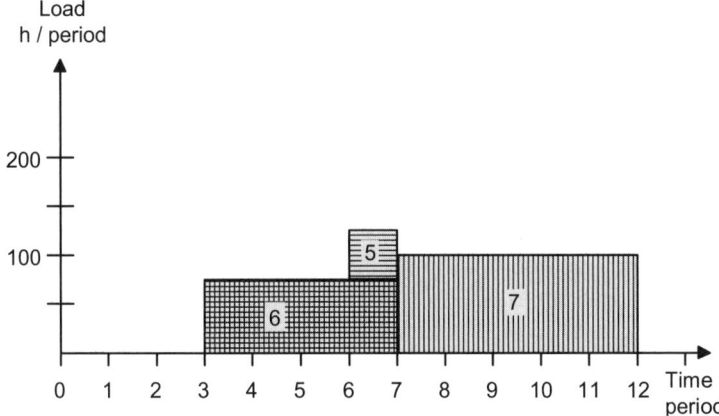

Fig. 13.4.1.3   Resource profile for rough-cut work center 2 as shown in Figure 13.4.1.1.

Finally, Figure 13.4.1.4 shows how they are combined to form a single rough-cut work center. For the sake of simplicity, in rough-cut planning we can regard the load as a rectangular distribution over the duration of the process. Indeed, this interpretation is also common in detailed planning.

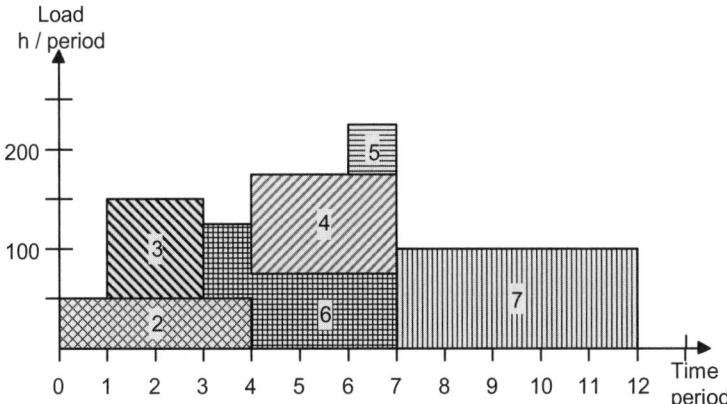

Fig. 13.4.1.4   Resource profile for the combination of rough-cut work centers 1 and 2.

If we chose the technique shown in Section 1.2.5, using lead-time setoff as the data structure behind the resource profile, we lose the typical information concerning operations before and after each operation in the network. Keeping the information in the data model is conceivable, however, and it would make the load and adjustment algorithms more flexible. However, the algorithms would also be more difficult to implement, which could result in longer response times.[11]

The problem of taking account of demand derived from bids, described in Section 4.2.1, also arises in rough-cut capacity planning. Regardless of whether we are planning for limited or infinite loading, the procedure to deal with this problem entails the following steps:

- The simplest method multiplies the product load profile by the *probability of order success* ("devalues" it) and thus loads only the resulting reduced load. Validation of the order success probability is a key factor here.

- Bids must be confirmed at an early stage or must be unloaded in order to make room for orders requiring definitive planning. The bid should therefore be assigned an expiration date. From that date on, we designate the bid as inactive or defer the promised delivery date by a sufficient number of periods.

- If a very large number of bids have already been planned, it will be difficult to assign a reliable delivery date to new bids. The completion date determined in planning is only a possible completion date. Additional information is required, such as a "maximum" completion date, for example, which is calculated assuming that all bids (or a significant proportion thereof) will be accepted. We do this by adding together the unloaded portions of the bids after calculating the probability, and dividing this figure by the capacity available per period. This gives the number of periods that must be added to the probable date in order to arrive at the "maximum" date.

13.4.2 Rough-Cut Infinite Loading

Rough-cut infinite loading corresponds to infinite loading, in this case based on the resource profile for rough-cut work centers presented in Section 13.4.1.

Here, we multiply the product load profiles related to a particular batch size (generally = 1) by the batch size and add a desired completion date.

---

[11]   Rough-cut planning is extremely interactive, i.e., it requires the planner to intervene and make decisions. It is not surprising, therefore, that rough-cut planning often works using the simplest data models, i.e., ignoring the interdependencies among operations.

The orders thus defined are then considered in a particular planning order. The priority can be determined by:

- The latest completion date
- The latest start date
- The external priority (importance) of the order.

When all orders have been loaded in this way (with no intervention from the planner) onto an existing "preloading," we obtain a resource profile that is typical of infinite loading. Figure 13.4.2.1 shows, as an example, the resource profile presented in Section 13.4.1. with loading from the earliest start date.

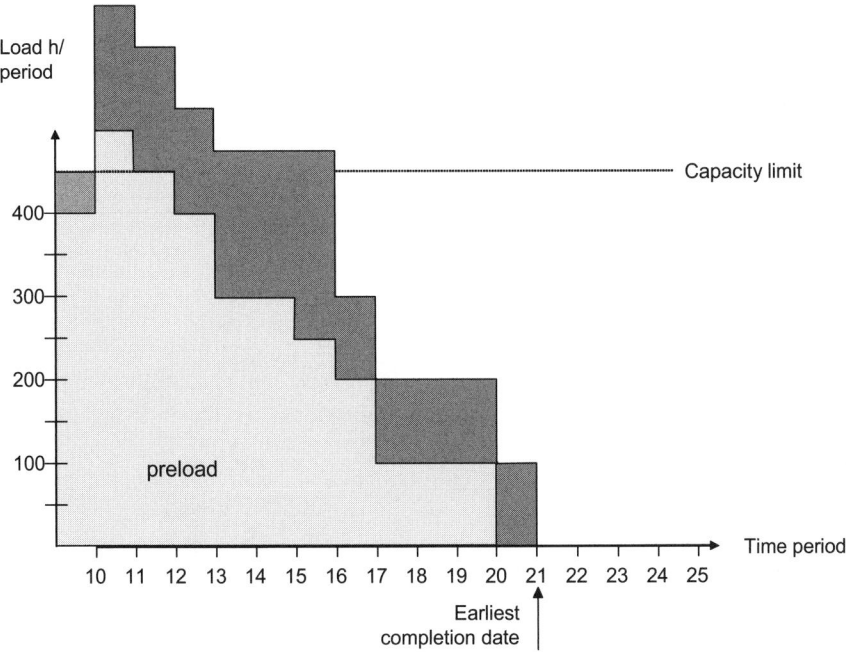

Fig. 13.4.2.1   Example of a resource profile for *one* rough-cut work center.

The planner then either defers the capacities or brings them into line with one another:

- If rough-cut planning is performed in the master planning, i.e., in the long term, capacities are flexible with respect to quantity. Indeed, determining such quantities is one of the objectives of long-term planning.

- If rough-cut planning is applied to the medium or short term, it provides decision support to accept, reject, or defer a waiting order. Capacity is then somewhat less flexible, which means that it will not always be possible to meet the desired completion date. In this case, the loading proceeds individually, order by order, with corresponding intervention by the planner after every order. If there are just one or two rough-cut work centers, this does not entail a lot of work, even if there are a lot of orders.

Figure 13.4.2.2 shows a possible response the planner can take to the overload shown in Figure 13.4.2.1. The planner can push the completion date back to the closest date that would produce an acceptable overload. Efficient algorithms highlight the order to be deferred by means of special graphical attributes (such as different colors) and automatically adjust the resource profile after rescheduling (generally using the mouse).

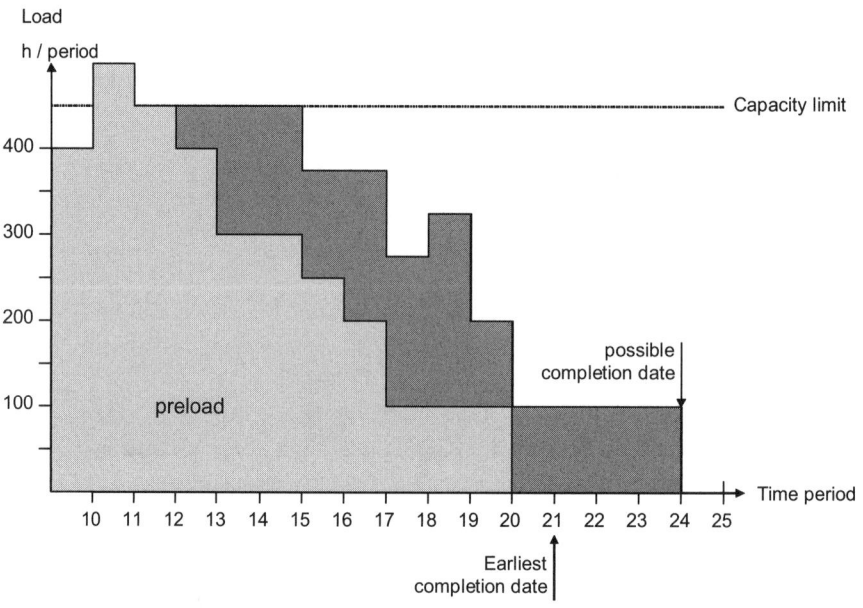

Fig. 13.4.2.2   Result of rough-cut capacity planning with deferred completion date.

Figure 13.4.2.3 shows the same resource profile, this time with two rough-cut work centers. The desired completion date causes an overload at rough-cut work center 2. In Figure 13.4.2.4 it has been brought into line by deferring the completion date by two periods.

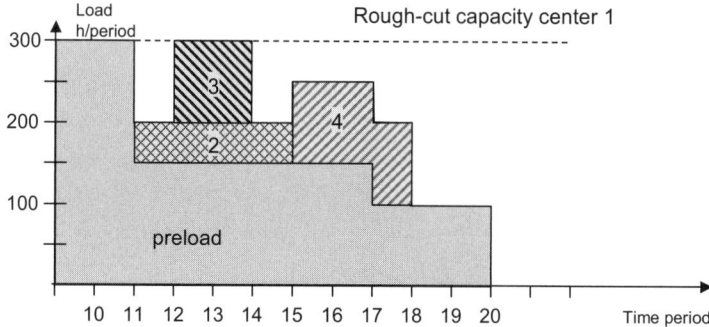

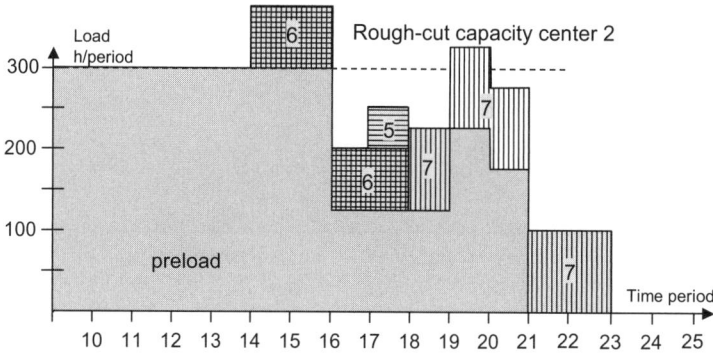

Fig. 13.4.2.3   Rough-cut capacity planning with two rough-cut work centers.

Detailed planning may nevertheless still be needed if we use short-term rough-cut planning. The individual rough-cut operations for the order under consideration can then be shown separately.

It is only by recording interdependencies between operations in the network plan that we are able to move the fifth operation forward from the period [19–20] (overload) to the period [18–19] (no overload), as shown in Figure 13.4.2.4. To be able to work efficiently and interactively, it must be possible to view all the work centers at the same time. The entire resource profile for an order can then be moved at all the work centers simultaneously.

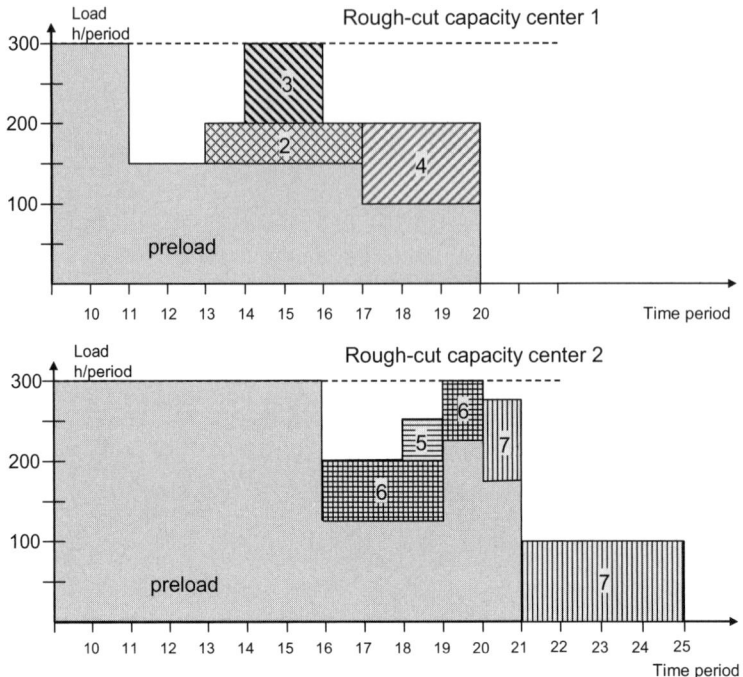

Fig. 13.4.2.4   Rough-cut planning: result after moving the completion date and operation 5.

13.4.3 Rough-Cut Finite Loading

Rough-cut finite loading corresponds to finite loading, but it is based on the resource profiles for rough-cut work centers presented in Section 13.4.1.

If order due dates are flexible or if variations in capacity are undesirable or unfeasible, we can also use planning with rough-cut finite loading. In this case, order-oriented techniques are relatively simple, since rough-cut planning places the emphasis on approximate, rather than exact maintenance of capacity. The sum of any over- and underloads should then be smoothed out over a sufficiently short time horizon.

It is always the cumulative capacity and cumulative "preload" that are considered. We also create a cumulative resource profile for the new order to be loaded. As an example, Figure 13.4.3.1 shows such a profile for one rough-cut work center. The important variable here is the cumulative load at the end of the profile.

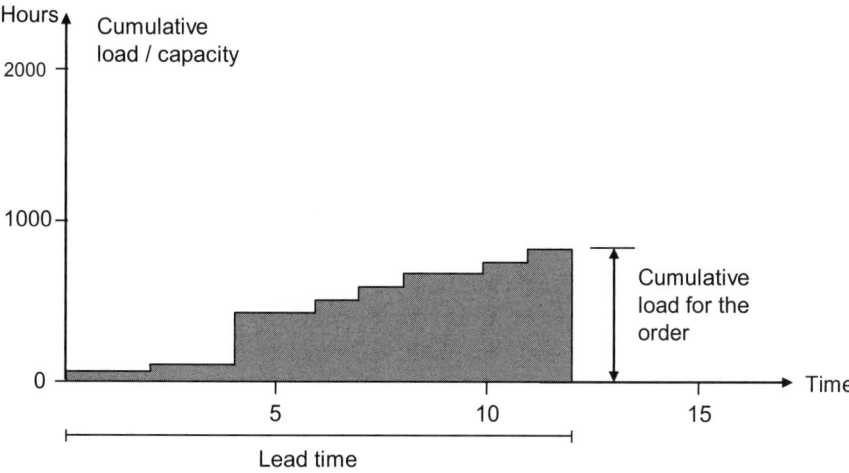

Fig. 13.4.3.1   Cumulative resource profile.

Figure 13.4.3.2 compares cumulative capacity and cumulative "preload" and yields the following result for the new order.

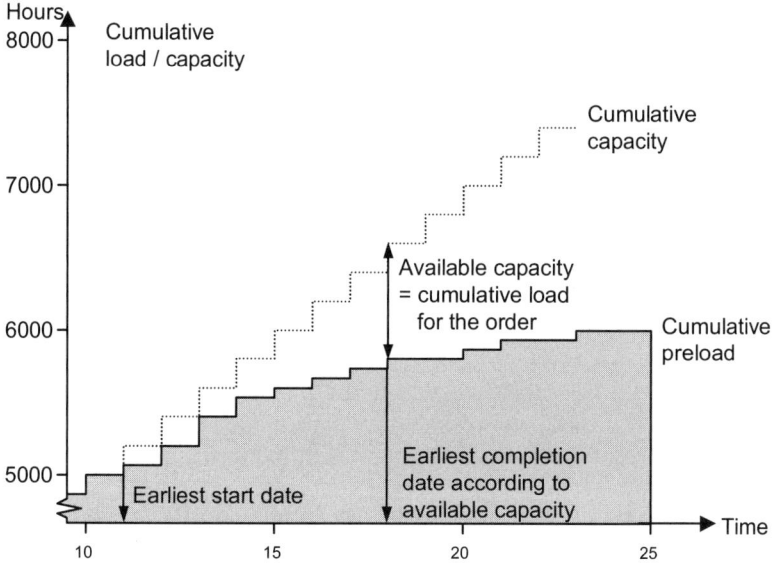

Fig. 13.4.3.2   Rough-cut planning: cumulative load and capacity before loading the order.

- The *earliest start date* is the period with the first available capacities that will not be used in subsequent periods.

- The *earliest completion date according to available capacity* is the end of the period in which, for the first time, the available capacity *permanently* exceeds the cumulative "preload" plus the cumulative load for the order, i.e., in which the available capacity is not less than this total.

Figure 13.4.3.3 also shows the newly loaded order.

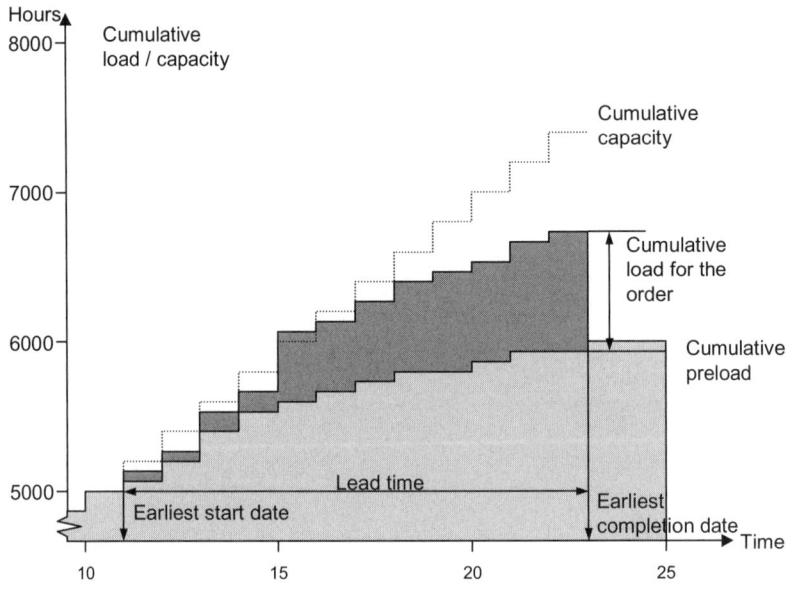

Fig. 13.4.3.3   Rough-cut planning: cumulative load and capacity after loading the order.

- The *earliest completion date* is the maximum total of the earliest completion date according to available capacity and the completion date obtained by adding the lead time to the earliest start date.

Capacities will be locally underused or exceeded. If the overload or underload frequency is relatively intense, i.e., continues over just a few periods, it can be compensated by means of control of operations. This is possible because we are dealing here only with rough-cut structures. The same applies to long-term infinite loading as described in Section 13.4.2, in this case simply because the loading is long term.

13.5 Summary

Capacities are workers or machines that can carry out work in order to produce goods or services. To calculate the rated capacity in order to add value, we have to know the utilization and the efficiency of a work center (or efficiency rate). Planning in two dimensions (time and quantity), as described in Section 4.3.3, is a fundamental problem when planning capacity requirements. Depending upon the situation, we must choose one of these dimensions to set the direction, which leads us to various classes of techniques.

Infinite loading is primarily a load profile calculation. The start date for an operation, which results from scheduling an order, determines the timing of an individual load. All the loads for each work center and time period are then added together to obtain the capacity requirement, which, in turn, is compared against rated capacity to obtain an overview. A closer look reveals a number of problems with the algorithms that have to be overcome. The load profile is then used for planning capacities, and the emphasis is placed on measures to alter capacity that are appropriate for the particular planning term. If there are only few orders to be planned, an additional measure — move the operations — is conceivable, although this can be difficult.

The chapter presented three finite loading techniques. The operations-oriented technique plans as many operations as possible for each work center from the perspective of the time axis. Priority rules are applied in order to decide among all the plannable operations in each time period. The result is high capacity utilization, but some orders will be kept waiting. On the other hand, use of the FIFO priority rule will distribute the delay equally among all the orders.

The order-oriented technique plans entire orders according to a particular priority and all the operations for each order. If there is no more capacity available for an operation, we can defer the remaining operations. The consequences for the performance indicators are similar to those of the operations-oriented technique. Another response is to unload such an order in its entirety. In this case the remaining orders will be executed on time (according to schedule), with a lower level of goods in process and less favorable capacity utilization than with the operations-oriented technique. However, we still need to find a later completion date for the unloaded orders, which may lead to long delays and possibly even to the loss of these orders. If there are only a few orders to be planned, we can also attempt to move individual operations forward or to defer other orders, although this can be a very time-consuming "manual" task.

The constraint-oriented method requires us to be able to identify a level of bottleneck capacities within the network of operations. The corresponding operations are planned by finite loading of the bottleneck capacities and by combining lots in order to minimize set-up times. We then perform backward planning for operations before the bottleneck capacities and forward planning for those that follow. The bottleneck capacities are thus fully utilized. For the others, the meeting of dates has higher priority.

For rough-cut capacity planning, we first create a rough-cut network plan for each product family and derive the resource profile for each rough-cut work center needed to manufacture the product family. Infinite loading is first applied, as in the detailed technique. Order by order planning then enables us to defer the entire profile, so we can decide whether to accept the order in the short term, for example. With finite loading, we first determine the earliest completion date according to available capacity and then add the lead time to the first date for which any capacity is available. The later of the two dates thus calculated is the earliest completion date for the order.

13.6   Keywords

activation, 688
actual capacity
    utilization, 686
availability (in
    capacity), 686
available work, 697
buffer management,
    712
capacity determination,
    685
capacity requirements
    planning (CRP), 691
constraint-oriented
    finite loading, 712
drum-buffer-rope, 712

finite loading, 700
firm planned load, 693
idle capacity, 688
infinite loading, 690
labor capacity, 685
load leveling, 698
load profile calculation,
    691
load traceability, 697
machine capacity, 684
operations sequencing
    (syn. operations-
    oriented finite
    loading), 700

optimized production
    technology (OPT),
    713
order-oriented finite
    loading, 705
order-wise infinite
    loading, 699
priority rule, 702
rough-cut finite
    loading, 724
rough-cut infinite
    loading, 720
subcontracting, 698
work on hand, 697

13.7 Scenarios and Exercises

13.7.1 Capacity Determination

The following exercise was developed on the basis of a communication from Barry Firth, CPIM, Melbourne, to whom we extend many thanks.

A plant runs 10 * 8 hour shifts per normal week. A work center in the plant has 5 identical machines, each requiring one operator to run it. This is a machine-paced work center (a machine capacity). Operators get a total of 1 hour for breaks, and they usually take their breaks at the same time. Each machine requires one episode of planned maintenance per week of three hours, scheduled by the planner. During the last 6 weeks, the performance data in Figure 13.7.1.1 were recorded:

Week No. ▶	1	2	3	4	5	6
Number of working days	5	4	5	5	5	5
Actual machine hours (setup+run)	260	200	280	320	260	280
Maintenance time in machine hours	15	12	18	15	15	15
Standard machine hours produced	220	160	240	280	220	220

Fig. 13.7.1.1 Capacity performance data.

Questions:

a. What is the *theoretical capacity* in machine hours *per normal week* (5 days)?

b. Taking into account scheduled non-production events, what is the *availability* (as a percentage) of machine time *per normal week*, without considering operator constraints?

c. What is the availability (as a percentage) of machine time *per normal shift*, taking into account the normal working conditions for operators?

d. If the tactical utilization is targeted to be 90%, what value should be used for the utilization factor of machine time for capacity rating purposes?

e. What is the *demonstrated capacity per normal week* of this work center? (Adjust the data for week 2 to correct for the short week.)

f. What was the *actual utilization* (as a percentage) through the 6 weeks in review?

g. What was the *actual work center efficiency* through the 6 weeks in review?

h. If *planned efficiency* is targeted to be 85%, and taking into account your answer to question (d), what was the *rated capacity per normal week*?

i. Compare your answers to questions (a), (e), and (h). What should we do now?

Solutions (see also the definitions in Section 13.1.1):

a. Theoretical   capacity   =   400   hours   per   normal   week = (5 machines) * (10 shifts) * (8 hours per shift and machine).

b. Downtime due to maintenance is 15 hours per week. Therefore, the availability factor is $(400 - 15)/400 = 96.25\%$.

c. Downtime due to operator breaks is 1 hour per shift of 8 hours. Therefore, the availability factor is $7/8 = 87.5\%$.

d. Assuming that maintenance can not be effected during operator breaks, the utilization factor is $87.5\% * 96.25\% * 90\% \approx 75.80\%$.

e. Demonstrated capacity is expressed as standard hours produced (row 4 in the table above). The adjusted output for week 2 is $160 * 5/4 = 200$ hours. Over 6 weeks, the mean is $(1340 + 40)/6 = 230$ standard hours per week.

f. During the 6 weeks in review, production has run for 1600 machine hours (row 2 in the table above) out of a possible 2320 hours (= 5*400 + 320). Therefore, actual utilization = $1600/2320 \approx 69.0\%$.

g. Actual efficiency – standard hours produced divided by actual hours worked = $1340/1600 = 83.75\%$.

h. Rated capacity = 400 hours * 75.8% * 85% ≈ 258 (standard) hours.

i. Demonstrated capacity (230 hours) is too low compared to rated capacity (258 hours). However, in week 4, the output (280 hours) exceeded 258 hours. Check whether the measurements are required still. If so, check for exceptional events, calculating actual utilization and efficiency for each week. Decide whether to make adjustments to planned utilization or efficiency.

13.7.2 Algorithms for Load Profile Calculation

One of the problems associated with the use of simple algorithms is that an operation can extend across several load periods (see Figure 13.2.2.2). This exercise will examine how manual or computer algorithms establish capacity and load in a load profile.

Use Figure 13.7.2.1 to enter the capacity or load curve (continuous or rectangular distribution within a time period) for a work center, given the problem outlined below.

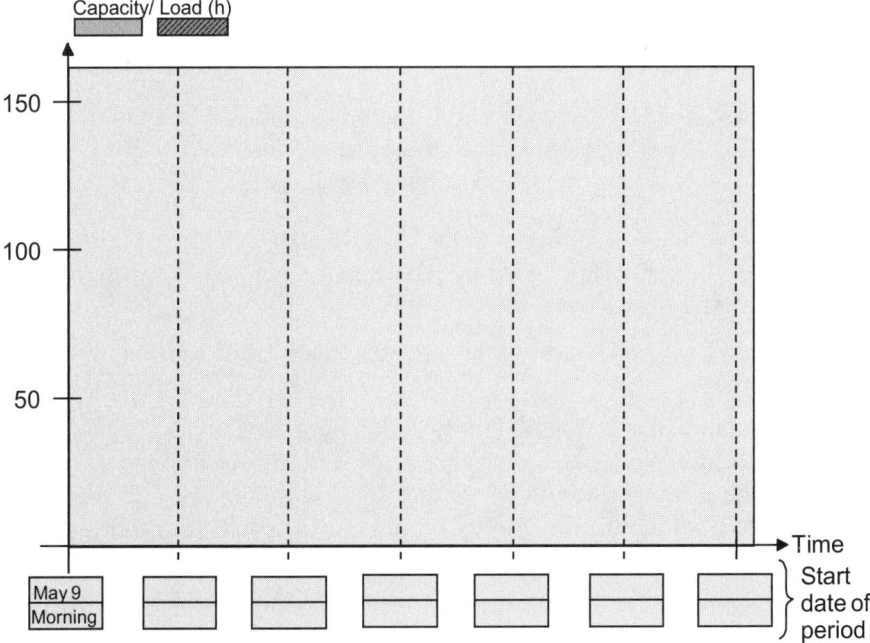

Fig. 13.7.2.1   Load profile calculation.

a. Determine the start date of each period and enter it into the figure above, given 2 weekly periods of 3.5 days each (½ calendar week): Sunday morning to Wednesday noon and Wednesday noon to

Saturday evening. The load profile starts with Sunday morning, May 9, (as indicated in the figure). The load profile covers 6 periods (3 weeks).

b. Allocate theoretical capacity to each of the 6 time periods, respecting the following data: At the work center, the plant runs one 8-hour shift per normal work day, (8 a.m. to 12 p.m., 1 p.m. to 5 p.m.). The work center has 5 identical machines. Saturdays and Sundays are off. Furthermore, May 13 and May 24 are public holidays (in practice, these dates would change each year). Note that "today," or the moment of the inquiry, is 7 a.m. on Wednesday, May 12.

c. Assume no existing load on the work center. For the following operation, allocate its standard load to the work center: Operation start date is Friday morning, May 14. Standard load (including setup) is 81 hours. The operation can be split on 2 machines, maximum.

Solutions:

a. The second period starts at Wednesday noon, May 12. The third period starts on Sunday morning, May 16. The fourth period starts at Wednesday noon, May 19. The fifth period starts on Sunday morning, May 23. The sixth period starts at Wednesday noon, May 26. The load profile ends before Sunday morning, May 30.

b. Note that there is either a Saturday or Sunday in each period of ½ calendar week. Thus, theoretical capacity per period with normal working days is

(5 machines) * (8 hours per day and machine) * (2.5 working days) = 100 hours.

Note that, in the first period, only 20 hours of capacity are left, because it is already Wednesday morning, May 12. Furthermore, in the second and the fifth periods there is one less working day due to public holidays, which results in only 60 hours of capacity for each of these periods.

c. The load has to be distributed to different periods. Only one working day is left during the period in which May 14 falls (the second period). Because only 2 machines can be used, a maximum of only 16 standard hours (note: not 40) can be loaded. During the third period, 2.5 working days on two machines allow the load of 40 hours. The same would be possible for the fourth period. However, only 25 hours are left to be loaded.

13.7.3 Rough-Cut Capacity Planning

Figure 13.7.3.1 shows the network plan for a production order.

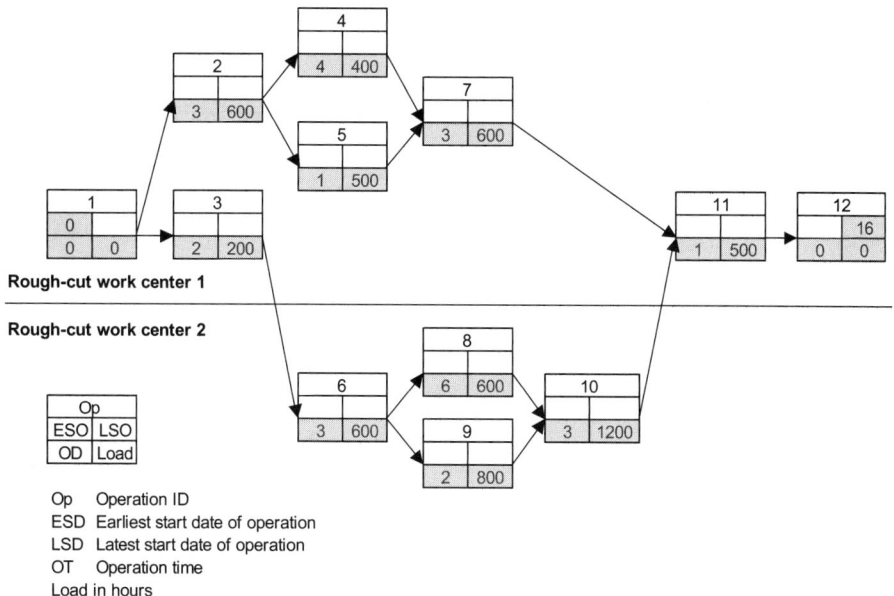

Fig. 13.7.3.1   Rough-cut network plan with two rough-cut work centers.

a. Complete the network plan: Calculate the earliest start date and the latest start date for each operation. What is the lead-time margin (the slack time), and what is the critical path? Determine the slack of all operations that are not on the critical path.

b. Following the technique introduced in Section 13.4.1, determine the resource profiles for rough-cut work centers 1 and 2, as well as the resource profile for the combination of rough-cut work centers 1 and 2.

c. Figure 13.7.3.2 shows the preload of rough-cut work center 2. Load the resource profile for rough-cut work center 2 with *infinite* loading. Determine the earliest completion date for the operations of rough-cut work center 2. Further, determine the load and the deferred earliest completion date for the operations of rough-cut work center 2 without overloading the capacities.

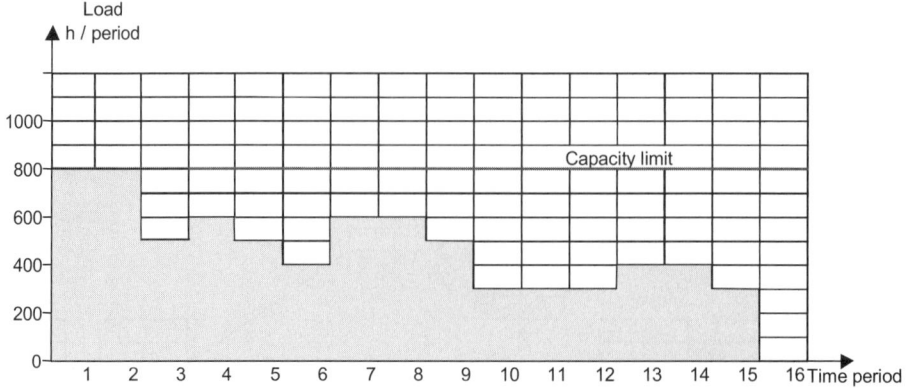

Fig. 13.7.3.2   Preload of rough-cut work center 2.

Solutions:

a.   Lead-time margin is 1. Operations 1, 3, 6, 8, 10, 11, and 12 make up the critical path. Operations 2, 4, 7, and 9 could be deferred by 4 time periods, operation 5 by 7 periods.

b.   The figure that follows shows the results for rough-cut work center 2 as well as for the combination of both rough-cut work centers 1 and 2. The length of the arrow indicates the number of time units for a possible deferring of the start date of operations that are not on the critical path.

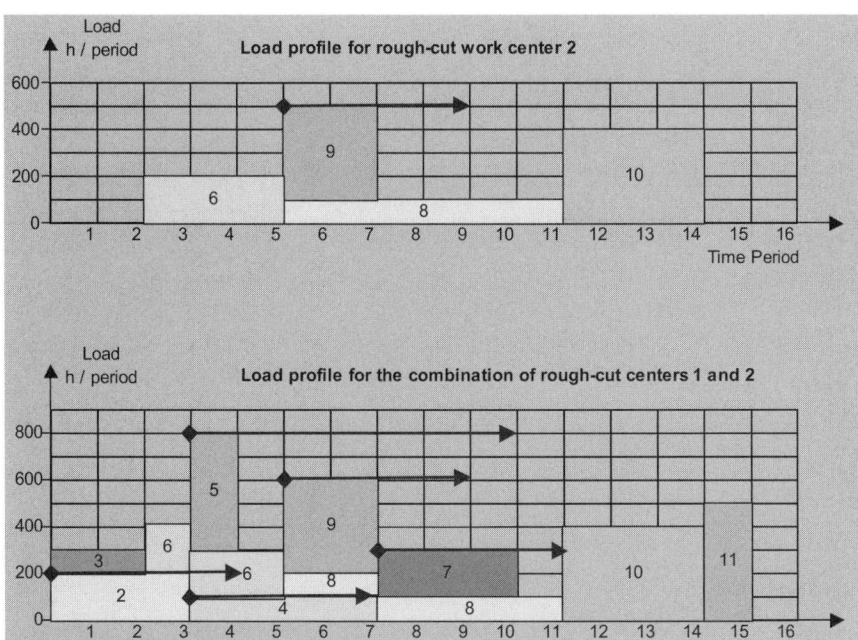

c.   The earliest possible completion date for the operations of rough-cut
     work center 2 using infinite loading is — as the above figure shows —
     at the end of period 14. For finite loading, the next figure shows the
     result: an earliest possible completion date at the end of period 15.
     Note: Because operation 9 is not on the critical path, parts of its load
     can be deferred to later periods in order to prevent overload.

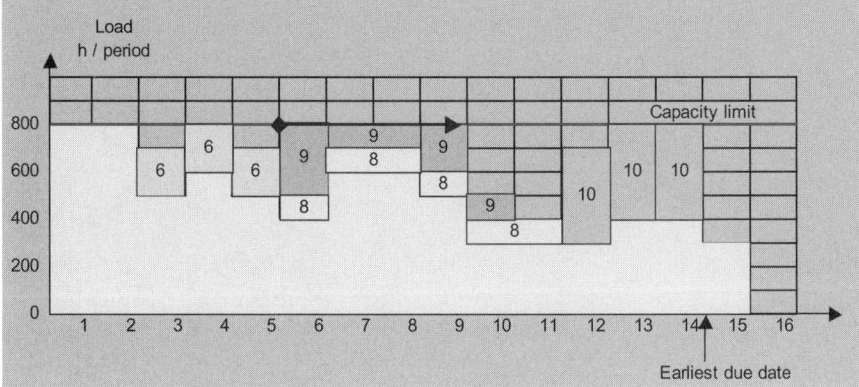

14 Order Release and Control

Chapters 10 and 11 on materials management showed the derivation of resource requirements for long-term and medium-term planning from independent demand (customer orders and forecasts). This results in *planned* order proposals for production and procurement. These are proposals for blanket orders or proposals for specific orders for a product, depending upon the temporal range. The present chapter now turns to planning & control tasks in the short-term planning horizon.

> *Control*, used here in a traditional sense, means the regulation and coordination of orders in order to achieve successful order completion, following the flow of goods from controlled release of order proposals through value-adding activities to manufacture and distribution of saleable products.

See the footnote on the term *control* in Section 1.3.3. Using the reference model for business processes and planning & control tasks from Figure 4.1.4.2, Figure 14.0.0.1 highlights the tasks and processes (darker background) that are the focus of this chapter. Sections 1.2.3, 4.3.3, and 4.3.4 also serve as introductions to this material.[1]

Each order release entails a *new* scheduling calculation and availability test of the needed resources using techniques of materials management, scheduling, and capacity management. If orders compete, there are techniques for choosing those that should be released.

The orders are then controlled through the areas (job shops for parts production, assembly, and so on, or for procurement). Electronic planning boards (*Leitstand*), or control boards, are also used here. Accompanying documents are prepared. Order control also includes the loading of infrastructures for picking and distribution. A shop floor data collection system records progress reports and the resources consumed. Finished products or received goods are inspected, supplied to further production, distribution, or stock and prepared for invoicing.

This chapter examines order release and control in the areas of distribution, production, and procurement only. Section 4.4 discussed possible concepts and methods in the area of research and development.

---

[1] We suggest that you review Sections 1.2.3, 4.3.3, and 4.3.4 before studying this chapter.

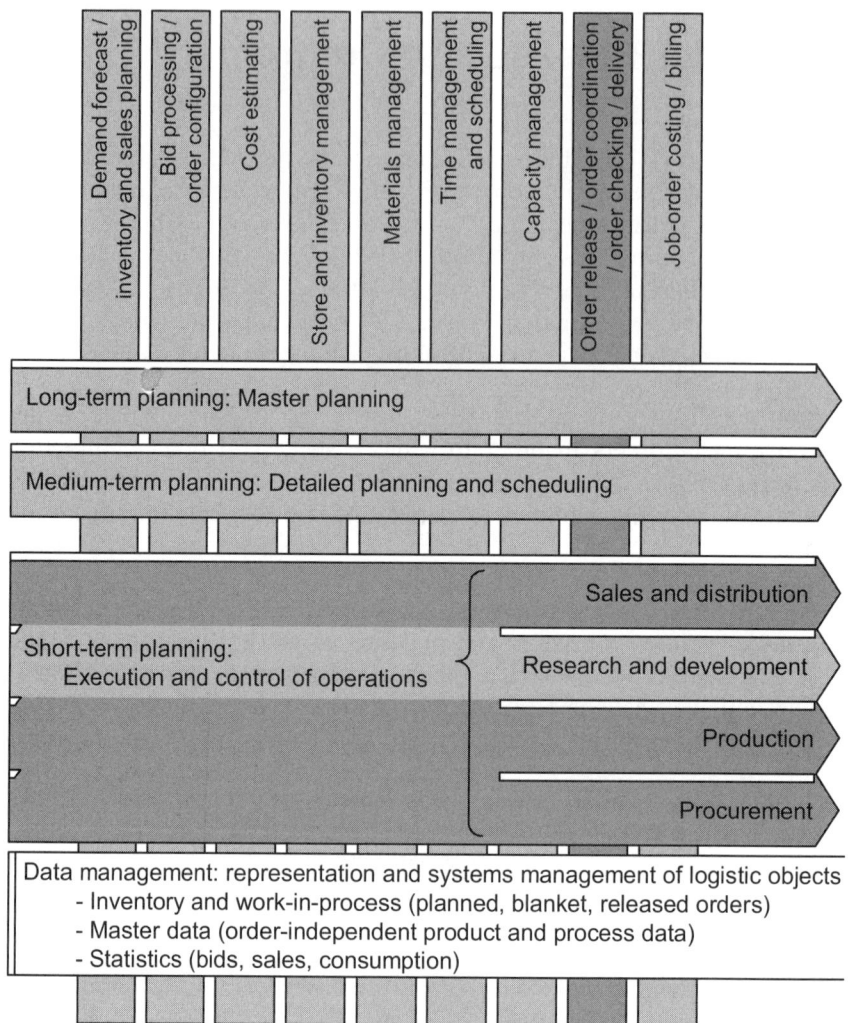

Fig. 14.0.0.1   The parts of the system treated in this chapter.

14.1   Order Release

The *order release* changes the status of an order from "proposed" to "released" and triggers the flow of goods to a procurement process or production process.

Generally, for an order release the availability of all resources needed to execute the order must be checked, in particular the availability of components and capacity.

14.1.1 Order Proposals for Production and Procurement and Order Release

The *order proposal*, or *planned order*, states the goods to be produced or procured, the order quantity, the proposed latest completion date, and — often given implicitly — the earliest start date.

The reasons for order proposals for production or procurement vary:

- An *unplanned demand is submitted*, that is, demand for customer or production orders not covered by projected available inventory or scheduled or planned receipts. In certain cases the proposal corresponds to the customer's demand in terms of quantity as well as delivery date. In other cases, order proposals stipulate production or procurement of a larger batch.

- A *purchase requisition is submitted.* This is an authorization to the purchasing department to purchase specified materials in specified quantities within a specified time, usually short term ([APIC04]).

- *Stock of an item falls below the order point.* Here the planned order proposal stems from *medium-term planning.* See also Section 10.3.1.

- *Net requirements planning specifies production or procurement of a lot of an item.* This type of order proposal stems from *long or medium-term planning.* See also Section 11.3.1.

There are two possible forms of presenting order proposals: either as simple lists of proposals or as planned orders in the order database. In the case of direct procurement for a customer order, the identification of the order proposal should refer directly to the identification of the order position in the customer order.

If there are only a few order proposals to release, or proposals based upon unplanned customer demand, planners will release these individually. Keeping track of orders to be released among numerous order proposals is difficult. It is useful to sort the orders by planner and weekly time window:

- An order proposal for C items in an ABC classification, particularly for goods to be purchased, can be released directly – with the proposed order quantity, proposed latest completion date, and standard supplier. Spot verifications will suffice for these automatically released orders.

- For other items the rhythm of selection, and thus ordering, depends upon the items' importance. This rhythm may be periodic, such as daily, weekly, bi-weekly, or monthly. However, an order may be released as soon as a demand event occurs.

In collective materials management, all items belonging to the same planning group are checked at the moment of order release. Joint ordering avoids procurement costs that are lot-size independent, but leads to additional carrying cost due to premature procurement.

Purchase order release does not necessarily have to be a formal procedure. According to specific agreements, certain suppliers can take on themselves the restocking of C items in the warehouse. This is common practice not only in the grocery retail trade, but also with suppliers of usage items in industrial production (compare the kanban technique in Section 5.3).

Production order release reasonably comprises, for every order, a check on availability, at least of critical resources. This also holds for order proposals stemming from long or medium-term planning, even if availability checks have been carried out earlier. The *availability test* consists of:

- *Calculation of lead time*, in order to determine the start dates for operations at critical work centers, as well as dates for the demand of critical components. We presented the techniques for calculating lead time in Sections 12.3 and 12.4.

- *Availability test of the components* on the start date of the operation for which they are needed. We outlined the techniques for this in Section 11.1. As an aside, in releasing contract work the availability of any accompanying materials that must be provided for the (external) operations must also be checked.

- *Availability test of required capacity* on the start date of operations using techniques that were outlined in Sections 13.2, 13.3, 14.1.2, and 14.1.3.

Production order release entails the following problems:

- Even with computer support, the checking of resource availability is a complicated and lengthy process. It is often impossible to gain rapid and exact results. As a common compromise solution, planners will test at least component availability *at the start date* of the order or the relevant partial order.

- The allocation of all the resources required for the order.

> An *allocation* is the classification of quantities of items that have been assigned to specific orders but have not yet been released from the stockroom to production.
>
> *Staging* is pulling material for an order from inventory before the material is required ([APIC04]).

If the availability of at least one resource is not guaranteed, the remaining components and production facilities nevertheless remain allocated for the order. Staging has the same effect: the order waits for missing resources and, moreover, blocks the plant.

- On the one hand, it would apparently be better to release all the operations for an order at the same time and only when all resources are completely available.

- On the other hand, it may be that some of the allocated resources of such unreleased orders could be used immediately in other production orders. Immediately available capacity may go unused, only to be lacking later. But assigning resources to other orders without procuring replacements to be used for the waiting order would lead to further problems.

In order to achieve an acceptable lead time for production order release as well as to make use of available capacity, a compromise — though less than optimal, since it leads to waiting work-in-process — can be reached through the following measures:

- Release only a partial quantity of the order lot.

- Release the first operations only, if the missing components are not required until later operations.

- Designate the planned order as *firm planned order*: With this, the allocation of components and production facilities on hand is also designated as "firm allocated." The necessary organizational discipline then ensures that the "firm allocated" resources are not withdrawn for other orders. In addition, it is important that computer programs, such as the MRP technique (material requirements planning), do not change this type of orders automatically.

There are different kinds of accompanying documents in production and procurement. The two following cases can be distinguished:

1. The contents of an order change remain the same each time, with the possible exception of the order quantity.

- With a *traveling card* a variable order quantity can be set. The due date automatically results, in relation to the date on which the traveling card is sent.

If the entire inventory of an item can be carried in two bins, a visual control system can be installed, namely, the following efficient "traveling" system with fixed order quantity:

- With a *two-bin inventory system*, the replenishment quantity is ordered as soon as the first bin (the working bin) is empty. During replenishment lead time, material is used from the second (reserve) bin, which has to contain enough items to cover the demand during lead time, plus a safety demand. At receipt of the replenishment quantity, the reserve bin is filled up. The excess quantity is put into the working bin, from which stock is drawn until it is used up again.

The traveling card and the two-bin inventory system have come into renewed favor with the kanban technique and its two-card kanban system.

2. The contents of an order change each time. In this case, a formal order from the ordering party (the sales department or the production management) to the order recipient (production or the supplier) is necessary:

- A *purchase order*, for procurement both of goods and work (see Section 1.2.1), essentially corresponds in form and structure to a customer order. As the current trend is to shorten administrative times between manufacturer and supplier, techniques supported by information technology are coming into increasing use. The detailed order data structures behind the "order" business object in Section 1.2.1 have undergone increasing standardization. This has led to the development of the EDI/EDIFACT interface. Thanks to Java programming and the CORBA standard (Common Object Request Broker Architecture), an increasing number of organizations are now making use of transmissions via the Internet.

- For a *production order,* the people at the shop floor responsible for execution require precise instructions as to the nature of the work to be executed and the components to be built in. See Section 14.2.1.

14.1.2 Load-Oriented Order Release (Loor)

Load-oriented order release (Loor) [Wien94] has — for *planning of limited capacity* – high load as its *primary objective* (see Section 1.3.1). Equally important are its *secondary objectives* of low levels of work-in-process, short lead times in the flow of goods, and delivery reliability.

Principle of the technique: This heuristic technique, which was introduced in the early 1980s, is based on the funnel model (see also Section 12.2.1). Essentially, its aim is to adapt the load to the capacity actually available. It is a generalization of the technique that we presented in Section 13.3.2, variation (c), because thanks to a clever heuristic the matching of load to capacity can be limited to one time period.

Planning strategy: Planning releases only those orders that can actually be handled by the work center without resulting in excessive queues. Processing of waiting work-in-process, and thus production control, proceeds according to the *first in, first out* (FIFO) principle.

Technique: Figure 14.1.2.1 illustrates the technique using the analogy of the funnel model. Starting from the uppermost funnel containing all known orders, two filtering techniques are used to determine the orders to be released.

The *time filter* permits only those orders to flow into the urgent order book that fall within the *time limit*, that is, within the anticipation horizon.

The *load filter* releases only the amount of work that will maintain constant mean inventory, that is, the desired work on hand, for a work center. The *load limit* is equal to the product of capacity during the anticipation horizon and the *loading percentage*.

Although instructions are available for determining the anticipation horizon and the loading percentage, in the world of practice the values chosen are often based on experience or arbitrary.

Load-oriented order release is performed on a cyclical basis, perhaps weekly, and always for a specific planning horizon. It is comprised of the same steps that were outlined in Figure 13.3.2.1. We will now describe these in more detail.

- Determine the orders to be included in planning and rank them by priority. The candidates are:

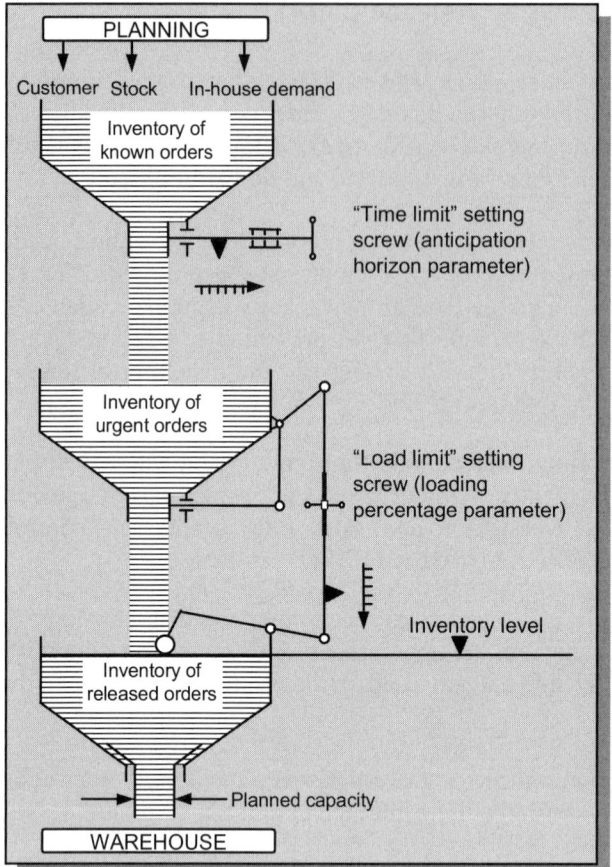

Fig. 14.1.2.1   Regulator analogy for load-oriented order release. (From: [Wien94].)

- All orders that have already been begun. The order progress report shows the next operation waiting to be performed. All remaining operations are to be planned.

- All orders that have not been begun, and for which the start date of the first operation lies within the time limit. Backward scheduling with standard lead times (see Section 12.3.3.) will determine the start date.

All of these candidates are classed "urgent" and are ordered by start dates, whereby already begun orders are loaded first.

- *Handle and load operations in series order*: The heuristic technique balances capacity for a single time period multiplied by the loading percentage against loads that will arise not only during this period, but also in later periods. This is the crucial idea of the generalization. To this end, subsequent operations are not loaded with full work contents.

> The *conversion factor* progressively converts the loads of subsequent operations.

For example, if the conversion factor is 0.5 (= 1 / 200%), then the cumulative conversion factor for the first operation of an order is 1, for the second 0.5, for the third 0.25 (= 0.5 · 0.5), for the fourth 0.125 (= 0.5 · 0.5 · 0.5), and so forth. If, on the other hand, the first operation of the order has already been completed, the second operation is next. Thus, the cumulative conversion factor for the second operation is 1, for the third 0.5, for the fourth 0.25, and so on.

- *Use the exception rule:* If one operation makes use of a work center whose load limit has already been exceeded (due to orders released earlier), unload the entire order, so that other orders are given priority.

- *Deal with all exceptions:* After having loaded all orders, list those orders that were unloaded or set aside. This list contains the identification of the order in question, the workload (e.g., in hours), and the work center that caused the order decline. Check whether the following possible measures can be applied:

  - Advance the start date of the order.

  - If there is flexibility in the timing of the order due date, postpone it.

  - If there is at least some degree of quantitative flexibility in the critical capacities, then deliberately increase the capacities.

By re-performing all the steps for the orders set aside, the orders can possibly now be released.

Figure 14.1.2.2 illustrates the steps using an example taken from [Wien94].

Assume that there are 5 orders to be added to an existing workload.

- In step 1 ("scheduling"), these 5 orders are shown together with their operations on the time axis. Each operation bears the work center (A, B, C, D, respectively) that is intended to execute the operation. Every order has its scheduled start date. The first idea of Loor is a time filter. This filter is in fact a time limit, calculated by a given anticipation horizon. It eliminates each order where the start date of the first operation is later than the time limit. In the example, the time filter eliminates order 5. This order is declared as not urgent. All the other orders are declared as urgent and passed to step 2.

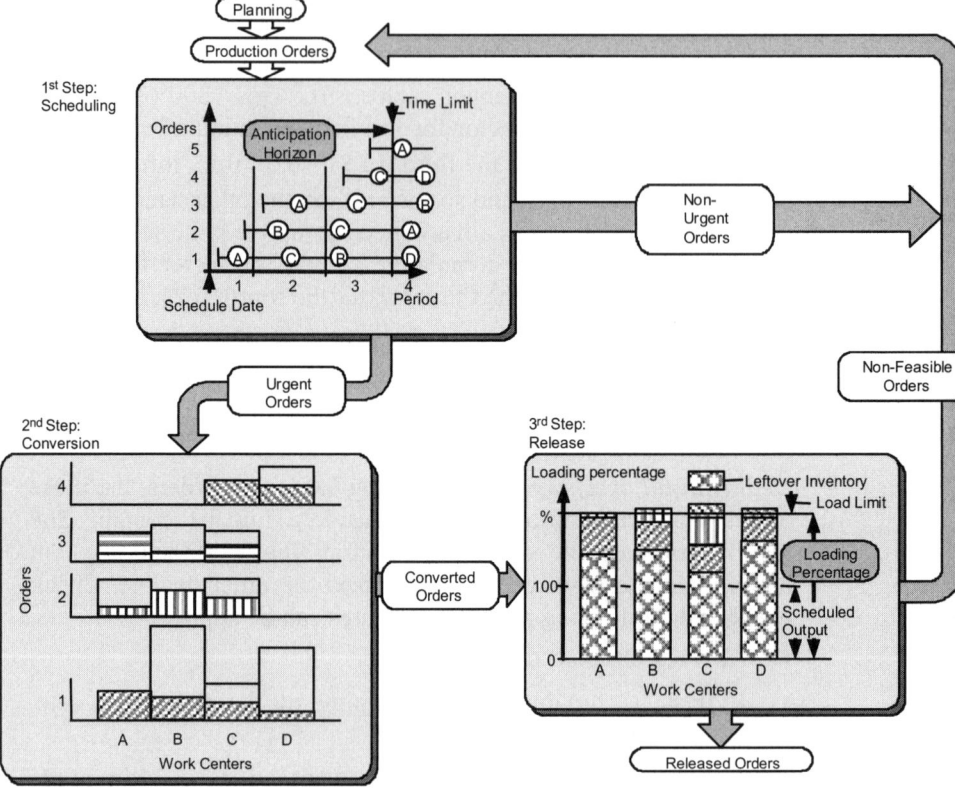

Fig. 14.1.2.2   Steps of load-oriented order release. (From: [Wien94].)

- In step 2 ("conversion"), the load of subsequent operations is converted progressively by the conversion factor, which in this example is 50%. That means that the load of the first operation is taken into consideration with 100%, the load of the second operation only with 50%, the load of the third operation only with 25%, and so on.[2] In the graph, every order is now shown by its

---

[2]   The further ahead you are trying to plan, the less certain you are that the planned load of an individual job will actually consume the planned capacity within the anticipation horizon. The conversion factor takes this into account by arguing that

load profile (original and converted). The operations do not appear in the sequence of their execution, but in the sequence of the work center. This is done in preparation for the next step.

Take now — as an example — order 2. In Figure 14.1.2.2 the load of this order is shown with vertical shading (not only in step 2, but also in step 3).

- Step 1 shows that the first operation will be executed at work center B. Therefore, the load is shown in step 2, converted by 100% (that is, the full load).

- Again, step 1 shows that the second operation will be executed at work center C. Therefore, the load is shown in step 2, converted by 50% (that is, half the load). The empty load (that is without shadings) corresponds to the other 50% of the load which will not been taken into account for step 3.

- Again, step 1 shows that the second operation will be executed at work center C. Therefore, the load is shown in step 2, converted by 50% (that is, half the load). The empty "load" (that is, without shadings) corresponds to the other 50% of the load, which will not been taken into account for step 3.

- Step 3 ("release") shows first the existing (pre-)load of all workstations before loading the four new orders. This preload stems from different periods on the time axis. This is why it can be greater than the scheduled output capacity for one time period. Arbitrarily, then, a loading percentage of 200% is chosen.[3] This factor yields the load limit for every work center. The orders are

---

in a multistep process, each manufacturing step reduces the probability that the next step will be completed on time (here, the definition of on time is within the anticipation horizon). While this is quite a reasonable assertion — the more steps that are involved, the less certain we are that we can keep to the plan as expected — there is no methodical proof.

[3] The loading percentage takes into account the aggregation of capacity of multiple periods (here about 3) over the anticipation horizon. This aggregation is important, as you can never be sure that a planned job will occur in precisely that time period that you expect. This concept is quite easy to explain: we use this reasoning routinely to explain that you can get a more precise view of a sales forecast when it is aggregated over many periods, compared to considering it over one period. Simple statistics show this by looking at the reduction in the forecast error with a normal distribution — and this reduction in forecast error can be used as a basis for choosing the loading percentage (Mark Bennet, CPIM, Perth, personal communication, 2001).

then loaded in the sequence of their start date.[4] The load of every operation is added to the preload. As soon as an operation has to be loaded on a work center whose load is already greater than the load limit, the whole order is unloaded. Thus, the load limit has the effect of a load filter.

- In the example, the load filter accepts first orders 1 and 2, with order 2 overloading work center B slightly (the algorithm accepts the first overload for each work center. But work center B is now declared to be unavailable for all subsequent orders).

- It then eliminates and unloads order 3 because of already fully loaded capacity at work center B by order 2.

- Finally, the load filter accepts order 4, for which work center B is not used.[5]

Orders 1, 2, and 4 can thus be released, whereas Order 3 is non-feasible and becomes an item for a further step, when exceptions are dealt with.

There is no relationship between the conversion factor and the loading percentage, and the values should not be linked. However, in the original literature on Loor, these values normally appear to be reciprocal. Furthermore, in the world of practice, the values chosen for anticipation horizon, loading percentage, and the conversion factor are often based on experience or are arbitrary.

Case example: The Siemens Electronics Plant in Amberg, Germany, manufactures electronic components in customer-independent production to stock. The comprehensive range of components allows the customer to obtain the optimal configuration of programmable SIMATIC control and monitoring operator panels for automated systems.

Approximately 500 components are manufactured and available for 24-hour delivery from stock. One production order consists of 10 to 20

---

[4]   Note that the height of the load might differ at each work center from that which is shown in the figure for step 2, because it has to be normalized with regard to the 100% of the capacity measure. However, the shading of the load of each order is the same as in step 2.

[5]   Note that order 4 overloads work centers C and D for the first time. Therefore, if there remained more orders to load, these two work centers would now also be unavailable.

operations. The number of machines in the area of load-oriented order release is 20.

The main objective in implementing Loor was to limit work-in-process inventory, thus reducing lead times and releasing no orders for production for which capacity was not available. The Amberg Electronic Plant itself took over the task of programming the algorithm. Implementing Loor has brought the expected advantages.

Evaluation of the technique and organizational aspects:

- The debate over the validity of this technique is highly polarized. Ardent defenders stand opposed to critical, rejecting voices. The misunderstanding apparently arises because load-oriented order release is readily presented as generally valid and scientific, as if it were a statistical technique. Thus, the conversion factor is often compared to a probability measure. Critics can easily take this to the point of absurdity. They construct an extreme case in which the technique loads operations that have an execution probability of 0 (zero). As a result, the technique does not release more urgent operations.

- Load-oriented order release is not an analytical technique; it is a cleverly chosen heuristic technique. It is simple and limited to just a few control parameters. It is quite robust, provided there is a certain quantitative flexibility in capacities and in order due dates. As with every heuristic technique, its applicability will depend upon an organization's strategies.

For implementation of the load-oriented order release technique, the following *prerequisites* must be met:

- Order due dates must be at least somewhat flexible in order to provide the scope for dealing with exceptions.

- Capacities must be at least somewhat flexible. Otherwise, the administrative effort to make the numerous deadline alterations will be prohibitive, or the calculations so imprecise that the capacities are only poorly loaded.

- It must be possible to determine the parameters of anticipation horizon, load percentage, and conversion factor in every organization empirically — in some cases through the aid of simulations. The parameters are dependent upon the desired work level and the size of the chosen planning period.

The following *limitations* result:

- Orders that fall outside the load limit are generally moved beyond the anticipation horizon, which may result in an unacceptable delay. Releases based on additional information (such as high external priority, rejections due to capacity overloads very far in the future, or similar information) are generally not provided for.

- In the medium term, the available capacity or the capacity that has been made available must be at least as large as the load. Otherwise, more and more orders will fall outside the load limit.

- Load-oriented order release only loads production with orders that can be processed. It thus leads to lower levels of work in process and to shorter lead times. Scheduled orders are finished on time. However, if the capacity is not flexible, load-oriented order release leads to low loading of capacity where completion dates must be pushed back in time. This is because the load that would have occurred far along on the time axis is now missing. If there are no other orders in line, the capacity is missed out.

- In cases of underload, the parameter "anticipation horizon" must not be altered in order to make the best use of the available capacity. Otherwise, it will result in too early completion dates and possibly unneeded warehouse stocks.

- In the literature, the following points are cited as problematic (see also [Knol92]):

  - Load-oriented order release does not coordinate operations that are interdependent but belong to different orders.

  - The funnel model on which load-oriented order release is based may oversimplify what actually occurs in production.

  - The FIFO control principle may not be reasonable under certain circumstances. The behavior of the load-oriented order release technique is questionable where work centers are fully loaded.

  - All components must be physically available at order release. Load-oriented order release does not account for the fact that certain components are only needed for later operations. Thus, higher stocks of components in inventory may negate reduction of work in process. On the other hand, with reduced lead time, components need only be available later. This can then reduce stocks.

The following *areas* lend themselves to *application* of the Loor technique:

- Given the prerequisites above, the technique can be applied in many branches of discrete manufacturing, particularly when there is a need for simplicity and robustness in the face of errors in planning dates or changes in order levels.

- In short-term planning and control, load-oriented order release provides a reliable work program that permits a considerable degree of situational planning on the spot.

14.1.3 Capacity-Oriented Materials Management (Corma)

Mixed manufacturing or *mixed production* is concurrent make-to-stock production and make-to-order production, using a single set of plant and equipment.

Mixed-mode manufacturers are manufacturing companies with mixed production.

Mixed-mode manufacturers produce and sell standard products whereby stocks are maintained at various levels of production, including the final product. Standard product manufacturing aims for *maximum possible utilization of capacity* (cost objective). At the same time, however, mixed-mode manufacturers also produce goods to customer order, often in one-of-a-kind production. Here, the manufacturer aims for the shortest possible lead times (delivery objective).

The main strategic objective of mixed-mode manufacturers is *on-time delivery*. The delivery of customer production orders to customers' required dates takes high priority. Stock replenishment orders must be fulfilled on time — as soon as stocks have been depleted. The volume of orders of both kinds of orders is about the same.

Simple logistics would call for separation and segmentation of the production resources. However, the very strength of some medium-sized organizations lies in their flexible planning & control of their resources, which allows them to make use of the one and the same production infrastructure. They manufacture a relatively wide range of products based on specialized competence in a relatively small number of production processes.

The products generally have short to medium lead times; processing time (or makespan) is a few hours or days, excluding interoperation times. With just a few production stages, a few dozen items in the bill of material, and a dozen operations per level, the products are of moderate complexity.

Planning strategy: Manufacturing firms with mixed production require a flexible planning strategy. By observing the natural logics of production management as practiced in medium-sized mixed-mode manufacturers, the following generic principle could be derived. For convenience, it is called capacity-oriented materials management, or Corma.

Capacity-oriented materials management (Corma) is an operations management principle that enables organizations to play off work-in-process against limited capacity and short lead times for customer production orders. See [Schö95].

Essentially, stock replenishment orders are viewed as "filler" loadings. The Corma principle makes intelligent use of critical capacity available short term, which leads to *balanced loading*. This helps to reduce queuing and thus lead times. Corma releases orders periodically, in "packages." This in turn provides for optimal order sequencing, which reduces setup times. The price of achieving flexible utilization of capacity is a higher level of work in process. The total costs of capacity, work-in-process, and warehouse stocks should be kept towards a minimum.

The *generic principle* consists of three parts:

1. A *criterion for order release* that releases stock replenishment orders earlier than needed, which means before inventory falls below the order point. An early order release is considered as soon as there is available capacity in otherwise well-utilized work centers.

2. A *scheduling technique for shop floor control* that for early released orders leads to work-in-process rather than early stock replenishment and still guarantees that orders will be completed on time. At the same time, customer production orders can be delivered with a minimum lead time. The key is continual reassigning of order priorities by estimating order slack time by (re-)calculation of either the critical ratio or a suitable lead-time-stretching factor of all orders.

3. A *mechanism that couples shop floor scheduling with materials management.* This is done by continually rescheduling stock replenishment orders according to the actual usage. The current physical inventory is converted into an appropriate latest completion date for the open replenishment order.

Thus, the Corma principle not only serves to release orders, but it also supports overall short-term planning & control from the order release to the moment when the goods either enter stock or are shipped to the customer. Long-term planning for goods and capacity is carried out independently of this. It can be based on traditional forecasting techniques: based on historical data for production with frequent repetition or based on future projections for one-of-a-kind manufacture, for example.

Technique: In general, the generic principle is implemented manually. To do this, the planner uses a set of known planning and control techniques. Each of these techniques can (but does not need to) be supported by functions of conventional PPC software, or simply by personal implementation using Microsoft Excel or similar software. The following describes the techniques of the three parts of Corma in greater detail.

Corma, Part 1: Criterion for early order release. The planner checks regularly the loading of *generally well-utilized capacity.* As soon as short-term unused capacity is discovered, he checks on the availability of the products that are manufactured using this capacity. It is as if capacity is on the lookout for an order (hence, the term *capacity-oriented materials management*). A work center where-used list can provide essential information for this first step. If an "agent" is assigned to each capacity, agent-based systems may also be applied here.

In practice, it often happens that a particular product family is manufactured in a group of just a few work centers. If one of the work centers — in particular the gateway work center[6] — of this group is not being utilized, quite often the others are not in use either. An early order release thus usually means that several operations can be performed in advance.

Which of the products thus identified are candidates for early order release? The planner finds the answer by calculating the anticipation time for each possible item.

> The *anticipation time* for an item is the time that will probably elapse before a production or procurement order must be released.

Figure 10.3.2.2 provides a formula for determining the articles that are candidates for an early release in the deterministic case. It takes into consideration all known transactions in the near future.

---

[6]   A *gateway work center* performs the first operation of a particular routing sequence.

Figure 14.1.3.1 shows a graphical representation of anticipation time in the stochastic case. This is the time expected to elapse before inventory falls below its order point, assuming average usage for the near future.

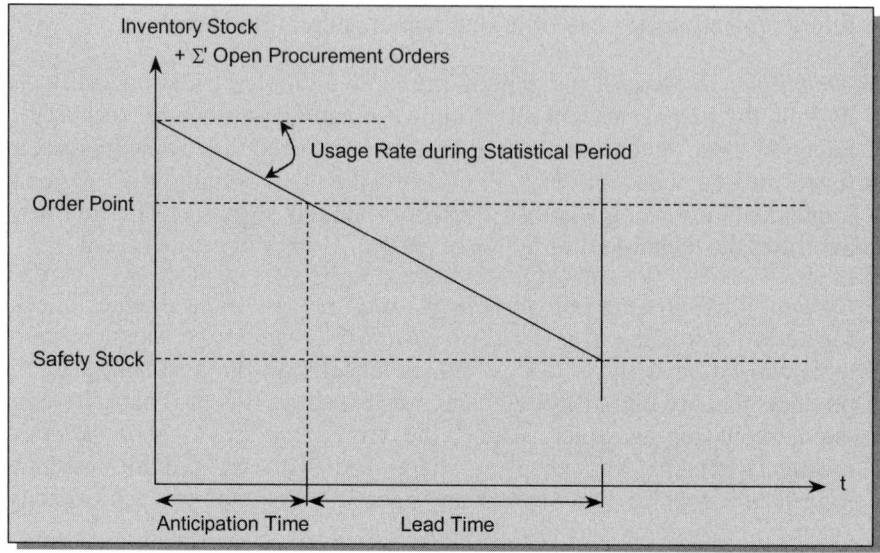

Fig. 14.1.3.1   Anticipation time in the stochastic case.

Figure 14.1.3.2 shows the formula for calculating the anticipation time.

$$\text{anticipation time} = \frac{\text{inventory stocks} + \sum \text{open procurement orders - order point}}{\text{usage rate during statistical period}}$$

Fig. 14.1.3.2   Calculating anticipation time in the stochastic case.

If there is more than one candidate for early order release, the product having the shorter anticipation time gains priority. Clearly, software can aid the planner in efficient calculation and decision-making.

Corma, Part 2: Scheduling technique for control of operations. New customer orders continually alter the workload. They also "hinder" the progress of stock replenishment orders, and vice versa. In this situation, the planner continually reassigns the priority of all orders in process by estimating order slack times.

A rough-cut estimation of order slack time is the following critical ratio.

> The *critical ratio of an order* is obtained by dividing the time left until the order due date by the standard lead time of work left on the order.

A ratio less than 1.0 indicates that the order is behind schedule; a ratio greater than 1.0 indicates that the job is ahead of schedule. The lower the result, the higher the order urgency in sequencing the operations of the order compared to those of other orders.

Generally, the critical ratios of the orders can be obtained by an inquiry of the order database. The planner transfers a resulting priority to the production order as soon as he considers the difference compared to the actual order priority to be significant. As a result, this technique either accelerates or slow downs the orders. It gives priority to early-released orders only when needed.

A more detailed and accurate measure of order urgency is obtained by implementing *probable scheduling* for shop floor control. Here, the key is the calculation of a suitable lead-time-stretching factor. See Section 12.3.6. This factor is a more accurate measure for the order slack time than the critical ratio of the order, as it is defined as a numerical factor by which only the non-technical interoperation times and the administrative times are multiplied. Since the technical process itself determines the duration of operations and the technical interoperation time, we can only modify slack time by increasing or reducing either the non-technical interoperation times or the administrative times.

Corma, Part 3: Mechanism that couples materials management with shop floor control. This is the transfer of actual inventory levels onto the latest completion date for the stock replenishment order, which then changes.

To do this, the planner checks the inventory on an ongoing basis and calculates the probable moment in time at which inventory will fall below safety stock (or, alternatively, at zero stock), assuming average use. To do this, he divides — roughly and in general — inventory stock less safety stock (alternatively without this deduction) by average use per time period. The resulting period of time added to the current date yields the probable date on which the replenishment order should arrive in stock. Clearly, software can provide for easy calculation here.

The planners (or software) transfer this date to become the latest completion date for the replenishment order as soon as they consider the difference between these two dates to be significant. The following situations may arise:

- The latest completion date will be pushed forward, if inventory stock is being depleted at a rate faster than the statistical average for the period up to the point of order release. Re-scheduling then calculates a smaller lead-time-stretching factor. This results in higher priority, and the order is accelerated.

- The latest completion date is postponed if inventory stock is being depleted at a rate slower than the statistical average for the period up to the point of order release. Rescheduling generates a higher lead-time-stretching factor. This results in lower priority, and the order is slowed down.

To show the effects of the Corma principle, let us look at a stock replenishment order with three production operations. Figure 14.1.3.3 shows four possible situations.

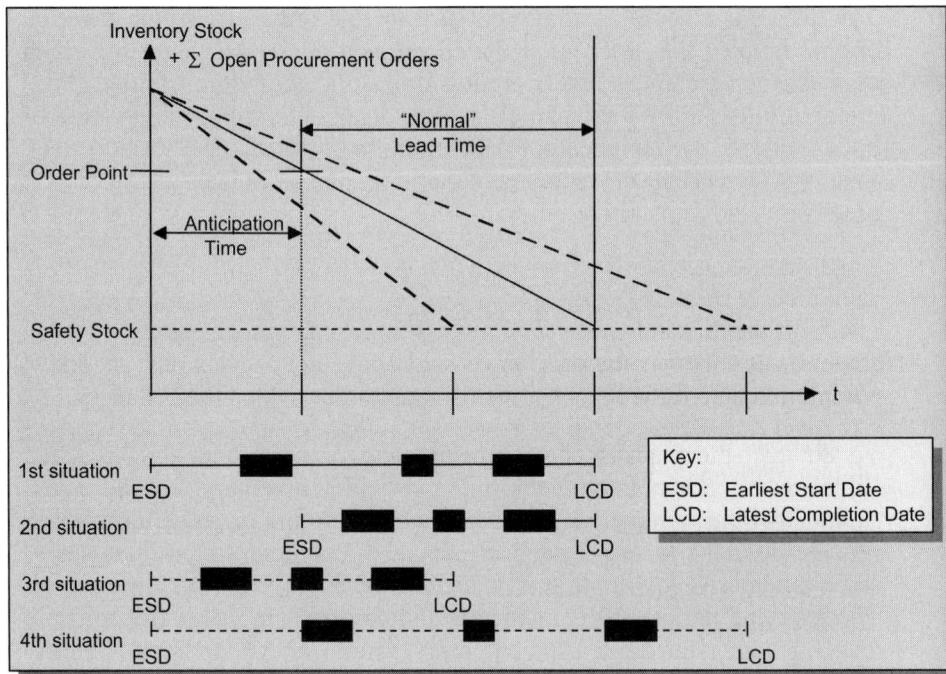

Fig. 14.1.3.3   Rescheduling of orders in process according to current materials management status.

- First situation: Due to the early order release, all three work operations are evenly distributed between the earliest start date (i.e., the earliest possible start date of the order, which is originally the date of the early release and then moves — in fact — forward along the time axis with the "today" date) and the latest (acceptable) completion date for the order (that is, the *order due date*). They are all scheduled, but — in this situation — without priority. As a result, they are performed as soon as there are no more urgent operations waiting to be processed at the work station.

- Second situation: Suppose now that the mixed-mode manufacturer accepts an unplanned customer order with a high priority. Then the stock replenishment order in process will wait. Not even the first operation is performed. However, the ongoing rescheduling "discovers" any order that has waited for too long, and the latest start date, i.e., "today," is being pushed closer and closer to the latest completion date. Rescheduling then calculates a smaller lead-time-stretching factor. This gives the order higher priority.

- Third situation: The inventory stocks fall faster than expected. The latest completion date is therefore brought forward. Rescheduling calculates a smaller lead-time-stretching factor, and the order is accelerated by expediting.[7]

- Fourth situation: The inventory stocks fall slowlier than expected. Thus, the latest completion date is postponed. Rescheduling calculates a higher lead-time-stretching factor, and the order is delayed.

The third and fourth situations in Figure 14.1.3.3 illustrate the most important aspect of the third part of Corma. Stock replenishment orders will receive the same priority as customer orders if stock falls below safety stock. If the demand is lower than expected, however, stock replenishment orders will not even start, and stock replenishment orders that have already been initiated will be halted.

Alterations in the due date of a customer order may also lead to rescheduling, with consequences similar to those in situations 3 and 4 above.

An interesting example is provided by *Trox Hesco Corp. (Rüti, CH-8630, Switzerland)*. Trox Hesco (200 employees) specializes in the development, production, and distribution of ventilation products, such as air diffusion lattices and fire dampers. Trox Hesco manufacturing is based on high

---

[7] To *expedite* means to rush or chase production or purchase orders that are needed in less than the normal lead time, to take extraordinary action because of an increase in relative priority ([APIC04]).

competency in a relatively small number of production processes. Five hundred different stock line items make up approximately 60% of sales volume. The same items, but made-to-order according to customer requirements with respect to dimension, color, and so on, make up the other 40% of sales. Product structures and routings are of moderate complexity, with one to two production stages and about a dozen items in the bill of material and fewer than a dozen operations per stage.

As responsiveness and on-time delivery are crucial, manufacturing planning & control gives high priority to special customer orders. At the same time, however, stock replenishment orders must also be completed on time to prevent shortages and depletion. Stock replenishment orders can therefore compete with special customer orders. As demand for stock items is variable, the stock depletion date estimated at the moment of order release must now be verified. This allows determination of the priority of the replenishment order.

While segmentation of the two production processes would make for simple logistics, this flexible planning & control of resources enables Trox Hesco to make use of the same production infrastructure for both modes of production.

Assessment of the technique and organizational considerations: The use of Corma demands the following prerequisites:

- The increase in work-in-process, which results from the early release of stock replenishment orders, must be feasible economically and manageable in terms of volume. Corma does not result in premature inventory in stock, however.
- Early order release has to be possible to a sufficient degree. Orders that are released early are stock replenishment orders or customer production orders that start in advance of the latest start date.

There are some *limitations* involved in applying Corma:

- The focus has to be on a *more balanced* utilization of capacity, not maximal utilization. Load fluctuations will remain.
- Planners "on site" must be able to deal with constantly changing order inventories. They have to understand how to make the best use of the Corma recommendations, which may entail changing the sequence of operations that Corma proposes to accommodate additional, situation-specific information known to the planner.

The following *areas* lend themselves to *application* of the technique:

- In addition to mixed production, Corma is applicable in all cases where due dates must be met and, nonetheless, the system must be robust in the face of errors in planning dates or alterations in orders on hand.

- Corma can be applied to self-regulating shop floor control (for mixed-mode manufacturers, for example), assuming that the data collected on order progress are precise enough. Because the basic premise of Corma is a constantly changing order backlog, it is robust enough to handle situational planning "on the spot," which in this case is desirable.

- Corma is useful as a self-regulating system for short-term materials management. Owing to its continuous coupling with materials management, an order may change its latest completion date multiple times. A stock replenishment order may change its completion date up to the moment when inventories fall below the safety stock. From that moment onwards, the replenishment order must be ranked directly among ongoing customer orders, since the replenishment order will serve to cover the customer orders. Since customer orders must have confirmed due dates that can no longer be changed, the replenishment order must also be given a *fixed, or definitive,* latest completion date.

14.2   Shop Floor Control

Shop floor control is comprised of the essential functions of production order processing, dispatching and sequencing, and order coordination and shop floor data collection (work-in-process, order progress checking, actual use of resources, performance indicators such as stock-inventory turnover, work-in-process-inventory turnover, work center efficiency, and capacity utilization).

Production activity control (PAC) is used synonymously for shop floor control.

14.2.1 Issuance of Accompanying Documents for Production

For a *production order,* people at the shop floor responsible for execution require precise instructions as to the nature of the work to be executed and the components to be built in. They require a *shop packet*, that is a set of comprehensive technical descriptions and administrative documents. Among the latter are:

- The *shop order routing*. This physically accompanies the products to be manufactured during the entire production process. It records the administrative course of the order in detail. It also often serves as a data collection document for the report of order termination and/or placement in stock. Figure 14.2.1.1 shows an actual shop order routing. It is printed for each partial order and includes all operations. Often it also lists reservations.

- An *operation card* for each operation to be performed, and thus for each position on the shop order routing. Generally speaking, the operation card will contain the same information that the shop order routing itself contains. Figure 14.2.1.2 shows examples of operation cards. Their primary purpose is shop floor data collection. A template for time stamps is on the reverse, so that it can serve as *time ticket*. If there is automated shop floor data collection, the operation card is often no longer necessary. See also Section 14.3.4.

- The *parts requisitions*. This relates to the reservation of an individual component of a production order and serves as the authorization for its issuance from stock. Parts requisitions are most often produced for raw materials or for components that cannot be itemized reasonably on a picking list. Figure 14.2.1.3 shows an example of a parts requisition.

- The *picking list*. This includes all components that are to be issued. It provides for efficient *(order) picking*, that is withdrawing the components in the warehouse for one or more production orders. It sorts reservations according to an issuance sequence that is optimal from a functional and technical perspective. Its identification also provides for the most efficient possible shop floor data collection. For an example, see Figure 14.2.1.4.

Order-Id.	Order-Id. (cont.)	Qty. Ordered	Unit	Product Description		Dimension		Start Date	Comple- tion date
040200	000103	4500	St	HEATER TRANSFORMER	CURRENT	035		07.01	09.06

Shop Order Routing

		Product-Id.	Type		Design-Id.	To Be Received By		Cost Center	
		365300	2/18-1001		09-053	STOCK GE-5		6	

Pos.	Quantity	Unit	Component Component-Id. Quality	Description	Dimension Design-Id.		Place of issue	Date of Issuance
Pos.	Department Quantity	Unit	Operation		Machine-Id. Work-Center-Id. Supplier-Id.	Cost Center.	Tot. Standard Load	Comple- tion date
100	157500	MM	E-I COMBINATION ECONO. 354953 4,2 W		103401701		GE-5	07.01
200	4500	PC	041/0304,5/0005,5 350761 E-COIL WINDING A)/C)		0,280 550000605		EX FAB	02.07
205	4500	PC	041/0310 350788 E-COIL WINDING B)		0,280 550000601		EX FAB	02.07
210	9000	PC	END CAP OUTSIDE 22442 -----------		- 5150029		GE-9	07.01
220	9000	PC	END CAP INSIDE 22443 -----------		- 5150030		GE-9	07.01
225	4500	PC	INSOLATION 22444 -----------		162304100		GE-5	07.01

*** CONTINUATION PAGE 02

Order-Id.	Order-Id. (cont.)	Qty. Ordered	Unit	Product Description		Dimension		Start Date	Comple- tion date
040200	000103	Page 2		HEATER TRANSFORMER	CURRENT	035		07.01	09.06

Shop Order Routing

		Product-Id.	Type		Design-Id.	To Be Received By		Cost Center	
		365300	2/18-1001		09-053	STOCK GE-5		6	

Pos.	Quantity	Unit	Component Component-Id. Quality	Description	Dimension Design-Id.		Place of issue	Date of Issuance
Pos.	Department Quantity	Unit	Operation		Machine-Id. Work-Center-Id. Supplier-Id.	Cost Center	Tot. Standard Load	Comple- tion date
230	27000	PC	CRIMP CONNECTION 30455 -----------		5262010		LH-ENN	07.01
255	4500	PC	ALU-INLAY STAMPED 3887 -----------		45MM 321303300		GE-5	07.01
650	CR 4500	PC	CRIMP, I.E. PLACE COIL(35 MM) IN END CAPS, PREWIRING, CRIMP (4 CONNECTIONS).			40	765 2 REPORT-ID:150495	4500
660	CR 4500	PC	CRIMP 2nd SIDE (2 CONNECTIONS).			41	465 2 REPORT-ID:150509	2070
700	PA 4500	PC	PREASSEMBLY: E-I-STAMP (DESIGN-ID 10 34 017/01), ASSEMBLE COIL SET FOLOW. DESIGN-ID 55 91 248 IN E- KERNEL, INSERT I-KERNEL			50	766 2 REPORT-ID:150517	1125 09.06

Fig. 14.2.1.1   Shop order routing.

Operation card / time ticket	Release Date 07.01	Complet. Date 09.06	Visa MI	Order Specification Card printed at 06.20		Order-Id. 040200 000103
Product Description			IND	**Quantity Released** 4500	**Product-Id.** 96878	**Remarks** Time ticket
2/18-1001 220V 50HZ	PERFEKT 2000					

CRIMP, I.E. PLACE COIL(35 MM) IN END CAPS, PREWIRING, CRIMP (4 CONNECTIONS).	650	Dept.: CR CostCtr.:765 WorkCtr: 40 Machine:		Time-ticket-Id.: 150495		
Operation Description	**Op. No.**	**Machine Group**		**Setup Time**	100 PE **Standard**	03 **Code** **Visa**
Name of Worker		**Paid Pieces**	**Register No.**	**Dept. Group**		**Work Hours**
	Date		Visa Foreman			

Operation card / time ticket	Release Date 07.01	Complet. Date 09.06	Visa MI	Order Specification Card printed at 06.20		Order-Id. 040200 000103
Product Description				**Quantity Released** 4500	**Product-Id.** 96878	**Remarks** Time ticket
2/18-1001 220V 50HZ	PERFEKT 2000		IND			

CRIMP 2nd SIDE (2 CONNECTIONS).	660	Dept.: CR CostCtr.:765 WorkCtr: 41 Machine:		Time-ticket-Id.: 150509		
Operation Description	**Op. No.**	**Machine Group**		**Setup Time**	46 PE **Standard**	03 **Code** **Visa**
Name of Worker		**Paid Pieces**	**Register No.**	**Dept. Group**		**Work Hours**
	Date		Visa Foreman			

Operation card / time ticket	Release Date 07.01	Complet. Date 09.06	Visa MI	Order Specification Card printed at 06.20		Order-Id. 040200 000103
Product Description				**Quantity Released** 4500	**Product-Id.** 96878	**Remarks** Time ticket
2/18-1001 220V 50HZ	PERFEKT 2000		IND			

PREASSEMBLY: E-I-STAMP (DESIGN-ID 10 34 017/01), ASSEMBLE COIL SET FOLOW. DESIGN-ID 55 91 248 IN E-KERNEL, INSERT I-KERNEL	700	Dept.: PA CostCtr.:766 WorkCtr: 50 Machine:		Time-ticket-Id.: 150517		
Operation Description	**Op. No.**	**Machine Group**		**Setup Time**	25 PE **Standard**	03 **Code** **Visa**
Name of Worker		**Paid Pieces**	**Register No.**	**Dept. Group**		**Work Hours**
	Date		Visa Foreman			

Fig. 14.2.1.2   Operation cards/time ticket.

Order-Id.	Order-Id. (cont.)	Order-Quantity	Unit	Product Description		Dimension	Start Date	Completion Date
040200	000103	4500	PC	HEATER CURRENT TRANSFORMER		035	07.01	09.06

Parts requisition

		Product-Id.	Type		Design-Id.		To Be Received By	Art	Ko.St./Kos KTG
Orderer	MILLER	365300	2/18-1001		09-053		STOCK	GE-5 6	20
Date	06.20				PRINTED AT		06.20		

Pos.	Picking Quantity	Unit	Actual Quantity	Unit	Component Description Type	Dimension	Design-Id. Warehouse Location	Place of issue Component-Id.	Date of Issuance
210	9000	PC		PC	END CAP OUTSIDE		5150029 322/	GE-9 022442	07.01

Order-Id.	Order-Id. (cont.)	Order-Quantity	Unit	Product Description		Dimension	Start Date	Completion Date
040200	000103	4500	PC	HEATER CURRENT TRANSFORMER		035	07.01	09.06

Parts requisition

		Product-Id.	Type		Design-Id.		To Be Received By	Art	Ko.St./Kos KTG
Orderer	MILLER	365300	2/18-1001		09-053		STOCK	GE-5 6	20
Date	06.20				PRINTED AT		06.20		

Pos.	Picking Quantity	Unit	Actual Quantity	Unit	Component Description Type	Dimension	Design-Id. Warehouse Location	Place of issue Component-Id.	Date of Issuance
220	9000	PC		PC	END CAP INTSIDE		5150030 322/	GE-9 022443	07.01

Order-Id.	Order-Id. (cont.)	Order-Quantity	Unit	Product Description		Dimension	Start Date	Completion Date
040200	000103	4500	PC	HEATER CURRENT TRANSFORMER		035	07.01	09.06

Parts requisition

		Product-Id.	Type		Design-Id.		To Be Received By	Art	Ko.St./Kos KTG
Orderer	MILLER	365300	2/18-1001		09-053		STOCK	GE-5 6	20
Date	06.20				PRINTED AT		06.20		

Pos.	Picking Quantity	Unit	Actual Quantity	Unit	Component Description Type	Dimension	Design-Id. Warehouse Location	Place of issue Component-Id.	Date of Issuance
225	4500	PC		PC	INSOLATION		162304100 120/	GE-5 022444	07.01

Order-Id.	Order-Id. (cont.)	Order-Quantity	Unit	Product Description		Dimension	Start Date	Completion Date
040200	000103	4500	PC	HEATER CURRENT TRANSFORMER		035	07.01	09.06

Parts requisition

		Product-Id.	Type		Design-Id.		To Be Received By	Art	Ko.St./Kos KTG
Orderer	MILLER	365300	2/18-1001		09-053		STOCK GE-5	6	20
Date	06.20				PRINTED AT		06.20		

Pos.	Picking Quantity	Unit	Actual Quantity	Unit	Component Description Type	Dimension	Design-Id. Location	Warehouse	Place of issue Component-Id.	Date of Issuance
230	27000	PC		PC	CRIMP CONNECTION		5262010 393/318		LH-ENN 030455	07.01

Fig. 14.2.1.3 Parts requisitions.

Picking List #2037			Date 07.14
Stock Location	Part-Id.	Description	Total Number of Pieces
A127 01	427413	snap ring	20
A127 02	290246	gasket	55
A127 01	427413	snap ring	20
A127 02	290246	gasket	55
A131 42	913222	snap ring	16
A171 29	160174	washer	10
	(160174	stockout	10)
B010 20	55243U7	valve	48
B017 24	167224	valve	3
B020 19	162221	tappet	27
B410 47	171222	valve	40
C202 29	204111	screw	1500
C210 29	204112	screw	450
C317 42	424324	nut	Inventory on floor stock
C416 19	917223	screw	250
Number of parts			12
Quantity of pieces			2409

Fig. 14.2.1.4   Picking list.

As to the point in time when accompanying documents should be printed:

- Individual execution deadlines for each operation as well as the assigned date of issuance for each reservation should not appear on the documents. This is because the execution dates are subject to change after the order release. Logically, it is not absolutely necessary to wait for the scheduling of individual operations and other time-intensive work in order to issue accompanying documents. Thus, they can be prepared immediately after the order release.

- Picking lists and parts requisitions are printed together with the shop order routing.

- Generally speaking, there are two possible ways to print operation cards:

  - They may be printed together with the shop order routing.

  - They may be printed at each work center within a particular window in time, in accordance with the results of the scheduling currently in effect.

14.2.2 Operations Scheduling, Dispatching, and Finite Forward Scheduling

> *Operations scheduling* is the actual assignment of starting or completion dates to operations or groups of operations ([APIC04]).

The result of operations scheduling shows when these operations must be done if the manufacturing order is to be completed in time. These dates are then used in the dispatching function.

> In *dispatching*, each operation is assigned to the individual workstations at a work center. At the same time, the work is assigned to employees, production equipment, and other work aids definitely and short term.

Dispatching is a part of production control. It is based on the inventory of work on hand or on the work program produced by detailed planning and scheduling (see Sections 13.2.3, 13.3.1, and 13.3.2). The latter is a time window, such as the coming week, for the inventory of work on hand at the work center.

Shop floor employees generally have the specific knowledge needed for dispatching. They know the secondary constraints in detail.

> A *secondary constraint* is a resource that can constrain the capacity of another resource.

Examples of secondary constraints are:

- The *individual pieces of equipment at a work center*: Not every machine in the work center can perform exactly the same jobs. Certain orders may require machine tools that can be mounted only on certain machines.

- The *qualification of employees*: Not all workers are qualified to perform exactly the same jobs. Certain orders may demand minimum qualifications that only certain employees possess.

Knowledge about secondary constraints can be used to further define the (constrained) utilization of each resource. In addition, dispatching draws upon large stores of fragmentary knowledge or knowledge by analogy to earlier cases. Such experience-based knowledge in the heads of supervisors or foremen is usually not structured or available in explicit form. Therefore, in the majority of cases the function of dispatching is a mental process — albeit supported by the algorithms of capacity planning (Sections 13.2 and 13.3). These algorithms show the probable consequences of prospective dispatching to individual machines in the context of the current situation.

Finite forward scheduling is a scheduling technique for production equipment and other aids, for the individual machines,[8] and possibly also for the workers and other resources, that builds a schedule by proceeding sequentially from the initial period to the final period while observing capacity limits. ([APIC04]).

Production equipment includes machine tools, devices, NC programs, and equipment for measuring and testing. Aids include drawings.

The current inventory of work on hand at the work center, from medium-term planning within a particular time window, serves as the basis for finite forward scheduling. Finite forward scheduling further requires detailed information on the availability of individual resources. For the needs of finite forward scheduling, any operations too roughly defined in medium-term planning must be broken down into individual operations and further detailed to individual workstations.

Just as in the case of dispatching, employees who work at the work centers have important knowledge of the situation in their heads. These people tend to be able to make the best decisions about control of operations. For precisely this reason, excessively detailed planning for the medium and long term makes little sense.

For representing the results of operations scheduling and finite forward scheduling, a Gantt chart is appropriate. A corresponding planning board permits the individual loads to be moved around among the workstations in a flexible way. Figures 14.2.2.1 and 14.2.2.3 show an example of finite forward scheduling with six work centers. The second work center has three workstations (WS), the fourth two. A calendar showing available days for these work centers is shown across the top; these work centers are available only five days per week.

Bold areas on the bars mark the related operations of a specific production order. In two cases, an interoperation time has to be respected.

---

[8]   Note: *Machine loading* is the accumulation by workstation, machine, or machine group of the hours generated from the scheduling of operations for released orders by time period ([APIC04]). Machine loading does not use the planned orders, but operates solely from released orders.

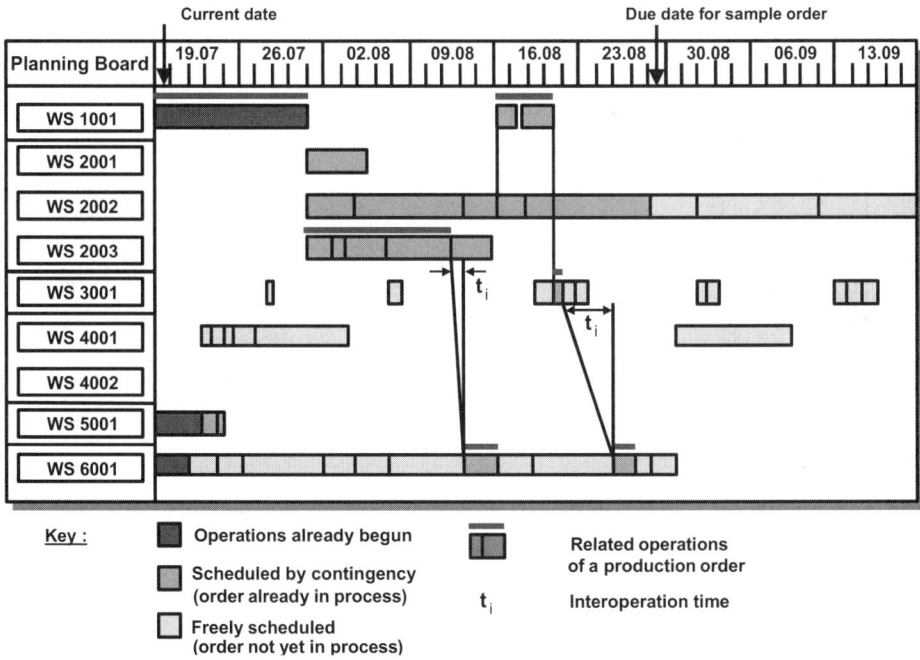

Fig. 14.2.2.1   Loading of production resources in the form of a planning board.

In the scenario in Figure 14.2.2.2, there is an additional order to load. The due date is "as soon as possible." Existing scheduled jobs are not to be changed. The result of finite forward scheduling of this order is shown in Figure 14.2.2.3.

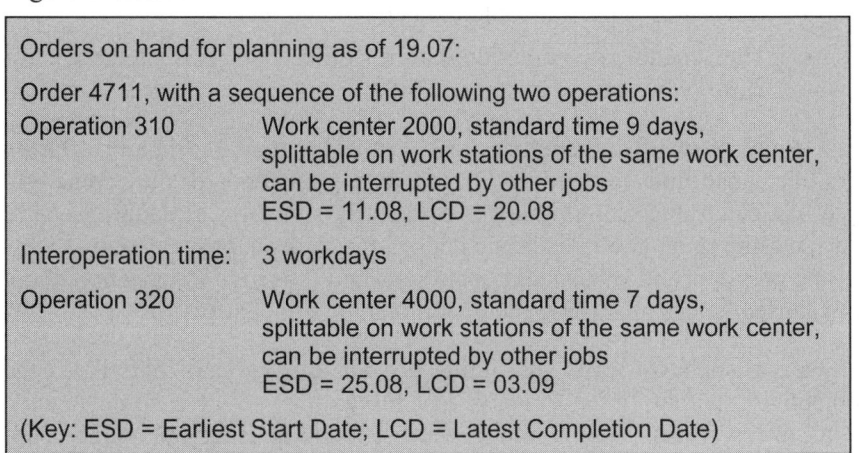

Fig. 14.2.2.2   New entry to orders on hand: order 4711.

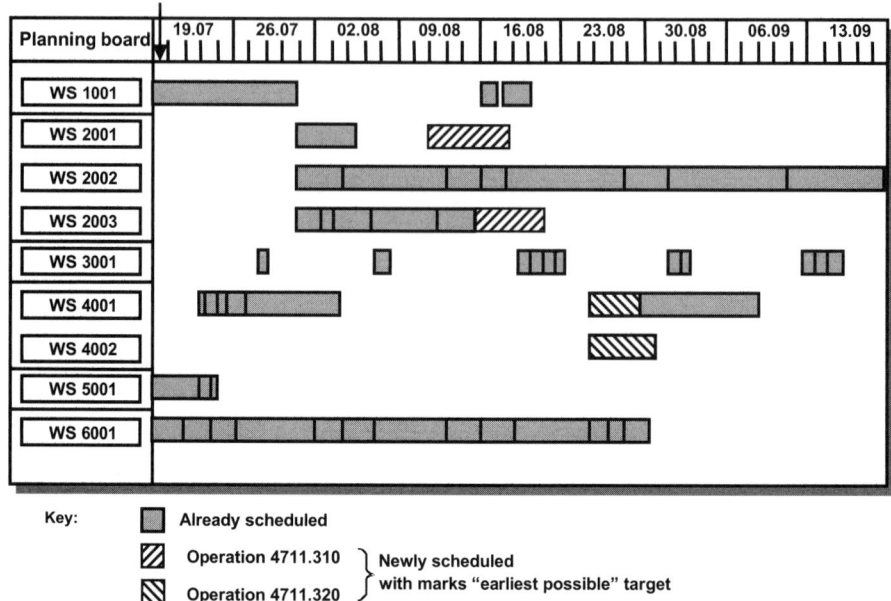

Fig. 14.2.2.3   Loading of production resources in the form of a planning board, situation following loading of the new order 4711.

Please note:

- The job is scheduled to start on August 11.

- Both operations are scheduled to run on two workstations.

- Operation 320 is scheduled to begin on August 25.

- The scheduled completion date for order 4711 is September 1 (or close of business day August 30).

For finite forward scheduling, an electronic planning board offering graphic capabilities (electronic *Leitstand*, or control board) may come into use. An electronic planning board essentially simulates a planning board. At the same time, good electronic control instruments provide an overview of the previous and subsequent operations and thus give information about the consequences of shifting the operations in various ways.

However, such software algorithms do not always lead directly to the objective, so that finite forward scheduling may involve some manual work or reworking. Thus, finite forward scheduling using a planning board is suitable only for production with operations of longer duration.

In summary, finite forward scheduling yields individually released operations together with their sequencing. It may cause aids to be made available and, in the case of disturbances in the process, provide suggestions for potential replanning, such as an altered assignment of personnel or orders to the individual workstation.

14.2.3 Sequencing Methods

Sequencing arranges the jobs in the inventory of work on hand in a particular series order.

A clever sequence of operations can reduce setup time. This is one of the essential objectives of sequencing. If the individual orders arrive randomly, in order to choose a sequence with minimal setup time there has to be a queue. However, this increases lead times, which is not an option with certain critical products. Frequently, however, one of the first operations, if not the first itself, often uses fully utilized capacities, so that saving setup time due to good sequencing can contribute significantly to reducing lead time. Here, it is appropriate to sort and combine the orders waiting for release right at the point of release according to the sequencing criterion for the corresponding operations. In other cases, the situation is more complex. Sequencing is thus often a compromise among the various aspects and criteria of shop floor control.

If setup time reduction is not the chosen strategy, other objectives and rules of priority (see Section 13.3.1) will be selected. In shop floor control these must be transparent and understandable for all persons involved. They can have the opposite effect, if they are applied incorrectly.

Detailed sequencing is indispensable for flexible manufacturing systems (FMS) under high load conditions, since the aim, due to costs and especially deadline reasons, is to avoid production interruptions due to order changes. Since information technology support in flexible manufacturing systems means that all data on the necessary time requirements are always available, a company may consider automating sequencing. This would still have to be an interactive process, however, since many decision-making rules arise on an *ad hoc* basis, grounded in the experience of the machine operators. These cannot be translated explicitly into rules that can be applied automatically.

Algorithms for sequencing constitute a field of study in operations research and in artificial intelligence and will not be presented here. Refer to [Sche98].

14.3   Order Monitoring and Shop Floor Data Collection

> *Shop floor data collection* provides for the reporting of all events relevant to planning and accounting during the value-added chain.

From this feedback, the exact state of orders can be derived, so that shop floor data collection additionally serves order monitoring and order checking as well as order coordination among orders that belong together in sales & distribution, R&D, production, and procurement logistics.

14.3.1 Recording Issues of Goods from Stock

As far as central warehouses are concerned, goods may be withdrawn only upon presentation of a parts requisition or a picking list. The data that appear on a parts requisition should include (see Figure 14.2.1.3):

- Order ID and order position
- Item ID
- Reserved quantity in stock units
- Reserved quantity in picking units. For example, an item may be carried in stock in kilos, but picked in meters (for example, materials in bars) or in number of sheets (sheet metal). The factor required for this conversion is maintained as an attribute of the bill of material position or, if it is the same for every possible issuance, as an attribute of the item master data.

For *unplanned issuances*, the parts requisition must be filled out in its entirety.[9] An availability check must precede every unplanned issuance, so that already confirmed reservations of physically available warehouse stocks for other orders can be taken into account (see Section 11.1).

For *planned issuances* from stock, the data that have to be collected are limited to the actually issued quantity, recorded either in converted units or in stock units. If the issued quantity corresponds to the reserved quantity, the only fact reported is that the material was "issued."

For a picking list, in a first step only those positions for which the issued quantity differs from the reserved quantity are recorded. Then the so-called backflush technique is used:

---

[9]   If there is an issue concerning overhead costs, the cost center ID should be given instead of the order ID.

The *backflush technique* reports the picking list itself as "issued," whereby every (remaining) position on it is reported as issued in the reserved (or produced) quantity.[10]

A *critical point backflush technique* is a backflush technique performed at a specific point in the manufacturing process, at a critical operation, or at an operation where key components are consumed ([APIC04]).

14.3.2 Recording Completed Operations

Among the data that are printed on an operation card are (see Figure 14.2.1.2):

- Order ID and order position
- ID of the assigned work center
- ID of the assigned machine or tool
- Quantity to be processed
- Standard setup load
- Standard run load
- Where applicable, the quantity to be produced in a unit that differs from the one on the order. For example, orders may be for pieces, but production is in meters (for sheet metal trimming, for example). The necessary conversion factor is an attribute of the *operation* object.

If the execution matches the standard, the only recorded fact is the execution of the operation. By collecting the number of finished items and the number of produced scrap items, rated capacity can be compared with demonstrated capacity.

Demonstrated capacity is proven capacity calculated from actual performance data, usually expressed as the average number of items produced by the standard load ([APIC04]).

Furthermore, actual operation load, measured in capacity units, can be collected, as well as effective times.

---

[10]   *Post-deduct inventory transaction processing* is used as a synonym for backflush. In contrast, *pre-deduct inventory transaction processing* reduces the book inventory of the components at the moment of the order release for the product.

> *Operation duration* is the total time that elapses between the start of the setup of an operation and the completion of the operation ([APIC04]).[11]

Standard operation time can then be compared with actual operation duration. In addition, downtime might be of interest:

> *Downtime* is time when a resource is scheduled for operation but is not producing for reasons such as maintenance, repair, or setup ([APIC04]).

For statistical and accounting purposes, the identification of the employees goes on record. In multiperson servicing, various operation cards are recorded. They all refer to the same operation. If the work center data or other planning data change during the execution of the job, the altered data must be registered. The order ID is also recorded for every unplanned executed operation.

Also conceivable is a separate recording of the actual quantities and the fact that the operation was completed. This may be necessary due to the legal situation (labor unions). In this case, recording includes only the number of produced items (good items and scrap) on the operation card. Separate collection documents then keep note of the actual loads. These summarize the activity of the personnel along with their other activities (training, illness, vacation, and so on).

14.3.3 Progress Checking, Quality Control, and Report of Order Termination

> *Progress checking* monitors the execution of all work, in terms of quantity and delivery reliability, according to a plan.

---

[11] "Operation time and operation duration would be synonymous except in a situation where there was a delay, for whatever reason, between setup and run. In that case, actual operation duration would include the delay, whereas actual operation time would not" (Jim Greathouse, CFPIM, Huntington Beach, CA, personal communication, 2003). "Operation time is connotatively used to mean a manufacturing operation where each unit of production is measured in seconds, minutes, or a few hours, i.e., machining, stamp press operations, plastic molding, wire extruding, etc. Operation duration is used to measure construction or large machinery manufacturing where each operation of a unit of production may take hours, days, or weeks, i.e., high rise buildings, naval craft building, road building, etc. So while they both refer to the same measure of an operational unit of measure, the time being measured is significantly different in the amount of time being measured" (Quentin Ford, CFPIM, Palatine, IL, personal communication, 2003).

Progress checking allows determination of the position of a production order in process at a specific moment.

Every time a parts requisition or operation card is reported, the administrative status of the position changes into "issued" or "executed." A strictly maintained reporting system is the prerequisite for exact control. It is important to report every operation as "executed" immediately upon completion. This ultimately serves for order coordination. In turn, the meaningfulness of scheduling and capacity planning is maintained. The system is transparent and finds acceptance with the users.

The recorded actual load of an operation permits statistical evaluation and determination of the average efficiency of a work center overall. Modifications to the standard load for an operation may result.

> *Quality control* checks every produced or purchased product according to a more or less explicit or detailed quality control sheet.
>
> A *quality control sheet* is a routing sheet that holds the process for quality assurance.

With production orders, quality control can take place after each operation. Ideally, the person performing the operation should carry out quality control. However, quality control can also take place at the end of production. It may also serve to estimate process capability.[12] For purchase orders, the *receiving department* inventories incoming receipts as to identity and quantity before transferring them to the quality control unit.

The production resources that are used for quality control are called *quality control materials*. The produced lot is designated "finished" or "received," but also "in quality control" during the quality control period. The availability date is, for example, the received date plus the lead time for completion of the quality control sheet. During execution of the control operations, errors are recorded.

> An *anticipated delay report* is a report to materials management, regarding production or purchase orders that will not be completed on time.

---

[12] *Process capability* refers to the ability of the process to produce parts that conform to (engineering) specifications. *Process control* is the function of maintaining a process within a given range of capability by feedback, correction, etc. ([APIC04]).

Besides the new completion date, the anticipated delay report has to explain why the order is delayed.

The *order termination report* is the message that an order was completed. It contains the results and states that all resources used were recorded.

For logistics purposes, the final stage of the quality check judges the portions of the procured order lot as accepted or as rejected as scrap. The *scrap* (that is, the material outside of specifications) goes back to production for *rework* (that is, reprocessing to salvage the defective items, if this seems practical), or back to the supplier for replacement (or reduction of the total of the receipts).[13] The *yield* (or the *"good" quantity*, that is, the acceptable material) moves to its destination: to stock, to a production process, or to sales.

Order termination is reported only when:

- All resources used for a production order have been recorded,
- The accounting check for a purchase order has been performed. This is the comparison between the usable quantity of a shipment received and the corresponding purchase order position quantity.

14.3.4 Automatic and Rough-Cut Data Collection

Conventional shop floor data collection, which uses operation cards and parts requisitions or picking lists, is relatively slow, particularly for short operation times. Prompt recording of transactions requires the presence of administrative personnel in the job shops, which in most cases is to be avoided. In addition, there is a great danger of erroneous data entries. For these reasons, there have long been attempts to record shop floor data automatically. The following tools are in use:

Bar codes: Information is coded in a combination of thick and thin lines. A light-sensitive pen reads and transfers this information to a computer.

Radio Frequency Identification (RFID) is an automatic identification technique, relying on storing and remotely retrieving data using RFID tags as transponders. A *transponder* is an electronic transmitter. An *RFID tag* can be attached to or incorporated into an object product, animal, or person for the purpose of identification using radio waves.

---

[13]   The manufacturer may keep these items at his site as *inventory returns.*

Badges: A badge is generally a card with a magnetic strip. The strip contains information that can be read with a device and sent to a computer.

The solutions developed thus far focus on the following techniques:

- The use of *bar codes* or *RFID* to identify the operation or the allocation directly on the shop order routing or picking list. The use of operation and parts requisition cards is reserved for unplanned issuances or operations. The human operator is identified by means of his or her *badge*. This is usually the same magnetic card that is used for measuring the employee's work hours.

- A clock in the data processing system runs together with the transaction and determines the actual time used through automatic recording of the start time and end time for the operation. The difference between start time and end time yields time used. This is the time that was used, or the actual load. However, an unplanned issued quantity must still be recorded by hand. With this, a small source of error remains. In contrast to the grocery trade, for example, issuances in industrial production are not in units; under certain circumstances a large set of units may be issued instead.

- Linking the data collection system to sensors that automatically count the goods produced or taken from stock. Such systems can be of value for any kind of line production as well as for CNC or robot-supported production.

Rough-cut data collection takes into account the fact that the results of the entire operation are more important than the success of a single order.

The costs of data collection must stand in healthy relation to the benefits of data collection itself — namely, better control of the production and the procurement process. This condition is difficult to meet for all extremely short operations where the administrative time needed to record the operation is in the same range as the operation time itself:

- Collective data collection for entire groups of short operations is possible. However, this requires the recording of the operations represented by this group or by collective data collection, so that the time recorded can ultimately be distributed among the individual operations according to a key. Since we often cannot determine this grouping in advance, it must be recorded at some point during the process. This quickly results in a quantitative data collection problem.

For group work, the recording of the actual processing time is often possible only for rough-cut operations, i.e., for a combination of individual operations. This can only deal with all participating persons together and includes interoperation times as well.

- This combination may correspond to a rough-cut operation, which is sufficient for long- or medium-term planning. It may, however, be even rougher and cover operations for multiple orders, as was shown above for short operations. In all these cases, accounting for individual orders is questionable. Instead, accounting for the entire group over one time period replaces this; the presence times of the group members and the actual times for the rough-cut jobs delivered are placed in relation to the corresponding standard times. This is also precise enough for payroll purposes (compensation); moreover, "success" is measured not only in terms of actual processing times, but also includes interoperation times.

- For the detailed operation, it is not possible in this way to compare the standard load to the actual load. In the case of well-tuned production — or procurement — with frequent order repetition this is actually not necessary, not even for cost estimating. The measure of success becomes the efficiency rate of the entire group (which is all the standard load divided by all the actual load; see Section 1.2.4), and not the costing of single jobs.

For machine-oriented work centers, especially for NC, CNC, and flexible manufacturing systems (FMS), as well as for automated stock transport systems, the solution for the future will lie in inexpensive sensors and in the link to the computer that performs shop floor control.

For manual work centers it is important that the workers do not need to leave their posts for data entry purposes and that they do not need to enter their identification anywhere. The company can introduce inexpensive data collection units that make use of barcode readers or transponders. These data collection units should be located right at the workstation and linked to an Intranet. The employee badge identifies the individual employee.

There is an observation with all the techniques that are used for measuring job shop processes: collection of excessively detailed data can influence processes to such an extent that without measurement the outcome as a whole would be different. This type of measurement falsifies the process (by slowing it down, for example) and should not be implemented.

14.4   Distribution Control

Distribution or distribution control comprises the logistics tasks involved in distributing (moving) finished goods from the manufacturer to the customer.

The shipping department readies finished products for delivery according to sales orders. Sales orders are transmitted to distribution logistics in the form of delivery proposals. Where appropriate, sales and distribution handling monitors production or procurement orders and transfers finished goods or received incoming goods directly to the shipping department.

The sales orders are readied for shipment according to delivery notes.[14] They are handled in sequence or grouped together for one-time picking depending mainly upon the confirmed delivery date. Determination of delivery dates depends to a significant extent upon the available distribution system. Decisions on the type of distribution network are made in the context of facilities location planning.

Warehousing describes the activities related to receiving, storing, and shipping materials to and from production or distribution locations ([APIC04]).

The distribution network structure (see Figure 2.4.4.1) determines the shipping distances for delivery of orders and the likely means of transportation for delivery. Although operations planning of shipments will take place later on (see Section 14.4.3), it is important to take operations into account as early as delivery confirmation, for it will affect the delivery date. Depending on the means of transportation, delivery dates are not arbitrary, for deliveries are grouped together, or collated, in delivery "tours" that are usually served cyclically.

Flexible distribution control is capable of monitoring customer orders, or the confirmed delivery dates of individual positions on orders, by continuous checks on the progress of production and procurement orders. This is similar to the "freight train" of customer order processing described in Section 1.3.3, which halts at particular stations to monitor the supply of goods and information from other trains. Changes in production or procurement completion dates require adjustments of the planned transports.

The actual shipping process encompasses order picking, packaging, assembling the shipment, and transport to the receiver. This is accompanied

---

[14]   A delivery note more or less corresponds to the customer order form

by administrative activities, such as preparation of supporting documents and packing slips; maintaining transport statistics; complaints handling of hauling (damage) claims, and much more.

14.4.1 Order Picking

Order picking, or simply *picking* is the issuance of items from stocking locations for delivery. Items are issued according to a particular picking strategy.

The *picking strategy* is the type of order picking chosen.

The order picking process typically includes the following steps: making goods available in storage units, picking the required quantities of goods, consolidating the picked goods according to the picking sequence, transport of the picking unit to shipping, and return of part-picked storage units to storage.

Order picking facilities find implementation mainly in the distribution of finished goods and in the shipping of spare parts, but they are also needed internally for supplying assembly or production. There are four picking strategies depending on the type of stocking system and the replenishment techniques employed, as shown in Figure 14.4.1.1:

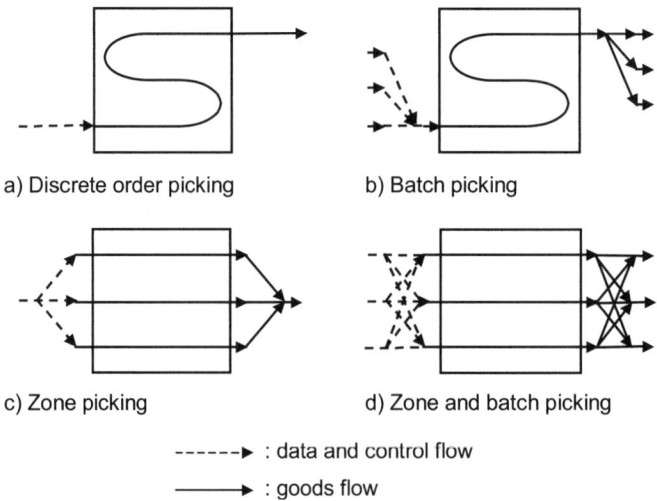

a) Discrete order picking   b) Batch picking

c) Zone picking   d) Zone and batch picking

------▶ : data and control flow

——▶ : goods flow

Fig. 14.4.1.1   Picking strategies. (Following [RKW].)

- In *discrete order picking*, orders are picked one after the other. The required accompanying document is a delivery note with the positions sorted in an optimal picking sequence. This optimal sequence is the shortest driving route through the warehouse. Accordingly, the specific sorting of the items of the delivery note is called a *picking list* (see also Section 14.2.1).

- *Batch picking* pools a number of orders and sorts the positions of all the corresponding items of the delivery notes together in an optimal sequence. The resulting picking list then permits all the products for delivery to be picked up in one trip through the warehouse. The individual shipments are then put together following the single, completed trip in a special secondary warehouse, in an *order picking store*, or in a *commissary*. This procedure makes high- performance order picking possible, but it entails higher costs than discrete order picking, as both higher capital and operating costs result. Only where the range of products is very large and there is a high volume of orders with few positions, such as in mail order businesses, is batch picking a cost-effective solution.

There are further picking strategies that are dependent upon both the size of the warehouse and the product structure:

- *Sequential picking*: A trip is made through the warehouse for each single order or batch of orders in its entirety.

- *Zone picking*, or *parallel picking*: The warehouse is segmented into a number of picking zones, and the single order or batch of orders is split into partial orders that are picked in parallel. In a further operation in a separate area of the warehouse, all partial orders are then placed together. This makes sense for very large warehouses in order to shorten the routes of individual pickers. There is also segmentation of the warehouse according to product, such as segmentation into different temperature zones for refrigerated and frozen goods or separate areas for flammable or hazardous chemicals or for products that should not be stored together in close proximity.

Other distinguishing criteria are the type of storage and the movement of the picker:[15]

---

[15]   The "picker" can be the person removing the goods or various technical aids such as stacker crane, grab, or picking robot.

- In *decentralized goods preparation*, the goods are stored at constant locations, and the picker moves from one picking position to the next (called routing "people to the product"). The picker then moves the picked goods to an order consolidation area. Depending on the warehouse layout, the picker moves back and forth, or — in the case of multilevel storage with platforms that can be elevated and lowered or mezzanines with materials elevators — back and forth and up and down. This very common picking method is relatively simple to realize.

- In *centralized goods preparation*, goods are conveyed from storage to a permanent picking station, or kitting area (called routing "product to the people"). Conveyor belts, rack operation equipment, or stacking cranes move the goods. An important decision criterion for this type of goods storage is the issue of how to handle part-picked storage units from which items have been picked for an order. Part-picked pallets of product, for example, can remain at the pick station, but for space reasons they often must be transported back to storage or to a special storage area. In planning & control in modern picking systems, the solution depends upon the frequency of demand for the item (for example, using an ABC classification). Frequently demanded goods remain at the pick station, while other goods return to storage until needed.

Picking can range from manual to fully automated, depending upon warehouse layout and type of picking system. Automation is possible for retrieving storage units, transporting them back to storage, dividing storage units (multiple-unit cartons or pallets) for single item picking, and finally, transporting the commissioned unit. Automation does not always require the use of robots. Separating single items can be accomplished by "automatic moving" rather than by gripping robots, whereby goods are lifted from a carton flow channel or caused to slide out of the channel.

Fully automated picking is a special case that is typically found in the pharmaceuticals industry and in mail order businesses. For order consolidation, picking robots, automated conveyors, and other technical devices replace people entirely. This is only possible, however, if the items to be picked have similar dimensions (geometry) and are stable in shape (stiffness). In addition, the goods must be stored in precise arrangements, meaning that items must be stored in predetermined and dedicated storage locations and particular orientations in order to allow retrieval by automated equipment. Full automation is cost effective, however, only with high turnover and steady load of the facility.

For optimum processing of order picking, increasingly complex computer-aided control systems are being implemented. Warehouse management systems collate orders, create picking lists, calculate optimum picking routes, control and monitor traffic in the picking system (for example, the movements of picking robots), and, finally, document completion of the order. Modern systems also shorten retrieval times and retrieval routes by calculating the optimum design for the warehouse (that is, minimization of routes and replenishment efforts, with good utilization of floor space) and, when capacity is available, automatically trigger restocking of piles for faster goods retrieval.

The picking process ends when the item quantities have been consolidated to fulfill the order. The goods, usually not yet packaged, must now be prepared for shipment by the packaging department. Exceptions, however, are "pick and pack" operations, where goods are packaged during the picking process.

If picking is incomplete, that is, not all the positions on a delivery note can actually be issued — whether foreseeable from the start or due to errors in inventory information — then the remaining positions of the order waiting for delivery can be split and put on a separate backorder.[16]

Order picking should choose an analogous procedure for putting accompanying materials together for *contract work*, that is, external operations. The delivery of accompanying materials is a legally binding event, just as true sales orders are. The only difference is that no invoicing results from this, since the accompanying materials ultimately remain the property of the company and are only temporarily "loaned out."

14.4.2 Packaging and Load Building

Packaging is the enclosure of goods for protection or other functions.

The *packaged good* is the packaged product or product to be packaged.

The packing unit is the quantity of packaged items per package, with reference to the item unit (for example, a case of 12 bottles).

The *packaging function* is the reason for packaging.

Packaging plays a crucial role in logistics, as it is often only through packaging that the goods produced are divided into single units. Packaging

---

[16]   Split orders may have to be recombined for invoicing purposes.

has no function on its own; it is the goods packaged that determine the function. As soon as the product arrives at the place of consumption, packaging has fulfilled its purpose and becomes waste or material for re-use and recycle. The many possible functions of packaging can be grouped into five areas (see Figure 14.4.2).

Function of packaging		Demands on packaging
Protection function		withstand heat or cold
		air- and watertight
		resist corrosion
		dust-free
		chemically inert
		preserve contents
		non-combustible
	Distribution function	stable in form (stiffness)
		resist impact
		withstand impact, shock
		withstand pressure
		resist tearing
		stackable
		non-slip
		standardized
		facilitate handling
		automation friendly
		creates (standard) units
		space saving
		area saving
Sales function		economical
	Information function	product promotion
		informative
		identifiable
		distinctive
	Use function	easy-open
		resealable
		reusable, recyclable
		environmentally friendly
		disposal friendly
		hygienic, aseptic

Fig. 14.4.2.1   Conceptual framework to handle the diverse functions and requirements of packaging. (Following [JuSc00].)

- The most important function of packaging is to protect contents. *Active protective functions* assure that the product reaches the end user undamaged. Packaging must protect packaged goods from inner and outer stresses: mechanical, chemical, physical, and biological. In addition, packaging can reduce pilfering. *Passive protective functions* protect the people, facilities, and other goods that are involved in distribution of the products.

- The *distribution function* of packaging supports storage, transport, and trans-shipment/reloading. The type of packaging has a significant effect on handling in the warehouse and utilization of storage and transport space. Well-thought-out packaging decisions can improve stackability, optimize space utilization, and simplify the implementation of technical devices. Reduction of the weight of packaging can reduce freight costs. The right packing — for example, the use of standardized load carriers like pallets and containers — can considerably improve cargo trans-shipment from one means of transportation to another at loading stations. For the most efficient packing, the dimensions of packaging will conform to standardized load carriers (for example, the 800 times 1200-mm European pool pallet).[17]

- Labeling and stamping produce the *information and sales promotion functions* of packaging. Legally required declarations of contents for foodstuffs or hazardous materials belong here, as do also printed instructions for transport, handling, or storage. Moreover, packaging can serve marketing purposes. This promotion function gains in significance the closer a product comes to being a consumer good. Self-service sales, for example, where there is no contact at all between producer and customer, rely on modern packaging, and it is the most significant component of the company's product-market positioning policy. Packaging attracts the attention of the customer and creates an association to the product. It is increasingly common for manufacturers to mark products with EAN or UCC/UPC identification numbers[18] or suggested retail prices for easier handling on the part of retailers and customers.

- The *use function* refers to two things: the customer's handling of the packaging and the reusability and recyclability of packaging.

---

[17] The European pool pallet is a standardized block pallet introduced by the European railroads after World War II. This is the only pallet that should be referred to as a "EuroPallet." These pallets are produced by licensed manufactures and bear the "EUR" logo.

[18] EAN is the European Association of Numbers. In the United States, retail items are identified with UPC codes (Uniform Product Code), which are created using a membership number provided by the UCC (Uniform Code Council). The 12-digit-long UPC-A barcodes were for a long time not the same as 13-digit EAN13 bar codes used in retail point of sale everywhere else in the world.

Environmentally friendly packaging is becoming ever important. Multi-way, or return, packaging is gaining customer acceptance.

- The *sales function* overlaps with all the other functions listed above but adds the demand for economical design of packaging for cost-reduction purposes. There is increasing cooperation between industry and commercial enterprises in the area of sales and retail packaging. This is particularly important for self-service sales, because unpacking shipping cartons, stocking the shelves of the store, and labeling products and display shelves are extremely labor intensive. For this reason, packaging is becoming much more store-friendly (store-ready shipments for better flowthrough) and is even being designed to fit the dimensions of store shelving units (shelf-ready for better presentation).

> The *packaging system* is comprised of the packaged good, the packaging or packaging materials, and the packaging process.

The three elements of the packaging system are closely intertwined. The choice of packaging is determined by the characteristics of the packaged goods and the functions that packaging must fulfill. The packaging materials in turn determine the packaging process. For example, they determine the type of machine that is required for forming, filling, and sealing. Conversely, to allow automated processing at all, packaging machines place much higher demands on the packaging materials than manual packing does.

> Packaging is produced from *packaging materials.*

Various materials are used for packaging: paper, cardboard, corrugated board, plastics, metal (steel), aluminum, glass, wood, rubber, textiles, and multilayer materials (composites). Each packaging material has its own unique properties that can be utilized in order to fulfill the packaging function. The choice of packaging materials is also determined by recycling and return packaging considerations. Return and recycling can engender additional costs that may be prohibitive.

> *Packing and marking* is made up of all necessary activities to package the good.

These activities include supplying empty packaging and the goods to the packing facilities, setting up and filling the packaging, marking and labeling, and preparation of the packaged units for transport. Support through packaging machines is common. Some examples are bagging machines, filling machines, form–fill–seal machines, can-filling machines, cartoning machines, palletizing machines, and overwrapping machines.

Load building is the grouping and consolidating of items for transport.

The *load unit* is the grouping of packing units for transport.

Packing units are placed on or in unit-load supports, such as pallets, trays, or containers, and secured with load stabilizers (bands, lashing belts, adhesives, stretch wrap, and so on), in order to facilitate handling, storage, and transport. The choice of the unit loading aid is highly dependent upon the specific means of transportation (see Section 14.3). For truck trailer transport, for example, pallets are used, whereas containers are frequently used for air or sea freight.

The *transport unit* is the number of load units per unit of the means of transportation (container, truck, rail wagon, etc.).

This process of successive consolidating is shown in Figure 14.4.2.2.

The necessary accompanying documents must be readied during the packaging process or, at the latest, during load building. These may include item-related instructions for use or transport-related documents such as bills of delivery, export authorization, export transfer notes, certificates of origin, international customs declarations, and the like.

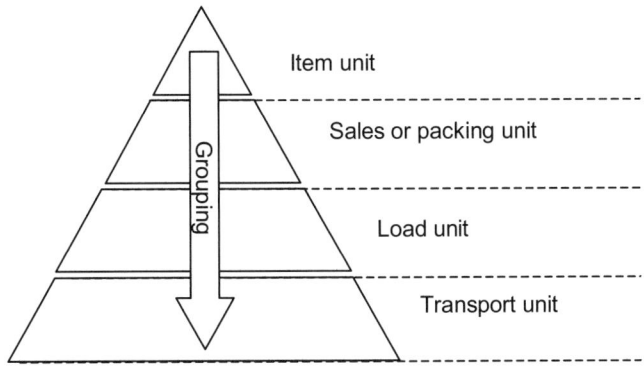

Fig. 14.4.2.2   Levels of aggregation in load building.

Interactions between packing units, load units, transport units, and the logistics system will significantly influence economic efficiency. For example, optimal packaging allows improved and more cost-effective transport, savings in (intermediate) storage costs, and even improved sales of the packaged product. Understanding and taking into account all of these factors can result in satisfactory economic efficiency.

14.4.3 Transportation to Receiver

Following picking of the goods to be shipped and packing, the next step is planning the transport of the goods to the receiver. Transport itself is often outsourced to a third-party logistics provider. The specific distribution network structure resulting from storage locations planning determines the distances of the routes and the choice of modes of transportation.

> *Transport planning and scheduling* involve finding solutions in three problems areas: transport mode selection, shipping route planning, and loading space optimization.

Fair and Williams (in [Ross04], p. 580) define a number of objectives that should be achieved through transport planning and scheduling. The most important objectives are most continuous flow of goods through the distribution network; optimal, load-specific transport mode selection; minimization of number of vehicles; standardization of loading aids (pallets, containers); and maximization of capacity utilization (capital, equipment, personnel).

Figure 14.4.3.1 shows interactions and mutual influences among the three main transport planning and scheduling tasks.

- The type of load largely determines the *transport mode selection.* Bulk goods loads, i.e., unpackaged substances in the form of solids, liquids, or gases, entail other requirements as to the mode of transport than loads that are made up of discrete standard loads like containers, packages, pallets, or sea containers. The specific nature of the goods to be shipped stipulates further requirements: The goods may be perishable, combustible, explosive, sensitive, or prone to shrinkage.

  Possible modes of transport away from the company are road motor vehicles, railways, ships, and aircraft. The transport chain may integrate both company-owned vehicles (such as trucks) and public modes of transport. For bulk goods, pipeline systems are possible. Bowersox (in [Ross04], p. 590) outlines six criteria that influence the decision on transport mode: speed, "completeness" (using the least possible number of different modes within one distribution channel), dependability, capability (not all goods can be transported via all modes of transport), transport frequency, and costs.

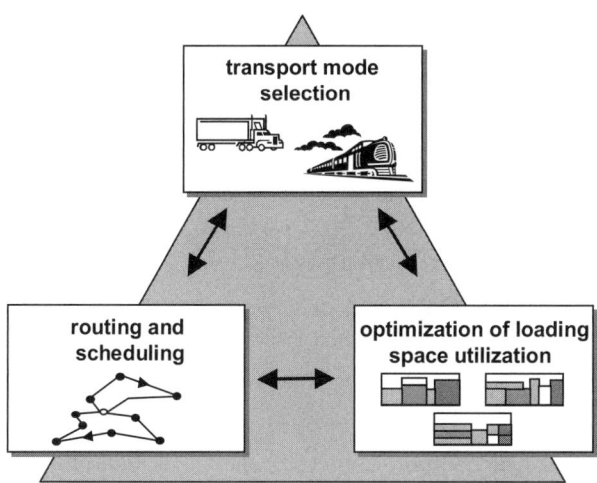

Fig. 14.4.3.1   Problems of transport planning and scheduling. (Following [FIR00], p. 254.)

For the delivery of a transportation order, a combination of transportation modalities can form a transport chain. A distinction is made among *direct course* (no interruption from supplier to receiver), *"pre" course* (from supplier to trans-shipment point), *"post" course* (from trans-shipment point to receiver), and *main course* (from trans-shipment point to trans-shipment point). The advantages of individual modes of transport can be utilized for the various legs of the transport. Due to their flexibility, trucks are often used for *"pre"* and *"post" course*, whereas for the main course over great distances the choice falls on air or water transport. Figure 14.4.3.2 shows some examples of transport chains.

When changing the means of transportation, there is the problem of getting the goods from one modality to another. While the transfer of the goods can be simplified through the use of standardized loading aids like containers or pallets, transferring goods entails special handling equipment (gantry crane, winch, lifting platform, chute, and so on), time and personnel, and associated costs. The following concepts are gaining in importance:

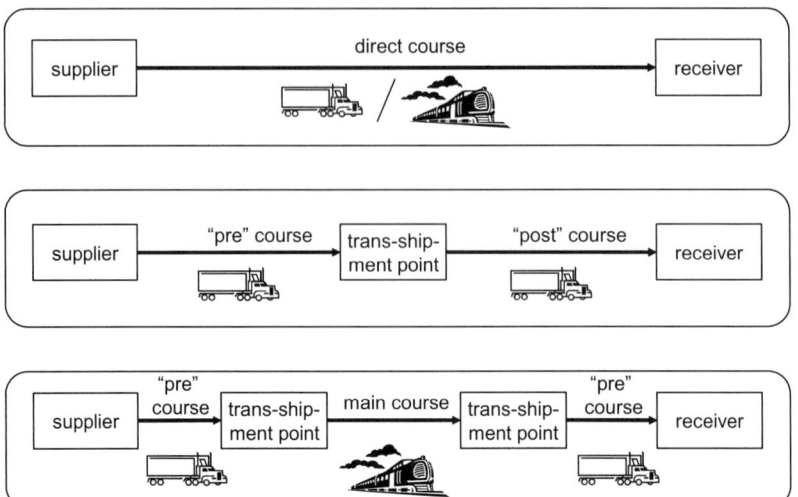

Fig. 14.4.3.2   Transport chain from supplier to receiver.

- *Cross-docking*, or *direct loading* is the concept of load building on the incoming vehicle so that the packaged goods can be easily carried at the trans-shipment point to the outgoing vehicle, without being stored in intermediate inventory ([APIC04]).

- The objective of *combined transport* is to transport goods using two modes of transport in combination, such as rail/road transport, in the best way possible so as to utilize the advantages of each. This is achieved through the use of intermodal transport units (container, swap body, or semi-trailer/goods road motor vehicle).

- *Trailer on flat car [TOFC] transport* is a synonym for road transport that is in part moved by rail. Semi trailers or entire road trains (drawbar–trailer combinations) are loaded onto trains. The major part of the journey is by rail; the final leg for delivery to the customer is carried out by road.

- *Routing and scheduling* determine the order in which a means of transportation will reach the individual stations (customer, trans-shipment stations, warehouses, and so on). The objective is to deliver to all customers in a delivery area at minimal cost. Strategic route optimization is required. The return movements of empty road vehicles must also be planned (direct return following delivery, loading of a return load, empty load minimization). Routing and scheduling are complex optimization problems that must be solved taking account of numerous constraints and restrictions, such as weight and volume constraints, distances, delivery time windows, and more. Planners often implement algorithms from "operations research." Using so-called "opening heuristics," an initial tour is scheduled and then optimized through the use of "improving heuristics." For a detailed description of this procedure, see, for example, [Doms97].

- *Optimization of loading space utilization* is closely connected to the two problems outlined above. Selection of the means of transportation and scheduling of the tour results in the assignment of a definite number of load units to each means of transportation (for example, truck or rail wagon). The next task is to load the goods into the units with optimal utilization of the loading space, leaving the least possible space unused. Planners may again use heuristic methods from the field of "operations research" to achieve optimization of the loading space.

Transport planning and scheduling produces transportation orders, which trigger the physical transportation of goods.

The *transportation order* stipulates the time and place for pickup of a particular number of load units and the time and place they will be delivered.

This order can contain a single load unit, several load units referring to a unique delivery order, or the optimized, combined transportation of several delivery orders. The transportation order usually sets a delivery time window or a maximum delivery lead time.

Consolidation is a term for packages and lots that move from suppliers to a carrier terminal and are sorted and then combined with similar shipments from other suppliers for travel to their final destination (see [APIC04]).

For the supplier, the advantage of this trans-shipment is daily deliveries of various goods to various receivers. This is to the customer's advantage, as well. However, the advantage must be weighed against the costs of trans-shipment. Routing and scheduling with consolidation is usually a job for the transport company, freight forwarder, or third-party logistics provider. Simple cases of consolidation are called *milk runs*, or regular routes for pickup of mixed loads from several suppliers (see [APIC04]).

> *Transportation control* consists in monitoring the route movements of the transport units, monitoring traffic conditions and delays, and registering and evaluating disturbances.

Transport controlling of external transport systems is usually managed via a control center that controls, monitors, and coordinates transports in dependency on actual conditions and contingencies. Today, drivers can communicate with central control via mobile data terminals, cellular phones, and personal digital assistants. The wireless Internet allows for the use of small handheld devices for interfacing with central control and accessing traffic and weather information. Some vehicles are also equipped with satellite navigation systems, such as global-positioning-system (GPS) receivers, that compute the location of vehicles in real-time and allow tracking by central control.

Whereas the delivery note used to suffice as the supporting document, today the entire goods flow is usually managed electronically. This makes standardization of communication means essential, so that uniform monitoring is possible in intermodal transport chains.

- Via scanning of the *bar code* on the goods, the legal "passing of the risk" that occurs at trans-shipment is documented.

- *EDIFACT* (electronic data exchange for administration, commerce, and transport) is one of the format standards that have been created for information technology support of transport control.

- *RFID* or another transponder technique for worldwide self-identification of goods.

- *Tracking and tracing* of package deliveries is now offered by many transport service providers. Using the World Wide Web via the Internet, customers can view information on their shipments (identified by transponders, for example).

Transport planning must also consider outsourcing logistics tasks to specialized distribution companies (self-owned or third-party logistics providers). With their focus on core competency and due to consolidation effects, the result can be a significant reduction in operating costs as well as improved efficiency, service, and flexibility. Companies can put these advantages to good use, for they stand under the growing pressure to lower costs and, at the same time, to meet higher demands from customers regarding service, price, and delivery capability. Courier services and express carriers are more and more becoming parts of logistics chains, in particular to fulfill just-in-time deliveries. For an extensive discussion of distribution tasks, see, for example, [Ross04], [Pfoh03], and [MarA96].

14.5 Summary

In the short-term time horizon, the company releases order proposals that stem from long- or medium-term planning. In same time horizon, unplanned sales are also realized that have to be delivered as soon as possible. If the items are available, they can be delivered from stock. Otherwise, creation and release of production or procurement orders is necessary.

An order release generally includes a test of resource availability. In addition, the techniques of materials, scheduling, and capacity management are put to use, independently of the type of data processing support available or the person performing the function. Scheduling calculations provide the necessary start dates for the operations. The components and the capacity must be available at the start date.

Specific techniques were developed for the release of multiple orders. *De facto*, they are techniques of control of operations as well. Load-oriented order release (Loor) is a generalization of order-by-order planning with limited capacity. For each work center, the capacity of a planning period is first multiplied by a loading percentage and then balanced with the load for all future periods. The load of later operations is thereby subject to a conversion. Operations that cannot be scheduled due to lead time calculations result in rejection of the order. Capacity-oriented materials management (Corma) provides an early release of stock replenishment orders when critical capacities are available. More urgent customer production orders may interrupt the processing of these orders. Continual rescheduling, which uses the technique of probable scheduling, is meant to speed up or slow down the orders in timely fashion. Furthermore, completion dates for stock replenishment orders are adapted to the actual consumption on an ongoing basis.

Shop floor control includes the issuing of accompanying documents for procurement and production. At the very least there is an order document, possibly in electronic form. In production there are also shop floor routings, picking lists, parts requisitions, and operation cards. The scheduling of detailed operations, the allocation of work to the individual persons and machines, the assignment of production equipment, and the sequencing of the orders for each workstation then follow. Ideally, the person executing the operation should perform these functions.

Shop floor data collection records the use of resources. It includes the issuance of goods and the executed (internal and external) operations. Thus it also yields information the progress of orders, if this is not tracked separately. Shop floor data collection is necessary in order to ensure updated planning of the availability of goods and capacities. It also serves as a preparation for order costing, readjusting load standards, and quality assurance. Completed or incoming orders undergo quality control, sometimes using a quality control sheet. Results determine whether parts of the lot are accepted or rejected and sent on to rework or replacement.

Automatic shop floor data collection offers speed, but it usually incurs higher costs as well. The benefits gained through precise data collection, which lie in better knowledge and control of the production processes, must justify the cost. For short operations or in group-work organization, the actual time can be measured at reasonable expense only for rough-cut operations. The measure of performance is then the efficiency rate for the group as a whole, and not the costing of a single job.

Distribution control encompasses the logistics tasks involved in distributing finished goods to the customer. Once the distribution network structure has been chosen, the tasks include order picking, packaging and load building, and transport to the receiver. Picking can follow various strategies and may be order or item oriented. Packaging serves a number of functions, such as protection, distribution, information and promotion, use, and sales. Load building is the successive grouping of production units in packing units, load units (on pallets, for example) depending on the transport mode, and finally in transport units. For transport to the receiver, solutions must be found for choice of transportation mode, routing and scheduling, and optimization of the loading space.

14.6   Keywords

14.7   Scenarios and Exercises

14.7.1 Load-Oriented Order Release (Loor)

The first table in Figure 14.7.1.1 shows five orders with their sequence of operations. The data for each operation include the work center, the standard load (e.g. setup plus run time), and a blank column for entering the converted load.

Or-der no.	Start-date	1st operation			2nd operation			3rd operation			4th operation		
		Work center	Standard load	Converted load	Work center	Standard load	Converted load	Work center	Standard load	Converted load	Work center	Standard load	Converted load
1	16.06.	A	100		B	60		C	480		D	240	
2	18.06.	B	40		C	120		A	120				
3	22.06.	A	40		C	30		B	20				
4	29.06.	C	40		D	60		A	20				
5	06.07.	A	30		B	40		D	100		C	120	

Today:	14.06.
Time period:	1 week
Anticipation horizon:	3 weeks
Loading percentage:	200%
Conversion factor:	50%

Work center	Weekly capacity	Cap. with loading %	Pre-load	Summarized load including orders				
				1	2	3	4	5
A	200		265					
B	100		150					
C	300		340					
D	100		160					

Fig. 14.7.1.1   Given data for a Loor problem.

The second table in Figure 14.7.1.1 shows parameters for load-oriented order release, as introduced in Section 14.1.2, as well as their values given for this exercise. The third table holds data for each work center, namely, the weekly capacity, the existing (pre-)load before loading the five orders, a blank column for entering the capacity upgraded by the loading percentage, and blank columns for the summarized load after releasing orders 1 to 5 (that is in the sequence given by the Loor algorithm).

a.   Load the five orders according to the Loor algorithm.

b.   What would have happened if for operation 3 of order 2 the standard load had been 200 units of time instead of 120?

c.   Discuss whether in your solution the treatment of order 3 was efficient.

d.   What would have happened if order 3 had been loaded before order 2?

Solutions:

a.   The time filter eliminates order 5. This order is declared as not urgent. For the other orders, the conversion factor is applied to their operations. In the third table, the loading percentage multiplies the weekly capacity. Then, order 1 is loaded, followed by order 2. Order 2 is accepted, but it overloads work center B (220 units of time against 200 units resulting from the loading percentage). Hence, order 3 cannot be loaded, because its last operation is at work center B. However, order 4 can be loaded, since it has no operation at work center B.

b.   Order 2 would have overloaded work center A. Hence, order 4 would not have been loaded.

c.   The converted load of order 3 on work center B had only 5 units of time. This would have changed the total load only very slightly. As there was no overloading of other work centers by orders 1, 2, and 4, it might have been wise to release order 3 as well.

d.   Order 3 would have overloaded work center A (405 units of time against 400 units resulting from the loading percentage). Therefore, the algorithm would formally reject both orders 2 and 4. This would result in a low utilization of the other work centers B, C, and D.

14.7.2 Capacity-Oriented Materials Management (Corma)

Applying the capacity-oriented materials management (Corma) principle has which of the following results?

I Evenly distributed extension of the manufacturing lead time for all the orders

II Minimum amount of work in process

III Maximum utilization of the generally well-utilized work centers

a. II only

b. III only

c. I and II only

d. II and III only

Solution:

The answer is (b), or "III only". In fact, the early release of an order implies an extension of its lead time, because it will wait as soon as there are (unplanned) customer orders. The latter will be performed with minimal lead time. Thus, I is not true. II is not true, either, because of the very presence of early released orders. However, III is true: A bottleneck capacity is loaded with non-urgent (i.e., early released) orders as soon as there is available capacity.

14.7.3 Finite Forward Scheduling

Your company owns one lathe (M1), one milling machine (M2), and one drilling machine (M3). A working day lasts eight hours. As Figure 14.7.3.1 shows, eight products (P1, P2, P3, ..., P8) are manufactured on these machines. Each product loads these machines in a different sequence. For simplicity, assume that there is no interoperation time.

Product	1st operation		2nd operation		3rd operation	
	Ma-chine	Load (h)	Ma-chine	Load (h)	Ma-chine	Load (h)
P1	M1	3	M2	4	M3	5
P2	M2	2	M1	3	M3	2
P3	M3	4	M1	3	M2	1
P4	M2	3	M3	2	M1	4
P5	M3	3	M2	3	—	—
P6	M2	4	M1	3	M3	3
P7	M3	1	M1	2	—	—
P8	M1	3	M3	4	M2	3

Fig. 14.7.3.1   Eight products manufactured on three machines.

Perform finite forward scheduling for the next three days. The normal working time of 8 hours per day has to be respected, as do the sequence of the operations for each order given by Figure 14.7.3.1 and the following three priority rules:

1. No idle time on the machine

2. Operation with the shortest processing time

3. Longest remaining lead time for the order

The Gantt-type chart planning board in Figure 14.7.3.2 will help you to perform the task. Note the first orders on each machine. The order for product P1 has been chosen for machine M1 because of the third priority rule.

	Working day 1 (8 hours)	Working day 2 (8 hours)	Working day 3 (8 hours)
M1	P1		
M2	P2		
M3	P7		

Fig. 14.7.3.2   Gantt-type chart for finite forward scheduling.

Discuss whether other priority rules would result in a better solution with regard to work in process.

Solution:

The total load is 21 hours on machine 1, 20 hours on machine 2, and 24 hours on machine 3. Thus, machine 3 is fully loaded, and priority rule 1 makes full sense. There are solutions for this problem that schedule the other two machines without idle time, respecting the sequence of operations for all eight orders. One of these solutions can be found by simply following the priority rules.

Replacing the second and the third priority rule by the rule *shortest remaining lead time* would result in considerably less work in process. However, strict application of this rule not only results in idle time on machine 3, but also creates delays for order 3 and order 6: They cannot be finished at the end of the third day. Both effects cannot be tolerated. They are due to the fact that these orders are started too late. As a consequence, there must be some rule giving them priority at some time, thereby augmenting work in order.

14.7.4 Order Picking

As depicted in Figure 14.4.1.1, discrete order picking, batch picking, sequential picking, and parallel, or zone, picking result in four common picking strategies. Point out the main characteristics of the following picking strategies. List the advantages and disadvantages of each. Derive possible fields of application:

a. Sequential, discrete order picking

b. Zone, or parallel, batch picking

Solution:

a. Sequential, discrete order picking

   Characteristics:
   - Most common method of picking
   - Pickers fill all open positions of an order before work on picking the next order can begin
   - Based on a picking list that contains an optimal routing

   Advantages:
   - Maintains order integrity

- Minimum of organizational efforts
- Simple to execute and easy to control
- Direct fill responsibility

Disadvantages:
- Required time for picking
- Decreasing efficiency with growing order size
- Large number of pickers needed

Possible fields of application:
- Small warehouses, low inventory turnover, low performance, small orders

b. Zone, or parallel, batch picking

Characteristics:
- Several orders are aggregated by product (as batch), the entire batch withdrawn, and the discrete orders reassembled in a consolidation area
- Batches are picked parallel in different zones of the warehouse and then merged in the consolidation area

Advantages:
- Reduced travel and fill times
- Low picking time due to parallel zones
- Improved supervision of order completion in consolidation area
- Increased picking accuracy and productivity due to zones
- Picker familiarity with zone products

Disadvantages:
- Double handling and sorting in the consolidation area
- Space and labor for consolidation area
- Difficult tracing and control of orders
- Requires high-volume picking

Possible fields of application:
- Large orders, high number of orders, large warehouses, products with different storage requirements (e.g., flammable goods, refrigerated goods)

15 Cost Estimating, Job-Order Costing, and Activity-Based Costing

Figure 15.0.0.1 shows the reference model for business processes and planning & control tasks from Figure 4.1.4.2 and highlights the tasks and processes that we will examine in this chapter.

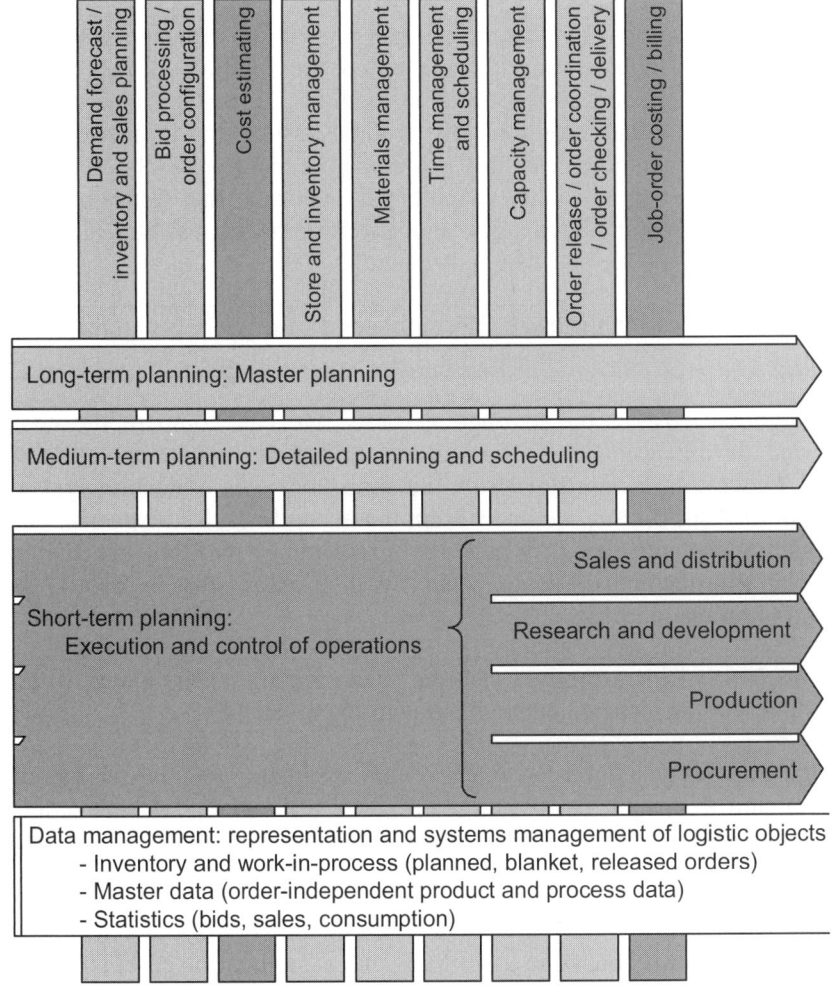

Fig. 15.0.0.1   The parts of the system discussed in Chapter 15 (shown on darker background).

Section 4.1.2 provides an overview of the topic discussed here. The reader may find it useful to go back over that section before reading this chapter.

Information on costs and pricing is vital in order to improve managerial decision-making in the area of sales and marketing:

- What is the cost of goods manufactured? How large is the profit resulting from an order, or, at the least, what fixed costs contribution margin does the order generate?

- How will varying the consumption of resources affect the costs of individual products or the total costs for the organization?

This chapter does not aim to provide an overview of financial and cost accounting, nor does it provide a detailed presentation of the various financing, costing, and cost accounting methods. However, since all cost object accounting, and therefore also product costing and project costing, is based on the planning & control system — or more precisely on master data or order data — the chapter will address the issue of how administrative logistics manages and determines the various elements needed to calculate the cost of goods manufactured.

> *Job-order costing* identifies and accumulates all the costs generated by an order.

By job-order costing on an ongoing basis, we can compare the costs incurred during production or procurement against target, or estimated costs. *Feedback*, or data flow from the shop floor data collection system, immediately signals any variances from these standards. Retrospective cost accounting systems generally have the disadvantage that they are applied too long after the actual events, when it is often impossible to identify the causes of the variances.

> *Cost estimating* for a product or order identifies and accumulates all the costs likely to be incurred when manufacturing a batch.

As the most detailed master data is captured in the planning & control information system, it is possible to perform a simulation of the orders. With computer-supported information systems, it is easy to perform preliminary calculations in advance for any variations in bills of material, routing sheets, or cost elements.

One of the major problems in identifying and accumulating costs is how to assign fixed costs, or indirect costs, to cost objects. Conventional cost systems assign these costs in relation to the number of product units manufactured, using for example direct-labor hours or direct material costs as a basis to assign production overhead. Activity-based costing, or activity-based cost accounting (ABC), is an instrument that focuses on the fixed costs (overhead) of repetitive processes. It is a more accurate costing method, for it traces expense categories to the particular cost object, making "indirect" costs "direct." ABC is based on management of the highly detailed master data in the planning & control system. The chapter will provide a detailed example in order to show what introducing ABC as a costing method entails.

15.1   Costs, Cost Elements, and Cost Structures

15.1.1 Actual, Direct, and Indirect Costs

The *actual costs* of an item are the costs that were incurred when that item was last produced or procured. They refer to the item's unit of measure.

The revenue generated by a customer order can be compared against its costs. This allows determination of the profitability of the order. This is particularly useful if the sales price fluctuates greatly or the cost of procured materials used in production varies — such as when the purchasing department takes advantage of large quantity discounts or special offers.

In contrast to costs, the revenue generated by a sale is often easy to identify. Cost accounting subdivides expenditures into a number of alternative pairs, such as direct and indirect costs.

Direct costs are the costs that can be identified specifically with or traced to a given cost object (a product, service, or order, for example).

Direct costs are, for example, costs for *direct labor*, such as wages or external operations, or for *direct material*, such as purchased components needed to produce the order.

Overhead costs or *indirect costs* are costs that cannot be identified specifically with or traced to a given cost object. Indirect costs must be allocated across the various cost objects (products, services, or orders, for example).

Typical examples of overhead include the costs of plant and operating equipment (machinery, devices, tools), depreciation, rent, lighting and heating, and management and administration costs.

In practice, actual costs may change frequently over the course of a year. Irregularities in procurement (breakdowns, scrap, discounts, special promotions) cause the actual costs to fluctuate considerably. There are also fundamental problems associated with calculating the cost of a sales order on the basis of the actual costs:

1. Many of the costs incurred within an organization are of an indirect nature, even overhead costs. Conventional cost accounting allocates overhead more or less equally to the individual orders (cost apportionment) to allow a meaningful comparison against revenue.

   - To allocate overhead costs to the individual products or orders, we need some sort of "fair" distribution formula as a basis for apportionment. This is often a percentage of sales, measured against direct costs. An alternative is to base allocation on cost rates per labor or machine hours, based on forecasts.

2. When items are issued for sale or for assembly in a higher level end product, it is important to specify the associated production or procurement order to allow further calculation of the actual costs of the orders.

   - To be able to do this, inventory management must keep accounting records according to production or procurement batch or charge. Issues are then always allocated to a particular batch. Lot control will then provide the necessary documentation (indeed, this procedure is mandatory in the process industry).

3. Job-order costing must be carried out as soon as possible after the order is completed.

   - Invoices, the source of information on actual costs for external operations and for components purchased directly for the order, must be received within a reasonable period. If this period is too long, then there will be a relatively long delay before the costs can be compared against revenue. Analysis of variances from budgeted costs becomes more difficult as more time elapses between the cost event and cost control. Data regarding the event are often not registered and are thus no longer available at the time of the analysis.

15.1.2 Average Costs and Standard Costs

Many organizations have introduced standard cost accounting systems because of the difficulties associated with actual costing systems.

> *Standard costs* are an estimate, a prediction, of actual costs.

Standard costs are used as the basis for budgeting and for analyzing variances (the differences that arise between targeted and actual results) in job order costing. Standards for costs, quantities, and times are also a useful means of cost estimating for a new product, particularly if it is comparable to previous products. In general, standard costs are determined on the basis of the average costs.

> The *average costs* for an item are the average last-in costs of this item. They refer to the item's unit of measure.

Average costs can be determined using the same techniques that were described for historically oriented forecasting in Section 9.2.

At the end of the budget period, such as at the end of every year, the average costs are carried over as the new standard costs. Here it is important to consider factors similar to those outlined in Chapter 9 for forecasting techniques, in particular for trend forecasting.

At this point, cost accounting also determines the new standard cost rates.

> *Standard cost rates* for labor costs per work center include,
>
> - As direct costs, the expected wage rate for the workers.
> - Overhead costs, for which cost accounting establishes the depreciation requirements and divides them by the load forecast — expressed in capacity units, that is, units of measure of the capacity for the work center (mostly hours) — for the new budget period.

For every operation, the same principle applies: calculation of the average values for the standard load of an operation, the setup load of an operation, the setup time, the run load of an operation, and the run time (see Section 12.1.2 for an explanation of these terms) on the basis of the actual load recorded during the processes. These values are then combined with other measurements to determine standard quantities and standard times.

As far as possible, standard costs, cost rates, quantities, and times should not change over the course of a budget period. However, it may be necessary to modify standard values over a budget period if the average values vary widely from these standard values.

As a *prerequisite* for calculating standard costs and quantities, the processes must be easy to measure and occur sufficiently frequently to allow the calculation of a statistical mean. They must also exhibit a degree of continuity, so that the predetermined standard quantities, times, costs, and cost rates will still be meaningful in the future.

15.1.3 Variable Costs and Fixed Costs

The *variable costs* for a product or order change with the number of products produced or procured. The company does not incur variable costs unless it actually makes and sells a unit of production.

Variable costs include the wages of production workers or salespeople, the cost of raw materials or purchased components, subcontracted operations, electric power to run machines during production, and so on. As a rule of thumb, the following statement applies:

"Variable costs are all those costs that would not be incurred if we did not produce or procure anything."

The *fixed costs* for a product or order are the costs that are not variable; they remain the same regardless of the level of production and sales.

Fixed costs remain constant even when activity levels change. Some typical examples include the production infrastructure (buildings, depreciation, property taxes, mortgage payments, insurance, salaries of foremen or departmental managers, heating), R&D, and so on.

Of course, fixed costs are "fixed" only for a certain period of time. Above this time threshold, they show step-wise jumps.

Step-function costs or *semifixed costs* have a habit of jumping in a step-wise fashion over time. For example, demand — and thus production — may increase and require a company to purchase new production equipment or to rent or purchase an additional building. Investments in infrastructure improvement or the hiring of new personnel will result in smaller step-wise jumps in the cost curve.

It is common practice to capitalize and depreciate investments that will be used for more than one year. Depreciation costs and ongoing fixed costs per year must then be allocated to individual orders using a formula or measure as the basis of apportionment. See also Section 15.1.4.

In most cases, direct costs are variable costs as defined above. Overhead costs are normally fixed costs.

However, costs are defined as fixed or variable with respect to specific cost objects. Therefore, some *overhead costs* can be *variable*, such as the cost of the energy used directly for the production process. A (rare) example of *direct fixed costs* is the capital costs that can be allocated directly to a production contract, such as fixed annual license fees.

Full costs for a product or order are the sum of the variable costs plus a reasonable portion of the fixed costs.

This reasonable allocation of fixed costs to products or orders entails the same problem as the "fair" distribution of fixed costs does. It is not possible in this chapter to go into the advantages and disadvantages of *variable costing* (fixed overhead not included in computation of unit product cost) or *full costing* (also called *absorption costing*, includes portion of fixed costs); a large body of literature is available on the topic. In general, though, it is important that the company can perform calculations using both of these costing principles. Furthermore, there are specific requirements for external financial reporting.

15.1.4 Cost Accumulation Breakdown: The Cost Breakdown Structure of a Product

For calculating the product costs, the product structure is used.

The *cost accumulation breakdown*, or *cost breakdown structure of a product*, is the accumulation of manufacturing costs in various subdivisions of costs, or *cost types*, according to the product structure.

Figure 15.1.4.1 shows an example cost accumulation breakdown. It is a breakdown of costs for managerial accounting used by a manufacturing company.

Material costs are the costs associated with purchased components.

Material costs are subdivided into two cost subtypes:

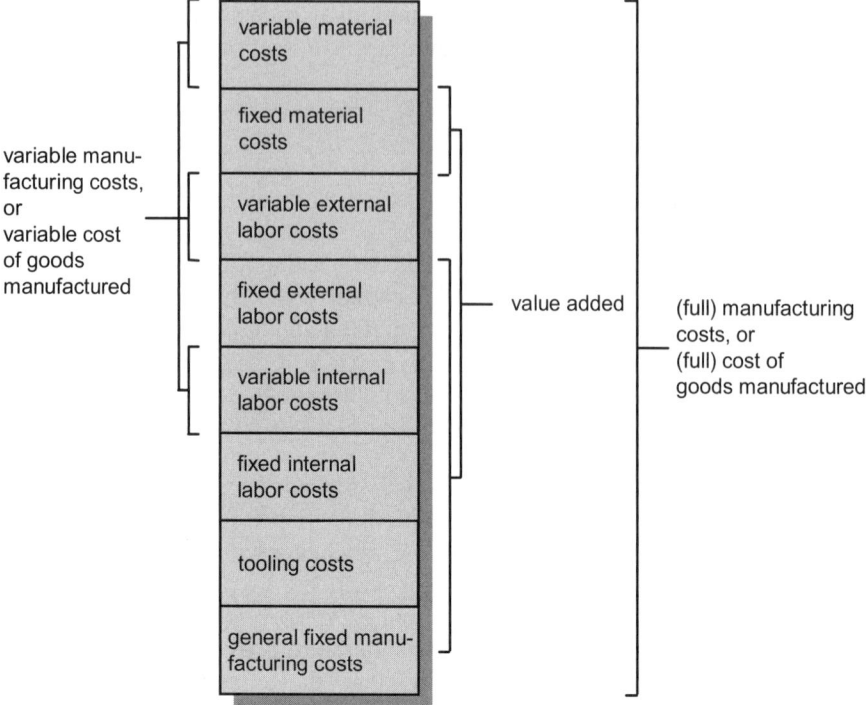

Fig. 15.1.4.1   Example cost accumulation structure, or cost breakdown structure of a product.

- The *variable material costs* for a product are the sum of:
    - The cost of purchased components (the true procurement costs)
    - The variable material costs for all components produced in-house

    Note: This definition is narrower than that utilized by many American costing systems, where material costs also include the full cost of goods manufactured for components produced in-house (variable and fixed), rather than just the variable material costs (principle of the "make or buy" decision).[1]

- The *fixed material costs*, comprised of

---

[1]   In that case, the term *component costs* would be more appropriate than *material costs* (see the definition of the terms *material* and *components* in Section 1.1.1).

- Costs of supplier and component qualification
- Purchasing costs
- Carrying costs
- Costs of receiving and inspecting purchased goods

The simplest way to account for fixed material costs is to calculate a percentage of the variable material costs by dividing the total fixed costs by the total turnover of goods with variable costs. This calculation is always carried out at the end of a budget fiscal period, using the data for the period just ended. It serves as the forecast for the next period.

It is also possible to use different percentages as a function of the stock location (different buildings, refrigerators, special packaging, etc.) or as a function of the type or value of the goods (such as iron, gold, wood). This means, however, that the fixed costs must be recorded separately for the various categories.[2]

External labor costs are the costs associated with the subcontracting of work.

Work may be subcontracted because the necessary production techniques, infrastructure (special machines), or capacity are not available in-house. For financial accounting, special cost centers are defined for such operations. The identification used for the cost center may be the same as the supplier identification. External labor costs are further subdivided into two subtypes:

- *Variable external labor costs* are the sum of all invoices arising from work subcontracted to suppliers, and they contain the suppliers' fixed costs. For the subcontracting company, on the other hand, these costs are variable costs.

- *Fixed external labor costs* are the various costs generated by the subcontracting of work, particularly:
  - Cost of shipping and transporting goods to and from the supplier

---

[2] This type of costing becomes more time consuming if a very precise percentage is required in order to allocate costs more "fairly" to products. Here, measuring the costs may even raise product prices. This also holds for activity-based costing (Section 15.4).

- Cost of receiving and inspecting the goods processed by subcontractors
- Administrative expenses associated with subcontracting work (evaluation, writing the order, and so on)

Just like fixed material costs, fixed external costs are also expressed as a percentage in relation to the total invoiced amount for subcontracted work. Again, we can apply different percentages to different categories of suppliers, in which case the fixed costs must be recorded separately for each of the categories. As with material costs, the percentages are calculated at the end of a budget period and then serve as forecasts for the next budget period.

Internal labor costs are the sum of the costs for all in-house operations to manufacture the product.

Every internal operation is assigned to a work center,[3] for which two cost rates are established. A cost rate is related to a capacity unit, that is, the unit of measure of the capacity for a work center (mostly an hour).

- The *cost rate for variable internal labor costs*. This includes the costs for wages, plant utilities, plant supplies used, and so on that are needed in order to carry out the operation. The cost rate is essentially determined either directly or by measurement.

- The *cost rate for fixed internal labor costs*. This includes the depreciation costs for both machinery and infrastructure and tools and devices, provided that tools and devices are not depreciated independently of the machinery. It also includes ongoing costs, such as operations management. The cost rate is always calculated at the end of a budget period and is used as the forecast for the next period. The total fixed costs are then divided by the forecast load quantity for the next budget period for each work center.

The variable and fixed costs of an operation are calculated by multiplying the *standard load of an operation* (see Figure 12.1.2.2) by the cost rate for variable or fixed costs.

The *tooling costs* for an operation are the costs incurred by the use of tools during that operation.

---

[3] In some cases, the operation is assigned to two work centers: the machine and the person.

In the past, tooling costs were regarded as part of the fixed costs for a capacity unit. Today, they represent such a large proportion of the costs and often differ so widely for each manufactured product that it is more sensible to set them out separately. The following technique, which accords with the activity-based costing approach (see Section 15.4), provides an illustration:

- The tooling costs per operation are calculated by multiplying the batch size by the cost rate per tool use, which is part of the master data for the tool (see also Section 16.2.7). We calculate the cost rate per tool use by dividing the amount to be depreciated by the expected number of uses of the tool.

- The actual number of uses of the tool (a cost driver) is recorded by the shop floor data collection system during the operation in question and is then stored in the master and inventory data for the tool. We can thus compare the actual number of uses against the budgeted number of uses for the tool. The cost rate can then be adjusted depending on the results of the comparison.

The *general fixed manufacturing cost* are the (fixed) costs for everything not associated directly with the design and manufacturing process or production infrastructure.

Typical general fixed manufacturing costs include:

- Licenses
- R&D costs
- General planning & control, manufacturing process development, and production management

These are usually calculated using one or more percentages that relate to the sum of these costs. The sum of all of the general fixed manufacturing costs is divided by the full cost of goods manufactured mentioned above. Again, this calculation takes place at the end of a budget period and serves as the basis for the forecast for the next period.

Variable cost of goods manufactured, or *variable manufacturing costs*, are the sum of all the variable cost for the product.

(Full) cost of goods manufactured, or *(full) manufacturing cost* for the product, is the sum of all the variable and fixed costs for the product.

In addition to the fixed costs mentioned above, there are also:

Sales and administration costs, which are the costs incurred by marketing, sales and distribution, finance and accounting, personnel, and company management.

Sales and administration costs are expressed as a percentage in relation to the full cost of goods manufactured. This percentage is calculated by dividing the accumulated fixed sales and administration costs by the full cost of goods manufactured during the budget period, again at the end of the budget period. The result is used as the basis for the forecast for the next period.

The *cost of sales* of a product is the sum of the manufacturing costs and the sales and administrative costs for the product.[4]

Another important concept is that of the *value added* of a product. This is defined as the full cost of goods manufactured minus

- Variable material costs
- Variable external production costs
- A part of the general fixed manufacturing costs (such as licenses)

Value-added is thus an organization's own output.[5] Its complement are purchased products or services. This definition of added value also serves as the basis for some aspects of taxation.

The variable costs of goods manufactured serve as the short-term lower limit for the sales price (variable, costing) or partial costing, while the full cost of goods manufactured can be regarded as the medium-term lower limit for the sales price (full costing, absorption costing). The sales price then — ideally — includes a profit margin in addition to the cost of sales.

For complete costing, costs must be broken down into all eight cost types for each item. The full manufacturing costs can then be derived simply by adding the cost types together.

---

[4]   *General and administrative expenses (G and A)* are the sum of general fixed manufacturing costs and sales and administration costs.

[5]   This is the added value from the point of view of the manufacturer, in contrast to added value from the customer's viewpoint (see Section 3.1.2).

15.2   Cost Estimating

15.2.1 An Algorithm for Cost Estimation of Goods Manufactured

Cost estimating for cost of goods manufactured is based on the master data. We can illustrate this using an example product, a *ball bearing*, according to Figure 15.2.1.1.

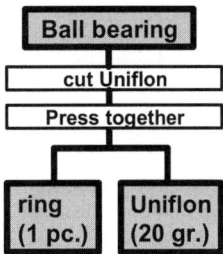

Fig. 15.2.1.1   A ball bearing as an example product.

- The product *ball bearing* (Item ID 83569) consists of two components, a *ring* (Item ID 83593, a semifinished product manufactured in-house) and *Uniflon* (Item ID 83607, a purchased raw material). The bill of material for the product thus has two positions.

- The ball bearing (Item ID 83569) is produced in two operations: *cut Uniflon* (position 250 at work center ID 907501, "manual production") and *press together* (position 270 at work center ID 908301, "special pressing"). The routing sheet for the product thus contains two operations.

In the case under consideration, there are other components, or operations. For the sake of simplicity, however, only these two components (respectively these two operations) are listed here.

In order to obtain the *costs per unit produced*, we must:

- Add together the costs for the entire batch and divide them by the batch size, or

- Divide the setup load of an operation by the batch size.

To estimate the costs, we must then calculate the costs for each of the cost types in Section 15.1.4. For the sake of simplicity, the algorithm in Figure 15.2.1.2 uses only three cost types as illustrations.

1 Variable material costs

- Treat each component of the bill of material for the product as follows:
  - Determine the *item* object associated with each component and determine the cost rate for the variable material costs for one unit of measure of that item.
  - Calculate the component costs by multiplying the quantity of the component incorporated into the product by this cost rate.
- Add together the component costs of all the components in the bill of material.

2 Internal labor costs per unit of measure at this structure level

- Treat each operation on the route sheet for the product as follows:
  - Determine the standard load for the operation.
  - Determine the *work center* object associated with each operation and determine the cost rate for the variable internal labor costs and the fixed internal labor costs for one capacity unit.
  - Calculate the variable and fixed operation costs by multiplying the standard load for the operation by the relevant cost rate.
- Add together all the variable and fixed operation costs for all operations on the routing sheet.

3 Internal labor costs per unit of measure at all structure levels

- Calculate the labor costs per unit produced at all lower production structure levels as follows:
  - Handle every component of the bill of material for the product as follows:
    - Determine the *item* object associated with each component and determine the cost rate for the variable internal labor costs and the fixed internal labor costs for one unit of measure of that item.
    - Calculate the variable and fixed labor costs for the component by multiplying the quantity of the component built into the product by the relevant cost rate.
  - Add together the variable and fixed labor costs of all components on the bill of material.
- Add to these the variable and fixed operation costs of all operations on the routing sheet for this level, as specified in step 2.

End of algorithm

Fig. 15.2.1.2   Algorithm for estimating the cost of a product (shown for three cost types).

Figure 15.2.1.3 shows the data flow of the cost-estimating algorithm described above.

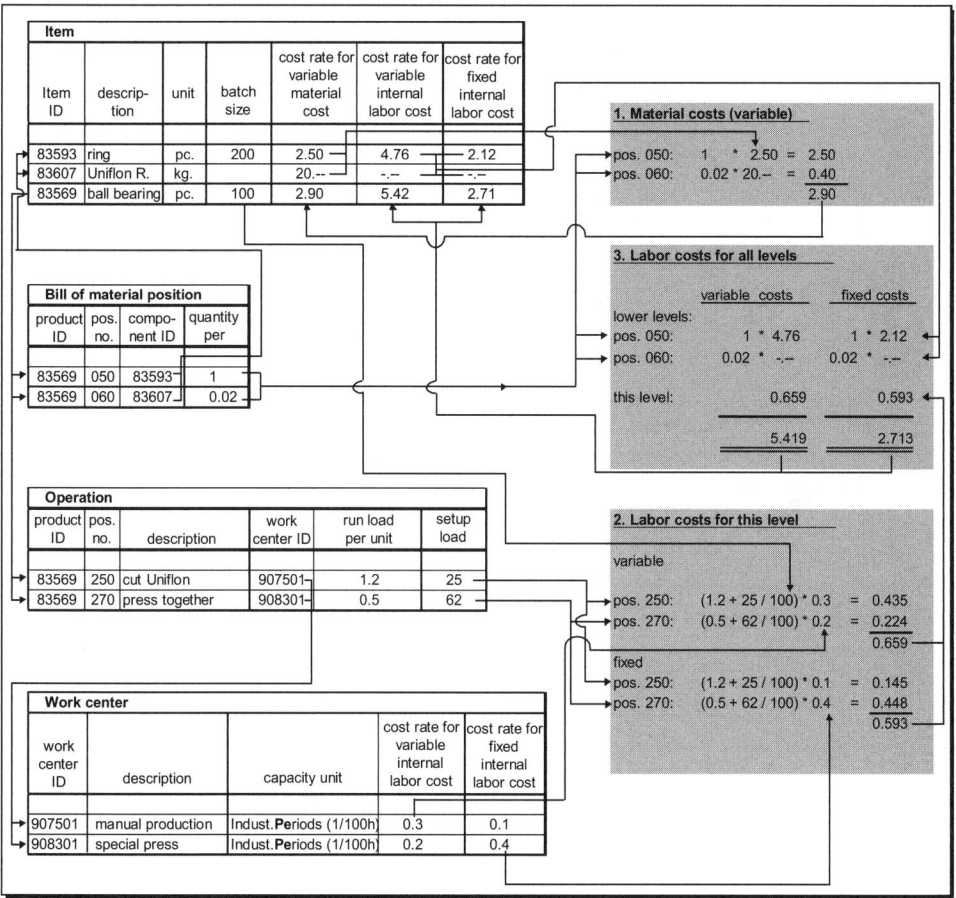

Fig. 15.2.1.3   Algorithm for estimating the cost of a product.

The three steps outlined above are shown in the gray section. The spreadsheet section shows the *item* (first table with three objects) and *work center* (fourth table with two objects) business objects. The *bill of material* business object (second table) is divided into detailed logistics objects, specifically into bill of material positions corresponding to the components. The operations are shown for the *routing sheet* business object (third table). See also the detailed description of the object and entity classes in Sections 16.2.1 to 16.2.8, in particular the Figures 16.2.1.1 and 16.2.8.1. The arrows in Figure 15.2.1.3 indicate the sources and usage of the data in the individual calculations.

15.2.2 Representation of the Cost Accumulation and Comprehensive Calculation for a Product Line

Figure 15.2.2.1 shows one possible way of representing the results of the (single-stage) *cost accumulation* for an individual product. Here, again, the *ball bearing* product from Section 15.2.1 is used as an example.

Cost Accumulation

Product ID: 83569   Description: Ball bearing   Batch size (order quantity): 5000   Actual quantity: 5000

pos.	text	fix. var.	comp. ID Wrk.-C. ID	setup load	quantity per / run load per unit	total qty. / load target	total qty. / load actual	unit	cost per unit	cost target	cost actual
1	ring (materials)	var.	83593		1	5000	0	pc.	2.50	12500.–	0
2	ring (labor)	var.	83593		1	5000	0	pc.	4.76	23800.–	0
3	ring (labor)	fix.	83593		1	5000	0	pc.	2.12	10600.–	0
4	Uniflon (materials)	var.	83607		0.02	100	0	kg.	20.00	2000.–	0
5	cut uniflon	var.	907501	25	1.2	6025	0	Pe	0.3	1807.50	0
6	cut uniflon	fix.	907501	25	1.2	6025	0	Pe	0.1	602.50	0
7	press together	var.	908301	62	0.5	2562	0	Pe	0.2	512.40	0
8	press together	fix.	908301	62	0.5	2562	0	Pe	0.4	1024.80	0

costs per batch / order quantity		costs per batch / actual quantity			costs per batch	
target	actual	target	actual	cost type	target	actual
2.90	0	2.90	0	variable material costs	14500.–	0
5.22	0	5.22	0	variable internal labor costs	26119.90	0
8.12	0	8.12	0	variable cost of goods manufactured	40619.90	0
2.45	0	2.45	0	fixed internal labor costs	12227.30	0
10.57	0	10.57	0	(full) cost of goods manufactured	52847.20	0

Fig. 15.2.2.1   Graphical representation of the cost accumulation for a product.

In this graphical representation, you can see that this is an *estimated-cost accumulation*, as only the *target costs* column has been completed. For *on-going job-order cost accumulation*, we would enter data collected from the shop floor into the *actual* column. Division by the batch size is performed only at the very end. However, first the run load per unit must be multiplied by the batch size. Compare the results of the calculation for batch size 5000 with the calculation in Figure 15.2.1.3 (where batch size is 100).

If the bill of material for a product contains components produced in-house, the costs must be estimated for these items first. Only then should we calculate the costs for the product itself into which the components are built. This is best achieved by estimating the costs for all components manufactured in-house, vertically along the tree structure, using a depth-first search. Once we have estimated the costs for all the components at one level, we can estimate the costs for the higher level product when we return to the next highest level of the tree structure.

If the entire line of products for sale has to be recalculated, it is more efficient to take the individual items in descending order of their low-level code. We start by calculating the costs for individual parts and subassemblies at the lowest possible level and end with the finished product. We can proceed in this order, because we have already calculated the level codes.

For components produced to order, which are produced on demand for the higher level product rather than being stored, we can integrate the cost accumulation for each component directly into the cost accumulation for this product. Since the batch that is produced depends on the product batch, the result will be different every time.

If the end product is a product family with many variants, rather than a stock item, we can combine different parameter values in the estimated-cost accumulation. In this way, we can calculate various points of support for product costs in the n-dimensional parameter space. These combinations of parameter values should then be stored in parameter value lists under the *item* object and introduced into the estimated-cost accumulation as shown in Figure 15.2.2.1.

15.3   Job-Order Costing

15.3.1 Actual Quantities and Actual Costs

The *actual quantities* are the quantities of components and capacity used for an order.

The shop floor data collection system (see Section 14.3) provides the data on the actual quantities for a production, procurement or R&D order. The actual quantities are generally used as a factor in calculating actual costs:

The *actual order costs* are the costs generated by an order.

In simple cases, we can determine the actual order costs as follows:

> *Backflush costing* is the application of costs based on the output of a process. It works backward to flush out the costs for the units produced, applying costs using standard costs. Backflush costing is usually associated with repetitive manufacturing environments.

In all other cases, we determine actual order costs by an accumulation of job-order costs according to the following *cost identification techniques*:

- *Standard costing* or *standard cost (accounting) system*: actual (used or consumed) quantities times standard cost rates for variable and fixed costs.

- *Normal costing* or *normal cost system*: invoiced amounts or actual cost of wages for variable costs, actual (used or consumed) quantities times standard cost rates for fixed costs.

- *Actual costing* or *actual cost system*: invoiced amounts or actual cost of wages for variable and fixed costs.

We thus obtain a total for each of the individual cost types in correspondence to the cost accumulation breakdown shown in Figure 15.1.4.1. The algorithm for job-order costing corresponds to the procedure illustrated in Figure 15.2.2.1. Here, the data are taken from the business object *order*, rather than from the master data (see Section 16.1 for further details). In the costing method shown in Figure 15.2.2.1, the *actual values* are entered into the columns on an ongoing basis (ongoing job-order cost accumulation). The values listed correspond to usage by the reported operations and the parts issued. In this way, we can continuously track the costs of every production order and compare them against the *target values*. Continuous comparison is particularly important for production according to customer orders, since these are subject to a budget. This will identify the likely profit or loss at a relatively early stage, enabling us to take corrective action in good time.

For the comparison to be meaningful the cost identification techniques used for cost estimating and job-order costing must be the same. However, for some types of costs this may not be the case:

- For actual costing, the invoices for materials or external operations may arrive much too late for efficient control of internal operations. If this is the case, we can then fall back on the standard load or the actual quantities valued at standard cost rates.

- Global invoicing may sometimes make it difficult to assign costs fairly to individual resources obtained externally, which means that standard cost rates may prove to be just as accurate. These standard cost rates are again multiplied by the actual quantities.

- The valuation of material costs on the basis of standard cost rates may be inaccurate due to large fluctuations in the cost of purchased items. Under these circumstances it may be necessary to use the average costs as a basis or to value certain materials at the actual cost of the procurement batches.

If actual costing is chosen as the cost identification technique, then the estimated-cost accumulation essentially reflects the most recent order. We may, however, impose a budget on the individual cost types that does not necessarily correspond to the total standard costs for the underlying operations or individual items issued. If the budgets correspond to the expected revenue, then the ongoing comparison of estimated cost (budget) against job-order cost accumulation leads directly to the expected revenue from the order.

15.3.2 Cost Analysis

Cost analysis seeks to reveal *significant variances* (i.e., variances that exceed established thresholds) of actual costs of an order (the actual order costs) from target costs.

Volume variances occur when the resources consumed deviate in quantity from planned quantities.

There are various causes for volume variances:

- *Volume variances in an internal operation.* Here, the actual load differs from the standard load because:
    - Unanticipated incidents occur during production.
    - The work center efficiency or efficiency rate (in a time period) is better or worse than expected.
    - The specified quantity of standard capacity requirement is wrong, or the quantity consumed is recorded incorrectly.
    - Additional operations are needed for reworking.

- *Volume variances for a component* or *an external operation.* The quantities consumed differ from the quantities specified on the bill of material or route sheet, because:
    - The wrong standards (estimates) were used.

- Goods are lost or scrapped.

- *Variances in the costs per unit produced.* If scrap is produced, the quantity actually produced may be less than the quantity ordered, in which case the cost of goods manufactured *per unit produced* will be higher than expected, because most of the components and resources were used for the initial operations in accordance with the original quantity ordered.

Standard costing reveals all these variances through a simple comparison of the job-order cost against the estimated cost accumulation. Since the underlying cost rates remain the same, the job-order cost accumulation highlights any volume variances.

Cost variances are deviations between actual and standard costs.

Cost accounting analyzes the various cost variances, namely:

- Variances between the actual costs of the purchased components and the standard costs for the same items.
- *Variances of the actual costs of a capacity unit of a work center.* The costs per capacity unit are predicted for the future based on past values in the form of a forecast. At the end of the budget period, this reveals variances arising from undercapacity or overcapacity, meaning that fixed costs should actually have been divided by a different load.

When basing costing on the actual costs, comparison of job-order and estimated-cost accumulations yields variances that encompass both volume and cost variances. In order to show these variances separately, we must add a third column that captures "actual quantities at standard cost rates." However, we can only do this if we know the cost rates when we carry out the estimated-cost accumulation. However, if we specify only the total budget for each cost type, then we cannot show volume variances separately from cost variances.

15.3.3 The Interface from Order Management to Cost Accounting

---

Carried out in the context of production order management, *cost object accounting*, e.g., *product costing* or *project costing*, is in essence job-order costing as described above.

Cost accounting also performs cost object accounting. Other outputs from cost accounting are cost center accounting and cost object group accounting. To be accurate, all costing systems, in particular, *costing software*, require a regular input of production order data and shop floor data. These data-capturing systems provide the interface to the cost accounting system and allow accumulation of the necessary cost data.

Costing software also manages the value of work in process. The cost accounting department requires a report of every transaction associated with a production order. These transactions include:

- Release or amendment of a production order.

- Every stock issue. Each stock issue increases the value of the work-in-process and reduces the value of inventory by the actual costs.

- Every execution of an operation. The actual cost of the operation is added to the value of the work-in-process. The load on the corresponding work center is reduced.

- Every invoice for delivery of goods or external subcontracting of work. We can also allocate the costs to a dummy inventory account or cost center, rather than the work-in-process, which will then be unloaded by a corresponding issue at standard cost rates.

- Completion of the order. The accumulated value for work-in-process for the order, together with the fixed costs, is charged either to the inventory account or directly to the expense account for customer production orders.

Transactions can be carried over every day. If cost accounting is carried out on a monthly basis, however, the data are transferred immediately before the accounting starts.

Note: At the end of every accounting period — at month's end, for example — all the actual values (such as the quantity consumed or actual costs) must be stored temporarily in a "quantity consumed to end of accounting period" attribute. This can be accomplished by a program that is run at the end of each accounting period. In this way, when the cost accounting department receives the data on the fifth of the month, for example, it receives the values stored in the temporary attributes. This is because the actual "quantity consumed" attribute now contains the usage that has accumulated in the new accounting period.

15.4   Activity-Based Costing

15.4.1 Limits of Traditional Product Costing

Job-order costing allocates fixed costs (overhead) by an extra charge, expressed as a percentage of the variable costs of labor and materials.

In the simplest case, this percentage is either a single percentage or multiplication factor for the variable cost of goods manufactured or two different percentages for material costs and labor costs, as shown in Figure 15.4.1.1. This traditional overhead-cost-allocation process thus allocates overheads to products using direct material and labor costs (for example, labor hours or machine hours) as the basis for allocation.

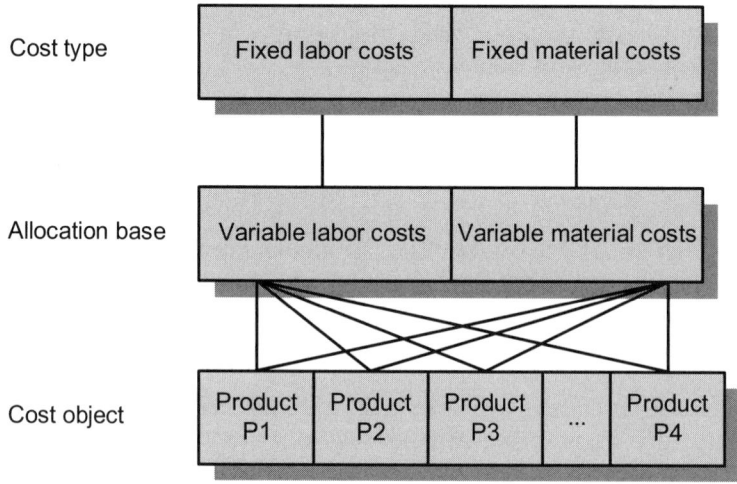

Fig. 15.4.1.1   Allocating fixed costs to products with conventional cost accounting using two cost types.

There has been a rapid explosion of the value of these simple job-order costing factors over the past two decades, mainly because internal labor costs have moved rapidly in the direction of fixed internal labor costs (machines, tools, etc.). Today, there are some companies with a ratio of fixed to variable costs of 10 to 1, meaning that variable costs represent just 10% of the manufacturing costs for the entire organization. The remainder is made up of fixed costs of various types (see also Figure 15.1.4.1), specifically:

- Material procurement and storage costs

- The cost of managing subcontracted operations
- Machinery, tool, production facility, and infrastructure costs
- The costs of research, development, licensing, product and process design, planning & control, etc.

Problems arise with conventional costing, for the focus remains on the variable costs. Often, the reduction in variable costs will merely increase the multiplication factor, since the same fixed costs are then simply distributed among fewer variable costs. If the organization has a broad product concept, such as mixed manufacturing with products ranging from products made to customer specification (which may change from one order to the next) through to standard products with no variants, this results in the distortion shown in Figure 15.4.1.2.

As a result, too much overhead is attributed to products produced with high variable costs — often standard products — and too little overhead is attributed to products with low variable costs — often products according to (changing) customer specification. In the example, P1 — having high variable costs (the black portion) — is over-costed with fixed costs (the white portion), and P2 — having low variable costs, is under-costed with fixed costs.

Since the cost of goods manufactured is used as the basis for pricing, this misallocation of fixed costs would tend to result in less complex products (technically and logistically) being put on the market at too high a price, while too low a price would be charged for complex products. This would mean that a company could lose its competitive edge for series and mass-produced items — not because of the high cost of wages or other factors, but due to the costing system itself!

The problems with conventional costing came to light with respect to investment in qualification of employees and machinery. These investments raised the fixed costs and had a disproportionately large effect on the very product range for which the investments had targeted more efficient production. It is not surprising that the new production methods resulted in a demand for a new way of thinking about costs. The new type of costing system proposed and developed was activity-based costing (ABC).

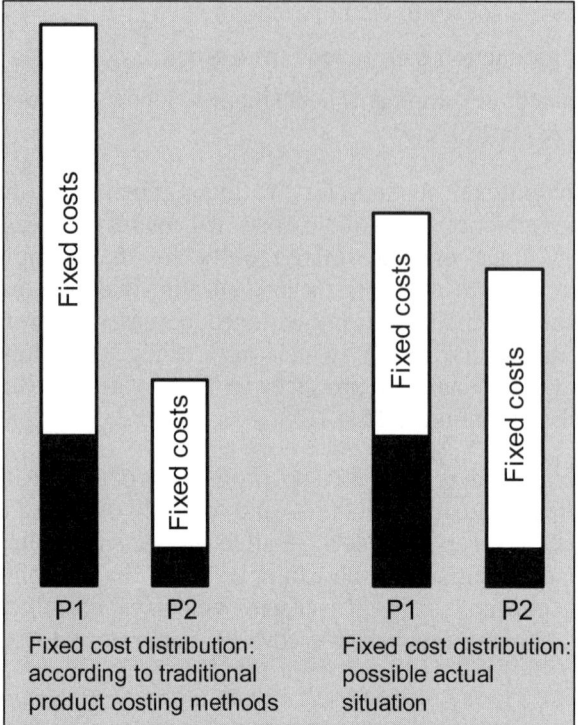

Fig. 15.4.1.2   Potential for error in traditional product costing.

15.4.2 Introducing Activity-Based Costing: Aim, Basic Premise, Requirements, and Technique

Activity-based costing, or activity-based cost accounting (ABC), is a cost accounting system designed to allocate fixed costs (overhead) as fairly and realistically as possible to the business processes.

The *aim* of activity-based costing is thus essentially not new. However, achievement of the aim means better performance on the following tasks:

- *Process management:* Planned investments can be linked to specific processes right from the outset. The resulting investment costs can be converted into corresponding process costs and then compared with the previous process costs.

- *Support for decision making in product development:* Developers are informed of the consequences of their choice of purchased components or new design and manufacturing processes at a very early stage. This information usually provides a comparison of different technologies or shows the consequences of changing the product design. This type of information is very important, for cost of a product has essentially been determined by the end of the design phase. After that, very little can be done to influence cost.

- *Product cost estimation:* Activity-based costing, just like conventional costing, is a useful technique for estimating costs. Pricing will be much more accurate if the costs are estimated correctly.

With respect to the *basic premise* behind activity-based costing, the need for a "fair" distribution formula for overhead also means finding a suitable measurement, or allocation base. For this reason, we need to examine our fixed costs in greater detail, tracing them back to the underlying processes — or even subprocesses or individual activities. In Section 15.1.4 we demonstrated how fixed material costs can be calculated differently for different groups of materials or cost centers. This is one step towards the principle illustrated below.

An *ABC process* is a process or activity that incurs extensive fixed costs in the company and thus is allocated to business processes using ABC.

The *process variable* is a unit against which we can measure the costs for the ABC process or activity in a suitable manner. This is called the *activity cost driver*. ABC uses activity cost drivers to allocate the costs to cost objects, such as products, in relation to the resources consumed.

In most cases, the activity cost driver is not associated with variable costs or an underlying time unit. Instead, activity cost drivers are, for example, the number of purchase orders, the number of items received, or the number of components for an assembly. If business processes or activities are identified and broken down with sufficient detail into subprocesses, the cost driver is usually easy to identify the fixed costs can now be related to the products by using the cost drivers. The methods used here are similar to those that were used in traditional *time studies* in process planning for establishing *time standards*: count, measure, and calculate average.

The *process cost rate* or *planned cost rate* for every ABC (sub-)process is the cost rate for an activity cost driver.

An ABC process or subprocess thus not only represents an actual process. Together with its process cost rate, it also represents a traditional work center or cost center and the associated cost rate. Processes can also be recorded in this way, especially in computer-supported systems.

The *ABC process plan* for each product is a list of all the ABC processes (activities) that a product requires while it is being produced or procured.

The *process quantity* is the quantity as measured by the activity cost drivers that is likely to be used in an ABC process for the product.

The structure of an ABC process plan is similar to that of a routing sheet (see Section 1.2.3).[6] One ABC process plan position is assigned to every ABC process required to produce or procure the product. These positions correspond to the operations. The process quantity corresponds to the standard load of an operation. This means that we can keep ABC process plans in exactly the same way as routing sheets, particularly if the system is computer supported.

Activity-based costing is thus based on the calculation of standard cost rates. The *requirement* for such activity-based costing is that the ABC processes must be clearly measurable and repetitive (see Section 15.1.2). Such processes can be found in the operational management of an organization, in logistics, and in accounting. It is in these areas that activity-based costing can be implemented successfully. The technique is more difficult to implement at the strategic level, since few repetitive ABC processes can be identified at this level (or, if they do exist, they relate to an extremely long period of time). Even if we could identify an activity cost driver, it would still not be possible to accurately determine the process quantity per product, i.e., the usage of process variables.

Figure 15.4.2.1 shows several examples of processes (activities) and process variables (activity cost drivers) in the areas of purchasing and production.

---

[6]   The term *ABC process plan* is used here mainly to emphasize that this is not the same as the process plan introduced in Section 1.2.3. The latter process plan includes the product structure and the time axis in addition to the routing sheet.

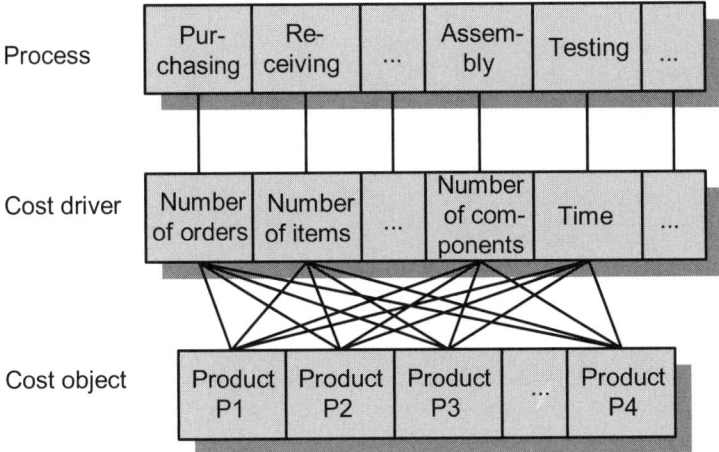

Fig. 15.4.2.1 Allocating fixed costs using activity-based cost accounting.

Examples of process cost rates associated with the process variables in Figure 15.4.2.1 are

- x dollars per order
- y dollars per item in receiving
- z dollars per component in assembly
- u dollars per run time unit in the testing process

The separation of tooling costs from fixed internal manufacturing costs described in Section 15.1.4 is one example of activity-based costing. There, the (ABC) process of tool utilization is considered separately. The activity cost driver may be the same as the tool utilization time or even, as suggested, simply the use of that tool to manufacture one unit of the batch.

To *introduce activity-based costing into the company,* the following steps are necessary:

1. *Determine the areas* in which activity-based costing is to be used.

2. *Determine the ABC processes, broken down into subprocesses (activities).* A meaningful ABC (sub-)process has at least the following characteristics:
   - The costs of the process are significant.
   - The process corresponds to a specific task within the process organization.
   - The various products (cost objects) should use the process to varying degrees (different process quantities).

3. *Determine the process variable (activity cost driver) for each process.* A good process variable has at least the following characteristics:

   - It is so closely related to the process costs that the process quantities can be based upon this unit variable.
   - It is self-explanatory to the people concerned within the organization, since it appears to be a natural variable within the operational process.
   - It should also appear to be a natural variable when options for different design variants or production methods are compared against one another.
   - The process quantities and cost rate per unit (process cost rate or process rate) can, as far as possible, be automatically calculated from the operational data.

4. *Determine the process cost rate for each ABC process.* This is done by dividing the fixed costs resulting from the process by the likely future process quantities.

5. *Specify the ABC process plan for each product and the process quantity for each ABC process in the ABC process plan.*

6. *Calculate the process costs for the product* by analyzing the ABC process plan (and the bill of material, of course) with the same algorithm used for production or procurement costs calculated using the traditional order costs or job order costing technique (see Section 15.2).

7. *Job-order costing and analyzing variances:* As in conventional costing, the volume variance can now be calculated for a particular order by recording the actual usage of process variables. Activity-based costing should thus identify any deviation from planned unit cost rates and compare actual process costs against the budgeted costs. This type of measurement is rather illusory, however, since small process quantities would take much too long to measure.

15.4.3 Typical Processes (Activities) and Process Variables

The following example, taken from [Schm92], shows how ABC is used in practice in the areas of production and purchasing. Figure 15.4.3.1 shows assembly of a printed circuit board, together with the main processes and subprocesses (activities), as well as the associated process variables.

Production: circuit board assembly

Main process	Subprocess, activity	Process variable
Automatic assembly	DIP insertion AXIAL insertion ROBOTIC insertion SMT insertion	Insertions Insertions Insertions Insertions
Manual insertion	Setup Manual insertion IC programming	Components Insertions Seconds
Soldering	Wave soldering Infrared	Piece (circuit board) Piece (circuit board)
Testing	ATS operation ATS engineering	Tested components Test adapter
Reworking		Time

Fig. 15.4.3.1   Determining main processes and subprocesses; example: circuit board assembly.

Figure 15.4.3.2 shows activities in a conventional purchase department.

Purchasing

Main process	Cost distribution %	Subprocess, activity	Process variable
Inventory management	50 50	Order management Inventory management	Order Item
Materials purchasing	70 30	Supplier management Order management	Supplier Order
Trade goods	70 30	Order management Inventory management	Order Product
Parts specification	100		Bill of material entry
Materials engineering	50 50	Supplier qualification Component qual.check.	Supplier Component
Planning	70 30	Assembly management Order planning	Assembly Production order
Warehouse	50 50	Stock room issues/receipts	Number of item ID transactions
Integration	100		Products
Shipping	100		Crates / boxes
Freight		International/ local freight	Distance / weight

Fig. 15.4.3.2   Determining main processes and subprocesses; example: procurement.

15.4.4 Activity-Based Product Cost Estimation

Figure 15.4.4.1 shows another example, taken again from [Schm92]. Here, "supplier management" is a subprocess of the main process "materials purchasing."

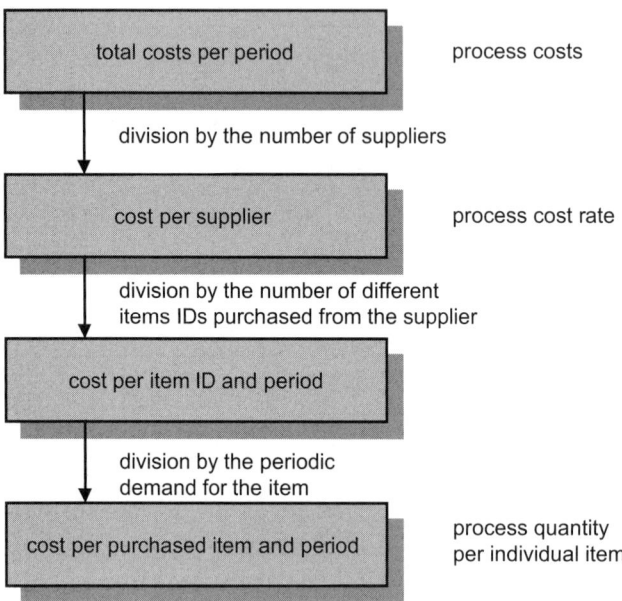

Fig. 15.4.4.1   Determining the process cost rate and process quantity for supplier management.

The process costs are recorded for a period of time (in this case, six months). The process variable is the supplier. The process cost rate, i.e., the process rate, is determined by simply dividing the process costs by the number of suppliers. The number of different items procured from the supplier and the usage for each of these items over the time period determines process quantity. This provides the process quantity of each component that is incorporated into one product.

Figure 15.4.4.2 provides a quantitative example using simple data for illustrative purposes. It reveals the difference between the process costs for supplier management with just one supplier and a large number of purchased items with a high turnover and the process costs for one supplier with just a few purchased items and a correspondingly lower turnover.

		standard component	exotic component
process costs	500 000 . -		
number of suppliers	100		
process cost rate	5 000 . -		
		standard component	exotic component
number of different purchased item IDs		200	5
∅ periodic requirements per article		1000	50
process quantity per individual purchased item		1	1
		200·1000	5·50
process costs per individual purchased item		0.025	20 . -

Fig. 15.4.4.2   Determining the process cost rate for a single item in the "supplier management" process: "standard component" versus "exotic component."

Figure 15.4.4.3 extends the supplier management example to include a costing for the entire purchasing process.

Here, again, the difference in process costs mentioned above stands out clearly. With conventional costing, in contrast, if the same additional percentage for material costs is applied to both the standard component and the exotic component, the loaded fixed material costs will be the same, even though the one is much more expensive to purchase than the other.

The next two examples show the *activity-based product cost estimation* for a manufactured item and a purchased item, each based on an ABC process plan. Figure 15.4.4.4 relates to the main processes and subprocesses of a product *manufactured in-house* that were shown in Figure 15.4.3.1. The individual positions are very similar to those that would be found on a normal routing sheet. In this case, however, "Process ID" replaces the work center. The administrative process plan positions for order management and stock issues/receipts, for example, would also be shown in addition to the operations. To calculate the cost of goods manufactured, we would also normally include the operations found on the normal routing sheet. They would be used only to calculate the variable costs, however.

Main process / sub process / Divisors for process quantities	Cost driver	Process for a standard component (Quantity · cost rate = costs)			Process for an "exotic component" (Quantity · cost rate = costs)		
Divisors for process quantities:							
- Number of different purchased item IDs per supplier			200			5	
- Ø Periodic requirements for each item			1000			50	
- Ø Number of items per inventory transaction			50			10	
- Number of orders per period			2			1	
Materials purchasing:							
- Supplier management	Supplier	$\frac{1}{200 \cdot 1000}$	5000	0.025	$\frac{1}{5 \cdot 50}$	5000	20
- Purchase order management	Order	$\frac{2}{1000}$	30	0.06	$\frac{1}{50}$	30	0.6
Materials engineering:							
- Supplier qualification	Supplier	$\frac{1}{200 \cdot 1000}$	2000	0.01	$\frac{1}{5 \cdot 50}$	2000	8
- Component quality check	Part ID	$\frac{1}{1000}$	300	0.30	$\frac{1}{50}$	300	6
Warehouse:							
- Store room	Part ID	$\frac{1}{1000}$	100	0.10	$\frac{1}{50}$	100	2
- Issues/Receipts	Trans-action	$\frac{1}{50}$	4	0.08	$\frac{1}{10}$	4	0.4
Total process costs for each individual item				0.575			37.0

Fig. 15.4.4.3   Determining the process costs for external procurement of a single item: "standard component" versus "exotic component."

Figure 15.4.4.5 represents the ABC process plan and the activity-based product cost estimation for a *purchased* item. Main process and subprocesses correspond to those shown in Figure 15.4.3.2, using the example in Figure 15.4.4.3. According to Figure 15.4.4.3, we should allocate $37 to fixed material costs for each built-in "power supply" component. The similarity to a routing sheet is obvious. Standard logistics software can be used to store the ABC process plan.

Item ID: "PC Board"

SEQ	Operation	Description	Process ID	Process quantity	Process cost rate	Process costs
010	4411	Preform	4311	48.0000	0.05	2.40
020	4401	DIP Insertion	4312	110.0000	0.15	16.50
030	4402	Axial Insertion	4313	163.0000	0.10	16.30
050	4400	Manual Insertion	4315	109.0000	0.20	21.80
060	4404	IC Programming	4316	0.1210	200.00	24.20
070	4405	Process Solder	4317	1.0000	1.50	1.50
080	4407	ATS Engineering	4324	0.0050	5000.00	25.00
090	4408	Board Repair	4322	0.0500	40.00	2.00
095	4409	ATS Operating	4318	459.0000	0.01	4.59
Total process costs						114.29

Fig. 15.4.4.4   A typical ABC process plan and activity-based product cost estimation for a produced item.

Item ID: "Power Supply"

Divisors for process quantities: Number of different purchased item IDs per supplier: 5
Average periodic requirements: 50
Number of orders per period: 1
Number of items per stock transaction: 1

SEQ	Operation	Description	Process ID	Process quantity	Process cost rate	Process costs
540	2400	Supplier management	4460	0.004	5000.00	20.00
545	2405	Purchase order management	4460	0.020	30.00	0.60
530	2300	Supplier qualification	4451	0.004	2000.00	8.00
535	2305	Component quality check	4452	0.020	300.00	6.00
550	2500	Store room	4520	0.020	100.00	2.00
555	2505	Receipts / issues	4520	0.100	4.00	0.40
Total process costs						37.00

Fig. 15.4.4.5   A typical ABC process plan and activity-based product cost estimation for a procured item.

15.5   Summary

In a sense, estimated cost and job-order cost accumulations are "by-products" of master data and production order management. The job-order cost accumulation is always current, which is not always the case where costing software is run on a monthly basis, for example. This is just one of the reasons why estimated and job-order cost accumulations are incorporated into computer-supported planning & control systems.

The actual costs cannot always be determined early on. We therefore have to use average costs and standard costs when estimating product costing. These also provide more robust estimates along the time axis. For short-term and long-term pricing purposes, we classify costs as variable and full, i.e., variable and fixed costs.

A cost accumulation breakdown is made up of the cost types associated with a product, such as material costs, labor costs, and general costs, and differentiates between the fixed and variable parts of each type. These costs can also be used to calculate added value.

Cost estimating for a product is thus an algorithm. It calculates the cost of materials from the positions on the bill of material (and the associated component entities) as well as the labor costs from the operations (and the associated work centers) and bill of material positions (for components produced in-house). This means that every component that goes to make up a product is included in the estimated-cost accumulation.

For job-order cost accumulation, we must compare the actual quantities and actual costs collected from the shop floor against target quantities and costs. It is not always possible to determine the actual costs, however. For fixed internal manufacturing costs, "only" standard cost rates are available, and these have to be predetermined at the start of an accounting period. Generally, at least part of the standard cost rate has to be extrapolated from the past. Using standard costs instead of actual costs enables us to distinguish variances in cost and variances in quantity. Every transaction that affects value must be passed on to the costing function. If costing is carried out only on a periodic basis, it is absolutely essential to identify precisely those transactions that belong to a previous period.

Activity-based costing (ABC) is designed to assign fixed costs (overhead) to individual items in a targeted manner. Blocks of fixed costs are subdivided into main processes and subprocesses (or activities) to a level of detail that allows identification of a characteristic activity cost driver (or process variable) for each activity. The activity cost driver is the measure that allows us to relate costs to products. The block of fixed costs is broken down into costs per activity for each of these activities by the shop floor data collection system. This provides a process cost rate for each activity cost driver. The number of item IDs and ultimately the number of items affected by a cost driver unit also have to be determined. The reciprocal of the product of these two numbers is thus the process quantity per item.

An ABC process plan is then assigned to every item in the master data. The ABC process plan contains as many "operations" as there are ABC processes needed in order to produce or procure the item. The standard load is thus the process quantity per "operation." The actual ABC process itself plays the part of a "work center," since it has a unit, an activity cost driver, and a process cost rate. The algorithm for calculating product costs otherwise corresponds to the algorithm used for job-order costing.

ABC is less likely than conventional costing to under-cost or over-cost products and may lead to improvements in pricing. Experience shows that ABC is successful wherever there are repetitive fixed cost processes that are comparable over a long period (that is, at the operational level). If this is not the case, calculating process cost rates and process quantities on an ongoing basis as well as the amount of resources required to keep the ABC database current would be disproportionately expensive relative to the benefit gained from allocating the fixed costs to cost objects more correctly.

15.6   Keywords

ABC (activity-based
    costing), 822
activity cost driver, 823
actual costing, 816
actual quantity, 815
average costs, 803
backflush costing, 816
component costs, 806
cost accumulation, 814
cost accumulation
    breakdown, 805
cost analysis, 817
cost estimating, 800
cost identification
    technique, 816

cost object accounting,
    818
cost of goods
    manufactured, 809
cost of sales, 810
direct costs, 801
general fixed
    manufacturing cost,
    809
indirect costs, 801
job-order costing, 800
labor costs, 807
material costs, 805
normal costing, 816
overhead costs, 801
planned cost rate, 823

process cost rate, 823
process quantity, 824
process variable, 823
product costing, 818
project costing, 818
sales and
    administration costs,
    810
standard cost rate, 803
standard costing, 816
step-function costs, 804
tooling costs, 808
variable cost of goods
    manufactured, 809
variable costs, 804

15.7   Scenarios and Exercises

15.7.1 Job-Order Costing

Two products A and B are produced from material Z with a batch size of 40. Consumption is the same for each product: 50 g per product A or B. The cost of 1 kg of material Z is $20.

For the sake of simplicity and comparison in our example, the *manufacturing process* is the same for products A and B: two operations (1 and 2) at two work centers (WC1 and WC2). The standard time for each operation is 1 hour per 40 units. Assume that setup time is negligible.

To calculate the costs of the manufacturing process, it is important to take into account the costs of the two work centers WC1 and WC2 in addition to the standard times. As Figure 15.7.1.1 shows, WC1 is more machine intensive, while WC2 is more employee intensive. The investments will be depreciated in 5 years, assuming 1000 productive hours per year. Further, assume that these costs make up the full manufacturing costs.

	Work center 1	Work center 2
Variable costs	$20.- / hour (labor cost)	$40.- / hour (labor cost)
Fixed costs	$300,000.- (investitures in machines and tools)	$150,000.- (investitures in machines and tools)

Fig. 15.7.1.1   Work center costs data.

Following the principle of job-order costing, determine the cost accumulation values for products A and B marked "?" in the tables in Figures 15.7.1.2 and 15.7.1.3 (compare Figure 15.2.2.1.)

Hint: The full cost of goods manufactured will be the same for both product A and B (why?): $4.75 per unit produced, or $190 for a batch size of 40.

Cost Accumulation

Product ID: 4711   Description: Product A   Batch size (order quantity): 40   Actual quantity: 0

pos.	text	fix. var.	comp. ID Wrk.-C. ID	setup load	quantity per / run load per unit	total qty./ load target	actual	unit	cost per unit	cost target	actual
1	Material	var.	Z		?	?	0	?	?	?	0
2	Operation 1	var.	WC 1	0	?	?	0	?	?	?	0
3	Operation 1	fix.	WC 1	0	?	?	0	?	?	?	0
4	Operation 2	var.	WC 2	0	?	?	0	?	?	?	0
5	Operation 2	fix.	WC 2	0	?	?	0	?	?	?	0

costs per batch/order quantity		costs per batch/actual quantity			costs per batch	
target	actual	target	actual	cost type	target	actual
?	0	?	0	Variable material costs	?	0
?	0	?	0	Variable internal labor costs	?	0
?	0	?	0	Variable cost of goods manufactured	?	0
?	0	?	0	Fixed internal labor costs	?	0
?	0	?	0	(Full) cost of goods manufactured	?	0

Fig. 15.7.1.2   Graphical representation of the cost accumulation for product A.

Cost Accumulation

Product ID: 4712   Description: Product B   Batch size (order quantity): 40   Actual quantity: 0

pos.	text	fix. var.	comp. ID Wrk.-C. ID	setup load	quantity per / run load per unit	total qty. / load target	actual	unit	cost per unit	cost target	actual
1	Material	var.	Z		?	?	0	?	?	?	0
2	Operation 1	var.	WC 1	0	?	?	0	?	?	?	0
3	Operation 1	fix.	WC 1	0	?	?	0	?	?	?	0
4	Operation 2	var.	WC 2	0	?	?	0	?	?	?	0
5	Operation 2	fix.	WC 2	0	?	?	0	?	?	?	0

costs per batch/order quantity		costs per batch/actual quantity			costs per batch	
target	actual	target	actual	cost type	target	actual
?	0	?	0	Variable material costs	?	0
?	0	?	0	Variable internal labor costs	?	0
?	0	?	0	Variable cost of goods manufactured	?	0
?	0	?	0	Fixed internal labor costs	?	0
?	0	?	0	(Full) cost of goods manufactured	?	0

Fig. 15.7.1.3   Graphical representation of the cost accumulation for product B.

15.7.2 Activity-Based Costing

Think again about products A and B described above. After reading Section 15.1.4, you know that tooling costs make up a sizeable proportion of the fixed costs. If the costs of the tools used for products A and B are different, this should be apparent in the cost accumulation. However, that can only be achieved if we view tool utilization as a process in its own right. Following the principle of ABC and the steps involved (see Section 15.4.2), the characteristic variables for this process are defined as follows:

- *ABC process:* tool utilization, or use.

- *Process costs:* the manufacturing or procurement costs of the tool.

- *Activity cost driver:* the number of units produced with the tool. Why? Usually, it is not the length of time that a tool is utilized that determines its wear, but rather production of a certain number of units of the product. A good example would be pressing tools.

- *Process cost rate:* process costs divided by the total quantity of product units that are produced using the tool until the tool is used up or worn out.

Figure 15.7.2.1 shows a breakdown of the fixed costs in machine costs and costs for tools and devices.

	Work center 1	Work center 2
Variable costs	$20/hour (labor cost)	$40/hour (labor cost)
Fixed costs: investitures in machines	$200,000.-	$100,000.-
Fixed costs: investitures in tools and devices	Tool T1: $4000 (used to manufacture product A) Tool T2: $16000 (used to manufacture product B)	Tool T3: $2000 (used to manufacture product A) Tool T4: $8000 (used to manufacture product B)

Fig. 15.7.2.1   Work center costs data.

As in exercise 15.7.1 above, the investitures in machines will be depreciated in 5 years, whereby 1000 productive hours are assumed annually. It is further assumed that a tool can be used to manufacture 20,000 products A or B before it is used up or worn out, no matter whether it is an expensive or inexpensive tool.

Since one hour of capacity is utilized for 40 units of products A or B, 200,000 products can be manufactured in 5000 productive hours. This means that, in that period, 10 tools will be required.

In the following, assume also that the same number of units of products A and B is manufactured. In this case, work center 1 will use 10 tools (5 T1 and 5 T2 tools), which represents an investment of $100,000. Work center 2 uses 10 tools (5 T3 and 5 T4 tools), which represents an investment of $50,000. The sum of fixed costs is thus the same as in exercise 5 above.

Determine the values marked "?" in the cost accumulation tables in Figures 15.7.2.2 and 15.7.2.3 below (compare Figure 15.2.2.1).

Cost Accumulation

Product ID: 4711   Description: Product A   Batch size (order quantity): 40   Actual quantity: 0

pos.	text	fix var.	comp. ID Wrk.-C. ID	setup load	quantity per / run load per unit	total qty./ load target	actual	unit	cost per unit	cost target	actual
1	Material	var.	Z		?	?	0	?	?	?	0
2	Operation 1	var.	WC 1	0	?	?	0	?	?	?	0
3	Operation 1	fix.	WC 1	0	?	?	0	?	?	?	0
4	Tool use for op. 1	fix.	T1	0	?	?	0	?	?	?	0
5	Operation 2	var.	WC 2	0	?	?	0	?	?	?	0
6	Operation 2	fix.	WC 2	0	?	?	0	?	?	?	0
7	Tool use for op. 2	fix.	T3	0	?	?	0	?	?	?	0

costs per batch/order quantity		costs per batch / actual quantity			costs per batch	
target	actual	target	actual	cost type	target	actual
?	0	?	0	Variable material costs	?	0
?	0	?	0	Variable internal labor costs	?	0
?	0	?	0	Variable cost of goods manufactured	?	0
?	0	?	0	Fixed internal labor costs	?	0
?	0	?	0	(Full) cost of goods manufactured	?	0

Fig. 15.7.2.2   Graphical representation of the cost accumulation for a product A.

To calculate the process cost of the tool, use the following:

- The process quantity or quantity per for the ABC process "tool use for operation 1 (or 2)" is 1 (one use per unit produced).
- The total (target) quantity is the number of units produced.
- The process variable, or activity cost driver, is the "use of the tool"
- The process cost rate (or cost per unit) is the cost of the tool divided by the number of units that can be produced until the tool is used up.
- The process costs (target) are the product of the total (target) quantity times the cost per unit.

Cost Accumulation

Product ID: 4712   Description: Product B   Batch size (order quantity): 40   Actual quantity: 0

pos.	text	fix. var.	comp. ID Wrk.-C. ID	setup load	quantity per / run load per unit	total qty./ load target	total qty./ load actual	unit	cost per unit	cost target	cost actual
1	Material	var.	Z		?	?	0	?	?	?	0
2	Operation 1	var.	WC 1	0	?	?	0	?	?	?	0
3	Operation 1	fix.	WC 1	0	?	?	0	?	?	?	0
4	Tool use for op. 1	fix.	T2	0	?	?	0	?	?	?	0
5	Operation 2	var.	WC 2	0	?	?	0	?	?	?	0
6	Operation 2	fix.	WC 2	0	?	?	0	?	?	?	0
7	Tool use for op. 2	fix.	T4	0	?	?	0	?	?	?	0

costs per batch / order quantity target	costs per batch / order quantity actual	costs per batch/actual quantity target	costs per batch/actual quantity actual	cost type	costs per batch target	costs per batch actual
?	0	?	0	Variable material costs	?	0
?	0	?	0	Variable internal labor costs	?	0
?	0	?	0	Variable cost of goods manufactured	?	0
?	0	?	0	Fixed internal labor costs	?	0
?	0	?	0	(Full) cost of goods manufactured	?	0

Fig. 15.7.2.3   Graphical representation of the cost accumulation for a product B.

Problem-solving hints:

The full cost of goods manufactured will *not* be the same for products A and B (why?): In fact, we calculate $4.30 per unit produced of product A (or $172 for a batch size of 40), and $5.20 per unit produced of product B (or $208 for a batch size of 40).

15.7.3 Comparing Job-Order Costing and Activity-Based Costing

a.   Why is the cost per unit produced in the conventional job order costing exercise 15.7.1 ($4.75) exactly the mean of the costs per unit of the two products in the ABC exercise 15.7.2 ($4.30 and $5.20)?

b.   What product pricing considerations would you take into account on the basis of the results when calculating manufacturing costs by ABC?

c.   Would a change of the batch size (40 in both exercises) imply different results? Is this generally the case in the world of practice? What assumption made in the problem description for the sake of simplicity led to the special case of the two exercises?

16   Representation and System Management of Logistic Objects

In Figure 16.0.0.1, the dark shaded box contains the logistical objects associated with the tasks and processes of the reference model for business processes and planning & control tasks in Figure 4.1.4.2.

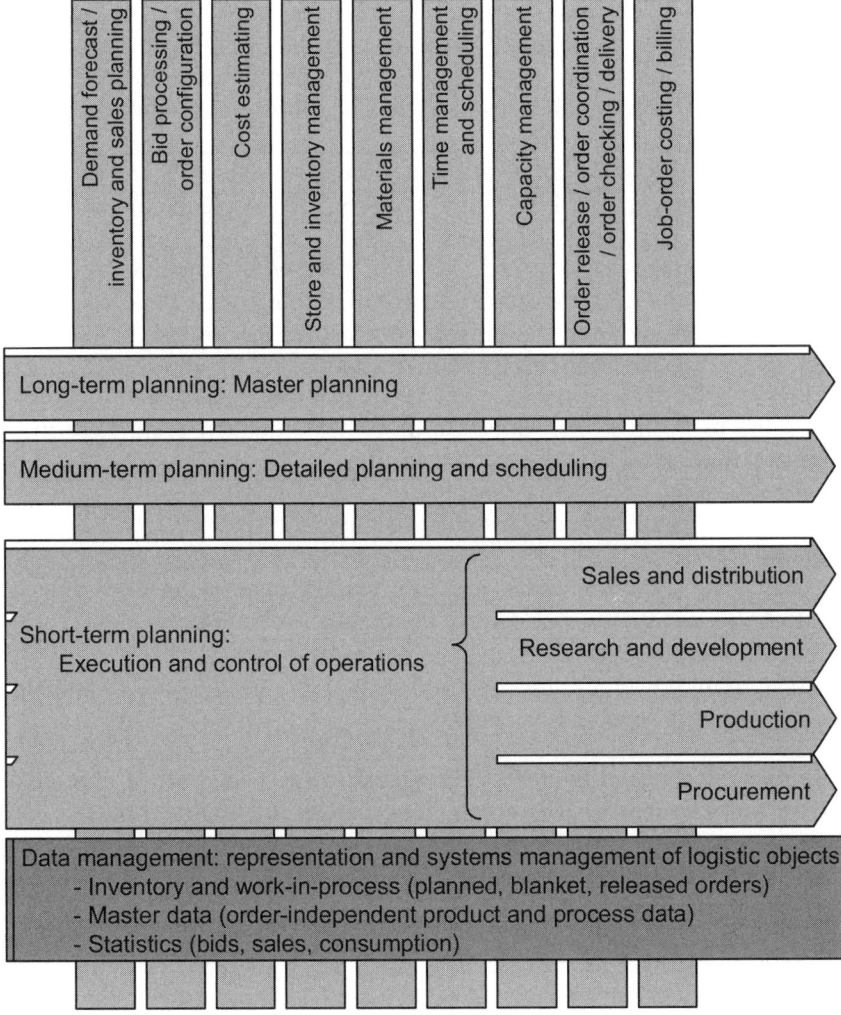

Fig. 16.0.0.1   The subject covered in this chapter is shown against a darker background.

This chapter describes in detail the business objects introduced in Sections 1.2 (order and master data), 10.1 (inventory), and 10.2 (statistics).[1] The discussion is also structured from the viewpoint of an information system with a view to computerization. In addition, the chapter covers tasks that can be summarized as obtaining information from an information system using suitable queries. It also discusses some additional logistical objects that are needed for the tasks described in Chapters 4 to 15, but do not appear in a broad-brush description of business objects, such as objects used to coordinate orders.

We shall start by defining some terms from the language of information systems, that are also generally used in everyday language. This means that they are easy to understand and should therefore facilitate communication between the users and producers of information systems.[2]

According to [Long03], an *entity* is a formal something that exists as a single and complete unit. It is, more precisely, "the existence of a thing."

This definition is closely linked to that of the *object*, as shown in Figure 3.1.2.1. The entity describes the existence of a thing, while the object is the thing under consideration. In logistics, one aspect cannot exist without the other, so the two terms are used synonymously.

According to [Long03], an *attribute* describes a quality, feature, or more precise definition of something (of an entity).

Each object or entity thus has a set of attributes.

According to [Long03], *data* are information concerning real objects, events, facts, etc. that is encoded for the purposes of analysis.

The data of an object are thus the attributes of an object to which concrete values have been assigned.

An *object class* or *entity class*, abbreviated to *class*, is a set of entities or objects whose essential qualities are described by the same attributes.

A *primary key* is the minimum set of attributes that combine to unambiguously identify an object.

---

[1]   You may find it useful to go back over Sections 3.1, 10.1, and 10.2 before reading the rest of this chapter.
[2]   Planning & control can also be understood as an information system.

16.1   Order Data in Sales, Distribution, Production, and Procurement

The *order* business object was introduced in Section 1.2.1. It describes all types of order within the logistics network. This section describes in detail the order objects used in distribution, production, and procurement logistics. Section 16.5 (The Management of Product and Engineering Data) describes the R&D order in greater depth. Stock status and statistics are also discussed in this section since they are related to order objects.

16.1.1 Customers and Suppliers

The *business partner* business object of a company was introduced in Section 1.2.1 as a general term to describe an internal or external customer or supplier. In terms of their property as business objects, both *customer* and *supplier* may be defined as a specialization of *business partner*.

The customer and supplier classes are thus both specializations of the business partner class. Most of the attributes of the customer object class correspond to those of the supplier object class. The most important common attributes are:

- The *business partner ID*. This is generally a dummy identification. Changes to the identification should be avoided during the life of the business partnership. The business partner ID is unique and also acts as the primary key for the class.

- *Business partner name, address*, and *country*, and optionally a *delivery address*: these attributes act as "secondary keys" enabling a particular customer to be quickly and easily traced within the class.

- Communication details (telephone, fax, e-mail and web site).

- Various codes used to classify the business partner.

- Credit limit, bank details.

- Codes for handling the business partner with respect to the tax authorities.

- Codes for order processing, shipping, and incoming goods.

Various types of sales statistics are kept for each business partner. These are generally administered in separate object classes.

Business partners may be incorporated into an overall company hierarchy.

> A *combined bill of material* is the set of all business partners belonging to a combined business partner.

This bill of material structure enables general analyses (consolidations), for example, to be carried out for all the companies in exactly the same way as for the individual business partners.

Aspects of *computerized administration*: The business partner is normally identified by a dummy identification which is allocated by the information system. A business partner entity, as a data set, may not be physically deleted while it continues to appear in an order or in statistics. A business partner ID is normally allocated for many years, even if the connection with that business partner no longer exists.

16.1.2 The General Structure of Orders in Sales and Distribution, Production, and Procurement

The examples in Figures 1.2.1.1 and 1.2.1.2 show that the *order* is a relatively complex business object. The individual *order data* that combine to form the *order* business object include:

- The *order header*: This is the data that appear at the top or bottom of each order, including the principal, contractor, and the order validity date. Each order has precisely one order header.

- The *order line* or *order position*. An order may contain any number of this object. Each is assigned a suitable position number and appears in a specific order. Every line describes an object that must be scheduled or controlled within a company's logistics, or may be used for text only.

    - In Figure 1.2.1.1 these objects are, without exception, *order positions (of the) item (type)* that pass from the supplier to the customer. From the supplier's viewpoint they are *(item) issues*, whereas the customer regards them as *(item) receipts* or *entries*.

    - Figure 1.2.1.2 also shows item issues, although in this case the contractor — the garage — also supplies *order positions (of the) work* or *order operation (type)*. This means individual pieces of work that the customer purchases as part of the service, but which never assume the character of a product. In this case, they are carried out directly on the object that characterizes the order, i.e., the car. The other positions listed under the "Work" heading are an item issue (small items and cleaning materials) and an *order position (of the) production equipment (type)*. A courtesy car was provided in order to fulfill the order. The courtesy car is an investment on the part of the garage, just like any other device, machine, or tool.

Figure 16.1.2.1 shows the general structure of an order in sales and distribution, production, or procurement that arises from these observations.

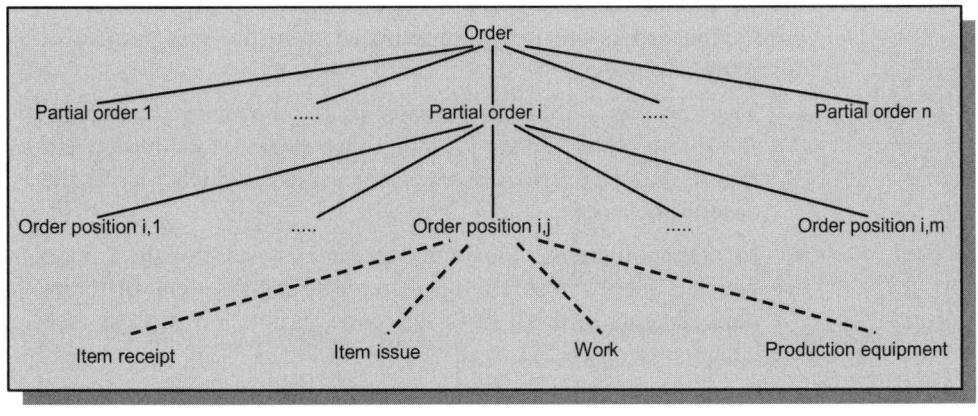

Key: ————— : "consists of"   – – – – · : "is either ... or ..."

Fig. 16.1.2.1   The general structure of an order in sales and distribution, production or procurement.

Here, the observations from the examples in Figures 1.2.1.1 and 1.2.1.2 are supplemented with a further level.

> A *partial order* is an order object within an order, which is complete with respect to content but is not regarded as a separate business object.

Several partial orders may logically be combined under a single order.

- For example, the partial orders in a sales or procurement order may be sets of order positions that will be procured at different times, but together form a whole, e.g., with respect to order billing.

- In addition, certain partial orders in a production order may result in semifinished goods which, in turn, may appear as item issues in other partial orders. In this case, a first partial order is used to produce a lower structure level, for example. Its result is not stored temporarily, but rather is immediately used in the partial orders for the upper structure levels. This creates a network of partial orders.

In principle, all types of order position may appear in sales, production, and procurement orders.

- Sales orders generally relate to item issues, although in service companies they may also involve work and the production equipment used.

- Procurement orders generally contain *item receipts*, although purchased services can also involve the *work* and *equipment* types.

- Production orders are more complicated from the viewpoint of a company's logistics:

  - There is often only one item receipt, i.e., the manufactured and saleable product. This goes either into store or to shipping and thus is passed on to the sales department, which placed the order.

  - In other situations, the item receipt is a semifinished good which is placed in stock. It is also possible for several different item receipts to arise from the same production process (see Chapter 7).

  - From the logistics viewpoint, the commodities used in the production process are also item issues, e.g., issues from the raw materials or semifinished goods store.

  - A production order is characterized by operations and the production equipment used, i.e., tools, devices, and machines.

Figure 16.1.2.2 contains a formalized order structure with the same content as Figure 16.1.2.1, in this case as an entity or object model for an information system (see [Schö01]).[3] The special graphical structures are defined as follows:

---

[3]   The illustration in Figure 16.1.2.2 originates from the modeling of objects in information systems. Such a model is suitable for use as the interface between organizers and the IT experts. Other modeling formats are also used, however. Essentially, they do not differ very much from one another.

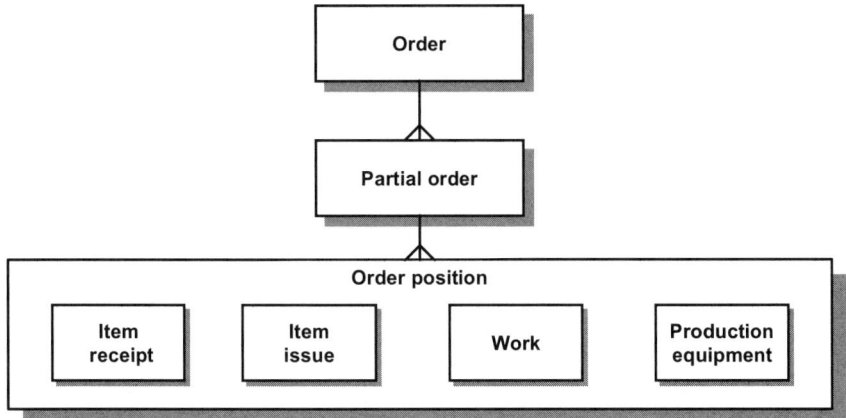

Fig. 16.1.2.2   The basic object classes in an order database.

The "fan" symbol describes a hierarchy between objects.

> In a *hierarchy* or *hierarchical association*, an object of the higher level class "has" n objects of the lower level class.[4]

In the situation illustrated in Figure 16.1.2.2, the fan symbol expresses a *"consists of"* association, called a *composition*.

> In a *composition*, an object of the higher level class consists of n objects of the lower level class.[5]

An object of the *order* class consists of n different objects of the *partial order* class, while an object of the *partial order* class consists of n objects of the *order position* class.

The way in which the *item receipt*, *item issue*, and *work* and *production equipment* class symbols are nested within the *order position* class describes a specialization.

> In a *specialization* or *specialization association*, an object of the specialized class "is" also an object of the generalized class.[6]

---

[4]   Rather than a hierarchy, we also speak of a special *"1 to n association"* between objects from the two classes.

[5]   A *composition* is a special type of hierarchy, a strong type of an aggregation, also called *whole-part*.

Conversely, a certain order position *is* also an item receipt, item issue, or work or production equipment.[7]

The individual object classes that make up the *order* business object are discussed in depth later in this chapter.

16.1.3 The Order and Partial Order Header

The order header class combines all the data that represent the order as a whole. Its attributes can essentially be divided into the following subsets:

1. *Attributes that describe the business partner.* For a sales order, this is the customer. For a procurement order, it is the supplier; for a production order, it is the sales, R&D, or even logistics department. These attributes include:

   - *Business partner ID* and the address of the business partner

   - Business partner's object for which the order is used

2. *Attributes used to administer the order.* These are attributes associated with the status of an order, typically:

   - *Order ID*, that is, the order identification

   - *Validity date* of the order (tender date, date on which order was issued, etc.)

   - *Kind of order* (e.g., customer order, procurement order, production order for finished or semifinished goods, overhead order, etc.)

   - *Costing unit* of the order (in order to combine orders to compare costs against profits) and other attributes to prepare for job-order costing

   - *Billing address*

   - *Order status*, i.e., the administrative status of the order (e.g., in preparation, scheduled, released, started, cancelled, completed, inspected, deletable)

---

[6]   There is thus a special *1 to 1 association* between the objects of the specialized class and those of a generalized class.

[7]   For the definition of specialization given above, the order item could also be a different specialization or a number of specializations simultaneously. The optional rules of completeness and disjunction within a specialization provide an *is exactly* association.

- *Order conditions* and other information that appears at the bottom of the order; allocation to the order header means that a separate *order footer* class may be omitted

3. *Attributes that concern planning & control of the order.* These include:
   - A *flag* to indicate whether it is a *simulated* or *effective* order
   - The *order priority*
   - The *order urgency*
   - The *order start date* and the *order end date* or *order completion date*
   - A *flag* to indicate whether the *dates* are *firm* or may be postponed

The *partial order header* object class essentially incorporates the same attributes as the third subset of attributes for the *order header* class, plus the order ID, partial order ID (generally a consecutive number that supplements the order ID), and a brief description of the partial order.

16.1.4 The Order Position

The *order position* class is comprised of all the attributes (information) that appear on each line of an order. One object is stored in each order position. The attributes may be divided into the following subsets:

1. The identifying attributes, which include
   - *Order ID*
   - *Partial order ID*
   - *Order position ID*, is generally a number; for work, it may correspond to the sequence in the routing sheet, whereas for items or production equipment it is a relative position within a picking list determined using suitable logic (e.g., the order in which they are taken from stock)
   - *Type of order position*: item receipt, item issue, work or production equipment
   - *Position status*, i.e., the administrative status of the position (e.g., scheduled, reserved, released, partly executed, fully executed, administration complete)

- *Flag* to indicate whether the *dates* are *firm* or may be postponed

2. Specific attributes which differ according to the type of order position. For the *item* order position, i.e., for item receipts or item issues, these include:

- *Item ID*

- *Reserved* or *allocated quantity*

- *Quantity issued* or *effective quantity*

- *Billed quantity*

- *Reservation date* or the *earliest start date*

- *Item description*, a set of attributes that may be used for more detailed identification and classification (see also Section 16.2.2)

- *Position-specific item description* within the current order, i.e., the position of an electronic component

- Information for stockkeeping and accounting, which generally means a set of the attributes described in detail in Section 16.2.2.

- *Work order position ID*, i.e., the operation ID for which an item issue is required or which results in an item receipt

The following attributes apply to the *work* order position (or *order operation*):

- *Work center ID* (or capacity ID), i.e., the identification of the location or group of machines where or with which this operation is used for production

- *Work description*

- *Standard load* in capacity units (defined in the same way as the load specification for an operation in Sections 1.2.4 and 12.1.2)

- *Setup load* and *run load*

- *Actual load* in capacity units

- *Billed load* in capacity units

- *Lead time* and, if necessary, lead time components

- *Start date* (that is, the *operation start date*), e.g., the earliest, latest, or probable date

- *End date* (that is, the *operation due date*), e.g., the earliest, latest, or probable date

- *Work center description* and other data used to identify and classify the organizational unit carrying out the work; see also Section 16.2.4.

- *Costs* and *availability data* for the work center; this is a set of the attributes described in detail in Section 16.2.4

For a *production equipment* order position, it relates to the specific attributes of:

- *Production equipment ID*

- *Reserved* or *allocated quantity*

- *Quantity issued* or *effective quantity*

- *Billed quantity*

- *Production equipment description* and other attributes for identifying and classifying the production equipment

- *Work order position ID*, i.e., the operation ID for which the production equipment is used

- *Costs per issued quantity* and other attributes used for billing

- *Start date*, e.g., the earliest, latest, or probable date

- *End date*, e.g., the earliest, latest, or probable date

- *Quantity of available production equipment*, their *costs*, and other attributes used for billing; see also Section 16.2.6

Any amount of text may be assigned to each *order position* object.

16.1.5 Inventories and Inventory Transactions

The following objects are grouped into logical units (object classes) for the purposes of administering inventories:

- *Storage location* for administering the various stock locations within the company. The attributes of this object class are the storage location ID, storage location description, various classifications and attributes for modeling the different features described in Section 10.1.1, etc.

- *Physical inventory* for administering the various stocks of storable items for accounting purposes. The attributes of this object class are the identification of the administered item, identification of the stock location, the quantity stocked expressed in the unit of measure for the item, date of the last receipt into and issue from stock, etc.

These two classes are not sufficient on their own to represent stocks of batches or variants, however. The extensions required for the processing industry and for production with a wide range of variants are discussed in Section 16.4.2. According to [Schö01], Ch.8, a stock of batches or variants ultimately becomes a specialization of an order position.

All item movements, particularly the inventory transactions, are defined in a *transaction* class. See also Section 10.1. This class may be analyzed using any number of criteria, e.g., for consumption, sales, or bid statistics (see Section 10.2). The attributes of this class include:

- *Transaction date*
- *Item ID* or *item family ID*
- *Moved quantity*
- *Persons responsible* for recording the transaction
- *Two* customers, production, or procurement order positions or stock level positions concerned ("from" and "to" positions associated with the transaction)

16.2   The Master Data for Products and Processes

The generic term *master data* covers all the order-independent business objects discussed in Section 1.2 (see Section 4.1.4).

This section first introduces the master data for the conventional MRP II concept, which is intended for products with convergent product structures. Section 16.4 discusses the extensions arising from processor-oriented concepts (divergent product structures). The extensions arising from variant-oriented concepts are described in Section 16.5.

16.2.1 Product, Product Structure, Components, and Operations

Master data are created as the result of product and process development that is not associated with a specific customer order. A suitable customer, production or procurement order can then be repeatedly derived from these master data if an order quantity and date are added to the product and process description.

This can be compared to a recipe in a cookbook since the recipe is developed on its own, i.e., independently of the subsequent cooking processes. Such a recipe may be used repeatedly for preparing meals, and different order quantities (= number of people) may be applied. The cookbook contains the following information:

- The ingredients are shown in a list (recipe).
- The sequence of individual working tasks is also given in the form of a list that describes how to arrive at the result, i.e., the finished meal, starting from the ingredients.
- The cooking utensils, such as knives, pans, etc., are mentioned in the description of the work. They are sometimes also summarized in a list.
- The cooking device required, e.g., stove, oven, sink, etc., is mentioned in the description of the work.

The same concept can be applied to the description of the product and production process within a company, using generalized or specific terminology:

- The result is a *product* or a *parent item*.
- The ingredients become components and the recipe becomes a bill of material.
- The work becomes operations and the sequence of operations becomes a routing sheet or process plan.
- The cooking device and other cooking utensils become machinery and other production equipment.
- The actual kitchen becomes a work center with one or more workstations at which the individual operations are carried out.

Figure 16.2.1.1 shows, by way of example, the composition of master data in the form of a production order of the ball bearing of Fig. 15.2.1.1. It specifies an order quantity (a lot) of 100 units of measurement (in this case "piece"). No dates are specified, however. The only other information is certain characteristic data and positions. [8]

PRODUCT (POTENTIAL ITEM RECEIPT)					
Product ID		Order quantity or lot	U/M	Description	Dimension
83569		100	Pce	Ball bearing	12 mm
BILL OF MATERIAL WITH POSITIONS (COMPONENTS OR POTENTIAL ITEM ISSUES)					
Position	Component ID	Total usage quantity	U/M	Description	Dimension
050	83593	100	Pce	Ring	12 mm
060	83607	2	KG	Uniflon-R	67/3000 mm
⋮	⋮		⋮	⋮	⋮
ROUTING SHEET WITH POSITIONS (OPERATIONS OR POTENTIAL WORK TASKS)					
Position	Work description	Standard time	U/M	Work center / Description	
250	10.5 x 67 mm Cut Uniflon	1.45	H	907501/Manual production	
270	Press together	1.12	h	983001/Special presses	
⋮	⋮		⋮	⋮	

Fig. 16.2.1.1   The production order as a collection of master data.

- The *ball bearing* product (item ID 83569) is a potential item receipt and consists of the two components *ring* (item ID 83593, a semifinished good made in-house) and *Uniflon* (item ID 83607, a purchased raw material). The bill of material for the product thus has at least the two specified positions. These are potential item issues.

- The ball bearing (item ID 83569) is produced by the two operations *Cut Uniflon* (position 250 at work center ID 907501, "Manual production") and *Press together* (position 270 at work center ID 908301, "Special presses"). The routing sheet for the product thus has at least the two specified operations. These are the potential *work* order positions (or order operations).

Figure 16.2.1.2 shows the simple, single-level *convergent product structure* that occurs in the initial stages. See also Figures 16.1.2.1 and 1.2.2.2.

All the resources needed to manufacture the product are listed as positions in the product structure. Such a position may thus be a component, an operation, or production equipment.

---

[8]   In the case under consideration, there are other components and operations. For the sake of simplicity, however, only two components are listed here.

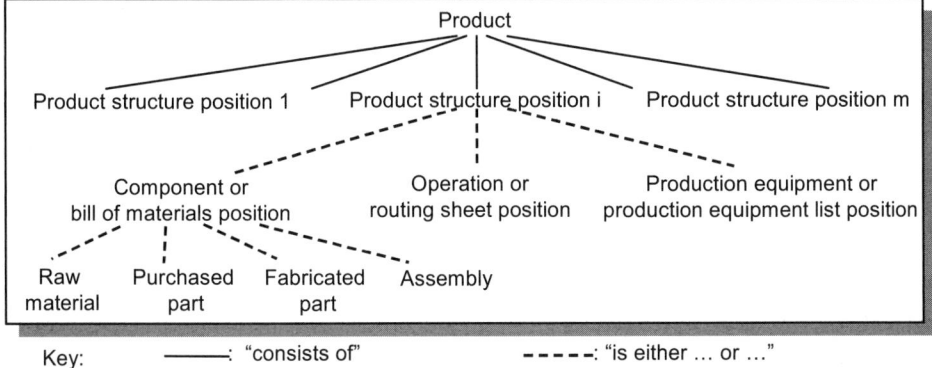

Fig. 16.2.1.2   A simple product structure.

According to Figure 1.2.2.1, a component may first be a raw material or a purchased part. In reality, a product often has hundreds, or even thousands, of such components. These are grouped into (product) modules or intermediate products (in-house parts [that is, parts produced in-house], semifinished goods, or assemblies). This takes place for various reasons:

- A module may be used in several different products. Under certain circumstances, it is sensible to produce or procure this inter-mediate product with a logistics characteristic different from that of the higher level products.

- A module may be either produced in-house or purchased and thus acts as a point of differentiation for logistics purposes.

- A module corresponds to a design structure level or production structure level.

An intermediate product may itself be made up of different components and may also be used as a component of various higher level products. Figure 16.2.1.3 formalizes this fact in two different hierarchies,[9] which refer to the upper and lower levels of the multilevel bill of material. See also the two intermediate products in Figure 1.2.2.2.

The creation of intermediate products may be repeated in several levels. Intermediate products lead from the simple, single-level product structure

---

[9]   Both cases refer to *"component is simultaneously an intermediate product"* as an association class. The "lower" case is also a composition ("whole-part" association).

to a multilevel product structure. To illustrate this, the cookbooks of a professional cook will contain multilevel recipes, i.e., semifinished goods as components of the menu that are prepared in advance or purchased.

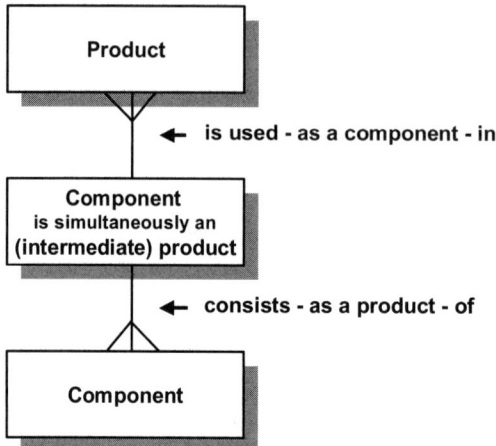

Fig. 16.2.1.3   The intermediate product used simultaneously as a component in higher level products.

16.2.2 Item Master

The various specializations of the *item* business object are summarized in Figure 1.2.2.1. This section provides a detailed description of the object, particularly its most important attributes.

An *item master record* contains the master data for an item.

An *item master file* is a file containing all item master records.

Each record contains three different types of information: technical information, stockkeeping information, and information on costs and prices. The three types are often administered by different offices within the company. If this is the case, they must be coordinated by an organizational procedure (e.g., using workflow techniques).

The *technical information* has at least the following attributes:

- The *item ID*, that is, the item identification. If computerized, this should, if possible, be a dummy identification that is allocated by the information system. The item ID is a primary key and is thus unique. It must not be changed during the product life cycle.

- The *EAN/UPC -code*. This is a re-identification of the item ID for automatic shop floor data acquisition, and its structure is based on international standards.

- The *drawing number* or *technical reference number*. This also helps people within the company to identify the item. As a *secondary key*, however, it does not necessarily have to be unique. Its value can also change over the product life cycle, which may be necessary if the drawing numbers are reorganized, for example.

- The *item description*. This often has different attributes, which also act as secondary keys for quick and easy searching, e.g.,

  - A verbal description which may be in different languages

  - The item abbreviation or acronym used to describe the item within the company

  - The item's dimension or dimensions

- The *item type*, i.e., its specialization (end product, semifinished good, raw material, document, information, etc.).

- A flag to indicate whether the item is *purchased* or *produced in-house.*

- *Classification codes* which group items together for certain statistics.

- The *low-level code*; see Section 1.2.2.

- A flag to indicate a *by-product* or a *waste product*

- The *units of measure*, e.g., the storage unit, the unit to which costs and prices relate, the purchasing unit, or the weight unit.

- *Conversion factors* for converting from one unit of measure to another.

The *stockkeeping information* has at least the following attributes:

- The *reason for order release* (see Section 3.4.4), order release by demand (technique: MRP), order release by prediction (technique: MRP), order release by consumption (technique: order point or kanban).

- The stock location or stockkeeping location. A separate class is needed for administering the storage locations of an item with *multiple stock organization* (see Section 10.1.1). See also Section 16.1.5.

- The *lead time.*

- The *production or procurement size*. This is a quantity (batch size), a time period, or a number of requests, etc., depending on the *batch-sizing policy* (see also Section 11.4.1).
- The *mean consumption* and the attributes used to update this value (see Section 9.2.1). Cumulative past consumption values are generally administered using separate classes (see Section 10.2.1).

Attributes for *information on costs and prices* are generally as follows (see also Chapter 15):

- The *manufacturing* or *procurement costs*: full or variable, standard, average, real or updated, simulated
- The *cost types* taken from the cost breakdown structure of a product (the cost accumulation structure): cost of materials, direct labor costs and overheads or fixed and variable labor costs, etc.
- The various *selling prices*: Different prices for each market segment; Previous, current, and future price (and optionally the date of validity)

Aspects of computerized administration:

- For certain large-scale modifications, however, it may be sensible to record the amendments in advance and then to run them in background mode using a batch procedure. A typical example is a change of selling prices: If the new prices are not derived from the old prices using a formula, the only possible solution is to record the new prices for each item online as separate attributes. At the key date, all the prices will then be changed in a few seconds by overwriting the "Price" attribute with the value of the "New price" attribute.
- It is necessary to record the latest modifications in the item master data if different users are able to modify the same data. It will thus be possible to identify who modified which data and when.
- When entering the data for a new item into the item master data, it is generally convenient first to copy all the attribute values of an existing item to the attributes of the new item and then to change the values.
- An item may not be physically deleted while it still occurs as a component, product, or reservation in an order or consumption statistics. An item ID is normally reserved for several years, even if the associated item is no longer physically present within the company.

16.2.3 Bill of Material, Bill of Material Position, and Where-Used List

By way of example, Figure 1.2.2.2 shows a bill of material, i.e., a convergent product structure with two structure levels. The conventional method used to model the *bill of material* business object does not represent the object as a whole. Instead, it defines a detailed logistical object for that business object.

A *bill of material position* is a product ↔ component connection within a bill of material.

Here is an example. Figure 16.2.3.1 contains five items — the three components x, y, and z, each of which occurs in products 1 and 2.

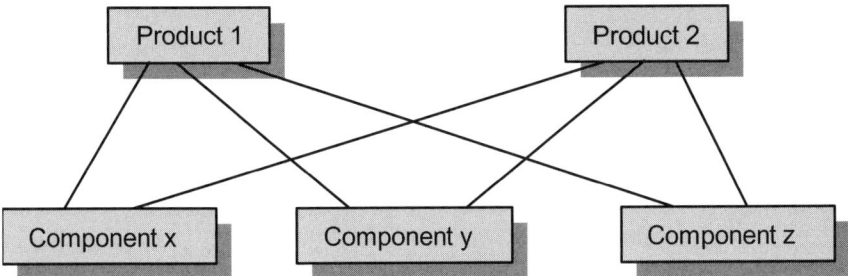

Fig. 16.2.3.1   Representation of two bills of material, each with three components.

The two bills of material lead to detailed objects, i.e., *six* bill of material positions. These represent the six connections shown in Figure 16.2.3.2 from the product viewpoint and from the component viewpoint.

Product viewpoint	Component viewpoint
Product 1 ↔ Component x	Component x ↔ Product 1
Product 1 ↔ Component y	Component x ↔ Product 2
Product 1 ↔ Component z	
	Component y ↔ Product 1
Product 2 ↔ Component x	Component y ↔ Product 2
Product 2 ↔ Component y	
Product 2 ↔ Component z	Component z ↔ Product 1
	Component z ↔ Product 2

Fig. 16.2.3.2   Detailed logistical objects: the six bill of material positions as connections in two bills of material, each with three components.

Breaking down bills of material into their individual positions leads directly to further logistical objects. They are all derived from the bill of material positions by means of algorithms.

A *where-used list* indicates the way in which a component is used in different products, taking the structural levels into account (see Section 1.2.2).

The component viewpoint in Figure 16.2.3.2, that is, the bottom to top viewpoint in Figure 16.2.3.1, leads to three where-used lists — for the components x, y, and z, each with two uses in products 1 and 2.

Different forms of these bills of material and where-used lists are needed, depending on the application. Each "product ↔ component" connection should only be defined or stored once, however. The only exception to this rule is for components that occur several times in the same product (but are different each time). These occurrences can be differentiated using a relative position number (see below).

A *single-level bill of material* shows all the components of a product.

Figure 16.2.3.3 shows the three single-level bills of material, each with two bill of material positions, as implicitly defined by the example in Figure 1.2.2.2.

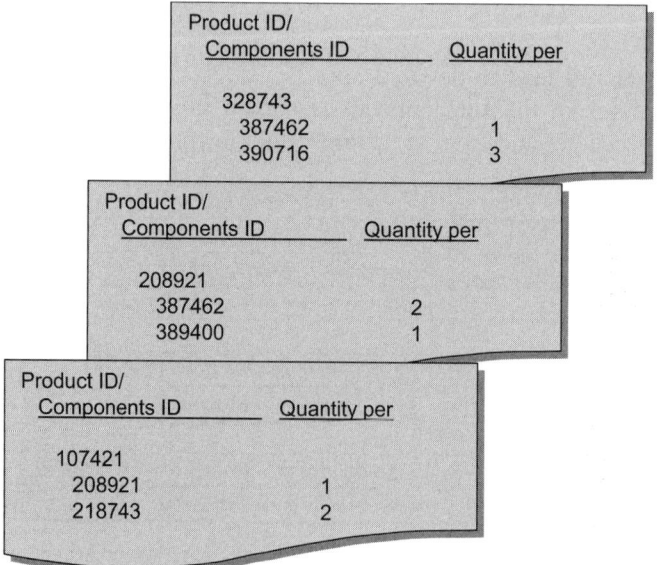

Fig. 16.2.3.3   Single-level bills of material.

The *multilevel bill of material* or *indented bill of material* shows the structured composition of a product, across all the levels.

Figure 16.2.3.4 shows the indented bill of material for the example in Figure 1.2.2.2.

Product ID/ Components ID	(Cumulative) Quantity per
107421	
208921	1
387462	2
389400	1
218743	2
387462	2
390716	6

Fig. 16.2.3.4   Indented bill of material (multilevel bill of material).

In this form, the content corresponds exactly to the graphical representation of a product as a tree structure, again as shown in Figure 1.2.2.2.[10] The quantity per is always the cumulative quantity of the component used at this point in the product (by way of contrast to the graphical form in Figure 1.2.2.2).[11] An algorithm can also be used to generate a multilevel bill of material from the single-level bills of material.

The *summarized bill of material* is a condensed multilevel bill of material in which each component occurs only once, although the total quantity per is specified.

Figure 16.2.3.5 shows the summarized bill of material for the example in Figure 1.2.2.2.

The quantity per is the cumulative quantity of components used in the product. A summarized bill of material is used for manual cost estimating or for quickly calculating the number of components to be bought in for a

---

[10]   This tree structure occurs naturally for a product with an assembly orientation as orientation of product structure.

[11]   Of course, the cumulative quantity per can also be shown in the graphical form.

lot of end products. A summarized bill of material can also be generated from the single-level bills of material using an algorithm.

Product ID/ Components ID	(Total) Quantity per
107421	
208921	1
218743	2
387462	4
389400	1
390716	6

Fig. 16.2.3.5   Summarized bill of material (condensed multilevel bill of material).

Similar algorithms can also be used to create various types of where-used lists from the bill of material positions.

The *single-level where-used list* shows all the products that are integrated directly into a component.

Figure 16.2.3.6 shows the five single-level where-used lists implicitly defined by the example in Figure 1.2.2.2.[12]

Figure 16.2.3.6 contains exactly the same number of connections as Figure 16.2.3.3, i.e., six. Although these are the same connections, here they are taken from the component view in Figure 16.2.3.2. In this case, the quantity per is the quantity of components integrated directly into the product. The single-level where-used list is useful because it provides a picture of a certain component.

The *multilevel where-used list* or *indented where-used list* shows, in structured form, how a component is used across all the levels, right down to the end products.

Figure 16.2.3.7 shows the multilevel where-used list for the component with item ID 387462 from the example in Figure 1.2.2.2.

---

[12]   The where-used list for an end product is empty; that is, there is no where-used list.

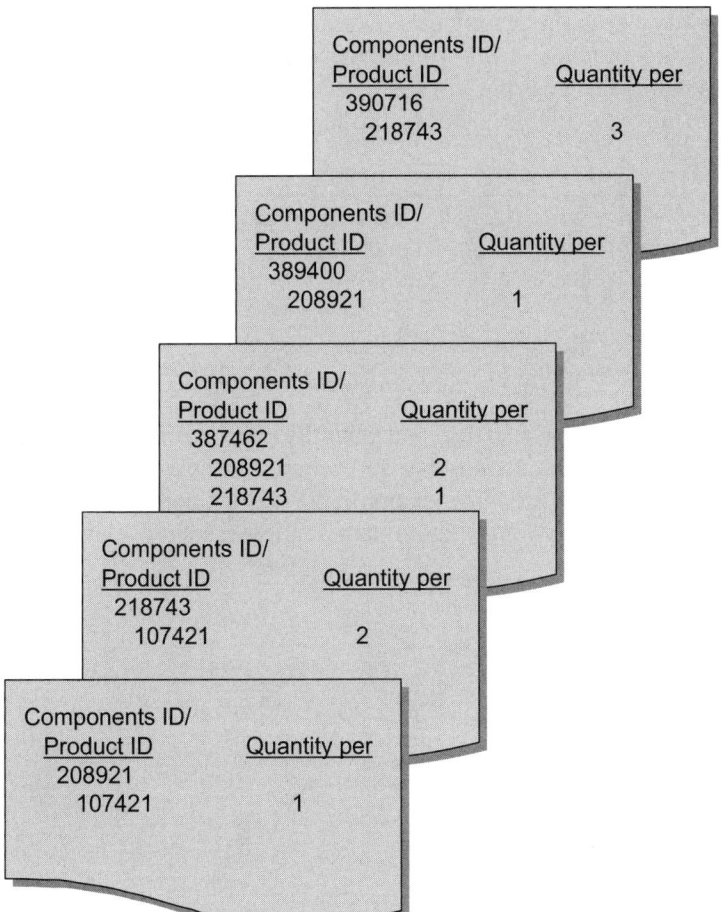

Fig. 16.2.3.6   Single-level where-used list.

Components ID/ Product ID	(Cumulative) Quantity per
387462	
208921	2
107421	2
218743	1
107421	2

Fig. 16.2.3.7   Indented where-used list (multilevel where-used list).

Here, the quantity per is the cumulative quantity of this component that is integrated into the product at this point. An indented where-used list is useful for assessing the possible consequences of a *substitution*, i.e., the replacement of an unavailable primary product or component by a non-primary item.

The *summarized where-used list* is a condensed multilevel where-used list in which each product occurs only once, together with the cumulative quantity of that component incorporated into the product.

Figure 16.2.3.8 shows the summarized where-used list for the component with item ID 387462 from the example in Figure 1.2.2.2.

In this case, the quantity per is the total quantity of components that are integrated into the product. A summarized where-used list is needed to draw up a procurement plan, for example, or to estimate which end products will be affected by replacing an item at a lower level.

Components ID/ Product ID	(Total) Quantity per
387462	
208921	2
218743	1
107421	4

Fig. 16.2.3.8   Summarized where-used list (condensed multilevel where-used list).

The *bill of material position* logistical object appears in the type of formalized product structure shown in Figure 16.2.3.9.

The left-hand side of Figure 16.2.3.9 shows the content of Figure 16.2.1.3, as shown in Figure 1.2.2.1. The *item* class is thus in an "n to n" association with itself.

- A product may have different components. Expressed formally, this means that an object of the *item* class, in its specialization *as a product*, *consists of* n different objects from the item class, *component* specialization.

- A component may occur in different products. Expressed formally, this means that an object of the *item* class, in its specialization *as a component, is used in* n different objects from the item class, *product* specialization.

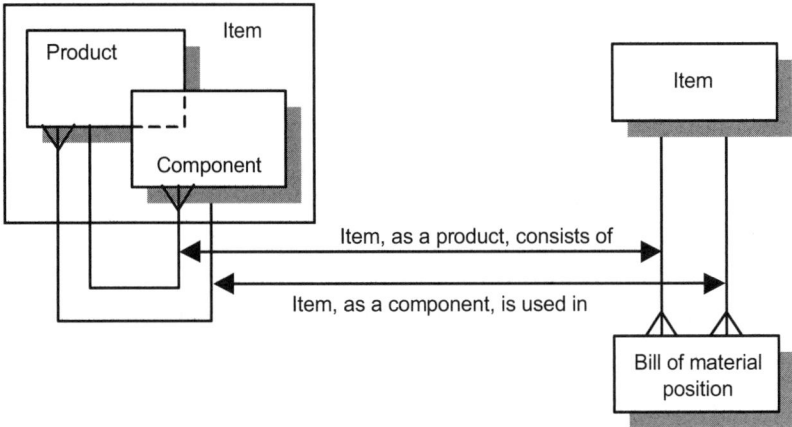

Fig. 16.2.3.9 The bill of material position logistical object.

This "n to n" association is then shown on the right-hand side of Figure 16.2.3.9, broken down into the two corresponding "1 to n" associations. This results in an additional object class, namely, the bill of material position, which determines the "product ↔ component" connection or association between two items. This association may be either *"item, as a product, consists of"* or *"item, as a component, is used in,"* depending on which side we start. A bill of material position is thus simultaneously a where-used list position.

> The *where-used list position* is a different view of the bill of material position.

The view of the bill of material can be described as follows:

- All n bill of material positions can be reached from a product, and all these positions lead to a component that is incorporated into the product. Taken together, all the bill of material positions with the information they contain on the component form the bill of material.

The view of the where-used list can be described as follows:

- All n where-used list positions can be reached from a component, and all these positions lead to a product in which the component is used. Taken together, all the positions of the where-used list with the information they contain on the product form the where-used list.

The most important attributes that have to be administered for a bill of material position are:

- *Product ID* (the product identification); this is an item ID

- *Component ID* (the component identification); this is an item ID

- *Quantity per*, i.e., the number or quantity of components that is needed to produce a single unit of the product

- *Sequential number of the position within the bill of material* (for sorting and identification purposes)

- *Operation ID* for which the component is needed (see Section 16.2.6)

- *Lead-time offset*, i.e., the difference in time relative to the product completion date before which the components must be made available (see Section 1.2.3)

- *Effectivity (dates)* or *effective dates (start and stop)*, that are the dates on which a component is to be added or removed from the bill of material; effectivity control may also be by engineering change number or serial number rather than date

Again, these are only the most important attributes for the elementary functions associated with the bill of material and where-used list. Additional attributes and even additional logistical objects must be represented for more complex applications, e.g., bills of material for a *product family with many variants*. See also Chapter 6 and Section 16.3.

In historic and generic terms, the *bill of material position ID* (bill of material position identification) combines the *product ID* and *component ID* attributes. Today, it is more often the union of the *product ID* and *sequential number of the position within the bill of material* attributes, however.

The advantage of the second definition is that the same component can occur more than once in the same bill of material. The components may also be sorted into a logical order that does not correspond to the component ID. This does have the disadvantage that the number of possible components of a product is limited by the number of possible relative position numbers. In addition, in order to keep a certain degree of order, any "holes" must be filled in the order of relative position numbers. This can be done by first allocating every tenth number and then periodically reorganizing the numbering.

Aspects of *computerized administration*:

- Certain transactions enable whole or partial bills of material for one assembly to be copied to another assembly. There are also transactions that allow large-scale modifications to be carried out, e.g., by replacing a certain component with a different component in every bill of material (batch procedure running in background mode).

- Another algorithm periodically calculates the *low-level code* of all items. It can also check whether a multilevel bill of material is actually a product structure without loops. This test is often rather time consuming and is difficult to carry out online while administering the bills of material. See also Section 7.3.3.

16.2.4 Work Center Master Data

The *work center* business object is introduced in Figure 1.2.4 together with the other business objects. This section provides a detailed description of the object, particularly its most important attributes.

The *work center* object class is generally comprised of different types of information relating to capacity and costs, plus information used for scheduling, particularly for calculating lead times. These different types of information may, in turn, be administered by different people, depending on how the company is organized.

The *information relating to capacity* includes the following attributes:

- *Work center ID*
- *Work center description*
- *Position within the hierarchy of workshops* (see also Section 16.2.5)
- *Work center type* (store, parts production, assembly, external, etc.)
- *Number of work centers or machines*
- *Number of working hours per shift and per day* (often measured in 1/100 hour or industrial periods)
- *Capacity unit* (see Section 1.2.4)
- *Number of capacity units per shift and per day* (machine capacity or labor capacity, depending on the work center type
- *Number of shifts per day*

- Various factors: *capacity utilization, work center efficiency*, or the *efficiency rate*; see Section 1.2.4)

Capacity may change its value after a certain date. Capacities that change over the course of time are administered in a separate object class.

The *information concerning costs* includes at least the following attributes (see also Section 15.1.4):

- *Fixed labor costs* per capacity unit *for personnel*
- *Variable labor costs* per capacity unit *for personnel*
- *Fixed labor costs* per capacity unit *for machinery*
- *Variable labor costs* per capacity unit *for machinery*

This information is needed in order to analyze the standard or actual times for cost estimating or job-order costing. Conversion factors and different overhead rates are also needed when operating multiple machines or if the machines are operated by several people. It may also be necessary to specify different overhead rates for the setup time.

The following attributes are administered for time management (see Section 12.1), particularly for calculating the *lead time* (see Section 12.3.2):

- The move time from and to the work center. This time incorporates both the actual handling time (administration and transportation) needed to move a commodity from one work center and another and the time needed to move it between two successive operations. See also Section 12.1.5.
- The *non-technical wait time before the operation* or *queue time*, i.e., the average time a job remains in the queue upstream of the work center before being processed.

Other attributes concern alternative work centers, for example. As for the *item*, it is also possible to record the most recent modifications.

16.2.5 The Work Center Hierarchy

Figure 16.2.5.1 shows an example of a work center hierarchy within a company. It often corresponds to the company's structural organization.

As already mentioned, a work center is comprised of several similar or identical workstations or machines.

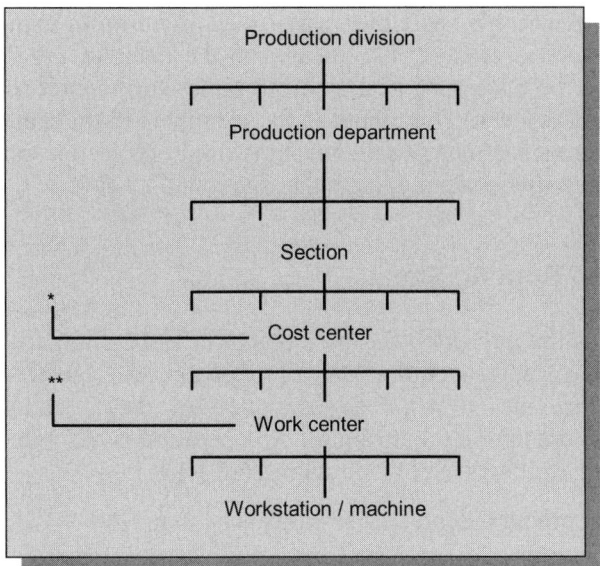

Notes:

* A cost center may occur in several sections.
** A work center may occur in different cost centers.

Fig. 16.2.5.1   The work center hierarchy.

A *cost center* is a unit made up of work centers with the same costs.

The work centers of a cost center are also often of the same type. Work centers are defined by the production carried out at them, while the cost center is an accounting term and is therefore defined for financial purposes.

A *section* is made up of several cost centers or work centers. It is managed by a foreman.

A *production department* is a factory, for example, which is managed by a production director.

The *production division* is comprised of all the factories of a company.

The levels described above are needed for various analyses with different levels of compression (reserve capacity, comparison of capacity and load). The same analysis may be needed for a work center considered in isolation and for a group of work centers at any level in the work center hierarchy.

The simplest structure is that of a strict hierarchy (tree structure). In many cases, however, a network is created, as indicated in the notes to Figure 16.2.5.1. In fact, it may be necessary to define the same work center for several sections or cost centers. This applies, for example, if the same machine is used in different sections and the machine from one section can easily be used as an alternative machine in another section.[13]

16.2.6 Operation and Routing Sheet

Section 1.2.3 introduces the *operation* business object in association with the routing sheet and resource requirement or process plan business objects. This section provides a detailed description of the operation object, particularly its most important attributes. An operation is described by at least the following attributes (See also Figure 16.2.1.1):

- *Product ID* (the product identification); this is an item ID
- *Sequential* or *operation number*; this defines the order in which the operations are carried out
- *Work center ID* of the *primary work center*, that is, where the operation is normally scheduled to be performed
- *Work center ID* of the *alternate work center*, that is, where the operation is not normally scheduled to be but can be performed
- *Operation description*, which may consist of several lines; this is ideally a typical concise description, followed by detailed information
- Standard *setup load* (see Section 12.1.2)
- Standard *run load per unit* (see Section 12.1.2)
- *Setup time* and *run time per unit* or the *formulas for converting* from setup load and run load to setup time and run time
- *Technical wait time after the operation* (see Section 12.1.3)
- *Effective dates (start and stop)*. On these dates the operation is to be added or removed from the routing sheet; effectivity control may also be by engineering change number or serial number rather than date

---

[13]   In this case, the identification or primary key for the *work center class* is made up from the identifications for the work center, cost center, and section classes. The load and capacity can then be compared for each combination of "section – cost center – work center," as well as for identical work centers in the various sections.

The *operation ID* is the union of the *product ID* and *operation number* attributes.

The *routing sheet* or *routing* can be derived from its operations, just as the bill of material can be derived from its bill of material positions. A product forms a "1 to n" association with its operations.

An *alternate routing* is a routing, usually less preferred than the primary routing, but resulting in an identical item.

An *alternate operation* is a replacement for a normal step in the manufacturing process.

Alternate routings and operations may be maintained in the computer or offline via manual methods, but the computer software must be able to accept alternate routings and operations for specific jobs (see [APIC04]).

A *work center where-used list* provides an indication of how a work center is used in products, or more precisely in the operations for products.

As with the where-used list for components, the work center where-used list addresses the operations from the work center viewpoint, as a supplement to the product viewpoint. See Figure 16.2.3.2. A work center also forms a "1 to n" association with the operations.

Aspects of *computerized administration*:

- There are transactions which allow the entire routing sheet for an assembly or a partial routing sheet to be assigned to another assembly. There are also transactions that allow large-scale modifications to be carried out, e.g., by replacing a certain work center with a different work center in every operation (batch procedure running in background mode).
- A batch procedure can periodically calculate the sum of certain elements of the lead time and insert the results into the operation in order to quickly recalculate the rough-cut planning (see Figure 12.3.2.4):
    - Sum of the setup times
    - Sum of the run times for each product, related to an average batch size
    - Sum of the interoperation times

16.2.7 Production Equipment, Bill of Production Equipment, and Bill of Tools

The *production equipment* business object was introduced in Section 1.2.4 together with the work center and routing sheet objects. This section provides a detailed description of the production equipment object, together with some additional logistical objects and their most important attributes.

Production equipment means machines, devices (e.g., jigs, fixtures), and tools, objects that are becoming increasingly important and can no longer simply be mentioned in passing in a work instruction. We are now interested in, for example,

- How a certain tool will be used in the operations, e.g., in order to plan an alternative for that tool or to determine the load on a tool
- Utilization of a tool, in order to calculate depreciation and to schedule maintenance

The *technical information* for production equipment is essentially the information that is administered as attributes for the item.

The *information concerning depreciation* of production equipment uses attributes similar to the cost attributes of the item. Additional specific attributes must also be administered, such as the depreciation rate and planned and effective utilization.

The *information concerning the capacity of a tool or device* uses attributes similar to those for the work center. Today, however, a tool is no longer necessarily associated with just one machine or work center. Flexible work cells often allow tools to be used flexibly.

The load and capacity of a machine are subsets of the load and capacity of the entire work center to which the machine belongs.

A *bill of production equipment* for a product is made up of various bill of production equipment positions. A *bill of production equipment position* is production equipment that is used in a specific operation.

A production equipment position has roughly the same attributes as a bill of material position.

A *production equipment where-used list* shows the usage of production equipment within products, more correctly within operations, for manufacturing products.

In analogy to the where-used list of components, the production equipment where-used list is a view of the production equipment on the operations, thus complementing the view of the product. A production equipment is in a "1 to n" association with the operations.

A *collective tool* or *toolkit* is the combination of a set of tools.

A *bill of tools* describes the individual tools that make up a toolkit.

Collective tools are particularly important in machining centers, for example. The structure of a bill of tools is similar to that of a bill of material with its bill of material positions (see Section 16.2.3).

A *tool where-used list* shows the usage of a tool within collective tools.

Bills of tools and tool where-used lists can be compared to bills of material and where-used lists of items. The possible variants of such bills and lists (single-level, multilevel, etc.) correspond to those in Section 16.2.3.

16.2.8 Overview of the Basic Master Data Objects

Figure 16.2.8.1 shows, by way of example, a breakdown of the master data for the ball bearing shown in Figure 16.2.1.1 into the four most important classes, namely item, bill of material position, work center, and operation.

The arrows point to the associations between the logistical objects discussed above, i.e.,

- To the two "1 to n" associations shown in Figure 16.2.3.9 between the item and the bill of material position which determines the "product ↔ component" connection between two items. These connections are *"as a product, consists of"* (product viewpoint) or *"as a component, is used in"* (component viewpoint), depending on which side we start. See also Figure 16.2.3.2.

- To the two "1 to n" associations between the item and work center to the operation (see Section 16.2.6). These connections are *"is produced by"* (product viewpoint) or *"as a work center, is used in"* (work center viewpoint), depending on which side we start.

Figure 16.2.8.2, as a generalization of Figure 16.2.8.1, shows all the fundamental logistical object classes for the master data, together with their associations, for products with *a convergent product structure*. This representation corresponds to the type of data model used in logistics software today.

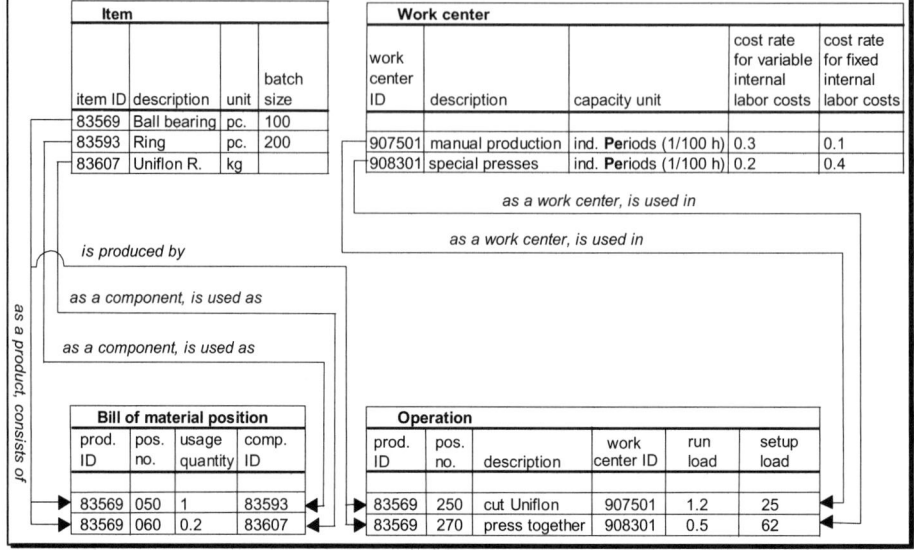

Fig. 16.2.8.1   Breakdown of the master data into individual classes and their associations using the example of the ball bearing (see Figure 16.2.1.1).

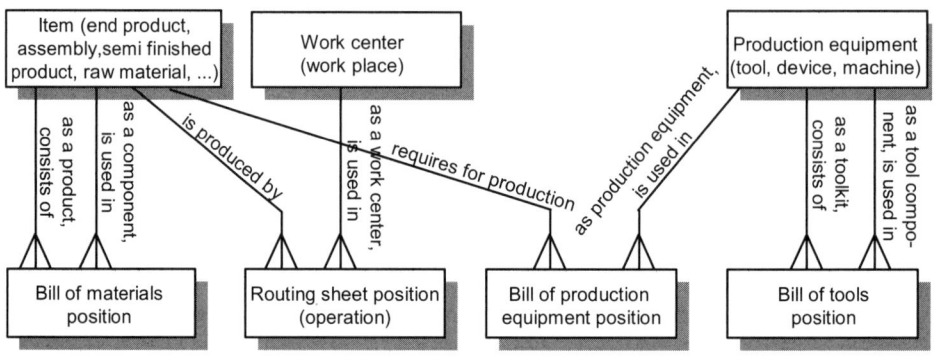

Fig. 16.2.8.2   The basic object classes for planning & control.

Depending on how it is organized, the master data are administered partly by a central standardizing committee and partly directly by the sections in which the data concerned arise, i.e., design or production equipment.

It should be noted that the objects relating to production equipment are similar to the objects relating to the item (see Section 16.2.7). Collective tools or toolkits and their tool bills of material behave in the same way as products and their bills of material. Their use in operations, however, is similar to the use of a work center.

16.3   Extensions Arising from Variant-Oriented Concepts

Variant-oriented concepts were introduced in Section 3.5.3 as an extension of the MRP II and lean / just-in-time concepts. Chapter 6 covered the various techniques for planning & controlling product concepts such as product families and products produced to customer specification, first the process network plan must be refined.

Variants in bills of material and routing sheets were introduced in Section 6.3 as the production rules of an expert system for handling product families with many variants. This section explains the extensions arising from this approach in detail, i.e., the associated tools and objects.

16.3.1 Expert Systems and Knowledge-Based Systems

It is difficult to find a precise definition of the term *expert system* in the literature (see [Apel85]). One practical definition relates, in particular, to the way in which an expert system works:

Expert systems are *knowledge-based information systems*. Such systems:

- Attempt to represent large amounts of knowledge concerning a limited application in a form that is suitable for the particular problem.

- Help to acquire and modify this knowledge.

- At the user's request, draw conclusions from the knowledge and make the result available to the user.

Here, the term *knowledge* incorporates all the stored information that is needed in order to answer queries. Most expert systems differentiate among:

- Facts

- Rules, i.e., knowledge about the facts
- Metarules, i.e., knowledge about the rules

The term *fact base* is used to describe the rules as a whole.

The term *rule base* designates the rules as a whole.

The *inference engine* is a programming logic that applies rules to facts in order to derive new facts in order to answer questions.

Figure 16.3.1.1 illustrates the interaction between the various components of an expert system and its users for the purposes of design and operation.

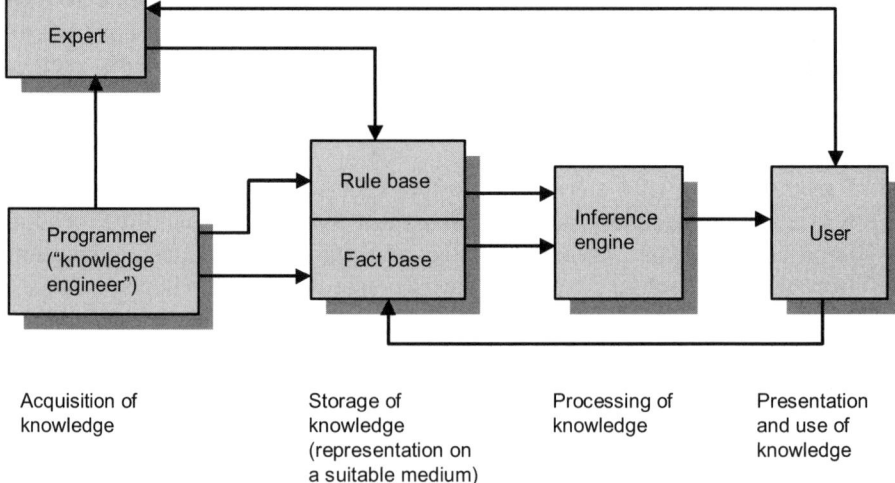

Fig. 16.3.1.1 Organization of an expert system (or knowledge-based information system).

- A programmer is responsible for designing the system.
- An expert drafts and maintains the rules and any metarules.
- The user records and maintains the facts.
- The user starts the inference engine in order to make a query.

The following requirements must be met before we can really speak of an expert system:

- It must be possible to operate an expert system without the help of programmers.

- It must be possible to make queries on the expert system without the help of experts. In practice, however, there is periodic contact between the users and experts in order to supplement or modify the rule base.

- There is clear separation between the rule base and fact base. In practice, however, the rule base is also represented by entities in a database.

- The inference engine is independent of knowledge and facts. If the knowledge changes, the inference engine must not change in any way.

The *rules* of a knowledge base can be presented in different ways. The simplest and the most intuitive form is the production rule.

> A *production rule* is a statement of the "if (condition), then (action)" type, i.e.,
>
> - *If* a certain situation is true (a number of facts), *then* conclude (infer) various actions (a certain number of facts)

The structure of positions in a bill of material and routing sheet, which is made conditional though the use of IF clauses (see the example in Figure 6.3.2.1), precisely corresponds to the structure of production rules in an expert system expressed regressively (from effect to cause): Here, a *production rule in the true sense of the word*, i.e., of a product to be manufactured, corresponds to a *production rule within the expert system* in the applied sense.

The *facts* of the expert system are formed by the item, production equipment, and work center logistical objects and by the values assigned to the query parameters (e.g., for an existing order). The *experts* are the designers and process planners within the company. The *users* are the people who issue, monitor, and produce the orders. See Section 6.3.2.

The *inference engine* works on the chaining principle: The inferred facts can in turn occur in rules (e.g., in the IF clause of a production rule). Further facts can be inferred if the engine is then applied iteratively, particularly to this type of rule. In this case, the inference engine is generally only needed for forward chaining. By analyzing production rules containing IF clauses with the relevant parameters, it is able to return the order bill of material and order routing sheet applicable to the specified parameter values.

A more complex expert system also contains a *declaration component* which makes the rules that are applied transparent to the user. These may be linked to a production rule in text form, for example. In practice, however, most bill of material positions and operations are self-explanatory.

More complex expert systems also suggest methods for handling incomplete knowledge or knowledge arising from conclusions by analogy.

16.3.2 Implementation of Production Rules

The following structure with three objects illustrates a production rule using object classes (see Sections 16.2.1, 16.2.3, 16.2.6, and 16.2.8):

a. The conventional item business object for items and item families, for products and components.

b. The *bill of material position variant* or *operation variant*. This is the conventional object bill of material position or operation, plus a variant number, which also belongs to the bill of material position ID or operation ID.

   The assembly has, for example, u positions, where $u \geq 1$. For each position x, $1 \leq x \leq u$, there are thus v_x variants, $v_x \geq 1$. If there is only one variant, then there is equality; this is the conventional situation with an unconditional bill of material.

c. The IF clause. This is a logical expression in parameters such as "type," "length," etc.

The three objects — product family, position variant, and IF clause — are linked together to form a production rule.

• "If product (a) and IF clause (c) are true, then the position variant (b) applies in the bill of material or routing sheet. In the case of the bill of material, it is thus true (or "is inferred") that the component in (b) is a (new) fact."

If analysis of the rule then "infers" a component and thus adds to the original fact bank, and this component is an intermediate product, then a further pass of the inference engine can activate all the rules and process those that are assigned to the intermediate product (a). Such forward chaining thus corresponds to the processing of a multilevel bill of material (see Section 16.2.3).

The structure shown below is an extension of the traditional bill of material and routing sheet. The generalized structure and special case often encountered in the past are shown in graphical form in Figure 16.3.2.1 for ease of understanding.

Position . Variant		Condition
1.1	if	{Clause 1.1}
or ⋮		
or 1.v_1	if	{Clause 1.v_1}
⋮ ⋮		
u.1	if	{Clause u.1}
or ⋮		
or u.v_u	if	{Clause u.v_u}

Fig. 16.3.2.1   Representation of the bill of material or routing sheet for a product with options (thick lines: standard version without variants).

If we select $v_x = 1$ and no clause for all x, $1 \leq x \leq u$, then we obtain the conventional case of the "unconditional" bill of material or routing sheet position.

Figure 16.3.2.2 shows the conventional bill of material position or operation object supplemented with the variant number with respect to bill of material positions.

	Assembly	Position	Variant	Component	Quantity per	etc.
Before	69015	040		16285	2	
	69015	050		14216	15	
	⌞__Primary key__⌟					
After	69015	040	01	16285	2	
	69015	040	02	16285	1	
	69015	050	01	14216	15	
	69015	050	02	14216	18	
	⌞__Extended primary key__⌟					

Fig. 16.3.2.2   Extended primary key for a bill of material with options.

The simplest version of the IF clause is a succession of simple logical expressions, e.g., connections such as type = 2, order quantity > 100, etc., linked with "and" or "or" in the manner of the disjunctive or conjunctive normal form. See also [Schö88], p. 49 ff. For more complicated connections, it is better to use a formula scanner, which will create the logical expression in free form using the rules of Boolean algebra.

In practice, most bill of material positions and operations are self-explanatory, and a declaration would ideally be a repetition of the rule. In the cases where this does not apply, text linked to a production rule may be used as a *declaration component*, in addition to its true function as a means of storing the operation description and any other comments concerning a position. A special text format differentiates the declaration component from other text, so it can be transferred to the result during the query, as required. This rudimentary form of declaration component is quite sufficient for the problem at hand.

Reference is again made to Section 6.3.3, particularly Figure 6.3.3.1, in order to demonstrate the *way the inference engine works*. It keeps the variants within a position in the best order for the query by counting the variants selected in previous queries and periodically rearranging these variants, sorting them by frequency of occurrence. For his part, the expert selects a criterion, e.g., a lexicographical criterion, suitable for administering and arranging the variants.

16.3.3 A Data Model for Parameterized Representation of a Product Family (*)

The production rules introduced in Section 6.3.2 as an extension of conventional bill of material and operation positions form the basic idea behind the generative technique for product families with many variants.[14] Additional object classes are needed for a complete model. With respect to the information system see also [Pels92], p. 93 ff, [Veen92], [Schö01], Section 12.3, or [Schi01]. See also [SöLe96] for a comprehensive application in the insurance industry. For an application in the banking industry and in the event of uncertainty, see [Schw96].

The master data model introduced in Section 16.2 must be supplemented with at least the following object classes:

---

[14]   In addition to rule-based techniques for product and process configurators, there also are case-based and constraint-based techniques.

- *Parameter* or *product feature*: This is used to define the distinctive characteristics of an item, e.g., dimensions, options, etc.
- *Parameter class*: A product family is described by an "item" entity. The specific products are also characterized by parameters or features. These are combined to form parameter classes for structuring the set of all parameters. The item ID of the product family, together with a value for each parameter of the assigned parameter classes, then defines a product as a specific feature of the product family.

Parameters may be subdivided into:

- *Primary parameters,* which directly characterize the product family.
- *Secondary parameters,* which can be derived from the primary parameters using a rule or formula whose range of values is thus totally dependent on the primary parameters. Secondary parameters are always needed if facts expressed by primary parameters can be better or more simply expressed for certain people using a different term.

The range of values that a parameter can assume may also be partly dependent on other parameters of the same class. In this case, we speak of:

- A plausibility or compatibility test. This can take the form "If …", e.g., "If width > 1000, then height < 500," or "If type = 2, then width ≤ 1500 and height ≤ 1500." The simple logical expressions in the IF and THEN clauses may, however, become very complex.

The components of product families may, in turn, belong to a product family, even one with different parameter classes. It must therefore be possible to transfer parameter values from one parameter class to another, so parameter classes are declared in the form of bills of material:

- *Bill of parameter class position*: This defines how a parameter from a (lower level) class is derived from the parameters of another (higher level) class. As with a secondary parameter, the parameter is derived using a rule or formula. The rule or formula may also be directly linked to the bill of material position that links the component to the product. If this is the case, the rule or formula can only be used to transfer the parameter values of this component from those of the higher level product family.

It has been demonstrated in practice that, for complex connections, the quantities used, setup loads and loads per piece, and setup times and times per piece are dependent on the parameters, rather than being constant. Each of these master data attributes should therefore be linked to an arithmetical formula that expresses this dependency.

The *formula* is a logistical object for defining expressions that are dependent on parameters.

These *formulas* are maintained by the users and must therefore be easy to use. There are *formulas* for:

- *IF or THEN clause, a production rule, and a compatibility test.* If these contain only one parameter, then they can be represented by a table. Otherwise, they are logical expressions in disjunctive or conjunctive normal form or free form, which can be evaluated using a formula interpreter using the rules of Boolean algebra.

- *Range of values.* This may be a table or a general free-form logical expression.

- *Free-form numerical or alphanumerical expression, which nevertheless uses a standardized syntax.* Such an expression may be part of a logical expression or a formula for calculating attributes. A formula interpreter analyzes the algebraic expression using the basic operators, brackets, functions, and constants, with variable parameters, in accordance with the rules of arithmetic.

An object class that saves the parameter values of a specific product from a product family for an order or query is needed as an extension of the object classes for representing orders described in Section 16.1.

- *The parameter value* object is linked to an item receipt order position and defines the value of a parameter for a product family. The parameter value is taken from a range of values. The representation of this range by a formula is discussed further below. Sets of frequently recurring parameter values, e.g., for a cost estimating of "interpolation points" for a product family, may also be defined as part of the master data.

A model defined in this way may be regarded as an expert system. As already mentioned, no one has yet provided a generally applicable definition of this term. Lists of characteristics are normally used to decide whether a system satisfies the requirements of an expert system. A typical list is given on page 7 of [Apel85], which states that "the list should be interpreted such that … the quantitative and qualitative fulfillment of the list is a good gauge of the degree of complexity of an expert system."

Researchers tend only to recognize systems with a high degree of complexity as expert systems. This is certainly not the case for product configuration: The facts can be clearly separated from the rules, a clear application reference is given, and it provides a user-friendly dialog. On the other hand, the inference engine only uses simple deduction mechanisms and the declaration capacity is limited to commenting upon the rules. Nevertheless, the product configuration has become important when using knowledge-based techniques, particularly since the product with a wide range of variants has become a significant marketing strategy.

16.4   Extensions Arising from Processor-Oriented Concepts

Processor-oriented concepts were introduced in Section 3.5.3 as an extension of the MRP II and lean/JIT concepts. The various planning & control techniques for process industries were discussed in Chapter 7.

This section covers processor-oriented production structures in detail. In fact, these can actually be regarded as an extension of the conventional production structure described in Sections 1.2.3 and 16.2.8. This extension is very important since it is likely that the processor-oriented production structure will become the most common model in the future. The conventional, convergent production structure, which is thus linked to a (single) product with its bill of material and routing sheet, will then become an important special case.

In the future, even lot control will become the general administration of stock statuses. Proofs of origin are an increasingly common requirement in the field of logistics and in assembly-oriented systems.

16.4.1 Process, Technology and the Processor-Oriented Production Structure

As already mentioned in Section 7.2.1, product development requires a knowledge of the technologies that can be used in manufacturing processes. Such technologies and processes must be defined in a suitable manner. Figure 16.4.1.1 contains a simple structure.

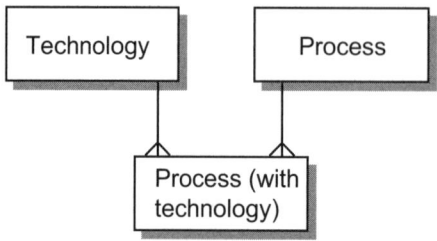

Fig. 16.4.1.1   Technology and process.

A *processor-oriented production structure* (or a *process train*) is a combination of the objects described in Section 7.2.2, such as process stage, basic manufacturing step, and resource.

Figure 16.4.1.2 contains a data model for the processor-oriented production structure.

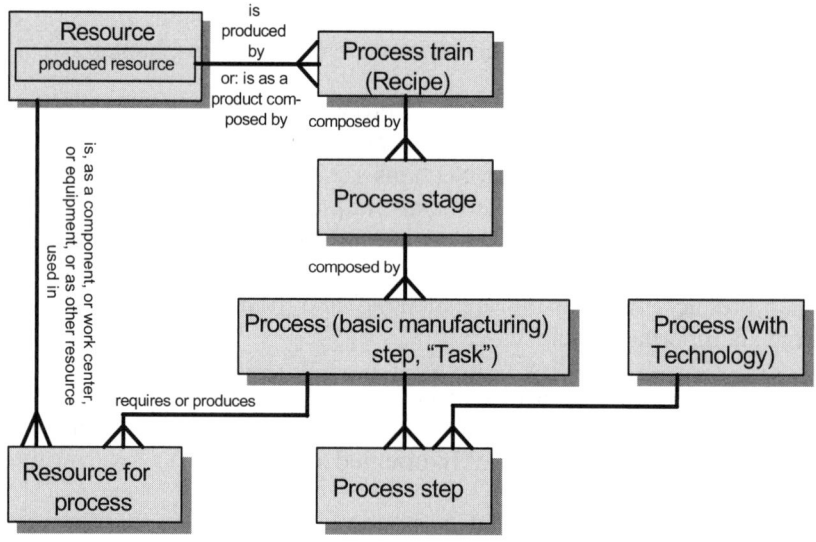

Fig. 16.4.1.2   Process train (processor-oriented production structure, recipe): objects for master data and order data.

The processor-oriented production structure defined in this way may be regarded as an extension of the model of a convergent product structure in

Figure 16.2.8.2. Interestingly, the processor-oriented production structure also corresponds to the processor-oriented order structure.[15] In this case, a stage corresponds to a partial order. An order position is now always work (an operation) to which the other order positions (resources) are assigned.

16.4.2 Objects for Lot Control

Figure 16.4.2.1 shows the objects used for lot control (see Section 7.2.3).

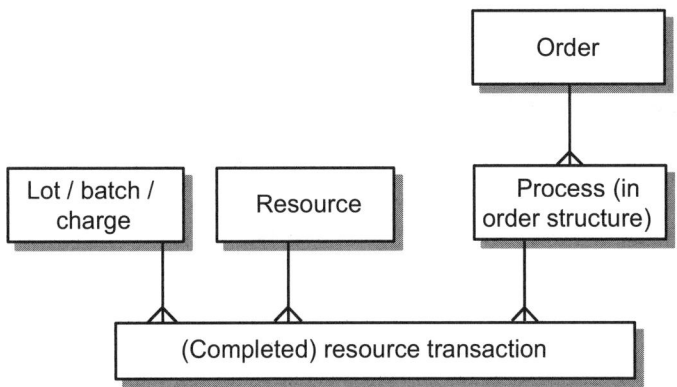

Fig. 16.4.2.1   Objects for lot control in inventory management.

The objects introduced in Section 16.4.1 must therefore be supplemented with the two objects *batch* and *completed resource transaction*. The latter object is still associated with traditional order administration. Transactions are not only used for legal reasons. They also ensure data integrity and are used in statistics concerning inventory transactions.

With this model, the structures of the two stock status and order objects increase in similarity: in fact, the batch may also be regarded as the re-identification of an order ID. Placing a batch in stock simply means placing a production or procurement order in stock, where it remains identifiable as such.

---

[15]   However, the conventional production structure in Figure 16.2.8.2 (bills of material and routing sheet) does *not* correspond to the associated order structure in Figure 16.1.2.2.

16.5   The Management of Product and Engineering Data

Section 4.4 discusses business methods for planning & control in the field of research and development. This essentially means project management for integrating the various tasks that take place during the business process. The interesting aspect here is the simultaneous engineering during both time to market and delivery lead time. Integration is more difficult because the various people involved have different views of the business objects. The CIM concept relates to the computerization of integrated business processes, in which the logistics software and CAx software should be linked to one another.

16.5.1 Engineering Data Management

Figure 16.5.1.1 shows an initial concept for integrating those areas in which the common data should ideally flow in both directions by programming interfaces between every pair of areas.

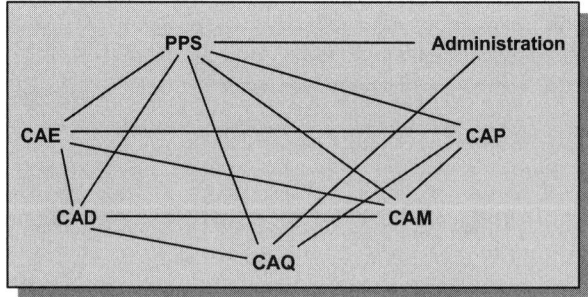

Fig. 16.5.1.1   The EDM concept with interfaces.

Section 4.4.1 and Figure 4.4.4.1 suggest a comprehensive concept.

Engineering data management (EDM) is a concept that enables a company's procedures to be integrated — all across the company. This makes the data available to anyone involved in a business process via an engineering database.

Product data management (PDM) and *CIM handler* are synonymously used terms.

> A *product database* or *engineering database* is a database for commonly used information which can communicate with all information systems in the various areas.

Figure 16.5.1.2 shows the concept of engineering data management.

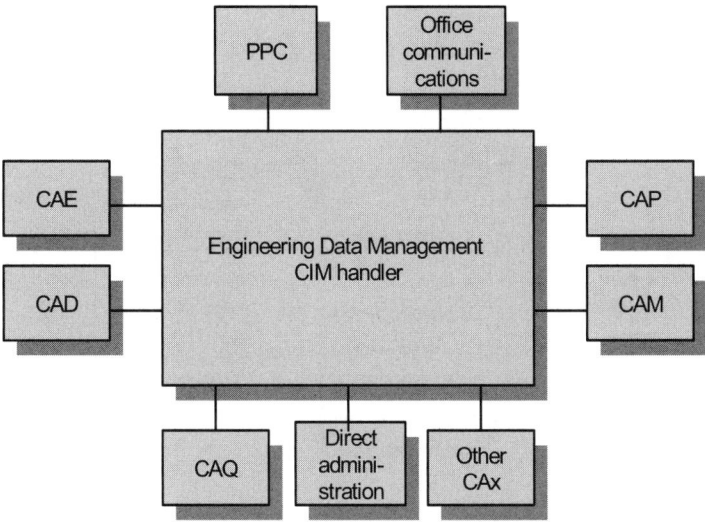

Fig. 16.5.1.2   The concept of engineering data management or the CIM handler.

The product database contains all the information which is used by various CIM areas or components or has to be transported from one CIM component to another, e.g., the master data and technical product descriptions. Most data in the product database are managed directly by a CAx or the PPC software in the engineering database and then referred to by the same or another software. The CIM handlers can also be associated with general office communications. This enables information and proposed action to be passed on to other areas, particularly to the company management and the planning and administration departments.

If is often possible to agree on an *outline model* for the conceptual (logical) aspect of integrated order processing in the R&D area (see Figure 4.4.1.4). The CIM handlers support the important tasks that occur in all CIM areas. Figure 16.5.1.3 shows a possible structure.

For a *detailed EDM model*, the basic idea behind CIM also means that the technical and commercial areas of the company must agree on a common functional and data model to represent the company's products. For example, if the design department requires a certain functionality, then it must be comprehensible to planning & control, and vice versa. Viewed pragmatically, EDM, computerized planning & control, and CAD must ultimately be adapted to one another (see also Figure 4.4.3.2). This will often already apply since, ultimately, the same products are represented and handled in each case.

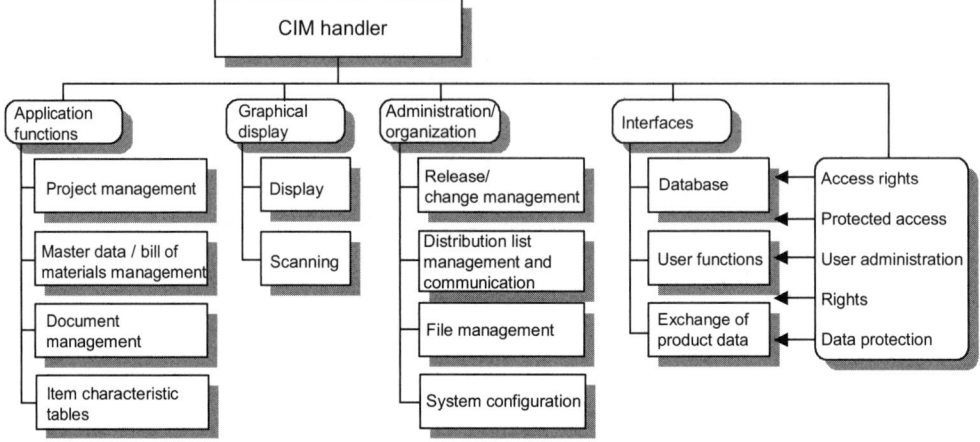

Fig. 16.5.1.3   CIM handlers. (See [EiHi91].)

16.5.2 The Engineering Database as Part of a Computerized System

When implementing CIM, there are and always have been various options concerning the conceptual and technical aspects (see Figure 4.4.1.4). Three concepts are particularly worthy of mention. These have grown up historically. All three concepts involve the use of ideal types that have emerged in hybrid forms from the available software and where it is installed. The third is still applied to prototypes. However, all concepts must have a clear logical structure, and the scope of functions must meet the requirements of users within the company, regardless of how they are implemented physically. The functionality of the individual links may differ greatly, depending on the direction of each link.

1. Point-to-point connections with direct interfaces between the individual CIM components. If there are m CIM components (as shown in Figure 16.5.1.1), then there will be up to m * (m − 1) different interfaces. One relatively old example of an interface

between individual packages is CADMIP, which links CADAM and COPICS. These direct links are still very important today.

2.   Functional integration using an EDMS.

An *engineering data management system* (EMDS) is a database management system that links physically separate databases using the principle of a *data warehouse* as shown in Figure 16.5.2.1. The principle works as follows:

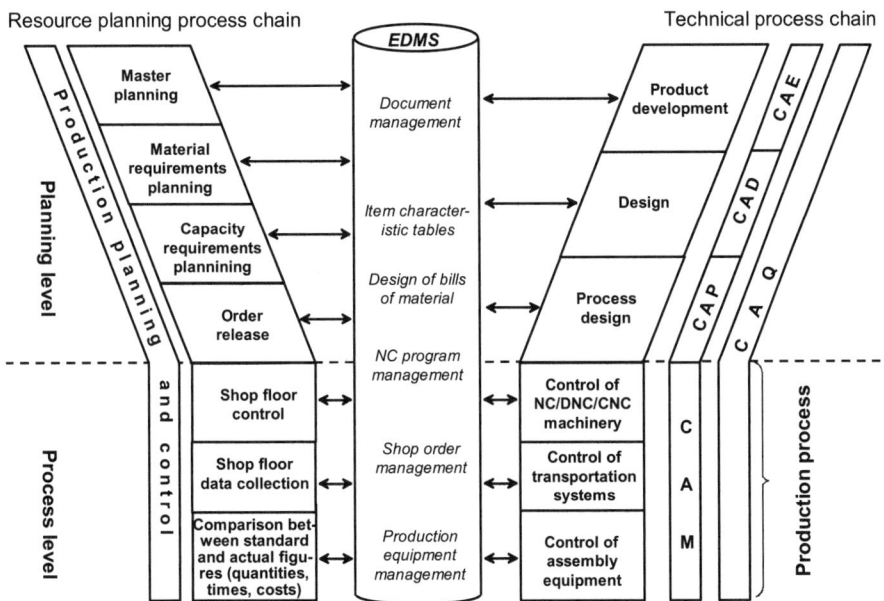

Fig. 16.5.2.1   Integration of order processing by an EDMS (engineering data management system). (From [EiHi91].)

Data are stored in the databases provided by the local software. Whenever data are modified, the changes are transferred to the local database. When a department requests data from the EDMS, it knows the location of all the data in the local databases, but is not aware of the values. The EDMS queries the local database to determine the value of the data and transfers the answers to the system. If there are m CIM components, then there will be up to m interfaces. Frequently requested data is also kept in a redundant central database which is connected to the EDMS. If there is no online interface, the data are transferred in batch mode by extraction programs and declared free format files.

3. Functional integration by creating a common logical and physical *product database*. This results a database management system as shown in Figure 16.5.2.2, which links physically separate databases as follows:

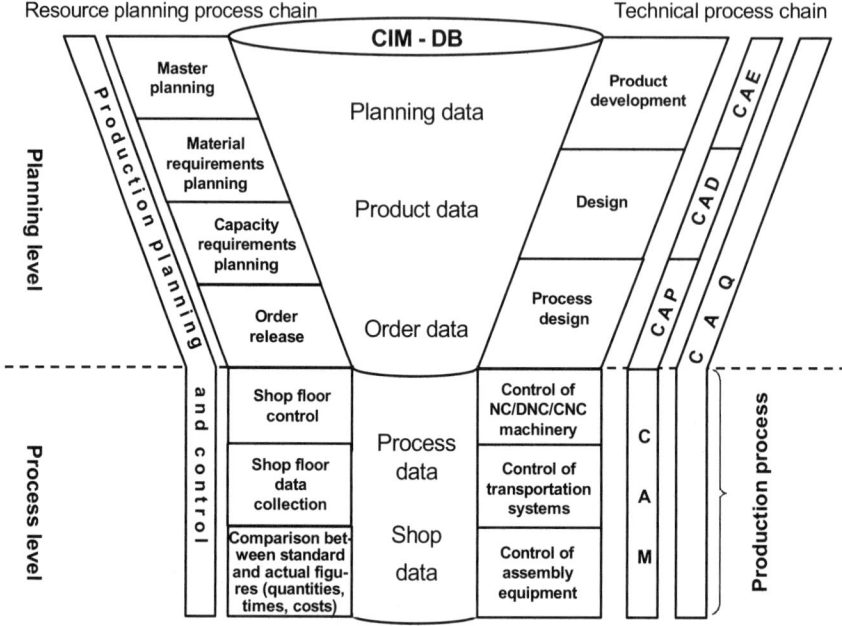

Fig. 16.5.2.2   Integration of order processing functions using a common product database.

Data are stored in the central database. Whenever the data in one CIM component are changed, the data in the central database must change as well. The data are then immediately available to all the other CIM components. Under certain circumstances, the individual applications also have their own, local databases. These are used to store data that are used almost exclusively by the application concerned. For example, the geometric data for a CAD application are located in the local database, while the master data (item, bill of material, etc.) are stored centrally.

16.5.3 Data and Functional Model for General EDM Tasks

The CIM handler is used to manage the technical data that describe a product, together with the relevant standards and classification. Many of these classes can be compared to the master data for planning & control described in Section 16.2:

- *Item master file*: All the technical data used to describe and classify items. This category includes data for defining the release and transfer of data to the corresponding CIM components. Search criteria are used to find items on the basis of different attributes. The item ID may first be assigned provisionally by the designer. However, the standardizing committee within the company must define an appropriate identification before the item may be definitively released. This ID is then used for planning & control.

- *Drawing directory*: This contains additional, item-related data, i.e., data that are usually shown in the drawing header. The attributes are a description; the date on which the drawing was created, checked, or printed; and the people responsible for all these actions. A list of revisions is also provided.

- Special object classes for works standards, e.g., DIN standards, may be kept in separate object classes.

- *Bill of material* (actually the *bill of material position*): This is comprised of the attributes described in Section 16.2.3. These include the "relative position in the drawing," which generally incorporates the relative position number. This forms the bill of material position ID together with the product ID. Other attributes include the date and person responsible for all this information.

- *Work center*, with the attributes shown in shown in Section 16.2.4

- *Production equipment* and *bill of tools* (see Section 16.2.7)

- *Operation* (see Section 16.2.6)

There is also a classification guide to aid the designer's work. This enables an item to be traced using a standardized, hierarchical classification. An example is shown in Figure 16.5.3.1.

The classification guide shown here should ideally be filled in using standardized information, e.g., conforming to DIN 4000. The bottom level of this classification guide corresponds to an item family and is linked to the item characteristic table.

An *item characteristic* is a parameter or criterion that is typically associated with this item family.

An *item characteristic table* is a set of typical attributes for an item family, i.e., a description of a specific item from an item family using values for various item characteristics.

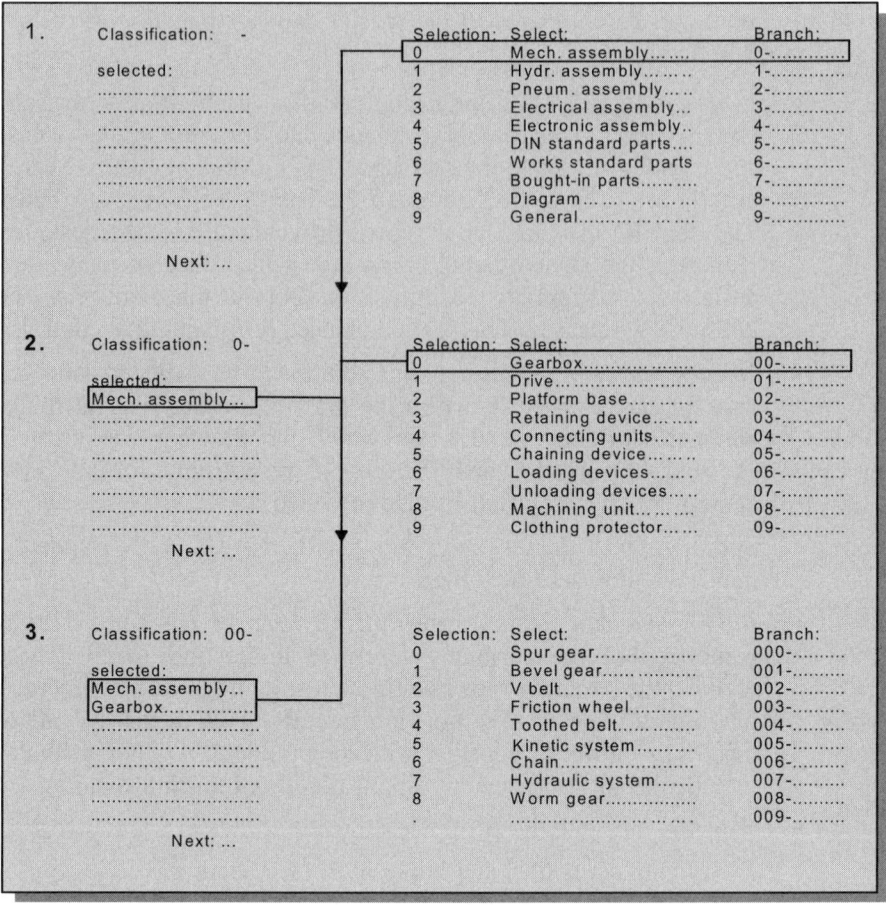

Fig. 16.5.3.1   Standardized classification system. (From [ADIC90].)

The item characteristics and item characteristic table should ideally follow standards, e.g., in Europe, in accordance with DIN 4000. Figure 16.5.3.2 shows the item characteristic table for the item family "shafts."

The top half shows the names of the individual item characteristics for a specific item family. In the bottom part are various items that belong to the same item family. New item characteristics can be added or existing characteristics modified for each item.

Multilevel bills of material or where-used lists would be needed in order to search the bill of material, as would tests for product structures with loops Queries will also be needed for the standardized classification system and item characteristics table hierarchies.

ITEM CHARACTERISTIC TABLE										

Item group: Shafts_____   Classification: 010_____
DIN designation: Shaft-shaped parts_____

Name Designation	Name Designation
1 ___ Item ID _____	F ___ Shoulder length, right _____
A ___ Shaft diameter _____	G ___ Shoulder diameter, right _____
B ___ Total length _____	H ___ Material _____
C ___ Number of shoulders _____	I ___ Material / DIN _____
D ___ Shoulder length, left _____	J ___ Number of turned / relief grooves
E ___ Shoulder diameter, left____	

1	A	B	C	D	E	F	G	H	I	J
120003	40.0	650.0	2	50.0	35.0	125.0	31.0	C60Pb K	DIN1652	1
120004	50.0	550.0	1	50.0	35.0	120.0	41.0	X40Cr	DIN1657	1
120005	30.0	500.0	1	50.0	40.0	125.0	20.0	C60Pb K	DIN1654	1
120007	20.0	450.0	1	40.0	40.0	120.0	20.0	C60Pb K	DIN1654	1
120023	40.0	450.0	2	40.0	40.0	125.0	20.0	C60Pb K	DIN1654	1
	mm	mm	mm	mm	mm	mm	mm			

Fig. 16.5.3.2   Item characteristic table: modification and query. (From [ADIC90].)

16.5.4 Object Classes and Functions for Release and Engineering Change Control (*)

The *EC number* or *engineering change number* is a standard concept in release and engineering change control (ECC). This is a unique and *ascending* number that is assigned to every modification or redesign project.

In principle, a new object is defined for every item belonging to a certain release. This new object has the *same item ID* but is suffixed with a new EC number.[16] A new item should be defined as soon as the function's forward compatibility can no longer be guaranteed. This means that the new item cannot replace the old item in every situation. On the other hand, backward compatibility is not required, i.e., it does not have to be possible to install the old item in place of the new item.

_____

[16]   The EC number can thus be regarded as a mandatory parameter for a product. Depending on this parameter, different bill of material positions and operations can be defined.

The following object classes could be used for administrative checking by the project manager for release and engineering change control (ECC):

- *Project header*, with attributes such as a description of the release, EC number, status and other data for staggered release, in each case indicating the person responsible.

- *Project operation*, defining one of the various stages and works required for release, with attributes such as the EC number, position, description, status, start date, and end date, in each case indicating the person responsible.

- *Project bill of material position*, specifying all the items belonging to the release, in each case with the status, date, and personnel responsible for release of the item; as well as its drawing, bill of material, and routing sheet. There are different pairs of "date / person responsible" attributes for different release stages.

The following functional model could be used for *release control*:

1. Definition of a new version, i.e., of a new release or EC (engineering change):

    - Enter in the project header the date and person responsible.

    - Enter the items belonging to the release, each with date and person responsible for the various tasks, e.g., creating or modifying drawings, bill of material, routing sheet, and item as a whole.

    - Enter the various tasks involved in the release, each with start date, end date, and person responsible.

2. Progress and release:

    - Enter the progress (with status changes) and the end of individual activities, plus correction of the status at a higher level.

    - Allow for (staggered) release of bills of material, routing sheets, the actual item or entire release (of the new version), with automatic correction of the higher level activity list.

3. Queries:

    - Sort work in process by person responsible or various statuses.
    - Monitor deadlines.
    - Indicate the content of a release (of the associated items and activities).

The data could be transferred from and to the CIM components, e.g., for linking CAD and logistics software via the engineering database, using the following functions:

1. Transfer bills of material and any variants online:

   - From the CAD to the engineering database by a "drawing release" process or in the opposite direction by a revision process

   - From the engineering database to the logistics software by a "production release" process or in the opposite direction by a revision process

2. Transfer all: Transfer any data that has not yet been transferred.

3. Similar functions for the item master data, often in the opposite direction — from the logistics software via the engineering database to the CAD system. One example would be the transfer of all item descriptions modified after a certain date, but which have not yet been transferred to the engineering database or other CIM components.

4. Transfer order data from the logistics software to the CAD system: Transfer the item and order ID, optionally with lists of parameter values (see Section 16.3.3), as a request to create a drawing.

16.6   Summary

Orders are the primary instrument of a company's logistics. Order data are thus the fundamental information for logistics. An order is a complex business object. It is made up of an object for data that is entered once only for each order (order header or footer), various partial orders for each order, and various order positions for each partial order. An order position is an item receipt, an item issue, work, or an order operation or production equipment.

A product or process design process creates order-independent data, known as master data. The most important object classes are the item, work center, and production equipment. The bill of material position, operation, and production equipment position object represent links between objects of the specified classes, thus enabling products and processes to be represented. Single-level or multilevel bills of material or where-used lists can be derived from the bill of material positions. Operations can be combined to form routing sheets or work center where-used lists.

Extensions arising from variant-oriented concepts concern knowledge-based techniques for representing conditional positions in the bill of material and routing sheet. Product families can thus be suitably represented in a data model. Many software packages already contain such models.

Extensions arising from processor-oriented concepts concern processor-oriented production structures and lot control objects, in particular. These are particularly important because they form the future standard for modeling logistics software.

Engineering data management (EDM) brings together the organizational, conceptual (logical), and technical (physical) aspects: The organization of structures and procedures is considered in the conceptual (logical) question, while the technical (physical) aspects involve the networking of computer operating systems. The conceptual (logical) aspect also involves agreeing on common data and functional models, known as CIM handlers for general EDM tasks. These include item characteristic tables and object classes and functions for release and change management. This can be implemented in at least three ways: (1) direct interfaces, (2) interposition of an EDMS linked to "local" systems at every stage of the adding value process, and (3) creation of a common logical and physical database installed on every platform that carries out logistical order administration.

16.7   Keywords

16.8   Scenarios and Exercises

16.8.1 Different Forms of Representing Bills of Material

Figure 16.8.1.1 shows the bill of material for products A and K represented in the form of the familiar arborescent structure.

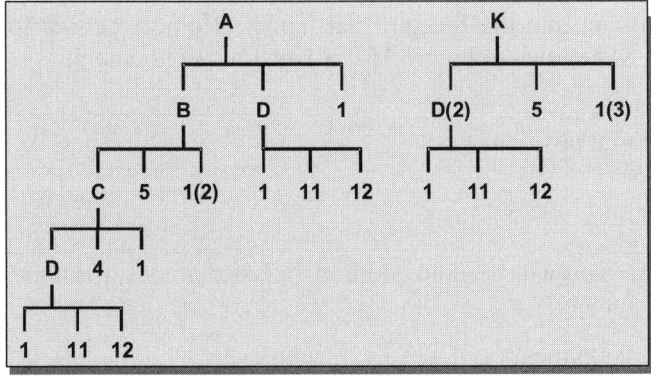

Fig. 16.8.1.1   Graphical representation of the bill of material of products A and K.

In parentheses you see the quantity per of a component, if it is not equal to one. For example, product K is assembled from two units of component D, one unit of component 5, and three units of component 1.

From the two bills of material above, derive the following forms of representation, as described in Section 16.2.3:

- All single-level bills of material

- Two multilevel bills of material for final products A and K

- Two summarized bills of material for final products A and K

16.8.2 Where-Used Lists

On the basis of Figure 16.8.1.1, derive all types of where-used lists following the forms of representation in Section 16.2.3:

- All single-level where-used lists
- Multilevel where-used list for component 1
- Summarized where-used list for component 1
- Arborescent structure of the multilevel where-used list of component 1 (*hint*: it looks similar to Figure 16.8.1.1)

16.8.3 Basic Master Data Objects

Take products A and B, as they were defined in the exercise in Section 15.7.2 (in other words, with the individual tools).

Transfer the given data into the fundamental logistical object classes for the master data, as was shown in Figure 16.2.8.1 or 15.2.1.3, namely:

- Item
- Bill of material position
- Work center
- Operation

To enter all the data, you will need an additional class that was mentioned in Figure 16.2.8.2, namely:

- Production equipment (tool, device, machine)

Determine all the necessary attributes and their values for the individual objects (entities) in these five classes.

Hints: The number of objects per class is as follows:
- Item: 3
- Work center: 2
- Production equipment: 6   (2 machines and 4 tools / devices)
- Bill of material position: 2
- Operation: 4

Part C. Overview of Further Management Systems in the Enterprise

In the following, the enterprise is understood as a sociotechnical system. The individual components of the system as well as their relationships, both within the system and to surrounding systems, are complex in nature. Accordingly, various interested parties have an impact on the company. Each of these interests has a different idea of company goals. The company must fulfill all of these requirements, which makes management of the organization a complex task. Integrated company management means building simultaneous management systems from different enterprise views and fulfilling interlocking management tasks. Figure 17.0.0.1 shows these views in three dimensions of business activity.

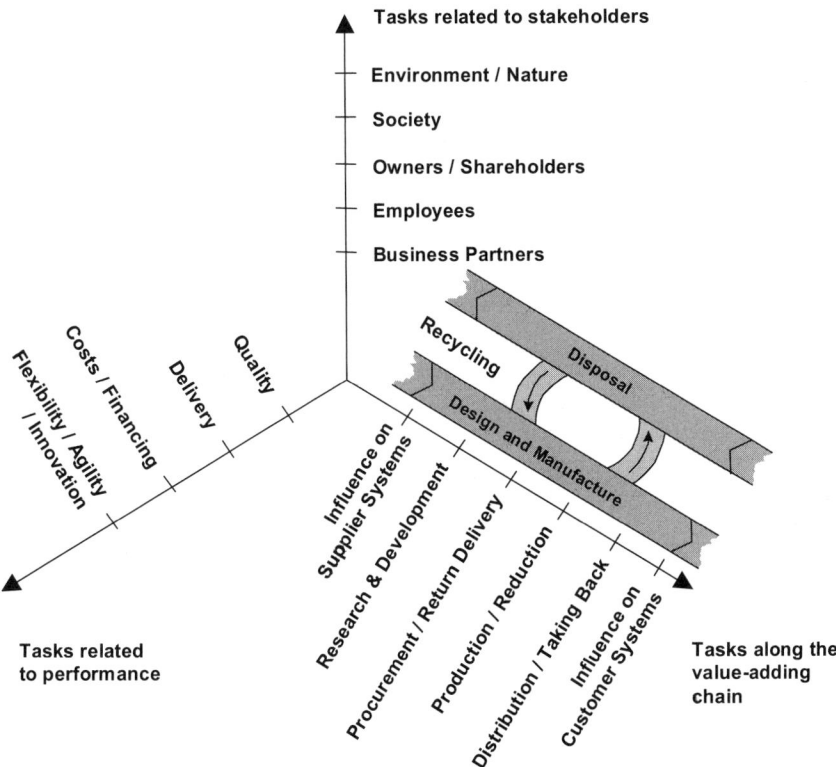

Fig. 17.0.0.1   Three dimensions of business activity.

Management systems in the company can be built along these dimensions. Thus, there are management systems for

- Tasks along the *value-adding chain*: These management systems encompass both short-range and long-range tasks. Today, advanced logistics partnerships are required in order to meet customer goals. For instance, the company's own management systems should affect customers and especially suppliers, just as customers and suppliers influence the management systems. This close partnership is necessary also from the perspective of the comprehensive product life cycle. Today, product returns from the customer, disassembly, recycling, and returns to suppliers have to be considered as part of value-adding and paid for accordingly.

- Tasks in connection with the *stakeholders* of the enterprise: Customers especially, but also suppliers, must be seen as business partners. Depending on market conditions with regard to supply and demand, customers and suppliers are treated differently, of course. Individual stakeholders, such as employees and owners (shareholders) stand opposite the collective stakeholders in the form of society – that is, the macro-economic system in which the company as a microcosm is embedded. In the figure, the environment (nature) is shown as a personified stakeholder. In practice, of course, the demands of the environment become manifest only through the environmental consciousness of the other stakeholders mentioned.

- Tasks related to company *performance*: Here are the management systems that focus on company objectives in various areas. See here also Section 1.3.1. Priority areas are the expected quality and delivery as well as required costs and financing. The degree of goal attainment in these areas generally has a direct effect on business results. Then there is also the area that can be called flexibility, agility, and innovation. These are usually potentials. In these cases, the extent of goal attainment in this area has an indirect impact on business results, via future performance in the other three areas. Tasks related to company performance influence each other mutually and function as tasks that cut across the tasks along the value-adding chain and the tasks related to stakeholders.

The chapters in Part A and Part B treat logistics and operations management as the management system in the enterprise that focuses in particular on expected delivery – on goals such as customer service ratio, delivery reliability, and short lead times. There is no other management system within the company that focuses to this extent on these objectives.

Thus, logistics and operations management is a task oriented to company performance. In order to achieve the objectives, not only do the persons involved have to be in command of appropriate methods, techniques, and tools, but also the corresponding way of thinking has to be successfully anchored in all of the management systems along the entire value-adding chain. For logistics and operations management as supply chain management, it is particularly important that this way of thinking is also anchored across companies, in the whole supply chain. Integral logistics management monitors value-adding over the entire product life cycle, but considers just as much the impact on the various stakeholders, especially the business partners.

Logistics and operations management and also supply chain management are closely interconnected with various other management systems in the enterprise. In addition to strategic management, these systems include in particular technology and product innovation management, the financial and cost accounting system, information management, knowledge and know-how management, and system and project management. For this reason, it makes sense to provide an overview of some of these management systems, in Part C of this edition and continuing in future editions of this book, and, most especially, to show why and where the linkages exist. In any case, the information provided here is meant to serve as a summary, which is why no scenarios or exercises are provided. References are provided for readers who wish to consult works that treat the topics in greater depth.

Our overview of further management systems in the enterprise begins here with quality management. The reason is that there is a special interconnection between logistics, or operations, management and quality management, particularly in their extended forms, meaning integral logistics management and total quality management or Six Sigma. Both management systems focus on fulfillment of concrete customer needs and thus belong to the area of operational management of the enterprise. The famous Japanese approaches give priority to a combination of concepts from both systems. The Toyota Production System, for example, combines the lean / just-in-time concept with the jidoka concept, which a concept for quality management.

Systems engineering and project management are also very strongly connected with logistics and operations management. *First*, the associated tasks in their entirety can be understood as management systems. The design, development, and continuous improvement of these systems must be approached using the methods of systems engineering and project management. *Second*, some tasks are unique (one-of-a-kind), e.g. in facility location planning, in the project business, or in customer-specific services (production and procurement without order repetition). *Third*, some techniques are used in both areas. These are, among others, scheduling techniques, such as the Critical Path Method CPM and the Gantt chart, and methods of financial evaluation of investments, such as the payback or Net Present Value methods.

17 Quality Management – TQM and Six Sigma

This chapter provides an overview of the management system called TQM (*total quality management*). In recent years, the Six Sigma program has come to the fore in the quality movement. Figure 17.0.0.1 showed that "quality" must always be seen relative to what is happening in the entire company. Quality management is therefore a task that is oriented to company performance.

To achieve goals in the area of quality, it is necessary to master the specific elements of the management concept for quality and to integrate these goals appropriately in all management systems along the value chain. Beyond that, comprehensive quality management and Six Sigma are systems within comprehensive company management, which like probably no other management system focuses on the needs and expectations of internal and external stakeholders.

The first section in this chapters deals with the concept of quality, its measurability. The second part provides a summary of the tasks of quality management at the operations level. Part three looks at the more strategic tasks as related to total quality management and Six Sigma.

17.1 Quality: Concept and Measurement

The historical development of the topic of quality management resulted in very different ideas about what the term means. In common usage, quality means the good characteristics of an object. For instance, we speak of a "quality object" and mean that an object is well-made. In that usage, quality is equated with good quality, the term being used to indicate a positive value. However, particularly in the field of economics, it has become customary to use the term quality as a neutral term, following its original definition.

> The term *quality* originated in the sixteenth century, derived from the Latin "qualis," meaning to be made in some way or being in a certain condition or state. According to dictionaries, quality always refers to an object and stands for its state, feature characteristic, or nature.

It is only according to the sense of this definition that degrees of quality (excellence) can be stated, that we can speak of "quality improvement." However, in many discussions on quality, it is apparent that people have certain angles of vision or standpoints. There are indeed different ways to view quality. For example, Joseph M. Juran defines quality as "fitness for use" [Jura88, see also www.juran.com]. Consumers and suppliers have different understandings of quality, as do usually the different organizational units within a company. "Quality" is hence a multilayered term. It is not by chance that the following four disciplines, among others, have dealt with the concept of quality: philosophy, business sciences, marketing, and operations management.

In the company environment, quality can relate to various objects. At the foreground stand the processes and the products of an enterprise or a service-providing public organization. In the sense of total quality, however, the company or service provider as a whole is such an object.

17.1.1 Quality of Processes

A *process* comprises certain activities that lead from a beginning state to an end state and thus to certain functions. Examples of processes include:

- An assembly process, through which an assembly is built from various components
- A procurement process, through which various materials are purchased
- A quality control process, through which procured or manufactured parts are tested and verified for features and characteristics to specified requirements.

Processes come in different degrees of complexity. A process may be an individual, elementary activity or a large-scale business process that is designed to produce a significant business outcome, called a product. Certain processes have a special structure.

> A *service* is a process that a customer views as the performance of some useful function.

Examples of services include:

- Installing equipment and bringing it into service at the customer location
- Service and maintenance during use of a product

- Business consultancy in the broadest sense, particularly also sales advising and the sale itself

It makes a difference to the customers whether they buy a finished product and can judge only the quality of the outcome or whether they experience the processes themselves and thus can judge the quality of the process. With a view to quality management, it is of interest that customers buying products increasingly want to observe exactly the processes that result in the products. For this reason, Figure 17.0.0.1 postulates also a supplier management system, which among other objectives aims towards knowledge of the supplier's processes.

Services provided to dependents is a process in which the customer is not only the object upon which the process occurs; the customer also ends up with a limited capacity to act to which the service provider has contributed.

Examples of these processes include:

- Processes in training and education
- Processes in connection with patients in health care
- Treatment of delinquents by the justice system.

In these cases, the affected persons have restricted free will, which can lead to their treatment not as customers, but more as the objects of guardianship. However, the affected persons in this situation are particularly positioned to form judgments about the quality of a service.

Process quality is the quality of processes.

Process quality is judged according to certain subjective or objective characteristics of quality of processes. To these belong the features shown in Figure 17.1.1.1:

- Accuracy: precision in meeting expectations
- Reliability: consistency, for example, of same process when repeated
- Safety: For example, as related to undesirable side-effects
- Competence: skill, expertise, professionalism in execution (sovereignty)
- Courtesy: friendliness and comfort (for example, of a service)
- Load: amount of work content required (often measured in time units)

Fig. 17.1.1.1   Characteristics of the quality of processes.

Process time is the period of time during which the process runs.

> *Process load*, that is, the burden that the process places on the customer, is the work or effort content through which the characteristic effect of the process is achieved.

Process load should not be confused with process time:

- Process time can be shortened, for example by putting more people to work (splitting) or by executing sequential work steps in an overlapping fashion. The process load is higher, but for a shorter time.

- Process time also encompasses waiting times: When are people ready to begin the service? When is a means of transport available to take a person from A to B?

Process time, which is of interest to the customer in addition to process load, is influenced by factors that lie outside of the nature of the process, namely, in the area of logistics management.

Increasing quality with regard to individual process characteristics can lead to greater work content. Increased work content as a rule results in longer process times. Here a conflict between the target areas quality and delivery becomes apparent.

17.1.2 Quality of Products

> *Product quality* is the quality of products

Products can be either of material or non-material nature, for example:

- Raw materials, purchased parts, semi-processed items, finished items in an industrial or commercial enterprise
- Insurance products, banking products, consulting products, travel arrangements in service industries.

Generally, a product represents the outcome of processes. Here we are not interested in the quality of the processes, but rather only the quality of the product according to the characteristics listed below.

The second group of examples above also shows that services performed, that is, the outcome of the process with the customer, can be viewed as products. In this kind of process, products can also be used as components. Consider a trip by train or plane. Here various products can complement the primary service, such as meals or travel items. In some cases, especially when various service providers have the same process quality, these products – although secondary at first glance – can be deciding factors.

In a buyer's market, a product provider has to offer ever more services and advice along with the product. The product supplier in this way becomes a real systems supplier of a general contractor type. The outputs of the company are then the products as well as the processes that provide the products to the customer. The product concept shifts more and more to a product in a broad sense. In the insurance industry, for instance, the core product is a specifically assembled insurance policy. But it is complemented by services, so that in the end there is a package that is being offered as a product and perceived by the customer as such (see here Section 1.1.1.) Product and process thus stand ultimately in a dual relationship.

Product quality is judged according to certain subjective or objective *characteristics of quality of products*. Figure 17.1.2.1 shows several features of quality.

- Resource consumption
- Effect, function
- Consistency, durability, and reliability
- Conformance to pre-established or expected standards
- Features, workmanship
- Ease of use and aesthetics
- Recyclable, disposability

Fig. 17.1.2.1   Characteristics of the quality of products.

Targets in the area of quality are derived from these characteristics. Costs and delivery lead time, in contrast, do not belong to the characteristics of the product, as long as we are not viewing the product in its most comprehensive sense. Costs and delivery lead time can be influenced in particular by logistics management, for example by type of stockkeeping or type of resource use.

17.1.3 Quality of Organizations

Interested and affected parties have a perception of an enterprise that goes beyond the company's products or processes. This is the perceived quality of the company's work as a whole. This is true for any type of organization, including organizations in the public sector.

> *Organizational quality*: is the quality of organizations, meaning the quality of the organization as a whole.

The quality of organizations can be evaluated comprehensively, as was shown in Figure 17.0.0.1. Anyone who has an interest or stake in a business is a stakeholder. Stakeholders include employees, suppliers, creditors, customers, shareholders, local communities, and anyone else who is affected by the operations of the business. A stakeholder will have a subjective – frequently also self-centered – perception of the quality of an organization. Generally, the stakeholders described here define their requirements of the organization independently of one another.

Organizational quality also is judged according to certain subjective or objective *characteristics of the quality of organizations*. Figure 17.1.3.1 assigns the various characteristics to meaningful groups. The interested parties standing behind these groups are the *stakeholders*.

- Quality in view of business partners
- Quality in view of employees of the organization
- Quality in view of shareholders
- Quality in view of society and environment / nature

Fig. 17.1.3.1   Quality towards the stakeholders of an organization.

- *Quality in view of business partners.* What is the customer's perception of the company's performance? Some criteria of the processes are already listed in Figure 17.1.1. Additional criteria apply to the organization as a whole, such as responsiveness, credibility, accessibility and communication, and understanding the customer. The characteristics of products are mentioned in Section 17.1.2. Moreover, customer satisfaction is more than satisfaction with the products and processes offered; there is a higher level of customer satisfaction that is the perception of receiving total care. In sellers' markets, the company must treat its suppliers similarly, attending to what is called "supplier satisfaction."

- *Quality in view of employees in the organization.* Employees also have expectations of the organization. The summary criterion of "employee satisfaction" encompasses a whole host of characteristics, such as compensation, the type of leadership in the organization, executability of tasks, flexibility and options for creativity in plans-of-work and work hours, material safety, and so on.

- *Quality in view of shareholders.* Certainly owners and shareholders will judge the quality of their company mainly according to financial results. On closer inspection, however, money stands also for deeper needs, such as owners' individual financial security or independence.

- *Quality in view of society and the environment.* Society as a whole places requirements on an enterprise even if it is not the owner of the company in the literal sense. These requirements are often set down in laws or codes of conduct. The quality of a company is proportionate to how well its processes, products, and conduct fit into the given framework. The characteristics are, for example, the safety of society and the protection of the integrity and property of its citizens. In the general sense, the same holds for the environment, where laws are given as natural laws. In practice, the requirements of the environment become manifest only in the consciousness of the other stakeholders mentioned. The quality of an enterprise is then evaluated according to whether it adheres to these laws as society demands. Characteristics are, for example, protection of the environment and responsible use of resources.

17.1.4 Quality and Its Measurability

The International Organization for Standardization (ISO) provides a formal definition of quality.

> "*Quality* is the totality of characteristics of an entity that bear on its ability to satisfy stated and implied needs" [ISO 8402].

In contrast to quantities (amounts), measurability is not contained in the term quality (nature, quality, character) from the start. But the nature, quality, character of an object is nevertheless assessed. The measurability of quality could be advantageous for quality management: "you can only improve what you measure," say some executives. However, measurability requires a measurement system.

> The *measurement system* contains goal or target that is to be achieved through the measurement (*measurement objective*), from which a *metric* must be derived.

The metric must be scaled appropriately, that is, divided into units of measure, and sensors collecting data to obtain a measurement in these units of measure must be made available. Moreover, the metric must be of a kind that can be translated into concrete corrective actions. Figure 17.1.4.1 shows well-known problems that arise with this endeavor.

> • Easily measurable metrics can be disadvantageous in that it is not clear what caused the measurements obtained and therefore not clear what actions and measures should be taken for improvement.
>
> • The other way round, metrics can be identified based on potential corrective actions for improvement. However, their measurement can exceed the budget and resources available, or the budget and resources required may be unforeseeable.

Fig. 17.1.4.1   Problems of the measurability of metrics and the step from measurement to corrective actions.

Characteristics that are relatively easy to measure are the physical characteristics of products and processes. This is the realm of traditional quality inspection and quality assurance. Both favorable outcomes and failures can be measured.

If the quantitative measures and the desired values are laid down in the product requirement specifications, the object can be measured accordingly. It is more difficult to determine whether the measurements obtained also satisfy stakeholders. It can happen that certain characteristics that are of crucial importance to stakeholders have not even been identified.

In connection with people, the measures are frequently combined and are general in content. Take, for instance, the characteristic *customer satisfaction*. Here it is not sufficient to measure some general value. The problem to be mastered is assessment of the customer's judgment of performance as to individual quality characteristics, while keeping cost and effort within reasonable bounds. On the time axis, the assessment should take place, where possible, in an events-related manner (for example, in reference to products or services sold). However, in the area of consumer goods particularly, many characteristics of customer satisfaction lie within the individual realm of the customer and may even be subconscious on the part of the customer. Measurement that provides objective and interpretable cause and effect analyses is thus often an illusion.

Similarly difficult is the measurement of *employee satisfaction*. People are not easily willing or even capable of openly explaining their conscious or unconscious needs. However, the effort that is required should not prevent us from measuring that which is feasible to measure.

It is interesting that frequently there will be some employees that have exact knowledge of their own needs and the needs of other stakeholders. It is therefore very important that these people be involved in the development and use of measurement systems in those areas.

17.1.5 Quality Measurement and Six Sigma

Six Sigma had its origins in the 1970s in Japan, in ship-building and in the electronics and consumer goods industry. In the second half of the 1980s, Six Sigma – pioneered first by Motorola – was introduced as a program to reduce defects in the manufacturing of electronic components. It included a set of methods and techniques focused on quality improvement. Later, the Six Sigma philosophy came to be applied to other business processes as well and for the same purpose, namely, in order to achieve reliable processes. The aim is to reduce variation and defects and to do so in all areas of company performance. Today, Six Sigma is important

- as a metric
- as a problem solving methodology, or method for improving performance
- as a management system.

This section focuses on the first definition.

The term "sigma" is often used as a scale for levels of 'goodness' or quality.

Sigma, the 18th letter of the Greek alphabet used as a mathematical symbol, was employed for many years by statisticians, mathematicians, and engineers as a unit of measurement for the standard deviation.

Six Sigma as a metric is a specific scale for measuring the number of successful products, events, processes, operations, or opportunities.

Figure 17.1.5.1 shows the conversion table for one to Six Sigma.

Sigma	Rate of successful opportunities in %	Failure rate per million opportunities
1	30.9	691462
2	69.1	308538
3	93.3	66807
4	99.4	6210
5	99.98	233
6	99.99966	3.4

Fig. 17.1.5.1   The sigma conversion table.

The conversion table shows an exponential scale, which does not, however, accord with the standard deviation of the normal distribution, as it is often assumed (a glance at the tables in Section 10.3.3 provides easy confirmation of this). Motorola defined the Six Sigma level as equal to 3.4 DPMO. In the world of practice, however the mathematical explanation of the conversion table does not stand at the center of attention.

Six Sigma Quality is defined as a level of quality that represents no more than 3.4 DPMO (defect parts per million opportunities).

Figure 17.1.5.2 compares Three Sigma and Six Sigma process reliability, considering examples given by Motorola.

Reliability 99% (~ Three Sigma)	Reliability 99,9999% (~ Six Sigma)
20000 pieces of mail lost every hour	7 pieces of mail lost every hour
Unsafe drinking water almost 15 min. every day	1 min. unsafe drinking water every 7 month
5000 incorrect surgical procedures every week	1.7 incorrect surgical procedures every week
2 critical landings at major airports each day	2 critical landings at major airports every 5 years
200 000 incorrect drug prescriptions filled / year	68 incorrect drug prescriptions filled every year
Almost 7 hours without electricity every month	Almost 1 hour without electricity every 34 years

Fig. 17.1.5.2   Three Sigma and Six Sigma process reliability.

17.2   Quality Management Tasks at the Operations Level

Quality management is a set of actions of the general management function which determines the quality policy and aims and responsibilities and realizes them through means of quality planning, quality control, quality assurance, and quality improvement within the framework of the quality management system [ISO 8402].

Six Sigma of quality management focuses on the objects.

Six Sigma as a problem solving methodology, or method of improving performance is a method for improving products, procedures, processes, operations, or opportunities.

Within this context, the aim is to understand customer requirements and to improve the business processes that fulfill those requirements as rapidly and as sustainable as possible. Beyond the methods of quality management, the Six Sigma methodology attaches great importance to utilizing rigorous data analysis to minimize variation in business processes. The improvement processes are more precisely specified in measures of Six Sigma; this allows standard implementation.

17.2.1 The Deming Cycle (PDCA Cycle) and the Shewhart Cycle

The Deming cycle, or PDCA cycle (also known as PDSA cycle), was an early means of representing the task areas of traditional quality management. The cycle is sometimes referred to as the Shewhart/Deming cycle since it originated with physicist Walter Shewhart at the Bell Telephone Laboratories in the 1920s. W. Edwards Deming modified the Shewart cycle in the 1940s and subsequently applied it to management practices in Japan in the 1950s.

> The Shewhart cycle ([Shew39], p.45) is defined in Figure 17.2.1.1.

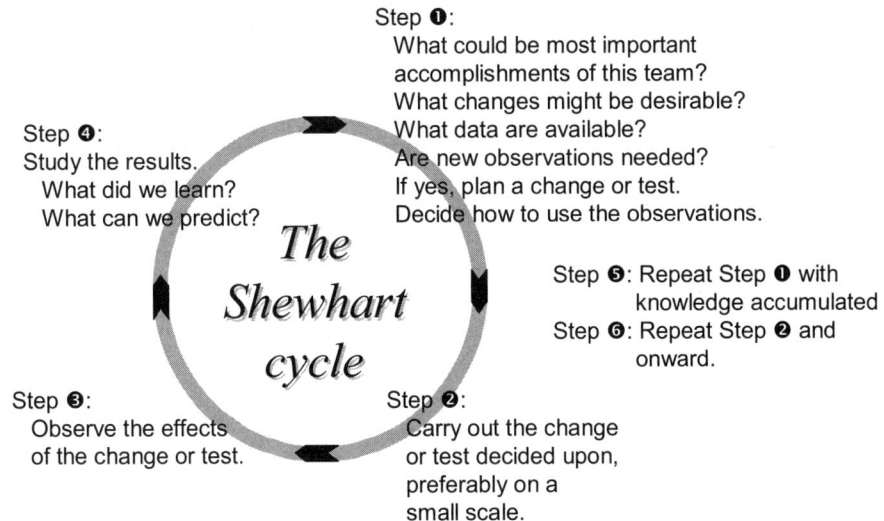

Step ❶:
What could be most important accomplishments of this team?
What changes might be desirable?
What data are available?
Are new observations needed?
If yes, plan a change or test.
Decide how to use the observations.

Step ❹:
Study the results.
What did we learn?
What can we predict?

The Shewhart cycle

Step ❺: Repeat Step ❶ with knowledge accumulated
Step ❻: Repeat Step ❷ and onward.

Step ❸:
Observe the effects of the change or test.

Step ❷:
Carry out the change or test decided upon, preferably on a small scale.

Fig. 17.2.1.1   The Shewhart cycle developed in statistical quality control.

> The *Deming cycle* ([Demi86], p. 88), shown in Figure 17.2.1.2, is the application of the Shewhart cycle.

The Deming cycle is also called the Plan, Do, Check, Act cycle (PDCA cycle). Figure 17.2.1.3 describes in greater detail the logical sequence of the four cyclical tasks in the spirit of continuous quality improvement.

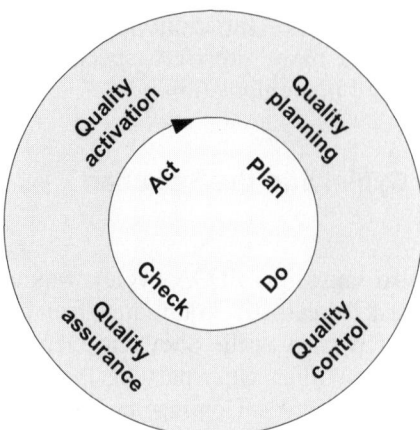

Fig. 17.2.1.2   Quality management tasks in the Deming cycle.

- Plan: Develop plan for quality improvement. In the value chain, this takes place mainly during product and process development.

- Do: Execute the plan in order to control quality. Implement change measures that impact the flow of goods along the value-added chain, that is, during procurement, production, and distribution.

- Check: Check and study the effects of implementation. This involves the tasks of measurement and testing in classical quality assurance.

- Act: Take action to standardize or improve the process. The focus is on acting on what was learned from the changes. The results lead to an improvement in quality. The result may require small refinements, but this is confirmation of the results found and equals quality improvement.

Fig. 17.2.1.3   Description of quality management tasks in the Deming cycle.

The fourth task in particular gives an indication of why, in total quality management, this same model is applied not only to systems in the value chain, but also to systems that impact stakeholders (see Figure 17.0.0.1). In those cases, the behavioral aspect – that is, making the changes a routine part of activity – has special significance (see here Section 17.3).

17.2.2 The Six Sigma Phases

The Six Sigma methodology is a sequence of phases, that is usually called DMAIC.

> *DMAIC* is an acronym for process improvement consisting of the following phases: Define, Measure, Analyze, Improve, and Control.

These phases are usually depicted with a beginning and an end, as shown in Figure 17.2.2.1.

Fig. 17.2.2.1   DMAIC, the Six Sigma phases.

These phases consist in the tasks shown in Figure 17.2.2.2

- Define: Define the project goals and the needs and expectations of internal and external customers
- Measure: Measure the performance of the process involved.
- Analyze: Analyze the data collected to determine root causes of defects
- Improve: Improve the process by elimination of the defects
- Control: Control the improvements to keep the process on the new course

Fig. 17.2.2.2   Description of tasks in the Six Sigma phases.

As compared to the Shewhart or Deming cycle, it is noticeable that the Six Sigma phases are not arranged in a circular form. This is in accordance with the view that a Six Sigma project is run through once to achieve a result. A further rotation of the Deming cycle type forms a new Six Sigma project of its own. Overall, the effect achieved is similar to the continuous improvement type of management system.

In the following, we will see that the five Six Sigma phases can be assigned quite well to the four tasks in the Deming cycle. However, the Six Sigma phases provide additional action catalogues and checklists that make operationalization generally easier. For each phase, there is a list of results and control questions that is intended to assure the comprehensiveness of the approach.

There are a number of important variants of DMAIC:

> *RDMAIC* is an acronym that stands for a DMAIC process that adds Recognize as an additional, initial phase.

As a part of the Recognize phase, company management seeks to identify opportunities for improvement. In many cases, this phase is a part of the Define phase.

> *DMAICT* is an acronym for a DMAIC process with a subsequent Transfer phase.

In the Transfer phase, best practices are transferred, or spread, to other areas of the organization.

An important variant of the DMAICT process focuses on the product development process.

> *DMADV* is an acronym for an improvement process that proceeds through the phases Define, Measure, Analyze, Design, and Verify.
>
> *DFSS (Design for Six Sigma)* comprises methods and instruments for ensuring that products and processes are designed at the outset to meet Six Sigma requirements.

Through DFSS and DMADV, the aim is to make later DMAIC processes less frequently necessary. As the two initial Ds indicate, the methods and tools largely correspond to those in DMAIC.

17.2.3 Quality Planning – Define Phase

> *Quality planning* is a term used today for all planning activities prior to the start of production; quality planning sets goals and works towards achieving the goals and preventing failures.

Analogously to this definition, in the Six Sigma Define phase the project team identifies what is important to the customer (captures the "voice of the customer"[1]), the goals, and the scope and boundary of the project.

Inclusion of stakeholders in quality planning means that for all of these tasks and activities, the quality of the outcome must be evaluated to determine if it satisfies stakeholders' needs. Figure 17.2.3.1 shows potential discrepancies between stakeholder needs and product characteristics that can arise during execution of the whole task from subtask to subtask.

Discrepancies can arise due to the following:

1. Assumed or implied needs have to be translated into words or symbols – that is, identified and established – in the language used

---

[1]   *Voice of the customer* (VOC) is the term for customer descriptions in words for the functions and features customers desire for goods and services. See [APIC04].

by stakeholders. Here there is the danger that the translation will fail to be accurate.

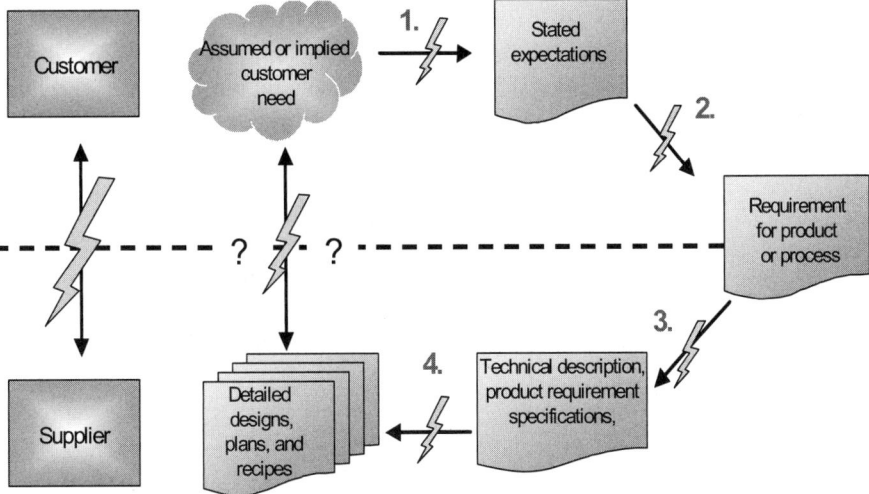

Fig. 17.2.3.1   Cause of differences between stakeholders' expectations and actual product or process characteristics.

2. The stated expectations determined have to be broken down into ideas or expectations concerning requirements for the product to be developed and for the process to be developed. This is often connected with a transition from relatively general quality characteristics to more specific characteristics. The result is a detailed, functional picture or functional model, which again is expressed in the language used by stakeholders.

3. The functional pictures or models determined for the product and the process are translated into specific quality requirements, but now in the language used by the provider/supplier. Finally, the requirements are described in specifications, called product requirement specifications, which are more technical descriptions.

4. The technical descriptions are transferred into designs, plans, and recipes. This is the actual development and design of product and process. The output then undergoes validation, which is the process of ensuring that the product conforms to the original stakeholder needs and requirements.

A typical method used in the quality planning phase is Quality Function Deployment, or QFD.

> *Quality Function Deployment* is *step-by-step development of quality functions.* The QFD process uses matrices to translate customer requirements into technical design parameters or characteristics.

To do this, a quality chart called the *"House of Quality"* is employed as a correlation matrix linking quality characteristics and target values and their variation and tendency. See Figure 17.2.3.2.

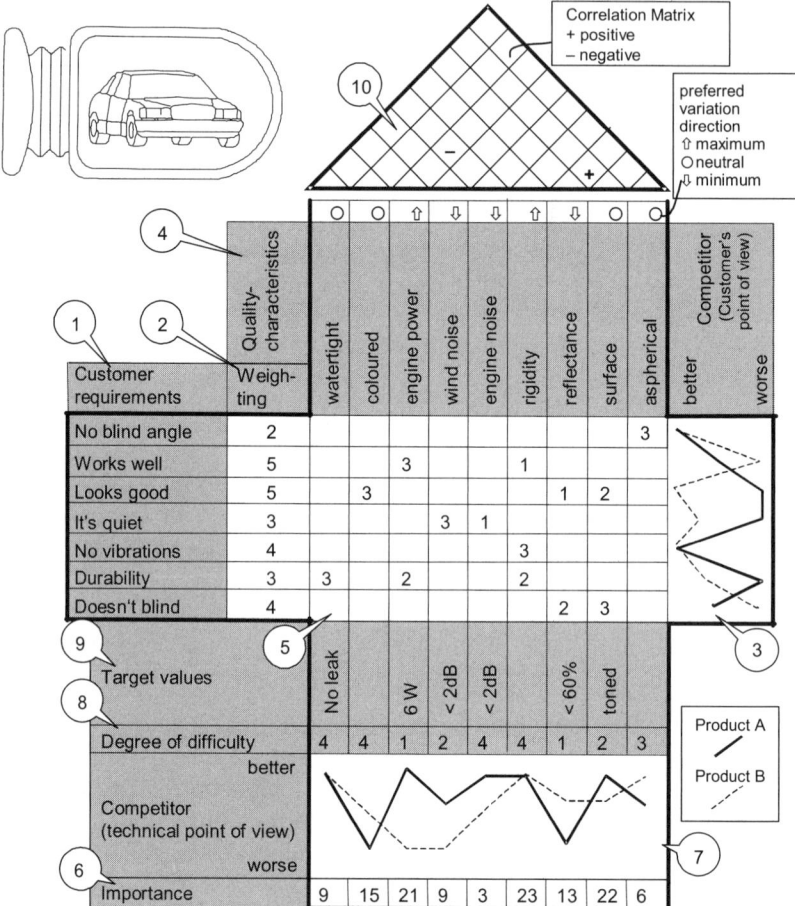

Fig. 17.2.3.2   Quality Function Deployment: House of Quality and ten steps of implementation (Source: [Guin93]).

The ten steps of implementation in Figure 17.2.3.2 are taken from [Guin93]:

1. Gather customer requirements for the product or service.
2. Customers weight the importance of each of the requirements.

3. Customer rating of the competition. Ask customers to rate competitors' products or services.
4. Technical descriptors. Translate customer requirements into quality characteristics.
5. Relationship matrix. Determine relationship between customers' needs and technical descriptors.
6. Estimation of the importance of the technical descriptors.
7. Technical analysis of competitor products. Conduct analysis of competitor technical descriptors.
8. Estimate degree of difficulty, technical feasibility.
9. Determine target values for each technical descriptor.
10. Determine variation and tendency for each technical descriptor and examine how each of them impacts the others.

> The *First pass yield* (FPY) is the percentage of results (i.e., units) that pass on first test – that is, without requiring rework.

An increased FPY entails reduced costs due to rework. Development is successful if the defect rate can be rapidly reduced once the product is introduced or if it is zero from the start (*zero-defect rate*). As the development process is essentially a creative one and can contain errors, defects can always be expected with an innovation. The need to reduce development time and development costs also speaks against a zero-defect rate. For these reasons, defects will be accepted at first, and importance will be placed on reducing this rate rapidly once the product is introduced. Particularly in the initial phase, then, it is important to have sufficient capacity for rapid revision as well as a comprehensive information system for capturing the responses of the first customers.

For example, during quality planning, quality requirements – together with the original ideas about the requirements – are translated into an offer to customers that describes the company's product or service. This description, which is often a component of a contractual agreement, can already deviate decisively from the customer's expectations, so that at this point in time at the latest, a decision must be made as to whether the individual steps of quality planning should be repeated (non first pass yield).

With this, the Define, or quality planning, phase entails capturing the relevant processes. In Six Sigma, this is represented in SIPOC diagrams.

> The SIPOC diagram shows the system with Inputs, Process, and Outputs as well as the Suppliers and the Customers. See Fig. 17.2.3.3.

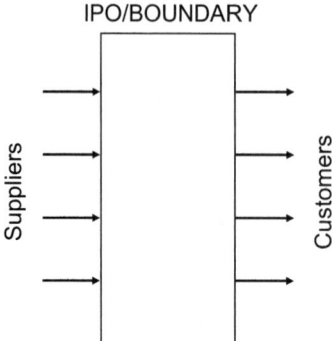

IPO/BOUNDARY

Suppliers

Customers

Fig. 17.2.3.3   SIPOC diagram.

In this phase, the diagrams show the actual state, before all work begins. On the basis of the diagramming of the process, the critical elements will then be worked out.

CTQs (Critical to Quality) are the key measurable characteristics (for example, regarding quality, costs, or delivery), elements of the process, or practices that have a great and direct effect on the customer's perception of the quality of a product or service. See Fig. 17.2.3.4.

	Product							
	Sub-Product A				Sub-Product B			
	CTQ1	CTQ2	CTQ3	CTQ4	CTQ5	CTQ6	CTQ7	
Process 1								ITEMS UNDER OUR CONTROL
Process 2								
Process 3								
Process 4								
	Important To Our Customer							

Fig. 17.2.3.4   CTQ matrix.

CTQs are usually represented in a matrix, or CTQ tree, that shows the products or sub-products and their critical attributes on the horizontal axis. The processes that can lead (or not lead) to these critical characteristics, process elements, or practices are shown on the vertical axis.

In the Six Sigma method, the outcomes to be delivered (the deliverables) of the Define phase are revisited again and again:

- Are the project teams well-trained and motivated?
- Have the customers been identified and CTQs defined?
- Has the project management handbook been drawn up?
- Have the business processes been diagrammed appropriately (for example, using SIPOC)?

Each of these questions is revisited repeatedly throughout the entire phase in greater detail in order to ensure that they are handled comprehensively.

17.2.4 Quality Control, Part 1 – Measure and Analyze Phases

Quality control encompasses the operational techniques and the activities used to fulfill and verify requirements of quality [ISO 8402]. It is also defined as a set of activities or techniques such as measurement and inspection of one or more characteristics of a unit and comparison of the results with set requirements in order to ensure that conformance with quality requirements is being met.

Quality control is the attempt to implement the predefined targets from quality planning in reality; that is, it measures for conformance to quality requirements. The techniques of quality control can be used for both monitoring a process and correcting or eliminating defects or failures. In the Six Sigma method, quality control comprises several phases, namely, Measure, Analyze, and (in part) Improve.

In the Measure phase, the task is to determine how the spoken needs of the customers, the CTQs, will be specified in measurable terms using tools. The appropriate measurement system is then installed or an existing system improved. See here Section 17.1.4. Further, actual current performance is quantified and the target goal determined (for example, increase process stability from 3 sigma to 4 sigma).

Some quality control tools and tests for this task are, for example, ABC or Pareto analyses, sampling plans, and *statistical process control* to determine process capability and process performance.

The deliverables of the Measure phase can be reviewed and revisited as follows:

- Is there agreement on the critical characteristics, and is there a detailed description of their measurability?

- Has a plan been drawn up showing what data will be captured and what measurement system will be used? Have the data been gathered?
- Has the current variation of the process (current sigma level) been calculated and opportunities for improvement defined?

In the Analyze phase, the task is to identify root causes of variation and defects. Now it is important to provide statistical evidence of current deviations and to then formulate options for improvement (improvement goals). Thus, the Measure and Analyze phases both encompass activities of quality control.

Quality control in its original usage stems from production engineering. The tools that are used include risk analysis, such as Failure Mode and Effects Analysis (FMEA), Design of Experiment (DOE), and hypothesis testing, such as analysis of variance (ANOVA) and multivariate analysis of variance (MANOVA).

Further tools for this step are Cause and Effect diagram (Fishbone, or Ishikawa diagram), histograms, quality control charts, correlation diagrams, checklists, and general graphical representations, such as time series diagrams, pie charts, bar charts, Gantt charts, or network diagrams.

The deliverables of the Analyze phase can be reviewed and revisited as follows:

- Were data and process analysis conducted and the gaps between actual and target process performance determined?
- Have the root causes of variation and defects been found and prioritized according to importance?
- Were the performance deficits communicated and converted to financial quantities (see here the discussion in Section 1.3.1 on opportunity costs)?

17.2.5 Quality Control, Part 2 – Improve Phase, Part 1

The first part of the Improve phase in the Six Sigma method can also be regarded as belonging to, and as the most creative part of, quality control; namely, solution finding. The task is to generate a number of possible solutions that counteract the root causes of variations and defects.

In the manufacture of physical products, the individual process steps are usually described in quite great detail. The process step instructions often include measures with tolerances that must be adhered to during machining. The same should hold for processes in the information flow of a company, for example for order processing. Exact descriptions are just as necessary for service processes, even though here it can be considerably more difficult to determine targets and variations.

For this creative process, the following principles hold (these are realized, for example, in the jidoka concept; see definition in Section 5.1.1):

- Possible defects should be identified at the source of origin as early as possible in the process. The problems or defects can be identified by the human eye or by specialized sensors.

- All components and units should be checked 100% in order to ensure complete faultlessness.

- Direct intervention prevents further subsequent mistakes. With jidoka, any worker can stop the line by pulling a cord; this is then signaled on visual display devices called andon boards that are visible to all.

- The processes must be made "foolproof" (poka yoke).

Andon is a visual signal, or visual control system. With jidoka, andon are electronic display boards that show the status of the processes in a job shop or production line as well as information for coordination of the connected work stations. Commonly used colors to indicate status are green (OK) / yellow (needs attention) / red (stop). See here [Toyo98].

Figure 17.2.5.1 shows an example of numbered andon lights.

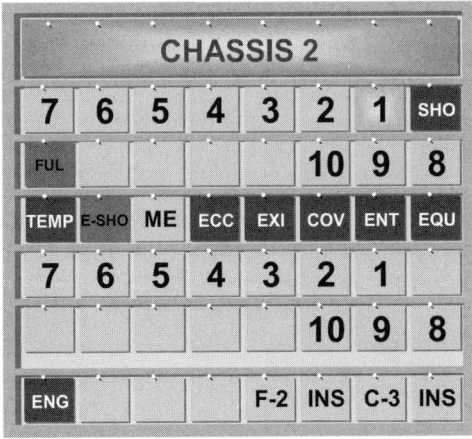

Fig. 17.2.5.1   Andon: visual control system in a job shop.

The yellow light shows a problem at work station 1. There the worker has pulled the cord to stop the line.

Poka yoke, or *failsafe techniques*, means to avoid (yokeru) inadvertent errors (poka). The basic principles of poka yoke advocate designing or developing tools, techniques, and processes to detect defects, thus relieving people of error-prone tasks such as repetitive monitoring of the same states or the checking of a great many details [Kogy90].

Some examples of such simple mechanisms and devices are:

- Sensors that detect missing or defective components and shut down the process automatically
- Guide pins on parts that prevent assembly in the wrong orientation
- Construction of parts and corresponding clamping and mounting apparatuses that prevent backwards insertions.

Applying poka yoke to information flows represents a considerable challenge. However, for the area of order processing, computer-supported, computer programs are conceivable that can monitor the completeness of information and the correct sequence of functions. Indeed, computer programs have always had the task of recognizing and preventing all possible defective constellations of data. Workflow techniques are now used to ensure correct implementation of additional sequences of ordered tasks, even where several people are involved in the process. Due to the many unforeseeable influences on information processes, however, these techniques are likely to be of help only for simple and highly repetitive processes.

17.2.6 Quality Assurance – Improve Phase, Part 2

Quality assurance as it was used originally corresponds to today's term quality inspection (see Section 17.2.4).

Use of the term *quality assurance* – like use of the term *quality management* – has changed over time as shown in Figure 17.2.6.1.

	Aspect Defined	ISO Vocabulary (International Organization for Standardization)
Up to 1987	Wider term	quality assurance
Since 1987	Wider term Quality management system demonstration	quality management quality assurance

Fig. 17.2.6.1   Changing definitions of terms over time (Source: [Verb98]).

- Up until 1987, the term *quality assurance* was used as generic term for all activities with regard to quality.

- After 1987, the term *quality management* was introduced as the wider term. Quality assurance was now used for concrete quality management system demonstration.

> *Quality assurance* can be understood today as *active* risk management for the purpose of reducing the probability of quality defects and of mitigating the consequences of defects (passive risk management would be insuring or covering against risk).[2]

Quality assurance as defined today first of all involves quality inspection to determine whether the quality targets for the individual quality characteristics are actually met. Such inspection measures include:

- Tests of incoming goods to ensure that procured goods are free of defects

- Supplier ratings, based on delivery quality

- Design reviews during the research and development process

- Early warning systems that detect defects in new products at an early stage

- Testing of administrative processes, in particular of completeness of information and delivery reliability

In analogy, the task in the second part of the Improve phase in the Six Sigma method is implementation of one or more of the solutions found. There must then be a check providing statistical evidence that the solutions are achieving the desired results.

---

[2]   Where *risk* is defined as venture, danger, or possible losses in an insecure action, specifically as the product of the probably of occurrence of an event times the probable extent of the effect, that is, deviation from a goal.

For the quality assurance step, all of the tools used in quality control (see Section 17.2.4) are available. Although these tools were developed for the production of material goods, they can also be applied to the production of nonmaterial goods and to services. However, for quality assurance of organizations or of complex sequences of processes – especially whole business processes – evaluation methods in the form of assessments stand in the foreground. Assessments are used in the evaluation of the quality management system itself. They will be discussed in connection with TQM models in Section 17.3.

As for any type of organization, quality assurance, or the Improve phase, must also not be simply a control mechanism; the point is to enable and motivate people appropriately to deliver defect-free products and processes. The focus today is usually on self-inspection. To avoid unnecessary slowing down of the value-adding processes, quality tasks, as far as possible, should be carried out by the same persons who are also responsible for the operational added value. For this they require training in the relevant quality techniques.

To complement self-inspection, third parties (superiors, other internal parties, or external parties) conduct suitable inspections. The task of a company-wide post for quality is to advise the persons accountable for producing the goods and services as to selection of the quality assurance tools and, in difficult cases, to take on an advising and coordinating function in the quality assurance process.

The deliverables of the Improve phase can be reviewed and revisited as follows:

- Have sufficient solutions been generated in the first part of this step?
- Were the solutions tested, and has the best solution been selected based on these tests?
- For the selected solution, were target processes and cost-benefit analyses drawn up?
- Was a plan drawn up for introducing the selected solution?

17.2.7 Quality Activation – Control Phase

Quality activation means activation of quality improvement.

This means active follow-up: the changes introduced have to be evaluated. The knowledge gained during the quality assurance phase must be compared to the targets set in the planning phase. Afterwards, the decision can be made as to whether the change was good and should be continued, or whether it should even be applied to further activities, products, or processes, and what improvements must be made before doing so. This can possibly mean continuing on as before without implementing the change or making it standard work practice. Furthermore, the results have to be communicated, so that any subsequent iteration of the Deming Cycle will be higher-level and thus achieve improvement a priori.

Analogous with this, the task in the Control phase of the Six Sigma method is to integrate the results into daily operations and document and communicate them within the organization. In addition, however, Six Sigma demands that measures be taken in order to maintain the gains of the processes in future. Here again, statistical evidence that the improvements are maintained is required.

The representation tools listed in Sections 17.2.3 to 17.2.6 can be applied. These include affinity diagrams: (meaningful groupings of ideas to refine when brainstorming or moderating), relationships diagram (such as mind maps), matrix diagrams, decision trees, network plans, decision tables, and flowcharts of some type, such as Process Decision Program Charts (PDPC). See here also [Mizu88]. These tools and methods are general in nature, that is, they are also utilizable in other management systems.

The deliverables of the Control phase can be reviewed and revisited as follows:

- Has a system for monitoring consistent use of new method been documented and implemented?
- Have the new process steps, standards, and documentations become standard work practices?
- Has the knowledge gained regarding the new processes been documented and shared in the organization?
- Have responsibilities and accountability been identified, understood, and communicated in the organization?
- Has ownership and knowledge been handed over to the process owner and his or her team and the project officially closed down?

17.2.8 Project Management, Continuous Improvement, and Reengineering

Responsibility for projects in quality management can be assigned to everyone involved in the process, the "process team." It is advantageous to define a "process owner" as a coordinator. Well-oiled teams of persons that comprehensively master all tasks related to performance capability (see Figure 17.0.0.1) are preferable to individual specialists that work on the process independently and sequentially. The observation is generally valid that defects in the process arise particularly if process execution is beset with interfaces, where the process is handed over from one person to another person who acts independently of the first. Experience has shown that even if the interface is defined as specifically as possible, errors occur here, alone due to the tendency of people integrated in one organizational unit to close themselves off from other organizational units.

The proponents of Six Sigma recognized early on that for successful project management for quality improvement, people must be trained and awarded special certification. Attractive names that acknowledge Japanese origins were chosen for the different levels of certification.

Green Belts are Six Sigma team members that have been trained in Six Sigma at this level and work part-time in Six Sigma projects under the guidance of a team leader.

Black Belts are team leaders that have specific training and experience in guiding Six Sigma projects.

Master Black Belts are experienced, qualified Six Sigma experts that implement strategic quality initiatives, which includes training Black Belts and Green Belts at all levels of the organization.

Champions and sponsors are owners of the processes for which projects are being carried out. They support the projects at decisive positions within the company, carry out implementation, and thus help the results achieve breakthroughs.

The first Black Belts acquired certification in the early 1990s, thus marking the beginnings of formalization that led to accredited certification programs in Six Sigma methods.

Because in Europe the Deming cycle for a long time did not catch on as an advantageous method, a new term was sought that would express an understanding of the Deming cycle as a permanent task. For this, the term continuous process improvement was coined.

> *Continuous process improvement (CPI)*, or simply *continuous improvement*, is a never ending effort, a culture, in which improvement – usually in small steps – becomes the guiding principle: The journey is the objective!

With the introduction of continuous process improvement, the Deming cycle was pushed forward as the basic insight, in that the cycle, once understood in a more static way, was made into a dynamic circle. The aim was to utilize the entire potential within the organization. Ultimately, the greatest potential can be set free only through influencing the behavior of the collaborating persons. Organizational measures can promote collaborative behavior, such as the collecting of proposals and suggestions in the firm, quality circles of employees, periodical goal and measures planning, campaigns, and so on. However, implementing the concept of continuous process improvement and the culture connected with it is difficult. Moldaschl [Mold97] pointed out this and similar issues when he reported that in some companies, continuous process improvement came to be called the "cooperation interruption program."

In connection with the quality of organizations or of complex business processes, benchmarking has recently come to the fore as an efficient tool. We will take a closer look at benchmarking in Section 17.3 in connection with TQM models.

As customer needs change sooner or later, the demand for improvement of company performance also implies that products and processes must change over time. Each change, however, entails the risk of errors. While quality control and quality assurance promote stability in the company, they are a priori hostile to change and therefore also hostile to improvement. The compromise solution may be to continuously improve performance through continuous incremental changes, without having to take too great a risk. For this, the Japanese use the term *Kaizen* [Imai86]. In the Kaizen philosophy, the focus is not on achieving a specific level of quality, but rather a certain degree of improvement of quality ("the journey is the reward").

Continuous improvement as a whole is, therefore, much a question of company culture. With this, it is a continuous task over an open-ended period of time, and it does not have the character of a project. Within this continuous improvement, however, the individual, incremental improvement measures as such are usually carried out in the form of projects. For example, a project of this kind may attempt to

- Increase customer benefit. The additional expenditure has to be able to be covered by either higher prices or lower costs. Higher prices can usually be realized only if customer satisfaction can also be improved long-term.

- Reduce the defect rate. The expenditure for the project and the connected investments must be covered by continuous cost savings created by fewer defects.

In the place of continuous process improvement, what happens in reengineering, or new development, is innovation on a grand scale.

Reengineering means fundamentally rethinking the company's options for designing products and processes.

The same holds for reengineering business processes.

Business process reengineering (BPR) is improvement of business processes in big steps by fundamentally redesigning the processes.

Improvement in big steps through radical changes is then the task of quality planning in the first iteration of the corresponding Deming cycle. In the course of the further product and process life cycle, continuous incremental changes serve improvement of company performance.

17.3   Quality Management Systems

Whereas for a long time the term *quality* was understood in America and in Europe as quality assurance in production, a management-oriented quality concept achieved dominance early on at the highest levels of management in Japan. This concept was developed in the 1950s by two Americans, W. E. Deming and J. M. Juran.

Total quality management is defined as a management approach of an organization centered on quality, based on the participation of all its members, and aiming at long-term success. This is achieved through customer satisfaction and benefits to all members of the organization and to society [ISO 8402].

There is a corresponding management-oriented understanding also for Six Sigma. Motorola, for instance, learned early on that disciplined application of metrics and the improvement methodology alone are not sufficient in order to achieve big breakthroughs and sustainable improvements.

Six Sigma as a management system is a framework for assigning resources with priority to projects that result in rapid and sustainable improvement of business results.

Here metrics and improvement methodology are implemented in order to tackle the important problems in connection with company strategy in the correct sequence. In this way, the results should be evident at all levels of the company and ultimately in company results. In 1989, Motorola received the Malcolm Baldrige National Quality Award, which will be described in more detail in the following.

17.3.1 Standards and Norms of Quality Management: ISO 9000:2000

Because of extensive criticism of the ISO 9000 family of standards, they were revised at the end of the year 2000. The current standards are known as the ISO 9000:2000 Standards.

The *ISO 9000:2000 Standards* are shown in Figure 17.3.1.1.

The new standards pay greater attention to the ability of the organization to fulfill the requirements of various stakeholders, such as customers, employees, and investors. The new standards also place greater emphasis on the need for continuous improvement.

Today there exist two strategies for deriving a quality management system. The two strategies can also be seen as paradigms:

- The *fulfillment paradigm*: This leads to systems that contain a set number of quality assurance standards, or rules and measures. With *certification*, that is, confirmation of the measures by an impartial third party, the aim is to guarantee mutual trust among business partners as to the demanded quality of products or services. Under this paradigm, all organizations that achieve a specified level of quality receive certification. ISO 9000:2000 is a quality management system of this type.

- The *optimization paradigm*: This leads to comprehensive concepts that aim for outstanding performance in the achievement of quality. The degree to which this is met is evaluated by means of Quality Awards (QA) awarded by independent associations. What is evaluated here is the degree to which a company recognizes quality to be the crucial factor for all its activities and makes it the focus of attention of business activity. Under this paradigm, only the best organizations receive an award. Corresponding quality management systems are introduced in Section 17.3.2.

ISO 9000:2000	QM – Systems – Fundamentals and vocabulary
ISO 9001:2000	QM – Systems – Requirements
ISO 9004:2000	QM – Systems – Guidelines for performance improvements
ISO 19011	Guidelines on Quality and/or Environmental Management Systems Auditing (currently under development)
ISO 10005:1995	QM - Guidelines for quality plans
ISO 10006:1997	QM - Guidelines to quality in project management
ISO 10007:1995	QM - Guidelines for configuration management
ISO/DIS 10012	Quality assurance requirements for measuring equipment Part 1: Metrological confirmation system for measuring equipment
ISO 10012-2:1997	Part 2: Guidelines for control of measurement of processes
ISO 10013:1995	Guidelines for developing quality manuals
ISO/TR 10014:1998	Guidelines for managing the economics of quality
ISO 10015:1999	Quality management - Guidelines for training
ISO/TS 16949:1999	Quality systems- Automotive suppliers- Particular requirements for the application of ISO 9001:1994

Fig. 17.3.1.1   Standards in the DIN ISO 9000:2000 series.

The advantage of awards over certification is that the demands to be met for awards actually increase over time, as the companies applying for the award improve. This means that awards result in best practices instead of merely sufficient levels. Awards are the embodiment of a continuous improvement philosophy (optimization relating to goals), whereas certification according to a standard in the ISO 9001-9003 family of quality system standards results "only" in achievement of a specific level (fulfillment of requirements).

In connection with the optimization paradigm, it quickly became apparent that long-term improvement of all management systems in a company is a question of company culture, and thus of the behavior of the individual, the individual organizational units, but also the organization as a whole. The desired culture and the corresponding behavior are generally laid down in a strategy or policy. Strategic management then builds up the corresponding management systems ("structure follows strategy"), such as, for example, a quality management system. The aim of establishing such management systems is to influence the individual and thus to achieve the desired behavior ("culture follows structure").

17.3.2 The Optimization Paradigm: Models and Awards for Total Quality Management

In the 1950s, together with the development of the management-oriented quality concept, the Union of Japanese Scientists and Engineers established a national prize to provide an incentive for the continued development of total quality management in Japan, the annually awarded Deming Prize.

The *Deming Prize* uses the examination criteria shown in Figure 17.3.2.1.

- Understanding and enthusiasm
- Policies
- Organization and operation
- Information
- Standardization
- Human resources development and utilization
- Quality assurance activities
- Maintenance and control activities
- Improvement activities
- Implementation and evaluation
- Social responsibilities
- Effects
- Future plans

Fig. 17.3.2.1   Deming Prize examination criteria.

The first Deming Prize was awarded in September 1951 in Osaka. Today, total quality management thinking is firmly established in the Japanese business world. See here also "The Deming Prize and Development of Quality Control/Management in Japan" at http://www.deming.org.

The reaction of the American government, science, and economy to the ever stronger Japanese competition occurred with about a 30-year delay in the form of various initiatives and agreements under the lead of Malcolm Baldrige, who served as United States Secretary of Commerce. This resulted in the creation of Public Law 100-107, the Malcolm Baldrige

National Quality Improvement Act of 1987, which was signed into law in August, 1987, under President Ronald Reagan. The Act established the *Malcolm Baldrige National Quality Award* (MBNQA).

Figure 17.3.2.2 shows the *Malcolm Baldrige National Quality Award* (MBNQA) criteria for performance excellence.

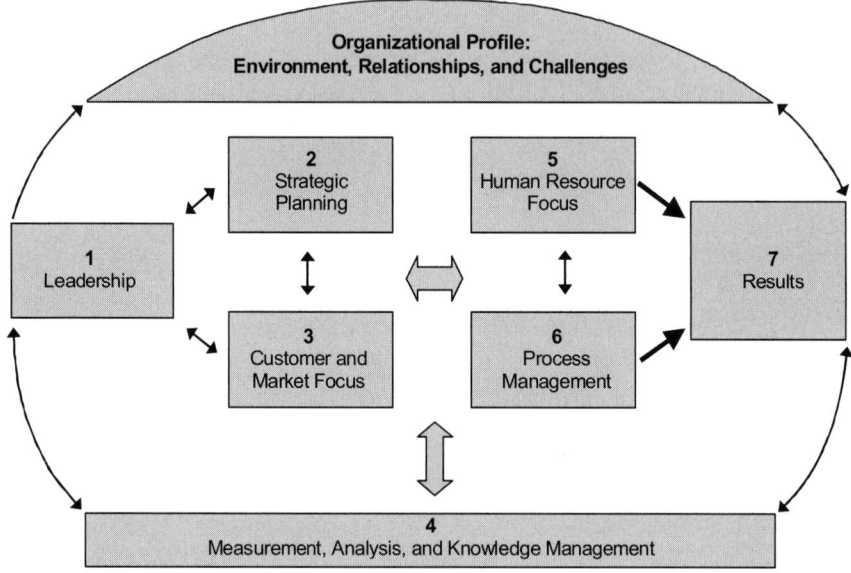

Fig. 17.3.2.2   Structure of the Malcolm Baldrige National Quality Award (based on [NIST06]).

See here also http://www.quality.nist.gov/Business_Criteria.htm and www.baldrige.org, as well as – for the award winners – Figure 17.3.2.3. The MBNQA evaluation model gives the company a good opportunity to determine its own standing with regard to quality management.

The European response to the challenge is the *European Foundation for Quality Management (EFQM.)*. The EFQM was founded in 1989 by the CEOs of 14 prominent European businesses. As one of its main activities, the EFQM presents the EFQM Excellence Award (formerly, "European Quality Award" EQA) to organizations that excel in "Fundamental Concepts of Excellence" based on the EFQM Excellence Model.

The EFQM Excellence Model and the EFQM Excellence Award are based on the evaluation elements shown in Figure 17.3.2.4.

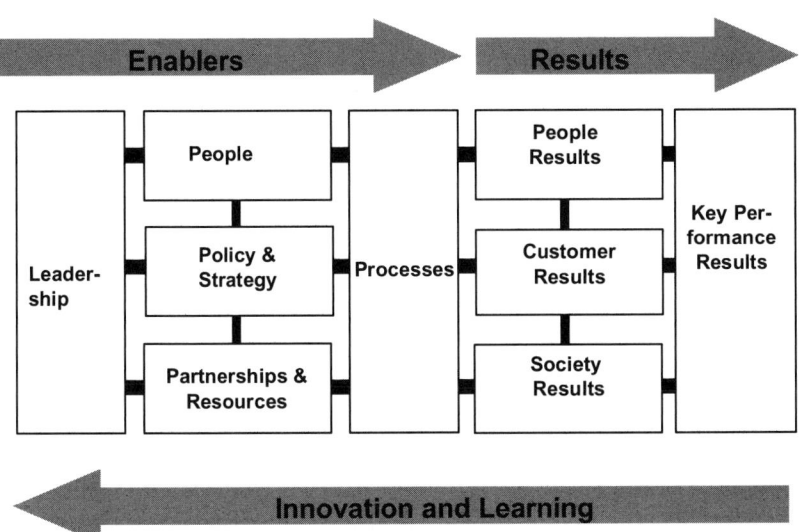

Baldrige National Quality

	Manu-facturing	Service	Small Business	Education	Health Care
2005	Sunny Fresh Foods, Inc.	DynMcDermott Petroleum Operations Company	Park Place Lexus	Jenks Public Schools / Richland College	Bronson Methodist Hospital
2004	The Bama Companies, Inc.		Texas Nameplate Company, Inc	Kenneth W. Monfort College of Business	Robert Wood Johnson University Hospital Hamilton
2003	Medrad, Inc.	Caterpillar Financial Service Corporation / Boeing Aerospace Support	Stoner, Inc.	Community Consolidated School District 15	Saint Luke's Hospital of Kansas City / Baptist Hospital, Inc.
2002	Motorola Commercial, Government & Industrial Solutions Sector		Branch-Smith Printing Division		SSM Health Care
2001	Clarke American Checks, Inc.		Pal's Sudden Service	Chugach School District / Pearl River School District / University of Wisconsin-Stout	

Fig. 17.3.2.3   Baldrige National Program. Excellence Award Winners.

Fig. 17.3.2.4   The EFQM Excellence Model (Source: EFQM, "The EFQM Excellence Award - Information Brochure for 2006," available at http://www.efqm.org/uploads/EEA2006Brochure.pdf).

The first EFQM Excellence Award was presented in 1992. The award recognizes excellence in the organization's ability to realize outstanding quality and comprehensive customer benefit. See more at http://www.efqm.org, as well as – for the award winners – Figure 17.3.2.5.

EFQM Excellence Award

EFQM	Category for Large Businesses and Business Units	Category for Operational Units	Category for Public Sector	Category for SME	Category for Independent SME	Category for Subsidiary SME
2005		TNT, Express Information & Communication Services, UK				FirstPlus Financial Group Plc, UK
2004	YELL, UK		Kocaeli Chamber of Industry, TUR			
2003		Bosch Sanayi ve Ticaret AS, TUR	Runshaw College, UK		Maxi Coco-Mat SA, GRC	Edinburgh International Conference Centre, UK
2002					Springfarm Architectural Mouldings, UK	
2001		St Mary's College Northern Ireland, UK				Zahnarztpraxis, CHE
2000	Nokia Mobile Phones, FIN		Inland Revenue, Acc.Office, Cumbernauld, UK			Burton-Apta Refractory Manufacturing, HUN

Fig. 17.3.2.5   EFQM Excellence Award winners.

Based on the EFQM Excellence Model, excellent leadership is seen as a prerequisite for customer satisfaction, employee satisfaction, and positive results for society. To this purpose, the organization must develop a quality-conscious policy and strategy, utilize resources efficiently, and choose an employee-oriented way of proceeding. Only in this way, under consideration of all processes, can sustainable performance results be achieved. The strong mutual dependency of the individual factors makes it clear that quality refers to each and every employee and that everyone must work together towards the highest goal, customer satisfaction.

17.3.3 Audits and Procedures for Assessing the Quality of Organizations

An *audit* is a formal examination [MeWe03]. This is generally understood as an act of hearing that is conducted by third parties according to well-defined criteria and rules.

ISO 8402 [ISO 8402] defines a quality audit as a "systematic and independent examination to determine whether quality activities and related results comply with planned arrangements and whether these arrangements are implemented effectively and are suitable to achieve objectives."

Assessing the quality of organizations is fundamentally different from measuring physical properties of products or processes. However, individuals and also organizations are accustomed to periodically taking stock of where they stand, deriving opportunities and goals for improvement, and checking progress towards achieving these objectives. This is probably true for all areas of life. One of the difficulties involved is the lack of uniform standards that are universally recognized.

Possibilities for conducting an assessment include external procedures of the audit type on the one hand and self-assessment on the other. Self-assessment results in strong identification, strong learning effects, and considerable self-motivation ([Henn95]). The disadvantage of self-assessment can be that people, especially if they have little experience in assessing, can tend towards misjudgments and can consciously distort the facts. But external audits also have some fundamental disadvantages:

- the subjectivity of the persons that establish the measurement criteria
- the subjectivity of persons that perform the assessment, that is, the evaluation according to those measurement criteria

For this reason, the culture of the assessors appears to be the greatest factor influencing the assessment process.

Three types of audits provide an option for more formal assessments (see [Pira97] for further details):

- A *first-party* or *internal audit* is performed by trained auditors who assess individual company areas. The auditors are selected from within the company but are independent of the area being audited.
- A *second-party audit* is performed by customers who evaluate their suppliers. Customers are typically interested in details of the product and process design. If the supplier has a quality management system in place, this type of audit can be limited to assessing that system.
- A *third-party audit* is performed by external agencies that are specialized in this task. This type of audit can be conducted in connection with quality awards, but this is not generally recom-

mendable due to insufficient sustainability. Instead, company-internal employees should be trained in assessment. External agencies can then, for example, participate in the company's internal audit in an advising role on methodology, especially if the company does not yet have much experience with auditing methods.

17.3.4 Benchmarking

Benchmarking means identifying best practices that result in outstanding performance.

Comparison of companies based on the number of points achieved for an award allows for a general comparison of the overall management of companies. If at this level companies compare themselves to companies in very different industries and of different sizes, they will discover that they have strengths in different areas. A company can in this way obtain information about the improvement strategies set by very different companies. Occasionally, this can give rise to ideas on how practices in other industry sectors and companies might be applied to their own business activities. Nevertheless, benchmarking on too broad a base has only limited effectiveness.

Just as important, therefore, are comparisons with other companies in the same industry sector. Once comparable processes, products, or organizational units are available, criteria and measurement categories can be set up that should be included in the comparison procedure. Benchmarking is then not restricted to quality aspects, but can in principle extend to any aspect of the company that represents a best practice. Once the benchmarking partners and the objects to be compared have been established, it is possible to examine how the reference partner achieves outstanding performance. What key processes are involved? What is the company culture behind this? On the basis of the answers to these questions, companies can derive their own new goals (for a detailed discussion on implementation, see, for example, [Camp94]).

The above shows relatively quickly the limits of benchmarking with competitors within the same branch of industry. If these are direct competitors, they will hardly be willing to reveal the secrets of their success. Information on competitors' best practices should probably be acquired from third parties. Direct collaboration in benchmarking among competitors only makes sense if it results in a win-win situation for both partners. This can be the case when otherwise competing suppliers in one geographic region decide to take on the suppliers in another geographic region.

For these reasons, the tendency is for groups of companies to form that are not competitors on the market and thus do not produce the same products but that have essentially comparable processes, company structures, and stakeholders.

- *Functional benchmarking* is benchmarking of similar processes or functions. Here a rather broad spectrum of companies can be examined. For example, companies might compare logistics and information management.

- *Generic benchmarking* is comparing not only individual functions, but whole business processes, such as the R&D process. Here, the selection of comparable companies will, of course, be smaller.

17.4   Summary

Quality management encompasses a number of concepts, methods, tools, procedures, and techniques that aim to improve the quality of company performance. Quality in the company can refer to its processes and products but also the organization as a whole. Organizational quality must be oriented to the various company stakeholders. Here a specific challenge is the measurement of quality, especially when it comes to people's perceptions. Easily measurable quantities can have the disadvantage that it is not clear what, exactly, led to the test results and thus not clear what actions must be taken. In reverse, the quantities to be measured can be determined on the basis of possible actions for improvement. But their measurement can entail excessive or unforeseeable expense.

The Deming cycle, or Shewhart cycle, gathers together the traditional tasks of quality management, namely, quality planning, quality control, quality assurance, and quality activation (Plan, Do, Check, Act). Today, in addition, the Six Sigma method is also very well-known. The Six Sigma method is divided into steps that, taken together, correspond with the tasks of the Deming cycle. For each task, there is a set of tools. Particularly well-known tools are the House of Quality in quality planning and *poka yoke* in quality control. For quality assurance, besides the statistical methods, a wealth of representation tools is available. These and further tools can also be utilized in quality activation. When the Deming cycle is conducted repeatedly, or a number of Six Sigma projects are carried out, this leads ultimately to continuous process improvement. However, innovation on a grand scale, such as new development of products, breaks with that process, and a new process of continuous improvement begins.

Total Quality Management (TQM) is a management-oriented quality concept. Quality management systems aim to influence the individual in order to achieve desired behaviors. In the case of management systems that follow the fulfillment paradigm, all organizations that achieve a certain level of quality receive certification. The ISO 9000:2000 series belong here. In the case of management systems that follow the optimization paradigm, only the best organizations receive an award. The various prizes here include the Deming Prize, the Malcolm Baldrige National Quality Award (MBNQA), and the EFQM Excellence Award awarded by the European Foundation for Quality Management. In comparison, awards have the advantage that they promote best practices, which are found in very few organizations, whereas certification indicates a satisfactory level at many organizations. In order to determine the standing of a company in quality management, there are various assessment methods. The main method is self-assessment. Using benchmarking, companies compare their performance with others in their search for best practices.

17.5   Keywords

18   Systems Engineering and Project Management

System is defined in [MeWe03] as a regularly interacting group of items (or set of elements) forming a unified whole.[1]

In the narrower sense, a system describes complex phenomena in the real world, such as the solar system or the periodic table of the chemical elements. But also abstract phenomena can be described as systems, such as

- Numerical systems or systems of equations in mathematics
- Theories and models
- Electrical, pneumatic, or hydraulic systems
- Social systems
- The organization of a company or the national economy

In the following, a company is understood as a sociotechnical system. The elements themselves – that is, the people, production machines, materials, and so on – and their relationships both within the system and with the surrounding systems (environment) are complex in nature. Parts of a company, for example production, can also be viewed as systems.

Systems theory deals with general characteristics of systems. For example, a *dynamic system* refers to a system with interactions among the elements of the systems. *Open dynamic systems* refers to systems in which the elements also interact with other elements in the system environment (as opposed to closed systems). Systems thinking in general systems theory can be applied to the special company systems theory. Production in an industrial company, for example, is typically an open dynamic system. The interactions are formed through the flows of goods, data, and information. See here also [Züst04] and [HaNa02].

In analogy to the product life cycle, the system "company," or its part systems, also has a life cycle. What makes up the system life cycle? What problem-solving techniques are used? These questions will be covered in the section below on systems engineering.

---

[1]   *Merriam-Webster* lists further definitions, which all revolve around "arrangement," or "organization." The definition underlying the sociotechnical system "company" is, however, the one shown above.

> *Systems engineering* (SE) is a method, based on some models and procedural principles, for enabling appropriate and efficient realization of complex systems, to which also systems in a company explicitly belong [HaNa02].

Systems engineering is thus a *systemic* method for the realization of systems.

> A *project* is a scheme, plan, or planned undertaking (from the Latin *projectum*, or that which is thrown forward) [MeWe03]. For use of the term in practice, [PMBOKD] defines project as a temporary endeavor undertaken to create a unique product, service, or result. [APIC04] defines a project as an endeavor with a specific objective to be met within the proscribed time and dollar limitations and that has been assigned for definition or execution.

In contrast to operations or processes in the company, which are recurrent and ensure "normal" business operation, such as, for example, the processing of sales orders, projects are undertakings that

- have a definite start and end
- create something new and in that sense are unique
- require resources (such as persons, equipment, money) that are most often limited in availability, absolutely and also often on the time axis.

Some examples of projects from business life and personal life are

- Introduction of a new business process
- A change in structural organization
- Development of a new product
- A research project to investigate a certain phenomenon
- Planning a trip around the world
- Redecoration of a room in your house

While a project may contain parts that were already parts of other projects, the result of a project as a whole is unique. For instance, any single bridge can be seen as a unique construction, although some components can be identical in many bridges.

> *Project management* is the organizing, planning, scheduling, directing, controlling, monitoring, and evaluating of prescribed activities to ensure that the stated objectives of the a project are achieved ([APIC04]).

Project management is thus a systematic approach to ensure the effectiveness of a project and the efficient use of resources.

On the basis of these definitions, we can derive the following connections:

- The realization of a system in a company virtually always has a unique character, creates in addition something new, and requires limited resources. The realization of a system can be seen as a set of projects, which can be handled – in particular where system complexity is high – by project management.

- Not every project has to be seen as realization of a system. The planning of a world trip or a research project investigating a specific phenomenon, for example, utilize methods and techniques of project management but not necessarily the methods and techniques of systems engineering.

- Simple projects do not necessarily have to be accompanied by project management. In private life especially, the project may affect only one single person. A person redecorating a room at home – this being the realization of a system, even – often takes a less systematic approach.

The two sections that follow below look at the methods of systems engineering for the realization of systems and the methods of project management for effective and efficient execution of projects.

18.1   Systems Engineering

In all realizations of systems, typical problems arise. These problems are dealt with by systems engineering, independently of the type of system. Figure 18.1.0.1 shows the characteristics of systems engineering following [HaNa02], [HaWe05], or [Züst04]. The most important principles are then summarized below.

The essential, core ideas in systems engineering can also be applied without difficulty to the life cycle phases of all types of systems. In quite a lot of cases, however, there are specific differences. Section 18.1.4

provides an example: the development of computer-aided information systems, or software engineering. Software engineering differs from classical systems engineering in some important aspects.

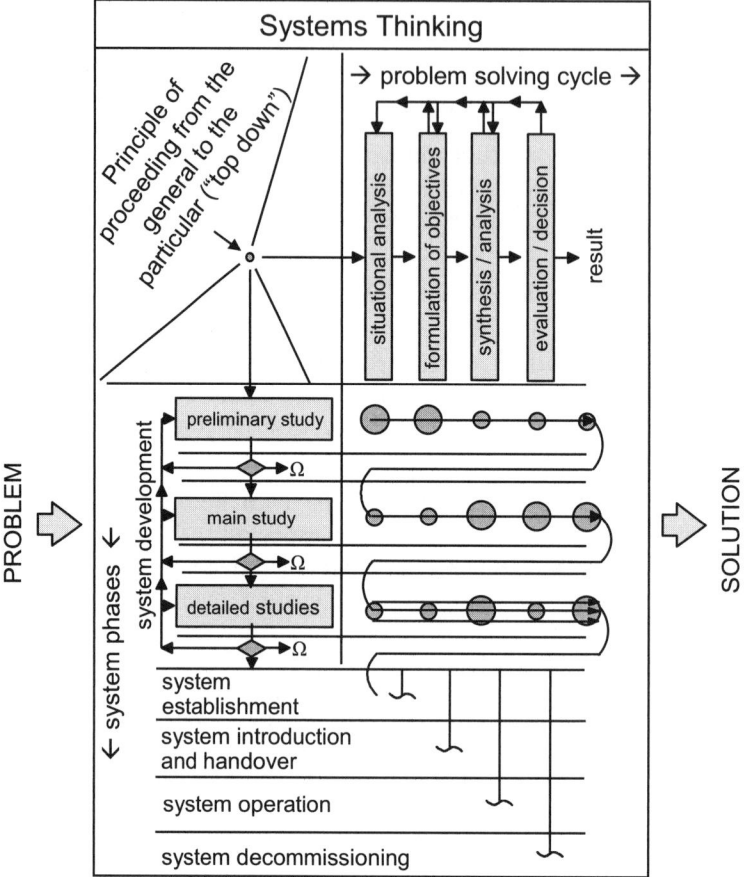

PROBLEM ⇨ ... ⇨ SOLUTION

Fig. 18.1.0.1   Systems engineering: overview based on [HaNa02]. The symbol Ω stands for end, that is, termination of system development.

18.1.1 Systems Thinking and the Top Down Approach

In *systems thinking*, or *systems-related thinking*, the goal is to understand the issue to be solved as a system with its elements and interactions both within the system and with the *surrounding systems* – that is, the system environment.

> The basic idea of *proceeding from the general to the particular* (top down approach) demands that the system be observed at different levels. This can be at the highest level, meaning the whole system, or within *subsystems*, that is at lower levels.

Also of interest are *part systems*, such as for example the flow of goods, data, or information. Figure 18.1.1.1 illustrates the terms.

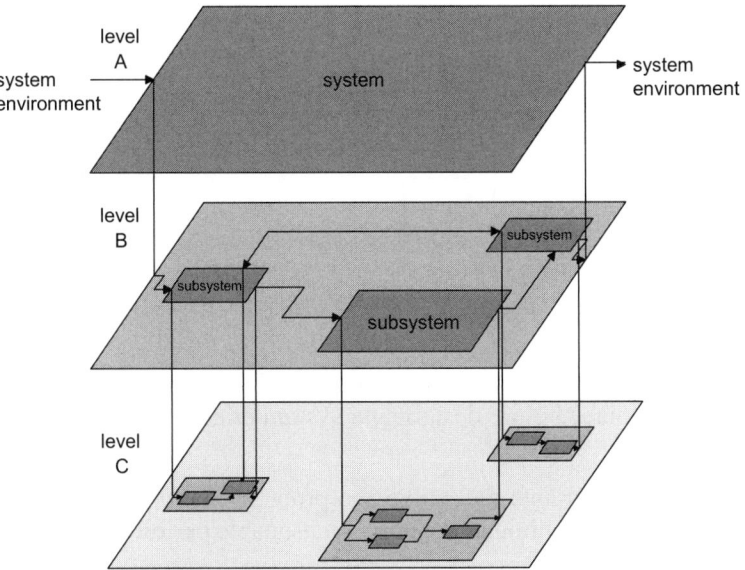

Fig. 18.1.1.1   Proceeding from the general to the particular (top down approach).

First, the whole system at the highest level has to be formulated in its interaction with the systems in the system environment. At this point the subsystems remain "black boxes," meaning that input, output, and the function of the black box are specified but not the mechanisms by which the function will be realized. In a subsequent phase, each subsystem, or black box, will be handled in the same way as the system. The highest level or levels generally describe the generalist's point of view on solving the problem, while the lower levels refer more to the structure of the problem and therefore resemble the specialist's point of view. For each aspect that is to be considered, it is important that the discussion is conducted at the correct system level.

Usually there are various possible ways to design the system at each level, especially regarding definition of the subsystems. These possibilities result in a range of variants at each level, as Fig. 18.1.1.2 shows.

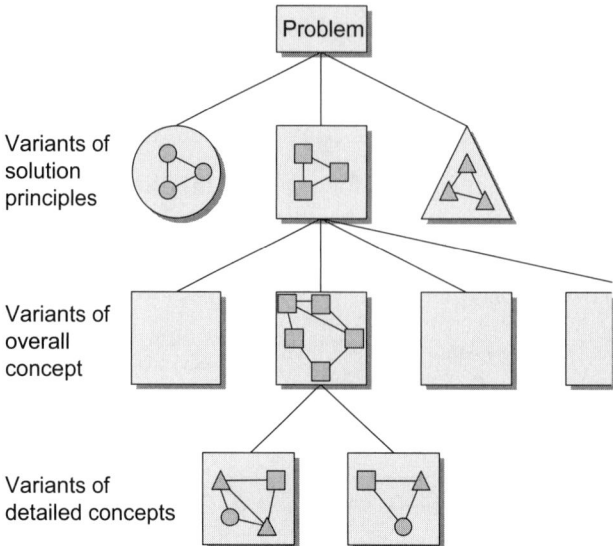

Fig. 18.1.1.2   Creating and evaluating variants at each level of the system.

Ideally, evaluation of variants and selection decision on which variants to retain should take place before designing a system or subsystem at a lower level:

- *Advantage:* Variants that solve the problem insufficiently can be determined and eliminated within a reasonable period of time.

- *Disadvantage:* Whether the postulated mechanism for a black box at a lower level can actually be realized can sometimes be determined only through detailed study at the lower system level.

Therefore, the effort required to work out a variant at a lower level stands opposite to the risk of making an erroneous decision at a higher level.

18.1.2 System Phases and System Life Cycle

The *phases of a system* encompass three concept phases and four implementation phases as shown in Figure 18.1.0.1. The *system life cycle* comprises all of the life-cycle phases of a system.

In *system development* there are three concept phases:

1. The *preliminary study*, where the goal is, within a reasonable time frame, to acquire insights regarding whether there exists a real need for a new system or modification of a system

- whether there exits a real need for a new system or modification of a system,
- whether the approach to the problem is correctly selected,
- what the boundaries of the given system are,
- what the most important functions of the system are,
- what the principle solution variants for the problem are.

The client's decision regarding feasibility and thus continuation or termination of the project and decision regarding the variants to be selected form the end of the preliminary study.

2. The *main study*, which comprises study of the whole system. If a subsystem can be assessed only with great difficulty, it can be necessary to conduct a detailed study already at this point. The result of the main study is a comprehensive concept of the system, and – depending on the type of system – it is in the form of a plan of tasks or activities, of construction plans, of a verbal description, or of other suitable means. With these results, it is now possible to make decisions regarding the investments, to define the subsystems, and set priorities in the realization of the detailed studies.

   This last point is particularly important, as the task is now to evaluate and plan project resources (financial and human resources). In addition, it is necessary to first develop the important subsystems to which the less important subsystems are oriented. While this may reduce the degrees of freedom in the realization, it does accelerate the realization of the other subsystems, through, for example, possibly copying relevant subsystems developed first.

   The result of the main study may require a return to the previous concept phase, for example if the requirements are not precise or not feasible.

3. *Detailed studies*. The result of detailed studies encompass, for one, the detailed concept for the subsystems and the final decision on the variants to be selected, and, for another, specification of the description of the individual part systems. The description will be precise enough to allow the system to be built without interpretation problems.

   Because there are various detailed studies, namely, detailed studies of the individual subsystems, at different levels, the next task is to reintegrate the individual systems, proceeding from the particular to the general (bottom up). With this, it is now possible to test the entire function and the interplay of the subsystems in their supersystems. This is a process that can reveal ways in which the detailed studies or also the main study should be modified.

During each of the concept phases, decisions must be made regarding the selection of the variants, end of the study, or return of the project to the next higher-level phase. Important factors in these decisions are – in addition to the factors that relate to the functional objectives of the project – the expected costs and benefits. Costs and benefits often determine the variant that is to be selected among variants that appear to be equally good functionally. Or they may provide impetus to search for other variants, to terminate system development (the symbol Ω in Figure 18.1.0.1), or to continue on to the next life cycle phase of the system.

In *system implementation* there are four life cycle phases:

1. *System establishment*, describes elaboration of the system functions, for example:
   - production of a machine and its documentation
   - drawing up of a process or an organization
   - coding and documentation of the programs in a computer-cased information system
   - elaboration of the organization to operate the system. In the example of an information system, what is needed are, among other things, documentation for the user, exact description of the procedures for data acquisition – especially from and to the surrounding systems – and the procedures for the use of information, actions to be taken in the case of system crisis, and training of users.

2. *System introduction and handover* is the transition to the production phase of the system. Often, especially with large projects, one subsystem is introduced after another, as there are always various unforeseeable factors to allow for. In this usually relatively short phase of introducing the system, systems corrections are often required that are very time-critical. It is also possible to put some subsystems into operation while keeping others in the detailed concept phase, especially if the concept of thc latter subsystems can be influenced by experience gained during operation of subsystems already introduced. In classical systems engineering, at the least the entire main study should be completed in all cases before beginning the building of the first part system.

3. During *system operation* there must be periodic and constructive review of the following points:

   - Is the system really functioning as conceptualized? The answer to this question can serve as a source of experience for later, similar projects and provide the basis for a process of modification/correction.

   - Are the commercial objectives being met as foreseen? Any deviations observed can aid improved assessment of costs and benefits in future projects.

4. Usually, the decision of *system disposal*, or of *system decommission* is made concurrently with the introduction of a replacing system. For systems that are highly intertwined with daily operations, such as software systems at the operations level of a company, system replacement is often no light matter. Generally the requirements are

   - that daily processes in the real world must not be interrupted for longer than a very short period

   - that the data should be transferred from the old system to the new system automatically, if possible.

   System decommissioning for hardware systems (for example, computers, terminals) involves also physical disposal of the individual components. This can be a big challenge, both technically and in terms of costs. For this reason, system disposal should be a part of systems engineering from the start.

If the system will be in operation for a certain period of time only, all of the life cycle phases of the system can be seen as and conducted as one single project. Otherwise, the concept phases can be taken together with elaboration of the system and introducing the system as one project, and system decommissioning as a new project.

18.1.3 The Problem Solving Cycle

As seen in Fig. 18.1.0.1, the three concept phases (during system development) stand alongside the problem solving cycle.

The *problem solving cycle* is defined as the six steps described in the following, which are conducted during the three concept phases of system development.

The importance of each step is indicated in Fig. 18.1.01 by small versus large circles, and the required expense and effort is indicated by single versus triple arrows.

1. The purpose of *situational analysis* is to understand the situation and identify the problem and its causes and consequences. Situational analysis distinguishes among at least four aspects:

    - System-related: Determination of the system and subsystems, with their elements and interactions

    - Diagnostic: Determination of the symptoms of the unsatisfactory solution, derivation of the causes

    - Therapeutic: Finding of possible corrections and applying corrections to the relevant elements

    - Time-related: Does the situation develop on the time axis with or without correction?

    During situational analysis, the bounds and constraints for a possible solution have to be defined, such as

    - Bounds and constraints arising from the system environment (social, technological, regulatory, and so on)

    - Bounds and constraints stemming from decisions made earlier, which can not be modified at present

    - Bounds and constraints comings from fixed parts of the situation, that is, parts that for some reason must remain as they are

    It is advantageous to summarize the situational analysis in an analysis of strengths, weaknesses, opportunities, and threats, often abbreviated as *SWOT analysis*. The analysis of strengths and weaknesses refers to the system under review at the present time. The analysis of opportunities and threats refers to the system environment: How will changes in the environment expected in the future impact the system, if it is left *unchanged*?

2. *Formulation of objectives* generally comprises functional, commercial, and time-related objectives. The objectives must be solution-neutral, complete, precise, understandable, and realistic. They must relate to the elements in the SWOT analysis; that is, they must be coherent with the system analysis. Generally, two classes of objectives are distinguished:

    - *Mandatory objectives*, that is, objectives that must be achieved in any case to solve the problem ("need to have").

- *Preferred objectives*, that is, objectives that are to be achieved if possible ("nice to have"). These goals will eventually serve as a catalogue of criteria for decision-making among several acceptable variants.

- In the end, the client has to approve the formulation of objectives. This is because unanticipated factors may make it necessary to change the formulation of objectives.

3. *Synthesis of solutions* is conception of the possible solutions. Synthesis has to be sufficiently precise to allow comparison of the various variants. All required functions and available resources have to be taken into account. Synthesis is the creative part of the work, and therefore it is usually also the most difficult part of the problem solving cycle.

4. *The analysis of solutions* is a kind of test of the synthesis. Is the solution concept comprehensive (that is, does it meet all objectives)? Is it realizable (that is, have all conditions and constraints been complied with)? It is sometimes difficult to differentiate between the two steps of synthesis and analysis in the problem solving cycle. That is because analysis often begins already at the birth of an idea for a solution concept.

5. In *evaluation of solutions*, quantitative methods are selected for measuring the efficiency or quality of a possible solution and of a possible solution as compared to other variants. The methods chosen are usually similar to the methods otherwise used for comparing benefits, such as cost-benefit analysis. The criteria come from the catalogue of objectives, possibly with the addition of more detailed technical criteria.

6. The *decision in the problem solving cycle* step refers to both selection of the variants and the decision to repeat this or a preceding concept phase. The decision is made jointly by specialists, the people responsible for the system, and the client. Reasons for repeating a concept phase are, among others:
   - The situational analysis is insufficient or not precise enough for derivation of a solution.
   - The results of the analysis show that the concept does not in all parts meet the need and the constraints.
   - New objectives are added.
   - The objectives are changed, as no solution is possible.
   - New variants should be developed for evaluation.

- New weightings are given to the criteria used for evaluation of the variants.

18.1.4 Differences between Software Engineering and Classical Systems Engineering

The majority of experiences in the past have shown that software engineering can not be executed with exactly the same strictness of the *sequence* of life cycle phases that classical systems engineering likes to stipulate. There are two reasons for this:

1. The organizers and industrial engineers, with their often incomplete knowledge of what can be done on the information technology side, can not formulate system objectives precisely and understandably enough to allow the software developers, who are not sufficiently familiar with the business processes, to design the correct information technology view of the system. As a result, the formulation of objectives is unstable through the course of the project. In the literature, this challenge is called the evolutionary character of software engineering.

2. A critical factor is the customer or sponsor contracting the project. Customers want "to see something." However, the system development for complex software systems is very long; it can take months or even a year or more. In the end, customers have little possibility to closely evaluate the quality of the work.

In both of these cases, therefore, the attempt is to solve the problem, for example, by what is called iterative system development.

> *Iterative system development* means that software engineers break up the traditional systems engineering, so that not each life cycle phase of the system must be strictly completed before the next is initiated. For certain system functions in the preliminary, main, and detailed studies, *prototyping* is done, that is, a provisional and rough version of the system is built.

Iterative system development does not, however, shorten the system development as compared to the traditional sequential model. On the contrary, time is lost in the process. But this loss can be made up for by the following advantages:

1. The user interface and process scenarios can be shown early on. This helps to avoid misunderstandings that can occur already in systems analysis – that is, in an early phase of the system, and this

increases certainty. Often, business people and software developers only come to recognize that they have different understandings when they can "see the thing."

2. The prototype strengthens users' and client's trust in the project and in the project actors. This creates a boost in motivation.

In software engineering, system development following the *sequence* of life cycle phases is also called the *waterfall model*, as shown in Figure 18.1.4.1.

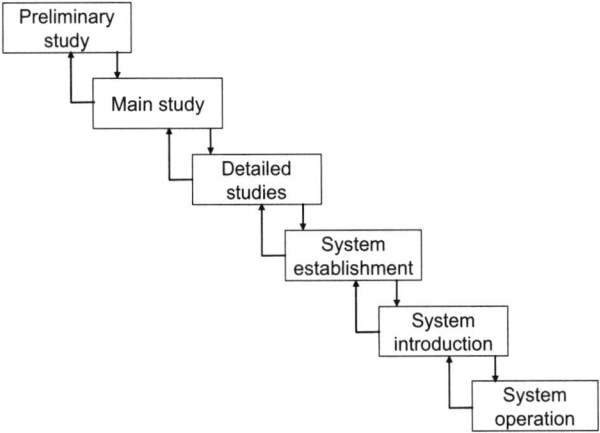

Fig. 18.1.4.1   The waterfall model.

Opposed to that, the *spiral model* is a cyclic process, as shown in Figure 18.1.4.2. Here, the system is built, through prototyping, in every phase. In each cycle, the results of earlier phases are refined and extended.

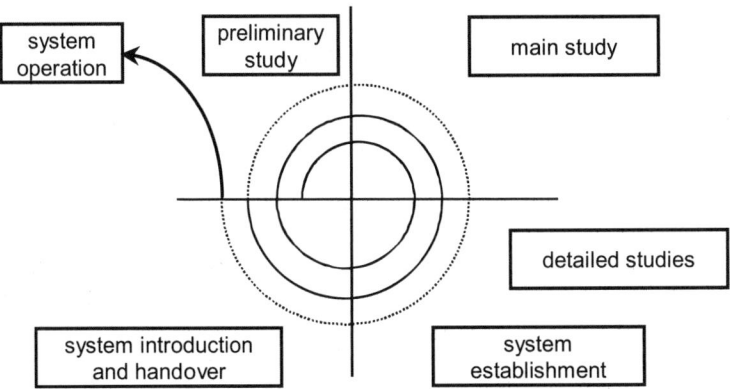

Fig. 18.1.4.2   The spiral model.

In the iterative development process following the spiral model, the software is not specified, programmed, and taken on as a "complete" product but instead is developed in functional capability increments. The main advantage of the spiral model is that the application of successive increments provides future users with results that they can evaluate, so that the software developers can incorporate their feedback. The trend towards the spiral model developed not least also due to advances in programming techniques, in particular in connection with CASE (computer-aided software engineering) tools.

18.2   Project Management

The following overview of project management is limited to project goals and constraints, nature and content of a project, organization and process planning, and project costs, benefits, profitability, and risk. For details of the areas presented here in overview, the reader may want to refer to specific works on project management and on tasks such as project cost management, project human resources and project quality management, project information and communications management, and project procurement management (see, for example, [Kerz06], [KuHu06], [PMBOKD], and [PMBOK]).

18.2.1 Goals and Constraints of a Project

Every project has certain goals and objectives; these the project performs.

Project performance comprises achievement of the project objectives in the areas of quality, cost, delivery, and flexibility.[2]

The following describes target areas both generally and taking the example of developing and preparing a machine for marketing:

- In the target area of quality, the goals include functional objectives, such as the use of product and process technologies, or the way that the organization functions. Examples: exact specifications of the functions of the machine, decisions regarding the principles of construction and production.

---

[2]   Compare here the definition of company performance in Section 1.3.1.

- In the target area of delivery, the goals include, for example, realization by the planned date to meet the "time to market".

- In the target area of cost, the goals are commercial, such as meeting the cost budget, or realization of expected financial benefit. Example: determining cost per unit and the sales price of the machine, setting the development budget.

The goals themselves are expressed as what are called deliverables.

> A *deliverable* is a tangible result created by the work of a project.

Deliverables are, for example, a product prototype, a software package introduced to the market, or a new organization of an area in the company. But a deliverable can also be a study, guidelines, or documents.

Generally, projects have to be performed and delivered under certain constraints.

- *External constraints* are constraints in the project environment over which one can have little or no influence. In the case of system development, these are mainly the surrounding systems. External constraints of business projects can be legal/regulatory but also political, sociological, environmental, or economic. External constraints are also the scarcity of goods or customers' quality requirements.

- *Internal constraints* are issues in the world of the project that can be influenced and changed – sometimes easily. Internal constraints can be aspects of business and business management but also qualitative abilities and quantitative availability of persons involved in the project. Internal constraints are also the complexity of the project and the technologies implemented, or the quality and delivery reliability of procured goods.

Once project goals and deliverables have been defined and approved, in principle they may not be changed, even if the constraints change. This is one of the main tasks of project management.

18.2.2 Project Phase, Project Life Cycle, and Work Breakdown Structure

Deliverables are produced at the end of a project but also as the result of individual phases within the project.

A *project phase* is a major part of a project. Collectively, the project phases are called the *project life cycle*.

Figure 18.2.2.1 shows the project phases in a sample generic project life cycle. See here [PMBOKD or PBMOK, Section 2.1].

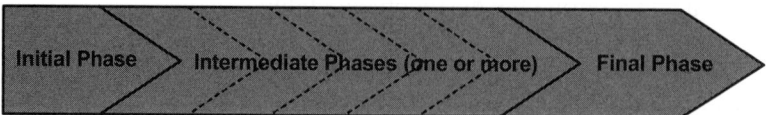

Fig. 18.2.2.1   Project phases in a generic project life cycle (Source: PMBOK).

The intermediate phases will differ depending on the type of project. For example, if the goal is realization of a system, the different life cycle phases shown in Fig. 18.1.0.1, from preliminary study to establishment of the system can be seen as system development. Fig. 18.1.4.1 showed the life cycle phases of a project in software development. Possible life cycle phases of classical *product development* are concept development, product planning, process planning, building prototypes, pilot production, and ramp up.

The product life cycle in Fig. 1.1.1.2 can be accompanied by several project life cycles. An initial project handles product development and a further project the development of services that is, additional services connected with the product. Another project can aim at further development.

In project management, a *program* is a group of related projects. The term is then synonymous with a project, mostly a large project.

An example of a program is the NASA Space Shuttle program. The project itself is subdivided into smaller units.

A *(project) task* is a subset of a project, having a duration of a number of months, for example, and carried out by a certain group or organization. A task can also be subdivided into a number of subtasks.

A *work package* is a set of activities assigned to the manager of a component of the project and, if possible, also to an organizational unit. Work packages are deliverables, defined in as much detail as possible, at the lowest level of the *Work Breakdown Structure*. A work package has a cost budget, scheduled start date, scheduled finish date, and *project milestones*, that is, the specific events in the project – usually completion of major deliverables.

Whenever possible, a project should begin with a statement of work.

A *statement of work* is the "first project planning document that should be prepared. It describes the purpose, history, deliverables, and measurable success indicators for a project. It captures the support required from the customer and identifies contingency plans for events that could throw the project off course" [APIC04].

The statement of work thus serves management as the basis for decision-making. The logical relationships of a project, that is, the tasks and work packages, are called the Work Breakdown Structure.

Work Breakdown Structure (WBS) is a hierarchical description of tasks and work packages of a project, whereby "each descending level represents an increasingly detailed definition of a project component" [PMBOK].

Figure 18.2.2.2 shows a formal representation of a WBS.[3]

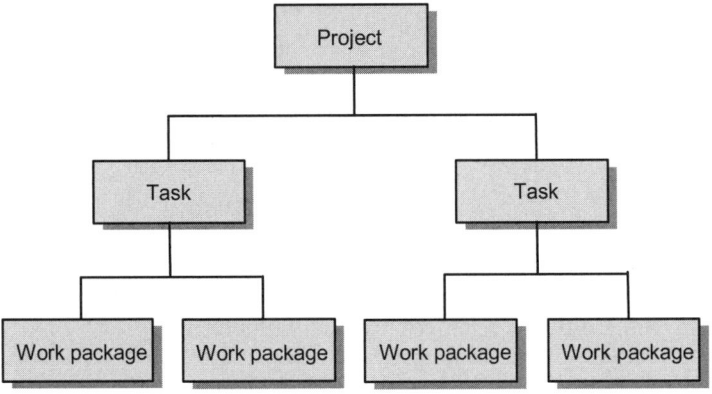

Fig. 18.2.2.2   Increasing degree of detail in a Work Breakdown Structure.

This representation corresponds to the product structure (bill of material) in Figure 1.2.2.2, or more precisely, a convergent product structure, or tree structure. In the place of manufacturing components in the product structure, the Work Breakdown Structure in Figure 18.2.2.2 has tasks or work packages, which are processes. Fig. 18.2.2.3 shows a Work Breakdown Structure for a part of a sample project, here the preliminary study for the conversion of a building.

---

[3]   In other standards (for example, in European Union (EU) projects), work packages are placed above tasks.

```
Building Conversion Project
 Task
  Work package                      Identification
 Develop plans                      1
   Generate ideas                   1.1
    Describe work                   1.2
 Select suppliers                   2
   Conduct supplier research        2.1
   Solicit bids                     2.2
 Secure financing                   3
   Estimate financial requirements  3.1
   Obtain credit                    3.2
     Evaluate credit institutions   3.2.1
     Apply for credit               3.2.2
 Obtain building permit             4
   Determine applicable regulations 4.1
   Construction stakeout            4.2
     Procure materials              4.2.1
     Stakeout proposed construction 4.2.2
   Prepare application for building
     permit                         4.3

                                    ...
```

Fig. 18.2.2.3   Excerpt from a work breakdown structure for the preliminary study for a building conversion.

This representation corresponds to the multilevel bill of material in Fig. 16.2.3.4. Again, in the place of components, here there are tasks and work packages. Instead of item IDs, there are task and work package IDs; in the example in Fig. 18.2.2.3 this is a lexicographical numbering.

With a view to project scheduling and rapid project completion, it is advantageous when tasks and work packages are defined such that as many as possible can run concurrently. In addition, they should be allocated the necessary resources, and there should be measurable indicators for success of the tasks and packages.

18.2.3 Project Scheduling and Effort Planning

Most representations used in project scheduling are graphic displays.

A *Gantt chart* is a planning board of schedule-related information, showing scheduling of tasks, work packages, or operations in the form of a bar chart.

Figure 18.2.3.1 shows a possible Gantt chart for the project "preliminary study for building conversion."

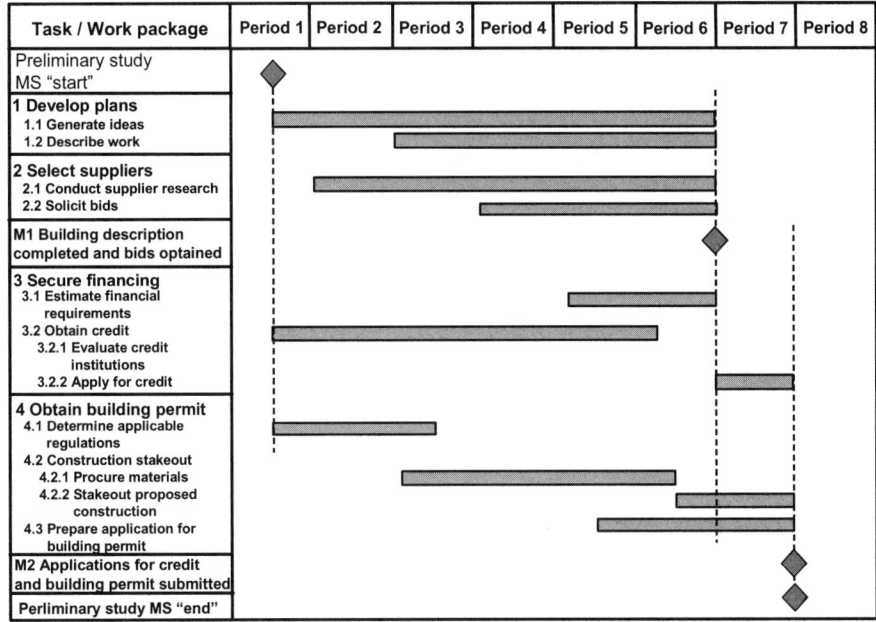

Fig. 18.2.3.1   Gantt chart for the project "preliminary study for building conversion" (excerpt).

This Gantt chart also shows the project milestones MS (start), M1, M2, and ME (end). A master schedule in the form of a Gantt chart that identifies milestones only is called a milestone chart.

A *milestone chart* shows the major deliverables on the time axis.

Under certain conditions, which do not have to apply in every project, a *network planning* technique can be used to aid project *scheduling* and control:

- For every task or every work package, early start date and early finish date, as well as late start date and late finish date can be calculated.

- For every activity within a task or work package the durations can be determined precisely enough.

- The activities can be ordered in sequence, that is, for each activity the logical relationships (reflecting chronology: what activities logically precede and follow an activity) can be displayed schematically. In Figure 18.2.3.1, starting out from start, it must be determined for each activity what other activity triggers it and what activities it may trigger or whether it leads to the end (the same is done for work packages).

Network planning techniques mainly determine the *critical path*. The critical path is the series of activities that determines the earliest completion of the project [PMBOK]. The critical path may change with time, especially when certain tasks, which lie on paths that were not yet critical in the first estimate calculated, are completed behind schedule.

Well-known network planning techniques are the *Critical Path Method* (CPM), the *Program Evaluation and Review Technique* (PERT), and the *Critical Chain Method*. These network planning techniques are described in more detail in Section 12.3.4.

Fig. 18.2.3.2 shows a simple schematic display of *project effort*, which can be expressed in staff months.

Task / Work Package	Effort Group A	Effort Group B	Effort Group C	Effort Work Package
1 Develop plans				
1.1 Generate ideas	1	2	4	7
1.2 Describe work	3	1	1	5
L1.2 Building description	1	5		6
2 Select suppliers				
2.1 Conduct supplier research	1	2	3	6
2.2 Solicit bids	5	1	1	7
L2.2 List of suppliers and bids	2	1		3
3 Secure financing				
3.1 Estimate financial requirements	1	1	1	3
L3.1 Budget		2		2
3.2 Obtain credit				
3.2.1 Evaluate credit institutions		2		2
3.2.2 Apply for credit	1	1	1	3
L3.2.2 Credit application		1		1
4 Obtain building permit				
4.1 Determine applicable regulations	1		5	6
4.2 Stakeout proposed construction				
4.2.1 Procure materials		3	1	4
4.2.2 Stakeout proposed construction	1		4	5
	2			2
L4.2.2 Baugespann	1	4	1	6
4.3 Prepare building permit application		2		2
L4.3 Building permit application				
Total effort	**20**	**28**	**22**	**70**

Fig. 18.2.3.2   Effort per organizational unit.

This schematic representation also lists the deliverables L1.2, L2.2, and so on, as positions in project effort. This is in accordance with the fact that the completion of a deliverable can be connected with particular effort. In the example of Figure 18.2.3.2, this is almost always the effort required for the preparation of a document that requires the consent of all parties involved. Another example is the effort required for the stakeout of the proposed construction.

Effort is measured, for example, in staff days and can be added up for each task or work package. In the present example, the effort for subproject management for a task could be, for example, assigned to the group that has the greatest effort. In this case, that would be Group A for task 2, Group B for tasks 1 and 3, and Group C for task 4.

Based on the schematic representation, project resources, for example, can be released, in whole or part, for example after completion of milestones, possibly in dependency on the quality of the deliverables. The consumption of resources can be measured accordingly.

18.2.4 Project Organization

There are various possibilities for the organization of a project. Similar descriptions of the variants mentioned in the following are found in [PBMOK]. Figure 18.2.4.1 shows project organization in a functional, or line, organization.

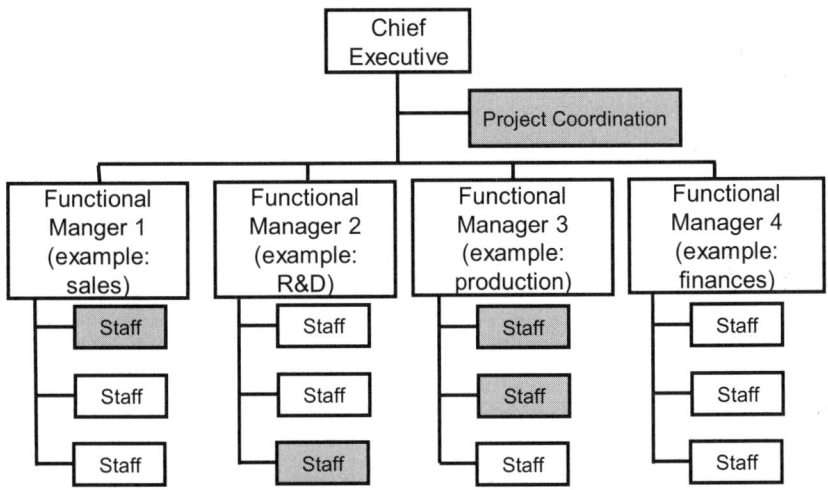

Fig. 18.2.4.1   Project coordination in a functional, or line, organization.

In this type of project organization, which is typical in small and medium-sized companies (SME), the project manager (see shaded box) has little authorization. The project manager usually works on the project part-time, alongside his or her other tasks. The authority of the project manager is more or less limited. Various staff members from different functional areas (also shown in shaded boxes) are involved in the project. However, line managers always give priority to their original functional tasks. The connection among the people involved is given by the definition of the project. The project manager coordinates the project activities and the line managers.

As a variant of this type of project organization, there is also what is called the weak matrix organization, in which project organization is conducted by the persons involved in the project only. Here, the role of the project coordinator, or project leader, is mostly only coordination. Another variant is what is called the balanced matrix, in which the project manager, or project officer, answers to one of the line managers and from there acts with low to moderate authority across the organization. In Figure 18.2.4.1, one of the "staff" boxes would be labeled "project management."

A second possibility is the organization of the entire company based on projects, as shown in Figure 18.2.4.2.

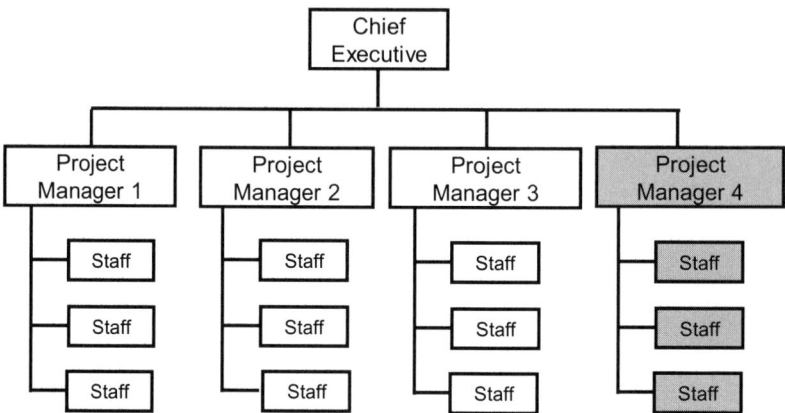

Fig. 18.2.4.2   Project management in a project-based organization.

This organizational structure is typical for a company that primarily sells and implements projects, such as, for example, in consulting businesses or in engineering. A *project manager* – usually assigned full-time to project work – manages all persons and the other resources that are required to complete the project within the project area (shaded boxes).

A further possibility is the strong matrix organization shown in Figure 18.2.4.3.

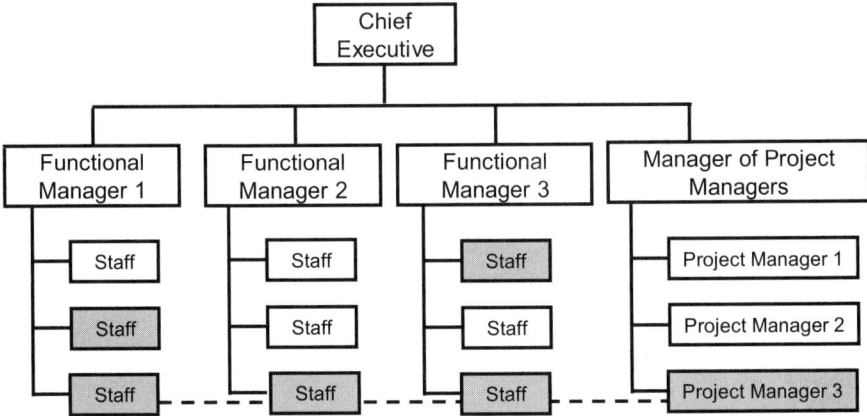

Fig. 18.2.4.3   Project management in a strong matrix organization.

This organization is found in larger companies. Again, the company areas that are involved in a particular project are seen in the shaded boxes in the figure. Important resources are allocated to the project manager as well as a moderate to high authority to issue instructions in the horizontal organization, which is indicated in the figure by the broken line. Other people may also be involved in the project, but – as was the case in Fig. 18.2.4.1 – their first work priority is assigned to their line tasks. With this, also composite forms are possible, especially if several projects are being conducted simultaneously, some of them possibly with a weak matrix organization.

Depending on the type of project organization, the project leader or manager has varying responsibilities and resources at his or her disposal. In any case the project manager is responsible for motivating and inspiring people in relation to the project. The issues are after all unique, whereby usually a project team made up of people from different company areas must work together. For this, the project manager has to have a high degree of social competency, a wealth of ideas, and good communication abilities. For a *high-performance project team*, the same is required of all team members. For a detailed discussion of this aspect of project management, see, for example, [Kerz06] or [KuHu06].

18.2.5 Project Cost, Benefits, Profitability, and Risk

For the decision to be made to conduct a project, generally the benefits have to be greater than the costs. A profitability calculation is also a basis for prioritizing several possible projects. As the projects of interest here are mostly the realization of systems, the general decision techniques described below are illustrated taking the example of the introduction of an ERP software system.

> *Project costs*, also called *total cost of ownership of a project*, encompasses all costs, both for the initial investment and for running costs incurred in accomplishing work during a given time period.

The difficulty of estimating the different project costs varies. Relatively good estimates can be made of the *initial investment*. In the software system example, the initial costs include, in the normal case

- the required hardware, system software, and application software
- premises and installations for machines and people
- internal startup costs for the persons assigned to the project
- decommissioning of the existing, old system
- first training of users in mastering the selected business processes, that is, the organizational solution
- first training of users in mastering computer support of the business processes
- external startup costs, for example, for consultants

Running costs of maintaining the operation of the IT system should not be underestimated. In the case of introducing software, these include

- service and maintenance of hardware and software
- ongoing training of users

Estimation of expenses to avoid opportunity costs is not simple. These expenses arise through evaluation of customer requirements for the new system in the target areas of quality and delivery. They therefore concern *system risks* and are sometimes difficult to estimate. In the case of investment in information technology, the costs are also called "*total cost of computing.*" System risks include the costs of non-accessibility for one, and faultiness of hardware and software, for another. The opportunity costs include lost profit contributions from customer business. Depending on the application, opportunity costs are very high as compared to other costs, or they are inconsequential. Examples:

- A bank that deals in online stock trading has to equip the system for extreme loads that can unexpectedly and rapidly occur if there are new issues or the stock market crashes. System overload or even system failure at this time inevitably leads to a loss of a large part of the customers. To reduce system risks, and thus avoid opportunity costs, the information technology system can at best be duplicated, that is, mirrored, as a backup, which leads to increased investment costs.

- Tax collection agencies do not have to deal with the problem of losing "customers." A system failure of short duration is unproblematic does not result in opportunity costs. In other words, no additional costs arise in order to avoid opportunity costs.

> *Project benefit* is the financial return that arises through the realization of the project.

As with project costs, the difficulty of determining project benefit can vary. A fundamental difficulty here is the following problem: many aspects of benefit – particularly in the target areas of quality and delivery – are not expressed primarily in monetary terms and therefore have to be converted in the end to financial quantities, that is, returns.

This is also the case with introduction of a new software system. The following description is taken from [IBM75]. It can be applied easily to other types of projects. Here, three types of benefit are distinguished:

1. *Direct benefit through savings*: Example: Reduction of administrative personnel by one job, reduction of the expensive maintenance costs of previous machines requiring higher maintenance.

2. *Direct benefit through additionally achieved profit contributions:* For example, higher business volume through the processing of additional contracts with customers via EDI (Electronic Data Exchange) or via the World Wide Web, improved payment practices by customers through the charging of 0.5% interest on the invoiced amount for late payment.

3. *Indirect benefit:* For example: Reduction of physical inventory by 3% through more exact, complete, and detailed information, 2% increase in utilization achieved in the same way, faster lead times in the flow of goods.

Figure 18.2.5.1 shows these three types of benefit in a matrix in comparison, with high, medium, or low probability of realization.

	Probability of Realization		
	high	medium	low
1. Direct benefit through savings	1	2	4
2. Direct benefit through additionally achieved profit contributions	3	5	7
3. Indirect benefit	6	8	9

Fig. 18.2.5.1   Matrix for estimating the benefit of an investment in a software system.

The idea is to enter all expected benefits into the nine cells of the matrix, together with the year in which the respective benefit will occur (that is the year of its realization), calculated from the time of introducing the software system. Sometimes, two or more cells must be used.

- For example, it is estimated that a 1% reduction in physical inventory will occur starting in year 2 with high probability, 1% starting in year 3 with medium probability, and 1% starting in year 4 with low probability. In this case the value and the year are entered into cells 6, 8 and 9.

This technique takes the observation into account that benefits – in greater variation than costs – can be estimated pessimistically, realistically, or optimistically. The numbers from 1 to 9 indicate the sequence in which the expected benefits will be included in the calculation of the cumulative benefit.

Cumulative benefit with degree of realization d, $1 \leq d \leq 9$, is defined as the addition of the benefits in cells 1 to d.

The different degrees of realization allow estimation of risk in the form of a sensitivity analysis.

Project profitability is comparison of the costs and benefits of a project.

This calculation is also called capital budgeting.

Following [IBM75], the cumulative benefits with degree of realization 1 to 9 are entered on the time axis, as shown in Figure 18.2.5.2. This results in nine different benefit curves. The cost curve is entered into the same graph. At time point 0, this is the initial investment; in the following years, this is initial investment plus running costs. The result obtained is the *payback period,* or, in other words, the *breakeven point* of the investment: (and this is what makes the technique intuitively simple) de facto for nine profitability calculations shown in overlay.

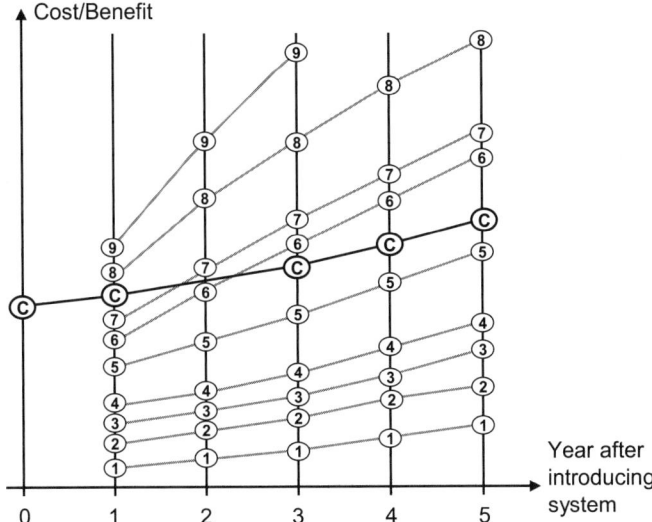

Fig. 18.2.5.2   Graphic representation in overlay of nine profitability calculations, for cumulative benefits with degrees of realization 1 to 9.

According to the example graph in Figure 18.2.5.2, for degree of realization 6, the payback period is approximately two years. For cumulative benefits with degree of realization 7, the payback period is approximately one and a half years.

Up to now, costs and benefits were included in the comparison without adjustment. However, tallying up the costs and benefits can also be done with *discounting*, which means converting all costs and benefits to their present value (at the time of introducing the system). For this, standard methods for analyzing the profitability of investments can be used. The

Net Present Value (NPV) formula, shown in Figure 18.2.5.3 is one. See here also [Kerz06, Ch. 14].

$$NPV = \sum_{t=0}^{T} \frac{(B_t - C_t)}{(1+r)^t}$$

NPV: Net present value
t: Period of realization (e.g., year after system introduction)
C_t: Sum of costs in period t (C_0: initial investment)
B_t: Sum of benefits in period t ($B_0 = 0$, in general)
r : Investment interest rate (e.g. 10% = 0.1)

Fig. 18.2.5.3   NPV, net present value technique.

The Net Present Value formula takes into account the fact that one Euro is worth more today than one Euro a year from now. This is because of interest payments on capital. At an interest rate of 10%, one Euro today is equal in value to 1 Euro · (1+0.1) = 1.1 Euro a year from now. Vice versa, one Euro one year from now is only worth 1 Euro / (1+0.1) = 0.909 Euro today. Projects with a net present value greater than zero are profitable. As most projects have many of the investment costs up-front or in year one, the NPV formula favors de facto projects with a short payback period.

Project risk refers to events that impact the profitability of a project.

In accordance with Figure 18.2.5.3, the project risk can be that the cost objectives of the project or the expected benefits are not achieved. As the costs of the projects are generally far better known than the project benefits, the risk analysis is usually restricted to the amount of the benefit and the year in which it occurs (realization). One way to estimate the risks is sensitivity analysis, which becomes possible by performing several profitability calculations with inclusion of cumulative benefits with different degrees of realization, as is the case in Figure 18.2.5.2.

In practice, for most investments with strategic importance, the big benefits are often seen only with cumulative benefits with degree of realization 6 and higher – that is, they include indirect benefits. In these cases, project management must take caution. The realization of an indirect benefit depends namely not only on realization of the actual investment, but also and primarily on whether the selected organizational solution as such is appropriate for handling the business task and whether staff know how to use it. When an IT system to support business processes is introduced, for example,

- the physical inventory level also depends on the general situation concerning orders and the competitiveness of the company. The inventory that results from these influencing factors can surpass by far any possible reduction of inventory due to the software investment.

- the lead time for goods also depends on whether information made available by a software application can also be implemented on time. Rapid information flow – information concerning a late order, for example – is no use, if there is no one at the workplace to process the information.

If the choice is to be made among a number of possible projects, varying risk behavior is seen in the degree of realization of the cumulative benefits that one wants to include.

The reasons for project risk are many and diverse. The fundamental difficulty of estimating costs and benefits is made even more difficult, among other things, by inadequately define project objectives, poor project organization, inadequate human resources and other resources, inadequate project management and insufficient motivation on the part of the people. Appropriate *project risk management* includes the use of methods such as assessments or audits, which are discussed in Section 17.3.3.

18.3 Summary

Systems engineering is a systemic method of realizing systems. The basic idea of proceeding from the general to the particular (top down approach) requires that the system be viewed at different levels, that is, with its subsystems and environment. The system life cycle encompasses three concept phases (system development) called preliminary study, main study, and detailed studies and four implementation phases – establishment of the system, introducing the system and handing it over, operation of the system, and disposal, or decommissioning, of the system. The three concept phases run through the problem solving cycle with the following six steps: situational analysis, formulation of objectives, synthesis, analysis, evaluation, and decision. In the preliminary study this is predominantly system analysis and formulation of objectives; in the main study an din the detailed studies, this is synthesis, analysis, evaluation, and decision.

Individual phases in the system life cycle can be viewed as projects. Here, project management is a systematic approach to ensure project effectiveness and the efficient use of resources. A project follows certain objectives, the achievement of which often culminates in deliverables and is subject to external constraints and conditions from the environment, such as regulatory requirements, and internal constraints and conditions, such as deadlines and cost and capacity limitations. The project life cycle encompasses initiation, a number of intermediate phases, and an end phase. A Work Breakdown Structure subdivides a project in levels of tasks and work packages, whereby the degree of detail increases with each descending level. For project scheduling, the durations for each task or work package in the Work Breakdown Structure can be graphically shown as date-placed along horizontal bars. The resulting Gantt chart also contains the project milestones. Under certain conditions, network analysis techniques, such as the Critical Path Method, can be used for scheduling. The role of the project manager can be that of coordination in a line organization, or direct management in a project-based organization, or one of limited authority in a matrix organization. Project costs can generally be determined relatively easily. Estimating benefits, however, is difficult in many cases. Often, project profitability can be established only when indirect benefit is included. Profitability itself can be determined using the payback period method or the Net Present Value (NPV) formula. Multiple profitability calculations with inclusion of cumulative benefits with different degrees of realization can provide the required basis for decision-making. This procedure also yields a sensitivity analysis that can be used in the estimation of project risk.

18.4 Keywords

deliverable, 953
detailed study, 945
Gantt chart, 956
main study, 945
phases of a system, 944
preliminary study, 944
problem solving cycle, 947
project, 940
project benefit, 963

project costs, 962
project life cycle, 954
project management, 941
project phase, 954
project profitability, 965
project risk, 966
system, 939
system disposal, 947

system establishment, 946
system introduction and handover, 946
system life cycle, 944
system operation, 947
systems engineering, 940
work breakdown structure, 955

References

Chapter 1

Albe95 Alberti, G., "Erarbeitung von optimalen Produktions-infrastrukturen und Planungs- und Steuerungssystemen", Dissertation ETH Zurich, No. 11841, Zurich, 1996

APIC04 APICS, Dictionary 11th Edition, APICS — The Association for Operations Management, Alexandria, VA, 2004

FoBl91 Fogarty, D.W., Blackstone, J.H., Hoffmann, T.R., "Production & Inventory Management", 2nd Edition, South Western Publishing, 1991

GoNa94 Goldman, S.L., Nagel, R.N., Preiss, K., "Agile Competitors and Virtual Organisations, Strategies for Enriching the Customer", Van Nostrand-Rheinhold, New York, 1994

Gots06 Gottschalk, L., "Flexibilitätsprofile – Analyse und Konfiguration von Strategien zur Kapazitätsanpassung in der industriellen Produktion", Dissertation ETH Zurich, No.16333, Zurich, 2006

Hieb01 Hieber, R., "Supporting Transcorporate Logistics by Collaborative Performance Measurement in Industrial Logistics Networks", vdf-Verlag, Zurich, 2001

HuMe95 McHugh, P., Merli, G., Wheeler, W.A., "Beyond Business Process Reengineering — Towards the Holonic Enterprise", Wiley, New York, 1995

KaNo92 Kaplan, R., Norton, D., "The Balanced Scorecard — Measures That Drive Performance", *Harvard Business Review*, Jan./Feb. 1992, pp. 71–79

Long03 Longman, "Dictionary of Contemporary English", 4th Edition, Longman Group, Harlow, England, 2003

MeWe03 Merriam-Webster, "Merriam Webster's Collegiate Dictionary", 11th Edition, Merriam-Webster, Inc., Springfield, MA, 2003

OdLa93   Oden, H.W., Langenwalter, G.A., Lucier, R.A., "Handbook of Material & Capacity Requirements Planning", McGraw-Hill, New York, 1993

PrGo97   Preiss, K., Goldman, S.L., Nagel, R.N., "Cooperate To Compete — Building Agile Business Relationships", Van Nostrand-Rheinhold, New York, 1997

RuTa05   Russell, R.S., Taylor III B.W., "Operations Management", 5th Edition, Wiley John + Sons, 2005

Schn07   Schnetzler, M.J.; Sennheiser, A.; Schönsleben, P., "A decomposition-based approach for the development of a supply chain strategy", International Journal of Production Economics, Vol. 105 (2007), No. 1, pp. 21-42

Shef05   Sheffi, Y., "The Resilient Enterprise: Overcoming Vulnerability for Competitive Advantage", The MIT Press, Cambridge MA, 2005

Chapter 2

AbKl06   Abele, E., Kluge, J., Näher, U. (Hrsg.), "Handbuch Globale Produktion", Hanser, München, 2006

Alar02   Alard, R., "Internetbasiertes Beschaffungsmanagement direkter Güter – Konzept zur Gestaltung der Beschaffung durch Nutzung internetbasierter Technologien", Dissertation ETH Zurich, No.14772, Zurich, 2002

AlFr95   Alberti, G., Frigo-Mosca, F., "Advanced Logistic Partnership: An Agile Concept for Equitable Relationships between Buyers and Suppliers", *Proceedings of the 1995 World Symposium of Integrated Manufacturing*, APICS, Auckland, 1995, pp. 31–35

AlHi01   Alard, R., Hieber, R., "Electronic Procurement Solutions for Direct Materials", International Conference on Industrial Logistics, July 9-12, 2001, Okinawa, Japan

APIC04   APICS, Dictionary 11th Edition, APICS — The Association for Operations Management, Alexandria, VA, 2004

BeHa00   Berrymann, K., Harrington, L.F., Layton-Rodin, D., Rerolle, V., "Electronic Commerce: Three Emerging Strategies", *The McKinsey Quarterly*, 2000, Number 3 Strategy, pp. 129–136

Bens99   Bensaou, M., "Portfolios of Buyer-Supplier Relationships", MIT Sloan Management Review, No. 40, pp. 36-44, Cambridge, 1999

Brue98   Bruetsch, D. et al., "Building up a Virtual Organization", in Schönsleben, P., Büchel, A., Eds., "Organizing the Extended Enterprise", Chapman & Hall, London, 1998

Coas93   Coase, R.H., "The Nature of the Firm", in Williamson, O., Winter, S., "The Nature of the Firm — Origins, Evolution, and Development", Oxford University Press, London, 1993, p. 18

DaHe05   Davis, M., Heineke, J., "Operations Management – Integrating Manufacturing and Services", 5th Edition, McGraw Hill, 2005

DaMa93   Davidow, W.H., Malone, M.S., "The Virtual Corporation", Harper-Collins, New York, 1993

DoBu02   Dobler, D.W., Burt, D.N., "Purchasing and Supply Management", 7th Edition, McGraw-Hill, New York, 2002

FIR00   Forschungsinstitut für Rationalisierung FIR (Hrsg.), "Industrielle Logistik", 6th Edition, Eigenverlag, Aachen, 2000

Fish97   Fisher, M.L., "What Is the Right Supply Chain for Your Product?", *Harvard Business Review*, March–April 1997, pp. 105–116

Forr58   Forrester, J.W., "Industrial Dynamics: A Major Breakthrough for Decision Makers", *Harvard Business Review*, 36(4) 1958, pp. 37-66

Frau04   Fraunhofer ISI, "Produktionsverlagerungen ins Ausland und Rückverlagerungen", Fraunhofer Institute for Systems and Innovation Research, Karlsruhe, Germany, 2004

GoNa94   Goldman, S.L., Nagel, R.N., Preiss, K., "Agile Competitors and Virtual Organisations, Strategies for Enriching the Customer", Van Nostrand-Rheinhold, New York, 1994

GuGa00   Gulati, R., Galino, J., "Get the Right Mix of Bricks and Clicks", *Harvard Business Review*, May–June 2000

Gull02   Gulledge, T.R., "B2B eMarketplaces and Small- and Medium-Sized Enterprises", *Computers in Industry*, Vol. 49 (2002), 47-58

Hand95   Handy, Ch., "Trust and the Virtual Organization — How Do You Manage People You Don't See?", *Harvard Business Review*, 5/6 1995, pp. 40–50

Hart04   Hartel, I., "Virtuelle Servicekooperationen – Management von Dienstleistungen in der Investitionsgüterindustrie", BWI-Reihe Forschungsberichte für die Unternehmenspraxis, vdf Hochschulverlag an der ETH Zurich, 2004

HuMe95   McHugh, P., Merli, G., Wheeler, W.A., "Beyond Business Process Reengineering — Towards the Holonic Enterprise", Wiley, New York, 1995

Kral83   Kraljic, P., "Purchasing must become supply management", Harvard Business Review, No. 61, pp. 109-117, 1983

LePa97   Lee, H.L., Padmanabhan, V., Whang, S., "Information Distortion in a Supply Chain: The Bullwhip Effect", *Management Science*, 43(4) 1997, pp. 546–558

MaSc04   Manecke, N., Schönsleben, P., "Cost and benefit of Inernet-based support of business processes", Int. Journal of Production Economics, Vol 87, 2004, pp. 213-229

MeFa95   Mertens, P., Faisst, W., "Virtuelle Unternehmen, eine Organisationsstruktur der Zukunft", Festschrift Universität Erlangen, Deutschland, 1995

Merl91   Merli, G., "Co-Makership: The New Supply Strategy for Manufacturers", Productivity Press, Cambridge, MA, 1991

MeWe03   Merriam-Webster, "Merriam Webster's Collegiate Dictionary", 11th Edition, Merriam-Webster, Inc., Springfield, MA, 2003

Pico82   Picot, A., "Transaktionskostenansatz in der Organisationstheorie: Stand der Diskussion und Aussagewert", *Die Betriebswirtschaft*, 42. Jahrgang, pp. 267–284, 1982

Port98a   Porter, M., "Competitive Strategy", The Free Press, New York, 1998

Port98b   Porter, M., "Competitive Advantage", The Free Press, New York, 1998

Port01   Porter, M., "Strategy and the Internet", *Harvard Business Review*, March 2001, pp. 63–78

Ross97   Ross, D.F., "Competing Through Supply Chain Management", Chapman & Hall, London, 1997

Schö01   Schönsleben, P., "Integrales Informationsmanagement", 2. Auflage, Springer-Verlag, Berlin, 2001

SöLö03   Schönsleben, P., Lödding, H., Nienhaus, J., "Verstärkung des Bullwhip-Effekts durch konstante Plan-Durchlaufzeiten – Wie Lieferketten mit einer Bestandsregelung Nachfrage- schwankungen in den Griff bekommen", PPS Management (2003) 1, pp. 41-45; english translation forthcoming

SiKa03   Simchi-Levi, D., Kaminsky, P., Simchi-Levi, E., "Designing and Managing the Supply Chain. Concepts, Strategies, and Case Studies", 2nd Edition, Irwin McGraw-Hill, 2003

Ulic05   Ulich, E., "Arbeitspsychologie", 6. Auflage, vdf Hochschulverlag an der ETH, Zurich, 2005

WaJo04   Wagner, S.M., Johnson, J.L., "Configuring and Managing Strategic Supplier Portfolios", in: Industrial Marketing Management, Vol. 33, No. 8, November, pp. 717-730, 2004

Chapter 3

Albe95   Alberti, G., "Erarbeitung von optimalen Produktions- infrastrukturen und Planungs- und Steuerungssystemen", Dissertation ETH Zurich, No. 11841, 1996

APIC04   APICS, Dictionary 11th Edition, APICS — The Association for Operations Management, Alexandria, VA, 2004

ArCh03   Arnold, T., Chapman, S., "Introduction to Materials Management", 5th Edition, Prentice Hall, Englewood Cliffs, NJ, 2003

Dave93   Davenport, T., "Process Innovation — Reengineering Work Through Information Technology", Harvard Business School Press, Cambridge, MA, 1993

FoBl91   Fogarty, D.W., Blackstone, J.H., Hoffmann, T.R., "Production & Inventory Management", 2nd Edition, South Western Publishing, 1991

Grul28   Grull, W., "Die Organisation von Fabrikbetrieben", Gloeckners Handelsbücherei BD.11/12, 3. Auflage, Gloeckner, Leipzig, 1928

HaCh01   Hammer, M., Champy, J., "Reengineering the Corporation — A Manifesto for Business Revolution", Harper Business, School Press, Cambridge, MA, 2001

Hart04   Hartel, I., "Virtuelle Servicekooperationen – Management von Dienstleistungen in der Investitionsgüterindustrie", BWI-Reihe Forschungsberichte für die Unternehmens-praxis, vdf Hochschulverlag an der ETH Zurich, 2004

Hieb01   Hieber, R., "Supporting Transcorporate Logistics by Collaborative Performance Measurement in Industrial Logistics Networks", vdf-Verlag, Zurich, 2002

JoHu93   Johansson, H.J., McHugh, P., Pendlebury, A.J., Wheeler, W.A., "Business Process Reengineering — Breakpoint Strategies for Marketing Dominance", Wiley, 1993

Long03   Longman, "Dictionary of Contemporary English", 4th Edition, Longman Group, Harlow, England, 2003

LuEv01   Luczak, H., Eversheim, W., "Produktionsplanung und -steuerung – Grundlagen, Anwendungen und Konzepte", 2. Auflage, Springer, Berlin, 2001

MeWe03   Merriam-Webster, "Merriam Webster's Collegiate Dictionary", 11th Edition, Merriam-Webster, Inc., Springfield, MA, 2003

PtSc03   Ptak, C.A., Schragenheim, E., "ERP: Tools, Techniques, and Applications for Integrating the Supply Chains", 2nd Edition, St. Lucie Press, Boca Raton, FL, 2003

Senn04   Sennheiser, A., "Determinant based selection of
          benchmarking partners and logistics performance
          indicators", Dissertation ETH Zurich, No. 15650, Zurich,
          2004

Shin89   Shingo, S., "A Study of the Toyota Production System from
          an Industrial Engineering Viewpoint", revised Edition,
          Productivity Press, Cambridge, MA, 1989

Stew97   Stewart, G., "Supply Chain Operations Reference Model
          (SCOR): The First Cross-Industry Framework for Integrated
          Supply Chain Management", *Logistics Information
          Management*, 10(2) 1997, pp. 62–67.

Ulic05   Ulich, E., "Arbeitspsychologie", 6. Auflage, vdf
          Hochschulverlag an der ETH, Zurich, 2005

VoBe04   Vollmann, T.E., Berry, W.L., Whybark, D.C.,
          "Manufacturing Planning and Control Systems", 5th Edition,
          McGraw-Hill, New York, 2004

Wigh95   Wight, O.W., "MRP II: Unlocking America's Productivity
          Potential", Revised Edition, Oliver Wight, New York, 1995

Chapter 4

APIC04   APICS, Dictionary 11th Edition, APICS — The Association
          for Operations Management, Alexandria, VA, 2004

ArCh03   Arnold, T., Chapman, S., "Introduction to Materials
          Management", 5th Edition, Prentice Hall, Englewood Cliffs,
          NJ, 2003

Bern99   Bernard, P., "Integrated Inventory Management", Wiley,
          New York, 1999

BoGa00   Boutellier, R., Gassmann, O., von Zedtwitz, M., "Managing
          Global Innovation", 2nd Edition, Springer, Berlin, 2000

Chap06   Chapman, S., "The fundamentals of production planning
          and control", Pearson Education, Upper Saddle River, NJ,
          2006

DuCa98   Duffuaa, S., Campbell, John D., Raouf A, "Planning and
          Control of Maintenance Systems: Modeling and Analysis",
          Wiley, New York, 1998

GoCo04   Goldratt, E., Cox, J., "The Goal: A Process of Ongoing Improvement", 3rd rev. Edition., North River Press, Norwich, CT, 2004

IBM75   IBM, "Executive Perspective of Manufacturing Control Systems", Brochures IBM G360-0400-12, 1975

IBM81   IBM, "Communications Oriented Production Information and Control System (COPICS)", Vols. 1–8, Brochures IBM G320-1974-0 to G320-1981-0, 1981

Ross04   Ross, D.F., "Distribution: Planning and Control", 2nd Edition, Chapman & Hall, London, 2004

Sche95   Scheer, A.-W., "CIM, Computer Integrated Manufacturing — Towards the Factory of the Future", Springer, Berlin, 1995

Scho96   Schonberger, R.J., "World Class Manufacturing", Free Press, New York, 1996

Schö95   Schönsleben, P. (Hrsg.), "Die Prozesskette 'Engineering', Beiträge zum Stand von Organisation und Informatik in produktionsvorgelagerten Bereichen Schweizerischer Unternehmen 1995", vdf Hochschulverlag an der ETH, Zurich, 1995

Schö01   Schönsleben, P., "Integrales Informationsmanagement", 2. Auflage, Springer-Verlag, Berlin, 2001

VoBe04   Vollmann, T.E., Berry, W.L., Whybark, D.C., "Manufacturing Planning & Control Systems", 5th Edition, McGraw-Hill, New York, 2004

Wigh90   Wight, O.W., "Production and Inventory Management in the Computer Age", Wiley, John & Sons, Inc., 1990

Chapter 5

APIC04   APICS, Dictionary 11th Edition, APICS — The Association for Operations Management, Alexandria, VA, 2004

HaAn90   Harmon, R.L., Anderson, L., "Reinventing Manufacturing", Free Press, New York, 1990

Imai94   Imai, M., "Kaizen: The Key to Japan's Competitive Success", Random House, New York, 1994

Kogy90   Kogyo, N., "Poka-Yoke", Productivity Press, Cambridge,
            MA, 1990

Maas92   Maasaki, I., "Kaizen, La clé de la compétitivité", Eyrolles,
            Paris, 1992

Ohno88   Ohno, T., "Toyota Production System: Beyond Large-Scale
            Production", Productivity Press, Cambridge, MA, 1988

Schu89   Schuh, G., "Gestaltung und Bewertung von Produkt-
            varianten", Fortschritt-Berichte VDI, Reihe 2,
            Fertigungstechnik, No. 177, 1989

Shin85   Shingo, S., "A Revolution in Manufacturing: The SMED
            System", Productivity Press, Cambridge, MA, 1985

Shin89   Shingo, S., "A Study of the Toyota Production System from
            an Industrial Engineering Point", Productivity Press,
            Cambridge, MA, 1989

Suza87   Suzaki, K., "The New Manufacturing Challenge:
            Techniques for Continuous Improvement", Free Press, New
            York, 1987

Suza89   Suzaki, K., "The New Manufacturing Challenge", Free
            Press, New York, 1989

Toyo98   "The Toyota Production System", Toyota Motor Corpora-
            tion, Public Affairs Divison, Toyota City, Japan, 1998

Voss87   Voss, C.A., "Just-in-Time Manufacture", Springer, Berlin,
            1987; IFS Publications, Bedford, 1987

Wien04   Wiendahl, H.P., "Betriebsorganisation für Ingenieure",
            5. Auflage, Hanser, München, 2004

Wild89   Wildemann, H., "Flexible Werkstattsteuerung durch
            Integration von Kanban-Prinzipien", CW-Publikationen,
            München, 1989

WoJo91   Womack, J.P., Jones, D.T., Roos, D., "The Machine That
            Changed the World", Macmillan Publishing, New York,
            1991

Chapter 6

Apel85   Appelrath, H.J., "Von Datenbanken zu Expertensystemen",
            Informatik Fachberichte 102, Springer, Berlin, 1985

APIC04   APICS, Dictionary 11ᵗʰ Edition, APICS — The Association
          for Operations Management, Alexandria, VA, 2004

GuNo95   Gu, P., Norrie, D. H., "Intelligent Manufacturing Planning",
          Chapman & Hall, London, 1995

Pels92   Pels, H.J., Wortmann, J.C., "Integration in Production
          Management Systems", North-Holland, Amsterdam, 1992

Schi01   Schierholt, K., "Process Configuration — Mastering
          Knowledge-Intensive Planning Tasks",vdf-Hochschul-
          verlag, Zurich, 2001

Schö88   Schönsleben, P., "Flexibilität in der computergestützten
          Produktionsplanung und -steuerung", 2. Auflage, CW-
          Publikationen, München, 1985; 2. Auflage, AIT,
          Hallbergmoos, 1988

Schö88b   Schönsleben, P., "Expertensysteme als Hilfsmittel der
          variantenreichen Produktkonfiguration", in Informatik,
          Forschung und Entwicklung, Springer, Berlin, 1988

Schw96   Schwarze, S., "Configuration of Multiple Variant Products",
          vdf-Hochschulverlag, Zurich, 1996

SöLe96   Schönsleben, P., Leuzinger, R., "Innovative Gestaltung von
          Versicherungsprodukten: Flexible Industriekonzepte in der
          Assekuranz", Gabler, Wiesbaden, 1996

SwLe03   Swaminathan, J.M., Lee, H., "Design for Postponement", in
          Kok, A.G., Graves, S.C., "Handbooks in Operations
          Research & Management Science", Vol. 11, Elsevier, 2003

Wem84   Wemmerlöv, U., "Assemble-to-Order Manufacturing:
          Implications for Materials Management", Journal of
          Operations Management, no. 4, pp. 347-68, 1984

Chapter 7

APIC04   APICS, Dictionary 11ᵗʰ Edition, APICS — The Association
          for Operations Management, Alexandria, VA, 2004

FiCo87   Finch, B.J., Cox, J.F., "Planning and Control System
          Design: Principles and Cases for Process Manufacturers",
          APICS — The Association for Operations Management,
          Alexandria, VA, 1987

Hofm92   Hofmann, M., "PPS – nichts für die chemische Industrie?",
              io Management Zeitschrift Bd. 61, No. 1, Zurich, 1992

Hofm95   Hofmann, M., "Konzeption eines Prozessinformations- und
              Managementsystems", Gabler Edition, Wissenschaft,
              Wiesbaden, 1995

Hübe96   Hübel, S., "Unterstützung zeitkritischer Dokumentations-
              prozesse in der Pharmaindustrie", BWI-Reihe
              Forschungsberichte für die Unternehmenspraxis, vdf
              Hochschulverlag an der ETH, Zurich, 1996

HüTr98   Hübel, S., Treichler, J., "Organizational Concepts for
              Production Planning and Resource Allocation in a Multi-
              national Pharmaceutical Enterprise", in Brandt, D., Cernetic,
              J., Eds., "Automated Systems Based on Human Skills",
              IFAC/Pergamon Press, Oxford, 1998

Kask95   McKaskill, T., "Process Planning – In Search of a
              Standard", *Proceedings of the APICS World Symposium*,
              Auckland, Australasian Production and Inventory Control
              Society, 1995

Loos95   Loos, P., "Information Management for Integrated Systems
              in Process Industries", in Brand, D., Martin, T., Eds.,
              "Automated Systems Based on Human Skills",
              IFAC/Pergamon Press, Oxford, 1995

Namu92   NAMUR-Recommendation, Standardization Committee for
              Measuring and Control Engineering in the Chemical
              Industry, 1992

Sche95   Scherer, E., "Approaches to Complexity and Uncertainty of
              Scheduling in Process Industries", in Brand, D., Martin, T.,
              Eds., "Automated Systems Based on Human Skills",
              IFAC/Pergamon Press, Oxford, 1995

Schö88   Schönsleben, P., "Flexibilität in der computergestützten
              Produktionsplanung und -steuerung",
              2. Auflage, AIT, D-8055 Hallbergmoos, 1988

TaBo00   Taylor, S.G., Bolander, St.F., "Process Flow Scheduling
              Principles", APICS — The Association for Operations
              Management, Alexandria, VA, 2000

Chapter 8

IBM81   IBM, "Communications Oriented Production Information and Control System (COPICS)", Brochures Vol. 1–8, IBM G320-1974-0 to G320-1981-0, 1981

IBM83   IBM, copied from Hollerith-Mitteilungen, No. 3 (June 1913), copied and translated from IBM-Nachrichten 33, 1983

Mart93   Martin, R., "Einflussfaktoren auf Akzeptanz und Einführungsumfang von Produktionsplanung und -steuerung (PPS)", Verlag Peter Lang, 1993

MöMe96   Möhle, S., Weigelt, M., Braun, M., Mertens, P., "Kann man ein einfaches PPS-System mit Microsoft-Bausteinen entwickeln?", 12(5) 1996, pp. 47–52

Nien04   Nienhaus, J., "Modeling, analysis, and improvement of supply chains – a structured approach", Dissertation ETH Zurich, No. 15809, Zurich, 2004

Sche94   Scheer, A.-W., "Architecture of Integrated Information Systems: Foundations of Enterprise Modelling", Springer, Berlin, 1994

Sche98   Scheer, A.-W., "Business Process Engineering: Reference Models for Industrial Enterprises", Springer, Berlin, 1998

Schö01   Schönsleben, P., "Integrales Informationsmanagement", 2. Auflage, Springer-Verlag, Berlin, 2001

Chapter 9

Many of the recent, comprehensive works referred to in Chapter 4 contain at least one chapter on each of the subjects demand and demand forecast. The following lists specialized and also earlier works that treat these subjects.

APIC04   APICS, Dictionary 11th Edition, APICS — The Association for Operations Management, Alexandria, VA, 2004

BoJe94   Box, G.E.P., Jenkins, G.M., "Time Series Analysis: Forcasting and Control", 3rd Edition, Prentice-Hall, New York, 1994

Eilo62   Eilon, S., "Industrial Engineering Tables", Van Nostrand, London, 1962

Fers64   Ferschl, F., "Zufallsabhängige Wirtschaftsprozesse", Physica, 1964

Gahs71   Gahse, S., "Mathematische Vorhersageverfahren und ihre Anwendung", Verlag Moderne Industrie, München, 1971

GaKe89   Gardner, E.S, Jr., McKenzie, E., "Seasonal Exponential Smoothing with Damped Trends", *Management Science* (Note), 35(3) 1989, pp. 372–375

IBM 73   IBM, COPICS, "Communications Oriented Production Information and Control System, Bedarfsvorhersage", IBM, Deutschland, 1973

KrSn94   Kress, G.J., Snyder, J., "Forecasting and Market Analysis Techniques: A Practical Approach", Greenwood Publishing, 1994

Levi98   Lewis, C., "Demand Forecasting and Inventory Control", Wiley, New York, 1998

Lewa80   Lewandowski, R., "Prognose- und Informationssysteme und ihre Anwendungen", de Gruyter, Berlin, 1980

Mari85   de Maricourt, R., "La prévision des ventes", Presses Universitaire de France, Paris, 1985

MaWe97   Makridakis, S.G., Wheelwright, S.C., Hyndman, R.J., "Forecasting: Methods and Applications", 3rd Edition, Wiley, New York, 1997

TrLe67   Trigg, D.W., Leach, A.G., "Exponential Smoothing with an Adaptive Response Rate", *Operations Research Quarterly*, 1967, pp. 53–59

WhMa97   Wheelwright, S.C., Makridakis, S., "Forecasting Methods for Management", 3rd Edition., Wiley, New York, 1997

Chapter 10

Many of the recent, comprehensive works referred to in Chapter 4 contain at least one chapter on each of the subjects inventory management and stochastic materials management. The following lists specialized and also earlier works that treat these subjects.

APIC04   APICS, Dictionary 11ᵗʰ Edition, APICS — The Association
            for Operations Management, Alexandria, VA, 2004

Bern99   Bernard, P., "Integrated Inventory Management", Wiley,
            New York, 1999

Brow67   Brown, R.G., "Decision Rules for Inventory Management",
            Holt, Rinehart and Winston, New York, 1967

Cole00   Coleman, B.J., "Determining the Correct Service Level
            Target", *Production and Inventory Management Journal*,
            41(1) 2000, pp. 19–23

Eilo62   Eilon, S., "Industrial Engineering Tables", Van Nostrand,
            London, 1962

Foga83   Fogarty, D.W., "Inventory Management: Basic Models and
            Systems", APICS, — The Association for Operations
            Management, Alexandria, VA, 1983

Nyhu91   Nyhuis, P., "Durchlauforientierte Losgrössenbestimmung",
            Fortschrittberichte VDI, Reihe 2, No. 225, Düsseldorf, 1991

Stev02   Stevenson, W.J., "Principles of Inventory and Materials
            Management", 7ᵗʰ Edition, Irwin, Boston, 2002

Chapter 11

Many of the publications mentioned in Chapter 4 contain at least one
chapter that refers to deterministic materials management. The literature in
which this subject is discussed in detail is therefore listed below.

APIC04   APICS, Dictionary 11ᵗʰ Edition, APICS — The Association
            for Operations Management, Alexandria, VA, 2004

BlKr86   Blackburn, J.D., Kropp, D.H., Millen, R.A., "A Comparison
            of Strategies to Dampen Nervousness in MRP Systems",
            Management Science 32(4) 1986

Gläs95   Glässner, J., "Modellgestütztes Controlling der
            beschaffungslogistischen Prozesskette", Fortschritt-Berichte
            VDI Reihe 2 No. 337, VDI, Düsseldorf, 1995

Orli75   Orlicky, J., "Material Requirements Planning", McGraw-
            Hill, New York, 1975

Plos94   Plossl, G.W., "Orlicky's Material Requirements Planning",
            2nd Edition, McGraw-Hill, New York, 1994

Ross04   Ross, D.F., "Distribution: Planning and Control", 2nd
            Edition, Kluver Academic Publishers, Norwell, 2004

Schö88   Schönsleben, P., "Flexibilität in der computergestützten
            Produktionsplanung und -steuerung", 2. Auflage, AIT, D-
            8055 Hallbergmoos, 1988

Stee75   Steele, D.C., "The Nervous MRP System: How To Do
            Battle", *Production and Inventory Management*, 16, 1975

WaWh58   Wagner, H.M., Whitin, T.M., "Dynamic Version of the
            Economic Lot Size Model", *Management Science*, 1958, pp.
            89–96

Wien97   Wiendahl, H.-P., "Fertigungsregelung: Logistische
            Beherrschung des Fertigungsablaufs auf Basis des
            Trichtermodells", Hanser, München, 1997

Chapter 12

APIC04   APICS, Dictionary 11th Edition, APICS — The Association
            for Operations Management, Alexandria, VA, 2004

Alba77   Albach, H. (Hrsg.), "Quantitative Wirtschaftsforschung", in
            Ferschl, F., Ed., "Approximationsmethoden in der Theorie
            der Warteschlangen", p. 185 ff., Verlag Mohr, Tübingen,
            1977

CoMa03   Conway, R.W., Maxwell, W.L., Miller, L.W., "Theory of
            Scheduling", Addison-Wesley, Reading, MA., 2003

Coop90   Cooper, R.B., "Queueing Theory", Chap. 10, in Heyman,
            D.P., Sobel, M.J., Eds., "Stochastic Models", North-
            Holland, Amsterdam, 1990

Fers64   Ferschl, F., "Zufallsabhängige Wirtschaftsprozesse",
            Physica, 1964

GrHa98   Gross, D., Harris, C.M., "Fundamentals of Queueing
            Theory", 3rd Edition, Wiley-Interscience, New York, 1998

Hill05   Hillier, F.S., Liebermann, G.J., "Introduction to Operations
            Research", 8th Edition, McGraw-Hill, New York, 2005

IBM75   IBM, "Executive Perspective of Manufacturing Control
            Systems", IBM Brochure G360-0400-12, 1975

LyMi94   Lynes, K., Miltenburg, J., "The Application of an Open
            Queueing Network to the Analysis of Cycle Time,
            Variability, Throughput, Inventory and Cost in the Batch
            Production System of a Microelectronics Manufacturer",
            International Journal of Production Economics, 37, 1994

Wien94   Wiendahl, H.P., "Load-Oriented Manufacturing Control",
            Springer, Berlin, 1994

Chapter 13

APIC04   APICS, Dictionary 11th Edition, APICS — The Association
            for Operations Management, Alexandria, VA, 2004

BeJa90   Bechtold, S.E., Jacobs, L.W., "Subcontracting, Coordina-
            tion, Flexibility, and Production Smoothing in Aggregate
            Planning", *Management Science*, 36(11) 1990, pp. 352–363

Bigg85   Biggs, J.R., "Priority Rules for Shop Floor Control in a
            Material Requirements Planning System Under Various
            Levels of Capacity", *International Journal of Production
            Research*, 23(1) 1985, pp. 33–46

Friz89   Frizell, G.D.M., "OPT in Perspective, Advanced
            Manufacture Engineering", Vol.1, Butterworths, U.K., 1989

GoCo04   Goldratt, E., Cox, J., "The Goal: A Process of Ongoing
            Improvement", 3rd rev. Edition, North River Press, Norvich,
            CT, 2004

Jaco84   Jacobs, F.R., "OPT Uncovered", *Industrial Engineering*,
            16(10) 1984

RuTa85   Russell, R.S., Taylor III, B.W., "An Evaluation of
            Sequencing Rules for an Assembly Shop", *Decision
            Sciences*, 16(2) 1985

SmFo86   Smith, S.F., Fox, M.S., Ow, P.S., "Constructing and
            Maintaining Detailed Production Plans: Investigations into
            the Development of Knowledge-Based Factory Scheduling
            Systems", *AI Magazine*, 1986

Wemm80   Wemmerlov, U., "A Note on Capacity Planning", *Produc-
            tion and Inventory Management*, 21(3) 1980, pp. 85–89

Chapter 14

APIC04   APICS, Dictionary 11th Edition, APICS — The Association for Operations Management, Alexandria, VA, 2004

Arno98   Arnold, D., "Materialflusslehre", 2. Auflage, Vieweg-Verlag, Braunschweig/Wiesbaden, 1998

BaBr94   Bauer, S., Browne, S., Bowden, M., Duggan, A., Lyons, J., "Shop Floor Control Systems", 2nd Edition, Chapman & Hall, London, 1994

Doms97   Domschke, W., "Rundreisen und Touren", 2. Band der Reihe Logistik, 2. Auflage, Oldenbourg-Verlag, München, 1997

FIR00   Forschungsinstitut für Rationalisierung FIR (Hrsg.), "Industrielle Logistik", 6th Edition, Eigenverlag, Aachen, 2000

JuSc00   Jünemann, R., Schmidt, T., "Materialflusssysteme: Systemtechnische Grundlagen", 3. Auflage, Springer-Verlag, Berlin, 2000

Kass96   Kassel, S., "Multiagentensysteme als Ansatz zur Produktionsplanung und –steuerung", *Information Management*, 11(1) 1996, pp. 46–50

Knol92   Knolmayer, G., "A Widely Acclaimed Method of Load-Oriented Job Release and its Conceptual Deficiencies", Arbeitsbericht No. 29 des Instituts für Wirtschaftsinformatik, University Bern, 1992

Marr72   Marrei, K. A., "A Dynamic Programming Approach to Production Smoothing Problems in Single and Small Batch Production", Dissertation ETH Zurich, No. 4713, Zurich, 1972

MarA95   Martin, A., "Distribution Resource Planning", Oliver Wight, New York, 1995

Pfoh03   Pfohl, H.-Ch., "Logistiksysteme: Betriebswirtschaftliche Grundlagen", 7. Auflage, Springer-Verlag, Berlin, 2003

RKW   RKW-Handbuch Logistik, "Integrierter Material- und
            Warenfluss in Beschaffung, Produktion und Absatz",
            ergänzbares Handbuch für Planung, Einrichtung und
            Anwendung logistischer Systeme in der
            Unternehmenspraxis, Erich Schmidt Verlag

Ross04   Ross, D.F., "Distribution: Planning and Control", 2nd
            Edition, Kluver Academic Publishers, Norwell, 2004

Sche98   Scherer, E., "Shop Floor Control — A Systems Perspective:
            From Deterministic Models Towards Agile Operations
            Management", Springer, New York, 1998

Schö95   Schönsleben, P., "Corma: Capacity Oriented Materials
            Management", *Proceedings of the APICS World
            Symposium*, Auckland, Australasian Production and
            Inventory Control Society, 1995

Scho98   Schorr, J.E., "Purchasing in the 21st Century: A Guide to
            State-of-the-Art Techniques and Strategies", 2nd Edition,
            Wiley, New York, 1998

VoBe04   Vollmann, T., Berry, W., Whybark, D.C., "Manufacturing
            Planning & Control Systems", 5th Edition, McGraw-Hill,
            New York, 2004

Wien94   Wiendahl, H.P., "Load-Oriented Manufacturing Control",
            Springer, Berlin, 1994

Chapter 15

CoSt93   Cokins, G., Stratton, A., Helbling, J., "An ABC Manager's
            Primer – Straight Talk on Activity-Based costing", Institute
            of Management Accountants, 1993

Habe04   Haberstock, L., "Kostenrechnung I", 12. Auflage, Erich
            Schmidt Verlag, Berlin, 2004

KeBu93   Keller, D.E., Bulloch, C., Shultis, R.L., "Management
            Accountant Handbook", 4th Edition, Wiley, New York, 1993

Schm92   Schmid, R., "Activity-based costing im praktischen Einsatz
            bei Hewlett Packard", Practitioners Meeting, Production and
            Information Management, BWI/ETH Zurich, Nov. 26, 1992

Chapter 16

ADIC90   ADICAD, "Dokumentation der Ingenieurdatenbank ADICAD", ADI D-7500, Karlsruhe, 1990

Apel85   Appelrath, H.J., "Von Datenbanken zu Expertensystemen", Informatik Fachberichte 102, Springer, Berlin, 1985

APIC04   APICS, Dictionary 11th Edition, APICS — The Association for Operations Management, Alexandria, VA, 2004

EiHi91   Eigner, M., Hiller, C., Schindewolf, S., Schmich, M., "Engineering Database: Strategische Komponente in CIM-Konzepten", Hanser, München, 1991

Long03   Longman, "Dictionary of Contemporary English", 4th Edition, Longman Group, Harlow, England, 2003

MeWe03   Merriam-Webster, "Merriam Webster's Collegiate Dictionary", 11th Edition, Merriam-Webster, Inc., Springfield, MA, 2003

Pels92   Pels, H.J., Wortmann, J.C., "Integration in Production Management Systems", North-Holland, Amsterdam, 1992

Schi01   Schierholt, K., "Process Configuration — Mastering Knowledge-Intensive Planning Tasks", vdf-Hochschulverlag, Zurich, 2001

Schö01   Schönsleben, P., "Integrales Informationsmanagement", 2. Auflage, Springer-Verlag, Berlin, 2001

Schö88   Schönsleben, P., "Flexibilität in der computergestützten Produktionsplanung und -steuerung", 2. Auflage, CW-Publikationen, München, 1985; 2. Auflage, AIT, Hallbergmoos, 1988

Schw96   Schwarze, S., "Configuration of Multiple Variant Products", BWI-Reihe Forschungsberichte für die Unternehmenspraxis, vdf-Hochschulverlag, Zurich, 1996

SöLe96   Schönsleben, P., Leuzinger, R., "Innovative Gestaltung von Versicherungsprodukten: flexible Industriekonzepte in der Assekuranz", Gabler, Wiesbaden, 1996

Veen92   Veen, E.A., "Modelling Product Structures by Generic Bills of Material", Elsevier Science, Amsterdam, 1992

Chapter 17

Camp94   Camp, R.C., "Benchmarking", Carl Hanser Verlag, München, 1994

Demi86   Deming, W.E., "Out of Crisis", Center for Advanced Engineering Study, MIT, Cambridge Mass., 1986

Garv88   Garvin, David A., "Managing Quality: The Strategic and Competitive Edge", The Free Press, New York, 1988

GrJu00   Gryna, F.M., Juran, J.M., "Quality Planning and Analysis: From Product Development through Use", 4th Edition, McGraw Hill, New York, 2000

Guin93   Guinta, L.R., Praizler, N.C., "The QFD Book - The Team Approach to Solving Problems and Satisfying Customers Through Quality Function Deployment", American Management Association, New York, 1993

Henn95   Henning, R., Winzer, P., "Qualitätsmanagement - Erfolg am Markt", QZ 40/1, S.8 bis 10, Carl Hanser Verlag, München, 1995

Imai86   Imai, M., "Kaizen, The Key to Japan's Competitive", Random House, New York, 1986

ISO8402   International Organization for Standardization, "ISO 8402:1994: Quality management and quality assurance; Vocabulary", 1994

Jura88   Juran, J.M., "The Quality Control Handbook", McGraw Hill, New York, 1988

Kogy90   Kogyo, N., "Poka-Yoke", Productivity Press, Cambridge Mass., 1990

Masi99   Masing, W. (Hrsg.), "Handbuch Qualitätsmanagement", 4. Auflage, Carl Hanser Verlag, München Wien, 1999

MeWe03   Merriam-Webster, "Merriam Webster's Collegiate Dictionary", 11th Edition, Merriam-Webster, Inc., Springfield, MA, 2003

Mizu88   Mizuno, S., "Management for Quality Improvement: the 7 new QC Tools", Quality Press, Milwaukee, 1988

Mold97   Moldaschl, M., "KVP als Kooperations-Verhinderungs-Programm", QZ 42/4, S.403 bis 408, Carl Hanser Verlag, München, 1997

NIST06   National Institute of Standards and Technology, "Malcolm Baldrige National Quality Award: 2006 Criteria for Performance Excellence", ASQC Customer Service Department, Milwaukee, Wi., 2006

Pfei01   Pfeifer, T., "Qualitätsmanagement: Strategien, Methoden, Techniken", 3. Auflage, Carl Hanser Verlag, München Wien, 2001

Pira97   Pira, A., "A Self-Assessment Approach for Implementing Total Quality Management (TQM) in Hospitals", Proceedings of the 9th Quest for Quality & Productivity in Health Services Conference, St. Louis, September 1997.

Shew39   Shewhart, W. A., "Statistical Method from the Viewpoint of Quality Control", Graduate School, Department of Agriculture, Washington, 1939

Ohno88   Ohno, T., "Toyota Production System: Beyond Large-Scale Production", Productivity Press, Cambridge, MA, 1988

Toyo98   "The Toyota Production System", Toyota Motor Corporation, Public Affairs Divison, Toyota City, Japan, 1998

Verb98   Verbeck, A., "TQM versus QM - Wie Unternehmen sich richtig entscheiden", vdf Hochschulverlag AG an der ETH Zurich, 1998

Zink94   Zink, K.J., "Business Excellence durch TQM - Erfahrungen europäischer Unternehmen", Carl Hanser Verlag, München, 1994

Chapter 18

APIC04   APICS, Dictionary 11th Edition, APICS — The Association for Operations Management, Alexandria, VA, 2004

HaNa02   Haberfellner, R., Nagel, P., Becker, M., von Massov, H., "Systems Engineering" (Hrsg. Daenzer,W.F., Huber, F.), 11. Auflage, Verlag Industrielle Organisation, Zurich, 2002

HaWe05   Haberfellner, R., De Weck, O., "Agile Systems Engineering versus Engineering Agile Systems", INCOSE 2005 World Conference, Rochester, NY, 2005

IBM75   IBM (Hrsg.), "Datenverarbeitung - Gewinnquelle des Unternehmens - Nutzenanalyse einer Wirtschaftlichkeitsrechnung für Datenverarbeitungsanlagen", IBM Form GE 12-1307-01, p. 23, 1975

Kerz06   Kerzner, H., "Project Management", 9th Edition, Wiley, Hoboken NJ, USA, 2006

KuHu06   Kuster, J., Huber, E. et al., "Handbuch Projektmanagement", Springer Berlin, 2006

PMBOKD   "A guide to the project management body of Knowledge: PMBOK Guide", Deutsche Übersetzung, Project Management Institute, PMI Publications, Newton Square, PA, USA, Ausgabe 2000, 2003

PMBOK   "A guide to the project management body of Knowledge: PMBOK Guide", Project Management Institute, PMI Publications, Newton Square, PA, USA, 3rd Edition, 2004

MeWe03   Merriam-Webster, "Merriam Webster's Collegiate Dictionary", 11th Edition, Merriam-Webster, Inc., Springfield, MA, 2003

Züst04   Züst, R., "Einstieg ins Systems Engineering", 3. Auflage, Verlag Industrielle Organisation, Zurich, 2004

Index

- **Page numbers in bold type** indicate the page on which a definition of the term can be found.
- <u>Underlined page numbers</u> refer to passages that contribute to an understanding of the term.
- Page numbers in normal type refer to important passages in which the term is used.
- "syn." refers to a synonym, used instead of the term.

1

1 to 1 association, **846**
1 to n association, **845**, 863, 869, 871

A

A item, 81, **542**
ABC (activity-based costing), 56, **822**, 836
ABC category, **544**, 581
ABC classification, 183, 342, **542**, 565, 581, 620, 780, 919
ABC process, **823**
ABC process plan, **824**, 826, 829
abnormal demand, 516, **541**
acceptance of logistics software, 466
accompanying document, 233, 737, 779
  shop packet, **760**
accounting
  cost center, 819
  cost object, 800, **818**
  cost object group, 819
  inventory, **537**
accuracy
  classification of demand according to, **264**
  record, **538**
act (tasks in the Deming cycle), **912**
action message, 618, **619**
action state, **156**
activation, **688**
activity cost driver, **823**
activity-based cost accounting (ABC) (syn. activity-based costing), **822**
activity-based costing, 56, 475, 565, **822**, 836

activity-based product cost estimation, <u>829</u>
actual capacity utilization, **686**
actual cost system, **816**
actual costing, **816**
actual costs, 534, **801**, 817
actual cumulative production figures diagram, **345**
actual demand, **10**, 600
actual load, **29**, 30, 686, 848
  of an operation, **29**
actual order costs, **815**, 817
actual quantity, **815**, 848
actual time, **24**, 772, 866
adaptive smoothing, **503**
adaptive technique, **375**
additive seasonality, **506**
administration cost rate, **56**
administration time, **25**, 316, 629, <u>634</u>
administrative logistics, **46**, 800
advanced logistic partnership (ALP), **98**
advanced planning and scheduling (APS) concept, **215**, 449
affinity diagram, 925
agency costs, **75**
agent-based system, 753
aggregate demand, **248**
aggregate forecast, **248**
aggregate lead time (syn. cumulative lead time), **26**
aggregate plan, **248**
agile company, **42**, 114
agile competitor, **42**
agile manufacturing, **42**
agility, **42**, 164
allocated quantity, 259, 548, **588**
allocation, **741**

Author's Note

For our interactive elements, as well as for additional teaching material, please refer to http://intlogman.ethz.ch/. In addition, a visit to my web site could be helpful: www.lim.ethz.ch/schoensleben/index_EN. Please refer to Paul.Schoensleben@ethz.ch for questions and comments.

Section 4.5.3 mentions the important role played by APICS, the Association for Operations Management (the former American Production and Inventory Control Society). This society of business persons maintains the body of knowledge on planning & control in logistics and transmits it to people from all over the globe.

In view of the current need for globalization, APICS makes a significant contribution through supporting the development of standard terminology and a shared understanding of issues and problem-solving approaches.

APICS can be accessed at their web site at http://www.apics.org/ or contacted at the following address:

> APICS
> 5301 Shawnee Road,
> Alexandria, VA 22312-2317
> USA

The APICS Educational and Research Foundation programs (CIRM, CPIM, and BSCM certification programs) are supported in the German-speaking world by its associate in Germany:

> PRODUCTION MANAGEMENT INSTITUTE
> Lena-Christ-Str. 50
> D-82152 Planegg bei München,
> Tel. +49 89 857 61 46, Fax +49 89 859 58 38
> www.pmi-m.de

In the French-speaking part of Europe, the APICS programs are supported by its associate in France:

> MGCM
> Tour Aurore
> 18, place des Reflets
> F-92975 Paris la Défence Cedex
> Tél. +33 1 49 67 06 06
> www.mgcm.com